Gender, Race, and Class in Media

Fourth Edition

Gender, Race, and Class in Media

A Critical Reader

Fourth Edition

Gail Dines
Wheelock College

Jean M. Humez
University of Massachusetts, Boston

Editors

Los Angeles | London | New Delhi
Singapore | Washington DC

Los Angeles | London | New Delhi
Singapore | Washington DC

FOR INFORMATION:

SAGE Publications, Inc.
2455 Teller Road
Thousand Oaks, California 91320
E-mail: order@sagepub.com

SAGE Publications Ltd.
1 Oliver's Yard
55 City Road
London EC1Y 1SP
United Kingdom

SAGE Publications India Pvt. Ltd.
B 1/I 1 Mohan Cooperative Industrial Area
Mathura Road, New Delhi 110 044
India

SAGE Publications Asia-Pacific Pte. Ltd.
3 Church Street
#10-04 Samsung Hub
Singapore 049483

Acquisitions Editor: Matthew Byrnie
Production Editor: Laura Barrett
Copy Editor: Megan Granger
Typesetter: C&M Digitals (P) Ltd.
Proofreader: Theresa Kay
Indexer: Wendy Allex
Cover Designer: Anthony Paular
Marketing Manager: Liz Thornton

Copyright © 2015 by SAGE Publications, Inc.

Printed in the United States of America

Library of Congress Cataloging-in-Publication Data

Gender, Race, and Class in Media : A Critical Reader / editors, Gail Dines, Wheelock College, Jean M. Humez, University of Massachusetts, Boston. — Fourth Edition.

pages cm
Includes bibliographical references and index.

ISBN 978-1-4522-5906-2 (paperback : acid-free paper)

1. Mass media and culture—United States. 2. Mass media and sex—United States. 3. Mass media and race relations—United States. 4. Social classes in mass media. 5. Mass media—Social aspects—United States. 6. Popular culture—United States. 7. United States—Social conditions—1980- I. Dines, Gail. II. Humez, Jean McMahon, 1944-

P94.65.U6G46 2014
302.23'0973—dc23   2013039084

This book is printed on acid-free paper.

14 15 16 17 18 10 9 8 7 6 5 4 3 2

CONTENTS

PREFACE

In this fourth edition of *Gender, Race, and Class in Media,* our overall goal remains the same as in previous editions: to introduce undergraduate students to some of the richness, sophistication, and diversity that characterizes contemporary media scholarship, in a way that is accessible and builds on students' own media experiences and interests. We intend to help demystify the nature of **mass media** entertainment culture and **new media** by examining their production, analyzing the **texts** of some of the most pervasive forms or **genres**, and exploring the processes by which audiences make meaning out of media imagery or texts—meaning that helps shape our economic, cultural, political, and personal worlds.[1] We start from the position that, as social beings, we construct our realities out of the cultural norms and values that are dominant in our society. The mass media are among the most important producers and reproducers of such norms and values.

We have designed this as a volume to help teachers (1) introduce the most powerful theoretical concepts in contemporary media studies; (2) explore some of the most influential and interesting forms of contemporary media culture; and (3) focus on issues of **gender** and **sexuality**, **race**, and **class** from a **critical** perspective. Most of the readings in this book take an explicitly critical perspective that is also informed by a diversity of approaches, such as **political economy**, **feminism**, **cultural studies**, **critical race theory**, and **queer theory**. We have chosen readings that make the following assumptions, as we do: (1) that industrialized societies are stratified along lines of gender and sexuality, race, and class; (2) that everyone living in such a society "has" gender and sexuality, race, and class, and other aspects of social identity that help structure our experience; and (3) that economic and other resources, advantages, and privileges are distributed inequitably in part because of power dynamics involving these categories of experience (as well as others, such as age, ethnicity, ability, or disability).

Our selection of material has been guided by our belief that an important goal of a critical education is to enable people to conceptualize social justice clearly and work toward it more effectively. For us, greater social justice would require a fairer distribution of our society's economic and cultural resources.

Our book is situated within both media studies and cultural studies. When we started working on the first edition of *Gender, Race, and Class in Media* in the early 1990s, cultural studies was a relatively new academic field in the United States, although it had been popular for some time in England (where it originated at The Center for Contemporary Cultural Studies at the University of Birmingham). The cultural studies approach has now been dominant in U.S. media studies for more than a generation. Several other interdisciplinary fields concerned with social issues and representation, such as American studies and women's studies, have been heavily influenced by cultural studies.

The field of cultural studies is actually **multidisciplinary**, drawing on insights and approaches from history, critical race studies, literary studies, philosophy, sociology, and psychology. Because of its **progressive** politics and because it offers a much broader and apparently more democratic definition of culture than was used in humanistic studies such as literary criticism in the past, many scholars and students particularly interested in race, gender, and class have been attracted to its theories and **activist** potential. (For a more extended discussion of the development of multiculturalism and cultural studies in the last decades of the 20th century, see Douglas Kellner's reading in Part I.)

In this fourth edition, we continue to emphasize, with Kellner, three separable but interconnected areas of analysis: **political economy, textual analysis,** and **audience reception.** For Kellner, it is crucial to link all three to provide a full understanding of the entire media culture communication process, from production through consumption. Indeed, one of the initial goals of cultural studies was to contextualize the media text within the wider society that informs its production, construction, consumption, and, more recently, distribution along a range of **media platforms.**

Traditionally, political economy has looked at the ways the profit motive affects how texts are produced within a society marked by class, gender, and racial inequality. Who owns and controls the media? Who makes the decisions about content? How does financing affect and shape the range of texts produced? In what other ways does the profit motive drive production? These are central questions asked by political economists. Examining this economic component is still essential to an understanding of what eventually gets produced and circulated in the mainstream commercial mass media industries. However, with the advent of new media technologies that enable consumers to produce and widely distribute their own content, we must broaden our view of production, as many of the readings in this book do.

Media representations are never just mirrors or "reflections of reality" but, rather, always artfully constructed creations designed to appeal to our emotions and influence our ideas, and especially our consumer behavior. Therefore, to educate ourselves as consumers, we need tools to help us closely examine the ways all cultural texts—from TV sitcoms, dramas, or reality shows to fan-produced music videos—are structured, using complex combinations of words, sounds, and visual languages. Critical textual analysis provides a special focus on how to analyze the **ideological** significance of media texts— that is, to look at how, through the use of certain codes and conventions, they create or transmit meanings that generally support the economic, social, and political status quo.

Media studies has long acknowledged that audiences also have a role in creating the meanings of media texts, and for at least a generation, **ethnographic** audience reception research has focused on this dimension. By observing and talking with actual consumers of media texts—as opposed to critics—much has been learned about how we are active as we interpret, make sense of, understand, and use such texts within our everyday social and private lives. These studies have played an important role in complicating the older view of media audiences as passive, or even brainwashed, recipients of prepackaged meanings. Clearly, gender, race, ethnicity, class, sexuality, political beliefs, and age are important factors that can help explain the different meanings that various audiences appear to take away from an advertisement, movie, or sitcom. Studies of **fans**—those dedicated consumers of media texts who build community around their experiences of consumption—go even further in exploring how consumers of media texts can produce meanings quite different from those intended by the original text producers. With the advent of new media aided by the Internet, the debate over audience exploitation versus empowerment has only intensified.

However we conceptualize the media audience in the age of the Internet, it is still vital to study all three components of media representations—production, text, and consumption—to understand how such texts can and do strengthen—or perhaps in some ways undermine—our dominant systems and ideologies of gender, race, and class inequality.

In this fourth edition, we have maintained our thematic focus on gender (including sexuality), race, and class, since we believe that media studies need to address the issues of social inequality that continue to plague our society and undermine its democratic potential. Some of the readings in this book employ an **intersectional** analysis—that is, one that complicates each of these social categories by examining how they interact with one another. Whenever possible, we have selected articles that give voice to the multiple levels of analysis needed to make media studies a truly **multicultural** endeavor. We acknowledge the ever-intensifying interrelationships among media cultures globally while continuing to focus primarily on the North American examples of media texts that we see as most likely to be familiar to instructors and students working with this book.

For the fourth edition, we again located, read, and discussed many new journal articles and book chapters. We consulted with colleagues who teach media courses, and we spoke to students to see what they found compelling in former editions. Thirty readings in this edition are either new or substantially updated. This reflects both the rapid evolution of the field and our desire to provide analysis of relatively recent and current media texts likely to be familiar to students. Several "classic" readings reprinted from earlier editions of this book were at one time key to highly significant developments in the field, and they still offer important and clearly articulated historical and theoretical insights into media analysis.

We've grouped our selections into thematic parts that highlight some of the important changes that have taken place in the worlds of entertainment mass media and new media over the past several years and that also reflect our experience of student interest. As in the third edition, we include an index of individual reading topics, which will allow instructors to create alternative groupings of readings to suit their own course designs. We hope that instructors and students will find the themes and genres represented in this collection provocative, stimulating, and an invitation to engage in further thinking, research, and perhaps even media activism.

In condensing previously published journal articles and book chapters, we have often had to omit quite a lot of detail from the originals, while preserving central arguments and challenging ideas. The omissions are carefully noted with the use of ellipses (. . .). By judiciously cutting the overall length, we have aimed to make cutting-edge scholarship as accessible as possible for undergraduate and graduate students alike. Our brief introductory essays to each part highlight key concepts and identify some interesting connections we see among the readings in that section. Of course we welcome comments from users of this book about our selections, about what worked well in the classroom and what did not. We especially invite suggested articles for future editions.

At the end of the book, we have provided some supplementary resources for the teacher. In addition, we have included a selective list of the many media activist organizations easily located on the Internet. We hope this will be useful for those who, inspired by the progressive ideals espoused by many of the writers in this collection, would like to explore this kind of grassroots consumer and citizens' activism on behalf of a more democratic media culture in the future.

Ancillary Material

Visit www.sagepub.com/dines4e to access online resources including articles from previous editions, video links, web resources, eFlashcards, recommended readings, SAGE journal articles, and more.

Note

1. Throughout our book, key concepts important for students to discuss and digest appear in boldface. These are defined in more detail in the Glossary at the end of the volume. Some instructors have found it useful to assign the Glossary itself as a reading early in a course, for the benefit of students new to media theory and critical cultural studies.

ACKNOWLEDGMENTS

We would like to thank the many colleagues and students who have contributed over the years to our thinking about the questions raised in this book. They are too many to be mentioned individually, but they include faculty and students at the University of Massachusetts Boston and Wheelock College, as well as colleagues and associates with whom we have worked in multiple other locations.

Both authors would especially like to thank Susan Owusu, director of the Communications and Media Literacy Program at Wheelock College, for her insights, advice, and help with developing the new edition.

We appreciate all the writers whose essays and edited articles have been included in the four editions, for their original insights and their willingness to allow us to shorten their texts.

We gratefully acknowledge Matt Byrnie, Nancy Loh, Laura Barrett, and Megan Granger at SAGE Publications, for their belief in the book and their careful work in bringing the fourth edition into print.

We are indebted to the external reviewers of all four editions of the book, and most recently to the reviewers of this edition: Jennifer Brayton (Ryerson University), Kenneth Campbell (University of South Carolina), Bobbie Eisenstock (California State University, Northridge), Breanne Fahs (Arizona State University), Ted Gournelos (Rollins College), Heloiza G. Herscovitz (California State University, Long Beach), Kristyn E. Hunt (Lamar University), Cynthia P. King (Furman University), Suzanne Leonard (Simmons College), Heather McIntosh (Boston College), Melinda Messineo (Ball State University), Erin A. Meyers (Oakland University), Margaret Montgomerie (De Montfort University), Amy Kiste Nyberg (Seton Hall University), Robert Rabe (Marshall University), Robin L. Riley (Syracuse University), Tracy M. Robison (Michigan State University), Margaret Schwartz (Fordham University), and Phyllis S. Zrzavy (Franklin Pierce University).

And again, we salute the members of our families, who provided much-needed moral support as we pursued our research and editorial labors.

PART I

A CULTURAL STUDIES APPROACH TO MEDIA: THEORY

In this book, we offer a selection of **critical** discussions of mass media entertainment culture and **new media** to exemplify a powerful method of analysis you will be able to apply on your own to other examples. In this way, we hope to promote and support critical **media literacy**. While there are many ways to think about media literacy, for the purposes of this book, we argue that in a postindustrial society in which public regulation of a for-profit media system is weak, media literacy can be one tool to help limit the **discursive** power of media in our lives. While a sophisticated level of media literacy cannot replace other efforts to democratize our society's economic and cultural resources, in our view, it does give audiences the skills necessary to analyze and question the ideologies that often work at a subtextual level within media texts.

We begin with media theory because we think students will find it useful to have a good grasp of several central concepts illustrated in an introductory way here, before going on to tackle later readings in which an understanding of these concepts is often presumed. In the media theory section, we especially highlight the central concepts and terms of the field of **cultural studies** as applied to **mass media**. As in all the other sections of this book, the chapters in this section are in dialogue with one another in many ways. In these opening comments, we give only one possible reading of the ways their main themes connect.

We open with "Cultural Studies, Multiculturalism, and Media Culture," by Douglas Kellner (I.1). This sets out the three-part approach to cultural studies (**political economy**/production, **textual analysis**, and **audience reception**/consumption) that characterizes this field. With Kellner, we believe that to understand a media product such as a TV show, advertising image, or online digital game, one must be able to understand the socioeconomic context in which it is created (political economy/production); analyze its constructed meaning(s) through careful attention to its particular visual/verbal/auditory languages, or **codes** (textual analysis); and determine through **ethnographic** research what its real-world audiences contribute to the meaning-making process, and even to the production and distribution of cultural products (audience consumption/production). In addition, Kellner points to the importance of better integrating considerations of gender, race, and class as categories of social analysis in cultural studies work in the future.

In "The Meaning of Memory" (I.2), an important historical background piece that sheds light on how and why corporations came to dominate media culture so heavily in the United States, George Lipsitz shows how the needs of the national economy in the post–World War II period facilitated the development of mass television production. He explores how the increase in the sale of televisions and the development of a group of situation comedies were used to transform a traditional, ethnic immigrant ideology that stressed values of community, thrift, and commitment to labor unions into an **American Dream ideology** that stresses **individualism, consumerism**, and suburban domesticity—values consistent with the needs of the expanding postwar **capitalist** economy.

In subsequent decades, media industries have changed dramatically as a result of mergers and buyouts. Commercial entertainment today is a highly profit-oriented business controlled for the most part by a small number of giant corporations. In "The Economics of the Media Industry" (I.3), David P. Croteau, William D. Hoynes, and Stefania Milan focus on the concentration of ownership in these industries, showing why this is an important problem in a democratic society.

Giant media **conglomerates** are able to "assemble large portfolios of magazines, television stations, book publishers, record labels, and so on to mutually support one another's operations" (a process called "horizontal integration"). They also use "vertical integration"—"the process by which one owner acquires all aspects of production and distribution of a single type of media product"—to gain further control over the market. As the authors point out,

> In this era of integrated media conglomerates, media companies are capable of pursuing elaborate cross-media strategies, in which company-owned media products can be packaged, sold, and promoted across the full range of media platforms. Feature films, their accompanying soundtracks and DVD/Blu-ray Disc releases, spin-off television programs, and books, along with magazine cover stories and plenty of licensed merchandise can all be produced and distributed by different divisions of the same conglomerate. (p. 34)

In these ways, the owners of the media giants benefit economically from conglomeration and integration and, arguably, make it "more difficult for smaller media firms to compete," but even more worrisome is the potential for such conglomerates to translate media ownership into political power. Giving examples from the United States (Mayor Bloomberg of New York), Europe (Italy's Berlusconi), and the United Kingdom and Australia (Rupert Murdoch), the authors warn that "owners can systematically exclude certain ideas from their media products." Building on political economist Herb Schiller's concept of "the corporate voice," they ask us to consider whether "the corporate voice" has been generalized so successfully that most of us do not even think of it as a specifically corporate voice: [That is, the corporate view has become "our" view, the "American" view,] even though the interests of the corporate entities that own mass media are far from universal. (p. 37)

One way of thinking about how the corporate view becomes woven into the dominant ways of thinking about the world is the theory of **hegemony** that James Lull explores in his chapter (I.4). While Karl Marx was one of the first major theorists to explore how the ideologies of the ruling class become the mainstream ideas of the time, theorists such as Antonio Gramsci, Louis Althusser, and Stuart Hall helped develop the more nuanced concept of hegemony that Lull defines as "the power or dominance that one social group holds over others" (p. 39). As Lull points out,

Owners and managers of media industries can produce and reproduce the content, inflections, and tones of ideas favorable to them far more easily than other social groups because they manage key socializing institutions, thereby guaranteeing that their points of view are constantly and attractively cast into the public arena. (p. 40)

Though many critical studies of media owned by private companies use the concept of hegemony, at first it seems more difficult to apply this notion to the Internet, which has been seen as a kind of "public sphere" in which many voices are heard, because there is an often-obscured, profit-oriented entity in control of production and distribution of media products. Indeed, somewhat grandiose and utopian claims were made in some circles about the new era of free expression and democratic cultural production the Internet would bring with it. But as John Bellamy Foster and Robert W. McChesney remind us in "The Internet's Unholy Marriage to Capitalism"

(I.5), there is a need to think more critically about the relationship between the Internet and capitalism. They argue: "There was—and remains—extraordinary democratic and revolutionary promise in this communication revolution. But technologies do not ride roughshod over history, regardless of their immense powers. They are developed in a social, political, and economic context" (p. 44).

The authors provide an account of the Internet's origins and an extensive analysis of the ways its development has been shaped by market forces. They conclude:

In a world in which private riches grow at the expense of public wealth, it should not surprise us that what seemed at first the enormous potential of the internet—representing a whole new realm of public wealth, analogous to the discovery of a whole new continent, and pointing to the possibility of a vast new democratic sphere of unrestricted communication—has vaporized in a couple of decades. (p. 48)

Like the Internet, reality television was once seen as an innovative media sphere where noncorporate voices could potentially predominate—in this case, because the audience supposedly can view real people filmed in the midst of an unpredictable, unscripted situation, rather than a drama scripted by writers and performed by professional actors. However, as Gareth Palmer's chapter (I.6) on the reality show *Extreme Makeover: Home Edition* argues, reality TV is no less ideological than other forms of media storytelling in the way it constructs our ideas about market forces, individualism, and economic inequality. Palmer sees this show, in which individual homeowners are assisted by neighbors and businesses in their quest for a dream home, as a kind of fairy tale with a happily-ever-after ending. According to Palmer's analysis, this television text tries to render invisible what he calls "the massive cracks . . . in the American Dream" (p. 56).

It does this by **encoding** the idea that government assistance no longer has any significant role to play in improving the lives of its citizens, a **neoliberal** theme that is also apparent in other media entertainment discussed in this book.

Textual analysis of the ideological dimension in media entertainment, such as that provided by Palmer, is an important component in understanding how the text works, especially when linked with background knowledge about the producers' political and economic interests; however, there is another element that students of media culture need to take into account. Irrespective of whether the media text appears to encode dominant or subversive cultural ideas, Kellner reminds us that as students of media culture, we cannot simply assume that we know how consumers of media texts actually read or **decode** them (constructing meaning from texts for themselves). For that piece of the equation, we must turn to studies of **audience reception**—how particular media consumers understand and use media texts.

Scholars widely agree that consumers of the media should not be conceptualized as passive pawns of media imagery, completely controlled by the dominant culture, but there are several different ways of understanding audience activity. First, according to the influential concept of **oppositional readings,** initiated by Stuart Hall (and also discussed by Kellner in I.1), the meaning of media texts cannot be established by only one critic's decoding of the text—no matter how subtle and full— because all texts are to some degree "open" (**polysemic,** or capable of multiple meanings). Therefore, we must also seek to know how audiences, both as individuals and as members of various communities, bring different experiences and complex identities to the processes of reading/viewing by which they actually feel, think about, and come to understand these texts.

According to Hall's paradigm, readers or audience members may do one of three things in relation to the intended or preferred meanings encoded in the text: (1) accept them uncritically and read the text as its producers intended, (2) produce a **negotiated reading** (partially **resisting** the encoded meaning), or (3) create an **oppositional** reading of their own, completely rejecting the preferred meaning of the text.

Janice Radway's classic ethnographic research into the audience reception of romance novels was an early and influential study of how specific readers actually engage with a mass media text. In "Women Read the Romance" (I.7), Radway looks closely at how a group of White lower-income women in the 1970s and 1980s negotiated with the genre of the romance novel, in terms of both the books they selected and the ways they actually read the text and appropriated and changed its meanings. Radway acknowledges that "romance reading . . . can function as a kind of training for the all-too-common task of reinterpreting a spouse's unsettling actions as the signs of passion, devotion, and love" (p. 65). Yet she sees, in these women's selection of certain books as favorites and their rejection of others, an active tendency to critique certain patriarchal masculine behaviors, substituting an ideal of the "nurturing" male that might have been missing in their own family lives. Through the act of reading itself, she argues, this group of women romance readers escaped temporarily from familial demands on their time, and Radway interprets this action as potential **resistance** to, or refusal to accept completely, the patriarchal restrictions on their lives. While encouraging respect for women's own experiences as cultural consumers, however, Radway warns that we should not confuse modes of resistance that reside in textual consumption with more practical, real-world modes of resistance (such as organized protest against the patriarchal abuses women such as these meet in real life).

Radway's work helped establish the field of audience studies, which has since developed into a rich body of research and interpretation. At the same time, over the past two decades or so, a distinct subfield of audience study has emerged, devoted to one particularly active kind of text consumer—the **fan**. In an early and influential essay, "*Star Trek* Rerun, Reread, Rewritten: Fan Writing as Textual Poaching" (I.8), Henry Jenkins III drew our attention to "a largely unexplored terrain of cultural activity, a subterranean network of readers and writers who remake [media texts] in their own image." For Jenkins and many who have been influenced by his work,

> "fandom" is a vehicle for marginalized subterranean groups (women, the young, gays, etc.) to pry open space for their cultural concerns within dominant representations; it is a way of appropriating media texts and rereading them in a fashion that serves different interests, a way of transforming mass culture into popular culture. (p. 70)

Drawing on his studies of fans organized around their mutual appreciation of the long-running television series centered on space exploration by a team of diverse characters, Jenkins brought to light a fascinating body of fan fiction written for the most part by female fans, whom he conceptualized as

> reluctant poachers who steal only those things that they truly love, who seize televisual property only to protect it against abuse by those who created it and who have claimed ownership over it. In embracing popular texts, the fans claim those works as their own, remaking them in their own image. . . . Consumption becomes production; reading becomes writing; spectator culture becomes participatory culture. (p. 76)

Following Jenkins's lead, contemporary fandom studies foreground the **agency** and creativity of culture consumers who go on to produce their own cultural materials, often through such "poaching" of ideas and materials from the original mass-produced texts. New digital technologies have clearly added to the opportunities available to do-it-yourself cultural producers outside of the commercial world of the media industries, including fans. Moreover, some fans have taken advantage of **social networking** sites on the Internet to facilitate not only their own fan networking but also a more politicized fan activism to protect favorite mass media culture texts from fates such as cancellation. (See Part VIII for examples of these kinds of fan activity and fan activism.)

Some critical media theorists have warned (as Kellner does) of the dangers of overemphasizing the power of media audiences to resist or effectively challenge the dominant ideologies that normalize social and economic inequities, simply through their activities as consumers—even if they become active fans. Mark Andrejevic, in "Watching Television Without Pity: The Productivity of Online Fans" (I.9) complicates our understanding of **active audiences** by examining the unpaid productive labor of fans who provide extensive viewer feedback to television writers and producers through an ostensibly independent and often highly critical website. As this ethnographic study of the fan forums argues, the producers have learned how to profit from this unpaid labor:

> As in the case of other forms of interactive commerce, the information provided by the viewers does not just add value to the product; it doubles as audience research. . . . TWoPpers [Television Without Pity contributors] may be working for free, but that does not mean they are not producing value. The work they do—the work of making their preferences transparent, of allowing themselves to be watched as they do their watching—is an increasingly important component of the emerging interactive economy. (p. 82)

The study found that many of the posters on this website see themselves as savvy, sophisticated media consumers/critics and often enjoy exercising their analytical and writing skills, as well as their ability, if limited, to influence the future development of their favorite shows. But Andrejevic points out,

> It is one thing to note that viewers derive pleasure and fulfillment from their online activities and quite another to suggest that pleasure is necessarily either empowering for viewers or destabilizing for entrenched forms of corporate control over popular culture. (p. 84)

He concludes that "a savvy identification with producers and insiders facilitated by interactive media fosters an acceptance of the rules of the game" (p. 85).

Throughout this section, the notion of resistance has already frequently surfaced, as it will throughout the rest of the book. Richard Butsch provides us with a detailed and challenging discussion of this notion in our final chapter of the section, "Reconsidering Resistance *and* Incorporation" (I.10). Some strands of cultural studies work on the media tend to ignore the more structured analysis of political economy, which foregrounds the inequality of access to media resources. Butsch's chapter is both a critique of an overly celebratory use of the idea of audience resistance and a call for a more nuanced understanding of how resistance and "incorporation" (the process by which resistance is co-opted and contained within hegemony) work together. In this way, he works to bridge competing paradigms within media studies.

We have aimed in this book to contribute to the project Butsch calls for. We invite you, the reader, to engage in a critical analysis of your own media consumption, exploring how you may be at times resisting the dominant ideologies while at other times unwittingly internalizing the "corporate voice" and seamlessly weaving it into your own social construction of reality.

1

Cultural Studies, Multiculturalism, and Media Culture

Douglas Kellner

Radio, television, film, popular music, the Internet and social networking, and other forms and products of media culture provide materials out of which we forge our very identities, including our sense of selfhood; our notion of what it means to be male or female; our conception of class, ethnicity and race, nationality, sexuality; and division of the world into categories of "us" and "them." Media images help shape our view of the world and our deepest values: what we consider good or bad, positive or negative, moral or evil. Media stories provide the symbols, myths, and resources through which we constitute a common culture and through the appropriation of which we insert ourselves into this culture. Media spectacles demonstrate who has power and who is powerless, who is allowed to exercise force and violence and who is not. They dramatize and legitimate the power of the forces that be and show the powerless that they must stay in their places or be oppressed.

We are immersed from cradle to grave in a media and consumer society, and thus it is important to learn how to understand, interpret, and criticize its meanings and messages. The media are a profound and often misperceived source of cultural pedagogy: They contribute to educating us how to behave and what to think, feel, believe, fear, and desire—and what not to. The media are forms of pedagogy that teach us how to be men and women. They show us how to dress, look, and consume; how to react to members of different social groups; how to be popular and successful and how to avoid failure; and how to conform to the dominant system of norms, values, practices, and institutions. Consequently, the gaining of critical media literacy is an important resource for individuals and citizens in learning how to cope with a seductive cultural environment. Learning how to read, criticize, and resist sociocultural manipulation can help one empower oneself in relation to dominant forms of media and culture. It can enhance individual sovereignty vis-à-vis media culture and give people more power over their cultural environment.

In this chapter, I will discuss the potential contributions of a cultural studies perspective to media critique and literacy. From the 1980s to the present, cultural studies has emerged as a set of approaches to the study of culture, society, and politics. The project was

This piece is an original essay that was commissioned for this volume. It has been updated from an earlier version that appeared in the third edition.

inaugurated by the University of Birmingham Centre for Contemporary Cultural Studies, which developed a variety of critical methods for the analysis, interpretation, and criticism of cultural artifacts. Through a set of internal debates, and responding to social struggles and movements of the 1960s and 1970s, the Birmingham group came to focus on the interplay of representations and ideologies of class, gender, race, ethnicity, and nationality in cultural texts, including media culture. They were among the first to study the effects on audiences of newspapers, radio, television, film, advertising, and other popular cultural forms. They also focused on how various audiences interpreted and used media culture differently, analyzing the factors that made different audiences respond in contrasting ways to various media texts, and how they made use of media in their personal and social lives in a multiplicity of ways.[1]

Through studies of youth subcultures, British cultural studies demonstrated how culture came to constitute distinct forms of identity and group membership for young people. In the view of cultural studies, media culture provides the materials for constructing views of the world, behavior, and even identities. Those who uncritically follow the dictates of media culture tend to "mainstream" themselves, conforming to the dominant fashion, values, and behavior. Yet cultural studies is also interested in how subcultural groups and individuals resist dominant forms of culture and identity, creating their own style and identities. Those who obey ruling dress and fashion codes, behavior, and political ideologies thus produce their identities as members of specific social groupings within contemporary U.S. culture, such as White, middle-class, conservative American men, or lesbian African American women, for instance. Persons who identify with subcultures, such as punk culture or Latino subcultures, dress and act differently than those in the mainstream and thus create oppositional identities, defining themselves against standard models.

Cultural studies insists that culture must be studied within the social relations and system through which culture is produced and consumed and that the study of culture is thus intimately bound up with the study of society, politics, and economics. Cultural studies shows how media culture articulates the dominant values, political ideologies, and social developments and novelties of the era. It conceives of U.S. culture and society as a contested terrain, with various groups and ideologies struggling for dominance (Kellner, 1995, 2010). Television, film, music, and other popular cultural forms are thus often liberal or conservative, or occasionally express more radical or oppositional views—and can be contradictory and ambiguous as well in their meanings and messages.

Cultural studies is valuable because it provides some tools that enable individuals to read and interpret culture critically. It also subverts distinctions between "high" and "low" culture by considering a wide continuum of cultural artifacts, from opera and novels to soap operas and TV wrestling, while refusing to erect any specific elite cultural hierarchies or canons. Earlier mainstream academic approaches to culture tended to be primarily literary and elitist, dismissing media culture as banal, trashy, and not worthy of serious attention. The project of cultural studies, in contrast, avoids cutting the field of culture into high and low, or popular versus elite. Such distinctions are difficult to maintain and generally serve as a front for normative aesthetic valuations and, often, a political program (i.e., either dismissing mass culture for high culture/art or celebrating what is deemed "popular" while scorning "elitist" high culture).

Cultural studies allows us to examine and critically scrutinize the whole range of culture without prior prejudices toward one or another sort of cultural text, institution, or practice. It also opens the way toward more differentiated political, rather than aesthetic, valuations of cultural artifacts in which one attempts to distinguish critical and oppositional from conformist and conservative moments in a given cultural artifact. For instance, studies of Hollywood film show how key 1960s films promoted the views of radicals and the counterculture and how film in the 1970s was a battleground between liberal and conservative positions; late 1970s films, however, tended toward conservative positions that helped elect Ronald Reagan as president (see Kellner & Ryan, 1988). During the Bush–Cheney era, there were many oppositional films, such as the work of Michael Moore, and liberal films that featured black heroes and anticipated the election of Barack Obama (Kellner, 2010). For instance, African American actor Will Smith was the top grossing U.S. actor during the Bush–Cheney era, Denzel Washington won two Academy Awards and played a wide range of characters, and Morgan Freeman played a president, corporate executive, crime figure, and even God, attesting that U.S. publics were ready to see African Americans in major positions in all arenas of society. This is not to say that Hollywood "caused" Obama's surprising victory in 2008 but that U.S. media culture anticipated a black president.

There is an intrinsically critical and political dimension to the project of cultural studies that distinguishes it from objectivist and apolitical academic approaches to the study of culture and society. British cultural studies, for example, analyzed culture historically in the context of its societal origins and effects. It situated culture within a theory of social production and reproduction, specifying the ways cultural forms served either to further social domination or to enable people to resist and struggle against domination. It analyzed society as a hierarchical and antagonistic set of social relations characterized by the oppression of subordinate class, gender, race, ethnic, and national strata. Employing the Italian sociologist Antonio Gramsci's (1971) model of hegemony and counterhegemony, it sought to analyze "hegemonic" or ruling, social, and cultural forces of domination and to seek "counterhegemonic" forces of resistance and struggle. The project was aimed at social transformation and attempted to specify forces of domination and resistance to aid the process of political struggle and emancipation from oppression and domination.

For cultural studies, the concept of ideology is of central importance, for dominant ideologies serve to reproduce social relations of domination and subordination.[2] Ideologies of class, for instance, celebrate upper-class life and denigrate the working class. Ideologies of gender promote sexist representations of women, oppressive ideologies of sexuality promote homophobia, and ideologies of race use racist representations of people of color and various minority groups. Ideologies make inequalities and subordination appear natural and just and thus induce consent to relations of domination. Contemporary societies are structured by opposing groups who have different political ideologies (liberal, conservative, radical, etc.), and cultural studies specifies what, if any, ideologies are operative in a given cultural artifact (which could involve, of course, the specification of ambiguities and ideological contradictions). In the course of this study, I will provide some examples of how different ideologies are operative in media cultural texts and will accordingly provide examples of ideological analysis and critique.

Because of its focus on representations of race, gender, sexuality, and class, and its critique of ideologies that promote various forms of oppression, cultural studies lends itself to a multiculturalist program that demonstrates how culture reproduces certain forms of racism, sexism, and biases against members of subordinate classes, social groups, or alternative lifestyles. Multiculturalism affirms the worth of different types of culture and cultural groups, claiming, for instance, that Black; Latino; Asian; Native American; lesbian, gay, bisexual, transgendered, and questioning (LGBTQ); and other oppressed and marginalized voices have their own validity and importance. An insurgent multiculturalism attempts to show how various people's voices and experiences are silenced and omitted from mainstream culture, and struggles to aid in the articulation of diverse views, experiences, and cultural forms from groups excluded from the mainstream. This makes it a target of conservative forces that wish to preserve the existing canons of White male, Eurocentric privilege, and thus attack multiculturalism in cultural wars raging from the 1960s to the present over education, the arts, and the limits of free expression.

Cultural studies thus promotes a critical multiculturalist politics and media pedagogy that aims to make people sensitive to how relations of power and domination are "encoded" in cultural texts, such as those of television and film, or how new technologies and media such as the Internet and social networking can be used for oppositional pedagogical or political purposes (Kahn & Kellner, 2008). A critical cultural studies approach also specifies how people can resist the dominant encoded meanings and produce their own critical and alternative readings and media artifacts, as well as new identities and social relations. Cultural studies can show how media culture manipulates and indoctrinates us and thus can empower individuals to resist the dominant meanings in media cultural products and produce their own meanings. It can also point to moments of resistance and criticism within media culture and thus help promote development of more critical consciousness.

A critical cultural studies approach—embodied in many of the articles collected in this reader—thus develops concepts and analyses that will enable readers to analytically dissect the artifacts of contemporary media culture and gain power over their cultural environment. By exposing the entire field of culture and media technology to knowledgeable scrutiny, cultural studies provides a broad, comprehensive framework to undertake studies of culture, politics, and society for the purposes of individual empowerment and social and political struggle and transformation. In the following pages, I will therefore indicate some of the chief components of the

type of cultural studies I find most useful for understanding contemporary U.S. society, culture, and politics.

Components of a Critical Cultural Studies Approach

As a theoretical apparatus, cultural studies contains a threefold project of analyzing the production and political economy of culture, cultural texts, and the audience reception of those texts and their effects in a concrete sociohistorical context. This comprehensive approach avoids too narrowly focusing on one dimension of the project to the exclusion of others. To avoid such limitations, I propose a multiperspectival approach that (a) discusses production and political economy, (b) engages in textual analysis, and (c) studies the reception and use of cultural texts.[3]

Production and Political Economy

Since cultural production has been neglected in many modes of recent cultural studies, it is important to stress the importance of analyzing cultural texts within their system of production and distribution, often referred to as the political economy of culture.[4] Inserting texts into the system of culture within which they are produced and distributed can help elucidate features and effects of the texts that textual analysis alone might miss or downplay. Rather than being an antithetical approach to culture, political economy can actually contribute to textual analysis and critique. The system of production often determines, in part, what sorts of artifacts will be produced, what structural limits will determine what can and cannot be said and shown, and what sorts of audience effects the text may generate.

Study of the codes of television, film, or popular music, for instance, is enhanced by studying the formulas and conventions of production, which are shaped by economic and technical, as well as aesthetic and cultural, considerations. Dominant cultural forms are structured by well-defined rules and conventions, and the study of the production of culture can help elucidate the codes actually in play. Because of the demands of the format of radio or music television, for instance, most popular songs are 3 to 5 minutes long, fitting into the format of the distribution system, just as the length of content on YouTube or Twitter has technical constraints. From the early years of the Internet to the present, there have been legal and political conflicts concerning file sharing of music, other forms of media culture, and information, situating media culture in a force field of political conflict. Because of their control by giant corporations oriented primarily toward profit, film and television production in the United States is dominated by specific genres such as talk and game shows, soap operas, situation comedies, action/adventure series, reality TV series, and so on, which are familiar and popular with audiences. This economic factor explains why there are cycles of certain genres and subgenres, sequelmania in the film industry, crossovers of popular films into television series, and a certain homogeneity in products constituted within systems of production marked by relatively rigid generic codes, formulaic conventions, and well-defined ideological boundaries.

Likewise, study of political economy can help determine the limits and range of political and ideological discourses and effects. My study of television in the United States, for instance, disclosed that the takeover of the television networks by major transnational corporations and communications conglomerates in the 1980s was part of a "right turn" within U.S. society, whereby powerful corporate groups won control of the state and the mainstream media (Kellner, 1990). For example, during the 1980s, all three networks were

taken over by major corporate conglomerates: ABC was taken over in 1985 by Capital Cities, NBC was taken over by GE, and CBS was taken over by the Tisch Financial Group. Both ABC and NBC sought corporate mergers, and this motivation, along with other benefits derived from Reaganism, might well have influenced them to downplay criticisms of Reagan and generally support his conservative programs, military adventures, and simulated presidency.

Corporate conglomeratization has intensified further, and today Time Warner, Disney, Rupert Murdoch's News Corporation, Viacom, and other global media conglomerates control ever more domains of the production and distribution of culture (McChesney, 2000, 2007). In this global context, one cannot really analyze the role of the media in the Gulf War, for instance, without also analyzing the production and political economy of news and information, as well as the actual text of the Gulf War and its reception by its audience (see Kellner, 1992). Likewise, the ownership by conservative corporations of dominant media corporations helps explain mainstream media support of the Bush–Cheney administration and its policies, such as the wars in Afghanistan and Iraq (Kellner, 2003, 2005).

Looking toward entertainment, female pop music stars such as Madonna, Britney Spears, Beyoncé, and Lady Gaga deploy the tools of the glamour industry and media spectacle to become icons of fashion, beauty, style, and sexuality, as well as purveyors of music. And in appraising the full social impact of pornography, one needs to be aware of the immense profits generated by the sex industry and the potential for harm endemic to the production process of, say, pornographic films and videos, and not just dwell on the texts themselves and their effects on audiences.

Furthermore, in an era of globalization, one must be aware of the global networks that produce and distribute culture in the interests of profit and corporate hegemony. The Internet and new media link the globe and distribute more culture to more people than at any time in history, yet giant media conglomerates and institutions, such as the state, that can exert censorship continue to be major forces of cultural hegemony (see McChesney 2013). Yet political economy alone does not hold the key to cultural studies, and important as it is, it has limitations as a single approach. Some political economy analyses reduce the meanings and effects of texts to rather circumscribed and reductive ideological functions, arguing that media culture merely reflects the ideology of the ruling economic elite that controls the culture industries and is nothing more than a vehicle for capitalist ideology. It is true that media culture overwhelmingly supports capitalist values, but it is also a site of intense struggle between different races, classes, genders, and social groups. It is also possible in the age of new media and social networking for consumers to become producers of their own media content and form, including oppositional voices and resistance. Thus, to fully grasp the nature and effects of media culture, one needs to develop methods to analyze the full range of its meanings and effects that are sensitive to the always mutating terrain of media culture and technology.

Textual Analysis

The products of media culture require multidimensional close textual readings to analyze their various forms of discourses, ideological positions, narrative strategies, image construction, and effects. "Reading" an artifact of media culture involves interpreting the forms and meanings of elements in a music video or television ad as one might read and interpret a book. There has been a wide range of types of textual criticism of media culture, from quantitative content analysis that dissects the number of,

say, episodes of violence in a text to qualitative study that examines representations of women, Blacks, or other groups, or applies various critical theories to unpack the meanings of the texts or explicate how texts function to produce meaning. Traditionally, the qualitative analysis of texts attended to the formal artistic properties of imaginative literature—such as style, verbal imagery, characterization, narrative structure, and point of view. From the 1960s on, however, literary-formalist textual analysis has been enhanced by methods derived from semiotics, a system for investigating the creation of meaning not only in written languages but also in other, nonverbal codes, such as the visual and auditory languages of film and TV.

Semiotics analyzes how linguistic and nonlinguistic cultural "signs" form systems of meanings, as when giving someone a rose is interpreted as a sign of love or getting an A on a college paper is a sign of mastery of the rules of the specific assignment. Semiotic analysis can be connected with genre criticism (the study of conventions governing long-established types of cultural forms, such as soap operas) to reveal how the codes and forms of particular genres construct certain meanings. Situation comedies, for instance, classically follow a conflict/resolution model that demonstrates how to solve certain social problems with correct actions and values, and they thus provide morality tales of proper and improper behavior. Soap operas, by contrast, proliferate problems and provide messages concerning the endurance and suffering needed to get through life's endless miseries, while generating positive and negative models of social behavior. And advertising shows how commodity solutions solve problems of popularity, acceptance, success, and the like.

A semiotic and genre analysis of the film *Rambo* (1982), for instance, would show how it follows the conventions of the Hollywood genre of the war film that dramatizes conflicts between the United

States and its "enemies" (see Kellner, 1995). Semiotics describes how the images of the villains are constructed according to the codes of World War II movies and how the resolution of the conflict and happy ending follow the tradition of Hollywood classical cinema, which portray the victory of good over evil. Semiotic analysis would also include study of the strictly cinematic and formal elements of a film such as *Rambo*, dissecting the ways camera angles present Rambo as a god or how slow-motion images of him gliding through the jungle code him as a force of nature. Formal analysis of a film also includes how lighting is used to code characters as "good" or "evil," or how any of the technical features of film production can help generate meanings.

Similarly, a semiotic analysis of James Cameron's *Avatar* (2009) would reveal how the images in the film present an anti-militarist and pro-ecological agenda, although the narrative form celebrates a White, male savior, replicating more conservative narratives. *Avatar* also demonstrates how fantasy artifacts can project a wealth of political and ideological meanings, often ambiguous or contradictory. Discussions of *Avatar* have also generated heated debates in the politics of representation, concerning how the film has represented gender, sexuality, race, the military, and the environment, as well as other themes and dimensions of the film (see Kellner, 2010).

The textual analysis of cultural studies thus combines formalist analysis with critique of how cultural meanings convey specific ideologies of gender, race, class, sexuality, nation, and other ideological dimensions. Ideologies refer to ideas or images that construct the superiority of one class or group over others (i.e., men over women, Whites over people of color, ruling elites over working-class people, etc.) and thus reproduce and legitimate different forms of social domination. Ideological textual analysis should deploy a wide range of methods to fully explicate

each dimension of ideological domination across representations of class, race, gender, and sexuality, and other forms of domination and subordination and to show how specific narratives serve interests of domination and oppression, contest it, or are ambiguous (as with many examples of media culture). Each critical method focuses on certain features of a text from a specific perspective: The perspective spotlights, or illuminates, some features of a text while ignoring others. Marxist methods tend to focus on class, for instance, while feminist approaches highlight gender, critical race theory emphasizes race and ethnicity, and gay and lesbian theories explicate sexuality. Yet today, the concept of "intersectionality" is often used, and many feminists, Marxists, critical race scholars, and other forms of cultural studies depict how gender, class, race, sexuality, and other components intersect and co-construct each other in complex cultural ways (see Crenshaw, 1991).

Various critical methods have their own strengths and limitations, their optics and blind spots. Traditionally, Marxian ideology critiques have been strong on class and historical contextualization and weak on formal analysis, while some versions are highly "reductionist," reducing textual analysis to denunciation of ruling class ideology. Feminism excels in gender analysis and in some versions is formally sophisticated, drawing on such methods as psychoanalysis and semiotics, although some versions are reductive, and early feminism often limited itself to analysis of images of gender. Psychoanalysis in turn calls for the interpretation of unconscious contents and meaning, which can articulate latent meanings in a text, as when Alfred Hitchcock's dream sequences project cinematic symbols that illuminate his characters' dilemmas or when the image of the female character in *Bonnie and Clyde* (1967), framed against the bar of her bed, suggests her sexual frustration, imprisonment in middle-class family life, and need to revolt.

Of course, each reading of a text is only one possible reading from one critic's subjective position, no matter how multi-perspectival, and may or may not be the reading preferred by audiences (which themselves will be significantly different according to class, race, gender, ethnicity, ideology, and so on). Because there is a split between textual encoding and audience decoding, there is always the possibility for a multiplicity of readings of any text of media culture (Hall, 1980b). There are limits to the openness or polysemic nature of any text, of course, and textual analysis can explicate the parameters of possible readings and delineate perspectives that aim at illuminating the text and its cultural and ideological effects. Such analysis also provides the materials for criticizing misreadings, or readings that are one-sided and incomplete. Yet to further carry through a cultural studies analysis, one must also examine how diverse audiences actually read media texts and attempt to determine what impact or influence they have on audience thought and behavior.

Audience Reception and Use of Media Culture

All texts are subject to multiple readings depending on the perspectives and subject positions of the reader. Members of distinct genders, classes, races, nations, regions, sexual preferences, and political ideologies are going to read texts differently, and cultural studies can illuminate why diverse audiences interpret texts in various, sometimes conflicting, ways. Media culture provides materials for individuals and communities to create identities and meanings, and cultural studies work on audiences detects a variety of potentially empowering uses of cultural forms. One of the merits of cultural studies is that it has focused on audience reception and fan appropriation, and this focus provides one of its major contributions, although there are also some limitations and problems with the standard cultural studies approaches to the audience.[5]

Ethnographic research studies people and their groups and cultures and is frequently used in an attempt to determine how media texts affect specific audiences and shape their beliefs and behavior. Ethnographic cultural studies have indicated some of the various ways audiences use and appropriate texts, often to empower themselves. For example, teenagers use video games and music television to escape from the demands of a disciplinary society. Males use sports media events as a terrain of fantasy identification, in which they feel empowered as "their" team or star triumphs. Such sports events also generate a form of community currently being lost in the privatized media and consumer culture of our time. Indeed, fandoms of all sorts, from *Star Trek* fans ("Trekkies"/"Trekkers") to devotees of various soap operas, reality shows, or current highly popular TV series, also form communities that enable them to relate to others who share their interests and hobbies. Some fans, in fact, actively re-create their favorite cultural forms (see examples in Jenkins, 1992; Lewis, 1992; and Gray, Sandvoss, & Harrington, 2007). Other studies have shown that audiences can subvert the intentions of the producers or managers of the cultural industries that supply them, as when astute young media users laugh at obvious attempts to hype certain characters, shows, or products (see de Certeau, 1984, for more examples of audiences constructing meaning and engaging in practices in critical and subversive ways).

The emphasis on active audience reception and appropriation, then, has helped cultural studies overcome the previously one-sided textualist orientations to culture and also has directed focus to the actual political effects texts may have. By combining quantitative and qualitative research, audience reception and fandom studies—including some of the chapters in this reader—are providing important contributions to how people interact with cultural texts.

Yet I see several problems with reception studies as they have been constituted within cultural studies, particularly in the United States. Importantly, there is a danger that class will be downplayed as a significant variable that structures audience decoding and use of cultural texts. Cultural studies in England were particularly sensitive to class differences—as well as subcultural differences—in the use and reception of cultural texts, but I have noted many dissertations, books, and articles in cultural studies in the United States in which attention to class has been downplayed or is missing altogether. This is not surprising, as a neglect of class as a constitutive feature of culture and society is endemic in the American academy in most disciplines.

There is also the reverse danger, however, of exaggerating the constitutive force of class and downplaying, or ignoring, such other variables as gender and ethnicity. Staiger (1992) noted that Fiske, building on Hartley, lists seven "subjectivity positions" that are important in cultural reception—"self, gender, age-group, family, class, nation, ethnicity"—and proposes adding sexuality. All these factors, and no doubt more, interact in shaping how audiences receive and use texts and must be taken into account in studying cultural reception, for audiences decode and use texts according to the specific constituents of their class, race or ethnicity, gender, sexual preference, and so on.

Furthermore, I would warn against a tendency to romanticize the "active audience" by claiming that all audiences produce their own meanings and denying that media culture may have powerful manipulative effects. There is a tendency within the cultural studies tradition of reception research to dichotomize between dominant and oppositional readings (Hall, 1980b). "Dominant" readings are those in which audiences appropriate texts in line with the interests of the dominant culture and the ideological intentions of a text, as when audiences feel pleasure in the restoration of male power, law and order, and social stability at the end of a film such as *Die Hard,* after the hero and representatives of authority eliminate the terrorists who had taken over a high-rise corporate headquarters. An "oppositional" reading, in contrast, celebrates the resistance to this reading in audience appropriation of a text. For example, Fiske (1993) observed (and implicitly approved) resistance to dominant readings when homeless individuals in a shelter cheered the violent destruction of police and authority figures during repeated viewings of a videotape of *Die Hard.*

Fiske's study illustrates a tendency in cultural studies to celebrate resistance per se without distinguishing between types and forms of resistance (a similar problem resides with indiscriminate celebration of audience pleasure in certain reception studies). For example, some would argue that the violent resistance to social authority valorized in this reading of *Die Hard* glamorizes brutal, masculinist behavior and the use of physical violence to solve social problems. It is true that theorists of revolution, including Jean-Paul Sartre, Frantz Fanon, and Herbert Marcuse, among others, have argued that violence can be either emancipatory, when directed at forces of oppression, or reactionary, when directed at popular forces struggling against oppression. In contrast, many feminists and those in the Gandhian tradition see all violence against others as a form of brutal, masculinist behavior, and many people see it as a problematic form of conflict resolution. Thus, audience pleasure in violent resistance cannot be valorized per se as a progressive element of the appropriation of cultural texts. Instead, difficult discriminations must be made as to whether the resistance, oppositional reading, or pleasure in a given experience should be understood as progressive or reactionary, emancipatory or destructive.

Thus, while emphasis on the audience and reception was an excellent correction to the one-sidedness of purely textual analysis, I believe that in recent years, cultural studies has overemphasized reception and textual analysis while underemphasizing the production of culture and its political economy. This type of cultural studies fetishizes audience reception studies and neglects both production and textual analysis, thus producing populist celebrations of the text and audience pleasure in its use of cultural artifacts. This approach, taken to an extreme, would lose its critical perspective and put a positive gloss on audience experience of whatever is being studied. Such studies also might lose sight of the manipulative and conservative effects of certain types of media culture and thus serve the interests of the cultural industries as they are presently constituted.

No doubt, media effects are complex and controversial, and it is the merit of cultural studies to make the analysis of such effects an important part of its agenda. Previous studies of the audience and reception of media privileged ethnographic studies that selected slices of the vast media audiences, usually from the sites where researchers themselves lived. Such studies are invariably limited, and broader effects research can indicate how the most popular artifacts of media culture have a wide range of effects.

One new way to research media effects is to use Google, or databases that collect media texts, to trace certain effects of media artifacts through analysis of references to them in the journalistic media. Likewise, a new terrain of Internet audience research studies how fans act in chat rooms or on fansites devoted to their favorite artifacts of media culture. New media such as Facebook, YouTube, Twitter, and other social networking sites produce forums for more active audiences, as well as new sites for audience research. As audiences critically discuss or celebrate their preferred artifacts of media culture and, in some cases, produce their own versions, disseminated to audiences throughout the Internet and via new digital technologies, media culture expands its reach and power while audiences can feel that they are part of their preferred cultural sites and phenomena. Studies are proliferating in this field, examining how Facebook, YouTube, Twitter, and other new media are used by individuals and groups in diverse ways, from sharing pictures and media content to social networking to political expression and organizing and pedagogical purposes (Kellner & Kim, 2010).

Toward a Cultural Studies That Is Critical, Multicultural, and Multiperspectival

To avoid the one-sidedness of textual analysis approaches or audience and reception studies, I propose that cultural studies itself be multiperspectival, getting at culture from the perspectives of political economy, text analysis, and audience reception, as outlined above. Textual analysis should use a multiplicity of perspectives and critical methods, and audience reception studies should delineate the wide range of subject positions, or perspectives, through which audiences appropriate culture. This requires a multicultural approach that sees the importance of analyzing the dimensions of class, race and ethnicity, and gender and sexual preference within the texts of media culture, while also studying their impact on how audiences read and interpret media culture.

In addition, a critical cultural studies approach attacks sexism, heterosexism, racism, and bias against specific social groups (i.e., gays, intellectuals, seniors, etc.) and criticizes texts that promote any kind of domination or oppression. As an example of how considerations of production, textual analysis, and audience readings can fruitfully intersect in cultural studies, let us reflect on the Madonna phenomenon.

Madonna came on the scene in the moment of Reaganism and embodied the materialistic and consumer-oriented ethos of the 1980s ("Material Girl"). She also appeared in a time of dramatic image proliferation, associated with MTV, fashion fever, and intense marketing of products. Madonna was one of the first MTV music video superstars who consciously crafted images to attract a mass audience. Her early music videos were aimed at teenage girls (the Madonna wannabes), but she soon incorporated Black, Hispanic, and minority audiences with her images of interracial sex and multicultural "family" in her concerts. She also appealed to gay and lesbian audiences, as well as feminist and academic audiences, as her videos became more complex and political (e.g., "Like a Prayer," "Express Yourself," "Vogue," etc.).

Thus, Madonna's popularity was in large part a function of her marketing strategies and her production of music videos and images that appealed to diverse audiences. To conceptualize the meanings and effects in her music, films, concerts, and public relations stunts requires that her artifacts be interpreted within the context of their production and reception, which involves discussion of MTV, the music industry, concerts, marketing, and the production of images (see Kellner, 1995). Understanding Madonna's popularity also requires focus on audiences, not just as individuals but as members of specific groups—such as teenage girls, who were empowered by Madonna in their struggles for individual identity, or gays, who were also empowered by her incorporation of alternative images of sexuality within popular mainstream cultural artifacts. Yet appraising the politics and effects of Madonna also requires analysis of how her work might merely reproduce a consumer culture that defines identity in terms of images and consumption. It would make an interesting project to examine how former Madonna fans view the superstar's evolution and recent incarnations, such as her many relationships and marriages and ongoing world tours, as well as to examine how contemporary fans view Madonna in an age that embraces pop singers such as Beyoncé and Lady Gaga.

Likewise, Michael Jackson's initial popularity derived from carefully managed media spectacles, first in the Jackson Five and then in his own career. Jackson achieved his superstar status, like Madonna, from his MTV-disseminated music videos and spectacular concert performances, in which promotion, image management, and his publicity apparatus made him the King of Pop. While, like Madonna, his frequent tabloid and media presence helped promote his career, media spectacle and tabloids also derailed it, as he was charged with child abuse in well-publicized cases. After his death in 2009, however, Jackson had a remarkable surge in popularity as his works were disseminated through the media, including new media and social networking sites.

Cultural Studies for the 21st Century

As discussed above, a cultural studies that is critical and multicultural provides comprehensive approaches to culture that can be applied to a wide variety of media artifacts, from advertising and pornography to Beyoncé and the *Twilight* series, from reality TV and *World of Warcraft* to Barbie and *Avatar*. Its comprehensive perspectives encompass political economy, textual analysis, and audience research and provide critical and political perspectives that enable individuals to dissect the meanings, messages, and effects of dominant cultural forms. Cultural studies is thus part of a critical media pedagogy that enables individuals to resist media manipulation and increase their freedom and individuality. It can empower people to gain sovereignty over their culture and struggle for alternative cultures and political change. Thus, cultural studies is not just another academic fad but, rather, can be part of a struggle for a better society and a better life.

Notes

1. For more information on British cultural studies, see Agger (1992); Durham and Kellner (2012); During (1992, 1998); Fiske (1986); Grossberg (1989); Grossberg, Nelson, and Treichler (1992); Hall (1980b); Hammer and Kellner (2009); Johnson (1986–1987); O'Connor (1989); and Turner (1990). The Frankfurt school also provided much material for a critical cultural studies approach in its works on mass culture from the 1930s through the present; on the relation between the Frankfurt school and British cultural studies, see Kellner (1997).

2. On the concept of ideology, see the Centre for Contemporary Cultural Studies (1980), Kellner (1978, 1979), Kellner and Ryan (1988), and Thompson (1990).

3. This model was adumbrated in Hall (1980a) and Johnson (1986–1987), and guided much of the early Birmingham work. Around the mid-1980s, however, the Birmingham group began to increasingly neglect the production and political economy of culture (some believe that this was always a problem with their work), and the majority of their studies became more academic, cut off from political struggle. I am thus trying to recapture the spirit of the early Birmingham project, reconstructed for our contemporary moment. For a fuller development of my conception of cultural studies, see Kellner (1992, 1995, 2001, 2010).

4. The term *political economy* calls attention to the fact that the production and distribution of culture take place within a specific economic system, constituted by relations between the state and economy. For instance, in the United States, a capitalist economy dictates that cultural production is governed by laws of the market, but the democratic imperatives of the system mean that there is some regulation of culture by the state. There are often tensions within a given society concerning how many activities should be governed by the imperatives of the market, or

economics, alone and how much state regulation or intervention is desirable to ensure a wider diversity of broadcast programming, for instance, or the prohibition of phenomena agreed to be harmful, such as cigarette advertising or pornography (see Kellner, 1990; McChesney, 2007).

5. Influential cultural studies that have focused on audience reception include Ang (1985, 1996), Brunsdon and Morley (1978), Fiske (1989a, 1989b), Jenkins (1992), Lewis (1992), Morley (1986), and Radway (1983). On "fandom," see Gray, Sandvoss, and Harrington (2007).

References

Agger, B. (1992). *Cultural studies*. London: Falmer.

Ang, I. (1985). *Watching* Dallas. New York: Methuen.

Ang, I. (1996). *Living room wars: Rethinking media audiences for a postmodern world*. London: Routledge.

Brunsdon, C., & Morley, D. (1978). *Everyday television: "Nationwide."* London: British Film Institute.

Centre for Contemporary Cultural Studies. (1980). *On ideology*. London: Hutchinson.

Crenshaw, K. W. (1991). Mapping the margins: Intersectionality, identity politics, and violence against women of color. *Stanford Law Review, 43*(6), 1241–1299.

de Certeau, M. (1984). *The practice of everyday life*. Berkeley: University of California Press.

Durham, M. G., & Kellner, D. (Eds.). (2012). *Media and cultural studies: Key works* (Rev. 2nd ed.). Malden, MA: Blackwell.

During, S. (1992, 1998). *Cultural studies*. London: Routledge.

Fiske, J. (1986). British cultural studies and television. In R. C. Allen (Ed.), *Channels of discourse* (pp. 254–289). Chapel Hill: University of North Carolina Press.

Fiske, J. (1989a). *Reading the popular*. Boston: Unwin Hyman.

Fiske, J. (1989b). *Understanding popular culture*. Boston: Unwin Hyman.

Fiske, J. (1993). *Power plays, power works*. London: Verso.

Gramsci, A. (1971). *Selections from the prison notebooks of Antonio Gramsci* (Q. Hoare & G. Nowell Smith, Eds.). New York: International.

Gray, J., Sandvoss, C., & Harrington, C. L. (Eds.). (2007). *Fandom: Identities and communities in a mediated world.* New York: New York University Press.

Grossberg, L. (1989). The formations of cultural studies: An American in Birmingham. *Strategies, 22,* 114–149.

Grossberg, L., Nelson, C., & Treichler, P. (1992). *Cultural studies.* New York: Routledge.

Hall, S. (1980a). Cultural studies and the Centre: Some problematics and problems. In S. Hall, D. Hobson, A. Lowe, & P. Willis (Eds.), *Culture, media, language: Working papers in cultural studies, 1972–79* (pp. 15–47). London: Hutchinson.

Hall, S. (1980b). Encoding/decoding. In S. Hall, D. Hobson, A. Lowe, & P. Willis (Eds.), *Culture, media, language: Working papers in cultural studies, 1972–79* (pp. 128–138). London: Hutchinson.

Hammer, R., & Kellner, D. (2009). *Media/cultural studies: Critical approaches.* New York: Peter Lang.

Jenkins, H. (1992). *Textual poachers.* New York: Routledge.

Johnson, R. (1986–1987). What is cultural studies anyway? *Social Text, 16,* 38–80.

Kahn, R., & Kellner, D. (2008). Technopolitics, blogs, and emergent media ecologies: A critical/reconstructive approach. In B. Hawk, D. M. Rider, & O. Oviedo (Eds.), *Small tech: The culture of digital tools* (pp. 22–37). Minneapolis: University of Minnesota Press.

Kellner, D. (1978, November–December). Ideology, Marxism, and advanced capitalism. *Socialist Review, 42,* 37–65.

Kellner, D. (1979, May–June). TV, ideology, and emancipatory popular culture. *Socialist Review, 45,* 13–53.

Kellner, D. (1990). *Television and the crisis of democracy.* Boulder, CO: Westview.

Kellner, D. (1992). *The Persian Gulf TV war.* Boulder, CO: Westview.

Kellner, D. (1995). *Media culture: Cultural studies, identity, and politics between the modern and the postmodern.* London: Routledge.

Kellner, D. (1997). Critical theory and British cultural studies: The missed articulation. In J. McGuigan (Ed.), *Cultural methodologies* (pp. 12–41). London: Sage.

Kellner, D. (2001). *Grand Theft 2000.* Lanham, MD: Rowman & Littlefield.

Kellner, D. (2003). *From September 11 to terror war: The dangers of the Bush legacy.* Lanham, MD: Rowman & Littlefield.

Kellner, D. (2005). *Media spectacle and the crisis of democracy.* Boulder, CO: Paradigm.

Kellner, D. (2010). *Cinema wars: Hollywood film and politics in the Bush/Cheney era.* Malden, MA: Blackwell.

Kellner, D., & Kim, G. (2010). YouTube, critical pedagogy, and media activism. *Review of Education/Pedagogy/Cultural Studies, 32*(1), 3–36.

Kellner, D., & Ryan, M. (1988). *Camera politica: The politics and ideology of contemporary Hollywood film.* Bloomington: Indiana University Press.

Lewis, L. A. (1992). *Adoring audience: Fan culture and popular media.* New York: Routledge.

McChesney, R. (2000). *Rich media, poor democracy: Communications politics in dubious times.* New York: New Press.

McChesney, R. (2007). *Communication revolution: Critical junctures and the future of media.* New York: New Press.

McChesney, R. (2013). *Digital disconnect: How capitalism is turning the Internet against democracy.* New York: New Press.

Morley, D. (1986). *Family television.* London: Comedia.

O'Connor, A. (1989, December). The problem of American cultural studies. *Critical Studies in Mass Communication, 6,* 404–413.

Radway, J. (1983). *Reading the romance.* Chapel Hill: University of North Carolina Press.

Staiger, J. (1992). Film, reception, and cultural studies. *Centennial Review, 26*(1), 89–104.

Thompson, J. (1990). *Ideology and modern culture.* Cambridge, UK: Polity Press and Stanford University Press.

Turner, G. (1990). *British cultural studies: An introduction.* New York: Unwin Hyman.

2

The Meaning of Memory

Family, Class, and Ethnicity in Early Network Television Programs

George Lipsitz

The Meaning of Memory

. . . In the midst of extraordinary social change, television became the most important discursive medium in American culture. As such, it was charged with special responsibilities for making new economic and social relations credible and legitimate to audiences haunted by ghosts from the past. Urban ethnic working-class situation comedies provided one means of addressing the anxieties and contradictions emanating from the clash between the consumer present of the 1950s and collective social memory about the 1930s and 1940s.

The consumer consciousness emerging from economic and social change in postwar America conflicted with the lessons of historical experience for many middle- and working-class American families. The Great Depression of the 1930s had not only damaged the economy, it also undercut the political and cultural legitimacy of American capitalism. Herbert Hoover had been a national hero in the 1920s, with his credo of "rugged individualism" forming the basis for a widely shared cultural ideal. But the depression discredited Hoover's philosophy and made him a symbol of yesterday's blasted hopes to millions of Americans. In the 1930s, cultural ideals based on mutuality and collectivity eclipsed the previous decade's "rugged individualism" and helped propel massive union organizing drives, anti-eviction movements, and general strikes. President Roosevelt's New Deal attempted to harness and co-opt that grass roots mass activity in an attempt to restore social order and recapture credibility and legitimacy for the capitalist system (Romasco 1965). The social welfare legislation of the "Second New Deal" in 1935 went far beyond any measures previously favored by Roosevelt and most of his advisors, but radical action proved necessary for the Administration to contain

Reproduced by permission of the American Anthropological Association from *Cultural Anthropology*, Volume 1, Issue 4, pp. 355–387, 1986. Not for sale or further reproduction.

the upsurge of activism that characterized the decade. Even in the private sector, industrial corporations made more concessions to workers than naked power realities necessitated because they feared the political consequences of mass disillusionment with the system (Berger 1982).

World War II ended the depression and brought prosperity, but it did so on a basis even more collective than the New Deal of the 1930s. Government intervention in the wartime economy reached unprecedented levels, bringing material reward and shared purpose to a generation raised on the deprivation and sacrifice of the depression. In the postwar years, the largest and most disruptive strike wave in American history won major improvements in the standard of living for the average worker, both through wage increases and through government commitments to insure full employment, decent housing, and expanded educational opportunities. Grass roots militancy and working-class direct action wrested concessions from a reluctant government and business elite—mostly because the public at large viewed workers' demands as more legitimate than the desires of capital (Lipsitz 1981).

Yet the collective nature of working-class mass activity in the postwar era posed severe problems for capital. In sympathy strikes and secondary boycotts, workers placed the interests of their class ahead of their own individual material aspirations. Strikes over safety and job control far outnumbered wage strikes, revealing aspirations to control the process of production that conflicted with capitalist labor-management relations. Mass demonstrations demanding government employment and housing programs indicated a collective political response to problems previously adjudicated on a personal level. Radical challenges to the authority of capital (like the 1946 United Auto Workers' strike demand that wage increases come out of corporate profits rather than from price hikes passed on to consumers), demonstrated a social responsibility and a commitment toward redistributing wealth,

rare in the history of American labor (Lipsitz 1981:47–50).

Capital attempted to regain the initiative in the postwar years by making qualified concessions to working-class pressures for redistribution of wealth and power. Rather than paying wage increases out of corporate profits, business leaders instead worked to expand the economy through increases in government spending, foreign trade, and consumer debt. Such expansion could meet the demands of workers and consumers without undermining capital's dominant role in the economy. On the presumption that "a rising tide lifts all boats," business leaders sought to connect working-class aspirations for a better life to policies that insured a commensurate rise in corporate profits, thereby leaving the distribution of wealth unaffected. Federal defense spending, highway construction programs, and home loan policies expanded the economy at home in a manner conducive to the interests of capital, while the Truman Doctrine and Marshall Plan provided models for enhanced access to foreign markets and raw materials for American corporations. The Taft-Hartley Act of 1947 banned the class-conscious collective activities most threatening to capital (mass strikes, sympathy strikes, secondary boycotts); the leaders of labor, government, and business accepted as necessity the practice of paying wage hikes for organized workers out of the pockets of consumers and unorganized workers, in the form of higher prices (Lipsitz 1981).

Commercial network television played an important role in this emerging economy, functioning as a significant object of consumer purchasers as well as an important marketing medium. Sales of sets jumped from three million during the entire decade of the 1940s to over five million a *year* during the 1950s (*TV Facts* 1980:141). But television's most important economic function came from its role as an instrument of legitimation for transformations in values initiated by the new economic imperatives of postwar America. For Americans to accept the new world of 1950s' consumerism, they had to make a break with the past. The depression years had helped generate fears about installment buying and excessive materialism, while the New Deal and wartime mobilization had provoked suspicions about individual acquisitiveness and upward mobility. Depression era and war time scarcities of consumer goods had led workers to internalize discipline and frugality while nurturing networks of mutual support through family, ethnic, and class associations. Government policies after the war encouraged an atomized acquisitive consumerism at odds with the lessons of the past. At the same time, federal home loan policies stimulated migrations to the suburbs from traditional, urban ethnic working-class neighborhoods. The entry of television into the American home disrupted previous patterns of family life and encouraged fragmentation of the family into separate segments of the consumer market.[1] The priority of consumerism in the economy at large and on television may have seemed organic and unplanned, but conscious policy decisions by officials from both private and public sectors shaped the contours of the consumer economy and television's role within it.

Commercial Television and Economic Change

Government policies during and after World War II shaped the basic contours of home television as an advertising medium. Government-sponsored research and development during the war perfected the technology of home television while federal tax policies solidified its economic base. The government allowed corporations to deduct the cost of advertising from their taxable incomes during the war, despite the fact that rationing and defense production left business with few products to market. Consequently, manufacturers kept the names of their products before the public while lowering their tax obligations on high wartime profits. Their advertising expenditures supplied radio networks and advertising agencies with the capital reserves and business infrastructure that enabled them to dominate the television industry in the postwar era. After the war, federal antitrust action against the motion picture studios broke up the "network" system in movies, while the FCC sanctioned the network system in television. In addition, FCC decisions to allocate stations on the narrow VHF band, to grant the networks ownership and operation rights over stations in prime markets, and to place a freeze on the licensing of new stations during the important years between 1948 and 1952 all combined to guarantee that advertising-oriented programming based on the model of radio would triumph over theater TV, educational TV, or any other form (Boddy 1985; Allen 1983). Government decisions, not market forces, established the dominance of commercial television, but these decisions reflected a view of the American economy and its needs which had become so well accepted at the top levels of business and government that it had virtually become the official state economic policy.

Fearing both renewed depression and awakened militancy among workers, influential corporate and business leaders considered increases in consumer spending—increases of 30% to 50%—to be necessary to perpetuate prosperity in the postwar era (Lipsitz 1981:46, 120–121). Defense spending for the Cold War and Korean Conflict had complemented an aggressive trade policy to improve the state of the economy, but it appeared that the key to an expanding economy rested in increased consumer spending fueled by an expansion of credit (Moore and Klein 1967; Jezer 1982). Here too, government policies led the way, especially with regard to stimulating credit purchases of homes and automobiles.

During World War II, the marginal tax rate for most wage earners jumped from 4% to 25%, making the home ownership deduction more desirable. Federal housing loan policies favored construction of new single family detached suburban housing over renovation or construction of central city multifamily units. Debt-encumbered home ownership in accord with these policies stimulated construction of 30 million new housing units in just twenty years, bringing the percentage of home-owning Americans from below 40% in 1940 to more than 60% by 1960. Mortgage policies encouraging long term debt and low down payments freed capital for other consumer purchases, while government highway building policies undermined mass transit systems and contributed to increased demand for automobiles (Hartman 1982:165–168). Partly as a result of these policies, consumer spending on private cars averaged $7.5 billion per year in the 1930s and 1940s, but grew to $22 billion per year in 1950 and almost $30 billion by 1955 (Mollenkopf 1983:111).

For the first time in U.S. history, middle-class and working-class families could routinely expect to own homes or buy new cars every few years. Between 1946 and 1965 residential mortgage debt rose three times as fast as the gross national product and disposable income. Mortgage debt accounted for just under 18% of disposable income in 1946, but it grew to almost 55% by 1965 (Stone 1983:122). In order to insure eventual payment of current debts, the economy had to generate tremendous expansion and growth, further stimulating the need to increase consumer spending. Manufacturers had to find new ways of motivating consumers to buy ever increasing amounts of commodities, and television provided an important means of accomplishing that end.

Television advertised individual products, but it also provided a relentless flow of information and persuasion that placed acts of consumption at the core of everyday life. The physical fragmentation of suburban growth and declines in motion picture attendance created an audience more likely to stay at home and receive entertainment there than ever before. But television also provided a locus redefining American ethnic, class, and family identities into consumer identities. In order to accomplish this task effectively, television programs had to address some of the psychic, moral, and political obstacles to consumption among the public at large.

The television and advertising industries knew that they had to overcome these obstacles. Marketing expert and motivational specialist Ernest Dichter stated that "one of the basic problems of this prosperity is to give people that sanction and justification to enjoy it and to demonstrate that the hedonistic approach to life is a moral one, not an immoral one" (Jezer 1982:127). Dichter went on to note the many barriers that inhibited consumer acceptance of unrestrained hedonism, and he called on advertisers "to train the average citizen to accept growth of his country and its economy as *his* growth rather than as a strange and frightening event" (Dichter 1960:210). One method of encouraging that acceptance, according to Dichter, consisted of identifying new products and styles of consumption with traditional, historically sanctioned practices and behavior. He noted that such an approach held particular relevance in addressing consumers who had only recently acquired the means to spend freely and who might harbor a lingering conservatism based on their previous experiences (Dichter 1960:209). . . .

Family Formation and the Economy—The Television View

Advertisers incorporated their messages into urban ethnic working-class comedies through indirect and direct means. Tensions developed in the programs often found indirect resolution in commercials. Thus

Jeannie MacClennan's search for an American sweetheart in one episode of *Hey Jeannie* set up commercials proclaiming the abilities of Drene shampoo to keep one prepared to accept last minute dates and of Crest toothpaste to produce an attractive smile (*Hey Jeannie:* "The Rock and Roll Kid"). Conversations about shopping for new furniture in an episode of *The Goldbergs* directed viewers' attention to furnishings in the Goldberg home provided for the show by Macy's department store in exchange for a commercial acknowledgment (*The Goldbergs:* "The In-laws").

But the content of the shows themselves offered even more direct emphasis on consumer spending. In one episode of *The Goldbergs*, Molly expresses disapproval of her future daughter-in-law's plan to buy a washing machine on the installment plan. "I know Papa and me never bought anything unless we had the money to pay for it," she intones with logic familiar to a generation with memories of the Great Depression. Her son, Sammy, confronts this "deviance" by saying, "Listen, Ma, almost everybody in this country lives above their means—and everybody enjoys it." Doubtful at first, Molly eventually learns from her children and announces her conversion to the legitimacy of installment buying by proposing that the family buy two cars so as to "live above our means—the American way" (*The Goldbergs:* "The In-laws"). In a subsequent episode, Molly's daughter, Rosalie, assumes the role of ideological tutor to her mother. When planning a move out of their Bronx apartment to a new house in the suburbs, Molly ruminates about where to place her furniture in the new home. "You don't mean we're going to take all this junk with us into a brand new house?" asks an exasperated Rosalie. With traditionalist sentiment Molly answers, "Junk? My furniture's junk? My furniture that I lived with and loved for twenty years is junk?" But in the end she accepts Rosalie's argument—even selling off all her old furniture to help meet the down payment on

the new house, and deciding to buy new furniture on the installment plan (*The Goldbergs:* "Moving Day").

Chester A. Riley confronts similar choices about family and commodities in *The Life of Riley*. His wife complains that he only takes her out to the neighborhood bowling alley and restaurant, not to "interesting places." Riley searches for ways to impress her and discovers from a friend that a waiter at the fancy Club Morambo will let them eat first and pay later, at a dollar a week plus ten percent interest. "Ain't that dishonest?" asks Riley. "No, it's usury," his friend replies. Riley does not borrow the money, but he impresses his wife anyway by taking the family out to dinner on the proceeds of a prize that he received for being the one-thousandth customer in a local flower shop. Though we eventually learn that Peg Riley only wanted attention, not an expensive meal, the happy ending of the episode hinges totally on Riley's prestige, restored when he demonstrates his ability to provide a luxury outing for the family (*Life of Riley:* R228).

The same episode of *The Life of Riley* reveals another consumerist element common to this subgenre. When Riley protests that he lacks the money needed to fulfill Peg's desires, she answers that he would have plenty if he didn't spend so much on "needless gadgets." His shortage of cash becomes a personal failing caused by incompetent behavior as a consumer. Nowhere do we hear about the size of his paycheck, relations between his union and his employer, or, for that matter, the relationship between the value of his labor and the wages paid to him by the Stevenson Aircraft Company. Like Uncle David in *The Goldbergs*—who buys a statue of Hamlet shaking hands with Shakespeare and an elk's tooth with the Gettysburg address carved on it—Riley's comic character stems in part from a flaw which in theory could be attributed to the entire consumer economy: a preoccupation with "needless gadgets." By contrast, Peg Riley's desire for an evening out is portrayed as reasonable and modest—as reparation due her for the inevitable tedium of housework. The solution to her unhappiness, of course, comes from an evening out rather than from a change in her own work circumstances. Even within the home, television elevates consumption over production; production is assumed to be a constant—only consumption can be varied. But more than enjoyment is at stake: unless Riley can provide her with the desired night on the town, he will fail in his obligations as a husband (*Life of Riley:* R228; *The Goldbergs:* "Bad Companions"). . . .

"Mama's Birthday," broadcast in 1954, delineated the tensions between family loyalty and consumer desire endemic to modern capitalist society. The show begins with Mama teaching Katrin to make Norwegian potato balls, the kind she used long ago to "catch" Papa. Unimpressed by this accomplishment, Katrin changes the subject and asks Mama what she wants for her upcoming birthday. In an answer that locates Mama within the gender roles of the 1950s, she replies, "Well, I think a fine new job for your Papa. You and Dagmar to marry nice young men and have a lot of wonderful children—just like I have. And Nels, well, Nels to become president of the United States" (Meehan and Ropes 1954). In one sentence Mama has summed up the dominant culture's version of legitimate female expectations: success at work for her husband, marriage and childrearing for her daughters, the presidency for her son—and nothing for herself.

But we learn that Mama does have some needs, although we do not hear it from her lips. Her sister, Jenny, asks Mama to attend a fashion show, but Mama cannot leave the house because she has to cook a roast for a guest whom Papa has invited to dinner. Jenny comments that Mama never seems to get out of the kitchen, adding that "it's a disgrace when a woman can't call her soul her own," and "it's a shame that a married woman can't have some time to herself." The complaint is a valid one, and we can imagine how it

might have resonated for women in the 1950s. The increased availability of household appliances and the use of synthetic fibers and commercially processed food should have decreased the amount of time women spent in housework, but surveys showed that home-makers spent the same number of hours per week (51 to 56) doing housework as they had done in the 1920s. Advertising and marketing strategies undermined the potential of technological changes by upgrading standards for cleanliness in the home and expanding desires for more varied wardrobes and menus for the average family (Hartmann 1982:168). In that context, Aunt Jenny would have been justified in launching into a tirade about the division of labor within the Hansen household or about the possibilities for cooperative housework, but network television specializes in a less social and more commodified dialogue about problems like housework: Aunt Jenny suggests that her sister's family buy her a "fireless cooker"—a cast iron stove—for her birthday. "They're wonderful," she tells them in language borrowed from the rhetoric of advertising. "You just put your dinner inside them, close 'em up, and go where you please. When you come back your dinner is all cooked" (Meehan and Ropes 1954). Papa protests that Mama likes to cook on her woodburning stove, but Jenny dismisses that objection with an insinuation about his motive, when she replies, "Well, I suppose it *would* cost a little more than you could afford, Hansen" (Meehan and Ropes 1954). By identifying a commodity as the solution to Mama's problem, Aunt Jenny unites the inner voice of Mama with the outer voice of the sponsors of television programs. . . .

Prodded by their aunt, the Hansen children go shopping and purchase the fireless cooker from a storekeeper who calls the product "the new Emancipation Proclamation—setting housewives free from their old kitchen range" (Meehan and Ropes 1954). Our exposure to advertising hyperbole should not lead us to miss the analogy here: housework is compared to slavery, and the commercial product takes on the aura of Abraham Lincoln. The shopkeeper's appeal convinces the children to pool their resources and buy the stove for Mama. But we soon learn that Papa plans to make a fireless cooker for Mama with his tools. When Mama discovers Papa's intentions she persuades the children to buy her another gift. Even Papa admits that his stove will not be as efficient as the one made in a factory, but Mama nobly affirms that she will like his better because he made it himself. The children use their money to buy dishes for Mama, and Katrin remembers the episode as Mama's happiest birthday ever (Meehan and Ropes 1954).

The stated resolution of "Mama's Birthday" favors traditional values. Mama prefers to protect Papa's feelings rather than having a better stove, and the product built by a family member has more value than one sold as a commodity. Yet the entire development of the plot leads in the opposite direction. The "fireless cooker" is the star of the episode, setting in motion all the other characters, and it has unquestioned value even in the face of Jenny's meddlesome brashness, Papa's insensitivity, and Mama's old-fashioned ideals. Buying a product is unchallenged as the true means of changing the unpleasant realities or low status of women's work in the home.

This resolution of the conflict between consumer desires and family roles reflected television's social role as mediator between the family and the economy. Surveys of set ownership showed no pronounced stratification by class, but a clear correlation between family size and television purchases: households with three to five people were most likely to own television sets, while those with only one person were least likely to own them (Swanson and Jones 1951). The television industry recognized and promoted its privileged place within families in advertisements like the one in the *New York Times* in 1950 that proclaimed, "Youngsters today need television for their morale as much as they need fresh air and sunshine for their health" (Wolfenstein 1951). Like previous communications media, television sets occupied honored places in family living rooms, and helped structure family time; unlike other previous communications media, they displayed available commodities in a way that transformed all their entertainment into a glorified shopping catalogue....

Note

1. Nielsen ratings demonstrate television's view of the family as separate market segments to be addressed independently. For an analysis of the industry's view of children as a special market, see Patricia J. Bence (1985), "Analysis and History of Typology and Forms of Children's Network Programming From 1950 to 1980."

References

Allen, Jeanne. 1983. The Social Matrix of Television: Invention in the United States. In *Regarding Televison*. E. Ann Kaplan, ed. Pp. 109–119. Los Angeles: University Publications of America.

Berger, Henry. 1982. Social Protest in St. Louis. Paper presented at a Committee for the Humanities Forum. St. Louis, Missouri. March 12.

Boddy, William. 1985. The Studios Move Into Prime Time: Hollywood and the Television Industry in the 1950s. *Cinema Journal* 12(4):23–37.

Dichter, Ernest. 1960. *The Strategy of Desire*. Garden City: Doubleday.

Goldbergs, The. 1955. Moving Day. Academy of Television Arts Collection. 35F34I. University of California, Los Angeles.

———. 1955. The In-laws. Academy of Television Arts Collection. F32I8. University of California, Los Angeles.

———. 1955. Bad Companions. Academy of Television Arts Collection. F32I9. University of California, Los Angeles.

Hartmann, Susan. 1982. *The Home Front and Beyond*. Boston: Twayne.

Hey Jeannie. 1956. The Rock and Roll Kid. Academy of Television Arts Collection. University of California, Los Angeles.

Jezer, Marty. 1982. *The Dark Ages*. Boston: South End.

Life of Riley. 1953. Academy of Television Arts Collection. R228. University of California, Los Angeles.

Lipsitz, George. 1981. *Class and Culture in Cold War America: A Rainbow at Midnight*. New York: Praeger.

Meehan, Elizabeth, and Bradford Ropes. 1954. *Mama's Birthday*. Theater Arts Collection. University Research Library. University of California, Los Angeles.

Mollenkopf, John. 1983. *The Contested City*. Princeton: Princeton University Press.

Moore, Geoffrey, and Phillip Klein. 1967. *The Quality of Consumer Installment Credit*. Washington, D.C.: National Bureau of Economic Research.

Romasco, Albert U. 1965. *The Poverty of Abundance*. New York: Oxford University Press.

Stone, Michael. 1983. Housing and the Economic Crisis. In *America's Housing Crisis: What Is to be Done?* Chester Hartman, ed. Pp. 99–150. London and New York: Routledge and Kegan Paul.

Swanson, Charles E., and Robert L. Jones (1951). Television Ownership and Its Correlates. *Journal of Applied Psychology* 35:352–357.

TV Facts. 1980. New York: Facts on File.

Wolfenstein, Martha. 1951. The Emergence of Fun Morality. *Journal of Social Issues* 7(4):15–25.

3

The Economics of the Media Industry

David P. Croteau, William
D. Hoynes, and Stefania Milan

...Concentration of Ownership

One of the clearest trends in media ownership is its increasing concentration in fewer and fewer hands. In his widely cited book, *The New Media Monopoly*, Ben Bagdikian (2004) argues that ownership of media has become so concentrated that by the mid-2000s only five global firms dominate the mass media industry in the United States, operating like a cartel. The five companies are Time Warner, The Walt Disney Company, Viacom, News Corporation, and Bertelsmann AG. With the exception of the German company Bertelsmann, all of them are based in the United States. They are multimedia entertainment conglomerates that produce and distribute newspapers, magazines, radio, television, books, and movies. According to Bagdikian, "This gives each of the five corporations and their leaders more communication power than was exercised by any despot or dictatorship in history" (Bagdikian 2004: 3). Within each sector of the media industry, these large companies tower above their smaller competitors. For example, in book publishing, HarperCollins is owned by News Corporation, Simon & Schuster by Viacom, and Random House by Bertelsmann. Together with Hachette Book Group, Macmillan, and Penguin Group, they constitute the "Big 6" in the book industry and control the global English-language book market.

In the U.S. magazine industry, Time Inc. (property of Time Warner, which operates, among others, the premium cable television network HBO, Warner Brothers, and CNN) towers above its competitors, with its 22 U.S. print titles reaching over 100 million adults (nearly half the U.S. adult population) and controlling a 21% share of domestic magazine advertising spending (Time Warner 2010). Hearst Magazines, property of Hearst Corporation, publishes 14 titles in the U.S. and about 200 international editions (Hearst 2010).

The motion picture industry in the United States is dominated by six companies—NBC Universal's Universal Pictures, Viacom's Paramount Pictures, Time Warner's Warner Bros.,

From David P. Croteau, William D. Hoynes and Stefania Milan, "The Economics of the Media Industry," in *Media/Society: Industries, Images, Audiences* (2011). Reprinted with permission of SAGE Publications.

Walt Disney Studios, the News Corporation's 20th Century Fox, and Sony's Columbia Pictures. In 2009, Warner Bros. led the way with U.S. box office revenues of $2.1 billion, accounting for 20% of the domestic market. Its top film, *Harry Potter and the Half-Blood Prince,* made $302 million at the box office. Paramount's revenue amounted to $1.48 billion, and Sony/Columbia was third with $1.46 billion at the box office (Box Office Mojo 2010a). In addition, most of the leading "independent" film companies are owned by the industry giants—Focus Features (NBC Universal), Miramax (Walt Disney Company), Fox Searchlight (News Corporation), Sony Pictures Classics (Sony/Columbia), and New Line (Time Warner).

In the recorded music industry, only four companies account for the vast majority of U.S. music sales: Sony Music Entertainment, Vivendi/Universal Music Group, Warner Music Group, and EMI. Each controls a number of smaller labels and local subsidiaries . . . . At the same time, Clear Channel, with more than 800 radio stations in 2010, is the dominant player in the U.S. radio industry. With more than 150 million listeners, Clear Channel stations reach 75% of adults in the United States (Clear Channel 2010).

The live music industry is even more concentrated, with one single company, Live Nation, active in over 40 countries and producing over 22,000 events per year. Live Nation is a spin-off of radio industry giant Clear Channel, which then merged with Ticketmaster in 2010. It manages artists (including many well-known stars, such as Jay-Z, Shakira, and U2), owns and operates more than 140 concert venues (including more than a dozen House of Blues venues across the country), promotes shows, manages corporate sponsorship of tours, and handles ticket sales (livenation.com).

One exception to the concentration trend is the U.S. television industry, which became somewhat less concentrated in the 1990s as FOX joined ABC, CBS, and NBC to expand the number of major broadcast networks to four, along with the fledgling CW network. However, the major players in the television industry are leaders in other sectors of the media industry as well. In particular, there has been an increase in integration between television networks and movie studios. Four of the five broadcast networks are owned by media conglomerates with major film studios: ABC (Disney), NBC (Universal), Fox (Twentieth Century Fox), and CW (Warner Brothers). In addition, these major movie studios are also the leading producers of prime-time programming for network television, accounting for about 90% of the series on the major networks (Kunz 2009). This makes it very difficult for independent producers to ever get their programs on broadcast television.

The major media companies own vast portfolios of products, spanning the range of media formats and delivery systems. Indeed, the media giants own such a dizzying array of entertainment and news media that the scale of their operations may surprise many readers. Because most products carry a distinct name, rather than the label of the corporate owner, most media users are unaware that a large number of media outlets are actually owned by a single corporation. In the world of newspapers, for example, chains such as Gannett and MediaNews own newspapers all over the country. . . . Gannett owns 85 daily newspapers, including *USA Today,* the best-selling newspaper in the United States, alongside 130 news websites and 20 television stations in the United States. MediaNews Group, the second largest newspaper publisher in the country, owns 56 newspapers, including the *Denver Post* and the *Detroit News,* along with 210 websites and more than 200 specialty magazines (MediaNews Group 2010). At the newspaper chains, each paper has a different name, and it is not always apparent to readers that a paper is part of a national chain. Similarly, in book publishing, the major companies have so many different imprints that even a conscientious reader is unlikely to know the common owners of the different imprints . . .

Conglomeration and Integration

Concentration of media ownership means that fewer corporations own the media. At the same time that concentration of ownership has been occurring, conglomeration has been taking place. That is, media companies have become part of much larger corporations, which own a collection of other companies that may operate in highly diverse business areas (see Exhibit).

Much as in other industries, the largest media companies are growing in size and reach as they purchase or merge with their competitors. In the United States, media outlets are among the most attractive properties to both potential investors and buyers. While some high-profile mergers ultimately failed—including AOL-Time Warner (which split into two companies in 2009) and Viacom-CBS (split in 2005)—the process of conglomeration in the media industry continues. For example, Google purchased YouTube in 2006, the New Corporation bought Dow Jones, owner of *The Wall Street Journal* in 2007, and cable giant Comcast tried throughout 2010 to close a deal to purchase NBC Universal. Media—in both news and entertainment forms—have become a key segment of the American economy. The media industry is producing high visibility, high profits, and a major item for export to other countries.

Concentration has affected the relationships among various media organizations within a single conglomerate. Economic analysts have long used the terms *horizontal integration* and *vertical integration* to describe two types of ownership concentration in any industry. In the media industry, vertical integration refers to the process by which one owner acquires all aspects of production and distribution of a single type of media product. For example, a movie company might integrate vertically by acquiring talent agencies to acquire scripts and sign actors, production studios to create films, manufacturing plants to produce DVDs, and various venues to show the movies, such as theater chains, premium cable channels, broadcast television networks, and Internet-based streaming services. The company could then better control the entire process of creating, producing, marketing, and distributing movies. Similarly, a book publisher might integrate vertically by acquiring paper mills, printing facilities, book binderies, trucking firms, and bookstores chains. . .

Horizontal integration refers to the process by which one company buys different kinds of media, concentrating ownership across differing types of media rather than up and down through one industry. In horizontal integration, media conglomerates assemble large portfolios of magazines, television stations, book publishers, record labels, and so on to mutually support one another's operations. In a classic example, when Warner Bros. released the 2001 film *Harry Potter and the Sorcerer's Stone*, its then-parent company AOL Time Warner pursued an elaborate multimedia strategy to cash in on the Harry Potter franchise. AOL's online services provided links to various Harry Potter web pages, including sites for purchasing the Harry Potter merchandise that AOL sold. The company's movie information site, Moviefone, promoted and sold tickets to the film, while company magazines *Time, People,* and *Entertainment Weekly* featured prominent Harry Potter stories. In addition, AOL Time Warner used its cable systems and cable networks for massive promotion of the film, and the company-owned Warner Music Group released the Harry Potter soundtrack. More recent blockbusters such as *Avatar* employ similar strategies, taking advantage of new promotional channels, such as cell phones and social networking sites.

Exhibit 3.1   Anatomy of Media Conglomerates (Disney and Time Warner)

The Walt Disney Company, Select Holdings, 2010	

Film
Walt Disney Pictures
Walt Disney Animation Studio
Pixar Animation Studios
Touchstone Pictures
Hollywood Pictures
Miramax Films
Disneynature
Walt Disney Studios Home Entertainment
	Broadcast Television
	ABC Television Network
	ABC Daytime
	ABC News
	ABC Sports
	ABC Kids
	Television stations, including:
	  New York, NY WABC-TV/Channel 7
	  Los Angeles, CA KABC-TV/Channel 7

Music
Disney Music Group
Walt Disney Records
Hollywood Records
Lyric Street Records
	Chicago, IL WLS-TV/Channel 7
	  Philadelphia, PA WPVI-TV/Channel 6
	  San Francisco, CA KGO-TV/Channel 7
	  Houston, TX KTRK-TV/Channel 13

Radio
Radio Disney Network—41 radio stations
ESPN Radio—5 stations
	Raleigh-Durham, NC WTVD-TV/Channel 11
	  Fresno, CA KFSN-TV/Channel 30
	  Flint, MI WJRT-TV/Channel 12
	  Toledo, OH WTVG-TV/Channel 13

Theater Disney Theatrical Productions Disney Live! Disney on Ice	**Cable Television** ESPN & ESPN2 ESPN Classic ESPNEWS
Publishing Disney Global Book Group Global Children's Magazines *FamilyFun Magazine* Marvel Entertainment	ESPN Deportes ESPNU Disney Channel SOAPnet ABC Family
Parks and Resorts Walt Disney World & Disneyland Resorts Disneyland Paris, Hong Kong, & Tokyo Disney Vacation Club Disney Cruise Line	Jetix A&E The History Channel The Biography Channel Lifetime
Games and Software Propaganda Games Avalanche Software Black Rock Studio Junction Point Studios GameStar Wideload Games	**Interactive Media** Disney.com Disney Interactive Studios Club Penguin Disney Toontown Online Pirates of the Caribbean Online Disney Fairies Franchise Site

(Continued)

(Continued)

Consumer Products	World of Cars
Disney Store (231 in North America, 109 in Europe)	Disney Princess Franchise Site
	Playhouse Preschool Time Online
Disney Toys	Disney Family.com
Disney Home Furnishings	iParenting
Disney Stationary	Kaboose
DisneyShopping.com	Baby Zone
Disney Baby Einstein	

Time Warner, Select Holdings, 2010

Film	Magazines
Warner Bros. Pictures	Largest magazines publisher in the U.S. with 22 U.S. print titles & 26 U.S. websites . . ., including:
Warner Bros. Animation	
Warner Premiere	*All You*
New Line Cinema	*Coastal Living*
Warner Home Video	*Cooking Light*
Warner Bros. International Cinemas	*Entertainment Weekly*
	Essence
Television	*Fortune*
Warner Bros. Television	*Golf Magazine*
Producer of more than 40 network & cable television series for 2010–2011 season	*Health*
	InStyle
Warner Bros. Television Distribution	*Money*
The CW Television Network	*People*
Studio 2.0	*People Country*
Telepictures Productions	*People en Español*
Warner Horizon Television	*People StyleWatch*
	Real Simple
Cable Television	*Sports Illustrated*
HBO	*Sports Illustrated Kids*
Cinemax	*Southern Living*
Adult Swim	*Sunset*
Cartoon Network	*This Old House*
CNN	*Time for Kids*
Fashion TV	*Time*
HTV	IPC Media, a leading magazine publisher in the U.K., with more than 85 print and digital titles.
Infinito	
HLN	
Pogo	Grupo Editorial Expansión, a leading magazine publisher in Mexico, with 16 magazines.
TBS	
truTV	
Turner Classic Movies	
Turner Network Television	

Other	Interactive Media
Warner Bros. Consumer Products	Warner Bros. Interactive Entertainment
DC Entertainment/DC Comics	CNN.com
Warner Bros. Theatre Ventures	NASCAR.com
	PGA.com
	CelebrityBabyBlog.com
	CNNMoney.com
	FanNation.com
	LIFE.com

Source: Disney and Time Warner corporate websites.

In another example, Disney turned its sports cable channel ESPN into a multimedia cross-promotional vehicle, developing ESPN Classic, ESPN2, ESPN Deportes, ESPNU, ESPN International, ESPN radio, an ESPN magazine, an ESPN news service, ESPN 360 broadband, ESPN Mobile, an ESPN store, and the (now struggling) Restaurant/Sports Bar ESPN Zone, all working together to promote Disney's growing list of ESPN products. This kind of opportunity for cross promotion is one of the driving forces behind the growth of horizontally integrated media companies.

Consequences of Conglomeration and Integration

While the trends in media ownership may be of interest in themselves, our prime concern is with the relationship between ownership and the media product. What are the consequences of integration, conglomeration, and concentration of ownership?

INTEGRATION AND SELF-PROMOTION

The economic factors propelling both vertical and horizontal integration are clear: Owners perceive such arrangements as both efficient and profitable. The cultural consequences are more ambiguous. However, an institutional approach suggests that such ownership patterns are likely to affect the types of media products created. In particular, integrated media conglomerates seeking the benefits of what industry insiders refer to as "synergy" are likely to favor products that can best be exploited by other components of the conglomerate. (Synergy refers to the dynamic where components of a company work together to produce benefits that would be impossible for a single, separately operated unit of the company.) For example, horizontal integration may well encourage the publication of books that can be made into movies and discourage the publication of those that cannot. Or it might encourage of the creation of TV talent search programs because they can generate new musical acts who are contractually obligated to record for the company's music label, featured in the company's magazines, played on the company's radio stations, and showcased on their websites. More generally, promotion and marketing are likely to dominate the decision-making process within a horizontally integrated media industry.

Vertical integration becomes especially significant when the company that makes the product also controls its distribution. For example, a corporation that owns a mail-order book-of-the-month club is likely to prominently feature its own publications, limiting competitors' access to a lucrative segment of the book-buying market.

The possibilities for fully using horizontal and vertical integration are startling. In this era of integrated media conglomerates, media companies are capable of pursuing elaborate cross-media strategies, in which company-owned media products can be packaged, sold, and promoted across the full range of media platforms. Feature films, their accompanying soundtracks and DVD/Blu-ray Disc releases, spin-off television programs, and books, along with magazine cover stories and plenty of licensed merchandise can all be produced and distributed by different divisions of the same conglomerate—with each piece serving to promote the broader franchise. One consequence of integration, then, is an increase in media cross promotion and, perhaps, a decrease in media products that are not suitable for cross promotion. It also makes it more difficult for smaller media firms to compete with the major corporations who can use their vast and diverse holdings to saturate consumers during their promotional campaigns.

THE IMPACT OF CONGLOMERATION

What has the growth of large multimedia firms over the past two decades meant for the news, television, radio, films, music, and books we receive? In other words, to what extent does conglomeration affect the media product? The loudest warnings about the impact of conglomeration have come from within the news industry, in part because some news media had traditionally been sheltered from the full pressure of profit making. For example, for much of television history, respectable television news divisions were understood to represent a necessary public service commitment that lent prestige to the major broadcast networks. They were not expected to turn a

substantial profit. However, that changed with the takeover of news operations by major corporate conglomerates during the 1980s.

Ken Auletta's *Three Blind Mice* (1991) paints a vivid picture of the clash that ensued during this time, when new corporate owners took over the major television networks and their news divisions. For those who worked at NBC News, for example, the purchase of the network by General Electric led to conflicts about the meaning and role of television news. In most of these conflicts, the new corporate owners ultimately prevailed. As Auletta tells it, when General Electric took over as the new owners of NBC, they:

> emphasized a "boundaryless" company, one without walls between News, Entertainment, Sales, and other divisions. . . . At NBC's annual management retreat in 1990, many of the 160 executives questioned why Sales or Entertainment couldn't have more input into news specials, or why News tended to keep its distance from the rest of the company, as if it were somehow special. (p. 564)

General Electric chair Jack Welch even specified that *Today Show* weather reporter Willard Scott should mention GE lightbulbs on the program. According to former NBC news president Lawrence Grossman, "It was one of the perks of owning a network. . . . You get your lightbulbs mentioned on the air. . . . People want to please the owners" (Husseini 1994: 13).

Since that time, the network news programs have faced stiff competition from the 24-hour cable news channels, yet they are expected to turn a profit by attracting audiences that owners expect and advertisers demand. One result has been an increased emphasis on entertainment and celebrities on the network news. As CBS news anchor Dan Rather said, the Hollywoodization of the news is deep and abiding. It's been one of the more important developments of the last 20 to 25 years, particularly the last 10 to 15, that we run stupid celebrity stories. . . . It has become pervasive, the belief that to be competitive, you must run a certain amount of celebrity news. (*Brill's Content* 1998a: 117) . . .

Can concentrated media ownership be translated into undue political influence? Most people recognize the importance of such a question in examining the government's control of media in totalitarian nations. It is clear in such situations that state ownership and exclusive access are likely to affect media products. In the United States, most discussion about the First Amendment and free speech also focuses on the possibility of government censorship. This discussion is generally blind, however, to the impact of corporate ownership.

In addressing this concern, Bagdikian (2004) has argued that the United States has a "private ministry of information," metaphorically referring to the type of government-led propaganda system that exists in totalitarian societies. In the case of the contemporary United States, however, private interests, not the government, largely control this information system. Bagdikian suggests that when a small number of firms with similar interests dominate the media industry, it begins to function in a way similar to a state information system. It is hard to question the underlying argument that those who own large media conglomerates have at least the potential to wield a great deal of political power.

How might ownership of media translate into political power? It is possible that those building media empires could use their media outlets to promote a very specific political agenda. Furthermore, when media barons become candidates

for major office, their media holdings can be invaluable political resources. Perhaps the starkest example of this in a Western democracy is the case of Silvio Berlusconi in Italy, who managed to use ownership of private media to gain public office—which then enabled him to influence public media.

Silvio Berlusconi, a media magnate and the dominant force in Italian broadcasting and publishing, was elected prime minister four times (1994, 2001, 2005, and 2008). For Berlusconi, ownership of television and radio clearly had great political value; he owned strategic assets that were unavailable to other political actors. In the 2001 electoral campaign, he was given four times the exposure of his rival candidate on the television networks that he owns. After winning that election, he went on to effectively control 90% of Italian television programming (*The Economist* 2001). That's because Italian prime ministers have the right to replace the boards of directors of the three public television channels, known as RAI, and thus can influence RAI's editorial choices. In subsequent election campaigns, Berlusconi not only had his own private television networks as a political resource, he also influenced the public channels too.

Berlusconi's domination of television was so great that, after the 2001 election and again in 2004, the European Federation of Journalists called for new regulations limiting media ownership. In 2004, both the European Parliament and the Council of Europe condemned the open conflict of interest between Berlusconi's role as prime minister and that of media magnate. The corrosive effect of this arrangement on Italian democracy was so serious that Freedom House, an independent watchdog group that produces annual rankings of freedom and democracy around the world, downgraded Italian freedom of the press from "free" to "partially free" (Freedom

House 2004). After Berlusconi launched a series of attacks and lawsuits against the press, Reporters Without Borders (2009) declared that Berlusconi "is on the verge of being added to our list of Predators of Press Freedom," which would be a first for a European country (Ginsborg 2005; Hine 2001).

Though the media environment is quite different, private media ownership can be a huge political asset in the United States too. Media entrepreneur Michael Bloomberg amassed a fortune selling technology and media products to businesses. He drew on the widespread recognition of his brand-name line of Bloomberg business media products—and the enormous profits they have generated for him—in his successful campaign to become New York City mayor in 2001. In the process, he spent $69 million of his own money— more than $92 per vote. Bloomberg won reelection in 2005 then successfully had the term-limit law changed so he could run again (and win again) in 2009. There has long been speculation that Bloomberg, one of the 10 wealthiest men in the United States as of 2010 (Forbes 2010), will one day launch a presidential bid.

However, the situation in the United States is complicated, largely because of the vast size of the U.S. media industry. In some cases, owners of media companies have direct control over media products and thus are able to exert political influence by promoting ideas that enhance their interests. Conservative media magnate Rupert Murdoch, for example, has used a variety of his News Corporation's media holdings to advance his political and economic goals. In 1975, he had his Australian newspapers slant the news so blatantly in favor of his conservative choice for prime minister that Murdoch's own journalists went on strike in protest. His British papers played a crucial role in the 1979 election of British conservative Margaret Thatcher. In 1995, Murdoch financed the multimillion-dollar start-up of the

high-profile conservative U.S. magazine *The Weekly Standard*. In 1996, Murdoch's News Corporation initiated a 24-hour news channel, Fox News Channel (headed by Rush Limbaugh's former executive producer and long-time Republican Party political consultant, Roger Ailes), that prominently features commentary by well-known conservatives. Critics have long argued that the Fox News Channel promotes a consistent conservative agenda (Ackerman 2001; Aday 2010; McDermott 2010); indeed, Fox News is perhaps the only national television news outlet that is regularly applauded by conservative political activists.

However, some media outlets, especially news outlets, rely on a perception of objectivity or evenhandedness to maintain their legitimacy. Journalists often see themselves as members of a sort of fourth estate, complementing the executive, legislative, and administrative branches of government. Their job is to act as watchdogs over politicians (Louw 2010; Schultz 1998). As a result, with perhaps the exception of Fox News, most major news media outlets will not consistently and blatantly promote a single political agenda. Instead, viewers are more likely to find such an approach on specific cable programs or on the growing number of ideologically driven websites and blogs.

There are more subtle processes at work in mainstream media, though, and these do have serious political consequences. The process of using media to promote a political agenda is more complex than simply feeding people ideas and images that they passively accept. Owners can use media sites to disseminate a specific position on a controversial issue or to help legitimize particular institutions or behaviors. Just as important, owners can systematically exclude certain ideas from their media products. While control of information or images can never be total, owners can tilt the scales in particular directions quite dramatically.

Ownership by major corporations of vast portfolios of mass media gives us reason to believe that a whole range of ideas and images—those that question fundamental social arrangements, under which the media owners are doing quite well—will rarely be visible. This does not mean that all images and information are uniform. It means that some ideas will be widely available, while others will be largely excluded. For example, images critical of gridlock in the federal government are frequent; images critical of capitalism as an economic system are virtually nonexistent. There is no way of proving the connection, but the media's focus on the shortcomings of the government, rather than of the private sector, seems consistent with the interests of the corporate media owners.

This process is most obvious in products that directly address contemporary social and political events, but it also happens in entertainment products. Consider, for example, the depiction of gays and lesbians on prime-time television. For most of U.S. television history, there were virtually no gay or lesbian characters. As gay rights advocates made advances in the 1980s and 1990s, gay and lesbian characters began appearing, though infrequently and in often superficial depictions. Also, gay characters faced constraints that heterosexual characters did not; for example, they typically did not kiss, even as popular television continued to become more explicit in depictions of heterosexual sex. It was not until 2004 that the first television drama series to revolve around a group of lesbian, gay, bisexual, and transgendered characters appeared; *The L Word* ran from 2004 to 2009 on the premium cable channel Showtime. There is no conspiracy here. More likely, a small number of profit-making firms that rely on mass audiences and major advertisers simply avoided potential controversies that might threaten their bottom line. As network executives and major advertisers began to define such images as more

acceptable to mainstream audiences, lesbian and gay characters have become more commonplace in recent years (GLAAD 2010). We return to these issues in Chapters 5 and 6 when we explore the content of mass media.

The political impact of concentrated corporate ownership, however, is both broader and subtler than the exclusion of certain ideas in favor of others. Herbert Schiller (1989) argues that "the corporate voice" has been generalized so successfully that most of us do not even think of it as a specifically corporate voice. That is, the corporate view has become "our" view, the "American" view, even though the interests of the corporate entities that own mass media are far from universal. One example of this is the entire media-generated discourse—in newspapers, television, radio, and magazines—about the American economy, in which corporate success provides the framework for virtually all evaluations of national economic well-being. Quarterly profits, mergers and acquisitions, productivity, and fluctuations in the financial markets are so widely discussed that their relationship to the corporate voice is difficult to discern. The relationship between corporate financial health and citizen well-being, however, is rarely discussed explicitly—even in times of serious financial crisis. During the economic crises of 2008–2009, the U.S. news media were remarkably unquestioning of the message from both government and the private sector that a massive and immediate bailout of banks, Wall Street firms, and other corporate interests was absolutely essential.

A concentrated media sphere can also disempower citizens in monitoring their government's war-making powers. McChesney (2008: 98) argues that "those in power, those who benefit from war and empire, see the press as arguably the most important front of war, because it is there that consent is manufactured, and dissent is marginalized. For a press system, a war is its moment of truth." The 2003 U.S.-led invasion of Iraq was justified by the alleged presence of weapons of mass destruction (WMD) in Iraq. The news media reported these WMD charges uncritically, relying on official sources and without further investigating, effectively affirming the Bush administration's rationale for war. According to one study of U.S. news media coverage in the first three weeks of the Iraq war, pro-war U.S. sources outnumbered antiwar sources by 25 to 1, thus making it very difficult for citizens to access critical perspectives on the war (Rendall and Broughel 2003).

One possible political consequence of the concentration of media ownership is that, in some ways, it becomes more difficult for alternative media voices to emerge. Because mass media outlets in all sectors of the media industry are large mass-production and mass-distribution firms, ownership is restricted to those who can acquire substantial financial resources. In the age of multimillion-dollar media enterprises, freedom of the press may be left to those few who can afford to own what has become a very expensive press.

The Internet offers the possibility for small producers to create professional-looking alternative websites. However, without a means to effectively promote such sites, and without the budget to pay for staff to continuously produce substantive new content that continues to draw users, such sites are limited to relatively small niche audiences. Television and the major daily newspapers—along with the websites associated with them—are still the main sources of news for most of the population.

In the end, ownership of the means of information becomes part of larger patterns of inequality in contemporary societies, and large media conglomerates can use both cultural and financial strategies to try to influence public policy. In this sense, mass media institutions are no different from other social institutions; they are linked to the patterned inequality that exists throughout our society....

4

Hegemony

James Lull

Hegemony is the power or dominance that one social group holds over others. This can refer to the "asymmetrical interdependence" of political-economic-cultural relations between and among nation-states (Straubhaar, 1991) or differences between and among social classes within a nation. Hegemony is "dominance and subordination in the field of relations structured by power" (Hall, 1985). But hegemony is more than social power itself; it is a method for gaining and maintaining power.

Classical Marxist theory, of course, stresses economic position as the strongest predictor of social differences. Today, more than a century after Karl Marx and Friedrich Engels wrote their treatises about capitalist exploitation of the working class, economic disparities still underlie and help reproduce social inequalities in industrialized societies. . . . Technological developments in the twentieth century, however, have made the manner of social domination much more complex than before. Social class differences in today's world are not determined solely or directly by economic factors. Ideological influence is crucial now in the exercise of social power.

The Italian intellectual Antonio Gramsci—to whom the term *hegemony* is attributed—broadened materialist Marxist theory into the realm of ideology. Persecuted by his country's then fascist government (and writing from prison), Gramsci emphasized society's "super structure," its ideology-producing institutions, in struggles over meaning and power (1971; 1973; 1978; see also Boggs, 1976; Sassoon, 1980; and Simon, 1982). A shift in critical theory thus was made away from a preoccupation with capitalist society's "base" (its economic foundation) and towards its dominant dispensaries of ideas. Attention was given to the structuring of authority and dependence in symbolic environments that correspond to, but are not the same as, economically determined class-based structures and processes of industrial production. Such a theoretical turn seems a natural and necessary development in an era when communications technology is such a pervasive and potent ideological medium. According to Gramsci's theory of ideological hegemony, mass media are tools that ruling elites use to "perpetuate their power, wealth, and status [by popularizing] their own philosophy, culture and morality" (Boggs, 1976: 39). The mass media uniquely "introduce elements into individual consciousness that would not otherwise appear there, but will not be rejected by consciousness because they are so commonly shared in the cultural community" (Nordenstreng, 1977: 276). Owners and managers of media industries can produce and reproduce the content, inflections, and tones of ideas favorable to them far more easily than other social groups because they manage key socializing institutions, thereby guaranteeing that their points of view are constantly and attractively cast into the public arena.

Mass-mediated ideologies are corroborated and strengthened by an interlocking system of efficacious information-distributing agencies and taken-for-granted social practices that permeate every aspect of social and cultural reality. Messages supportive of the status quo emanating from schools, businesses, political organizations, trade unions, religious groups, the military and the mass media all dovetail together ideologically. This inter-articulating, mutually reinforcing process of ideological influence is the essence of hegemony. Society's most entrenched and powerful institutions—which all depend in one way or another on the same sources for economic support—fundamentally agree with each other ideologically.

Hegemony is not a *direct* stimulation of thought or action, but, according to Stuart Hall, is a "framing [of] all competing definitions of reality within [the dominant class's] range bringing all alternatives within their horizons of thought. [The dominant class] sets the limits—mental and structural—within which subordinate classes 'live' and make sense of their subordination in such a way as to sustain the dominance of those ruling over them" (1977: 333). British social theorist Philip Elliott suggested similarly that the most potent effect of mass media is how they subtly influence their audiences to perceive social roles and routine personal activities. The controlling economic forces in society use the mass media to provide a "rhetoric [through] which these [concepts] are labeled, evaluated, and explained"

(1974: 262). Television commercials, for example, encourage audiences to think of themselves as "markets rather than as a public, as consumers rather than citizens" (Gitlin, 1979: 255).

But hegemony does not mature strictly from ideological articulation. Dominant ideological streams must be subsequently reproduced in the activities of our most basic social units—families, workplace networks, and friendship groups in the many sites and undertakings of everyday life. Gramsci's theory of hegemony, therefore, connects ideological representation to culture. Hegemony requires that ideological assertions become self-evident cultural assumptions. Its effectiveness depends on subordinated peoples accepting the dominant ideology as "normal reality or common sense . . . in active forms of experience and consciousness" (Williams, 1976: 145). Because information and entertainment technology is so thoroughly integrated into the everyday realities of modern societies, mass media's social influence is not always recognized, discussed, or criticized, particularly in societies where the overall standard of living is relatively high. Hegemony, therefore, can easily go undetected (Bausinger, 1984).

Hegemony implies a willing agreement by people to be governed by principles, rules, and laws they believe operate in their best interests, even though in actual practice they may not. Social consent can be a more effective means of control than coercion or force. Again, Raymond Williams: "The idea of hegemony, in its wide sense, is . . . especially important in societies [where] electoral politics and public opinion are significant factors, and in which social practice is seen to depend on consent to certain dominant ideas which in fact express the needs of a dominant class" (1976: 145). Thus, in the words of Colombian communication theorist Jesús Martín-Barbero, "one class exercises hegemony to the extent that the dominating class has interests which the subaltern classes recognize as being in some degree their interests too" (1993: 74).

Relationships between and among the major information-diffusing, socializing agencies of a society and the interacting, cumulative, socially accepted ideological orientations they create and sustain is the essence of hegemony. The American television industry, for instance, connects with other large industries, especially advertising companies but also national and multinational corporations that produce, distribute, and market a wide range of commodities. So, for example, commercial TV networks no longer buy original children's television shows. Network executives only want new program ideas associated with successful retail products already marketed to children. By late 1990 more than 20 toy-based TV shows appeared on American commercial TV weekly. Television also has the ability to absorb other major social institutions—organized religion, for instance—and turn them into popular culture. The TV industry also connects with government institutions, including especially the federal agencies that are supposed to regulate telecommunications. The development of American commercial broadcasting is a vivid example of how capitalist economic forces assert their power. Evacuation of the legislatively mandated public service ideal could only have taken place because the Federal Communications Commission stepped aside while commercial interests amassed power and expanded their influence. Symptomatic of the problem is the fact that government regulators typically are recruited from, and return to, the very industries they are supposed to monitor. . . .

Hegemony as an Incomplete Process

Two of our leading critical theorists, Raymond Williams and Stuart Hall, remind us that hegemony in any political context is indeed fragile. It requires renewal and modification through the assertion and reassertion of power. Hall suggests that "it is crucial to the concept that hegemony is not a 'given' and permanent state of affairs, but it has to be actively won and secured; it can also be lost" (1977: 333). Ideological work is the winning and securing of hegemony over time. . . . Ideology is composed of "texts that are not closed" according to Hall, who also notes that ideological "counter-tendencies" regularly appear in the seams and cracks of dominant forms (Hall, 1985). Mediated communications ranging from popular television shows to rap and rock music, even graffiti scrawled over surfaces of public spaces, all inscribe messages that challenge central political positions and cultural assumptions.

Counter-hegemonic tendencies do not inhere solely in texts. They are formulated in processes of communication—in the interpretations, social circulation, and uses of media content. As with the American soldiers' use of military gas masks as inhaling devices to heighten the effect of marijuana smoke, or the homeless's transformation of supermarket shopping carts into personal storage vehicles, ideological resistance and appropriation frequently involve reinventing institutional messages for purposes that differ greatly from their creators' intentions. Expressions of the dominant ideology are sometimes reformulated to assert alternative, often completely resistant or contradictory messages. . . .

Furthermore, resistance to hegemony is not initiated solely by media consumers. Texts themselves are implicated. Ideology can never be stated purely and simply. Ways of thinking are always reflexive and embedded in a complex, sometimes contradictory, ideological regress. . . .

Audience interpretations and uses of media imagery also eat away at hegemony. Hegemony fails when dominant ideology is weaker than social resistance. Gay subcultures, feminist organizations, environmental groups, radical political parties, music-based formations such as punks, B-boys,

Rastafarians, and metal heads all use media and their social networks to endorse counter-hegemonic values and lifestyles. Indeed, we have only just begun to examine the complex relationship between ideological representation and social action.

References

Bausinger, H. (1984). Media, technology, and everyday life. *Media, Culture & Society*, 6, 340–52.

Boggs, C. (1976). *Gramsci's Marxism*. London: Pluto.

Elliott, P. (1974). Uses and gratifications research: A critique and a sociological alternative. In J. G. Blumler and E. Katz (eds.), *The Uses of Mass Communications: Current Perspectives on Gratifications Research*. Beverly Hills, CA: Sage.

Gitlin, T. (1979). Prime-time ideology: The hegemonic process in television entertainment. *Social Problems*, 26, 251–66.

Gramsci, A. (1971). *Selections from the Prison Notebooks*. New York: International.

Gramsci, A. (1973). *Letters from Prison*. New York: Harper and Row.

Gramsci, A. (1978). *Selections from Cultural Writings*. Cambridge, MA: Harvard University Press.

Hall, S. (1977). Culture, media, and the "ideological effect." In J. Curran, M. Gurevitch, and J. Woollacott (eds.), *Mass Communication and Society*. London: Edward Arnold.

Hall, S. (1985). Master's session. International Communication Association. Honolulu, Hawaii.

Martín-Barbero, J. (1993). *Communication, Culture and Hegemony*. Newbury Park, CA: Sage.

Nordenstreng, K. (1977). From mass media to mass consciousness. In G. Gerbner (ed.), *Mass Media Policies in Changing Cultures*. New York: Wiley.

Sassoon, A. S. (1980). *Gramsci's Politics*. New York: St. Martin's.

Simon, R. (1982). *Gramsci's Political Thought*. London: Lawrence and Wishart.

Straubhaar, J. (1991). Beyond media imperialism: Asymmetrical interdependence and cultural proximity. *Critical Studies in Mass Communication*, 8, 39–59.

Williams, R. (1976). *Key Words: A Vocabulary of Culture and Society*. New York: Oxford University Press.

5

The Internet's Unholy
Marriage to Capitalism

John Bellamy Foster and Robert W. McChesney

The United States and the world are now a good two decades into the Internet revolution, or what was once called the information age. The past generation has seen a blizzard of mind-boggling developments in communication, ranging from the World Wide Web and broadband, to ubiquitous cell phones that are quickly becoming high-powered wireless computers in their own right. Firms such as Google, Amazon, Craigslist, and Facebook have become iconic. Immersion in the digital world is now or soon to be a requirement for successful participation in society. The subject for debate is no longer whether the Internet can be regarded as a technological development in the same class as television or the telephone. Increasingly, the debate is turning to whether this is a communication revolution closer to the advent of the printing press.[1]

The full impact of the Internet revolution will only become apparent in the future, as more technological change is on the horizon that can barely be imagined and hardly anticipated.[2] But enough time has transpired, and institutions and practices have been developed, that an assessment of the digital era is possible, as well as a sense of its likely trajectory into the future.

Our analysis in this article will focus on the United States—not only because it is the society that we know best, and the Internet's point of origin, but also because it is there, we believe, that one most clearly finds the integration of monopoly-finance capital and the Internet, representing the dominant tendency of the global capitalist system. This is not meant to suggest that the current U.S. dominance of the Internet is not open to change, or that other countries may not choose to take other paths—but only that all alternatives in this realm will have to struggle against the trajectory now being set by U.S. capitalism, with its immense global influence and power. . . .

The Internet, or more broadly, the digital revolution is truly changing the world at multiple levels. But it has also failed to deliver on much of the promise that was once seen as implicit in its technology. If the Internet was expected to provide more competitive

From John Bellamy Foster and Robert W. McChesney, "The Internet's Unholy Marriage to Capitalism," *Monthly Review* online (2011). Volume 62, Issue 10. Reprinted with permission of *Monthly Review*.

markets and accountable businesses, open government, an end to corruption, and decreasing inequality—or, to put it baldly, increased human happiness—it has been a disappointment. ...

We do not argue that the initial sense of the Internet's promise was pure fantasy, although some of it can be attributed to the utopian enthusiasm that major new technologies can engender when they first emerge. (One is reminded of the early-twentieth-century view of the Nobel Prize-winning chemist and philosopher of energetics, Wilhelm Ostwald, who contended that the advent of the "flying machine" was a key part of a universal process that could erase international boundaries associated with nations, languages, and money, "bringing about the brotherhood of man."[3]) Instead, we argue that there was—and remains—extraordinary democratic and revolutionary promise in this communication revolution. But technologies do not ride roughshod over history, regardless of their immense powers. They are developed in a social, political, and economic context. And this has strongly conditioned the course and shape of the communication revolution.

This economic context points to the *paradox of the Internet* as it has developed in a capitalist society. The Internet has been subjected, to a significant extent, to the capital accumulation process, which has a clear logic of its own, inimical to much of the democratic potential of digital communication, and that will be ever more so, going forward. What seemed to be an increasingly open public sphere, removed from the world of commodity exchange, seems to be morphing into a private sphere of increasingly closed, proprietary, even monopolistic markets.

... We hope to provide a necessary alternative way to imagine how best to develop the Internet in contrast to the commodified, privatized world of capital accumulation. This does not mean that there can be no commerce, even extensive commerce, in the digital realm, but merely that the system's overriding logic—and the starting point for all policy discussions—must be as an institution operated on public interest values, at bare minimum as a public utility.

It is true that in any capitalist society there is going to be strong, even at times overwhelming, pressure to open up areas that can be profitably exploited by capital, regardless of the social costs, or "negative externalities," as economists put it. After all, capitalists—by definition, given their economic power—exercise inordinate political power. But it is not a given that all areas will be subjected to the market. Indeed, many areas in nature and human existence cannot be so subjected without destroying the fabric of life itself—and large portions of capitalist societies have historically been and remain largely outside of the capital accumulation process. One could think of community, family, religion, education, romance, elections, research, and national defense as partial examples, although capital is pressing to colonize those where it can. Many important political debates in a capitalist society are concerned with determining the areas where the pursuit of profit will be allowed to rule, and where it will not. At their most rational, and most humane, capitalist societies tend to preserve large noncommercial sectors, including areas such as health care and old-age pensions, that might be highly profitable if turned over to commercial interests. At the very least, the more democratic a capitalist society is, the more likely it is for there to be credible public debates on these matters.

However—and this is a point dripping in irony—such a fundamental debate never took place in relation to the Internet.

... The lack of debate about how the Internet should be developed was due, to a certain extent, to the digital revolution exploding at precisely the moment that neoliberalism was in ascendance, its flowery rhetoric concerning "free markets" most redolent. The core spirit was that businesses should always be permitted to develop any area where profits could be found, and that this was the most efficient use of resources for an economy. Anything interfering with capitalist exploitation was bad economics and ideologically loaded, and was usually advanced by a deadbeat "special interest" group that could not cut the mustard in the world of free market competition and so sought protection from the corrupt netherworld of government regulation and bureaucracy.[4] This credo led the drive for "deregulation" across the economy, and for the privatization of once public sector activities.

The rhetoric of free markets was adopted by all sides in the communications debate in the early 1990s, as the World Wide Web turned the Internet seemingly overnight into a mass medium. For the business community and politicians, the Internet was all about unleashing entrepreneurs, slaying monopolies, promoting innovation, and generating "friction-free capitalism," as Bill Gates famously put it.[5] There was great money to be made. Even those skeptical toward corporations and commercialism tended to be unconcerned, if not sanguine, about the capitalist invasion, as the power of this apparently magical technology could override the efforts of dinosaur corporations to tame it. There was plenty of room for everybody. The Internet bubble of the late 1990s certainly encouraged capitalism's embrace of the Internet, and U.S. news media could barely contain themselves with their enthusiasm for the happy couple. Capitalism and the Internet seemed a marriage made in heaven.

Internet Service Providers

A more sober analysis, however, can locate certain inconsistencies, if not contradictions, in ascribing so called "free markets" to the Internet, beyond the fact that the Internet's very existence was a testament to public sector investment. . . .

First, the dominant wires that would come to deliver Internet service provider (ISP) broadband access for Americans were and are controlled by the handful of firms that dominated telephone and cable television. These firms were all local monopolies that existed because of government monopoly licenses. In effect, they have been the recipients of enormous indirect government subsidies through their government monopoly franchises. . . . The telephone companies had lent their wires to Internet transmission and, over the course of the 1990s, they—soon followed by the cable companies—realized it was their future, and a very lucrative one, at that. All the more so, considering that ISP's are the only entry point to the Internet and digital networks.

These telephone and cable giants came to support the long process of what was called the "deregulation" of their industries that came to a head in the 1990s, not because they eagerly anticipated ferocious new competition, but because they suspected deregulation would allow them to grow ever larger and have more monopolistic power. . . .

Deregulation has led to the worst of both worlds: fewer enormous firms with far less regulation.[6] To top it off, the political power of these firms in Washington, D.C. and state capitals has reached Olympian heights. . . . Unlike firms in many other nations, U.S. telephone and cable firms are not required to allow competitor broadband ISPs access to their wires, so there is virtually no meaningful competition in the now crucial broadband ISP industry. Fully 18 percent of U.S. households have access to no more than a single broadband provider—a monopoly. . . . Meanwhile, four companies control the mushrooming U.S. wireless market, and the two leaders—AT&T and Verizon—are in the process of amassing one hundred million subscribers each. With dreams of converting the Internet into an expanded version of cable television, all of these firms have spectacular incentive to "privatize" the Internet as much as possible, and to use their control over broadband access as a bottleneck where they can exact additional tolls on users. Moreover, with little meaningful competition, as the FCC acknowledges, these firms have no particular incentive to upgrade their networks.[7]

Remarkably, the United States, which created and first developed the Internet, and which ranked, throughout the 1990s, close to first in world Internet connectivity, now ranks between fifteen and twenty in most global measures of broadband access, quality of service, and cost per megabit.[8] There is no incentive to terminate the "digital divide," whereby poor and rural Americans remain unconnected to broadband far beyond the rates in other advanced nations; a digital underclass encourages people to pay what it takes to avoid being unconnected. There is a striking comparison here to health care, where Americans pay far more than any other nation per capita, but get worse service, due to the parasitic existence of the health insurance industry. President Barack Obama said that if the United States were starting from scratch, it would obviously make more sense (from a public welfare standpoint) to have a publicly run health care system, and no private health insurance industry.[9] The same overall logic applies to broadband Internet access, in spades. . . .

Market Concentration in Multiple Areas

. . . Capitalist development of Internet-related industries has quickly, inexorably, generated considerable market concentration at almost every level, often beyond that found in non-digital markets. What this means is that there are multiple areas where private interests can get a chokehold on the Internet and seize monopoly profits, and they are all being pursued. Google, for example, holds 70 percent of the search engine market, and its share is increasing. It is on pace to challenge the market share that John D. Rockefeller's Standard Oil had at its peak. Microsoft, Intel, Amazon, eBay, Facebook, Cisco, and a handful of other giants enjoy considerable monopolistic power as well. The crucial Wi-Fi chipset market, for example, is a duopoly where two firms have 80 percent of the market between them.[10] Apple, via iTunes, controls an estimated 87 percent market share in digital music downloads and 70 percent of the MP3 player market.[11]

This, too, runs directly counter to the notion of the Internet as a generator of competition and consumer empowerment, and as a place for an alternative to the top-down corporate system to prosper. Writers like Clay Shirky and Yochai Benkler wax eloquent about the revolutionary potential for collaborative and cooperative work online. Some of this has carved out an important niche on the Internet, which stands as a tangible reminder of how different the Internet could look. They point to peer-to-peer activities, the Open Source movement, Mozilla Firefox, WikiLeaks, and the Wikipedia experience. We find this work illuminating and encouraging, and it points to the great potential of the Internet that we have only begun to tap.[12]

But this collaborative potential, arguably the democratic genius of the Internet, runs up against the pressure of capital to consolidate monopoly power, create artificial scarcity, and erect fences wherever possible. At nearly every turn, industries connected to the Internet have transitioned from competitive to oligopolistic in short order. To a large extent, this is a familiar story: any sane capitalist wants to have as much market power and as little competition as possible. By conventional economic theory, concentration in markets in general is bad for the efficient allocation of resources in an economy. Monopoly is the enemy of competition, and competition is what keeps the system honest.

. . . Most important, the Internet adds to the mix what economists term "network effects," meaning that just about everyone gains by sharing use of a particular service or resource. Information networks, in particular, generate "demand-side economies of scale," related to the capture of customers as opposed to supply-side economies of scale (prevalent in traditional oligopolistic industry) related to cost advantages as scale goes up.[13] The largest firm in an industry increases its attractiveness to consumers by an order of magnitude as its gets a greater market share—similar to how a hurricane picks up speed as it crosses the ocean on a hot summer day—and makes it almost impossible for competitors with declining shares to remain attractive or competitive. . . .

Google is a classic example of economies of scale and monopoly power; as it grows larger, its search engine becomes ever more superior to erstwhile competitors, not to mention it gains the capacity to build up traditional barriers-to-entry and scare away anyone trying to mess with it.[14] Its network effects are so large that it has drowned out all other search engines, allowing it to prosper by selling data derived from its network to others (as well as prominently positioning paid-for "sponsored links"), marketing the vast mine of data at its disposal. In the old days, such "winner take all" markets were termed "natural monopolies."[15]

Likewise, consider Microsoft, which has been able to exploit the dependence of a wide range of software applications on its underlying operating system in order to lock in its operating system seemingly permanently, allowing it to enjoy long-term monopoly-pricing power. Any competitor, seeking to introduce a new, rival operating system, is faced with an enormous "applications barrier to entry."[16] "Apps" have thus become key to the construction of barriers of entry and monopoly power, not only in relation to information technology in general, but also, more crucially today, in relation to the Internet.

Along these lines, new devices, such as the iPhone and the iPad, carry with them applications specific to a given device that are designed to lock customers in a whole commercial domain that mediates between them and the Internet—quite differently than the Web—and that generates "network effects" and rising sales for the producer. The more that a particular device becomes the interface for whole networks of applications, the more customers are drawn in, and the exponential demand-side economies of scale take over. This directly translates into enormous economic power, and the ability to determine much of the technological landscape. Once such economic power is fully consolidated and people become increasingly dependent on a new device, network prices can be leveraged up. . . .

Such monopolistic firms accrue huge amounts of cash with which they can gobble up any potential competitor or promising upstart attempting to create a new commercial sector on the Internet. These corporate giants use their monopoly base camps to make expeditions to conquer new areas in the Internet, especially those in proximity to their monopoly undertaking. Google, for example, has a purported $33 billion in cash to play with. It has spent many billions making several dozen key Internet acquisitions, averaging around one acquisition per month, over the past several years. In just the first three quarters of 2010, Google reported that it made forty distinct acquisitions.[17] Microsoft, with $43 billion in cash on hand, has a similar record. Apple is sitting on $51 billion in cash to play with.

The idea that new technological breakthroughs will create competition online is increasingly absurd, and if it does somehow happen, it will only be a temporary stop on the way to more monopoly. The exceptional case is not actual competition—that is not even in the range of outcomes—but, instead when a new application avoids being conquered by an existing giant and creates another new monopolistic powerhouse (a new Facebook, for example) because the upstart is able to escape the clutches or enticements of an existing giant laden with cash, and create its own "walled garden" of economic value. The name of the game in such "walled gardens" of value is to exploit what economists now sometimes call "an enhanced surplus extraction effect," that is, the increased ability to fleece those walled within.[18]

Even more dire by the standards of conventional economics is the manner in which this monopoly power permits giant Internet firms effectively to control the policy-making process and rigidify their power with minimal public "interference." To the extent there are genuine policy debates, it is because powerful firms and sectors—much like King Kong and Godzilla—square off against one another. The most striking manner in which this political power manifests itself is with regard to electromagnetic spectrum, which can be defined as "the resource on which all forms of electronic wireless communication rely—the range of frequencies usable for the transmission of information." There is an enormous amount of unused spectrum that could be put to use—greater than the amount actually in use—but the incumbent spectrum users prefer the artificial scarcity that rewards them, and the government obliges. In 2011 AT&T alone has license to $10 billion worth of spectrum that is laying fallow, while it lobbies to have more spectrum diverted to it.[19] . . .

In the realm of the Internet, a state-corporate alliance has developed that is matched perhaps only in finance and militarism. It makes a mockery of traditional economics, with its emphasis on an independent private sector responding to a competitive market. It also makes a mockery of the traditional liberal notion that capitalist democracy works because economic power and political power are in two distinct sets of hands, and that these interests have strong conflicts that protect the public from tyranny. Examples of how large communication corporations and the national security state work hand-in-hand are beginning to proliferate. The one that was exposed—and is singularly terrifying—concerned how, for much of the past decade, AT&T illegally and secretly monitored the communications of its customers on behalf of the National Security Agency.[20] . . .

This integration of corporations and the state leads us to reappraise one of the greatest claims for the Internet: the notion that the Internet was impervious to control or censorship, and is the tool of the democratic activist. The same Internet, for both commercial and political reasons, can provide an unparalleled instrument for surveillance.[21] This does not mean that activists cannot use the Internet to do extraordinary organizing, merely that this has to be balanced with the notion that the Internet can make individual privacy from state and corporate interests difficult, if not impossible. The monopoly-capitalist development of the Internet has given more weight to the antidemocratic tendency. . . .

THE PARADOX OF THE INTERNET

In a world in which private riches grow at the expense of public wealth, it should not surprise us that what seemed at first as the enormous potential of the Internet—representing a whole new realm of public wealth, analogous to the discovery of a whole new continent, and pointing to the possibility of a vast new democratic sphere of unrestricted communication—has vaporized in a couple of decades. Competitive strategy in this sphere revolves around the concept of the lock-in of customers and the leveraging of demand-side economies of scale, which allow for the creation of massive concentrations of capital in individual firms.

Like the elimination of free land in the United States, the Internet is being transformed into a few dominant spaces that are thereby able to exploit their scarcity value. The effective "closure" (or displacement) of much of the free public space on the Internet, which now seems to be occurring, means that what was once clearly a form of public wealth in new communicative possibilities, as measured by use values—that is, in the new, universal human capacities it seemed to promise—is giving way to a very different type of system. Here exchange value dominates, and the disappearance of those use values associated with relatively free communication comes to be registered as a gain in wealth, since it produces massive private riches overnight.

...An innovation is commercially developed, and a market created, only by finding a way to "wall" off a sector of public wealth and effectively privatize and monopolize it, leading to huge returns. Information, which is a public good—by nature available to all and, if consumed by one person, still available to others—is, in this way, turned into a scarce private commodity through the exercise of sheer market power.

All of this is possible, however, only with the cooperation of the public sector. The privatization and monopolization of the Internet requires a state, which, in partnership with capital, neither provides the population with the alternatives necessary to develop access to this public domain, nor protects it against Internet robber barons. The state, in effect, looks the other way when it sees new realms of economic wealth being made out of "nothing" (the value attributed to, say, the electromagnetic spectrum outside market exchange) and fails to move against rapid concentration of capital, even facilitating the latter.

The FCC's approval of the 2011 merger of Comcast and NBC Universal is a case in point. As FCC Commissioner Michael Copps stated, in his lone dissenting vote: the merger "opens the door to cable-ization of the Internet." According to Copps, this creates "the potential for walled gardens, toll booths, content prioritization, access fees to reach end users, and a stake in the heart of independent content production."[22] Public wealth, free access, net neutrality, and a democratic communicative sphere are all losers. In this way, the real wealth of the Internet, like a newly discovered land that has not yet been explored, is given away to private interests—before the population has been able to realize or even to imagine the full material use value of such a realm, if managed in the public interest.

Communication is more than an ordinary market. Indeed, it is properly not a market at all. It is more like air or water—a form of public wealth, a commons. When Aristotle said that human beings were "*social animals*," he might just as well have said that we are *communicative animals*. We know that the human brain coevolved with language (a social characteristic).[23] The development of social relations and democratic forms, as well as science, culture, etc., are all communicative. The rise of the Internet as a form of free communication, seemingly without limits, thus raises the prospect of vast new realms of human sociability and enhanced democratic possibilities. Yet, rather than a means of expanding human sociability, the Internet is being turned into the opposite: a new means of alienation. There is nothing natural in this process; at bottom it remains a social choice.

The moral of the story is clear. People in the United States and worldwide must redouble their efforts to address the paradox of the Internet at all levels of the analysis presented herein. The outcome is far from certain, and the issues are still very much in play. A global network of resistance is both necessary and feasible. Indeed, in view of the nature of the Internet and the stakes involved, it seems fair to say that these issues will only become more encompassing in coming years. How this battle plays out will go a long way toward determining our future as social animals.

Notes

1. For a discussion of this point, see Robert W. McChesney, *Communication Revolution* (New York: The New Press, 2007), ch. 3.

2. For important recent discussions of the negative implications of the digital revolution, see Nicholas Carr, *The Shallows: What the Internet Is Doing to Our Brains* (New York: W.W. Norton, 2010); Sherry Turkle, *Alone Together: Why We Expect More from Technology and Less from Each Other* (New York: Basic Books, 2011).

3. Wilhelm Ostwald, "Breaking the Boundaries," *The Masses* (February 1911), 15–16.

4. See Ha-Joon Chang, *23 Things They Don't Tell You About Capitalism* (New York: Bloomsbury Press, 2010) for a superb discussion of this point and debunking of the other ideological ballast underpinning neoliberal economics.

5. Bill Gates, *The Road Ahead* (New York: Viking, 1995), 180.

6. For a revealing discussion of the 1990s lobbying by the telephone companies, see Tim Wu, *The Master Switch: The Rise and Fall of Information Empires* (New York: Alfred A. Knopf, 2010).

7. The information in this paragraph comes from *Connecting America: The National Broadcasting Plan* (Washington, D.C.: Federal Communications Commission, 2010), 37–38.

8. For OECD data see OECD, Directorate for Science, Technology and Industry, OECD Broadband Portal, http://oecd. org. See also: James Losey and Chiehyu Li, *Price of the Pipe: Comparing the Price of Broadband Service Around the Globe* (Washington, DC: New America Foundation, 2010).

9. Lynn Sweet, "Obama on why he is not for single payer health insurance. New Mexico town hall transcript," *Chicago Sun Times*, May 14, 2009, http://blogs.suntimes.com. Of course, Obama's statement was partly meant to justify acceding to the demands of the insurance companies, since a truly rational course, he implied, was no longer possible. He was wrong. It would still make more sense today from a health care standpoint to move to a publicly run health care system, but vested interests, which benefit from the present system, stand in the way.

10. Sascha D. Meinrath, James W. Losey, and Victor W. Pickard, "Digital Feudalism: Enclosures and Erasures from Digital Rights Management to the Digital Divide," *CommLaw Conspectus,* vol. 19, no. 2 (2011).

11. Adam L. Penenberg, "The Evolution of Amazon," *Fast Company* (July 2009), 66–74.

12. Yochai Benkler, *The Wealth of Networks* (New Haven: Yale University Press, 2006); Clay Shirky, *Cognitive Surplus: Creativity and Generosity in a Connected Age* (New York: The Penguin Press, 2010).

13. Carl Shapiro and Hal R. Varian, *Information Rules* (Boston: Harvard Business School Press, 1999), 173.

14. Matthew Hindman, *The Myth of Digital Democracy* (Princeton: Princeton University Press, 2009), 84–86. Hindman does a superb job of demonstrating the immense capital expenses Google incurs to assure its dominance, and that all but guarantee no other firm can or will challenge it in the search engine market.

15. Jia Lynn Yang, "Google: A 'Natural Monopoly'?" *Fortune*, May 10, 2009, http://money.cnn.com.

16. Hal R. Varian, Joseph Farrell, and Carl Shapiro, *The Economics of Information Technology* (Cambridge: Cambridge University Press, 2004), 37, 49, 71–72; Richard Gilbert and Michael L. Katz, "An Economists's Guide to US v. Microsoft," *Journal of Economic Perspectives* 15, no. 2 (2001): 30.

17. Google, Inc., "Quarterly Report Form 10-Q," September 30, 2010. http://investor.google.com/ documents/20100930_google_10Q. html.

18. Anderson, "The Web Is Dead," 127; Varian, Farrell, and Shapiro, *The Economics of Information Technology*, 14.

19. Karl Bode, "AT&T Wants FCC to Free More Spectrum—For Them to Squat On," *Broadband DSL Reports*, January 14, 2011, http://dslreports.com.

20. See Wu, 249–52.

21. Evgeny Morozov, *The Net Delusion: The Dark Side of Internet Freedom* (New York: Public Affairs, 2011).

22. "FCC's Copps Fears 'Cable-ization of the Internet," January 20, 2011, http:// broadcastengineering.com.

23. Terence W. Deacon, *The Symbolic Species: The Co-evolution of Language and the Brain* (New York: W.W. Norton, 1997).

6

Extreme Makeover: Home Edition

An American Fairy Tale

Gareth Palmer

It's a fairy tale. It's a guaranteed happy ending (Forman 2005).

ABC's *Extreme Makeover: Home Edition* (hereafter *EMHE*) was one of the top ten programmes of the 2004/05 season in America and winner of the 2005 Emmy for Outstanding Reality TV Programme. *EMHE* tells a fascinating story about modern day America where the return of a strong right-wing ideology privileges the traditional family and the interests of business, yet also affords a glimpse of the crises affecting ordinary Americans. In the model of community proposed by the programme, the state has no role to play: in its place are people coming together out of fellow-feeling for their neighbours. But the repair work is so extreme it throws into relief the mundane quality of most American homes. In promoting such a perspective both in the programme and through its various affiliated enterprises with Sears etc., ABC are championing an America which resonates with its mythical past but which is utterly unrepresentative of family life for most Americans. The programme is, in short, a fairy tale where magic is represented by selfless communities, free goods, labour, and dreams coming true.

The Family

> ... Representations have become a critical battleground in the conflicts over family and family values leading to the spectacularization of the family as the platform on which society's profound debates about sexual and personal morality are performed. (Chambers 2001: 176)

From Palmer, G. (2007). *Extreme Makeover: Home Edition:* An American fairy tale. In D. Heller (Ed.), *Makeover TV: Realities remodelled* (pp. 165–176). London: I. B. Taurus.

EMHE starts every week with a sequence in which the assorted designers who will lead the re-design of the house are situated in a van watching the targeted family's videotape. Team Leader Ty Pennington gives the background to this family and the rest of this sequence involves reaction shots of all involved. What is remarkable about this sequence, at least for this British viewer, is that these video-diary sequences sent in by the family are all extraordinarily revealing about the state of America.

In many cases the desperation of families is a direct result of the fact that agencies of the state have abandoned them. For example, in one case a family had to watch their son die because ambulances and police refused to go into their neighbourhood for fear of their lives. In another video we see a family whose son is dying because he is ineligible for medical aid. In yet another typical episode, an Iraq War veteran has materials provided for him, as the state does not support veterans very generously. Week after week we see first hand video testimony that the state is in retreat and only those lucky enough to have many friends, family and neighbours are able to survive. . . .

After watching their tape for a few moments the crew arrive, and the family to be chosen is woken very early in the morning, on the doorstep of their home. This magical moment is only the first of many such other-worldly touches in the narrative. After meeting the team and crying tears of gratitude, the family is then whisked away for a week-long holiday while crew, enlisted community, and contractors go about the business of changing their home.

What follows is a monumental effort to effect the transformation. But why has all this energy been devoted to making the home so central? In the last ten years, makeover shows have become a mainspring of TV schedules in Britain and America. In each case a person with limited resources is assisted into a new look and given the confidence he or she needs to progress. However,

at the centre of these 'reveals' is the family. In examples ranging from *This Old House* to *The Swan* it is the family that has inspired the change and the family who are focused on in their reaction to it. In this way the home is remade as a machine for keeping families together, the place to retreat to. It need hardly be said that such an approach brings to mind long and powerful myths about the centrality of the family. In Anthony Giddens' formulation, 'The site for the democratisation of intimate relationships, the family becomes a major platform on which debates about moralities and ethics get staged' (Giddens 1999: 165).

The makeover show turns individuals into family members, foregrounds the family and makes it a part of the wider community. It is hard to imagine a clearer message about the centrality of the home and the importance of keeping the family together come what may. . . .

It might be argued that there are two families at work in *EMHE*—the subject of the makeover and the extended family of the design team. It is, after all, this latter family that we get to know every week through their work and their relationships with one another. It is they who represent a modern family with no fixed relationships and no permanent 'home' they can call their own. (We might also note that the five men exhibit some of the camp characteristics that are now a trademark of the makeover genre: only in this sense can the hint of homosexuality be tolerated, in a space marked off from ordinary life.) In a sense, the *EMHE* team represent the fluid upwardly mobile petit bourgeoisie against the time-worn virtues of the proletariat. This divide between the classes ensures that the working class are always receptive and thankful for the 'good taste' bestowed upon them by the middle class. But while it is the role of the working class to be properly grateful, the designers are all seen to be humbled by their experience, which extends beyond the show and is maintained through letters and notes pinned to a message board.

The coming together of these two family groupings is about 'learning'—a theme that dominates so much American television. While the working class learn taste, the petit bourgeoisie learn about 'real people' (i.e. the sort of people they would not normally ever encounter in their lives as designers for the rich and famous). This learning is a means of bringing groups together, the wider theme that animates the series and which keys it into the classic picture of an America constituted of families connected to communities making one nation (Morley and Robins 1995: 109).

At the end of the show the ramshackle house, held together by the depth of the bonds between the family members, is replaced by a magnificent home. . . . As we are led through the magically transformed home at the same time as the family, we, too, can be awestruck by the changes wrought by the designers and of course the wider community. In one sense, we marvel at the high quality of the work achieved, but perhaps more significant is the fact that we are reminded that this transformation is also a reward—it is because people have held the family together in very difficult situations that they deserve this home. In clips and segments that remind us of the past, we are moved to see that these people have got what they deserve. The home is an extension of the love that the family members hold for one another. By undergoing this transformation as a reward for their dedication to the family, the individuals go from being objects of our pity to ones of our envy. . . .

Community

'A better community—get involved and help—click here.' (ABC website)

Makeover programmes are the most overt sign of the ways television perceives itself to be engaged in a project of advising ordinary viewers about their transformation into happier, more satisfied, up-to-date versions of their selves. (Bonner 2003: 136)

The community plays a central role in *EMHE*. It is made clear throughout the programme and in all accompanying materials that it is the community that are responsible for making the whole thing come together. While it may be designers who provide the creative impetus, it is the community that are seen doing all the unglamorous heavy work. Unlike the virtual shadow-communities inspired to 'call the cops' in response to televised police appeals, which dissolve once their contribution is made, *EMHE* features real communities showing us all how to work together.

To begin with, the community has often been the sponsor of the families who are featured. As Forman has said: 'Most of the families we end up doing are nominations. The kind of families we're looking for don't say "Gee, I need help". They are quietly trying to solve their problems themselves and it's a neighbor or co-worker who submits and application on their behalf.' (Forman 2005)

We see the community, shortly after the programme begins, giving testimony to the deserving family, then later throughout the show at work in various jobs. They play small but significant roles in the drama as the glue in the cracks of the community holding everything together. And yet they are also there in the reveal. They 'star' here because of what they have done to bring about these changes. Whether as contractors, friends, tradesmen or simply labourers, all have a role to play and are defined not so much as individuals but as part of a greater whole. No individual pulls focus: it is always about the larger community. But what actually constitutes this community?

It is important to see the entire series in context as a trigger for activating a wide variety of communities. For example, the local press are often keen to highlight the series if a local family is involved. In Salt Lake City we learn of the '1,500 workers and volunteers working 24 hours a day to build a bigger home for the Johnson family.' In the *Boston Globe* we read about how residents had 'been rooting for more than a year for a family to be picked up by the show.' Once they had been selected, the community were all too keen to get involved.

Two allied supporters of this community effort are local businesses and the Church. John McMurria has pointed out how Sears has benefited from the programme (McMurria 2005). But plenty of other local services are represented in *EMHE*, not as profit-led businesses but as benevolent organizations. The value of PR here can be enormous as big cardboard cheques are presented to tearful local residents. As one business said of a veteran— 'He has such a sweet and humble spirit and we wanted to thank him for the way he loves for his country and his family.'

It is important also to note that American Christian groups have been generous in praising the show. As Evangelical journalist Holly Vincente Robaina wrote, 'It's a rare phenomenon. Believers of every age, ethnicity and denomination are embracing the primetime television show ABC's *Extreme Makeover: Home Edition*' (Robaina 2006).

Executive producer Tom Forman was specifically asked whether any plan was made to 'include elements that would connect specifically with Christian values.' Forman responded that the show appealed because 'good things happen to good people. That's possibly why it resonates with the Christian community and all of our viewers' (Forman, ABC interview).

Church leaders are quoted by the local press, such as Mr A. Wigston in the *Cass County Democrat of Missouri*. 'It was really neat to see God working through the hearts of the designers for people with disabilities.' Some other churches have set out on 'copy-cat' schemes in which members decorate or attempt mini-makeovers

of their own in just the way that producer Forman had hoped they would. Not only does this imitative practice privilege the role of the Church in the community, but the reporting and celebration of this role presents a clear ideological message on the centrality of helping heterosexual families. But is this at the expense of other communities?

These timeless myths of the American 'heartland', featuring the happy smiling community working for nothing but love, bring to mind classic American TV fictions such as *Little House on the Prairie* and *The Waltons*. These idealized versions of perfect family life may be instructive about nostalgia in the 1970s and 1980s, and for settled family life in a time of great upheaval. But of course these fictions were located in the past when such a myth may have been feasible. But what are we to make of *EMHE*'s portrait of American life, which suggests such ideals are here with us now? . . .

The Magical Market

. . . One of the most unusual factors about the programme for British viewers is the complete absence of cost. In contrast to many UK makeover shows, costs are never mentioned in *EMHE*. Why is this? The instinctual answer has to be that costs have no place in a fairy tale. Do we know where the Prince bought the glass slippers? Of course not—these are crass questions. It is our role simply to be enchanted by the transformations wrought. But, at the risk of breaking the spell, there are various economic elements that I think merit discussion, for they speak to the real and entirely non-magical base of the programme.

In the first place, we might consider the costs of labour. What would it cost to hire such designers or to employ upwards of 150 people for 24 hours a day, seven days a week? Secondly, we might look at the cost of the furnishings, the materials and the many other artful purchases that go into the ideal home. It is only at the end of the show that we have any sort of opportunity to calculate the cost of this transformation, but by then we are too emotionally involved to make such calculations. The point is that all of these costs are hidden in the service of repairing families. But not mentioning costs makes these repairs appear free or even magical. As most communities know, the economic is determining and not at all magical. The fact is that there are many who profit enormously from the show.

While it is clearly the case that one family will benefit from the makeover, the public relations benefits to others involved are extraordinary. The most obvious recipient of good PR is the Sears corporation. The programme's website makes it clear that the company is a major partner in the production of the show. It is worth noting that Sears also sponsor *EMHE* host Ty Pennington. Pennington's 'can-do' attitude represents something that Sears wants—as long as the 'can-do' he recommends is connected to Sears products. Pennington legitimates Sears as a caring company through his leadership of such obvious good works.

But Sears is only the most high profile of sponsors. Every week we hear of many other local organizations that have devoted their goods and services to the families in need. At this point we are encouraged to think of local businesses not as profit driven but as charitable organizations. The PR benefit of this publicity is enhanced when favourable coverage appears in the local papers about the *EMHE* projects in their town. This would be a good time for local businesses to place adverts reminding consumers of their modest role in the transformation.

Thirdly, and perhaps most obviously, the benefits to ABC will be very considerable. Firstly, there are the benefits in revenue that accrue to shows that are doing well. This factor is particularly important when competition from other stations and other media is more intensive than ever

before. During the show the families often thank ABC while the presenters and others also make subtle mention of how the programme has only been possible through the good offices of the station. Again, this will represent an invaluable opportunity for the station to define itself as family-driven in contrast to its more ruthless rivals CBS, Fox and NBC. This benefit sometimes informs the company's well-advertised outreach programmes and also helps to inspire other shows. The praise heaped on the programme by churches and other religious groups helps ABC reposition itself in the family market. (The station's owner, The Disney channel, has used gay-friendly corporate policies and has sponsored broadcast gay-themed sitcoms such as *Ellen,* resulting in criticism from Christian groups. *EMHE* redefines ABC as a wholesome family station.)

Finally, is it not also the case that the programme is of enormous benefit to the eight designers who appear on the show? The 'good works' they do here will drive business to their companies as well as raise their price in the celebrity market as guest speakers, seminar leaders, etc.

But what is crucial to all of this is that the market appears to be driven not by the hunt for profit but by the simple desire to do 'good works'. In this way, capitalism is sold to audiences as a warm and responsive mechanism reacting to community needs rather than a system for maximizing profits. It is not money that pulls people together, but a sort of magic. . . .

Television That Works

> An ethics of care as presented in lifestyle programmes is primarily about care and responsibility. . . good and bad way[s] to live their lives. (Hill 2005: 184)

EMHE is part of a growing number of television programmes that are not simply recording or reflecting on society but becoming active elements, working practically and ideologically to change the world. . . .

In one sense, television has always done this. Magical solutions to practical problems for everyday people have been the staple of quiz and games shows for decades. But the past twenty years have seen a distinct rise in the number of programmes that focus on intervening in the lives of the public. In a curious historical quirk, commercial television is engaging with the public in a way that PBS, public television, can no longer afford to do. But commercial interests inspire all these interventions. *Wife Swap, Big Brother* and *Temptation Island* are not there to help the public (despite the rhetoric) but to offer mutual exploitation opportunities. They work, however, and this fact is proved night after night in reality TV shows, makeover shows, talk shows, cosmetic surgery shows, and many other programmes made at the behest of commercial institutions. Like any other product maker, the apparatus of ABC has a vested interest in producing 'good' (i.e. repeatable) results. Furthermore, if it does this in a way which makes it look socially responsible, then it gets a double-whammy. Not only does this help to keep the profile of the medium high but it also foregrounds television as a site for the validation of the person. To be on television is now one of the highest honours that can be accorded someone.

There is another significant point underscoring and helping to guarantee the effects of *EMHE* and others in the lifestyle genre, and it is in the craft of performance. *EMHE* is a very polished production that pulls together emotionally moving performances with the use of music, lighting and photography. Not only does the styling of the show borrow creatively from drama, it also emphasizes a theatrical transformation that will impress children—the next generation whose devotion to the medium all stations need to cherish. . . .

It would be comforting to think that our own responses to the transformations, led by the families and designers, heralded some sort of emotional literacy, but even if we try to gain comfort from this we cannot escape the fact that this is all wrought for commercial profit (Littler 2004: 20). It is sad to reflect upon, but the radical changes to one family's life that we see in *EMHE* would simply not happen if it were not for television. Despite the powerful and manipulative devices that bring forth our involvement, at base the programme is a device for selling audiences to advertisers. It is not an engine for social change. . . .

Conclusion

Commercial culture does not manufacture ideology, it relays and reproduces and processes and packages and focuses ideology that is constantly arising set forth both from social elites and from active social groups and movements throughout the society. (Gitlin 1994: 518)

We have seen that *EMHE* produces a vision of America that has powerful emotional resonances. Its view of the world articulates connections with families, the Christian right and the neo-conservative policies of the Bush era. Yet the programme also provides gaps and fissures through which we can see massive cracks appearing in the American Dream. Although *EMHE* might seem like an unadulterated paean of praise to Capitalism, it fails to completely convince because of what it reveals as the inspirations to the makeover: things have got to be so bad because of the retreat of the state, that radical, even magical, consumer surgery is necessary. . . .

The fact is that in modern-day America many families and communities have been wrecked by policies that force them to uproot and look for work elsewhere. While the statistics attest to the breakdown of the family unit, ABC is doing the massive ideological labour of shoring it up. In the face of this breakdown *EMHE* deploys its excesses. The revamped houses look like sets because they are there to provide ideal templates for the performance of family roles.

As capitalism continues to deepen divisions between rich and poor, ABC offers the cold comfort of the *EMHE* fairy tale, the belief that if the family holds together despite everything that can be thrown against it, then the reward will eventually come.

Hope may be all they have.

References

Bonner, Frances. *Ordinary Television: Analyzing Popular TV*. London: Sage, 2003.

Chambers, D. *Representing the Family*. London: Sage, 2001.

Forman, T. Interview at official ABC website. (2005) www.abc.go.com/primetime/xtreme home/index.html

Giddens, Anthony. *Runaway World: How Globalisation Is Reshaping Our Lives*. London: Profile Books, 1999.

Gitlin, T. "Prime Time Ideology: The Hegemonic Process in Television Entertainment." In Horace Newcomb, ed., *Television: The Critical View*. Oxford: Oxford University Press, 1994.

Hill, Annette. *Reality TV: Audiences and Popular Factual Television*. London: Routledge, 2005.

Littler, J. "Making Fame Ordinary: Intimacy, Reflexitivity, Keeping It Real." *Mediactive*. 2 (2004): 8–25.

McMurria, John. "Desperate Citizens." Flow. 3.3 (2005). http://jot.communication.utexas.edu/f low/?jot=view&id+1047

Morley, D. and K. Robins. *Spaces of Identity: Global Media, Electronic Landscapes and Cultural Boundaries*. London: Routledge, 1995.

Robaina, Holly Vincente. "A Foundation of Faith." Christianity Today. www.christianity today.com. *Salt Lake City Tribune*. (2006) www.sltrib.com

7

Women Read the Romance

The Interaction of Text and Context

Janice Radway

The interpretation of the romance's cultural significance offered here has been developed from a series of extensive ethnographic-like interviews with a group of compulsive romance readers in a predominantly urban, central midwestern state among the nation's top twenty in total population.[1] I discovered my principal informant and her customers with the aid of a senior editor at Doubleday whom I had been interviewing about the publication of romances. Sally Arteseros told me of a bookstore employee who had developed a regular clientele of fifty to seventy-five regular romance readers who relied on her for advice about the best romances to buy and those to avoid. When I wrote to Dot Evans, as I will now call her, to ask whether I might question her about how she interpreted, categorized, and evaluated romantic fiction, I had no idea that she had also begun to write a newsletter designed to enable bookstores to advise their customers about the quality of the romances published monthly. She has since copyrighted this newsletter and incorporated it as a business. Dot is so successful at serving the women who patronize her chain outlet that the central office of this major chain occasionally relies on her sales predictions to gauge romance distribution throughout the system. Her success has also brought her to the attention of both editors and writers for whom she now reads manuscripts and galleys.

My knowledge of Dot and her readers is based on roughly sixty hours of interviews conducted in June 1980 and February 1981. I have talked extensively with Dot about romances, reading, and her advising activities as well as observed her interactions with her customers at the bookstore. I have also conducted both group and individual interviews with sixteen of her regular customers and administered a lengthy questionnaire to forty-two of these women. Although not representative of all women who read romances, the group appears to be demographically similar to a sizable segment of that audience as it has been mapped by several rather secretive publishing houses.

From Janice A. Radway, "Women Read the Romance: The Interaction of Text and Context," originally published in *Feminist Studies*, Volume 9, Number 1 (Spring 1983): 56–68, by permission of the publisher, *Feminist Studies*, Inc.

Dorothy Evans lives and works in the community of Smithton, as do most of her regular customers. A city of about 112,000 inhabitants, Smithton is located five miles due east of the state's second largest city, in a metropolitan area with a total population of over 1 million. Dot was forty-eight years old at the time of the survey, the wife of a journeyman plumber, and the mother of three children in their twenties. She is extremely bright and articulate and, while not a proclaimed feminist, holds some beliefs about women that might be labeled as such. Although she did not work outside the home when her children were young and does not now believe that a woman needs a career to be fulfilled, she feels women should have the opportunity to work and be paid equally with men. Dot also believes that women should have the right to abortion, though she admits that her deep religious convictions would prevent her from seeking one herself. She is not disturbed by the Equal Rights Amendment and can and does converse eloquently about the oppression women have endured for years at the hands of men. Despite her opinions, however, she believes implicitly in the value of true romance and thoroughly enjoys discovering again and again that women can find men who will love them as they wish to be loved. Although most of her regular customers are more conservative than Dot in the sense that they do not advocate political measures to redress past grievances, they are quite aware that men commonly think themselves superior to women and often mistreat them as a result.

In general, Dot's customers are married, middle-class mothers with at least a high school education.[2] More than 60 percent of the women were between the ages of twenty-five and forty-four at the time of the study, a fact that duplicates fairly closely Harlequin's finding that the majority of its readers is between twenty-five and forty-nine.[3] Silhouette Books has also recently reported that 65 percent of the romance market is below the age of 40.[4] Exactly 50 percent of the Smithton women have high school diplomas, while 32 percent report completing at least some college work. Again, this seems to suggest that the interview group is fairly representative, for Silhouette also indicates that 45 percent of the romance market has attended at least some college. The employment status and family income of Dot's customers also seem to duplicate those of the audience mapped by the publishing houses. Forty-two percent of the Smithton women, for instance, work part-time outside the home. Harlequin claims that 49 percent of its audience is similarly employed. The Smithton women report slightly higher incomes than those of the average Harlequin reader (43 percent of the Smithton women have incomes of $15,000 to $24,999, 33 percent have incomes of $25,000 to $49,999—the average income of the Harlequin reader is $15,000 to $20,000), but the difference is not enough to change the general sociological status of the group. . . .

When asked why they read romances, the Smithton women overwhelmingly cite escape or relaxation as their goal. They use the word "escape," however, both literally and figuratively. On the one hand, they value their romances highly because the act of reading them literally draws the women away from their present surroundings. Because they must produce the meaning of the story by attending closely to the words on the page, they find that their attention is withdrawn from concerns that plague them in reality. One woman remarked with a note of triumph in her voice: "My body may be in that room, but I'm not!" She and her sister readers see their romance reading as a legitimate way of denying a present reality that occasionally becomes too onerous to bear. This particular means of escape is better than television viewing for these women, because the cultural value attached to books permits them to overcome the guilt they feel about avoiding their responsibilities. They believe that reading of any kind is, by nature, educational.[5] They insist accordingly that they also read to learn.[6]

On the other hand, the Smithton readers are quite willing to acknowledge that the romances which so preoccupy them are little more than fantasies or fairy tales that always end happily. They readily admit in fact that the characters and events discovered in the pages of the typical romance do not resemble the people and occurrences they must deal with in their daily lives. On the basis of the following comments, made in response to a question about what romances "do" better than other novels available today, one can conclude that it is precisely the unreal, fantastic shape of the story that makes their literal escape even more complete and gratifying. Although these are only a few of the remarks given in response to the undirected question, they are representative of the group's general sentiment.

> Romances hold my interest and do not leave me depressed or up in the air at the end like many modern day books tend to do. Romances also just make me feel good reading them as I identify with the heroines.

> The kind of books I mainly read are very different from everyday living. That's why I read them. Newspapers, etc., I find boring because all you read is sad news. I can get enough of that on TV news. I like stories that take your mind off everyday matters.

> Different than everyday life.

> Everyone is always under so much pressure. They like books that let them escape.

> Because it is an escape, and we can dream. And pretend that it is our life. I'm able to escape the harsh world a few hours a day.

> It is a way of escaping from everyday living.

> They always seem an escape and they usually turn out the way you wish life really was.

I enjoy reading because it offers me a small vacation from everyday life and an interesting and amusing way to pass the time.

These few comments all hint at a certain sadness that many of the Smithton women seem to share because life has not given them all that it once promised. A deep-seated sense of betrayal also lurks behind their deceptively simple expressions of a need to believe in a fairy tale. Although they have not elaborated in these comments, many of the women explained in the interviews that despite their disappointments, they feel refreshed and strengthened by their vicarious participation in a fantasy relationship where the heroine is frequently treated as they themselves would most like to be loved.

This conception of romance reading as an escape that is both literal and figurative implies flight from some situation in the real world which is either stifling or overwhelming, as well as a metaphoric transfer to another, more desirable universe where events are happily resolved. Unashamed to admit that they like to indulge in temporary escape, the Smithton women are also surprisingly candid about the circumstances that necessitate their desire. When asked to specify what they are fleeing from, they invariably mention the "pressures" and "tensions" they experience as wives and mothers. Although none of the women can cite the voluminous feminist literature about the psychological toll exacted by the constant demand to physically and emotionally nurture others, they are nonetheless eloquent about how draining and unrewarding their duties can be.[7] When first asked why women find it necessary to escape, Dot gave the following answer without once pausing to rest:

> As a mother, I have run 'em to the orthodontist. I have run 'em to the swimming pool. I have run 'em to baton twirling lessons. I have run up to school because they forgot their lunch. You

know, I mean really. And you do it. And it isn't that you begrudge it. That isn't it. Then my husband would walk in the door and he'd say, "Well, what did you do today?" You know, it was like, "Well, tell me how you spent the last eight hours, because I've been out working." And I finally got to the point where I would say, "Well, I read four books, and I did the wash and got the meal on the table and the beds are all made and the house is tidy." And I would get defensive like, "So what do you call all this? Why should I have to tell you because I certainly don't ask you what you did for eight hours, step by step."

But their husbands do that. We've compared notes. They hit the house and it's like "Well, all right. I've been out earning a living. Now what have you been doin' with your time?" And you begin to be feeling, "Now, really, why is he questioning me?"

Romance reading, as Dot herself puts it, constitutes a temporary "declaration of independence" from the social roles of wife and mother. By placing the barrier of the book between themselves and their families, these women reserve a special space and time for themselves alone. As a consequence, they momentarily allow themselves to abandon the attitude of total self-abnegation in the interest of family welfare which they have so dutifully learned is the proper stance for a good wife and mother. Romance reading is both an assertion of deeply felt psychological needs and a means for satisfying those needs. Simply put, these needs arise because no other member of the family, as it is presently constituted in this still-patriarchal society, is yet charged with the affective and emotional reconstitution of a wife and mother. If she is depleted by her efforts to care for others, she is nonetheless expected to restore and sustain herself as well. As one of Dot's customers put it, "You always have to be a Mary Poppins. You can't be sad, you can't be mad, you have to keep everything bottled up inside."

Nancy Chodorow has recently discussed this structural peculiarity of the modern family and its impact on the emotional lives of women in her influential book, *The Reproduction of Mothering*,[8] a complex reformulation of the Freudian theory of female personality development. Chodorow maintains that women often continue to experience a desire for intense affective nurturance and relationality well into adulthood as a result of an unresolved separation from their primary caretaker. It is highly significant, she argues, that in patriarchal society this caretaker is almost inevitably a woman. The felt similarity between mother and daughter creates an unusually intimate connection between them which later makes it exceedingly difficult for the daughter to establish autonomy and independence. Chodorow maintains, on the other hand, that because male children are also reared by women, they tend to separate more completely from their mothers by suppressing their own emotionality and capacities for tenderness which they associate with mothers and femininity. The resulting asymmetry in human personality, she concludes, leads to a situation where men typically cannot fulfill all of a woman's emotional needs. As a consequence, women turn to the act of mothering as a way of vicariously recovering that lost relationality and intensity.

My findings about Dot Evans and her customers suggest that the vicarious pleasure a woman receives through the nurturance of others may not be completely satisfying, because the act of caring for them also makes tremendous demands on a woman and can deplete her sense of self. In that case, she may well turn to romance reading in an effort to construct a fantasy-world where she is attended, as the heroine is, by a man who reassures her of her special status and unique identity.

The value of the romance may have something to do, then, with the fact that women find it especially difficult to indulge in the restorative experience of visceral regression to an infantile state where the self is cared for perfectly by another. This regression is so difficult precisely because women have been taught to believe that men must be their sole source of pleasure. Although there is nothing biologically lacking in men to make this ideal pleasure unattainable, as Chodorow's theories tell us, their engendering and socialization by the patriarchal family traditionally masks the very traits that would permit them to nurture women in this way. Because they are encouraged to be aggressive, competitive, self-sufficient, and unemotional, men often find sustained attention to the emotional needs of others both unfamiliar and difficult. While the Smithton women only minimally discussed their husbands' abilities to take care of them as they would like, when they commented on their favorite romantic heroes they made it clear that they enjoy imagining themselves being tenderly cared for and solicitously protected by a fictive character who inevitably proves to be spectacularly masculine and unusually nurturant as well.[9]

Indeed, this theme of pleasure recurred constantly in the discussions with the Smithton women. They insisted repeatedly that when they are reading a romance, they feel happy and content. Several commented that they particularly relish moments when they are home alone and can relax in a hot tub or in a favorite chair with a good book. Others admitted that they most like to read in a warm bed late at night. Their association of romances with contentment, pleasure, and good feelings is apparently not unique, for in conducting a market research study, Fawcett discovered that when asked to draw a woman reading a romance, romance readers inevitably depict someone who is exaggeratedly happy.[10]

The Smithton group's insistence that they turn to romances because the experience of reading the novels gives them hope, provides pleasure, and causes contentment raises the unavoidable question of what aspects of the romantic narrative itself could possibly give rise to feelings such as

these. How are we to explain, furthermore, the obvious contradiction between this reader emphasis on pleasure and hope, achieved through vicarious appreciation of the ministrations of a tender hero, and the observations of the earlier critics of romances that such books are dominated by men who at least temporarily abuse and hurt the women they purportedly love? In large part, the contradiction arises because the two groups are not reading according to the same interpretive strategies, neither are they reading nor commenting on the same books. Textual analyses like those offered by Douglas, Modleski, and Snitow are based on the common assumption that because romances are formulaic and therefore essentially identical, analysis of a randomly chosen sample will reveal the meaning unfailingly communicated by every example of the genre. This methodological procedure is based on the further assumption that category readers do not themselves perceive variations within the genre, nor do they select their books in a manner significantly different from the random choice of the analyst.

In fact, the Smithton readers do not believe the books are identical, nor do they approve of all the romances they read. They have elaborated a complex distinction between "good" and "bad" romances and they have accordingly experimented with various techniques that they hoped would enable them to identify bad romances before they paid for a book that would only offend them. Some tried to decode titles and cover blurbs by looking for key words serving as clues to the book's tone; others refused to buy romances by authors they didn't recognize; still others read several pages *including the ending* before they bought the book. Now, however, most of the people in the Smithton group have been freed from the need to rely on these inexact predictions because Dot Evans shares their perceptions and evaluations of the category and can alert them to unusually successful romantic fantasies while steering them away from those they call "disgusting perversions."

When the Smithton readers' comments about good and bad romances are combined with the conclusions drawn from an analysis of twenty of their favorite books and an equal number of those they classify as particularly inadequate, an illuminating picture of the fantasy fueling the romance-reading experience develops.[11] To begin with, Dot and her readers will not tolerate any story in which the heroine is seriously abused by men. They find multiple rapes especially distressing and dislike books in which a woman is brutally hurt by a man only to fall desperately in love with him in the last four pages. The Smithton women are also offended by explicit sexual description and scrupulously avoid the work of authors like Rosemary Rogers and Judith Krantz who deal in what they call "perversions" and "promiscuity." They also do not like romances that overtly perpetuate the double standard by excusing the hero's simultaneous involvement with several women. They insist, one reader commented, on "one women—one man." They also seem to dislike any kind of detailed description of male genitalia, although the women enjoy suggestive descriptions of how the hero is emotionally aroused to an overpowering desire for the heroine. . . .

According to Dot and her customers, the quality of the ideal romantic fantasy is directly dependent on the character of the heroine and the manner in which the hero treats her. The plot, of course, must always focus on a series of obstacles to the final declaration of love between the two principals. However, a good romance involves an unusually bright and determined woman and a man who is spectacularly masculine, but at the same time capable of remarkable empathy and tenderness. Although they enjoy the usual chronicle of misunderstandings and mistakes which inevitably leads to the heroine's belief that the hero intends to harm her, the Smithton readers prefer stories that combine a much-understated

version of this continuing antagonism with a picture of a gradually developing love. They most wish to participate in the slow process by which two people become acquainted, explore each other's foibles, wonder about the other's feelings, and eventually "discover" that they are loved by the other.

In conducting an analysis of the plots of the twenty romances listed as "ideal" by the Smithton readers, I was struck by their remarkable similarities in narrative structure. In fact, all twenty of these romances are very tightly organized around the evolving relationship between a single couple composed of a beautiful, defiant, and sexually immature woman and a brooding, handsome man who is also curiously capable of soft, gentle gestures. Although minor foil figures are used in these romances, none of the ideal stories seriously involves either hero or heroine with one of the rival characters.[12] They are employed mainly as contrasts to the more likable and proper central pair or as purely temporary obstacles to the pair's delayed union because one or the other mistakenly suspects the partner of having an affair with the rival. However, because the reader is never permitted to share this mistaken assumption in the ideal romance, she knows all along that the relationship is not as precarious as its participants think it to be. The rest of the narrative in the twenty romances chronicles the gradual crumbling of barriers between these two individuals who are fearful of being used by the other. As their defenses against emotional response fall away and their sexual passion rises inexorably, the typical narrative plunges on until the climactic point at which the hero treats the heroine to some supreme act of tenderness, and she realizes that his apparent emotional indifference was only the mark of his hesitancy about revealing the extent of his love for and dependence upon her.

The Smithton women especially like romances that commence with the early marriage of the hero and heroine for reasons of convenience. Apparently, they do so because they delight in the subsequent, necessary chronicle of the pair's growing awareness that what each took to be indifference or hate is, in reality, unexpressed love and suppressed passion. In such favorite romances as *The Flame and the Flower, The Black Lyon, Shanna,* and *Made for Each Other,* the heroine begins marriage thinking that she detests and is detested by her spouse. She is thrown into a quandary, however, because her partner's behavior vacillates from indifference, occasional brusqueness, and even cruelty to tenderness and passion. Consequently, the heroine spends most of her time in these romances, as well as in the others comprising this sample, trying to read the hero's behavior as a set of signs expressing his true feelings toward her. The final outcome of the story turns upon a fundamental process of reinterpretation, whereby she suddenly and clearly sees that the behavior she feared was actually the product of deeply felt passion and a previous hurt. Once she learns to reread his past behavior and thus to excuse him for the suffering he has caused her, she is free to respond warmly to his occasional acts of tenderness. Her response inevitably encourages him to believe in her and finally to treat her as she wishes to be treated. When this reinterpretation process is completed in the twenty ideal romances, the heroine is always tenderly enfolded in the hero's embrace and the reader is permitted to identify with her as she is gently caressed, carefully protected, and verbally praised [with] words of love.[13] At the climactic moment (pp. 201–2) of *The Sea Treasure,* for example, when the hero tells the heroine to put her arms around him, the reader is informed of his gentleness in the following way:

> She put her cold face against his in an attitude of surrender that moved him to unutterable tenderness. He swung her clear of the encroaching water and eased his way up to the next level, with painful slowness. . . . When at last he had finished, he pulled her into his arms and held her against his heart for a moment. . . . Tenderly he lifted her. Carefully he negotiated the last of the treacherous slippery rungs to the mine entrance. Once there, he swung her up into his arms and walked out into the starlit night.

> The cold air revived her, and she stirred in his arms.

> "Dominic?" she whispered.

> He bent his head and kissed her.

> "Sea Treasure," he whispered.

Passivity, it seems, is at the heart of the romance-reading experience in the sense that the final goal of the most valued romances is the creation of perfect union in which the ideal male, who is masculine and strong, yet nurturant, finally admits his recognition of the intrinsic worth of the heroine. Thereafter, she is required to do nothing more than exist as the center of this paragon's attention. Romantic escape is a temporary but literal denial of the demands these women recognize as an integral part of their roles as nurturing wives and mothers. But it is also a figurative journey to a utopian state of total receptiveness in which the reader, as a consequence of her identification with the heroine, feels herself the passive *object* of someone else's attention and solicitude. The romance reader in effect is permitted the experience of feeling cared for, the sense of having been affectively reconstituted, even if both are lived only vicariously.

Although the ideal romance may thus enable a woman to satisfy vicariously those psychological needs created in her by a patriarchal culture unable to fulfill them, the very centrality of the rhetoric of reinterpretation to the romance suggests also that the reading experience may indeed have some of the unfortunate consequences pointed to by earlier romance critics.[14] Not only is the dynamic of reinterpretation an essential component of the plot of the ideal romance, but it also characterizes the very process of constructing its meaning because the reader is inevitably given more information about the hero's motives than is the heroine herself. Hence, when Ranulf temporarily abuses his young bride in *The Black Lyon*, the reader understands that what appears as inexplicable cruelty to Lyonene, the heroine, is an irrational desire to hurt her because of what his first wife did to him.[15] It is possible that in reinterpreting the hero's behavior before Lyonene does, the Smithton women may be practicing a procedure which is valuable to them precisely because it enables them to reinterpret their own spouse's similar emotional coldness and likely preoccupation with work or sports. In rereading this category of behavior, they reassure themselves that it does not necessarily mean that a woman is not loved. Romance reading, it would seem, can function as a kind of training for the all-too-common task of reinterpreting a spouse's unsettling actions as the signs of passion, devotion, and love.

If the Smithton women are indeed learning reading behaviors that help them to dismiss or justify their husbands' affective distance, this procedure is probably carried out on an unconscious level. In any form of cultural or anthropological analysis in which the subjects of the study cannot reveal all the complexity or covert significance of their behavior, a certain amount of speculation is necessary. The analyst, however, can and should take account of any other observable evidence that might reveal the motives and meanings she is seeking. In this case, the Smithton readers' comments about bad romances are particularly helpful.

In general, bad romances are characterized by one of two things: an unusually cruel hero who subjects the heroine to various kinds of verbal and physical abuse, or a diffuse plot that permits the hero to become involved with other women before he settles upon the heroine. Since the Smithton readers will tolerate complicated subplots in some romances if the hero and heroine continue to function as a pair, clearly it is the involvement with others rather than the plot complexity that distresses them. When asked why they disliked these books despite the fact that they all ended happily with the hero converted into the heroine's attentive lover, Dot and her customers replied again and again that they rejected the books precisely because they found them unbelievable. In elaborating, they insisted indignantly that they could never forgive the hero's early transgressions and they see no reason why they should be asked to believe that the heroine can. What they are suggesting, then, is that certain kinds of male behavior associated with the stereotype of male machismo can never be forgiven or reread as the signs of love. They are thus not interested only in the romance's happy ending. They want to involve themselves in a story that will permit them to enjoy the hero's tenderness *and* reinterpret his momentary blindness and cool indifference as the marks of a love so intense that he is wary of admitting it. Their delight in both these aspects of the process of romance reading and their deliberate attempt to select books that will include "a gentle hero" and "a slight misunderstanding" suggest that deeply felt needs are the source of their interest in both components of the genre. On the one hand, they long for emotional attention and tender care; on the other, they wish to rehearse the discovery that a man's distance can be explained and excused as his way of expressing love.

It is easy to condemn this latter aspect of romance reading as a reactionary force that reconciles women to a social situation which denies them full development, even as it refuses to accord them the emotional sustenance they require. Yet to identify romances with this conservative moment alone is to miss those other benefits associated with the act of reading as a restorative pastime whose impact on a beleaguered woman is not so simply dismissed. If we are serious about feminist politics and committed to reformulating not only our own lives but those of others, we would do well not to condescend to romance readers as hopeless traditionalists who are recalcitrant in their refusal to acknowledge the emotional costs of patriarchy. We must begin to recognize that romance reading is fueled by dissatisfaction and disaffection, not by perfect contentment with woman's lot. Moreover, we must also understand that some romance readers' experiences are not strictly congruent with the set of ideological propositions that typically legitimate patriarchal marriage. They are characterized, rather, by a sense of longing caused by patriarchal marriage's failure to address all their needs.

In recognizing both the yearning and the fact that its resolution is only a vicarious one not so easily achieved in a real situation, we may find it possible to identify more precisely the very limits of patriarchal ideology's success. Endowed thus with a better understanding of what women want, but often fail to get from the traditional arrangements they consciously support, we may provide ourselves with that very issue whose discussion would reach many more women and potentially raise their consciousnesses about the particular dangers and failures of patriarchal institutions. By helping romance readers to see why they long for relationality and tenderness and are unlikely to get either in the form they desire if current gender arrangements are continued, we may help to convert their amorphous longing into a focused desire for specific change. . . .

Notes

1. All information about the community has been taken from the 1970 U.S. Census of the Population *Characteristics of the Population,* U.S. Department of Commerce, Social and Economic Statistics Administration, Bureau of the Census, May 1972. I have rounded off some of the statistics to disguise the identity of the town.

2. See Table 1.

3. Quoted by Barbara Brotman, "Ah, Romance! Harlequin Has an Affair for Its Readers." *Chicago Tribune,* 2 June 1980. All

Table 1 Select Demographic Data: Customers of Dorothy Evans

Category	Responses	Number	%
Age	(42) Less than 25	2	5
	25–44	26	62
	45–54	12	28
	55 and older	2	5
Marital Status	(40) Single	3	8
	Married	33	82
	Widowed/Separated	4	10
Parental Status	(40) Children	35	88
	No children	4	12
Age at Marriage	Mean 19.9		
	Median 19.2		
Educational Level	(40) High school diploma	21	53

Category	Responses	Number	%
	1–3 Years of college	10	25
	College degree	8	20
Work Status	(40) Full or part time	18	45
	Child or home care	17	43
Family Income	(38) $14,999 or below	2	5
	15,000–24,999	18	47
	25,000–49,999	14	37
	50,000+	4	11
Church Attendance	(40) Once or more a week	15	38
	1–3 times per month	8	20
	A few times per year	9	22
	Not in two(2) years	8	20

Note: (40) indicates the number of responses per questionnaire category. A total of 42 responses per category is the maximum possible. Percent calculations are all rounded to the nearest whole number.

other details about the Harlequin audience have been taken from this article. . . .

4. See Brotman (1980), cited above. All other details about the Silhouette audience have been drawn from Brotman's article. . . .

5. The Smithton readers are not avid television watchers. . . .

6. The Smithton readers' constant emphasis on the educational value of romances was one of the most interesting aspects of our conversations, and chapter 3 of *Reading the Romance* discusses it in depth. Although their citation of the instructional value of romances to a college professor interviewer may well be a form of self-justification, the women also provided ample evidence that they do in fact learn and remember facts about geography, historical customs, and dress from the books they read. Their emphasis on this aspect of their reading, I might add, seems to betoken a profound curiosity and longing to know more about the exciting world beyond their suburban homes.

7. For material on housewives' attitudes toward domestic work and their duties as family counselors, see Ann Oakley, *The Sociology of Housework* (New York: Pantheon, 1975) and

Woman's Work: The Housewife, Past and Present (New York: Pantheon. 1975); see also Mirra Komorovsky, *Blue Collar Marriage* (New York: Vintage, 1967) and Helena Znaniecki Lopata, *Occupation:* Housewife (New York: Oxford University Press, 1971).

8. Nancy Chodorow, *The Reproduction of Mothering: Psychoanalysis and the Sociology of Gender* (Berkeley: University of California Press, 1978). I would like to express my thanks to Sharon O'Brien for first bringing Chodorow's work to my attention and for all those innumerable discussions in which we debated the merits of her theory and its applicability to women's lives, including our own.

9. After developing my argument that the Smithton women are seeking ideal romances which depict the generally tender treatment of the heroine, I discovered Beatrice Faust's *Women, Sex, and Pornography: A Controversial Study* (New York: MacMillan, 1981) in which Faust points out that certain kinds of historical romances tend to portray their heroes as masculine, but emotionally expressive. . . .

10. Daisy Maryles, "Fawcett Launches Romance Imprint with Brand Marketing

Techniques," *Publishers Weekly* 216 (3 Sept. 1979), 69.

11. Ten of the twenty books in the sample for the ideal romance were drawn from the Smithton group's answers to requests that they list their three favorite romances and authors. . . . I also added *Summer of the Dragon* (1979) by Elizabeth Peters because she was heavily cited as a favorite author although none of her titles were specifically singled out. Three more titles were added because they were each voluntarily cited in the oral interviews more than five times. . . . Seven were added because Dot gave them very high ratings in her newsletter. Because I did not include a formal query in the questionnaire about particularly bad romances, I drew the twenty titles from oral interviews and from Dot's newsletter reviews.

12. There are two exceptions to this assertion. Both *The Proud Breed* by Celeste DeBlasis and *The Fulfillment* by LaVyrle Spencer detail the involvement of the principal characters with other individuals. Their treatment of the subject, however, is decidedly different from that typically found in the bad romances. Both of these books are highly unusual in that they begin by detailing the extraordinary depth of the love shared by hero and heroine, who marry early in the story. The rest of each book chronicles the misunderstandings that arise between heroine and hero. In both books the third person narrative always indicates very clearly to the reader that the two are still deeply in love with each other and are acting out of anger, distrust, and insecurity.

13. In the romances considered awful by the Smithton readers, this reinterpretation takes place much later in the story than in the ideal romances. In addition, the behavior that is explained away is more violent, aggressively cruel, and obviously vicious. Although the hero is suddenly transformed by the heroine's reinterpretation of his motives, his tenderness, gentleness, and care are not emphasized in the "failed romances" as they are in their ideal counterparts.

14. Modleski has also argued that "the mystery of male motives" is a crucial concern in all romantic fiction (p. 439). Although she suggests, as I will here, that the process through which male misbehavior is reinterpreted in a more favorable light is a justification or legitimation of such action, she does not specifically connect its centrality in the plot to a reader's need to use such a strategy in her own marriage. While there are similarities between Modleski's analysis and that presented here, she emphasizes the negative, disturbing effects of romance reading on readers. In fact, she claims the novels "end up actually intensifying conflicts for the reader" (p. 445) and cause women to "reemerge feeling . . . more guilty than ever" (p. 447). While I would admit that romance reading might create unconscious guilt, I think it absolutely essential that any explanation of such behavior take into account the substantial amount of evidence indicating that women not only enjoy romance reading, but feel replenished and reconstituted by it as well. See Tania Modleski, "The Disappearing Act: A Study of Harlequin Romances," *Signs* 5 (Spring 1980), 435–48.

15. Jude Deveraux, *The Black Lyon* (New York: Avon, 1980), 66.

8

Star Trek Rerun, Reread, Rewritten

Fan Writing as Textual Poaching

Henry Jenkins III

In late December 1986, *Newsweek* (Leerhsen, 1986, p. 66) marked the 20th anniversary of *Star Trek* with a cover story on the program's fans, "the Trekkies, who love nothing more than to watch the same 79 episodes over and over." The *Newsweek* article, with its relentless focus on conspicuous consumption and "infantile" behavior and its patronizing language and smug superiority to all fan activity, is a textbook example of the stereotyped representation of fans found in both popular writing and academic criticism, "Hang on: You are being beamed to one of those *Star Trek* conventions, where grown-ups greet each other with the Vulcan salute and offer in reverent tones to pay $100 for the autobiography of Leonard Nimoy" (p. 66). Fans are characterized as "kooks" obsessed with trivia, celebrities, and collectibles; as misfits and crazies; as "a lot of overweight women, a lot of divorced and single women" (p. 68). . . .

Fans appear to be frighteningly out of control, undisciplined and unrepentant, rogue readers. Rejecting aesthetic distance, fans passionately embrace favored texts and attempt to integrate media representations within their own social experience. Like cultural scavengers, fans reclaim works that others regard as worthless and trash, finding them a rewarding source of popular capital. Like rebellious children, fans refuse to read by the rules imposed upon them by the schoolmasters. For fans, reading becomes a type of play, responsive only to its own loosely structured rules and generating its own types of pleasure.

Michel de Certeau (1984) has characterized this type of reading as "poaching," an impertinent raid on the literary preserve that takes away only those things that seem useful or pleasurable to the reader. "Far from being writers . . . readers are travelers; they move across lands belonging to someone else, like nomads poaching their way across fields they did not write, despoiling the wealth of Egypt to enjoy it themselves" (p. 174). De Certeau perceives popular reading as a series of "advances and retreats, tactics and games played with the text" (p. 175), as a type of cultural bricolage through which readers fragment texts and reassemble the broken shards according to their own blueprint, salvaging bits and pieces of found material in making sense of their own social experience. Far from viewing consumption as imposing meanings upon the public, de Certeau suggests, consumption involves reclaiming textual material, "making it one's own, appropriating or reappropriating it" (p. 166). . . .

In this chapter, I propose an alternative approach to fan experience, one that perceives "Trekkers" (as they prefer to be called) not as cultural dupes, social misfits, or mindless consumers but rather as, in de Certeau's term, "poachers" of textual meanings. Behind the exotic stereotypes fostered by the media lies a largely unexplored terrain of cultural activity, a subterranean network of readers and writers who remake programs in their own image. "Fandom" is a vehicle for marginalized subterranean groups (women, the young, gays, etc.) to pry open space for their cultural concerns within dominant representations; it is a way of appropriating media texts and rereading them in a fashion that serves different interests, a way of transforming mass culture into a popular culture.

I do not believe this essay represents the last word on *Star Trek* fans, a cultural community that is far too multivocal to be open to easy description. Rather, I explore some aspects of current fan activity that seem particularly relevant to cultural studies. My primary concern is with what happens when these fans produce their own texts, texts that inflect program content with their own social experience and displace commercially produced commodities for a kind of popular economy. For these fans, *Star Trek* is not simply something that can be reread; it is something that can and must be rewritten in order to make it more responsive to their needs, in order to make it a better producer of personal meanings and pleasures.

No legalistic notion of literary property can adequately constrain the rapid proliferation of meanings surrounding a popular text. Yet, there are other constraints, ethical constraints and self-imposed rules, that are enacted by the fans, either individually or as part of a larger community, in response to their felt need to legitimate their unorthodox appropriation of mass media texts. E. P. Thompson (1971) suggests that eighteenth and nineteenth century peasant leaders, the historical poachers behind de Certeau's apt metaphor, responded to a kind of "moral economy," an informal set of consensual norms that justified their uprisings against the landowners and tax collectors in order to restore a preexisting order being corrupted by its avowed protectors. Similarly, the fans often cast themselves not as poachers but as loyalists, rescuing essential elements of the primary text misused by those who maintain copyright control over the program materials. Respecting literary property even as they seek to appropriate it for their own uses, these fans become reluctant poachers, hesitant about their relationship to the program text, uneasy about the degree of manipulation they can legitimately perform on its materials, and policing each other for abuses of their interpretive license. . . .

Fans: From Reading to Writing

The popularity of *Star Trek* has motivated a wide range of cultural productions and creative reworkings of program materials: from children's backyard play to adult interaction games, from needlework to elaborate costumes, from private fantasies to computer programming. This ability to transform personal reaction into social interaction, spectator culture into participatory culture, is one of the central characteristics of fandom. One becomes a fan not by being a regular viewer of a particular program but by translating that viewing into some type of cultural activity, by sharing feelings and thoughts about the program content with friends, by joining a community of other fans who share common interests. For fans, consumption sparks production, reading generates writing, until the terms seem logically inseparable. In fan writer Jean Lorrah's words (1984, p. 1):

> Trekfandom . . . is friends and letters and crafts and fanzines and trivia and costumes and artwork and filksongs [fan parodies] and buttons and film clips and conventions—something for everybody who has in common the inspiration of a television show which grew far beyond its TV and film incarnations to become a living part of world culture.

Lorrah's description blurs all boundaries between producers and consumers, spectators and participants, the commercial and the home crafted, to construct an image of fandom as a cultural and social network that spans the globe.

Many fans characterize their entry into fandom in terms of a movement from social and cultural isolation, doubly imposed upon them as women within a patriarchal society and as seekers after alternative pleasures within dominant media representations, toward more and more active participation in a community receptive to their cultural productions, a community where they may feel a sense of belonging. . . .

For some women, trapped within low paying jobs or within the socially isolated sphere of the homemaker, participation within a national, or international, network of fans grants a degree of dignity and respect otherwise lacking. For others, fandom offers a training ground for the development of professional skills and an outlet for creative impulses constrained by their workday lives. Fan slang draws a sharp contrast between the mundane, the realm of everyday experience and those who dwell exclusively within that space, and fandom, an alternative sphere of cultural experience that restores the excitement and freedom that must be repressed to function in ordinary life. One fan writes, "Not only does 'mundane' mean 'everyday life,' it is also a term used to describe narrow-minded, pettiness, judgmental, conformity, and a shallow and silly nature. It is used by people who feel very alienated from society" (Osborne, 1987, p. 4). To enter fandom is to escape from the mundane into the marvelous.

The need to maintain contact with these new friends, often scattered over a broad geographic area, can require that speculations and fantasies about the program content take written form, first as personal letters and later as more public newsletters, "letterzines" or fan fiction magazines. Fan viewers become fan writers. . . .

Although fanzines may take a variety of forms, fans generally divide them into two major categories: "letterzines" that publish short articles and letters from fans on issues surrounding their favorite shows and "fictionzines" that publish short stories, poems, and novels concerning the program characters and concepts.[1] Some fan-produced novels, notably the works of Jean Lorrah (1976, 1978) and Jacqueline Lichtenberg (1976), have achieved a canonized status in the fan community, remaining more or less in constant demand for more than a decade.[2]

It is important to be careful in distinguishing between these fan-generated materials and commercially produced works, such as the series of *Star Trek* novels released by Pocket Books under the official supervision of Paramount, the studio that owns the rights to the *Star Trek* characters. Fanzines are totally unauthorized by the program producers and face the constant threat of legal action for their open violation of the producer's copyright authority over the show's characters and concepts. Paramount has tended to treat fan magazines with benign neglect as long as they are handled on an exclusively non-profit basis. Producer Gene Roddenberry and many of the cast members have contributed to such magazines. Bantam Books even released several anthologies showcasing the work of *Star Trek* fan writers (Marshak & Culbreath, 1978).

Other producers have not been as kind. Lucasfilm initially sought to control *Star Wars* fan publications, seeing them as a rival to its officially sponsored fan organization, and later threatened to prosecute editors who published works that violated the "family values" associated with the original films. Such a scheme has met considerable resistance from the fan community that generally regards Lucas' actions as unwarranted interference in its own creative activity. Several fanzine editors have continued to distribute adult-oriented *Star Wars* stories through an underground network of special friends, even though such works are no longer publicly advertised through *Datazine* or sold openly at conventions. A heated editorial in *Slaysu,* a fanzine that routinely published feminist-inflected erotica set in various media universes, reflects these writers' opinions:

> Lucasfilm is saying, "you must enjoy the characters of the *Star Wars* universe for male reasons. Your sexuality must be correct and proper by my (male) definition." I am not male. I do not want to be. I refuse to be a poor imitation, or worse, someone's idiotic ideal of femininity. Lucasfilm has said, in essence, "this is what we see in the *Star Wars* films and we are telling you that this is what you will see." (Siebert, 1982, p. 44)

C. A. Siebert's editorial asserts the rights of fanzine writers to consciously revise the character of the original texts, to draw elements from dominant culture in order to produce underground art that explicitly challenges patriarchal assumptions. Siebert and the other editors deny the traditional property rights of textual producers in favor of a right of free play with the program materials, a right of readers to use media texts in their own ways and of writers to reconstruct characters in their own terms. Once characters are inserted into popular discourse, regardless of their source of origin, they become the property of the fans who fantasize about them, not the copyright holders who merchandise them. Yet the relationship between fan texts and primary texts is often more complex than Siebert's defiant stance might suggest, and some fans do feel bound by a degree of fidelity to the original series' conceptions of those characters and their interactions.

Gender and Writing

Fan writing is an almost exclusively feminine response to mass media texts. Men actively participate in a wide range of fan-related activities, notably interactive games and conference planning committees, roles consistent with patriarchal norms that typically relegate combat—even combat fantasies—and organizational authority to the masculine sphere. Fan writers and fanzine readers, however, are almost always female. Camille Bacon-Smith (1986) has estimated that more than 90% of all fan writers are female. The greatest percentage of male participation is found in the "letter-lines," like *Comlink* and *Treklink,* and in "nonfiction" magazines, like *Trek* that publish speculative essays on aspects of the program universe. Men may feel comfortable joining discussions of future technologies or military lifestyle but not in pondering Vulcan sexuality, McCoy's childhood, or Kirk's love life.

Why this predominance of women within the fan writing community? . . .

A particular fascination of *Star Trek* for these women appears to be rooted in the way that the program seems to hold out a suggestion of nontraditional feminine pleasures, of greater and more active involvement for women within the adventure of professional space travel, while finally reneging on those promises. Sexual equality was an essential component of producer Roddenberry's optimistic vision of the future; a woman, Number One (Majel Barrett), was originally slated to be the Enterprise's second in command. Network executives, however, consistently fought efforts to break with traditional feminine stereotypes, fearing the alienation of more conservative audience members (Whitfield & Roddenberry, 1968). Number One was scratched after the program pilot, but throughout the run of the series women were often cast in nontraditional jobs, everything from Romulan commanders to weapon specialists. The networks, however reluctantly, were offering women a future, a "final frontier" that included them.

Fan writers, though, frequently express dissatisfaction with these women's characterizations within the episodes. In the words of fan writer Pamela Rose (1977, p. 48), "When a woman is a guest star on *Star Trek,* nine out of ten times there is something wrong with her." Rose notes that these female characters have been granted positions of power within the program, only to demonstrate through their erratic emotion-driven conduct that women are unfit to fill such roles. Another fan writer, Toni Lay (1986, p. 15), expresses mixed feelings about *Star Trek*'s social vision:

> It was ahead of its time in some ways, like showing that a Caucasian, all-American, all-male crew was not the only possibility for space travel. Still, the show was sadly deficient in other ways, in particular, its treatment of women. Most of the time, women were referred to as "girls." And women were never shown in a position of authority unless they were aliens, i.e., Deela, T'Pau, Natira, Sylvia, etc. It was like the show was saying "equal opportunity is OK for their women but not for our girls."

. . . Indeed, many fan writers characterize themselves as "repairing the damage" caused by the program's inconsistent and often demeaning treatment of its female characters. Jane Land (1986, p. 1), for instance, characterizes her fan novel, *Kista,* as "an attempt to rescue one of *Star Trek*'s female characters [Christine Chapel] from an artificially imposed case of foolishness." Promising to show "the way the future never was," *The Woman's List,* a recently established fanzine with an explicitly feminist orientation, has called for "material dealing with all range of possibilities for women, including: women of color, lesbians, women of alien cultures, and women of all ages and backgrounds." Its editors acknowledge that their publication's project necessarily involves telling the types of stories that network policy blocked from airing when the series was originally produced. A recent flier for that publication explains:

> We hope to raise and explore those questions which the network censors, the television genre, and the prevailing norms of the time made it difficult to address. We believe that both the nature of human interaction and sexual mores and the structure of both families and relationships will have changed by the 23rd century and we are interested in exploring those changes.

Telling such stories requires the stripping away of stereotypically feminine traits. The series characters must be reconceptualized in ways that suggest hidden motivations and interests heretofore unsuspected. They must be reshaped into full-blooded feminist role models. While, in the series, Chapel is defined almost exclusively in terms of her unrequited passion for Spock and her professional subservience to Dr. McCoy, Land represents her as a fiercely independent woman, capable of accepting love only on her own terms, ready to pursue her own ambitions wherever they take her, and outspoken in response to the patronizing attitudes of the command crew. Siebert (1980, p. 33) has performed a similar operation on the character of Lieutenant Uhura, as this passage from one of her stories suggests:

> There were too few men like Spock who saw her as a person. Even Captain Kirk, she smiled, especially Captain Kirk, saw her as a woman first. He let her do certain things but only because military discipline required it. Whenever there was any danger, he tried to protect her. . . . Uhura smiled sadly, she would go on as she had been, outwardly a feminine toy, inwardly a woman who was capable and human.

Here, Siebert attempts to resolve the apparent contradiction created within the series text by Uhura's official status as a command officer and her constant displays of "feminine frailty." Uhura's situation, Siebert suggests, is characteristic of the way that women must mask their actual competency behind traditionally feminine mannerisms within a world dominated by patriarchal assumptions and masculine authority. By rehabilitating Uhura's character in this fashion, Siebert has constructed a vehicle through which she can document the overt and subtle forms of sexual discrimination that an ambitious and determined woman faces as she struggles for a command post in Star Fleet (or for that matter, within a twentieth century corporate board room).

Fan writers like Siebert, Land, and Karen Bates (1982; 1983; 1984), whose novels explore the progression of a Chapel-Spock marriage through many of the problems encountered by contemporary couples trying to juggle the conflicting demands of career and family, speak directly to the concerns of professional women in a way that more traditionally feminine works fail to do. These writers create situations where Chapel and Uhura must heroically overcome the same types of obstacles that challenge their male counterparts within the primary texts and often discuss directly the types of personal and professional problems particular to working women. . . .

The fan community continually debates what constitutes a legitimate reworking of program materials and what represents a violation of the special reader-text relationship that the fans hope to foster. The earliest *Star Trek* fan writers were careful to work within the framework of the information explicitly included within the broadcast episodes and to minimize their breaks with series conventions. In fan writer Jean Lorrah's words (1976, p. 1), "Anyone creating a *Star Trek* universe is bound by what was seen in the aired episodes; however, he is free to extrapolate from those episodes to explain what was seen in them." Leslie Thompson (1974, p. 208) explains, "If the reasoning [of fan speculations] doesn't fit into the framework of the events as given [on the program], then it cannot apply no matter how logical or detailed it may be." As *Star Trek* fan writing has come to assume an institutional status in its own right and therefore to require less legitimization through appeals to textual fidelity, a new conception of fan fiction has emerged, one that perceives the stories not as a necessary expansion of the original series text but rather as chronicles of alternate universes, similar to the program world in some ways and different in others:

> The "alternate universe" is a handy concept wherein you take the basic *Star Trek* concept and spin it off into all kinds of ideas that could never be aired. One reason Paramount may be so liberal about fanzines is that by their very nature most fanzine stories could never be sold professionally. (L. Slusher, personal communication, August 1987)

Such an approach frees the writers to engage in much broader play with the program concepts and characterizations, to produce stories that reflect more diverse visions of human interrelationships and future worlds, to rewrite elements within the primary texts that hinder fan interests. Yet, even alternate universe stories struggle to maintain some consistency with the original broadcast material and to establish some point of contact with existing fan interests, just as more faithful fan writers feel compelled to rewrite and revise the program material in order to keep it alive in a new cultural context.

Borrowed Terms: Kirk/Spock Stories

The debate in fan circles surrounding Kirk/ Spock (K/S) fiction, stories that posit a homo-erotic relationship between the show's two primary characters and frequently offer detailed accounts of their sexual couplings, illustrates these differing conceptions of the relationship between fan fiction and the primary series text.[3] Over the past decade, K/S stories have emerged from the margins of fandom toward numerical dominance over *Star Trek* fan fiction, a movement that has been met with considerable opposition from more traditional fans. For many, such stories constitute the worst form of character rape, a total violation of the established characterizations. Kendra Hunter (1977, p. 81) argues that "it is out of character for both men, and as such comes across in the stories as bad writing. . . . A relationship as complex and deep as Kirk/Spock does not climax with a sexual relationship." Other fans agree but for other reasons. "I do not accept the K/S homosexual precept as plausible," writes one fan. "The notion that two men that are as close as Kirk and Spock are cannot be 'just friends' is indefensible to me" (Landers, 1986, p. 10). Others struggle to reconcile the information provided on the show with their own assumptions about the nature of human sexuality: "It is just as possible for their friendship to progress into a love-affair, for

that is what it is, than to remain status quo. . . . Most of us see Kirk and Spock simply as two people who love each other and just happen to be of the same gender" (Snaider, 1987, p. 10). . . .

What K/S does openly, all fans do covertly. In constructing the feminine countertext that lurks in the margins of the primary text, these readers necessarily redefine the text in the process of rereading and rewriting it. As one fan acknowledges, "If K/S has 'created new characters and called them by old names,' then all of fandom is guilty of the same" (Moore, 1986, p. 7). Jane Land (1987, p. ii) agrees: "All writers alter and transform the basic *Trek* universe to some extent, choosing some things to emphasize and others to play down, filtering the characters and the concepts through their own perceptions."

If these fans have rewritten *Star Trek* in their own terms, however, many of them are reluctant to break all ties to the primary text that sparked their creative activity and, hence, feel the necessity to legitimate their activity through appeals to textual fidelity. The fans are uncertain how far they can push against the limitations of the original material without violating and finally destroying a relationship that has given them great pleasure. Some feel stifled by those constraints; others find comfort within them. Some claim the program as their personal property, "treating the series episodes like silly putty," as one fan put it (Blaes, 1987, p. 6). Others seek compromises with the textual producers, treating the original program as something shared between them.

What should be remembered is that whether they cast themselves as rebels or loyalists, it is the fans themselves who are determining what aspects of the original series concept are binding on their play with the program material and to what degree. The fans have embraced *Star Trek* because they found its vision somehow compatible with their own, and they have assimilated only those textual materials that feel comfortable to them. Whenever a choice must be made between fidelity to their program and fidelity to their own social norms, it is almost inevitably made in favor of lived experience. The women's conception of the *Star Trek* realm as inhabited by psychologically rounded and realistic characters insures that no characterization that violated their own social perceptions could be satisfactory. The reason some fans reject K/S fiction has, in the end, less to do with the stated reason that it violates established characterization than with unstated beliefs about the nature of human sexuality that determine what types of character conduct can be viewed as plausible. When push comes to shove, as Hodge and Tripp (1986, p. 144) recently suggested, "Non-televisual meanings can swamp televisual meanings" and usually do.

Conclusion

The fans are reluctant poachers who steal only those things that they truly love, who seize televisual property only to protect it against abuse by those who created it and who have claimed ownership over it. In embracing popular texts, the fans claim those works as their own, remaking them in their own image, forcing them to respond to their needs and to gratify their desires. Female fans transform *Star Trek* into women's culture, shifting it from space opera into feminist romance, bringing to the surface the unwritten feminine countertext that hides in the margins of the written masculine text. Kirk's story becomes Uhura's story and Chapel's and Amanda's as well as the story of the women who weave their own personal experiences into the lives of the characters. Consumption becomes production; reading becomes writing; spectator culture becomes participatory culture. . . .

Notes

1. Both Lorrah and Lichtenberg have achieved some success as professional science fiction writers. For an interesting discussion of the relationship between fan writing and professional science fiction writing, see Randall (1985).

2. Although a wide range of fanzines were considered in researching this essay, I have decided, for the purposes of clarity, to draw my examples largely from the work of a limited number of fan writers. While no selection could accurately reflect the full range of fan writing, I felt that Bates, Land, Lorrah, and Siebert had all achieved some success within the fan community, suggesting that they exemplified, at least to some fans, the types of writing that were desirable and reflected basic tendencies within the form. . . .

3. The area of Kirk/Spock fiction falls beyond the project of this particular paper. My reason for discussing it here is because of the light its controversial reception sheds on the norms of fan fiction and the various ways fan writers situate themselves toward the primary text. For a more detailed discussion of this particular type of fan writing, see Lamb and Veith (1986), who argue that K/S stories, far from representing a cultural expression of the gay community, constitute another way of feminizing the concerns of the original series text and of addressing feminist concern within the domain of a popular culture that offers little space for heroic action by women.

References

Bacon-Smith, C. (1986, November 16). Spock among the women. *The New York Times Book Review,* pp. 1, 26, 28.

Bates, K. A. (1982). *Starweaver two.* Missouri Valley, IA: Ankar Press.

Bates, K. A. (1983). *Nuages one.* Tucson, AZ: Checkmate Press.

Bates, K. A. (1984). *Nuages two.* Tucson, AZ: Checkmate Press.

Blaes, T. (1987). Letter. *Treklink, 9,* 6–7.

de Certeau, M. (1984). *The practice of everyday life.* Berkeley: University of California Press.

Hodge, R., & Tripp, D. (1986). *Children and television: A semiotic approach.* Cambridge: Polity Press.

Hunter, K. (1977). Characterization rape. In W. Irwin & G. B. Love (Eds.), *The best of Trek 2* (pp. 74–85). New York: New American Library.

Lamb, P. F., & Veith, D. L. (1986). Romantic myth, transcendence, and *Star Trek* zines. In D. Palumbo (Ed.), *Erotic universe: Sexuality and fantastic literature* (pp. 235–256). New York: Greenwood Press.

Land, J. (1986). *Kista.* Larchmont, NY: Author.

Land, J. (1987). *Demeter.* Larchmont, NY: Author.

Landers, R. (1986). Letter. *Treklink, 7,* 10.

Lay, T. (1986). Letter. *Comlink, 28,* 14–16.

Leerhsen, C. (1986, December 22). *Star Trek's* nine lives. *Newsweek,* pp. 66–73.

Lichtenberg, J. (1976). *Kraith collected.* Grosse Point Park, MI: Ceiling Press.

Lorrah, J. (1976). *The night of twin moons.* Murray, KY: Author.

Lorrah, J. (1978). The Vulcan character in the NTM universe. In J. Lorrah (Ed.), *NTM collected* (Vol. 1, pp. 1–3). Murray, KY: Author.

Lorrah, J. (1984). *The Vulcan academy murders.* New York: Pocket.

Marshak, S., & Culbreath, M. (1978). *Star Trek: The new voyages.* New York: Bantam Books.

Moore, R. (1986). Letter. *Treklink, 4,* 7–8.

Osborne, E. (1987). Letter. *Treklink, 9,* 3–4.

Randall, M. (1985). Conquering the galaxy for fun and profit. In C. West (Ed.), *Words in our pockets* (pp. 233–241). Paradise, CA: Dustbooks.

Rose, P. (1977). Women in the federation. In W. Irwin & G. B. Love (Eds.), *The best of Trek 2* (pp. 46–52). New York: New American Library.

Siebert, C. A. (1980). Journey's end at lover's meeting. *Slaysu, 1,* 28–34.

Siebert, C. A. (1982). By any other name. *Slaysu, 4,* 44–45.

Snaider, T. (1987). Letter. *Treklink, 8,* 10.

Thompson, E. P. (1971). The moral economy of the English crowd in the 18th century. *Past and Present, 50,* 76–136.

Thompson, L. (1974). *Star Trek* mysteries— Solved! In W. Irwin & G. B. Love (Eds.), *The best of Trek* (pp. 207–214). New York: New American Library.

Whitfield, S. E., & Roddenberry, G. (1968). *The making of Star Trek.* New York: Ballantine Books.

9

Watching Television Without Pity

The Productivity of Online Fans

Mark Andrejevic

In an era in which the mass audience is becoming increasingly visible thanks to a variety of increasingly sophisticated monitoring technologies, viewers are increasingly encouraged to climb out of the couch to embrace a more "active" approach to their viewing experience. Fan culture is at long last being deliberately and openly embraced by producers thanks in part to the ability of the internet not just to unite far-flung viewers but to make the fruits of their labor readily accessible to the mainstream—and to producers themselves.

The digital embrace of viewer activity requires a rethinking of any approach to media audiences that seeks to orient itself through recourse to the opposition between passive and active viewership, where the former is associated with the straw man figure of the manipulated dupe and the latter with the subversive textual poacher (Jenkins 1992; Fiske 1987). Although Jenkins (1992, 287) once noted that fandom proves "not all audiences are passive," the advent of interactive media highlights what has been true all along: that *all* audiences are active, although perhaps not in the progressive sense the term has come to imply. What is perhaps distinctive about the advent of interactive media is the development of strategies for promoting, harnessing, and exploiting the productivity of this activity. To observe that such strategies are doubtless facilitated by celebratory portrayal of the creative, subversive potential of an active audience (as an antidote to the implied passivity of the mass audience) is not to discount or dismiss this potential. Rather, it is to attempt to understand and elucidate the ways in which creative activity and exploitation coexist and interpenetrate one another within the context of the emerging online economy. This article draws on a case study of the Television Without Pity (TWoP) web site to explore the role of mediated interactivity in facilitating what Terranova (2000, 45) has described as the "simultaneity of labor as something which is voluntarily given and exploited."

Drawn from Chapter 5 of *iSpy: Surveillance and Power in the Interactive Era* by Mark Andrejevic, published by the University Press of Kansas (2007), www.kansaspress.ku.edu.

The Productivity of TWoP: An Overview

For producers, fan sites such as TWoP can serve as an impromptu focus group, providing instant feedback to plot twists and the introduction of new characters even as they help to imbue the show with the kind of "stickiness" coveted in the online world by creating a virtual community as an added component of the show. As a *New York Times* article about online fan sites put it, "It is now standard Hollywood practice for executive producers (known in trade argot as 'show runners') to scurry into Web groups moments after an episode is shown on the East Coast. Sure, a good review in the print media is important, but the boards, by definition, are populated by a program's core audience—many thousands of viewers who care deeply about what direction their show takes" (Sella 2002, 62).

As in the case of other forms of consumption, viewer feedback promises to become increasingly integrated into the production process in a cybernetic cycle that offers to reduce uncertainty and, at least according to the marketing industry, increase customer satisfaction (Pine 1993). Indeed, many of those who visit TWoP, which includes forums devoted to some three dozen shows, are convinced that their feedback has had some sort of impact on writers or producers. As one respondent to my online survey of TWoP participants put it, "The decision makers can come and see what specifically the audience liked and disliked about the way they handled various things, and why . . . which, if they choose to pay attention, can help them to improve their work." Although the site, as its name suggests, encourages critical, "snarkastic" commentary, many of those who post do so in the spirit described by the respondent, adopting the viewpoint of assistants who can help producers and writers do their job better by providing detailed commentary not just on plot development but also on technical aspects of the show, including continuity, wardrobe, and makeup. The "recappers"— hired by TWoP to craft lengthy, detailed, and humorous summaries of the shows— often focus on production details including lighting and editing, thereby helping direct the attention to the formal aspects of the shows they describe.

The result is the merging of two forms of audience participation: the effort viewers put into making the show interesting to themselves and the effort they devote to taking on the role of production assistants and attempting to provide feedback to writers and producers. Part of the entertainment value of a site such as TWoP is the implicit promise to erode the boundaries between the sites of ostensibly passive consumption and those of the sequestered power of media producers—what Couldry (2000) has called the "place of media power." If interactive technologies help dedifferentiate sites of consumption and production according to this account, they also pose a challenge to the boundaries that reinforce the concentration of control in the hands of the few. In keeping with the celebratory predictions of those who champion the democratizing potential of new media (Gilder 1994; Kelly 1996), respondents to an online survey I posted to TWoP overwhelmingly agreed with the assertion that online fan sites will make TV producers more accountable to viewers. As one respondent put it, "I think producers/writers etc. would be well served to see what their 'constituents' want. TV should be more viewer driven and I think TWoP is a foundation for a movement toward that."

Interestingly, the promise of accountability seems to cut both ways: if TWoP provides producers with direct and immediate access to the viewpoints of the audience, it also fosters identification on the part of audiences with the viewpoint of producers. Market and production imperatives such as show promotion, mass audience appeal, and technical details are taken up in depth by TWoP posters, who, in elaborate postings directed to producers, suggest ways to more effectively tailor a particular show to its viewers. The promise of virtual participation in the production process, in short, invites viewers to adopt the standpoint of producers, and thereby facilitates the conversion of viewer feedback into potentially productive marketing and demographic information.

. . . The embrace of new media, interactive sites, and online communities by marketers does not go unacknowledged by posters, some of whom expressed concern that fan sites might be reduced to one more marketing strategy. As one poster put it, "The majority of producers/execs either fear the Internet community or feel that if they try hard enough, they can manipulate it right back." However, direct manipulation by producers is not necessary to make even a critical site like TWoP an effective form of promotion. Almost one-third of the 1,800 respondents to my online survey indicated that they felt they watched more television because of TWoP, and a large majority said that the site made television more entertaining to watch. Indeed, it is the collective effort of viewers to enlist the internet to enhance the entertainment value of their televisions that emerges as a recurring theme in the remarks of respondents. Interactivity, in short, allows the viewers to take on the work of finding ways to make a show more interesting.

. . . The responses referred to throughout the following argument are drawn from two online surveys posted to the TWoP web site for one week in May 2003. The first survey, which was largely quantitative, received more than 1,800 responses; the second, composed of open-ended questions, received more than 500 responses. Statistics in the remainder of this article come from the first survey, quotes from the second. About 87 percent of the responses to the first survey were from women, a fact that will be discussed in the following section. Seventy percent of the respondents indicated they were in the eighteen to thirty-four age range, which represents the demographic group most prized by advertisers and marketers. The respondents, of course, were self-selected—they represented visitors to the web site who clicked on a link to the survey—but the large number of responses provided a rich set of observations, and several clear trends, discussed below, that demonstrate the ways in which viewer participation, while providing perceived benefits to viewers, doubled as what I will characterize as a form of free labor for producers.

Talking Back to the TV

If, as Antonio Gramsci (1971, 286) suggested, the implementation of a new economic regime requires the elaboration of "a new type of man suited to the new type of work and productive process," the same might be said of the emerging interactive economy, and even for the advent of interactive television: it requires the creation of new, more active—or "interactive"—types of viewer and consumer. . . .

A site such as TWoP provides a neat transition to this era of interactive viewing. Many of my respondents told me that even if they were not online while watching TV, they often took notes as they watched, writing down choice morsels of dialogue and observations to help them prepare for their posts. The TWoP forums, in short, provide a pool of research expertise available not just to fellow fans but also to producers. The result is both a ready resource for fans and, at times, a resource for writers and producers who learn from attentive viewers that an upcoming script includes a continuity flaw or plot inconsistency.

TWoP contributors collectively put a significant amount of time and energy into the creation of a detailed and productive online resource. One-fourth of the survey respondents indicated that they spent between five and ten hours a week in the TWoP forums, and 13 percent said they spent more than ten hours a week on the site (much of which, according to several of the comments in the qualitative portion of the survey, takes place at work). In addition, many TWoPpers devoted time not just to watching (and sometimes taking notes on) particular shows but to gathering information about them from other sources. This is precisely the type of effort that Terranova (2000, 33) has described as the "free labor" characteristic of the relationship between the online economy and what, following the Italian autonomists, she terms "the social factory." She invokes this term to describe the process "whereby 'work processes have shifted from the factory to society, thereby setting in motion a truly complex machine.'"

The notion of the social factory coincides with the creation of an interactive consumer–viewer, one prepared to devote time and energy to developing the skills necessary to participate in an increasingly interactive media economy. . . . To the extent that such effort generates useful demographic feedback to producers (as in the case of interactive devices that record, save, and aggregate viewer preferences), it is productive not just in the sense that it facilitates the consumption of an increasingly technologically sophisticated array of media products and services but also insofar as it allows producers to, as one business futurist put it, "save costs by off-loading some of the duties of consumer interactions onto consumers themselves" (Mougayar 1998, 174). Work that used to be the province of producers is being redefined as that of the active consumer, who is increasingly becoming responsible for developing a unique demographic profile and relaying the information it contains to producers.

. . . The interactive consumer is the market analogue of the "active" citizen interpellated by the proponents of the neoliberal postwelfare state. As Rose (2001, 164) puts it, the model of the active citizen is that of the "entrepreneur of him- or herself" who "was to conduct his or her life, and that of his or her family, as a kind of enterprise, seeking to enhance and capitalize on existence itself through calculated acts and investments." It does not seem farfetched to extend this analysis into the realm of consumption, where the consumer is increasingly encouraged to make the investment of time and energy it takes to be an interactive consumer responsible for his or her own viewing and consumption practices and experiences.

Similarly, many TWoPpers suggest that the effort that they put into the shows they watch increases their own viewing pleasure. As one fan put it in a column about her passion for collecting behind-the-scenes and advance information about her favorite show, "At the most basic level, being plugged-in means becoming invested in the creation of the show, rather than simply a passive recipient" (Nussbaum 2002, 1). To the extent that such sites, even those that are ostensibly critical, promote this sense of investment, they consolidate a multiplatform involvement with the show, the type that producers covet in an era of multitasking and channel surfing. As one respondent put it, "TWoP has definitely made me pay closer attention to the shows I watch (ie script, direction, set decoration, etc.). While at times I can be more critical of a show, for example more aware of continuity errors and obvious audience manipulation, it also makes me more appreciative of the work that goes into creating a show, and insanely, more loyal to a show." This post and several similar ones suggested that the more the boundary between the "offstage" site of production and that of consumption is eroded, the greater the sense of participation-based loyalty.

Although TWoPpers pride themselves on belonging to a knowing and critical subset of viewers, many nonetheless find themselves captivated by those moments when producers, actors, or writers participate in the forums or agree to be interviewed online for the site. One respondent described the experience of hearing from those involved in a favorite show as "unbelievably weird and simultaneously wonderful. Their feedback and insights made my love for the show grow exponentially! If actors and other persons affiliated with shows regularly showed up, I might end up watching much more TV, simply because of the stronger connection I would feel." TV shows attempt to capitalize on such loyalty by creating official web sites, the savviest of which provide interactive interviews and the kind of behind-the-scenes information that gives fans the sense of at least partial entry into an inner circle of producers and writers.

Official sites, however, do not have the luxury of deliberately fostering the critical, sarcastic repartee that has become the staple of TWoP, which provides visitors with not just tightly monitored and witty forums but also lengthy, often sarcastic and savagely funny recaps of selected shows. . . . TWoP fans focus their attention on the lengthy recaps written by paid freelancers and on the ongoing discussions of fellow fans and critics in the forums. Within this context, the show is no longer the final product but rather the raw material to which value is added by the labor—some paid, some free—of recappers and forum contributors. Not only did roughly one-third of the respondents indicate that they watched more TV because of TwoP, but a similar number noted that there were shows that they would not have watched without the TWoP recaps. The most frequently mentioned of these shows were the reality shows *Joe Millionaire*, *Married by America*, *Are You Hot*, and *The Bachelor*. Respondents said that, taken on their own, such shows were too contrived and poorly produced to merit watching but that they provided wonderful raw material for the TWoP recaps and forums. As one respondent put it, "I watched parts of *Married by America* simply because Miss Alli [one of the favorite recappers] was recapping it and

I wanted to see what she was so hysterically mocking. . . . " . . . Interestingly, a few respondents said they followed some shows entirely online because the recaps were entertaining and thorough enough to stand on their own.

. . . As in the case of other forms of interactive commerce, the information provided by viewers does not just add value to the product; it doubles as audience research. . . . CBS spokesman Chris Ender said the power of the web-based fan groups first caught his attention during the airing of the smash hit reality series *Survivor*: "In the first season there was a groundswell of attention in there. . . . We started monitoring the message boards to actually help guide us in what would resonate in our marketing. It's just the best market research you can get" (Sella 2002, 68). TWoPpers may be working for free, but that does not mean they are not producing value. The work they do—the work of making their preferences transparent, of allowing themselves to be watched as they do their watching—is an increasingly important component of the emerging interactive economy.

One of the ancillary effects of the promise of shared control mobilized by producers who publicize the impact that their online fans have on a show is that of an implicit bridging of the production-consumption divide. If viewers are, to some limited extent, allowed to participate in the production process, then the notion that a new set of duties has devolved on them becomes much more palatable. Furthermore, the promise of shared control, the invitation to participate in the production process, doubles as an invitation to internalize the imperatives of producers. There are entire threads on TWoP devoted, for example, to the marketing of a favored show. Posters frequently bemoan the ineffectiveness of promotional ads for the shows they follow and offer suggestions as to which characters and images ought to be included to increase audience appeal and viewership. Even in the face of a still relatively nonresponsive industry, the formal introduction of an interactive element helps foster a sense of identification with producers. While there are instances in which the feedback seems to have had an impact, for the most part the impact from the boards is limited and indirect. The fun comes not so much from watching the implementation of viewer suggestions—since very few of these have any directly discern-able impact—as from embracing the modicum of interactivity that makes it possible to identify with the position of the producer.

The work that viewers do for producers emerges as a necessary corollary to their entrepreneurial activity: the work that they do for and on themselves. If, in other words, the advent of advanced neoliberalism is associated with the constellation of practices that promote the "responsibilization" of the citizen, a similar logic emerges in the realm of consumption, wherein viewers are invited to take on some of the "duties" associated with their media consumption. . . . Viewed within this context, the recurring refrain that TWoP promotes critical and intelligent viewing on the part of its participants appears as a form of self-optimization. If, as Rose (2001, 164) suggests, the emergent society of control operates on the assumption that "one is always in continuous training, lifelong learning, perpetual assessment, continual incitement to buy [and] to improve oneself," the imperative for consumers is to become not only more efficient but also more informed and even more critical viewers. To borrow some loaded terms from the political sphere, if the passive viewer is associated with the welfare "culture of dependency," the active viewer is associated with the post-welfare culture of individual responsibility and self-activation. If TV is low quality, unentertaining, or unintelligent, the viewer can take on the duty of making it more interesting, entertaining, and intelligent. As one respondent put it, "I would like my

TV to be smarter, better written, more intellectually stimulating, and more emotionally engaging. With TWoP, at least my watching of TV can be those things."

. . . The portrayal of interactivity as a means for revitalizing a self-actualizing form of participation parallels the marketing of the digital economy as one that counters the stultification and homogenization of mass society. Indeed, one of the recurring marketing strategies of the new economy is the suggestion that with the addition of the interactivity prefix—the telltale lower case *i*—forms of media that were once passive and mind numbing are transformed into means of creative self-expression and empowerment. Thus, as one survey respondent put it, a site such as TWoP "changes TV from a brain-dead pastime to an art and a science." Or, similarly, "bad TV becomes good TV when combined with TWoP." The element of reflexivity, combined with a "snarkastic" savvy, inoculates the viewer against the ostensible depredations of passivity.

The intriguing result is that, thanks to the inclusion of the formal element of interactivity, the character of a particular show changes from that of a mass-produced product of the culture industry into a tool to hone and develop one's critical thinking and viewing skills. As one response put it, "Being able to see through the stereotypes and clichés bad shows propagate is a useful skill, much like being able to deconstruct and analyze advertising. At least if you are able to hone your critical thinking skill during a tasteless show, it's not a total waste." . . .

Several respondents suggested that the development of critical viewing skills, combined with the feedback supplied by increasingly sophisticated viewers, might result in improved programming. However, even if such a result is not forthcoming, savvy reflexivity serves as a kind of coping mechanism, a strategy for salvaging the very same advertisements and programming that, viewed uncritically or nonreflexively, are relegated to the category of the shallow manipulations of the culture industry. In other words, it is not the content itself but the attitude taken by the viewers, the way in which they watch—or, more precisely, the way in which they are *seen* to watch (or see themselves watching)—that makes the difference. TWoPpers esteem savvy, critical posts highly, and those who are active contributors to the site say that while they like the idea that producers may be paying attention, they post mainly for the benefit of fellow posters and the moderator. The goal is not so much to influence the group of producers and production assistants referred to in posts as TPTB (the powers that be) as it is to entertain and impress the TWoP community with wit, insight, and, above all, "snark."

"Thanks for Listening (Or Not)!"

Despite the stories of shout-outs and other examples of the impact of the online community on producers and writers, the savvy attitude of TWoPpers includes a marked skepticism toward the notion that they might actually be making a difference. As one poster put it, "The producers are such prostitutes to advertisers and whatever other show may be popular that giving advice would be pointless. It is all about the Benjamins." Indeed, most of the respondents took pains to suggest that they did not have any illusions about transforming or improving the culture industry....

For those who claim to have few illusions about the impact they're having on the industry, the appeal of online critique is not just its entertainment value but also the recognition that they receive online. Respondents repeatedly emphasized the satisfaction they received from having their posts noticed and responded to in the online forums. A typical example was the observation by one regular poster that "when posting, my main goal is to make the other posters laugh, to be witty. If I get a 'word' out of the deal, my day's pretty much made." Another respondent, highlighting the work done by viewers in making the viewing experience more entertaining, wrote, "My 'job' on TWoP is the class clown—almost all of my posts are humorous in nature and I love it when posters respond to them in their posts. I guess I enjoy the validation that I can indeed be funny."...

...One of the apparent goals of posters is to be seen by others as not being duped, to make it clear to one another that they have not been caught up in the illusory, breathless promise of a kind of immaculate revolution, painlessly effected by technological developments.

Surely, there are those on TWoP who imagine a world in which producers will pay more attention to viewers and in which viewers may play an active and creative role in producing the culture they then turn around and consume. However, the characteristic attitude encouraged by the site and its posters is much more skeptical.... Rather than buying into the promise that interactive technology will fundamentally alter the power relations between consumer and producer, the interactive viewer enlists the proffered technologies to, if nothing else, let others know that he or she has not been taken in by the ruse....

Conclusion

...The point of exploring the ways in which the interactivity of viewers *doubles* as a form of labor is to point out that, in the interactive era, the binary opposition between complicit passivity and subversive participation needs to be revisited and revised. It is one thing to note that viewers derive pleasure and fulfillment from their online activities and quite another to suggest that pleasure is necessarily either empowering for viewers or destabilizing for entrenched forms of corporate control over popular culture. If, as Jenkins (1992, 278) observes, "fandom constitutes the base for consumer activism," it would be misguided to regard all viewer participation as activist. Activity and interactivity need to be clearly distinguished from activism. This becomes a particularly important distinction in an era when the simple equation of participation with empowerment serves to reinforce the marketing strategies of corporate culture. It is precisely the creative character of viewer activity that makes it more valuable to producers: the better the contributions to TWoP, the more likely viewers are to continue to tune in to a particular show; the more work viewers put into researching a program, the more likely they are to form an affective attachment to it.

Thus, to note with Baym (2000, 16), following Radway, noting that audience practices have the "potential" for empowerment is not to valorize audience practice "as is." Rather, Radway (1986, 116), in reflecting on her own work on women's romance novels, makes a clear distinction between the potential invoked by the contradictions in audience response and what would count as progressive action: not just transformations in romance narratives themselves but transformation of "real social and material relations as well as the way they are conceived within symbolic forms." By the same logic, fan activity that—even in the form of a communal activity with all of its attendant benefits—ends up reinforcing social and material relations might be considered a form of active participation in the constitution of those relations rather than a challenge to them. The workplace can be a site of community and personal satisfaction and one of economic exploitation. Thinking of these characteristics together is crucial to any critical approach to the current deployment of the promise of interactivity. The internet helping to promote the formation of communities of practice around TV shows in the era of

relationship marketing community is, as Fernback (2002, 11) notes, an increasingly valuable marketing apparatus. The advantage to marketers of online communities is that they help build allegiance to particular products, serving as forums for practices of self-disclosure that generate detailed information about consumers. As one company quoted by Fernback puts it, the systematic development of product-related sites represents "a trend toward the transformation of ad hoc e-communities into established forums that drive product innovation and contribute to profits."

TWoP, which remained an independent site for several years, was purchased by Bravo (whose parent company is NBC Universal) in early 2007, but its posters continue to make the most of its largely critical approach to the TV shows it recaps. The site may have the potential to serve as an instant focus group, as one respondent put it, but perhaps even more importantly, it helps draw viewers to particular shows and allows them to build up social and information capital that increases their commitment to viewing. Several posters noted that they continued to watch shows that they once enjoyed but no longer really liked because they wanted to participate in the ongoing online dissection of the program, its characters, and its writers. . . . A savvy identification with producers and insiders facilitated by interactive media fosters an acceptance of the rules of the game. In an era of interactive reflexivity, the media turn back on themselves: new media mock the old while tellingly failing to deliver on the promised transformative shift in power relations. It is perhaps possible to discern in the criticism of the commercial mass media a certain resentment over a failed promise, that information would double as a form of power sharing, that once the secret of power were exposed it would be shared. The perceived dissolution of the democratic promise of publicity, in an era in which information is increasingly available and in which power and wealth (and the media) are simultaneously becoming increasingly concentrated in the hands of the few, feeds a savvy attitude toward the media itself. The critical impetus shifts away from political leaders . . . and toward the media themselves. The result, however, is not a transformed media but participatory submission. As in the online world of TWoP, spectators take their pleasure in knowing—with the insiders—just why things are as bad as they are and why they could not be any different.

References

Baym, Nancy. 2000. *Tune in log on: Soaps, fandom, and online community.* London: Sage.

Fernback, Jan. 2002. Using community to sell: The commodification of community in retail web sites. Paper presented at the annual conference of the Association of Internet Researchers, Maastricht, the Netherlands, October.

Fiske, John. 1987. *Television culture: Popular pleasures and politics.* London: Methuen.

Gilder, George. 1994. *Life after television: The coming transformation of media and American life.* New York: Norton.

Gramsci, Antonio. 1971. Americanism and Fordism. In *Selections from the prison notebooks of Antonio Gramsci,* ed. and trans. Quintin Hoare and Geoffrey Nowell Smith, 279–318. London: Lawrence and Wishart.

Habermas, Jurgen. 1991. *The structural transformation of the public sphere: An inquiry into a category of bourgeois society.* Cambridge, MA: MIT Press.

Jenkins, Henry. 1988. Star Trek rerun, reread, rewritten: Fan writing as textual poaching. *Critical Studies in Mass Communication* 5:85–107.

———. 1992. *Textual poachers: Television fans & participatory culture.* New York: Routledge, Chapman and Hall.

Kelly, Kevin. 1996. What would McLuhan say? *Wired,* 4.10. http://www.wired.com (accessed April 5, 2005).

Lazarsfeld, Paul F., and Robert K. Merton. 1948. Mass communication, popular taste, and organized social action. In *The communication of ideas,* ed. Lyman Bryson, 95–118. New York: Harper and Row.

Mougayar, Walid. 1998. *Opening digital markets: Battle plans and business strategies for internet commerce.* New York: McGraw-Hill.

Nussbaum, Emily. 2002. Confessions of a spoiler whore: The pleasures of participatory TV. *Slate,* April 4. http://slate.msn.com/id/2063235/(accessed October 2, 2003).

Pine, Joseph. 1993. *Mass customization: The new frontier in business competition.* Cambridge, MA: Harvard University Press.

Plant, Sadie. 1997. *Zeros + ones: Digital women and the new technoculture.* London: 4th Estate.

Radway, Janice. 1986. Identifying ideological seams: Mass culture, analytical method, and political practice. *Communication* 6:93–123.

Robins, Kevin. 1999. Against virtual community: For a politics of distance. *Angelaki* 4 (2): 163–70.

Rose, Nikolas. 2001. *Powers of freedom: Reframing political thought.* Cambridge, UK: Cambridge University Press.

Sella, Marshall. 2002. The remote controllers. *New York Times Magazine,* October 20.

Terranova, Tiziana. 2000. Free labor: Producing culture for the digital economy. *Social Text* 63 (18): 33–57.

Witheford, Nick. 2004. Autonomist Marxism and the information society. *Endpage.* http://www.endpage.com (accessed April 20, 2005).

Zizek, Slavoj. 1999. *The ticklish subject.* London: Verso.

10

Reconsidering Resistance *and* Incorporation

Richard Butsch

For a century, American cultural elites and intellectuals have criticized commercial leisure for giving people the wrong ideas. Much of this has been criticism of commercial entertainment and media, that is, mass culture. The more widely used term "commercialization," as well as the more technical "commodification" have been used with negative connotations by social commentators, reformers, and researchers warning of mass culture's corrupting influences on aesthetics, community, and class consciousness.

Art and literary figures have long blamed commercialism, that is, commercial entertainment, amusements and media, for undermining artistic taste and support of the arts. Nathaniel Hawthorne's famous misogynous statement about "scribbling women" was directed at popular novels and magazines. Actors, playwrights, and drama critics bemoaned what they called the commercialization of theater in late nineteenth and early twentieth century America, blaming the Theater Syndicate, and its commercial success in particular, for low aesthetic standards in drama. Modernists and mass culture critics through the twentieth century abhorred commercialization for aesthetic degradation (Huyssen, 1986; Li, 1993), moral debasement (Boyer, 1978) and social disintegration (Giner, 1976; Kornhauser, 1959).

Political economists use the more technical term "commodification" to indicate an ongoing expansion of commercial exchange into all areas of human activity, gradually turning all of human intercourse into a "universal market" (Braverman, 1974). In recent years, journal articles have described commercial inroads into areas that most people consider inappropriate. These include such personal areas as renting wombs and purchasing pregnancies (Resnik, 1998; Rothman, 1987), the patenting of genes and animals (Berlan, 1989), advertising in schools (Molnar, 1996), the packaging of ethnic identity (Castile, 1996; Lee, 1992; Richer, 1988) and privatization of public services such as policing (Loader, 1999; McMullan, 1996). Commodification has also been dreaded in the choice between development and conservation of parks and wilderness (Swinnerton, 1999).

From Butsch, R. (2001). Considering resistance and incorporation. *Leisure Sciences*, (23)2, 71–79. Reprinted by permission of Taylor & Francis Ltd. (http://www.tandf.co.uk/journals).

Trading in identity, bodies, and personal or public services crosses a moral threshold and transforms social relations traditionally regulated by values that transcend money into exchange relations regulated by money. As part of this change, leisure, instead of being a haven from alienated wage work, now becomes like work, an environment of commodity consumption in which treasured aspects of social relations (based on attachment and commitment rather than self-interest) and personal identity (based on character rather than clothes) are lost.

During the twentieth century, criticism of commercialization and commodification has usually presumed that such processes and their agents control those who consume these products and services, shaping and corrupting people's thoughts, behavior and relationships as they participate in monetary exchanges and inhabit the cultural environments built for these purposes. Critics, in other words, tend to emphasize domination of the masses, and cast people as victims of commercial culture.

In the mid-1970s, the new field of cultural studies broke ranks with those who shared this premise. Cultural studies introduced the idea that, while commodity culture is powerful, the victory is never total, and people regularly resist the domination that is so feared. In particular, they saw this resistance in the leisure activities of working class youth—clubbing, dancing, dress, motorbiking, drug use, "hanging out" (Hall & Jefferson, 1976).

Cultural studies arose as a reaction to traditional Marxist criticism of popular culture. Orthodox Marxists as well as humanistic Marxists, such as the Frankfurt School, shared a base and superstructure model that presumed the unquestioned dominance of ideas legitimating the existing social structure (Williams, 1973). According to this deterministic model, the economic structure would inevitably generate a culture that justified it and its beneficiaries, and the mass of the population would be "duped" into false consciousness by these justifications (Jay, 1973; Swingewood, 1977). Popular culture and leisure were particularly problematic in this respect, the new "opiate of the masses." Working class resistance, which was presumed to occur in political and economic realms (political parties and labor unions), was prevented by cultural production of false consciousness in the realm of leisure. Workers did not "throw off their chains" because they were persuaded from watching television and enjoying their new car that capitalism was good for them. This was a rather pessimistic model since it left little room for popular resistance to evolve.

Cultural studies rejected this model and instead offered a more optimistic model in which people were not suffering from false consciousness, but rather contended against cultural institutions and elites, often reinterpreting commodities to produce their own subculture serving their own interests. Other scholars disputed the significance of such cultural resistance and continued to emphasize the overwhelming power of capitalist institutions to control culture and create false consciousness.

Since that time the concept of cultural resistance has been under regular attack from many quarters, including from within cultural studies, and there has been endless debate over commodification versus resistance, what Richard Johnson two decades ago called "intellectual ping-pong," in which sides have taken absolutist partisan positions, each oversimplifying the argument of the other side and dismissing it (Johnson, 1981, p. 386). In response to the rancorous debate there also arose recurring calls for an end to the debate and a search for a synthesis (Clarke, 1990; Grossberg, 1995; Johnson, 1981).

My purpose here is to repeat this call for a truce and suggest an avenue for synthesis of the foci of both sides of the debate. The path I propose first is to acknowledge the validity of both the strength of hegemony and of the significance of resistance. Second, I propose to seek a differentiated vocabulary for different levels of resistance. Third, I seek to reintegrate into the analysis a side of the dialectic of hegemony proposed by Raymond Williams, but generally neglected in cultural studies. That side is "incorporation," a process that in many ways reflects the concerns of those critical of resistance studies and that overlaps the process of commodification. To describe this path I will retrace some of the theoretical roots of cultural studies to retrieve this concept of incorporation and reinstate it in the framework as originally conceived.

Retracing Forgotten Paths

Studies of the ideological power of monopoly capital and studies of resistance both have contributed greatly to our understanding of modern society. At the same time, domination studies have focused too narrowly on the (admittedly great) power of corporations and media monopoly; and resistance studies have been too singularly focused on resistance or alternate readings. Now, we need to take the next step, to analyze the *relationship between* resistance and incorporation, to look at their interaction. We need to understand not simply domination or resistance, but domination and resistance.

Both concepts are central to Raymond Williams' essay, "Base and Superstructure in Marxist Cultural Theory," first published in *New Left Review* (1973) and later elaborated into his book, *Marxism and Literature* (1977). In this essay, Williams first introduces an idea of cultural opposition, though he does not use the term resistance. Williams' purpose in this essay is to critique the traditional Marxist concepts of base, superstructure and ideology as too deterministic. The base referred to the economic structure, the mode of production. The superstructure included the other institutions presumed to be derivative of the base (e.g., law,

education, arts, and leisure), institutions whose purpose was the production, dissemination, and application of ideas. Both their organization and the ideas they propagated were determined by the base. The base was material, the superstructure ideational. In the traditional model, the form of the superstructure and, thus, the dominant ideas of a society, are determined by the base. In other words, the predominant ideas are controlled by and justify the existing order and, thus, the existing power structures. Such ideas are so dominant that most people most of the time are duped into a false consciousness that prevents opposition. In more concrete terms, commercialized leisure dupes most people into acceptance and cooperation with the enterprise of monopoly capital.

Williams argued that this concept of ideological control was too rigid and too extensive. He did not dispute the power of monopoly capital to shape the prevailing ideas of an era. But he rejected the assumption of inevitability and totality. Instead he suggested a more flexible concept of cultural hegemony that acknowledged concentrated power, but also allowed for "space" in which people might create and sustain their own ideas different from or opposed to and, on occasion, prevailing over those promoted by concentrated power. He conceived of alternative and oppositional cultures resisting domination; he considered these cultures never to be a given, but always a contingency. In his own words,

> We have to emphasize that hegemony is not singular; indeed that its own internal structures are highly complex, and have to be continually renewed, recreated and defended; and by the same token, that they can be continually challenged and in certain respects modified. (1973, p. 8)

He argued that hegemony is always contingent and in a continual struggle that is never certain or final, that resistance (without using that word in his essay) is perennial, although the degree of it varies historically. The incompleteness, contingency, and struggle are necessary concepts to account for historical change.

Unlike later resistance studies, Williams continued to acknowledge the power of hegemonic forces. He began his explanation of his model with a description of hegemony as a central system of practices, meanings and values which we can properly call dominant and effective . . . which are organized and lived . . . a sense of reality for most people . . . beyond which it is very difficult for most people of the society to move, in most areas of their lives (1973, p. 9).

He cautioned that hegemony is not static and therefore is capable of countering resistance. He said, "We can only understand an effective and dominant culture if we understand the real social *process* on which it depends: I mean the process of *incorporation*" (p. 9), the process whereby resistances are corralled and rearticulated within the framework of hegemony. He argued that hegemony is "active and *adjusting*" (p. 9) and flexible. Incorporation is the dominant cultural response to challenges and the means to overcome them. Williams never lost sight of the power of hegemony, its dominance. Yet at the same time, he also insisted that there is also space, sometimes more, sometimes less, for "other senses of reality" (p. 9), alternative or oppositional.

Williams seems to have been thinking in terms of more self-consciously organized and overtly political movements when he conceived of alternative and oppositional cultures. In a subsequent book, *Culture* (1981), he described anti-establishment arts movements of the nineteenth and twentieth centuries, such as the Pre-Raphaelites and the Bloomsbury Group, as oppositional cultural movements. The new field of cultural studies was likewise concerned with opposition to hegemony, but they were focused on popular, commercial culture, on what youth in particular did with commodities, on leisure.

Early classics of cultural studies recognized the importance of incorporation, even when not pursuing it. Dick Hebdige's *Subculture: The Meaning of Style* (1979, pp. 92–99) is probably the most widely cited study of resistant subcultures, including mods, skinheads, punk, teddy boys, and reggae. It became the prototype of studies that celebrated subcultural style as resistance. Yet Hebdige also discussed their incorporation in commodity form back into the dominant culture. Quoting Henri Lefebvre (1971), Hebdige said that oppositional ideas, such as these subcultures, are often subverted by being commodified and resold as fashionable styles, stripped of their more dangerous content. At the same time, an ideological form of incorporation in other sectors, especially media, translates the messages of such subcultures into trivia or meaningless spectacle, again stripping away dangerous elements. News stories depict them as innocuous adolescent rebellion, blunting the class and political content of their message. (Other news stories characterize them as dangerous and to be repressed. Another study, *Policing the Crisis* [Hall, Critcher, Jefferson, Clarke, & Roberts, 1978], examined this aspect of dominant culture response.)

Unfortunately, Hebdige's treatment of incorporation was secondary and overshadowed by his more elaborate and persuasive presentation of resistance. Hebdige's emphasis and its reception is understandable in terms of the debate at the time, since resistance was the side of the equation that had been ignored and needed elaboration. Domination, the power of hegemony, was already a well-developed topic of study and needed little elaboration. The idea of resistance was new, exciting and eye-opening. Students and faculty at the University of Birmingham's Centre for Contemporary Cultural Studies (CCCS), birthplace of cultural studies, immersed themselves in projects on resistance.

The center's work on resistance was introduced in *Resistance Through Rituals*

(1976), a collective effort led by Stuart Hall along with several CCCS students who would later gain renown, among them Ian Chamber, John Clarke, Paul Corrigan, Chas Critcher, Simon Firth, Tony Jefferson, Angela McRobbie, Graham Murdoch, Paul Willis and Hebdige. Some of this work preceded Williams' original essay—though Williams had been talking about these ideas for some time before. *Resistance* was inspired more by sociologist Howard Becker's formulation of labeling theory and Phil Cohen's studies of East London subcultures than by Williams. It focused on deviance and proposed a then new interpretation of deviant subculture as an expression of subordinate class and generational resistance to labeling that denied the dominant culture as valid and themselves as deviant. Problematic for the authors was not the power of hegemony but the category of deviant. Hegemony was a given. They showed how deviance, understood as resistance, was a response to hegemony.

Like Williams, however, the authors of *Resistance* never forgot the significance of hegemonic power. Indeed the book presumed its dominance as something from which these subcultures were trying to "win space," to avoid suffocation so to speak. They used the term "resistance," instead of Williams' concept of alternative and oppositional culture, because they wanted to avoid Williams' suggestion of a fully formed culture and more developed class consciousness. Williams wrote of opposition in terms of the grand historical sweep of classes and modes of production supplanting each other, for example, the bourgeoisie of capitalism replacing the aristocracy of feudalism. At CCCS, they focused on the sources of change at the microsocial level—hence the interest in the American sociology of deviance—as people live their everyday lives surrounded by the dominant culture, but subverting it by adapting this culture to their own purposes. They had in mind something less grand in scope and less fully formed than

Williams did. Their idea was simply a "refusal" to be taken in, to succumb, to conform to the dominant. Unfortunately, usage of the term has gravitated toward a suggestion of something more forceful, self-conscious, politically motivated, fully formed, and *effective* than was originally intended.

Far from submissive, deviant subcultures such as the skinheads studied by John Clarke (1990, pp. 99–102) rebelled against the efforts to control and define them. These working class youth exhibited a fierce sense of "us," embattled against a society that described them with contempt and attempted to control their behavior and appearance. Instead of behaving as they were told in school, in reaction to government control of their daily lives through social workers' visits and to the unfavorable comparisons to middle class hippies, lower working class youth of the 1960s created their own identity and community in the form of violent rituals of football hooliganism. One skinhead quoted by Clarke summed it up.

All these dummoes at school who always do what they're told ... end up being Coppers ... social workers [are] really authority pretending to be your friend. They try to get you to do things and if you don't do them, they've got the law on their side. ... With all this lot against us, we've still got the yids, Pakis, 'ippies on our backs. (1990, p. 100)

The consciousness of belonging to a despised and dominated class and the refusal to submit is at the core of a third cultural studies work that first appeared as an essay in *Resistance*, Paul Willis' *Learning to Labor* (1977), centered on English working class adolescent boys' refusal to cooperate with school authorities from teachers on up, rejecting the values and promises the school made as false and as requiring a rejection of their own background. Willis deftly described the delicate and intimate interweaving of resistance and incorporation in the delinquent acts of the boys at school, leisure pursuits and work. He showed how the lads in and around Birmingham England incorporated themselves into the hierarchy of work and class through their very acts of resistance. In resisting they were "learning to labor." Their very rebelliousness helped to consign them to their place in the class structure. It did provide them some space to sustain their own self-constructed identities, something that can be very important to subordinate groups attempting to save their self-respect. Willis' book continues to be one of the best examples of attending to the relationship between resistance and incorporation. Unfortunately it did not inspire emulation or extension to other areas besides education and work.

The director of CCCS at the time, Stuart Hall, also consistently acknowledged the power of the dominant culture while arguing that this power was resisted. In "Encoding/Decoding" (1980, 1994), originally given as a talk in the 1970s, Hall included a category of "preferred reading," the intended meaning of media messages. Alternative or oppositional readings had to work against its grain. In "Deconstructing the Popular," presented in the late 1970s, Hall echoed Williams' words that popular culture is "partly where hegemony arises, and where it is secured . . . [but also] where struggle for and against a culture of the powerful is engaged" (1981, p. 239). His formulation begins and ends with recognizing the power of the dominant culture, as well as resistance to domination. He sees popular culture as an especially important arena where this struggle takes place in today's world.

Losing Our Path

Cultural studies began to go off the track when new converts neglected incorporation and failed to bring it back into the equation once we had established the existence of

resistance and the need to take it into account. This was made worse by the universal application of resistance as a single, undifferentiated concept of divergence from the dominant culture. Even Williams' original distinction between "alternative" and "oppositional" cultures faded into the background, as those two concepts were supplanted in the scholarly discourse by the undifferentiated "resistance." By the 1980s, lacking a nuanced vocabulary for different kinds of resistance (such as suggested by Butsch, 2000, pp. 292–294), some, even within cultural studies, began to criticize the use of a label that had been used to describe significant cultural actions for relatively trivial and self-indulgent behavior.

Some cultural studies scholars adopted Michel de Certeau's (1984) idea of "making do" to describe oppositional stances not significant enough to warrant being called resistance, but still constituting a refusal to complete subordination. According to de Certeau, people carve out space of their own in a cultural sense and make do with what cultural autonomy they can hold onto. They may live in a world of advertising and mass produced products, but they construct a world with these products in ways not predetermined by the products or producers. Nor are they duped by ads and media imagery. They do not overthrow this world of corporate power. But they do make a place of their own within it. A range of terms for different levels of refusal would help greatly to clarify analysis and reduce criticism.

Hall's *Resistance Through Rituals* (1976, pp. 42–45) talks about resistance in similar terms of "winning space" from the dominant culture, not in terms of explicit political opposition. Stuart Hall, in "Deconstructing the Popular" (1981), wrote about popular culture and leisure not so much as explicit opposition, but as a ground to prepare opposition. Resistance in these early formulations, then, was not proposed as some grand assault on the status quo, but as the ground from which might arise some political force. In Hall's words, popular culture is "not a sphere where socialism, socialist culture—already fully formed—might be simply expressed, but it is one of the places where socialism might be constituted" (1981, p. 239).

The failure of our vocabulary to differentiate levels of refusal made it easier to lump all resistance studies as exaggerated extremes, and left us to choose either political economy or cultural studies as mutually exclusive and hostile camps. This in turn closed off explorations of approaches incorporating both views.

There followed a genre of essays calling for a more balanced approach. I will mention only three. John Clarke (1990) characterized the two extreme positions as "populism versus pessimism." He presented a simple but clear map of the basic differences, noting positive and negative aspects of both positions, and then called for a synthesis that puts an end to our "oscillation" between the two. The same sensitivity to both forces was espoused by Justin Lewis and Sut Jhally (1994) and by Herman Gray (1994) in his response to them. All three claimed cultural studies as their ground, all agreed that one extreme or the other is inadequate and that we need take account of determination as well as semiotic space for resistance and evasion.

Yet years after several such calls for synthesis, we still lack an approach that integrates the two forces. We need to focus on this nexus instead of looking exclusively at the resistance or the domination side of the equation. We need to return Williams' concept of incorporation to its place in the equation without displacing some concept of resistance. We need a more nuanced concept of resistance, perhaps several distinct terms for different levels of refusal or opposition. Most important, we need to focus on the connection between resistance and incorporation, to transcend a focus on either one individually and look at how they operate together, how the balances and tensions between the two processes work, how the contradictions of their relationship operate. Incorporation

is akin to processes that are at the heart of analyses of commodification, but is also integral to the formulation of opposition by Raymond Williams and of resistance in early formulations of cultural studies. Hopefully such integrated studies will interest both sides to this debate and build common ground.

Tracing a New Path

What would such a combined approach look like? Consider, for example, the incorporation of resistive subcultures into fashionable new commodities. Incorporation often takes place through commodification, that is, incorporating an alternative or oppositional idea in a commodity, often using the idea to sell or advertise the product by presenting it as avant garde or different from the mass. The universal market is ever searching for new commodities and new packaging. Alternative and oppositional cultures are treated by corporations as simply sources of new products or styles.

The dialectic of resistance and incorporation, particularly in the form of commodification, has been explored in terms of the path of avant-garde art movements. Critiques of modernists have argued that the antibourgeois stance of modernism was incorporated quickly into commodity capitalism (Huyssen, 1986; Li, 1993; Williams, 1982). These studies have emphasized the victories of commodification over resistance.

Another example is the incorporation of two explicitly oppositional subcultures, classic examples of resistance, American hippie subculture in the 1970s and hip-hop subculture in the 1990s (Frank, 1997; Watkins, 1998). They were quickly commodified by corporations. The clothing industry adopted hippie and hip-hop dress styles, stripping or taming their original symbolism and substituting values compatible with consumption. Advertisements of large corporations co-opted their subcultural slogans. Music of both movements that advocated revolt was distributed by major record companies.

Most studies however continue to focus on either incorporation or resistance, but not the relation between the two. For example, Thomas Frank's *The Conquest of Cool* (1997) and S. Craig Watkins' *Representing* (1998) are outstanding new pieces of scholarship on incorporation, but they focus on one half of the relationship. As Hebdige's *Subculture* (1979) acknowledged, both books recognize resistance, but that is overshadowed by concentrating on incorporation. Neither takes as the central purpose understanding the relationship between resistance and incorporation. What is missing in most research is the next step of analysis after incorporation. We should not presume that incorporation is the end of the story of resistance, but should rather pose it as an empirical question. Is there a resistance to incorporation itself, a new stage of resistance, so to speak? Does one resistance die with its incorporation, with new resistances emerging elsewhere? Are they in turn incorporated, and so on? Wherever we leave off telling the story, we should not make it appear that this is the end, but leave open the possibility of continuation. As Williams said, hegemony is never complete, nor is resistance. Such research is daunting, but necessary to progress in understanding consumption, culture and power.

Another approach is to examine cases in which domination went awry, to discover the relation between domination and resistance, just as I have suggested for incorporation and resistance. One approach looks at the process beginning with domination and moving toward resistance; the other begins with resistance and moves toward domination (through incorporation).

In the 1980s, huge electronics corporations tried to introduce a new consumer product, the video disc. They failed because consumers simply refused to buy them (Butsch, 2000). People exercised economic power. Can cultural power be exercised against economic power? Isn't the decision to buy or not a cultural decision? How about resisting a heavily hyped cultural product like a movie, book, or music CD? Movie studios spend tens of millions on movie ads and yet success seems mostly determined by word of mouth. How does this work? Who's in control? Are there resistive and incorporative forces at work?

Here is where the future of leisure studies and cultural studies lies, weaving together the threads of domination, resistance, and incorporation in order to understand leisure and popular culture in an era of hyper commodification and consumption. We have examined the individual threads enough. They are conceptually and empirically sound. Now we can weave our tapestry of power and struggle.

Afterword: Changes in Media and Audience Studies Over the Past Decade

In 2001, I framed the issue as subcultural resistance of active audiences facing the framing power of centralized mass media, including its power to incorporate and co-opt audiences. Since then much has changed. The media landscape has changed remarkably. Digital convergence, the Internet, and mobile media have created an everywhere, ever-on environment and changed audiences into users, or what some have called "prosumers," both producing and consuming media content. Industrial convergences and concentration have created multimedia giants with global reach much greater than once envisioned by sociologist Herbert Schiller (1969). Politics have changed, too. Across the globe, neoliberal politics has privatized public media and supplanted the public service model with a market model to justify deregulation and enable media monopoly. In some cases, an older power-elite conspiracy theory seems more appropriate than Williams' (1977) concept of hegemony, which he conceived to explain a subtler form of domination in post-war Western democracies.

Our understanding of media industry and especially of audiences has grown as well, in ways that enable a synthesis of hegemony and resistance in the production and reception of media texts. The concept of active audiences that accompanied the idea of resistance has led us also to discover a good deal more. Resistance and its companion communication model of encoding/decoding (Hall, 1980) were largely conceived within the framework of "short-term" media effects, focusing on the impact of a single media message. More recent research into audience history, studies of entire genres (e.g., sitcom, telenovela, reality shows), and the impact of media per se has provided a picture of "long-term," cumulative effects of repetition across time and media that are presumed in the concept of hegemony and in critiques of media monopoly.

In hindsight, resistance can been seen as a conceptual passage that led from the study of effects to a broad theoretical and empirical plain with a far richer understanding of audiences and audiencing than either effects or resistance enabled. This new framework more readily allows structural and macro considerations that typify concerns about media monopoly and thus connect our understandings of audiences with those of media industry and production. Resistance was conceived in a culturalist framework and as a result lent itself to broader cultural explorations such as ideas of "embeddedness," "net locality," and collective concepts of audiences.

The first idea, that of embeddedness (Silverstone, 1994) grew from addressing family (Lull, 1990; Morley, 1986) and group structure at the micro level of television viewing. It places media experience within the living context of audiences, understanding media as part of the whole immediate social environment, and has notably contributed to this broadened

horizon in understanding audiences. What people do with media and their messages is influenced by the situation within which they do it, whether in the home or elsewhere, alone or with others, and often while focused or multitasking.

Second, the idea of "net locality" characterizes some new research on media companies that links the virtual and physical locations of audiences (Gordon & de Sousa e Silva, 2011) and has begun to interweave analysis of Internet users' (audience) behavior with studies of the organization and actions of media companies. This research potentially bridges the macro approach of corporate policies and the micro analysis of audiences' responses. It places the interface between audiences and media industries at the very center of its focus, and shows promise for further integration of ideas about hegemony and resistance.

A third new idea focuses on audiences on a macro level, as collectivities such as publics in a democratic polity, or as crowds that potentially contest government or corporate authority, or as communities (Butsch & Livingstone, 2013; Carpentier, 2011; Harindranath, 2009; Livingstone, 2005). This macro level is the same turf as political economy, thus presenting a possible convergence. It situates audiences in a larger framework where they are positioned vis-á-vis the centralized power of hegemony and domination.

Additionally, three new areas of research have begun to explore links between production, text, and consumption, connecting our knowledge of media industries, texts, and audiences: (1) cultural production studies, (2) global media studies, and (3) discourse studies. These show promise for further convergence of our understanding of active audiences with that of media monopoly's influence over audiences.

Critiques of cultural imperialism and media monopoly (Bagdikian, 2000; Baker, 2007; Schiller, 1976) have presumed that concentration of cultural production truncates the range of ideas to those that are consistent with the interests of power elites. However, research demonstrating how this actually happens, whether by conspiracy or by structural constraints, has been sparse. Yet we need such research to demonstrate not "short-term" effects of a single text, as might happen in the wake of a conspiracy, but "long-term" effects of organizational structures producing a steady stream of similarly themed texts that may shape the culture and widespread values and beliefs.

Earlier American sociological research linked production organization and process to specific cultural content (Tuchman, 1988). Studies of the production of news demonstrated how objectivism, dependence on sources, and time constraints resulted in much news composed of prearranged "routine events" (Molotch & Lester, 1974). Peterson and Berger (1975) explained how record industry oligopoly constrained the range of commercial recorded music. A new generation of cultural production studies (Hesmondhalgh, 2006; Holt & Perren, 2009; Mayer, Banks, & Caldwell, 2009) has wedded this older American research to cultural studies to reveal organizational processes by which outcomes grow as resolutions of strains and resistances within organizations. For example, Laura Grindstaff (2002) demonstrated how the reality show format produced an emphasis on manipulating participants into the emotional labor of the "money shot," and constructed a differential characterization of social class in the process. However, production studies linking the production process to the resulting texts remain sparse. Hesmondhalgh (2006) explains the importance of this link. Butsch (1989; Chapter VII.53 in this volume) has welded together insights of multiple studies of production processes for American domestic situation comedies to explain how these resulted in specific content about social class.

Global media studies has forged a connection between industry studies and audience studies, partly through the experience of actual global companies (Volkmer, 2012). The concept of "glocal" has been used to describe the failure of global media to reach cross-culturally to disparate audiences and the strategies by global corporations such as STAR TV to resolve this by revising production and distribution to tailor content to local cultures and audiences (Chadha & Kavoori, 2000).

Another new approach has examined hegemonic discourses about audiences that reveal institutional goals in relation to the social control of populations. One such example is Livingstone and Lunt (2011), on the "implied audience" in regulation. Looking at British regulation, they find a remarkably consistent framing of audiences as consumers, to the neglect of audiences as citizens. This seems a good example of corporate efforts to incorporate audiences into a hegemonic structure of consumption (bread and circuses) and to distract them away from their role as citizens. U.S. regulation took a similar path in abandoning the trustee model (also the basis of the BBC) to make good citizens in favor of a market model based on audiences as consumers buying the media they prefer. Butsch (2008) finds that American elite discourses over two centuries judged audiences against standards of good citizenship. Butsch and Livingstone (2013) compare such discourses about audience across diverse cultures and governing structures around the world.

In sum, we now have ways to understand audiences and industries that interweave audience and production studies; so we are moving toward a more holistic picture of production, texts, and reception.

References

Bagdikian, B. (2000). *Media monopoly* (6th ed.). Boston: Beacon Press.

Baker, C. E. (2007). *Media concentration and democracy: Why ownership matters.* Cambridge, UK: Cambridge University Press.

Berlan, J. P. (1989). The commodification of life. *Monthly Review, 41,* 24–30.

Boyer, P. (1978). *Urban masses and moral order in America, 1820–1920.* Cambridge, MA: Harvard University Press.

Braverman, H. (1974). *Labor and monopoly capital.* New York: Monthly Review Press.

Butsch, R. (1989). How does it happen: The television industry, the production process, and images of class. In L. Chorbajian (Ed.), *Introduction to critical sociology* (pp. 25–34). Boston: Ginn.

Butsch, R. (2000). *The making of American audiences.* Cambridge, UK: Cambridge University Press.

Butsch, R. (2008). *The citizen audience: Crowds, publics, and individuals.* London: Routledge.

Butsch, R., & Livingstone, S. (2013). *Meanings of audiences.* London: Routledge.

Carpentier, N. (2011). New configurations of the audience? In V. Nightingale (Ed.), *Handbook of media audiences* (pp. 190–212). Malden, MA: Wiley Blackwell.

Castile, G. P. (1996). The commodification of Indian identity. *American Anthropology, 98*(4), 743–749.

Chadha, K., & Kavoori, A. (2000). Media imperialism revisited: Some findings from the Asian case. *Media Culture Society, 22*(4), 415–432.

Clarke, J. (1990). Pessimism versus populism: The problematic politics of popular culture. In R. Butsch (Ed.), *For fun and profit: The transformation of leisure into consumption* (pp. 28–44). Philadelphia: Temple University Press.

de Certeau, M. (1984). *The practice of everyday life* (S. Rendall, Trans.). Berkeley: University of California Press.

Frank, T. (1997). *The conquest of cool: Business culture, counterculture and the rise of hip consumerism.* Chicago: University of Chicago Press.

Giner, S. (1976). *Mass society.* New York: Academic Press.

Gordon, E., & de Sousa e Silva, A. (2011). *Net locality: Why location matters in a networked World.* Malden, MA: Wiley Blackwell.

Grindstaff, L. (2002). *The money shot: Trash, class, and the making of TV talk shows.* Chicago: University of Chicago Press.

Grossberg, L. (1995). Cultural studies vs. political economy. *Critical Studies in Mass Communication, 12*(1), 72–81.

Hall, S. (1980). Encoding/decoding. In S. Hall, D. Hobson, A. Lowe, & P. Willis (Eds.), *Culture, media, language: Working papers in cultural studies, 1972–79* (pp. 128–138). London: Hutchinson.

Hall, S. (1981). Notes on deconstructing "the popular." In R. Samuels (Ed.), *People's history and socialist theory* (pp. 227–240). London: Routledge & Kegan Paul.

Hall, S. (1994). Reflections upon the encoding/decoding model: An interview with Stuart Hall. In J. Cruz & J. Lewis (Eds.), *Viewing, reading, listening: Audiences and cultural reception* (pp. 253–274). Boulder, CO: Westview Press.

Hall, S., Critcher, C., Jefferson, T., Clarke, J., & Roberts, B. (1978). *Policing the crisis: Mugging, the state, and law and order.* London: MacMillan.

Hall, S., & Jefferson, T. (1976). *Resistance through rituals: Youth subcultures in postwar Britain.* London: Hutchinson.

Harindranath, R. (2009). *Audience-citizens: The media, public knowledge, and interpretive practice.* New Delhi: Sage.

Hebdige, D. (1979). *Subculture: The meaning of style.* London: Methuen.

Hesmondhalgh, D. (2006). Media organizations and media texts. In D. Hesmondhalgh (Ed.), *Media production.* Berkshire, UK: Open University Press.

Holt, J., & Perren, A. (Eds.). (2009). *Media industries: History, theory and method.* Malden, MA: Wiley Blackwell.

Huyssen, A. (1986). *After the great divide: Modernism, mass culture, postmodernism.* Bloomington: Indiana University Press.

Jay, M. (1973). *The dialectical imagination: A history of the Frankfurt School.* Boston: Little, Brown.

Johnson, R. (1981). Against absolutism. In R. Samuels (Ed.), *People's history and socialist theory* (pp. 386–396). London: Routledge & Kegan Paul.

Kornhauser, W. (1959). *The politics of mass society*. New York: Free Press.

Lee, D. O. (1992). Commodification of ethnicity. *Urban Affairs Quarterly, 28*, 258–275.

Lefebvre, H. (1971). *Everyday life in the modern world*. New York: Harper.

Lewis, J., & Jhally, S. (1994). The politics of cultural studies; and Gray, H. Response. *American Quarterly, 46*(1), 114–121.

Li, V. (1993). Selling modernism: Resisting commodification, commodifying resistance. *English Studies in Canada, 19*(1), 35–44.

Livingstone, S. (Ed.). (2005). *Audiences and publics*. Bristol: Intellect Press.

Livingstone, S., & Lunt, P. (2011). The implied audience of communication policy making. In V. Nightingale (Ed.), *Handbook of media audiences* (pp. 169–189). Malden, MA: Wiley Blackwell.

Loader, I. (1999). Consumer culture and the commodification of policing and security. *Sociology, 33*(2), 373–392.

Lull, J. (1990). *Inside family viewing: Ethnographic research on television's audiences*. London: Routledge.

Mayer, V., Banks, M., & Caldwell, J. (Eds.). (2009). *Production studies: Cultural studies of media industries*. Abingdon, UK: Routledge.

McMullan, J. L. (1996). The new improved monied police. *British Journal of Criminology, 36*, 85–108.

Molnar, A. (1996). *Giving kids the business: The commercialization of America's schools*. Boulder, CO: Westview Press.

Molotch, H., & Lester, M. (1974). News as purposive behavior: On the strategic use of routine events, accidents, and scandals. *American Sociological Review, 39*(1), 101–112.

Morley, D. (1986). *Family television: Cultural power and domestic leisure*. London: Comedia.

Peterson, R. A., & Berger, D. (1975). Cycles in symbol production: The case of popular music. *American Sociological Review, 40*(2), 158–173.

Resnik, D. (1998). The commodification of human reproductive materials. *Journal of Medical Ethics, 24*(6), 388–393.

Richer, S. (1988). Fieldwork and the commodification of culture. *Canadian Review of Sociology and Anthropology, 25*, 406–420.

Rothman, B. K. (1987). Reproductive technology and the commodification of life. *Women and Health, 13* (1–2), 95–100.

Schiller, H. (1969). *Mass communications and American Empire*. New York: A. Kelley.

Schiller, H. (1976). *Communication and cultural domination*. White Plains, NY: International Arts and Science Press.

Silverstone, R. (1994). *Television and everyday life*. London: Routledge.

Swingewood, A. (1977). *The myth of mass culture*. Atlantic Highlands, NJ: Humanities Press.

Swinnerton, G. (1999). Recreation and conservation. In E. Jackson & T. Burton (Eds.), *Leisure studies: Prospects for the twenty-first century* (pp. 199–231). State College, PA: Venture.

Tuchman, G. (1988). Mass media institutions. In N. Smelser (Ed.), *Handbook of sociology* (pp. 601–626). Newbury Park, CA: Sage.

Volkmer, I. (2012). *The handbook of global media research*. Malden, MA: Wiley Blackwell.

Watkins, S. C. (1998). *Representing: Hip-hop culture and the production of Black cinema*. Chicago: University of Chicago Press.

Williams, R. (1973). Base and superstructure in Marxist cultural theory. *New Left Review, 82*, 3–16.

Williams, R. (1977). *Marxism and literature*. New York: Oxford University Press.

Williams, R. (1981). *Culture*. London: Fontana.

Williams, R. (1982). *Sociology of culture*. New York: Schocken Books.

Willis, P. (1977). *Learning to labor: How working class kids get working class jobs*. New York: Columbia University Press.

PART II

REPRESENTATIONS OF GENDER, RACE, AND CLASS

The chapters in this section apply many of the theoretical concepts that we isolated in Part I to the analysis of **gender** and **sexuality**, **race** and **class** within media production, text construction, and audience reception or consumption. This book insists on the need to develop and ground theory within an understanding of how media texts may either contribute to or undermine the inequalities that exist in post-industrialized societies like our own. The linkage of media theory and politics is particularly important within cultural studies, which, as indicated in Part I, is concerned with the lived experience of economically and socially subordinate groups and with making visible the ways in which media industries contribute to the continuation of inequalities.

What do we mean when we say that we view gender (and sexuality), race, and class as "social constructs"? To take this approach means to reduce the explanatory role of biology or "nature" in all our social arrangements and power imbalances. Instead, we shift our attention to the social, economic, and political forces that shape and reshape these conceptual categories over time and place. Many examples can be offered of the "instability" (changeable or shifting nature) of these concepts—some from recent history.

We begin with a brief overview of the ideas of **critical race theory.** In the 1960s, 1970s, and 1980s, the civil rights movement and subsequent antiracist organizing and institutions mobilized many vigorous campaigns focusing public attention on denigrating racial representations that buttressed an inequitable economic and political status quo. Academic fields such as Black studies, Africana studies, Asian American studies, and Native American studies developed important critiques of taken-for-granted but demeaning imagery originating from the "White imaginary" (the culturally dominant store of ideas and feelings about "race"). Building on this base, the 1990s saw the development of sophisticated studies in critical race theory and **postcolonial theory** that critiqued Western European and U.S. historical narratives of "progress" and "civilization" and assimilation. In such narratives, the politically and culturally dominant (White, Eurocentric) group defined the terms and projected simplicity, closeness to nature, and a host of other less desirable characteristics upon the racial "Other"—whether African, Arab, East or South Asian, Pacific Islander, or indigenous (Native American). Such historical studies help us understand the role of concepts of race both within U.S. culture and globally, in relation to international politics.

Thanks to the political work done by the civil rights movement, as a society we have developed some sensitivity to the more overt racist images of the past. But as Stuart Hall points out in the classic piece, "The Whites of Their Eyes" (II.11), we still need to educate ourselves about "inferential racism," which he defines as

> those apparently naturalized representations of events and situations referring to race, whether "factual" or "fictional," which have racist premises and propositions inscribed in them as a set of unquestioned assumptions. (p. 106)

Raka Shome (II.12) offers a compelling chapter that provides an example of such unquestioned racist assumptions underlying "apparently naturalized representations" of race. In her study of white femininity in the context of transnational "motherhood"

narratives in popular culture, she points to a phenomenon that is "simultaneously gendered, racialized, and heterosexualized": the pictorial or narrative representation of the White woman "saving, rescuing, or adopting international children from underprivileged parts of the world" (p. 108). Analyzing many examples of this phenomenon (featuring celebrities like Princess Diana, Angelina Jolie, and Madonna), she shows that the media construction of heroic maternal **Whiteness** is dependent upon, and further reproduces, the denigration of women of color as mothers. As she writes,

> The white mother can only occupy the position of a "global mother" by erasing the non-white maternal body from visions of global domesticity. The white mother's subject position is thus ironically dependent on the necessary failure of the non-white native mother. (p. 113)

Another underlying assumption about race that has historical resonance in U.S. media representations is that African Americans in particular are hypersexual. This imputed hypersexuality has played a part in the creation of "otherness" and has historically legitimized acts of violence such as the rape of Black women and the lynching of Black men. Drawing on sports media coverage of tennis athletic stars Serena and Venus Williams, McKay and Johnson (II.13) help contextualize what they call the "sexual grotesquerie" in these recent media texts, by placing them within a larger context of historic denigration of Black bodies by Europeans and Euro-Americans. Acknowledging that "the exceptional performances of the Williams sisters have provoked complex and ambivalent narratives of qualified praise and grudging approval, as well as subtle and overt racism and sexism" (p. 120), these scholars argue that contemporary socially constructed images of Black women need to be understood as linked to historically deep ideologies of Blacks as embodying a deviant sexuality.

Femininity in its **hegemonic** form (White, domesticated, heterosexual) is also a powerful ideological formation that seems "natural" until we begin to explore its historical evolution. The artificiality or "constructedness" of femininity is the focus of Mary Rogers's provocative brief chapter, "Hetero Barbie?" (II.14). As Rogers writes, the Barbie doll's femininity "entails a lot of artifice, a lot of clothes, a lot or props such as cuddly poodles and shopping bags, and a lot of effort." Indeed, Rogers playfully raises the possibility that Barbie may not be heterosexual and indeed may not even be a woman: Barbie may be a drag queen. Much in the tradition made widely visible by cross-dressing stars like RuPaul, Barbie's ultrafeminine presence may signal the ironic exaggeration that drag queen performances enact (p. 128).

As Rogers's chapter suggests, the term **gender** has acquired a whole new range of associations in light of the **queer theory** that has grown out of both activist politics and **postmodern** scholarship over recent years. Historians of gender and sexuality have pointed out that the very terms we use to describe the concept of fixed and opposite sexual orientations— "heterosexuality" and "homosexuality"— are only about a century old. These terms were produced within a late nineteenth-century medical **discourse** developed by the emerging professional health fields of psychology and sexology. Through the cultural dominance of the new medical discourse in the twentieth century, heterosexuality came into being as a norm against which same-sex attraction and love (as well as many other desires and sexual behaviors) could be defined as threateningly deviant or "other." A queer theory approach questions traditional ideas of "normal" and "deviant" in the realms of both gender and sexuality by arguing against the commonsense notion that there are only two genders (masculine and feminine) and two kinds of desire or attraction (straight and gay). In queer theory, gender, sexuality, and desire are all

seen as ambiguous, shifting, unstable, and too complex to fit neatly into **binary** (either/or) systems. Drag performance, cross-dressing, and a myriad of other types of gender-bending activities, behavior, and identities now highly visible in twenty-first century urban culture certainly suggest the futility of attempts to maintain that the once traditional categories are fixed by nature. The influential feminist philosopher and queer theorist Judith Butler has likened gender to a theatrical performance—a matter of gradually learned role-playing, with no necessary correlation to one's biological sex (Butler, 1999).

While the commercial entertainment media have on some level acknowledged that gender and sexual identities are more fluid than was once thought, and film and TV representations have become more diverse, Kay Siebler (II. 15) shows that there is still a strong tendency to caricature and stereotype, and in general to "reinforce gender rigidity" (p. 134). This is especially the case with **transgender** people who, according to Siebler, "are reduced to very un-queer definitions of masculinity and femininity, maleness and femaleness" (p. 135). As she points out, in the context of commercial media products, "the presence of a traditionally marginalized group does not necessarily equate to advancement" (p. 135).

Siebler also looks at how members of the transgender community construct their own identities, often influenced by the resources made available by commercial media and, most disappointingly, the Internet. She acknowledges that "the digital world has opened up communities for transgender people where none have existed before. There is less isolation and perhaps less struggle because of the resources, social networks, and virtual communities provided on the Internet" (p. 139). At the same time, Siebler offers an important critique of the ways in which some of these virtual communities and forums "also serve to create a codified version of limited ways of being transgender.

A transgender norm becomes established so that even transgender people are no longer queering gender . . . " (p. 139).

Our final category of analysis, social class, is unfortunately less well represented in media scholarship than gender and race. The comparative absence of class analysis in the scholarship reflects the fact that as a society, we're more attuned to unequal treatment based on race and gender than to economic inequality, and this in turn reflects the history of social movement activity in the twentieth and twenty-first centuries. A robust labor movement arose during the years of most intensive industrialization in the United States to challenge the absolute right of **capitalism** to exploit working people's labor, but the subsequent sharp decline in union membership and labor movement visibility have been accompanied by a corresponding decline in the national conversation about the disruptive social effects of a highly unequal distribution of wealth. In 2010, the Occupy Wall Street movement briefly highlighted the alarmingly increased gap in wealth between the top 1% of Americans and everyone else, but as of this writing very little has changed in national policies that support increasing inequality.

Despite our best efforts, we have been able to locate only a relatively small number of new media studies articles that foreground **class**. Among these is Michael J. Lee and Leigh Moscowitz's chapter, "The Rich Bitch" (II.16), an unusually strong discussion of the class dimension in the reality TV series *Real Housewives of New York City*, and one which also demonstrates the importance of considering the intersections of aspects of social identity often discussed in isolation from one another. This chapter is also notable for its focus on the wealthy, rather than the poor, and for its insight into the use of rich women as the target for a class-based hostility toward the rich that lies just below the surface of envy and admiration. As the authors write,

> According to the logic of *RHW-NYC*, rich women, not rich men, spend frivolously, project false appearances, backstab, gossip, and leave their children's care to paid staff. (p. 144)

While the authors point out that there is a "populist promise" underlying the sardonic portrait of the rich as unenviable "figures of scorn and pity," they see the promise as limited in part by the desired audience of the show, labeled "affluencers" by the Bravo network itself. (This audience can enjoy judging the badly behaved superwealthy, without having to reflect uneasily on their own material privilege.) Similarly problematic for Lee and Moscowitz is the fact that viewers of *RHW-NYC* are "invited to conclude that the rich are undeserving because these women violate traditional gender roles so flagrantly" (p.153).

The issue of traditional gender norms under threat is the focus of Jackson Katz's analysis of gendered political **discourse** on conservative talk radio, as best known through the Rush Limbaugh show (II.17). Katz looks closely at how during a period when "white men's unquestioned dominance in the family and workplace are in the process of a long-term decline," a media genre denying these changes provided listeners "with an alternate media universe where the old order of male dominance and white supremacy is still intact" (p. 157). Katz suggests that Limbaugh's critics have tended to miss the "gendered nature of Limbaugh and company's contempt for liberals," and draws attention to recent right-wing radio and TV discourse giving Republicans credit for superior "manhood"—including efforts to deprive President Obama of credit for the popular killing of Osama Bin Laden (p. 160). In Katz's view,

> Embedded firmly within the talk radio hosts' scathing critique of liberalism is a barely suppressed well of anger at the progressive changes in the gender

and sexual order over the past forty years and the concomitant displacement of traditional patriarchal power. (p. 160)

The issues related to gender, sexuality, race, and class ideology in media culture that have been highlighted here will be important to bear in mind throughout subsequent chapters, where a wide array of media cultural forms are examined in more depth, through our organization into thematic chapters that we hope will be of lively interest to you.

11

The Whites of Their Eyes

Racist Ideologies and the Media

Stuart Hall

W e begin by defining some of the terms of the argument. 'Racism and the media' touches directly the problem of *ideology*, since the media's main sphere of operations is the production and transformation of ideologies. . . .

I am using the term ideology to refer to those images, concepts and premises which provide the frameworks through which we represent, interpret, understand and 'make sense' of some aspect of social existence. Language and ideology are not the same—since the same linguistic term ('democracy' for example, or 'freedom') can be deployed within different ideological discourses. But language, broadly conceived, is by definition the principal medium in which we find different ideological discourses elaborated.

Three important things need to be said about ideology in order to make what follows intelligible. First, ideologies do not consist of isolated and separate concepts, but in the articulation of different elements into a distinctive set or chain of meanings. In liberal ideology, 'freedom' is connected (articulated) with individualism and the free market; in socialist ideology, 'freedom' is a collective condition, dependent on, not counterposed to, 'equality of condition,' as it is in liberal ideology. The same concept is differently positioned within the logic of different ideological discourses. One of the ways in which ideological struggle takes place and ideologies are transformed is by articulating the elements differently, thereby producing a different meaning: breaking the chain in which they are currently fixed (e.g. 'democratic' = the 'Free' West) and establishing a new articulation (e.g. 'democratic' = deepening the democratic content of political life). This 'breaking of the chain' is not, of course, confined to the head: it takes place through social practice and political struggle.

Second, ideological statements are made by individuals: but ideologies are not the product of individual consciousness or intention. Rather we formulate our intentions *within*

Extract from *Silver Linings: Some Strategies for the Eighties* (George Bridges and Ros Brunt, eds.), Lawrence & Wishart, 1981, "The Whites of Their Eyes: Racist Ideologies and the Media," by Stuart Hall, pp. 28–52.

ideology. They pre-date individuals, and form part of the determinate social formations and conditions into which individuals are born. We have to 'speak through' the ideologies which are active in our society and which provide us with the means of 'making sense' of social relations and our place in them. The transformation of ideologies is thus a collective process and practice, not an individual one. Largely, the processes work *unconsciously*, rather than by conscious intention. Ideologies produce different forms of social consciousness, rather than being produced by them. They work most effectively when we are not aware that how we formulate and construct a statement about the world is underpinned by ideological premises; when our formations seem to be simply descriptive statements about how things are (i.e. must be), or of what we can 'take-for-granted.' 'Little boys like playing rough games; little girls, however, are full of sugar and spice' is predicated on a whole set of ideological premises, though it seems to be an aphorism which is grounded, not in how masculinity and femininity have been historically and culturally constructed in society, but in Nature itself. Ideologies tend to disappear from view into the taken-for-granted 'naturalized' world of common sense. Since (like gender) race appears to be 'given' by Nature, racism is one of the most profoundly 'naturalized' of existing ideologies.

Third, ideologies 'work' by constructing for their subjects (individual and collective) positions of identification and knowledge which allow them to 'utter' ideological truths as if they were their authentic authors. This is not because they emanate from our innermost, authentic and unified experience, but because we find ourselves mirrored in the positions at the centre of the discourses from which the statements we formulate 'make sense.' Thus the same 'subjects' (e.g. economic classes or ethnic groups) can be differently constructed in different ideologies. . . .

Let us look, then, a little more closely at the apparatuses which generate and circulate ideologies. In modern societies, the different media are especially important sites for the production, reproduction and transformation of ideologies. Ideologies are of course, worked on in many places in society, and not only in the head. The fact of unemployment is, among other things, an extremely effective ideological instrument for converting or constraining workers to moderate their wage claims. But institutions like the media are peculiarly central to the matter since they are, by definition, part of the dominant means of *ideological* production. What they 'produce' is, precisely, representations of the social world, images, descriptions, explanations and frames for understanding how the world is and why it works as it is said and shown to work. And, amongst other kinds of ideological labour, the media construct for us a definition of what *race* is, what meaning the imagery of race carries, and what the 'problem of race' is understood to be. They help to classify out the world in terms of the categories of race.

The media are not only a powerful source of ideas about race. They are also one place where these ideas are articulated, worked on, transformed and elaborated. We have said 'ideas' and 'ideologies' in the plural. For it would be wrong and misleading to see the media as uniformly and conspiratorially harnessed to a single, racist conception of the world. Liberal and humane ideas about 'good relations' between the races, based on open-mindedness and tolerance, operate inside the world of the media. . . .

It would be simple and convenient if all the media were simply the ventriloquists of a unified and racist 'ruling class' conception of the world. But neither a unifiedly conspiratorial media nor indeed a unified racist 'ruling class' exists in anything like that simple way. I don't insist on complexity for its own sake. But if critics of the media subscribe to too simple or reductive a view of their operations, this inevitably lacks credibility and weakens the case they are making because the theories and critiques don't square with reality. . . .

Another important distinction is between what we might call 'overt' racism and 'inferential' racism. By *overt* racism, I mean those many occasions when open and favourable coverage is given to arguments, positions and spokespersons who are in the business of elaborating an openly racist argument or advancing a racist policy or view.

By *inferential* racism I mean those apparently naturalized representations of events and situations relating to race, whether 'factual' or 'fictional,' which have racist premises and propositions inscribed in them as a set of *unquestioned assumptions*. These enable racist statements to be formulated without ever bringing into awareness the racist predicates on which the statements are grounded. . . .

An example of *inferential* racist ideology is the sort of television programme which deals with some 'problem' in race relations. It is probably made by a good and honest liberal broadcaster, who hopes to do some good in the world for 'race relations' and who maintains a scrupulous balance and neutrality when questioning people interviewed for the programme. The programme will end with a homily on how, if only the 'extremists' on *either side* would go away, 'normal blacks and whites' would be better able to get on with learning to live in harmony together. Yet every word and image of such programmes are impregnated with unconscious racism because they are all predicated on the unstated and unrecognized assumption that the *blacks* are the *source of the problem*. Yet virtually the whole of 'social problem' television about race and immigration—often made, no doubt, by well intentioned and liberal minded broadcasters—is precisely predicated on racist premises of this kind. . . .

Recent critics of imperialism have argued that, if we simply extend our definition of nineteenth century fiction from one branch of 'serious fiction' to embrace popular literature, we will find a second, powerful strand of the English literary imagination to set beside the *domestic* novel: the male-dominated world of imperial adventure which takes *empire*, rather than *Middlemarch* as its microcosm. I remember a graduate student, working on the construction of race in popular literature and culture at the end of the Nineteenth Century, coming to me in despair—racism was so *ubiquitous*, and at the same time, so *unconscious*—simply assumed to be the case—that it was impossible to get any critical purchase on it. In this period, the very idea of *adventure* became synonymous with the demonstration of the moral, social and physical mastery of the colonizers over the colonized.

Later, this concept of 'adventure'—one of the principal categories of modern *entertainment*—moved straight off the printed page into the literature of crime and espionage, children's books, the great Hollywood extravaganzas and comics. There, with recurring persistence, they still remain. Many of these older versions have had their edge somewhat blunted by time. They have been distanced from us, apparently, by our superior wisdom and liberalism. But they still reappear on the television screen, especially in the form of 'old movies' (some 'old movies,' of course, continue to be made). But we can grasp their recurring resonance better if we identify some of the base image of the 'grammar of race.'

There is, for example, the familiar *slave-figure*: dependable, loving in a simple, child-like way—the devoted 'Mammy' with the rolling eyes, or the faithful field-hand or retainer, attached and devoted to 'his' Master. The best known extravaganza of all—*Gone With the Wind*—contains rich variants of both. The 'slave-figure' is by no means limited to films and programmes *about* slavery. Some 'Injuns' and many Asians have come on to the screen in this disguise. A deep and unconscious ambivalence pervades this stereotype. Devoted and childlike, the 'slave' is also unreliable, unpredictable and undependable—capable of 'turning nasty,' or of plotting in a treacherous way, secretive, cunning, cut-throat once his or her Master's or Mistress's back is turned: and inexplicably given to running away into the bush at the slightest opportunity. The whites can never be sure that this childish simpleton—'Sambo'—is not mocking his master's white manners behind his hand, even when giving an exaggerated caricature of white refinement.

Another base-image is that of the 'native.' The good side of this figure is portrayed in a certain primitive nobility and simple dignity. The bad side is portrayed in terms of cheating and cunning, and, further out, savagery and barbarism. Popular culture is still full today of countless savage and restless 'natives,' and sound-tracks constantly repeat the threatening sound of drumming in the night, the hint of primitive rites and cults. Cannibals, whirling dervishes, Indian tribesmen, garishly got up, are constantly threatening to overrun the screen. They are likely to appear at any moment out of the darkness to decapitate the beautiful heroine, kidnap the children, burn the encampment or threaten to boil, cook and eat the innocent explorer or colonial administrator and his lady-wife. These 'natives' always move as an anonymous collective mass—in tribes or hordes. And against them is always counterposed the isolated white figure, alone 'out there,' confronting his Destiny or shouldering his Burden in the 'heart of darkness,' displaying coolness under fire and an unshakeable authority—exerting

mastery over the rebellious natives or quelling the threatened uprising with a single glance of his steel-blue eyes.

A third variant is that of the 'clown' or 'entertainer.' This captures the 'innate' humour, as well as the physical grace of the licensed entertainer—putting on a show for The Others. It is never quite clear whether we are laughing with or at this figure: admiring the physical and rhythmic grace, the open expressivity and emotionality of the 'entertainer,' or put off by the 'clown's' stupidity.

One noticeable fact about all these images is their deep *ambivalence*—the double vision of the white eye through which they are seen. The primitive nobility of the ageing tribesman or chief, and the native's rhythmic grace always contain both a nostalgia for an innocence lost forever to the civilized, and the threat of civilization being over-run or undermined by the recurrence of savagery, which is always lurking just below the surface; or by an untutored sexuality, threatening to 'break out.' Both are aspects—the good and the bad sides—of *primitivism*. In these images, 'primitivism' is defined by the fixed proximity of such people to Nature.

Is all this so far away as we sometimes suppose from the representations of race which fill the screens today? These *particular* versions may have faded. But their *traces* are still to be observed, reworked in many of the modern and up-dated images. And though they may appear to carry a different meaning, they are often still constructed on a very ancient grammar.

12

"Global Motherhood"

The Transnational Intimacies of White Femininity

Raka Shome

In October 2005, ABC news published an online story about a Midwestern woman in Ohio who, inspired by images of Angelina Jolie's adoption of an Ethiopian child, expressed a desire to do the same.[1] The woman, Ann Charles Watt, recalled that: "I remember being at the store and seeing Angelina on the cover of, I think it was People magazine," and I said "Oh my gosh! We can do this" [i.e. adopt from Ethiopia]. Watt, along with her husband Jason Hillard, enthusiastically noted that "in the grand scheme of things, she changed our lives . . . Angelina . . . probably brought us an African child." Ann Watt's husband reinforced this enthusiasm by adding that *"we're inviting a whole new genealogy to our family line. We invite culture and diversity into our family* and those are things that inspired me to adopt" (emphasis added). Ann and Jason's enthusiasm here has to do not only with their decision of international adoption but also that they would be able to bring a "new genealogy" of "culture and diversity" into their "family."

This story is important because it is representative of a growing transnational phenomenon (that is simultaneously gendered, racialized, and heterosexualized) that is marking the late twentieth and early twenty-first century's media and cultural landscape. This is a phenomenon in which it is now becoming commonplace and even fashionable to see white Western women saving, rescuing, or adopting international children from underprivileged parts of the world, and rearticulating them through *familial* frameworks that recenter white Western (and especially North Atlantic) heterosexual kinship logics. From the exhaustive images of Princess Diana with children of the world in the 1990s, to more recent images of celebrity adoption (such as by Angelina Jolie, Madonna, Mia Farrow, and Meg Ryan), to representations of white women as U.N. "good will" ambassadors (such as Nicole Kidman, Susan Sarandon, Audrey Hepburn, and Angelina Jolie), to

From Shome, R. (2011). "Global motherhood": The transnational intimacies of white femininity. *Critical Studies in Mass Communication*, (28)5, 388–406. Copyright © National Communication Association, reprinted by permission of Taylor & Francis Ltd, www.tandfonline.com on behalf of The National Communication Association.

numerous websites of international adoption in nations such as the U.S. and U.K. that specifically target middle-and upper-class white women, a discourse of what I term *global motherhood* has surfaced as a logic through which white womens' bodies are spilling into the global community and offering visions and hopes of a multicultural global family. . . .

This essay examines the representational logics through which white women are represented as "global mothers" in popular culture, and how such representations manifest new transnational formations of whiteness (and race more broadly). It is particularly concerned with the visualities, myths, and desires that are spun as well as concealed through images of white women representing transnational maternity in popular culture. . . .

Representations of "Global Motherhood"

In order to examine the representational logics of global motherhood, I focus on a range of celebrity white women such as Princess Diana, Angelina Jolie, Madonna, and white female movie stars serving as United Nations' good will ambassadors. Although I address representations of many white women, much of my focus remains on Princess Diana, given that she was the first woman in the current neoliberal regime of the late twentieth century who was so extensively visualized as a global mother and imbricated in a logic of humanitarian borderlessness through which she was styled as a global caretaker. Indeed, no other white woman in history has been visualized as a site of global intimacies—of love, care, desire—to the extent that Diana has been; just to think of Diana is to think of her with children of the world. And it is these images that today make it commonplace for us to engage with other celebrity white women such as Angelina Jolie endlessly adopting and caring for children of

the world. Indeed, as Jolie herself recently stated (as reported by one of her friends) she wants to be the Diana of the twenty-first century. . . .

Rays of Light

In representations of white women as transnational mothers, we often find them moralized through visual logics that represent them as angelic figures emanating compassion, love, and healing. Dyer (1997) has written about the relationship between the aesthetics of photographic technology and whiteness. He has noted how in media culture white women are often bathed through soft white light that represents them as pure, divine, and angelic. "Idealised white women are bathed in and permeated by light. It streams through them and falls on to them . . . In short they glow" (p. 127). He further argues that the "angelically glowing white woman is an extreme representation precisely because it is an idealisation" in which white women become the symbol of "white virtuousness and the last word in the claim that what made whites special as a race was their non-physical, spiritual, and indeed ethereal qualities" (p. 127).

White women who come to signify transnational motherhood are not only bathed in a halo of virtuousness but they are also always beautiful. Beauty is frequently associated with the production of life; it serves as an "exemplary image for the furtherance of life" (Colebrook, 2006, p. 138).

We regard as beautiful anything that will serve to realize life's potential—anything that is fertile, productive, and conducive to self recognition and self maintenance (p. 138).

Women visually coded as ordinary looking generally do not grace our screens as carrying the potential for producing and sustaining life. Although this is not surprising—given that women who signify global motherhood tend to be celebrities and hence beautiful—such representations, however, highlight an underlying intersectional logic in which heterosexuality, race, class, gender, and internationality come together in constructing the "global mother" and highlighting her life giving abilities. Women whose bodies are "out of place"—the "white trash" woman, the lesbian woman, the non-white woman, the non-Western woman—are usually not celebrated as global mothers in popular culture. Lacking in desirability and civility, they do not glow and hence cannot "further life" and further it in a way that conforms to the purities and moralities associated with an idealized reproductive body.

Diana's images, for instance, are often saturated in visual codes that moralize her beautiful body. This is seen especially in lighting techniques. For instance, a famous image that circulated in many magazines was of Diana with children in Africa. Diana is sitting on a bamboo bench with hungry children who have probably just been handed food by Diana. The visual organization of the image is situated in a play of light and darkness. The sunlight falls on Diana; the photograph has been deliberately composed to emphasize Diana through that light. We notice that the light *flows up* to Diana's body, centralizing her and she literally glows. When reprinted in a popular commemorative book, *Diana: An extraordinary life* (1998, pp. 384385) this image is narratively positioned by the copy headline—"Lighting up the third world." This copy text positions Diana as the carrier of light; it invites us to view Diana's body through the trope of light (and life) and the "third world" around her through darkness and death. Many of the other visual components in the image are also in darkness—the background, for instance, is in darkness where we only see hazy ill-defined silhouettes of children. Some of the children sharing the bench with her, with eating bowls in their hands,

are in shadows that by contrast again visually emphasize the light on Diana. . . .

Verbal narratives often shore up the meanings imbedded in such visual techniques; for instance, Diana is frequently represented through the language of a healer. Reports describe her in terms such as:

> Diana used her power just like a magic wand, waving it in all kinds of places where there was hurt . . . And everywhere she used it, there were changes, almost like a fairy tale. (*People*, February 2, 1998, p. 84)

Or

> These children were victims of cancer, mines, Aids, leprosy or hunger. [. . . .] She would cuddle and stroke them. She would kiss them—whatever their condition. . . . *When she left, they would describe her as an angel.* (*Daily Mail*, 1997, September 6, p. xix) (emphasis added)

This theme, where Diana is seen as having some innate power to heal, is also dominant in other representations of white women. When controversies around Madonna's adoption of baby David in Malawi were exploding, Madonna justified her adoption saying that when she saw baby David in the clinic, she was "transfixed" by him. The sense one gets is that an inner spiritual pull drew her to this adoption. Meg Ryan also recently described her adoption of a baby from China as a "metaphysical kind of labor."[2] In such representations white femininity, associated with the spiritual/metaphysical, seems to transcend time and space as its transnational love becomes coded as something authentic, almost something that exists a priori in relation to the body. Constructing an inward "essence" for white femininity, such representations reproduce a universalism which equates whiteness with spirit and not corporeality.

And as Dyer (1997) has noted, historically this has been a classic mode through which whiteness has reproduced its universality and godliness.

Other visual assemblages also play a role in attributing goodness and spirituality to the white maternal body. Especially important is the *Madonna-Child trope* which functions as a significant representational framework. The Madonna-Child image, evoking associations of Mary with Jesus, has had significant visual power in Western religious discourses. Reproduced in the art of Raphael, DaVinci, Michelanglo, and Salvador Dali, it is saturated with connotations of salvation and love, and has historically functioned to represent white women through compassion and morality. Briggs (2003), for instance, has illustrated the prevalence of the Madonna/Child image in post–cold war U.S. narratives and has demonstrated how this trope informed foreign policy, international aid, and family values discourses.

Representations of global motherhood frequently draw on this Madonna/Child trope. Consider an image of Diana cradling a cancer-ridden baby in Pakistan (Owen, 1997). Diana's eyes are closed in compassion (notice again how the light falls on Diana). The child looks up at Diana with devotion. Diana's hand is touching the hand of the child as though giving it life. Similarly, in a recent image of Jolie in the British magazine *Hello* (May 2, 2006, p. 77) Jolie is carrying baby Zahara and looking out into the endless desert, a peaceful smile gracing her face. The starkness of the landscape confers an otherworldly quality to the mother/child image. Additionally, many international adoption agencies take on names such as *Adopt an Angel, Angels Haven Outreach, Adoption Blessings Worldwide,* and *Cradle of Hope* that rhetorically invoke religiosity imbedded in the Madonna/Child trope that then gets associated with white women's adoptive desires.

Discursive operations of the Madonna/Child image through which white women are positioned in relation to deprived children of the global south also manifest what Bashford (2006) calls "global biopolitics" (p. 67). For example, the children that Diana visits in "other worlds" are usually unhealthy—they are sick children, often abandoned by their families (read: the nation). Given the normalized assumption that a modern body is a healthy body, for it has the apparatus to attend to its care and development, the unhealthy body of the child signifies the non-modern future of its nation. And the rescue/healing of that unhealthy body from its nation, by white female cosmopolitan subjects such as Diana or Jolie, moralizes a movement from the darkness of non-modernity to the light of modernity. Such global biopolitics where health, race, and nation collide, manifest a larger phenomenon of late twentieth century in which the very battle over modern belonging is being fought out on the terrain of health. From AIDS to SARS, the social representations of diseases have played an important role in imperial cultural projects, in securing borders, prohibiting cross-national flows of populations, and framing nations through the language of disease whereby health becomes spatialized (Briggs, 2003; Bashford, 2006; Cartwright, 2003; Patton, 1992; Treichler, 1999). For instance, Madonna justified to Oprah her controversial adoption, stating that:

> "I beg all of those people to go to Africa" she said, "and see what I saw and walk through those villages . . . *To see mothers dying, with Kaposi sarcoma lesions all over their bodies. To see open sewers everywhere.* To see what I saw." (USA Today, 2006, emphasis added)

Singer Bono supported Madonna's actions to Britain's *Sun* newspaper, stating that "Madonna should be applauded for helping to take a child out of the worst poverty imaginable." He also despaired that "the situation is so desperate in the third world continent that parents are willing to give up their children if there is a chance for them to have a better life" (Exposay, 2006). Place and nation here begin to symbolize a crisis in hygiene that ultimately suggests a crisis in the modernity of such nations—a crisis which, however, conceals larger geopolitical struggles related to toxic dumping, environmental pollution, the need for cheap mobility of pharmaceutical products to the global south, the neoliberal destruction of local economies, the need for greater international aid, and the history of Western colonialisms.

The visual contrast between bodies reinforces this struggle that is fought out on the terrain of health. For instance, when the robust, toned, tall body of Diana (i.e. healthy) that has been built up with gym equipment, modern yoga, swimming, and other body-care technologies (technologies of the modern) is visually juxtaposed with the starving and undernourished bodies of children in the global south, the white female body's (read the nations) "built up" superiority in relation to the damaged bodies of the children becomes highlighted. Camera angles and lighting are often organized to inspire awe towards Diana's body: we often look *up* at Diana's body (or at least her body is at eye level with our gaze) while we look *down* at the native children around her body. . . .

Transnational Maternities and "Ethics of Care"[3]

Imperialism has always been about a struggle over maternities. Sometimes this struggle has been explicit, as during slavery in the U.S. when the black mothers body was regularly raped by white plantation owners and the child of the rape recirculated as plantation labor. At other times the struggle has silently informed grand narratives of imperial enlightenment, as with cases of white women in British imperialism supporting the empire's cultural mission as teachers, governesses, and missionaries by enculturating upper-class children of the colonized in manners of "civilization." If narratives of imperialism are also grand narratives about modernity, then underlying visions of the modern have always lurked in the politics of domesticity, home, and family (Stoler, 1997, 2002). To produce modern subjects is to ensure that the home as the basic unit of the nation is civilized, for home is the site for the production of the nation's future. In Western imperial discourses, where white heterosexual femininity functions as a signifier of "homeliness," the non-white non-Western mother by contrast often functions as a failure of civil "homeliness." In contemporary Anglo-centric discourses, for example, the non-white mother is often a failed mother. Within the U.S. black mothers are "crack mothers," Latina mothers are seen as overly breeding children while unable to look after them, and Native American mothers are seen as suffering from Fetal Alcohol Syndrome.

Imaginations about a "global family" that circulate in adoption discourses are often underpinned by such a logic of failed non-white, non-Western motherhood. For example, a U.S. adoption agency, International Adoption Help, invokes the trope of maternal abandonment to encourage U.S. families to adopt from Guatemala. It emphasizes that "the easiest way to understand the type of child/children that become available for adoption in Guatemala is to realize" the processes of "abandonment" and "relinquishment" at work. Abandonment, explains the text, is "when a child has been abandoned by his/her biological family, or when parental rights have been terminated by the Guatemalan government due to neglect" and "relinquishment" is when a Guatemalan mother relinquishes the child's care to a lawyer because of her inability to give maternal care. The invocation of a crisis in Guatemalan motherhood enables the invitation to white U.S. mothers to step in and rescue those children.

Such a logic of maternal abandonment also informs representations of Diana as a "global mother."[4] In a popular book *Diana: An extraordinary life* (1998) a particular chapter (from which an image was discussed earlier) is entitled "Lighting up the third world." The chapter offers a detailed description of the conditions of children in Brazil:

> As Diana quickly learned, Brazil, a spectacular country full of beautiful tourist sights had a *horrifying secret*—a mass of starving homeless children, many *abandoned by their mothers and their societies*. . . . When Diana arrived, she saw only the tiniest remnants of these human cast-offs: ten children aged from five months to five years *left in the streets by their mothers who were drug addicts or prostitutes* . . . (1998, p. 392, emphasis added)

Brazilian mothers here are failed mothers; metaphors of prostitution and drug addiction frame their bodies. Their bodies thus cannot nurture their children—the future of the nation and the world.

A BBC program, *The Diary of a Princess* (1997), that chronicles Diana's humanitarian work with British Red Cross in Angola, also invokes the logic of failed non-Western motherhood. The program is replete with images of sick and dying babies, and children with broken limbs from landmine explosions. A particular moment in the film captures Diana's arrival at a health clinic where local mothers are waiting with their babies. On Diana's arrival, a young mother hands over her highly overweight baby to Diana. Diana cuddles the baby, laughs, and then asks: "he weighs a ton. What has she been feeding him?" At this moment we see the baby's mother, partly eclipsed in the frame by Diana, standing in the background with a shy smile, not understanding the conversation.

While a humorous and affectionate moment, the image of a white mother examining a black baby while that baby's mother stands in the background, rendered into silence, is poignant and revealing. The poignancy emerges from the erasure of the African mother by the global motherhood of Diana. The passage of the highly overweight baby from the native mother to Diana is a performative moment through which competing visions of global domesticity are staged in which one (white maternal domesticity) negates the other (non-white maternal domesticity). The question "what has she been feeding him?" is addressed to the local male officials around Diana and not to the native mother as she cannot speak English. The male native officials become a point of mediation between the white woman and the native mother. A complex positionality of the third-world mother in relation to the white mother becomes visible here. As Diana addresses her query to the local official, this address situates the native men in a position that invites them to "speak for" the native mother. . . .

The white mother can only occupy the position of a "global mother" by erasing the non-white maternal body from visions of global domesticity. The white mother's subject position is thus ironically dependent on the necessary failure of the non-white native mother. . . .

United Colors of Children

Today, a continental collecting of impoverished children is becoming a way through which to represent a seamless global family in popular culture. In a 2006 interview, Angelina Jolie noted that she and Brad wanted to travel the world to find babies from different countries to adopt:

> I want to create a rainbow family. That's children of different religions and cultures from different countries. I believe I am meant to find my children in the

world and not necessarily have them genetically. (MailOnline, 2006)

Reports of how they were first planning to adopt in Russia but then adopted from Ethiopia, or how they were planning to adopt from India and name the child India "to honour its homeland" illustrate the pervasiveness of a "worldliness" in which collecting children becomes a way of engaging with different national cultures, and the children become a commodity through which race/culture can simply be bought, and engaged with, at will. As Jolie once stated: "do you balance the race, so there's another African person in the house for Zahara, after another Asian person in the house for Mad? . . . We think so" (Fox News, 2006). (Similarly, Madonna in an interview with Oprah reinforced such a history-blind and individualized cosmopolitan logic when she claimed that her natural children simply did notice the "difference" of the adopted baby from Malawi: "they've [her natural children] never once mentioned the difference in his skin colour or questioned his presence in our life" (Pilkington, 2006).

. . . Colorful visual regimes of "global motherhood" ultimately constitute a symbolic exchange between nations; how the child figures in this exchange becomes crucial to analyze, for the representation of the child makes a larger statement about the ways in which the relationality between nations and their domesticities are conceptualized in Western media discourses (Castaneda, 2002). . . . It is important to note that the figure of the child does not represent a threat to our sense of self in the (white) West. A child lacks agency. As Castaneda (2002) notes, a "child is not only in the making but is also malleable—and so can be made" (p. 3). This is unlike the adult—a fully formed human being—whose adultness cannot be so easily be stripped of its national history. In contrast, the child enables an easy dehistoricization and a *re-historicization*

that is non-threatening to the white national self.

There is also the issue of what Ahmed (2004) calls "affective economies" (p. 117). Feelings and emotions, argues Ahmed, are not merely psychological matters; rather they "mediate the relationship" between "the psychic and the social, and between the individual and the collective" (p. 119). They function as sites of bonding through which national and, in this case, transnational attachments are fostered. The child, as opposed to the adult, easily functions as a love object and thus inspires bonding in ways that the adult cannot. We can love the child of another nation *out of its history* in ways we cannot for the adult, for to be a child is to be (seemingly) without much of a history and memory. Consequently, feelings of affection that the figure of the child invites in the white mother are also feelings that can be mobilized in the larger imagination of a loving (and dehistoricized) global family. . . .

One reason why we in the West can feel pity and compassion for these starving, abandoned children is because we are simultaneously invited to hate the underlying conditions of their nations. We are meant to feel gratitude that we are not them. This underlying gratitude mobilizes our pity and speaks to our sense of superiority that then invites care from us. The irony is this: our hatred of the conditions that have produced the native child always interrupts our capacity to seriously love the child on *an equal cultural level*, for to love the child with dignity and equality is to love its nation and culture with dignity. Thus, romantic internationalism (Malkki, 1994) mobilizes our love in the West as conditions of attachment to underprivileged nations but it simultaneously reifies our underlying disgust for these nations.

. . . The Sponsor-a-child section of the adoption agency Children's International states:

We unite sponsors with children around the world—bringing different nations and cultures together. So take a peek by clicking below and learn about the children and their countries, their traditions and their lives.

When a potential sponsor clicks on the image of a child from a country, s/he is directed to a section that provides cultural descriptions of traditions of that particular country—from food and cultural festivals, to language and social norms. One could almost be shopping for a tourist place to visit. In choosing to adopt a child, one chooses to affiliate with a particular nation that takes one's fantasy. Jolie expresses this touristic logic when she notes to *People*: "there is something . . . about waking up and travelling somewhere and finding your family . . . Sooner or later, I'll end up everywhere" (*People*, January 11, 2006). In such language, the child becomes a route for the white woman to enter a particular nation/culture even while the child, in such representations, becomes rooted in that culture as it is often made to embody the markers of its exotic national difference. . . .

Such representations of internationally adopted children frequently contrast with representations of domestic trans-racial adoption (in the U.S. for instance). International adoption receives far greater attention in the media, especially made popular by celebrities; it is seen as more exciting than domestic adoption. U.S. adoption agencies note that "there is an idea that because these kids [domestic kids] come from unfortunate circumstances, that they are juvenile delinquents," a view confirmed by Rita Soronen, executive director of *Dave Thomas Foundation*, to Fox News.[5] Ortiz and Briggs (2003) explain that in discourses of transnational adoption there is greater sentimentalization attached to a child from an "other" nation than from within the nation. One reason for this, they argue, is that underclass children (usually children of color) within the U.S. are already racialized in ways that make their body threatening: they

are already coded as products of violent, drug cracking, antisocial families that have transgressed the bounds of proper citizenly belonging. Hence these children are often perceived as psychologically damaged or flawed in character. In contrast, international children while perceived as unhealthy and non-modern, do not represent delinquency or violence, and hence are less threatening. They are simply seen as needing rescuing by the modernizing Western family.[6] Although recent films such as *The Blind Side* (2009) have represented trans-racial domestic adoption, the film reinforces many of the stereotypes of black pathology that strengthen the perception that domestic kids are products of dangerous, toxic environments. To be sure, the film is based on a factual story, but the very selection of this content for representational purposes tends to reinforce anxieties around black pathology.

Conclusion

Contemporary representations of global motherhood make visible new logics of whiteness that are imbricated in a politics of the transnational, . . . The discussion offered in this essay for instance, invites us to ask how whiteness—in particular the white family form—today is being bolstered by, and remaking itself through, particular kinds of transnational flows—in this case of children who occupy positions of extreme global otherness. . . .

This essay has also underscored the importance of a transnational contextual analysis of whiteness. Given that whiteness is a contextual formation, and that national contexts today are shaped by, as well as shaping, transnational relations of power, ignoring transnational linkages in the production of whiteness is limiting, for it can potentially perpetuate a view that power relations of whiteness within the nation are somehow disconnected from larger transnational struggles and flows (see also Shome, 2010). Examining whiteness through the methodological lens of the transnational also enables us to avoid conceiving whiteness as though its logics are the same wherever and whenever. A transnational *contextual* analysis of whiteness recognizes that the power of whiteness lies precisely in its ability to constantly shift its strategies of reproduction in response to the changing contours of the nation, and that those contours are always imbricated in larger international and geopolitical relations.

Notes

1. http://www.femalefirst.co.uk/celebrity/MegRyan-22693.htm

2. I borrow the term from Michel Foucault.

3. See Dorow (2006) for a different discussion about maternal abandonment.

4. http://www.Foxnews.com/entertainment/2009/04/03/domestic-vs-international-adoption celebrities-overlooking-american-children.

5. http://www.Foxnews.com/entertainment/2009/04/03/domestic-vs-international-adoption celebrities-overlooking-american-children.

References

Ahmed, S. (2004). Affective economies. *Social Text, 22,* 117–139.

Anagnost, A. (2000). Scenes of misrecognition: Maternal citizenship in the age of transnational adoption. *Positions, 8,* 299–421.

Bashford, A. (2006). Global biopolitics and the history of world health. *History of the human sciences, 19,*67–88.

Berlant, L. (1991). *Anatomy of a national fantasy.* Chicago, IL: University of Chicago Press.

Berlant, L. (1997). *The queen of American goes to Washington city.* Durham, NH: Duke University Press.

Berlant, L. (2000). Intimacy: A special issue. In L. Berlant (Ed.), *Intimacy* (pp. 18). Chicago, IL: University of Chicago Press.

Blunt, A. (1999). The flight from Lucknow: British women travelling and writing home. In J. Duncan & D. Gregory (Eds.), *Writes of passage* (pp. 92–113). New York, NY: Routledge.

Briggs, L. (2003). Mother, child, race, nation: The visual iconography of rescue and politics of transnational and transracial adoption. *Gender and History, 15,* 179–200.

Briggs, L. (2006). Making "American" families: Transnational adoption and U.S. Latin America foreign policy. In A. Stoler (Ed.), *Haunted by empire: Geographies of intimacy in North American history* (pp. 344–364). Durham, NH: Duke University Press.

Colebrook, C. (2006). Introduction. *Feminist Theory* (special issue on Beauty), 7, 131–142.

Cartwright, L. (2003). Photographs of waiting children. *Social Text, 21,*83–109.

Castaneda, C. (2002). *Figurations: Child, bodies, worlds.* Durham, NH: Duke University Press.

Diana: An extraordinary life. (1998). London, UK: Orbis Publishing Limited.

Dorow, S. (2006). *Transnational adoption.* New York, NY: New York University Press.

Dyer, R. (1997). *White.* New York, NY: Routledge.

Eng, D.L. (2003). Transnational adoption and queer diasporas. *Social Text, 76,* 21,137.

Exposay (2006, November 13). Bono praises Madonna for African adoption. Retrieved from http:// www.exposay.com/bono-praises-madonna-for-adoption/v/6011

Fox News. (2006, December 14). Angelina Jolie: I'm on the pill. Retrieved from http://www.foxnews.com/story/0,2933,236522,00.html

Gilroy, P. (2005). *Postcolonial melancholia.* New York, NY: Columbia University Press.

Grewal, I. (1996). *Home and harem.* Durham, NH: Duke University Press.

Kaplan, C. (1995). A world without boundaries: The Body Shop's trans/national geographics. *Social Text, 43,*45–66.

Kaplan, C. (2001). Hillary Rodham Clinton's Orient: Cosmopolitan travel and global feminist subjects. *Meridians: Feminism, Race, Transnationalism, 2,* 219–240.

MailOnline (2006, October 26). Angelina set to adopt another baby. Retrieved from http://www.dailymail.co.uk/tvshowbiz/article-412751/Agenlina-set-adopt-baby.html

Malkki, L. (1994). "Citizens of humanity": Internationalism and the imagined community of nations. *Diaspora, 3,* 41–68.

Marre, D., & Briggs, L. (Eds.). (2009). *International adoption: Global inequalities and the circulation of children.* New York, NY: New York University Press.

Nakayama, T.K. & Krizek, R. (1995). Whiteness as strategic rhetoric. *Quarterly Journal of Speech, 81,* 291–309.

Nakayama, T.K., & Martin, J. (Eds.). (1999). *Whiteness: The communication of social identity.* Oakland, CA: Sage Publication.

Ortiz, A., & Briggs, L. (2003). The culture of poverty, crack babies, and welfare cheats: The making of the "healthy white baby crisis." *Social Text, 76,* 21, 39–57.

Owen, Nicholas (1997). *Diana: The People's Princess.* Carlton Books.

Patton, C. (1992). From nation to family: Containing African AIDS. In H. Abelove, D. Halperan, & M. Barale (Eds.), *Lesbian and gay studies reader* (pp. 127–138). New York, NY: Routledge.

People , January 11, 2006. Angelina Jolie Pregnant. Retrieved from: http://www.people.com/people/archive/article/0.20145123.000.html

Pilkington, E. (2006, October 26). Confessions on a TV show: Oprah hears Madonna's side of the story. The Guardian. Retrieved from http://www.guardian.co.uk/world/2006/oct/26/arts.usa

Ram, K., & Jolly, M. (1998). *Maternities and modernities.* Berkeley: University of California Press.

Shohat, E. & Stam, R. (1994). *Unthinking Eurocentrism: Multiculturalism and the media.* UK: Routledge.

Shome, R. (2006). Transnational feminism and communication studies. *Communication Review, 9*(4), 255–267.

Shome, R. (2010). Internationalizing critical race communication studies: Transnationality, space, and affect. In T. Nakayama & R. Halualani (Eds.), *Handbook of Critical Intercultural Communication* (pp. 149–170). Malden, MA: Blackwell Publishing.

Spivak, G. (1988). Can the subaltern speak? In L. Grossberg & C. Nelson (Eds.), *Marxism and the interpretation of culture* (pp. 271–313). Urbana: University of Illinois Press.

Stoler, A. (1997). *Race and the education of desire.* Durham, NH: Duke University Press.

Stoler, A. (2002). *Carnal knowledge and imperial power.* Berkeley: University of California Press.

Stoler, A. (2006). Tense and tender ties. In A. Stoler (Ed.), *Haunted by empire: Geographies of intimacy in North American history* (pp. 2367). Durham, NH: Duke University Press.

Treichler, P. (1999). How to have theory in an epidemic: Cultural chronicle of AIDS. Durham, NH: Duke University Press. USA Today (2006). Retrieved from http://www.foxnews.com/story/0,2933,236522,00.html

Volkman, T. (2003). Transnational adoption. *Social Text, 74,* 21, 1–5.

Wells, K. (2009). *Childhood in a global perspective.* Cambridge, MA: Polity.

Wiegma, R. (1999). Whiteness studies and the paradox of particularity. *Boundary, 2, 26,* 115–150.

13

Pornographic Eroticism and Sexual Grotesquerie in Representations of African American Sportswomen

James McKay and Helen Johnson

Go Back To The Cotten [sic] Plantation Nigger. (Banner in the stands when Althea Gibson walked on court to defend her US Open title in 1958)

That's the way to do it! Hit the net like any Negro would! (Racist male heckling Serena Williams before she served at the 2007 Sony Ericsson Championships in Miami)

In this paper we use sport to encourage 'white' people to deconstruct the privileged lens through which they construct and view 'black' people. More specifically, we analyse how sections of the media have framed tennis champions Serena and Venus Williams as threats to sport's racist and sexist regime. Like other sportswomen of colour, the Williams sisters have challenged racist and sexist stereotypes and inspired millions of females around the world (Hargreaves, 2000, 2007). However, given that Althea Gibson and Serena Williams were subjected to blatant racism at tennis tournaments nearly 50 years apart, we should not be sanguine about the social constraints that African American sportswomen still encounter. . . .

African American Sportswomen as Threats to Gender and Racial Hierarchies

Rowe (1990, p. 409) argues that gender hierarchies are threatened whenever women's bodies are deemed to be excessive: 'too fat, too mouthy, too old, too dirty, too pregnant, too sexual (or not sexual enough) for the norms of conventional gender representation.'

From McKay, J., & Johnson, H. (2008). Pornographic eroticism and sexual grotesquerie in representations of African-American Sportswomen. *Social Identities*, 14(4), 491–504. Reprinted by permission of Taylor & Francis Ltd., www.tandf.co.uk/journals

Following Schulze (1990, p. 198), we can add muscularity to this list of corporeal transgressions: '[t]he deliberately muscular woman disturbs dominant notions of sex, gender, and sexuality, and any discursive field that includes her risks opening up a site of contest and conflict, anxiety and ambiguity.' While muscularity in women and men is becoming an increasingly desirable body type, it is, in the twenty-first century, hyper-muscularity in women that threatens heteronormative gender relations (Heywood & Dworkin, 2003). . . .

Hyper-muscularity as both a new social phenomenon and a denigrating stereotype is especially evident in sport, which has embodied in the past the 'natural' superiority of men in contrast to the 'otherness' of female athletes as objects of ridicule, weakness, inferiority, decoration, passivity and as erotically desirable yet transgressive, but which is now searching for new ways to disparage the powerful and therefore 'uppity' African American sportswomen. . . .

A common strategy of reasserting masculine hegemony in sport is via 'pornographic eroticism,' in which sexuality is constructed as the 'primary characteristic of the person represented' (Heywood, 1998). Heywood distinguishes 'pornographic eroticism' from 'athletic eroticism,' in which sexuality is 'one dimension of human experience, as a quality that emerges from the self-possession, autonomy, and strength so evident in the body of a female athlete.' Although Heywood refers to bodybuilding, examples of 'pornographic eroticism' are prevalent in most sports (Glenny, 2006; Messner, Dunbar & Hunt, 2002; Messner, Duncan & Cooky, 2003).

While Heywood's concept of 'pornographic eroticism' is useful for explaining how female athletes in general are recuperated by the media, the negative coverage of the Williams sisters that we analyse below demonstrates that African American sportswomen also threaten racial hierarchies. Hence, we propose that the racialized anxieties that drive censorious responses to African American sportswomen are most effectively understood when situated within the historical context of black women's enslavement, colonial conquest, and exhibition as ethnographic 'grotesquerie.' The categorization of black women's bodies as hyper-muscular and their targeting for lascivious comment mirrors the public and pseudo-scientific response to nineteenth century exhibits of Saartjie Baartman, the South African woman labeled the 'Hottentot Venus' (Hobson, 2003, p. 87). Thus, we also use Hobson's concept of 'sexual grotesquerie,' which, in turn, was suggested by Morgan's (1997) analysis of European explorers' writings about Africa that depicted African women's bodies as mythic and monstrous. . . .

The 'Ghetto Cinderellas'

On Tuesday the story was Maria Sharapova's Swan Lake dress. On Wednesday it was Tatiana Golovin's red knickers. Yesterday it was Venus Williams' hot pants . . . [C]overage of men's tennis tends to focus on tennis. Not so the women's game, especially in the first week of a Grand Slam event when the lack of depth in the field means the opening rounds serve as a glorified warm-up for the 'big beasts.' (Moore 2007)

'Pornographic eroticism' is particularly prominent in media coverage of women's tennis, where many players' physiques and performances are the objects of a constant gaze and are monitored for 'excess' (Harris & Clayton, 2002; Kennedy, 2001; Miller, McKay & Martin, 1999; Stevenson, 2002). Anna Kournikova has been criticized for trading on her looks and displaying more style than substance; Amelie Mauresmo was reproached for being openly lesbian and having a strong body and powerful topspin backhand; former world number 1 Justine Henin is belittled for having a drab image, while Maria Sharapova has been nicknamed 'The Glamazon,' to describe her combination of conventional good looks, statuesque physique, and powerful forehand (she also has been dubbed 'Shriekapova' and 'Belle of the Decibel' and censured for having a 'banshee-like grunt'); Daniela Hantuchova has been accused of being an anorexic, while Casey Dellacqua and Marion Bartoli have been condemned for allegedly being overweight. For instance, journalist Sue Mott (2007) described 2007 Wimbledon singles finalist Bartoli as 'more Friar Tuck than Maid Marion.'

Matthew Syed (2008) contends that

there has always been a soft-porn dimension to women's tennis, but with the progression of Maria Sharapova, Ana Ivanovic, Jelena Jankovic and Daniela Hantuchova to the semi-finals of the Australian Open, this has been into the realms of adolescent (and non-adolescent) male fantasy.

He complains that Western society has not 'reached a place where heterosexual men can acknowledge the occasionally erotic dimension of watching women's sport without being dismissed as deviant' thus articulating the unreflective, heterosexual, white male-centred viewpoint that is normative in mainstream media.

The Williams sisters also have been subjected to the carping critical gaze that both structures and is a key discursive theme of 'pornographic eroticism.' Of great significance, however, is that they also have been constructed by derogatory racial, sexual and class stereotypes associated with African Americans. . . .

Since 1999 the Williams sisters have dominated international women's tennis by winning 14 Grand Slam singles titles (Serena eight, Venus six), five women's doubles and four mixed doubles Grand Slam titles, and gold medals in singles (Venus) and women's doubles at the Olympics. The Williams sisters began playing sport early while living in Compton, an economically impoverished area of Los Angeles, before moving to Florida while young. Whereas many tennis prodigies attend private tennis academies,

the Williams sisters trained under the unorthodox regime of their father, Richard, a sharecropper's son from Louisiana. Serena and Venus have become wealthy international sporting superstars and celebrities, with incomes estimated at over $US100 million from endorsement contracts with firms such as McDonald's, Nike, Wilson, Estée Lauder, and Reebok. Thus, they have been constructed within a 'ghetto-to-glory' narrative: a journalist referred to their ascent as a 'fairy tale, that astonishing narrative of the "ghetto Cinderella"' (Adams, 2005); one described Venus as a former 'teenage curio from a Los Angeles ghetto' (Muscat, 2007); and another stated that, 'Only in America would Venus have risen from her cradle of crack dealers and grunge courts to contest the women's singles final at Wimbledon' (Mott, 2000). Patton (2001, p. 122) refers to these sorts of narratives as 'an Africanized version of the Horatio Alger story in which athletics provides a route out of the ghetto.'

The exceptional performances of the Williams sisters have provoked complex and ambivalent narratives of qualified praise and grudging approval, as well as subtle and overt racism and sexism (Douglas, 2002, 2005; Schultz, 2002; Spencer, 2001, 2004). Media coverage of the Williams sisters is not always negative, because their performances are too extraordinary to be completely denigrated. For instance, in the lead-up to the 2003 French Open, Serena appeared in an action shot on the cover of *Sports Illustrated* with the caption 'Awesome.' Journalist Will Buckley (2007, p. 15) compared the Williams sisters to male legends like Pele, Muhammad Ali, Roger Federer, Tiger Woods, and Jack Nicklaus, rating them as the 'greatest duo' in sporting history. However, such praise co-exists with both subtle and overt racism and sexism. The Williams sisters have been criticized for lacking 'commitment' by refusing to conform to the Spartan training regime of professional tennis, restricting their playing schedules, having too many 'off-court interests' in acting, music, product endorsements, fashion and interior design, and their Jehovah's Witness religion. They have been accused of fixing matches against one another, cheating, and engaging in unsporting behaviour. They have been called arrogant, aloof, and self-absorbed; indicted for putatively ostentatious lifestyles and wearing expensive jewelry while not assisting African Americans affected by Hurricane Katrina; and disparaged for competing while wearing beaded cornrows and/or tinted hairstyles and 'tacky' outfits. At the 2002 US Open Serena was condemned for wearing a black 'catsuit,' and in 2003 her appearance at a public function was disparaged as a 'hooker look' by *The Washington Post*'s fashion writer:

> She wore an orange crochet hussy dress modeled after something that Wilma Flintstone might choose. The low-cut dress, with its embroidered bodice, had a hemline that looked like it had been gnawed by Dino. . . . Her admirers paint a picture of poise and exuberance, talent and physical grace. One only wishes that Williams would use her wealth and notoriety to paint herself in equally flattering terms. (PostWatch, 2002)

In an article about the 2007 Wimbledon tournament, entitled 'Street style gives Venus her deadly cutting edge,' Venus was compared poorly to her vanquished opponent Akiko Morigami:

> Williams the elder is urban hip-hop, a swirling, whirling, street babe who believes tennis is a sport best played at full volume. . . . With Williams wearing an ill-fitting vest and hot-pants outfit that might have been plucked off the *Primark* bargain rail, Morigami, the ultimate in femininity, won the consolation fashion stakes in her broderie anglaise skirt and scalloped sleeved top. (Philip, 2007)

The title of another article about Wimbledon condensed many of the above points. Although Venus was portrayed in an 'action shot,' the title was, 'Williams has designs on title despite host of outside distractions.' Much of the material was devoted to suggesting that Venus had played in her underwear, to her preoccupation with her interior design company, to the gold handbag she brings courtside, and to her guitar-playing skill (Smith, 2007). While Serena and Venus have been described as the 'Sisters Sledgehammer' (Bierley, 2004) and as having an 'Amazonian physique and piranha mentality' (Mott, 2000), Daniela Hantuchova, in contrast, was portrayed as playing tennis 'with grace and artistry, words that appeared to have been all but crushed by the blitzkrieg that was Venus and Serena Williams' (Viner, 2007).

Such commentary has often been anchored by the stereotypes to which we have alluded of black people being constructed as animalistic and closer to nature. Following Venus' victory at Wimbledon in 2000, a journalist hailed her as a 'role model for blacks' and lamented that black people had not been given more opportunities to participate in sport, because 'there is a natural physical superiority about those of African origin . . . only centuries of repression has prevented them becoming masters of so many sports' (Miller, 2000). Serena was described as a 'cat woman' at the 2002 US Open (Schutz, 2002), and Venus' quarterfinal victory over Sharapova at Wimbledon in 2007 was headlined 'Dying swan devoured as giant bird of prey returns to SW19,' with Barnes (2007) writing that, 'The dying swan [Maria Sharapova] slunk out in her tutu, savaged to death by a giant bird of prey—a Californian condor, if you like.' Marion Bartoli's loss to Venus in the final was attributed to the 'immense hard luck that Venus can chase from side to side like a cheetah on the run' (Mott, 2007), and Venus was also depicted as 'a panther, sensing a wounded animal' (White, 2007).

The Williams sisters arrived at the 2006 Australian Open in the unusual situation of being ranked lowly due to injuries and long lay-offs. Their commitment, fitness, and weight were targeted even before competition began. In 'Aussie defeat is the bottom line for overweight Serena,' British journalist Alix Ramsay (2006) claimed that

> Both Venus and Serena were unfit, unprepared and under-done as the Open began. . . . Swanning into Melbourne as only they can, the sisters were seen shopping and posing around town. They certainly acted the part of superstar athletes but they certainly did not look it. Serena, in particular, was patently overweight and pictures of her larger-than-life figure were splashed across every newspaper in the land. . . . Clearly the sisters, 'crossover celebrities' both, are too busy to devote their time exclusively to tennis.

Journalists' fixation with Serena's diet, weight, fitness, and appearance then shifted into categories of 'pornographic eroticism' and 'sexual grotesquerie.' Her breasts and bottom were fetishized via headlines such as, 'Size up Serena Williams at your own risk' (Stevens, 2006), 'Serena out to kick butt' (Epstein, 2006), and 'Easybeat? Fat chance' (Crawford, 2006a), and photographs of her allegedly abnormal gluteal muscles and weight. When asked about her physical status, Serena commented that: 'Honestly, I've never read any comments about my fitness. I don't read the papers. I saw (a picture) of me running. And I was like, "Wow, my hamstring muscle is that big?" I had no idea my muscle was like that. But that's about it' (Epstein, 2006). One newspaper used the headline 'Serena Shocked by Pictures,' but selectively printed Serena's comment about her hamstring being large, thereby suggesting she was alarmed (Crawford, 2006b). In one of Australia's 'quality' newspapers, journalist Stephen Gibbs (2006) compared Serena with Maria Sharapova in his article 'Big bum rap for Serena.'

> Serena Williams has this great big arse. Some tennis commentators seem able

to ignore the urge to record that for posterity and instead have concentrated on her career . . .

> Righto. This is the spot for a sentence that starts: 'Before the letters of complaint come flooding in from the hairy-armpit brigade . . . ' This may or may not be interesting but, in fact, they never do. Those sentences are written for female colleagues and partners rather than letter-writing lesbians.

> [But] Sharapova is a Russian glamour girl and can apparently play a bit, too. She is tanned, teenaged, firm of bottom and pert of breast. She has for some time been ranked No. 1 by the tennis world as the female player heterosexual males most want to up-end.

> But that is not how they put it in the media, just as we don't say Serena Williams has a big arse.

> . . . The authoritative discourse of 'science' was . . . used by a journalist, who consulted a sports medicine specialist about Serena's physique, and was advised that, 'It is the African-American race. They just have this huge gluteal strength. With Serena, that's her physique and genetics' (Stevens, 2006). The media attributed early upset losses by both Serena and Venus to excess weight, lack of commitment, and interest in 'frivolous' pursuits outside tennis, while an Australian journalist 'joked' that the quick exit of local hero Lleyton Hewitt was due to his dislike for the Rebound Ace courts, which were 'more dangerous than trying to steal Serena Williams's lunch box' (Hinds, 2006).

While Serena publicly stated during the 2007 Australian Open that her critics were haters who simply served to motivate her, such defiance intensified media attention. For instance, Hinds (2007a) wrote that Serena's game has always been about as subtle as a 'kick in the groin,' she had 'bludgeoned her way to seven grand slam titles with the swing of her executioner's blade,' and she had a 'chip on her shoulder.'

He also alluded to her displeasure over losing a challenge to the electronic officiating system, Hawk-Eye, by posing the rhetorical question: 'Is she a Hawk-Eye hater, too?' (Hinds, 2007a). Despite struggling in the preliminary rounds, Serena reached the final, only to receive ongoing criticism that her progress highlighted the inferior status of women's tennis:

> That she has reached the final speaks volumes for her competitive spirit and determination, while once again underlining the general lack of intelligence and creative ability of the other leading players. . . . Williams has played so few tournaments in the last 13 months that her success here rather makes a mockery of the circuit. Why play at all if you can get to a grand slam final with virtually no previous match-play? . . . Williams should not have been able to get to the final with such ease. The fact that she has must be deeply embarrassing. (Bierley, 2007)

Serena easily defeated top-seeded Maria Sharapova in the final, an outcome that could have been embedded in several stock heroic sporting narratives: 'Champion rises to the occasion,' 'Comeback Queen,' or 'Serena battles through adversity.' Instead, her triumph was narrativized in recurrent deprecating and sexualized scripts: 'Champ focused on retail therapy after responding to critics' (Scott, 2007); 'Serena ignores the knockers' (Pearce, 2007); 'Cyclone Serena slams Maria and her knockers' (in which Serena was described as 'the game's Alpha female'—Niall, 2007a); and 'Sharapova and the critics dealt a blow by Williams' sledgehammer' (in which Serena was said to resemble a 'wrecking ball' and to have an 'Exocet return'—Niall, 2007b). Hinds (2007b) reported her success via a mock attack on the behaviour of the highly respectable and respected men's champion, Roger Federer, with the sarcastic conclusion: 'See, Serena, you were right. We can hate anyone. It's just that you make it so much easier.' Serena's post-match response to the barrage of criticism was as powerful and as eloquent as her tennis:

> I have a large arse and it always just looks like I'm bigger than the rest of the girls, but I have been the same weight for I don't know how long. If I lost 20 pounds, I'm still going to have these knockers, forgive me, and I'm still going to have this arse.

While the narratives of 'pornographic eroticism' were used to portray Griffith-Joyner nearly 20 years earlier, a journalist described a match by Serena at Wimbledon in 2007 in terms that had hardened into those of 'sexual grotesquerie':

> Cartoonists would have been hard pressed to create Serena. First there was the body—all bosom, bottom and muscle. In her skintight faux leather bodysuit she gave Lara Croft a run for her money. (The great kinkster cartoonist Robert Crumb told me that she was his ideal woman; his idea of heaven was to be given a piggyback by Serena.) (Hattenstone, 2007)

At the 2008 Australian Open, the fixation turned to Venus with one newspaper article using the title, 'Venus Williams with a superior posterior' (Johnson, 2008). Jessica Halloran (2000), in a story entitled 'Venus win helps keep focus on bottom line,' reported that television commentator Roger Rasheed practically started salivating when admiring Venus's rear end during her first-round win. Venus then fielded questions about Rasheed's comment with grace and humor in the post-game interview.

Conclusion

Our study shows that despite their outstanding sporting achievements, the Williams sisters have been subjected to the 'gender-specific images that deem black bodies as less desirable if not downright ugly' (Collins, 2004, p. 284); that is, their bodies have been positioned by the 'sexually grotesque.' The complex and ambivalent ways in which the Williams sisters have been constructed—exotic/erotic yet deviant and repulsive, athletic yet animalistic and primitive, unfeminine yet hyperfeminine, muscular yet threateningly hyper-muscular—is a reinscription of the 'Hottentot Venus' genealogy. . . .

However, the very contradictions of their lived experiences as sportswomen provide some African-American sportswomen with the discursive tools to re-imagine and re-work their experiences in new ways, as the Williams sisters' responses to the media demonstrate. Paying attention to the multifaceted discourses and symbolic expressions through which African American people construct new forms of social identities has contributed to sociological understandings of marginalized people's responses to racism. Listening to the positive responses of African American women to negative readings of their corporeality could enable the sports industry to cultivate what Hobson (2003, p. 98) calls a black feminist aesthetic that recognizes the black female body as 'beautiful and desirable' in its distinction from stereotypes of white beauty.[1]

Of greater significance, however, is the need for 'white' people to deconstruct their privileged perspectives and the powerful lenses through which they construct and view 'black' people, to develop a new critical race consciousness that can inform sporting commentary and media narratives. Since sport both reinforces and reproduces the 'persistent,' 'resurgent,' and 'veiled' forms of white power that permeate society (King, Leonard & Kusz, 2007, p. 4), a systematic targeting and 'outing' of racist and sexist narratives in sport has the potential to enable African American women and men to envision and achieve equality within a broader framework of social justice.[2]

Notes

1. Creef (1993) and Fabos (2001) have shown how Asian and Asian-American women figure skaters have also been inscribed by racist and sexist narratives.

2. For alternatives to the prevailing able-bodied, racist, sexist, and commodified representations of sportswomen, see the book, exhibition, and educational outreach programs based on Jane Gottesman's collection of photographs, which emphasize diversity and inclusion (Gottesman, 2003; *Game Face: What Does a Female Athlete Look Like?*).

References

Adams, T. (2005, January 9). Selling the sisters. *The Observer*. Retrieved July 1, 2005 from http://observer.guardian.co.uk/osm/story/0,,1 383632.00.html

Barnes, S. (2007, July 5). Dying swan devoured as giant bird of prey returns to SW19. *Timesonline*. Retrieved July 5, 2007 from http://www.timesonline.co.uk/tol/sport/columnists/simon_barnes/article2028764.ece

Bennett, M., & Dickerson, V. (2001). Introduction. In M. Bennett & V. Dickerson (Eds.), *Recovering the black female body: Self-representations by African American women* (pp. 1–12). New Brunswick, NJ: Rutgers University Press.

Bierley, S. (2004, January 14). Sisters sledgehammer lured towards siren song of celebrity. *The Guardian*. Retrieved June 1, 2007 from http://sport.guardian.co.uk/columnists/story/0,,1122498,00.html

Bierley, S. (2007, January 26). Fighting Williams sets up Sharapova showdown. *The Guardian*. Retrieved January- 28. 2007 from http://sport.guardian.co.Uk/australianopen2007/story/0,, 1998879, 00.html

Buckley, W. (2007, September 16). Ali? Laver? Best? No, the Williams sisters. *The Observer*, p. 15.

Collins, P. H. (2004). *Black sexual politics: African Americans, gender, and the new racism.* New York: Routledge.

Crawford, C. (2006a, January 15). Easybeat? Fat chance. *The Sun-Herald,* p. 34.

Crawford, C. (2006b, January 15). Serena shocked by pictures. *The Sunday Mail,* p. 23.

Creef, E. T. (1993). Model minorities and monstrous selves: The winter Olympic showdown of Kristi Yamaguchi and Midori Ito; or: 'How to tell your friends apart from the Japs.' *Visual Anthropology Review, 9*(1), 141–146.

Douglas, D. D. (2002). To be young, gifted, black and female: A meditation on the cultural politics at play in representations of Venus and Serena Williams. *Sociology of Sport Online, 5*(2). Retrieved July I, 2006 from http://physed.otago.ac.nz/sosol/v5i2/v5i2_3 .html

Douglas, D. D. (2005). Venus, Serena, and the Women's Tennis Association (WTA): When and where 'race' enters. *Sociology of Sport Journal, 22*(3), 256–282.

Epstein, J. (2006, January 15). Serena out to kick butt. *MensTennisForums.com.* Retrieved January 16, 2006 from http://www.menstenn isforums.com/archive/index.php/t-63698 .html

Fabos, B. (2001). Forcing the fairy tale: Narrative strategies in figure skating competition coverage. *Sport in Society,* 4 (2), 185–212.

Game Face: What does a female athlete look like? Retrieved January 28, 2007 from http://www.gamefaceonline.org/4_5_press.html

Gibbs, S. (2006, January 21). Big bum rap for Serena. *The Age,* p. 63.

Gilman, S. (1985). *Difference and pathology.* Ithaca, NY: Cornell University Press.

Glenny, G. H. (2006). Visual culture and the world of sport. *The Scholar & Feminist Online.* Retrieved January 30, 2007 from http://www .barnard.edu/sfonline/sport/glenny_ 01.htm

Gottesman, J. (2003). *Game face: What does a female athlete look like?* New York, NY: Random House.

Hadfield, W. (1988, September 30). Fast as a cheetah but Flo-Jo no cheater. *The Australian,* p. 33.

Hadley Freydberg, E. (1995). Sapphires, spitfires, sluts, and superbitches: Aframericans and Latinas in contemporary American film. In K. M. Vaz (Ed.), *Black women in America* (pp. 222–243). Thousand Oaks, CA: Sage.

Halloran, J. (2008, January 18). Venus win helps keep focus on bottom line. *The Sydney Morning Herald.* Retrieved January 18, 2008 from http://www.smh.com.au/news/tennis/ venus-win-helps-keep-focus-on-bottom-line/2008/01/17/1200419971695.html

Hargreaves, J. (2000). *Heroines of sport: The politics of difference and identity.* London: Routledge.

Hargreaves, J. (2007). Sport, exercise, and the female Muslim body: Negotiating Islam, politics, and male power. In J. Hargreaves & P. Vertinsky (Eds.), *Physical culture, power and the body* (pp. 74–100). London: Routledge.

Harris, J., & Clayton, B. (2002). Femininity, masculinity, physicality and the English tabloid press: The case of Anna Kournikova. *International Review for the Sociology of Sport, 37*(3/4), 397–413.

Hattenstone, S. (2007, January 31). Serena's triumph over tragedy a weepy classic. *The Guardian.* Retrieved January 31, 2007 from http://sport.guardian.co.uk/columnists/ story/0,,2002277,00.html

Heywood, L. (1998). Athletic vs pornographic eroticism: How muscle magazines compromise female athletes and delegitimize the sport of bodybuilding in the public eye. *Mesomorphosis Interactive, 1*(1). Retrieved July 1, 2007 from http://www .mesomorphosis .com/exclusive/heywood/ eroticism01.htm

Heywood, L., & Dworkin, S. L. (2003). *Built to win: The female athlete as cultural icon.* Minneapolis, MN: University of Minnesota Press.

Hinds, R. (2006, January 30). Crocks, shocks and 'nots' did the Open proud. *The Sydney Morning Herald,* p. 54.

Hinds, R. (2007a, January 26). Surrounded by 'haters,' rampaging American plays angry. *The Age,* p. 62.

Hinds, R. (2007b, January 28). I hate to admit it, Serena, but we can even dislike Federer. *The Sun-Herald*, p. 59.

Hobson, J. (2003). The 'batty' politic: Toward an aesthetic of the black female body. *Hypatia*, 18(4), 87–105.

Johnson, M. (2008, January 18). Venus Williams with a superior posterior. *The Telegraph*. Retrieved January 18, 2008, from http:// www .telegraph.co.uk/sport/ main.jhtml?xml=/ sport/2008/01/18/ stjohn118.xml

Kennedy, E. (2001). She wants to be a sledge-hammer: Tennis femininities in British television. *Journal of Sport & Social Issues*, 25(1), 56–72.

King, C. R., Leonard, D. J., & Kusz, K. W. (2007). White power and sport: An introduction. *Journal of Sport & Social Issues*, 31, 3–10.

Messner, M. A., Dunbar, M., & Hunt, D. (2002). The televised sports manhood formula. *Journal of Sport & Social Issues*, 24, 380–394.

Messner, M. A., Duncan, C. M., & Cooky, C. (2003). Silence, sports bras, and wrestling porn: Women in televised sports news and highlights shows. *Journal of Sport & Social Issues*, 27, 38–51.

Miller, D. (2000, July 10). Victor deserves role model status. *The Sunday Telegraph*. Retrieved June 15, 2005 from www.tele graph.co.uk:80/et?ac=003087666203340 &rtmo=aq4CWX4J&atmo=99999999& pg-/et/00/7/9/strole09.html

Miller, T., McKay, J., & Martin, R. (1999). Courting lesbianism. *Women and Performance: A Journal of Feminist Theory*, 11(1), 211–234.

Moore, G. (2007, June 29). Williams' fashion statement the hot topic. *The Independent*. Retrieved June 29, 2007 from http://sport .independent.co.uk/tennis/article2720027 .ecc

Moore, K. (1988, July 25). Get up and go. *Sports Illustrated*. Retrieved June 12, 2005 from sportsillustrated.cnn.com/olympics/features/ joyner/flashback2.html

Morgan, J. L. (1997). 'Some could suckle over their shoulder': Male travelers, female bodies, and the gendering of racial ideology, 1500–1770. *William and Mary Quarterly*, 54, 167–92.

Morton, P. (1991). Introduction. *Disfigured images: The historical assault on Afro-American women*. Westport, CT: Greenwood Press.

Mott, S. (2000, December 14). Wimbledon: Triumph of American values. *The Daily Telegraph*. Retrieved June 30, 2006 from http://www.telegraph.co.uk/sport/main.jht ml;jsessionid=TP5GNFRXV0LFLQFIQM FSFFWAVCB00IV()?xml=/sport/tennis/ stmott08.xml

Mott, S. (2007, July 9). Star quality is no match for Venus. *The Daily Telegraph*. Retrieved July 9, 2007 from http://www.telegraph .co.uk/sport/main.jhtml?xml=/sport /2007/07/09/stmott 109.xml

Muscat, J. (2007, June 28). Molik stirs the lighting character in Williams. *Timesonline*. Retrieved June 29, 2007 from http://www .timesonline.co.uk/tol/sport/tennis/article 1996666.ece

Niall, J. (2007a, January 28). Cyclone Serena slams Maria and her knockers. *The Sydney Morning Herald*, p. 54.

Niall, J. (2007b, January 28). Sharapova and the critics dealt a blow by Williams' sledgehammer. *The Age*, p. 54.

Patton, C. (2001). 'Rock hard': Judging the female physique. *Journal of Sport & Social Issues*, 25(2), 118–140.

Pearce, L. (2007, January 24). Serena ignores the knockers. *The Sydney Morning Herald*. Retrieved January 25, 2007 from http:// www.smh.com.au/ncws/tennis/serena-ignores-the-knockers/2007/01/23/1169518 709298 .html

Peterson, C. (2001). Foreword: Eccentric bodies. In M. Bennett & V. Dickerson (Eds.), *Recovering the black female body: Self- representations by African American women* (pp. ix–xvi). New Brunswick, NJ: Rutgers University Press.

Philip, R. (2007, July 3). Street style gives Venus her deadly cutting edge. *The Daily Telegraph*. Retrieved July 3, 2007 from http://vvww .telegraph.co.uk/sport/main.jhtml?xml=/ sport/2007/07/03/Stphil 103.xml

PostWatch. (2002). *Defending the trashy.* Retrieved July 1, 2006 from http://post watch.blogspot.com/2002_08_25_post watch_archive.html

Ramsay, A. (2006, January 22). Aussie defeat is the bottom line for overweight Serena. *News.scotsman.com.* Retrieved August 14, 2006 from http://sport.scotsman.com/tennis .cfm?id=105902006

Rowe, K. (1990). Roseanne: Unruly woman as domestic goddess. *Screen, 31*(4), 408–419.

Schultz, L. (2002). Reading the catsuit: Serena Williams and the production of blackness at the 2002 US Open. *Journal of Sport & Social Issues, 29*(3), 338–357.

Schulze, L. (1990). On the muscle. In J. Gaines & C. Herzog (Eds.), *Fabrications: Costume and the female body* (pp. 59–78). London: Routledge.

Scott, B. (2007, January 28). Champ focused on retail therapy after responding to critics. *The Sun-Herald*, p. 57.

Sharpley-Whiting, T. D. (1999). *Black Venus: Sexualized savages, primal fears, and primitive narratives in French.* Durham, NC: Duke University Press.

Smith, G. (2007, June 29). Williams has designs on title despite host of outside distractions. *The Times*, p. 104.

Spencer, N. E. (2001). From 'child's play' to 'party crasher': Venus Williams, racism and professional Women's tennis. In D. L. Andrews & S. J. Jackson (Eds.), *Sport stars: The cultural politics of sporting celebrity* (pp. 87–101). London: Routledge.

Spencer, N. E. (2004). Sister Act VI: Venus and Serena Williams at Indian Wells: 'Sincere fictions' and white racism. *Journal of Sport & Social Issues, 28*(2), 115–135.

Stevens, M. (2006, January 12). Size up Serena Williams at your own risk. *The Sun-Herald*, p. 57.

Stevenson, D. (2002). Women, sport and globalization: Competing discourses of sexuality and nation. *Journal of Sport & Social Issues, 26*, 209–225.

Syed, M. (2008, January 24). They play great. They look great. So what, exactly, is the problem? *The Times.* Retrieved January 24, 2008 from http://www.timesonline.co.uk/ tol/sport/tennis/article3241414.ece

Vertinsky, P., & Captain, G. (1998). More myth than history: American culture and representations of the black female's athletic ability. *Journal of Sport History, 25*, 532–561.

Viner, B. (2007, June 15). There is way too much emphasis on how we look. Focus on my game. *The Independent.* Retrieved June 15, 2007 from http://sport.independent.co.uk/ tennis/article2659628.ece

White, C. (2007, January 28). Williams silences critics. *The Telegraph.* Retrieved January 28, 2007 from http://www.telegraph.co.uk/ sport/main.jhtml?xml=/sport/2007/OI/28/ stlina28.xml

14

Hetero Barbie?

Mary F. Rogers

As they enter their teenage years, if not before, most heterosexual females begin putting a boy or young man at the center of their lives. Moving through puberty toward adulthood, girls and young women find that their popularity at school, their feminine credibility, and much else hinge on their attractiveness to boys and their relationship with one particular boy.[1] As they get heterosexualized, then, girls and young women face pressures to give boys and dating a lot of priority. In turn, they pay increasing attention to the size and shape of their bodies, the range and contents of their wardrobes, the styling of their hair, and the making up of their faces. Barbie epitomizes, even exaggerates, these families mandates. She gives girls endless opportunities to costume her, brush and style her hair, and position her in settings like aerobics class, a school dance, or the shopping mall.

Yet Barbie escapes the typical outcomes of such activities. In the end she seems not to have her heart in her relationship with Ken, who in no way monopolizes her attention. Barbie exudes an independence that deviates from the codes of mainstream femininity. That she is insistently single and perpetually childless means that hers is no "normal" femininity. Again, one comes up short by looking for an explanation in Barbie's teenage status, for she is no teenager when it comes to occupations, travel, and other aspects of her lifestyle. The facts of Barbie's having neither a husband nor a child do not speak for themselves, then. Instead, these circumstances leave Barbie open to multiple, conflicting interpretations. They enlarge this icon's field of meanings and thus the range of consumers she can attract.

Within that field of cultural meanings stands the possibility that Barbie may not be heterosexual. Indeed, she may not even be a woman. Barbie may be a drag queen. Much in the tradition made widely visible by stars like RuPaul, Barbie may be the ultrafeminine presence that drag queens personify. Her long, long legs and flat hips suggest this possibility. So does her wardrobe, especially her shimmering evening gowns, high heels, heavy-handed makeup, and brilliant tiaras and other headpieces. Barbie's is a bright, glittery femininity never visibly defiled by a Lady Schick or Kotex. This exceptionally, emphatically feminine icon has some appeal among gay men.

From Rogers, M. F. (1999), *Barbie Culture*. London: SAGE Publications Ltd. Reprinted by permission of SAGE Publications Ltd.

That appeal shows up in diverse ways. I have no interest in whether or not this designer or that, this collector or that, this event or that is gay, however. My concern is with the *gay-themed* character of what one comes across in some corners of Barbie's far-reaching world. In many cultural worlds heterocentrism and heterosexism prevail in no uncertain terms. In the world of "Father Knows Best" or the feminine mystique, attention to gender and family center on heterosexuality strongly enough to snuff out alternative readings whereby "transgressive" sexualities such as lesbianism or bisexuality can enter the picture. Commonly intertwined with such heterocentrism are values celebrating heterosexuality as normal and natural while condemning or at least rejecting lesbigay sexualities. The world of Barbie is *relatively* free of such heterocentrism and heterosexism and thus holds *relative* appeal for nonheterosexual people, especially gay men. Lesbians, particularly those inclined toward feminism, are more likely to reject some of the central features of Barbie's world, as are bisexuals who might find her apparent monosexuality unappealing. In any case, Barbie's world allows for nonstraight readings, just as many other "straight" cultural products do.[2] I tap such possibilities here by treating Barbie's sexual identity as less than certain while arguing that her sweeping appeal revolves around such ambiguities.

As an icon of drag, Barbie illustrates what feminists and culture critics have been saying for some years. In no uncertain terms Barbie demonstrates that femininity is a manufactured reality. It entails a lot of artifice, a lot of clothes, a lot of props such as cuddly poodles and shopping bags, and a lot of effort, however satisfying at times.[3] If Barbie can join drag queens as an exemplar of the constructed character of femininity, she can also be an icon of nonheterosexual femininity. In the extreme Barbie might be a lipstick lesbian, a lesbian fem, or a lesbian closeted more tightly than most who choose

not to "come out." She might be a bisexual woman who once cared about and pursued a relationship with Ken but now prefers her "best friend" Midge. Most radically of all, Barbie might be asexual. She might be sexy without being sexual, attractive without being attracted. . . .

Not surprisingly, RuPaul sometimes shows up in Barbie's world. Scott Arend (1995) reports that Ivan Burton, who designs artist dolls, has done a "one-of-a-kind RuPaul." Jim Washburn (1994) says that Michael Osborne, a Barbie doll collector, wants to be buried with what he calls his "RuPaul Barbie, or Ru-Barbie for short." Osborne's favorite doll is made from a My Size Barbie, the 18-inch version of the doll, and has "brown skin, blue eyes and platinum hair."

The feature story on Osborne, which appeared in the *Los Angeles Times*, illustrates how a gay-themed text fits into a mainstream publication, that is, how a gay reading of a supposedly straight text involves little stretch of the nonheterosexual imagination. Twenty-four-year-old Osborne, who has been collecting Barbie dolls since he was thirteen, has nearly 300 of them and makes no attempt to hide his "love" for them. Osborne says he has friends employed by Mattel who help him acquire some of his more unusual dolls, such as a hairless Skipper, Barbie's little sister. Like other collectors, Osborne keeps a lot of his dolls in their original packaging. (NRFB, or Never Removed From Box, enhances the market value of a doll.) Osborne, however, has "play-with dolls, whose outfits he changes monthly." He also shampoos his dolls' hair and gives them permanents. Also, Osborne once dressed as Barbie at Halloween and claims to have "looked pretty darn snappy." Asked about the possibility that his sizable Barbie collection could be an obstacle to "finding a mate," Osborne responds in terms of "friends who have had rocky relationships with *people* because they did not really like Barbie." Washburn poses the more difficult question: What "if it came down to a choice between giving up the Barbies or the *person?*" Osborne answers, "It depends on the *person,* but probably the *person.*"

Where a heterocentrist text would talk about finding a wife or a woman, this one refers only to mates and people and persons. In view of its subject matter this text readily passes as gay-themed. Along those lines Osborne reports, "I had always liked fashion, always liked doing hair. When people asked what I wanted to be when I grew up, I said I wanted to be a hairdresser and president of Mattel." Osborne's interest in being a hairdresser expresses an interest in what queer theorists, who theorize about nonheterosexual or "transgressive" sexualities, call *non-normative occupations.* Such lines of work are those that attract disproportionate numbers of lesbigay people and are widely considered inappropriate for people of a given gender. The ballet and hairdressing for men and the military and auto mechanics for women are examples. In any event Osborne's interest in a non-normative occupation bespeaks a gay-themed text, as does his claim that "the best times of his life have been Barbie times." . . .

More generally, *Barbie Bazaar* often offers gay-themed fare for those attuned to it. Like most such material, it does not leap out to most readers as lesbigay even while leaving room for "queer" interpretations. . . . Often, too, gay-themed material shows up in comments about or articles on doll artists, most of whom appear to be men often working in conjunction with male "partners" to refashion Barbie in designs of their own. In one *Barbie Bazaar* article Pattie Jones (1995), for instance, mentions Jim Faraone, who once designed jewelry for Anne Klein but now "designs hand-beaded Barbie doll outfits." Faraone began collecting in 1986 and now has a thousand Barbie dolls. Two of his artist dolls are pictured in Janine Fennick's *The Collectible Barbie Doll* (1996). One is AIDS Awareness

Barbie where the AIDS-awareness red ribbon runs around the back of Barbie's neck, across her breasts, and then crosses at her waist. Also showing up in *Barbie Bazaar* are references to Mattel's participation with collectors and other Barbie fans in AIDS fundraisers, often targeting children with AIDS as beneficiaries. . . .

Barbie thus points to what Jesse Berrett (1996) sees as "mass culture's power to define, commodify, and mutate sexual identity." Put more queerly in terms used in *Out* magazine:

> RuPaul's larger-than-life, gayer-than-gay presence on runways, VH1, and New York radio and everywhere else . . . suggests that the mall of America has embraced him not as a novelty but as a genuine homo star. But it doesn't take a drag queen to have an impact. (1997: 96)

Mattel can unintentionally sponsor the same impact, it seems. . . .

Notes

1. For insights into this state of affairs, see Eder with Evans and Parker (1995), Fine (1992), and Walkerdine (1990).

2. See, for example, Valerie Traub, "The Ambiguities of 'Lesbian' Viewing Pleasure: The (Dis)Articulation of *Black Widow,*" in Julia Epstein and Kristina Straub (eds.), *Body Guards: The Cultural Politics of Gender Ambiguity* (New York, Routledge, 1991), pp. 304–9; Bonnie Zimmerman, "Seeing, Reading, Knowing: The Lesbian Appropriation of Literature," in Joan E. Hartman and Ellen Messer-Davidow (eds.), *(En)Gendering Knowledge: Feminists in Academe* (Knoxville, University of Tennessee Press, 1991), pp. 92–7.

3. Dorothy E. Smith is one of the best commentators on how pleasurable some of the projects of femininity can be. She talks, for example, about the pleasures of female community built up around such feminine pastimes as clothes

shopping. See *Texts, Facts, and Femininity: Exploring the Relations of Ruling* (London and New York: Routledge, 1990), p. 199.

References

Arend, S. (1994). Review of mondo Barbie. *Barbie Bazaar, 6,* 51.

Berrett, J. (1996). The sex revolts: Reading gender and identity in mass culture. *Radical History Review, 66,* 210–219.

Eder, D., with Evans, C., & Parker, P. (1995). *School talk: Gender and adolescent culture.* New Brunswick, NJ: Rutgers University Press.

Fennick, J. (1996). *The collectible Barbie doll: An illustrated guide to her dreamy world.* Philadelphia: Courage Books.

Fine, M. (1992). *Disruptive voices: The possibilities of feminist research.* Ann Arbor: University of Michigan Press.

Jones, P. (1995). Viva la Barbie. *Barbie Bazaar, 7,* 63–67.

Walkerdine, V. (1990). *Schoolgirl fictions.* London and New York: Verso.

Washburn, J. (1994). The man who would be Ken. *Los Angeles Times,* 2 August: 1: Life & Style Section.

15

Transgender Transitions

Sex/Gender Binaries in the Digital Age

Kay Siebler

Tim Curry, in a black corset, big-girl-cha-cha shoes, elbow-length black gloves, and sexy garters, will forever be the quintessential queer for a generation of Americans. But that generation, of which I proudly count myself a member, is now just a bunch of geezers. What Curry's character of Dr. Frank-n-Furter in the cult classic *Rocky Horror Picture Show* did for us was show us queerness that could be celebrated, queerness that could be embraced, queerness that was hip, and cool. If we did not want to be just like Curry *and* his character, we wanted to be his friend. In fact, many of us spent a better part of our teens and twenties learning to perform his specific brand of queer in our rooms, at parties, and in the front of movie theaters all over the country.

The Rocky Horror Picture Show (1975) provides a celebratory portrayal of a "Transvestite from Transylvania," although we never see Dr. Frank-n-Furter out of drag. The language of the time did not accommodate anything but transsexuals or transvestites. There was no such term as "transgender" or the umbrella term of "queer" other than as an epithet. Judith Butler's theories on gender as performance were yet to be written. Yet for the fans of this film and musical (the London musical *The Rocky Horror Show* debuted in 1973), Dr. Frank-n-Furter was not a drag queen—although the character self-identified as a transvestite. He was not trying to perform femaleness. He had a sexy bulge in his black briefs; there were no breasts in his laced-up bustier. He was the first media representation of a delightful transgender person before we had the language to describe him as thus. He was dancing on the grave of the oppressive systems that rigidly link sex with gender and sexuality; he remains a glorious model for people who play with gender. He thrilled us, even if—in the mid 1970s—we did not know exactly why. We knew he was bolder, different, and seemingly more fun and joyful than any other transvestite we had ever seen on the silver screen.

From Siebler, K. (2012). Transgender transitions: Sex/gender binaries in the digital age. *Journal of Gay & Lesbian Mental Health*, 16(1), 74–99. Reprinted by permission of Taylor & Francis Ltd., www.tandf.co.uk/journals.

At that time Dr. Frank-n-Furter's ambiguity was part of the appeal. Today we are far less comfortable with the sort of ambiguity embodied by transgender people. We want them to be either/or: pre-op or post-op, transvestite or transsexual. There are few representations in mainstream media of a transgender person who defies these categories. Characters or people may define themselves as transgender, but they are modifying their bodies into the accepted codes for masculine male or feminine female. Unfortunately, the Internet serves to reinforce these binaries. Locating a transqueer identity online, that is, a person who is not "transitioning" with hormones and surgery to a specific gender identity, is difficult. What the digital realm tells users and viewers is that "trans" means "transitioning," not moving outside of systems defining sex and gender. . . . For all the strides we have made as a culture of embracing and complicating queerness in the Digital Age—for all the communities and groups that the Internet offers to queer folks finding their way in the world—we have taken a step backwards in relation to breaking out of the gender/sex binaries. . . .

The Dangerous Moves of Definitions

Before we go any further, we need to first enter the prickly business of defining terms. . . . Queer is the umbrella term for people who resist the binaries. There are various identities within the context of identifying as queer. People who were, 20 years ago, described as "hermaphrodite" (people having biological characteristics of both sexes) now name themselves "intersex." Language shifted because the intersex community wanted to name themselves rather than being named by the medical profession. One will occasionally still encounter the term "hermaphrodite" in reference to a person who is intersex, but the preferred term of those claiming the identity is intersex.

Only in the past 20 years has the intersex community come out and talked about their experiences. Previously, when an intersex child was born, pediatric surgeons were called upon to "fix" the baby, that is, create a distinct penis or vagina. As the child grew and went through puberty, hormones were given to ensure the surgical assignment had been "correct." Most intersex babies grew up not knowing what had happened to them. Today, medical professionals are more attuned to the sensitivity of the intersex individual and counsel parents on letting their child decide who he or she will become. Yet in a world where gender is a primary way we interact with the world, raising a child to be gender-neutral is no small feat.

A transsexual may or may not come into the world intersex. A transsexual is an individual who undergoes hormones and surgery in an effort to feel at home in hir[1] body. Transsexuals are identified as Female-to-Male (FTM) or Male-to-Female (MTF). A transsexual may identify as intersex, but once zhe begins the transition to create a distinctly male or female body, zhe moves into the category of transsexual. Once a transsexual has transitioned for any period of time, he or she may no longer identify as trans as he or she feels zhe is now accepted as a masculine male or feminine female.

A transgender person is someone who occupies the borderlands between communities and identities. A transgender person may be intersex, but may not be. With the feminist and gay/lesbian rights movements of the 1970s, the term "transgender" was coined. At that time, most transgender people eschewed the idea that they needed surgery or hormones to modify their body. Today transgender people see hormones and surgery as a way to "pass" in a heteronormative world that mandates a rigid gender/sex binary. . . .

Genderqueer or transgender people reject the terms "transvestite" or "cross dresser" as ways of describing themselves because these terms imply a superficial or playful performance of gender. . . . The transgender/genderqueer person rejects and resists categorization: "The Genderqueer has an identity that is unrecognizable in the gender binary" (Saltzburg, 2010, p. 18). As Leslie Feinberg, a self-defined transgender warrior, describes the identity in the film, *Outlaw*, that profiles hir life (Lebow, 1994): "Not everybody who is differently gendered is gay."

Feinberg, as a gender warrior, defies the either/or categories and instead identifies as both/all. Saltzburg's research found this to be indicative of the transmasculine people she interviewed. "Many participants conceptualized genderqueer as a **'both/neither'** identity . . . This means there is a sense of being more than one gender at a time, or being in between genders" (*bold in original text*) (2010, p. 43). Feinberg describes this identity as a transgender warrior; Saltzburg defines it as genderqueer. Both are articulating the identity of those who actively resist and defy the gender binary. Therefore, this population is less likely to feel the need for hormones and surgery. These are the people whose perspectives and identities are disappearing or lost to us in the Digital Age. . . .

Passing on the Queer

. . . Where many media theorists have argued that the Internet offers a disembodiment—a way of transforming the physical body into a digital identity—that is liberating, the Internet more often serves to reinforce a rigid trans body type. For example, in his research regarding online ads by and for transgender people (2010), Daniel Farr discovered that there was very little play within the categories of trans people. Descriptors of identity were reduced to "FTM" and "MTF," using easy shorthand that simplifies, as opposed to

complicates, the gender system. Farr writes, "The use of MTF and FTM are problematic when engaging with transgender persons given the mélange of embodiment and social enactments, but were exceptionally common terms among the personal ads" (p. 91). Farr found that the majority of people posting ads included descriptors about their bodies, with the focus on convincing their audience they were "real" men or women (p. 93). . . .

There has been limited research on transgender people and online communities (Gauthier & Chaudoir, 2004). Despite the dearth of research, it makes sense that transgender people would seek out online communities more than other queer populations as they are a minority within a minority. Transgender people face disproportionate violence (Lombardi et al., 2001). People of minority communities find that the Internet provides a feeling of safety and anonymity (Farr, 2010, pp. 89–90). But as transgender people may seek out on-line communities to escape violence and find acceptance, these communities may only accept them if they have certain gender characteristics. The dominant narrative found in online queer spaces is one of reductive definitions of trans bodies and trans identity. . . .

The FTM Body: Our Right to Stare

Transgender bodies are discussed, displayed, and regulated much more rigidly on the Internet than the physical bodies of others within the queer community. . . . Popular television shows and films reinforce gender rigidity, and online fan sites debate and celebrate these representations. Max, the trans character on *The L Word*, is a fascinating example of how online fans expressed mixed responses to fictionalized trans people. In season four (2006), the character Moira was introduced, a slight, butch lesbian. By mid-season Moira was transitioning to Max with the help of hormones, cross-dressing, and crotch stuffing. Top surgery was discussed. Max has transitioned across three seasons. He is referred to as a "trans-man" instead of a "butch lesbian" because of his choice to use hormones. Max is no longer considered a lesbian because he uses hormones, but without surgery, Max still has the vagina and breasts that code him as female (Edwards, 2010, p. 167). Among the lesbian and trans communities there was much Internet discussion about the Max character. One online viewer expressed typical frustration with Max's gender ambiguity on the "After Ellen Forum" electronic bulletin board, writing: "Also, L word STILL has no butch characters. Moira/Max does not count because he's a transgender man which isn't the same thing! L word is making it look as if the natural progression for butch women is to eventually become transgender" (Edwards, 2010, p. 168). Many online lesbians expressed frustration that finally there was a butch lesbian on *The L Word* and she turned out to be trans, echoing what Judith Halberstam refers to at the "butch/FTM border wars" (Coogan, 2006, p. 18). It seems no one was willing to see Max as a transgender person, where binaries of sex and gender are queered. News media tells us there is either/or, we cannot see anything else, we cannot *be* anything else. Queer, in relation to transgender people, is not really queer in the Digital Age. Instead trans-gender people are reduced to very un-queer definitions of masculinity and femininity, maleness, and femaleness. . . .

Trannies Are the New Black/"Chicks With Dicks"

The cultural curiosity of trans identity permeates popular media. From Ru Paul's or Tyra Banks' talk shows to *Queer Eye for the Straight Guy* or *Law and Order*, the laptop screen and the television screen bring us images of MTF transgender people as an intriguing oddity or amusement. Transgender people, typically in various

stages of surgical and hormonal transitioning, are appearing on the "hip" television programs with predictable regularity: *Nip and Tuck* (Famke Janssen plays Ava Moore), *America's Next Top Model* (Isis King plays herself), VH1's *I Want to Work for Diddy* (Laverne Cox plays herself). ABC's *Dirty Sexy Money* (Candis Cayne plays Carmelita), *Ugly Betty* (Rebecca Romijn plays Alexis Meade), and *All My Children* (Jeffery Carlson plays Zoe) are popular television shows that have clamored onto the "Trannies are the New Cool" bandwagon. The Internet discussions (blog posts and comments on fan websites) regarding these characters connect these television shows to the digital world.

Some may argue that the mainstream presence of trans people is revolutionary, but as many media theorists have pointed out (Clark, 1969; Leifer, Gordon, & Graves, 1974; Berry, 1998; Hartley, 1999; Padva, 2007), the presence of a traditionally marginalized group does not necessarily equate to advancement. MTF people are typically portrayed as high drag. They have big hair, lots of make-up, push-up bras, and large implants that they are happy to display through low-cut bodices. They often carry the stereotypically gay catty (snap, snap, swish) attitudes that straight audiences love. The MTF transqueers can easily be read as gay men dressing in drag and playing to the stereotypes both of hyper-feminine females and comedic drag performers. A thread on a Facebook discussion board ("Nigel, is this your daughter/son?") focused on transgender people, making a direct connection between trans representations on television and "real world" trans people. The posts (presumably written by nontrans people) contained references to stereotypical trans identity. A person using the screen name of Jessica posted, "I've seen transgender people on television, and there's always something different about their voices and their body shape. I think MTV Real World had a chick with a d*** recently" ("Nigel," 2010). The vernacular of "chick with a dick" reflects how the complexity of trans identity is reduced to male/female—the genitalia; the physical manifestation of the body is what counts. To further codify the sex/gender connection, body aesthetics of MTF trans people *must* ascribe to hyper feminine ideals. Femininity costs money and means body modification.

In *Girl Inside* (Gallus, 2007), the filmmaker follows Madison, a college-aged transgender person, as she goes through the gradual steps of transitioning to female: first her Adam's apple is shaved, then she takes hormones, finally the genital surgery. The most interesting parts of this film are the relationships that are portrayed. Madison has a close and loving relationship with her 80-year-old grandmother who accepts her transition and attempts to teach her about the standards of femininity, and tutors Madison in the power that resides in being feminine. This hyper-feminine fixation can be attributed to a postfeminist cultural moment where people have been duped into believing that feminine sexual power is a form of real and sustained power within the culture. Rosalind Gill, in writing of cisfemales (women who were born female) and the effects of media on their bodies, states:

> One of the most striking aspects of post feminist media culture is its obsessive preoccupation with the body. . . . [f]emininity is defined as bodily property rather than (say) a social structural or psychological one. Instead of caring or nurturing or motherhood being regarded as central to femininity (all, of course, highly problematic and exclusionary) in today's media it is possession of a "sexy body" that is presented as women's key (if not sole) source of identity. (Gill, p. 255)

Transgender characters such as Laverne Cox on *I Want to Work for Diddy*, Carmelita on *Dirty Sexy Money*, and Isis King on *America's Top Model* all fit the "chick with a dick, gay Barbie" stereotype of MTF transqueers. Cox has an interview clip on the VH1 website where she talks about trans politics, the lack of portrayals of transqueers on television, and connects the struggles of transgender people with the Civil Rights movement ("Transgendered People on Television," 2008). She is articulate, smart, and politically astute. But these dynamics of her politics and intellect never make it to the *I Want to Work for Diddy* show where she plays a stereotypical "gay Barbie" with big hair, Valley Girl language, and glamorous fashion. This image is reiterated in Cox's casting in the reality show *TRANSform*. In *TRANSform*, Cox plays one of three Charlie's Angels-type trannies who do makeovers of cisgender women (VH1, 2010). The promotional materials for this show, entitled *TRANSform Me*, pose Cox and her two co-stars (Jamie Clayton and Nina Poon) with hair dryers and hair products instead of guns but striking a pose that calls back to the Charlie's Angels television show logo of the 1970s. The postfeminist illusion is that these transgender women are taking up the Charlie's Angels torch by doing makeovers instead of fighting crime because they are, after all, Barbie beautiful. One could argue that *all* women in pop culture media outlets, trans or not, manifest the Barbie Aesthetic. If they did not, they would not be on the screen. The interesting twist with *TRANSform Me* is that the trans women are so Stepford Wife feminine that they can give advice to cisfemales on how to be/become/buy-their-way to the ideal femininity.

The only MTF transqueers who are allowed to escape this hyper-feminine, make-up and product-dependent aesthetic that permeates the MTF representation in the Digital Age, are trans *children*. Tyra Banks on her talk show *The Tyra Show* aired an episode on transgender children in January 2010. Because the market has been saturated with MTF transgender adults, media puts a new edge on the topic by talking about children who identify as trans. On one episode of The *Tyra Show*, Banks brags that "*The Tyra Show* has the daytime exclusive" of airing interviews with transgender children. She follows that statement by interviewing two children, a six-year-old (Josie) and her transgender sister, Jade. The parents sit by the two tykes, smiling nervously. Jade describes being transgender as having a birth defect. Banks reduces that analogy to hinting that the birth defect is the child's penis that is "just not supposed to be there"—again distilling the trans identity to genitalia (2010). Although all the people (from the children to the parents) interviewed on this episode of *The Tyra Show* are articulate and on-the-mark in talking about the complexities of being transgender or having a trans-gender child, the format and Bank's own approach gives the program a sensational quality, as if the concept of a transgender child is bizarre. The focus is, if not an unveiling and displaying of the body, a discussion of body parts that define biological sex.

The above genres of reality shows or talk shows show trans people talking about their "real" lives for the consumption of the audience. Candis Cayne, a MTF transqueer, has made the cross-over from reality show to serialized drama. According to Ryan Baber at Reuters.com, ABC's *Dirty Sexy Money* was the first television show that cast a transgender person to play a transgender character in prime time. The character Carmelita (played by Cayne) is a transgender person who is involved with a married man. The actor Candis Cayne (a.k.a. Candi Cayne) blurs the line between drag queen and transgender person. She is often described as a "female impersonator" (ETonline, 2007) or "transsexual" (Roberts, 2007). Other web postings or online articles describe Cayne as transgender. Some interviews avoid the politics of naming altogether by simply referring to her as a spokesperson for an unnamed cause or describing her as having "transitioned" ("Access Extended,"

2010). Cayne's identity as a trans person cast to play a trans character is seen as a victory by many in the queer rights community. The issue of casting nontrans people to play trans people is an abiding critique, similar to the critique leveled against directors who cast straight actors to play gay and lesbian characters.

We see this in transfeminine representations where legs, cleavage, youth and the Barbie aesthetic are primarily portrayed. There are no other sorts of representations to counter this hyper-sexualized, hyper-feminine ideal that pivots on capitalist models of gender facilitated by product consumption. "The body is presented simultaneously as women's source of power *and* as always unruly and requiring constant monitoring, surveillance, discipline and remodeling (and consumer spending) in order to conform to ever narrower judgments of female attractiveness. . . . Women's bodies are evaluated, scrutinized and dissected . . . and are always at risk of 'failing'" (Gill, p. 255). In order *not* to "fail" at being female or feminine, both cisfemales and trans-feminine people must resort to surgery and consumption of more and more products that define femininity. The body, be it female or trans, is not acceptable in its natural state.

Digital Trans Bodies of Matter

Digital space, films and television shows serve to teach transqueers what the current standards are for being trans in this world. These texts codify just one version of trans identity that transqueers must manifest to be accepted. Angela McRobbie and Janice Winship analyzed the discourses in women's magazines and how a highly restrictive femininity is constructed, centering on romance, domesticity, and caring (2004). As a result, females of all ages in the culture internalize that restrictive femininity and aspire to it by dieting, buying beauty products, and dressing to accommodate. To an even larger degree, this is true of trans people who feel they have to be über-feminine or hyper-masculine to prove their identity as "real" or true females/males. The standards of beauty and the standards of body are hooked into the capitalistic culture of consumption: consuming undergarments made specifically for trans "passing," consuming clothing, makeup, and beauty products, consuming various types of surgeries. Without this consumption mandate, would there be these rigid gender standards of how to be trans? Most media theorists argue that the capitalist culture creates the *need* for body modification or body insecurity. If there were no body insecurity, there would be no need for the products. Therefore, it is the goal of the marketers to make the viewing public feel insecure enough to buy.

We trust our screens to inform us how we should be, perceiving it as "real." Zizek writes, "The postmodern universe is the universe of naive trust in the screen which makes the very quest for what lies behind it irrelevant" (*Plague,* p. 134). The technology of this postmodern moment creates both disillusionment and the idea that technology is reality; objective reality and technology become blurred. What technology delivers to us, we believe to be real; the virtual reality of the computer screen is confused with the physical world in which we live. Therefore, the information, language, and representations encountered in that virtual world are seen as truth. The ramifications of new media reinforcing the rigidity of the sex/gender systems results in the demand for more hormones and more surgeries. Zizek believes the virtual world inside the screen "jeopardizes our most elementary perceptions of our own bodies. It cripples our own phenomenological attitudes toward the bodies of others. We suspend our knowledge of what actually exists and conceive of that surface (the computer interface) as directly expressing the soul"

(1997, p. 137). Yet we believe we are not affected by the cyber-texts we consume.

In research conducted by Bryson et al., regarding queerness and digital texts, they found people were in denial about how much they folded the digital world into their own. Bryson et al. write, "It was relatively common for participants to describe daily practices of living as highly mediated by a range of Internet technologies and spaces, and their lives as relatively insulated from any cybercultural 'effects' or 'affects'" (Bryson et al., 2006, p. 798).

Websites, films, and television are making gender more rigid. New media may support alternative genders, but only those alternative genders that require the assistance of hormones and surgery. Carroll and Gilroy (2002) wrote about treatment approaches for transgender people. Rather than counseling patients to assume either a male or female role, counselors are more likely to encourage patients to explore other identities and options even as the screen-mediated world sends the opposite message. Carroll and Gilroy challenge counseling educators and counselors to embrace a "trans positive" approach, affirming various gender identities. These counselors will have little chance of success against the digital onslaught of gender/sex binaries.

The Internet feeds trans people the notion that gender means capitalist consumption with images, banner ads on web pages, and websites that exist only to sell products to transqueers. The website *Susan's Place Transgender Resources* is an example of a hybrid site that initially purports to provide "resources," but getting products to help one pass is the dominant function of the site. The name suggests that there may be some support groups listed or organizations that advocate for trans people. And there are, but there are also various links to surgeons, places to buy clothing, where to shop, what kind of surgery is available, and where to buy prostheses. The "academic" link is empty. The *Transgender Care* website is one that focuses on surgery, hormones, and hair removal; the "care" advertised has a cost, both literally and figuratively.

. . . Buck Angel, a muscular, tattooed, bald man who harkens back to Mr. Clean, has a well-known body that matters in the digital space. Angel is not afraid to queer his image by letting us know that he does not have a penis. The line Angel is most known for is, "It isn't what is between your legs that makes your gender" (*Buck Angel Entertainment,* 2010). Angel resists the mandate of being fully female or male, although Angel has had top surgery and presumably is taking hormones. Angel has a web site devoted to his own brand of queer politics and his "Public Cervix Announcement" is popular on YouTube (2010). Angel's web-site *Buck Angel Entertainment's* (http://buckangelenter tainment.com/) tag line promises "Agency, Advocacy, Lectures, Workshops and Media Projects." His public service announcement (PSA) about cervical cancer screenings advises transmen to continue to get annual pap and pelvic exams. Responses posted by viewers are overwhelmingly hostile, calling Angel a "monster" and a "synthetic male" (among other things). He also has a YouTube PSA on transgendered women getting prostate exams.

Buck Angel's website, as well as websites such as *Transgender Law and Policy Center, Transgender Forum Community Center*, and *National Association of Gay, Lesbian, Bisexual, and Transgender Centers,* offer essential information on where a transgender person can go to find community, information, and support. There are more websites peddling products, surgery, and testimonials of the one "true" trans way. The Internet offers a singular and unified pedagogy of transgender identity: be who you are, but you need to spend money to align your body with who you really are; your natural state is one that is unnatural and needs remediation. . . .

The digital world has opened up communities for transgender people where none have existed before. There is less isolation and perhaps less struggle because of the resources, social networks, and virtual communities provided on the Internet. However, these virtual communities and forums also serve to create a codified version of limited ways of being transgender. A transgender norm becomes established so that even transgender people are no longer queering gender in the way that Dr. Frank-n-Furter did in the 1970s. The Transgender Warrior that Leslie Feinberg describes is being co-opted by the capitalist culture so that a buck—and a Buck Angel—can be made. This commodification of queerness is not exclusive to transgender people, but this group seems the most vulnerable because the "products" they are persuaded to purchase are not new wardrobes or cars. Instead, the capitalist culture has successfully convinced transgender people that they must purchase surgeries and hormones, body parts or the removal of them, to embody their "true" identity. In a culture where consumption is a way of life, a way to validate one's existence, a way to display one's status and worth, queerness has been co-opted. The Digital Age has obliterated the transqueers who embrace the borderlands of gender fluidity and replaced it with "gender as consumption."

Note

1. A note on pronouns: when the person I am referring to has designated a specific pronoun for himself or herself, I use that pronoun. If the person I am referring to has not designated a pronoun, or if I am generally speaking about trans people, I will use the gender-neutral pronouns of "hir" and "zhe." These terms are embraced by many activists in the trans community as a way of shaping language to reflect their reality. Standard Written English does not allow for a gender-neutral third person singular or gender-neutral pronoun referring to a person.

References

Access Extended: Candis Cayne Talks Chastity (Chaz) Bono's Transgender Transformation. (2010). *Access Hollywood.* Retrieved from www.accesshollywood.com

Anderson, J. (Writer/Director). (2003). *Normal* [Television movie]. United States: Avenue Picture Productions.

Angel, B. (2010, February 23). Buck Angel's public cervix announcement. *You Tube.* Retrieved from http://www.youtube.com/watch?v=X uNFmZHvO0& feature=related

Applegate, K., Chermol, C., Medina, B., Miskowiec, B., Moriarity, J., & Redmann, R. (Executive Producers). (2010, January 27). *The Tyra Banks Show* [Television broadcast]. New York, NY: Warner Brothers Broadcasting Company.

Babenco, H. (Director). (1985). *Kiss of the Spider Woman* [Motion picture]. United States: HB Films.

Baber, R. (2008, April 25). TV has never seen more transgender characters. *Reuters.* Retrieved from http://www.reuters.com/article/idUSN2534139520080425

Bastian, R., Cooper, L., Dungan, S., Macy, W., & Moran, L. (Producers), & Tucker, D. (Writer/Director). (2005). *Transamerica* [Motion picture]. United States: Belladonna Productions.

Becker, A. E. (1995). *Body, self, and society: The view from Fiji.* Philadelphia, PA: University of Pennsylvania.

Berlanti, G. (Producer). (2007, October 31). *Dirtysexymoney* [Television broadcast]. Los Angeles, CA: ABC.

Berry, G. (1998). Black family life on television and the socialization of the African American child: Images of marginality. *Journal of Comparative Family Studies, 29*(2), 233–242.

Bryson, M., MacIntosh, L., Jordan, S., & Lin, H.-L. (2006). Virtually queer? Homing devices, mobility and un/belongings. *Canadian Journal of Communication, 31,* 791–814.

Buck Angel Entertainment. (2010). Available from http://buckangelentertainment. com/

Butler, J. (1999). *Gender trouble* (First ed.). London, England: Routledge.

Carroll, L., & Gilroy, P. J. (2002). Transgender issues in counselor preparation. *Counselor Education and Supervision, 41,* 233–242.

Carstarphen, M., & Zavoina, S. (Eds.). (1999). *Sexual rhetoric: Media perspectives on sexuality, gender, and identity.* Westport, CT: Greenwood Press.

Clark, C. (1969, Spring). Television and social controls: Some observations on the portrayals of ethnic minorities. *Television Quarterly,* 18–22.

Collins, D., Eric, R., Metzler, D., Panzanaro, J., & Williams, M. (Producers). (2006, August 1). *Queer eye for the straight guy* [Television broadcast]. New York, NY: Bravo.

Coogan, K. (2006). Fleshy specificity: (Re)considering transsexual subjects in lesbian communities. *Journal of Lesbian Studies, 10*(1/2), 17–41.

De Lauretis, T. (1989). *Technologies of gender: Essays on theory, film, and fiction.* Basingstoke and London, England: Macmillan.

Edwards, M. (2010). Transconversations: New media and community. In C. Pullen & M. Cooper (Eds.), *LGBT identity and online new media* (pp. 159–172). London, England: Routledge Press.

Eonline. ETonline. (2007, September 26). Retrieved from http://www.etonline.com/news/2007/09/54395/

Farr, D. (2010). A very personal world: Advertisement and the identity of transpersons on craigslist. In C. Pullen & M. Cooper (Eds.), *LGBT identity and online new media* (pp. 87–99). London, England: Routledge Press.

Feder, S., & Hollar, J. (2006). *BoyI am* [Film].

Feinberg, L. (1993). *Stone butch blues.* Ithaca, NY: Firebrand Books.

Feinberg, L. (2004, January 12). Reading my author afterward. *WBAI.org.* Retrieved from http://wbai.org/index.php?option=com content&task=view& id=741&Itemid=127

Gallus, M. (Director). (2007). *Girl inside* [Motion picture]. United States: Women Make Movies.

Gauthier, D. K., & Chaudoir, N. K. (2004). Tranny boyz: Cyber community supports in negotiating sex and gender mobility among female to male transsexuals. *Deviant Behavior, 25,* 375–398.

Gill, R. (2007). *Gender and the media.* Cambridge, England: Polity.

Gray, M. L. (2010). From websites to Wal-Mart: Youth, identity work, and the queering of boundary publics in small town USA. In C. Pullen & M. Cooper (Eds.), *LGBT identity and online new media* (pp. 288–298). London, England: Routledge Press.

Hansbury, G. (2005). The middle men: An introduction to the transmasculine identities. *Studies in Gender and Sexuality, 6,* 241–264.

Harrison, D. (2010). No body there: Notes on the queer migration to cyberspace. *The Journal of Popular Culture, 43*(2), 286–310.

Hartley, J. (1999). *Uses of television.* New York, NY: Routledge.

Hichon, J., & Reaves, S. (1999). Media mirage: The thin ideal as digital manipulation. In M. Carsarphen & S. Zavoina (Eds.), *Sexual rhetoric* (pp. 65–76). Westport, CT: Greenwood Press.

Hill, R. J. (2004, Summer). Activism as practice. *New Direction for Adult and Continuing Education, 102,* 85–96.

Hudson's FTM Resource Guide. (2004). Retrieved from http://www.ftmguide.org/

Jordan, N. (Writer/Director). (1992). *The Crying Game* [Motion picture]. United States: Miramax Films.

Kimball, M. M. (1986). Television and sex-role attitudes. In T. M. Williams (Ed.), *The impact of television: A natural experiment in three communities* (pp. 265–301). New York, NY: Academic Press.

Lebow, Alisa. (Writer/Director). (1994). *Outlaw* [Documentary]. United States: Women Make Movies.

Leifer, A. D., Gordon, N. J., & Graves, S. B. (1974). Children's television: More than mere entertainment. *Harvard Educational Review, 44*(2), 213–245.

Lombardi, M., Wilchins, R., Priesing, D., & Malouf, D. (2001). Gender violence: Transgender experiences with violence and discrimination. *Journal of Homosexuality, 42*(1), 89–101.

McCarthy, M. (1992). The thin ideal, depression and eating disorders in women. *Behavioral Research Therapy, 28,* 205–215.

MacDonald, K. (Writer/Director) (2006). *Black and white* [Documentary]. United Kingdom: Women Make Movies.

McGee, M. (2005). *Self-help Inc.: Makeover culture in American life.* Oxford, England: Oxford University Press.

Nevins, S. (Executive Producer), & Davis, K. (Director). (2001). *Southern Comfort* [Motion picture]. United States: Home Box Office (HBO).

Nigel, is that your daughter/son? (2010). *Facebook.* Retrieved November 17, 2010, from www.facebook.com

Padva, G. (2007). Media and popular culture representations of LGBT bullying. *Journal of Gay & Lesbian Social Services, 19*(3–4), 105–118.

Roberts, G. (2007, September 25). Transsexual actress joins mainstream American drama. *Pink News.* Retrieved from http://www.pinknews.co.uk/news/ articles/2005-5553.html/

Roen, K. (2002). Either/or and both/neither: Discursive tensions in transgender politics. *Signs, 27,* 501–522.

Ross, K. (2010). *Gendered media: Women, men and identity politics.* Lanham, MD: Rowman and Littlefield.

Rosskam, J. (Writer/Director). (2005). *Transparent* [Documentary]. San Francisco, CA: Frameline.

Saltzburg, N. (2010). Developing a model of transmasculine identity. (Unpublished doctoral dissertation). University of Miami, Coral Gables, FL.

Sawyer, T. (2003). Hail the Prada-worshipping queer. *Alternet.* Retrieved from www.alternet.org

Shernoff, M. (2000). Cyber counseling for queer clients and clinicians. *Journal of Gay & Lesbian Social Services, 11*(4), 105–113.

Stasi, L. (2003, August 26). Flame out! Linda isn't happy with how gay TV turned out.

New York Post. Retrieved August 13, 2010, from nypost.com

Stice, E. M., & Shaw, He. E. (1994). Adverse effects of the media portrayed thin-ideal on women and linkages to bulimic symptomatology. *Journal of Social and Clinical Psychology, 13*(3), 288–308.

Tan, A. S. (1977). TV beauty ads and role expectations of adolescent female viewers. *Journalism Quarterly, 56,* 283–288.

TransBucket. (2010). Retrieved from http://www.transbucket.com

Transgendered People on Television. (2008, September 11). *VHI.* Retrieved from http://www.vh1.com/video/misc/275123/transgendered-people-on-tv.jhtml

Veneruso, T. (2001). Interview with Max from Southern Comfort. *New Wave Films.* Retrieved from http://www.nextwavefilms.com/ulbp/max.html

Ward, L. M. & Harrison, K. (2005). The impact of media use on girls' beliefs about gender roles, their bodies, and sexual relationships: A research synthesis. In E. Cole & J. Henderson Daniel (Eds.), *Featuring females: Feminist analysis of media* (pp. 3–23). Washington, DC: American Psychological Association.

Zizek, S. (1989). *The sublime object of ideology.* London, England: Verso.

Zizek, S. (1997). *The plague of fantasies.* London, England: Verso Press.

16

The "Rich Bitch"

Class and Gender on the
Real Housewives of New York City

Michael J. Lee and Leigh Moscowitz

As the US economy collapsed in 2008 and 2009, a record number of viewers tuned in to Bravo each week to gawk at the consumptive, ostentatious lives of six Manhattan socialites. Bravo perfected its formula for "recession-proof television" in its reality docudrama series, the *Real Housewives of New York City* (*RHW-NYC*), which puts the lives of Alex, Jill, Bethenny, Ramona, LuAnn, and Kelly on display as objects of fascination, envy, and scorn (Guthrie 2009, p. 3). Between the characters' summer homes in the Hamptons, banter about the size of strangers' "p.p.'s" (private planes), $30,000-per-year pre-schools with full-time nutritionists on staff, and week-long jaunts to St. Bart's, *RHW-NYC* is not focused on how the "fortunate few make their fortunes but on how they spend them" (Stanley 2008, p. E1). As *Broadcasting & Cable* magazine reported, "The poster girls for conspicuous consumption are scoring record ratings while Americans are losing their jobs in record numbers" (Guthrie 2009, p. 4).

The *Real Housewives* franchise, which includes five additional shows set in Orange County, Atlanta, New Jersey, Washington DC, and Beverly Hills, is one of the most popular of a bevy of reality television programs about conspicuous consumption. *RHW-NYC* is, at its core, a show about rich women and, as such, resembles television forerunners about lives lived in luxury's lap such as MTV's *Cribs* or *Lifestyles of the Rich and Famous*. However, as we argue in this essay, *RHW-NYC* complicates the scholarly conversation about the role of class on television (Gans 1995; Grindstaff 2002; Kendall 2005). Rather than valorizing the rich and demonizing the poor like its predecessors, *RHW-NYC* takes aim at the consumptive lives of its arriviste heroines.

From Michael J. Lee and Leigh Moscowitz (2012), "The 'Rich Bitch,'" *Feminist Media Studies*. Vol. 12, No. 4, 1–19. Reprinted by permission of the publisher (Taylor & Francis Ltd., www .tandf.co.uk/journals).

Nevertheless, the populist scorn the show provokes is not gender-neutral; its sights are set on the rich, to be sure, but only rich women, especially those who transgress the traditional gender roles of supportive friend, nurturing mother, doting wife, and ceaseless caretaker. According to the logic of *RHW-NYC*, rich women, not rich men, spend frivolously, project false appearances, backstab, gossip, and leave their children's care to paid staff. Indeed, the failure of a different reality series about status-obsessed men reveals that when it comes to casting wealthy, out-of-touch villains, female socialites are hard to beat. Fox Reality channel's short-lived *Househusbands of Hollywood* could not leave its viewers aghast like the housewives could. Describing the "chasm in watchability" between the househusbands and housewives series, one entertainment writer quipped, "I found myself wondering what their wives were doing" (Alston 2009, p. 75).

In this essay, we employ the concept of irony to analyze how *RHW-NYC* creates rich women as objects of cultural derision, well-heeled jesters in a populist court. *RHW-NYC* primes its savvy, upscale audience to judge the extravagance of female scapegoats harshly in tough economic times. In failed quests to perform the public role of esteemed aristocrats, these women are shown as neglecting their private duties as mothers. In ironic scenes dubbed "winks" by the show's producers, *RHW-NYC* primes cultural expectations about class and gender behaviors only to show a "housewife" failing to measure up to the standard on both accounts. Their class and gender flops are inter-related; the lure of class status produces inconsiderate mothers. In the world of *RHW-NYC*, money destroys, rather than enables, self-awareness, friendships, and, most importantly, competent mothering. Ultimately, *RHW-NYC* uses ironic "winks" to produce a provocative, recession-era, post-feminist drama about rich women too crass to be classy, too superficial to be nurturing, and too

self-obsessed to be caring. These are self-professed "working mothers" who work little and mother even less.

Building on feminist media scholarship about portrayals of class and gender, this project offers the opportunity to examine the ways in which normative conceptions of class and gender cohere to produce an archetypal, trans-historical villain typified by the mythology around historical figures like Marie Antoinette, fictional television characters like *Dynasty*'s Alexis Carrington, and cinematic villains like Cruella Deville, a performance we term the "rich bitch." Sacrificing motherhood, empathy, and altruism, the rich bitch, a bourgeois feminine character done up as a cartoonish trope, pursues selfish material gains single-mindedly. Always gendered (female), always classed (leisure), and almost always racialized (white), she functions at a cultural crossroads where class antagonisms can be articulated and traditional gender roles can be reasserted. The figure of the rich bitch fuels class-based contempt by reinforcing anti-feminist tropes. . . .

Ironic Portrayal and "The Bravo Wink"

RHW-NYC depicts the lives of five New York City "real housewives" whose day-to-day lives are comprised of gala events, high-profile charity auctions, see-and-be-seen functions, and, to a far lesser extent, motherhood and familial bonds. Each program is divided into vignettes that accentuate the cultural type each housewife occupies. Ramona Singer, to provide one example, the entrepreneur and self-described "MILF," frequently organizes "girls-only" events such as group Botox trips. Jill Zarin, the established "Jewess" socialite whose husband oversees a family-owned fabric company, obsesses about the remodeling of her posh Manhattan apartment. Bethenny Frankel, the youngest of the housewives and now subject of her own spin-off reality series, is tagged the "runaway bride" whose celebrity chef career complicates her personal relationships with men. LuAnn de Lesseps, a former model and countess by marriage, is cast as the stereotypical, if unconvincing, "classy" socialite: wealthy, snooty, and judgmental. Alex McCord, a graphic designer whose marriage to an eccentric hotelier is a topic of ridicule among the housewives, is marked as a social climber on the outside of the elite circle of the fabulously wealthy. Kelly Bensimon, the author, model, equestrian, and, in her words, Manhattan "tastemaker," was a second-season addition to *RHW-NYC*.

These wealthy characters violate, both consistently and flagrantly, the performative conventions of wealth and femininity. Disrupting long-held linkages between wealth and manners, economic class and behavioral class, these wealthy characters are rough and rude even though their cultural type suggests formality and urbanity. We use the concept of irony both to make sense of how *RHW-NYC* is a vivid postfeminist narrative in which wealthy stars contravene class and gender norms out of indifference or ignorance.

. . . What generally signifies an ironic move is the violation of an audience assumption that is deeply engrained or has been recently primed (Booth 1974; Burke 1969). . . . Irony is a code that invites participation in the completion of a communicative act. Sarcastic irony is an illustrative example. When a friend declares *Desperate Housewives* to be "the greatest show in television history," auditors are prodded to discern whether the speaker's hyperbolic formulation, peculiar over-emphasis of "greatest show," or sly smirk are evidence that the intended meaning was the exact opposite of the statement's literal meaning. . . . Given its utility in shaming, ridiculing, inducing laughter, and exposing hypocrisy, some cultural critics have even heralded irony's potential in "creating the conditions of possibility for a genuine

democratic environment to develop" (Tabako 2007, p. 27; Rorty 1989).

Irony is central to the production, composition, and narrative of *RHW-NYC*. Even the show's basic premise, showing audiences the lives of "real housewives," is itself a layered irony. These so-called "real housewives" live lives most would find surreal, and none are actual housewives. Two of the six women, moreover, are not even married. Beyond these fundamental ironies, the show depicts several other, but no less galling, ironies: a group of friends who are not actually friends, rich people with no class, and wealthy who profess, but do not conduct, hard work.

Ironic framing is, in fact, the Bravo producers' chief métier. Andy Cohen, Bravo executive and host of the Real Housewives reunion specials, explains that the show is intentionally coded to highlight hypocrisy: "We do something with the editing that is called the Bravo wink. We wink at the audience when someone says 'I'm the healthiest person in the world' and then you see them ashing their cigarette. We're kind of letting the audience in on the fun" (Cohen 2009). This ironic viewing is only possible because the show is framed for Bravo viewers, television's most educated and upscale audience that considers itself "'hip to television'" (Dominus 2008).

Such ironic scenes are, nevertheless, not unique to Bravo. Some reality television shows, as Dubrofsky notes, gain dramatic purchase in climactic scenes in which female contestants, previously portrayed as well-mannered contenders, are overcome by uncontrollable emotions and display them "in a way that is unexpected and breaks social norms" (2009, p. 356). Such scenes are structured as acts of unmasking in which a hidden truth about a person is revealed in a surprising, even shocking, way. Even without the emotional spasm, "wink" scenes are of a similar species in the sense that they are designed to expose and reduce female characters and engage the viewing audience in the process. As a housewife brags about being a doting mother or a hard worker, *RHW-NYC* cuts to images of ignored children and a luxuriating mother. These are scoff-inducing scenes in which a housewife says something so patently false, so comically contradicted by several shows' worth of evidence, that the housewife becomes ridiculous and other-worldly, someone who must have descended from another planet ill-equipped to manage life on this one.

Class Transgressions

Economic class, of course, is definable in strictly economic terms: as personal income, as familial wealth, as net worth, or, in Marxist terms, as the relationship of an individual to the mode of production (Kendall 2005, pp. 12–13). Class, nevertheless, is also definable as a cultural construct tethered to a range of behavioral expectations. As Laura Grindstaff clarifies, "Class, especially in the context of television, is also a performance, a social script involving, among other things, language use, mannerisms, and dress" (2002, p. 31). Although the recent scholarly focus on class as a performance is often indebted to contemporary theorists, foundational thinkers about class were also sensitive to issues of culture and identity. Writing in 1899, Thorstein Veblen notes how the "consumption" of "excellent goods" signified wealth whereas a lack, in either quantity or quality, of such goods was viewed as a "mark of inferiority or demerit" (1967, p. 74). The enactment of personal taste, nevertheless, would collapse minus the delicate, polished manners useful in projecting an "apparently natural" image of effortless class (Lane 2000, p. 52). What Veblen calls "manners and breeding," decorousness and etiquette befitting social hierarchies, were vital when exhibiting a "reputable degree of leisure" (1967, p. 46).

Extending Veblen's focus on the repertoire of upper-class signifiers, Pierre Bourdieu explores how the performance of upper class-ness is more a symphony than a solo; it requires the integration of seemingly disparate elements into a fluent whole. Typical conversational "banalities" about art or literature, for example, are "inseparable from the steady tone, the slow, casual diction, the distant or self-assured smile, the measured gesture, the well-tailored suit and the bourgeois salon of the person who pronounces them" (Bourdieu 1984, p. 174). These status markers are, in Bourdieu's terms, cultural capital, the means of reifying class hierarchy. As he explains, the "manner" in which "symbolic goods" are employed is an "ideal weapon in strategies of distinction, that is, as Proust put it, 'the infinitely varied art of marking distances'" (Bourdieu 1984, p. 66).

Veblen was an early chronicler of the process by which the cultural meaning of wealth was disciplined in the late nineteenth century. Gentility and refinement, two markers of behavioral class, became strongly correlated with the upwardly mobile economic classes during the period (Veblen 1967, pp. 48–49). The expectation that the wealthy would be well-mannered and personally reserved was popularized in etiquette manuals, finishing schools, and broader social and educational trends in the nineteenth century (Grindstaff 2002, p. 268). Such socialization was not uniform across social stratas, however; the expectation of etiquette "was especially true for upper-class white women, whose participation in public life was precarious, and for whom the stakes of transgression were high" (Grindstaff 2002, p. 268).

Whereas the management and suppression of public emotion has been construed as a middle and upper-class phenomenon, the embodiment of emotion has been construed as a working and lower-class phenomenon; this perception has been persistently reinforced by myriad talk shows and reality television programs (Grindstaff 2002, p. 246). It is un-ironic to see the impoverished inhabitants of a trailer park come to blows on a nationally tele-vised daytime talk show because public displays of physicality and emotionality are associated with poverty. The link between "class and emotional expressive-ness" rests on the faulty assumption that the working poor are innately predisposed toward public paroxysms and that the rich are naturally geared toward private, man-nered dispute resolutions (Grindstaff 2002, p. 143). By this cultural logic, it would be highly ironic for hedge fund managers to throw chairs at one another on the same daytime program. Rich people, quite sim-ply, do not publicize their hysterics because they do not profit from social scorn; they do not televise their outbursts because they do not need the money. It is one thing for even the newly moneyed to commit a social indelicacy that would attract the judging eyes of an elite strata within the upper class and quite another to participate in a shout-ing match at a charity dinner (Season Two, Episode Four). The latter behavior might be judged as boorish across classes. . . .

Wealth and Social Class

Nearly every aspect of the characters' eco-nomic lives is framed ironically in ways that lampoon a character as bumbling, mindless, or disgraceful. Typically, an *RHW-NYC* episode is edited to couple audio of a character's platitudinous pontifications about "class" or "grace" with video of the character's tactlessness. The characters defy nearly every image of the poised, high-society sophisticate com-mitted to social graces and well-mannered to a fault. . . .

LuAnn is coded as the prototypically pre-tentious socialite. When this code is coupled with the show's ironic frame, LuAnn is exposed before viewers as a judgmental hypocrite. *RHW-NYC* becomes a prosecu-torial vehicle. Much like the cigarette-ashing health nut described by the show's producer, audiences are presented video

evidence of LuAnn's professed values followed by images of her contradictory behavior. The producers pursue this ironic line through much of the second season as LuAnn parlays her new, Bravo-driven celebrity status into a book deal, *Class With the Countess*. The dramatic irony, demonstrated unsubtly in "wink" scenes, is that the joke is on LuAnn. With Bravo's assemblage of audacious quotations about class and footage of her behavioral record, viewers can see her missteps, point out her hypocrisies, and evaluate her class perfor-mance. As Bethenny quips about LuAnn's repeated gaffes, "Not very countess-like. It's dis-countess" (Season Two, Episode Nine). Ultimately, LuAnn has performed her class incorrectly.

Like LuAnn, the show paints the other housewives as obsessed by questions of personal authenticity. Each housewife frets over whether she projects a "real," "genu-ine," "ladylike," "down-to-earth," and, of course, "classy" image. Of equal impor-tance, *RHW-NYC* depicts these women as militant enforcers and harsh critics of the ways in which their acquaintances live up to these standards of authenticity as well. The women become the class police who misunderstand the concept they attempt to enforce. Ramona, for example, polices other characters' class performances while violating her own standards. After Jill refuses her second-row seat at a fashion event—"This is bullshit," Jill exclaims—Ramona stares intently into the camera and snidely isolates a point of difference between them: "I'm not into that kind of status. I could care less who sits where. It was not a normal reaction, or ladylike, or classy, or elegant, more importantly" (Season One, Episode Four). Ramona states that she and Bethenny are united as friends because each is "anti-hypocrisy" (Season Two, Episode Five). Ramona dismisses Alex and Simon for similar reasons: "They aren't real, and I don't have time for people who aren't real." (Season Two, Episode Three). Bravo frames these class ironies as perpetrated by women with no shame, women whose money obstructs self-examination. The characters are highly conscious of the high-ideal of the poised socialite yet framed as doubly incapable of attaining the ideal or of realizing the disparity.

Wealth and Social Life

A second irony of class performances on *RHW-NYC* is that money precludes a rewarding social life. *RHW-NYC* dramatizes the housewives' relational difficulties by implying that wealth and anomie among women are linked. To be sure, several principal characters on the show espouse basic feminist bromides. All of the housewives profess to be strong, independent women. All of the housewives have successful careers. "In New York, women work. Women have to work," Jill instructs (Season Two, Episode Nine). All of the women profess a desire to bond with other women and maintain an active social life. The original cast members later berate the newcomer, Kelly, for fixating on men. "You are not a girl's girl," Bethenny yells. "I am a girl's girl," Kelly protests (Season Two, Reunion One). In the same vein, all are suspicious, in some senses more than others, of traditional gender roles with regards to household duties like cooking, cleaning, and child-rearing. Viewers even witness Ramona, in several scenes, use painful examples from her childhood to teach her daughter feminist lessons. Ramona urges her daughter to avoid relying on men, exhorting her "to make her own money" to achieve "the greatest self-worth" and "independence as a woman" (Season One, Episode Six).

The cast members speak a language of women's empowerment; nevertheless, in their relationships with other women, their consumerist lifestyles, and their obsession with personal appearance, the characters become post-feminist cautionary tales rather than feminists. Put differently, the characters dress consumerist desires in a feminist idiom. . . . The housewives figure plastic surgery, losing weight, looking youthful, going out, and dressing provocatively as the liberation of their essential womanhood. Ramona, for instance, sees plastic surgery as sisterly bonding. She says to her friends in a plastic surgeon's office, "I believe women should share . . . and I have this friend who is a doctor who has some new machines to make us look beautiful." "To good girlfriends and a great doctor," she toasts in a scene typifying the Bravo "wink." Same-sex closeness between women is achieved by indulging their common desire to look "eighteen forever" (Season One, Episode Eight).

Conflict is not a prelude to greater interpersonal connectedness; it is the basis of their relationships. In many cases, the housewives' competitive tensions bubble over into televised catfights, produced and edited for the delight of audiences. When Ramona and LuAnn offer Bethenny competing dating advice at a cancer benefit, Ramona dismisses LuAnn's comments as nonsense: "What do you know? You got married very young. You married a man twice your age" (Season Two, Episode Four). Similarly, a spat between Kelly and Bethenny at an arthritis event reveals their animosity to be mutual and visceral. Kelly establishes social hierarchy: "We're not the same." "This is you," she says holding her left hand low, and "this is me," she concludes raising her other hand above her head (Season Two, Episode Four). When asked about the incident at the reunion show, Bethenny is direct; Kelly is a "piece of shit" (Season Two, Reunion Two).

On the surface, *RHW-NYC* shares much with *Sex and the City*, another show that addressed issues of class, sex, and inter-personal relationships by conjuring consumerist and post-feminist narratives about a group of affluent white women in Manhattan (Arthurs 2003; Brasfield 2006; Gerhard 2005). Several of the New York housewives make sense of their social lives in terms of iconic *Sex and the City* images (Season Two, Episodes 11 and

12). Nevertheless, *RHW-NYC* can be productively read as the anti–*Sex and the City*. The *Sex and the City* characters live fabulously in Manhattan; they maintain strong inter-personal bonds and buy Jimmy Choo shoes. They can "have it all," and even though they may fight, they can have each other too. In *RHW-NYC*'s ironic portrayal of class, the housewives' drive for material possessions and social status destroys the sisterhood; the cattiness overwhelms the camaraderie. In *Sex and the City*, class facilitates social fulfillment. In *RHW-NYC*, women become so consumed by class that their inter-personal connections suffer. . . .

Bad Mommies in Manhattan

These real housewives may not be housewives, but four of the five are mothers, and the fifth regrets not having children. (The fifth housewife, Bethenny, became a mother after these shows aired.) One central dynamic in the *Real Housewives* is the collision of the temptations of the housewives' glamorous lives with their motherly obligations. The housewives are shown consistently choosing socializing over mothering and self-maintenance over nurturing, inviting a harsh criticism of mothering which only serves to justify misogynistic gender divisions that presume that "women remain the best primary caretakers of children" (Douglas & Michaels 2004, p. 4). *RHW-NYC* uses gender stereotypes to re-signify the upper class and uses catty and conspicuously consumptive behaviors to reinscribe the notion that mommy should be at home with the kids.

Producers direct much of the audience's attention toward instances of failed mothering, as opposed to failed parenting, participating in a larger overall trend of what Ruth Feldstein (2000) refers to as "mother-blaming." Susan Douglas and Meredith Michaels (2004) have written extensively about the ways in which media culture construct our common-sense notions of how mothers ought to behave, celebrating the "best" mothers and punishing the "worst" mothers. Recent mediated "mommy wars" between falsely polarized "working moms" and "stay at home moms" have turned motherhood into the latest "competitive sport" (Douglas & Michaels 2004, p. 11). As images of intensive mothering drown out notions of egalitarian parenting, "ridiculous, honey-hued ideals of perfect motherhood" dominate popular culture (Douglas & Michaels 2004, p. 2).

In direct violation of these standards of "new momism," viewers of *RHW-NYC* are invited to critique these women as mothers who have chosen their superficial lives over the development of their children (Vavrus 2007). Consistent with the show's cultivation of irony, the mothers' behavior, in some cases, becomes so egregious that the mother-daughter relationship is upended; the mother is childish and the child is authoritative. In a role reversal exemplifying the show's ironic frame, Ramona's twelve-year-old daughter, Avery, adopts the motherly role and scolds her mother about her revealing outfits, her lewd language, and her "embarrassing" behavior. Avery, who is asked in interview segments to critique her mother's behavior, repeatedly refers to her mother's hyper-sexualized dress and conduct as "ewww," "disgusting," "gross," and "unlady like." After witnessing her mother start a poolside bikini-wrestling match, Avery screams at Ramona: "Oh my god mom, don't! You're such an evil woman," before storming off. Ramona laughs away her daughter's concerns in sexual terms: "We're just a bunch of MILFs" (Season One, Episode Two).

When mothering is prominently featured, producers employ the "Bravo wink" to construct these real mothers as ineffective, neglectful, selfish, superficial, and juvenile. The housewives' relationships with their children are depicted as empty, built on consumptive behaviors and unsolicited, shocking, and even dangerous advice. Excess means are blamed tacitly for the shortage of mothering; a life brimming with extravagance and temptation provides the "pull" that draws mothers outside the home, away from their rightful duties of child-rearing. . . .

Neglecting Home Life for Social Life

The housewives' home lives and social lives are framed as forced choices, rearticulating post-feminist tensions in leisure-class terms. In a standard scene, a housewife dresses for a night out at a charity events or drinks with friends, and the children are left behind, sullen and abandoned. The scene depicts the glitzy housewife leaving the house and, as a melodramatic score plays, a close-up shot of a sad child fills the screen. The forced choice these women face is not between parenting and work (production), but between mothering and consumptive socializing (consumption): "me-time." What makes their choices even more transgressive of social expectations of mothers is that the "work" they perform at the perceived expense of competent mothering is not really work, but pretend. The housewives are cast as worse than working moms because they choose social obligations and maintaining their external beauty over motherhood, all under the guise of "hard work."

This trope is exemplified by LuAnn, who is often shown siding with sociality over her two children. Noel, her ten-year-old son, at one point begs to come out with his mother and she lies and explains that "children don't go to this restaurant" (Season One, Episode Seven). In the following scene, viewers witness what LuAnn "deserted" her children for: a "girls night out" of drinking, clubbing, and "window shopping" for dildos at a sex shop with her twenty-three-year-old niece, violating not only her responsibilities as mother and nurturer, but normative boundaries assigned by her age and social status. LuAnn arrives at

the "bohemian" bar clearly exasperated, greets her niece who is half her age, and directs the bartender who is pouring her cocktail to "make it on the stronger side." To her niece, Nicole, she exclaims, "Yippee! You don't know how happy I am to get out of the house because it has been so grueling" (Season One, Episode Seven). Employing the "wink," producers juxtapose these scenes that mount evidence of absentee mothering with LuAnn's admission to viewers that it "feels great to get out" of the house when her husband is out of town and "forget about being a mom." Rather than identify with and celebrate LuAnn's "escape" from her motherly duties, viewers are primed to jeer at her pathetic attempt to reclaim her youth as she buys gaudy trinkets, giggles girlishly at dildos in a sex shop window, and pretends to enjoy the band playing at the "bohemian" dive bar. . . . Her desperation to drink from the fountain of youth is not only rendered a failure but an unworthy diversion from her legitimate role of familial caretaker.

Outsourcing Motherhood

Highlighting another irony of "working motherhood" on the *Real Housewives* series, the housewives' children are not nurtured by their mothers but by an expensive array of *au pairs*, live-in nannies, wellness centers, and high-end pre-schools. Motherhood is outsourced. LuAnn's children are "raised" by their second mother, a Pilipino housekeeper named Rosie. In one telling scene, LuAnn is busily preening for an evening out with a girlfriend and ordering Rosie what to make for the kids' dinner. Noel, clearly upset, accuses his mother of neglect: "All my friends, their parents are home every single night. Are you going to be back early?" In a separate interview, LuAnn justifies to viewers: "They [the children] always try to pull the guilt trip on me. I, of course, feel for him, but I don't let it override me and what I have to do in my own social life." It is up to Rosie to counsel Noel: "When he asks 'When are my parents going to be back?' I just say 'They love you very much,' and he says, 'I love you, Rosie'" (Season One, Episode Five). Rosie directly addresses LuAnn's absenteeism and the consequences of outsourcing motherhood in a personal interview. Rosie says to viewers, "I want them [LuAnn and the Count] to spend more quality time with the kids. I don't want the children growing up saying, 'You weren't there.'"

In this family, viewers are repeatedly reassured that Rosie plays the role of the substitute mother. Rosie, LuAnn explains, "is like mom when I'm gone." While LuAnn socializes, she employs quality paid labor to provide the nurturing, care, and love the children are otherwise missing from their relationship with their parents. Rosie explains, "I raise them how I raise my kids. They treat me like a second mother. I am always there for them whenever to give them whatever they need." In contrast to negative working class depictions on television, viewers are invited to empathize with Rosie's plight, to "side" with her and see her as the true motherfigure in the household. Rosie does the heavy-lifting in the household, not only in terms of the care and upkeep of the home, but also in the rearing and nurturing of the children.

As LuAnn farms out the domestic work of parenting and housework to Rosie, Jill attempts to solve problems facing her thirteen-year-old daughter Ally by sending her to a posh "detox" center in Martha's Vineyard. Through careful editing, it becomes evident that "detox" is code for "weight loss," despite Jill's failed attempts to mask the trip as being primarily about curing Ally's "arthritis." The center is run by the author of *How to Lose 21 Pounds in 21 Days*, and video footage of her time there makes it clear the program focuses on purge dieting made up entirely of liquid meals. Jill is thrilled when Ally returns a week later eleven pounds thinner, drastic weight loss

for a young teen. In a scene intended to make audiences squirm uncomfortably, Jill pokes at her daughter's mid-section while she screams in delight at the prospect of weight loss, "Oh my god! Where'd my daughter go?" (Season One, Episode Three).

Classing Children

The housewives' failures as mothers are not limited to absenteeism or substituting shoe shopping for emotional intimacy. Alex's failures, in particular, stem from her attempts to manufacture worldly, learned adults out of young children. Her class anxieties have infiltrated her parenting style, and frequent scenes of Johan and Francois running, screaming, and defiant attest to her limitations as a mother.

. . . As involved, hyper-attentive parents, one narrative arch involves Alex and Simon's often barely concealed attempts to break into the right social circle, and the importance of their children in that quest. They named them pretentiously (Johan and Francois); they employ a French *au pair*; they try to cajole the children to order food in French at fancy restaurants; they tour fifteen Manhattan preschools.

Alex, of all the characters, hews most closely to popular media representations of "new momism," a logic that naturalizes "intensive mothering" (Douglas & Michaels 2004). But in this social climate, this kind of doting only serves to destroy effective parenting practices. These children are spoiled, and even the best, most well-intentioned attempts to set boundaries, instill work ethic, and inspire a fulfilled life inevitably fail. Johan and Francois are shown violating the standards of good behavior expected from children of such a wealthy family. At the formal dinner party that concludes Season One, Alex and Simon sit idly as the children scream incessantly and poke guests' food, ruining a thirty-dollar hamburger in one instance.

The camera focuses intently on the other housewives as they exchange judgmental glances, eye rolls, and catty commentary. Ramona scolds: "My daughter would never be able to do that . . . I've never seen that before in my life." This dinner party footage is replayed repeatedly, slowed down for dramatic effect, and colored in sepia tone to place it in the past. It serves as ammunition for another powerful "Bravo wink" whenever the Van Kempens espouse their views on effective parenting, especially in Season Two when they reveal they are writing a book of their "collection of experiences" they gleaned from raising their children. The Van Kempens are subjected to the ridicule of their show-mates, as producers juxtapose the footage of the dinner party as LuAnn makes a mockery of their book: "The way the Van Kempen children behave, I wouldn't say they would be the authority on writing a book about childhood behavior." Just as the housewives police one another's class performances, they also criticize each other's mothering skills; they fail to adhere to the standards they preach in both instances. Not only are viewers invited to level harsh criticisms against the characters' failed attempts at mothering. Often these criticisms are channeled through the characters themselves, who act out their own version of the "mommy wars" for the delight of TV audiences.

Conclusion: The Downside of the Populist Promise

The ironies of the housewives' performances of class and gender alienate viewers from identifying with the six women of *RHW-NYC* on two levels. First, the characters, through some outlandish display of wealth or an ill-considered comment about another character's looks, spouse, or parenting, mark themselves as poorly behaved. In these instances, any judgment viewers make about the characters' excessive purchases

or materialistic values draws upon the audience's latent senses of class consciousness and social decorum. Such judgments are primed by displays of the characters' deviant behaviors. Second, these primed judgments are reinforced by standards the characters set for themselves. That is, the show uses outlandish behavior to mark these characters' difference, and deviance, from an audience's most basic aspirations of tactful consumption and social grace, but it also highlights through "winks" their failure to live up to their own criteria. By juxtaposing the characters' stated behavioral ideals with their numerous televised transgressions, *RHW-NYC* compounds many viewers' latent judgments with an explicit invitation to label these women as hypocrites. In the end, these women are a far cry from hegemonic conceptions of motherhood perpetuated by popular media forms. The show is entertaining precisely because they fail to meet these standards. As one reality producer said, "*Housewives* isn't as much about them being rich as it is about them being spoiled, senseless and self-obsessed. No matter what the economy is, people are always going to tune in that" (Guthrie 2009, p. 4).

The show, of course, is not a cultural phenomenon solely because it broadcasts rich bitch villains; that is only part of its force. Fans of *RHW-NYC* are empowered as judges and invited to conclude that those with the most deserve the least. Many viewers delight in witnessing "the women on the show program bicker nakedly, flaunting diamonds—and talons— with equal hauteur" (La Ferla 2009, p. 2). On *RHW-NYC*, as with other reality TV formats, viewer-judges are supplied evidence of repeated violations of class performances: vulgar behavior, conspicuous consumption, poor relationships, and bad mothering. The host of the season-ending reunion episodes showcases this audience empowerment by reading viewers' condemnatory emails and blog posts on air. For instance, regarding Jill's consumptive lifestyle, the host says, "We got thousands of viewer emails, many of them very pointed," before asking, "Do you feel any responsibility for the [economic] crash?" (Season Two, Reunion One). Another email read during the reunion show illustrates how the producers feature emails that are pointed and personal. One viewer tells Kelly, "You need to seek professional help." Many of these emails feature an accusation of hypocrisy by an angered viewer. One viewer, for example, emailed Kelly: "If you're so private, why would you do a reality show?" (Season Two, Reunion Two).

On these season-finales-as-trials, the characters have to explain themselves and atone for bad behavior. Such scenes, when coupled with hours of footage of the rich defiling themselves in numerous ways, reflect deep class anguish within the US political culture and express a potentially powerful populist sentiment. The upper-class is not evidence of an economic system that rewards hard labor or elite education. They are neither models for imitation or spectacles for amazement. Reading critical emails that identify the hypocrisy of these rich women is the mass mediation of a leveling of social hierarchy. The rich not only become accessible and accountable for their behavior, they become less than the audience. They are scapegoats for economic crises, figures of scorn and pity, morality tales of lives led wastefully. Their Manhattan social lives, their profligate purchases, the location of their summer homes, and the baroque renovations of their high-rises are motivated by status anxiety. They appear as simple rats unaware of their unnecessary race, rich automatons enslaved by extravagance. . . .

RHW-NYC, to be sure, is not overt, class-based vitriol, but it has an antagonistic undertone. Historically, images of villainous or buffoonish elites have fueled progressive class politics in which the downtrodden, priced-out farmers, and even the forgotten middle class has exposed a fat cat banker or a corrupt robber-baron to highlight gross inequalities in the social conditions produced by industrial capitalism. Whether motivated by Marx, the Christian social gospel, or simple egalitarianism, whether decried as the "super-rich," in Huey Long's words, or the "economic royalists," in Franklin Roosevelt's language, a critique of the rich as too rich has accompanied calls for income redistribution, social safety nets, progressive taxation, workers' rights, and, ultimately, social democracy (Kazin 1995, p. 110).

Considering Bravo's upscale branding to some of the most desirable audience demographics on television, however, the populist promise of *RHW-NYC* may be limited. It is not the downtrodden, laid-off worker who is empowered but a relatively affluent and well-educated audience that is encouraged to see themselves as superior to the extremely wealthy. The show's themes may nourish class antagonisms, but Bravo's audience is not exactly the working-class heroes of Left fables. Bravo dubs its audience "affluencers," a catchy name for its young, chic, stylish, and upward-aspiring demographic, a quarter of whom make over $100,000 a year (Dominus 2008). The show's mockery and prosecution of tremendously wealthy women may also let the merely affluent Bravo audience off the hook. In their role as viewer-judge, they may conclude that some rich people do their class comically wrong and nothing more politically potent than that. As one television programmer explained, "Viewers can enjoy all the vapid consumerism . . . without imagining that they're falling sway to the very forces that make that show catnip for advertisers" (Dominus 2008).

Potentially empowering though this critique may be, its seductiveness also exists at the intersection of populist class ideals and anti-feminist gender tropes. Viewers of *RHW-NYC* are invited to conclude that the rich are undeserving because these women violate traditional gender roles so flagrantly. The housewives are convicted for failing to live up to the June Cleaver image of mom as an omnipotent nurturer. Moreover, parental mistakes on the show are consistently framed as maternal mistakes. When the children act up, the ostensible judgment is that the mother should become a better disciplinarian. In the world of *RHW-NYC*, strong fatherly figures are noticeably absent, but only mothers, not fathers, are persecuted for their absence. This economic morality tale mirrors other vaguely Faust-ish tales in which individuals sell their souls for social status. Money, so the bromide goes, is the root of all evil. In the case of *RHW-NYC*, however, the evil that money engenders is specific to women, specific to the stereotype of the pampered rich wife, and specific to six women transgressing their roles as mothers and caregivers. Although *RHW-NYC* offers the viewing public a wealthy villain to judge, scapegoating women during an unfolding economic crisis smacks of retrograde gender politics.

References

Alston, Joshua. (2009) 'The limp factor', *Newsweek*, 23 & 31 Aug., p. 75.

Arthurs, Jane. (2003) '*Sex and the City* and Consumer Culture: Remediating Postfeminist Drama', *Feminist Media Studies*, vol. 3, no. 1, pp. 83 –99.

Baym, Geoffrey. (2010) *From Cronkite to Colbert: The Evolution of Broadcast News*, Paradigm Publishers, Boulder, CO.

Booth, Wayne A. (1974) *A Rhetoric of Irony*, University of Chicago Press, Chicago.

Bourdieu, Pierre. (1984) *Distinction: A Social Critique of the Judgment of Taste*, trans. Richard Nice, Harvard University Press, Cambridge, MA.

Brasfield, Rebecca. (2006) 'Rereading sex and the city: exposing the hegemonic feminist narrative', *Journal of Popular Film & Television*, vol. 34, no. 3, pp. 130 –139.

Brown, Laura S. (2005) 'Outwit, outlast, out-flirt? the women of reality TV', in *Featuring Females: Feminist Analyses of Media*, eds

Ellen Cole & Jessica H. Daniel, American Psychological Association, Washington, DC.

Burke, Kenneth. (1961) *The Rhetoric of Religion*, University of California Press, Berkeley, CA.

Burke, Kenneth. (1969) *Grammar of Motives*, University of California Press, Berkeley.

Butsch, Richard. (2003) 'Ralph, Fred, Archie, and Homer: Why television keeps re-creating the white male working-class buffoon', in *Gender, Race and Class in Media*: a *Text-Reader*, eds Gail Dines & Jean M. Humez, 2nd edn, Sage Publications, Thousand Oaks, CA, pp. 575–585.

Class Dismissed: How Tv Frames the Working Class. (Videorecording) (2005) Media Education Foundation, Northampton, MA.

Cohen, Andy. (2009) 'Bravo exec on the art of creating "reality"', *National Public Radio*, 19 Aug.

Dominus, Susan. (2008) 'The Affluencer', *The New York Times Magazine*, 2 Nov., pp. MM38–48, [Online] Available at: http://www.nytimes.com/2008/11/02/magazine/02zalaznick-t. html?pagewanted=all .

Douglas, Susan & Michaels, Meredith. (2004) *The Mommy Myth: The Idealization of Motherhood and How It Has Undermined All Women*, Free Press, New York.

Dubrofsky, Rachel E. (2009) 'Fallen women on reality TV: a pornography of emotion', *Feminist Media Studies*, vol. 9, no. 3, pp. 353 –368.

Dubrofsky, Rachel E. & Hardy, Antoine. (2008) 'Performing race in Flavor of Love and the Bachelor', *Critical Studies in Media Communication*, vol. 25, no. 4, pp. 373 – 392.

Fairclough, Kirsty. (2004) 'Women's work? *Wife Swap* and the reality problem', *Feminist Media Studies*, vol. 4, no. 2, pp. 344–360.

Feldstein, Ruth. (2000) *Motherhood in Black and White: Race and Sex in American Liberalism*, 1930–1965, Cornell University Press, Ithaca, NY.

Fernandez, James W. & Huber, Mary T. (2001) 'The anthropology of irony', in *Irony in Action: Anthropology, Practice, and the Moral Imagination*, eds James W. Fernandez & Mary T. Huber, University of Chicago Press, Chicago, pp. 1–40.

Galewski, Elizabeth. (2007) 'The strange case for women's capacity to reason: Judith Sargent Murray's use of irony in 'on the Equality of the Sexes' (1790)', *Quarterly Journal of Speech*, vol. 93, no. 1, pp. 84–108.

Gans, Herbert. (1995) *The War Against the Poor: The Underclass and Antipoverty Policy*, BasicBooks, New York.

Gerhard, Jane. (2005) '*Sex and the city*', *Feminist Media Studies*, vol. 5, no. 1, pp. 37 – 49.

Gies, Lieve. (2008) 'Reality TV and the jurisprudence of Wife Swap', in *Law and the Media: the Future of an Uneasy Relationship,* ed. Lieve Gies, Routledge-Cavendish, New York.

Gill, Rosalind & Arthurs, Jane. (2006) 'Editors' introduction: new femininities?', *Feminist Media Studies*, vol. 6, no. 4, pp. 433–451.

Gill, Rosalind. (2007) 'Postfeminist media culture: elements of a sensibility', *European Journal of Cultural Studies*, vol. 10, no. 2, pp. 147 – 166.

Grindstaff, Laura. (2002) *The Money Shot: Trash, Class, and the Making of TV Talk Shows*, University of Chicago Press, Chicago.

Guthrie, Marisa. (2009) 'VH1 working on reality concept about upscale Aspen ski bunnies', *Broadcasting & Cable,* 23 Feb., pp. 3– 4, [Online] Available at: http://www.broadcastingc able.com/article/174568-VH1_Working_on_Reality_Concept_About_Upscale_Aspen_ Ski_Bunnies.php (6 January 2011).

Heider, Don. (ed.) (2004) *Class and News,* Rowman & Littlefield, Lanham, MD.

Hendershot, Heather. (2009) 'Belabored Reality: Making It Work on *the Simple Life and Project Runway*', in *Reality TV: Remaking Television Culture*, eds Susan Murray & Laurie Ouellette, New York University Press, New York, pp. 243–259.

Hofstadter, Richard. (1996) *The Paranoid Style in American Politics: and other Essays*, Harvard University Press, Boston.

Kazin, Michael. (1995) *The Populist Persuasion: an American History*, Cornell University Press, Ithaca, NY.

Kendall, Diana. (2005) *Framing Class: Media Representations of Wealth and Poverty in America*, Rowman & Littlefield, New York.

La Ferla, Ruth. (2009) 'TV royalty, but no longer a housewife', *the New York Times*, 15 Apr., p. E1.

Lane, Jeremy F. (2000) *Pierre Bourdieu: a Critical Introduction*, Pluto Press, London.

Lauzen, Martha M., Dozier, David M. & Cleveland, Elizabeth. (2006) 'Genre matters: an examination of women working behind the scenes and on-screen portrayals in reality and scripted prime-time programming', *Sex Roles: a Journal of Research*, vol. 55, no. 7–8, pp. 445 –456.

Martin, Christopher. (2004) *Framed: Labor and the Corporate Media*, Cornell University Press, Ithaca, NY.

Mcrobbie, Angela. (2004) 'Post-feminism and popular culture', *Feminist Media Studies*, vol. 4, no. 3, pp. 255–264.

Mills, C. Wright. (1956) *The Power Elite*, Oxford University Press, New York.

Olson, Kathryn M. & Olson, Clark D. (2004) 'Beyond strategy: a reader-centered analysis of irony's dual persuasive uses', *Quarterly Journal of Speech*, vol. 90, no. 1, pp. 24 –52.

Ouellette, Laurie. (2003) 'Inventing the cosmo girl', in *Gender, Race and Class in Media: a Text-Reader*, eds Gail Dines & Jean M. Humez,, 2nd edn, Sage Publications, Thousand Oaks, CA, pp. 116–128.

Ouellette, Laurie & Hay, James. (2008) *Better Living through Reality TV,* Blackwell Publishing, Malden, MA.

Ringrose, Jessica & Walkerdine, Valerie. (2008) 'Regulating the abject: the TV make-over as site of neo-liberal reinvention toward bourgeois femininity', *Feminist Media Studies*, vol. 8, no. 3, pp. 227–246.

Rorty, Richard. (1989) *Contingency, Irony, and Solidarity*, Cambridge University Press, New York.

Skeggs, Beverly. (1997) *Formations of Class and Gender*, Sage, London.

Skeggs, Beverly. (2005) 'The making of class and gender through visualizing moral subject formation', *Sociology*, vol. 39, no. 5, pp. 965 – 982.

Sgroi, Renee M. (2006) '*Joe Millionaire* and women's positions: a question of class', *Feminist Media Studies*, vol. 6, no. 3, pp. 281–294.

Stanley, Alessandra. (2008) 'New Yorkers sure love to spend. Who knew?', *the New York Times*, 15 Mar., p. E1.

Tabako, Tomasz. (2007) 'Irony as a pro-democracy trope: Europe's last comic revolution', *Controversia*, vol. 5, no. 2, pp. 23 – 53.

The Real Housewives of New York City. (television series) (2008–2010) Bravo, USA.

Vavrus, Mary D. (2007) 'Opting out moms in the news', *Feminist Media Studies*, vol. 7, no. 1, pp. 47 –63.

Veblen, Thorstein. (1967) *The Theory of the Leisure Class*, the Viking Press, New York.

Waggoner, Catherine Egley. (2004) '*Disciplining female sexuality in Survivor*', *Feminist Media Studies,* vol. 4, no. 2, pp. 217–220.

Wray, Matt. (2006) *Not Quite White: White Trash and the Boundaries of Whiteness*, Duke University Press, Durham, NC.

17

Big Talkers

Rush Limbaugh, Conservative Talk Radio, and the Defiant Reassertion of White Male Authority

Jackson Katz

Rush Limbaugh and the Rise of Conservative Talk Radio

The rise of militantly antigovernment conservatism in the 1990s was catalyzed in part by White men's continuing loss of economic power and an accompanying loss of familial and cultural authority, especially in the working and middle classes. Not coincidentally, the 1990s was also the decade in which the influence of conservative talk radio increased dramatically. Over the past two decades, Rush Limbaugh and a number of charismatic White male radio talk and cable TV hosts have risen to cultural prominence—and they have done so by selling a brand of authoritarian, bellicose, and at times verbally abusive White masculinity, which for reasons of identity politics and history has touched a nerve with millions of listeners—especially White men.

In the real world of the 21st century, White men's unquestioned dominance in the family and workplace is in the process of a long-term decline. But not when you turn on right-wing AM talk radio or Fox News Channel. People don't generally travel to those precincts to seek out new ideas about the possibilities of democratic governance and citizenship in an increasingly diverse and interconnected world—and they don't get it there. Instead, Limbaugh and his colleagues and imitators speak with an old-school masculine authority that recalls an idealized past, when (White) men were in control in the public and private spheres, and no one was in a position to actively challenge their power. They provide their listeners with an alternate media universe where the old order of male dominance and White supremacy is still intact, even if they've (sometimes) cleaned up the cruder rhetorical expressions of sexism and racism. It is both fitting and revealing that one of the signature on-air promotions for Rush Limbaugh's top-rated radio program features an announcer

---

This piece is an original essay that was commissioned for this volume.

boldly proclaiming that Rush is "America's anchorman," slyly invoking association with the memory (if not the liberal politics) of the late Walter Cronkite, a paternal and authoritative television presence as the chief anchor of the *CBS Evening News* in the 1960s and 1970s who was known as the "most trusted man in America."

Of course, not all conservative talk hosts are White men. There are women, such as Laura Ingraham, a former law clerk for Supreme Court Justice Clarence Thomas, and a handful of men of color, such as the African American conservative libertarian Larry Elder. The Los Angeles–based Elder's signature characteristic, and perhaps the key feature of his popularity with a largely White male audience, is his performance of an "angry Black man" persona. But unlike the angry Black man who elicits fear and resentment in the White racist imagination, Elder's anger typically is targeted at the usual objects of conservative scorn: antiracist White liberals, feminists, and progressives of all stripes. Elder is the Black man who literally gives voice to sentiments—especially about race—that White conservatives are reluctant to say out loud, for fear of being labeled as racists.

But women and Black men are the exceptions on conservative talk radio, which remains a bastion of White men's power and center stage for the airing of myriad cultural and political grievances on the part of conservative White men. On the air and in their public personae, the (White) men who personify the genre—such as Rush Limbaugh and Sean Hannity—typically shun nuance and rarely concede points in arguments, or even acknowledge the validity of opposing viewpoints. This is, arguably, less a result of their personal stubbornness than it is an occupational imperative: the simplicity of their arguments and their exaggerated self-confidence are the very source of their popularity. In the midst of a society in transition, in which the old *Father Knows Best* certainties are a figment of the idealized past, these men provide a comforting patriarchal presence, just as the reactionary ideology they champion seeks to roll back the democratizing social changes that have disrupted White men's cultural centrality.

It is notable—although hardly surprising—that Rush Limbaugh's audience is 72% male, more than 90% White, and skews 50+ years old. Presumably, a key part of the appeal of conservative talk radio to its predominantly older White male audience resides in its reinforcement of traditional masculinity in the face of a culture where epochal economic transformations and progressive social movements have shaken old certainties about what constitutes a "real man." Limbaugh not only articulates a set of conservative moral precepts and reactionary politics, but he also performs a kind of cartoonish masculinity from a bygone era. For example, Limbaugh loves to talk about football, and he is frequently photographed smoking expensive cigars. He champions the military and was a prominent defender of the conduct of U.S. service members in the disgraceful episode of the Abu Ghraib prison in Iraq, which he dismissed as a "fraternity prank." According to his biographer, the thrice-divorced Limbaugh has "a fair amount" of Hugh Hefner in him (Chafets, 2010, p. 204). In the media persona he has constructed for himself, his unrestrained narcissism drives him to broadcast to his audience an inflated sense of himself as a "man's man," while his political agenda seeks to reinforce the link between manly strength and political conservatism. He accomplishes this rhetorically, in part, by relentlessly attacking the femininity of feminist women and the masculinity of men who support gender equality.

Since the early 1990s, Limbaugh's astounding political influence on the right—and in the Republican Party—has been an open secret. He has been the top-rated radio talk show host in America since *Talkers* magazine started the rankings in 1991. His weekly audience is estimated at about 15 million listeners. Over the past two decades, Limbaugh's influence has grown to the point that he was described by David Frum as the "unofficial spokesman for the Republican Party." Limbaugh's audience is made up not only of casual listeners and die-hard "dittoheads" but also includes a significant percentage of the political class in and outside of the Washington Beltway, especially conservatives. In 1994, dubbed "The Year of the Angry White Male," when Republicans gained control of Congress for the first time in 40 years, Limbaugh was asked to address the new GOP legislators and was named an honorary member of the freshman class (Chafets, 2010). As Karl Rove said of Limbaugh, "He's a leader. If Rush engages on an issue, it gives others courage to engage" (Wilson, 2011, p. 252).

For two decades Limbaugh has regularly been the subject of mainstream media interest—and concern. One *Time* magazine cover story that appeared as far back as 1995 was headlined, "Is Rush Limbaugh Good for America? Talk radio is only the beginning. Electronic populism threatens to short-circuit representative democracy" (*Time*, 1995). A 2008 cover story in the *New York Times Magazine* profiled Limbaugh's political influence, as well as offering readers a glimpse of the lavish lifestyle afforded him due to his financial success (Chafets, 2008). But not everyone recognizes his political influence. When the controversy over Limbaugh's misogynous tirade against Georgetown law student Sandra Fluke erupted in 2012, Al Neuharth, founder of *USA Today*, wrote that "The real problem with Rush Limbaugh is that people take him seriously. He's a clown. If you listen to his radio program regularly, it should be to get your daily laugh" (Neuharth, 2012).

In recent years, bloggers, journalists, and scholars have begun to move beyond dismissive caricatures of talk radio as merely entertainment or simplistic populist chatter and to pay closer attention to its cultural and political influence. This is long overdue. But with the exception of ongoing feminist criticism of the crude sexism that persists among too many male political commentators in media, there has been very little gendered analysis of talk radio's role in establishing and enforcing a certain kind of old-school White manhood. What follows is a brief sketch of several areas in which conservative talk radio—and Rush Limbaugh in particular—functions as a mass media vehicle for the defiant reassertion of a kind of traditional White male authority.

Gendered Rejection of Empathy

On conservative talk radio, qualities such as compassion and empathy are typically equated with weakness and femininity; a major theme of Rush Limbaugh's social commentary is that the "chickification" of American society is linked to our cultural decline (Limbaugh, 2011). In fact, one of the most popular rhetorical techniques used by conservative talk hosts is a variation of the rational–public sphere/emotional–private sphere binary. Men in patriarchal cultures have employed this binary for centuries to justify the perpetuation of their familial, religious, economic, and political control over women. The idea is that men are more rational and hence better equipped to handle public matters of the economy and foreign policy than women, who are said to be more "emotional" and thus more suited to the private sphere of caregiving and maintaining relationships. Feminist theorists and popular writers have critiqued—and discredited—this falsely gendered dichotomy for decades, but it continues to animate conservative talk radio—one of the chief sources of news and political commentary for millions of White men.

On his nationally syndicated radio program, the Los Angeles–based conservative talk show host Dennis Prager regularly declares that liberal thought is based on the heart, not on the mind. In his book *Still the Best Hope: Why the World Needs American Values to Triumph*, Prager (2012) outlines what he calls the "feelings-based nature" of liberalism. Of course the "feeling" of empathy or compassion that Prager and other conservatives deride as incapable of competing with conservative "logic" has long been devalued in public discourse as feminine. In fact, conservative polemicists have so thoroughly feminized the word *liberal* that in recent years few Democratic candidates of either sex wanted to claim the label. Male candidates feared being unmanned; women candidates didn't want to be seen in narrow, stereotypical terms as merely a "woman's candidate."

Antifeminism

Rush Limbaugh has a long history of making explicitly sexist and dismissive statements about women—especially feminists. Early in his career, he published his "Undeniable Truths of Life," which included this: "Feminism was established so as to allow unattractive women easier access to the mainstream of society" (Limbaugh, 2008b). He is also the media personality most responsible for popularizing the term *feminazi*, which links feminists, who are among those at the forefront of democratic advocacy and nonviolence, with Nazis, the embodiment of masculine cruelty and violence. In Limbaugh Land, Democratic women who demand to be treated as men's equals are castrating "feminazis," and Democratic men are either neutered wimps or gay. This antiwoman and antifeminist anger finds expression in the commercial world of talk radio in a way that is inconceivable in other forms of mainstream political discourse.

In fact, the source of Limbaugh's immense popularity on AM radio has some interesting parallels to Howard Stern's popularity on FM and later satellite radio. Under the guise of self-consciously constructed personae—Limbaugh as the fun-loving conservative truth teller, Stern as naughty rock-and-roll bad boy—both men function as the id of their respective audiences. They say

things that men in more responsible or respectable contexts may believe but would never say *out loud*. For example, few men in public life—particularly Republican candidates and officeholders—would dare criticize sexual harassment laws when women make up 53% of the electorate. But Rush Limbaugh—who repeatedly refers to accomplished women, including women in politics, as "babes"; female journalists as "infobabes" and "anchorettes"; and lesbians as "lesbos"—boasts that a sign on his door reads, "Sexual harassment at this work station will not be reported. However, ... it will be graded" (Edsall, 2006, p. 183).

Heterosexism and Rhetorical Bullying of Progressive Men

Critics of Limbaugh and other right-wing talk radio hosts often point to the coarsening of political discourse to which the talkers have contributed. Former Vice President Al Gore (2007) describes what he terms the "Limbaugh-Hannity-Drudge axis" as a kind of "fifth column in the fourth estate" that is made up of "propagandists pretending to be journalists" (p. 66). Gore claims that what most troubles him about these right-wing polemicists is their promotion of hatred as entertainment—particularly their mean-spirited hostility toward liberals and progressives. But what most of right-wing radio's progressive critics overlook or downplay is the gendered nature of Limbaugh and company's contempt for liberals. Embedded firmly within the talk radio hosts' scathing critique of liberalism is a barely suppressed well of anger at the progressive changes in the gender and sexual order over the past 40 years, and the concomitant displacement of traditional patriarchal power. Limbaugh is perhaps the most overt in his open hostility not only toward feminist women but also toward the men who support them. He calls these men the "new castrati" and ridicules them for having "lost all manhood, gonads, guts, and courage throughout our culture and our political system" (Media Matters, 2011).

Limbaugh likes to dismiss liberal presidential candidates as feminine, such as when he labeled former Senator John Edwards the "Breck Girl" because of his famously stylish hair, or when he traded in a popular stereotype about the supposed effeminacy of the French by derisively referring to Senator John Kerry as "Looks French" Kerry. During the presidential contest of 2008, he repeatedly stated, "I don't even think Barack Obama is half the man Sarah Palin is" (Limbaugh, 2008a). Also in 2008, similarly targeting Democratic men, Limbaugh reported a news item about how business at Denver strip clubs was supposedly slow during the Democratic National Convention, held the previous week. Taking the opportunity to ridicule their manhood and—presumably—their heterosexuality, he boasted: "This is easily understood by me. . . . How many real men were in Denver this past week? That's the question you need to ask" (Limbaugh, 2008b).

Unmanning Obama After the Bin Laden Killing

Talk radio plays an important role in national debates about military spending and foreign policy because, in many thousands of hours of on-air discussion and debate, it helps define what course of action "manly" men should support. This, in turn, helps define the political space in which politicians, especially presidents, have to operate. As many observers have noted, Democrats have often supported or acquiesced in the advancement of militaristic policies in part out of fear of being accused of being "soft" on defense. This is why when the news broke on the evening of May 1, 2011, that a team of Navy Seals had killed Osama Bin Laden, it was the right's biggest nightmare. One of their main narratives about President Obama had been

dealt a devastating blow. Even before he was elected president, Barack Obama had been the target of relentless mockery and ridicule on conservative talk radio. The line of attack varied from issue to issue, but its essence was usually the same: Obama was Jimmy Carter II—a weak and vacillating leader who (in Obama's case) gave good speeches but was in way over his head.

The Bin Laden killing posed a problem for Limbaugh because the man whom Limbaugh and others on the right had relentlessly mocked and ridiculed as a lightweight and a wimp had quietly and systematically led and authorized the killing of Bin Laden in such a militarily impressive way that crowds in sports stadiums cheered, "USA! USA!" and spontaneous rallies erupted in front of the White House. In another era, conservatives would have been measured and even generous in crediting Obama with a job well done—but not in the era of conservative talk radio and not on *The Rush Limbaugh Show*. When he went on-air, Limbaugh—who avoided military duty in the Vietnam era by claiming an anal boil rendered him unfit for service—attempted to strip Obama of any military/manhood credentials he might have earned from his leadership in the killing of Public Enemy No. 1 (Greenwald, 2008, p. 110).

Limbaugh and other conservative talk radio hosts desperately tried to downplay Obama's accomplishment with a series of arguments, summarized as follows:

1. Obama was taking personal credit for the actions of others, especially George W. Bush, a decisive, risk-taking conservative who made the tough choices.

2. Obama had opposed the hard-line, hyperaggressive policies that made the successful raid possible.

3. Obama had no choice but to authorize the raid.

4. Obama's failure to release the photos of a dead Bin Laden proved that he's a wimp.

In summary, they argued that the killing of Bin Laden coincidentally happened on Barack Obama's watch, asserted that Obama had to be kicked dragging and screaming into authorizing it, and finally claimed that, even then, he made lots of mistakes (MacNicol, 2011; Politico, 2011).

Conclusion

This chapter outlined some of the ways conservative talk radio is not simply "entertainment." Rather, it has a profound influence on public discourse and, thus, ultimately on public policy on issues from women's health to climate change. Until now, little attention has been paid in cultural studies scholarship to the important cultural and political role of conservative talk radio, and even less to how this cultural phenomenon functions in the gender order. Considering the important "public pedagogical" role that charismatic hosts play in their embodiment and modeling of an influential version of conservative White masculinity, and the influence this has on contemporary American political dialogue and debate, much more empirical research and analysis of conservative talk radio's social impact is necessary.

References

Chafets, Z. (2008, July 6). Late-period Limbaugh. *New York Times Magazine*. Retrieved from http://www.nytimes.com/2008/07/06/magazine/06Limbaugh-t.html?pagewanted=all&_r=0

Chafets, Z. (2010). *Rush Limbaugh: An army of one*. New York: Sentinel.

Edsall, T. (2006). *Building red America: The new conservative coalition and the drive for permanent power*. New York: Basic Books.

Gore, A. (2007). *The assault on reason*. New York: Penguin.

Greenwald, C. (2008). *Great American hypocrites:Toppling the big myths of Republican politics*. NY: Crown Publishers.

Limbaugh, R. (2008a, September 3). Attack on Palin shifts from experience to trailer trash. Retrieved from http://www.rushlimbaugh.com/daily/2008/09/03/attack_on_palin_shifts_from_experience_to_trailer_trash

Limbaugh, R. (2008b, August 29). Drive-bys scramble to destroy her. Retrieved from http://www.rushlimbaugh.com/daily/2008/08/29/drive_bys_scramble_to_destroy_her

Limbaugh, R. (2011). Chickification of America: NFL cancels game because of snow. RushLimbaugh.com. Retrieved from http://www.rushlimbaugh.com/daily/2011/01/04/chickification_of_america_nfl_cancels_game_because_of_snow

MacNicol, G. (2011, May 2). Rush Limbaugh MOCKS the idea that Obama is responsible for capture of Bin Laden: "Thank God for President Obama!" *Business Insider*. Retrieved from http://www.businessinsider.com/rush-limbaugh-thank-god-for-president-obama-2011-5

Media Matters for America. (2011, March 8). Limbaugh describes "the new castrati": "You're like geishas—you gesticulate like you're effeminate" [Video]. Retrieved from http://mediamatters.org/video/2011/03/08/limbaugh-describes-the-new-castrati-youre-like/183385

Neuharth, A. (2012, March 19). Column: Limbaugh is a clown so let's laugh at him. *USA Today*.

Politico. (2011, May 2). Limbaugh mocks Obama for bin Laden hit. Retrieved from http://www.politico.com/blogs/onmedia/0511/Limbaugh_mocks_Obama_for_bin_Laden_hit.html

Prager, D. (2012). *Still the best hope: Why the world needs American values to triumph*. New York: Broadside Books.

Time. (1995, January 23). Cover.

Wilson, J. (2011). *The most dangerous man in America: Rush Limbaugh's assault on reason*. New York: St. Martin's Press.

PART III

READING MEDIA TEXTS CRITICALLY

Media scholars have recognized that media **texts** are never simple, however obvious they may seem. According to the view of media texts as "open" or **polysemic** (discussed in the introduction to Part I) there is frequently room to make readings that go at least partially against dominant ideologies (**counterhegemonic** readings). However, in our everyday media text consumption, we don't always attend closely to the mechanisms and techniques that are helping to influence the way we make meanings out of these texts. This inattention makes us more likely to internalize the messages encoded in the texts and to become passive rather than active and possibly resistant consumers

In this section, we have assembled a group of articles that provide a variety of models for how to **deconstruct** or get underneath the surface of media texts, in order to understand better how they are **encoding ideologies** of gender, sexuality, race, and class. We acknowledge that some student readers may find that doing close analysis interferes with the pleasure of consuming media texts. But if you are in this situation, we would invite you to join media scholars in finding the special pleasure (and power) available to those who become critical readers of texts. As audiences build **media literacy** skills, a dual consciousness can develop, enabling us both to enjoy reading the text somewhat uncritically and simultaneously take pleasure in decoding its more subtle and nuanced meanings.

We begin with a particularly good example of how one might do a close reading of a **polysemic** media text—one with multiple possible meanings. Emily Drew's chapter, "Pretending to be 'Post Racial': The Spectacularization of Race in Reality TV's *Survivor*" (III.18) discusses a television show that has brought pleasure not only to its U.S.-version audience but also, in other locally customized versions, to audiences all over the world. Drew offers an analysis of the **representation** of race in the thirteenth season, when the producers boldly aimed to represent what they saw as a **postracial** society, "in which race was not important to forming relationships or shaping life chances"(p. 167).

> In fact, it seems that *Survivor: Cook Islands* producers were so confident that race would not play a role in people's interactions or survival, they spectacularized it by imposing racial segregation on the cast and required that the racial tribes compete against one another to literally and metaphorically survive. (p. 167)

By carefully deconstructing the "racial wars" narrative developed by the producers over the fifteen episodes of the season, Drew shows that what she calls "essentialist notions of race" were used to explain the behavior of the initially ethnically segregated groups of contestants. While she commends the producers for "calling attention to **Whiteness** as an identity, a worldview, and a set of cultural norms," she ultimately offers a strong critique:

> Rather than showing society's transcendence of race, *Survivor* demonstrated its own reliance on the significance of race for exploiting conflict to attract audiences. . . . Furthermore, it blamed the problem of race on people of color. . . . (p. 172).

Another media text that reveals itself as multilayered, requiring reading at different levels, is the popular television dramas of the past two decades: *Law & Order: Special Victims Unit*, a show that began broadcasting in 1999 as a spin-off of the widely acclaimed earlier series *Law &*

Order. At first reading, as Cuklanz and Moorti (III.19) point out, this show appears politically progressive, in that it has encoded a **feminist** understanding of sexual assault. In addition, it is notable among police dramas in that one of its main characters is a woman who is not afraid to stand up to the men in her team and who repeatedly advocates for rape victims. Moreover, as these writers point out, "By showcasing women who survive their sexual assaults *SVU* asserts a key feminist idea: There is life after rape—that is, the raped woman is a survivor with agency" (p. 177).

However, as these scholars look more deeply into patterns of character and plot in the text of this series, they make a more critical reading and assessment. Noting that on the show, "numerous storylines depicted families that produce criminal children," in many cases casting mothers as "either criminals in their own right" or responsible for the criminality of their children, Cuklanz and Moorti assess the show's political content as problematic for feminists:

> The monstrous maternal storylines show *SVU* grappling with the limits of the detective-cop show genre. In this genre, traditionally associated with masculinity, the vilification of feminine qualities and the association of women with horrific crimes within the family counterbalances the feminist perspective presented in many episode narratives in relation to rape and rape reform. (p. 184)

Motherhood is also on the mind of hip-hop feminist and critic Marlo David (III.20), who highlights African American women's perspectives, both as cultural producers and as critics of the genre. David first points to the complexity and urgency of the task of learning to read hip-hop culture in more nuanced ways than most people do:

> Reading hip-hop culture is a messy business. While we must resist simplistic readings that force us to assess what is good or bad, positive or negative for the black community, it is also possible and

desirable to understand how hip-hop disrupts racist, sexist, classist culture. . . . (p. 189)

From her own perspective as a hip-hop feminist, David explores the problematic theme of motherhood in hip hop, even within Black female rappers' lyrics. Motherhood is a particularly fraught concept for the African American community, given the history of public blaming of Black mothers as the "matriarchs" whose excessive power in the traditional Black family was said in the infamous Moynihan Report of 1965 to have "emasculated" Black men, which in turn led to the endemic poverty of single-parent families. From David perspective, in the "body politics" articulated by much of masculinist hip hop and even by some female rappers "talking back," the female body is represented as strong only through heterosexual sexiness. The black mothering body, by contrast, is associated with weakness and vulnerability. David's goal is to show that "there is room at the table for black feminists, womanists and hip-hop feminists to address the representations of black motherhood and their importance to our communities" (p. 191).

David's article reminds us that there is no one completely dominant perspective encoded throughout mass media. As cultural studies scholars often emphasize, drawing upon the complex concept of power famously articulated by Michel Foucault, competing voices and alternative perspectives always arise to contest the **hegemonic** formulations, in an ongoing and decentralized struggle for superiority. Thus, even in a socially conservative time and place, there is always some space for more progressive ideologies to be expressed.

In the early 21st century, one place within mass media production where arguably **counterhegemonic** views can be found is in the more narrowly targeted commercial entertainment media such as cable TV channels. For example, the Comedy Channel's *The Daily Show with Jon Stewart,* featuring comedian Jon Stewart, slyly conveys dissident political views

through parodying the conventions of the mainstream television news format. Jamie Warner (III.21) compares Stewart's show's tactics to those practiced by activist "culture jammers," who are "rebelling against the hegemony of the messages promoting global capitalism." In Stewart's case, the target is frequently the "branding techniques" used by politicians and political parties "to drown out dissident messages," and the method for subverting these "brand" messages is "dissident humor":

Like other culture jammers, *The Daily Show* subversively employs emotional and aesthetic modalities similar to those employed by political branding itself, thus interrupting it from within. Unlike many culture jammers, however, *The Daily Show*'s reliance on a humorous version of parody means that they can add their voices to the conversation in a seemingly innocuous way. (After all, it is *just* a joke.) (p. 195)

Another example of a potentially subversive TV show is *The Simpsons,* the long-running edgy satirical animation series on the Fox Network that has been very popular with young people. Gilad Padva (III.22) situates *The Simpsons* within "the popular subgenre of animated TV sitcoms in the late 1990s and 2000s," which "integrates semi-anarchistic humor and spectacular imagery that often challenge conventional ethnic, social, gender and sexual patterns of representation." Using an episode from *The Simpsons* called "Homer Phobia," which lampoons the leading character Homer Simpson for knee-jerk antigay attitudes, Padva deconstructs the text, showing how it can be understood to **encode** a celebration of "queer counter-culture" and to be susceptible of different readings for those "in the know."

Although straight audiences too enjoy this episode, its hyperbolic scenes particularly empower gay viewers, who likely identify the linguistic maneuvers and decode the queer meanings. (p. 208)

Candace Moore (III. 23) presents another example of a media text in which forbidden truths rupture the smooth surface of social harmony. Ellen DeGeneres, the stand-up comic who famously "came out" as a lesbian on her sitcom in 1997, has since adopted what is called "an everywoman approach" on her talk show, launched in 2003. According to Moore, DeGeneres has been critiqued for failing to embrace her lesbian identity in her post-sitcom media work. However, by closely analyzing the persona and self-presentation of DeGeneres on this show, Moore is able to see a strategy more subtle than simply denying her lesbianism or returning to the closet, as some of her critics would have it. Moore argues that "she performs queerness through what implicitly 'exceeds' her stand-up jokes and sit-down talk, and, physically, through the ritual action of her daily dance sequence" (p. 211). Through these methods, perhaps DeGeneres escapes being such a "convenient screen" for hate-mongers or bearing the responsibility of being a spokesperson for all of gay America, while she still maintains a *televisibility* of **queer** identity.

The complexity of gay media visibility is also discussed in Chong-suk Han's chapter (III.24), which critiques mainstream gay print media. Reading the gay journals closely to document both gay Asian invisibility and the presence of race-related stereotypes, Han provides evidence for his argument that gay masculinity in mainstream gay media has reflected the traditional hegemony of White **masculinity** by marginalizing men of color. In his view,

> While 'gay' masculinity can never be hegemonic, it can, nonetheless, position

itself closer to the hegemonic ideal by pitting the more feminized masculinity of Asian men as a counter balance. (p. 225)

Han continues by arguing that what constitutes masculinity is under constant negotiation and that "all forms of media produce and reproduce inequality to varying degrees and by extension are sites of contested identity formation" (p. 221).

Without doubt, sports radio is a major producer of hegemonic masculinity, yet even here, according to David Nylund's chapter (III.25), there are spaces for contesting homophobia. Interestingly, Nylund found that well-known sports radio talk show host Jim Rome unexpectedly critiqued the use of homophobic slurs by callers, thus opening up space through his show for questioning dominant social ideas. Nylund is careful to point out, however, that "Rome's location of the problem of homophobia in a few bigoted, intolerant individuals leaves unchallenged the larger societal structures that perpetuate heterosexism" (p. 234).

Decoding media texts is never simple, because they work on multiple levels of meaning and have polysemic potential. Once you learn to read them with a critical eye, of course it makes them even more interesting. Students usually find courses that develop critical media literacy "eye-opening" and intellectually transforming—but as you share your new insights into the depths of the texts with friends who just want to be entertained, be prepared to face some eye-rolling as well!

18

Pretending to Be "Postracial": The Spectacularization of Race in Reality TV's *Survivor*

Emily M. Drew

During the thirteenth season of the reality show *Survivor* (CBS, 2000–), one of television's most consumed programs, the producers made an unprecedented move to draw the "color line" explicitly and to use race as a central organizing principle. The program's creators explained that their decision to divide the show's twenty contestants into four "tribes" based on racial group membership was part of a larger attempt to grapple with the seemingly unspoken issue of race in society as well as race in reality television. They acknowledged that producing a season in which racial tribes compete against one another would result in criticism. But the producers stood by their "good intentions" to depict a wider range of people of color in prime-time television, to increase the racial diversity of applicants for reality television programming, and to boost and diversify the consumer audience for their show. And despite protests from communities of color and media watch groups and a decrease in corporate sponsorship, the show enjoyed some of its highest ratings ever and won its time period every week (Carter 2006). Survivor's executive producer insisted that he "knew people would never judge each other by skin color" (Carter 2006, 2).

In fact, it seems that *Survivor: Cook Islands* producers were so confident that race would not play a role in people's interactions or survival, they spectacularized it by imposing racial segregation on the cast and required that the racial tribes compete against one another to literally and metaphorically survive. By quickly desegregating the competition in its third week, producers hoped to entice viewers with the "postracial" premise that race would be insignificant in shaping the politics of competition, survival, and reality television. Even the program's first-ever Asian American winner said the show proved "that people's individual values, not ethnicity, make up what kind of people they are" (Crooks 2007).

On its surface, this season's metaphor for the "race wars" told an explicit narrative of a postracial society in which race was not important to forming relationships or shaping life chances and that race would lose its currency if we would just choose to not pay it

From Emily M. Drew (2011), "Pretending to be 'Post-Racial': The Spectacularization of Race in Reality TV's *Survivor*." *Television and New Media*, Vol. 12, No. 4, 326–346. Reprinted with permission of SAGE Publications.

any attention. Presumably, when humans are stripped to the bare essentials of life and must work for their survival, race will not emerge as a salient means of doing life together. However, by digging beneath the program's racially enlightened veneer, viewers got a glimpse into the failure of "postracial" logic in reality television. . . .

How *Survivor* Works

For nearly a decade, CBS has assembled a cast of twenty people who are relocated to a remote location where they build a micro society together and compete to be the last person standing to win the prize of one million dollars. Each week, "tribes" compete in physical and mental challenges against each other, ranging from rigorous athletic activities or puzzle solving to eating local foods or being tested in knowledge about fellow contestants. Teams that lose the competitions must face a "tribal council" in which they vote off a team member, using a variety of rationale, including who caused the loss, who contributes the least to community life, or who poses the greatest help or threat to individual success later in the competition. Once these eliminations have whittled the cast to half, people then compete as individuals to "survive" to the final week, when a winner is voted on by contestants eliminated previously.

During this *Cook Islands* season, producers placed the twenty competitors in distinct "tribes" (teams) organized by racial group membership. People from diverse ethnic groups were lumped into major U.S. racial classifications, resulting in four racially classified groups, each with five people: Latino, Asian American, African American, and white.[1] Each racial tribe had a near gender balance, and other social identities, such as social class, sexuality, ethnicity, and occupation, were strategically revealed by contestants over the course of the season. Although the tribes were organized by racial groups, the host of the show used only the word *ethnicity* (and sometimes *culture* or *color*) to refer to what was

clearly a *racial* classification.[2] . . . Each tribe built its own shelter, provided its own food, and competed for three weeks against other racial tribes for rewards and the ability to avoid a teammate's elimination. During the third week of the season, the program's producers desegregated the racial tribes and created two racially diverse tribes that continued in the competition. Despite the white contestants making up only one-fourth of the cast, only one white person was eliminated during the first three-fourths of the season. Conflict within and among people of color groups allowed white people to remain in the competition relatively unnoticed and eventually represent equal numbers with people of color in the final weeks.

Representing Essentialist Notions of Race

Central to *Survivor*'s racial representations was an assertion of the biological and cultural primacy of race. People of color, as individuals and group members, were presented as essentialized Others by the program's host, white tribe members, and, very often, one another. The show's narrative attributed individuals' feelings, interactions, and chances of survival as rooted in an essentialized racial identity. Despite creating a social experiment to demonstrate how insignificant race is, every racial group was represented in ways that are consistent with dominant racial ideology in the United States and with the prevailing representations in television.

BLACK CULTURE: KEEPIN' IT REAL

After being divided along racial group membership, the African American tribe was presented as feeling no awkwardness about being separated along racial lines and did not seem to be bothered by being black together. They began their time as a racialized tribe by cheering for themselves and lifting up a desire to "keep it real" and to "represent" (yelling this word loudly as a cheer). Having a language to speak about their racial identity, tribe members discussed their desire to represent blackness to the viewing audience in ways that could offer alternatives to the negative stereotypes that the media frequently portray. One of the men noted how pleased he was to not be "the only token black brother anymore," commenting on how unusual it was to be among other black people rather than an "only" in a reality show competition.

African Americans' comfort with one another was shown as being a comfort with an essentialized blackness. Right away, four of the five tribe members made reference to their group as "family" and often to being "the black community," even calling themselves "blood." The tribe was shown deploying what they essentialized as "black humor" and laughing a great deal with one another, from cracking jokes about "having a dream," to building their shelter on the island and referring to it as "low-income housing," to commenting on one another's inability to swim. After their first loss in a boat competition in the water, the remaining team members called themselves "a bunch of city kids," and the producers cut to an image of them struggling to use their boat. After they eventually gave up, one remarked that "our people had bad experiences with boats," and the group laughed about this reference to the Middle Passage of the slave trade. Blackness got culturally defined by the producers and black tribe members themselves, as being "headstrong" ("black people don't like to be told what to do"), "tough" (in their resilience and ability to survive), and having musical talent (from one woman praying over the group singing "Amazing Grace" to a man's comedic dance performance to the *Fresh Prince of Bel-Air* song).

LATINOS AS HARDWORKING AND ANIMAL-LIKE

During their first week on the island, the Latino tribe was also represented as having an awareness about the significance of being racially categorized and quickly launched into discourse that essentialized themselves, biologically and culturally. This began with a claim and subsequent agreement about how equipped they were to do well in the competition since they are "used to Caribbean environment and heat." In fact, one shared that his family came to the United States on boats, so the survival experience was nothing new. After the tribe worked together to establish a comfortable campsite, in advance of the other teams, one member heralded that Latinos were good workers because it was in their blood and heritage. Similarly, the Latinas were reduced to essential identities in which they were named as "hot tempered" and always "clashing"; both racially gendered markers were used as the justification for their elimination.

Since four of the five Latino competitors were eliminated during the first third of the season, the diversity within the Latino community, in terms of ethnicity, culture, class, generation, and other axes of identity, was not adequately represented. However, the one remaining Latino survived the entire season and captured a great deal of essentialist and dehumanizing attention from the host and fellow competitors. He was described early in the season as a "picture out of jungle book and Mogley climbing the tree." The cameras showed at least one shot each week of him climbing up a tree with bare hands or single-handedly accomplishing a task that likely required several people. He dominated most of the competitions physically, and because of his hard labor at the team's campsite, he was primarily responsible for their ability to eat and drink each day. Meanwhile, the host biologized him through animalistic frameworks, saying he was "a dolphin" or noting that he was standing in a "monkey pose." One white contestant referred to this Latino as a "little jungle boy," while another white player commented to the camera, after this Latino won an individual competition, that he was "half animal, half man" and in another episode called him "part fish and part monkey."

ASIAN AMERICANS AS "MODEL MINORITIES" AND "PERPETUAL FOREIGNERS"

Upon their racial grouping, Asian American tribe members were not initially shown discussing the racial segregation of the teams. Instead, their focus was largely on the one team member: an elder and immigrant from Vietnam. (He was also the producers' focus, receiving more camera time than any other competitor, despite being on the island for only six weeks.) *Survivor* fetishized Asian identity by highlighting his behaviors, while giving very little airtime to the other four Asian Americans who seemed to do only "American" things. This elder Asian American man was shown essentializing Asians as having "slanted eyes, small bodies, and refugee status"; he was presented dancing "wildly" with fire sticks (getting labeled a "Zen fire master" by a white woman) and as a "healer" who cured two teammates of ailments using Eastern medicine. He was shown celebrating his broken English (which appeared to be done intentionally, as it was otherwise perfect) and berating the younger Asian Americans for their emphasis on technology, hailing this as a marker of their being out of touch with their homelands.

The season's Asian American winner was represented as several major racial archetypes, being depicted simultaneously as the brilliant model minority, the untrustworthy foreigner, and the asexual male. The host and competitors were shown commenting repeatedly on his hard work and intelligence, as he was called "smart guy" or the "Harvard Stanford brain guy." He also contributed to the viewers consuming him as a "model minority" in characterizing himself as a "very complex, intellectual guy who came out of [his] shell" and was shown to pass the time on the island by doing things such as calculating the total surface area of his feet for "fun."

Asian Americans were also represented as "perpetual foreigners" (Wu 2002), as not being from the United States, as having cultural practices that are not "American," and as embodying loyalty to a home country over the United States. This was shown when the host asked the perennial question of "where are you *really* from" to one and when another explained to the audience that most people do not believe he speaks English. During the concluding episode of the show, many players revealed that they believed the Asian American man was untrustworthy, that he was secretly "calling the shots," and that he manipulated everyone else as "puppets." While he worked to counter his racialization as a "perpetual foreigner" by repeatedly pointing out how "American" he felt, he could also not escape being feminized in the representation. His masculinity was called into question as he sat awkwardly in a hot tub with young flirty heterosexuals and wanted to use this luxury "reward" time to strategize rather than have fun. Another Asian American man was also feminized by a white woman and a black man, who referred to him using the emasculating term of "Nancy boy."

MAKING WHITENESS INVISIBLE AND NORMAL

Unlike the explicit racial discourses that emerged in the people of color tribes, members of the white team began their time in a tribe together without even noticing that they had been grouped by race. It was not until the entire cast of twenty members was called together for a competition that they are shown observing the racial categorization of each team. In this way, they played out racial scripts that demonstrated the ability of whiteness to mask itself (Dalton 2008) and to become so normalized (Brown et al. 2003) that it took "encountering" people of color for white tribe members to notice their own race. One white competitor's initial reaction to this lumping was to note that racial grouping "wouldn't make a difference... that people don't live their lives according to race." White tribe members used the language of normalcy to articulate how being among only white people felt to them. However, one disagreed, noting that that she felt strange to be separated by color and that she did not like being segregated. The white tribe spent almost no time discussing race, their own racial status (with the exception of a white American Jew who often noted his own liminal status in the group of whites), or the significance of this grouping in the game of *Survivor*. The show's white host reinforced blindness to and silence about whiteness by narrating that "ethnicity has nothing to do with how alliances are formed, kept or broken in this game."

Even after the racial tribes integrated, the white players continually used the word *they* to describe a now dispersed and amorphous group of people of color. Three of the four whites, in talking about strategy and their own positions, constructed an "us versus them" dichotomy, despite the fact that both tribes included multiple races. This us–them divide was shown through white players giving hugs and high fives only to other white players, despite racial "integration" and no longer constituting a white "tribe." Ironically, these same whites who were allied with each other on the basis of race articulated that it was the people of color who "play[ed] the race card." One white woman described the Latino tribe as "fiercely loyal," despite that fact that 80 percent of the team has been voted out (usually by each other) before the season was even one-third complete. If "fierce loyalty" was measured in outcomes rather than intentions, it would be only the whites who demonstrated it.

The most salient feature of whiteness that surfaced during the season was a narrative of white fear and white perceptions of victimization by people of color. Consistent with the characteristics of the new racial structure—not a postracial society—in which whites came to view whiteness as a disadvantage and social liability (O'Brien 2000; McKinney 2003), white people were shown to be angst-ridden about being outnumbered and fearful about being dominated in competitions, and they perceived themselves as victims

of the racism people of color unleashed on them. After one white man stole food from a tribe of color, he was confronted and articulated being "shocked" (his word) that they would "gang up" on him; in this way, he reveals feelings of victimization, despite having been the perpetrator of theft. For the duration of the season, white people either were not asked or were not shown speaking about the significance of race in shaping their strategic choices in the competition. They were largely silent about the subject of race, until the end of the season when people of color coalesced and united against them. Only then did white people pay explicit attention to race. The last white man standing criticized people of color's unity and elimination of white players, saying that they "have blinders on" for using race as a determinant. Such comments to the camera highlighted the white imaginations of the contestants but also of the white producers and audiences who view white racialized behaviors as decidedly "nonracial."

Conclusion: "Race Wars" in a Postracial Society?

For ten years *Survivor* has represented race, produced racial logics, and promoted what Hunt (1999, 9) calls "raced ways of seeing" that perpetuate the new racial structure. In all of its seasons, both before and since this decision to make race an explicit organizing principle, the television program uses the power of representation to "both promote and mask the complicated social realities of the inequitable distribution of political power" and has done so with significant consequence (Wall 2008, 1044). . . . In this season, *Survivor* produced race as the primary—at times the only—frame of analysis through which to interpret competitors' ability to outwit, outplay, and outlast one another. Although the content is presented as simply reflecting "reality," producers' interview questions remain invisible, hundreds of hours of footage go unused, and all of the images and commentary that do not fit the season's narrative remain invisible. It is quite possible that the competitors used other narratives such as gender, education and social status, or sexuality to guide their strategy in the competition. . . . So while the diversity of discourses the contestants used to frame their experiences is not known, what is apparent is the significance that *Survivor* placed on race as the central organizing principle, all the while espousing a postracial politic. . . .

. . . How did *Survivor*'s "race wars" season produce cultural meanings, reproduce racism, and provide alternative conceptions for the future of reality television? How did spectacularizing race redraw the "racial rules of reality television" in new and complicated ways?

To begin with, the season did resist some of the prevailing representational strategies in prime-time and reality television. Instead of racial "tokens" that come to represent their entire race in monolithic and narrow ways, having five competitors from each racial group suggested that there is ethnic and cultural difference—and even disagreement—*within* races, not just between them. While television often highlights the differences and disagreements among racialized groups, having multiple competitors from each racial group illuminated the differences and diversity *within* racial groups. For example, almost without exception, Latinos and Asian Americans are represented in prime time by one person whose ethnicity, class, generation, and social status are minimized or erased to narrowly represent the *racial* group. This season of *Survivor* demonstrated the ethnic and generational hierarchies within racialized groups and the complex ways in which identity politics and internalized racism operate inside racialized groups, particularly the Latino and Asian American communities, neither of which gets represented as complex, diverse, or dynamic in television depictions. Similarly, African Americans, while shown to unite around blackness, were revealed to have real

fissures within the community, based on social class, skin color, and perceptions of a narrowly defined authenticity. Since an "us–them" dichotomy is so often drawn in television, the dividing lines were shown to be far more complicated than television usually presents.

By producing a season with explicitly racialized tribes, *Survivor* also defied the significant and normalized practice in prime-time television of making whiteness invisible. Through constructing a "white" tribe and calling attention to whiteness as an identity, a worldview, and a set of cultural norms, the program named the reality that white is not simply the universal, neutral, or default state of being. Competitors and the viewing audience alike were forced to grapple with the "reality" that white is not simply "unraced" but that the group itself has "tribal" affinity and racialized ways of seeing, experiencing, and articulating life. Unfortunately, the only times *Survivor* represented whites as grappling with whiteness in any meaningful way was once group members began to experience their whiteness as a liability, as the reason for their perceived victimization by people of color. In this way, the white contestants ceased their color-blind rhetoric and began constructing their racial group membership as a liability, conceiving of themselves as victims, rather than beneficiaries, of the status quo (McKinney 2003, 39). . . .

. . . Rather than showing society's transcendence of race, *Survivor* demonstrated its own reliance on the significance of race for exploiting conflict to attract audiences, consolidating white fears regarding impending "race wars," and emphasizing the postracial logic that racial categorization, not historical racial formations and unequal access to institutionalized power, causes racial inequality in the United States. Furthermore, it blamed the problem of race on people of color, whose insistence on racial solidarity and racialized ways of seeing the world keep racism in place.

After stripping individuals down to the bare essentials of life, *Survivor* produced representations that both reflect and maintain racial misunderstanding and inequality, in exchange for the higher ratings and profits derived from this televisual spectacle. Its producers sought to create a television program that could demonstrate the postracial premise that a society could "get beyond" race and racism if more important things such as "survival" were what really mattered. Through this veneer of racial enlightenment, they claimed that race was so insignificant its significance could be mocked. Such spectacularization ended up backfiring since racial groups (whether segregated or integrated) were presented as always in competition with one another for limited resources rather than in cooperation with one another about how to use resources responsibly. If the goal of *Survivor* was to represent an unscripted reality in which race and racism did not matter, what the program actually produced was a narrative about the durability of the "racial contract" (Mills 1997). In fact, the season represents a bit of a "cautionary tale" about what *not* to do, about how *not* to deal with race in reality TV, if the goal is to use representational tools to transcend—or at least make less damaging— the realities of racial inequality in society.

References

Andrejevic, Mark, and Dean Colby. 2006. Racism and reality TV: The case of MTV's *Road Rules*. In *How real is reality TV? Essays on representation and truth*, ed. David Escoffery, 195–211. Jefferson, NC: McFarland.

Bell-Jordan, Katrina. 2008. *Black. White.* and a *Survivor* of *The Real World*: Constructions of race on reality TV. *Critical Studies in Media Communication* 25:353–72.

Bonilla-Silva, Eduardo. 2001. *White supremacy & racism in the post–civil rights era*. Boulder, CO: Lynne Rienner.

Bonilla-Silva, Eduardo. 2003. Racism without racists: Color-blind racism and the persistence of racial inequality in the United States. Lanham, MD: Rowman & Littlefield.

Brown, Michael K., Martin Carnoy, Elliott Currie, Troy Duster, David Oppenheimer, Marjorie Shultz, and David Wellman. 2003. *White-washing race: The myth of a color-blind society*. Berkeley: University of California Press.

Carter, Bill. 2006. Segregated *Survivor* teams turn out to be temporary. *New York Times*, October 5, 2.

Chidester, Phil. 2008. May the circle stay unbroken: *Friends*, the presence of absence, and the rhetorical reinforcement of whiteness. *Critical Studies in Media Communication* 25: 157–74.

Churchill, Ward. 2003. *Acts of rebellion: The Ward Churchill reader*. New York: Routledge.

Crew, Richard. 2006. Viewer interpretations of reality television: How real is *Survivor* for its viewers? In *How real is reality TV? Essays on representation and truth*, ed. David Escoffery, 61–77. Jefferson, NC: McFarland.

Crooks, Peter. 2007. *Survivor*'s newest millionaire. *Diablo Magazine*, February. http://www.diablomag.com/Diablo-Magazine/February-2007/Survivors-Newest-Millonaire.

Croteau, David, and William Hoynes. 2006. *The business of the media*. Thousand Oaks, CA: Pine Forge Press.

Dalton, Harlon. 2008. Failing to see. In *White privilege: Essential readings on the other side of racism*, ed. Paula Rothenberg, 15–18. New York: Worth.

Dubrofsky, Rachel, and Antoine Hardy. 2008. Performing race in flavor of love and the bachelor. *Critical Studies in Media Communication* 25:373–92.

Entman, Robert, and Andrew Rojecki. 2000. *The black image in the white mind: Media and race in America*. Chicago: University of Chicago Press.

Friedman, James. 2002. *Reality squared: Televisual discourse on the real*. New Brunswick, NJ: Rutgers University Press.

Gallagher, Charles. 2003a. Color blind privilege: The social and political functions of erasing the color line in post-race America. *Race, Gender & Class* 10 (4): 22–37.

Gallagher, Charles. 2003b. Miscounting race: Explaining Whites' misperceptions of racial group size. *Sociological Perspectives* 46:381–96.

Gray, Herman. 2004. *Watching race: Television and the struggle for blackness*. Minneapolis: University of Minnesota Press.

Hall, Stuart. 1997. Representation: Cultural representations and signifying practices. London: SAGE.

Hasinoff, Amy. 2008. Fashioning race for the free market on America's Next Top Model. *Critical Studies in Media Communication* 25:324–43.

Hill Collins, Patricia. 2004. Black sexual politics: African Americans, gender and the new racism. New York: Routledge.

hooks, bell. 1992. Eating the other. In *Black looks: Race and representations*, 21–40. Boston: South End.

Hunt, Darnell. 1999. O. J. Simpson facts and fictions: New rituals in the construction of reality. New York: Cambridge University Press.

Kelley, Robin D. G. 1997. Yo mama's DisFUNKtional: Fighting the culture wars in urban America. Boston: Beacon.

Larson, Stephanie. 2006. Media & minorities: The politics of race in news and entertainment. Lanham, MD: Rowman & Littlefield.

Lewis, Justin, and Sut Jhally. 2001. Television and the politics of racial representation. In *Multiculturalism in the United States*, ed. Peter Kivisto and Georganne Rundblad, 149–60. Thousand Oaks, CA: Pine Forge Press.

Li, Jieli. 1999. Exploring Asian Americans: The myth of the "model minority" and the reality of their lives. In *Perspectives in social problems*, ed. Robert McNamara, 134–41. St Paul, MN: Coursewise.

Lichter, S. Robert, and Daniel Amundson. 1997. Distorted reality: Hispanic characters in TV entertainment. In *Latin looks: Images of Latinas and Latinos in the U.S. media*, ed. Clara Rodriguez, 57–72. Boulder, CO: Westview.

Lippard, Lucy. 1990. Mixed blessings: New art in multicultural America. New York: Pantheon.

McKinney, Karyn. 2003. "I feel whiteness when I hear people blaming whites": Whiteness as cultural victimization. *Race & Society* 6:39–55.

McMurria, John. 2008. Desperate citizens and good Samaritans: Neoliberalism and makeover reality TV. *Television & New Media* 9:305–32.

Mills, Charles W. 1997. *The racial contract*. Ithaca, NY: Cornell University Press.

Murray, Susan, and Laurie Ouellette. 2004. *Reality TV: Remaking television culture*. New York: New York University Press.

O'Brien, Eileen. 2000. Are we supposed to be colorblind or not? Competing frames used by whites against racism. *Race & Society* 3:41–59.

Orbe, Mark. 2008. Representations of race in reality TV: Watch and discuss. *Critical Studies in Media Communication* 25:345–52.

Perez, Richie. 1997. From assimilation to annihilation: Puerto Rican images in US films. In *Latin looks: Images of Latinas and Latinos in the U.S. media*, ed. Clara Rodriguez, 142–63. Boulder, CO: Westview.

Riggs, Marlon. 1995. Black is, black ain't: A personal journey through black identity. San Francisco: California Newsreel.

Ryan, William. 1971. *Blaming the victim*. New York: Pantheon.

Santos, Carla, and Christine Buzinde. 2007. Politics of identity and space: Representational dynamics. *Journal of Travel Research* 45:322–32.

Smith, Debra. 2008. Critiquing reality-based televisual black fatherhood. *Critical Studies in Media Communication* 25:393–412.

Taylor, Lisa, and Andrew Willis. 1999. *Media studies: Texts, institutions and audiences*. Oxford, UK: Blackwell.

Wall, David. 2008. It is and it isn't: Stereotypes, advertising and narrative. *Journal of Popular Culture* 41:1033–50.

Wright, Christopher. 2006. *Tribal warfare: Survivor and the political unconscious of reality television*. Lanham, MD: Rowman & Littlefield.

Wu, Frank. 2002. *Yellow: Race in America beyond black & white*, New York: Basic Books.

19

Television's "New" Feminism

Prime-Time Representations of Women and Victimization

Lisa M. Cuklanz and Sujata Moorti

I n the fall of 1999, NBC debuted its second program in the *Law & Order* franchise, *Law & Order: Special Victims Unit* (hereafter *SVU*), a scripted series devoted to crimes of sexual assault and rape. Although the runaway success of the original *Law & Order* helped assure an eager audience for the new venture, the seemingly narrow focus on a subject as emotionally and politically charged as rape took the television crime genre in an unexpected direction. *SVU*'s popularity over the last five years raises questions about the series' ability to introduce the topic of sexual violence into the prime-time arena and sustain viewership. How does a prime-time fictional chronicling of sexual violence, trauma, and victimization operate within the confines of the traditionally masculine genre of detective fiction? What forms of feminism, if any, does such a prime-time focus on sexual violence enable?

With its "ripped from the headlines" storylines *SVU* centers on cases undertaken by a police unit modeled after the New York Police Department's Special Victims Unit.[1] In the tradition of television crime dramas, the series spotlights the detective duo of Olivia Benson (Mariska Hargitay) and Elliot Stabler (Christopher Meloni), and an ensemble cast of characters that include Odafin Tutuola (Ice-T) and John Munch (Richard Belzer), Captain Donald Cragen (Dann Florek), Assistant D. A. Casey Novak (Diane Neal), medical examiner Melinda Warner (Tamara Tunie), and police psychologist George Huang (B. D. Wong).[2] *SVU* is both similar to and different from the original title series, *Law & Order*, which combines the genres of the cop show and the legal drama. *SVU* episodes rarely include a trial and although most of its narratives end with the positive identification of the perpetrator, some conclude with the criminal still at large.[3] Producer Dick Wolf characterizes it as a "compelling" cop drama that tracks the emotional effects of the crimes on its two protagonist detectives and on victims. Like the original title series, *SVU* begins with a voice-over that provides the program with a sense of verisimilitude:

> In the criminal justice system, sexually-based offenses are considered especially heinous. In New York City, the dedicated detectives who investigate these vicious felonies are members of an elite squad known as the Special Victims Unit. These are their stories. (http://www.tvtome.com/lawandorder/svu)

Shot on location in New York City, *SVU* shares several of the signature elements of the title series: scene-setting labeling, staccato music, edgy camerawork, sudden shifts in scenes, and use of street argot. Airing originally on NBC, episodes are shown nine days later on the cable channel USA, following a unique syndication policy termed "repurposing."

SVU is distinguished by its subject matter, which reprises decades-long feminist discussions of violence against women. If rape provides a foundational feminist allegory for women's subordinated status in society (Sielke, 2002), *SVU*'s decision to base an entire prime-time series on this topic locates it within the limited body of programming that can be characterized as feminist television. However, *SVU*'s depictions mark a new stage in the trajectory of televisual feminism. Analysis of the first five seasons of *SVU* suggests that its representations of rape facilitate a feminism that is markedly different both from the lifestyle feminism that dominated 1970s and 1980s prime-time entertainment and the postfeminism of the 1990s. We will show that, in a seemingly contradictory move, *SVU* storylines couple feminist premises and assumptions with an indictment of so-called female traits.

The storylines on *SVU* thematize and elaborate key elements of feminist understandings of sexual violence. However, paradoxically, this feminist take on the subject of rape is not carried through in *SVU*'s treatment of women. Some of the storylines condemn aspects of feminine behavior and character, including empathy and intuition. Female characters seldom can or do form bonds with each other. Female criminals are manipulative and use relationships to harm others; numerous storylines explore narratives of moral depravity and extreme violence on the part of women. While criminal women are nothing new in popular cultural products, *SVU*'s particular construction of the dangerous woman takes an unusual turn. The criminal women on *SVU* use their power in the domestic realm to harm those closest to them, particularly their own children. Their criminality is often linked with misguided maternalism. We contend that the feminist elements of the storylines appear primarily in the depiction of sexual assault; at the level of the deep structure the narratives articulate an anxiety about feminine characteristics and the power women possess within the private sphere. Thus, in *SVU* narratives the home—the primary arena of women's activities and the site of the feminine qualities of nurturing, care-giving, and affect—is presented repeatedly as the site within which a dangerous maternal instinct motivates women to commit heinous crimes. . . .

SVU's claims of feminism are encouraged by press quotes given by the show's cast. After completing two months of victim advocate training with the Sexual Assault and Violence Intervention Program at Mount Sinai Hospital, New York City, Mariska Hargitay told reporters she hoped to incorporate the perspectives of the police and of victim advocates (Beck & Smith, 2003). Hargitay is known for her work with rape survivors and for her "Joyful Heart" foundation, which Hargitay's website indicates is "committed to helping victims of rape and sexual assault heal—mind, body, and spirit" (http://www.joyfulheart-foundation.org/). Like other cast members, Hargitay emphasizes the show's commitment to realistic representations of sexual assault and to presenting victim/survivor perspectives. One news article noted her assertion that *SVU* writers "don't try to sensationalize the stories," and quoted her comment that "rape . . . is not about sex, it's about anger and violence towards women, and we really go into what that's all about" (Fidgeon, 2003). Her character is often regarded as a feminist heroine. For example, a *New York Times* television review noted that her character is one of just a few who "mirror the feminist ethos of the past—dedicated, seasoned, and tough" (Stanley, 2005). Reporters also cite Hargitay's volunteer work outside the show to emphasize the commitment of both *SVU* the program and Benson the character to victims' perspectives and experiences. . . .

Demystifying Rape Myths

SVU's feminist depiction of rape is clearest when the episodes are viewed cumulatively. Following a trend since the late 1980s, *SVU* does not objectify sexual assault victims. The series rarely depicts the sexual assault itself, thus omitting titillating and objectifying details common in previous media representations. The majority of storylines track events after a rape so the sexual assault itself remains beyond the diegetic space of the series. This "post-rape" narrative strategy permits *SVU* to sidestep the problematic of rape's resistance to representation (Bal, 1992). Simultaneously, by showcasing women who survive their sexual assaults *SVU* asserts a key feminist idea: There is life after rape—that is, the raped woman is a survivor with agency (Rajan, 1993).

While the series, in title and content, pays silent homage to the achievements of the women's movement of the 1970s, storylines are more overt in highlighting the rape law reforms initiated by feminists. *SVU* also underscores the continuing shortcomings of the judicial system. *SVU* episodes often are limited to investigation of the crime and apprehension of the criminal. That said, storylines that include a trial segment often underscore the juridical hurdles that preclude more systematic prosecution of criminals. For example, some episodes exploring the legal definition of consent emphasized how slippery the term becomes during trial. The episode "Consent" featured a female college student who was raped while under the influence of a date rape drug. The rapists were exonerated after the lawyer exploited the murky definition of consent. Other episodes highlighted definitions of statutory rape as well as more complicated ethical dimensions of consent. In "Waste," detectives pondered the possibility of filing a rape charge when a comatose patient was suddenly discovered to be six weeks pregnant. The episode parsed the meaning of consent in a complex manner by introducing a subplot where the fetus was aborted, but the patient's mother filed charges since she did not consent to the termination of the pregnancy. Some storylines showcased the troubling questions of who can press charges and who can offer evidence in rape cases, while other episodes highlighted how often rapists invoke the spousal confidentiality clause to halt the disclosure of crucial evidence. In each of these instances, *SVU* episodes revealed some of the rape law reforms such as rape shield laws, but also gave voice to feminist concerns about the lacunae that remain.

The absence of on-screen depictions of sexual assault and the critique of existing legal practices are the two predominant axes along which *SVU* introduces feminist understandings of sexual assault into the arena of prime-time entertainment. Even as these feminist insights are introduced unproblematically as a meta-discourse, individual episodes spell out more carefully the numerous rape demystification strategies that have been central to the women's movement. Most significantly, storylines highlight myths and misunderstandings that continue to surround the topic of sexual assault.

Feminists have insisted on dismantling the categories of "good" and "bad" victims that have dominated common sense (and media) definitions of the crime (Benedict, 1992). Unequivocally asserting that consent—rather than the conduct of the victim—is central to definitions of rape, *SVU* narratives repeatedly showcase assaults on prostitutes. In "Hysteria," an African-American teenager's rape and murder was treated lightly by police officers who assumed she was a prostitute. *SVU* detectives, however, managed to set the record straight, tracking down her murderer, a policeman, and unraveling the unsolved murders of at least 18 prostitutes. Storylines have presented the rape of police officers. While most victim-survivors are depicted as "normal" everyday people, some episodes have centered on "sexually adventurous" women. The detectives might make awkward jokes about these women's kinky sexual habits, but they do not discount the possibility of sexual violation. *SVU* narratives repeatedly declare that a person's sexual practices must not be used to undermine the person's credibility. The series rejects the assumption that only virtuous and sexually chaste women can be violated.

Apart from showcasing a range of survivor-victims including gay men and an MTF transsexual, storylines have contested the myth that women are assaulted when they are alone in "unsafe" public places. *SVU* narratives have depicted the sexual assault of women in public and private spaces with equal levels of complexity. "Remorse" depicted an attractive reporter who was raped by two strangers in an abandoned swimming pool. "Contact" provided a different valence to the term "public space" with the rapist assaulting women in crowded subway cars. Other *SVU* episodes featured assaults in "safe spaces" such as the home. "Limitations" tracked a serial rapist who attacked women in their beds and used a hair dryer as a "fake" gun, while "Disappearing Acts" featured an executive raped in her office. Thus the series does not categorize public and private spaces as safe or unsafe. By insistently inscribing the presence of sexual assault in all spaces, perpetrated by strangers and acquaintances, the series helps forward a pivotal feature of feminist definitions of rape.

As the key female protagonist, Benson is a singular figure through which the show espouses identifiably feminist attitudes toward rape and police work. When a reporter Benson dates said he would like to "playfully" re-enact the subway rapes they had been discussing, Benson's reaction was swift and categorical. After telling the reporter his suggestion was disgusting, she locked herself in the bathroom with the instruction that he'd better be gone when she returned. The scene provided an unambiguous model for dealing with unwanted sexual behavior. Likewise, when a vice cop remarked that prostitutes cannot really be raped, Benson made clear that she did not mind offending him to make explicit her belief that the definition of rape does not depend on a victim's identity or profession. In "Limitations," she was angered by a retired SVU detective whose failure to document and take seriously a rape claimant's information resulted in multiple repeat offenses by a perpetrator at large for years. When the retired detective said it was "clear" that the alleged victim was just fantasizing about the rape, Benson confronted him with his sexism and incompetence and stomped away in disgust. The scene clearly differentiated between the traditional police view of rape and Benson's more feminist understanding, clearly taking a side in her favor.

The storylines also work to demystify the black male rapist myth. Walk-on characters often include interracial couples, heterosexual and gay; but rarely are people of color depicted as assailants (and often these are foreigners). Several narratives raised the prospect of the black male rapist. Inevitably, though, once arrested, the black male was found innocent, thus highlighting how racist assumptions of criminality shape policing practices. For instance, a black athlete was initially assumed to be the rapist in "Sophomore Jinx," but the narrative instead offered an eloquent assessment of the stereotypes and racist assumptions that shape the everyday lives of African Americans. People of color are rarely depicted as criminals in interracial crimes. This, too, is a departure from the history of popular culture representations. The series also manages to render visible the victimization of women of color. In storylines featuring interracial couples the victim-survivor is always a woman of color. Perhaps these racialized depictions of criminality and victimization might be shaped by the network's standards department (Gitlin, 1983). In any case they help articulate concerns of feminists regarding the ways in which fears of black male sexuality have shaped cultural definitions of sexual assault (Brownmiller, 1975; Davis, 1978) and of critical race theorists, who highlighted the historical silencing of black female victimization. *SVU*'s depiction of racialized victims thus helps correct the dominant tropes of black femininity in popular culture (Collins, 2005; Crenshaw, 1995).

SVU offers an unequivocally feminist understanding of sexual assault in its depiction of power imbalances as causing rape. Thus, while the majority of the episodes in the first season focused on the victimization of "classic" powerless subjects—women and children—storylines have increasingly drawn attention to other violated bodies, those gendered subjects who occupy the space of the female body in "rape scripts" (Marcus, 1992). Several *SVU* narratives featured the rape of men—heterosexual and gay—in a manner akin to that of their female counterparts, highlighting how the broader social climate of homophobia helps render this particular brand of sexual assault either invisible or sensational. In effect, the series does not prioritize the victimization of one sex over the other. Rather, it asserts that sexual violence pivots on power imbalances.

Portrayals of perpetrators of sexual assaults are as heterogeneous as the victim-survivors. They include authority figures (judges, doctors, and police officers), working-class men, those that are "mentally retarded," and felons. *SVU* storylines have depicted men and women as child molesters, but only once were women presented as rapists. In "Ridicule," three women raped a male stripper; they were not prosecuted for this crime, although one of them was convicted of murder. This ecumenical presentation of sexual assault criminals echoes the feminist slogan that rape is not sex but is the assertion of power.

SVU storylines often go beyond offering an individual-centered explanation for sexual assault. They reiterate feminists' claim that violent masculinity is facilitated by society at large. Dworkin (1976), Griffin (1986), MacKinnon (1987), and other scholars have identified an interlocking web of social factors—such as the prevalence of pornographic representations that perpetuate the sexual objectification of women—as constituting a climate that makes possible men's assault of women. Storylines point out factors such as pornography, beauty pageants, and an overall "sexual objectification of women" that promote a rape culture. Thus, for instance, "Care" explored how young boys might learn and replicate the misogyny depicted in video games. "Appearances," featuring a 10-year-old beauty pageant participant, indicted the broader social milieu that normalizes the sexual objectification of all females, young and adult. Several *SVU* storylines evocatively described the complicated manner in which female college students are victimized by fraternity culture and institutional practices that facilitate the expression of male violence.

The New Televisual Feminism

Within these feminist elements, however, is enfolded a demonization of feminine characteristics. We do not assume that televisual representations should follow or develop only one perspective on controversial issues related to rape and sexual assault, or even of women. *SVU*'s depictions of violent and criminal women are not necessarily unrealistic or inherently anti-feminist. We recognize that competing elements and themes, as well as a range of reading positions, characterize televisual detective fiction. Nonetheless, we find that *SVU*'s representations of violent women present female power in the domestic sphere as not only dangerous, but as a cause of crime in general. Having analyzed the specific ways that *SVU* tells the stories of criminal women, we offer below some instances that highlight how the narratives castigate feminine characteristics even as the episodes adhere to a feminist understanding of sexual violence.

SVU's strategy of granting legitimacy to some feminist ideas about rape while subtly condemning feminine characteristics is exemplified in the character development of Detective Elliot Stabler. A proto-feminist family man, Stabler has from the first season been seen as encountering the limits of his male-centered understanding of sexual assault. With the assistance of his female partner he realizes a key feminist insight that sexual crimes often defy rationality. This process of coming into consciousness was demonstrated in *SVU*'s debut episode, "Payback." This storyline drew Stabler and Benson into a gruesome investigation of a cab driver who was posthumously castrated. The forensic trail allowed the detectives to identify the taxi driver as a Serbian war criminal who had committed numerous atrocities, including participation in rape camps.[4] The detectives eventually located three survivors of the rape camps who now resided in New York City, two of whom collaborated to murder the taxi driver/war criminal. Stabler pursued the rule of law; he insisted that the two women be prosecuted for murder. However, Benson used the women's narratives to make the case that such acts of violence are the only recourse available to women victims of civil war atrocities, in the absence of viable international institutions

of justice. While Stabler never abandoned his faith in U.S. law and order institutions, by the narrative's end he showed remorse because one of the accused women committed suicide and the other was imprisoned.

Through similar narrative strategies, Stabler became the vehicle for the enunciation of a nuanced feminist idea. He often understands the cases he is investigating through a connected mode of reasoning reminiscent of Gilligan's (1982) understanding of female knowledge acquisition patterns. Stabler's professional successes do not always stem from a rule-orientation. Rather, the male detective arrives at a better and more accurate sense of sexual crimes when he imagines one of his four children in the place of the actual victims. For instance, in "Or Just Look Like One," a storyline about the rape and murder of teenage models, Stabler understood, with Benson's prompting, that they were not investigating a "simple" crime. Rather, he better understood the rape culture engendered by the beauty business in coming to terms with his older daughter's struggles with her body image. In particular, Benson instructed Stabler on the stakes women have in their looks, and the anger and insecurities that follow the loss of one's looks. Armed with this knowledge the detectives tracked down the criminal, a former female supermodel.

While the main storyline in this episode elaborated on the unrealistic body image promoted by the fashion industry, a secondary storyline depicted Stabler comprehending his daughter's battles with anorexia only after he recognized the physical, psychological, and material price the cult of thinness exacts from women. *SVU* storylines repeatedly present Stabler as blurring the public and domestic realms in the sense that his professional conduct is informed by insights from the domestic realm. This narrative choice underscores a key feminist idea that separating the public and private arenas is an untenable ideological device. Notably, *SVU* enacts a gender role reversal in articulating this idea. Stabler is presented repeatedly as a concerned father who is successful in his detective work when he projects his children as victims of the crimes he is asked to pursue. While other television shows deprecated female characters who cannot separate their public conduct from the domestic realm, *SVU* has normalized Stabler as a concerned father who brings his domestic life and concerns into the workplace. Benson, meanwhile, maintains a rigid separation of the two arenas. She is rarely shown outside the professional realm; often she is depicted as having no private life.

The proto-feminist gestures enacted by Stabler's character, however, also impede his work. Understanding cases by imagining his children in the place of the victims makes Stabler too emotionally invested in his cases. For instance, in "Wanderlust," Stabler was convinced that a teenage girl must be a victim of sexual crime. Picturing his teenage daughter at the crime scene, he refused to follow Benson's hunch that the teenager was the murderer. It was left to Benson to explain that young teenagers can fall in love with father figures and commit crimes of passion. Benson finally convinced Stabler that all adolescent girls are not innocent and always-already victimized. Thus, Stabler's tendency to see his job through the prism of his family often hinders his work. Stabler is blinded by his concern for his family and his identification with women. Stabler's feminine characteristics of empathy and emotionality prevent him from apprehending female criminality.

Since the 1970s, feminists have worked actively with the police to alter the ways in which rapes are investigated, including by forming special victims' units, and ensuring that detectives are less skeptical and cynical about women's rape claims. So, it is striking that *SVU* has featured a number of storylines with false rape charges. We do not question the possibility of false rape claims but draw attention to the cultural work accomplished by the many storylines that focus on women who fabricate rape charges.

In the series as a whole, survivors are relatively rare, since most victims die during or after their attacks; this narrative strategy enables *SVU* to avoid titillating representations of rape and to concentrate on the aftermath. Nevertheless, the fact that *SVU* storylines position several survivors as false claimants of rape makes this a provocative and weighted strategy, one that cannot be dismissed as a twist intended to produce a "fresh" angle.[5] Often the most eloquent survivors, those who can coherently and poignantly reconstruct their assault and the trauma they have experienced, turn out to be dissemblers. The false rape episodes are never depicted as "imagined" assaults; rather, the women are portrayed as maliciously and willfully fabricating the false charge. The female claimant's manipulative staging of false crimes, her ability to wield dangerously controlling interpersonal power over accomplices, and efforts to fool detectives become the focus of these storylines. . . .

Women as Victimizers

We have identified an archetypal "family" scenario where anti-women sentiments are present in the deep structure of the narrative. These stories center on the recurrent manifestation of what we call the monstrous maternal. Since these scenarios draw attention to the family as a site of violence, at first glance these storylines appear to articulate feminist concerns about a patriarchal space where male power is exercised and sometimes abused. Yet the limits of the detective genre come into visibility in these narratives, which tend to reflect an anxiety about feminine qualities and women's power.

During the first five seasons, numerous storylines depicted families that produce criminal children, or couples without children who are the source of crimes. When all of the "damaged families" narratives are totaled, over 40 episodes (approximately one third of the episodes aired in the first five seasons) focused largely on family problems that result in crime. With a few notable exceptions that featured innocent victims who cannot ultimately be helped by law and order institutions ("Wrong Is Right" centered on a young boy adopted by a pedophile; in "Disrobed" a judge abused domestic violence survivors and then extorted them), the direction of cause and effect in nearly all of these suggests that damaged families create damaged individuals who become criminals. The episodes reiterate a simple causal logic—that individual "sick" families cause social problems, and that "the system" fails some families that it should help. The dysfunctional family is a cause of crime, rather than the symptom or result of larger institutions and social problems. In *SVU* narratives, mothers often are either criminals in their own right or they cause the criminal behavior of their children. *SVU* women misuse their domestic power in the commission of crime as often as men do. Women's abuse of their power in the domestic realm is presented as more dangerous in its physical immediacy as well as more psychologically damaging than that of men. Bad mothering is much more frequently depicted as the cause of criminal behavior by adult children than is bad fathering.

The Monstrous Maternal

In *Motherhood and Representation* (1992) Kaplan identified two primary—and predominating—types of "bad" or "evil" mothers in popular culture. The so-called "fusional" mother is the "possessive and destructive all-devouring one," while the second is over-indulgent and vicariously satisfies her own needs through the child (p. 47). These mothers "project on to the child [their] resentments, disappointments and failures for which the child is also to

suffer" (p. 47). Kaplan explained that much less attention has been given to abusive fathers than to abusive mothers because of prevailing mother-constructs dictating that mothers be gentle and self-sacrificing. "Their deviation is then all the more reprehensible" (p. 193). Men's/father's abuse is "more socially acceptable" (p. 193), because they are not held up to the same standard of gentleness and self-sacrifice. Kaplan added that mothers are usually "blamed as individuals, rather than blame being placed on social structures and governmental priorities" (p. 192). Although Kaplan is primarily referring to news coverage, her description of popular representations of abusive mothers is borne out in *SVU*'s ripped-from-the-headlines fictional world as well. Here, mothers commit a range of horrific crimes related to their maternal role (such as withholding food, failing to nurture, or psychologically manipulating their children). They are also implicated much more often than are fathers in the crimes of rapists, sociopaths, pedophiles, and a range of extreme criminals who are their children.

The numbers of abusive mothers and abusive fathers in the first five seasons of *SVU* are almost identical. We analyzed more than two dozen episodes featuring criminally insane, violent, or otherwise dangerous mothers, referred to here as monstrous maternal figures. The monstrous maternal involves women who fail in their parental roles so grievously as to cause serious harm or even death to their children or others. The monstrous maternal storylines contend that violent women are often more dangerous and harmful than male victimizers; mothers are implicated in crimes committed by their children, whereas fathers are implicated almost exclusively in psychological damage that harms the children.

Our concept of the monstrous maternal differs somewhat from Creed's (1993) "monstrous feminine." Creed focused on the horror film genre. For example, her discussion of "Alien" treated non-human elements such as the Alien monster and its mode of attack as cases of the "monstrous feminine." Often, women's sexuality is depicted as the underlying problem in horror films, revealing male fears of women's sexual power. Working from a psychoanalytic model in order to understand the relationships between the human and non-human in horror film, Creed focused on women as victims. Our "monstrous maternal," while she may pose as victim, is always the aggressor. However, with both concepts, the texts emphasize the threat posed to men by women, particularly mothers, and suggest that it is women who pose the real threat to the social order. In *SVU*, the monstrous mother particularly focuses on children or others under her care as her victims, but her crimes may also represent a misdirection of the maternal role.

In many episodes about dysfunctional families, mothers' crimes were violent and immediate. Three episodes centered on mothers who had murdered their own children, and two others involved mothers who either accidentally or sympathetically killed their own children. No episodes featured fathers who murder their own children (although in "Monogamy," a man attacked his wife and killed the fetus they conceived). In three episodes maternal figures (two mothers and a grandmother with full guardianship) murdered their children through some variation of Munchausen by Proxy syndrome, physically abusing or poisoning them secretly in order to gain sympathy as caretakers of sick children.

Mothers are frequently the perpetrators of ongoing violence, whereas fathers' abuse is usually located in the distant past. Significantly, female perpetrators often utilize the domestic sphere as their means of committing crime. In addition to committing straightforward physical abuse (in "Careless," a foster mother murdered a child in her care), women poison their children's food, commit psychological abuse by seducing or dominating their sons, fail to nurture and love their children, abandon

sick children, and murder (others) to assure their children's happiness. Women's crimes are thus associated with misdirections of caregiving (poisoning not nourishing, murdering to protect, abusing rather than loving). Women's crimes are generally motivated by greed, jealousy, competition, and materialism, while men's serious crimes are committed for simple pleasure and covering up sexual wrongdoing. The worst female criminals are nearly always mothers of some kind. . . .

Repeatedly, *SVU*'s dysfunctional families present the monstrous maternal as resulting from a misguided sense of caring and nurturing or a pathological selfishness. The mother-child bond itself is presented as profoundly dangerous. Often the episodes do not feature women as mothers but surrogates who within the domestic sphere occupy the role of caregivers and nurturers. *SVU* episodes feature women criminals as loving grandmother, devoted wife, sister ("Painless" depicted a woman whose resentment against her own mother turned to sociopathy; she murdered dozens of elderly nursing home patients who, she recalled, "were all called mother"), or long-suffering mother. In "Sacrifice" a porn star mother played the part of rape victim while she framed her husband for murder and abandoned her daughter to pursue an acting career. In "Shaken," a single mother was overwhelmed by her infant daughter's crying and suffocated her. . . .

Feminism in a New Era

SVU departs from most other prime-time fare in several important ways. It fits solidly within the historically masculine detective genre while deliberately focusing on a subject of primary interest to women. It positions itself as a dramatic series with feminist sympathies, addressing a subject that was long a focus of feminist activism. It is uniquely issue-oriented, building its emotional and dramatic appeal from a political issue rather than focusing on an eponymous protagonist (such as *Cagney and Lacey*). *SVU* highlights power in gender relations, including within the family, and provides evidence of "rape culture" as a potential factor in the commission of the crime. Yet in many instances the real victims are men and patriarchal institutions. Enfolded in the feminist perspectives on sexual assault are problematic depictions of feminine characteristics. . . .

We argue that *SVU*'s co-dependent linkage of a critical view of feminine qualities with a feminist understanding of sexual assault and rape reform constitutes a new brand of televisual feminism, distinct from the lifestyle feminism of the 1970s and 1980s and the postfeminism of the 1990s. *SVU*'s misogynist feminism includes false claims of rape; negative portrayals of feminine characteristics such as intuition, emotion, and manipulation; criminal use of interpersonal power by women; and the figure of the monstrous mother. Feminine characteristics such as empathy, intuition, passion, and nurturance are deployed in the conduct of crimes, but even in these episodes that "criminalize" feminine characteristics, *SVU* maintains a feminist understanding of sexual assaults. This self-contradictory double-movement comes to the forefront in episodes dealing with female criminality within the family. Episodes with female criminals not only inveigh against feminine characteristics such as nurturance, but also give voice to anxieties about women's power within the domestic sphere. The monstrous maternal storylines show *SVU* grappling with the limits of the detective-cop show genre. In this genre, traditionally associated with masculinity, the vilification of feminine qualities and the association of women with horrific crimes within the family counterbalances the feminist perspective presented in many episode narratives in relation to rape and rape reform. We contend that the cumulative effect of the anti-feminine traits makes the series appear more misogynist rather than feminist.

This new brand of televisual feminism may be spreading to other television genres, particularly those that have not traditionally been understood as "women's" genres (such as the soap opera) and those that have not historically been on the cutting edge of progressive politics (such as the situation comedy). Meanwhile, the new brand of televisual feminism emerging in crime dramas shows a retrenchment of a traditional gendered split between public and private spheres. Crime drama has drifted toward realism, including the inclusion of more and more powerful professional women in the public sphere. *SVU* is no exception. However, its construction of crime and criminals maintains a gender division between public and private spheres. Male criminality is portrayed primarily as an ambiguous, lurking threat from unknown strangers who attack from outside the family. Female criminality is primarily depicted as an insidious interpersonal dysfunction that destroys the family and society from within.

Notes

1. The *Law & Order* franchise pivots on storywriters' ability to cull news stories for ideas about crime and criminality. This "ripped-from-the-headlines" technique provides an aura of newness and contemporaneity. Simultaneously, the news origins of these storylines replicate journalism's reliance on the unique and the exceptional. Special victims units were added to real-world police forces starting in the late 1970s in response to feminist activists who vehemently decried the severe mishandling of all stages of rape investigation. See Fairstein (1993) for an insider's view on these units' functioning.

2. Several characters reprise roles from other series, such as Detective Munch from *Homicide* and Captain Cragen from the original *Law & Order* series. *SVU* relies on and plays on audiences' television archives—memories of past programs and surrounding discourses that frame their interpretations of programming (Deming,

1992). While the criminals may appear mono-chromatic, the officers themselves are cast to present an appropriately multicultural rainbow. Ice-T's character had a walk-on role in several episodes of the first season but in the second season Odafin Tutuola became an integral part of the ensemble cast. During an interview with Tavis Smiley, Ice-T exclaimed that only in America can someone who raps about being a cop killer become a police officer in another media outlet. Similarly, B. D. Wong's character began as a recurring figure but was formally included in the fourth season's cast. Monique Jeffries, Alexandra Cabot, Dr. Audrey Jackson, and Dr. Emil Skoda were replaced after the first season by new cast members.

3. Television representations of sexual violence sometimes involve a trial, such as in *L.A. Law*; the crime drama genre generally does not include trials.

4. "Rape camps" refers to specially-designated areas where women are raped systematically during wars by military personnel. While estimates vary, most human rights organizations estimate that at least 20,000 women were raped and tortured during the Bosnia-Herzegovina war. Rape camps are not unique to the former Yugoslavia but have been established in various conflict zones. See Salzman (1998).

5. Feminists say that false rape claims, about two percent of filed charges, are similar to false claims in other crimes.

References

Bal, M. (2001). *Looking in: The art of viewing.* Amsterdam: G & B Arts International.

Beck, M., & Smith, S. J. (2003, May 26). *Lifestyle* (p. D4). Chattanooga Times Free Press.

Benedict, H. (1992). *Virgin or vamp: How the press covers sex crimes.* New York: Oxford University Press.

Brownmiller, S. (1975). *Against our will: Men, women, and rape.* New York: Simon & Schuster.

Collins, P. H. (2005). *Black sexual politics: African Americans, gender, and the new racism.* New York: Routledge.

Creed, B. (1993). *The monstrous-feminine: Film, feminism, psychoanalysis.* New York: Routledge.

Crenshaw, K. W. (1995). Mapping the margins: Intersectionality, identity politics, and violence against women of color. In C. Crenshaw, N. Gotanda, G. Peller, & K. Thomas (Eds.), *Critical race theory: The key writings that formed the movement* (pp. 357–383). New York: The New Press.

Cuklanz, L. M. (1998). The masculine ideal: Prime time representations of rape, 1976–1978. *Critical Studies in Mass Communication, 15,* 423–448.

Cuklanz, L. M. (2000). *Rape on prime time: Television, masculinity, and sexual violence.* Philadelphia: University of Pennsylvania Press.

Davis, A. (1978). Rape, racism, and the capitalist setting. *Black Scholar, 9*(7), 24–30.

Deming, R. (1992). Kate and Allie: New women and audiences' television archives. In L. Spigel & D. Mann (eds.), *Private screenings: Television and the female consumer* (pp. 203–214). Minneapolis, MN: University of Minnesota Press.

Dworkin, A. (1974). *Woman hating.* New York: Dutton.

Fairstein, L. (1993). *Sexual violence: Our war against rape.* New York: William Morrow & Company.

Fidgeon, R. (2003, July 16). Boom or Bust. *Herald Sun,* p. H08.

Gilligan, C. (1982). *In a different voice: Psychological theory and women's development.* Cambridge, MA: Harvard University Press.

Gitlin, T. (1983). *Inside prime time.* New York: Pantheon Books.

Griffin, S. (1986). *Rape, the power of consciousness* (3rd ed.). San Francisco: Harper & Row.

Kaplan, E. A. (1992). *Motherhood and representation: The mother in popular culture and melodrama.* London: Routledge.

MacKinnon, C. (1987). *Feminism unmodified: Discourses on life and law.* Cambridge, MA: Harvard University Press.

Marcus, S. (1992). Fighting bodies, fighting words: A theory and politics of rape prevention. In J. Butler & J. Scott (Eds.), *Feminists theorize the political* (pp. 385–403). New York: Routledge.

Moorti, S. (2002). *Color of rape: Gender and race in television's public spheres.* Albany, NY: State University of New York Press.

Projansky, S. (2001). *Watching rape: Film and television in postfeminist culture.* New York: New York University Press.

Rajan, R. S. (1993). *Real and imagined women: Gender, culture, and postcolonialism.* New York: Routledge.

Salzman, T. (1998). Rape camps as a means of ethnic cleansing: Religious, cultural, and ethical responses to rape victims in the former Yugoslavia. *Human Rights Quarterly, 20,* 348–378.

Sielke, S. (2002). *Reading rape: The rhetoric of sexual violence in American literature and culture, 1790–1990.* Princeton, NJ: Princeton University Press.

Stanley, A. (2005, June 13). Cracking cases (and superiors) with more than good looks. *New York Times,* p. E9.

http://www.joyfulheartfoundation.org

http://www.tvtome.com/lawandorder/svu

20

More Than Baby Mamas

Black Mothers and Hip-Hop Feminism

Marlo David

For nearly two decades scholars, activists and artists have broken new ground in regard to the ways we think about women and hip-hop. Through a number of necessary interventions, these artists and intellectuals have moved from critiquing the popular phallocentric swagger of hip-hop to critiquing this very critique. It is no longer appropriate to simply identify hip-hop as patriarchal and complain that its favorite son, rap music, is misogynist. Instead, our post-soul, post-modern, post-black sensibilities have allowed us to complicate how we situate women within this self-reflexive organism called hip-hop. We understand more about the ways in which black women contribute to the contours and substance of hip-hop culture. The 1980s and early 1990s produced Roxanne Shante's groundbreaking raps and Queen Latifah's Kente-adorned embodiment of the Strong Black Woman, while the late nineties and new century have given way to what Imani Perry calls [the] rise of the "sexy MC," such as Lil' Kim and Eve.[1] Despite the individual critiques that each of these artists have garnered, they together represent two generations of women in hip hop who have carved a space for black women to vocalize their independence, sexual agency and lyrical mastery.

In response, early hip-hop critics from Tricia Rose, Nancy Guevara and Cheryl L. Keyes, as well as relative new-jacks such as Joan Morgan, Imani Perry and Gwendolyn Pough have explored the ways in which black women create a progressive, feminist space within hip-hop's hyper-masculine universe.* They intervene on behalf of complexity in order to analyze black women's embrace of hip-hop identity. They sharply critique the misogyny, violence and materialism of hip-hop. Meanwhile, they also show how black women navigate the conflicting, inconsistent gray areas of hip-hop to stand up and be heard. Each of these voices, often in harmony and discord with traditional black feminist theory, contribute to what we can now confidently call hip-hop feminism. This is a feminism that can read sexual objectification *and* agency within the same artist or textual production. It

From David, Marlo, "More than Baby Mamas: Black Mothers and Hip-Hop Feminism." In Gwendolyn Pough et al (eds) (2007), *Home Girls Make Some Noise: Hip Hop Feminism Anthology*. Mira Loma, CA: Parker Publishing, 345–367. Reprinted with permission of Parker Publishing.

articulates the racial and sexual tensions experienced by round-the-way sistas, ghetto princesses, college students and club hoppers through the vernacular ideology of hip-hop. While our black feminist foremothers such as Barbara Smith, Barbara Christian and Michelle Wallace fought to put race and gender on the table together in order to liberate black women from a myriad of oppressions, hip-hop feminists have argued that there are realities that traditional black feminists overlook. Hip-hop feminists offer a response to a contemporary backlash against feminism among young, intelligent, progressive black women. Joan Morgan, therefore, describes a new-school desire for a functional feminism

> that possesses the same fundamental understanding held by any true student of hip-hop. Truth can't be found in the voice of any one rapper but in the juxtaposition of many. The keys that unlock the riches of contemporary black female identity . . . lie at the magical intersection where those contrary voices meet.[2]

At the intersection of those contrary voices, female hip-hop artists have addressed major feminist issues: sexual agency, domestic violence and sexual assault, female economic survival, empowerment and the strength and beauty of black women. However, the hip-hop community has neglected one key aspect of black feminist theory—discourses on motherhood. Since the Moynihan Report was issued in 1965, pathologizing black matriarchy, black feminists have sought to redefine racist and sexist notions that construct black motherhood for the dominant society. These women were compelled to action not only because Moynihan misread the lives of black American women, but also because the implications of his "research" cleared the way for decades of violent and demoralizing public policy toward black people. In order to bring these issues to the forefront, black feminists had to distinguish themselves from

their white counterparts, whose feminism sought gender equality without concern for the entanglements of other oppressions. Womanists, such as Alice Walker and Sherley Anne Williams, began to articulate a desire to synchronize group survival and women's issues into a personal politics that women could use.[3] Among their concerns were the real and imagined intricacies of black motherhood. With that brief feminist history in mind, I am interested in where issues of motherhood and procreative power stand among young women today. As far as hip-hop culture is concerned, there seem to be few popular female rappers who speak openly about their procreative lives and choices. Few portray mothers in music videos or even rhyme about procreative issues affecting the black women they represent. Furthermore, scholars and journalists who write about hip-hop and gender politics do not often address how black women navigate this highly charged political space.

This is not to say that mothering—and its attendant procreative issues such as abortion, fertility, birth control, pregnancy and child rearing—does not receive attention in hip-hop. There are a number of "mama" narratives popular in the music. Think of the strong black mother trope best remembered in Tupac's "Dear Mama" or the cautionary teen mom genre exemplified in Slick Rick's "All Alone" or another Tupac classic, "Brenda's Got a Baby." While these narratives are significant, they often work to objectify the subject position of mother. Mothers are alternatively honored or pitied. Rarely does rap music offer the chance to examine how women perceive themselves as mothers or as potential mothers, nor is there much attention paid to the intense political implications of that subjectivity.

Political rhetoric as well as legislative and legal activity surrounding social welfare, education, criminal justice and health care in the United States remains highly enmeshed with the fact of black motherhood. Moreover, medical and political technologies conjoin to manipulate not only the physical bodies of black women but also the cultural intelligibility of motherhood at all. Patricia Hill Collins notes in *Black Feminist Thought:* "African-American women's experiences as mothers have been shaped by the dominant group's efforts to harness Black women's sexuality and fertility to a system of capitalist exploitation."[4] Certainly, this has been the case in terms of the use and abuse of black women for the purpose of reproducing a slave labor force in early American history. Yet Collins' insight begs for further application within contemporary U.S. society. Black women are no longer baby machines for a plantation economy, but what about a prison economy or a low-wage welfare economy? Post-slavery regulation of black women's fertility has been, in effect, one of the major tools with which capitalist class relations have been maintained.[5] How does the dominant society manipulate the sign of the black mother in order to subdue, fix and rank groups and bodies . . . ? How can black women reclaim control of the images that are used to perpetuate a neo-slave existence? It is with these "real-world" applications that this inquiry attempts to engage. Therefore, the consideration of black women's procreative power has implications beyond my personal attraction to the issue as a black feminist scholar and mother. These issues, in fact, should be central for any individuals who align themselves with progressive struggle and social justice in the academy and beyond. What I am interested in developing are ways of reading the procreative performativity of black women and their bodies, as they are presented to us through hip-hop. . . .

I am concerned that while many black women hip-hop artists strive to assert sexual freedom, they do not attend with as much vigor to the related issue of the mothering body and how that subject position is exploited to continue to oppress all black people. Women asserting sexual freedom and agency through the language of hip-hop often trade upon patriarchal notions of the female body as weak, vulnerable and ripe for exploitation, rather than strong, confident and in control. Lauryn Hill, I will argue, flips this script and refuses to trade in the masculine narratives and metaphors to make her claims to power. Instead, much of her early work draws upon feminist language to assert mastery of her life and procreative body. Hip-hop feminists must recognize how black mothering continues to be manipulated and provide new narratives of empowerment for women; otherwise our hopes for reproductive freedom and social justice will continue to fall short of the transformative potential held within hip-hop music and culture. . . .

Reading hip-hop culture is a messy business. While we must resist simplistic readings that force us to assess what is good or bad, positive or negative for the black community, it is also possible and desirable to understand how hip-hop disrupts racist, sexist, classist and homophobic discourses that are par for the course in American culture. This is not to remove all ethical judgment from hip-hop criticism. There are aspects of hip-hop that are sexist, misogynist, homophobic, racist and exploitative. . . . Hip-hop feminist critique makes space for the gray areas, the ironies, and contradictions that are part of hip-hop and life, but it should also provide a way out of the mire of postmodern detachment to invite women and men to get down to the business of "bringing wreck" against the social forces that control their lives. . . .

Lauryn Hill: Killing Them, Softly

Lauryn Hill, as a member of The Fugees and as a solo artist, has always stood her ground among the legions of male MCs. She consistently ranks among the upper echelon of the tightest rappers to ever hold a mic, and she has maintained that control through a carefully mixed blend of conscious lyrics, undeniable flow, reggae/dub influence and R&B foundations. Unlike her female contemporaries who often defer to the power of masculinity to carve out space of empowerment for female hip-hop audiences, Hill has maintained a strident feminist stance against the hyper-masculine aesthetics that dominate the industry. . . .

Lauryn Hill has offered her subjectivity as a mother to articulate a sense of possibility and empowerment for women. Her song "To Zion," a melismatic, stirring ode to her newborn son Zion, stands as her most direct testament to motherhood. I will discuss this song in the context of Hill's own comments about the song and how it describes her struggles with having a son. Beyond that, however, I will highlight a few other textual moments made before and shortly after Hill became a mother that suggest that she seeks to empower the female body, not as a sexy gangsta, but for its "female" attributes. For Lauryn Hill, being a woman is not a curse, it is a blessing. . . .

"To Zion" is Hill's meditation on her procreative choice to have a child at the pinnacle of her artistic career. Through the confessional narrative style that has been a signature of her writing, Hill explains to her audience how she felt when she found out that she was pregnant. For Hill, her bodily experience of pregnancy initially "overwhelmed" her. Like many women who discover that they are pregnant, Hill expresses the deep sense of apprehension she feels towards the function her body had "been chosen to perform." However, she comes to see the experience as a blessing, an opportunity to bring forth "an angel" and "a man-child." Through these lines, Hill participates in a reversal of the descriptions of female embodiment expressed by her contemporaries Eve and Missy Elliott. Hill's body, her "belly," is a space of hope and generosity. She does not see her body as necessarily vulnerable nor does she express a desire to use her body in order to entice or entrap the man in her life. She dwells on her personal connection with her body and the possibilities that it holds within.

She remains future oriented and positive. She furthers her hip-hop feminist narrative as she explains the choice she makes to become a mother at such a young age. As she describes her "crazy circumstance," Hill chronicles the daunting decision of whether to continue her pregnancy or to terminate it. Hill had just come off of the success of The Fugees' CD *The Score* and was in the process of embarking on her solo career. She was young and still in college. With all of these demands, it may have seemed to her, as it does to many women, that she could not handle the added physical and emotional responsibility of a baby. Hill clearly understands that she has access to procreative choice, what she describes as a choice between her "head" or her "heart." Regardless of how she characterizes this choice, she embraces the fact that there is a choice to be made. Then, despite legitimate concerns for her career, she chooses motherhood, not as a replacement for her career, but as another aspect of her life. She seems to recognize the inherent difficulty for women facing this choice, but she seems to argue for working through the struggle.[6]

Finally, Lauryn Hill intervenes within hip-hop discourse on motherhood by simply articulating the power of the maternal figure for group survival. Taking on a womanist perspective, Hill reminds her listeners that her reasons for rapping and singing have as much to do with personal fulfillment as they do with providing narratives of black empowerment through her work. She rhymes in the song "Everything is Everything": "Let's love ourselves and we can't fail." The lyrics of this song indicate a desire to promote love and progress to her audiences. Hill wants to be a catalyst for a "better situation," which can be read as better schools, better health-care, better jobs and better opportunities for black people. Hill argues for self-love as the fail-safe method toward empowerment. She then expresses her future orientation, which relies on the power of "our seeds." Seeds, within [the] hip-hop lexicon, refers to children. Therefore, Hill's claim that "our seeds will grow" does not refer only to a metaphorical seed, but rather literally to children. In other words, Hill sees black children as the potential for progressive change within black communities. Her final admonition—"all we need is dedication"—suggests that dedication to black children represents collective struggle.[7]

Lauryn Hill does not describe this devotion toward children as a space of weakness or vulnerability. She also does not sentimentalize this notion. While her vocals in "To Zion" certainly exhibit a tender side to Hill's perceptions of mothering, her lyrics in "Everything is Everything" shows that she does not sentimentalize the political implications of mothering. She also critiques systems that work to oppress black children and adopts the lyrical hyperbole of gunplay to designate her commitment to her cause. For example, in "Lost Ones," she rhymes that she "Can't take a threat to my newborn son." Hill, who refers to herself as L-Boogie in this song, adopts the rhetoric of the civil rights struggle to illustrate her commitment to her son, the seed for the new future, within the first two lines of this verse. Hill explains that she is both down for nonviolent and armed struggle depending on the situation. Threats to her "newborn son" are of the highest order, calling for the more violent response.[8]

Taken as a whole, lyrics from a number of songs by Lauryn Hill reflect an intense attention to motherhood as a legitimate contribution to the intersecting struggle for racial and gender equality. Her attention is reflected in at least three ways. First, she defends the power of the female body in and of itself against male and female rappers who render that body vulnerable and exploitable. Importantly, Hill also addresses the power of procreative choice in her song "To Zion." In this R&B song, Hill sings about the difficulty she faced in making this decision and how she ultimately finds another avenue to empowerment via the subject position of mother.

Finally, Hill places mothering and children within the framework of the collective struggle for justice. She takes the stance of the revolutionary—armed if necessary who will fight against the dominant social structures designed to take advantage of black children.

Conclusion

...What I hope is clear is that there is room at the table for black feminists, womanists and hip-hop feminists to address the representations of black motherhood and their importance to our communities. I would love to see more women artists, especially those blessed with mainstream and popular audiences, to bring these issues to light. When Lauryn Hill sings "if I ruled the world, I'd free all my sons," she attends to the emotional desire for a mother to see her own children free and speaks the reality that so many of our "sons"—and daughters—are locked up. The life and music of the multitextual entity of Lauryn Hill offers new narratives for young black women to relate to and explore feminism.

My desire to embark on this project emerges not out of an effort to reclaim black domesticity and respectability or to add to the debates between conscious and gangsta lyricists, but out of a personal interest in what it means to be a black woman steeped in hip-hop and a mother in the twenty-first century. It means that the bedtime story I tell my sons is as likely to be Slick Rick's morality tale from 1988 ("Children's Story") as anything by Hans Christian Anderson or the Brothers Grimm. It means that while I still love the music and the metaphors of hip-hop, I struggle to train my boys into men, not knuckleheads, ruffnecks or gangstas. And ultimately, it mean[s] walking the precarious line between raising the hope for generations to come—those black diamonds and pearls that Lauryn Hill sings about—or contributing to the cadre of workers/neo-slaves for a burgeoning U.S. prison and low-wage welfare economy that seeks to entrap our children within its snares. Therefore, I am arguing for a more nuanced and conscious use of hip-hop feminism, because in many cases our lives depend on it. By situating black procreative power and mothering as a theoretical space worth exploring—by contextualizing it historically as well as within its contemporary manifestations—those of us within hip-hop feminist discourse can continue to probe the possibilities and limits of the culture as a revolutionary genre.

Notes

*See references for selected critical readings [Ed.].

1. Imani Perry, *Prophets of the Hood: Politics and Poetics in Hip Hop* (Durham: Duke University Press, 2004), 155.

2. Joan Morgan, *When Chickenheads Come Home to Roost: A Hip Hop Feminist Breaks It Down* (New York: Simon & Schuster, 1999), 62.

3. Sherley Anne Williams, "Some Implications of Womanist Theory," *African American Literary Theory: A Reader*. Ed. Winston Napier. (New York: New York University Press, 2000), 219.

4. Patricia Hill Collins, *Black Feminist Thought: Knowledge, Consciousness, and the Politics of Empowerment* (New York: Routledge, 2000), 50.

5. Ibid., 51.

6. The Original Hip-hop Lyrics Archive. http://www.ohhla.com/all.html. (6 January 2006)

7. Ibid.

8. Ibid.

References

Bost, Suzanne. "'Be deceived if ya wanna be foolish'; (Re)Constructing Body: Genre and Gender in Feminist Rap." *Postmodern Culture*. 12.1, 1–31.

Collins, Patricia Hill. *Black Feminist Thought: Knowledge, Consciousness and the Politics of Empowerment*. New York: Routledge, 2000.

Doyle, Laura. *Bordering on the Body: The Racial Matrix of Modern Fiction and Culture*. New York: Oxford University Press, 1994.

Keyes, Cheryl L. "'We're More than a Novelty, Boys': Strategies of Female Rappers in the Rap Music Tradition." *Feminist Messages: Coding in Women's Folk Culture*. Ed. Joan Newlon Radner. Urbana: University of Illinois Press, 1993. 203–19.

Missy Elliot. Internet, http://www.missy-elliott.com/

Morgan, Joan. *When Chickenheads Come Home to Roost: A Hip-Hop Feminist Breaks It Down*. New York: Simon & Schuster, 1999.

Moynihan, D. *The Negro Family: A Case for National Action*. Washington, D.C.: Government Printing Office, 1965.

Perry, Imani. *Prophets of the Hood: Politics and Poetics in Hip-Hop*. Durham: Duke University Press, 2004.

Potter, Russell A. *Spectacular Vernaculars: Hip-Hop and the Politics of Postmodernism*. Albany: State University of New York Press, 1995.

Pough, Gwendolyn D. *Check It While I Wreck It: Black Womanhood, Hip-Hop Culture, and the Public Sphere*. Boston: Northeastern University Press, 2004.

Rose, Tricia. *Black Noise: Rap Music and Black Culture in Contemporary America*. Hanover: Wesleyan University Press, 1994.

The Original Hip-Hop Lyrics Archive. Internet. http://www.ohhla.com/all.html.

Wallace, Michele. "When Black Feminism Faces the Music, and the Music is Rap." *The New York Times* 29 July 1990, sec. 2:20.

Williams, Sherley Anne. "Some Implications of Womanist Theory." *African American Literary Theory: A Reader*. Ed. Winston Napier. New York: New York University Press, 2000.

Discography

Elliott, Missy. "Momniy." *The Cookbook*. Atlantic Records, 2005.

———. "Work It." *Under Construction*. Electra, 2002.

Eve. "Heaven Only Knows." *Let There Be Eve . . . Ruff Ryders' First Lady*. Interscope Records, 1999.

———. "Love is Blind." *Let There Be Eve . . . Ruff Ryders' First Lady*. Interscope Records, 1999.

———. "Who's That Girl?" *Scorpion*. Interscope Records, 2001.

Hill, Lauryn. "Everything is Everything." *The Miseducation of Lauryn Hill*. Ruffhouse Records, 1998.

———. "Lost Ones." *Miseducation of Lauryn Hill*. Ruffhouse Records, 1998.

———. "To Zion." *The Miseducation of Lauryn Hill*. Ruffhouse Records, 1998.

Ol' Dirty Bastard, Raekwon and Method Man. "Raw Hide." *Return to the 36 Chambers*. Electra, 1995.

Poor Righteous Teachers. "Shakiyla." *Holy Intellect*. Profile, 1990.

Queen Latifah and Monie Love. "Ladies First." *All Hail the Queen*. Tommy Boy, 1989.

Nas and Lauryn Hill. "If I Ruled the World." *It Was Written*. Sony, 1996.

Slick Rick. "All Alone (No One to Be With)." *Behind Bars*. Def Jam, 1994.

———. "Children's Story." *Great Adventures of Slick Rick*. Def Jam, 1988.

The Fugees. "Ready or Not." *The Score*. Sony, 1996.

Tupac. "Brenda's Got a Baby." *2Pacalypse Now*. Jive, 1992.

———. "Dear Mania." *Me Against the World*. Jive, 1995.

21

Political Culture Jamming

The Dissident Humor of
The Daily Show With Jon Stewart

Jamie Warner

Armed with branding techniques honed and perfected in the commercial marketplace, politicians and political parties have attempted to drown out dissident messages to better "sell" their own political policies, a dagger in the heart of deliberative democrats who argue that democracy cannot survive without open, ongoing, and rational political conversation. In fact, much of contemporary democratic theory rests on two propositions: (a) the public sphere is populated with multiple and disparate voices who can and will engage each other, and (b) these conversations will be rational. Jürgen Habermas's (1962/1989) *The Structural Transformation of the Public Sphere* is perhaps the most important of the recent statements of this position (Habermas, 1973/1975, 1998; see also Bennett & Entman, 2001; Carey, 1989; White, 1995). Indeed, many scholars posit some version of accessible, public, substantive, rational conversations among numerous and diverse participants as *the* prerequisite for a healthy democracy. . . .

Political elites and their consultants have no such concerns. Rather than fretting over possible barriers confronting marginal voices, politicians instead want their voices, agenda, and framing of issues to crowd out divergent voices because such dominant status helps contribute to the success of their specific political agendas (Lakoff, 2002, 2004). In the past two decades, politicians have increasingly utilized what are known as "branding" techniques of commercial marketers to just such an end, in the hopes of persuading the citizen/consumer to trust their "product"—their platform and policy positions—to the exclusion of all others. These branding techniques, relying on emotional rather than rational appeals, are used in the attempt to achieve automatic, unreflective trust in the branded product, whether that product is a Popsicle, a Palm Pilot, or a political party. Although such brand hegemony is obviously profitable in terms of money and/or power for the

From Warner, J. (2007). Political culture jamming: The dissident humor of *The Daily Show With Jon Stewart*. *Popular Communications, 5*(1), 17–36. Reprinted by permission of Taylor & Francis Ltd.

hegemon, it works to the detriment of the tenets of democratic theory, both by talking over viable voices and conversations in the public sphere, and by operating through calculated emotional appeals. How, in the name of the healthy democracy described previously, can one *disrupt* the transmission of the dominant political brand messages so that competing conversations can occur?

One intriguing model comes from the same realm as the original branding techniques, the media saturated world of consumer capitalism, where an insurgent movement known as "culture jamming" is at the forefront of this type of disruption. Culture jammers are a loose collection of media activists who are rebelling against the hegemony of the messages promoting global capitalism. Spearheaded by media activist Kalle Lasn of the Media Foundation and his *Adbusters* magazine, culture jammers utilize a wide variety of tactics to destabilize and challenge the dominant messages of multinational corporations and consumer capitalism. Rather than simply using factual information, rational argumentation, legal language, and traditional political tactics to oppose capitalist institutions directly, culture jamming turns the commercial techniques of image and emotion back on themselves through acts of what Christine Harold (2004) calls "rhetorical sabotage" (p. 190).

As politicians and political parties increasingly utilize the branding techniques of commercial marketers to "sell" their political agendas, it follows that similar jamming techniques could be employed to call those branding techniques into question. In this chapter, I argue that the comedian Jon Stewart and his fake news program, *The Daily Show With Jon Stewart,* act as *political* culture jammers. Through their own humorous version of news parody, *The Daily Show* writers and comedians disseminate dissident interpretations of current political events, potentially jamming the transmission of the dominant political brand message. Like other culture jammers, *The Daily Show* subversively employs emotional and aesthetic modalities similar to those employed by political branding itself, thus interrupting it from within. Unlike many culture jammers, however, *The Daily Show*'s reliance on a humorous version of parody means that they can add their voices to the conversation in a seemingly innocuous way. (After all, it is *just* a joke.) . . .

The Fetish of Political Branding

See, in my line of work you got to keep repeating things over and over and over again for the truth to sink in, to kind of catapult the propaganda. (George W. Bush, quoted in Froomkin, 2005)

. . . The basic assumption behind branding is simple: Consumers are not "rational" shoppers. Instead, they are busy people, possessing neither the time nor the inclination to do detailed comparisons of sneakers, sunglasses, or fabric softeners. This time crunch creates an opening for marketers. Knowing that many consumers cannot or will not do research based on quality and/or price, marketers instead strive to cultivate a *relationship* with consumers that inspires loyalty for that particular brand. Trust in a particular brand allows the consumer to take a time-saving shortcut at the supermarket or mall, as well as get the supposed value, and, hopefully, the status that marketers strive to attach to the brand. Thus, the key to establishing this lucrative connection with consumers is through the play of emotion, rather than the dissemination of information: "Marketing is no longer about selling. It's about creating relationships with customers that cultivate an emotional preference for your brand" (Travis, 2000, cited in Hiebert, 2001; see also Gobe, 2001, 2002). The particular relationship to be cultivated with consumers depends on the type of image that marketers believe will best sell their product to its target demographic: dependable, practical, good value for the price, safe, or the much coveted yet ever elusive "cool."

Politicians and their political consultants have fully embraced the logic and tactics of branding in the political arena. Although the normative value of the migration of these marketing tactics into the political sphere, via the media, has been widely disputed, its efficacy has not, at least from the point of view of the politicians themselves (Newman, 1999). It is obvious why parties and politicians would see brand loyalty as a desirable outcome. Citizens, like consumers, are busy people, and cultivating trust in the "Republican" or "Democratic" brand works to save the citizen/consumer time, in the form of information costs, while providing the politician or party a solid base of support. Many of the same branding techniques used to sell soap and MP3 players are exploited for political gain, including market research techniques, the proliferation of emotional messages across various media through the use of sound bites and talking points, and repetition/saturation strategies within each medium. In addition to creating a sense of familiarity, an important part of building trust, repetition of carefully researched emotional messages (e.g., talking points) helps locate a party or politician as one of the "top of mind" or "dominant" brands—the first or, hopefully, the only brand that comes to mind in response to a particular stimulus (Carter, 1999, cited in Karlberg, 2002, p. 7). The ultimate goal in political branding is the same as in commercial branding: the creation of such unquestioning trust in the brand that the citizen/consumer allows the brand [to] do the "thinking" for him or her.

Culture Jamming

How does one call these very effective branding techniques into question, so that alternative voices can get into the conversation?

The success of global consumer capitalism and the marketing techniques that go with it, specifically the branding techniques mentioned previously, have spurred many internal and external critiques and rebellions, often lumped together under the term culture jamming (e.g., Klein, 2000, 2002; Roddick, 1994; Talen, 2003). Current culture jammers, such as media activist Kalle Lasn, place themselves on a "revolutionary continuum" with anarchists, Dadaists, surrealists, the Situationists, the Sixties hippie movement, and early punk rockers, among others (Lasn, 1999, p. 99; see also Dery, 1993). According to Lasn, the primary goal of culture jammers is *détournement,* a French term borrowed from the Situationists of the 1950s and 1960s. Translated literally as a "turning around," Lasn (1999) defines the concept of *détournement* as "a perspective-jarring turnabout in your everyday life" (p. xvii), which is instigated by "rerouting spectacular images, environments, ambiences and events to reverse or subvert their meaning, thus reclaiming them" (p. 103).

Specifically, Lasn and his fellow culture jammers want to reverse, subvert, and reclaim our identity as brand-trusting pawns of consumer capitalism. For example, Lasn's Web site (www.adbusters.org) constantly runs multiple ongoing anti-brand campaigns, and these do utilize traditional, rational techniques such as boycotts and petition drives against heavily branded corporations such as Nike and Tommy Hilfiger. However, *Adbusters* is perhaps best known for its attempts to jam the dominant brand images with alternative images, what Lasn calls subvertisements. These images use the same branding technologies and design layouts that advertisers do, with a problematizing twist: "A well produced print 'subvertisement' mimics the look and feel of the target ad, prompting the classic double-take as viewers realize what they're seeing is the very opposite of what they expected" (Lasn, 1999, p. 131). Successful *Adbuster* subvertisments include those parodying alcohol, cigarettes, and the fast food industry, as well as the fashion establishment.

One of *Adbusters'* best-known subvertisements revolved around the Calvin Klein *Obsession* ads of the 1990s. The original and very successful print ads for the perfume featured close-ups of young, beautiful, tan, taut bodies with the words "Obsession for Men" or "Obsession for Women" across the top of the ad. Exploiting what Lasn calls "leverage points" or logical contradictions in the underlying logic of consumer capitalism, *Adbusters* attacks Calvin Klein, not with facts and figures demonstrating how the empty quest to buy beauty and status is dangerous, but instead with perverted mirror images (1999, p. 130)....

In what follows, I argue that *The Daily Show With Jon Stewart* functions as what I call "political culture jamming" by working in much the same way: disseminating dissident images with messages designed to provoke the same type of *détournement* or subversion of the dominant meaning that Lasn and his fellow culture jammers seek....

Political Culture Jamming: *The Daily Show With Jon Stewart*

In January 2004, the Pew Research Center for the People and the Press released the results of a survey designed to discover where Americans get their political news. One of the most interesting findings involved a relatively new phenomenon: 21% of those 18–29 regularly learned about the presidential campaign and its candidates on comedy programs (compared with 23% who said they regularly learned this information from network news). Overall, 50% of the 18–29 demographic said that they at least "sometimes" learn about the campaign from these shows, compared with 27% of the 30–49 demographic and 12% of people 50 and older....

One of the most popular of these comedy shows—with an estimated 1.3 million viewers per night—is *The Daily Show With Jon Stewart,* a 30-min "newscast"

that airs Monday through Thursday at 11:00 p.m. EST on the cable network *Comedy Central* (Hall, 2005)....

The Daily Show is a funny and often sharply critical parody of a television news broadcast; the entire cast is made of up of comedians. In fact, in his videotaped acceptance of the Television Critics Association Award, Stewart recommended that one of the other, legitimate nominees, *60 Minutes* perhaps, should investigate how a *fake* news program won the award for "Outstanding Achievement in News and Information" (Kurtz, 2003). It is this seeming lack of seriousness within the serious format of a cable/network news broadcast, however, that makes *The Daily Show* both a popular and a cogent critic. Like the *Adbuster* subvertisements, *The Daily Show* inserts its voice into the political conversation by plagiarizing the aesthetics of the media, in this particular case, the news media. It is a copy, but a copy that has been strategically altered to highlight political "leverage points": factual errors, logical contradictions, and incongruities in the dominant political brand messages and the media that disseminates them.

MATTER OUT OF
PLACE: PARODIC FORMAT

The first political culture jamming technique employed by *The Daily Show* is a metatechnique, one that most explicitly resembles the aesthetics of the *Adbusters'* subvertisements discussed previously: news parody format. This twisted mimicking of the newscast format is the first and most important jamming technique and the entire show makes sense only within this format. Just as the subversive parody of the *Obsession* ad must closely approximate the actual ad to be effective, the news parody must closely resemble an actual news television broadcast, and *The Daily Show* does. The anchor, Jon Stewart, presents the top stories of the day, complete with the video over his right shoulder, and conducts interviews. Correspondents, many of whom are now becoming celebrities in their own right, do segments and interviews on current events. Watching the show with the volume turned down might not alert you to the fact that this is anything other than one of the myriad news options now available. Turning the volume up should let you in on the secret. Here Stewart is interviewing "senior media analyst" Stephen Colbert about the media coverage of the U.S. invasion of Iraq in March 2003:[1]

Stewart: What should the media's role be in covering the war?

Colbert: Very simply, the media's role should be the accurate and objective description of the hellacious ass-whomping we're handing the Iraqis.

Stewart: Hellacious ass-whomping? Now to me, that sounds pretty subjective.

Colbert: Are you saying it's not an ass-whomping, Jon? I suppose you could call it an "ass-kicking" or an "ass-handing-to." Unless, of course, you love Hitler.

Stewart: [stammering] I don't love Hitler.

Colbert: Spoken like a true Hitler-lover.

Stewart: I'm perplexed. Is your position that there's no place for negative words or even thoughts in the media?

Colbert: Not at all, Jon. Doubts can happen to everyone, including me. But as a responsible journalist, I've taken my doubts, fears, moral compass, conscience, and all-pervading skepticism about the very nature of this war and simply placed them in this empty Altoids box. [Produces box] That's where they'll stay, safe and sound, until Iraq is liberated. (Miller, 2003)

This is obviously not a typical network or cable news interview. . . .

What are the consequences of choosing to intentionally misuse the newscast format? Parodying the sober and seemingly impartial language and layout of a newscast gives the content an air of legitimacy and respectability. This seemingly weighty format then allows an automatic contrast with the humorous content—out of which incongruity, a prerequisite for most humor, can flow.[2] . . .

MATTER OUT OF TIME: STRATEGIC USE OF VIDEO

The mimicking of the news format at a metalevel, however, is a necessary but not sufficient condition for the specific political culture jamming of *The Daily Show*. There is nothing inherently subversive about parody, which can just as easily be employed in the service of the dominant political message as in the critique of that message. Within the larger parodic format of the show, however, *The Daily Show* also presents the political content in a way that calls into question the *substantive* claims of the dominant brand message, as well as the media that unproblematically disseminates it.

The second technique employed by *The Daily Show*—the strategic use of video clips—thus works inside the metatechnique of the news parody. Similar to the parodic format of the show, the use of video is designed to disrupt the dominant political message by presenting various types of "matter out of time" using video clips. As previously stated, there is usually one video screen above Stewart's right shoulder just as there is on network and cable news shows. Often Stewart will turn his head and talk to the video clips, stopping the video to pose questions and make comments. . . . Stewart's own comments provide the matter that is out of time; news anchors do not usually interject such comments during "serious" news programs. . . . However, the most effective way *The Daily Show* uses video is to strategically juxtapose video clips to highlight leverage points. . . . The branding techniques are exposed as orchestrated techniques and so can be examined explicitly and critically, rather than operating in the background where they are most successful. . . .

Technically, the audience is left to draw their own conclusions, although those conclusions are channeled in a certain direction by the specific sequence of video, as the following 2003 segment demonstrates:

Stewart: . . . When you combine the new mandate that criticizing the Commander in Chief is off limits in wartime with last year's official disbanding of the Democratic Party, we're left at the all time low in the good old fashion debate category. Now I know you're thinking: But Jon, every time I want to have a calm, honest discussion about these kinds of issues, I'm shouted down and harassed by the Dixie Chicks and their ilk. Well, tonight it all changes. . . . So first, joining us tonight is George W. Bush, the 43rd President of the United States. . . . Taking the other side, from the year 2000, Texas Governor and presidential candidate, George W. Bush.

(Split screen of Governor Bush on the left and President Bush on the right. "Bush vs. Bush" logo between them.)

Stewart: Mr. President, you won the coin toss. The first question will go to you. Why is the United States of America using its power to change governments in foreign countries?

President Bush: We must stand up for our security and for the permanent rights and the hopes of mankind.

Stewart: Well, certainly that represents a bold new doctrine in foreign policy, Mr. President. Governor Bush, do you agree with that?

Governor Bush: Yeah, I'm not so sure that the role of the United States is to go around the world and say, "This is the way it's gotta be."

Stewart: Well, that's interesting. That's a difference of opinion, and certainly that's what this country is about, differences of opinion. Mr. President, let me just get specific: Why are we in Iraq?

President Bush: We will be changing the regime of Iraq for the good of the Iraqi people.

Stewart: Governor, then I'd like to hear your response on that.

Governor Bush: If we're an arrogant nation, they'll resent us. I think one way for us to end up being viewed as the ugly American is to go around the world saying, "We do it this way, so should you." . . . ("Bush vs. Bush," n.d.)

Again, Stewart makes no direct comment, simply presenting the matter out of time and allowing the audience to decide how to interpret this information. Is this an example of the notorious flip-flopping [of George W. Bush]? Or does this simply represent a wise policy change due to 9/11? Stewart does not say. He simply presides over the clips. Although Stewart will often alternate looking pained or amused, as the videos are playing, rarely does he directly offer his own opinion on the video clips. By customarily adhering to this tactic, *The Daily Show* manages to stay suggestive rather than didactic, provocative rather than sermonizing or moralizing.

DIALECTICS THAT MATTER: STEWART'S SOCRATIC INTERVIEW STYLE

. : . Although the interview is a common technique used on television news broadcasts, Stewart often employs what is called "Socratic irony" as a rhetorical tactic to point out incongruities, inconsistencies, and internal contradictions in the interviewee's argument, without directly offering his own opinion, as well as without appearing confrontational. In the Platonic dialogues, Socrates routinely adopted an ignorant or tentative tone, asking simple and direct questions to his often dense interlocutors, with the seemingly innocent goal of getting to the "truth." However, his questions were neither simple nor innocent, and Socrates would use his interlocutors' answers to suggest that they should not be quite so confident in their assertions, as well as to make his own substantive points (Colebrook, 2002, p. 87; see also Seery, 1990; Vlastos, 1991). In addition, Socrates' self-effacing demeanor and rather halting comments add to the perception of his sincerity, a mode of personal presentation that Stewart also utilizes.

Discussing the public's perception of the war in Iraq in the summer of 2005 with "senior military analyst" Stephen Colbert, Stewart, like Socrates, plays the straight man, strategically setting up the interviewee to make the substantive point for him:

Stewart: . . . When the Vice President says that the insurgency is in its last throes and Donald Rumsfeld says that that could mean 12 years, isn't that contradictory?

Colbert: Well, Jon, as a member of the cynical, knee-jerk reaction media, liberal, Ivy League, Taxachusetts elite, I can see how you would find a discrepancy between the words "last throes" and "12-year insurgency." But your mistake is looking at what's happening in Iraq on a human scale. The Administration is looking at it from a *geological* perspective. After all, it took a billion years for the earth to cool . . . ("Administrative Discrepancies," n.d.)

Here Stewart plays the calm, polite voice of reason to Colbert's vastly overstated and thus comical position. Like Socrates in the Platonic dialogues, he is *just* asking questions. . . .

By feigning ignorance and constantly insisting that *The Daily Show* is only for laughs, Stewart can operate stealthily. Unlike his culture jamming counterparts who are openly hostile to consumer capitalism and use the violent language of revolution in their fight to be heard, Stewart's self-effacing humor fosters both a sense of trust with those interviewed on the show and a sense of camaraderie with the audience. Further, any attempts by those who were the butt of the joke to attack *The Daily Show*'s credibility could easily falter, as Stewart would be the first one to agree that he is stupid and that the show means nothing. After all, it is *just* a joke.[3] Criticizing *The Daily Show* could come close to admitting that one had no sense of humor, something nobody, especially a politician, would be eager to admit. Employing this Socratic stance— one of Socrates' most famous quotations is "All I know is that I know nothing"— Stewart can create a dissident message that raises questions about both the dominant political and media brands (Colebrook, 2002, p. 87).

Notes

1. Colbert [who now has his own spinoff show: Ed.] is also senior war correspondent, senior religious correspondent, senior UN analyst, senior White House correspondent, senior psychology correspondent, senior "death" correspondent (for stories that report on the death penalty), and senior child molestation expert (for stories on the Catholic Church).

2. George Test (1991) calls this technique the "irony of misused form" (p. 169). For a detailed discussion of the role of incongruity in humor, see Morreall (1987).

3. In his book chronicling the "new political television" of comedians Bill Maher, Dennis Miller, and Jon Stewart, Jeffrey Jones (2005) argues that Stewart's persona is like that of the court jester or fool, speaking truth to power without fear of retaliation because he has the ability to make everyone laugh.

References

Administrative discrepancies. (n.d.). *The Daily Show with Jon Stewart.* Retrieved October 2, 2005, from http://www.comedycentral.com/shows/the_daily_show/videos/stephen_colbert_index.jhtml

Bauder, D. (2004, February 29). Stewart delivers news to younger viewers. *The Associated Press.* Retrieved October 19, 2005, from http://www.washingtonpost.com/wp-dyn/articles/AI6704–2004Feb29.html

Baym, G. (2005). *The Daily Show:* Discursive integration and the reinvention of political journalism. *Political Communication, 22,* 259–276.

Bennett, W. L., & Entman, R. (Eds.). (2001). *Mediated politics: Communication in the future of democracy.* New York: Cambridge University Press.

Bush vs. Bush. (n.d.). *The Daily Show with Jon Stewart.* Retrieved August 8, 2004, from http://www.comedycentral.com/tv_shows/thedailyshowwithjonstewart/videos_corr.jhtml?startIndex=25 &p=stewart

Carey, J. (1989). *Communication as culture: Essays on media and society.* Boston: Unwin Hyman.

Colebrook, C. (2002). *Irony in the works of philosophy.* Lincoln: University of Nebraska Press.

Dery, M. (1993). *Culture jamming: Hacking, slashing and sniping in the empire of the signs.* Westfield, NJ: Open Pamphlet Series.

Froomkin, D. (2005, May 25). The ostrich approach. *Washington Post.* Retrieved August 10, 2005, from http://www.washington post.com/wp-dyn/content/blog/2005/05/25/BL2005052501250.html

Gobe, M. (2001). *Emotional branding: The new paradigm for connecting brands to people.* New York: Allworth.

Gobe, M. (2002). *Citizen brand: 10 commandments for transforming brands in a consumer democracy.* New York: Allworth.

Habermas, J. (1975). *Legitimation crisis* (T. McCarthy, Trans.). Boston: Beacon. (Original work published 1973)

Habermas, J. (1989). *The structural transformation of the public sphere: An inquiry into a category of bourgeois society* (T. Burger, Trans.). Cambridge, MA: MIT University Press. (Original work published 1962)

Habermas, J. (1998). *Between facts and norms: Contributions to a discourse theory of law and democracy* (W. Rehg, Trans.). Cambridge, MA: MIT Press.

Hall, S. (2005). Colbert's "Daily Show" Spinoff. *Eonline.* Retrieved April 15, 2006, from http://www.eonline.com/News/Items/0,1,16481,00.html

Harold, C. (2004). Pranking rhetoric: "Culture jamming" as media activism. *Critical Studies in Media Communication, 21,* 189–211.

Hiebert, R. (2001). Review of *Emotional branding: How successful brands gain the irrational edge* and *Adbusters: Journal of the mental environment. Public Relations Review, 27,* 244–245.

Jones, J. (2005). *Entertaining politics: New political television and civic culture*. New York: Rowman & Littlefield.

Karlberg, M. (2002). Partisan branding and media spectacle: Implications for democratic communication. *Democratic Communique, 18,* 1–21.

Klein, N. (2000). *No logo*. New York: Picador.

Klein, N. (2002). *Fences and windows: Dispatches from the front lines of the globalization debate*. New York: Picador.

Kurtz, H. (2003, July 27). No holds barred: Alternative news outlets smack down convention coverage. *The Washington Post,* p. C1. Retrieved October 15, 2005, from LexisNexis database.

Lakoff, G. (2002). *Moral politics: How liberals and conservatives think* (2nd ed.). Chicago: University of Chicago Press.

Lakoff, G. (2004). *Don't think of an elephant!* White River Junction, VT: Chelsea Green.

Lasn, K. (1999). *Culture jam: How to reverse America's suicidal consumer binge—and why we must*. New York: Quill.

Miller, L. (2003, April 8). TV's boldest new show. Retrieved August 8, 2004, from http://archive.salon.com/ent/tv/feature/2003/04/08 stewart/index_np.html

Morreall, J. (1987). *The philosophy of laughter and humor*. Albany: State University of New York.

Newman, B. (1999). *Handbook of political marketing*. Thousand Oaks, CA: Sage.

Roddick, A. (1994). *Body and soul: Profits with principles—The amazing success story of Anita Roddick & The Body Shop*. Pittsburgh, PA: Three Rivers Press.

Seery, J. (1990). *Political returns: Irony in politics and theory, from Plato to the antinuclear movement*. Boulder, CO: Westview.

Talen, B. (2003). *What should I do if Reverend Billy is in my store?* New York: New Press.

Test, G. (1991). *Satire: Spirit and art*. Tampa: University of South Florida Press.

Vlastos, G. (1991). *Socrates: Ironist and moral philosopher*. Cambridge, UK: Cambridge University Press.

White, S. (Ed.). (1995). *The Cambridge companion to Habermas*. Cambridge, UK: Cambridge University Press.

22

Educating *The Simpsons*

Teaching Queer Representations in Contemporary Visual Media

Gilad Padva

T he visual media, mainly popular films and TV programs, offer an excellent tool for high
school and university educators to encourage sexual tolerance, and in particular to promote a supportive attitude towards queer students. . . . I have selected "Homer's Phobia" as a
case study here because of the significant popularity of this Emmy Award–winning 15th episode of the *Simpsons*' 8th season, aired on February 16, 1997. . . . I offer a scholarly counter-
cultural analysis of this episode in regard to its politics of sexuality and gay-straight alliance,
and to its visualized socio-linguistic strategies of subverting homophobia and sissy-phobia. . . .

Queering the Simpsons

. . . The popular subgenre of *animated* TV sitcoms in the late 1990s and 2000s . . . integrates semi-anarchistic humor and spectacular imagery that often challenge conventional
ethnic, social, gender *and* sexual patterns of representation. This subgenre includes, for
example, *Beavis & Butthead, King of the Hill, Daria, Family Guy, The Kid,* and *The
Simpsons. The Simpsons,* in particular, is one of the world's most successful American
television exports, syndicated in over 60 countries since 1991 (Chocano, 2001). In its
imaginative, disruptive, and even surrealistic way, this subgenre often criticizes conservatism, bigotry, and prejudice with humor. . . .

Jonathan Gray (2003) suggests that *The Simpsons* has turned on its family sitcom
brethren, situating its action within an anti-suburb that is depicted as xenophobic, pro-
vincial, and narrow-minded. Brilliantly parodying the traditional family sitcom neighborhood, *The Simpsons'* town of Springfield satirizes and challenges rather than extols the
American Dream. This series criticizes the hypocrisy within the American educational

From Padva, G. (2008). Educating *The Simpsons:* Teaching queer representations in contemporary
visual media. *Journal of LGBT Youth, 5*(3), 57–73. Reprinted by permission of Taylor & Francis
Ltd., www.tandf.co.uk/journals.

system, religious, political, and even economic systems (Tingleff, 1998). Notably, through Bart, Homer, and Grandpa, *The Simpsons* even challenges categories of male sexuality. Sam Tingleff notes that the relationship between the vicious, albeit decrepit Mr. Burns, who owns the local nuclear plant, and his younger assistant Smithers, is a consistent attack on male sexual norms. Smithers' loyalty comes not from monetary desires, but his quasi-sexual attraction towards Mr. Burns.

Furthermore, the males of *The Simpsons* challenge categories of male sexuality and demonstrate its flexibility. For instance, Homer shaves his "bikini zone" for a presumed swimsuit competition; he kisses his secretary Carl (voice of the gay icon Harvey Fierstein) on the lips, and later mistakenly calls his wife "Carl" in bed; his favorite song is "It's Raining Men"; and he says Oliver North was "just poured into that uniform." And in one episode, when Grandpa Simpson can't take his pills, the elder turns into a woman, later accepting flowers and a date from a male suitor (Tingleff, 1998). Moreover, when Lenny, Homer's co-worker, is dying, he sees a heaven full of Carls. On the other hand, Homer suggests that Lisa could win a class election over Nelson by starting a rumor that he's gay. And when a Gay Pride parade passes the Simpson's house, Homer disapproves of his dog's attempt to hook up with an effeminate, leather-clad dog.

In the gay classic episode "Homer Phobia" (written by Ron Hauge and directed by Mike B. Anderson, 1997), the Simpsons befriend "John," a mustachioed kitsch trader (resembling and voiced by the cult filmmaker and gay icon John Waters). The fact that he is gay makes Homer fear his potential effect on Bart. After a series of ridiculous attempts to turn Bart into a "real man" (and consequent arguments with his wife Marge), Homer assures his son that his love for him is unconditional, whether he is straight or gay.

The anti-homophobic contribution of this episode to the empowerment of GLBT young viewers is based on its three political premises: celebrating queer counter-culture, embracing straight-gay alliance, and promoting diversity and multiculturalism.

Celebrating Queer Counter-Culture

The Simpsons' friendship with John starts during their visit to the latter's "Cockamamie's" antique store. Marge tries to sell Grandma's Civil War doll to John in order to pay an exorbitant Springfield Gas Company bill. John tells her that the doll is nothing but a Johnny Reb bottle from the early 1970s. Homer counters that it's still better than the junk that John is selling, and he wonders how a grown man can love a nostalgic box or a toy. John replies: "It's camp! The tragically ludicrous? The ludicrously tragic?" Eventually, Homer invites John over to see their home, which is "full of valuable worthless crap." John is delighted.

Camp is defined in the *Oxford Dictionary* (1996) as "Affected, theatrically exaggerated; effeminate; homosexual." Susan Sontag (1999 [1964]) categorically defined camp as a vision of the world in terms of a particular kind of style.

> It is the love of the exaggerated, the "off," of things-being-what-they-are-not . . . The androgyne is certainly one of the great images of Camp sensibility . . . What is most beautiful in virile men is something feminine; what is most beautiful in feminine women is something masculine. (p. 56)

Jack Babuscio identified camp with queer subculture based on *gay* sensibility "as a creative energy reflecting a consciousness that is different from the mainstream; a heightened awareness of certain human complications of feeling that spring from the fact of social oppression" (1999 [1978], pp. 117–18). . . .

The *Simpsons* episode's visual vocabulary is dominated by camp. For instance,

John wears flamboyant, striped shirts from the 1970s and his store contains many telling artifacts: Godzilla toy, piggy bank, pink flamingo (echoing John Water[s]'s eponymous cult film), a statue of an Easter Island native head, cola bottle, floral wall decoration, etc. All these items are highly camp, as they are related to kitsch, extravagance, "good" bad taste, artificiality, style, and retrostyle, and also to feminine or "girly" behavior, demonstrated in John's clothing choices and his coy intonation and gestures.

Ironically, John finds the Simpsons extremely camp. He is thrilled by the corn-printed curtain in their kitchen, the color scheme, the rabbit ears antenna, the Hi-C soft drink and Lisa's necklace ("Pearls on a little girl! It's a fairy tale!"). Homer asks him if his records have camp value, and John flatters him: "You yourself are worth a bundle, Homer! Why I could wrap a bow around you and slap on a price tag." Homer laughs and starts dancing with John to an Alicia Bridges disco record ("I Love the Nightlife"). Marge comments that Homer has "certainly taken a shine to him."

The next morning, Homer decides to invite John and his wife over for drinks. But Marge does not think John is married. In fact, she tells Homer that "John is a ho-mo-sexual" (adopting the apparently scientific/medical definition). In response, Homer shouts hysterically.

Soon afterwards, Homer sees Bart wearing a Hawaiian shirt, choosing a pink cake over a brown one and dancing to Cher's "Shoop Shoop Song (It's In His Kiss)," wearing a large black wig with a pink bow. Bart's drag show is traumatic for his father. No confusion is allowed over his child's sexual identity and orientation (two concepts Homer repeatedly mixes up). Homer suspects that his son is gay, not because Bart is attracted to boys, but because he does not behave manly enough. Homer sees Bart's dance, not as innocent child's play, but as a *camp* performance, identified (even in Homer's presumably straight mind) with

"transvestite" gay identity, and therefore, as extremely, "problematic." He consequently resolves to "normalize" his son. . . .

While Homer is threatened by John's (homo)sexuality and its "effeminizing" influence on Bart, the female protagonists— wife Marge, their individualistic pre-adolescent daughter Lisa, and baby Maggie—sympathize with their new friend. Marge, in particular, likes gossiping with John, who demonstrates his impressive knowledge of celebrities' secret lives, and she adores him for his sense of humor, creativity, friendship, stylishness and delicacy. These qualities are contrasted to her husband's stupidity, egocentricity, misbehavior, clumsiness and machismo. It is no wonder that Marge immediately becomes John's best (female) friend, his devoted "fag hag."

Embracing Straight-Gay Alliance

The term "fag hag" dates back to the United States in the late 1960s, dismissively directed at women who were considered not attractive enough to socialize with "real men." But like so many derogatory terms, it was reclaimed in the 1990s as a stereotypic term to be worn with pride. In the ideal, gay men introduced their female friends into a world free from sexual harassment, where the emphasis was on fun and where, more often than not, they would find themselves the center of flattering and unthreatening attention. Hence, "[F]ag haggery was in fashion" (Button, 2000, p. 46). . . .

Marge's "sistership" with John is a bonding between a straight woman and a gay man who enjoys his own stylishness, neatness and effeminacy. In contrast to many straight men *and* some sissy-phobic gay men, John celebrates rather than mocks male femininity, sissiness and stylishness. He and Marge share "feminine" insights and feelings in a friendship that signifies an alternative, equal and respectful relationship between a man and a woman in conservative small Springfield.

After Bart points a giant, phallic and colorful plastic pistol at him, Homer's worry becomes stronger. He suspects that his wife is ignoring John's malicious homosexualization of Bart, and he makes foolish attempts to save his son from gayness. For instance, he forces his Bart to look at a huge sexist advertising billboard, showing two female models in bathing suits smoking cigarettes; after a long look at the models, Bart only (homo)erotically wishes for "anything slim."

Homer decides that if he is to turn the boy into a man, Bart will need manhood and virility in his environment. During their visit to the local steel mill, Roscoe, the muscular and mustachioed manager, asks the ultravirile, muscular workers to say hello to the Simpsons. In response, they wave effeminately, "Hello-o." Homer wonders if the whole world has gone insane, watching a slender worker running-in-place while his mate theatrically slaps his back: "Stand still, there's a spark in your hair!" and the worker replies: "Get it! Get it!" Then a tanned bodybuilder in hot pants walks past Homer holding a vat of hot steel and announcing "Hot stuff, comin' through!"— a phrase that echoes gay pornography. Roscoe states, "We work hard. We play hard" and pulls a chain. Surprisingly, a high-tech disco ball descends and the entire mill turns into a nightclub called "The Anvil," with flickering spotlights, smoke effects, dance floors, mustachioed body builders, and muscular young men at work, proudly exposing their torsos. All the workers dance to "Everybody Dance Now," except Homer, who is in shock and leaves this male-only enclave, shading Bart's eyes.

Edmund White (2000 [1980]), in his discussion of the political vocabulary of homosexuality, notes that in the past, feminization, at least to a small and symbolic degree, seemed a necessary initiation into gay life. Today, almost the opposite seems to be true. Many gay men sport beards, army fatigues, work boots, etc. They build up their bodies or are "busy arraying themselves in these castoffs and becoming cowboys, truckers, telephone line-men, football players (in appearance and sometimes also in reality)" (p. 192). In this way, the ultra-virile spectacle at the gay steel mill can be perceived as a high-camp drag show. . . .

Earl Jackson (1995) suggests that a truly subversive gay representational practice must contest not only the gay subject's experience of heterosexist persecution, but also his experience of patriarchal privilege. He notes that certain gay male cultural practices that transvalue deviance as a positive mode of self-identification contain at least an implicit critique of the normative male ideal (and the dominant heterosexual sex/gender system) from which the gay male deviates. Sam Fussell (1999 [1994]) contends that even apparently straight male bodybuilding signs a *reversal* of sex roles, with the bodybuilder taking a traditionally female role: body as object. Further, Fussell observes, "whether it be beefcake or cheesecake, it's still cake . . ." (p. 46).

David Halperin (1995) contends that gay muscles, in particular, deliberately flaunt the visual norms of straight masculinity, which impose discretion on masculine self-display and require that straight male beauty exhibit itself only casually or inadvertently. Brian Pronger (2000) also contends that gay muscles, commercialized as they are, have at least one significant character of drag performances: they are ironic. "Musculature," he notes, "within a gay ironic sensibility signifies the *subversion* of patriarchal power by acting as homoerotic *enticements* to other men" (pp. 689–690).

Homer is not only surprised by the muscular men's queerness. He is also astonished by their proud cultural identity: their dress (and undress), language ("Hot stuff, comin' through!"), behavior (dancing and having fun), and mood (happy), which contradict his image of gays as low-life, dubious and miserable people. This lively discotheque is a demonstration of power, as it presents an alternative culture, part of an alternative camp lifestyle. Homer feels threatened by the spectacular: "This is a nightmare! You're all sick!" He pathologizes gayness as deviation from the "natural" order. Camp, as a queer counter-cultural political praxis, uses its innovative and inspirational deviancy to contest the oppressive social order. This deviation is also political because camp reflects an aesthetic and ethical refusal to be visually hetero-normalized or silenced by dominance (Meyer, 1994; Padva, 2000).

Promoting Diversity and Multiculturalism

Homer's phobia primarily derived from ignorance. His negative reaction towards the gay workers/clubbers is caused by guilt for what he considers his son's deviancy. Pointedly, Homer is not demonized. From this perspective, not only gays but also straight Homer are victims of the same oppressive "natural" sexual order that stigmatizes and discriminates against sexual minorities and imposes restricting hetero-masculine codes of visibility, behavior and sexual expression on men. Although he does not recognize it, Homer too transgresses the (hetero)sexual representational regime, by wearing Hawaiian shirts, dancing with another man, etc.

Homer wonders how it could be possible that a gay son has developed in a straight family. As Eve Kosofsky Sedgwick pointed out (1990), the double-edged potential for injury in the scene of gay coming out results partly from the fact that the erotic identity of the person who receives the disclosure is also apt to be implicated in, and hence perturbed by, it.

In an earlier scene, Homer blames Marge for being "too feminine around the boy" and she replies that if there is actually a problem with Bart worth worrying over, it must be that he's not spending time with his dad. But Homer's own transgressive masculinity might be implicated in his son's suspected homosexuality.

Michael Kimmel (2001) contends that homophobia is a central organizing principle of our cultural definition of manhood. He suggests that homophobia is more than the irrational fear of gay men, more than the fear that straights might be perceived as gay men. David Leverentz (1986) points out that the word "faggot" has nothing to do with homosexual experience or even with fear of homosexuals. Rather, it arises from the depths of manhood: a label of ultimate contempt for anyone who seems sissy, untough, uncool.

Homer, horrified by the gay steel mill/dance club, decides to socialize his son into the hetero-masculine world through a male brotherhood that putatively includes himself, the paranoid local bar-owner Moe, and the town's notorious drunk Bernie—three unappealing male role models. When Bart hears about his dad's plan to go hunting with him and his friends, he whispers: "Something about a bunch of guys alone together in the woods . . . seems kinda gay." The three (straight and narrow) losers get drunk and fall asleep near the bonfire. Homer is shown gently and compassionately holding his sleeping son. Desperate to provide Bart with an animal to kill, the hunting group breaks into a reindeer pen. Homer orders him to shoot a reindeer after Bernie has assured him (ironically) that shooting a reindeer is like killing a beautiful man. Suddenly, the deer attack the unwelcome guests, who are rescued at the last moment by John's Japanese Santa Claus robot.

John has earned Homer's gratitude: "Hey, we owe this guy, and I don't want you calling him a sissy. This guy's a fruit, and a . . . no, wait, wait, wait: queer, queer, queer! That's what you like to be called, right?" and John wittily replies, "Well, that or John." Lisa remarks that this is about as tolerant as her dad gets, so John should be flattered. Here, language demonstrates the change that has occurred in Homer's thinking, when he agrees to use the other's terminology as a sign of respect.

The word "queer," as Cherry Smith (1996) points out, defines a strategy, an attitude, a reference to other identities, and a new self-understanding. "Both in culture and politics," Smith notes, "queer articulates a radical questioning of social and cultural norms, notions of gender, reproductive sexuality and the family" (p. 280).

Embracing the idea of unconditional love, Homer tells Bart in the final scene that he loves him because he is his son, gay or not. Bart looks quite surprised to be identified by his parent as gay, before he has recognized *himself* to be gay. This presents the whole identification process as questionable and contradicts Homer's (and some of the viewers') fixation over gender roles and sexual identities.

The hit song "Everybody Dance Now" (associated with the disco in the steel mill) forms the sound track for the final scene, as John's car drives off and Bart's face is shown in increasing close-ups, matching the rhythm and lyrics, "I've got the power." The makers of the "Homer Phobia" episode dedicated it to the steelworkers of America and, winking, exhorted them to "Keep reaching for that rainbow," metaphorically liberating their hyper-masculine territory from its monologic perception.

This episode's multicultural perspective, embracing diversity and open-mindedness, is based on universal ideas of freedom, liberty, equality, justice, tolerance, solidarity and compassion. The outwardly naive medium of animation here mediates sexual pluralism through (unexpected) comic situations that parody homophobia rather than homosexuals. The creators have knowingly encoded many gay expressions (e.g., "Dad, you are the living end!"), erotic innuendos (e.g., the gay steel workers' dance club is called "The Anvil"), intertextual hints (e.g., Homer recalls the hit song "It's Raining Men"; and John's car beeper plays Judy Garland's "Somewhere Over the Rainbow"). Although straight audiences too enjoy this episode, its hyperbolic scenes particularly empower gay viewers, who

likely identify the linguistic maneuvers and decode the queer meanings. In "Homer's Phobia"'s Utopian vision, homophobia is just a phase; the hysterical drama queens are primarily Homer and his bigoted straight friends; and an amplified machismo is as theatrical as a flamboyant drag show.

References

Babuscio, J. (1978). The cinema of camp (aka Camp and the gay sensibility). *Gay Sunshine Journal, 35*; reprinted in Cleto, F. (Ed.). (1999). *Camp: Queer aesthetics and the performing subject* (pp. 117–135). Edinburgh: Edinburgh University Press.

Button, S. (2000). Best friends. *Attitude* 75 (July 2000), 46–48.

Chocano, C. (2001). Matt Groening. *Salon*. Retrieved April 2, 2005, from hitp://www.salon.com/people/bc/2001/01/30/groening/print.html

Fussell, S. (1994). Bodybuilder americanus. In Goldstein, L. (Ed.), (1999). *The male body: Features, destinies, exposures* (pp. 43–60). Ann Arbor: The University of Michigan Press.

Gray, J. (2003). *Imagining America: The Simpsons and the anti-suburb go global.* Paper presented at Communication in Borderlands: The 53rd Annual Conference of the International Communication Association, San Diego, California, USA. May 23–27.

Halperin, D. (1995). *Saint Foucault: Towards a gay hagiography.* New York: Oxford University Press.

Jackson, E., Jr. (1995). *Strategies of deviance: Studies in gay male representation.* Bloomington: Indiana University Press.

Kimmel, M. (2001). Masculinity as homophobia: Fear, shame, and silence in the construction of gender identity. In Whitehead, S. M. & Barrett, F. J. (Eds.), *The masculinities reader* (pp. 266–287). Cambridge: Oxford and Malden, MA: Polity.

Leverentz, D. (1986). Manhood, humiliation and public life: Some stories. *Southwest Review,* 71.

Meyer, M. (1994). Introduction: Reclaiming the discourse of camp. In *The politics and poetics of camp* (pp. 1–23). London and New York: Routledge.

The Oxford Dictionary. (1996). Oxford and New York: Oxford University Press.

Padva, G. (2000). *Priscilla* fights back: The politicization of camp subculture. *Journal of Communication Inquiry,* 24(2), 216–243.

Pronger, B. (2000). Physical culture. In Haggerty, G. (Ed.), *Gay histories and cultures: An encyclopedia* (pp. 688–690). New York: Garland Publishing.

Sedgwick, E. K. (1990). *Epistemology of the closet.* Berkeley and Los Angeles: University of California Press.

The Simpsons (1997). Homer Phobia. Created by M. Groening; episode written by R. Hauge; directed by M. Anderson. Distributed by Gracie Films in association with 20th Century Fox Television: retrieved on June 22, 2008, from http://www.snpp.com/epidoses/4F11 .html

Smith, C. (1996). What is this thing called queer? In Morton, D. (Ed.), *The material queer: A lesbigay cultural studies reader* (pp. 227–285). Boulder, Colorado and Oxford: Westview Press.

Sontag, S. (1964). Notes on camp. *Partisan Review,* 31(4), 515–530; reprinted in Cleto, F. (Ed.), *Camp: Queer aesthetics and the performing subject* (pp. 53–65). Edinburgh: Edinburgh University Press.

Szalacha, L. (2004). Educating teachers on LGBTQ issues: A review of research and program evaluations. *Journal of Gay & Lesbian Issues in Education* 1(4), 67–79.

Tingleff, S. (1998). "I will not expose the ignorance of the faculty": *The Simpsons* as a critique of consumer culture. *The Simpsons Archive.* Retrieved on April 2, 2005, from http://www.snpp.com/olher/papers/st .paper.html

White, E. (1980). The political vocabulary of homosexuality. In Michaels, L. & Ricks, C. (Eds.), *The state of the language* (pp. 235–246). Berkeley and Los Angeles: University of California Press; reprinted in Burke, L., Crowley, T. & Girvin, A. (Eds.), *The Routledge language and cultural theory reader* (pp. 189–196). London and New York: Routledge.

23

Resisting, Reiterating, and Dancing Through

The Swinging Closet Doors of Ellen DeGeneres's Televised Personalities

Candace Moore

Gushing to *The Advocate* about her new girlfriend, comedian Ellen DeGeneres, *Arrested Development* star Portia De Rossi says: "She was so courageous and loud in '97, and now she is doing something that is more subliminal. She's changing the world, she really is" (Kort, "Portia," 40). De Rossi subtly articulates a difference between Ellen's 1997 "coming out" and Ellen's current daily dance into America's living rooms as a beloved daytime talk show host who "happens to be" gay. LGBT activists and media critics slightly disagree, asserting that Ellen may be "softpedaling her lesbianism" on *Ellen: The Ellen DeGeneres Show* to find widespread acceptance (Lo, "The Incredible Story"; Heffernan, "The Perils" E5). As *New York Times* critic Virginia Heffernan puts it: "Ms. DeGeneres no longer wants to talk about being gay, so she discusses pleasant [topics]: décor, holidays and the fridge" (E5). Host of a mainstream variety show that has wowed NBC network executives by pulling in impressive numbers of its targeted demographic—women ages 25–54 (Deeken 30; Schnuer S1)—and hyped as an "every-woman approach" ("The Ellen DeGeneres Show"), DeGeneres avoids the topic of her own homosexuality and actively closes down conversation in which the very word or concept comes up.

. . . Not verbally addressing queer identity on her talk show is understandable from DeGeneres's personal perspective. Her career all but collapsed not long after the glow of her public coming-out party died down.

From Moore, C. (2008). Resisting, reiterating, and dancing through: The swinging closet doors of Ellen DeGeneres's televised personalities. In R. Beirne (Ed.), *Televising queer women: A reader* (pp. 17–31). New York: Palgrave Macmillan. Reproduced with permission of Palgrave Macmillan.

"To come out," according to [queer theorist David M.] Halperin,

> is precisely to expose oneself to a different set of dangers and constraints, to make oneself into a convenient screen onto which straight people can project all the fantasies they routinely entertain about gay people, and to suffer one's every gesture, statement, expression, and opinion to be totally and irrevocably marked by the overwhelming social significance of one's openly acknowledged homosexual identity. (30)

Following Ellen DeGeneres's self-outing, her private life (with ex-girlfriend Anne Heche) became unbearably public—their love affair's ups and downs became unending fodder for gossip columnists and paparazzi, who stalked the new couple. Ellen's groundbreaking sitcom was also summarily canceled the next year, due to advertiser pullouts, public attacks from the religious right, and, arguably, sabotage by the ABC network itself in imposing parental advisories because of the show's portrayals of same-sex romance. (Such advisories were not, of course, placed on programs that tackled more explicitly sexual subjects with heterosexual leads) (Gross 162). Throughout these trials, DeGeneres became an important icon of political courage for the LGBT community, even though she candidly expressed that she had neither intended her coming out as a political statement nor wished to become a poster-woman for the queer cause. . . .

Since its launch in 2003, Ellen has crafted herself a talk-show persona on *Ellen: The Ellen DeGeneres Show*, who linguistically sidesteps the word or concept of homosexuality. However, she performs queerness through what implicitly "exceeds" her stand-up jokes and sit-down talk, and, physically, through the ritual action of her daily dance sequence. Through these methods, perhaps DeGeneres escapes being such a "convenient screen" for hate-mongers or bearing the responsibility of being a spokesperson for all of gay America, while she still maintains a *televisibility*[1] of queer identity. Demonstrating how Ellen's coming out and her return to the closet become enacted again and again, ad infinitum, on television, my textual analysis involves queer ruptures on the primarily heterosexual text of Ellen's current Emmy-winning daytime talk show. Seeing "being in the closet" and "being out" as performances that are constantly negotiated socially—either actively resisted or reinscribed—rather than one-time denials or declarations of sexuality that hold, this chapter highlights ambiguous moments in DeGeneres's daily show. In specific instances that I explore, DeGeneres gestures rhetorically or symbolically to her sexual preference, absurdly omits or redirects possible discussions of homosexuality, or is subtly or not-so-subtly "called out" as gay by her celebrity guests. . . .

Repetition and reiteration is a central theme in Ellen's show, with her daily dances, recurring verbal noises and catch phrases. I ultimately argue that Ellen's many repetitious behaviors also serve as multiple self-outings. Anna McCarthy suggests that perhaps queer visibility on television is only permissible as spectacle; such televisibility becomes dangerous to heteronormativity when it presents queer lives and loves as "quotidian" ("Ellen: Making Queer Television History" 597). By repeatedly dancing to the same songs and expressing the same verbal ticks over and over again, Ellen seeks in the opening sequences of her talk show to present the out-of-the-ordinary repeatedly, until its very performance, occurring daily, becomes un-alarming and even infectiously celebratory.

During her ritual opening dance, Ellen looks into the camera, directly addressing the audience, and then follows by breaking the proscenium arch, dancing out into the pulsating, cheering, similarly dancing live studio audience. Her daily dances, set to a handful of uplifting disco, hip hop, and R&B songs, with their awkward, non-choreographed moves, together with her wide, toothy grin, seem to proclaim a message of self-acceptance: *This is me! I'm great just the way I am, and you can be great just the way you are too!* Her dance moves themselves evoke nostalgia for the gay-steeped, 1970s-era culture of disco. While Ellen does not remind her audience of her queerness over and over again verbally, Ellen does repeat acts that are both absurd and permissible, causing the most bizarre squawks and awkward dance moves to become a commonplace sight, and a site for pleasure.

Subliminal Rituals

While De Rossi's claim that Ellen is "changing the world" might represent the overstated rhetorical flourish of the lovestruck, De Rossi's use of the word "subliminal," meaning "below the threshold of conscious perception" (*Webster's II New Riverside University Dictionary* 1994: 1154), to describe what Ellen is "doing," does astutely point out the very *liminality* of Ellen's ritualistic daily performances.[2] To put it in other terms, De Rossi is here distinguishing between a media *event* and a repeated media *ritual*. A media *event* is a one-time, idiosyncratic phenomenon that acts as an exception to the usual rules of both television flow and content, and, if planned, is often surrounded by quite a bit of promotional hype (Hubert 31; McCarthy, "Ellen: Making Queer Television History" 593). A repeated media *ritual* also temporarily upends or stretches convention (only to reinstate it); however, it is less outwardly eventful; in fact, it gradually becomes perceived as a part of the normal flow, and signifies through repetition, over time, or through multiple broadcasts (Couldry 24). One punctuates the Nielsen's ratings, the other has the potential to slowly, rather than rapidly, shift consciousnesses through a process of slow audience acclimation to, and reinforcement of, difference.

Encoding/Decoding the Dance

When asked why Ellen DeGeneres does not address her homosexuality on her talk show, lesbian actress and screenwriter Guinevere Turner (*Go Fish, The L Word*) declared emphatically "How could you dance like that and not be gay? That's a way of saying with every opening representation, I'm gay!" ("Personal Interview" 2005). Marusya Bociurkiw, in a recent critical essay published in *Canadian Woman Studies*, concurred with Turner's view that Ellen's lesbianism is palpable in her dancing: "As the music, usually hip hop, is played, Ellen's body is on display in a manner that is decidedly not heteronormative. Here DeGeneres displays the grace and confidence that her accessible, self-deprecating, 'kook' act disavows. DeGeneres looks like a butch lesbian dancing alone, in a club" (176).

However, these interpretations are just that, individualized readings of a polysemic text, and sometimes we see what we want to see. Furthermore, "what a dyke dancing looks like" is a nearly impossible thing to put one's finger on. Just as lesbians are a diverse, rather than homogeneous group, comprising women of varying ethnicities, cultural backgrounds, styles, classes, gender presentations, and so on, their dance moves likely vary enormously. So while a general consensus remains among these readings, that "something's queer" here, I try to show, through examining prior precedents of Ellen expressing herself physically—whether through physical humor or through dance—that not only does her opening "dance with herself" (and thus the viewer) represent a daily declaration of queer identity, but that she has previously coded it to mean exactly that.

Rather than revisit the coming-out media event of Ellen's "Puppy Episode" (4.22 and 4.23, April 30, 1997), which has been explored in depth by Anna McCarthy, Susan J. Hubert, and Steven Capsuto, among others, I concentrate instead on two pre-coming-out episodes from the second season of *Ellen*—texts, which, like her talk show, operate "doubly." In "The Fix Up" (2.5, October 19, 1994), Ellen's dance moves are first foregrounded, and in "Thirty Kilo Man" part 1 and 2 (2.23, May 10, 1995; 2.24, May 17, 1995), her character has a heterosexual love affair that reads as unmistakably queer.

Elevator Music on Early *Ellen*

Early *Ellen* is best described as ABC's version of *Seinfeld*'s sitcom about nothing, since both half-hour shows center around known stand-up comedians and their witty banter about insignificant, repetitive, or everyday matters with friends. During the three seasons prior to Ellen DeGeneres's/Ellen Morgan's doubly momentous 1997 coming out, Ellen's character on the middling-rated sitcom was consistently stuck in a weekly cycle of dates-gone-wrong with guys, that, for an array of incidental and sometimes extravagantly bizarre reasons, just do not fit. In "The Gladiators" (2.19, March 1, 1995) for instance, Ellen's new beau, Nitro, a gladiator from the then-popular television show, *American Gladiators*,[3] is snapped away from her by an ultra-buff woman (Ice), leading the bookstore owner to jealously beat the pumped-up woman to a pulp with a padded lance.

The sitcom's season with the most overtly heterosexual storylines, the second, is also the season with the most queer subtext. Disney would not okay the idea of Ellen Morgan's coming out until more than a year later, when blatant hints began to be worked into the weekly scripts (Gross 157). Ellen's obsessive man-shopping in season two is painted by the writers and producers as downright absurd, but what will serve as the alternative (asexuality, in most of season three, before facing her queer identity), is not quite clear yet. Journalist for *The San Francisco Examiner,* Joyce Millman, caught

on early. In the spring of 1995, in a column entitled "The Sitcom that Dare Not Speak Its Name," the television critic prematurely outed Ellen Morgan: "As a gal sitcom, *Ellen* doesn't make any sense at all, until you view it through the looking glass, where the unspoken subtext becomes the main point. Then is Ellen is transformed into one of TV's savviest, funniest, slyest shows. Ellen Morgan is a closet lesbian" (B1).

In "The Fix Up" (2.5, October 19, 1994) of season two, the episode opens with Ellen inside an elevator—the enclosed space that arguably acts as the show's metaphorical stand-in for a closet. Ellen's adventures in (or waiting for) an elevator are a reoccurring trope on the show. Given the sitcom's frequent meta-references to sitcom history (see McCarthy, "Ellen: Making Queer Television History" 607–614), perhaps this trope, seen throughout the second season, is also a tip of the hat to the historically common "meat locker" sitcom scenario, wherein people with differences get stuck in a small space, often a meat locker or an elevator, and overcome differences (Sconce 104–105). In this case, the elevator's only other passenger exits, and finding herself alone, Ellen openly acknowledges the song playing over the loud speakers, Aretha Franklin's "Respect," by first tapping her feet, then swinging from side to side and lip-synching. As the song builds to crescendo, Ellen is observed flailing, rocking her head along to the words, and jumping into the air, landing with thumps. As audience members, we are in anticipation for the elevator doors to suddenly open and or Ellen to be "found out." Instead, Franklin's rousing tune halts abruptly and a male authoritarian voice comes over the loud speakers: "Excuse me, ma'am, this is security" the voice interrupts. "Please refrain from jumping in the elevator." The camera offers a shot from above, looking down at Ellen, as she immediately looks up to the speaker, with a petrified deer-in-the-headlights acknowledgment that she is being surveyed. She then cradles her head down in her hand, in embarrassment, before the camera cuts away.

This scene might be read divorced from any queer subtext, as mere silliness in an elevator, with Ellen as the 1990s Lucy Ricardo, always getting herself into a new kind of trouble. However, the larger text of the sitcom suggests the elevator as a contained closet, within which Ellen Morgan can finally release herself, be happy with who she is, until she is again reminded, reprimanded by a voice from outside, that others do not approve of her lifestyle. This is particularly suggested by the content of the dialogue between Ellen and her mother that immediately follows, and furthermore by the theme (failed heterosexual daring, what else?) of "The Fix Up."

In the scene that follows, Ellen's mother asks her a question over coffee that reoccurs, rephrased, throughout the series: "So, are you seeing anyone these days?" When Ellen's answer implies no, her mom continues in full fuss mode: "I just worry about you. You're not immortal . . . I just want you to be happy." Ellen retorts, "You know it's possible to be happy without a man." "Must you joke about everything?" her mom returns, and then promptly tries to fix Ellen up with someone she grew up with. Described by Ellen as the "weird" kid in the neighborhood who ate bugs, he has matured into an adult man who is not peculiar at all; in fact, Ellen seems to find him quite charming. In a plot reversal, he ends up finding Ellen entirely "weird," through the usual comedy of errors. "The Fix Up" is a stereotypical example of the pre-coming-out plotline, wherein events beyond Ellen's control, but generally propelled at least partially by her neurotic behavior, spiral, causing Ellen ultimately to be rejected by her possible heterosexual love interest, rather than force the thirty-something to own up to the fact that she is not truly interested in the first place. There are also instances where Ellen rejects men; these generally involve Ellen's discovery that the man she thought was a dreamboat has an impossible-to-stand trait.

The "date that always goes wrong" plot is finally frustrated and complicated in the two-part season two finale, "Thirty Kilo Man" (2.23 and 2.24, May 10, 1995, and May 17, 1995). The first part of the finale opens in Ellen's apartment, with Ellen's mother asking her about her plans for the weekend. When Ellen makes a joke about getting a "Chia Date," so that she can sprinkle it and "watch it grow," Ellen's mom pulls out the claws: "You know what the problem with you is, Ellen? You're too picky. You always look for a man's faults. Greg was too nice, Roger watched too much TV, Carl was a drag." "Drag king, mother," Ellen corrects, "I know I nitpick . . ." As the episode continues, Dan, a man she was interested in during an earlier episode but rejected after discovering that he delivered pizza for a living, returns from Italy with a new, more prestigious job. The first ever return "beard" is also the one that actually ends up in bed with Ellen. A "next day" scenario finds Ellen strutting out from her bedroom in a robe, hair mussed, puffing on an imaginary cigarette. Dan emerges fully dressed and primped, and she kisses him, mumbling, "No fair, you brushed your teeth." "Sorry," he practically sings. They touch their way into the living-room, and in full soap-opera pitch, Dan gushes: "I never want this feeling to end. Ellen Morgan, I think I'm falling in love with you." In this scene, Ellen is scripted and choreographed into the position of the stereotypical man in a classic romance, who swaggers out of the bedroom, while Dan is the stereotypical woman, who rushes to say effusive things, to say "I love you" right away.

Later, when Dan comes back from work, Ellen backs him into the couch and gets on top, kissing him. His beeper starts to vibrate in his pants, she pauses to say, "What's that?" and then keeps kissing him, pressing into him, moaning "You are such a considerate man!" She grabs the cordless phone from the coffee table. "Okay, it stopped. What's your number?" This joke on his beeper as vibrator, a device implied as more pleasurable than perhaps his penis, again with the classic roles switched (her as the "horny" one), plays on the notion that, although he is a man, they are in a "lesbian" affair. This joke is toyed with even further in part two of the finale, when he figuratively "brings a U-Haul," moving in with her right away, and they spend all waking moments together. In their every dialogue and physical interaction, Ellen plays butch to Dan's femme, and the season uses the potential of their hetero-homo romance continuing as a cliff-hanger to the next season. Here the sitcom *Ellen* playfully *queers* heterosexual scenarios, since it cannot yet show a queer one. Ellen's otherness is continually the underlying gag.

In "Three strikes" (2.21, March 29, 1995), Ellen, forced under court order to live with her parents, is made, by her mother, to wear a dress. As she walks through work, the laugh track goes wild; Ellen in a flowery dress in which she looks awkward is a joke in and of itself. Ellen Morgan's (and, really, Ellen DeGeneres's) queerness is what always exceeds the text, both with her dates that do not work, and with the one, Dan, that does.

Heterosexual Talk

Ellen's closeted verbal discourse around the topic of her sexuality on *Ellen: The Ellen DeGeneres Show* functions similarly to the coded scripting of her pre-out counterpart, Ellen Morgan, on *Ellen*. . . .

Generally, when the topic of her own sexuality is broached, live, Ellen DeGeneres defers the question within a heterosexual paradigm, in which straight desire is always the point-of-reference, the norm. Like a pre–"Puppy Episode" Ellen Morgan, who cannot seem to find the right man, Ellen DeGeneres never enunciates the nature of her desire on air, but always enunciates, rather, *what her desire is not*.

Two live tapings of *Ellen: The Ellen DeGeneres Show* demonstrate this point. In a November 10, 2005, interview with Jake Gyllenhaal, the young actor comes out on stage with 400 white roses for Ellen, to congratulate her on her 400th live talk show (3.49, November 10, 2005). When they sit down together, Ellen immediately declares Jake "cute" and gives him a publicity suggestion: "More shots with your shirt off," showing a clip of him naked from the waist up in *Jarhead*. Her studio audience, mostly women, cheer at the top of their lungs. "You should take it off right now," Ellen urges. "You don't have to . . . It's only going to help you." Gyllenhaal unbuttons his top button then closes it again. "It's my 400th show," begs Ellen. "Roses are sweet and everything . . . I'll give 'em back if you'll take your shirt off." Gyllenhaal becomes bright red and laughs, clearly bashful.

Ellen here mimics Rosie O'Donnell's "passing" as straight. Rosie O'Donnell, who came out as a lesbian *after* her popular television talk show wrapped, perfected "passing" by regularly harping on her ambiguously sexualized obsession with *Top Gun* star Tom Cruise. Gyllenhaal is verbally worshiped like Cruise; however, Ellen camps the faked crush even further, demonstrating her "passing" clearly as shtick. Acting similarly as a facilitator for straight women in their fantasies, DeGeneres's play act has a distinct difference from O'Donnell's: DeGeneres's homosexuality is a known secret—a secret the audience knows in an iconic way—and she trades on this knowledge to make her interaction funny.

"It's not for me," Ellen asserts, looking Gyllenhaal in the eye, smiling. He can barely talk; he refuses to budge, but good naturedly. "It's not for me!" she insists again, making it clear, as if he did not get it the first time, that she is not trying to sexually harass him; *besides, she's gay*. They share an understanding glance. "Are you single right now? I should ask that.

Not for me, again, *I don't care,* but the women in the audience want to know." After the commercial break, Gyllenhaal loosens the collar of his shirt and exposes the top of his chest.

The sustained tease of Gyllenhaal's potential strip that never happens acts as a promotional para-text for the film *Jarhead.* Ellen even spells this out: "If you want to see what the rest of that looks like, you have to go see the movie *Jarhead."* Ellen focuses entirely on *Jarhead* and on her flirtation with Gyllenhaal about taking off his shirt. She gives his other about-to-release-film, *Brokeback Mountain,* an ever-so-quick mention at the end, but does not ask Gyllenhaal one question about this "film with Heath Ledger" (as she summarizes it), nor does she mention that the film deals with a homosexual romance between Gyllenhaal's and Ledger's characters. While implying that her own homosexuality gives her the social mobility to be so openly cheeky with him, without it constituting any kind of gender upheaval or sexual come-on, Ellen has, in this exchange, played butch to Gyllenhaal's femme, much like Ellen Morgan did with Dan, placing him in the position of the looked at, the desirable. . . . She insists, however, on her non-desire, and does not name why it is that she is not attracted to him—that is supposedly "understood," it goes without saying. Gyllenhaal gets visibly uncomfortable with his position as object, but becomes visibly more comfortable when Ellen finally asks whether he is single, since "the women in the audience want to know," because she is offering him the space of normal heterosexual identity by default. Therefore, she intelligently also skirts the question of *his* sexuality. Ellen comes out through negation, although a denial of a heterosexual desire for one person does not necessarily imply homosexuality. The way she addresses the subject matter is very crafty—to those that do not want to be reminded of the nature of her desires, she does not dare speak its name; to those that do, she is, at least, honest.

In a special event edition of *Ellen: The Ellen DeGeneres Show* that aired on November 30, 2005, celebrating Ellen's twenty-fifth anniversary as a stand-up comedian, a similar incident takes place (3.63). Ellen's "anniversary" special revolves around clips shown from Ellen's career as a stand-up comedian, allowing her to poke fun at her many bad haircuts. Guest celebrities visit to reminisce about Ellen's start in "show biz." Jay Leno, for instance, discusses getting Ellen her first gig on the *Johnny Carson Show,* a show that obviously inspired her own. Her first Carson appearance was featured most prominently during the hour, and the fact that she was the first female comedian ever invited to be interviewed by Carson after her act was underscored. . . . Strangely, however, her sitcom was conspicuously missing from this retrospective. (Consider, for example, a retrospective on Jerry Seinfeld that fails to mention *Seinfeld . . .*) By focusing only on Ellen's stand-up career, not only was her sitcom and her "coming out" conveniently occluded from the history of Ellen that the talk show offers, but no clips with *any* gay content were shown. Ellen rehistoricizes herself as a stand-up comedian first and fore-most, and an asexual one at that.

David Spade joins Ellen on this episode, and we learn through their conversation that they met twenty years ago when the two traveled comedy circuits together, Spade opening for Ellen's headlining act. Spade admits a secret: "We used to do some of these gigs together . . . I had a big crush on her . . . then I got the news." Ellen becomes visibly embarrassed and just laughs for a long while, while Spade turns it into a joke: "What it was, was the fact that you had a Walkman . . . and a *sweet* mullet." "I thought you were adorable," Ellen finally responds, "No interest, other than the fact that you were adorable. Although I did . . . I had a crush on you and you know it." She goes right from this statement into a clip of David Spade's vintage comedy. Those of us that are "in" on the joke, read David's crush on Ellen as real, and Ellen's crush on David as purely platonic. Again here Ellen discursively frames her queerness through expressing what she *does not desire,* and even that in a very mixed-up way, as is evident in the statement, "No interest, other than the fact that you were adorable." *What does that mean?* Ellen does not outright deny her homosexuality; when it comes up, she deflects mention of "gayness" with the double-speak and coded strategies of her pre-coming-out sitcom character. DeGeneres is comfortable expressing her nonheterosexuality (in a specific instance— so that it could be read as follows: she just does not like *him*) on air, but not her *homosexuality* directly.

John Limon points out that DeGeneres's strategy of "skirting" is not only admitted, but defined, in her book *My Point . . . and I Do Have One:*

> Someone recently wrote a letter . . . asking "Why does Ellen DeGeneres always wear pants and never skirts?" I'm guessing that the person who wrote that letter meant skirt, a noun signifying an article of clothing, and not skirt, a verb defined as, "to evade or elude (as a topic of conversation) by circumlocution." Because, if they mean the verb skirt, well, they're dead wrong. I'm always skirting. (DeGeneres 93; quoted in Limon 115)

Limon identifies DeGeneres's "skirting" as a form of "escapist art" that refuses "to put all kidding aside," and where "what is made visible . . . is evasion" (116–117). Her verbal skirts act as denials of reality that constantly rely on reality as their vanishing point. Rather than expressing information that can be pinned down or literally understood, she replaces objective "truths" with tangential flights of fancy, distractions, wordplay, while presenting the journey of the skirt itself as having *subjective* and transient values—of imagination, pleasure, possibility.

Limon lyrically asks of DeGeneres's skirting: "Is knowledge of the body repressed or unlearned? Is the body itself decoded or disclaimed?" (121). He dubs DeGeneres "an inverse Lenny Bruce, whose shame existed to be displayed as pride" (121). The notion that DeGeneres's *pride* (with all of the meanings attached to that word) exists to be *displayed* as shame, as the case may be, is a savvy way to view beneath her linguistic skirts. If skirting is DeGeneres's verbal strategy for, at least on the surface, distancing her comedy from the bodily, from *her body* and the material consequences of the world, while leaking other meanings, DeGeneres's physical displays, especially her dances, convey and rely on utter embodiment: the body engaged in ritual.

Interpretive Dance

. . . . Ellen's choice to deflect or redirect the question of her homosexuality in potentially heterosexual discursive terms on her talk show is one strategy to remove herself from the confessional paradigm, wherein an implied authority outside of herself (like the voice in Ellen Morgan's elevator), "the one who listens" (in the case of her show, the audience), is the implied judge or cheerleader of her private life. Instead, Ellen *performs* her daily dances—illustrating both her control over what is expressed and her pleasure in expressing it. Here Ellen presents her queerness, individuality, difference, otherness, in an expressive act that broadcasts her self-love, and as part of a daily ritual that is ultimately not all about her. Her daily dance also becomes a boundary-crossing ritual shared with all, where she encourages others (her studio audience and viewers at home) to join her—to get up and dance *themselves.* For Ellen, dancing with oneself becomes dancing with the watching world, fulfilling the wish of the final refrain of the 1980s Billy Idol tune, "Dancing With Myself": "If I had a chance, I'd ask the world to dance." Dancing with oneself on television *presents* a dance *of oneself* to be received, shared, and potentially reciprocated.

Opening the stand-up special *Ellen DeGeneres: The Beginning,* which first aired on cable channel HBO on July 23, 2000, Ellen briefly addresses her coming-out saga before performing a dance about the very subject (set to disco music that devolves into chants of "nah nah, nah nah, nah"). A comedy special such as this one, on a pay cable network such as HBO, offers DeGeneres a markedly less censored venue in which to express herself than on network television, daytime or prime time. In her introduction, Ellen offers an extremely telling speech that I end this chapter with, because I believe it not only introduces Ellen's specific dance performance that night, but frames both her discursive closet and her soon-to-be-daily dance as "out." Speaking her mind about what should now be said, or not said, about her sexuality, Ellen successfully encodes the media ritual of dancing, later to appear on *Ellen: The Ellen DeGeneres Show,* as a performance of queerness that expresses meaning where words have been found to fail:

> Since I made the decision to come out three years ago, my life has been very interesting . . . I knew that people would want me to talk about it. Some people may not want me to talk about it. So I went back and forth, trying to decide should I talk about it, should I not talk about it, and ultimately I decided: No, I don't want to talk about it. It's been talked about enough, what can I say? I feel it would be best expressed through interpretive dance.

Notes

1. I use the word *televisibility* to refer to instances of visibility on television by queer subjects.

2. [Liminality refers to an in-between, or transitional, phase or state of consciousness. Ed.] . . .

3. *American Gladiators* (1989–1997, CBS) featured body builders competing against contestants on an obstacle course. Nitro was a regular gladiator and sometime co-host on the sensationalistic game show. Featuring *American Gladiators* on *Ellen* obviously served as an ABC-CBS cross-promotion.

References

Bociurkiw, Marusya. "It's Not About the Sex: Racialization and Queerness in Ellen and The Ellen DeGeneres Show." *Canadian Woman Studies* 24:2–3 (2005): 176–182.

Couldry, Nick. *Media Rituals: A Critical Approach.* London: Routledge, 2003.

Deeken, Aimee. "Syndies Score in February." *Mediaweek* March 14, 2005: 30.

DeGeneres, Ellen. *My Point . . . And I Do Have One.* New York: Bantam, 1996.

"The Ellen DeGeneres Show: About the Show." Warner Bros.com. December 31, 2006. http://ellen.warnerbros.com/showinfo/about.html.

Gross, Larry. *Up from Invisibility: Lesbians, Gay Men and the Media in America.* New York: Columbia University Press, 2001.

Halperin, David M. *Saint Foucault: Towards a Gay Hagiography.* New York: Oxford University Press, 1995.

Heffernan, Virginia. "The Perils of Pleasant, or Spacey, on Talk Shows." *New York Times,* September 16, 2003. E5

Hubert, Suan J. "What's Wrong with This Picture? The Politics of Ellen's Coming Out Party." *Journal of Popular Culture* 33:2 (1999): 31–37.

Kort, Michele. "Welcome Back to the L World." *The Advocate* February 1, 2005: 40–45.

———. "Portia Heart & Soul." *The Advocate,* September 13, 2005: 40–46.

Limon, John. *Stand-up Comedy in Theory, or, Abjection in America.* Durham and London: Duke University Press, 2000.

Lo, Malinda. "Does the L Word Represent? Viewer Reactions Vary on the Premiere Episode." *AfterEllen.com: Lesbian and Bisexual Women in Entertainment and the Media.*

January 2004. May 3, 2006. http://www.afterellen.com/tv/thelword/reaction.html.

McCarthy, Anna. "Ellen: Making Queer Television History." *GLQ* 7:4 (2001): 593–620.

———. "Must-see Queer TV: History and Serial Form in Ellen." *Quality Popular Television: Cult TV, the Industry and Fans*. Ed. Mark Jancovich and James Lyons. London: BFI, 2003. 88–102.

Millman, Joyce. "The Sitcom that Dare Not Speak Its Name." *San Francisco Examiner* March 19, 1995: B1.

Schnuer, Jenna. "The Ellen DeGeneres Show: Upbeat Host Gains Fans, Feel-Good Marketers." *Advertising Age* May 16, 2005: S1.

Sconce, Jeffrey. "What If? Charting Television's New Textual Boundaries." *Television After TV: Essays on a Medium in Transition*. Eds. Lynn Spiegel and Jan Olsson. Durham: Duke University Press, 2004. 93–112.

Turner, Guinevere. "Lipstick Los Angeles." *OUT Traveler Magazine*. December 2004. September 7, 2006. http://www.thelwordonlin.com/lipstick_LA.html.

———. *Personal Interview with Candace Moore*. March 28, 2005.

Turner, Victor. *From Ritual to Theatre: The Human Seriousness of Play*. New York: PAJ Publications, 1982.

24

"Sexy Like a Girl and Horny Like a Boy"

Contemporary Gay "Western" Narratives About Gay Asian Men

Chong-suk Han

In this chapter, I analyze the *Advocate* and *OUT* magazines from 2005, employing methods of critical discourse analysis (CDA), 'a neo-Marxist turn to the study of discourse which examines language and its usage to understand their social and political import' (Park, 2005: 11), in order to examine how images of gay Asian men are constructed and maintained within larger Western gay narratives. I argue that the response of mainstream 'gay' publications has been to marginalize gay Asian men by simply ignoring their existence or employing existing stereotypes about Asian men in general, thereby maintaining 'gay' as largely a 'white' category and relegating gay Asian men to the margins of the gay 'community.' By looking at mainstream gay publications and the way these publications marginalize gay Asian men, I hope to add another dimension to Bérubé's (2001) argument of how 'gay stays white.' More generally, I hope to contribute to the literature on the intersection of race and sexuality and how these intersections contribute to the development of various identities among multiply marginalized groups. . . .

Given the inherent power dynamics in the creation and dissemination of media images, it is not surprising to find that representations of the 'East' have a long and lurid history in the Western imagination. Through various historical periods, Asian men have routinely been portrayed as meek houseboys, asexual deviants, or domestic servants who fill 'female' roles when women are scarce (Hamamoto, 1994). It is clear that taken as a whole, these stereotypical images have worked to construct Asian men (and women) as fundamentally foreign, threatening, and perhaps most importantly, as inferior to white

From Chong-suk Han, "'Sexy Like a Girl and Horny Like a Boy': Contemporary Gay 'Western' Narratives about Gay Asian Men." *Critical Sociology* (2008), 34 (6), 829–850. Reprinted with permission of SAGE Publications, Ltd.

men (and women). For Asian men, both in the USA and abroad, stereotypes have often taken on an explicit sexual tone (Eng, 2001) as the need to ease the twin fears of the growing 'yellow peril' and miscegenation came crashing into the need to justify Western imperial thrusts into Asian territories (Lee, R., 1999). In addition, as Lowe (1996: 11) points out, 'racialization along the legal axis of definitions of citizenship has also ascribed "gender" to the Asian American subject.' Denied the ability to become citizens, the scarcity of Asian women, rigid laws barring miscegenation, and labor laws barring Asian men from the more 'masculine' trades reserved for white men, Asian men took on a decidedly feminine aura in the Western imagination.

While it is true that there have been competing images of Asian men, as Fung (1996) points out, even the 'masculine' images of Asian men have been desexualized in American media. As Nguyen Hoang points out:

> Despite the recent critical attention and popularity of Asian male actors in Asian cinema and its successful crossover into Hollywood (represented by such actors as Jackie Chan, Jet Li, and Chow Yun Fat, and directors such as Ang Lee and John Woo), the representation of Asian men as sexually appealing scarcely figures into mainstream American popular culture. (Hoang, 2004: 225)

As such, even Asian 'action' heroes who are highly sexual in Asian films are de-sexed for the American market. A stark example is in the movie 'Romeo Must Die,' where Jet Li spends the entirety of the movie 'negotiating' a romantic affair with Aalyiah. However, the two are never shown engaging in any real act of romance. The omission of any 'real' romantic interlude between Li and Aalyiah is in stark contradiction to the normal action hero narrative when the hero virtually always ends up with the leading female character.

Clearly, all forms of media produce and reproduce inequality to varying degrees and by extension are sites of contested identity formation. Yet while narratives from novels and images on screens are often perceived to be 'fictional,' there continues to be a strong belief that narratives found in newspapers and magazines are 'factual,' and reflective of an objective 'reality.' While the 'official' goal of journalism is to provide an objective truth, in reality, journalism is a site of storytelling whereby a subjective version of reality is actually presented (Dahlgren, 1992; Storey, 1996). In fact:

> [Journalistic] texts foster specific ways of seeing the world, hinder other ways, and even structure specific ways of relating to the text itself. The net outcome could in many cases be judged as ideological; that is, the ways of seeing [serve] certain social interests at the expense of others, while at the same time appearing to be neutral and natural. (Dahlgren, 1992: 13)

The subjective storytelling found in 'journalistic' pieces reinforces social inequalities by '[fostering] such feelings of collective belonging—based on class, gender, sexual preference, subcultural lifestyle or whatever' (Dahlgren, 1992: 17). On the flip side, they also foster feelings of marginalization and non-belonging along the same basis as they foster collectivism. In this way, journalistic text defines who belongs in certain categories and what that membership entails. It also works to highlight what/who is valued, and how we should think about those who are not included or valued. Given 'journalism's centrality in politics and culture, as well as its vested economic and occupational interests, [these] make questions regarding its boundaries, uses and contingencies of more than idle concern' (Dahlgren, 1992). Rather, it becomes critical to examine the role that journalism plays in maintaining and promoting social inequality by exposing journalistic practices that add to further marginalization of subaltern groups. . . .

Where Are All the Gay Asian Men?

Looking at gay media, it is evidently clear that the strategy deployed by gay publications to maintain white male privilege is one of exclusion. Asian men, and other men of color, rarely appear as subjects of a story and are rarely represented as contributors to the debates. As such, gay print media often speaks only to white men. Advertising that 'targets' the gay community is often no better. Ads that feature white men seem to be marketing to them, while ads that feature Asian men seem to be marketing them as commodities. The invisibility of Asian men in gay media is most evident between the pages of *The Advocate*, the largest gay and lesbian news magazine in the USA.

As Bérubé (2001) would expect, gay Asian men (and other gay men of color) are virtually non-existent within the pages of *The Advocate*. During the entire year [2005], gay Asian men were the subjects of one feature story, ironically enough, about the invisibility of gay Asian men in the larger gay community. The images and narratives about gay Asian men that do make it between the covers are a reflection of their 'place' within the larger gay community, marginal members at best, commodified objects at worst. . . .

Issue 943 (July 19) of *The Advocate* featured a gay Asian man on the cover of the magazine, making him the only Asian person, man or woman, to appear on the cover of *The Advocate* in 2005. Voice-over actor James Sie, featured with his partner, musician Douglas Wood, was featured as a part of the magazine's coverage of gay parenting and adoption. In both the photos, one on the cover and the other with the story, Wood is shown holding their adopted son, while Sie is in the background. Given the 'theme' of the piece on parenting, presenting Wood as the active parent and Sie as the passive parent blatantly gives Wood primacy in the article, while relegating Sie to the background.

In addition, Sie's work as a voice-over actor is only given a brief mention, while a story box promotes Wood's recently released music CD. [Thus] Wood's occupation, and by extension his role as family provider, is given primacy, while Sie's work is merely a footnote. The narrative is also symptomatic of the way the larger society, both gay and straight, views Asian Americans and other racial minorities.

In the second paragraph, the author quotes Sie as stating: 'We wanted to adopt an Asian child, and that's hard to do domestically . . . There are very few Asian women here who give their children up for adoption. It seemed like an international adoption was our best bet' (Lehoczky, 2005: 47). Later, Lehoczky explains: 'The couple were also introduced to a homophobic government from which they needed to hide their relationship . . . The adoption could be blocked if local officials found out that Sie was not in fact single' (Lehoczky, 2005: 47). While other countries are mentioned as being unfriendly towards potential gay parents, Lehoczky specifically points out China, by quoting Adam Pertman, executive director of the Evan B. Donaldson Adoption Institute, as stating: 'When Chinese officials see a single person, they grimace and start asking questions . . . They changed their rules to accommodate more married couples, which was largely a way of cutting instances of gay and lesbian adoptions' (Lehoczky, 2005: 48).

While presenting Chinese officials as being overly homophobic, and Asian women as unwilling to 'give up' their children, the article makes no mention of laws in the USA that forbid gay men and women from adopting any children, or the scarcity of white babies available for adoption. In fact, the trials endured by Wood and Sie in having to seek a child outside of the USA are blamed on Asian American women's unwillingness to 'give up' their children and the Chinese government's homophobic attitudes. Contrasted to this homophobia in 'Asian' cultures, whites, whether in the USA or elsewhere, are given a pass from blame. . . .

Adding Insult to Injury

While the treatment of gay Asian men by *The Advocate* may be lacking, at least it is not outright degrading. In fact, given the relatively small number of gay Asian men in the USA compared to gay white men, a few articles that represent the needs of a small portion of their potential readers might be expected. However, articles in *OUT* magazine seem to actively degrade gay Asian men for entertainment value, while relegating them to the margins of the gay community or placing them outside of the 'gay' community altogether. For example, the February 2005 issue of *OUT* magazine ran a column titled, 'How to Gab in Gaysian.' A pitiful and unfortunate attempt at comic relief, *OUT* magazine introduced the column in this way: 'Sometimes members of a group pepper their conversations with sexual euphemisms, saucy slang terms, and just flat-out un-PC parlance. Since there isn't an official English-Gaysian dictionary, *OUT* offers you a small menu of words you might want to know in order to verbal-vogue it like a queer Asian' (Lee, 2005, 28). Included in the list of words to be 'translated' into 'English' were *FOBulous*, an adjective meaning 'fresh off the boat and fabulous' and *dogeater*, a noun to describe a 'gaysian who unapologetically uses men for all their emotional, sexual, and financial worth, because they feel men are dogs by nature.'

First, the column works to highlight the 'foreignness' of gay Asian men compared to gay white men. From its outset, it marks gay Asians as being members of a 'group' that is outside of the gay mainstream. In implying that readers of *OUT* magazine would need an 'English-Gaysian dictionary,' the column presupposes that such readers are white. It is the implied gay white reader who is provided with a lesson on how to decipher the 'foreign' language

of gay Asian men and it is the implied gay white reader who is to receive a 'lesson' about a 'foreign' group.

In addition, the column plays upon old stereotypes of Asian Americans. One, Asian men are perpetually foreign, and as such are outside of the gay mainstream. While an adjective to describe a recent immigrant is provided, there is no attempt to define slang terms that describe American born Asians. Not surprising is the inclusion of 'dogeater,' meant to conjure up stereotypical images of Asians and perceived dietary patterns. It goes without saying that such caricatures are not new. . . .

Commodifying Asian Bodies

. . . While virtually invisible in feature stories and profiles, gay Asian men are amply present in advertisements placed in gay periodicals. Full page advertisements for pornographic films with all-Asian casts are scattered generously within the pages of gay publications, all the while Asian men are excluded from the features. While advertisements in gay periodicals seem to advertise to gay white men, they advertise gay Asian men as a commodity for consumption. Perhaps nowhere is this more evident than between the pages of *Oriental Guys Magazine*. Originally published in Sydney, the recently defunct *Oriental Guys Magazine* was a nine-year advertisement of gay Asian men for white men. As Hagland (1998) notes, the Asian men who grace the pages of *Oriental Guys Magazine* and other such 'rice queen magazines'—named in reference to 'rice queens,' gay white men who prefer Asian sex partners—are meant for white male consumption, and sexual narratives regarding the men who are pictured are almost always written by white men. . . .

This commodification of gay Asian men can also be observed at gay community events. For example, the 'Mr' and 'Miss' pageants put on by the Long Yang Club (LYC)—an organization with a global network of nearly four dozen chapters that purport to cater to 'gay Asians and interested non-Asians . . .'—involve exclusively Asian contestants who are on display for white male enjoyment (Long Yang Club, 2005). Asian contestants compete with each other largely by putting their bodies on display for the approval of white judges who 'score' them and 'select' a winner. Given the true purpose of LYC, to promote inter-racial dating among gay Asian men and their 'admirers,' one wonders why only Asian men are on display. Within this structure, it becomes clear that within the inter-racial dating relationship between white men and Asian men, as facilitated by the LYC, white men have the power to objectify and select, while Asian men are objectified and selected.

Discussion

It is not surprising that the feminine image of all Asian men has been easily superimposed onto gay media. Contrasting the 'feminine' gay Asian man to the 'masculine' gay white man places gay white men in the dominant position in a society and culture that values masculinity over femininity, active over passive, and virile over submissive. In doing so, gay publications create a hierarchy of those who 'belong' in the gay 'community' and those who are simply marginal members.

Many would argue that gay publications generally tend to present only one type of image, that of young, attractive, muscular, and successful men. Certainly, in this way, gay publications are little different from 'mainstream' publications hoping to attract advertising dollars. Also, it is likely that the focus on lean, muscular bodies has negative consequences for gay white men as well (Lorenzen et al., 2004). At the same time, these images of young, attractive white men—while problematic for other reasons—do not relegate other

white men to the margins of the gay community nor actively construct them as being outside of the gay community. Rather, it works to highlight their privileged racial status allowing non-young, non-muscular, and non-successful gay white men to racially identify with the privileged position within the gay community, thereby allowing them to practice a complicit model of masculinity (Connell, 1995). As such, the results of the 'typical' images found in gay publications are different for white men who do not 'fit' the norms, and men of color.

In recent years, gay Asian American men have been active in creating their own images that go beyond the stereotypes that seem to be regurgitated in the popular 'gay' press. Sadly, *Noodle Magazine,* the only such publication produced entirely by gay Asian American men, closed after publishing just six issues between summer of 2002 and fall of 2003. In its inaugural issue, *Noodle Magazine* declared:

> What you have in your hands is something that we thought was missing in all of our lives. Sure, we've seen Asian and Pacific Islander men in a magazine or two in the past, but we kind of feel that they weren't really about us, and they talked more about us than toward us. Hey, we like the attention as much as anyone, but we don't think we've ever actually seen who we really are in print before. Not in a token article in a gay magazine, not as a sidebar in an Asian American magazine, and not as a human interest story in the newspaper. We thought it was about time we tell the stories that we want to tell. (*Noodle Magazine,* 2002: 5)

While it is clear that the producers of *Noodle Magazine* were aware of the negative stereotypes about gay Asian men within the gay community, they relied on a strategy of compensation whereby they attempted to undermine the stereotypes by 'conforming par excellence to the hegemonic ideal'

(Chen, 1999: 592). By using images of muscular, and masculine, gay Asian men that mimicked the images found in magazines such as *OUT*, the producers of the magazine attempted to present gay Asian men as being similar to the hegemonic norm found within the gay press. While doing so clearly provides an alternative to the images of gay Asian men found in mainstream gay publications, and provides gay Asian men with alternative images of themselves, the same action may have unfortunate consequences. As Chan (2001: 13) notes, the desire to 'disinherit emasculating representations' simply 'reflects a willingness to adhere to a predominantly white model of masculinity.' Thus, by promoting the images of masculinity and desirability found in mainstream gay publications, these images give credit to the dominant view of 'gay' masculinity that allowed for the existence of the negative stereotypes about gay Asian men in the first place. After all, as Michael Kimmel (1994) points out, masculinity is constructed on racism, homophobia, and sexism. I would argue here that 'gay' masculinity is largely founded on transposing 'white' masculinity over that of men of color. While 'gay' masculinity can never be hegemonic, it can, nonetheless, position itself closer to the hegemonic ideal by pitting the more feminized masculinity of Asian men as a counter balance. As such, I would argue that that very masculinization of gay identity as discussed by Levine (1998) relies, to some extent, on the feminized gay Asian representations. At the same time, the entire notion of 'masculinity' is socially constructed, with the very definition of what is and is not masculine constantly negotiated and altered. Even the 'gay macho' discussed by Levine can be seen as in flux as new models of masculinity come to dominate the gay press.

The real goal needs to be an attempt at changing the dominant view of 'masculinity' within the gay community rather than buying into the existing model provided by the gay mainstream. Doing so, however, is hardly an easy task. Rather than focusing on reproducing the dominant gay images of masculinity with Asian faces, I believe, as Chan (2000: 385) suggests, that 'an ambivalent or ambiguous model of masculinity is a more effective way to counter a hegemonic model of masculinity.' Yet as Chan (2000) finds, doing so is a daunting task. But at the same time, what other options are there if the ultimate goal is to dismantle the very system of gendered expectations that continually places gay men of color in the subordinate position to gay white men?

References

Bérubé, A. (2001) How Gay Stays White and What Kind of White It Stays. B.B. Rasmussen et al. (eds) *The Making and Unmaking of Whiteness,* pp. 234–65. Duke University Press: Durham.

Caldwell, J. (2005) Invisible No More. *The Advocate.* 15 March 2005: 28–30.

Chan, J. (2000) Bruce Lee's Fictional Model of Masculinity. *Men and Masculinities* 2(4): 371–87.

Chan, J. (2001) *Chinese American Masculinities: From Fu Manchu to Bruce Lee.* Routledge: New York.

Chen, A. (1999) Lives at the Center of the Periphery, Lives at the Periphery of the Center: Chinese American Masculinities and Bargaining with Hegemony. *Gender and Society* 13(5): 584–607.

Connell, R. (1995) *Masculinities.* University of California Press: Berkeley.

Dahlgren, P. (1992) Introduction. P. Dahlgren and C. Sparks (eds) *Journalism and Popular Culture,* pp. 1–23. Sage: London.

Eng, D. (2001) *Racial Castration: Managing Masculinity in Asian America.* Duke University Press: Durham.

Fung, R. (1996) Looking for My Penis. R. Leong (ed.) *Asian American Sexualities,* pp. 181–98. Routledge: New York.

Hagland, P. (1998) Undressing the Oriental Boy: The Gay Asian in the Social Imagination of the Gay White Male. D. Atkins (ed.) *Looking Queer: Body Image and Identity in Lesbian, Bisexual, Gay and Transgender Communities,* pp. 277–93. Harrington Park Press: New York.

Hamamoto, D. (1994) *Monitored Peril: Asian Americans and the Politics of TV Representation.* University of Minnesota Press: Minneapolis.

Hoang, N.T. (2004) The Resurrection of Brandon Lee: The Making of a Gay Asian American Porn Star. L. Williams (ed.) *Porn Studies,* pp. 223–70. Duke University Press: Durham.

Kimmel, M. (1994) Masculinity as Homophobia: Fear, Shame, and Silence in the Construction of Gender Identity. H. Brod and M. Kaufman (eds) *Theorizing Masculinities,* pp. 119–141. Sage: Thousand Oaks.

Kumashiro, K. (ed) (2004) *Restoried Selves: Autobiographies of Queer Asian/Pacific American Activists.* Harrington Park Press: New York.

Lee, D. (2005) How to Gab in Gaysian. *OUT* (February): 28.

Lee, R. (1999) *Orientals: Asian Americans in Popular Culture.* Temple University Press: Philadelphia.

Lehoczky, E. (2005) Rough Going Overseas. *The Advocate.* 19 July 2005: 47–8.

Levine, M. (1998) *Gay Macho: The Life and Death of the Homosexual Clone.* New York University Press: New York.

Long Yang Club (2005) www.longyangclub.org

Lorenzen, L., Grieve, F. and Thomas, A. (2004) Exposure to Muscular Male Models Decreases Men's Body Satisfaction. *Sex Roles* 51(11/12): 743–8.

Lowe, L. (1996) *Immigrant Acts.* Duke University Press: Durham.

Noodle Magazine (2002) Hello, My Name is Noodle. *Noodle* (Summer): 5.

Park, Y. (2005) Culture as a Deficit: A Critical Discourse Analysis of the Concept of Culture in Contemporary Social Work Discourse. *Journal of Sociology and Social Welfare* 32(3): 11–33.

Storey, J. (1996) *Cultural Studies and the Study of Popular Culture.* University of Georgia Press: Atlanta.

25

When in Rome

Heterosexism, Homophobia, and Sports Talk Radio

David Nylund

*T*he *Jim Rome Show* reflects a growing cultural trend in the United States—sports talk radio. According to sportswriter Ashley Jude Collie (2001), Jim Rome is the "hippest, most controversial, and brutally honest voice" (p. 53) in mediated sports. In addition to his nationally syndicated radio program that airs on more than 200 stations, the 40-year-old hosts ESPN's *Rome Is Burning,* a weekly 1-hr television sports talk show (and his second show on ESPN). Rome began his radio career broadcasting University of California, Santa Barbara (UCSB), basketball games. After graduating from UCSB in 1986 and serving seven non-playing radio internships, Rome earned a local weekend job at XTRA in San Diego, a powerful 77,000-watt station. The "clever fashioning of a streetwise persona" (Mariscal, 1999), his raspy voice, staccato delivery, and fiercely independent opinions separated him from the talk radio crowd, and he soon moved into hosting a primetime radio show. Eventually, his popularity earned him a television spot on ESPN2, *Talk2,* a cable show that Rome hosted in the early 90s. The Noble Sports Network syndicated Rome's radio show in 1995, and Premiere Radio Networks acquired the rights to the show 1 year later. Rome also hosted Fox Sports Net's *The Last Word,* a sports talk television program that ran from 1997 to 2002.

However, despite the variety of venues in which he plays, it is the radio show's format that contributes to Rome's controversiality and popularity. Loyal callers, whom he calls "clones," phone in with their opinion (referred to as a "take") on what's happening in the world of sports. Rome listens intently and either "runs" the caller with a buzzer (meaning he disconnects the call) or he allows them to finish their take and says, "rack 'em" (meaning he saves the call as an entry into the huge call-of-the-day contest). As opposed to other talk radio programs where there is some dialogical interaction between the caller and hosts,

From David Nylund, "When in Rome: Heterosexism, Homophobia, and Sports Talk Radio." *Journal of Sport and Social Issues* (2004), 28 (2), 136–168. Reprinted with permission of SAGE Publications.

Rome and his callers do not engage in a back-and-forth interchange. The caller's comments are highly performative, full of insider language, and monological. Rome silently listens to the call and only comments when the caller is finished with his or her monologue or Rome disconnects the call. Rarely, if ever, does a caller disagree with Rome.[1] "Huge" calls are those that Rome considers good "smack" speech—his term for sports talk that is gloatful, uninhibited, and unbridled. According to Rome, only the strong survive in this 3-hr dose of smack and irreverence. Rome's in-group language and his unique interaction (or lack thereof) make his radio show distinctive. His "survival of the fittest" format is responsible for the show's reputation as sports version of hate-speech radio (Hodgson, 1999).

The Jim Rome Show epitomizes the growing trend of talk radio. Presented as a medium in which citizens/callers can freely "air their point of view," talk radio has become a very popular forum for large numbers of people to engage in debate about politics, religion, and sports. The media culture, with talk radio as a prominent discourse, plays a very powerful role in the constitution of everyday life, shaping our political values, gender ideologies, and supplying the material out of which people fashion their identities (Kellner, 1995). Hence, it is crucial for scholars to furnish critical commentary on talk radio; specifically, we should critique those radio texts that work to reinforce inequality.

Talk radio formats, particularly political talk radio, exploded in the 1980s as a result of deregulation, corporatization of radio, and niche marketing (Cook, 2001).[2] Deregulation, which loosened mass-media ownership and content restrictions, renewed interest in radio as a capitalist investment and galvanized the eventual emergence of its two 1990s prominent showcase formats: hate radio talk shows and all-sports programming (Cook, 2001). By the late 1990s, there were more than 4,000 talk shows on 1,200 stations (Goldberg, 1998).[3] Sports talk radio formats have,

according to cultural studies scholar Jorge Mariscal (1999), "spread like an unchecked virus" (p. 111). Currently, there are more than 250 all-sports stations in the United States (Ghosh, 1999).

As a result of deregulation and global capitalism, new media conglomerates emerged as the only qualified buyers of radio programming.[4] Infinity Broadcasting, the largest U.S. company devoted exclusively to owning and operating radio stations, owns WFAN[5] and Sacramento's local all-sports station, 1140 AM. Its competing company, Premiere Radio Network, owns the popular nationally syndicated programs hosted by Howard Stern, Rush Limbaugh, Dr. Laura, and Jim Rome.... Talk radio is aimed at a very desirable demographic: White middle-class men between the ages of 24 and 55 years. Research shows that talk-radio listeners are overwhelmingly men who tend to vote Republican (Armstrong & Rubin, 1989; Hutchby, 1996; Page & Tannenbaum, 1996). The most popular program, the *Rush Limbaugh Show*, has 20 million daily listeners who laugh along with the host as he rants and vents, opening a channel for the performance of the angry White male.... Douglas (2002) argued that although most of the research on talk radio is on the threat it poses to democracy, what is obvious, but far less discussed, is talk radio's central role in restoring masculine hegemony:

> Talk radio is as much—maybe even more—about gender politics at the end of the century than it is about party politics. There were different masculinities enacted on the radio, from Howard Stern to Rush Limbaugh, but they were all about challenging and overthrowing, if possible, the most revolutionary of social movements, feminism. The men's movement of the 1980s found its outlet—and that was talk radio. (Douglas, 2002, p. 485)

Similarly, sports talk radio, according to Goldberg (1998), enacts its White hegemony via hypermasculine posing, forceful opinions, and loudmouth shouting. Sports talk radio "pontificates, moralizes, politicizes, commercializes, and commodifies—as it entertains" (p. 213). Although Rome's masculine style is different from Limbaugh's and Stern's, all three controversial hosts have built reputations through their rambunctious, masculinist, and combative styles (Farred, 2000). With White male masculinity being challenged and decentered by feminism, affirmative action, gay and lesbian movements, and other groups' quest for social equality, sports talk shows, similar to talk radio in general, have become an attractive venue for embattled White men seeking recreational repose and a nostalgic return to a prefeminist ideal (Farred, 2000).

This chapter offers a critical analysis of the most prominent sports talk-radio program, *The Jim Rome Show*. My study does not critique and dissect *The Jim Rome Show* in isolation from other media texts or discourses about sports; rather, I aim to provide a historicized and contextualized study based in cultural studies methodology. I show how *The Jim Rome Show* is situated within a broader set of social, gender, racial, political, economic, and cultural forces. In particular, I examine the ways in which the show reinforces and (less obviously) calls into question heterosexism as well as what gender scholars call hegemonic masculinity. . . .

As a casual listener to *The Jim Rome Show* over the past 3 years, I have noticed themes of misogyny, violence, and heterosexual dominance appear to recur with considerable frequency. Rome's persona embodies an aggressive masculinity with unassailable expertise and authority. This aggressive persona climaxed in 1994 on the set of Rome's ESPN show *Talk 2* while interviewing NFL quarterback Jim Everett. During the interview, Everett knocked Rome off his chair after Rome taunted Everett by calling him "Chris" (i.e., female tennis star, Chris Evert), a veiled reference to the quarterback's reputed lack of toughness.

Rome's reference to Everett as "Chris" on the show was not the first time he had done so. In fact, Rome has used this term on Everett throughout the 1993 NFL season on his local radio show on XTRA 690 AM. This hypermasculine event increased Rome's fame and reputation among some of his audience as a host who "tells it like it is" even if it means insulting someone. However, many in the media criticized Rome's lack of professionalism and predicted the end of his career (Sports Illustrated Editors, 1994). Although Rome left ESPN2 soon after the Everett incident, his radio career slowly continued to grow to the prominence it now holds. Rome's reputation as intolerant and abusive continues to this day because his rapid-fire, masculinist-laden opinion on sports provoked OutSports.com—a Web site that caters to gay and lesbian sports fans—to refer to him as "the commentator who makes a name for himself by saying stupid things with an obnoxious style, that for some reason, attracts many straight sports fans" (Buzinski, 2000, p. 5).[6]

As a cultural studies scholar and committed sports fan, I am compelled to study *The Jim Rome Show* to examine the sexism and homophobia present in the show. When in Rome, do the clones do as the Romans do? This question led me to conduct a textual analysis that identifies those features that appear to reinforce or promote homophobia and sexism. I also researched audiences in various sports bars in the United States to achieve a better understanding of what *The Jim Rome Show* means to listeners. I was particularly curious whether certain audience members resist the dominant, hegemonic, textual themes. . . .

Hegemonic Themes

My analysis of the text confirms that much of the discourse on the show contains themes of misogyny, violence, and heterosexual dominance including themes that reinforced sexism and lesbian baiting. The following examples highlight these instances.

The first is from an infamous program dated July 23. On this date, Rome was commenting on the breaking story that several professional male athletes (Patrick Ewing, Terrell Davis, and Dekembe Motumbo) had testified in an Atlanta court that they regularly attended a strip club (The Gold Club) and engaged in sex acts with some of the club's dancers.[7] This tabloidlike story was a great opportunity for Rome to engage in his sardonic "smack" talk. Here are Rome's acerbic comments on Patrick Ewing's admission that he received free oral sex at the Gold Club:

> Want some free oral sex Patrick [Ewing]? Nah, I'm good. Maybe next time! Come on! He said he'd been there 10 times. He said he had free oral sex 2 times. And by the way, who's going to say "no" to free oral sex? I mean, clones, would you like some free oral sex? Who's going to say no to that [laughing]? Most athletes go to a club or restaurant and get comped some free drinks, chicken wings. . . . not Patrick, he gets comped free oral sex.
>   [later in his monologue] Meanwhile, a former stripper testified. And it's a good thing. We finally have some good testimony. She testified that she performed sex acts or witnessed other dancers perform sex acts on celebrities including Terrell Davis and Dekembe Motumbo. So in response to the proverbial question, "who wants to sex Motumbo?" The answer obviously is whichever skank's turn it is at the Gold Club.

In this section of the transcript, Rome employs a very common, taken-for-granted discourse—"the heterosexual male sexual drive discourse" (Hare-Mustin, 1994). This dominant ideology is predicated on the notion that women are objects (Rome misogynistically refers to the dancers as "skanks") who arouse men's heterosexual urges, which are assumed to be "natural and compelling" (Hare-Mustin, 1994, p. 24). Accordingly, men cannot control their primitive sexual yearnings, and women are blamed for inflaming them. This assumption, reproduced by Rome's rhetorical question, "who is going to turn down 'free' oral sex," reinforces women's subjugation as they become defined as existing solely for men's pleasure.

Rome's language takes on homophobic tones later in the same program. In this excerpt, Rome ridicules a former dancer's testimony:

> Finally we are getting somewhere. I thought Ewing's testifying of getting "hummers" was going to be the best that the trial had to offer. Thankfully, it's not in fact, not even close! After Patrick was done humiliating himself, one of the hookers got on the stand. That's when it really got good. A former dancer at the club starting naming names! This is just the beginning. This "tramp" also testified that she went back to the hotel room of a former wrestling executive, to perform sex acts, not on him, but on his wife! Now, we are getting somewhere. Sex with athletes; lesbian sex acts with the wives of executives. That's what I was hoping for from the beginning! And this tramp also added that she and another dancer performed a lesbian sex show for Ewing and some friends before he was given free oral sex by other dancers. And perhaps the most amazing thing, this tramp that ratted everybody out, is now working at a day care center in Georgia. Wonderful. Who wouldn't want to leave their kids with a woman who used to be a hooker? There's no one I would trust my kids with more than a woman who used to perform lesbian sex shows for NBA centers and had sex with wrestling executives' wives. What a perfect person to have around children! Man, I can't wait to see what happens today in the trial. I wonder who else's life will be ruined today?

Many of the callers on the September 9 program also reproduced male hegemony during their takes. Here is the call of the day:

Dan: [Contemptuously] I feel sorry for those skanks. I mean Ewing, Motumbo![8] Hopefully, the dancers got time and a half! I guess America has finally found a job worse than Assistant Crack Whore. About the only thing good to come out of this sordid mess is that Motumbo finally found a bar where his pickup line works.

Rome: [Laughing] Good job Dan!

Rome and his production staff chose this take as the call of the day, and in doing so, they support offensive, masculinist humor.[9] Dan's behavior reflects a common social practice for many men—the desire to earn the homosocial approval of other, more powerful men such as Jim Rome. Rome has power over the discourse and decides that Dan's wit gives him the right to enter the homosocial space of male privilege. Yes, Dan attempts to hold the players accountable for their behavior. However, the underlying tone of Dan's comments—"crack whore" and "skanks"—are racialized and sexist.

Rome's comments on athletes receiving oral sex at a strip club references the Clinton/Lewinsky affair and the increasing media focus on sex scandals in the lives of public figures. Although the "tabloidization" of the media has many negative consequences, Lumby (2001) posited that it is not completely destructive. In fact, the increased media attention on private sexuality is because of, in part, the "feminist project of politicizing the private sphere and its attendant issues, such as sexual harassment, domestic violence, and child care" (p. 234). "Bad" tabloid style press may actually stem from some "good" political motives that have focused on issues that were once seen as merely personal. Yet the media focus on Clinton and Rome's focus on athletes at the Gold Club elides a feminist analysis of structures of power (Clinton with an intern or famous athletes with female sex workers). Hence, the entertainment value of sex scandals undermines the feminist goal of politicizing the private and reinforces "patriarchal sexuality morality: a proscription of sexual behavior outside the bounds of heterosexual monogamous marriage and the violation of that proscription by powerful and privileged males" (Jakobsen, 2001, p. 307).

Entertainment and Male Hegemony

How do fans themselves make sense of and respond to Rome's problematic masculinist commentary? Not surprisingly, many of the fans I spoke to found it humorous; "It's entertaining" was the most common response. In fact, 2 days after Rome's acerbic comments about the incidents at the Gold Club, the topic came up with George (all the names of my research participants have been changed to preserve anonymity), a 27-year-old White male, in a sports bar in Sacramento. While inquiring about what he finds appealing about Rome, he replied,

> I listen every day. He tells like it is. He lets it rip. He doesn't hold back. I like that! And he's entertaining! He pokes fun at people like the other day when Rome went off about the Ewing (Gold Club incident). It's funny! It reminds me of locker room humor. Yes, I get a kick out of his smack talk. It's pure entertainment. Like when he trashes NASCAR and the WNBA.

His friend, John (a 26-year-old White male), echoed similar sentiments:

> Yeah, Rome is hilarious. I thought it was hilarious when he called Jim Everett, "Chris." That's what sticks in my head when someone says something about Rome. He's kind of like the Rush Limbaugh or Howard Stern of sports talk radio. Like he thinks he's God. But I don't mind it because he's entertaining. And it's a way for him to get the ratings

and the market share. I admire that because I am a stockbroker. You need to market yourself to stand out. You need to be aggressive and controversial to be successful in today's society. The show makes men cocky—like the clones. I listen to it for the entertainment. And he does know his sports.

Such comments are fairly representative of the participants that I interviewed. Many men valorize Rome's "transnational business masculinity," a term coined by Council (2000) to describe egocentrism, conditional loyalties, and a commitment to capital accumulation. In addition, as stated above, many participants found the program pleasurable because Rome is knowledgeable, authoritative, and comedic. Implied here is the notion that listening to Rome is a natural as well as an innocent pleasure. One person, when asked about the so-called harmlessness of the program, said, "If you don't like it, turn the radio dial. No one is forcing you to listen. It's just entertainment!" This is a common response to critiques of the negative effects of media culture and audience pleasure. Yet amusement is neither innate nor harmless. Pleasure is learned and closely connected to power and knowledge (Foucault, 1980). As media scholar Douglas Kellner (1995) observed,

> We learn what to enjoy and what we should avoid. We learn when to laugh and when to cheer. A system of power and privilege thus conditions our pleasures so that we seek certain socially sanctioned pleasures and avoid others. Some people learn to laugh at racist jokes and others learn to feel pleasure at the brutal use of violence. (p. 39)

The media industry, therefore, often mobilizes pleasure around conservative ideologies that have oppressive effects on women, homosexuals, and people of color. The ideologies of hegemonic masculinity, assembled in the form of pleasure and humor, are what many of my participants found most enjoyable about *The Jim Rome Show,* including Rome's aggressive, masculinist, "expert" speech that ridicules others. Thus, many of the pleasurable aspects of the program may encourage certain male listeners to identify with the features of traditional masculinity.

Calling *The Rome Show:* Homosociality and Approval

I was also interested in what listeners of the program thought of callers' comments and if they had ever called the program themselves. Many enjoyed listening to callers such as Dan and found their commentary to constitute comical moments of the show. I was particularly interested in what calling in to the show might mean for men who subscribe to traditional masculinity. One of the main aspects of traditional masculine homosociality involves men's striving and competing for prestige and approval within their peer groups (Wenner, 1998). This striving provides the basis for an affiliation. Many people I interviewed stated that the ultimate compliment would be for Jim Rome to approve of their take if they called. To have your call "racked" by the leading sports media personality would be a revered honor. What's more, from within the terms of hegemonic masculinity, having one's call rejected may signify a "failure" of masculinity. The following dialogue occurred between me and Fred (a 44-year-old Black male):

David: Have you called the program before?

Fred: No, I never have called. I thought about calling but I would hate to get run [Rome disconnecting the call]. Man that would hurt! I sometimes think, "Man, I could give a good take ... but if I call and "suck" ... you know ... get run, start stuttering ... man that would be embarrassing.

David: What would be embarrassing about getting run?

Fred: It's embarrassing 'cause it's Jim Rome. He's the man [laughing]! He's the pimp in the box![10] Man, if you get racked and are the caller of the day, you're the man!

. . . When asked why *The Jim Rome Show* and other sports talk radio programs are so popular among heterosexual men, about one half of the men told me that they feel anxious and uncertain because of the changes in men's work and women's increasing presence in the public sphere. Moreover, several participants believed that sports talk provides a safe haven for men to bond and reaffirm their essential masculinity. Here's what a 27-year-old White male said in a bar in Tampa:

It's [*The Jim Rome Show*] a male bonding thing, a locker room for guys in the radio. You can't do it at work, everything's PC (politically correct) now! So the Rome Show is a last refuge for men to bond and be men. It's just in your car, Rome, and it's the audience that you can't see. I listen in the car and can let that maleness come out. I know its offensive sometimes to gays and women . . . you know . . . when men bond . . . but men need that! Romey's show gives me the opportunity to talk to other guy friends about something we share in common. And my dad listens to Romey also. So my dad and I bond also.

This comment is telling about the mixed effects of sports talk. On one hand, sports talk radio allows men to express a "covert intimacy"[11] (Messner, 1992) and shared meaning about a common subject matter. This bonding can bring forth genuine moments of closeness and should not necessarily be pathologized or seen as completely negative. However, much of the bonding is, as the interviewee stated, "offensive sometimes to gays and women."

Many of the men I interviewed were speaking in a group context in the presence of other male peers. The gender displays (sexist and homophobic jokes, for example) by the men I interviewed in the homosocial space of a sports bar were interesting to observe as they confirmed Messner's (2002) point that men in groups define and solidify their boundaries through aggressive misogynistic and homophobic speech and actions. Underneath this bonding experience are homoerotic feelings that must be warded off and neutralized through joking, yelling, cursing, and demonizing anybody who does not conform to normative masculinity. Pronger (1990) argued the arena of sports is paradoxical: on one hand, sports is a primary site for the expression of heterosexual masculinity, and on the other hand, there is a powerful homoerotic undercurrent subliminally present in sports. Sports radio operates similarly as an extension of this paradoxically homosocial and homoerotic space. Shields (1999), in his analysis of sports radio, stated, "It would be impossible to overstate the degree to which sports talk radio is shadowed by the homosexual panic implicit in the fact that it consists almost entirely of a bunch of out-of-shape White men sitting around talking about Black men's buff bodies" (p. 50). . . .

Counterhegemonic Themes

As the above analysis illuminates, *The Jim Rome Show* reinforces male hegemony. However, a close reading of the show reveals some contradiction and fissures to hegemony. The following transcripts of the program exemplify times when the text and its voices (Jim Rome, audience members) partially subvert hegemonic masculinity and homophobia. The first example is from the show dated April 30 when the topic of bigotry was raised by Rome. Here, Rome, in his belligerent vocal style, is taking issue with the homophobic comments made by Chicago Cubs pitcher, Julian Tavarez, about San Francisco Giants fans:

Julian Tavarez, a pitcher for the Cubs said this about San Francisco Giants fans—his words not mine—"they are a bunch of a-holes and faggots"... You know, it would be nice to go a week without some racist or bigot comment... but no, Julian. Nice job Julian.... And here's a thought, Julian Rocker [reference to John Rocker, a pitcher who became famous for making racist and homophobic comments during an interview in *Sports Illustrated*], just because San Francisco has a significant gay population, I would be willing to bet that not everybody at a Giants game is a homosexual. Maybe. Can't document that. Just a thought... I feel pretty secure in saying that? How do you come up with this garbage? I mean how do you get to the point where the proper response to heckling fans is to drop racist, anti-Semitic, or homophobic bombs on people? And even if you had those bigoted views, you would have the sense to keep it [to] yourselves. They might realize that not everybody hates everybody else. I think there is only one solution to this problem of overcrowding in the racist frat house. We are going to have to have honorary members.

In this instance, the host clearly positions himself as antiracist and antihomophobic. This stance is noteworthy and a possible contradiction to dominant sports talk discourse. Rome uses his masculine authority to stand against the intolerance often engendered by homophobia.

Rome's comments on the subject appear to be progressive and reasonable.[12] On closer examination, however, Rome's location of the problem of homophobia in a few bigoted, intolerant individuals leaves unchallenged the larger societal structures that perpetuate heterosexism. The stance taken up by the host is rooted within liberal discourse, which reduces analysis to an individual, private endeavor (Kane &

Lenskyj, 2000; Kitzinger, 1987) and forecloses any serious discussion of homophobia as structural and political issues related to power, gender, and sexuality. When Rome denounces a few athletes as "bigots," it prevents a wider analysis of the link between the institution of organized sports and its heterosexual, masculinist, and homophobic agenda. Addressing the thorny questions of sexuality, politics, power, and privilege would be a risky and bold move for *The Jim Rome Show,* as it would offer a more radical challenge to the institution of heterosexual privilege and sports.

The next seemingly subversive segment relates to an editorial letter in the May 2001 issue of *Out* magazine. In that issue, the editor in chief, Brendan Lemon, stated that his boyfriend was a Major League baseball player. Lemon did not give names, but hinted that the player was from an East Coast franchise. Rome and other mainstream media programs reacted quickly to the editorial. A media firestorm resulted in a rumor mill: Players, fans, owners, and sports talk radio hosts swapped guesses and anxieties over the athlete's identity.

On May 18, Rome's monologue pondered the questions. What would happen if that person's identity became public? What would it mean for baseball, gays, and lesbians in sports in general, and for the man himself? Given that Lemon's boyfriend would be the first athlete in one of the "big four" major league team sports (baseball, football, basketball, and hockey) to come out "during" his career, what effect would this have on the institution of sport? Rome decided to pose this question to one of his interview participants that day, well-respected baseball veteran Eric Davis.

Rome: What would happen if a teammate of yours, or any baseball player, would come out of the closet and say, "I am gay"? What would the reaction be like? How badly would that go?

Eric: I think it would go real bad. I think people would jump to form an opinion because everybody has an opinion about gays already. But I think it would be a very difficult situation because with us showering with each other . . . being around each other as men. Now, you're in the shower with a guy who's gay . . . looking at you . . . maybe making a pass. That's an uncomfortable situation. In society, they have never really accepted it. They want to come out. And if that's the case, fine, but in sports, it would definitely raise some eyebrows. . . . I don't think it should be thrown at 25 guys saying, "yeah I am gay."

[Rome changes the subject . . . no follow-up]

Rome asks a pointed question to Davis whose predictable homophobic response warrants more follow-up questions. Yet Rome shifts the subject to something less problematic, letting Davis off the hook. After Rome ends the interview, he addresses Davis's comments in another monologue:

That's [Eric Davis] a 17-year respected major league ballplayer. And I think that's a representative comment of a lot of these guys. . . . He is [a] very highly regarded guy. This is why I asked him the question. And he answered it very honestly. He would be concerned about having gay teammate. . . . For instance, when he's showering. Personally, I don't agree with the take. It's my personal opinion. However, I posed the question to see what the reaction would be. And this is what I have been saying since this story broke. This is why it would not be a good thing. This is why the editor of that magazine clearly was wrong and has never been in a locker-room or clubhouse. That's why it hasn't happened. Eric Davis' reaction is what you would expect. Not everybody would feel that

way, but a large majority would. It would make it nearly impossible for a gay player to come out.

Here, Rome is aware of the difficulties that would occur for an openly gay ballplayer. However, he shares his opinion in the safety of his "expert" monologue, not in the presence of Eric Davis. He does not risk compromising his masculinity or his relationship with Davis by endorsing this unusually progressive stance in the presence of a famous ballplayer such as Davis. However, when a listener calls immediately after the Davis interview, Rome responds differently:

Joe: I never imagined my first take would be on gays but I had to call. Being gay, it matters to no one but gays themselves. Why don't you guys, girls or gays . . . whatever you guys are. Just do us a favor, do yourselves a favor and keep it to yourselves. I mean . . . [Rome runs the caller with the buzzer and disconnects the call]

Rome: I think that's a very convenient response—"It's an issue only because you make it an issue." I don't agree with that, frankly. It's an issue because they are often persecuted against, harassed, assaulted, or killed in some cases. That's why it is an issue. They are fired from jobs, ostracized. It's not only an issue because they are making it an issue. What you are saying is keep your mouth shut, keep it in the closet; you are not accepting them for who they are and what they are. It's not an issue because they are making it an issue. It's an issue because of people saying things like, "keep your mouth shut. . . . We don't want you around. . . . We don't want to know you people exist." That's why it's an issue because of that treatment.

Again, Rome takes a strong stance against homophobia and demonstrates a fairly nuanced appreciation of the injustices of homophobia and heterosexism. This position is worth mentioning, particularly in the context of a program referred to as "The Jungle," with an audience of mostly men steeped in traditional masculinity and for whom heterosexuality is the unquestioned norm. Rome's antihomophobic stance represents a fissure in hegemonic masculinity. It can potentially foster a new awareness in Rome's listeners and invite new voices into this important conversation about masculinity and sexuality, potentially spurring a rethinking of masculinity and sports. Cutting off the first-time caller because of his homophobic comment could be viewed as a productive accountable maneuver, which is notable because straight men do not have a rich history of holding other straight men responsible for homophobic slurs.[13]

The historic May 18 radio show generated further substantive discussion on the issue of sports and heterosexual dominance in various media sites. This included a two-part show on Jim Rome's Fox TV show, *The Last Word,* titled "The Gay Athlete." The show's guests included two out athletes: Diana Nyad and Billy Bean. The show's discussion was very rich, with the host asking fairly nuanced and enlightened questions. Since this show, Rome has interviewed other athletes who have come out since they left professional sports, including football players, Esera Tuaolo and David Kopay. In these interviews, Rome asked perceptive questions about the prevalence of homophobia in male sports and applauded their courage in coming out. ESPN also addressed the same topic and conducted a poll that showed that a substantial number of sports fans would have no problem with a gay athlete (*Outside the Lines,* 2001). What's more, the *Advocate* magazine published an article by cultural critic Toby Miller (2001) where he argued that the media firestorm generated by Brendan Lemon's article could potentially create a moment "for unions and owners of the big four to issue a joint statement in support, to show that queers are a legitimate part of the big leagues" (p. 3). . . .

It is important to note that Rome's interviewing of out athletes such as Billy Bean and David Kopay is a unique outcome in the world of heteronormative sports. To allow visibility of the gay athletes cannot be taken lightly in terms of its potential ramifications. Yet it is equally important to ask which athletes are allowed to become visible? What is their social location? How is their sexuality represented? Virtually all the gay athletes who have been on *The Jim Rome Show* are White males (an exception is Esera Tuaolo who is Samoan) who define homosexuality as an essentialist identity. Foucault (1980) contended that although visibility opens up some new political possibilities, it is also "a trap" because it creates new forms of surveillance, discipline, and limits. Sure, Bean and Kopay are given space to discuss their experience as a gay athlete, however it must be contained within a very limited, private discourse. Scholar Lisa Duggan (2001) claimed that much of the recent visibility of gays and lesbians is framed within a post-Stonewall, identitarian, private discourse. She referred to this discourse as homonormativity—"a politics that does not contest dominant heteronormative assumptions and institutions, but upholds and sustains them, while promising the possibility of a demobilized gay constituency and a privatized, depoliticized gay culture anchored in domesticity and consumption" (p. 179). According to Duggan, homonormativity is privatizing, much as heteronormativity is, and each lends support to the other. As much as Rome's recognition of gays in the sporting world is noteworthy, it is very much contained with a homonormative frame that reproduces the sex and gender binary. Hence, Rome's show, although it may be influenced by traditional gay and lesbian identity polities, is not a queer space.

Athletes, including women who perform a more transgressive, non-normative sexuality, are invisible in sports radio. . . .

Notes

1. Rome's relationship with his caller, similar to most talk-show power relations between caller and host, is quite asymmetrical. Hutchby (1996) in his study of the discourse in talk radio stated that although the host has an array of discursive and institutional strategies available to him or her to keep the upper hand, occasionally callers have some resources available to resist the host's powerful strategies. Hence, Hutchby argued that power is not a monolithic feature of talk radio. Hutchby's argument does not appear to work with *The Jim Rome Show* as callers hardly ever confront Rome's authority. Rather, Rome's callers want his approval.

2. Deregulation was championed by then FCC chairman Mark Fowler who sold it as a form of media populism and civic participation. However, this public marketing campaign masked increased economic consolidation and increased barriers to entry into this market for all but very powerful media conglomerates such as Infinity Broadcasting and Premiere Radio. Commenting about the success of conservative White male talk radio due to deregulation of the 1980s, Douglas (2002) claimed that Reaganism was successful by "selling the increased concentration of wealth as move back toward democracy" (p. 491).

3. In 1960, there were just two radio stations in the United States that were dedicated to talk radio formats (Goldberg, 1998).

4. The other significant deregulatory move in the 1980s was the abandonment of the Fairness Doctrine, which the FCC announced it would no longer enforce. The doctrine required stations to offer access to air alternative opinions when controversial issues were discussed. The goal of the doctrine was to promote a balance of views. Opponents of the doctrine, including Fowler and Reagan, felt it inhibited freedom of speech. Stations, they argued, avoided giving airtime to opinionated individuals because of the requirement to broadcast competing points of view. Unrestricted by the Fairness Doctrine's mandate for balance, Limbaugh and a legion of ultraconservative imitators took off the gloves and revived the financial state of AM radio.

5. The largest sports station in the United States, based in New York, WFAN is also the largest ad-billing radio station in the United States.

6. In a recent interview in *Sports Illustrated,* Rome stated he regrets the Everett interview and has matured into a well-reasoned interviewer. In the article, Rome stated that he was "wiser" because of being married and having a child (Deitsch, 2003).

7. The court in Atlanta was prosecuting the owner of the Gold Club for mob connections and other illegalities. This event received a great deal of media attention.

8. Ewing and Motumbo are Black men. The caller of the day, Dan, is implying that they are unattractive men. Dan's disdainful "smack talk" could be understood to reproduce racist representations of Black athletes.

9. As a sidebar, Cook (2001) challenged the common notion that radio talk shows are a natural two-way dialogue between the caller and host that allow the caller to "freely air their point of view" (p. 62). The production process reveals that it is a complex, mediated process that constrains the dialogue through a range of in-studio control techniques. These hidden maneuvers include off-air talk decisions on what gets included on the program, what gets omitted, and time control cues. Cook argued that examining the complex relational politics in radio talk is important to examine to contest its negative power and influence.

10. The term *pimp in the box* refers to Rome's "pimping" of NHL hockey in Los Angeles during 1992–1993 when the Los Angeles Kings made it to the Stanley Cup Finals. Rome's show was the first in Los Angeles to actively talk about hockey on sports talk stations and book hockey players as guests. This made national news as Wayne Gretzky was to appear on the show following every playoff game the Kings played that season to the point where Gretzky thanked Rome during a televised interview after the Kings won Game 7 of the

Western Conference Finals to advance to the finals. After thanking Kings management and players he said, "To my friend Jim Rome, we've got the karma going."

11. Messner (1992) defined "covert intimacy" as doing things together rather than mutual talk about inner lives.

12. When I refer to Rome in this section, I am referring not to Rome, the individual person. Rather, I am referring to Rome's discourse.

13. However, it is important to note that Rome asserts his authority over a person with less power—a first-time caller. Rome doesn't take this strong a stance with Eric Davis, a high-status person who likely has more influence within the sports world. This textual example reveals the power relations of talk radio; hosts and famous athletes have more authority than callers.

References

Armstrong, C. B., & Rubin, A. M. (1989). Talk radio as interpersonal communication. *Journal of Communication, 39*(2), 84–93.

Buzinski, J. (2000, July 13). *Week in review.* Available at www.outsports.com

Buzinski, J. (2001, May 20). *Give the media good marks: Coverage of closeted gay baseball player was positive and non-judgmental.* Available at www.outsports.com

Collie, A. J. (2001, August 8). Rome rants. *American Way*, pp. 50–54, 56–57.

Connell, R. W. (2000). *The men and the boys.* Berkeley: University of California Press.

Cook, J. (2001). Dangerously radioactive: The plural vocalities of radio talk. In C. Lee & C. Poynton (Eds.), *Culture and text: Discourse and methodology in social research and cultural studies* (pp. 59–80). New York: Rowman & Littlefield.

Deitsch, R. (2003, May 12). Under review: Rome returning. *Sports Illustrated, 98*, 28.

Douglas, S. J. (2002). Letting the boys be boys: Talk radio, male hysteria, and political discourse in the 1980s. In M. Hilmes & J. Loviglio (Eds.), *Radio reader: Essays in the cultural history of radio* (pp. 485–504). New York: Routledge.

Duggan, L. (2001). The new homonormativity: The sexual politics of neoliberalism. In R. Castronovo & D. D. Nelson (Eds.), *Materalizing democracy: Toward a revitalized cultural politics* (pp. 175–194). Durham, NC: Duke University Press.

Farred, G. (2000). Cool as the other side of the pillow: How ESPN's Sportscenter has changed television sports talk. *Journal of Sport & Social Issues, 24*(2), 96–117.

Foucault, M. (1980). *Power/knowledge: Selected interviews and other writings, 1972–1977* (Colin Gordon, Ed. & Trans.). New York: Pantheon.

Ghosh, C. (1999, February 22). A guy thing: Radio sports talk shows. *Forbes*, p. 55.

Goldberg, D. T. (1998). Call and response: Sports, talk radio, and the death of democracy. *Journal of Sport & Social Issues, 22*(2), 212–223.

Hare-Mustin, R. T. (1994). Discourses in the mirrored room: A postmodern analysis of therapy. *Family Process, 33*, 19–35.

Hodgson, E. (1999, August 18). King of smack. *Fastbreak—The Magazine of the Phoenix Suns*, pp. 1–5.

Hutchby, I. (1996). *Confrontation talk: Arguments, asymmetries, and power on talk radio.* Mahwah, NJ: Lawrence Erlbaum.

Jakobsen, J. K. (2001). He has wronged America and women: Clinton's sexual conservatism. In L. Berlant & L. Duggan (Eds.), *Our Monica, ourselves: The Clinton affair and the national interest* (pp. 291–314). New York: New York University Press.

Kane, M. J., & Lenskyj, H. J. (2000). Media treatment of female athletes: Issues of gender and sexualities. In L. W. Wenner (Ed.), *Mediasport* (pp. 186–201). New York: Routledge.

Kellner, D. (1995). *Media culture: Cultural studies, identity, and politics between the modern and postmodern.* New York: Routledge.

Kimmel, M. (1994). Masculinity as homophobia. In H. Brod & M. Kaufman (Eds.), *Theorizing masculinities* (pp. 119–141). Thousand Oaks, CA: Sage.

Kitzinger, C. (1987). *The social construction of lesbianism.* Newbury Park, CA: Sage.

Lumby, C. (2001). The President's penis: Entertaining sex and power. In L. Berlant &

L. Duggan (Eds.), *Our Monica, ourselves: The Clinton affair and the national interest* (pp. 225–236). New York: New York University Press.

Mariscal, J. (1999). Chicanos and Latinos in the jungle of sports talk radio. *Journal of Sport & Social Issues, 23*(1), 111–117.

Messner, M. A. (1992). *Power at play: Sports and the problem of masculinity.* Boston: Beacon.

Messner, M. A. (2002). *Taking the field: Women, men, and sports.* Minneapolis: University of Minnesota Press.

Miller, T. (2001, June). Out at the ballgame. *Advocate,* pp. 1–3.

Outside the lines: Homophobia and sports. (2001, May 31). ESPN.com. Available at http://espn.go.com/otl

Page, B. I., & Tannenbaum, J. (1996). Populistic deliberation and talk radio. *Journal of Communication, 46*(2), 33–53.

Pronger, B. (1990). *The arena of masculinity: Sports, homosexuality, and the meaning of sex.* New York: St. Martin's.

Shields, D. (1999). *Black planet: Facing race during an NBA season.* New York: Crown.

Sports Illustrated Editors. (1994, April). The fall of Rome. *Sports Illustrated, 80,* 14.

Wenner, L. W. (1998). The sports bar: Masculinity, alcohol, sports, and the mediation of public space. In G. Rail & J. Harvey (Eds.), *Sports and postmodern times: Gender, sexuality, the body, and sport* (pp. 301–322). Albany: State University of New York Press.

PART IV

ADVERTISING AND CONSUMER CULTURE

A central theme of the articles in this section is the role of the media industries in the production and maintenance of an overwhelmingly consumption-oriented cultural environment in postindustrial economies like our own. Critics of such a **culture** point to a long list of social and political costs related to unchecked consumption of world resources, including environmental degradation, the dangerously increasing gap between rich and poor nations, erosion of political democracy, and even global warming—but the global corporate drive to increase levels of product consumption seems largely unaffected by these warnings.

In the **consumer** culture, we live in a world saturated with advertising **imagery** urging us to buy and consume products as a path to future happiness and self-transformation. As Sut Jhally says in "Image-Based Culture" (IV.26), which introduces this section, "In the contemporary world, messages about goods are all pervasive—advertising has increasingly filled up the spaces of our daily existence . . . it is the air that we breathe as we live our daily lives." Any discussion of the role of media within a **capitalist** economy has to foreground the role of advertising, both as an industry in its own right and, in Jhally's words, as a "discourse through and about objects." Because advertising legitimizes and even sacralizes consumption as a way of life, it is critical to our ability to think for ourselves that we learn to analyze not just the meanings of advertising **texts** but also the place of the advertising industry in our society.

As Jhally points out, "Fundamentally, advertising talks to us as individuals and addresses us about how we can become happy" (p. 242). In the past, advertisements told us that the key to happiness was our ability to keep up with the consumption patterns of our neighbors. But economist Juliet Schor, in "The New Politics of Consumption" (IV.27), points to the "upscaling of lifestyle norms" that characterizes "the new consumerism." Schor argues that a by-product of the recent economic boom times in the United States is that "luxury, rather than mere comfort, is a widespread aspiration." She shows the role of television, in particular, in contributing to this "upscaling of lifestyle norms."

> Because television shows are so heavily skewed to the "lifestyles of the rich and upper middle-class," they inflate the viewer's perceptions of what others have, and by extension what is worth acquiring—what one must have in order to avoid being "out of it." (p. 253)

Feminist scholars interested in the ways that the consumption of products plays a central role in constructing **hegemonic** femininity have traced several important changes in media culture over the past half century through the present, using women's magazines and advertising directed at women as windows into this topic. We begin with an essay by Laurie Ouellette (IV.28) on Helen Gurley Brown, author of the best-selling book *Sex and the Single Girl* (1962) and later the editor who made *Cosmopolitan* magazine such a major success in the 1960s and 1970s. Ouellette shows how Brown, in her book and in the advice columns of her magazine, took on the cultural mission of showing working-**class** White women the path to upward mobility. According to Ouellette,

> Brown's advice offered a gendered success myth to women who found themselves

taking on new roles as breadwinners, but who lacked the wages, education, professional skills, and social opportunities to recognize themselves in more conventional, male-oriented upward-mobility narratives. (p. 267)

For these White working-class women in the prefeminist 1960s, learning to fake a middle-class version of femininity was the key to real class mobility, through ensnaring a well-off man.

At the same time Brown was urging this traditional path to success on her magazine's readers, the early women's movement was beginning to critique the very institution of marriage as an agency of women's subordination in a male-dominated social order. Advertising images that confined women either to roles as wives and mothers or treated women's bodies as sex objects were an early and continuing target of feminist organizing and calls for change. Recounting her experience seeking advertisers to support the pioneering feminist *Ms* magazine in its early days, Gloria Steinem reminds us, in "Sex, Lies, and Advertising" (IV.29), how advertisers targeting women as consumers subscribed to very limited notions of what constitutes femininity (i.e., dependency, concern with beauty, fixation on family and nurturance, fear of technology) and consequently "feminine" buying patterns. Feminist efforts to redefine **gender** ideals for advertisers in the 1970s and 1980s met with disbelief, resistance, and downright hostility. Steinem's essay reveals the extent to which advertisers also assumed the right to control editorial content of the media—citing, among other practices, efforts to censor feature stories that might conflict with the interests of advertisers.

Thanks in large part to the feminist **activist** work to raise awareness about **sexism** in advertising representations, as well as to social and occupational changes since the 1970s, it is no longer acceptable for advertisers to depict women in such a narrow range of occupations, nor primarily as wives and mothers. However, there is a proliferation today of fashion advertising that employs a **hypersexualized** representation of the female body (for more on hypersexualization in pop culture generally, see Part V, below). Feminist scholars are not in agreement over what such hypersexualization means for women's lives. Some would argue that such **representations** are merely updated versions of traditional exploitation for profit ("sex sells"); others maintain that such representations depict sexual empowerment.

Rosalind Gill takes on this debate in "Supersexualize Me!" (IV.30). She questions the degree to which representations of young women aggressively emulating a media-constructed hypersexuality are truly about female **agency**. At the same time Gill points to the categories of women who are still denied any visibility in the world conjured up by advertising imagery: "older women, disabled women, fat women and any woman who is unable to live up to the increasingly narrow standards of female beauty and sex appeal that are normatively required" (p. 281).

One series of ads that would seem at first sight to make visible a much wider range of female body types and ages was produced by the much-discussed "Dove Campaign for Real Beauty." Dove developed a branding strategy that included apparently non-conventional ad images featuring "real women" rather than models, and a linked so-called "Movement for Self-Esteem," based on a corporate website and launched in 2010 at a convention of young women from the G20 countries. As Dara Persis Murray argues (IV.31), this was a strategy that **co-opted** popular feminist critical perspectives and discourse, encouraging consumers of beauty products "to think of themselves as insurgents" without actually having to do the work and pay the price of "true non-conformity and dissent" (p. 288). After analyzing both the ad **texts** and the

branding strategy as a whole, Murray concludes critically that "Real Beauty" can be seen as yet another "oppressive beauty ideology." By signing the online declaration ("Join the Movement")—and incidentally providing the company with a list of consumers—Murray argues,

> Girls and women work to become neoliberal subjects who accept responsibility to develop and perform Dove-approved "self-esteem" behaviors (requiring self-judgment and self-monitoring of one's emotional state) that are integral to the pursuit of "real beauty." (p. 292)

Such an **ideology** "reinforces the value of female beauty and its pursuit by garnering women's agreement with its values of ideological and material consumption" (p. 293).

Advertising is not the only media **genre** that generates and reinforces scrutiny of **gendered**, racialized and sexualized bodies in order to generate **consumerism** and thereby profit. In recent years, there has been a massive growth in gossip industry magazines and websites, which spectacularize every aspect of celebrities' lives, including their diets, clothing, sexual antics, "baby bumps" and children. As Kirsty Fairclough shows in her chapter on gossip blogs (IV.32), female celebrities in particular come in for what she terms "hyperscrutiny" in today's media. In Fairclough's view,

> Female celebrities have become the chief site upon which contemporary tensions and anxieties surrounding femininity, motherhood, body image, cosmetic surgery, marriage and ageing are now played out. (p. 297)

Reminding us that "in popular culture the older female body is particularly vilified" (p. 298), Fairclough is attentive to the spotlight the current gossip media industries shine on female ageing. Although there has been a trend in recent years for Hollywood to allow older women some visibility in film, she notes that the gossip discourses about these women "are always structured in terms of how well the actress is managing her ageing process." In the context of **postfeminist** ideology, as well as the hyperscrutiny of the new gossip culture, Fairclough points to "a new beauty norm ... that suggests youth must be held in limbo through the use of cosmetic procedures throughout adult life and for as long as possible" (p. 304).

An indispensable part of celebrity in today's media world is the construction and management of a persona that can provide **fans** with an illusion of authenticity and the possibility of intimacy, however limited, with the famous personality. Marwick and boyd, in their chapter on celebrities' use of Twitter (IV.33), show how "Networked media is changing celebrity culture, the ways that people relate to celebrity images, how celebrities are produced, and how celebrity is practiced."

Because celebrities are now branded "products" that help generate enormous profit for both the companies that use their names, and for themselves, they can be viewed both as both commodities and as producers of media texts. According to Marwick and boyd, who have studied data from the 300 most-followed Twitter accounts, actors, musicians, reality tv stars and other "highly followed people" are adapting their self-presentation practices to the demands of the new social media world, expending "must emotional labor maintaining a network of affective ties with their followers." As the authors point out, "even the famous must learn the techniques used by 'regular people' to gain status and attention online" (p. 315).

Athletes are also often branded commodity celebrities, and in the case of Olympic Games athletes, Rahman and Lockwood (IV. 34) show that their job is to present an authentic persona of heroic athleticism, so that the increasingly commercialized spectacle of the Games can be "enjoyed primarily for its demonstration of human endeavor rather than as another form of consumption" (p. 320). The authors analyze institutional **discourses** related to the Olympic Games held in London in the summer of 2012, against the backdrop of the ideal of noble athletic amateurism associated with the Games since the nineteenth century. As they argue,

> ... Reiterations of amateurism have become a central part of the modern Olympic discourse, and indeed provide a distinctive Olympic dimension to the 'authenticity' that is foregrounded to distract audiences from the commercialization of the Games. (p. 325)

We end this part with Jonathan Hardy's chapter (IV.35) on the HBO vampire series *True Blood*. Hardy's "mapping" of all the ways in which online and social **media platforms** were used to create a buzz around this cable TV program, and to help it "establish both cult status and popular appeal" (p. 332), brings together many of the themes of this part: advertising, marketing, consumerism, celebrity, and new media.

This chapter is also a particularly good example of new directions in **political economy** analysis, taking account of the new proliferation of media outlets and the ways in which they now operate synergistically—to create a greater impact through interlinked operation than could be achieved by each outlet working on its own. In Hardy's words,

> **Commercial intertextuality** is used to describe the production and interlinking of texts like blockbuster films or TV series with allied paratexts and products, such as spin-offs, reversionings, promos, online media, books, games and merchandise. (p. 327)

Hardy points out the "blurring and hybridization" between categories once considered separate in media studies, including "corporate/independent, professional/amateur, and as *True Blood* illustrates, . . . commercial/autonomous textuality" (p. 328). The research in this chapter highlights "the increasing diversity of transmedia intertextual space and its tensions and contradictions" (p. 333). It is these very tensions and contradictions that make necessary the kind of complex and nuanced analysis of media texts that Kellner calls for in chapter I.1. Production, textual analysis, and audience reception or consumption have become far less discrete, separable categories than ever before.

26

Image-Based Culture

Advertising and Popular Culture

Sut Jhally

Because we live inside the consumer culture, and most of us have done so for most of our lives, it is sometimes difficult to locate the origins of our most cherished values and assumptions. They simply appear to be part of our natural world. It is a useful exercise, therefore, to examine how our culture has come to be defined and shaped in specific ways—to excavate the origins of our most celebrated rituals. For example, everyone in this culture knows a "diamond is forever." It is a meaning that is almost as "natural" as the link between roses and romantic love. However, diamonds (just like roses) did not always have this meaning. Before 1938 their value derived primarily from their worth as scarce stones (with the DeBeers cartel carefully controlling the market supply). In 1938 the New York advertising agency of N.W. Ayers was hired to change public attitudes toward diamonds—to transform them from a financial investment into a *symbol* of committed and everlasting love. In 1947 an Ayers advertising copywriter came up with the slogan "a diamond is forever" and the rest, as they say, is history. As an N.W. Ayers memorandum put it in 1959: "Since 1939 an entirely new generation of young people has grown to marriageable age. To the new generation, a diamond ring is considered a necessity for engagement to virtually everyone."[1]

This is a fairly dramatic example of how the institutional structure of the consumer society orients the culture (and its attitudes, values, and rituals) more and more toward the world of commodities. The marketplace (and its major ideological tool, advertising) is the major structuring institution of contemporary consumer society.

This of course was not always the case. In the agrarian-based society preceding industrial society, other institutions such as family, community, ethnicity, and religion were the dominant institutional mediators and creators of the cultural forms. Their influence waned in the transition to industrial society and then consumer society. The emerging institution of the marketplace occupied the cultural terrain left void by the evacuation of

From Jhally, Sut. "Image-Based Culture." *The World and I*, July 1990, 506–519. Reprinted by permission of *The World & I*.

these older forms. Information about products seeped into public discourse. More specifically, public discourse soon became dominated by the "discourse through and about objects."[2]

At first, this discourse relied upon transmitting information about products alone, using the available means of textual communication offered by newspapers. As the possibility of more effective color illustration emerged and as magazines developed as competitors for advertising dollars, this "discourse" moved from being purely text-based. The further integration of first radio and then television into the advertising/media complex ensured that commercial communication would be characterized by the domination of *imagistic* modes of representation.

Again, because our world is so familiar, it is difficult to imagine the process through which the present conditions emerged. In this context, it is instructive to focus upon that period in our history that marks the transition point in the development of an image-saturated society—the 1920s. In that decade the advertising industry was faced with a curious problem—the need to sell increasing quantities of "nonessential" goods in a competitive marketplace using the potentialities offered by printing and color photography. Whereas the initial period of national advertising (from approximately the 1880s to the 1920s) had focused largely in a celebratory manner on the products themselves and had used text for "reason why" advertising (even if making the most outrageous claims), the 1920s saw the progressive integration of people (via visual representation) into the messages. Interestingly, in this stage we do not see representations of "real" people in advertisements, but rather we see representations of people who "stand for" reigning social values such as family structure, status differentiation, and hierarchical authority.

While this period is instructive from the viewpoint of content, it is equally fascinating from the viewpoint of *form;* for while the possibilities of using visual imagery existed with the development of new technologies, there was no guarantee that the audience was sufficiently literate in visual imagery to properly decode the ever-more complex messages. Thus, the advertising industry had to educate as well as sell, and many of the ads of this period were a fascinating combination where the written (textual) material explained the visual material. The consumer society was literally being taught how to read the commercial messages. By the postwar period the education was complete and the function of written text moved away from explaining the visual and toward a more cryptic form where it appears as a "key" to the visual "puzzle."

In the contemporary world, messages about goods are all pervasive—advertising has increasingly filled up the spaces of our daily existence. Our media are dominated by advertising images, public space has been taken over by "information" about products, and most of our sporting and cultural events are accompanied by the name of a corporate sponsor. There is even an attempt to get television commercials into the nation's high schools under the pretense of "free" news programming. Advertising is ubiquitous—it is the air that we breathe as we live our daily lives.

Advertising and the Good Life: Image and "Reality"

I have referred to advertising as being part of "a discourse through and about objects" because it does not merely tell us about things but of how things are connected to important domains of our lives. Fundamentally, advertising talks to us as individuals and addresses us about how we can become happy. The answers it provides are all oriented to the marketplace, through the purchase of goods or services. To understand the system of images that constitutes advertising we need to inquire into the definition of happiness and satisfaction in contemporary social life.

Quality of life surveys that ask people what they are seeking in life—what it is that makes them happy—report quite consistent results. The conditions that people are searching for—what they perceive will make them happy—are things such as having personal autonomy and control of one's life, self-esteem, a happy family life, loving relations, a relaxed, tension-free leisure time, and good friendships. The unifying theme of this list is that these things are not fundamentally connected to goods. It is primarily "social" life and not "material" life that seems to be the locus of perceived happiness. Commodities are only weakly related to these sources of satisfaction.[3]

A market society, however, is guided by the principle that satisfaction should be achieved via the marketplace, and through its institutions and structures it orients behavior in that direction. The data from the quality of life studies are not lost on advertisers. If goods themselves are not the locus of perceived happiness, then they need to be connected in some way with those things that are. Thus advertising promotes images of what the audience conceives of as "the good life": Beer can be connected with anything from eroticism to male fraternity to the purity of the old West; food can be tied up with family relations or health; investment advice offers early retirements in tropical settings. The marketplace cannot directly offer the real thing, but it can offer visions of it connected with the purchase of products.

Advertising thus does not work by creating values and attitudes out of nothing but by drawing upon and rechanneling concerns that the target audience (and the culture) already shares. As one advertising executive put it: "Advertising doesn't always mirror how people are acting but how they're *dreaming*. In a sense what

we're doing is wrapping up your emotions and selling them back to you." Advertising absorbs and fuses a variety of symbolic practices and discourses, it appropriates and distills from an unbounded range of cultural references. In so doing, goods are knitted into the fabric of social life and cultural significance. As such, advertising is not simple manipulation, but what admaker Tony Schwartz calls "partipulation," with the audience participating in its own manipulation.

What are the consequences of such a system of images and goods? Given that the "real" sources of satisfaction cannot be provided by the purchase of commodities (merely the "image" of that source), it should not be surprising that happiness and contentment appear illusory in contemporary society. Recent social thinkers describe the contemporary scene as a "joyless economy,"[4] or as reflecting the "paradox of affluence."[5] It is not simply a matter of being "tricked" by the false blandishments of advertising. The problem is with the institutional structure of a market society that propels definition of satisfaction through the commodity/image system. The modern context, then, provides a curious satisfaction experience—one that William Leiss describes as "an ensemble of satisfactions and dissatisfactions" in which the consumption of commodities mediated by the image-system of advertising leads to consumer uncertainty and confusion.[6] The image-system of the marketplace reflects our desires and dreams, yet we have only the pleasure of the images to sustain us in our actual experience with goods.

The commodity image-system thus provides a particular vision of the world—a particular mode of self-validation that is integrally connected with what one *has* rather than what one *is*—a distinction often referred to as one between "having" and "being," with the latter now being defined through the former. As such, it constitutes a way of life that is defined and structured in quite specific political ways. Some commentators have even described advertising as part of a new *religious* system in which people construct their identities through the commodity form, and in which commodities are part of a supernatural magical world where anything is possible with the purchase of a product. The commodity as displayed in advertising plays a mixture of psychological, social, and physical roles in its relations with people. The object world interacts with the human world at the most basic and fundamental of levels, performing seemingly magical feats of enchantment and transformation, bringing instant happiness and gratification, capturing the forces of nature, and acting as a passport to hitherto untraveled domains and group relationships.[7]

In short, the advertising image-system constantly propels us toward things as means to satisfaction. In the sense that every ad says it is better to buy than not to buy, we can best regard advertising as a *propaganda* system for commodities. In the image-system as a whole, happiness lies at the end of a purchase. Moreover, this is not a minor propaganda system—it is all pervasive. It should not surprise us then to discover that the problem that it poses—how to get more things for everyone (as that is the root to happiness)—guides our political debates. The goal of *economic growth* (on which the commodity vision is based) is an unquestioned and sacred proposition of the political culture. As the environmental costs of the strategy of unbridled economic growth become more obvious, it is clear we must, as a society, engage in debate concerning the nature of future economic growth. However, as long as the commodity image-system maintains its ubiquitous presence and influence, the possibilities of opening such a debate are remote. At the very moment we most desperately need to pose new questions within the political culture, the commodity image-system propels us with even greater certainty and persuasion along a path that, unless checked, is destined to end in disaster. . . .

The visual image-system has colonized areas of life that were previously largely defined (although not solely) by auditory perception and experience. The 1980s [saw] a change in the way that popular music commodities (records, tapes, compact discs) were marketed, with music videos becoming an indispensable component of an overall strategy. These videos were produced as commercials for musical commodities by the advertising industry, using techniques learned from the marketing of products. Viewing these videos, there often seems to be little link between the song and the visuals. In the sense that they are commercials for records, there of course does not have to be. Video makers are in the same position as ad makers in terms of trying to get attention for their message and making it visually pleasurable. It is little wonder then that representations involving sexuality figure so prominently (as in the case of regular product advertising). The visuals are chosen for their ability to sell.

Many people report that listening to a song after watching the video strongly affects the interpretation they give to it—the visual images are replayed in the imagination. In that sense, the surrounding commodity image-system works to fix—or at least to limit—the scope of imaginative interpretation. The realm of listening becomes subordinated to the realm of seeing, to the influence of commercial images. There is also evidence suggesting that the composition of popular music is affected by the new video context. People write songs or lines with the vital marketing tool in mind.

Speed and Fragmentation

In addition to issues connected with the colonization of the commodity image-system of other areas of social life (gender socialization, politics, children's play, popular cultural forms), there are also important broader issues connected with its relation to modes of perception and forms of consciousness within contemporary society. For instance, the commodity information-system has two basic characteristics: reliance on visual modes of representation and the increasing speed and rapidity of the images that constitute it. It is this second point that I wish to focus on here. . . .

The visual images that dominate public space and public discourse are, in the video age, not static. They do not stand still for us to examine and linger over. They are here for a couple of seconds and then they are gone. Television advertising is the epitome of this speed-up. There is nothing mysterious in terms of how it arose. As commercial time slots declined from sixty seconds to thirty seconds (and recently to fifteen seconds and even shorter), advertisers responded by creating a new type of advertising—what is called the "vignette approach"—in which narrative and "reason-why" advertising are subsumed under a rapid succession of lifestyle images, meticulously timed with music, that directly sell feeling and emotion rather than products. As a commercial editor puts it of this new approach: "They're a wonderful way to pack in information: all those scenes and emotions—cut, cut, cut. Also they permit you a very freestyle approach—meaning that as long as you stay true to your basic vignette theme you can usually just drop one and shove in another. They're a dream to work with because the parts are sort of interchangeable."[8]

The speed-up is also a response by advertisers to two other factors: the increasing "clutter" of the commercial environment and the coming of age, in terms of disposable income, of a generation that grew up on television and commercials. The need for a commercial to stand out to a visually sophisticated audience drove the image-system to a greater frenzy of concentrated shorts. Again, sexuality became a key feature of the image-system within this.

The speed-up has two consequences. First, it has the effect of drawing the viewer into the message. One cannot watch these messages casually; they require undivided attention. Intensely pleasurable images, often sexual, are integrated into a flow of images. Watching has to be even more attentive to catch the brief shots of visual pleasure. The space "in between" the good parts can then be filled with other information, so that the commodity being advertised becomes a rich and complex sign.

Second, the speed-up has replaced narrative and rational response with images and emotional response. Speed and fragmentation are not particularly conducive to *thinking*. They induce *feeling*. The speed and fragmentation that characterize the commodity image-system may have a similar effect on the construction of consciousness. In one series of ads for MTV, a teenage boy or girl engages in a continuous monologue of events, characters, feelings, and emotions without any apparent connecting theme. As the video images mirror the fragmentation of thoughts, the ad ends with the plug: "Finally, a channel for the way you think." . . .

Notes

1. See Edward Epstein, *The Rise and Fall of Diamonds* (New York: Simon & Schuster, 1982).

2. This is discussed more fully in William Leiss, Stephen Kline, and Sut Jhally, *Social Communication in Advertising* (Toronto: Nelson, 1986).

3. See Fred Hirsch, *Social Limits to Growth* (Cambridge: Harvard University Press, 1976).

4. Tibor Scitovsky, *The Joyless Economy* (New York: Oxford University Press, 1976).

5. Hirsch, *Social Limits*.

6. William Leiss, *The Limits to Satisfaction* (Toronto: Toronto University Press, 1976).

7. See Sut Jhally, *The Codes of Advertising* (New York: St. Martin's Press, 1987) and John Kavanaugh, *Following Christ in a Consumer Society* (New York: Orbis, 1981).

8. Quoted in Michael Arlen, *Thirty Seconds* (New York: Penguin, 1981), 182.

27

The New Politics of Consumption

Why Americans Want So Much More Than They Need

Juliet Schor

In contemporary American culture, consuming is as authentic as it gets. Advertisements, getting a bargain, garage sales, and credit cards are firmly entrenched pillars of our way of life. We shop on our lunch hours, patronize outlet malls on vacation, and satisfy our latest desires with a late-night click of the mouse.[1]

Yet for all its popularity, the shopping mania provokes considerable disease: many Americans worry about our preoccupation with getting and spending. They fear we are losing touch with more worthwhile values and ways of living. But the discomfort rarely goes much further than that; it never coheres into a persuasive, well-articulated critique of consumerism. By contrast, in the 1960s and early 1970s, a far-reaching critique of consumer culture was a part of our political discourse. Elements of the New Left, influenced by the Frankfurt school, as well as by John Kenneth Galbraith and others, put forward a scathing indictment. They argued that Americans had been manipulated into participating in a dumbed-down, artificial consumer culture, which yielded few true human satisfactions.

For reasons that are not hard to imagine, this particular approach was short-lived, even among critics of American society and culture. It seemed too patronizing to talk about manipulation or the "true needs" of average Americans. In its stead, critics adopted a more liberal point of view and deferred to individuals on consumer issues. Social critics again emphasized the distribution of resources, with the more economistic goal of maximizing the incomes of working people. The good life, they suggested, could be achieved by attaining a comfortable, middle-class standard of living. This outlook was particularly prevalent in economics, where even radical economists have long believed that income is the key to well-being. While radical political economy, as it came to be called, retained a powerful critique of alienation in production and the distribution of property, it abandoned the

Reprinted by permission of Juliet Schor.

nascent intellectual project of analyzing the consumer sphere. Few economists now think about how we consume, and whether it reproduces class inequality, alienation, or power. "Stuff" is the part of the equation that the system is thought to have gotten nearly right.

Of course, many Americans retained a critical stance toward our consumer culture. They embody that stance in their daily lives—in the ways they live and raise their kids. But the rejection of consumerism, if you will, has taken place principally at an individual level. It is not associated with a widely accepted intellectual analysis, and an associated *critical politics of consumption*.

But such a politics has become an urgent need. The average American now finds it harder to achieve a satisfying standard of living than 25 years ago. Work requires longer hours, jobs are less secure, and pressures to spend more intense. Consumption-induced environmental damage remains pervasive, and we are in the midst of widespread failures of public provision. . . . Many Americans have long-term worries about their ability to meet basic needs, ensure a decent standard of living for their children, and keep up with an ever-escalating consumption norm.

In response to these developments, social critics continue to focus on income. In his impressive analysis of the problems of contemporary American capitalism, *Fat and Mean*, economist David Gordon emphasized income *adequacy*. The "vast majority of U.S. households," he argues, "can barely make ends meet. . . . Meager livelihoods are a *typical* condition, an *average* circumstance." Meanwhile, the Economic Policy Institute focuses on the distribution of income and wealth, arguing that the gains of the top 20 percent have jeopardized the well-being of the bottom 80 percent. Incomes have stagnated and the robust 3 percent growth rates of the 1950s and 1960s are long gone. If we have a consumption problem, this view implicitly states, we can solve it by getting more

income into more people's hands. The goals are redistribution and growth.

It is difficult to take exception to this view. It combines a deep respect for individual choice (the liberal part) with a commitment to justice and equality (the egalitarian part). I held it myself for many years. But I now believe that by failing to look deeper—to examine the very nature of consumption—it has become too limiting. In short, I do not think that the "income solution" addresses some of the most profound failures of the current consumption regime.

Why not? First, consuming is part of the problem. Income (the solution) leads to consumption practices that exacerbate and reproduce class and social inequalities, resulting in—and perhaps even worsening—an unequal distribution of income. Second, the system is structured such that an *adequate* income is an elusive goal. That is because adequacy is relative and defined by reference to the incomes of others. Without an analysis of consumer desire and need, and a different framework for understanding what is adequate, we are likely to find ourselves, twenty years from now, arguing that a median income of $100,000—rather than half that—is adequate. These arguments underscore the social context of consumption: the ways in which our sense of social standing and belonging comes from what we consume. If true, they suggest that attempts to achieve equality, or adequacy of individual incomes, without changing consumption patterns will be self-defeating.

Finally, it is difficult to make an ethical argument that people in the world's richest country need more, when the global income gap is so wide, the disparity in world resource use so enormous, and the possibility that we are already consuming beyond the Earth's ecological carrying capacity so likely. This third critique will get less attention in this essay—because it is more familiar, not because it is less important—but I will return to it in the conclusion.

I agree that justice requires a vastly more equal society, in terms of income and wealth. The question is whether we should also aim for a society in which our relationship to consuming changes, a society in which we consume *differently*. I argue here for such a perspective: for a critique of consumer culture and practices. Somebody needs to be for quality of life, not just quantity of stuff. And to do so requires an approach that does not trivialize consumption, but accords it the respect and centrality it deserves.

The New Consumerism

A new politics of consumption should begin with daily life, and recent developments in the sphere of consumption. I describe these developments as "the new consumerism," by which I mean an upscaling of lifestyle norms; the pervasiveness of conspicuous, status goods and of competition for acquiring them; and the growing disconnect between consumer desires and incomes.

Social comparison and its dynamic manifestation—the need to "keep up"—have long been part of American culture. My term is "competitive consumption," the idea that spending is in large part driven by a comparative or competitive process in which individuals try to keep up with the norms of the social group with which they identify—a "reference group." Although the term is new, the idea is not.

Thorstein Veblen, James Duesenberry, Fred Hirsch, and Robert Frank have all written about the importance of relative position as a dominant spending motive. What's new is the redefinition of reference groups: today's comparisons are less likely to take place between or among households of similar means. Instead, the lifestyles of the upper middle class and the rich have become a more salient point of reference for people throughout the income distribution. Luxury, rather than mere comfort, is a widespread aspiration.

One reason for this shift to "upscale emulation" is the decline of the neighborhood as a focus of comparison. Economically speaking, neighborhoods are relatively homogeneous groupings. In the 1950s and 1960s, when Americans were keeping up with the Joneses down the street, they typically compared themselves to other households of similar incomes. Because of this focus on neighbors, the gap between aspirations and means tended to be moderate.

But as married women entered the work-force in larger numbers—particularly in white-collar jobs—they were exposed to a more economically diverse group of people, and became more likely to gaze upward. Neighborhood contacts correspondingly declined, and the workplace became a more prominent point of reference. Moreover, as people spent less time with neighbors and friends, and more time on the family-room couch, television became more important as a source of consumer cues and information. Because television shows are so heavily skewed to the "lifestyles of the rich and upper middle class," they inflate the viewer's perceptions of what others have, and by extension what is worth acquiring—what one must have in order to avoid being "out of it."

Trends in inequality also helped to create the new consumerism. Since the 1970s, the distribution of income and wealth has shifted decisively in the direction of the top 20 percent. The share of after-tax family income going to the top 20 percent rose from 41.4 percent in 1979 to 46.8 percent in 1996. The share of wealth controlled by the top 20 percent rose from 81.3 percent in 1983 to 84.3 percent in 1997. This windfall resulted in a surge in conspicuous spending at the top. Remember the 1980s—the decade of greed and excess? Beginning with the super-rich, whose gains have been disproportionately higher, and trickling down to the merely affluent, visible status spending was the order of the day. Slowed down temporarily by the recession during

the early 1990s, conspicuous luxury consumption intensified during the recent
boom. Trophy homes, diamonds of a carat
or more, granite countertops, and sport
utility vehicles became the primary consumer symbols of the late 1990s. Television,
as well as films, magazines, and newspapers, ensure that the remaining 80 percent
of the nation is aware of the status purchasing that has swept the upper echelons.

In the meantime, upscale emulation had
become well established. Researchers
Susan Fournier and Michael Guiry found
that 35 percent of their sample aspired to
reach the top 6 percent of the income distribution, and another 49 percent aspired
to the next 12 percent. Only 15 percent
reported that they would be satisfied with
"living a comfortable life"—that is, being
middle class. But 85 percent of the population cannot earn the six-figure incomes
necessary to support upper-middle-class
lifestyles. The result is a growing aspirational gap, and with desires persistently
outrunning incomes, many consumers find
themselves frustrated. One survey of U.S.
households found that the level of income
needed to fulfill one's dreams doubled
between 1986 and 1994, and by 1999 it
was more than twice the median household income.

. . . The new consumerism, with its
growing aspirational gap, has begun to
jeopardize the quality of American life.
Within the middle class—and even the
upper middle class—many families experience an almost threatening pressure to
keep up, both for themselves and their
children. They are deeply concerned about
the rigors of the global economy, and the
need to have their children attend "good"
schools. This means living in a community
with relatively high housing costs. For
some households this also means providing
their children with advantages purchased
on the private market (computers, lessons,
extra-curriculars, private schooling).
Keeping two adults in the labor market—
as so many families do, to earn the incomes
to stay middle class—is expensive, not
only because of the second car, child-care

costs, and career wardrobe. It also creates
the need for time-saving—but costly—
commodities and services, such as take-out
food and dry cleaning, as well as stress-
relieving experiences. Finally, the financial
tightrope that so many households walk—
high expenses, low savings—is a constant
source of stress and worry. While precise
estimates are difficult to come by, one can
argue that somewhere between a quarter
and half of all households live paycheck-
to-paycheck.

These problems are magnified for low-
income households. Their sources of
income have become increasingly erratic
and inadequate, on account of employment instability, the proliferation of part-
time jobs, and restrictions on welfare
payments. Yet most low-income households remain firmly integrated within
consumerism. They are targets for credit
card companies, who find them an easy
mark. They watch more television, and
are more exposed to its desire-creating
properties. Low-income children are
more likely to be exposed to commercials
at school, as well as at home. The growing prominence of the values of the market, materialism, and economic success
make financial failure more consequential and painful.

These are the effects at the household
level. The new consumerism has also set in
motion another dynamic: it siphons off
resources that could be used for alternatives to private consumption. We use our
income in four basic ways: private consumption, public consumption, private
savings, and leisure. When consumption
standards can be met easily out of current
income, there is greater willingness to support public goods, save privately, and cut
back on time spent at work (in other
words, to "buy leisure"). Conversely,
when lifestyle norms are upscaled more
rapidly than income, private consumption
"crowds out" alternative uses of income.
That is arguably what happened in the
1980s and 1990s: resources shifting into
private consumption, and away from free
time, the public sector, and saving. Hours

of work have risen dramatically; saving rates have plummeted; and public funds for education, recreation, and the arts have fallen in the wake of a grassroots tax revolt. The timing suggests a strong coincidence between these developments and the intensification of competitive consumption. . . . Indeed, this scenario makes good sense of an otherwise surprising finding: that indicators of "social health" or "genuine progress" (i.e., basic quality-of-life measures) began to diverge from Gross Domestic Product in the mid-1970s, after moving in tandem for decades. Can it be that consuming and prospering are no longer compatible states? . . .

Americans did not suddenly become greedy. The aspirational gap has been created by structural changes—such as the decline of community and social connection, the intensification of inequality, the growing role of mass media, and heightened penalties for failing in the labor market. Upscaling is mainly defensive, and has both psychological and practical dimensions.

Similarly, the profoundly social nature of consumption ensures that these issues cannot be resolved by pure acts of will. Our notions of what is adequate, necessary, or luxurious are shaped by the larger social context. Most of us are deeply tied in to our particular class and other group identities, and our spending patterns help reproduce them.

Thus, a collective, not just an individual, response is necessary. Someone needs to address the larger question of the consumer culture itself. But doing so risks complaints about being intrusive, patronizing, or elitist. . . .

Consumer Knows Best

The recent consumer boom rested on growth in incomes, wealth, and credit. But it also rested on something more intangible: social attitudes toward consumer decision making and choices. Ours is an ideology of noninterference—the view that one should

be able to buy what one likes, where one likes, and as much as one likes, with nary a glance from the government, neighbors, ministers, or political parties. Consumption is perhaps the clearest example of an individual behavior that our society takes to be almost wholly personal, completely outside the purview of social concern and policy. The consumer is king. And queen.

This view has much to recommend it. After all, who would relish the idea of sumptuary legislation, rationing, or government controls on what can be produced or purchased? The liberal approach to consumption combines a deep respect for the consumer's ability to act in her own best interest and an emphasis on the efficiency gains of unregulated consumer markets: a commitment to liberty and the general welfare.

Cogent as it is, however, this view is vulnerable on a number of grounds. Structural biases and market failures in the operation of consumer markets undermine its general validity; consumer markets are neither so free nor so efficient as the conventional story suggests. The basis of a new consumer policy should be an understanding of the presence of structural distortions in consumers' choices, the importance of social inequalities and power in consumption practices, a more sophisticated understanding of consumer motivations, and serious analysis of the processes that form our preferences. . . .

A Politics of Consumption

. . . But what should a politics of consumption look like? To start the discussion—not to provide final answers—I suggest seven basic elements:

1. *A right to a decent standard of living.* This familiar idea is especially important now because it points us to a fundamental distinction between what people need and what they want. In the not very distant past, this dichotomy was not only well

understood, but the basis of data collection and social policy. Need was a social concept with real force. All that's left now is an economy of desire. This is reflected in polling data. Just over 40 percent of adults earning $50,000 to $100,000 a year, and 27 percent of those earning more than $100,000, agree that "I cannot afford to buy everything I really need." One third and 19 percent, respectively, agree that "I spend nearly all of my money on the basic necessities of life." I believe that our politics would profit from reviving a discourse of need, in which we talk about the material requirements for every person and household to participate fully in society. Of course, there are many ways in which such a right might be enforced: government income transfers or vouchers, direct provision of basic needs, employment guarantees, and the like. For reasons of space, I leave that discussion aside; the main point is to revive the distinction between needs and desires.

2. *Quality of life rather than quantity of stuff.* Twenty-five years ago quality-of-life indicators began moving in an opposite direction from our measures of income, or gross domestic product, a striking divergence from historic trends. Moreover, the accumulating evidence on well-being, at least its subjective measures (and to some extent objective measures, such as health), suggests that above the poverty line, income is relatively unimportant in affecting well-being. This may be because what people care about is relative, not absolute income. Or it may be because increases in output undermine precisely those factors that do yield welfare. Here I have in mind the growing worktime requirements of the market economy, and the concomitant decline in family, leisure, and community time; the adverse impacts of growth on the natural environment; and the potential link between growth and social capital.

This argument that consumption is not the same as well-being has great potential to resonate with millions of Americans. Large majorities hold ambivalent views about consumerism. They struggle with ongoing conflicts between materialism and an alternative set of values stressing family, religion, community, social commitment, equity, and personal meaning. We should be articulating an alternative vision of a quality of life, rather than a quantity of stuff. That is a basis on which to argue for a restructuring of the labor market to allow people to choose for time, or to penalize companies that require excessive hours for employees. It is also a basis for creating alternative indicators to the GNP, positive policies to encourage civic engagement, support for parents, and so forth.

3. *Ecologically sustainable consumption.* Current consumption patterns are wreaking havoc on the planetary ecology. Global warming is perhaps the best known, but many other consumption habits have major environmental impacts. Sport utility vehicles, air conditioning, and foreign travel are all energy-intensive and contribute to global warming. Larger homes use more energy and building resources, destroy open space, and increase the use of toxic chemicals. All those granite countertops being installed in American kitchens were carved out of mountains around the world, leaving in their wake a blighted landscape. Our daily newspaper and coffee are contributing to deforestation and loss of species diversity. Something as simple as a T-shirt plays its part, since cotton cultivation accounts for a significant fraction of world pesticide use. Consumers know far less about the environmental impacts of their daily consumption habits than they should. And while the solution lies in greater part with corporate and governmental practices, people who are concerned about equality should be joining forces with environmentalists who are trying to educate, mobilize, and change practices at the neighborhood and household levels.

4. *Democratize consumption practices.* One of the central arguments I have made is that consumption practices reflect and perpetuate structures of inequality and power. This is particularly true in the "new consumerism," with its emphasis on luxury,

expensiveness, exclusivity, rarity, uniqueness, and distinction. These are the values that consumer markets are plying, to the middle and lower middle class. (That is what Martha Stewart did at Kmart.)

But who needs to accept these values? Why not stand for consumption that is democratic, egalitarian, and available to all? How about making "access," rather than exclusivity, cool, by exposing the industries such as fashion, home decor, or tourism, which are pushing the upscaling of desire? This point speaks to the need for both cultural change and policies that might facilitate it. Why not tax high-end "status" versions of products while allowing the low-end models to be sold tax-free?

5. *A politics of retailing and the "cultural environment."* The new consumerism has been associated with the homogenization of retail environments and a pervasive shift toward the commercialization of culture. The same mega-stores can be found everywhere, creating a blandness in the cultural environment. Advertising and marketing are also pervading hitherto relatively protected spaces, such as schools, doctors' offices, media programming (rather than commercial time), and so on. In my local mall, the main restaurant offers a book-like menu comprising advertisements for unrelated products. The daily paper looks more like a consumer's guide to food, wine, computer electronics, and tourism and less like a purveyor of news. We should be talking about these issues, and the ways in which corporations are remaking our public institutions and space. Do we value diversity in retailing? Do we want to preserve small retail outlets? How about ad-free zones? Commercial-free public education? Here too public policy can play a role by outlawing certain advertising in certain places and institutions, by financing publicly controlled media, and enacting zoning regulations that take diversity as a positive value.

6. *Expose commodity "fetishism."* Everything we consume has been produced. So a new politics of consumption must take into account the labor, environmental, and other conditions under which products are made, and argue for high standards. This argument has been of great political importance in recent years, with public exposure of the so-called global sweatshop in the apparel, footwear, and fashion industries. Companies fear their public images, and consumers appear willing to pay a little more for products when they know they have been produced responsibly. There are fruitful and essential linkages between production, consumption, and the environment that we should be making.

7. *A consumer movement and governmental policy.* Much of what I have been arguing for could occur as a result of a consumer's movement. Indeed, the revitalization of the labor movement calls out for an analogous revitalization of long dormant consumers. We need independent organizations of consumers to pressure companies, influence the political agenda, provide objective product information, and articulate a vision of an appealing and humane consumer sphere. We also need a consumer movement to pressure the state to enact the kinds of policies that the foregoing analysis suggests are needed. These include taxes on luxury and status consumption, green taxes and subsidies, new policies toward advertising, more sophisticated regulations on consumer credit, international labor and environmental standards, revamping of zoning regulations to favor retail diversity, and the preservation of open space. There is a vast consumer policy agenda that has been mainly off the table. It's time to put it back on.

Note

1. Sources for much of the data cited in this [chapter] can be found in the notes to *The Overspent American: Why We Want What We Don't Need* (Harper Perennial, 1999) or by contacting the author.

28

Inventing the Cosmo Girl

Class Identity and Girl-Style American Dreams

Laurie Ouellette

I am a materialist, and it is a materialistic world.

—Helen Gurley Brown[1]

In February 1997, a former secretary named Helen Gurley Brown stepped down from her position as the editor-in-chief of *Cosmopolitan,* the hugely successful consumer magazine she developed for the "single girl" market in the mid-1960s. Still an American cultural icon, Brown was suddenly back in the media spotlight, espousing her credo on topics ranging from sex and the workplace to the Cosmo Girl, the fictionalized woman she invented to characterize the magazine's imagined 18- to 34-year-old female reader. Just as feminist historians have recognized Brown's role in partly subverting patriarchal sexual ideologies (Douglas, 1994; Ehrenreich et al., 1986), media commentators framed the departure by casting Brown as the feminine piper of the sexual revolution.[2] What cannot be explained by a singular focus on sexual politics, however, are the class-specific dimensions of Brown's message and popular appeal.

This chapter analyzes Helen Gurley Brown's early advice to women as a cultural discourse that managed some of the social and economic tensions of the 1960s and early 1970s, while also offering certain women the symbolic material to enable them to think about themselves as historical subjects in new ways. John Fiske's understanding of discourse is especially helpful for making sense of Brown's position as a capitalist media maven and an immensely popular spokeswoman for everygirl. As Fiske argues, discourse is a "system of representation that has developed socially in order to make and circulate

From Laurie Ouellette, "Inventing the Cosmo Girl." *Media, Culture and Society* (1999), 21, 359–383. Reprinted with permission of SAGE Publications.

a coherent set of meanings about an important topic area" (1987: 14). Discourses are ideological insofar as their "meanings serve the interests of that section of society within which the discourse originates and which works ideologically to naturalize those meanings into common sense," but they are not conspiratorial or "produced" by individual authors or speakers (1987: 14). Rather, discourses are socially produced and often institutionalized ways of making sense of a certain topic that "preexist their use in any one discursive practice," and that construct "a sense, or social identity, of us" as we speak them (Fiske, 1987: 14–15).

. . . I wish to show how Brown's advice spoke to major changes in women's economic and sexual roles, while also constructing a suggested social identity for her "working girl" readers. . . . The cultural discourse Brown articulated legitimated sexism and the capitalist exploitation of women's labor, while simultaneously expressing hardships and desires in a voice that spoke with credibility to an expanding class of pink-collar women.

Based on my examination of *Cosmopolitan* magazine (1965–75) as well as Brown's books, recordings and interviews during this period, I am suggesting that she articulated a girl-style American Dream that promised transcendence from class roles as well as sexual ones. Brown was one of the first mainstream figures to free women from the guilt of premarital sex by advising them to disregard the patriarchal double standard. But she was also concerned with shaping and transforming the class position of the Cosmo Girl through a combination of self-management strategies, performative tactics, sexuality, and upwardly mobile romance.[3] At a time when the term often seems in danger of slipping from the critical vocabulary, Brown's advice to women offers a case study in the cultural construction of class—not as an economic category or even a relationship in the Marxist sense, but as a fragmented and sexualized identity. As Brown explained,

> There are girls who . . . don't want to be that driven, to have that many affairs; they don't want more than one man or one dress at a time. They don't care about jewelry and they don't want a sable coat or Paris for the weekend. . . . But "my girl" wants it. She is on the make. Her nose is pressed to the glass and she does get my message. These girls are like my children all over the country. Oh, I have so much advice for them. . . . (Quoted in *Guardian Weekly*, 1968)

Inventing the Cosmo Girl

In 1962, at the age of 42, Brown wrote the bestseller *Sex and the Single Girl* (1962) and became an overnight celebrity. According to Brown, the book was an unabashed self-help credo for "the girl who doesn't have anything going for her . . . who's not pretty, who maybe didn't go to college and who may not even have a decent family background" (quoted in Didion, 1965: 35). Drawing partly from Brown's experience as a woman who held 18 secretarial jobs before she was promoted to an advertising copywriter and then married at the age of 37, the book offered step-by-step advice on personal appearance, budget apartment dwelling, working, and, above all, flirting. Brown guided women through encounters with men who were not their husbands, instructing them how to attract the best ones, date them, cajole dinners and presents out of them, have affairs, and eventually marry the most eligible man available. In a year when "married people on television slept in twin beds" (Douglas, 1994: 68) and the sexual revolution remained the prerogative of men and student counterculture types, *Sex and the Single Girl* suggested that ordinary women could lead fully sexual lives outside marriage (Brown, 1962: 11).

Brown critiqued mandatory motherhood, advised birth control, condoned divorce, encouraged women to work outside the home, and recommended sexual and financial independence within boundaries. However, the book was by no means anti-marriage: As Brown explained, it was a response to the "man shortage," a guide to attracting desirable men while remaining "single in superlative style" ("A Proposal for Cosmopolitan," n.d.).

Sex and the Single Girl was mocked by intellectuals, reviewed, as one journalist observed, "only to provide a fixed target for reviewers eager to point up (amid considerable merriment) the superiority of their own perceptions over those of Mrs. Brown" (Didion, 1965: 36). But the book appealed to hundreds of thousands of women who were living out a growing gap between "girlhood and marriage" made possible by shifting urban migration patterns and the expanding pink-collar labor force (Ehrenreich et al., 1986: 54). *Single Girl* sold more than two million copies in three weeks, due to extensive publicity and Brown's rigorous efforts to get in touch with the kind of women critics derided as "subliterate and culturally deprived" (Didion, 1965: 36). Following the book's initial success, Brown was interviewed extensively in the press, appeared as a frequent guest on radio and television talk shows, and sold the motion-picture rights to *Single Girl* to Hollywood. She wrote a series of follow-up books, including *Sex and the Office* (1964) and *Sex and the New Single Girl* (1970a), recorded best-selling lectures with names like *Lessons in Love* (1963), and wrote a syndicated newspaper column called "Woman Alone." While early feminist leaders like Betty Friedan found Brown's message "obscene and horrible," few could deny that she had developed an "astonishing rapport with America's single-girldom" (quoted in Welles, 1965: 65).

In 1965, Brown took her credo and her phenomenal sales figures to Hearst Publications, owners of *Cosmopolitan* magazine, and became the magazine's new editor-in-chief. With close monitoring by Hearst, she transformed *Cosmopolitan* from a fledgling intellectual publication into a "compendium of everything I know about how to get through the emotional, social and business shoals that confront a girl, and have a better life" (Brown, 1970a: 7). Brown maintained such strict control over the magazine that critics began to ridicule the singular, gushy voice that permeated article after article, but the editorial formula she devised drew new readers (Brown, 1965). Circulation rose by more than 100,000 the first year alone, advertising sales grew 43 percent (*Newsweek*, 1966: 60), and a series of self-help books distributed through the *Cosmopolitan* Book-of-the-Month Club were equally successful. By the mid-1970s, *Cosmopolitan* was reaching more than two million readers, advertising sales were still soaring, 12 foreign-language editions had been launched, and Brown was a celebrity who claimed to embody much of the advice she distributed through her media enterprise.[4] Due to Brown's characterizations and the "I'm that Cosmopolitan Girl" advertising campaign, which she helped write, the fictionalized Cosmo Girl had entered the cultural lexicon as a sexualized symbol of pink-collar femininity. Before elaborating on her construction, it is useful to sketch out the historical context during which she arose.

As the economist Julie Matthaei has shown, the growth of the service sector has been "central in the absorption of female labor" (1982: 282). In the 1960s, as the U.S.A. moved rapidly toward a post-Fordist economy, women entered the paid workforce in greater numbers, and began to stay there for longer periods of time, earning approximately 59 cents on the male dollar (Howe, 1977: 3). According to the U.S. Department of Labor, between 1962 and 1974, the number of employed women rose by 10 million, or 45 percent. Some women entered the male-dominated professions, but the majority entered "feminine" pink-collar jobs, and the largest gain occurred in secretarial and clerical occupations that often required no college education (Howe, 1977: 10–11). Women were already the mainstay of these occupational fields, but the capitalist expansion of the service sector was a new development, as was the growing number of women working for prolonged periods of time to support themselves (and families) in these positions.[5] *Sex and the Single Girl* spoke directly to unmarried working women, and *Cosmopolitan* was the first consumer magazine to target single "girls with jobs" with feature articles, advice columns, budget fashions and advertisements for mainly "feminine" consumer items, such as cosmetics, personal care products, lingerie, and clothing.[6] The magazine also featured advertisements for temporary employment agencies, training centers and correspondence schools where women could learn stenography, typing, and dictation and similar clerical skills. Hearst's interest in hiring Brown to address self-sufficient working women was thus linked to their emergence as a consumer market capable of purchasing certain goods and services with their own wages.[7]

Cosmopolitan's pink-collar orientation and economic base is especially clear when compared to that of its nearest competitor, *Ms.* magazine. Critics have observed that when *Ms.* debuted in 1972 as a voice of the women's movement, it tended to emphasize the goals and aspirations of liberal feminism and college-educated women. Editorial material aimed at pink-collar women was less typical, and the female consumer hailed by "dress-for-success" fashions and durable consumer goods differed from the one hailed by *Cosmopolitan* (McCracken, 1993: 278–80; Valverde, 1986: 81). Both magazines claimed to serve independent working women, but market research found *Ms.* readers had higher incomes and were more than twice as likely to have attended college. More than a third of *Ms.* readers (as opposed to virtually no *Cosmopolitan* readers) also held advanced degrees

(Harrington, 1974). Critics, however, downplayed the social and economic basis of the skew and blamed Brown for the "Two Faces of the Same Eve," explaining that intelligent women with graduate degrees were not apt to be called "little Cosmo Girl" or buy a magazine whose editor insists that ideas be made "baby simple" (Harrington, 1974: 12). With considerable scorn, Brown was characterized as the "working girl's Simone de Beauvoir" of her era (*Newsweek,* 1966: 60).

In the U.S.A., women's mass entry into the workforce is often attributed to the second wave of the women's movement. However, when we consider the stratification within the female labor force, Barbara Ehrenreich's thesis that "male revolt" from the traditional breadwinning role was an earlier and more significant catalyst seems highly plausible. Breadwinning, according to Ehrenreich, was an informal economic contract rooted in the family wage system, and as such it was dependent upon the voluntary cooperation of men:

> Men are favored in the labor market, both by the kinds of occupations open to them and by informal discrimination within occupations, so that they earn, on the average, 40 percent more than women do. Yet nothing compels them to spread the wealth to those—women and children—who are excluded from work or less generously rewarded for it. Men cannot be forced to marry; once married, they cannot be forced to bring home their paychecks, to be reliable job holders, or, of course, to remain married. In fact, considering the absence of legal coercion, the surprising thing is that men have for so long, and, on the whole, so reliably, adhered to what might be called the "breadwinner" ethic. (1983: 11)

Once held together by popular culture, expert opinion and religious expectations, the breadwinning ethic began to unravel around the time the Beats, with their flagrant celebration of male freedom, appeared on the scene, says Ehrenreich (1983: 12; 52). When *Playboy* magazine debuted in 1953, she argues, "male revolt" was expressed in a broader context. While *Playboy* is often associated with the mainstreaming of soft-core pornography, it also promoted a "Dale Carnegie–style credo of male success" rooted in free enterprise, a strong work ethic and materialistic consumption. The only difference between conventional success mythology and Hugh Hefner's message was that men were not encouraged to share their money, says Ehrenreich. Wives and single women were depicted as shrews and "gold-diggers," while bachelors were advised to pursue sex on a casual basis to avoid getting snared in a "long term contract" (1983: 46). By the 1970s, alimony reductions and no-fault divorce laws—however progressive in the feminist sense—had legitimated male revolt at the official level of the state. For the first time in U.S. history, observed sociologist Jane Mansbridge, "society was beginning to condone a man leaving his family on the sole grounds that living with them and providing for them made him unhappy" (1986: 108).

Brown's advice spoke to the social and economic flux generated by these shifts by offering a modified sexual contract, and by presenting certain women, who may no longer have recognized their place in male-oriented American Dream mythology, with the discursive material to envision themselves as upwardly mobile sexual agents. Brown was clear in her wish for women to see themselves in the fictionalized persona of the Cosmo Girl. "A guy reading *Playboy* can say, 'Hey, That's me.' I want my girl to be able to say the same thing," she explained (quoted in *Providence Journal*, 1965). While her advice was often antagonistic, the social structure that was the cause of the dilemma was never challenged. . . .

The Beautiful Phony

. . . Brown's credo required an understanding of identity as something that could always be reworked, improved upon, and even dramatically changed. *Sex and the Single Girl* promised every girl the chance to acquire a stylish and attractive aura by copying fashion models and wealthy women (Brown, 1962: 189–94). Expenditures on clothing, cosmetics, and accessories were presented as necessary investments in the construction of a desirable (and thus saleable) self. *Cosmopolitan* columns with names like "So You're Bored to Death with the Same Old You" (1972) extended these possibilities by offering women the ability to construct a "whole new identity," defined in terms of fashion and style. According to the column, "A new lipstick will really not work a sudden transformation, but have you considered going further? Perhaps even to the point of changing everything (hair, makeup, clothes, manner), in short, changing your type?" (*Cosmopolitan*, 1972: 172). Other articles with names like "Yes, You Can Change Your Image" (De Santis, 1969) stressed the fluidity of female subjectivity, encouraging readers to make themselves over and even construct multiple selves, often to meet the demands and opportunities of prolonged courtship.

To "get into the position to sink a man" it was not necessary that a woman be beautiful, but she had to know how to create "an illusion of beauty" (Brown, 1962: 204). Phoniness was often celebrated as a form of trickery—a way to create a prettier, sexier, and more desirable self beyond one's allotted means. Even the *Cosmopolitan* cover girl was exposed as a "fake," her breasts made to appear more alluring with masking tape and Vaseline (Kent, 1972; Reisig, 1973). According to another column called the "The Beautiful Phony" (*Cosmopolitan*, 1966a), "naturalness" was an imposed value that destroyed the possibility of such illusions. Taking sides with the imagined reader, it opened with the advice:

They're always telling you to be the most natural girl in the world and you want to cooperate but, well, they just ought to see you in your natural state. Pale, lash-less, lusterless, bustless and occasionally, after a grinding day at the typewriter, almost fingernail-less! Darling, not another apology! (1966a: 104)

Instead, "new looks" created with wigs, and false eyelashes, tinted contact lenses, fake beauty spots, false toenails, false fin-gernails, nose surgery, padded bras, false derrieres, and fake jewelry were recom-mended. Another article explaining "Why I Wear My False Eyelashes to Bed" (Cunningham, 1968) presented the prob-lem of a shower with a lover, a situation where the investments of a highly produced femininity (and hence its material rewards) might be erased. Recommending hurling soap suds in his eyes so "he won't be able to see how you look" (Cunningham, 1968: 18), it got to the core of Brown's advice by linking femininity to the modified sexual contract she espoused.

The aspirations of the Cosmo Girl were white, heterosexual, and upper-middle class. "Other" women were sometimes acknowledged in *Cosmopolitan* articles like "What It Means to Be a Negro Girl" (Guy, 1966), but they were not presented as models for emulation, primarily because Brown's mobility credo forbade it. White working-class culture appeared more often, but as a reference point for make-over and improvement. Similar to feminin-ity, class was presented as a malleable identity that could be easily changed through performative tactics, covert strate-gies, and cultural consumption.

Unlike her feminist contemporaries who believed in the possibilities of a female sex class (Firestone, 1970; Millett, 1970), Brown was especially concerned with improving the lot of women stuck lower on the economic ladder. While her most radical suggestion may have been to carry Karl Marx's *Das Kapital* as a way to meet potential eligibles (1962: 63), the Cosmo Girl was often addressed as a have-not, and was offered instructions to remedy

the situation. Instead of critiquing the capitalist distribution of resources or the politics of wage labor, reworking one's identity was presented as an individual route to mobility. The extent to which these narratives constructed a feminine version of American Dream mythology is revealed by Brown's own version of the Horatio Alger story:

We have two Mercedes-Benzes, one hun-dred acres of virgin forest near San Francisco, a Mediterranean house over-looking the Pacific, a full-time maid and a good life. I am not beautiful, or even pretty . . . I didn't go to college. My fam-ily was, and is, desperately poor and I have always helped support them. . . . But I don't think it's a miracle that I mar-ried my husband. I think I deserved him! For seventeen years I worked hard to become the kind of woman who might interest him. (Brown, 1962: 4–5)

Drawing from John Berger (1972), Ellen McCracken has shown how commercial women's magazines trade on female inse-curities by offering a temporary "window to a future self" rooted in male visions of idealized femininity and consumer solu-tions (1993: 13). Jackie Stacey discusses something similar in her analysis of women and film stars, but proposes that the per-petual gap between "self and ideal" is the subjective space where female identities are negotiated (1993: 206). In *Sex and the Single Girl,* Brown extended these pro-cesses by constructing an idealized, but never fully realized, class subjectivity for her readers, which then manifested in the fragmented identity of the fictionalized Cosmo Girl. Although rooted in upper-class reverence and materialistic desires, her advice is difficult to dismiss as entirely co-optive or advertising-driven, because it was presented as a guide to overcoming the gendered class barriers Brown encoun-tered. Her path to success stressed the conventional motto of hard work and con-spicuous consumption, but it also required covert strategies and performative behaviors on the part of the Cosmo Girl. As I see it, the tenuous sense of agency Brown's advice offered is central to the tension between class fluidity and class consciousness in the politicized sense.

Women were essentially advised to "pass" as members of the bourgeoisie, by studying and copying its presumably superior tastes, knowledges, and cultural competencies. This performative strategy was rooted in the unauthorized acquisition of what Pierre Bourdieu (1984) calls "cultural capital," or the symbolic resources that signify and legitimate class dominance in capitalist democracies. In the U.S.A., the myth of equality of opportunity proposes that anyone can gain access to economic capital (what wealth buys) through individual effort and talent, while the cultural capital that breeds success is inherited via "proper" family socialization or acquired through extended years of schooling (Jhally and Lewis, 1992: 69). Brown subverted these intersecting mythologies in a roundabout way by revealing pink-collar barriers to the American Dream, and by partly subverting the uneven distribution of cultural capital. According to Brown's girl-style American Dream, anyone—even the Cosmo Girl—could appropriate the surface markers of cultural capital. Once acquired, these surface markers of class position could be traded for economic capital (or access to it) on the dating and marriage market.

The credibility of this advice was rooted in the fact that women who may have married directly into the lower classes were spending longer periods of time working as office workers. Under the ambiguous label "pink collar," they encountered men with more education, money, and resources. Brown's advice encouraged women to exploit these opportunities, and prepared them to do so by offering a basic introduction to upper-class customs and cultural traditions. "Some girls have it . . . some don't. But that elusive little quality separating the haves from the [have-]

nots is within everyone's grasp," claimed one *Cosmopolitan* article (Geng, 1970: 92).

Since the advice was always tempered to the experience of the Cosmo Girl, the reader was allowed to participate in two class cultures simultaneously, which encouraged a fragmented class subjectivity. However, the point of the lessons was to conceal one's working-class lineage. Thus, *The Cosmo Girl's Guide to the New Etiquette* warned women about common phrases that were "instant lower-class betrayals" (Brown, 1970b: 55). Similarly, *Cosmopolitan* articles with names like "Poor Girl Paintings" (*Cosmopolitan*, 1966c), "If You Don't Know Your Crepes From Your Coquilles" (Matlin, 1969), "Go Ahead, Pretend You're Rich" (Barnes and Downey, 1968), "Good Taste" (Johnson, 1974), and "Live Beyond Your Means" (de Dubovay, 1975) presented lessons on the ways of the educated, wealthy, and culturally sophisticated.

This advice often involved appropriating cultural signifiers of class, particularly European cuisine, art, foreign languages, and good books. One especially vivid example here was "A Handbook of Elegant Starvation," a *Cosmopolitan* guide to maintaining a "desirable image" while pursuing the arts and getting by on unemployment insurance (Dowling, 1966). According to the article, which offered detailed instructions for serving "Bogus Beef Bourguignon" to a male dinner guest, "The clue to faking it on $12.50 a week is a front. You've got to keep up a front—an aura of prosperity—at all times" (1966: 30). Another article proposed that an ordinary secretary, who "would probably expire from malnutrition if she didn't have a dinner date at least two nights a week," could easily pass as a member of the New York "jet set" or a corporation president's daughter (Tornabene, 1966: 43). By extending the aura of cultural capital to the female masses, this discourse subverted the myth that class is inevitable or natural. However, it also upheld the class pyramid and reproduced social and cultural hierarchies. . . .

Pink-Collar Sexuality

Feminist historians have suggested that what was potentially transforming about *Cosmopolitan* magazine was the emphasis placed on female sexuality (Douglas, 1994; Ehrenreich et al., 1986).[8] Features on female orgasm, birth control, masturbation, casual sex, and sexual experimentation appeared under Brown's editorship, while quizzes with names like "How Sexy Are You?" (*Cosmopolitan*, 1969) invited ordinary women into the sexual revolution, and *Cosmopolitan's Love Book* (Brown, 1972) offered them instructions on the new sexual protocol. At the close of the 1970s, Brown hired a sociologist to survey the sexual practices of *Cosmopolitan* readers, and they were found to be the most experienced group in western history (Wolfe, 1981). However, what a focus on sexual politics cannot fully explain are the class dimensions of Brown's discourse on female sexuality, as epitomized by her credo "Poor girls are not sexy!" (1962: 108).

. . . Sexual fantasies presented in *Cosmopolitan* fiction excerpts and in *Cosmopolitan's Love Book* encouraged women to identify with female heroines whose male sexual partners (or desired partners) were above them socially and economically. . . . Female desire was linked to what the male object represented socially and economically. As Brown explained in *Sex and the Single Girl,* a woman is "more favorably disposed toward a man who is solvent and successful than someone without status. She prefers a tycoon to a truck driver no matter how sexy the latter looks peering down at her from the cab of his chrome chariot" (1962: 227).

Cosmopolitan's "Bachelor of the Month" column was similarly constructed. This sought-after eligible was always solvent and socially established, as were the men presented as desirable in articles like "It's Just as Easy to Love a Rich Man" (Lilly, 1965), "How Much Will He Earn?"

(Sloane, 1966), "The Big Catch" (Blyth, 1972), and "Used Men: A Definitive Guide for the Selective Shopper" (Price, 1972). When acknowledged, working-class men were almost always presented as undesirable, as epitomized by the juxtaposition in February 1966 of two *Cosmopolitan* profiles, one featuring "Six Current (But Perennial) Fascinators" (1966d), the other featuring "10 Most Wanted Men (by the FBI)" (Reed, 1966). While the first roster was comprised of men characterized as rich, famous, successful, charming, and attractive, the second opened with the warning "You've seen the most fascinating men, now read about the most feared" (Reed, 1966: 72). Police mug shots were accompanied by one-liners detailing the physical characteristics of the men as well as their occupations, which included clerk, dishwasher, hospital orderly, tractor driver, and mason's helper.

While female sexual desire was linked to upward mobility through men, the construction of female sexual desirability in *Cosmopolitan* was linked to the cultural codes of the working-class prostitute. Indeed, sexually explicit representations of women were the only places readers were encouraged to forge positive identifications with working-class traditions. Bourgeois tastes were transgressed by these images, especially on the cover, where the desirability of the model was constructed through class-coded signifiers such as exposed cleavage, teased hair, heavy make-up, and flamboyant and suggestive costumes.[9] The sexualized Cosmo Girl was not the wholesome middle-class sex object of the era, and she appeared to contradict Brown's discreet schemes for mobility. However, the sexualized imagery also offered an entry point into the modified sexual contract Brown espoused.

In the 1960s, when college-educated women were beginning to demand and sometimes secure equality in the professional workplace, most pink-collar office workers were not so fortunate. Brown articulated an alternative way to get men to part with their disproportionate share of power and resources. She subverted the moral shame surrounding sex and reframed the sexual code as an individual ethic and a commodity exchange. In this sense, her advice was rooted in the history of working-class women's sexual practices.

Kathy Peiss, for example, has shown how a turn-of-the-century system of "treating" allowed young, unmarried workers to trade "sexual favors" ranging from flirting and kissing to sexual intercourse for small presents, meals, and admissions to amusement parks, which they could not otherwise afford (1983: 78). Some "charity girls" appropriated the look of a prostitute, using "high-heeled shoes, fancy dresses, costume jewelry, elaborate pompadours and cosmetics" to attract male attention (1983: 78). The system of treating was also present in the workplace, says Peiss, where sexual harassment was rampant (1983: 78–9). Brown's advice articulated an updated sexual barter system, by encouraging the Cosmo Girl to never go dutch, but to instead coax gifts, dinners, vacations, groceries, and cash presents from male dates, bosses, colleagues, and partners. Her revised sexual contract promoted women's sexual freedom and financial independence, while also encouraging the exchange of sexual "favors" for material comforts and luxuries. Perhaps the most significant difference between the system Peiss describes and what Brown articulated is that the Cosmo Girl was encouraged to pursue men who may have been off limits in earlier eras. . . .

While the mainstream women's movement strove for equality in the workplace, Brown often framed sexual activity in terms of work and achievement. "Sex is a powerful weapon for a single woman in getting what she wants from life," she explained to an interviewer (quoted in San Francisco, 1962). A similar message was conveyed in her memoir, where Brown described the ability to bring a man to orgasm as a "specialty" every upwardly mobile girl should

acquire (1982: 212). Occasionally, Cosmopolitan explained the advantages of being "kept" and "slightly kept" girls (Baumgold, 1970; Condos, 1974), and articles glamorizing upscale prostitution were not uncommon. However, these explicit cases of sexual trading were not nearly as prevalent as the sexualization of the office, especially the relationship between male superiors and female secretaries. Again, this pattern drew from and reworked historical assumptions about the role of women in offices. . . .

By the 1960s, office work was a rapidly growing occupational field, and women were an expanding part of the labor force. By the time Sex and the Single Girl appeared, almost one of every three employed women worked in clerical and secretarial jobs (Matthaei, 1982: 282), and by 1974 women held four out of five jobs in this category (Howe, 1977: 10). The capitalist expansion of the service sector opened the field to women outside the middle class, while women with college degrees were struggling to move into male-dominated professions. What remained was the middle-class respectability of office work compared to factory work and other working-class wage labor (Matthaei, 1982: 282). Despite the low pay and dead-end nature of most pink-collar jobs, this made it easier for women to see themselves as upwardly mobile. . . .

Cosmopolitan elevated the sexual worth of the secretary by suggesting that "a secretary is not necessarily rich, beautiful or brilliant, but she is the most sought-after female since King Kong chased Fay Wray" (Lewis, 1969: 133). Likewise, the rewards for working for women were defined through the types of men one encountered. In Sex and the Single Girl, Brown promoted secretarial jobs because they were "all-time great spots" for meeting men (1962: 37). Cosmopolitan articles with titles like "Secretaries Who've Made Very, Very Good" (James, 1969), "Be a 9-to-5 Show Off" (Fisher, 1970), and

"Hollywood Secretaries" (*Cosmopolitan*, 1975a) also glamorized secretarial jobs as excellent places to meet well-connected bosses, dreamy executives, and traveling salesmen with expense accounts. One article even recommended "A Different Job Every Day" (Fahey, 1966), contracted through temporary employment agencies, as a chance to meet dozens of eligible men in a single week. The low pay, insecurity, and lack of benefits offered by the growing temporary workforce were obscured. . . .

Brown clearly understood women's subordination in the office, but she did not directly challenge it because "in an ideal world, we might move onward and upward by using only our brains and talent, but since this is an imperfect world, a certain amount of listening, giggling, wriggling, smiling, winking, flirting and fainting is required in our rise from the mailroom" (1964: 3). . . .

There were exceptions to these patterns, especially after 1970, when Brown proclaimed herself a friend of women's lib and *Cosmopolitan* began to negotiate feminist discourse, however haltingly. Several feminist articles were published, including an excerpt in November 1970 from Kate Millett's book *Sexual Politics* (1970) critiquing the gendered aspects of economic inequality and the ideology of heterosexual romance. As was typical, however, it was shockingly out of place, juxtaposed with a fashion spread proclaiming "Be His Fortune Cookie in Our Gala Gypsy Dress" (*Cosmopolitan*, 1970). Liberal feminist demands for professional equality had a more lasting impact on Brown's thinking, and on the partial incorporation of conventional success mythology in *Cosmopolitan*. While she continued to value street smarts over a college degree and to promote the sensational opportunities offered by secretarial work, Brown modified her credo to suggest that the Cosmo Girl might be both a sex object and a "high powered" executive (Brown, 1982: 19–20).

Girl-Style American Dreams

Many pink-collar women may have found the Cosmo Girl's fragmented identity as an upwardly mobile sexual agent more attractive and even more feasible than what the mainstream women's movement offered. Brown's advice offered a gendered success myth to women who found themselves taking on new roles as breadwinners, but who lacked the wages, education, professional skills, and social opportunities to recognize themselves in more conventional, male-oriented upward-mobility narratives. She articulated, in feminine terms, the materialistic desires that so often underpin popular structures of feeling in a consumer-oriented nation where the class structure is officially denied. Brown's reworking of American Dream mythology involved the construction and reconstruction of a desirable self, the presentation of identity as self-made, the valorization of femininity as a creative production, the partial subversion of natural class distinctions, the refusal of Victorian sexual norms, and the expression of multiple hardships and frustrations—all within a framework that legitimated capitalism, consumerism, and patriarchal privilege. However, to dismiss the fragmented, sexualized class identity she promoted as wholly co-optive or less than "real" would be to lose touch with the way social beings construct a sense of self.

As Stuart Hall suggests with his theory of articulation, there is no necessary link between economics and class. Class awareness is a social construct, produced in a political sense only when individual experiences are articulated as a "political force," enabling subjects to enter the stage as historical agents (Hall, 1986: 55). Brown's advice encouraged women to rework their identities on the basis of upper-class ideals, and to assess their current situations and future possibilities on the basis of those constructions. One of the consequences of the discourse may have been the way it positioned women as individual competitors in the quest for mobility, rather than part of a growing female labor force with many differences, to be sure, but with collective interests and bargaining power. Characterizing her own self-transformation, for example, Brown explained that "early on you have to separate yourself in the head from those people (friends, family, colleagues) you don't want to be like . . . be one of the girls, but also don't be one of the girls" (1982: 38).

Helen Gurley Brown's historical resonance as the "working girl's Simone de Beavoir" suggests the need to take the cultural construction of class seriously. . . .

Notes

1. Quoted in *Time* (1965: 60).

2. See, for example, Brown's appearance, 25 January 1997, on CNN's *Larry King Live*.

3. Mariana Valverde (1986) also observed the promotion of mobility in *Cosmopolitan*, arguing that what both the Cosmo Girl and the Ms. woman of the 1980s wanted, despite their different paths to achievement (e.g., getting a man vs. merit), was to be white, upper-middle class, and heterosexual. While she sees both magazines imposing unified capitalist and patriarchal ideologies on women (a view similar to early feminist Marxist criticism), I see Brown's advice in poststructuralist terms, as a contradictory, historically specific and productive discourse that constructed a social identity for pink-collar women.

4. Harrington, 1974. In 1997, *Cosmopolitan* had a U.S. circulation of 2.5 million, resulting in $156 million in estimated annual advertising revenue (Pogrebin, 1997).

5. In 1940, about one-third of employed Americans were in white-collar occupations, while in 1959 nearly half were due to the expanding service economy and the growing number of women who joined the "white-collar ranks." However, many of these jobs were "essentially manual" in that they were routine, repetitive, and sometimes minimally

skilled. They paid less than the professions and often less than skilled blue-collar work, but were "rated" above traditional working-class wage labor because they were perceived as "cleaner" and more "dignified" (Packard, 1959: 25–6). Advertisers played on the social ambiguity, promising status through consumer goods. In this [chapter] I refer to non-professional white-collar jobs taken up predominantly by women as pink-collar. For more on the post-Fordist economy see Harvey (1990: 121–97).

6. Brown envisioned the "untapped" market for *Cosmopolitan* as single women, divorcees, and widows, separated, and "otherwise neglected wives" who worked outside the home. Working married women who were (because of their independent attitude) "women on their own" were considered a secondary market ("A Proposal for *Cosmopolitan*," n.d.; "Statement for Advertisers," n.d.). Early marketing discourse inflated the spending power of the magazine's readers, describing them as well educated, high income, and "working in top occupations," despite statistic[s] that contradicted these generalizations. Thus, there was overlap between the class performativity Brown encouraged and the strategies used to court advertisers. While the Cosmo Girl was constructed as single and sexually free, a high percentage of readers were married. This would suggest that they too were drawn to the magazine's guide to changing sexual and economic roles.

7. Products and services said to be bought by *Cosmopolitan* readers included cosmetics, perfumes, fashion and personal products, wines and liquors, travel, miscellaneous, and mail order (*Cosmopolitan* Advertising Kit, 1965). The first three categories comprised most of the advertising according to my research.

8. Ehrenreich et al. note that Brown championed independence and guiltless sex at a time when few women "could imagine options other than marriage and full-time motherhood" (1986: 56). Susan Douglas (1994) also cites Brown as a key figure in the transformation of female sexuality.

9. As McCracken argues, "If the *Cosmopolitan* cover photo presents women with an ideal image of their future selves, it is an image

at the other end of the social spectrum from that of the affluent *Vogue* or *Bazaar* cover" (1993: 158). While she sees this image as an invitation to male fantasy and sexual voyeurism, I see it rooted in the class dimensions of Brown's revised sexual code.

References

Barnes, J. and M. Downey (1968) "Go Ahead—Pretend You're Rich," *Cosmopolitan* (July): 54–5.

Baumgold, J. (1970) "The Slightly Kept Girl," *Cosmopolitan* (Sept.): 154.

Berger, J. (1972) *Ways of Seeing*. London: Penguin Books.

Blyth, M. (1972) "The Big Catch," *Cosmopolitan* (Jan.): 128–36.

Bourdieu, P. (1984) *Distinction: A Social Critique of the Judgment of Taste*. Cambridge, MA: Harvard University Press.

Brown, H. G. (1962) *Sex and the Single Girl*. New York: Bernard Geis Associates.

Brown, H. G. (1963) *Lessons in Love*. New York: Crescendo Records.

Brown, H. G. (1964) *Sex and the Office*. New York: Bernard Geis Associates.

Brown, H. G. (1965) "New Directions for *Cosmopolitan*," *The Writer* (July): 20.

Brown, H. G. (1970a) *Sex and the New Single Girl*. New York: Bernard Geis Associates.

Brown, H. G. (ed.). (1970b) *The Cosmo Girl's Guide to the New Etiquette*. New York: Cosmopolitan Books.

Brown, H. G. (ed.). (1972) *Cosmopolitan's Love Book: A Guide to Ecstasy in Bed*. New York: Cosmopolitan Books.

CNN Television. (1997) Interview with Helen Gurley Brown, *Larry King Live* (25 Jan.).

Condos, B. (1974) "I Was Kept," *Cosmopolitan* (May): 60, 66–74.

Cosmopolitan Advertising Kit, July 1965, HGB papers, Box 8, Folder 12.

Cosmopolitan (1966a) "The Beautiful Phony" (March): 104–7.

Cosmopolitan (1966b) "*Cosmopolitan* Interviews Hugh M. Hefner" (May): 76–81.

Cosmopolitan (1966c) "Poor Girl Paintings" (Aug.): 88.

Cosmopolitan (1966d) "Six Current (But Perennial) Fascinators" (Feb.): 66–71.

Cosmopolitan (1969) "How Sexy Are You?" (April): 54–6.

Cosmopolitan (1970) "Be His Fortune Cookie in Our Gala Gypsy Dress" (Nov.): 104.

Cosmopolitan (1975a) "Hollywood Secretaries" (Aug.): 36.

Cosmopolitan (1975b) "How to Sink into a Man" (Nov.): 48–9.

Cunningham, L. (1968) "Why I Wear My False Eyelashes to Bed," *Cosmopolitan* (Oct.): 46–51.

de Dubovay, D. (1975) "Live Beyond Your Means," *Cosmopolitan* (Aug.): 132–4.

De Santis, M. (1969) "Yes, You Can Change Your Image," *Cosmopolitan* (April): 91–3.

Didion, J. (1965) "Bosses Make Lousy Lovers," *Saturday Evening Post* (30 Jan.): 34–8.

Douglas, S. (1994) *Where the Girls Are: Growing Up Female with the Mass Media*. New York: Time Books.

Dowling, C. (1966) "A Handbook of Elegant Starvation," *Cosmopolitan* (Oct.): 30–2.

Ehrenreich, B. (1983) *The Hearts of Men*. New York: Anchor Books.

Ehrenreich, B. et al. (1986) *Re-Making Love: The Feminization of Sex*. New York: Anchor Books.

Fahey, P. (1966) "A Different Job Every Day," *Cosmopolitan* (Oct.): 128–31.

Ferguson, M. (1983) *Forever Feminine: Women's Magazines and the Cult of Femininity*. London: Heinemann.

Firestone, S. (1970) *The Dialectic of Sex*. New York: Quill Press (repr. 1993).

Fisher, K. (1970) "Be a 9-to-5 Showoff," *Cosmopolitan* (Nov.): 150–1.

Fiske, J. (1987) *Television Culture*. New York: Routledge.

Geng, V. (1970) "A Little Bit of Class," *Cosmopolitan* (Oct.): 92–7.

Greller, J. (1966) "Night School Isn't All Education," *Cosmopolitan* (July): 87–8.

Guardian Weekly (1968) newspaper clipping (12 Nov.) HGB papers, Box 7, Folder 3.

Guy, R. (1966) "What It Means to Be a Negro Girl," *Cosmopolitan* (July): 76–81.

Hall, S. (1986) "On Postmodernism and Articulation: An Interview," *Journal of Communication Inquiry* 10(2): 45–60.

Harrington, S. (1974) "Two Faces of the Same Eve: *Ms.* Versus *Cosmo*," *New York Times Magazine* (11 Aug.): 10–11, 36, 74–6.

Harvey, D. (1990) *The Condition of Postmodernity*. London: Blackwell.

Hennessy, R. (1993) *Materialist Feminism and the Politics of Discourse*. New York: Routledge.

Howe, L. (1977) *Pink Collar Workers*. New York: G. P. Putnam's Sons.

James, T. (1969) "4 Secretaries Who've Made Very, Very Good," *Cosmopolitan* (June): 134–5.

Jhally, S. and J. Lewis (1992) *Enlightened Racism: The Cosby Show, Audiences and the Myth of the American Dream*. Boulder, CO: Westview.

Johnson, N. (1974) "Good Taste!" *Cosmopolitan* (Feb.): 122–31.

Joyce, P. (ed.) (1995) *Class*. New York: Oxford University Press.

Kent, R. (1972) "Cover Girl: Behind the Scenes," *Cosmopolitan* (Aug.): 94–117.

Lewis, B. (1969) "Today's Secretary—Wow!" *Cosmopolitan* (June): 133.

Lilly, D. (1965) "It's Just as Easy to Love a Rich Man," *Cosmopolitan* (July): 66–9.

Mansbridge, J. (1986) *Why We Lost the ERA*. Chicago: University of Chicago Press.

Matlin, P. (1969) "If You Don't Know Your Crepes From Your Coquilles, Or How to Order From a French Restaurant," *Cosmopolitan* (April): 96–9.

Matthaei, J. (1982) *An Economic History of Women in America*. New York: Schocken.

McCracken, E. (1993) *Decoding Women's Magazines*. New York: St Martin's.

Millett, K. (1970) *Sexual Politics*. Garden City, NY: Doubleday.

Newsweek (1966) "Down with "Pippypoo" (18 July): 60.

Packard, V. (1959) *The Status Seekers: An Exploration of Class Behavior in America*. New York: David McKay.

Peiss, K. (1983) "'Charity Girls' and City Pleasures: Historical Notes on Working-Class Sexuality, 1880–1920," pp. 74–87 in Ann Snitow et al. *Powers of Desire*. New York: Monthly Review Press.

Pogrebin, R. (1997) "Changing of Guard at Cosmo," *New York Times* (13 Jan.): D1.

Price, R. (1972) "Used Men: A Definitive Guide for the Selective Shopper," *Cosmopolitan* (Aug.): 68–73.

"A Proposal for Cosmopolitan from Helen Gurley Brown" (n.d.) Helen Gurley Brown papers, Sophia Smith Collection, Smith College, Northampton, MA (hereafter HGB papers), Box 14, Folder 4.

Providence Journal (1965) newspaper clipping (1 July) HGB papers, Box 8, Folder 1.

Reed, R. (1966) "10 Most Wanted Men (by the FBI)," *Cosmopolitan* (Feb.): 72–81.

Reisig, R. (1973) "The Feminine Plastique," *Ramparts* (March): 25–9, 53–5.

San Francisco News Call Bulletin (1962) "Single Gal's Quandary" (6 July) HGB papers, Box 8, Folder 3.

Sloane, L. (1966) "How Much Will He Earn?" *Cosmopolitan* (Feb.): 30–7.

Stacey, J. (1993) *Star Gazing: Hollywood Cinema and Female Spectatorship*. London: Routledge.

"Statement from Helen Gurley Brown for Advertisers" (n.d.) HGB papers, Box 14, Folder 3.

Time (1965) "Big Sister" (9 Feb.): 60.

Tornabene, L. (1966) "How to Live Beautifully on $100 a Week," *Cosmopolitan* (Aug.): 42–7.

Valverde, M. (1986) "The Class Struggles of the Cosmo Girl and the Ms. Woman," *Heresies* 18: 78–82.

Welles, C. (1965) "Soaring Success of the Iron Butterfly," *Life* (19 Nov.): 65–6.

Wolfe, L. (1981) *The Cosmo Report*. New York: Arbor House.

29

Sex, Lies, and Advertising

Gloria Steinem

When *Ms.* began, we didn't consider *not* taking ads. The most important reason was keeping the price of a feminist magazine low enough for most women to afford. But the second and almost equal reason was providing a forum where women and advertisers could talk to each other and improve advertising itself. After all, it was (and still is) as potent a source of information in this country as news or TV and movie dramas.

We decided to proceed in two stages. First, we would convince makers of "people products" used by both men and women but advertised mostly to men—cars, credit cards, insurance, sound equipment, financial services, and the like—that their ads should be placed in a women's magazine. Since they were accustomed to the division between editorial and advertising in news and general interest magazines, this would allow our editorial content to be free and diverse. Second, we would add the best ads for whatever traditional "women's products" (clothes, shampoo, fragrance, food, and so on) that surveys showed *Ms.* readers used. But we would ask them to come in *without* the usual quid pro quo of "complementary copy."

We knew the second step might be harder. Food advertisers have always demanded that women's magazines publish recipes and articles on entertaining (preferably ones that name their products) in return for their ads: clothing advertisers expect to be surrounded by fashion spreads (especially ones that credit their designers); and shampoo, fragrance, and beauty products in general usually insist on positive editorial coverage of beauty subjects, plus photo credits besides. That's why women's magazines look the way they do. But if we could break this link between ads and editorial content, then we wanted good ads for "women's products," too....

I thought then that our main problem would be the imagery in ads themselves. Carmakers were still draping blondes in evening gowns over the hoods like ornaments. Authority figures were almost always male, even in ads for products that only women used. Sadistic, he-man campaigns even won industry praise. (For instance, *Advertising Age* had hailed the infamous Silva Thin cigarette theme, "How to Get a Woman's Attention: Ignore Her," as "brilliant.") Even in medical journals, tranquilizer ads showed

From Steinem, Gloria. "Sex, Lies and Advertising." *Ms. Magazine*, July/August 1990. Reprinted with permission of Gloria Steinem and Ms. Magazine.

depressed housewives standing beside piles of dirty dishes and promised to get them back to work.

Obviously, *Ms.* would have to avoid such ads and seek out the best ones—but this didn't seem impossible. *The New Yorker* had been selecting ads for aesthetic reasons for years, a practice that only seemed to make advertisers more eager to be in its pages. *Ebony* and *Essence* were asking for ads with positive black images, and though their struggle was hard, they weren't being called unreasonable. . . .

The fact that *Ms.* was asking companies to do business in a different way meant our saleswomen had to make many times the usual number of calls—first to convince agencies and then client companies besides—and to present endless amounts of research. I was often asked to do a final ad presentation, or see some higher decision maker, or speak to women employees so executives could see the interest of women they worked with. That's why I spent more time persuading advertisers than editing or writing for *Ms.,* and why I ended up with an unsentimental education in the seamy underside of publishing that few writers see (and even fewer magazines can publish).

Let me take you with us through some experiences, just as they happened:

1. Cheered on by early support from Volkswagen and one or two other car companies, we scrape together time and money to put on a major reception in Detroit. We know U.S. carmakers firmly believe that women choose the upholstery, not the car, but we are armed with statistics and reader mail to prove the contrary: a car is an important purchase for women, one that symbolizes mobility and freedom.

But almost nobody comes. We are left with many pounds of shrimp on the table, and quite a lot of egg on our face. We blame ourselves for not guessing that there would be a baseball pennant play-off on the same day, but executives go out of their way to explain they wouldn't have

come anyway. Thus begins ten years of knocking on hostile doors, presenting endless documentation, and hiring a full-time saleswoman in Detroit: all necessary before *Ms.* gets any real results.

This long saga has a semi-happy ending: foreign and, later, domestic carmakers eventually provided *Ms.* with enough advertising to make cars one of our top sources of ad revenue. Slowly, Detroit began to take the women's market seriously enough to put car ads in other women's magazines, too, thus freeing a few pages from the hothouse of fashion-beauty-food ads.

But long after figures showed a third, even a half, of many car models being bought by women, U.S. makers continued to be uncomfortable addressing women. Unlike foreign carmakers, Detroit never quite learned the secret of creating intelligent ads that exclude no one, and then placing them in women's magazines to overcome past exclusion. (*Ms.* readers were so grateful for a routine Honda ad featuring rack and pinion steering, for instance, that they sent fan mail.) Even now, Detroit continues to ask, "Should we make special ads for women?" Perhaps that's why some foreign cars still have a disproportionate share of the U.S. women's market.

2. In the *Ms.* Gazette, we do a brief report on a congressional hearing into chemicals used in hair dyes that are absorbed through the skin and may be carcinogenic. Newspapers report this too, but Clairol, a Bristol-Myers subsidiary that makes dozens of products—a few of which have just begun to advertise in *Ms.*—is outraged. Not at newspapers or newsmagazines, just at us. It's bad enough that *Ms.* is the only women's magazine refusing to provide the usual "complementary" articles and beauty photos, but to criticize one of their categories—*that* is going too far.

We offer to publish a letter from Clairol telling its side of the story. In an excess of solicitousness, we even put this letter in the

Gazette, not in Letters to the Editors where it belongs. Nonetheless—and in spite of surveys that show *Ms.* readers are active women who use more of almost everything Clairol makes than do the readers of any other women's magazine—*Ms.* gets almost none of these ads for the rest of its natural life.

Meanwhile, Clairol changes its hair coloring formula, apparently in response to the hearings we reported.

3. Our saleswomen set out early to attract ads for consumer electronics: sound equipment, calculators, computers, VCRs, and the like. We know that our readers are determined to be included in the technological revolution. We know from reader surveys that *Ms.* readers are buying this stuff in numbers as high as those of magazines like *Playboy*, or "men 18 to 34," the prime targets of the consumer electronics industry. Moreover, unlike traditional women's products that our readers buy but don't need to read articles about, these are subjects they want covered in our pages. There actually *is* a supportive editorial atmosphere.

"But women don't understand technology," say executives at the end of ad presentations. "Maybe not," we respond, "but neither do men—and we all buy it."

"If women *do* buy it," say the decision makers, "they're asking their husbands and boyfriends what to buy first." We produce letters from *Ms.* readers saying how turned off they are when salesmen say things like "Let me know when your husband can come in."

After several years of this, we get a few ads for compact sound systems. Some of them come from JVC, whose vice president, Harry Elias, is trying to convince his Japanese bosses that there is something called a women's market. At his invitation, I find myself speaking at huge trade shows in Chicago and Las Vegas, trying to persuade JVC dealers that showrooms don't have to be locker rooms where women are made to feel unwelcome. But as it turns out, the shows themselves are part of the problem. In Las Vegas, the only women around the technology displays are semi-nude models serving champagne. In Chicago, the big attraction is Marilyn Chambers, who followed Linda Lovelace of *Deep Throat* fame as Chuck Traynor's captive and/or employee. VCRs are being demonstrated with her porn videos.

In the end, we get ads for a car stereo now and then, but no VCRs; some IBM personal computers, but no Apple or Japanese ones. We notice that office magazines like *Working Woman* and *Savvy* don't benefit as much as they should from office equipment ads either. In the electronics world, women and technology seem mutually exclusive. It remains a decade behind even Detroit.

4. Because we get letters from little girls who love toy trains, and who ask our help in changing ads and box-top photos that feature little boys only, we try to get toy-train ads from Lionel. It turns out that Lionel executives *have* been concerned about little girls. They made a pink train, and were surprised when it didn't sell.

Lionel bows to consumer pressure with a photograph of a boy *and* a girl—but only on some of their boxes. They fear that, if trains are associated with girls, they will be devalued in the minds of boys. Needless to say, *Ms.* gets no train ads, and little girls remain a mostly unexplored market. By 1986, Lionel is put up for sale.

But for different reasons, we haven't had much luck with other kinds of toys either. In spite of many articles on child-rearing—an annual listing of nonsexist, multiracial toys by Letty Cottin Pogrebin; Stories for Free Children, a regular feature also edited by Letty; and other prizewinning features for or about children—we get virtually no toy ads. Generations of *Ms.* saleswomen explain to toy manufacturers that a larger proportion of *Ms.* readers have preschool children than do the readers of other women's magazines, but this industry can't believe feminists have or care about children.

5. When *Ms.* begins, the staff decides not to accept ads for feminine hygiene sprays or cigarettes: they are damaging and carry no appropriate health warnings. Though we don't think we should tell our readers what to do, we do think we should provide facts so they can decide for themselves. Since the antismoking lobby has been pressing for health warnings on cigarette ads, we decide to take them only as they comply.

Philip Morris is among the first to do so. One of its brands, Virginia Slims, is also sponsoring women's tennis and the first national polls of women's opinions. On the other hand, the Virginia Slims theme, "You've come a long way, baby," has more than a "baby" problem. It makes smoking a symbol of progress for women.

We explain to Philip Morris that this slogan won't do well in our pages, but they are convinced its success with some women means it will work with *all* women. Finally, we agree to publish an ad for a Virginia Slims calendar as a test. The letters from readers are critical—and smart. For instance: Would you show a black man picking cotton, the same man in a Cardin suit, and symbolize the antislavery and civil rights movements by smoking? Of course not. But instead of honoring the test results, the Philip Morris people seem angry to be proven wrong. They take away ads for *all* their many brands.

This costs *Ms.* about $250,000 the first year. After five years, we can no longer keep track. Occasionally, a new set of executives listens to *Ms.* saleswomen, but because we won't take Virginia Slims, not one Philip Morris product returns to our pages for the next 16 years.

Gradually, we also realize our naiveté, in thinking we *could* decide against taking cigarette ads. They became a disproportionate support of magazines the moment they were banned on television, and few magazines could compete and survive without them: certainly not *Ms.*, which lacks so many other categories. By the time statistics in the 1980s showed that women's rate of lung cancer was approaching men's, the necessity of taking cigarette ads had become a kind of prison.

6. General Mills, Pillsbury, Carnation, Del Monte, Dole, Kraft, Stouffer, Hormel, Nabisco: you name the food giant, we try it. But no matter how desirable the *Ms.* readership, our lack of recipes is lethal.

We explain to them that placing food ads *only* next to recipes associates food with work. For many women, it is a negative that works *against* the ads. Why not place food ads in diverse media without recipes (thus reaching more men, who are now a third of the shoppers in super-markets anyway), and leave the recipes to specialty magazines like *Gourmet* (a third of whose readers are also men)?

These arguments elicit interest, but except for an occasional ad for a convenience food, instant coffee, diet drinks, yogurt, or such extras as avocados and almonds, this mainstay of the publishing industry stays closed to us. Period.

7. Traditionally, wines and liquors didn't advertise to women: men were thought to make the brand decisions, even if women did the buying. But after endless presentations, we begin to make a dent in this category. Thanks to the unconventional Michel Roux of Carillon Importers (distributors of Grand Marnier, Absolut Vodka, and others), who assumes that food and drink have no gender, some ads are leaving their men's club.

Beermakers are still selling masculinity. It takes *Ms.* fully eight years to get its first beer ad (Michelob). In general, however, liquor ads are less stereotyped in their imagery—and far less controlling of the editorial content around them—than are women's products. But given the underrepresentation of other categories, these very facts tend to create a disproportionate number of alcohol ads in the pages of *Ms.* This in turn dismays readers worried about women and alcoholism.

8. We hear in 1980 that women in the Soviet Union have been producing feminist *samizdat* (underground, self-published books) and circulating them throughout the country. As punishment, four of the leaders have been exiled. Though we are operating on our usual shoestring, we solicit individual contributions to send Robin Morgan to interview these women in Vienna.

The result is an exclusive cover story that includes the first news of a populist peace movement against the Afghanistan occupation, a prediction of *glasnost* to come, and a grass-roots, intimate view of Soviet women's lives. From the popular press to women's studies courses, the response is great. The story wins a Front Page award.

Nonetheless, this journalistic coup undoes years of efforts to get an ad schedule from Revlon. Why? Because the Soviet women on our cover *are not wearing makeup.*

9. Four years of research and presentations go into convincing airlines that women now make travel choices and business trips. United, the first airline to advertise in *Ms.*, is so impressed with the response from our readers that one of its executives appears in a film for our ad presentations. As usual, good ads get great results.

But we have problems unrelated to such results. For instance: because American Airlines flight attendants include among their labor demands the stipulation that they could choose to have their last names preceded by "Ms." on their name tags—in a long-delayed revolt against the standard, "I am your pilot, Captain Rothgart, and this is your flight attendant, Cindy Sue"— American officials seem to hold the magazine responsible. We get no ads.

There is still a different problem at Eastern. A vice president cancels subscriptions for thousands of copies on Eastern flights. Why? Because he is offended by ads for lesbian poetry journals in the *Ms.* Classified. A "family airline," as he explains to me coldly on the phone, has to "draw the line somewhere."

It's obvious that *Ms.* can't exclude lesbians and serve women. We've been trying to make that point ever since our first issue included an article by and about lesbians, and both Suzanne Levine, our managing editor, and I were lectured by such heavy hitters as Ed Kosner, then editor of *Newsweek* (and later of *New York Magazine*), who insisted that *Ms.* should "position" itself *against* lesbians. But our advertisers have paid to reach a guaranteed number of readers, and soliciting new subscriptions to compensate for Eastern would cost $150,000, plus rebating money in the meantime.

Like almost everything ad-related, this presents an elaborate organizing problem. After days of searching for sympathetic members of the Eastern board, Frank Thomas, president of the Ford Foundation, kindly offers to call Roswell Gilpatrick, a director of Eastern. I talk with Mr. Gilpatrick, who calls Frank Borman, then the president of Eastern. Frank Borman calls me to say that his airline is not in the business of censoring magazines: *Ms.* will be returned to Eastern flights.

10. Women of color read *Ms.* in disproportionate numbers. This is a source of pride to *Ms.* staffers, who are also more racially representative than the editors of other women's magazines. But this reality is obscured by ads filled with enough white women to make a reader snowblind.

Pat Carbine remembers mostly "astonishment" when she requested African American, Hispanic, Asian, and other diverse images. Marcia Ann Gillespie, a *Ms.* editor who was previously the editor in chief of *Essence,* witnesses ad bias a second time: having tried for *Essence* to get white advertisers to use black images (Revlon did so eventually, but L'Oréal, Lauder, Chanel, and other companies never did), she sees similar problems getting integrated ads for an integrated magazine. Indeed, the ad world often creates black and Hispanic ads only for black and Hispanic media. In an exact parallel of the fear that marketing a product to women will endanger its appeal to men, the response is usually, "But your [white] readers won't identify."

In fact, those we are able to get—for instance, a Max Factor ad made for *Essence* that Linda Wachner gives us after she becomes president—is praised by white readers, too. But there are pathetically few such images.

11. By the end of 1986, production and mailing costs have risen astronomically, ad income is flat, and competition for ads is stiffer than ever. The 60/40 preponderance of edit over ads that we promised to readers becomes 50/50; children's stories, most poetry, and some fiction are casualties of less space: in order to get variety into limited pages, the length (and sometimes the depth) of articles suffers; and, though we do refuse most of the ads that would look like a parody in our pages, we get so worn down that some slip through. . . . Still, readers perform miracles. Though we haven't been able to afford a subscription mailing in two years, they maintain our guaranteed circulation of 450,000.

Nonetheless, media reports on *Ms.* often insist that our unprofitability must be due to reader disinterest. The myth that advertisers simply follow readers is very strong. Not one reporter notes that other comparable magazines our size (say, *Vanity Fair* or *The Atlantic*) have been losing more money in one year than *Ms.* has lost in 16 years. No matter how much never-to-be-recovered cash is poured into starting a magazine or keeping one going, appearances seem to be all that matter. (Which is why we haven't been able to explain our fragile state in public. Nothing causes ad-flight like the smell of nonsuccess.)

My healthy response is anger. My not-so-healthy response is constant worry. Also an obsession with finding one more rescue. There is hardly a night when I don't wake up with sweaty palms and pounding heart, scared that we won't be able to pay the printer or the post office;

scared most of all that closing our doors will hurt the women's movement.

Out of chutzpah and desperation, I arrange a lunch with Leonard Lauder, president of Estée Lauder. With the exception of Clinique (the brainchild of Carol Phillips), none of Lauder's hundreds of products has been advertised in *Ms.* A year's schedule of ads for just three or four of them could save us. Indeed, as the scion of a family-owned company whose ad practices are followed by the beauty industry, he is one of the few men who could liberate many pages in all women's magazines just by changing his mind about "complementary copy."

Over a lunch that costs more than we can pay for some articles, I explain the need for his leadership. I also lay out the record of *Ms.*: more literary and journalistic prizes won, more new issues introduced into the mainstream, new writers discovered, and impact on society than any other magazine: more articles that became books, stories that became movies, ideas that became television series, and newly advertised products that became profitable: and, most important for him, a place for his ads to reach women who aren't reachable through any other women's magazine. Indeed, if there is one constant characteristic of the ever-changing *Ms.* readership, it is their impact as leaders. Whether it's waiting until later to have first babies, or pioneering PABA as sun protection in cosmetics, *whatever* they are doing today, a third to a half of American women will be doing three to five years from now. It's never failed.

But, he says, *Ms.* readers are not *our* women. They're not interested in things like fragrance and blush-on. If they were, *Ms.* would write articles about them.

On the contrary, I explain, surveys show they are more likely to buy such things than the readers of, say, *Cosmopolitan* or *Vogue.* They're good customers because they're out in the world enough to need several sets of everything: home, work, purse, travel, gym, and so on. They just don't need to read articles about these things. Would he ask a men's magazine to publish monthly columns on how to shave before he advertised Aramis products (his line for men)?

He concedes that beauty features are often concocted more for advertisers than readers. But *Ms.* isn't appropriate for his ads anyway, he explains. Why? Because Estée Lauder is selling "a kept-woman mentality."

I can't quite believe this. Sixty percent of the users of his products are salaried, and generally resemble *Ms.* readers. Besides, his company has the appeal of having been started by a creative and hardworking woman, his mother, Estée Lauder.

That doesn't matter, he says. He knows his customers, and they would *like* to be kept women. That's why he will never advertise in *Ms.*

In November 1987, by vote of the Ms. Foundation for Education and Communication (*Ms.*'s owner and publisher, the media subsidiary of the Ms. Foundation for Women), *Ms.* was sold to a company whose officers, Australian feminists Sandra Yates and Anne Summers, raised the investment money in their country that *Ms.* couldn't find in its own. They also started *Sassy* for teenage women.

In their two-year tenure, circulation was raised to 550,000 by investment in circulation mailings, and, to the dismay of some readers, editorial features on clothes and new products made a more traditional

bid for ads. Nonetheless, ad pages fell below previous levels. In addition, *Sassy,* whose fresh voice and sexual frankness were an unprecedented success with young readers, was targeted by two mothers from Indiana who began, as one of them put it, "calling every Christian organization I could think of." In response to this controversy, several crucial advertisers pulled out.

Such links between ads and editorial content was a problem in Australia, too, but to a lesser degree. "Our readers pay two times more for their magazines," Anne explained, "so advertisers have less power to threaten a magazine's viability."

"I was shocked," said Sandra Yates with characteristic directness. "In Australia, we think you have freedom of the press—but you don't."

Since Anne and Sandra had not met their budget's projections for ad revenue, their investors forced a sale. In October 1989, *Ms.* and *Sassy* were bought by Dale Lang, owner of *Working Mother, Working Woman,* and one of the few independent publishing companies left among the conglomerates. In response to a request from the original *Ms.* staff—as well as to reader letters urging that *Ms.* continue, plus his own belief that *Ms.* would benefit his other magazines by blazing a trail—he agreed to try the ad-free, reader-supported *Ms.* you hold now, and to give us complete editorial control.

30

Supersexualize Me![1]

Advertising and the "Midriffs"

Rosalind Gill

●●● **F**or the last four decades the notion of objectification has been a key term in the feminist critique of advertising. Its centrality to the feminist critical lexicon lay in its ability to speak to the ways in which media representations help to justify and sustain relations of domination and inequality between men and women. In particular, processes of objectification were held to be the key to understanding male violence against women:

> Adverts don't directly cause violence . . . but the violent images contribute to the state of terror. Turning a human being into a thing, an object, is almost always the first step towards justifying violence against that person . . . This step is already taken with women. The violence, the abuse, is partly the chilling but logical result of the objectification. (Kilbourne, 1999: 278)

It is difficult to over-estimate the importance of this argument for feminism (and also for understandings of racism and other relations of brutality); it has been central to feminist activism around advertising and media representations more generally. However, I want to suggest that a number of significant changes have taken place in the regime of representation that mean that the notion of objectification no longer has the analytic purchase to understand many contemporary constructions of femininity. Increasingly, young women are presented not as passive sex objects, but as active, desiring sexual subjects, who seem to participate enthusiastically in practices and forms of self-presentation that earlier generations of feminists regarded as connected to subordination. . . .

This shift was emblematic of a wider transformation happening in advertising in the early 1990s. Robert Goldman (1992) has argued that advertisers were forced to respond to three challenges at this time. First, there was the growing experience of 'sign fatigue' on the part of many media audiences fed up with the endless parade of brands, logos and consumer images. Like its millennial sibling, compassion fatigue,

---

From Rosalind Gill, "Supersexualize Me! Advertising and the 'Midriffs.'" In Feona Attwood (ed) (2009), *Mainstreaming Sex: The Sexualization of Western Culture*. New York: I. B. Taurus, 93–99.

sign fatigue showed itself in what we might call a weariness of affect, an ennui and a disinclination to respond. Secondly, advertisers had to address increasing 'viewer scepticism,' particularly from younger, media-savvy consumers who had grown up with fast-paced music television and were the first generation to adopt personal computers and mobile phones as integral features of everyday life. To get through to this generation, who regarded themselves as sceptical and knowing in relation to commercial messages, advertisers had to adapt. They increasingly came to produce commercials that mocked the grammar and vocabulary of advertising and effaced their own status as advertisements. Thirdly, advertisers needed to address feminist critiques of advertising and to fashion new commercial messages that took on board women's anger at constantly being addressed through representations of idealized beauty.

Goldman argued that advertisers' response to this third challenge was to develop what he called 'commodity feminism'[2]—an attempt to incorporate the cultural power and energy of feminism whilst simultaneously domesticating its critique of advertising and the media. Commodity feminism takes many different forms. It consists of adverts that aim to appease women's anger and to suggest that advertisers share their disgruntlement with images of thin women, airbrushed to perfection. It is found in adverts that attempt to articulate a rapprochement between traditional femininity and characteristics which are coded as feminist goals; independence, career success, financial autonomy. It may be identified in gender-reversal adverts or in revenge adverts that mock or turn the tables on men. Elsewhere I have considered a number of shifts in the representation of gender in advertising in some detail (Gill, 2007a).[3] In the remainder of this chapter, however, I will turn my attention to perhaps the major contemporary shift in the sexual representation of women: the construction of a young, heterosexual woman who knowingly and deliberately plays with her sexual power and is forever 'up for it': the midriff.

Sexualization and the Midriffs

The midriff is a part of the body between the top of the pubis bone and the bottom of the rib cage. This part of the female body has been the site of erotic interest in many non-Western cultures for a long time. In the West, the recent upsurge of interest in the midriff can be traced back to the visual presentation of Madonna in the late 1980s in which her pierced belly button and toned abdomen became features for erotic display in dance routines. For almost a decade, between the mid-1990s and the mid-2000s, revealing the midriff was central to young women's fashion in the West, with low-hung hipster jeans and cropped or belly top, exposing a pierced navel at the front and the familiar 'whale back' (visible g-string) from behind. Increasingly, the lower back has also become a site for elaborate tattoos.

This style was so widespread for such a long time that the term 'midriffs' has become a shorthand employed by advertisers and marketing consultants (Quart, 2003). In one sense it signals a generation—primarily women in their 20s and 30s, but sometimes also girls in their teens and women in their early 40s—defined by their fashion tastes. More tellingly, the midriffs can be understood in relation to a particular sensibility: a sensibility characterized by a specific constellation of attitudes towards the body, sexual expression and gender relations.

Advertising aimed at the midriffs is notable for its apparently 'sexualized' style but this is quite different from the sexual objectification to which second-wave feminist activists objected. In today's midriff advertising, women are much less likely to be shown as passive sexual objects than as empowered, heterosexually desiring sexual subjects, operating playfully in a sexual marketplace that is presented as egalitarian or actually favourable to women.

Midriff advertising has four central themes: an emphasis on the body, a shift from objectification to sexual subjectification, a pronounced discourse of choice and autonomy, and an emphasis upon empowerment.

Perhaps the most striking feature of midriff advertising is the centrality of the body. If in the 1950s the home was the ideal focus for women's labour and attention, and the sign used to judge their 'worth,' in the new millennium it is the body. Today, a sleek, controlled figure is essential for portraying success, and each part of the body must be suitably toned, conditioned, waxed, moisturized, scented and attired. In advertising, more and more parts of the body come under intense scrutiny: Dove's summer 2006 campaign alerts us that the newest must-have accessory is beautiful armpits, lest we forget to use all the products necessary to render this part of the body acceptable.

Today, the body is portrayed in advertising and elsewhere as the primary source of women's capital. This may seem obvious and taken-for-granted, but it is, in fact, relatively new. Surveillance of women's bodies constitutes perhaps the largest type of media content across all genres and media forms. Women's bodies are evaluated, scrutinized and dissected by women as well as men and are always at risk of 'failing.' This is most clear in the cultural obsession with celebrity which plays out almost exclusively over women's bodies. . . . In the very recent past, women's cooking, domestic cleanliness or interior design skills were the focus of advertisers' attention to a much greater extent than the surface of the body. But there has been a profound shift in the very definition of femininity so that it is now defined as a bodily property rather than a social or psychological

one. Instead of caring or nurturing or motherhood, it is now possession of a 'sexy body' that is presented as women's key source of identity. . . .

There has also been a shift in the way that women's bodies are presented erotically. Where once sexualized representations of women in the media presented them as the passive, mute objects of an assumed male gaze, today women are presented as active, desiring sexual subjects who choose to present themselves in a seemingly objectified manner because it suits their liberated interests to do so. . . . The notion of objectification does not seem to capture this; a better understanding would come from the Foucaultian idea of (sexual) subjectification, which speaks to the way that power operates through the construction of particular subjectivities.

A crucial aspect of both the obsessional preoccupation with the body and the shift from objectification to sexual subjectification is that this is framed in advertising through a discourse of playfulness, freedom, and, above all, *choice*. Women are presented not as seeking men's approval but as *pleasing themselves*; in doing so, they just happen to win men's admiration. . . .

Dee Amy-Chinn (2006) eloquently captures this double-edged postfeminist emphasis on women pleasing themselves, in the title of her article about lingerie advertising: 'This is just for me(n).' Such advertising hails active, heterosexual young women, but does so using a photographic grammar directly lifted from heterosexual pornography aimed at men. The success—and this is what is novel about this—is in connecting 'me' and 'men,' suggesting there is no contradiction—indeed no difference—between what 'I' want and what men might want of 'me.' This is clearly complicated. There is no necessary contradiction or difference between what women and men want, but equally it cannot be assumed that their desires are identical. What is most interesting is the sophisticated 'higher' development of ideology and power relations, such that the ideological is literally made real. This takes the form of constructions of femininity that come straight out of the most predictable templates of male sexual fantasy, yet which must also be understood as authentically owned by the women who produce them. Part of their force lies precisely in the fact that they are not understood as ideological, or indeed are understood as *not* ideological. . . .

Almost as central to midriff advertising as the notions of choice and 'pleasing one's self,' is a discourse of feminine *empowerment*. Contemporary advertising targeted at the midriffs suggest, above all, that buying the product will empower you. . . . What is on offer in all these adverts is a specific kind of power—the sexual power to bring men to their knees. Empowerment is tied to possession of a slim and alluring young body, whose power is the ability to attract male attention and sometimes female envy. . . . A US advert for lingerie dares to make explicit that which is usually just implied. Showing a curvaceous woman's body from the neck down, clad in a black basque and stockings, the advert's text reads, 'while you don't necessarily dress for men, it doesn't hurt, on occasion, to see one drool like the pathetic dog he is.'[4] This is 'power femininity': a 'subject-effect' of 'a global discourse of popular post-feminism which incorporates feminist signifiers of emancipation and empowerment, as well as circulating popular postfeminist assumptions that feminist struggles have ended, that full equality for all women has been achieved, and that women of today can "have it all"' (Lazar, 2006).

Supersexualize Me: Midriff Advertising and Postfeminism

What, then, are we to make of the shift in the way that women are presented sexually? In offering up representations of women who are active, desiring sexual subjects, who are presented as powerful and playful, rather than passive or victimized, has advertising pointed to more hopeful, open or egalitarian possibilities for gender relations? I do not think so. On the contrary, I want to argue that midriff advertising re-sexualizes women's bodies, with the excuse of a feisty, empowered postfeminist discourse that makes it very difficult to critique.

Let us examine first some of the exclusions of midriff advertising. Most obviously this includes anyone living outside the heterosexual norm. Contemporary midriff advertising operates within a resolutely hetero-normative economy, in which power, pleasure and subjectivity are all presented in relation to heterosexual relationships. Indeed, the parallel growth of a kind of 'queer chic' (Gill, 2008) seems to locate homosexuality in terms of style and aesthetics rather than sexuality. A cynic might suggest that the greater visibility of hyper-feminine/hyper-sexualized lesbians in advertising may be a way for advertisers to evade charges of sexism, whilst continuing to present women in a highly objectified manner.

Others excluded from the empowering, pleasurable address of midriff advertising are older women, disabled women, fat women and any woman who is unable to live up to the increasingly narrow standards of female beauty and sex appeal that are normatively required. These women are never accorded sexual subjecthood. The figure of the 'unattractive' woman who seeks a sexual partner remains one of the most vilified in popular culture. . . .

Sexual subjectification, then, is a highly specific and exclusionary practice, and sexual pleasure is actually irrelevant here; it is the power of sexual attractiveness that is important. Indeed, the two are frequently and deliberately confused in midriff advertising.

The practice is also problematic for what it renders invisible, what Robert Goldman has called the 'diverse forms of terror experienced by women who objectify themselves.' He explains:

> There is the mundane psychic terror associated with not receiving 'looks' of admiration—i.e., not having others validate one's appearance. A similar sense of terror involves the fear of 'losing one's looks'—the quite reasonable fear that ageing will deplete one's value and social power. A related source of anxiety involves fear about 'losing control' over body weight and appearance . . . and there is a very real physical terror which may accompany presentation of self as an object of desire—the fear of rape and violence by misogynist males. (1992: 123)

Midriff advertising is notable not only for its success in selling brands but also—much more significantly—for its effective rebranding or reconstruction of the anxieties and the labour involved in making the body beautiful, through a discourse of fun, pleasure and power. The work associated with disciplining the feminine body to approximate the required standards is made knowable in new ways that systematically erase pain, anxiety, expense and low self-esteem. See, for example, the way that the application of boiling wax to the genital region and then its use to pull out hairs by their roots can be discursively (re) constructed as 'pampering' (Sisters, I don't think so!).

Goldman is correct, too, to point to the erasure of violence in such advertising. It seems literally to have been conjured away. In one advert, an attractive young woman is depicted wearing just a bra, her arm stretched high in the internationally recognized gesture for hailing a taxi. 'I bet I can get a cab on New Year's Eve 1999,' she declares, laughing. Here, again, exposed breasts are a source of male attention-grabbing power, a way to defeat the notorious concerns about taxi queues on the millennium eve. But the representation is entirely shorn of any suggestion of the violence that might threaten a woman so scantily attired, late at night, in the midst of large numbers of men who are drinking heavily. More generally, the depiction of heterosexual relations as playful, and women as having as much—if not more—power as men in negotiating them, is at odds with statistics, which give an extraordinarily sobering picture of the levels of violence by men against women.[5] . . .

Midriff advertising articulates a thoroughgoing individualism in which women are presented as entirely autonomous agents, no longer constrained by any inequalities or power imbalances. The pendulum swing—from a view of power as something obvious and overbearing which acts upon entirely docile subjects, towards a notion of women as completely free agents who just 'please themselves'—does not serve feminist or cultural understandings well. It cannot explain why the look that young women seek to achieve is so similar. If it were the outcome of everyone's individual, idiosyncratic preferences, surely there would be greater diversity, rather than a growing homogeneity organized around a slim, toned, hairless body. Moreover, the emphasis upon choice sidesteps and avoids all the important and difficult questions about how socially constructed ideals of beauty are internalized and made our own.

The notion of choice has become a postfeminist mantra. The idea that women are 'pleasing themselves' is heard everywhere: 'women choose to model for men's magazines,' 'women choose to have cosmetic surgery to enhance the size of their breasts,' 'women choose to leave their children in Eastern Europe or in the Global South and come and make a better life in the rich countries.' Of course, at one level, such claims have some truth: some women do make 'choices' like this. However, they do not do so in conditions of their own making, and to account for such decisions using only a discourse of free choice is to oversimplify, both in terms of analysis and political response. We need urgently to complicate our understandings of choice and agency in this context (Gill, 2007b).

Finally, I would argue that midriff advertising involves a shift in the way that power operates: it entails a move from an external, male-judging gaze, to a self-policing, narcissistic gaze. In this sense it represents a more 'advanced' or pernicious form of exploitation than the earlier generation of objectifying images to which second-wave feminists objected—because the objectifying male gaze is internalized to form a new disciplinary regime. Using the rather crude and clunky language of oppression, we might suggest that midriff advertising adds a further layer of oppression. Not only are women objectified, as they were before, *but through sexual subjectification they must also now understand their own objectification as pleasurable and self-chosen.* If, in earlier regimes of advertising, women were presented as sexual objects, then this was understood as something being done to women. In contemporary midriff advertising, however, some women are endowed with the status of active subjecthood so that they can 'choose' to become sex objects, because this suits their liberated interests. One of the implications of this shift is that it renders critique much more difficult.

. . . Goldman's analysis of commodity feminism discussed earlier in this chapter . . . stresses the ongoing struggle between advertising and feminism, . . . that, so far, . . . has largely been resolved in favour of the advertising industry, with feminist ideas ransacked, cannibalized, incorporated, and 'domesticated.' To contest this, there are three fronts on which feminists must engage: first, to articulate a language and cultural politics of resistance to midriff advertising, preferably one that is funny, feisty, sex-positive and inclusive; second, to rethink agency and choice in more sophisticated terms that reject the existing dualisms; and finally, to push for—or create—more diverse representations of gender and sexuality.

Notes

1. This title owes a debt to Morgan Spurlock's powerful critique of the fast-food industry, *Super Size Me* (2004).

2. Commodity feminism is, of course, an homage to Marx and Engels's notion of commodity fetishism.

3. See also Gill (2008) for a discussion of sexualization that looks at the rise of 'queer chic' in advertising, the erotic depiction of men's bodies, and the increasing use of the grammars of heterosexual pornography in advertising.

4. Elsewhere (2007a) I have considered the offensive depiction of male sexuality in such adverts.

5. It is estimated that there were 190,000 incidents of serious sexual assault and 47,000 female victims of rape in 2001 in England and Wales. Research by Amnesty International in the UK published in November 2005 found that a blame culture exists against women who have been raped, with up to one-third of people who were questioned seeing a woman as responsible if she was wearing revealing clothing, had been drinking or had had a number of sexual partners.

References

Amy-Chinn, D. (2006). "This is just for me(n): Lingerie advertising for the post-feminist woman." *Journal of Consumer Culture* 6(2).

Gill, R. (2007a). "Critical respect: Dilemmas of choice and agency in feminism (A response to Duits and Van Zoonen)." *European Journal of Women's Studies* 14(1).

Gill, R. (2007b). "Postfeminist media culture: Elements of a sensibility." *European Journal of Cultural Studies.*

Gill, R. (2008). "Beyond 'sexualization': Sexual representations in advertising." *Sexualities.*

Goldman, R. (1992). *Reading ads socially.* London; New York, Routledge.

Kilbourne, J. (1999). *Can't buy my love: How advertising changes the way we think and feel.* New York, London, Touchstone.

Lazar, M. (2006). "'Discover the power of femininity!' Analysing global 'power femininity' in local advertising." *Feminist Media Studies* 6(4).

Quart, A. (2003). *Branded: The buying and selling of teenagers*. London, Arrow Books.

Rushkoff, Douglas. (2001). *The Merchants of Cool*. Documentary film aired on Frontline, PBS.

Spurlock, Morgan. (2004). *Super Size Me*. Documentary film.

Walby, Sylvia and Jonathan Allen. (2004). *Domestic Violence, Sexual Assualt and Staulking: Findings from the British Crime Survey*. Home Office Study 276. Home Office Research, Development and Statistics Directorate.

31

Branding "Real" Social Change in Dove's Campaign for Real Beauty

Dara Persis Murray

In June 2010, the Dove Movement for Self-Esteem launched at the G(irls) 20 Summit. Modeled after the G20 Summit, this convention brought together young women from the same countries[1] represented at the G20 Summit to discuss education, health, and economic initiatives that could stimulate girls' activism and advancement in their communities. The ideological intersection of the Movement (a brand extension of Dove's Campaign for Real Beauty, or CFRB) and the G(irls) 20 Summit reflects the complex and often problematic meanings of feminism that circulate in popular culture: the blending of active female citizenship with empowerment via consumption in the marketplace.

This chapter explores CFRB's branding strategy, wherein its "real beauty" messaging merges co-opted feminist discourse and "a postfeminist sensibility" (Gill 2007, p. 254). A feminist semiotic analysis suggests that, under a guise of corporate altruism that democratizes female beauty, CFRB endorses global postfeminist citizenship. The findings suggest that CFRB may reflect a social change in the relationship between corporations and audiences that carries perilous meanings for the future roles of feminists and practices of female citizenship in global consumer culture. CFRB offers a rich site for unpacking the production and consumption of popular meanings of feminism, social change, female citizenship, and female beauty at this cultural moment.

Dove Gets the Word Out

Dove is a brand of personal care products such as soaps, body washes, and body lotions manufactured by the Unilever Corporation. Since 1957, Dove's mainstay product has been

From Murray, D. P. (2012). Branding "real" social change in Dove's campaign for real beauty. *Feminist Media Studies*, 12(4), 1–19. Reprinted by permission of Taylor & Francis Ltd., www.tandf .co.uk/journals.

the Beauty Bar. In 2002, Unilever reassessed Dove's marketing strategy with its public relations firm, Edelman, and its advertising/marketing agency, Ogilvy & Mather, to create a unified global image to generate brand loyalty. Discussing her view of the global brand, Ogilvy's Chairman and Chief Executive Officer Shelly Lazarus stated, "It means figuring out what is universal about the brand-those things that transcend where it happens to be manufactured, or where it started" (O'Barr, Lazarus & Moreira 2008). Lazarus's statement indicates that in today's market, a brand needs to reach audiences' emotions by building a platform that drives ideological alliance with the corporate identity before the act of material consumption.

CFRB was largely shaped by women in industry and as research subjects. Female members of Ogilvy & Mather's CFRB team included Lazarus, two creative directors, an art director, a writer, and producer. Lazarus is a graduate of Smith College (an all-women's institution listing numerous feminist icons among its alumni), where she sat on its Board of Trustees. Although Lazarus has not publicly aligned herself with feminism, others have identified her as "a strong feminist . . . Yet Lazarus's feminist love of economic empowerment prevents her from acknowledging the ways in which capitalism can hurt the powerless" (Dyer 2004, p. 191). Moreover, Dove commissioned women[2] to direct its foundational research and conduct much of the Campaign's research.

The construction of CFRB was based on Dove's 2003 global research study, "The Real Truth About Beauty." This research involved the participation of thirty-two hundred women, ages eighteen through sixty-four, in ten countries, in a twenty to twenty-five-minute long telephone interview. The study found that less than 2 percent of women feel beautiful; 75 percent want representations of women to reflect diversity through age, shape, and size; and 76 percent want the media to portray beauty as more than physical (Etcoff, Orbach, Scott & D'Agostino

2004). These responses suggested a market for a new philosophy of beauty that was "a great opportunity to differentiate the brand from every [other] beauty brand" (Fielding, Lewis, White, Manfredi & Scott 2008), according to Alessandro Manfredi, Dove's Global Brand Director. CFRB has been identified as a cause marketing effort (Lachover & Brandes 2009), which associates corporate identities with social problems to benefit the corporate image, "distracting attention from their [the corporation's] connections as to why these social problems continue to exist" (Stole 2008, p. 21). This article advances that CFRB is a *cause branding* strategy that merges messages of corporate "concern and commitment for a cause" (Cone 2000) with the participation of women and girls for the same social goals, further concealing corporate aims.

In line with their findings, Dove announced its challenge to the dominant ideology of beauty: it would feature "real" women and girls of "various ages, shapes and sizes" (Campaign for Real Beauty 2008). The campaign launched in England in 2004, and was soon exported to Canada and the United States; CFRB is currently marketed in thirty-five countries.[3] The branding strategy was executed through television and print advertising, billboards, new media, and national and grassroots outreach. The Dove Self-Esteem Fund is a brand extension that serves as the site for in-person and online workshops that provide "self-esteem toolkits" for girls and "parent kits" for mothers/mentors. In the United States, the Fund has partnered with multiple national nonprofit girls' organizations (Girl Scouts, Girls Inc., and Boys & Girls Clubs of America) to facilitate these workshops. As an example of CFRB's international events that engage female audiences, Dove "call[ed] on women from the Middle East to write about someone they find beautiful and the reasons they see a different kind of 'real beauty.' Participants could be treated to a luxury five-star treatment for two" (Dove Exposes the Beauty Myth 2007) in return. The Dove

Movement for Self-Esteem launched in Canada and the United States in Fall 2010.
. . .

A Feminist Perspective on Beauty

In the twentieth and twenty-first centuries, the beauty and fashion industries have produced powerful media images communicating the dominant ideology of female beauty as ultra-thin, tall, sexual bodies. Consumption of these images has resulted in a cultural norm of women and girls disciplining their bodies (Bordo 2003). The beauty industry's discourse connects ideological and physical nonconformity to the dominant ideology with a woman's inability to fulfill her gender role or experience happiness (Bartky 1990). The struggle of women and girls to physically emulate media images has manifested itself in eating disorders and body image issues, while the lack of a fulfilled identification may result in low self-esteem (Kilbourne 1999).

Dove's stated call to arms echoes feminist and feminist media studies scholarship that addresses how representations in popular culture convey often-problematic meanings of gender and beauty. In its advocacy of women's rights and egalitarian roles, the feminist position argues for social change of oppressive social structures (Dworkin 1974). By contrast, the postfeminist position contends that gender equality and female empowerment have been achieved in the public sphere. Postfeminism has immense power in western culture, as noted by feminist media studies scholar Rosalind Gill, who names our current time a "postfeminist media culture" (2007, p. 249). Significantly, she advances that postfeminism can be interpreted as "a sensibility" (2007, p. 254) whose messaging includes:

the notion that femininity is a bodily property; the shift from objectification to subjectification; the emphasis upon self-surveillance, monitoring and discipline; a focus upon individualism, choice and empowerment; the dominance of a makeover paradigm; the articulation or entanglement of feminist and antifeminist ideas . . . and an emphasis upon consumerism and the commodification of difference. (Rosalind Gill 2007)

The postfeminist position easily aligns with corporate interests, situating messages of women's freedom in the marketplace as "empowered consumer[s]" (Tasker & Negra 2007, p. 2). This identity lies at the intersection of consumerism and neoliberal governmentality, thereby separating meanings of female citizenship from civic engagement (McRobbie 2008, p. 533). The emergent neoliberal postfeminist citizen links meanings of empowerment and choice to ideological and material consumption.

The postfeminist citizen's pursuit of beauty engages her consumer power and self-governance, aligning her identity with the goals of institutional power. In postfeminist media culture, the body is a site of attention for the postfeminist citizen since it is promoted as integral to female identity (Gill 2007, p. 255). Consumption of the dominant ideology of beauty involves absorbing representations and meanings of hypersexual women and, increasingly, girls. Agreement with these messages may make it difficult for postfeminist citizens to understand their sexuality in "healthy, and progressive ways" (Durham 2008, p. 39). This feminist analysis will consider the political, social, and economic meanings in CFRB's texts and address how female identity may be shaped as postfeminist citizenship through the myth of "real beauty."

Self-Branding by Embracing Popular Feminism

A strategy for accomplishing audience identification with texts is the co-option of discourse; importantly, such appropriation highlights social issues as a means of generating sales (Danesi 2002). Alignment with co-opted subcultural signs allows consumers to think of themselves as insurgents; yet, since their rebellion occurs through consumerism, they do not "pay the social price of true non-conformity and dissent" (Danesi 2002, p. 197).

Sociologist Robert Goldman terms this tactic "commodity feminism," wherein advertisers attempt "to reincorporate the cultural power of feminism" (Goldman 1992, p. 130) and, in so doing, depoliticize the feminist message. . . .

Branding enlists audiences to support a corporate brand identity that is managed by the corporation to produce its desired outcome. . . . Importantly for this study, cause branding is a specific type of branding that blends corporate and individual identities through brand communication and audience participation. Cause branding "falls at the intersection of corporate strategy and citizenship and is fast becoming a 'must do' practices [sic] for the 21st century" (Cone 2000), therefore positioning corporations to implement their identities to attract and retain consumers through a depth of involvement that draws on their emotions, actions, and identities to drive brand commitment.

It is important to consider the practice of self-branding when thinking about girls and women who consume cause branding messages. While media studies scholars have examined the meanings of textual signs, a study of current consumer culture entails an exploration of the ways in which individuals are encouraged to become a self-branded "commodity sign" (Hearn 2008, p. 201) using "the narrative and visual codes" (Hearn 2008, p. 198) promoted by institutional power (corporations, advertisers, and so on). . . . This analysis considers how CFRB's meanings of popular feminism and social change convey the message that audiences should self-brand as postfeminist "real" beauties. . . .

ANALYSIS OF DOVE'S "REAL BEAUTY" PRINT TEXTS

CFRB's texts integrate feminist politics from the three waves[4] through the pictorial signs of "real" women and the use of feminist discourse to foster audience identification based on physical attributes, age, and generational feminist politics. The pictorial signs of women signify their age, which corresponds with a feminist wave, and all the women are photographed against a white background. These images inaugurate the campaign's mission with representations of five women of distinctly varied ages, signifying a unification of women from the three waves. The first word of CFRB—"Campaign"—acknowledges a political intention. Linguistic signs in the CFRB texts connote the politics of the feminist waves: specifically, the first wave's focus on suffrage; the second wave's focus on collective—"we"—political action by women; and the third waves focus on individual difference—in gender, ethnicity, race, etc.—or micro-politics. The print launch comprised six images: portraits of five women (three close-ups of faces and two body shots at a distance) and one composite picture of them. The five women pose with questions that address the dominant ideology of beauty; each question offers two options as a response. The CFRB manifesto accompanies the composite image, stating:

> For too long, beauty has been defined by narrow, unattainable stereotypes. It's time to change all that. Because Dove believes real beauty comes in many shapes, sizes, colors and ages. It's why we started the campaign for real beauty. And why we hope you'll take part. Together, let's think, talk, debate and learn how to make beauty real again. Cast your vote at campaignforreal beauty.com. (Dove Manifesto 2004)

The three close-up photos represent women from each wave. Their images are accompanied by ballot boxes next to descriptive labels, posed as questions: "wrinkled? wonderful?" (First Wave), "gray? gorgeous?" (Second Wave) and "flawed? flawless?" (Third Wave). The dark-skinned ninety-ish woman wearing a colorful headscarf smiles, with the text beside her asking, "Will society ever accept old can be beautiful?" This query signifies the difficulties involved in changing societal views regarding the role of women (First Wave). The smiling fifty-ish Caucasian woman wears a black turtleneck and, looking over her shoulder at the audience, the text beside her raises the only question of those in this set that invites discussion, rather than a yes/no response: "Why aren't women glad to be gray?" This question signifies the consciousness-raising ideology of dialogue relevant to her era (Second Wave). The text beside the twenty-ish, red-haired Caucasian woman, wearing a white tank top, poses a question that seemingly derives from her freckled appearance, "Does beauty mean looking like everyone else?" This inquiry signifies the ideology of difference in her wave (Third Wave).

Additionally, two women belonging to the Third Wave are photographed from head to thighs and are presented next to the ballot box signifier. One image ("half empty? half full?") depicts a slim, smiling, short-haired, small-breasted black woman in a white tank top and jeans with her hands in her back pockets; the text beside her breast questions, "Does sexiness depend on how full your cups are?" This phrasing suggests optimism or pessimism, an intertextual reference to the rhetorical expression, "Is the glass half empty or half full?" The other image ("oversized? outstanding?")[5] depicts a full-figured, smiling, large-breasted Caucasian woman in a strapless black cocktail dress with hands crossed behind her head; the text, positioned at her hips, asks, "Does true beauty only squeeze into a size 6?" Both of their confidently smiling visages connote an optimistic, "real beauty" answer to the ballot box question posed next to them. . . .

The composite representation of all five women is accompanied by the CFRB manifesto. . . . The corporate message is visually constructed as more important than the women: the paragraph of copy occupies more space on the page than all the women together, the text occupies more vertical space than the strip of photos, and the copy concludes with a blue color whose length and vibrancy are more visually compelling than the women. Further, this blue copy relays information about Dove and CFRB: the campaign website, the Dove icon, and a request to "Cast your vote." The copy emphasizes Dove as the organizer, catalyst, and vehicle for change: "it's time to change all that . . . it's why we started the campaign for real beauty." . . .

SELF-ESTEEM FUND: TELEVISION AND VIRAL VIDEO TEXTS

Dove took CFRB's messaging "a step further and [focused on] talk about self-esteem" (Branding Evolution 2007) by launching two texts in 2006 to brand the Dove Self-Esteem Fund, which was established by and is primarily financed by Unilever/Dove. These texts encourage ideological identification for girls and adult female audiences (mentors/mothers). Girl audiences may identify with the "real" girls in CFRB's television advertisement and viral video through sharing their physical attributes, ages, and, significantly, their emotional states. These texts are designed to arouse emotions against the dominant ideology of beauty and garner support for "real beauty." The mentors /mothers identification is mobilized through acceptance of the Fund's leadership and mission: to save girls' psychological and physical health via an emphasis on "self-esteem" (a crucial component of the "real beauty" ideology). Women can also economically bond with Dove by making donations to the Fund.

"True Colors" debuted during the February 2006 Superbowl XL Game, at a cost of $2.4 million dollars for forty-six seconds. The spot ran during this time to make contact with the largest audience possible, in keeping with Dove's goal (which was achieved) of reaching one million young girls by 2008. In "True Colors," Dove represents itself as a facilitator and problem-solver, declaring: "let's change their minds/we've created the Dove self-esteem fund/because every girl deserves to feel good about herself/and see how beautiful . . . she really is/ help us . . . get involved at" the CFRB website. . . .

"True Colors" offers a range of emotions in the expressions of "real" girls of various sizes and ethnicities. The emotional song, "True Colors," is performed by The Girl Scouts Chorus. At first, the girls' faces reflect innocence or ambivalence, bolstered by linguistic signs connoting feelings of victimization—"hates her freckles," "thinks she's ugly," "wishes she were blonde," "afraid she's fat"—because they do not meet the dominant ideology of beauty. The lyrics simultaneously elevate the poignant portraits and offer an intimate relationship with the person ("I") in the music and the girls in the text: "Show me a smile then, don't be unhappy, can't remember when, I last saw you laughing, If this world makes you crazy and you've taken all you can bear, You call me up, because you know I'll be there." Halfway through the video, an emotional shift occurs following the encouraging syntagm, "Let's change their minds" against a white background. The lyrics also become positive: "And I'll see your true colors shining through." Accompanying this phrase is a group of smiling girls euphorically pumping their hands in the air, an intertextual reference to the feminist iconic image of "Rosie the Riveter," whose slogan was "We Can Do It!" Another phrase, "We've created the Dove Self-Esteem Fund," appears next, also against a white background. Smiling girls appear throughout the rest of the text, accompanying Dove's

announcement of leadership via the Fund and the lyrics: "I see your true colors, And that's why I love you, So don't be afraid, To let them show, You're beautiful like a rainbow." The white background on which the pivotal text for the film's message appears signifies light, symbolizing Dove as the caring narrator ("I") and the ray of light illuminating the public perception of female beauty and girls' "real beauty."

"Evolution" launched on YouTube at no cost to Dove or Ogilvy & Mather other than its production expenses. Near its commencement, a screen displays the words "a Dove film." . . .

"Evolution" depicts a woman's makeover using the tools (physical, technological) that are employed by the beauty industry to transform a "real" woman into a supermodel. The subject appears to be in her twenties and sits on a stool, staring without affect into the camera. Bright lights suddenly turn on; the footage speeds up in a choppy, fast-forward simulation; and music plays in synchrony with the rapid projection of images. The woman is presented as a site of work for make-up artists and hair stylist. During the transformation, the camera zooms in on her face, removing any indicators of her tank top to imply a state of undress. The image is manipulated through Photoshop, and her final representation as the dominant beauty appears on a billboard that two girls walk past and briefly acknowledge, connoting acceptance of the manufactured image as a cultural norm. . . .

At the conclusion of the film, [the tagline] "no wonder our perception of beauty is distorted," implicitly acknowledges a social problem that relates to the dominant ideology. . . . The logo that appears, "the Dove self-esteem fund," shows the upward flight of three blue doves in ascending size (from small to large). . . . Their upward direction connotes unity and positive direction for the future. However, this optimistic sign diverts from the messaging, which positions the corporation to usurp the feminist role of engendering social change for women and displaces the influential role of the women who share girls' everyday lives onto institutional power. Moreover, through the Fund, Dove asks mothers/mentors and girls to endorse the oppressive female role as an ideological and material consumer.

*DOVE MOVEMENT
FOR SELF-ESTEEM WEBSITE*

The Dove Movement for Self-Esteem is primarily an online branding strategy through social media and the corporate website. Achieving online popularity (over ten million views) and more popular discourse for the brand than "True Colors" (and for minimal cost), The Movement may be an effort drawing on the success of "Evolution" as a low cost, high impact text. It is a site of interactivity, a critical process for understanding the agency and subjectivity of users.

... The Movement brings together the "real beauty" ideology from CFRB's print texts with the Fund's positioning of Dove as the site for women's and girls' activism. The centerpiece of the Movement is acceptance of its mission, which is executed when women and girls acknowledge their participation by signing a "declaration" to "Join the Movement." A declaration denotatively affords power to the audience by offering the opportunity to make a choice and assert oneself. Yet the Movement's language communicates a hegemonic relationship between the corporate leader and its followers, asking users to join "our Movement," "our vision," and "our cause." The declaration itself amounts to providing their email address, first and last name, zip code, and age, as well as an answer to an "optional" question: "What advice would you give to your 13 year old self? We'll collect these messages and deliver them to girls to build self-esteem in the next generation" (Our Vision: Join Us 2010). . . .

That the Movement may be using the declaration to create a list of consumers under the guise of participation for social change is not surprising: CFRB was formulated on the findings from a global research study and Dove has conducted numerous global and national studies[6] throughout the Campaign. The Movement can be seen as a form of market research, and the Movement's participants are its research subjects. The work of media studies theorist Mark Andrejevic is of particular importance here, as he contends that it is critical to question the politics of participation by users, who may be involved in "the labor of detailed information gathering and comprehensive monitoring . . . in the name of their own empowerment . . . and to view such participation as a form of power sharing" (2007, p. 15). Scholarship on Dove's user-generated marketing raises issues of users' labor on behalf of the brand (Duffy 2010) and users' discourse may support the patriarchal view that women's role is to pursue the dominant ideology (Lachover & Brandes 2009). In light of these voices, the Movement's declaration serves as a contractual agreement between audiences and the "real beauty" ideology, whose potential for the liberation of women and girls is questionable. . . .

Producing a Postfeminist Campaign and Self-Branded Postfeminist Citizenship

CFRB and its brand extensions (the Fund and the Movement) created and advanced a myth of "real beauty." This ideology mandates female audiences to practice psychological self-improvement and physical subjectification as a means of liberation from the dominant ideology of beauty. This section explores the production (concentrating on the politics of women's participation in CFRB) and potential consumption (in connection with self-branded identity and postfeminist citizenship) of "real beauty" to consider its promise to facilitate audience liberation.

In addition to the aforementioned participation of women from Ogilvy & Mather, CFRB's partnership with the Woodhull Institute for Ethical Leadership further highlights women s involvement in this branding strategy. Woodhull is a nonprofit women's organization named after feminist Victoria Woodhull. Its website describes its partnership by employing the key words of feminist activism—"social change": "The Woodhull Institute of Ethical Leadership has partnered with the Dove CFRB to share success building tools through online training sessions that promote ethical development and empower women to act as agents of positive social change" (Woodhull 2007). Of note, Woodhull's co-founder and most public figure is Naomi Wolf, who may be known to popular audiences for her bestselling critique of the beauty industry, *The Beauty Myth*. Three years later, Wolf advocated a postfeminist position in her subsequent (and lesser known) book. However, for audiences who remember Wolf from her argument in *The Beauty Myth* and are not versed in postfeminism, this partnership may pose conflicting meanings of feminist involvement with the beauty industry. As one journalist notes, "To go from writing *The Beauty Myth* to touring with Dove and singing its praises is a big jump" (M.K. Johnson 2008). At the same time, the author optimistically queries whether Wolf is actually "spreading her message about the hypocrisy of the beauty industry, all on Dove's dime? Savvy audience members would certainly catch the irony, and Dove can laugh all the way to the bank. Everybody wins" (M.K. Johnson 2008).

Several "self-esteem" partners (nonprofit girls' organizations that draw on feminist ideologies) similarly bolster CFRB/Dove's credibility to audiences. The participation of these female-focused groups extends the brand into community spaces in a grassroots way that may read as "feminist" for popular audiences. These groups thereby function as a kin network that aids in the development of a CFRB community. The strategy surrounding Dove with these partnerships may operate to reduce popular attention to Unilever's other brands; after all, Unilever manufactures Slimfast (a diet plan), Fair & Lovely Fairness Cream (a skin lightening product), and Axe deodorant (whose advertisements, targeted at men, portray objectified women). Unilever's ownership structure suggests it is a site of fractured ideological credibility that circulates knotty popular meanings of feminism and social change.

By asking girls and women to partner with the corporate ideology in a similar manner as the aforementioned organizations, The Movement potentially enlists global postfeminist citizenship through the support of yet *another* oppressive beauty ideology. By signing the declaration, girls and women work to become neoliberal subjects who accept responsibility to develop and perform Dove-approved "self-esteem" behaviors (requiring self-judgment and self-monitoring of one's emotional state) that are integral to the pursuit of "real beauty."

. . . Becoming "a real beauty" necessitates ideological and material labor on the self that originates from acceptance of the "real beauty" myth: support of CFRB's hegemonic views of female beauty, agreement with Dove as the site for social change and female activism about beauty (even if it displaces the roles of feminists, mothers, and mentors in individuals' lives and in cultural ideology), work to achieve Dove's meaning of self-esteem, and embrace of women's traditional role as consumers.

. . . The rationale for women's and feminists' support of CFRB may lie in the postfeminist belief that contemporary women are consumers with agency. Or, feminists might welcome CFRB's representations as a positive change in a mediascape that is otherwise saturated with the dominant ideology of beauty. It is important to stress, however, that the feminist task is to realize social change that revolutionizes social structures, not to support corporate strategies that seek audiences' brand attachment.

. . . Ultimately, it seems that "who wins" in CFRB's effort is the corporation. At first, CFRB resulted in enormous financial success for Dove and industry acclaim for Ogilvy & Mather and Edelman Public Relations, which spearheaded CFRB's marketing. Sales figures indicate that Dove's revenues increased following its launch: 12.5 percent in 2005 and 10.1 percent in 2006 (Neff 2007). In 2006, CFRB swept the highest awards[7] in the advertising industry and its sister industry, public relations. In 2007, however, sales growth dwindled to 1.2 percent (Neff 2007), and industry pundits questioned whether sales were connected to advertisements for Dove's Pro-Age product line (featuring unclothed women over age fifty) that perhaps "went a step too far in embracing aging in all its naked, wrinkled and sagging glory" (Neff 2007). The same year, controversy over the realness of CFRB's texts may have impacted sales when retoucher Pascal Dangin implied in an interview that he had altered the Pro-Age texts (Collins 2008). While Dove denied any textual modifications and Dangin retracted his statements, the public realization that there had (or could have) been retouching may have generalized to a lack of textual and brand authenticity. In 2008, although the "brand reportedly gained $1.2 billion in value" (Molitor 2008) since CFRB's launch, Dove's unhappiness with its sales led to a re-assessment of CFRB. The Movement may be CFRB's tactic to restore its integrity with audiences to bolster sales. More than previous CFRB strategies, the Movement incites ideological brand commitment through focusing on women's "depth of involvement, the engagement, the participation and the commitment of moving people to take action" (Molitor 2008). The Movement may also be a way for Dove to publicly emphasize the brand bond with consumers, thereby minimizing the role of industry insiders.

"Real beauty" is an oppressive ideology that reinforces the value of female beauty and its pursuit by garnering women's agreement with its values of ideological and material consumption. At its core is a paradox: while apparently decrying it, "real beauty" embraces conformity to hegemonic beauty standards through both corporate instigation for brand attachment and women s striving to be part of what they may feel is a positive beauty ideology. "Real beauty," then, is "diluted by its contradictory imperative to promote self-acceptance and at the same time increase sales by promoting women s consumption of products that encourage conformity to feminine beauty ideology" (Johnson & Taylor 2008, p. 962). CFRB's "real" women, whose beauty deviates from the beauty norm in size and/or color, lend credibility to the campaign and invite female audiences to self-brand as a "real beauty"; yet, this identity aligns with being a consumer of a corporate brand strategy that positions itself in the feminist role as an advocate for social change that promises to empower women. The stakes are high for audiences who agree with CFRB's meanings of "real beauty," and may intensify when such popularized meanings of empowerment are drawn on and reinforced as cultural norms by future brands. . . . Like cause marketing, this cause branding strategy "is merely a cleverly disguised ploy to mask some of the fundamental problems for which the very same marketing forces are directly or indirectly responsible" (Stole 2008, p. 34). Within this consumer context, commercial connotations are attached to popular messages and practices of philanthropy (Stole 2008).

There is much work to be done to arrive at a strong collective feminist voice of what empowering female beauty means for current and future audiences. As feminist media studies scholar Angela McRobbie suggests, this action may "entail the resuscitation and re-conceptualization of feminist anti-capitalism" (2008, p. 548). . . . CFRB s partnership between female cultural producers and a corporation is problematic at best.

Notes

1. Countries represented at The G(irls) 20 Summit and the G20 Summit are Argentina, Australia, Brazil, Canada, China, France, Germany, India, Indonesia, Italy, Japan, Mexico, Russia, Saudi Arabia, South Africa, South Korea, Turkey, UK, USA and the European Union.

2. Women who participated included Dr. Jennifer Scott and Heidi D'Agostino of research firm StrategyOne; Dr. Nancy Etcoff, Harvard psychologist; and Dr. Susie Orbach, author of *Fat Is a Feminist Issue.*

3. See "Welcome to Dove" for a list of countries.

4. Industry insiders confirmed that there is no single database for global CFRB texts. A search of texts in the major markets where CFRB was created (the UK, the US, and Canada) found minor differences in the images and language that did not substantially alter the messaging. The US texts were selected since they are among the first set of texts, the United States is a major market, and they were accessible. This analysis thus focuses on the US texts.

5. The feminist movement is generally regarded as comprising three "waves" whose dates are as follows: the first wave occurred from the late nineteenth century to the 1930s; the second wave occurred from the 1960s to the 1980s; the third wave began in the 1990s and characterizes the present time.

6. The author was granted permission to reproduce the First-Wave and Third-Wave portraits and Third-Wave body shots, but not the Second-Wave portrait and composite portrait of the women (these images, accordingly, are not included in the article).

7. The UK version says, "fat? fit?" and the Canadian version asks, "fat? fab?" These sentiments are strikingly similar to the US version.

8. "Beyond Stereotypes" (2005) collected information from 3,300 girls and women from ten countries; "Beauty Comes of Age" (2006) surveyed 1,450 women from nine countries; and "Real Girls, Real Pressure" (2008) surveyed 1,029 American girls.

9. Awards include: Cannes Advertising's Grand Effie Award, Cannes' Film Grand Prix and Cyber Grand Prix, Global Campaign of the Year by Advertising Age, Consumer Launch Campaign of the Year by PR Week, and Best of Silver Anvil Award from the Public Relations Society of America.

References

About The Movement (WEB PAGE) (2010) *Dove/Unilever,* [Online] Available at: http://www. dovemovement.com/movement/about (1 November 2010).

Andrejevic, Mark (2007) *iSpy: Surveillance and Power in the Interactive Era*, University Press of Kansas, Lawrence.

Arvidsson, Adam (2006) *Brands: Meaning and Value in Media Culture,* Routledge, New York.

Bartky, Sandra Lee (1990) *Femininity and Domination: Studies in the Phenomenology of Oppression*, New York, Routledge.

Bignell, Jonathan (1997) *Media Semiotics: An Introduction,* St. Martin's Press, New York.

Bordo, Susan (2003) *Unbearable Weight: Feminism, Western Culture, and the Body*, University of California Press, Berkeley.

Branding Evolution: The Dove Story (Web Page) (2007) *The Manufacturer*, [Online] Available at: http://www.themanufacturer.com/us/ content/5640/Branding_evolution%3A_ the_Do- ve_story (10 October 2010).

Byerly, Carolyn M. & Ross, Karen (2006) *Women & Media: A Critical Introduction,* Blackwell Publishing, Malden.

Campaign For Real Beauty (Web Page) (2008) *Dove/Unilever,* [Online] Available at: http://www.dove.us/#/CFRB/arti_cfrb. aspx[cp-documentid=7049726]/ (1 April 2008).

Collins, Lauren (2008) 'Pixel perfect: Pascal Dangin's virtual reality', *The New Yorker*, [Online] Available at: http://www.newyorker .com/reporting/2008/05/12/fa_fact_ collins?currentPa- ge=all (14 May 2008).

Color Wheel Pro (Web Page) (2010) *QSX Software Group,* [Online] Available at: http://www.color-wheel-pro.com/color-meaning.html (2 June 2008).

Cone, Carol L. (2000) 'Cause branding in the 21st century', *Public Service Advertising Research Center,* [Online] Available at: http://www.psaresearch.com/causebranding .html (5 October 2010).

Cruikshank, Barbara (1993) 'Revolutions within: self-government and self-esteem', *Economy and Society,* vol. 22, no. 3, pp. 327–344.

Danesi, Marcel (2002) *Understanding Media Semiotics,* Oxford Publishing Press, New York.

Dove Exposes The Beauty Myth To Reveal 'Real Beauty' To Women In The Middle East (Press Release On Web Page) (2007) *Dove/Unilever,* [Online] Available at: http://www.campaignforrealbeauty.ae/press .asp?url=press.asp&section=news&id=7221 (3 June 2008).

Dove Manifesto (Print) (2004) [Online] Available at: http://www.coloribus.com/adsarchive/prints/dove-skincare-products-dove-manifesto-6606505/ (5 June 2008).

Duffy, Brooke Erin (2010) 'Empowerment through endorsement? Polysemic meaning in Dove's user-generated advertising', *Communication, Culture & Critique,* vol. 3, pp. 26–43.

Durham, Meenakshi Gigi (2008) *The Lolita Effect: The Media Sexualization of Young Girls and What We Can Do About It,* The Overlook Press, New York.

Dworkin, Andrea (1974) *Woman Hating,* E.P. Dutton, New York.

Dyer, Stephanie (2004) 'Lifestyles of the media rich and oligopolistic', in *Censored 2005: The Top 25 Censored Stories,* ed. Peter Phillips, Seven Stories Press, New York.

Etcoff, Nancy, Orbach, Susie, Scott, Jennifer & D'agostino, Heidi (2004) 'The real truth about beauty: a global report: findings of the global study on women, beauty and well-being' [Online] Available at: http://www.campaignforrealbeauty.com/uploadedfiles/dove_white_paper_final.pdf (5 June 2008).

Evolution. (videorecording) (2006) [Online] Available at: http://www.youtube.com/watch?-v=iYhCn0jf46U (10 October 2010).

Fielding, Daryl, Lewis, Dennis, White, Mel, Manfredi, Alessandro & Scott, Linda (2008) 'Dove campaign roundtable, *Advertising & Society Review,* vol. 9, no. 4 [Online] Project MUSE, Available at: http://muse.jhu.edu.proxy.libraries.rutgers.edu/ (22 October 2010).

Fiske, John (2000) 'The codes of television , in *Media Studies: A Reader,* eds Paul Marris & Sue Thornham, New York University Press, New York, pp. 220–230.

Gill, Rosalind (2007) *Gender and the Media,* Polity, Cambridge.

Goldman, Robert (1992) *Reading Ads Socially,* Routledge, New York.

Hearn, Alison (2008) '"Meat, mask, burden:" probing the contours of the branded "self,"' *Journal of Consumer Culture,* vol. 8, no. 2, pp. 197–217.

Jenkins, Henry (2006) *Convergence Culture: Where Old and New Media Collide,* New York University Press, New York.

Jhally, Sut (2003) 'Image-based culture: advertising and popular culture', in *Gender, Race, and Class in Media: A Text-Reader,* eds Gail Dines & Jean M. Humez, Sage Publications, Thousand Oaks, CA.

Johnson, M. K. (2008) 'Is Naomi wolf pulling punches for Dove's real beauty campaign?', *Lucire,* [Online] Available at: http://lucire.com/insider/20080215/is-naomi-wolf-pulling-punches-for-doves-real-beauty-campaign (10 June 2010).

Johnston, Josee & Taylor, Judith (2008) 'Feminist consumerism and fat activists: a comparative study of grassroots activism and the dove real beauty campaign', *Signs: Journal of Women in Culture and Society,* vol. 33, no. 4, pp. 941–966.

Kilbourne, Jean (1999) *Can't Buy My Love: How Advertising Changes the Way We Think and Feel* Simon & Schuster, New York.

Lachover, Einat & Brandes, Sigal Barak (2009) 'A beautiful campaign? Analysis of public discourse in Israel surrounding the dove campaign for real beauty', *Feminist Media Studies,* vol. 9, no. 3, pp. 301–316.

McRobbie, Angela (2008) 'Young women and consumer culture: an intervention', *Cultural Studies,* vol. 22, no. 5, pp. 531–550.

Molitor, Dori (2008) 'In dove we trust', *The Hub Magazine*, [Online] Available at: http://www.hubmagazine.com/html/2008/may_jun/womanwise.html (1 October 2010).

Neff, Jack (2007) 'Soft soap', *Advertising Age*, vol. 78, no. 38, p. 1.

O'barr, William M., Lazarus, Shelly & Moreira, Marcio (2008) 'Global advertising', *Advertising & Society Review*, vol. 9, no. 4 [Online] Project MUSE, Available at: http://muse.jhu.edu.proxy.libraries.rutgers.edu/ (1 October 2010).

Our Vision: Join Us (Web Page) (2010) Dove/Unilever, [Online] Available at: http://www.dovemovement.com/declaration/sign (5 October 2010).

Seiter, Ellen (1992) 'Semiotics, structuralism, and television', in Channels of Discourse, *Reassembled: Television and Contemporary Criticism*, ed. Robert C. Allen, The University of North Carolina Press, Chapel Hill.

Stole, Inger L. (2008) 'Philanthropy as public relations: a critical perspective on cause marketing', *International Journal of Communication*, vol. 2, pp. 20–40.

Tasker, Yvonne & Negra, Diane (2007) '*Introduction: feminist politics and postfeminist culture*', in Interrogating Postfeminism: Gender and the Politics of Popular Culture, eds Yvonne Tasker & Diane Negra, Duke University Press, Durham, pp. 1–25.

True Colors (videorecording) (2006) [Online] Available at: http://video.google.com/videoplay?-docid=1731400614466797113# (2 June 2008).

Welcome To Dove (web page) (2010) [Online] Available at: http://www.dove.com/?ref=dove (1 October 2010).

Williamson, Judith (1978) *Decoding Advertisements: Ideology and Meaning in Advertising*, Marion Boyars Publishers, New York.

Woodhull (Web Page) (2007) *The Woodhull Institute for Ethical Leadership*, [Online] Available at: http://www.woodhull.org/gallery/index.php (20 June 2008).

32

Nothing Less Than Perfect

Female Celebrity, Ageing, and Hyper-Scrutiny in the Gossip Industry

Kirsty Fairclough

Introduction

... Female celebrities have become the chief site upon which contemporary tensions and anxieties surrounding femininity, motherhood, body image, cosmetic surgery, marriage and ageing are played out. The corporeal is the principal means by which the famous women are now represented; it is the celebrity's face and body that become the locus for discussion in both printed and online discourse. These bodies are still revered and aspired to, but they are also exposed, examined and scrutinised in order to reveal their corporeal construction. In an increasingly individualistic culture, a woman's outward appearance represents her entire selfhood, and it is both pertinent and timely to examine the flow of discourses about ageing and cosmetic surgery that circulate in and out of celebrity culture.

Popular discourses surrounding female celebrities and cosmetic surgery most often emerge from a post-feminist perspective. Post-feminism is a term made up of multiple and conflicting meanings, and in this context, I refer to Rosalind Gill's conception of post-feminism as a distinctive sensibility consisting of a number of interrelated themes. These include 'Femininity as a bodily property; the shift from objectification to subjectification; an emphasis upon self surveillance, monitoring and self-discipline; a focus on individualism, choice and empowerment; the dominance of a makeover paradigm; and a resurgence of ideas about natural sexual difference' (Gill 2007, p. 148). These themes have provided the basis for analysis by some feminist scholars and are a useful touchstone from which to ground this analysis. In celebrity culture, transgression of post-feminist norms is subject

From Fairclough, K. (2012). Nothing less than perfect: Female celebrity, ageing and hyperscrutiny in the gossip industry. *Celebrity Studies*, 3(1), 90–103. Reprinted by permission of Taylor & Francis Ltd., www.tandf.co.uk/journals.

to excoriating attack, particularly in the case of ageing and cosmetic surgery. The age narrative is a central trope in gossip culture where the perpetual discussion of the age of female celebrities and whether their behaviour, lifestyle and look are 'age appropriate' reflects a deeply entrenched double standard.

Gossip Tropes and Ageing

Celebrity gossip is of course nothing new. Gossip mavens such as Louella Parsons and Hedda Hopper were prolific during the Hollywood Studio System and often operated in conjunction with the studios. Later, the gossip industry began to provide the public with more salacious rumour and scandal about Hollywood stars through magazines such as *Confidential*. In the digital era, the gossip industry is thriving. From well-known gossip mavens such as *Perezhilton* and *Laineygossip* to spin-off sites associated with tabloid and gossip magazines such as *US Weekly* and *Heat,* the celebrity gossip blog is now firmly embedded within celebrity culture and is hinged on the hyper-scrutiny of the famous. . . .

The gender politics of contemporary celebrity is highly visible through the gossip blog, often a more derisive alternative to the printed gossip magazine, which actively deconstructs the female celebrity image in ways that are distinctly post-feminist in that they encourage and privilege hyper-femininity and perpetual transformation, and often espouse conservative views regarding gender roles. Celebrity gossip magazines and blogs lock women in a seemingly endless process of reinventing the neo-liberal self, providing sites to negotiate this self through evaluating celebrities and their lifestyle choices, allowing the facade of choice to be deeply inscribed within it. In this context, gossip bloggers have the ability to essentially eradicate the carefully crafted image that

the entertainment industry works to cultivate and maintain. As Anne-Helen Petersen suggests, 'As new media technology makes New Hollywood's mechanisms visible, gossip bloggers utilise this visibility to influence consumption. Bloggers illuminate the star system, and in so doing, alter our expectations and understanding of stars and their importance in society today' (Petersen 2007).

It is certainly not new to suggest that ageing as represented in the mainstream media is linked to a range of negative connotations. In popular culture the older female body is particularly vilified. Ageing is configured in contemporary society as a kind of narcissistic problem and exists as an embarrassing reminder to a celebrity-obsessed transformation focused society that ultimately there is no successful way to fight it. Audiences are constantly bombarded with ways to overcome the ageing 'problem' through advertising, marketing, the visibility of youthful older people in celebrity culture and through the promotion of a lifestyle trajectory that suggests there is no need to succumb to old age any longer, as the technologies exist to stave it off or at least keep it at bay. . . .

To this end, there has been both an intensification of the visibility and sexual objectification of the older woman in popular culture, particularly on US and UK television with series such as *Desperate Housewives* (Channel 4 2004–present), *Cougar Town* (ABC 2009–present) and *Mistresses* (BBC 2008–2010) . . . , all of which feature the relationships between groups of women post-forty. This may be seen as a positive shift in the representation of 'older' women and is in line with more general societal attitudes, where representations of ageing have undergone seismic shifts in recent years. More active populations, lifestyle industries creating an idealised older age and cosmetic surgery developments and its accessibility have contributed to a perceived 'ageless' society. This idea became entrenched in popular culture as the baby boomer generation aged. . . . Yet as a consequence of these shifts, and especially in a post-feminist context, women are not allowed to grow old naturally and are encouraged to fight the ageing process at every turn, as there is apparently no reason not to engage with technologies to stave off ageing when they are seemingly available to all. This places further responsibility on the individual in a neo-liberal context, where they must be in complete control of their own lives and ageing process. Indeed, in a post-feminist, neo-liberal society, ageing is not something to be feared, but must be both celebrated and fought; women must battle nature in order to look much younger to adhere to and maintain the fantasy of the sexualised middle-aged woman. In this stage of life, women are encouraged to adopt strict regimes in order to be considered still attractive and youthful. . . .

Ageing in the Spotlight

It has long been stated that male-dominated Hollywood is notoriously ageist against women. Men can continue long and successful careers in the film industry as they age, and yet their women peers struggle to continue to secure lead roles and are rendered almost invisible. Actors, such as Harrison Ford, Michael Douglas, Sylvester Stallone and Clint Eastwood, continue to undertake major roles whilst moving beyond middle age. Women are far less visible in major roles as they age, and the normative structure for women in roles post-fifty is that their ageing is part of the narrative, as seen in recent films such as *Mamma Mia* (2008), *The Women* (2008), *Sex and the City* 1 (2008), *Sex and the City* 2 (2010) and *It's Complicated* (2009). For men, ageing is rarely considered part of the nexus of their characters. Indeed, the male is often portrayed as the ageless 'hero', where the film disregards

their age, imagining that time has stood still for the character, especially in reference to a sequel or franchise. Hollywood has long fed age anxieties and it has become an oft-repeated exhortation that there are few interesting roles for older actresses in Hollywood. However, the recent visibility of older women on screen and the greater coverage of older women in the gossip industry in general has been posited as a progressive move towards inclusivity. Yet, discourses surrounding these women are first and foremost framed in terms of narratives of ageing, which are always structured in terms of how well the actress is managing her ageing process.

This utopian ideal of transcending time through cosmetic surgery is firmly ensconced in celebrity culture and its seductive aura is one that has been routinely criticised by feminists and cultural studies scholars alike. Cosmetic surgery in celebrity culture attempts to judge women by a particular beauty norm. This norm aims to construct women as ageless, the face must be taut and smooth, but must no longer adhere to the often-mocked early advances in face lift technologies, such as the 'wind tunnel' look of the 1980s and 1990s, it must be devoid of wrinkles and the body must be toned and slender, with evidence of the disciplined, yet discreet work that has been undertaken to achieve it. Indeed, it would appear that the older woman may well be visible in gossip culture, but she should never look her age.

Gossip, Surgery and Hyper-scrutiny

. . . The culture of hyper-scrutiny that exists within the gossip industry is explicit and contradictory. Aside from well-known gossip mavens, sites such as awfulplasticsurgery.com and famousplastic.com track alleged celebrity surgery in minute detail and allow readers to view detailed images of celebrity surgery. Such sites present categories such as *Bad Brow Lift, Bad Cheekbone Implants* and *Awful Plastic Surgery Victims* and simultaneously deride and revere the processes of surgical transformation, both mocking the celebrity but offering the reader advice and guidance on surgical procedures, where to gain advice, and so on . . .

Sites such as these present their versions of 'appropriate' and 'inappropriate' age maintenance with sections featuring 'monstrous' examples of surgery, those that congratulate celebrities for getting their surgery 'right' and those that deride the celebrity for attempting to transcend time or more pertinently, making visible the signs of labour involved in maintaining a youthful look. They highlight the perceived difficulties in attempting to maintain an appropriately feminine public image, career and private life. . . .

Many gossip sites offer the reader paths of negotiation regarding staving off the ageing process where correct and incorrect versions of celebrity ageing are presented and justified. This kind of discourse is not exclusive to individual bloggers: in August 2010 the following discussion of Madonna appeared on *Femail*, the UK's *Daily Mail* newspaper online site and was widely disseminated across a number of gossip sites:

> With her fresh complexion and taut skin, she would have been the envy of many women half her age. In fact, Madonna looked so youthful as she arrived at her 52nd birthday party in London at the weekend that some even drew favourable comparisons with her 13-year-old daughter Lourdes. Sadly for the singer, however, there was one telltale sign that she has not been immune to the ageing process. A look at her hands as she clutched her black bag and a chunky gold crucifix showed that there are some things that even careful make-up and a tough gym regime can't hide. (www .mailonline 2010a)

Here Madonna is both praised for her 'fresh complexion' and 'taut skin', usually represented as the result of numerous cosmetic interventions, and she is then compared with a teenager. The strict regime that Madonna undergoes to maintain her look is commended, but it is also made clear that not *even* Madonna, the foremost example of extreme health and beauty discipline, is 'immune' to ageing and that this is a 'sad', but inevitable state. In gossip culture these discourses can be deeply contradictory where not to engage in practices of transformation means certain descent into career oblivion and engaging in too 'obvious' a way suggests desperation. Famous women are not considered 'true stars' if they make the signs of labour too obvious in the gossip industry. Female celebrities have long been hounded by the media for attempting to remain youthful by utilising the technologies available to them. British actress Lesley Ash was one of the first high-profile women to experience such vitriolic responses. In 2003 Ash underwent a collagen lip filler procedure that went wrong, giving her unnaturally large lips, which was deemed the 'Trout Pout' by British tabloid newspapers. She was then vilified in the press and gossip industry as an example of selfish indulgence; a desperate woman trying to stave off ageing.

Surgical and Ageing Typologies in the Gossip Industry

I want now to consider how typical discourses in the gossip industry and blog in particular, generally place female celebrities into surgical and ageing categories, which I shall identify here as the 'gruesome', the 'desperate' and the 'sanctioned'. These categories effectively outline the flow of discourse that pervades gossip culture in relation to female celebrity and place women into particular groups, which are then often integrated into their star images and become part of the circulation of discourse in relation to their celebrity status.

THE GRUESOME

Most apparent is the celebrity as gruesome object. . . . These gruesome women are positioned as abject freaks, who lie outside the boundaries of appropriate and acceptable feminine selves. They possess a macabre and morbid look, which operates as a reminder of the perils of both ageing and indulging in excessive cosmetic surgery. Celebrities such as Cher, Lil' Kim, Joan Rivers, Priscilla Presley, Joan Van Ark, LaToya Jackson, Alicia Douvall, Janice Dickinson, Melanie Griffith, Courtney Love, Lara Flynn Boyle and, most notoriously, Jocelyn Van Wildenstein are routinely discussed in these terms. . . .

Cher regularly features in discourses surrounding the gruesome version of the celebrity face. She has been perceived as the poster girl for cosmetic surgery since the 1990s, and formerly her look was praised in terms of how well she appeared to transcend her age. More recently, however, the tone of coverage in gossip culture has become increasingly malicious. At the December 2010 premiere of her film *Burlesque,* Cher was described as looking glamorous and youthful on the red carpet (Daily Mail 2010b). However, close ups later revealed face lift tape hidden just beneath her jaw line. She was predictably vilified across the gossip industry and was seen as desperately attempting to cling on to youth, but this moment was also widely seen as an acceptable improvement on her 'natural' look when she was photographed shortly after in natural daylight. Cher's *faux pas* was perceived as bizarre, gruesome and monstrous, a rather pathetic attempt to hold back, literally, her already heavily surgically enhanced face. Indeed, the celebrity that makes their cosmetic surgery too obvious, as in Cher's case, and becomes cast as gruesome is rejected by culture and becomes

a spectacle to be ridiculed rather than revered. . . . Despite her seemingly following all the 'acceptable' paths, the result is that of a face that embodies both horror and fascination. As with all cosmetic surgery narratives in gossip culture, this is deeply problematic and contradictory and these women then become part of the carnivalesque matrix of post-feminist makeover culture, operating as both spectacle and caveat, warning the reader that there is a price to pay for overindulging in technologies of cosmetic surgery.

THE DESPERATE

The second category constructed by the gossip industry is the 'desperate'. Celebrities in this group are generally over forty and have often had successful careers. They are configured as desperate to remain youthful in order to suspend time and reclaim their once glittering careers and images, but are often constructed as failing at both. Examples of such women include Nicole Kidman, Meg Ryan, Sharon Stone and Pamela Anderson. They are positioned as rarely, if ever, making any public acknowledgement of cosmetic surgery and are pursued by the gossip industry on precisely these terms. Here the celebrity is both maligned and praised, often treated as anxiously attempting to remain relevant to the extent that the reconfiguring of their celebrity through cosmetic surgery becomes more visible than their actual work. A pertinent example of this is Nicole Kidman who appears regularly in the gossip industry and whose star image has been altered considerably by gossip culture. Generally considered a serious and accomplished actress, her star image is becoming more tenuous and is at times located in the category of 'has-been' in some quarters of the gossip industry. High-profile bloggers such as Perez Hilton and Lainey Liu of *Laineygossip* have been scathing in their discussion of Kidman. Both appear to hinge their dislike on

Kidman's lack of authenticity, based on the fact that she appears to have undergone various cosmetic procedures but refuses to acknowledge them. *Laineygossip* has taken particular issue with this invisibility of the 'authentic' self by renaming Kidman 'Granny Freeze'. Subsequently, *Laineygossip* has also named Kidman's body parts and has given them a particular narrative of their own. Kidman's supposedly collagen-enhanced lips are now deemed by the blogger as 'Third Lip'. Hilton regularly states that she has a 'frozen face' and discussion surrounding Kidman suggests that she is no longer relevant to the industry, having become old and inauthentic. Consider the following 2010 post from *Perezhilton. com*:

> Nicole Kidman is a stickler for denying that she has had any work done, even though you could build an ice rink on her forehead. But it's actually another part of her anatomy that got people's attention at Wednesday's CMA Awards — her lips! Sources are claiming that the actress showed up at the event with hubby Keith Urban looking like she had just had her lips done. One witness said she looked 'freakish' and compared her to Meg Ryan! Ouch! It is obvious she has had massive amounts of Botox put in her face, but the lips . . . we're not sure. They sure look like they've been plumped, but we wouldn't go as far to call them freakish. Maybe it's just because we've seen worse. What do you think? *(PerezHilton.com)*

Here Hilton suggests Kidman should be open with the public regarding cosmetic surgery in order to gain approval and popularity. Kidman is compared with Meg Ryan, whose star image has plummeted in recent years, post lip augmentation. No longer perceived as America's favourite romantic comedy sweetheart, she is repeatedly represented as a bitter older woman. These celebrities operate in a difficult space: they are considered fraudulent, yet appealing, ugly yet beautiful, has-beens, yet in demand.

These are the women who face the most vitriol, represented as oscillating between nostalgic notions of a better version of themselves and a reinvented youthful version of middle age that is balanced precariously between the beautiful and the grotesque.

THE SANCTIONED

Lastly, the sanctioned refers to those celebrities who are positioned by the gossip industry as ageing well and who have purportedly employed the technologies of cosmetic surgery in 'acceptable' ways according to the post-feminism and who are held up as beautiful, womanly and appropriately feminine. Examples in this category include Demi Moore, Halle Berry, Charlize Theron, Cindy Crawford, Andie McDowell and Sandra Bullock.

What links these women is their ability to remain 'ageless', as if they have frozen middle age and left it somehow suspended. This is widely praised in gossip culture, but is of course precarious.

Demi Moore is a particularly good example of a celebrity who is depicted as engaging in such practices, since she is often held up as the epitome of cosmetic surgery 'done right'. Moore starred in a number of successful films during the 1990s including *Ghost* (1990), *A Few Good Men* (1992) and *Indecent Proposal* (1993), resulting in her being one of the highest paid Hollywood actresses of the decade. More recently she has repositioned herself in the industry. She is married to actor Ashton Kutcher, 15 years her junior, and is consistently featured in the gossip industry as a celebrity who has managed to negotiate the ageing process skilfully. Rather than entering the category of the abject, freakish or desperate, despite her repeated denial of surgery, she is desirable and 'appropriately' feminine . . .

Moore also became an early Twitter user, demonstrating her knowledge of the mechanisms of the blogosphere and social networking, regularly posting commentary in response to particular stories about her look, age and surgery rumours in the gossip industry and also cementing her status as youthful. Her ability to suspend time and her visibility and participation in gossip culture have both revived her star image and brought her to the attention of a new generation of fans.

Yet, this group is not immune to derogatory discussion. Perez Hilton routinely comments upon Moore's image and suggests that she is ageing well, whilst behaving in ways that are age inappropriate. In a 2010 post, for example, he commented:

> Isn't she a little old for this?! Demi Moore may have felt the need for everyone to look at her because the 47-year-old actress took to her Twitter to post pics of her bikini body. The photos were given the caption, 'Maybe this is more like summer!' It's not that she doesn't look great, but we're starting to understand where her daughters get the need to let their goods hang out. Grow up, honey! (*PerezHilton.com*)

In gossip culture, discourse surrounding cosmetic surgery is most concerned with the celebrities' visible management of ageing and how well they tap into technologies that will allow youth to be extended through the face. This linking of age and surgery becomes the nexus of post-feminist rhetoric, assuming that the reader can become as beautiful and youthful as Moore if they only use the technologies available to become an empowered and appropriately feminine older woman. It is these markers of femininity that are linked with Moore and her youthful look, the long, glossy hair, the lean body, the wrinkle-free face.

She is often pitted against other actresses of her generation such as Meg Ryan, who is represented as desperate, old and frumpy because she failed to employ cosmetic technologies successfully, whilst Moore is youthful, fun and hyper-feminine. . . .

Botox Babies

There are other types of discourse reverberating around female celebrity and ageing in gossip culture. Recently, media attention has focused on the issue of much younger women undergoing cosmetic procedures before they reach an age where the visible signs of ageing are even present. It must be recognised that many have never known anything but a culture where cosmetic surgery is performed on women routinely. There has been growing 'concern' in the gossip industry regarding the use of cosmetic surgery on women and young girls who are deemed too young, certainly propelled by the 23-year-old star of MTV's reality series *The Hills* (2006–2010) Heidi Montag and her much publicised cosmetic procedures. The term 'Botox Babies' has been used to describe young women who undergo surgical enhancement, such as singer Charice Pempengco, who recently appeared on television having Botox at 18 years old, as she reportedly wanted to look 'fresh' for her appearance on the hit US television show *Glee*. Heidi Montag represents the results of the era's cultural pressure and appears to have succumbed to the crippling images of beauty that abound in popular culture.

Montag reportedly underwent 10 surgical procedures in a single day including a chin reduction, liposuction and rhinoplasty, resulting in an extreme physical transformation that was unveiled through the gossip industry. The work prompted widespread condemnation from the media who were quick to label her 'Franken-Heidi' and 'Franken-Barbie', relating her surgeries to mental health problems. . . .

Montag's face is now a composite of what is culturally coded as beautiful, sexual and feminine. Her almond-shaped eyes, petite nose, full lips, large breasts and tightly sculpted body are constructed from a set of norms that are valued culturally, yet they appear at odds with an individual in early womanhood. Indeed, Heidi seems to be gazing out, trapped from underneath her face, her surgeries speaking for her, telling her that she is her 'best self.' Montag may well function as the epitome of a post-feminist culture that places so much emphasis on the image that a woman so young felt she had to conform, to make her, in her words, 'like Barbie' (www.people .com 2010) and assist her in reclaiming some sense of agency, now she has become effectively a living embodiment of a Barbie doll. Montag has been widely condemned because her surgery appears far removed from the current prescribed look, which in order to remain within the boundaries of acceptability should not reveal the work. The trickery lies in the ability to disguise the labour involved in order to maintain the alignment of the inner self and the outer self.

However, the contradictory nature of the ways in which cosmetic surgery is represented in popular culture, as indulgent, excessive and unnecessary, pitted against desirable, necessary and normal, complicates and fragments the ideal self so it becomes hopelessly unstable. The juxtaposition of fear and desire associated with cosmetic surgery and the complexity and intertwined nature of celebrity and makeover cultures makes the boundaries of acceptable and desirable cosmetic surgery even narrower and ever more elusive.

Youthful beauty as evidenced in celebrity culture now appears to be the only type of beauty to aspire to. Weber suggests celebrity functions as a playing field on which a fascinated and perplexed culture negotiates sites of identity (Weber 2009, p. 235). Indeed individuals use celebrity as a nexus of identity negotiation. Through the matrix of post-feminism and gossip culture, a new beauty norm has been created advocating the use of cosmetic procedures on younger women, a norm that suggests youth must be held in limbo through the use of cosmetic procedures throughout adult life and for as long as possible. . . .

References

A Few Good Men, 1992. Film. Directed by Rob Reiner. USA: Castle Rock Entertainment.

Blum, V., 2003. *Flesh wounds: the culture of cosmetic surgery.* Berkeley, CA: University of California Press.

Cougar Town, 2009–present. Film. Directed by Michael McDonald. USA: Doozer/Coquette Productions.

Daily Mail, 2010a. Madonna, still a smooth operator at 52 as she celebrates birthday with daughter Lourdes. *Daily Mail* 16 Aug. [online]. Available from: http://www.daily mail.co.uk/tvshowbiz/article-1303369/ Madonna-smooth-operator-52--hands-havent-stood-test-time-face.html [Accessed 20 August 2010].

Daily Mail, 2010b. So that's why you need face tape, Cher... 24 hours after red carpet appearance, 64-year-old shows her natural side. *Daily Mail* 15 Dec. [online]. Available from: http://www.dailymail.co.uk/tvshowbiz/ article-1338296/Cher-64-shows-needed-facelift-tape-Burlesque-premiere.html [accessed 15 December 2010].

Desperate Housewives, 2004–present. Film. Directed by Larry Shaw. USA: Cherry Alley Productions.

Ghost, 1990. Film. Directed by Gerry Zucker. USA: Paramount Pictures.

Gill, R., 2007. Postfeminist media culture: elements of a sensibility. *European journal of cultural studies,* 10, 147–166.

Gilleard, C., 2005. Cultural approaches to the ageing body. *In:* J. Bengtson, V. Coleman, and P. Kirkwood, eds. *The Cambridge handbook of age and ageing.* Cambridge: Cambridge University Press, 156–163.

Good Morning America, 1975–present. Film. Directors various. USA: ABC News.

Hills, 2006–2010. Film. Directed by Hisham Abed. USA: Reel Security/ MTV.

Indecent Proposal, 1993. Film. Directed by Adrian Lyne. USA: Paramount Pictures.

It's Complicated, 2009. Film. Directed by Nancy Meyers. USA: Universal Pictures.

Jones, M., 2008. *Skintight: an anatomy of cosmetic surgery.* London: Berg.

Mamma Mia!, 2008. Film. Directed by Phylilda Lloyd. USA: Universal Pictures.

Mistresses, 2008–2010. BBC.

Negra, D. and Holmes, S., 2008. Going cheap? Female celebrity in the reality, tabloid and scandal genres. *Genders special issue* [online], 48. Available from: http://www.genders.org/g48/ g48_negraholmes.html [accessed 10 April 2011].

Petersen, A., 2007. Celebrity juice, not from concentrate: Perez Hilton, gossip blogs, and the new star production. *Jump cut: A review of contemporary media,* Spring, 49.

Sex and the City 1, 2008. Film. Directed by Michael Patrick King. USA: New Line.

Sex and the City 2, 2010. Film. Directed by Michael Patrick King. USA: New Line.

Shildrick, M., 2002. *Embodying the monster: encounters with the vulnerable self.* London: Sage.

The Hills, 2006–2010. MTV.

The Women, 2008. Film. Directed by Diane English. USA: Picture house Entertainment.

Wearing, S., 2007. Subjects of rejuvenation: aging in postfeminist culture. *In:* Y. Tasker and D. Negra, eds. *Interrogating postfeminism; gender and the politics of popular culture.* Durham, NC: Duke University Press, 277–311.

Weber, B., 2009. *Makeover TV: selfhood, citizenship and celebrity.* Durham, NC: Duke University Press.

Woodward, K., 2006. Performing age, performing gender. *NWSA journal,* 18 (1), 162–189.

www.abcnews.com, 2010. Heidi Montag interview prompts huge response. *www.abcnews .com* 20 Jan. [online]. Available from: http://abcnews.go.com/GMA/Entertainment/heidi-montag-interview-plastic-surgery-prompts-huge-response/story?id=9610622 [accessed 12 April 2011].

www.people.com, 2010. Heidi Montag; my surgeries aren't an addiction. *www.people.com* 19 Jan. [online]. Available from: http://www.people.com/people/artic1e/0,,20337744,00 .html [accessed 12 April 2011].

Available from: www.laineygossip.com

Available from: www.perezhilton.com [accessed 16 December 2010].

33

To See and Be Seen

Celebrity Practice on Twitter

Alice Marwick and danah boyd

Introduction

Networked media is changing celebrity culture, the ways that people relate to celebrity images, how celebrities are produced, and how celebrity is practiced. Gossip websites, fan sites, and blogs provide a plethora of new locations for the circulation and creation of celebrity, moving between user-generated content and the mainstream media. The fragmented media landscape has created a shift in traditional understanding of 'celebrity management' from a highly controlled and regulated institutional model to one in which performers and personalities actively address and interact with fans.

Celebrity Theories

. . . Although famous people represent an increasingly significant part of mass media, for many academics, they personify the trivial, dangerous decadence of American culture (Ewen, 1989; Lowenthal, 1961). In keeping with this viewpoint, people who enjoy consuming celebrity culture have been pathologized, portrayed as miserable or lonely, or seen as cultural dupes (Feasey, 2008; Jensen, 1992). However, celebrity images are culturally pervasive; they have become part of our day-to-day lives (Turner, 2004: 17) and part of the raw material through which we construct identities and engage in public discourse (Feasey, 2008; Gamson, 1994). More recently, fandom has become a subject of study in its own right (Baym, 2000; Jenkins, 1992, 2006b). In the tradition of active audience studies, theories of 'participatory culture' examine how people draw from media texts to create and produce their own cultural products (Jenkins, 2006a; Lessig, 2004). Understanding not only how the celebrity construct functions as a product within media industries, but how

From Alice Marwick and danah boyd (2011), "To See and Be Seen: Celebrity Practice on Twitter," *Convergence*, 17: 139–158. Reprinted with permission of SAGE Publications, Ltd.

and why people make meaning from celebrity culture in their daily lives, is essential as we see the process of celebrification trickling down to blog writers, social network site participants, YouTube stars, and other social media users (Senft, 2008). Celebrity can now be practiced by a greater number of people.

... Reality TV popularized a behind-the-scenes, self-conscious examination of celebrity construction; online, this goes one step further. Theresa Senft defines 'micro-celebrity' as a technique that 'involves people "amping up" their popularity over the Web using techniques like video, blogs, and social networking sites' (2008: 25). 'Micro-celebrity' describes a prevailing style of behavior both online and off, linked to the increase in popularity of 'self-branding' and strategic self-presentation (Hearn, 2008; Lair et al., 2005). This phenomenon was first noted in camgirls, young women who broadcast images of themselves 24/7 to interested audiences (Snyder, 2000). Their strategic micro-celebrity is distinct from the inadvertent fame resulting from internet memes, such as the 'Star Wars Kid' and 'Tron Guy'. Micro-celebrity involves viewing friends or followers as a fan base; acknowledging popularity as a goal; managing the fan base using a variety of affiliative techniques; and constructing an image of self that can be easily consumed by others. As we will see, these resemble techniques that extremely famous people use to manage audiences on Twitter, rather than relying on formal access brokers like managers and agents to maintain the distance between themselves and fans.

While the distinction between micro-celebrity and 'real' celebrity might once have been a question of popularity, approachability, or mainstream status, this article looks at how 'traditional' celebrities have adopted techniques formerly characterized as 'micro-celebrity'. We view celebrity practice as a *continuum* that can be practiced across the spectrum of fame rather than a schism. This essay examines how celebrity is practiced by the very

famous, yet we are interested in the larger cultural shifts indicated by these celebrity performances and recognize the need for research on the daily practice of celebrity by non-famous individuals.

In this chapter, we define celebrity as a *practice*. Whenever possible, we refrain from referring to people as celebrities, preferring to use 'celebrity practitioners' or 'famous people' to avoid the binary implications of the noun. However, since celebrity-as-noun is the prevalent usage within both scholarly and public discourse, we use it in reference to other works and discourses.

Twitter and Method

The microblogging site Twitter lets people post quick 140-character updates, or 'tweets', to a network of followers. Twitter asks participants 'What's happening?' resulting in a constantly-updated stream of short messages ranging from the mundane to breaking news, shared links, and thoughts on life. In Twitter's directed model of friendship, users choose others to 'follow' in their stream, and each user has his or her own group of 'followers'. There is neither a technical requirement nor social expectation of reciprocity (particularly with famous people, although this differs by user group). Tweets can be posted and read from the web, SMS, or third-party clients for desktop computers, smartphones, and other devices. This integration allows for instant postings of photos, on-the-ground reports, and quick replies to other users. The site launched in 2006 and broke into the mainstream in 2008–2009, when user accounts and media attention exponentially increased. Twitter had approximately 18.2 million users in May 2009 (Nielsen Company, 2009), increasing to 27.2 million by January 2010 (Quantcast Corporation, 2010). As of 2010, the most-followed Twitter users are well-known organizations like CNN and Whole Foods, very famous people and public figures, from President

Barack Obama to actor Ashton Kutcher and pop star Britney Spears. While Twitter can be used as a broadcast medium, the dialogic nature of Twitter and its ability to facilitate conversation has contributed substantially to its popularity.

This popularity has contributed to media fascination with the site. Unlike individuals famous primarily for their affiliation with social media properties, such as Tila Tequila on MySpace or Tay Zonday on YouTube, Twitter attracts actors, pop stars, authors, politicians, and others with established fame, such as Oprah Winfrey, Senator John McCain, Shaquille O'Neal and Weird Al. Although people known primarily for their online presence, like marketer Pistachio and video blogger iJustine, are well-represented on Twitter, the most-followed Twitter users are, for the most part, the conventionally famous.

Given this, we used Twitter to understand how celebrity is practiced through interactions between famous people and fans, friends, and other practitioners on Twitter. Part of the appeal of Twitter, as we will discuss, is the perception of direct access to a famous person, particularly 'insider' information, first-person pictures, and opinionated statements. Those celebrities who use Twitter primarily to 'broadcast' publicity information are seen as less authentic than those using the tool for dialogue and engagement with fans. One of our first methodological tasks was to work out who authored accounts of famous people.

We collected data from all people in the 300 most-followed Twitter accounts (as measured by Twitterholic.com during May and June 2009), including actors, musicians, technologists, politicians, reality television stars, and so forth for a total of 237 individuals; the remaining 63 accounts were media, companies, and organizations. . . . All the accounts we looked at were public. The messages we analyzed are also public; we use the actual usernames of both fans and highly followed people in this article, since the tweets are publicly searchable and accessible (while tweets are

only publicly searchable for 21 days, they can always be directly accessed from the user's page). Twitter allows for private, person-to-person tweets that do not appear on public pages, called direct messages (DMs). This chapter references several practices that Twitter users have developed to facilitate conversation on the site, namely @replies, retweets, and hashtags. @ replies, or 'at-replies', are public tweets that use a '@+username' convention to refer to other Twitter users; these can be used to identify people, address tweets to particular users and attribute quotes (Honeycutt and Herring, 2009). @replies are common on Twitter and 42 per cent of tweets in our sample are @replies.

The second type of common user practice we tracked was the retweet (RT), a repost of another person's tweet (see boyd et al., 2010, for a comprehensive look at retweeting). This is less common, and only 5 per cent of tweets in our sample were retweets. Hash tags, or the # sign followed by a word, mark tweets with descriptive terms. On sites like Delicious, Amazon.com, and Flickr, tags are used for many purposes, only one of which is classifying the tweet's subject matter (Golder and Huberman, 2006). On Twitter, tags are typically used to group tweets together by subject, such as a conference or meme; 6 per cent of the tweets in our sample included hashtags.

Performing Celebrity on Twitter

Like other public genres of social media, Twitter requires celebrity practitioners to negotiate a complicated social environment where fans, famous people, and intermediaries such as gossip columnists co-exist. These multiple audiences complicate self-presentation, since people present identity differently based on context. Erving Goffman's 1959 work *The Presentation of Self in Everyday Life* suggested that people, like actors, navigate 'frontstage' and 'backstage' areas in any given social situation.

This can be understood in terms of place. For instance, a restaurant's floor is frontstage, since employees must interact in front of an audience of bosses and customers. More candid talk between servers can take place backstage, away from the watchful eye of the employer. These concepts can also be understood in terms of content. For instance, intimate details about one's life are understood as part of the 'backstage' while professional communications can be seen as a 'frontstage' performance. However, frontstage and backstage are always relative as they depend on audience, context, and interpretation.

Goffman's work is related to symbolic interactionism, a sociological perspective which maintains that meaning is constructed through language, interaction, and interpretation (Blumer, 1962; Strauss, 1993). Symbolic interactionists claim that identity and self are constituted through constant interactions with others —primarily, talk. Individuals work together to uphold preferred self-images of themselves and their conversation partners, through strategies like maintaining (or 'saving') face, collectively encouraging social norms, or negotiating power differentials and disagreements. What Goffman refers to as 'impression management' takes place through ongoing adjustment to perceptions of audience judgment (1959).

Very famous people constantly navigate complex identity performances. The ostensible disconnect between a famous person's public persona and 'authentic' self is fueled by tabloid magazines, paparazzi photos, and gossip columns that purport to reveal what a particular starlet is 'really' like. Celebrity scandals often involve the exposure of personal information to the public, such as outing someone as queer or the dissemination of photos, 'sex tapes', answering machine messages, emails, and other purportedly backstage documents. This tricky territory has traditionally been navigated with the help of assistants, agents, public relations personnel, bodyguards, and other mechanisms that broker access between famous person and fan. On Twitter, however, this infrastructure is not available. As we will see, celebrity practice involves the appearance and performance of backstage access to the famous, presuming that the typical celebrity persona involves artifice. . . . Determining whether readers are watching an 'authentic' individual or a performed 'celebrity' persona is not entirely the point; it is the uncertainty that creates pleasure for the celebrity-watcher on Twitter.

Simultaneously, celebrity practice reinforces unequal power differentials. While Twitter users who do not use the site instrumentally may think of their followers as friends or family (Marwick and boyd, 2010), celebrity practice necessitates viewing followers as fans. Performing celebrity requires that this asymmetrical status is recognized by others. Fans show deference, creating mutual recognition of the status imbalance between practitioner and fan. In return, fan–practitioner relationships move beyond parasocial interaction, the illusion of a 'real', face-to-face friendship with a performer created through watching television shows or listening to music (Horton and Wohl, 1956). In parasocial relationships, or what John Thompson calls 'mediated quasi-interaction' (J Thompson, 1995: 98), a fan responds to a media figure 'as if s/he was a personal acquaintance' (Giles, 2002: 289); in contrast, Twitter suggests the possibility of interaction. There is no singular formula for celebrity practice; it consists of a set of learned techniques that are leveraged differently by individuals.

PUBLIC RECOGNITION AND FAN MAINTENANCE

Like much social media, Twitter creates a 'context collapse' (boyd, 2008) in which multiple audiences, usually thought of as separate, co-exist in a single social context. The practice of celebrity involves negotiating these multiple audiences to successfully maintain face and manage impressions. Celebrity practitioners use public acknowledgment, in the form of @replies, to connect with others. Fans @reply to famous people not only in the hope of receiving a reply, but to display a relationship, whether positive or negative. If fans receive @replies back, they function as a mark of status and are publicized within the fan community. Celebrity practitioners' public acknowledgment of friends, peers, and colleagues is rarely critical, primarily adhering to frontstage norms of public appearance. Famous people mention fans to perform connection and availability, give back to loyal followers, and manage their popularity.

Celebrity practice requires constant interaction with fans to preserve the power differentials intrinsic to the performed 'celebrity' and 'fan' personas. Celebrity practitioners approach this in different ways. . . . For example, when Mariah Carey tweets about her friend Jasmine Dotiwala, an MTV producer and gossip columnist, she chooses to identify her by her Twitter username:

> MariahCarey: @jasminedotiwala just sang the Vegas remix of "these are a few of my favorite things and did a little dance in a terry cloth robe" hilarious

This establishes intimacy between Carey and her followers by sharing personal details from her life while publicly identifying jasminedotiwala as a friend—a performance of backstage access—and inviting her followers to check out Jasmine's Twitter stream. This maintains the power differential between an average fan and the singer's intimate friend, since Jasmine is marked as someone who spends time with Mariah in person. It also provides a public endorsement of Jasmine's Twitter stream.

While some highly followed users reference others without being prompted, others will acknowledge friends as a favor to direct attention their way. This is particularly visible through the practice of retweeting:

> KevinRose: RT: @garyvee announcing my 1st business book http://tinyurl.com/garyveebook – congrats to @garyvee, crush it!

> Greggrundberg: RT @WilfridDierkes "watch My Name is Earl tonite cause if it gets canceled my family is moving in w/you." Peeps please watch. Save us all!!

Both these tweets demonstrate publicly articulated relational ties: between Digg founder Kevin Rose and motivational speaker Gary Vaynerchuk, and between actor Gregg Grunberg and producer Greg Garcia. This practice suggests insiderness between the participants, but it also highlights the dynamics of attention on Twitter.

Public acknowledgment, of either friends or fans, is not always positive. Twitter user Leproff sends an angry tweet to Republican politician Newt Gingrich about Reagan, who responds tersely:

> Leproff: @newtgingrich I do not agree when you say that USSR collapsed because of Ronald Reagan. This is a historical lie!

> NewtGingrich: @Leproff do you really believe the soviet union would have disappeared without rea-gab. Read peter schweizers book reagans war

Gingrich's tweet reinforces his image as an ornery conservative, but the act of responding also shows that he takes time to talk directly with followers. The potential of such interactions implies that fans are faced with accountability to the actors and singers they gossip about. Some famous people directly address gossip, for instance:

> LilyRoseAllen: and no i didnt say that stuff, ive never met cheryl, or her husband , noe david beckham. please dont believe that rubbish.

> NewtGingrich: A false story was planted this morning about my sueing twitter. This is totally false and we have repudiated it with the media

Hollymadison123: @PerezHilton Criss and i r not back together.. lol!

Rumor-mongering, whether by follower or gossip columnist Perez Hilton, can theoretically be directly corrected. Of course, fans may choose to believe the rumor even if the famous person chooses to reject it and not all fans read all tweets written by a celebrity. As with any other medium, correcting a rumor on Twitter can be more challenging than starting one. . . .

INTIMACY

Twitter allows celebrity practitioners to create a sense of closeness and familiarity between themselves and their followers. Highly followed accounts vary in performed intimacy; while some mostly broadcast information about an upcoming tour or book, others write about personal subjects, post exclusive content, or chat about their daily lives. This type of strategic revealing found on confessional talk show appearances, tell-all autobiographies, and magazine interviews has been criticized as 'second order intimacy' (Rojek, 2001: 52) or the 'illusion of intimacy' (Schickel, 1985: 4; Turner, 2004). This point of view maintains that performed intimacy is synonymous with parasocial interaction and a poor substitute for actual interaction.

While it is true that the practice of celebrity involves strategically managed self-disclosure, we should not be so quick to judge the closeness created by Twitter as false and second-best. First, Twitter does provide the possibility of actual interaction with the highly followed person, in the form of a direct message or @reply. Second, the 'lifestreaming' function of Twitter encourages 'digital intimacy' (C Thompson, 2008). The many seemingly insignificant messages serve as phatic communication (Miller, 2008); rather than sharing meaningful information, many tweets serve a social function, reinforcing connections and maintaining social bonds (Crawford, 2009). If we accept that Twitter creates a sense of ongoing connection with one's real-life acquaintances and friends, following a famous person's tweets over a period of time may create an equally valid feeling of 'knowing' them. Finally, as we will see in the following case studies, users can and do let things slip via Twitter that would never be revealed in an interview with *People* magazine.

On Twitter, performative intimacy is practiced by posting personal pictures and videos, addressing rumors, and sharing personal information. Picture-hosting services, such as YFrog and Twitpic, allow users directly to post cameraphone pictures to Twitter. Famous people frequently use these services, creating the illusion of first-person glimpses into their lives. . . . Similarly, streaming video services like uStream are used by musicians like Bow Wow and Snoop Dogg to broadcast studio recordings and live performances, while others post funny videos, take questions from fans, or host live events. Shaquille O'Neal, for instance, filmed himself lipsynching and tweeted the link to his followers. While these pictures and videos add a visual dimension, they are still strategically chosen by the practitioner, in contrast to the unauthorized candids found in tabloids and gossip blogs.

As we have seen, other famous people use Twitter to directly address rumors. The same technique is used to respond to fan criticism or comments. For instance, Shaq retorted to a follower who said his sneakers were ugly:

@Naimthestar yea dats why I sold 80 million pair since 1992 at 3 dollars per pair comn to me, do the math

In addition to publicly recognizing and responding to a fan concern, this information makes the fan feel that they possess insider, candid knowledge about the sports star. Contentious discussions are not uncommon:

Jake_Banks: @ddlovato the Jonas Brothers, are just a disney fabrication who did not earn their fame and thusly are undeserving of such a large spotlight

Ddlovato: @Jake_Banks It's funny that you call them a "disney fabrication" but they have fans of ALL ages and they do deserve the spotlight.

Ddlovato: They've been touring and working extremely hard for years and they still haven't stopped. They're the hardest working people I know of. . . .

These exchanges demonstrate how Twitter has contributed to changes in the parasocial dynamic. While parasocial interaction is largely imaginary and takes place primarily in the fan's mind, Twitter conversations between fans and famous people are public and visible, and involve direct engagement between the famous person and their follower. The fan's ability to engage in discussion with a famous person de-pathologizes the parasocial and recontextualizes it within a medium that the follower may use to talk to real-life acquaintances. As we have seen, Twitter makes fans accountable for rude comments, taking the subjects of gossip out of the realm of fantasy and repositioning them as 'real people'. Traditional settings for in-person celebrity–fan interactions, such as autograph signings and award ceremonies, are highly managed and limited in scope. In contrast, although Twitter conversations are mediated, they appear off-the-cuff, contributing to a sense that the reader is seeing the real, authentic person behind the 'celebrity'.

AUTHENTICITY AND SINCERITY

In *Sincerity and Authenticity*, Lionel Trilling (1972) distinguishes authenticity from sincerity. He conceptualizes authenticity as a display of the hidden inner life, complete with passions and anguish, while sincerity is the opposite of hypocrisy— honesty without pretense. Both these elements matter on Twitter. The intimacy engendered by celebrity tweets provide the glimpse into the inner life that fans want, while at the most basic level, fans want to ensure that the person tweeting is sincerely who they claim to be. Twitter is generally a site where personal disclosure and intimacy are normative (Marwick and boyd, 2010), so access, intimacy, and affiliation are valueless if an account is fake or written by an assistant. The process involved in vetting whether a person is really who they claim to be reveals the appeal of celebrity practice for fans: the potential for disclosing the 'truth', the uncensored person stripped of PR artifice and management.

Users frequently debate whether Twitter accounts are written by who they claim to be. The site truthtweet.com verifies or debunks accounts like Tina_Fey and The_Pitts. During our research, accounts for Seth Rogen, Michael Phelps, and Tina Fey were identified as impostors and subsequently shut down (Tina_Fey was renamed 'FakeTinaFey' and the comedian Tina Fey took over Tina_Fey). Some of these demonstrably false accounts are valued for their satirical value or effective impersonation, such 'FakeSarahPalin' whose tweets include things like 'This "death panel" thing is really taking off! Suck it, Luntz, you got p0wned Palin style. Srsly!!!' In June 2009, Twitter introduced verified accounts that certify 'genuine' famous people. Not all 'celebrity' accounts are written by the purported individual. In our own efforts to account for authenticity of Twitter accounts, we focused on the signals of authenticity. Judith Donath discusses how subtle online signals function as identity cues, given the dearth of physical evidence (1998). Given the presence of typos in most participants' tweets, we expect that 'real' celebrity practitioners will make grammatical or spelling mistakes. Tweets that are personal, controversial, or negative—in other words, that contradict the stereotype of the overly managed 'celebrity' account—signal greater authenticity than safely vetted publicity messages. If the writer interacted with fans, used the first-person voice, and posted candid snapshots, they seemed more authentic, as did their use of mobile clients such as Tweetie or Twitterberry. Of course, our assessment is only based on the available signals; we have no way of validating our best guesses. Similarly, fans carefully evaluate the *sincerity* of celebrity accounts.

Trilling's alternative meaning of authenticity, as passion and interiority, is also crucial to Twitter's appeal. 'Authenticity' is a social construct that is ultimately always relative and context dependent (Bendix, 1997; Cheng, 2004); it seems that self-disclosure, and therefore what it means to be authentic, is expected more on Twitter compared to other venues. While we accept that a *Cosmopolitan* cover story on pop star Katy Perry will probably be a bit boring, we anticipate that Perry's Twitter feed will be in keeping with her glamorous, wacky image. Celebrity practice that sticks to the safe and publicly consumable risks being viewed as inauthentic, while successful celebrity practice suggests intimacy, disclosure, and connection. . . .

MARIAH CAREY: FAN RELATIONSHIPS WITH CELEBRITIES

The pop singer Mariah Carey has been releasing successful albums for 20 years, and has a devoted, loyal fan following which she calls her 'lambs'. While Carey is the best-selling female artist in the USA, her volatile career has included two highly publicized marriages, a divorce, the failed film *Glitter*, and a televised mental breakdown. Perhaps because of these personal tribulations, her fans send her intimate public messages that often resemble a quick text to a friend:

OMJitsReva: @MariahCarey On my way to NYC be there in 21 hours, yep I'm catchin teh greyhound... hope ur in town and i c u

halima12: @MariahCarey hey, been in the garden with sugapie dunking her in the pool & givin her a ride on the lilo. been playin E¼MC2 :) watcha up 2?

ShayneFly: @MariahCarey Had to put our family dog to sleep tonight. I know you know how it hurts. Im missing a piece and my stupid face is all wet :(

These messages both demonstrate the power of parasocial interaction and how Twitter changes it. Fan LaurenDayMakeUp responded to our question about her Twitter interaction with Mariah, 'I follow @MariahCarey becoz she has been with me through her music everyday of my life 4 the last 15 years! She inspires me!' But unlike listening to music, social media suggests the possibility of the media figure responding, which intensifies the interactive credibility.

MariahCarey: Trying to DM as many nice folks as possible. Thanks for all the love as always. I love twitter cos I can really stay in touch w/you.(Cont)

Fans know that Mariah uses Twitter to communicate directly with friends and fans, meaning she may potentially respond to them. As a result, fans directly ask for responses:

Rochyta: @Mariahcarey We miss you, Mariah! I had a terrible day today. It would be great to read a "hi" from you. Te quiero muchísimo. Rocío-Spain.

OriginalJengsta: @MariahCarey Today is my birthday and my birthday wish is to get a Twitter shout-out from MC -can you swing it?? -Nancy Jeng

Receiving a message from a highly followed individual is a status symbol in itself. User OMJitsReva writes on her profile, 'Check my FAVs [favorite tweets] for celebs that have tweeted me back! I feel like a mini-celebrity.' This is also a public performance of access. Users tweet to Mariah not only to feel a sense of connection with her, but also to publicly acknowledge the lack of distance between themselves and the singer.

> AviHBF: @dieguitoLAMB Mariah DM'd me today!

> DieguitoLAMB: @AviHBF OM*G!!! YOU LUCKY GURL!

> LoyalLamb88: @AviHBF Wow! That's awesome...

AviHBF brags about receiving a direct message; the responses show the value of this within the fan community. One fan, MiMiGreat, posted 'Mariah wrote me a DM!!!!!!!!!!!!!!!!!' upon receiving her own message. Notably, Mariah uses private direct messages rather than public @replies. This could be a way to avoid public accountability, but it also means that fans can claim that Mariah wrote to them even if she did not. Mariah's tweet about 'loving Twitter' and the excited responses from fans comprise a performance of fan interaction. Mariah could claim to interact with fans privately without actually doing so, or could have an assistant write DMs. For Mariah Carey and her fans, Twitter seems to be about the perception of availability and fan access.

MILEY CYRUS: CELEBRITY RELATIONSHIPS WITH CELEBRITIES

Celebrity practitioners also interact with other famous people on Twitter, creating revealing performances of what appear to be intimate interactions. Truly private interactions between famous people, with no public audience, are invisible to fans. Highly publicized romantic relationships and friendships covered by gossip magazines create the illusion of insider access, but are still public. Twitter allows the public visibility of casual friendships between famous people,

which both creates a sense of insiderness for fan observers and requires celebrities to navigate carefully. Celebrities must constantly shift between performing their stage persona, concealing or revealing personal information, and creating intimacy and authentic self-presentation for the benefit of their fans. At times, it becomes difficult to discern what is performance and what is 'real'; this is precisely the kind of juxtaposition that fans love.

Teen star Miley Cyrus began a public feud with fellow singer/actors Demi Lovato and Selena Gomez after posting a mocking parody of the girls' home-made video series on YouTube (Beer and Penfold-Mounce, 2009). Speculations on the origin of the feud include internal Disney rivalry; conflict over Gomez being labeled the 'Next Miley Cyrus' by the press; and tension after Lovato dated Cyrus' ex-boyfriend, teen idol Nick Jonas. The feud was heavily covered by the entertainment press, fueled by Nick's brother Kevin wearing a 'Team Demi and Selena' t-shirt in public. Cyrus, Lovato, and Gomez have publicly denied a feud and were photographed in late 2008 having dinner, presumably a staged event as damage control to counteract fallout from the rumors (Kidzworld, 2009). While Lovato and Gomez are publicly 'best friends' who continue to present themselves as such, Cyrus and Lovato engaged in a somewhat surprising ongoing series of public interactions on Twitter:

> Ddlovato: Now I'm with my other two best friends in the entire world... @selenagomez and @mileycyrus. What an amazing day. :D

> MileyCyrus: @ddlovato is one of the bestest friends in the world :)

> Ddlovato: @mileycyrus I'm comin'! You better visit me on tour!!! Idk how long I can go without seeing you :)

> MileyCyrus: @ddlovato I dont know if I've ever needed someone as badly as I need you right now.... I miss you sweet girl.

Ddlovato: @mileycyrus awww :(make me tear up why don't ya?! I love you so much. I've ALWAYS got your back.

These tweets can be viewed as strategic frontstage performances. It's irrelevant whether or not Miley, Demi and Selena actually are friends, since the frequency and emotional tone of the messages mark them as performative—Cyrus and Lovato want their fans to know that they are friends. . . .

While an agent or manager may have been the impetus for Lovato and Cyrus's public declarations of friendship, similar public declarations take place on social network sites among non-celebrities every day. Interactions between users create publicly visible relationship lines, marking friendship, romantic entanglements, break-ups, flirtations, rivalries, and alliances. It is not surprising that celebrities—particularly teenage girls whose peer group conduct their social lives via social media—do the same thing. The scrutiny may become too much; in October 2009, Miley Cyrus left Twitter in a whirlwind of publicity, stating in a home-made rap video posted on YouTube 'Everything that I type and everything that I do, all those lame gossip types take it and they make it news' (MandyMiley 2009).

The Cyrus–Lovato 'feud' demonstrates that reading conversations as performative or real is neither neat nor easy. Celebrity is practiced through scripted attempts to give backstage access. But just as actually getting backstage at a rock show does not provide true access to the band, neither does reading tweets provide insider access. The performance of celebrities interacting with no thought of fans, press, or managers on Twitter is actually managed interaction that creates the perception of intimacy. That is not to say that celebrities do not let things slip on Twitter; this is precisely why studios such as Disney and Dreamworks see Twitter as a liability (Wallenstein and Belloni, 2009). There is indeed a tension between deliberate self-presentation—what Erving Goffman called impressions 'given'—and unintentional self-presentation, or information 'given off' (1959). It is the inability to tell what is strategic and what is accidental, as well as what is truthful and what is not, that makes Twitter so enjoyable for fans.

Significance

. . . New media not only provides new outlets for the exploration of celebrity, but complicates the dynamics between celebrity practitioners, their audiences, and those who occupy spaces in-between. Interactions between famous people are typically brokered through entertainment media or kept from public view; Twitter allows famous people to make their conversations publicly visible. This requires celebrity practitioners to navigate skillfully the performative friendships, feuds, and negotiations with others, all in front of their fans and the mainstream media. Twitter also disrupts the expectation of parasociality between the famous person and the fan. The study of celebrity culture has primarily focused on fans as separate from celebrities, but the ability of famous people to read and reply to fans has given rise to new sets of practices and interactions. Celebrity practitioners must harness this ability to maintain ongoing affiliations and connections with their fans, rather than seem uncaring or unavailable. Thus, Twitter creates a new expectation of intimacy. Rather than handing off fan management to an agent or fan club, celebrity practitioners must expend emotional labor maintaining a network of affective ties with their followers. Thus, even the famous must learn the techniques used by 'regular people' to gain status and attention online. Twitter demonstrates the transformation of 'celebrity' from a personal quality linked to fame to a set of practices that circulate through modern social media.

References

Baym N (2000) *Tune In, Log On: Soaps, Fandom, and Online Community.* Thousand Oaks, CA: SAGE.

Becque S (2007) Big Damn Fans: Fan Campaigns of Firefly and Veronica Mars. Senior thesis, Departments of Sociology and Anthropology, Mount Holyoke College, MA, USA.

Beer D and Penfold-Mounce R (2009) Celebrity gossip and the new melodramatic imagination. *Sociological Research Online* 14(2–3). URL (consulted July 2009): http://www.socresonline.org.uk/14/2/2.html

Bendix R (1997) *In Search of Authenticity: The Formation of Folklore Studies.* Madison: University of Wisconsin Press.

Blumer H (1962) Society as symbolic interaction. In: Rose AM (ed.) *Human Behavior and Social Processes.* Boston, MA: Houghton Mifflin, 179–192.

Boorstin D (1961) *The Image: A Guide to Pseudo-Events in America.* New York: Athenaeum.

boyd d (2008) Taken out of Context: American Teen Sociality in Networked Publics. PhD dissertation, University of California, Berkeley.

boyd d, Golder S and Lotan, G (2010) Tweet, tweet, retweet: Conversational aspects of retweeting on Twitter. HICSS–43. IEEE: Kauai HI, 6 January.

Braudy L (1986) *The Frenzy of Renown: Fame and Its History.* New York: Oxford University Press.

Cheng VJ (2004) *Inauthentic: The Anxiety over Culture and Identity.* New Brunswick, NJ: Rutgers University Press.

Cohen N (2009) When stars Twitter, a ghost may be lurking, *The New York Times*, 26 March. URL (consulted December 2009): http://www.nytimes.com/2009/03/27/technology/internet/27twitter.html

Crawford K (2009) These foolish things: On intimacy and insignificance in mobile media. In: Goggin G and Hjorth L (eds) *Mobile Technologies: From Telecommunications to Media.* New York: Routledge, 252–265.

Donath J (1998) Identity and deception in the virtual community. In: Kollock P and Smith M (eds) *Communities in Cyberspace.* London: Routledge, 29–59.

Donath J (2007) Signals in social supernets. *Journal of Computer-Mediated Communication* 13(1). URL (consulted July 2009): http://jcmc.indiana.edu/vol13/issue1/donath.html

Dunbar RIM (1996) *Grooming, Gossip, and the Evolution of Language.* Cambridge, MA: Harvard University Press.

Dyer R (1986) *Heavenly Bodies: Film Stars and Society.* London: BFI Macmillan.

Ewan S (1989) *All Consuming Images: The Politics of Style in Contemporary Culture.* New York: Basic Books.

Feasey R (2008) Reading Heat: The meanings and pleasures of star fashions and celebrity gossip. *Continuum: Journal of Media & Cultural Studies* 22(5): 687–699.

Gamson J (1994) *Claims to Fame: Celebrity in Contemporary America.* Berkeley: University of California Press.

Giles DC (2002) Parasocial interaction: A review of the literature and a model for future research. *Media Psychology* 4(3): 279–305.

Goffman E (1959) *The Presentation of Self in Everyday Life.* Garden City, NY: Doubleday Anchor Books.

Golder S and Huberman BA (2006) Usage patterns of collaborative tagging systems. *Journal of Information Science* 32(2): 198–208.

Hearn A (2008) 'Meat, mask, burden' Probing the contours of the branded 'self'. *Journal of Consumer Culture* 8(2): 197–217.

Honeycutt C and Herring SC (2009) Beyond microblogging: Conversation and collaboration via Twitter. Proceedings of the Forty-Second Hawaii International Conference on System Sciences (HICSS–42). Los Alamitos, CA: IEEE Press.

Horton D and Wohl RR (1956) Mass communication and para-social interaction: Observations on intimacy at a distance. *Psychiatry* 19(3): 215–229.

Jensen J (1992) Fandom as pathology. In: Lewis L (ed.) *The Adoring Audience: Fan Culture and Popular Media.* New York: Routledge, 9–29.

Jenkins (1992) *Textual Poachers.* New York: Routledge.

Jenkins (2006a) *Convergence Culture*. New York: New York University Press.

Jenkins (2006b) *Fans, Bloggers, and Gamers: Exploring Participatory Culture*. New York: New York University Press.

Kachka B (2008) Have we reached the end of book publishing as we know it? *New York Magazine*, 14 September. URL (consulted July 2009): http://nymag.com/news/media/50279/

Kidzworld (2009) *Miley timeline: Nick Jonas and Miley Cyrus relationship 2009*. Kidzworld.com. URL (consulted June 2009): http://www.kidzworld.com/article/18635-niley-timeline-nick-jonas-and-mileycyrus-relationship–2009

Knoppner S (2009) *Appetite for Self Destruction: The Spectacular Crash of the Record Industry in the Digital Age*. New York: Simon & Schuster.

Lair D, Sullivan K and Cheney G (2005) Marketization and the recasting of the professional self. *Management Communication Quarterly* 18(3): 307–343.

Lessig L (2004) *Free Culture*. London: Penguin Books.

Lowenthal L (1961) *The triumph of mass idols. Literature, Popular Culture, and Society*. Englewood Cliffs, NJ: Prentice-Hall, 109–140.

MandyMiley (2009). *Goodbye Twitter*. YouTube.com 9 October. URL (consulted October 2009): http://www.youtube.com/watch?v=2tSOTQPUQoU

Marshall PD (1997) *Celebrity and Power: Fame in Contemporary Culture*. Minneapolis: University of Minnesota Press.

Marshall PD (2006) *The Celebrity Culture Reader*. New York: Routledge.

Marwick A and boyd d (2010) I tweet honestly, I tweet passionately: Twitter users, context collapse, and the imagined audience. *New Media and Society*. Published online before print, 7 July.

McLeod K (2002) *The private ownership of people*. In: McLeod K Owning Culture, New York: Peter Lang, ch. 6.

Miller V (2008) New media, networking, and phatic culture, *Convergence* 14(4): 387–400.

Murray S (2004) 'Celebrating the story the way it is': Cultural studies, corporate media and the contested utility of fandom. Continuum 18(1): 7–25.

Nielsen Company, the (2009) Nielsens Social Media QuickTake: May 2009. *Nielsen.com*. URL (consulted June 2009): http://blog.nielsen.com/nielsenwire/wp-content/uploads/2009/06/nielsen_pr_090619.pdf

Quantcast Corporation (2010). Twitter.com. *Quantcast.com*. URL (consulted March 2010): http://www.quantcast.com/twitter.com

Rahman M (2006) Is straight the new queer? David Beckham and the dialectics of celebrity. In: Marshall PD (ed.) *The Celebrity Culture Reader*. New York: Routledge, 223–228.

Rojek C (2001) *Celebrity*. Chicago, IL: Reaktion Books.

Schickel R (1985) *Intimate Strangers: The Culture of Celebrity*. New York: Doubleday.

Senft T (2008) *Camgirls: Celebrity and Community in the Age of Social Networks*. New York: Peter Lang.

Snyder D (2000) Webcam women: Life on your screen, In: Gauntlett D (ed.) *Web. Studies: Rewiring Media Studies for the Digital Age*. London: Arnold, 68–73.

Sternbergh A (2004) Cruise control: The publicist behind the movie star. *Slate*, 5 April. URL (consulted December 2009): http://www.slate.com/id/2098277/

Strauss AL (1993) *Continual Permutations of Action*. New York: Aldine De Gruyter.

Thompson C (2008) Brave new world of digital intimacy. *The New York Times* 7 September. URL (consulted February 2009): http://www.nytimes.com/2008/09/07/magazine/07awareness-t.html?r=1

Thompson JB (1995). *The Media and Modernity*. Stanford, CA: Stanford University Press.

Trilling L (1972) *Sincerity and Authenticity*. Cambridge, MA: Harvard University Press.

Turner G (2004) *Understanding Celebrity*. Thousand Oaks, CA: SAGE.

Wallenstein A and Belloni M (2009) Hey, showbiz folks: Check your contract before your next tweet. *The Hollywood Reporter: THR Esquire*, 15 October. URL (consulted December 2009): http://www.thresq.com/2009/10/check-your-contract-before-your-next-tweet.html

34

How to "Use Your Olympian"

The Paradox of Athletic Authenticity and Commercialization in the Contemporary Olympic Games

Momin Rahman and Sean Lockwood

Introduction

... Drawing on research on sports celebrity and modern celebrity culture, we discuss how the transformation of the Olympics into a media entertainment event affects the authenticity of the athletes who literally embody the positive aspects of 'Olympism'; the ideals that underpin the event and movement or, in more commercial terms, the meaning of the Olympic brand. The following is an example of the commercial use of Olympic athletes:

> The British Olympic Association is delighted that you have visited the britisholympians site and we hope that you take the next step of making a booking and using one of our Olympians to help you achieve your business objectives ... (From *Guidelines on the Use of Olympians*, British Olympic Association)[1]

To illustrate the role of authenticity within this commercialization, we investigate a range of institutional discourses drawn from the International Olympic Committee (IOC), London 2012, the British Olympic Association (BOA), and Lloyds TSB Bank, a major corporate sponsor of the London 2012 Games. ... We argue that the tension between authenticity and commercialization is inevitable given that media and corporate finances are necessary to fund the Games, and therefore that this paradox must be managed to

From M. Rahman and S. Lockwood (2011), "How to 'use your Olympian': The Paradox of Athlete Authenticity and Commercialization in the Contemporary Olympic Games." *Sociology*, 45, 815–829. Reprinted with permission of SAGE Publications, Ltd.

emphasize the positive side of this dialectic —the authenticity of motivation and fans' enjoyment of the same. Central to this management is the promotion of Olympic athletes as embodiments of the authentic Olympic ideal, which includes their construction as 'heroic' individuals who participate to excel rather than make money. However, this discourse is contradictory because the representation of athletes occurs within and draws on a celebrity and commodity culture that primarily serves the accumulation strategies of corporations. Moreover, the tacit assumption within this contemporary discourse of sporting heroism is that the Games of antiquity provide a precedent for authentic motivation based on athletic amateurism. We demonstrate, however, that this appeal was driven first by the requirements of legitimizing the modern Games, and subsequently by the need to manage the paradox of commercialization. The ancient Olympics have therefore become part of the wider discourse of authenticity that is deployed in contemporary times to facilitate the continued commercial and cultural viability of the Games in a mediatized and commodity culture.

The Olympics and Entertainment Culture: Paradoxes in the 'Brand' through Commercialization

Whilst the modern Games began in 1896 in modest fashion, their international impact was established by Stockholm 1912 (Barney, 2007). However, the only media available to these and other pre-Second World War Games were the contemporary forms of radio, press, and cinema newsreel. The subsequent modern Olympic Games developed concurrently with the growth of television and its relationship with sport in general (Smart, 2005; Wenn and Martyn, 2007; Whannel, 2009). Whannel explains that 'The emergence of television in the

1930s enabled a combination of the immediacy and uncertainty of live sport, the domestic context of radio, and the drama and spectacle of newsreel' (2009: 208). He describes how television was first used to broadcast the 1936 Berlin Olympics in local cinemas, and how public broadcast was expanded during the London Olympics of 1948, albeit to a limited audience of those with sets in the London area. In contrast, the London 2012 Olympics was a global 'mega-event' experienced not only through television but also through other forms of media such as print and websites that commented on the events and, moreover, create a simultaneous, communal global audience that is increasingly rare in the on-demand and subscription formats of most televised sport (Whannel, 2009). Television media technology is therefore a distinct aspect of the context in which the modern Olympic Games has existed since the mid-20th century (Smart, 2005; Whannel, 2002, 2009).

This mediatization is, however, fundamentally about commercialization, primarily the impact that the availability of media finances has had on the organization of sport. According to Whannel:

> Television transformed sport into a set of commodified global spectacles, producing huge audiences and massive new sources of income. Sport in turn provided television with an endless supply of major spectacular events and an enduring form of pleasurable and popular viewing. (2009: 206)

When a sport is popular enough, guaranteeing a significant audience, the governing bodies can demand huge monies for the broadcast rights both at national levels and internationally for 'mega-events'.[2] In the case of the Olympics, this process began in 1960 when the IOC licensed television rights for both summer and winter Games for the first time, in partnership with the local organizing committees. The

IOC took direct control of negotiations starting with Barcelona in 1992, allowing considerations of the Olympic Movement and brand to outweigh specific local or national agendas and local attempts to keep the majority of revenues (Wenn and Martyn, 2007: 311).

The mediatization and commercialization are linked because the media provide larger audiences who are also potential consumers, not only of the sporting event as media product, but also of associated advertising and branding. This media/commercial equation has clearly influenced the activities of the Olympic Movement, specifically transforming it into a more explicitly corporate operation, as characterized by Wenn and Martyn:

Fuelled by the revenues generated from television rights, the activities commonly associated with corporate enterprise flourished inside the halls of power of the organisation's Lausanne headquarters. Television matters aside, it was in the areas of product advertising and consumer sales, often identified as *marketing*, that the IOC became linked to what is commonly referred to as *commercialism*. (2007: 315)

This commercialization has been inevitable, largely because of the wider development of sport as a commercialized leisure and entertainment industry that is dependent on both corporate media and commodity corporate finances. Since the latter part of the 20th century, sport has increasingly become a central component of the wider media entertainment industry that consists of globalized transnational and multi-corporate organizations which deploy cross-media and cross-national delivery (Law et al., 2002; Maguire, 1999; Smart, 2005). The Olympic Movement has not only become drawn into these economic structures, but it has also been able to promote its unique identity to capitalize on funding sources: there is clearly a positive 'branding' effect of the Olympic discourse, both in hosting the event and for companies associated with it through sponsorship. In the case of the former, Zhang and Zhao detail the specific and concerted efforts of the Chinese authorities to secure the Games for Beijing and to use them to 'rebrand' the city (2009: 251). Although the authors remain sceptical as to whether economic or rebranding efforts were successful in this case, this example does demonstrate the attraction of the Olympic Games as a globally recognized mega-event that has specific, positive brand associations. Moreover, the IOC is aware of this power and commissioned research to define, refine, and promote its brand, resulting in an advertising campaign in 2000 called 'Celebrate Humanity', which was 'the first fully global marketing campaign to attempt to communicate the values embodied within the Olympic movement' (Maguire et al., 2008a: 70). The researchers comment, however, that:

. . . the 'message' becomes embedded in a broader process of commerce whereby the media/marketing/advertising/corporate nexus is concerned less with the values underpinning Olympism *per se* . . . and more with how such values can help build markets, construct and enhance brand awareness and thus create 'glocal' consumers/identities. (2008a: 74)

. . . Within the context of this inevitable commercialization, however, remains the perceived 'authenticity' of the Olympics as an athletic event and a brand, one that can therefore be enjoyed primarily for its demonstration of human endeavour rather than as another form of consumption. Broadly speaking, the Olympics are seen to represent a combination of the following: sport for its own sake; the pursuit of achievement and self-improvement through sport but also through associated cultural and educational programmes; and national pride but in a spirit of peace, mutual understanding, and friendship. This discourse of the Olympics is expressed in various ways by the institutions of the movement, primarily through the IOC's mission statements and in the promotion of specific games such as London 2012.

... Specific iterations are derived from the concept of 'Olympism' that is defined in the Olympic Charter thus:

1. Olympism is a philosophy of life, exalting and combining in a balanced whole the qualities of body, will and mind. Blending sport with culture and education, Olympism seeks to create a way of life based on the joy of effort, the educational value of good example and respect for universal fundamental ethical principles.

2. The goal of Olympism is to place sport at the service of the harmonious development of man, with a view to promoting a peaceful society concerned with the preservation of human dignity. (http://www. olympic.org/Documents/ Olympic%20Charter/Charter_ en_2010.pdf)

In the context of the Olympics as part of sports media entertainment culture, a paradox exists wherein the commercialization of the Games is potentially undermining its brand power, the meanings of which are antithetical to consumerism. For example, the key messages of the Celebrate Humanity campaign in 2000 mentioned above focus on issues such as 'hope', 'dreams' and inspirations', 'friendship', 'fair play', and 'joy in effort' (Maguire et al., 2008a), echoing the ideals of modern Olympism which emphasize peaceful international relationships, education through sport, and a focus on human greatness.[3] Indeed, a critical perspective

on contemporary IOC marketing efforts would suggest that they are there simply to veil the commercialism behind the Games, or at the very least to justify it as necessary for the Games to exist by providing the funds required to facilitate the rarefied Olympic atmosphere in which such ideals can still be pursued (Maguire et al., 2008a)....

The Contemporary Context for Sports Stars: Celebrity and Authenticity

... Sport has increasingly become part of the wider media entertainment structure of globalized transnational and multi-corporate organizations (Law et al., 2002; Maguire, 1999; Smart, 2005). Moreover, the media broadcasts themselves have been joined by commercial sports commodity products, associated with specific individuals, teams and nations, as well wider commodity branding through endorsement and sponsorship deals (Andrews and Jackson, 2001; Smart, 2005). This media-driven commercialization of sport has converged with the emergence of modern celebrity as a historically distinct form of fame, dependent on the development of mass media technologies throughout the 20th century and the significant expansion of mass consumption in late capitalism (Marshall, 1997; Rojek, 2001; Turner, 2004). In his critique of the consumerist and individualist society of the post-war period, Lasch (1979) bemoans the 'degradation of sport' into entertainment show business culture. One consequence of this 'degradation' has been an increasing emphasis on individual 'stars', and so sporting figures have been transformed into sporting celebrities. The status of celebrity beyond their own sport is a distinctive aspect of contemporary sports stars, derived from the transformation of sport from amateur community-based leisure into a globalized and mediatized 'entertainment' industry. Moreover, this industry uses the technologies and strategies of wider celebrity culture to provoke consumption of its own media products, associated sports commodities, and, crucially, wider commodity brands. Thus:

> ... commercial corporations have come to recognize that sport and sporting figures offer a rare, if not unique, quality of authenticity from which their brands can derive substantial benefit by association ... From the 1980s, sport events and sporting figures have been increasingly valued as the means through which all sorts of products and services, including those not related to sport at all could be marketed to consumers. (Smart, 2005: 144)

However, this branding is potentially a threat to the athletes' cultural resonance because it can make them seem more like corporate functionaries than genuinely motivated enthusiasts for their sport (Smart, 2005). The premise of the threat is that commercialization is a negative aspect of contemporary sports industries because it renders sport as just another indistinct form of consumerism, removing any enthusiasm from its audience. This argument, however, must be understood in terms of historical scale given that some level of economic burden has always been part of organized sport, both for players requiring equipment and wages if they were professionals, and for fans to buy tickets to events. The issue in contemporary times has become the large-scale finances available in many sports through commercialization and mediatization, requiring an associated increase in economic burdens for fans, and rewarding athletes to the extent that 'Making money is now an important part of sport and professional participants have to work hard at their games because it is their job to do so' (Smart, 2005: 5). Furthermore,

the commercialization of teams and sport industries has removed the close identification of traditional fan and team, whereby the latter, collectively and individually, 'were the apotheosis of the culture of their cities, symbolizing not only the heart and soul of the spectators who watched them but the spirit of the associated community' (Rojek, 2006: 684). The separation of fans from their teams through mediatization and the consequent positioning of fan as consumer and athletes as highly paid wage labourers are seen as less genuine than either an emotional identification with a team or sports star, or the athlete as motivated by the opportunity to excel. This tension is managed by emphasizing the genuine basis of emotional attachment in fans, focused on the authenticity of their heroes (Smart, 2005: 194–8). The inevitability of commercialization is therefore alleviated by promoting the authenticity of the sporting event, not only at the level of the event as brand as described in the previous section, but also through its particular sports stars. Authenticity is a key issue here precisely because it serves two symbiotic purposes: its presence is seen to promote brands and products through positive association, and it can also be deployed to manage the potentially disruptive consequences of this commercialization. We suggest that this latter function is more relevant to the Olympics: athletes' 'authenticity' is invoked to emphasize the purity of the event, distracting fans and audiences from their overt interpellation as consumers (Maguire et al., 2008b), and reiterating the actual Games as an arena for human achievement rather than a global media and commercial mega-event (Whannel, 2009).

The construction of the authenticity of sports stars is two fold: first, they are seen to achieve status through their talent and hard work at training that talent, rather than through inherited or class privilege. This resonates with the democratization of fame during the 20th century, whereby media 'stars' have been increasingly drawn from 'ordinary' backgrounds, or at least have celebrity personae that emphasize their ordinary origins (Rojek, 2001; Turner, 2004). This serves to model the idea that 'ordinary' people—from the newly enfranchised masses in democracies—do matter in mass capitalist society, and may even one day become rich, powerful and famous using their talents. As Rojek argues, sporting heroes have become part of the mediatized celebrity elite partly because 'In societies based around the meritocratic ideal, sport is also one of the paradigmatic institutions that articulate and elaborate the meritocratic ideal and reinforce achievement culture' (2006: 680–1). Rojek argues that the 'achievement culture' modelled by sports stars serves social integration by reinforcing the values needed for the discipline of work, but it does so by focusing our attention on heroic or exceptional individuals. Nike's reinvention and global expansion drew precisely on this achievement culture in both its advertising and branding, and in its sponsorship of athletes who embodied the hard-working and heroic ethos, most notably Michael Jordan (Goldman and Papson, 1998). Moreover, Nike's promotion of athletic celebrity illustrates a central point about celebrity culture: the pivotal affinity between consumer culture and the emergence of contemporary celebrity culture. Sports stars make great 'celebrity-commodities' (Turner, 2004: 34) precisely because they fulfil the function of modelling desire for their fans as consumers: sports celebrities embody both the work ethic of achievement culture *and* luxurious and exceptional lifestyle consumerism.

The second dimension of athletes' authenticity is the potential for heroism that is seen to underpin their professional activities. In his study on footballers in Britain and how they became media stars during the 1990s, Whannel argues that the 20th century saw more emphasis on sports as an arena for heroism (2002). He challenges arguments that describe a gradual erosion of 'authentic' heroism during the 20th century in favour of an emphasis on mass media entertainment stars, exemplified by Daniel Boorstin's (2006) characterization of the decline of heroes in favour of celebrities. Boorstin suggests that the interest in 'greatness' of achievement has gradually been replaced by the media-driven interest in the banalities of celebrities' lives, and hence we no longer have true heroes in our culture. Whannel argues, however, that while sports stars have replaced more traditional 'heroes' such as explorers, adventurers, scientists, and military men, athletes retain some of the authenticity of such extraordinary figures because 'the cultures of sport still depend in part on a constant re-enacting of the heroic' (2002: 46). The unpredictability of sporting contests is a key dimension of this authenticity in that it allows for 'heroic' or extraordinary performances in specific, limited, and never to be repeated time frames, resulting in both urgency and demands on participants to excel beyond expectations, to achieve 'greatness' (Smart, 2005). The 2010 World Cup demonstrates this in full measure, with many favoured teams knocked out at the league stage or surviving only through penalty kick deciders. Spain, a team that had perpetually missed the finals, eventually won the competition, but only through a last-minute goal in extra time, providing dramatic tension and finally matching long-held national expectation. Earlier in 2010 at the Winter Olympics, the Canadian men's hockey team beat their eternal American rivals in the gold medal game, but only after their youthful captain Sidney Crosby scored in overtime, provoking an outpouring of Canadian media stories on these national heroes. Goodman et al. (2002) demonstrate that adverts using Olympians also draw predominantly on narratives of heroism, illustrating that the commercial use of these celebrities relies directly on the perceived authenticity of athletic heroism. . . .

The Modern Construction of Olympism and the Appeal to Ancient Authenticity

As already discussed, heroism is a dominant discourse in the construction of sport (McKay et al., 2000; Whannel, 2002), but this heroism is often based on archetypes, many of which are drawn from eternal cultural myths (Goodman et al., 2002). In the case of the Olympics, an important archetype has been the ancient amateur athlete and his participation purely for the sake of sport—rather than for economic gain—which is certainly echoed in the contemporary discourses described above. . . .

The modern Olympics were established under the leadership of Pierre Frédy, Baron de Coubertin, a wealthy French aristocrat. Coubertin's original aim was to reform the French educational system to include athletic training, based on the model of the British public school system. When, however, he was unable to raise interest in this scheme, he turned his attention to establishing the international Olympics. Support for this was sought through an appeal to his fellow aristocrats and their contemporary notion of amateur sport. At a congress held in 1894 in Paris, delegates voted to re-establish the Olympic Games under the leadership of an already-formed IOC, restricting participation to amateurs, defined as those who received absolutely no monetary gain from athletics (and thereby impeding the participation of the working class, who would be discouraged by the expense involved in training and travelling to the games) (Young, 1984). The first Games held in 1896 in Athens were a moderate success, and Coubertin decided that the second should be staged in Paris. The IOC was reformed at this time, including nine new members of the European titled aristocracy. Also at this time, Coubertin began to promote the idea that ancient Greek Olympians were both aristocratic and amateur, and that their competition was based on the ideal of sport for its own sake (Young, 1984: 73). . . .

The simple truth, however, is that Greek athletes who participated in the Olympic Games and other athletic festivals were not amateurs but professionals, at least in the modern sense of the terms. . . . Victorious athletes were lavishly rewarded on their return home, as best demonstrated by evidence from Athens which shows that an Athenian Olympic victor would receive an immediate cash award and free meals for life at public expense (Kyle, 1987: 127, 146–7).[4] There is evidence that other cities took things a step further, paying Olympians to compete for them rather than their own home towns (Young, 1984: 141–2). The acceptance of monetary awards and particularly payment would have made any of these athletes professional, by modern definition, and disqualified all from competing in the pre-1980s Olympics. . . .

Although professional athletes are now an accepted presence in the modern Olympic Games, the authenticity of amateurism has become so ingrained that it is still, if only tacitly, invoked. If we turn to the example of the Lloyds TSB 'Local Heroes' programme, we can see attempts to emphasize the amateurism central to sporting authenticity that still exists. The programme:

> . . . is an initiative to support the future stars of Team GB and Paralympics GB in the lead up to London 2012 and beyond. Follow their journey as they pursue their sporting dreams. For every Olympic and Paralympic medalist, there are thousands of genuine hopefuls struggling without recognition or funding. (http://www.facebook.com/lloydstsblocalheroes)

These 'local heroes' need the financial support of the bank's donations to achieve their goals, suggesting that they are not yet established enough to have significant commercial sponsorship and that they are, therefore, amateurs who do not receive direct payment for their athletic activities. The ancient Greek Olympics have been used to legitimize and authenticate ideals of amateurism in the modern Games, but this discourse is based on the misinterpretation and occasional falsification of historic evidence. Nonetheless, the reiterations of amateurism have become a central part of the modern Olympic discourse, and indeed provide a distinctive Olympic dimension to the 'authenticity' that is foregrounded to distract audiences from the commercialization of the Games. . . .

Notes

1. The British Olympic Association's website http://www.britisholympians.com/guidelines .aspx was accessed on 14 January 2011, but the site was folded into the London 2012 preparations and these guidelines deleted.

2. The other major sporting mega-event is, of course, the World Cup. The global television rights in 2002 and 2006 were sold for almost USD$2 billion (Smart, 2005: 90) and, more recently, FIFA completed the worldwide sale of television rights for the 2010 World Cup, 18 months before the tournament began (http://www.fifa.com/aboutfifa/ tv/index.html). No details of the revenue are provided on FIFA's official website, but various media news reports USD$2.7 billion as the price of broadcast rights for South Africa 2010.

3. All institutions of the Olympic movement are governed by the Olympic Charter and contain many references to promoting the fairness, equality, and friendship of sporting contests, see http://multimedia.olympic.org/pdf/en_ report_122.pdf

4. The intrinsic monetary value of these awards has been debated (e.g. Instone, 1986).

References

Andrews DL and Jackson SJ (2001) *Sports Stars: The Cultural Politics of Sporting Celebrity*. London: Routledge.

Barney RK (2007) The Olympic Games in modern times. In: Schaus GP and Wenn SR (eds) *Onward to the Olympics: Historical Perspectives on the Olympic Games*, Part II. Waterloo, ON: Wilfred Laurier University Press.

Barney RK, Wenn SR and Martyn SG (2002) *Selling the Five Rings: The International Olympic Committee and the Rise of Olympic Commercialism*. Salt Lake City, UT: University of Utah Press.

Boorstin DJ (2006) From hero to celebrity: The human pseudo-event. In: Marshall PD (ed.) *The Celebrity Culture Reader*. New York and London: Routledge.

Chatziefstathiou D (2007) The history of marketing an idea: The example of Baron Pierre de Coubertin as a social marketer. *European Sport Management Quarterly* 7(1): 55–80.

Christensen P (2007) The transformation of athletics in sixth-century Greece. In: Schaus GP and Wenn SR (eds) *Onward to the Olympics: Historical Perspectives on the Olympic Games*, Part I. Waterloo, ON: Wilfred Laurier University Press.

Crowther NB (2007) The Ancient Olympic Games through the centuries. In: Schaus GP and Wenn SR (eds) *Onward to the Olympics: Historical Perspectives on the Olympic Games*, Part I. Waterloo, ON: Wilfred Laurier University Press.

Evjen HD (1987) Review of Young. *The Classical Journal* 82(3): 268–71.

Gardiner EN (1910) *Greek Athletic Sports and Festivals*. London: Macmillan.

Gardner P (1892) *New Chapters in Greek History*. London: Putnam's and Sons.

Goldman R and Papson S (1998) *Nike Culture: The Sign of the Swoosh*. London: Sage.

Goodman JR, Duke LL and Sutherland J (2002) Olympic athletes and heroism in advertising: Gendered concepts of valor?

Journalism and Mass Communication Quarterly 79(2): 374–93.

Instone S (1986) Review of Young. *The Journal of Hellenic Studies* 106: 238–9.

Kyle DG (1987) *Athletics in Ancient Athens*. Leiden: E.J. Brill.

Lasch C (1979) *The Culture of Narcissism*. New York: Warner Books.

Law A, Harvey J and Kemp S (2002) The global sport mass media oligopoly. *International Review for the Sociology of Sport* 37(3–4): 279–302.

McKay J, Messner MA and Sabo D (2000) *Masculinities, Gender Relations and Sport*. Thousand Oaks, CA: Sage.

Maguire J (1999) *Global Sport: Identities, Societies, Civilisations*. Cambridge: Polity.

Maguire J, Barnard S, Butler K and Golding P (2008a) 'Celebrate humanity' or 'consumers?': A critical evaluation of a brand in motion. *Social Identities* 14(1): 63–76.

Maguire J, Barnard S, Butler K and Golding P (2008b) Olympism and consumption: An analysis of advertising in the British media coverage of the 2004 Athens Olympic Games. *Sociology of Sport Journal* 25(2): 167–86.

Mahaffy JP (1879) Old Greek athletics. *Macmillan's Magazine* 36: 61–9.

Marshall PD (1997) *Celebrity and Power: Fame in Contemporary Culture*. Minneapolis, MN: University of Minnesota Press.

Miller SG (2004) *Ancient Greek Athletics*. New Haven, CT: Yale University Press.

Olympic.org (n.d.) *Revenue Sources and Distribution*. Available at: http://www.olympic.org/en/content/The-IOC/Financing/Revenues/?Tab=1

Poliakoff MB (1989) Review of Young. *The American Journal of Philology* 110(1): 166–71.

Rojek C (2001) *Celebrity*. London: Reaktion Books.

Rojek C (2006) Sports celebrity and the civilizing process. *Sport in Society* 9(4): 674–90.

Smart B (2005) *The Sport Star: Modern Sport and the Cultural Economy of Sporting Celebrity*. London: Sage.

Turner G (2004) *Understanding Celebrity*. London: Sage.

Wenn SR and Martyn SG (2007) Juan Antonio Samaranch's score sheet: Revenue generation and the Olympic Movement, 1980–2001. In: Schaus GP and Wenn SR (eds) *Onward to the Olympics: Historical Perspectives on the Olympic Games*, Part II. Waterloo, ON: Wilfred Laurier University Press.

Whannel G (2002) *Media Sports Stars: Masculinities and Moralities*. London: Routledge.

Whannel G (2009) Television and the transformation of sport. *The Annals of the American Academy of Political and Social Science* 625: 205–18.

Young DC (1984) *The Olympic Myth of Greek Amateur Athletics*. Chicago: Ares.

Zhang L and Zhao SX (2009) City branding and the Olympic effect: A case study of Beijing. *Cities* 26: 245–54.

35

Mapping Commercial Intertextuality

HBO's *True Blood*

Jonathan Hardy

Commercial intertextuality is used to describe the production and interlinking of texts like blockbuster films or TV series with allied paratexts and products, such as spin-offs, reversionings, promos, online media, books, games and merchandise. For critical political economists such commercial intertextuality is mainly read in terms of synergistic corporate communications that seek to maximize profits by cultivating and exploiting audiences and fans (Meehan, 1991, 2005). Corporate transmedia storytelling, such as the Matrix franchise, serve to create 'narratively necessary purchases' (Proffitt et al, 2007: 239). For scholars working in a cultural studies tradition—culturalists—commercial intertextuality can be read quite differently, as material that is fashioned in autonomous and creative ways for self-expression and social communication, generating new forms of participation, and collaboration amongst prosumers (Jenkins, 1992, 2002, 2006). While such divergent readings have reflected underlying clashes between 'critical' and culturalist scholarship, this article explores scope for more integrative approaches through a case study of cross-media promotion and intertextuality in HBO's vampire drama *True Blood*.[1]

Discussing *Star Wars: the Phantom Menace* (Lucasfilms 1999) Nick Couldry writes (2000:70):

> If we place *The Phantom Menace* in its own wider context (the Star Wars series, all the associated fan literatures and practices, the whole history of cross-marketed merchandise-saturated Hollywood blockbuster films), it is clear that we need to understand not one discrete text but a vast space of more or less interconnected texts, and how that space is ordered.

Couldry's notion of the ordering of textual space is usefully synthesizing, encouraging consideration of ordering as shaped by corporations but also other media practices. . . .

From Jonathan Hardy (2011), "Mapping Commercial Intertextuality: HBO's *True Blood*." *Convergence*, 17: 7–17. Reprinted with permission of SAGE Publications, Ltd.

. . . Textual 'space' includes various kinds of discourse, from corporate 'speech' to the discourses of critics and commentators, intergroup and interpersonal communication. Yet there is blurring and hybridization across each category, corporate/independent, professional/amateur, and, as *True Blood* illustrates, across commercial/autonomous textuality.

True Blood: Mapping Corporate Intertextual Space

True Blood is a fantasy horror entertainment series on HBO, the premium cable/multiplatform service owned by Time Warner. HBO, a quality brand ('It's not television. It's HBO'), was seeking a new hit on Sunday evenings, the traditional showcase for original material. The failure of series like *John From Cincinnati* and *Lucky Louie* had left HBO (dubbed 'HB-over') without a replacement for previous hits such as *Sex and the City* and *The Sopranos*. Promoting shows meant encouraging new subscribers to pay premium monthly fees. The first series aired in September 2008 shortly before the USA officially entered recession, when such subscriptions were vulnerable to household cutbacks. This was the context for HBO's investment in an extensive, expensive and innovative cross-media marketing campaign.

True Blood is a television show based on novels, *The Southern Vampire Mysteries,* by Charlaine Harris. The stories, the tenth of which was published in 2010, were bestsellers, providing a rich source of (inter-corporate) intertextuality. The *Twilight* franchise and later the CW's *The Vampire Diaries,* added to the resonance and intertextual reworking of vampire myths and iconography, whose rich cultural history continues to provide malleable resources for contemporary storytelling. Harris's nine books featured in *USA Today's* top 100 US book sales in 2009, while 17 per cent of total book sales that year were related to vampires or the paranormal (DeBarros et al., 2010). The stories and *True Blood* envision a world in which vampires 'live' alongside humans, able to feed off a synthetic blood product marketed as Tru Blood (discovered in Japan two years before the events in the drama begin). Set in Louisiana, the story has a powerful resonance of segregation, racism and bigotry, as well as 'Deep South' ingredients of swamps, sex, and religious fervour. There is a Vampire Rights Amendment being debated at the start of the series; with pronounced connotations of civil rights and gay liberation, Tru Blood has enabled Vampires to 'come out of the coffin'. Described by *USA Today* (Bianco, 2010: 9) as a 'blood-spattered, sex-obsessed, fabulously wild camp-vamp funfest', the show succeeded in building a large, majority female, audience, averaging 6.8 million per week for the first series, with a young, mainly college-educated and upscale profile. The central character, Sookie Stackhouse, is a telepathic woman attracted to a supernatural lover whose mind she cannot read and who is a mix of old-style, 'Southern' gentility (being 173 years old) and sexually charged, predatory animal. The lead writer and executive producer for the show is Alan Ball, who produced HBO's earlier hit *Six Feet Under.* Describing the show's appeal, Ball stated 'women love the storytelling and the romance, and men love the sex and violence' (Carter, 2009). Ball said he had pitched *True Blood* to HBO as 'popcorn television for smart people' (Associated Press, 2008a; *Rolling Stone,* 2008).

True Blood engages a complex mix then of intertextuality from the broadest cultural levels to the more proprietary and 'authorially' inflected, such as contemporary culture wars. The title sequence used 'handheld' and art-house cinema styles to provide an unsettling montage of images including Klu Klux Klansmen and signage ('God Hates

Fangs'), identifying vampires with themes of otherness, eroticism, miscegenation, danger and intolerance. Corporate intertextuality ranged across the various branded and co-branded elements, including that of producer, actors, visual images used across marketing, and sound, notably the music tracks used in promos and show. There was extensive inter-firm cross-promotion: Harris's publishers Orion, and retailers, cross-promoted the HBO series, while Harris herself cross-promoted the show via interviews, her official website and other fan sites.

PROMOTING *TRUE BLOOD*

HBO and its enlisted marketers have won awards and industry acclaim for an inventive campaign that has combined traditional and cutting edge marketing techniques for promotions in the USA and HBO's international markets. Most of these techniques, as distinct from treatments, are traceable to earlier innovation and comparable campaigns such as Showtime's *Dexter* (Young, 2010) or Fox's *24* (Scolari, 2009), however the campaign exemplified a highly developed cross-media strategy. HBO has a privileged site for its own self-/cross-promotion, and trailers and promos have been intensively used to promote the series on HBO channels. During the first series, these included explicitly intertextual trailers; one featured enthusiastic notices from professional media critics, another appreciation from fan sites and bloggers. Both highlight core brand features: confirming quality, promoting a cult-fan engagement, while also appealing to a broader audience. Another promotional theme has been to play, in startling and creative ways, with the conceit of vampires 'living' alongside humans, and thus as 'consumers' for marketed services from coffin fittings to dating agencies. Audiovisual promotions included a pre-launch mockumentary (disguised as a news show),

together with documentaries on vampire (inter)texts and cultural representation.

All contemporary 'event' television promotion is cross-platform, but HBO, seeking to make sense of a proprietary, non-advertising TV service and a franchise attractive to its other sales divisions, media partners and advertisers, had particular incentives to launch a cross-channel campaign, one which made innovative use of online and social media platforms. Promos and trailers were run across HBO's broadcast channel, its non-linear VOD service HBO On Demand, and online. For series 3, HBO produced six 'minisodes', first shown as webisodes on Yahoo! TV, then posted on HBO.com (n.d.) and subsequently shown on HBO following repeats of series 2. Exemplifying transmedia storytelling, and 'overflow' (Brooker, 2001), the minisodes were also posted to the official *True Blood* Facebook page with over 1.4 million fans. At a tertiary promotional level, a promo for the minisodes proclaimed (voice-over):

> You crave new blood. You're hungry for more of the story. Now sink your teeth into six *True Blood* mini episodes. Not from last season—won't been seen in the new season. All New. Written by *True Blood* creator Alan Ball. Beginning May 2, every Sunday night right after a season 2 encore presentation at eight. Get ready for the new season with a drop of *True Blood*.

Against the textual bias of 'intertextuality', the visual and aural dimensions must be reincorporated. A Depeche Mode track was used for a celebrated series 2 promotion, for series 3 a trailer was re-edited with the track 'Teeth' by Lady Gaga, while Snoop Dog crafted a cross-promotional rap homage, 'Oh Sookie'. Jace Everett's track 'Bad things' from the title sequence, climbed the alt-country sales charts, and the soundtracks were sold alongside the DVDs. Featured music and episode titles also add layers of inter-aural resonance, such as title use of the Cowboy Junkies' song 'To love is to bury'.

Marketing—using print, TV, radio and outdoor advertising, competitions and sweepstakes—was used extensively, but often in innovative ways. In New Zealand, outdoor billboard posters featured marked-out wooden stakes and stencilled instructions reading 'In case of Vampires, snap here'. In the USA, guerrilla marketing tactics included street teams with fake petitions for and against vampires (with heightened resonance in a presidential election year), as well as stunts involving 'Fangbanger' girls (the pejorative term used in *True Blood* for women who sleep with vampires) appearing in bars. However, amongst the most innovative aspects was an extensive cross-platform campaign, with significant investment online. This began with a teaser campaign in May 2008 involving viral outreach to a few influential bloggers amongst fantasy and horror fans and gamers. The strategy was contracted to Campfire NYC, a small marketing firm specializing in online and guerrilla marketing whose founders had developed the successful strategy for *The Blair Witch Project* (Marshall, 2002). Such viral strategies can overcome resistance to conventional media marketing and benefit from fans' own marketing efforts (Murray, 2004). For *True Blood,* Campfire (2009) pursued a similar strategy of distributing teaser material, alternate reality game (ARG) puzzles, and even posting capsules of *'blood'* in unmarked envelopes. In fact, there was no corporate branding for HBO at all in the first phase of the online campaign, a feature repeated in some later promotions. Bloodcopy.com (n.d.) was launched as the main site for stories and activity.

For the first series a cross-media marketing campaign for Tru Blood was developed using the iconography of an adult drink, with taglines such as 'Real blood is for suckers' 'All flavor. No bite'. Videos spread virally some three months before the series aired explaining how Tru Blood enabled

vampires to 'come out', while faux TV spots appeared on cable and late-night network TV advertising vampire-targeted products (Stanley, 2008). HBO also developed elaborate fake websites to support the concept. A fully functioning website for vampires, the American Vampire League, was modelled on such progressive organizations as the American Civil Liberties Union. In contrast to sites' multi-ethnic diversity, the other fake site, the Fellowship of the Light, features the iconography of a fundamentalist Christian organization. Opposing 'interspecies' relationships, the site displays a near exclusive array of white Anglo-Saxon models. Common to all these campaigns was a sophisticated, and knowing, intertextuality, from the graphic layout of websites to the images and text.

More overt programme promotions appeared towards launch. Time Warner's deal with You-Tube (and subsequently with Yahoo! TV) led to advertisements, trailers and proprietary clips being made available online, hyperlinked and copied by numerous emergent fan sites. HBO's vp advertising and promotions, Zach Enterlin, told *Brandweek,* 'From the start, we knew this was just so much bigger than print ads and 30-second spots. We wanted a campaign that's as rich as the series . . . The whole campaign has been about popping through in a really crowded environment, and using promotional content to tell a story' (Stanley, 2008). According to Gregg Hale, a partner at Campfire, 'We built this on solid storytelling and the idea of immersing people in this world . . . We never tried to fool anybody; we wanted to give them an entertaining experience and a way down the rabbit hole' (cited in Stanley, 2008).

By the time the second series was promoted in 2009, HBO was working with six different creative and media-buying agencies. Campfire produced Bloodcopy. com (n.d.), a fake vampire blog and news site, and viral videos for the campaign; Digital Kitchen, crafted 'vampire product' tie-in ads; Ignition produced radio ads; Red Creative did the same for online ads; Omnicom Group's PHD placed media advertising, while Deep Focus organized online media buying for parts of the campaign (Steinberg, 2009). For the second series, Tru Blood was marketed to fans, manufactured by Omni Consumer Products, a company specializing in creating 'real' products from fictional ones (Stanley, 2009a). A striking series of fake ads for vampire products featuring real brands were produced by Digital Kitchen, who had created the acclaimed title sequence for the first series (Alston, 2008). Ecko Unlimited, Geico, Gillette, Harley-Davidson, MINI and Monster. com all signed up to the HBO co-funded campaign, with taglines including 'Dead Sexy' (Gillette), 'Feel the wind in your fangs' (Mini), and 'Outrun the Sun' (Harley-Davidson).

HBO's campaign included faux evening weather reports on radio stations for vampires; a cinema advertisement made to look like local business ads; a weekly news magazine shown on HBO platforms that included a segment called 'The Vampire Report'. PHD won awards for its media campaign that included an 8-page vampire insert in *am New York* newspaper, a first-ever cover wrap-around for *The Los Angeles Times,* and a 12-page intra-firm advert in *Entertainment Weekly* (Moses, 2010). *Vanity Fair* featured party-photos of celebrities with fangs. Inter-firm cross-promotion included Warner Home Video's tie-up with fashion label Saint Augustine Academy for a vampire-inspired show at the Australian Fashion Week to promote the season 2 DVD.

There was extensive intra-firm advertising and editorial cross-promotion across Time Warner's holdings. *Entertainment Weekly* (2009), owned by Time Warner, featured *True Blood*'s star Stephen Moyer on the cover for a special feature on vampires, and numerous celebratory news, reviews and feature articles, such as 'Bring on the Blood' (Spines et al., 2009; Stack,

2009). Amongst extensive coverage for the third series in 2010 were a six-page cover story (18 June), previews (8 January, 9 April), and reviews (25 June). The corporate 'texts' produced and heavily cross-promoted included an original comic book, merchandise and series releases on DVD and Blu-ray. The series 2 release (involving another agency, BBDO) incorporated social media features so that, for the minority with internet linked Blu-ray players, users could post viewing status updates directly to their Facebook and Twitter accounts, share favourite scenes with friends, access the live feeds and receive gifts (Lezzie, 2010). For series 3, HBO launched new teaser posters, the minisodes, cross-promotional inserts in Time Warner's *Entertainment Weekly* and third-party media, including sponsorship (with 3D glasses) of the centrefold model in *Playboy* magazine. IDW Publishing produced a comic-book adaptation of the show, written by Ball. Mobile marketing specialists Medialets worked with PHD to launch an iPhone app that generated bloody fingerprints when users touched the screen.

This was a highly successful promotional strategy. *True Blood* was a domestic hit in the USA, becoming HBO's most successful show since *The Sopranos* and boosting subscriptions (Associated Press, 2008b). Extending the franchise, the first series DVD, released in May 2009, was the best-selling TV programme in June, while the series topped the iTunes chart for purchased TV episodes that month and remained a bestseller. The audience built steadily, increasing to 2.4 million for series 1 (Steinberg, 2009; Stelter, 2008). The second series premiered with a record-setting 3.7 million audience (Hibberd, 2009) peaking at 5.3 million, the largest audience HBO had achieved for five years since *The Sopranos* (Toff, 2009). The second series attracted weekly audiences of 10–12 million (made up of the Sunday show, repeat screenings, VOD and online access), from a subscription base around a third of the size of free-to-air TV. *True Blood* also sold successfully overseas. In Britain it was shown on News Corporation's FX channel on BSkyB, and then on free-to-air when the public service broadcaster Channel Four screened the first series in Autumn 2009.

True Blood and the Ordering of Textual Space

HBO's strategy involved a sophisticated effort to establish both cult status and popular appeal. Through the targeting of fan networks, buzz marketing and invitations for immersion, HBO's corporate strategy sought to cultivate fan engagement and use this as a tool to generate interest and publicity amongst wider audiences. There was a revealing moment of collision and controversy, however. In May 2009 the business and news weblog network site Gawker Media featured Bloodcopy, the fake blog purporting to be written by a vampire. Campfire and HBO staged Gawker Media's 'acquisition' of Bloodcopy as part of a paid sponsorship deal, and promoted it via a public relations strategy to business and technology reporters. Described as an adverblog (Steinberg, 2009), Bloodcopy was syndicated through Gawker sites such as the gadget site Gizmodo and gaming site Kotaku. Under the deal, Gawker was to create six original posts for the blog per day. However, this marketing—masquerading as vampire news—generated a backlash from users whose complaints eventually led to suspension of the blog. Some Gawker users complained that marketing discourse was not being adequately identified. In response, Chris Batty, Gawker's vp of sales and marketing, dismissed critics of the advertorial as 'humorless' (Seward, 2009), while Courteney Monroe, who led HBO's marketing, welcomed the exposure, commenting 'it contributed to the noise' (Stanley, 2009b). However, beyond the

issue of disclosure, the incident highlighted broader issues concerning corporate speech masquerading as autonomous speech, and the boundaries between 'interested' and 'independent' speech. If the fake vampire advertisements were playful masquerades, the corporate masquerading of autonomous textual production was more troubling, marking the complex friction between top-down (corporate) and bottom-up autonomous media practices. HBO closed Bloodcopy in September 2009, but resurrected it as a microsite for series 3, enabling fans to participate in live conversations on Twitter.

The online intertextual space for *True Blood* stretches from corporate sites to autonomous fan sites, some organized around the series, stars and characters, some around the novels, and others with greater distance from the megatext, connected to fantasy, gaming, horror and other networks. The off-air relationship between co-stars Anna Paquin and Stephen Moyer generated other intertextual connections. HBO has six official dedicated sites, while there are more than 30 major fan sites, together with Facebook and Twitter sites, forums and message boards. *True Blood* has also generated numerous fan sites around the world, notably in the UK, Italy, Spain, France, Germany, Poland, Serbia and Brazil. One of the leading fan sites True-blood.net (n.d.) has a predominantly US audience (57%) but with significant traffic from the UK (11%) and Canada (7%), followed by Australia, Sweden and Norway. The site's demographic profile (February 2009 to 2010) was 55 per cent women, 39 per cent 18-34, 44 per cent college educated and 11 per cent from graduate school (Quantcast, 2010).

As other studies show (Hills, 2002; Jenkins, 1992), there is evidence of a textual hierarchy in which some fans favour more independent sites over corporate ones, and sites declare their independence with varying intensity. Yet, while only a full study can do justice to the multiplicity of fan/audience texts, there is evidence that the boundaries between corporate/autonomous and commercial/non-commercial blur and merge. Already, in *Textual Poachers* (1992) Jenkins feared that division between fan autonomy and corporate directedness was breaking down, expressing in the final pages fears that the fan autonomy and authenticity which structures his account was being undermined by growing commercialism. Popular fan sites such as True-Blood.tv (n.d.), financed by advertising, contain prominent links to HBO merchandise. The commercial intertextuality of official merchandise is prominent across all the most popular 'independent' sites. Commodified intertextual flows thus extend into more 'autonomous' textual spaces. Yet a counter-flow is also discernible. Enabled by media corporations efforts to encourage online participation is the space created within 'controlled' sites such as HBO's Trueblood.wiki (n.d.) for critical fan discussions, for instance on the show s double standards in regard to male and female nudity.

The spectrum from corporate to autonomous texts is important for normative-critical analysis but also complex, often opaque, at points of intersection. *True Blood* Twitter, for instance, is 'officially endorsed' but not 'affiliated' to HBO. The corporate wiki's textual space is polyvocal, official promotions run alongside 'autonomous', albeit policed, exchanges. Leading fan sites, part-supported by advertising, incorporate HBO promotions, link to official merchandise, and in various ways 'trade' with HBO to secure privileged access to stars (interviews), news, and materials. Commercial intertexuality ranges from authorized texts/merchandise in official sites to unlicensed products, such as t-shirts. *True Blood* illustrates the increasing diversity of transmedia intertextual space and its tensions and contradictions. Online sites and allied promotions provided opportunities for immersion in story elaboration. For its architects, the strategy sought to engage with perceived audience demand for complexity, sophistication and subtlety, across both brand communications and media texts. This created space for participation, pleasure, creativity and play. However, this agency needs to be examined in the context of the shaping influence on reading and consumption from those managing such narrative brands.

Conclusion

This discussion has argued for the importance of examining how corporate activity seeks to order (inter)textual space, while emphasizing that this requires analysis of the multiple sites and contending forces of communicative exchange. HBO invested heavily in shaping textual space and extended commercial intertextuality through cross-media promotion, online and social media engagement. An important focus, as the Bloodcopy incident reveals, concerns the manner in which boundaries are negotiated as commercial speech extends into spaces governed by expectations of independence. Yet, an integrative analysis is required of the plural dynamics of textual production and interaction along a corporate-autonomous axis. Far from diminishing critical accounts, this strengthens attention to the power dynamics structuring textual space, the manner in which economic structures, imperatives of commodification and corporate interests impose constraints on that space, and the manner in which these are negotiated and contested. It requires efforts to reincorporate 'control' and 'pleasure' narratives (Meyrowitz, 2008), overcome the divide between 'contextual' and 'textual' analysis (Caldwell, 2006:104), and remain alert to the articulation of creativity and meaning as well as commerce. How the problems of synergistic corporate speech and commercialism might be evaluated alongside the pleasures of the (inter)texts is beyond the scope of this piece. Yet, both critical political economy and cultural studies are needed to trace the increasing complexity, and implications, of corporate (inter)textual proliferation.

Note

1. For more general discussion on political economy and cultural studies integration see Babe (2008), Kellner (1998, 2009), Hesmondhalgh (2007, 2009), Hardy (2010b).

References

Alston J (2008) Give HBO Some Credit. *Newsweek* 152(12) 22 September: 14.

Associated Press (2008a) Vampires, well, come to life in 'True Blood' (3 September), URL (accessed 12 February 2010): http://today.msnbc.msn.com/id/26513974

Associated Press (2008b) 'True Blood' a well-timed hit for HBO, MSNBC. (23 November) URL (accessed 12 February 2010): http://today.msnbc.msn.com/id/27821649

Babe RE (2008) *Cultural Studies and Political Economy: Towards a New Integration.* Lanham, MD: Lexington Books.

Bennett T and Woollacott J (1987) *Bond and Beyond: The Political Career of a Popular Hero.* Basingstoke: Macmillan.

Bianco R (2010) Wild, weird *True Blood* packs full-throated fun. *USA Today, Life* section (11 June): 9.

Bloodcopy.com (n.d.) URL (accessed October 2010): http://www.bloodcopy.com/

Brooker W (2001) Living on Dawson's Creek: Teen viewers, cultural convergence, and television overflow. *International Journal of Cultural Studies* 4(4): 456–472.

Caldwell J (2004) Convergence television: Aggregating form and repurposing content in the culture of conglomeration. In: Spigel L and Olsson J (eds) *Television After TV: Essay on a Medium in Transition.* Durham, NC: Duke University Press, 41–74.

Caldwell J (2006) Critical industrial practice: Branding, repurposing, and the migratory patterns of industrial texts. *Television & New Media* 7(2): 99–134.

Campfire (2009) Campfire wins four IAB MIXX awards for HBO's *True Blood.* News release 24 September. New York: Campfire. URL (accessed 27 September 2010): http://campfirenyc.com/press.html

Carter B (2009) With a little 'True Blood', HBO is reviving its fortunes. *New York Times-Business* (12 July): 1.

Couldry N (2000) *Inside Culture.* London: SAGE.

De Barros A, Donahue D, Memmott C, Minzesheimer B and Wilson C (2010) Trends, triumphs of 2009 book year. *USA Today, Life* section (14 January): 4.

Entertainment Weekly (2009) 20 greatest vampires of all time (31 July): cover, 30-33.

Fiske J (1987) *Television Culture.* London: Routledge.

Grey J (2010) *Show Sold Separately: Promos, Spoilers, and other Media Paratexts.* New York: New York University Press. Gripsrud J (1995) *The Dynasty Years.* New York: Routledge.

Hardy J (2010a) *Cross-Media Promotion.* New York: Peter Lang.

Hardy J (2010b) The contribution of critical political economy. In: Curran J (ed.) *Media and Society.* London: Bloomsbury, 186-209.

HBO.com (n.d.) URL (accessed October 2010): http://www.hbo.com/

Heszmondhalgh D (2007) *The Cultural Industries* (2nd edition). London: SAGE.

Hesmondhalgh D (2009) Politics, theory and method in media industries research. In: Holt J and Perren A (eds) *Media Industries: History, Theory, and Method.* Malden, MA: Wiley-Blackwell, 245–255.

Hibberd J (2009) 'True Blood' returns to biggest HBO audience in years. *Hollywood Reporter* (16 June). URL (accessed 15 February 2010): http://livefeed.hollywoodreporter.com/2009/06/true-blood-season-two-premiere-ratings.html

Hills M (2002) *Fan Cultures.* London: Routledge.

Jenkins H (1992) *Textual Poachers: Television Fans and Participatory Culture.* New York: Routledge.

Jenkins H (2002) Interactive audiences? In: Harries D (ed.) *The New Media* Book. London: BFI, 157–170.

Jenkins H (2006) *Convergence Culture.* New York: New York University Press.

Kellner D (1998) Overcoming the divide: Cultural studies and political economy. In: Ferguson M and Golding P (eds) *Cultural Studies in Question.* London: SAGE, 102–120.

Kellner D (2009) Media industries, political economy and media/cultural studies: An articulation. In: Holt J and Perren A (eds)*Media Industries: History, Theory, and Method.* Chichester: Wiley-Blackwell, 95–107.

Levine E (2005) Fractured fairy tales and fragmented markets: Disney's weddings of a lifetime and the cultural politics of media conglomeration. *Television & New Media* 6(1): 71–88.

Lezzie T (2010) The Work. *Advertising Age* 81(22) 31 May: 23.

Marshall PD (2002) The new intertextual commodity. In Harries D (ed.) *The New Media Book.* London: BFI, 69–81.

Marshall PD (2004) *New Media Cultures.* London: Arnold.

Meehan E (1991) 'Holy commodity fetish, Batman!' The political economy of a commercial intertext. In: Pearson RE and Uricchio W (eds) *The Many Lives of the Batman: Critical Approaches to a Superhero and his Media.* New York: Routledge, 47–65.

Meehan E (2005) *Why TV Is Not Our Fault.* Lanham, MD: Rowman and Littlefield.

Meyrowitz J (2008) Power, pleasure, patterns: Intersecting narratives of media influence. *Journal of Communication* 58(4): 641–663.

Moses L (2010) PHD: HBO's *True Blood. Brandweek* 51(24) 14 June: 22.

Murray S (2004) Celebrating the story the way it is : Cultural studies, corporate media and the contested utility of fandom. *Continuum,* 18(1): 7–25.

Ono KA and Buescher DT (2001) Deciphering Pocahontas: Unpacking the commoditization of a Native American woman. *Critical Studies in Media Communication* 18(1): 23–43.

Proffitt JM, Yune Tchoi D and McAllister MP (2007) Plugging back into the matrix: The intertextual flow of corporate media commodities. *Journal of Communication Inquiry* 31(3): 239–254.

Quantcast (2010) true-blood.net audience profile. URL (accessed 2 February 2010): www.quantcast.com/true-blood.net

Rolling Stone (2008) 'True Blood'. *Rolling Stone* 1061 (18 September): 101.

Sandvoss C (2005) *Fans.* Cambridge: Polity.

Scolari CA (2009) Transmedia storytelling: Implicit consumers, narrative worlds, and branding in contemporary media production.*International Journal of Communication* 3: 586–606.

Seward ZM (2009) Gawker VP says sponsored posts will bring in majority of revenue one day. *Nieman Journalism Lab* (27 May). URL (accessed 10 July 2009): http://www .niemanlab.org/2009/05/gawker-vp-says-sponsored-posts-will-bring-in-majority-of-revenue-one-day/

Spines C, Bentley J and Semingran A (2009) Bring on the blood. *Entertainment Weekly* (26 June): 23–24.

Stack T (2009) 'True Blood'. *Entertainment Weekly* 1063 (4 September 2009): 22–23.

Stanley TL (2008) HBO tempts consumers with 'trublood'. *Brandweek* (18 July). URL (accessed 6 December 2009): http://www .brandweek.com/bw/content_display/news-and-features/promotion/e3i3a2b5d0d04f5 fd1cba7c2bcb81329ccd#

Stanley TL (2009a) HBO markets bloodsucker beverage. *Brandweek* 50(29) 3 August: 21.

Stanley TL (2009b) Courteney Monroe. *Brandweek* 50(32) 14 September: 18.

Steinberg B (2009) Advertising for HBO's 'True Blood' bends truth a bit. *Advertising Age* (28 May). URL (accessed 6 February 2010): http://adage.com/mediaworks/article?article_ id=136942

Stelter B (2008) 'True Blood' renewed. New York Times 19 September: 6.

Toff B (2009) ARTS, BRIEFLY, 'True Blood' is boiling for HBO, New York Times 27 August: 2.

True-blood.net (n.d.) URL (accessed October 2010): http://true-blood.net/ True-Blood.tv (n.d.) URL (accessed October 2010): http://true-blood.tv/

Trueblood.wiki (n.d.) URL (accessed October 2010): http://truebloodwiki.hbo.com

Waetjen J and Gibson TA (2007) Harry Potter and the commodity fetish: Activating corporate readings in the journey from text to commercial intertext. Communication and Critical/Cultural Studies 4(1): 3–26.

Young A (2010) 'Dexter' vs. 'True Blood': The battle of two killer media plans. Advertising Age (20 May). URL (accessed 1 July 2010): http://adage.com/mediaworks/article?article_id=144011

PART V

REPRESENTING SEXUALITIES

A s a way of foregrounding the different ways media scholars analyze mainstream **representations** of heterosexuality, we begin this section with two chapters analyzing the immensely popular series of vampire romance novels, *The Twilight Saga*, by Stephenie Meyer. The first chapter, by Anne Helen Petersen (V.36), is based on a qualitative **audience-reception** study of "a very specific demographic—adult, female, feminist readers of *Twilight*," undertaken "to garner a more nuanced understanding of the ways in which feminists experience and negotiate pleasure derived from reading **postfeminist** texts" (p. 343). In the second chapter (V.37), Collins and Carmody offer a **content analysis** of instances of abusive behavior directed toward Bella, the heroine of the series. They also argue that the series must be seen as an example of the way entertainment media still represent violence against women as "an acceptable expression of love in adolescent relationships" (p. 356).

Petersen's chapter does not claim to be a comprehensive interpretation of the **text** or of the perplexing cultural phenomenon of the rejuvenation of the vampire romance **genre**. Rather, she focuses on the ambivalent pleasure that some self-identified feminists in her study reported:

> Having voiced immediate pleasure in the narrative, these readers were nonetheless deeply troubled by it—incensed and repulsed by several elements of the text that were readily labeled by readers as culturally regressive, non-feminist, and affirmative of patriarchal values. (p. 349)

In Petersen's view, during a "**postfeminist**" period, when consensus on many of the earlier feminist critiques of traditional heterosexuality is lacking, "the question remains: how can we approach tension-ridden texts in a way that is at once critical and constructive?" (p. 343).

While there might be many possible answers to this question, the next chapter provides one that is important to consider. For Collins and Carmody, located in the disciplines of sociology and criminal justice, and writing in a journal aimed at social workers, although "critics disagree about the presentation of adolescent relationships in the Twilight series" their own study "examined the book series with special attention to behaviors that are commonly associated with dating and intimate partner violence" (p. 356). They conclude by calling for the use of these books in "programs to prevent dating violence" and more generally in the education of teens about the mythology of "romantic dominance" in traditional heterosexuality:

> To recognize behaviors that were previously presented as chivalrous and romantic as clear examples of control, stalking, abuse, and intimidation may offer young people new insights into the insidious and often-subtle nature of abuse and control. In this way, the *Twilight* series could continue to influence young lives, but in a new way. (p. 363)

No contemporary book on popular culture can ignore what some scholars are calling the "**pornification**" of the culture. Although this term is controversial, many scholars use it to describe the ways that the **codes** and conventions of pornography have seeped into the wider culture, often to the point that such representations are so normalized that they are rendered invisible. In the next two chapters, we provide a brief and selective introduction to both a particular type of heterosexual pornographic representation and to the way in which soft-core pornographic conventions have moved inexorably into mainstream commercial media culture. These chapters are intended to help students think and debate about this important feature of our contemporary world.

Pornography itself has been held up to feminist scrutiny and divisive debate for many years, and it is not our intent to represent these heated debates here. However, it is worth pointing out a frequently ignored aspect of hardcore pornography in these earlier discussions: the way **race** works to intensify and sexualize the **gender** domination that is threaded through hardcore pornography. As Gail Dines (V.38) writes, "Analyzing the role of racial representations in pornography is . . . key to understanding how pornography works as a discourse."

> If, as radical feminists argue, pornography is pleasurable because it sexualizes inequality between women and men, then the more degraded and abused the woman, the greater the sexual tension and thrill for the male viewer. (p. 366)

By exploring the ways that pornography harnesses racist **ideologies** to sexualize the debasement of people of color, Dines argues that pornography is one of the few media genres that still trade on the explicit and overt racist images that were commonplace during the pre-civil rights era.

Jane Caputi (V.39) further explores the theme of eroticized sexual degradation in pornography-inspired pop culture imagery in her article, "The Pornography of Everyday Life." Closely analyzing mostly advertising images in fashion magazines targeted to women consumers, Caputi argues that when the codes from "degradation porn" filter into mainstream culture, "these are not generally perceived as humiliation and torture; rather they are perceived as sex." Even when "everyday" porn is not representing sexuality as entwined with female degradation, according to Caputi, it is still "founded in very conventional notions of gender: women and men are said to be opposites and unequal, with specific gendered attributes such as masculine aggression and female-identified passivity" (p. 374).

Some would argue that hip-hop representations of women as "bitches and hoes" clearly contribute to the degradation of Black women, within a society that already has a long and ugly history of sexualized racism. In a section from *The Hip Hop Wars,* Tricia Rose (V.40) engages with the longstanding and contentious debates within the Black community over representations of African American women and sexuality within hip-hop narratives, language, and visual imagery. For Rose, "although hip hop isn't primarily responsible for America's **sexism,** it is the most visible and extreme engine for it in black popular culture, which means that it has a special impact on black women and men who, because of the racist and sexist world in which they live, rely on black culture as a source of reflection, support, and affirmation." Complicating this discussion, Rose looks at how some hip-hop celebrities attempt to deflect accusations of sexism by asserting that many young Black women freely comply with their own sexist treatment, as both participants in music videos and as fans of hip-hop's street culture. But as Rose points out,

> For many young black women, the language of commercial hip hop about black sexuality has influenced their understanding of black women, not just reflected it. (p. 387)

To criticize representations of women as "bitches and hoes" within hip-hop culture is not to be "anti-sex," from Rose's perspective, but simply to offer a thoughtful analysis of the way sex is packaged and consumed within commercial pop culture. She argues for what she calls "a genuine sexual freedom of expression," but one that is not "tied to sexist male fantasies or to male-dominated sex trades in which women are demeaned and degraded in order to appear to be sexually free" (p. 389).

Problematic sexual representations in media culture are also of strong concern within the GLBT (gay, lesbian, bisexual, **transgender**) community. Despite some important advances in gay and lesbian visibility in media culture in recent years, representations of sexuality in mainstream pop culture continue to be, for the most part, rampantly heterosexual. Part of the reason for this is the continuing homophobia that producers assume continues to characterize the majority of media consumers in most targeted audiences. Although progress has been made by **activists** in raising awareness of new audiences for complex representations of nonnormative sexuality and gender, producers of mainstream media culture still shy away from representing sexual and gender minorities in richly textured ways.

Jay Clarkson (V.41) studies "the politics of gay representation" through an examination of "the discourse of the discussion board of StraightActing.com, an Internet discussion board for self-identified straight-acting gay men." He argues that in their discussions about "the nature of their and other gay men's visibility . . . they demonize an effeminate gay stereotype, which they perceive as dominating media representations of gay men" (p. 392). Viewing "the flamer" and other gender transgressives as limiting the progress of full **gay and lesbian** integration into the society's mainstream, they "argue that increased visibility of straight-acting gay men has the potential to undo what they see as the negative consequences of the prevalence of effeminate gay stereotypes" (p. 396). But for Clarkson, such a conservative and defensive visibility strategy is wrongheaded and would only contribute to the narrowing of public understanding of the complexities of gender and sexuality.

Even in the place where one might expect more openness and greater capacity for gender fluidity, the "virtual worlds" of cyberspace enabled by the Internet, it has proved difficult to re-envision gender and sexuality in ways that transcend the cultural norms and values of our real-life society. Brookey and Cannon (V.42), in their chapter on sexual representation within the massively multiplayer online role-playing game (MMORPG) *Second Life,* question the liberatory potential many early proponents of cyberspace celebrated, in this case with respect to representations of gender and sexuality.

In the virtual world created online by *Second Life* players, "users are able to build their own buildings, create their own clothing and accessories, and are usually at liberty to shape this virtual world in any way they see fit" (p. 398). Brookey and Cannon looked specifically at the ways in which players "are taking advantage of this liberty to refigure gender and sexuality"— or not. Focusing in particular on how players are enabled to construct their own *avatars* (the in-game embodiments or self-representations of the players themselves), the researchers looked at in-game stores selling clothing as well as sexual and fetish ware and found an emphasis on traditional femininity and female sexual submissiveness. While **queer** sexuality was not invisible in *Second Life,* they noted that in "queer spaces and 'islands,'" while sexual content was not restricted, many of the spaces were firmly gender segregated. Most restrictive was a voice verification system set up to make sure that players who patronize virtual "escorts" within *Second Life* are not inadvertently dating a transgender avatar.

Our final chapter in this part, by E. Tristan Booth (V.43), is a challenging exploration of the positive effect of "disruption" of "conventional process and behavior" caused by the mere presence of a transgender individual in a commercial cultural text, in this case, through the analysis of a particular episode of the cable TV makeover "reality" series, *Queer Eye for the Straight Guy.* The chapter employs anthropologist Victor Turner's concept of **liminality** to identify something or someone who is "betwixt and between" conventional or customary states of being—which is seen as

a useful way of thinking about transgendered bodies. Booth argues that the transman character who was included in this episode offered "an educational opportunity" to both the regular gay male characters of the show and to the audience, "by triggering self-reflexiveness and pushing the boundaries of hegemonic structures." (p. 415) In his deconstruction of the text of this episode, Booth carefully analyzes features such as the ways in which the "Fabulous Five" gay men interact verbally and physically with the transman, and contrasts these with how they treat their usual guests, heterosexual males "in need" of a fashion makeover. Pointing to one instance in the episode where sexuality "is directly addressed" in a joke made by one of the Fab Five, Booth points out that

> From the perspective of the nontrans-gender audience, the very suggestion that [the transman] would one day have sex with *anyone* could be read as transgressive, since it brings to mind questions regarding who that partner would be, what types of bodies would be involved, and how the activity would commence. (p. 412)

Though not uncritical, Booth found much to celebrate in this episode of a show which, "despite its name . . . had never been particularly queer in the theoretical sense." Indeed, in his view, the episode "shook the very foundation of a series premised on binary, essentialist conceptions of sex, gender and sexuality" (p. 410). Booth concludes that while "all marginalized bodies, including those of the Fab Five, face a certain amount of risk,"

> . . . ultimately, it took the liminality of a transman's body, as well as the corresponding liminality of his gendered social status, to bring an embodied, vulnerable queerness to *Queer Eye.* (p. 415)

Since the first edition of *Gender, Race, and Class in Media* in 1994, there has been a proliferation of images in pop culture that make non-hegemonic genders and sexualities visible through a range of representations that are, as Booth argues, nuanced and complex. In large part this increased nuanced visibility is due to the organization of activists on local and national levels to both educate and agitate for media representations that speak to the diversity of gendered identities and sexualities that are embodied in the contemporary world. Several examples of such grassroots media activism, along with examples of fan productivity, are to be found in Part VIII of this edition.

36

That Teenage Feeling

Twilight, Fantasy, and Feminist Readers

Anne Helen Petersen

Introduction

Like several feminist media critics before me, I find myself troubled by a "dirty" pleasure: I love *Twilight*. I fully recognize the numerous feminist objections to this particular text, yet I was completely swallowed by the four books one summer, devouring all 2,500 pages in a period of two weeks. *Twilight*'s narrative is simple and familiar: Bella, a passive, soft-spoken, plain, loner of a 17-year-old girl encounters Edward Cullen, a vampire forever frozen in the glory and strength of age eighteen. They fall immediately and irrevocably in love, but Edward must fight his overpowering urges to bite the object of his desire, effectively enacting a very thinly veiled allegory for the suppression of sexual desire. Over the course of the *Twilight* saga, Bella forsakes her future as an adult subject and her human identity in order to become a vampire with Edward, who refuses to allow her to join him until she agrees to marriage. Her love and desire lead her to acquiesce to Edward's demands; she marries at age eighteen, attends the prom she always hated, and enters into the paternalistic sphere of the Cullen "household." Conservative, regressive, decidedly postfeminist values are espoused throughout. Yet I love it. Indeed, I lose myself to the story with a depth of feeling last experienced in middle school.

The familiar conundrum, then, is how can a feminist take pleasure in media that explicitly contradicts my goals and aims as a feminist? What types of fantasy are enlisted in the process of said pleasure? Perhaps more importantly, in recognizing this persistent feminist problem, how can we understand and express the complicated set of pleasures, disavowals, acknowledgements, and sublimations that take place during the "indulgence" in such media? It is quite simple to dismiss the pleasure of others as juvenile, escapist, or elementary. But what happens when the pleasures are our own? When self-declared feminists—thousands of them!—are reading the text? This is difficult, contradictory, and personal

From Anne Helen Petersen (2012), "That Teenage Feeling: *Twilight*, Fantasy and Feminist Readers." *Feminist Media Studies*, Vol. 12, Issue 1, pp. 51–67. Reprinted by permission of the publisher (Taylor & Francis Ltd, http://www.tandf.co.uk/journals).

work, but I do not think that means that we should shy from it. The question remains: how can we approach tension-ridden texts in a way that is at once critical and constructive?

I have thus turned to a very specific demographic—adult, female, feminist readers of *Twilight*—to garner a more nuanced understanding of the ways in which feminists experience and negotiate pleasure derived from postfeminist texts. I recruited participants using a method known as "snowballing," garnering responses from approximately thirty women between the ages of eighteen and forty of varying educational backgrounds, geographical location, and ethnicity. These women all self-identified as feminists, but their means of engagement—as well as their overarching attitude towards the text—is by no means uniform. . . . Participants are PhD candidates, undergraduate students at private and public colleges, teachers, stay-at-home moms, and "young professionals"; they enjoy parts of the text, but are likewise troubled by aspects of the narrative and their own absorption therein.

Feminism Versus Postfeminism

. . . To be clear: I do not intend this article to function as an interpretation or critique of the *Twilight* phenomenon *writ large*—a project whose scope is beyond the limits of a single article. Rather, it uses the range of feminist responses as a lens through which we might gain better insight into the state of contemporary feminism.

For the uninitiated, the *Twilight* saga is a set of four published novels (*Twilight, New Moon, Eclipse, Breaking Dawn*) and one unfinished draft (*Midnight Sun*), readily accessible on the Internet. The first of the books was released in 2005; following initial success, Stephenie Meyer published three books in quick succession. *Twilight* frenzy hit its fever pitch in the summer of 2008, as anticipation grew for the August

publication of the series-concluding *Breaking Dawn*, with its initial printing of 3.7 million copies, and the release of the filmic version of the first book, simply named *Twilight* (2008). At the time of this writing, the books have sold over one hundred million copies worldwide, while the first three films have grossed $1.799 billion internationally (Boxofficemojo.com).

The books are labeled Young Adult fiction. A large portion of *Twilight* readers—and initial readers in particular—are indeed teenage girls. But the reason *Twilight* has morphed into a veritable phenomenon is rather simple: unlike *Hannah Montana*, The Jonas Brothers, or *High School Musical*, whose fan bases have remained solidly within the "tween and teen" demographic, moms, sisters, and friends began to pick up this "teen" text, in turn, recommending it to their friends, sisters, and mothers. In this way, *Twilight* became an inter-generational female sensation, as reinforced by the enormously popular site Twilightmoms.com.

The *Twilight* phenomenon has taken place against the backdrop of what many feminist scholars have termed "postfeminism." As Yvonne Tasker and Diane Negra explain, postfeminism "broadly encompasses a set of assumptions, widely disseminated within popular media forms, having to do with the 'pastness' of feminism, whether the supposed pastness is merely noted, mourned, or celebrated" (2007, p. 1). This ideological attitude of "pastness" suggests, despite ample evidence to the contrary, that the battle for gender equality has been won; feminism is thus unnecessary, superfluous, and/or a total buzz kill. Postfeminist rhetoric and texts commodify the language and attributes of feminism, coopting catchphrases like "Girl power!" as advertising slogans as they frame the "freedom to choose" as the freedom to choose one's lipgloss color. . . .

The effects of postfeminism are tangible: each year, fewer and fewer girls and young women are willing to identify themselves as "feminists," even when their beliefs, life philosophies, and politics align with those of the feminist agenda. In this way, the ubiquity of postfeminist rhetoric and texts have transformed "feminism" into the "F-word" for a new generation of women, painting feminists as a group of angry, bra-burning, lipstick-hating, middle-aged crones. But postfeminism has also proven a wedge within the women's movement itself, further exacerbating pre-existing rifts concerning what goals feminists should pursue and how those pursuits should be enacted. As Susan Faludi explains in "American electra: feminism's ritual matricide," the women's movement continues to be divided according to age, as "mothers" (generally affiliated with second and third wave feminism of the 1960s–1980s) find themselves at odds with their literal and figurative "daughters," whose goals, pleasures, and articulations of feminism may diverge from their own (2010, p. 29). . . .

For many of these younger women, including many participants of this ethnography, feminism means the ability to choose: to go to graduate school or be in control of one's own body, certainly, but also to not feel shame for staying at home, showing cleavage, finding pleasure in "postfeminist" objects, or rejecting any prescriptive definition of "true feminism."

Stephenie Meyer, author of the *Twilight* series, is one such woman. Meyer, a stay-at-home mother of two when she first began writing the books, is also a Mormon. While neither Mormonism nor religion is mentioned in the books, the series' general ethos and moral universe are in line with the conservative Mormon belief system, which forbids sex before marriage and encourages women to take a place in the home. According to Meyer, her lifestyle choices— or the life choices she has written for her heroine—do not render her anti-feminist. As she explains on her website, feminism is "being able to choose." She continues:

One of the weird things about modern feminism is that some feminists seem to be putting their own limits on women's choices. That feels backward to me. It's as if you can't choose a family on your own terms and still be considered a strong woman. How is that empowering? Are there rules about if, when, and how we can love or marry and if, when, and how we have kids? Are there jobs we can and can't have in order to be a "real" feminist? To me, those limitations seem anti-feminist in basic principle. (Meyer 2010)

Meyer's definition of feminism and critique of its "modern" form reproduces postfeminist rhetoric, emphasizing the "freedom of choice with respect to work, domesticity, and parenting" (Tasker & Negra 2007, p. 2).

Indeed, within the text of *Twilight*, Bella is "free" to "choose" to give up her human life—including college, a job, independence—for eternity with Edward. Bella's postfeminist traits become especially clear when compared to Buffy, another teen heroine grappling with her place in the vampire universe. Buffy has several romantic interests and dilemmas, but "her story always belonged to *her*" (Laura Miller 2008). She is likewise surrounded by a strong, supportive network that mirrors the multi-cultural ethos of third wave feminism. In contrast, Bella is hopelessly clumsy and incapable of physical coordination; she eschews the friendship of the girls at her school, opting instead for the thrall of her love for Edward. She plays helpmate to her father, cooking square meals every evening.

Meyer endows Bella with few distinctive traits, talents, or interests—there is little to sustain or define her apart from her all-consuming devotion to a man. She may attend high school, but few of the elements of teenage girldom concern her. At seventeen, Bella is already figured as an adult, ready to participate in the rituals of traditional female adulthood, including marriage and motherhood. Bella's very lack of distinguishing characteristics facilitates reader identification; through this identification, the reader is effectively encouraged to feel Bella's overwhelming desire to sacrifice all for a man. In this way, *Twilight* offers what Elena Levine terms a "post-feminism fantasy," "bend[ing] the notion of feminist empowerment so that it becomes feminine devotion" (2010, p. 283).

Meyer may not be *anti*-feminist. But she, her texts, and their stunning success form one of the most striking manifestations of postfeminist culture in recent years. Levine cautions, however, that just because "such a fantasy is so appealing to so many girls and women," it does not mean that *Twilight* fans are "dupes of patriarchy." Rather, "it means that they are so fully immersed in contemporary post-feminist culture that both feminist empowerment and feminist fulfillment have taken on new meanings" (2010, p. 284). Here is where this article intervenes, attempting to ascertain what empowerment and fulfillment mean to feminist readers—and whether they are, in fact, locating it in *Twilight*. If they are, how is the process accomplished? Is it negotiated? And if they are not, what else are they finding in the text that compels them to engage further? . . .

Fantasy and Pleasure

If readers were not finding pleasure in a feminist hero, or through rewriting the text themselves or other fan practices, what did they find so pleasurable and attractive about the text? The most frequently voiced form of pleasure was in response to *Twilight*'s cultivation of fantasy—but a very particular brand of fantasy, best explained by Elizabeth Cowie. Cowie's nuanced theorization of female fantasy speaks directly to a greater understanding of female desire, particularly as it pertains to fantasy spaces such as an ostensibly regressive vampire narrative. Cowie posits fantasy as a "mise-en-scène of desire": a setting forth of an elaborate scene of

drawn-out pleasure, of almosts and near-misses, of denial and the controlling of masculine and feminine subject positions. In her words, "fantasy depends not on particular objects, but on their setting out; and the pleasure of fantasy lies in the setting out, not in the having of the objects" (Elizabeth Cowie 1984, p. 79). Within this scenario, pleasure is not linked to consummation but rather to "the happening and the continuing to happen; in how it will come about, and not in the moment of *having happened*, when it will fall back into loss, the past" (1984, p. 80).

Yet what might lead a feminist to pursue distinctly non-feminist fantasies as roundabouts to pleasure? Following Freud and Lacan, Cowie explains fantasy as a manifestation of early, even pre-Oedipal desires, through which the present context is mapped with future desires. Fantasies bring pleasure through the representation of a wish, "but also by presenting the failure of a wish if the latter has undergone repression" (Cowie 1984, p. 81). Desires that have been repressed—as socially unacceptable, untenable within a functioning family unit, or discouraged by a feminist politics—rise to the surface in the form of the fantasy scenario. Crucially, personal fantasies often speak to a wide audience, thus explaining how a fantasy scenario like *Twilight* (the premise for which occurred to Meyer in a dream) can resonate with a broad swath of readers. Fantasies are likewise "contingent": viewers may simply translate the basic architecture of the fantasy to form their own mise-en-scene of desire, adorning it with the specifics of their own experience (Cowie 1984, p. 85).

What, then, are the original fantasies of *Twilight* for feminist readers? One might expect the answer to fixate on Edward, yet most readers were not necessarily attracted to the character, per se, but to the rituals of courting, love and devotion he represents. According to one respondent, "As a formerly outsider-ish teenage girl, I liked seeing the new girl in town become the object of desire of the hot outsider guy who nobody has managed to land" (Gillian, thirty-two, Graduate Student). For some, it is a matter of "being chosen," or offering the pleasure of first love: as a 20-year-old reader explains, "I can't believe how well Stephenie Meyer brought back all of those butterflies of falling in love for the first time!" (Jen, twenty, Undergraduate Student).

These original fantasies—Edward's devotion to Bella, the evocation of first love—combine to structure *Twilight*'s dominant mise-en-scene of desire. Importantly, many of these fantasies are rooted in an emotional return to feelings first felt as a teenager—a time when passions were unfettered by reason. Yet it is the way in which these fantasies are "laid out" that truly define reader's engagement: feelings of absorption, forestalled pleasure, and disappointment with the series' culmination run throughout the responses— emotions that associate strongly with "the happening and continuing to happen" of Cowie's framework. The pleasure of the series, it seems, is very much rooted in the extended escape to the world of Edward and Bella—and the equally extended time it takes for the couple to consummate their relationship. This "strategy," as one respondent cleverly explains, is one of the "slow-burn" (Gillian, thirty-three, Graduate Student).

The books may be about sex, but they certainly do not depict it. There is relatively little description of kissing or making-out; the text is clean enough for Meyer's Mormon readers. At the same time, the text is imbued with the romance and tension that attend abstinence: yearning and unfulfilled passion far more exciting than any amount of raw pornography. The passion within and produced by the books may be likened to a form of "rapture"—a term that connotes the extreme pleasure and joy of orgasm. The pleasure, as Cowie emphasizes, comes not in the conclusion; in fact, most readers express extreme dissatisfaction with the depiction of the eventual culmination. Rather, it is the tossing and turning in between, the pages upon pages of dithering over how, and when, sex will occur, that most clearly constitutes *Twilight*'s mise-en-scène of desire.

Cultural critic Caitlin Flanagan (2010) argues that the resonance of "super reactionary love stories," whether *Twilight*, *High School Musical*, or the bestselling songs of Taylor Swift, is this generation of women's way of demanding *more*. Having spent the last decade "being hectored—via the post-porn, Internet-driven world— toward a self-concept centering on the expectation that the very most they could or should expect from a boy is a hookup," girls and young women are rejecting the "low" romantic expectations set by their parents' generation (Flanagan 2010). In their place: "boyfriend stories" reminiscent of their *grandparents*' texts, inflected with the very cultural mores against which many of these girls' parents were rebelling.

Respondents' attraction to the traditional and "true love" aspects of *Twilight* highlight a yearning for traditional courtship and delay of sexual activity, even on the part of feminists. For these women, the gradual destigmatizeation of sexual activity and promiscuity (and the concurrent rise of "hook-up culture") has had an unfortunate sideeffect: the end of romance. One reader elaborated on this point at length, contrasting the depiction of romance to the complicated "reality" of relationships today:

> The books resonated a lot with me and perhaps other women because of [their] absolute simplicity. Bella and Edward's love story is intense, focused, and unmediated. What I mean by that is that in contemporary society, relationships are tempered by all sorts of "considerations"—work, distance, "timing," finances, etc. There's a mediocre, cynical view of love these days, down to when to "hook up" with someone or who should pay a bill, etc, etc. I think a lot of women long for those days when there was a magic to the mere thought of

kissing someone and being madly, deeply destabilized by love. Where just one look from the parties involved can be enough to make you swoon. (Gloria, thirty, Graduate Student)

For Gloria, the lifestyle afforded by the advances of the women's movement—including the right to work, to have an independent lifestyle, even the "right" to pay the bill—have obviated the simple pleasures of love and passion. Another reader underlines the ways in which the romance read, to her, as a subversion of contemporary relationship norms, even as it confirmed traditional notions of true love:

Bella and Edward represent the fantasy of subverting normative heterosexuality, and allow us to find faith in the existence of such a thing as true, passionate romantic love. In our everyday lives, we as twenty-something women getting older and more "responsible," feel pressure to date the Mike Newmans [Bella's other, "normal," human suitor] of the world; we want to date men who have jobs, who can pay their rent, who can function socially with our friends and family, who can keep their apartment somewhat clean, not the "bad boy," or brooding boy with whom many of us had passionate romantic flings in our younger days. Bella doesn't choose Mike Newman, she subverts the pressure to do that, and instead chooses Edward. And the fling isn't just a fling. It's true love that lasts, we imagine, through the banalities of a long-term relationship [. . .] And I took great pleasure in rooting for that. (Kate, twenty-seven, PhD Student)

For these women, *Twilight* provides a romance and experience for feminists that the realities of contemporary culture and living as an adult, responsible, woman do not. Yet the attraction to this type of traditional romance is fraught with ambivalence. In part due to their feminist beliefs, almost all respondents articulate an initial hesitancy to engage with the text. "I was highly skeptical," says one; "there was no way I thought that I could get into a vampire book"; "I was not interested at all"; "I was vehemently anti-*Twilight*." Yet akin to a classic tale of seduction, each reader was compelled, almost against her will, to engage in the fantasy of Edward and Bella's relationship. Once "seduced," the "slow burn" of the story took control. Readers articulate the resultant pleasure in varied fashion:

[The] physical tension between [Bella and Edward] was really unlike anything I'd read in a long time. Their fingers can brush against each other and it takes half a page and you're on the edge of your seat the whole time. (Ally, twenty-three, Master's Student)

The best reason I can come up with for having been completely glued to the story is that it reminded me of falling in love, or of being younger and thinking that love was about to happen. That is a fun feeling, whether you're experiencing it immediately or remembering it from years past. (Laura, thirty, Teacher's Assistant)

I think that (to generalize) a lot of people our age have settled into some sort of stability, whether it is a relationship, a job, a social group, and it was exciting to feel a little bit of the way we did when we were young, when a word, a gesture, or a look could make a huge impact on you. (Alex, twenty-nine, Marketing Specialist)

In other words, the books were transportive: like all fantasy, they allowed readers to vacate their own lives, however temporarily, and inhabit a different space, with different rules, many of which might not be termed feminist. Importantly, envelopment and submission to these fantasy scenarios is facilitated, and perhaps even contingent, upon a specific form of engagement with the text: that of "girl reading."

The Pleasures of Girl Reading

As evidenced above, the books inspire a sort of rapture—and as pleasurable as rapture may be, it also connotes a certain sense of surrender and danger. Indeed, for a number of respondents, the text, and the obsession that accompanied it, treads a knife-edge between satisfaction and a frightening loss of self. The shame of indulging, both in the romance and in absorbing texts in general, is nothing new. Building on Freud, Cowie explains how such shame stems "not only for being childish (and hence for a denial of reality) . . . but also surely because of the cathexis deriving from the archaic, original wishes involved" (1984, p. 85). *Twilight*-based cathexis—the process of focusing all energy on one person, idea, or thing—is, for some respondents, laughable, or a point of exclamatory pride:

It was an immediate obsession. I could not put the book down, and even with chasing my daughter ALL day, I finished reading the first book within three days (two nights)! (Courtney, twenty-five, Stay-at-home Mother)

My girlfriend and I read them out loud to each other, and we literally inhaled the first book. We couldn't get enough. (Dena, twenty-eight, Veterinary Assistant)

I found the experience, as is typical with my previous experience with romance and/or suspense novels, to be immersive, exciting, and pleasurable. I read the books [. . .] over the course of about a week and a half, sacrificing precious late-night and early-morning sleep hours just to be able to finish them. (Meredith, twenty-four, PhD Student)

I was devoured into the story. (Mandy, twenty-five, Stay-at-home Mother)

I read it in huge bouts—a couple hours at a time, uninterrupted—and I remember getting frustrated when my *Twilight* reading was interrupted by the important stuff like assembling furniture. (Ellen, twenty-eight, PhD Student)

For others, however, the obsession, however pleasurable, was lined with shame and chaos:

As soon as I started the first book I knew I was a goner . . . I read them all in a week, and was totally lost to the world. This does happen to me from time to time with a book, movie, or series, I'll get very involved in it and escape for a bit, but nothing has ever affected me like this. I couldn't talk, it was hard for me to focus on real life, I went grocery shopping for the week and only got milk . . . I am usually a very prepared, planned person, and after a bit it was hard to be so wound up—by the middle of third book, I just wanted it to end so I could have my life back! Of course, I also wanted it to never end, and missed it when it was done. (Ann, thirty-three, Preschool Teacher)

I truly hate to admit it, but I did find myself caught up in the swoon of the romance. (Lindy, twenty-six, Yoga Instructor)

I feel so sad that a book about a teenage girl and her vampire boyfriend could drag me in so far, so quickly, so (as Bella would put it) irrevocably. (Meghan, twenty-eight, Fundraising Manager)

For these readers, the fantasy space and engagement with the mise-en-scène of desire became so intense and detailed that it began to challenge the *non*-fantasy space of the outside world. In this way, consumption produced feelings of inadequacy—as if something must be wrong with one's life to seek such shelter in another.

Loving a vampire did not generate this shame. Rather, the shame resulted from the way the narrative overtook everyday life. Put differently, adult readers are ashamed of reading in a style usually associated with young girls. On this point, Flanagan provides essential insight. Recollecting her personal history, she nears an explanation of the appeal of reading for the adolescent girl. In her words,

> The salient fact of an adolescent girl's existence is her need for a secret emotional life—one that she slips into during her sulks and silences, during her endless hours alone in her room, or even just when she's gazing out the classroom window ... This means that she is a creature designed for reading the way no boy or man, or even grown woman, could ever be so exactly designed, because she is a creature whose most elemental psychological needs—to be undisturbed while she works out the big questions of her life, to be hidden from view while still in plain sight, to enter profoundly into the emotional lives of others—are met precisely by the act of reading. (Caitlin Flanagan 2008)

As for *Twilight*, Flanagan echoes several of this study's respondents: "It's the first book that seemed at long last to rekindle something of the girl-reader in me. In fact, there were times when the novel ... stirred something in me so long forgotten that I felt embarrassed by it" (2008). Again, *Twilight* is responsible and capable of stirring something—an impulse, a "teenage feeling," the stomach-punch of first love, a keen sense of sexual desire, and, most importantly, an obsessiveness, both toward the characters and the act of reading itself.

Clearly, someone or something—parents, authority figures, boys, feminists, whomever—have informed readers, consciously or unconsciously, that they should no longer feel attracted to the relationship represented in the story or to the act of consumption the series presents. Respondents report defending themselves from ridicule on all sides: one exclaims "Of course I have to defend

myself! To my sister, some friends, my husband ... "(Courtney, twenty-five, Stay-at-home Mother). And yet, as one reader flatly states, "my fiancé thinks it's ridiculous that I like such an obviously sentimental and crowd-pleasing narrative. He will never understand why I want to read stuff like this, but that's because he's never been a teenage girl" (Gillian, thirty-two, PhD Candidate). Here, the pleasures of *Twilight* are strongly linked with the pleasures inherent to teenage girldom, including reading, first love, and the obsession and absorption accompanying both practices. Ultimately, these pleasures have less to do with the specifics of *Twilight* than with feelings of envelopment, dedication, and intense emotion that many women associated with their pre-adult lives.

Ambivalence and Affirmation of the Feminist Project

Notwithstanding the various pleasures in the fantasy scenario and "girl reading," the single best way to characterize feminist readers' response to *Twilight* is ambivalence. Having voiced immense pleasure in the narrative, these readers were nonetheless deeply troubled by it—incensed and repulsed by several elements of the text that were readily labeled by readers as culturally regressive, non-feminist, and affirmative of patriarchal values. Objections generally centered on two issues critical to feminism today: girl-power (more specifically, the complete lack thereof) and the overarching conservative, pro-life agenda.

Respondents repeatedly critiqued the characterization of Bella, her lack of autonomy, and her traditional relationship with Edward:

> Bella is a weak character who is incapable of defining herself without Edward or a man in her life ... she's obsessed with the overprotective and fatherly Edward. (Dena, twenty-eight, Veterinarian's Assistant)

Bella's personality is completely sub-sumed by Edward. She's willing to give up anything, even her life (possibly her soul), to be with him. I said above that I (and most women) can somewhat relate to this feeling, but that doesn't mean that the level of her obsession is healthy and it probably isn't. The problem with the books is that the author never really makes any commentary on the unhealthy nature of this relationship . . . (Wendy, twenty-five, Administrative Assistant)

I was most disturbed in the second book when Bella gives up her desire to live when Edward leaves . . . For Bella to stop living because of a man is the worst message possible to deliver to young women just entering their roman-tic lives. Heartbreak can be overwhelm-ing, sure, but that is why we need messages about strength, self-sufficiency, and self-esteem. (Barbara, thirty-four, Graduate Student)

I continued to resent the character of Bella because I think she is a disempow-ered role model for young girls, and I think her relationship with Edward is disturbing. (Katherine, twenty-eight, Communications Director)

Bella, the feeble damsel in distress, is always either obsessing over her one, true love or is under his protection from the big, bad world. Her goal throughout the entire series is to be made a vampire so she can never be away from Edward. She has no other ambition. And she only achieves this goal by getting married and giving birth. (Maggie, twenty-six, Pastry Chef)

I think Bella is lame and the emphasis on childbearing/marriage is completely off-putting. It's also ridiculous that she needs to be pressured by her boyfriend to go to college. (Bethany, twenty-eight, PhD Candidate)

All of these readers had previously expressed appreciation for the text overall, yet each maintains a critical distance from the depiction of a submissive girl in a rela-tionship which may be readily portrayed as manipulative and controlling.

Respondents also expressed general dismay concerning its thinly veiled conser-vative allegories. For many readers, the developments of *Breaking Dawn*, the final book in the series, were most distressing:

When Bella becomes pregnant in *Breaking Dawn* . . . the narration switches to Jacob's point of view. The teenage bride pregnant with a monster baby literally loses her voice in the narrative. (Ally, twenty-three, Master's Student)

The fourth book is the epitome of pro-life politics—Bella has a baby who literally breaks her spine, and she loves the kid so much that she's will-ing to bear it. (Gillian, thirty-two, Graduate Student)

Several readers were wary of what they and other critics have termed the "absti-nence porn" that permeates the series. For these readers, what began as the "slow burn" within the mise-en-scène of desire eventually revealed itself to be the ideo-logical structuring of an author with an obvious agenda:

The feminist in me was annoyed and at times disturbed (not actually about the crazy birth, but the abstinence porn that went hog wild in the books). (Marissa, twenty-five, Master's Student)

Okay, the writing's not terrible, the plot's entirely predictable but wouldn't be if I was twelve, it's kind of strange how hot a description of hand holding can be, but why is no one talking about how much these books are abstinence-only propaganda? (Annabelle, twenty-one, Undergraduate Student)

The sexual politics are the most troubling, for me. Bella's sexuality is constantly denied an outlet—it's hard not to see a connection to cultural valuation of virginity, and the related association of women with temptation or impurity. The explicit construction of her desired male partner as dangerous is equally problematic, as he is both held up as more powerful and given control over the progression of their relationship, and capable of destroying her. The connection to conservative views in which a man is both the guard and the vandal of a woman's purity is pretty explicit. (Ellen, twenty-eight, PhD Student)

. . . Feelings of ambivalence led many to articulate a secondary reason for reading, thinking, and talking about *Twilight*, for as Ien Ang has pointed out, some find pleasure in a text in part because its very existence and popularity opens discursive doors. . . . Many women found the popularity of *Twilight* as clear evidence that the need for feminists was not, as postfeminism assumes, a thing of the past. As one respondent demonstrates, *Twilight* has the potential to facilitate conversations with younger readers who may not have been exposed to feminist thought:

I have thought many times about the assignments I would give to high school students who wanted to do a book report, etc. on *Twilight*. How do you get a teenage girl to consider the idea that this fantastical love story is actually sending a potentially dangerous message? How do you get her to consider the idea that Edward and Bella's obsession with each other involves emotional and psychological manipulation and abuse? How do you get teenage girls to notice all that's missing from Bella, and how much richer their own lives are? (Laura, thirty, Teacher's Assistant)

According to another reader, the books provide an avenue through which feminists and non-feminists of multiple generations may begin to form a discourse community. In her words,

The fandom of young girls strikes me as a largely positive, and potentially feminist, thing—it's bringing girls together with one another in a context of reading and discussing books and films. I'd rather see that happen than not, however problematic the text. (Ellen, twenty-eight, PhD Student)

Ellen values the text's community-building function, even if the text around which girls and women rally lacks an explicit feminist message. Some might label her opinion postfeminist— shouldn't communities also be charged with action and change? Yet as Ellen points out, *Twilight* inspires girls to read and discuss, and while that discussion may focus on whether one is "Team Edward" or "Team Jacob," even superficial discussion can lead to larger questions. Put differently, talking about *Twilight* can be a way for girls to work through issues and ideas that are otherwise difficult to articulate: What type of partner do I want? What kind of respect and freedom would I prefer? What sort of woman do I want to be? What about this particular romance makes me uncomfortable or excited? These type of introspective questions may not be explicitly feminist, but the answers girls find, especially if reading with mothers, friends, and mentors who are feminist, can guide them towards the women's movement. Ultimately, the majority of respondents see the *Twilight* phenomenon not as a problem, but an opportunity—a "media phenomenon that opens up a space where dialogue about feminism and patriarchy can take place with the next generation's feminists" (Ally, twenty-three, Master's Student).

Conclusion

As I mention above, my initial impulse to theorize *Twilight* was driven by my personal consternation with my pleasure in the text. Through the researching, surveying, and writing process, however, I have become acutely aware of the potential of *Twilight*—and other texts like it—to divide our already fragile and informal coalition of feminist scholars, thinkers, and activists. Women's pleasures have long been at the center of feminist debates, and here I would re-emphasize that its position within feminist debates is nothing new. . . .

Ultimately, feminists, whether at home in academia, mainstream media, or the domestic sphere, disparage and lampoon the pleasures of *Twilight*, or any other fantasy, at our peril. Because feminists, including this one, do love *Twilight*. And while I am not a likely candidate to "turn to the right," I do know many other women who, already wary of the label of feminist, are only further alienated through an attack on the cultural texts, artifacts, and practices, whether marriage, motherhood, or *Twilight* fandom, which grant them satisfaction. This is not to say that we should simply adopt the definition of feminism proffered by Meyer and other postfeminist texts. Instead, we might use texts such as *Twilight* to create dialogue with women drawn to such a definition, working to fortify, rather than fracture, feminism's overarching projects.

. . . Whether in the form of good old fashioned consciousness raising, mentoring girls and teenagers, leading book groups, or teaching in the classroom, feminism needs voices—voices that do not decry or dismiss, but encourage thought, critique, and examination. *Twilight* can serve as one of these points of discussion, but only if we recognize its potential alongside its problems. . . .

References

Ang, Ien (1985) *Watching Dallas: Soap Opera and the Melodramatic Imagination*, Muthean, New York.

Ang, Ien (2003) 'Living room wars: rethinking audiences for a postmodern world', in *The Audience Studies Reader*, eds W. Brooker & D. Jermyn, Routledge, New York, pp. 226–234.

Click, Melissa A., Stevens Aubrey, Jennifer & Behm-Morawitz, Elizabeth (eds) (2010) *Bitten by Twilight: Youth Culture, Media, and the Vampire Franchise*, Peter Lang, New York.

Cowie, Elizabeth (1984) 'Fantasia', M/F, vol. 9, pp. 71–105.

Faludi, Susan (2010) 'American electra: feminism's ritual matricide', *Harper's,* Oct. pp. 29–42.

Flanagan, Caitlin (2008) 'What girls want', *The Atlantic Monthly*, Nov, [Online] Available at: http:// www.theatlantic.com/ doc/200812/*twilight*-vampires (15 Apr. 2009).

Flanagan, Caitlin (2010) 'Love, actually', *The Atlantic Monthly*, Jun., [Online] Available at: http:// www.theatlantic.com/magazine/ archive/2010/06/love-actually/8094/ (15 Nov. 2010).

Hellekson, Karen (2009) 'Fan studies 101', *SFRA Review*, Winter, pp. 5–7.

Hills, Matt (2002) *Fan Cultures*, Routledge, New York.

Jenkins, Henry (1992) *Textual Poachers: Television Fans & Participatory Culture*, Routledge, New York.

Jenkins, Henry (2006) *Convergence Culture: Where Old and New Media Collide*, NYU Press, New York.

Levine, Elena (2010) 'Afterword', in *Bitten by Twilight: Youth Culture, Media, and the Vampire Franchise*, eds M. Click, J. Aubrey & E. Behm-Morawitz, Peter Lang, New York, pp. 281–286.

Levy, Ariel (2005) *Female Chauvinist Pigs*, Free Press, New York.

Meyer, Stephenie (2010) 'Frequently asked questions: *Breaking Dawn*', [Online] Available at: http:// www.stepheniemeyer.com/bd_faq.html (15 Nov. 2010).

Miller, Laura (2008) 'Touched by a vampire', *Salon*, 30 Jul., [Online] Available at: http:// www.salon.com/books/review/2008/07/30/ *Twilight*/ (15 Apr. 2009).

Modleski, Tania (1979) 'The search for tomorrow in today's soap operas', *Film Quarterly*, vol. 22, no. 1, pp. 12–21.

Negra, Diane (2009) *What a Girl Wants?: Fantasizing the Reclamation of Self in Postfeminism*, Routledge, New York.

Radway, Janice (1984) *Reading the Romance: Women, Patriarchy, and Popular Literature*, University of North Carolina Press, Chapel Hill, NC.

Tasker, Yvonne & Negra, Diane (eds) (2007) *Interrogating Postfeminism: Gender and the Politics of Popular Culture*, Duke University Press, Durham, NC.

Twilight (film) (2008) Catherine Hardwicke (dir.), Summit Entertainment, USA.

37

Deadly Love

Images of Dating Violence in the *"Twilight* Saga"

Victoria E. Collins and Dianne C. Carmody

Intimate Partner and Dating Violence

. . . In the past several decades, researchers have documented the prevalence and nature of violence that is perpetrated in the course of heterosexual relationships (Smith-Stover, 2005). Most of this research has focused on intimate partner violence by married or cohabitating partners, with a smaller collection of studies limited to violence among those in dating relationships, especially young people in high school and college (Eckhardt, Jamieson, & Watts, 2002; Gover, Kaukinen, & Fox, 2008). A greater understanding of the behaviors that are common to both intimate partner and dating violence may be gleaned from the following brief review of the literature.

Dating violence is gendered, with females suffering higher rates of victimization and injury than males (Centers for Disease Control and Prevention, 2000). At particular risk are adolescent males and females (Kim-Godwin et al., 2009). This vulnerability has been attributed to adolescents' tendency to exaggerate gender roles, as well as their subscription to fantastical ideals of romance (Prothrow-Stith, 1993). Estimates indicate that 2–9% of male adolescents and 4–20% of female adolescents in the United States have been victims of physical or sexual abuse at the hands their dating partners (Howard, Wang, & Yan, 2007). . . . Female adolescents have also reported greater levels of fear as a direct result of their victimization (O'Keefe, 2005).

Dating has traditionally been defined within the context of heterosexual relationships and is influenced by socially accepted forms of masculinity and femininity. Adelman and Kil (2007) described "conservative dating conflicts," characterized by dominant heterosexual comprehensions of masculinity and femininity, emphasizing the supremacy of intimate, romantic relationships over all other relationships. They noted

From Victoria E. Collins and Dianne C. Carmody (2011). "Deadly Love: Images of Dating Violence in the '*Twilight* Saga'." *Affilia* 26:382. Reprinted with permission of SAGE Publications.

that these conflicts occur when individuals become isolated from other societal relationships, including those with friends and family members, and can lead to the objectification of dating partners, jealously, and possessiveness. Bernard, Bernard, and Bernard (1985) also noted that strong patriarchal attitudes are linked to an increased risk of violence by men in dating relationships. Dating violence is strongly associated with dominant forms of masculinity and femininity (Black & Weisz, 2003; Feldman & Gowen, 1998).

Researchers have long noted the similarities between dating violence and intimate partner violence, both of which are linked to issues of power and control (Gover et al., 2008). The feminist perspective purports that intimate partner violence results from a social structure that is inherently male dominated and the socialization of males and females into specific gender roles (Pagelow, 1984; Prospero, 2007). These socialization processes reinforce socially appropriate behaviors for both sexes in a patriarchal society that promotes male privilege (Prospero, 2007). Social norms support the use of relationship violence as a means for the male to remain in control of the female (Marin & Russo, 1999).

Tactics that are designed to exert power and control have been identified as strong predictors of dating violence (Kaura & Allen, 2004; Riggs & O'Leary, 1996). In relationships in which power differentials exist and decision making is not shared, dating violence is more likely to occur (Felson & Messner, 2000). Instances of violence result from struggles over who is going to make important decisions in the relationship and dissatisfaction over the perceived level of power that each partner possesses (Hendy et al., 2003; Pulerwitz, Gortmaker, & DeJong, 2000; Ronfeldt, Kimerling, & Arias, 1998). Behaviors, such as stalking and threats of homicide and suicide, have been found to be strongly correlated with future violence and homicide

(McFarlane et al., 1999; Roehl, O'Sullivan, Webster, & Campbell, 2005). Research has also indicated that 75–90% of femicide victims were stalked prior to their murder (McFarlane et al., 1999), and in a high proportion of femicide cases, the perpetrator committed suicide following the act of homicide (Roehl et al., 2005).

It has been estimated that between 20% and 96% of dating relationships contain psychologically abusive behavior (James, West, Deters, & Armijo, 2000; Jezl, Molidor, & Wright, 1996). The presence of psychological abuse in dating relationships is positively related to the risk of physical violence (Kasian & Painter, 1992). Foshee (1996) identified four types of psychological abuse in adolescent dating relationships: Threatening behavior, which includes threats of physical violence; behavior monitoring, in which the perpetrator forces the victim to communicate where they are physically located; personal insults; and emotional manipulation. In addition, interpersonal violence has been found to be strongly associated with suicide and suicidal ideations for both the perpetrator and the victim of the dating violence (Swahn, Lubell, & Simon, 2004).

Research has also demonstrated that violence and love often become intertwined in adolescent relationships (Black & Weisz, 2003; James et al., 2000; Vezina, Lavoie, & Piche, 1995). In a 1990 study, Carlson found that the majority of adolescents supported the use of violence against a dating partner in some situations. In addition, Bergman's (1992) study of high school students showed that more than 79% of the girls who had experienced dating violence continued to date the perpetrators of that violence.

Dating Violence and the Media

The media have been found to have an impact on a wide range of adolescent issues, such as sexual activity, smoking, substance abuse, body image, obesity, and violence

(Brown et al., 2006; Brown & Witherspoon, 2002; Collins et al., 2004). Although causality has not been established, the media have been found to influence teenagers' attitudes and indirectly to affect behaviors (Brown et al., 2006; Collins et al., 2004). Teenagers are well aware of the way the media shape their attitudes and behaviors (Lavoie, Robitaille, & Hébert, 2000), and they turn to media sources for information on dating and romantic relationships. Borzekowski and Rickert (2001) found that 23% of teenagers used the Internet-accessed information about dating violence.

Violence is not exclusive to television or the Internet and can be found in other forms of media that have a teenage audience. Certainly, movies that are popular among teenagers include considerable violence (Sargent et al., 2002), as do music lyrics and videos (Haynes, 2009; Strasburger, 1995). A large proportion of the media, including music, movies, television, and books, specifically target a teenage audience.

Because violence has been recognized as being an acceptable expression of love in adolescent relationships (Vezina et al., 1995), it is necessary to examine the social messages that teenagers are receiving through the media. Of particular interest is Stephenie Meyer's Twilight Saga. This four-book series has a core target audience of teenage girls (Stone, 2009; Young, 2009) and has sold an estimated 40 million copies worldwide since its debut in 2005 (Memmott & Cadden, 2009). The series is centered on the relationship between a 17-year-old girl (Bella) and a 17-year-old vampire (Edward) and has sparked much controversy over the modeling of a healthy relationship for teenagers (McCulloch, 2009; Stone, 2009; Young, 2009). The series also includes a teenager named Jacob, who competes with Edward for Bella's affections.

The series has been said to be attractive to teenage girls because it portrays a "traditional, romantic relationship" and positively frames the issue of abstinence (Stone, 2009). Christian publications have heralded the book series, noting that the characters restrain from engaging in sexual intercourse until they are married (Smith, 2008) and portray themes of immense self-control in the face of temptation. Others, however, have criticized the series for modeling unhealthy, inequitable romantic relationships. In a 2009 article published by MSNBC, the relationship between the two main characters, Bella and Edward, was labeled "controlling" (Young, 2009). Others have argued that the books contain "a dark undercurrent of sexual assault and abuse" (Editorial, 2009), identifying unhealthy relationship behaviors that are synonymous with stalking, self-harm, and suicide (McCulloch, 2009). Clearly, critics disagree about the presentation of adolescent relationships in the Twilight series. The study presented here examined the book series with special attention to behaviors that are commonly associated with dating and intimate partner violence.

Theoretical Framework

The analysis was guided by feminist theories, which "analyze women's experiences, articulate the nature of social relations between women and men, and provide explanations that support efforts to transform these social relations" (Swigonski & Raheim, 2011, pp. 10–11). Specifically, gender-reform feminism provides the framework (Lorber, 2005). This approach focuses on gender inequality in the social order and its cultural and structural components. To be female in the United States brings a variety of disadvantages, such as lower pay than males for the same work and disproportionate exposure to sexual harassment, sexual assault, and other forms of gender-based violence (Tong, 2009). These disadvantages do not apply equally to all women; wealthy, white, attractive, heterosexual, and able-bodied women tend to have fewer disadvantages. In fact, more recent feminist theorists have argued that we must note the "complexities of multiple, competing, fluid, and intersecting identities" (Gringeri, Wahab, & Anderson-Nathe, 2010, p. 394).

Philaretou and Allen (2001) noted that under societally enforced, strict gender-role guidelines, men are pressured to use aggression and competition in romantic relationships. In this way, masculinity emphasizes sexualized violence and dominance. In an examination of adolescent masculinities, Messerschmidt (2000) also noted that under hegemonic masculinity, which is both youthful and heterosexual, force may be acceptable in romantic relationships. Such gender stereotypes, reinforced by mediated messages, may certainly encourage dating violence and perceptions of romance that reflect traditional gender roles.

Method

An ethnographic content analysis (Altheide, 1996) of the four books in the *Twilight* series provided the basis for the study. Table 1 presents brief overviews of the plots of the four books in the series. Prior to the coding, conceptual coding categories were identified, on the basis of previous research on predictors of dating violence (Felson & Messner, 2000; Hendy et al., 2003; Kaura & Allen, 2004). . . . These predictors included physical violence, which was defined as actual or threats of unwanted physical touching, pushing, and hitting; sexual violence, which was defined as unwanted or forced sexual behaviors, including physical harm and violence perpetrated during sexual acts; and controlling behaviors. Controlling behaviors were divided into three subcategories for the purpose of coding. These categories included (a) physical control, which included physically detaining, restraining, or preventing a character from moving in order to obtain compliance; (b) verbal orders, such as demanding that someone do something; and (c) emotional control, which involved one character controlling

the dissemination of information to another character, reacting with anger to threaten another character into compliance, or making threats to harm a loved one or himself if the character did not comply with his wishes. In addition, stalking behaviors, such as following and constantly monitoring a partner's location, were coded. Since jealousy is often used to justify such behaviors, it was also included in the analysis. Another category was male aggressiveness, which included the three subcategories of male territorial behavior that emerged during the analysis on the basis of the actor's intent. The first theme involved the display of male aggressiveness to exert territorial dominance over a female. The second theme was the use of aggressiveness or anger to obtain compliance from another character.

The last category involved the male characters' use of aggression as a means of defending a female character, namely, Bella. Finally, on the basis of the findings of Kettrey and Emery (2010), who found that traditional gender roles are a dominant theme presented in magazines for teenagers, particularly the central focus on finding a man, having a romantic relationship, and securing a home, the presentation of traditional gender roles was included in the analysis. During the process of coding the last category, secondary violence emerged, that is, violent acts or threats of violence against Bella that were a direct result of her being involved with Edward or his vampire family. . . .

Results

Situations involving physical violence or threats of immediate physical violence were identified 80 times across the series, and 30% of the physical violence was perpetrated by a male in the course of an intimate relationship. Within this category, 66.7% of the violence was perpetrated by Edward on Bella and 33.3% was perpetrated by Jacob

Table 1 Plot Overview of the Four Books in the *Twilight* Series

Book Title	Book Number	Number of Pages	Date of Publication	Plot Overview
Twilight	1	498	October 2005	Bella, a 17-year-old, moves to Forks, Washington, to live with her father. She meets and falls in love with Edward, a vampire. Edward is initially attracted to Bella because her blood smells especially good to him, and he desires to kill her and drink her blood. However, with significant restraint, he resists this impulse and pursues a romantic relationship with Bella. Bella finds out that Edward is a vampire, and instead of fearing him, she embraces him as he is. Because of her association with Edward and his family, Bella is exposed to other vampires, one of which tracks and attacks Bella to upset Edward. Edward saves Bella and kills the attacking vampire, James, but not before Bella is bitten by the other vampire. Edward is forced either to let Bella become a vampire herself or suck the venom from the bite, which involves sucking her blood. Edward chooses the latter course of action, preventing Bella from becoming a vampire.
New Moon	2	563	September 2006	On her 18th birthday, Bella receives a paper cut when opening her birthday presents. Edward's brother, Jasper, attacks Bella, but Edward intervenes, saving her. As a result, Edward and his family leave the area. Bella sinks into a depression that lasts months. Bella's depression is made bearable by her relationship with Jacob. Bella also finds that when she acts recklessly, subjecting herself to significant risk of harm, she suffers delusions that allow her to see Edward. Consequently her behavior becomes more reckless. When Jacob distances himself from Bella, she discovers he is a werewolf. Jacob reveals that another vampire is in the vicinity and that he has been protecting the area. It is revealed that the vampire is Victoria, James's disgruntled mate who is there to kill Bella. Following an extremely reckless stunt, in which Bella jumps off a cliff, Edward believes that Bella is dead and plans to kill himself by inciting anger from the vampires' governing body, the Volturi. Alice, Edward's sister, takes Bella to Italy to prevent him from taking such action. They are successful in preventing Edward from ending his life, but the Volturi agree to let them go only if Edward promises to turn Bella into a vampire.

Book Title	Book Number	Number of Pages	Date of Publication	Plot Overview
Eclipse	3	629	September 2007	Edward returns to Forks with Bella and promises never to leave again. He does not want Bella to spend time with her friend Jacob because he believes it is too dangerous for her. Victoria is still attempting to kill Bella and begins to create an army of new vampires for the purpose of killing her. Jacob and the wolf pack join forces with Edward and his vampire family to save Bella from Victoria and her newborn vampires. Jacob learns that Bella has agreed to marry Edward. The book ends with a fight in which Edward kills Victoria, and her newborns are defeated. Jacob suffers substantial injuries that require medical attention and significant respite.
Breaking Dawn	4	754	August 2008	Bella and Edward get married, and on their honeymoon they have sexual intercourse. As a result, Bella becomes pregnant. The pregnancy is accelerated because the fetus is not human. Edward wants to terminate the pregnancy because of the harm the baby can and does cause to Bella's body. Bella wants to carry the baby to term. Bella recruits Rosalie to ensure that no one attempts to take her baby from her. The baby causes Bella significant harm, including broken ribs. Jacob learns of the pregnancy and protects Bella from the wolf pack because they want to destroy her child. The pack splits into two, with those who support the protection of Bella siding with Jacob. The baby becomes so strong that it almost kills Bella. Edward has to cut the baby out of her and inject her with his venom to save her. Bella becomes a vampire, but the Volturi hear of Edward and Bella's child and come to Forks to kill the Cullens. The Cullens ask other vampires for help and create a small defensive force. Alice and Jasper disappear. The Volturi come and seek to find an excuse to exterminate the Cullen family. Alice and Jasper return with evidence that Edward and Bella's child is not a threat to vampire discovery and save the day. The Volturi return to Italy.

on Bella. Throughout the series, references are made to Edward's desire to drink Bella's blood, either as a mechanism that allows Edward to control both Bella's behavior and the course of their relationship or as a reminder of the power differential between the two characters. Physical violence also occurs when Edward attempts to protect Bella from harming herself or from being harmed by others. Although Edward's intention is not to harm Bella, she suffers physical harm on 16 (20%) occasions. For example, when Bella receives a paper cut while opening a birthday gift, another vampire lunges to attack her, and Edward jumps to her rescue, resulting in injury to Bella, "He threw himself at me, flinging me back across the table. It fell, as did I, scattering the cake and the presents, the flowers and the plates. I landed in the mess of shattered crystal" (Meyer, 2006, p. 28).

Bella is the victim of 96 instances of secondary violence in the book series. The most frequent perpetrators of this secondary violence are other vampires. The story involves a romantic relationship in which Bella's love for Edward repeatedly places her at risk of serious injury or death. In addition, Edward himself poses a threat because of his desire to drink her blood: "They have a name for someone who smells the way Bella does to me. They call her my singer—because her blood sings for me" (Meyer, 2006, p. 490). It is also interesting to note that in *Breaking Dawn*, the fourth book in the series, Bella is expecting Edward's child. Throughout the pregnancy, the nonhuman child causes significant injury to Bella, threatening both her health and her life.

We identified five cases of sexual violence in the four books. All were perpetrated against Bella by either Edward or Jacob. The following excerpt describes sexual violence perpetrated by Edward: "Under the dusting of feathers, large purplish bruises were beginning to blossom across the pale skin of my arm. My eyes followed the trail they made up to my shoulder, and then down across my ribs. I pulled my hand free to poke at a discoloration on my left forearm, watching it fade where I touched and then reappear" (Meyer, 2008, p. 89).

Although Edward and Bella do not engage in sexual intercourse until after they are married, which is in accordance with those who promote the series as advocating abstinence, the sexual relationship they do have is extremely violent.

Another instance of sexual violence involves Jacob and Bella. Jacob physically overpowers Bella and kisses her forcibly against her will. This act occurs twice in the series, and after the first time, Bella retaliates by punching Jacob, inadvertently breaking her hand. Bella's injury and distress are then the cause of amusement for both Jacob and Bella's father, Charlie, which trivializes both Jacob's perpetration of sexual violence and Bella's victimization.

With regard to cases of controlling behavior, 30 cases of the first type of controlling behavior, physical control, were detected, all but two of which involved either Edward or Jacob controlling Bella. The second type of controlling behavior, verbally ordering someone to comply, occurred exclusively between Edward and Bella, with Edward ordering Bella to do something a total of 31 times. For the last type of controlling behavior, emotional control, 58 cases were identified.

Examples of Edward's use of violence for the purposes of controlling Bella's behavior are illustrated by the following quotation, in which Edward intimates Bella, "'Where do you think you're going?' he asked, outraged. He was gripping a fistful of my jacket in one hand" (Meyer, 2005, p. 103), or through asking other characters to restrain her physically, "'Emmett,' Edward said grimly. And Emmett secured my hands in his steely grasp" (Meyer, 2005, p. 382), or by threatening violence to ensure that Bella complies with his wishes, "'No! No! NO!' Edward roared charging back into the room. He was in my face before I had time to blink, bending over me, his expression twisted in rage" (Meyer, 2006, p. 535).

Throughout the series, there are 60 references to self-harm or suicide. The majority of these thoughts and behaviors (60.67%) are Bella's. Within this category, three themes emerged. The first theme is Bella's desire to become a vampire and consequently to go through the process of becoming undead, a process that involves enduring intense pain and death. Bella is willing and eager to endure a painful death to be with Edward forever. The second theme is related to Bella's suicidal ideations when Edward leaves her. Bella's deep depression manifests itself through thoughts of suicide and subsequent reckless behaviors. The last suicidal theme is related to self-harm initiated in an effort to save another character. For example, during a fight with hostile vampires, Bella has the following thoughts, "If I had to bleed to save them, I would do it. I would die to do it" (Meyer, 2007, p. 539). Repeatedly, images of suicide or self-harm are romanticized in this book series.

We identified 14 instances of stalking behavior in the books, 11 (78.6%) of which were perpetrated by Edward against Bella. These behaviors included Edward breaking into Bella's room without her knowledge, listening to her conversations with other people, following her, and monitoring her interactions with others. For example, in *Eclipse* (Meyer 2007, pp. 131–132), Bella visits Jacob against Edward's orders. When she returns, the following ensues, "It came out of nowhere. One minute there was nothing but bright highway in my rearview mirror. The next minute, the sun was glinting off a silver Volvo right on my tail." Edward uses stalking techniques as a means of manipulating and controlling Bella. These behaviors are both minimized and romanticized throughout the series through Bella's response, or lack of response, to them: "'You spied on me?' But somehow I couldn't infuse my voice with the proper outrage. I was flattered" (Meyer, 2005, p. 292).

The content analysis also revealed 31 episodes involving jealousy in the series. Most of these episodes involved Edward's jealousy of Bella's interactions with another male (54.8%), and 41.4% were expressed by Jacob over Bella's interactions with another male. These behaviors manifested themselves in many ways: admitting jealously outright, acting aggressively toward other males, and physically fighting over Bella's attentions.

Edward and Jacob repeatedly express their feelings through anger and aggression.

We found 183 instances of male aggressiveness, machismo, or male privilege in the book series. The majority of these behaviors are perpetrated by Edward (44.3%), followed by Jacob (23.5%). Displaying male aggressiveness to exert territorial dominance over a female occurred 43 times (23.5%) and was either presented through expressions of possessiveness by Edward and Jacob toward Bella or establishing dominance when confronted by another male. For example, in *Eclipse*, when Jacob attempts to warm Bella up by getting into her sleeping bag with her, the following occurs:

> Edward snarled, but Jacob didn't even look at him. Instead, he crawled to my side and started unzipping my sleeping bag. Edward's hand was suddenly hard on his shoulder restraining, snow white against the dark skin. Jacob's jaw clenched, his nostrils flaring, his body recoiling from the cold touch. The long muscles in his arms flexed automatically. (Meyer, 2007, p. 490)

In addition, claims of ownership are made concerning Bella. On three occasions, Edward refers to Bella as if she is his property, as in the following example: "'She is mine.' Edward's low voice was suddenly dark, not as composed as before" (Meyer, 2007, p. 341).

We identified the use of aggressiveness or anger to obtain compliance from another character in 23 instances in the series, with 87% of the acts of aggressiveness perpetrated by Edward toward Bella and 13% by Jacob toward Bella. These acts vary from aggressive vocalizations, such as growling, snarling, or shouting, to threatening looks, physical intimidation, and physical restraint. There were also incidents involving the male characters' use of aggression to defend a female character, namely, Bella. These incidents occur 47 times (25.68%) in the series, most frequently by Edward (n = 37) and Jacob (n = 10). It is also interesting to note that the most common descriptive words used to convey expressions of male aggressive-ness throughout include "growl, snarl, and hiss." These words are animalistic, normalizing a primitive imagery of male dominance.

Of the 132 representations of tradi-tional gender roles in the four books that we identified, most involved Edward's behavior toward Bella (67.4%) or Jacob's behavior toward Bella (14.4%). Bella is physically saved from harm by male char-acters seven times (5.3%). Although these events occur relatively infrequently, they are often major events in the story. In one instance, Edward saves Bella from death by stopping a van that is speeding toward her, "Two long, white hands shot out pro-tectively in front of me, and the van shud-dered to a stop a foot from my face, the large hands fitting providentially into a deep dent in the side of the van's body" (Meyer, 2005, p. 56). Traditional gender roles are also emphasized in the chivalrous behaviors exhibited by both Edward and Jacob toward Bella (16.67%). These behaviors include opening doors, lending Bella clothes to ensure her warmth, carry-ing Bella when she is tired, and giving Bella comfort. Bella is repeatedly depicted as weak and dependent, requiring male protection from harm.

Discussion

Viewed through the lens of dating violence, the *Twilight* series offers many troubling examples of controlling behaviors and vio-lence. Many of these behaviors are mini-mized, justified, normalized, and sometimes romanticized. The majority of controlling and violent behaviors—physical and sex-ual violence, stalking, controlling, intimi-dating, and threatening—are exhibited by male characters. The central characters manifest behaviors that are consistent with traditional gender roles, with Edward and Jacob presenting as aggressive, territorial, and demanding, and Bella presented as subservient and weak. Considering the popularity of the books and the marketing of their stories to a predominantly teenage audience, these messages are counterintui-tive to the promotion of healthy, equitable, nonviolent relationships. This is especially true with regard to sexual violence since the representation of a sexually violent relationship seems to be in direct contra-diction to advocating abstinence.

Twilight, published in 2005, was ranked the best-selling book of 2008 by *USA Today*, closely followed by the book's sequels. In 2009, *New Moon*, published in 2006, was ranked number one on the U.S. best-seller list, again followed by the other three books in the series (DeBarros, Cadden, DeRamus, & Schnaars, 2010a). The books have reportedly sold more than 40 million copies worldwide (DeBarros, Cadden, DeRamus, & Schnaars, 2010b), with *Breaking Dawn*, published in 2008, selling 1.3 million copies in the United States the day it was released, debuting at the top of the best-seller lists in Britain, France, Italy, Ireland, and Spain. The books have also been printed in 37 languages, including Vietnamese, Croatian, Chinese, and Latvian (Parsons, 2008).

Given the widespread popularity of the series and the fact that the target audience is predominantly teenage girls (Young, 2009), it is of particular concern that the dominant romantic relationship is pre-sented with behaviors that are characteris-tic of relationship violence. The presentation of these behaviors in popular fiction clearly does not cause dating violence. However, it is troubling when one of the most popular book series in recent history repeatedly normalizes, minimizes, and romanticizes these behaviors. It reinforces cultural norms that condone men's use of force to obtain a variety of goals.

. . . Programs to prevent dating vio-lence and educational programs could certainly use examples from these books to illustrate behaviors and attitudes that are related to dating violence. To recognize behaviors that were previously presented as chivalrous and romantic as clear examples of control, stalking, abuse, and intimidation may offer young people new insights into the insidious and often-subtle nature of abuse and control. In this way, the *Twilight* series could continue to influence young lives, but in a new way.

References

Ackard, D., Eisenberg, M., & Neumark-Sztainer, D. (2007). Long-term impact of adolescent dating violence on the behavioral and psychological health of male and female youth. *Journal of Pediatrics*, 151, 476–481.

Adelman, M., & Kil, S. H. (2007). Dating conflicts: Rethinking dating violence and youth conflict. *Violence Against Women*, 13, 1296–1318.

Altheide, D. L. (1996). *Qualitative data analysis*. Thousand Oaks, CA: SAGE.

Bergman, L. (1992). Dating violence among high school students. *Social Work*, 37, 21–27.

Bernard, J. L., Bernard, S. L., & Bernard, M. L. (1985). Courtship violence and sex-typing. *Family Relations*, 34, 573–576.

Black, B., & Weisz, A. (2003). Dating violence: Help-seeking behaviors of African American middle schoolers. *Violence Against Women*, 9, 187–206.

Borzekowski, D., & Rickert, V. (2001). Adolescent cybersurfing for health information: A new resource that crosses barriers. *Archives of Pediatric and Adolescent Medicine*, 155, 813–817.

Brown, J. D., L'Engle, K. L., Pardun, C. J., Guo, G., Kenneavy, K., & Jackson, C. (2006). Sexy media matter: Exposure to sexual content in music, movies, television, and magazines predicts black and white adolescents' sexual behavior. *Pediatrics*, 117, 1018–1027.

Brown, J. D., & Witherspoon, E. M. (2002). The mass media and American adolescents' health. *Journal of Adolescent Health*, 31, 153–170.

Carlson, B. E. (1990). Adolescent observers of marital violence. *Journal of Family Violence*, 5, 285–299.

Centers for Disease Control and Prevention. (2000). Youth risk behavior surveillance—U.S. 1999. *Morbidity and Mortality Weekly Report*, 49, 1–96.

Centers for Disease Control and Prevention. (2007). Effectiveness of universal school-based programs for the prevention of violent and aggressive behavior, *Morbidity & Mortality Weekly Report*, 56, 1–11. Retrieved from http://www.cdc.gov/mmwr/preview/mmwrhtml/rr5607a1.htm

Collins, R., Elliott, M., Berry, S., Kanouse, D., Kunkel, D., Hunter, S. B., & Miu, A. (2004). Watching sex on television predicts adolescent initiation of sexual behavior. *Pediatrics*, 114, 280–289.

DeBarros, A., Cadden, M., DeRamus, K., & Schnaars, C. (2010a, January 14). The top 100 books of 2008. *USA Today*. Retrieved from http://www.usatoday.com/life/books/news/2009-01-14-2008-top-100titles_N.htm

DeBarros, A., Cadden, M., DeRamus, K., & Schnaars, C. (2010b, January 15). USA Today's best-selling books: The top 100 for 2009. *USA Today*. Retrieved from http://www.usatoday.com/life/books/news/2010-01-05top-books-2009_N.htm

Eckhardt, C., Jamieson, T. R., & Watts, K. (2002). Anger experience and expression among dating violence perpetrators during anger arousal. *Journal of Interpersonal Violence*, 17, 1102–1114.

Editorial: Frontline: Be critical of stalking, abuse in "Twilight" series. (2009, November 17). *The Western Front*. Retrieved from http://westernfrontonline.net/pdf/fall09/Nov17Final.pdf

Feldman, S., & Gowen, L. K. (1998). Conflict negotiation tactics in romantic relationships in high school students. *Journal of Youth and Adolescence*, 27, 691–717.

Felson, R. B., & Messner, S. F. (2000). The control motive in intimate partner violence. *Social Psychology Quarterly*, 63, 86–94.

Foshee, V. A. (1996). Gender differences in adolescent dating abuse prevalence, types, and injuries. *Health Education Research*, 11, 275–286.

Foshee, V. A., Benefield, T., Ennett, S., Bauman, K. E., & Suchindran, C. (2004). Longitudinal predictors of serious physical and sexual dating violence victimization during adolescence. *Preventive Medicine, 39,* 1007–1016.

Gover, A. R., Kaukinen, C., & Fox, K. A. (2008). The relationship between violence in the family of origin and dating violence among college students. *Journal of Interpersonal Violence, 23,* 1667–1693.

Gray, B. (2009, November 21). "New Moon" shatters opening day record. *Box Office Mojo.* Retrieved from http://www.boxofficemojo.com/news/?id=2626&p=.htm

Gringeri, C. E., Wahab, S., & Anderson-Nathe, B. (2010). What makes it feminist? Mapping the landscape of feminist social work research. *Affilia, 25,* 390–405.

Haynes, J. (2009). Exposing domestic violence in country music videos. In L. M. Cuklanz & S. Moorti (Eds.), *Local violence, global media* (pp. 201–217). New York, NY: Peter Lang.

Hendy, H. M., Weiner, K., Bakerofskie, J., Eggen, D., Gustitus, C., & McLeod, K. C. (2003). Comparison of six models for violent romantic relationships in college men and women. *Journal of Interpersonal Violence, 18,* 645–665.

Howard, D., Wang, M., & Yan, F. (2007). Psychosocial factors associated with reports of physical dating violence among U.S. adolescent females. *Adolescence, 42,* 311–327.

James, H. W., West, C., Deters, K. E., & Armijo, E. (2000). Youth dating violence. *Adolescence, 35,* 455–465.

Jezl, D., Molidor, C. E., & Wright, T. L. (1996). Physical, sexual, and psychological abuse in high school dating relationships: Prevalence rates and self-esteem issues. *Child & Adolescent Social Work Journal, 13,* 69–88.

Kasian, M., & Painter, S. L. (1992). Frequency and severity of psychological abuse in a dating population. *Journal of Interpersonal Violence, 7,* 350–364.

Kaura, S. A., & Allen, C. M. (2004). Dissatisfaction with relationship power and dating violence perpetration by men and women. *Journal of Interpersonal Violence, 19,* 576–588.

Kettrey, H. H., & Emery, B. C. (2010). Teen magazines as educational texts on dating violence: The $2.99 approach. *Violence Against Women, 16,* 1270–1294.

Kim-Godwin, Y. S., Clements, C., McCuiston, A. M., & Fox, J. A. (2009). Dating violence among high school students in southeastern North Carolina. *Journal of School Nursing, 25,* 141–151.

Lavoie, F., Robitaille, L., & Hébert, M. (2000). Teen dating relationships and aggression: An exploratory study. *Violence Against Women, 6,* 6–36.

Lorber, J. (2005). *Gender inequality.* Los Angeles, CA: Roxbury Press.

Marin, A. J., & Russo, N. F. (1999). Feminist perspectives on male violence against women: Critiquing O'Neil and Harway's model. In M. Harway & J. M. O'Neil (Eds.), *What causes men's violence against women?* (pp. 18–35). Thousand Oaks, CA: SAGE.

McCulloch, S. (2009, November 11). Star in Twilight vampire movies poor role model for girls says Victoria professor. *Times Colonist.* Retrieved from http://www2.canada.com/entertainment/movie-guide/starþtwilightþvampireþmovies+poor+role+model+girls+says+victoria+professor/2210174/story.html?id=2210

McFarlane, J., Campbell, J. C., Wilt, S., Sachs, C., Ulrich, Y., & Xu, X. (1999). Stalking and intimate partner femicide. *Homicide Studies, 3,* 300–316.

Memmott, C., & Cadden, M. (2009, August 5). Twilight series eclipses Potter records on best-sellers list. *USA Today.* Retrieved from http://www.usatoday.com/life/books/news/2009-08-03-twilight-series_N.htm

Messerschmidt, J. W. (2000). *Nine lives: Adolescent masculinities, the body, and violence.* Boulder, CO: Westview Press.

Meyer, S. (2005). *Twilight.* New York, NY: Little, Brown.

Meyer, S. (2006). *New moon.* New York, NY: Little, Brown.

Meyer, S. (2007). *Eclipse.* New York, NY: Little, Brown.

Meyer, S. (2008). *Breaking dawn.* New York, NY: Little, Brown.

O'Keefe, M. (2005). Teen dating violence: A review of risk factors and prevention efforts. *VAWnet: National Electronic Network on*

Violence Against Women Applied Research Forum. Retrieved from http://new.vawnet.org/Assoc_Files_VAWnet/AR_TeenDatingViolence.pdf

Pagelow, M. D. (1984). *Family violence.* New York, NY: Praeger.

Parsons, C. (2008, November 21). "Twilight" publisher sees film boosting book sales. *Reuter.* Retrieved from http://www.reuters.com/article/idUSTRE4AK03620081121

Pence, E., & Paymar, M. (1993). *Education groups for men who batter: The Duluth model.* New York, NY: Springer.

Philaretou, A. G., & Allen, K. R. (2001). Reconstructing masculinity and sexuality. *Journal of Men's Studies, 9*, 301–321.

Prospero, M. (2007). Young adolescent boys and dating violence: The beginning of patriarchal terrorism? *Affilia, 22*, 271–280.

Prothrow-Stith, D. (1993). *Deadly consequences.* New York, NY: Harper Perennial.

Pulerwitz, J., Gortmaker, S. L., & Dejong, W. (2000). Measuring sexual relationship power in HIV/STD research. *Sex Roles, 42*, 637–660.

Rennison, C. M. (2003, February). *Intimate partner violence 1993–2001: Bureau of justice statistics, crime data brief.* Retrieved from http://bjs.ojp.usdoj.gov/content/pub/pdf/ipv01.pdf

Riggs, D. S., & O'Leary, K. D. (1996). Aggression between heterosexual dating partners: An examination of a causal model of courtship aggression. *Journal of Interpersonal Violence, 11*, 519–540.

Roehl, J., O'Sullivan, C., Webster, D., & Campbell, J. (2005). *Intimate partner violence risk assessment validation study, final report.* Washington, DC: Unpublished manuscript, U.S. Department of Justice.

Ronfeldt, H. M., Kimerling, R., & Arias, I. (1998). Satisfaction with relationship power and the perpetration of dating violence. *Journal of Marriage and the Family, 60*, 70–78.

Sargent, J. D., Heatherton, T. F., Ahrens, M. B., Dalton, M. A., Tickle, J. J., & Beach, M. L.

(2002). Adolescent exposure to extremely violent movies. *Journal of Adolescent Health, 31*, 449–454.

Smith, C. (2008, July 9). "Twilight": A positive or negative influence for teens? *Christ and Pop Culture.* Retrieved from http://www.christandpopculture.com/featured/twilight-a-positive-or-negative-influence for-teens/

Smith-Stover, C. (2005). Domestic violence research: What we have learned and where do we go from here? *Journal of Interpersonal Violence, 20*, 448–454.

Strasburger, V. C. (1995). *Adolescents and the media: Medical and psychological impact.* Thousand Oaks, CA: SAGE.

Stone, L. (2009, November 19). Lack of sex attracts teen girls to Twilight series: Study. *The Vancouver Sun.* Retrieved from http://www.vancouversun.com/entertainment/Lack+attracts+teenþgirls+Twilightþseries+study/2238456/story.html http://www.crosswalk.com/blogs/liebelt/lack-of-sex-attracts-teen-girls-to-twi light-series-11617033.html

Swahn, M., Lubell, K., & Simon, T. (2004). Suicide attempts and physical fighting among high school students—United States, 2001. *Morbidity and Mortality Weekly Report, 53*, 474–476.

Swigonski, M. E., & Raheim, S. (2011). Feminist contributions to understanding women's lives and the social environment. *Affilia, 26*, 10–11.

Tong, R. (2009). *Feminist thought: A more comprehensive introduction.* Boulder, CO: Westview Press.

Vezina, L., Lavoie, F., & Piche, C. (1995, July). Adolescent boys and girls: Their attitudes on dating violence. Paper presented at the fourth International Family Violence Research Conference, Durham, NH.

Young, S. C. (2009, June 10). Bella no match for Sookie at vampire love: Subservient "Twilight" heroine a terrible model for preteen girls. *MSNBC.com.* Retrieved from http://www.msnbc.msn.com/id/31087539

38

The White Man's Burden

Gonzo Pornography and the Construction of Black Masculinity

Gail Dines

Recent articles in *Adult Video News* (*AVN*)[1] have called attention to the fact that the fastest growing and most bootlegged internet pornography is "interracial pornography" (IP). While web sites advertise a multicultural mix of males and females, by far the dominant performers are black men and white women. With titles such as *Black Poles in White Holes, Huge Black Cock on White Pussy,* and *Monster Black Penises* and *Tight White Holes,* the male viewer knows what to expect when he punches in his credit card numbers. Although there are sites that advertise Asian and Latina women, there are very few sites with Latino and Asian men and white women. Indeed, if the heterosexual male wants to gaze at Asian or Latino men, then he has to move into a truly forbidden world for straight pornography, namely gay pornography.

Analyzing the role of racial representations in pornography is, I argue, key to understanding how pornography works as a discourse, as it explicates taken-for-granted assumptions about what makes pornography pornographic. If, as radical feminists argue, pornography is pleasurable because it sexualizes inequality between women and men, then the more degraded and abused the woman, the greater the sexual tension and thrill for the male viewer. It is hard to conceive of a better way to degrade white women, in a culture with a long and ugly history of racism, than having them penetrated again and again by a body that has been constructed, coded, and demonized as a carrier for all that is sexually debased, namely the black male.

Pornography and Masculinity

In order to explore the way that race functions in pornography, it is important to first examine the contemporary world of internet pornography, since the explosion of electronic

Reprinted with permission of the *Yale Journal of Law and Feminism* from the *Yale Journal of Law and Feminism*, Vol. 18, No. 1, pp. 283–97.

pornography has had enormous implications for content as well as form. Mainstream pornography today looks nothing like the scrubbed, sanitized world of *Playboy*. In place of the "girl next door," smiling suggestively at the camera with her legs partially spread, is the girl that pornography consumers wish lived next door. Mainstream movies today are populated with what the male performers call "cum buckets," "sluts," and "cunts," who love pounding anal, oral, and vaginal sex, who enjoy being smeared with semen, and who see their lives' goals as breaking the record for the greatest number of "gang bangs" within a twenty four-hour period. Threaded throughout all these movies is an overt hatred for women that is evidenced in the dialogue and the fascination with body-punishing sex, such as frequent references to how much the woman can take before she breaks. Paul Little, AKA Max Hardcore, became famous (and rich) for his particular style of pornography that specializes in extremely violent and degrading sex. . . .

This type of violent pornography popularized by Max Hardcore helped to define the contours of present-day gonzo pornography.[2] By far the biggest moneymaker for the industry, this type of pornography makes no attempt at a storyline, but is just scene after scene of violent penetration in which the woman's body is literally stretched to its limit. . . . To argue that the pleasure of heterosexual pornography for men is not somehow wrapped up in the degradation of women is to ignore the multiple verbal and image-based cues that form the codes and conventions of mainstream pornography.[3] Moreover, failure to see pornography as a text about the elevation of men and the degradation of women also misses the role that pornography plays in the production of masculinity as both a category of material existence, and an identity that is contested, negotiated, and in need of constant reproduction.[4]

It is now a given in much of academic feminism that masculinity and femininity are social constructs that work together to produce a gender system that is fused with inequality, hierarchy and violence.[5] Until recently, much of the analysis of masculinity sought to explain how hegemonic masculinity is defined in opposition to femininity, where hegemonic masculinity is unproblematically coded as white. However, as many black scholars have argued,[6] white hegemonic masculinity is always in negotiation with black masculinity, as the two exist in what James Snead calls "a larger scheme of semiotic valuation,"[7] in that the elevation and mythification of white masculinity relies on the debasement of black men as sexual savages, Uncle Toms, and half-wits such as Stepin Fetchit. Patricia Hill Collins goes further by arguing that black masculinity is so debased by white culture that it becomes a fluid category whereby any man of color can become marked as black should he in any way fail to conform to the strict disciplinary practices of white masculinity.[8]

However, what constitutes hegemonic white masculinity is itself a moving target that depends on the socioeconomic dynamics of a given time and place. In the United States, and indeed most of the Western world, there is a general consensus that a real man (read: white) works hard, puts food on the table and an SUV in the driveway, shows some interest in his children's welfare, and exhibits a somewhat restrained set of sexual practices within state-sanctioned heterosexual marriage. On virtually every level, black men are defined by white culture as failing to meet the standards of white hegemonic masculinity. They are portrayed as shiftless, they need welfare to get food for their families, they drive pimp cars (when they can afford cars), and they engage in what Cornel West mockingly refers to as "dirty, disgusting, and funky sex."[9] And this is the problem for white men. While they would not swap their material privileges with black men, many white men would indeed like "black" sex as it is seen in the white racist imagination, as "more intriguing and interesting."[10] It is argued in this chapter that this white racist construction of black male sexuality is what drives IP and serves to heighten the sexual tension in the pornography, while simultaneously making this country an increasingly hostile and dangerous place for people (especially blacks) who fall outside the markers of whiteness. . . .

According to *AVN*, IP is emerging as the biggest single growing category, with nearly one in four new films fitting into this sub-genre.[11] A recent article quotes a producer, who says, "[r]ight now interracial gonzo is probably the strongest genre. . . . The demand for interracial far outweighs all the other formats of gonzo."[12] While there are both black and white pornography producers and directors, the audience for IP is overwhelmingly white, according to the on-going studies conducted by Dr. Robert Jensen.[13] The obvious question here is: why do white men want to gaze at, and masturbate to, black penises penetrating white women's vaginas, mouths, and anuses, given the historical coding of the black penis as defiler of white womanhood and emasculator of white masculinity?

Interracial Pornography: Looking for the Primitive (Black) Male

The most startling fact that jumps out at anyone who surfs these sites is the absence of men of color who are not black. A more precise term for interracial would be black men and white women, but in a society where the color line is defined by the binary black/white categorization, such precision would be redundant. This binary system has engaged many theorists who seek to interrogate how race has been constructed in American history against the backdrop of slavery. One insightful analysis is offered by James Snead, who writes, following W.E.B. Du Bois, that the "Negro" is "the metaphor . . . the major figure in which these power relationships of master/slave, civilized/primitive, enlightened/backward, good/evil, have been embodied in the

American subconscious."[14] This does not mean that other races don't exist in America, but that blacks are the "idealized" other, and different racial groups float between the two poles of the color line, depending on their economic, social, and cultural status.[15] And since pornography is not a genre known for its subtlety, when it deals with race, it deals with the clear, uncomplicated racial categories that define American society, ideologically if not materially.

Since the race of the performers is the key to marketing IP, it is not surprising that the black male tends to be very dark-skinned and the white woman very blonde. While skin color can vary among blacks, blonde hair is a clear signifier of white womanhood. . . .

One of the most popular series of IP movies is called Blacks on Blondes, which features blonde women with multiple black men. As in most IP, the blonde performer is "applauded" for being able to take a black penis in her white mouth, vagina, and anus. In one particular movie with "Liv Wylder," we see an example of a theme running through IP, namely the emasculation of the white man by the big black penis. The text on the site reads:

> Bring out the cuckold mask again! Time for another white couple to live out their naughtiest fantasy, and thanks to Blacks on Blondes for making it happen! Liv and Hubby have been married for a few years, and she wears her ring proudly. But lately the spark has left the bedroom, if you know what I mean. A few e-mails later, and we've got Hubby in a cage while Boz and Mandingo work Liv over. And when I say they work her over, we mean it. She takes so much black dick it amazed even us. The best part of this whole deal was the end: after Liv has about a gallon of cum all over her face and clothes, and grabs a plastic bowl—for Hubby to beat off in. He does, and his wad was weak, and Liv lets him know that.[16]

The white man's body is literally and metaphorically contained in this movie by both his whiteness and the physical cage in which he is locked during the sex scenes. References to his poor performance in bed ("the spark has left the bedroom") and his ineffectual semen ("his wad was weak") stand in sharp contrast to the size of the black men's penises, the skill of their sexual performance ("they work her over, we mean it") and the amount of semen they produce ("a gallon of cum"). And to illustrate where the white woman's allegiance lies, the last line lets us know that Liv is only too happy to ridicule the husband in front of the black men. Indeed, in many such movies, regular reference is made to the white woman's distaste for white penises after she has sampled a "real man's" penis. It is thus apparent why one popular series of IP films is called *Once You Go Black . . . You Never Go Back*.[17]

In heterosexual non-interracial pornography, it is the woman's body that is scrutinized, talked about, focused on, and visually interrogated. In IP it is the black penis that becomes the star of the show. Indeed, on one site where users post their reviews of movies, there is a debate going on about the apparent authenticity of the black penis in the movie, *White Meat on Black Street*.[18] Some of the viewers are clearly disturbed by what they see as the fake quality of the penis, while others express a desire to have such a penis. While the race of the user is not clear from the name (most use "anonymous"), the tone of the posts suggests white male readers. One particularly observant viewer, "ramjet" wrote on February 9, 2006:

> If you want the best available proof of the fake penis being used, check out the 5th MPEG video in respect of Ruby at the 1:30 mark. The dick is a different color to its "owner" and, more importantly, YOU CAN SEE WHERE IT ENDS AND HIS REAL COCK FITS IN TO IT. The fake has fully come away from his body and his real balls have fallen out underneath. Case closed.[19]

This "heterosexual" viewer seems more entranced by the black penis than by the white woman's body: his sense of betrayal at having paid to see a real black penis, and instead getting what he sees as a fake one, is palpable. . . .

In addition to the text that foregrounds the black penis, there are secondary themes that suggest that it is not just any black man who can perform. The black men are often described as thugs, pimps, hustlers, Hip-Hoppers, mofos, and bros who live in the "hood" and drive "pimp-mobiles." The class markers here make apparent that it is working class black men who are sexual savages, and the most esteemed is the "black pimp," who keeps his girls in line and has taught them all they need to know about being a "ho." Pimp-themed movies abound in IP, where the black pimp is defined as the "king of the hood," who uses the particular skill that black men "innately" have, of combining sex and violence, to turn black "bitches" into "hos." . . .

The pimp, thug/hustler black man of the "hood" with the out-of-control body is not only a favorite of white straight men, but also seems to be a popular object of desire for gay white men. Titles such as *Blacks on White Boys, Ebony Dicks in White Ass Holes,* and *Black Bros and White Twinks* make clear who does what to whom in interracial gay porn. The "hood" once again figures largely on the websites where users are encouraged to become site members by clicking the mouse, which will let them "Join Our MemberHood."[20] It seems that white gay men can buy their way into the hood for a short, and contained, time.

In his analysis of the visual and verbal clues that inform the fetishized and commodified black males in IP gay porn, Dwight A. McBride suggests that such images "presume a viewer who is other to the experience of the man represented in the films."[21] Moreover, the racial ideologies that make these images intelligible and pleasurable are the very ideologies that underscore mainstream white racism. As McBride argues:

> [H]ere in the form of typical images of black men in the mediated context of

black gay porn, the viewer can enjoy fantasies about his sexual relationship to blackness, without having to account for the possibly troublesome dimensions of the brand of thinking about race that he must necessarily bring to these images for them to work their magic, so to speak.[22]

These "troublesome dimensions" are what need to be explained, not only for gay IP but also straight IP, and indeed for many of the images that have circulated and continue to circulate in white-owned and white-consumed media. IP does not exist in a world of its own, but rather draws from, and contributes to, the hegemonic ideologies of race in America that have justified, legitimized, and condoned deeply-rooted systems of racial oppression. However, the way that IP articulates and rearticulates these ideologies is linked to the particular form of pleasure that it offers its readers, namely (white) masculinized sexual pleasure.

Interracial Pornography as the New Minstrel Show

The pleasure that white audiences receive from consuming images of blacks is complex and rooted in the politics of whiteness as an identity that affords status, privileges, and a sense of belonging to some mythical (glorified) racial group.[23] The above mentioned argument articulated by James Snead, that the debasement of blacks is linked to the elevation of whites, is not hard to grasp, given the vicious stereotypes of blacks as savages, Coons, half-wits, Mammies, and Jezebels. Whiteness, as an identity, is a meaningless concept outside of the constructed notions of blackness that whites have produced and circulated in popular culture. Thus, in this wholly mythical world, to be white is to be the opposite of black: hard-working, law abiding, intellectual, rational, and sexually restrained and controlled. These are all traits that in the everyday

world have very real currency, providing status to those who operate with a clear allegiance to the culture of whiteness.

However, the world of pornography is actually a parallel universe where, for at least the time it takes to get aroused and ejaculate, the currency is one that is in direct contradiction to whiteness. In this world, the traits of whiteness are indeed a burden for the white man, since restraint of any type threatens to undermine the full sexual pleasure that can be achieved with a bevy of "sluts," "whores," and "cum buckets," willing to do anything you want. In this world, the mythical black man, who is uncontrolled, unrestrained, animalistic, and savage, will always trump the uptight, contained, and penis-challenged white guy. Why, then, do white men who do not, in the real world, take kindly to seeing themselves as demasculinized by black men, buy IP?

To look for possible answers to this conundrum, I suggest we go back in time and examine another genre that poses similar questions for historians of race, namely, the blackface minstrel shows that swept through America in the 1830s and 1840s. Much has been written about the politics of these shows, the ways in which they encoded blackness, and the pleasures they afforded the white, mostly male, audiences through displays of white actors in blackface performing "blackness" by singing and dancing.[24] Gerald R. Butters suggests that once given the mask of blackness, white men could "sing, dance, speak, move, and act in ways that were considered inappropriate for white men."[25] While there is general agreement that these shows were unapologetically racist, historians suggest that multiple and contradictory pleasures were afforded to the audiences, in that they identified both with and against the white performers in black face.

Part of the identification process was facilitated by the fact that these shows did not employ unrecognizable songs or melodies; instead, the musical style and structure borrowed heavily from European patterns. What was different, however, according to

Deane Root, was the style of the performance of the songs, which was "much cruder. It was . . . foreign. Out of the culture. . . . They were trying to exaggerate and make [something] (sic) exotic."[26] In IP, the "songs or melodies"[27] are indeed similar to white-on-white porn, since the sex acts between black men and white women are the recognizable anal, vaginal, and oral penetrations. However, the style is, in a sense, exaggerated and cruder, in its focus on "big black dicks" pounding away at "small white orifices" that are stretched. . . to foreign proportions.[28] The aim here, however, is not so much to make the performance exotic as it is to make it erotic, since the sexual pleasure of IP is intensified by the increased sexual abuse of the woman, and the (partial) identification of the viewer with the hypersexual black male.

The fact that black men perform black pornography, rather than white men in blackface, speaks to the ways in which white ownership of media and pornography has defined, and continues to define, the contours of blacks playing blacks *as whites see them*. When black men were eventually allowed on to the stage in minstrel shows, they also had to cork their faces and behave as the whites did in black face.[29] The reason for this, argues Mel Watkins, is that whites assumed that the minstrel shows depicted something real and essential about blacks, because the shows "[w]ere advertised as the real thing. In fact, one group was called 'The Real Nigs' . . . they were advertised as 'Come to the theatre and get a real look into what plantation life was like' . . . It was advertised as a peephole view of what black people were really like."[30]

Rather than a peephole, IP porn is a peepshow for whites into what they see as the authentic black life, not on the plantation, but in the "hood," where all the conventions of white civilized society cease to exist. The "hood" in the white racist imagination is a place of pimps, ho's and generally uncontrolled black bodies, and the white viewer is invited, for a fee, to

slum in this world of debauchery. In the "hood," the white man can dispense with his whiteness by identifying with the black man, and thus can become as sexually skilled and as sexually out-of-control as the black man. Here he does not have to worry about being big enough to satisfy the white woman (or man), nor does he have to concern himself with fears about poor performance or "weak wads," or cages, like poor hubby in Blacks on Blondes. Indeed, the "hood" represents liberation from the cage, and the payoff is a satiated white woman (or man) who has been completely and utterly feminized by being well and truly turned into a "fuckee."

But before we celebrate the IP text as subversive and liberatory, we need to put the text in the context of the material world of racist America. The body that is celebrated as uncontrolled in IP is the very same body that needs to be controlled and disciplined in the real world. Just as white suburban teenagers love to listen to hip-hop and white adult males gaze longingly at the athletic prowess of black men, the white pornography consumer enjoys his identification with (and against) black males through a safe peephole, in his own home, and in mediated form. The real, breathing, living black man, however, is to be kept as far away as possible from these living rooms, and every major institution in society marshals its forces in the defense of white society. The ideologies that white men take to the pornography text to enhance their sexual pleasure are the very ideologies that they use to legitimize the control of black men: while it may heighten arousal for the white porn user, it makes life intolerable for the real body that is (mis)represented in all forms of white controlled media.

Notes

1. See, e.g., R. W. Connell, *Masculinities* (1995); Hazel Carby, *Race Men* (1998).

2. See, e.g., Dwight A. McBride, *Why I Hate Abercrombie and Fitch: Essays on Race*

and Sexuality in America (2005); Mark Anthony Neal, New Black Man (2005).

3. James Snead, *White Screens/Black Images: Hollywood from the Dark Side* 4 (1994).

4. Patricia Hill Collins, *Black Sexual Politics* 186–87 (2004).

5. Cornel West, *Race Matters* 83 (1993).

6. Ibid.

7. Ethnic Diversity in Adult: Can't We All Just Fuck Along?, *Adult Video News Mag.*, May 2003, http://www.adultvideonews.com/cover/cover0905_01.htmt (last visited Apr. 18, 2006).

8. Ibid.

9. Telephone Interview with Dr. Robert Jensen, Professor of Journalism, University of Texas at Austin (Apr. 3, 2006).

10. Snead, supra note 7, at 2.

11. The study of how different racial and ethnic groups became "white" illustrates the fluid nature of "race" and identity in this country. For a particularly insightful analysis, see Noel Ignatiev, *How the Irish Became White* (1995).

12. BlacksonBlondes.com, http//blacksonblondes.com/main.php?pg-6 (last visited Mar. 20, 2006).

13. For a description of the content of these movies, see searchextreme.com, *Once You Go Black . . . You Never Go Back,* http://www.searchextreme.com/series/Once_You_Go_Black . . . _You_Never_Go_Back/97899206841 (last visited Mar. 20, 2006).

14. See Sir Rodney's Guide to Online Erotica, http://www.sirrodney.com/singlereview/White+Meat+On+Black+Street#readerreviews (last visited Apr. 3, 2006).

15. Sir Rodney's Guide to Online Erotica, http://www.sirrodney.com/singlereview/White+Meat+On+Black+Street+#readerreviews (last visited Apr. 3, 2006).

16. *Twinks from the Hood,* http://www.twinksfromthehood.com/?revid=14522&pid=51&track (last visited Apr. 2, 2006).

17. McBride, supra note 6, at 103.

18. Ibid.

19. For a fuller discussion on how whiteness is socially constructed, see George Lipsitz, *The Possessive Investment in Whiteness: How White People Profit from Identity Politics* (1998); Ignatiev, supra note 15; and David R. Roediger, The *Wages of Whiteness* (1991).

20. For a fuller discussion of the politics of black face, see Gerald R. Butters, Jr., *Black Manhood on the Silent Screen* (2002); Eric Lott, *Love and Theft: Black Face Minstrelsy and the American Working Class* (1995); and Michael Rogin, *Blackface, White Noise: Jewish Immigrants in the Hollywood Melting Pot* (1998).

21. Butters, supra note 24, at 10.

22. Excerpts from the PBS program, *American Experience,* Stephen Foster, http://www.pbs.org/wgbh/amex/foster/sfeature/sf_minstrelsy_ 3.html (last visited Mar. 20, 2006).

23. For an analysis of how pornographic films can be likened to musicals, see Linda Williams, *Hard Core: Power, Pleasure and the 'Frenzy of the Visible'* 130–52 (1989).

24. See infra p. 284 and note 8.

25. This is not to argue that blacks simply mimicked the whites in black face as there were some real attempts by black actors to provide a more humanized, authentic version of black life. However, there were very real limits to this. Butters, supra note 24, at 11–12.

26. Excerpts from the PBS program, *American Experience,* Stephen Foster, http://www.pbs.org/wgbh/arnex/foster/sfeature/sf_minstrelsy_5.html (last visited Mar. 20, 2006).

27. See, e.g., DRM Versus P2P: Point, Counterpoint (Tripp Darnels ed.), *Adult Video News Mag.,* May 2003, http://www.avnon1ine.com/index.php?Primary_Navigation=Editorial&Action=Print_Artic1e&Contcnt_ID=105809 (last visited Apr. 10, 2006).

28. For a discussion of Max Hardcore's role in making pornography sexually violent, see Max Hardcore Porn Star, http://max- hardcore.excaliburfilms.com/AVN/Max-Hardcore-Biography.htm (last visited Apr. 16, 2006).

29. For a fuller discussion on the ways that the pornographic text constructs women as the degraded "other," see Robert Jensen, Cruel to be Hard: Men and Pornography, *Sexual Assault Report* 33 (2004), available at http://uts.cc.utexas.edu%7Erjensen/freelance/pornography&cruelty.htm.

30. For an analysis of how pornography is implicated in the construction of hegemonic masculinity, see John Stoltenberg, *Refusing to Be a Man* (1989).

39

The Pornography of Everyday Life[1]

Jane Caputi

The subject of sexualized degradation flooded world consciousness after May 2004, when trophy photos that American soldiers took of their abuse of Iraqi prisoners at Abu Ghraib prison were released to the public. The photos showed Iraqi men stripped, bound, and forced into situations both sides considered denigrating—simulating homosexual sex, crawling on the floor, posing for sexual display, and wearing women's underwear on their heads. In one photo, naked men were made to pile on top of one another, with their buttocks in the air (Image 1). Standing nearby, smiling and giving a "thumbs-up" gesture, is a pair of White soldiers, male and female. Shocked and appalled, many recognized the behavior in these photos as torture meant to break the prisoners' spirits.

What was not widely acknowledged, however, was how often we see women being posed and treated in precisely these ways and worse, not only in pornography but also in fashion magazines, music videos, and advertising. And these depictions are not generally perceived as humiliating, torturous, or spirit breaking; rather, they are perceived as "sexy."

For example, a photo in an issue of *Vibe* magazine (which appeared before the release of the Abu Ghraib photos) is structured around a scene eerily similar to the one I just described (Image 2). Two Black men are seated at a bar. To their left, a Black woman in a very short skirt and stiletto heels bends over the bar, exposing her "panties" and baring part of her buttocks. One man grins widely, and the other gives a "thumbs-up" gesture. In 2010, an ad for a new TV action series showed a White man posing on a ladder leading up into a helicopter (Image 3). In the photo, he stares out with an expression as firm as his chin, his outstretched hand brandishing a big gun. Higher up the ladder, we see a White woman getting into the helicopter. Well, we don't really see her—just her bare legs, red stiletto heels, and the red dress clinging to her protruding buttocks. In both of these displays, it's not hard to figure out who is in charge, and who is the "butt" of the misogynist joke.

As these examples indicate, this article is not about X-rated porn. Rather, it is about a "habit of thinking" (Williams, 1995, p. 123), an everyday pornographic discourse (including words and pictures) that sexualizes denigration, domination, and hierarchy itself, as it also genders all these—with "the man" on top and "the woman" on the "bottom," objectified, exposed, and denigrated (even when sometimes a woman plays the masculine role and vice versa).

This piece is an original essay that was commissioned for this volume. It has been updated from an earlier version that appeared in the third edition.

Catharine MacKinnon and Andrea Dworkin (1997, pp. 428–429) originally shifted the debate around pornography from the issue of morality to one of power relations. In so doing, they defined pornography as "the graphic, sexually explicit subordination of women," or men, children, or transsexuals "used in the place of women." Their extended discussion delineates specific elements, including women being put into "postures or positions of sexual submission, servility or display"; "scenarios of degradation, injury, abasement, torture"; "dehumanizing objectification"; and women being defined as "whores by nature" (that is, as incapable of ever saying *no* to sex, as they are made for sex). Pornography, in this view, is not about the "joy of sex" but about the domination and "denigration of women and a fear and hatred of the female body" (Kaplan, 1991, p. 322).

What is believed to be denigrating is contingent on social, religious, and moralistic systems. For example, nakedness is not a source of shame for many cultures, nor is being in a physically lower position, which really just puts one closer to the Earth. Patriarchal traditions, though, split underlying unities and then put everyone and everything in a top-down hierarchy, valuing men over women, mind over body, and Heaven over Earth. Everyone and everything that can be associated with the bottom half is stigmatized. Patriarchal cultures such as our own also associate nakedness and sex with shame and sin, and identify women with the essence of sex (in contrast, men can be viewed as sexual but are seen as having other attributes as well, such as intelligence). Patriarchal cultures also stigmatize male homosexuality because, in their view, this relationship necessarily reduces a man to the feminine, sexually subordinated position.

My plan in this chapter is to criticize select popular representations, especially those in advertising imagery, that transmit and normalize this patriarchal and pornographic paradigm. Some readers might see them the same way I do; others might not. Popular culture is not monolithic, and representations are open to interpretation. My intent is to suggest that the pornographic "habit of thinking" underlies and supports oppressions, including not only sexism but also homophobia, racism, colonization, and ecocide (wanton destruction of the Earth and nature). Pornography is an everyday occurrence, not just in the sense that coded versions of it populate mainstream images but also because its precepts underlie mainstream ideas and practices.

Gender Pornography

In conventional notions of gender, women and men are said to be opposites and unequal, with specific gendered attributes such as masculine aggression and feminine passivity. However different and unequal, the story goes, men and women still are (and should be!) attracted to each other, and *only* to each other. These gender norms thereby normalize and make "sexy" inequality, domination, and even violence, and are reflected in conventional representations of "ideal" *straight* (in the sense of heterosexual, non-"kinky," and non-comic) couples.

In many advertising images, for example, the man in the couple is situated as upright, taller, stronger, richer, older, bolder, and colder. He does not wear makeup or color his hair. He is self-contained, stands firmly on the ground, and is often dressed in a business suit or some other status-oriented and/or functional garb. In short, he is in the power position. The woman, however, often has glazed eyes and is unsteady, usually due to the shoes she is wearing and/or because she is tilting to one side, jutting out one hip, or turning one foot out and over. With great frequency, she is "put down" (often literally placed on the floor) or constrained (often up against a wall). She is shorter, warmer, weaker, vulnerable, and younger. Sometimes she is in a state of partial or even total undress, and what she does wear is coded as sexually alluring. She is accessible. Often, the man is holding her in some way that constrains her. In short, she is represented as socially powerless.

Even when both subjects in such common representations are undressed, the man is clearly the dominant partner. Gucci makes a fragrance called "Guilty," which it advertised in 2013 by showing (from the shoulders up) a naked White man and White woman embracing (Image 4). The man is unsmiling, steady, and looks directly at the viewer, while the woman is turned to the side, with her mouth partly open and her head tilted back, baring her throat (standard submissive body language). His hand comes around her neck, and his thumb presses up against it, suggesting that he could easily apply pressure there, while her arms are loosely draped over his shoulders.

Calvin Klein ads are especially known for their erotic tone. Consider a 2007 ad for "CK IN2U" fragrance. It shows a young White couple (Image 5). They are posed up against a gray concrete wall. He is taller and leaning over her, while her back is against the wall. His left hand presses into the wall, and his right tugs on her long hair. His look is determined, hers dazed. Both wear jeans, but hers are low-cut and show a good deal of skin. His belt is undone, and her hand is wrapped limply around its end. The situation is clearly sexual, but with an obvious power differential. He seems determined to get "into her," while she is passive. Moreover, he is backing her up against that unyielding barrier. The phrase "up against a wall" means literally to be trapped, cornered, and put into a situation with no escape and no options. Pressure and coercion, not consent, create the sexually charged dynamic here.

This same version of power over sex is more obvious in another fragrance ad from the same year. This one is for Sean Jean's "Unforgiveable Woman," a product line created by the hip-hop star Sean "P. Diddy" Combs (Image 6). An African American couple is featured in what appears to be a sexual situation, once again with a wall as the backdrop. This time, the man (Combs) crushes the woman, whose back is to him, up against the wall. Both of his arms are around her, holding her there. In profile, her eyes are closed, her right arm flails back as if in futile resistance. The perfume's name, "Unforgivable Woman," implies that she has done something to deserve this sexualized punishment. When taking in such images, we should know that from 2 to 4 million women are victims of domestic violence every year in the United States, that rape is a core element in that abuse, and that Black women are reported to experience domestic violence at a rate 35% higher than that of White women, and about 2.5 times the rate for women of other races (Rennison & Welchans, 2000). This is due to poverty, a continuing legacy of the U.S. history of enslavement and racism.[2]

The rightness of male sexual domination of women is assumed, even when there seems to be a challenge. A photo illustrating a 2007 Cosmopolitan article (Benjamin, 2007) shows a White woman lying on top and clearly over a White man in bed. The theme of the piece is that some men entertain a fantasy of a girlfriend playing the role of "boss lady" in bed. But nothing is really that different here. The sexuality is still focused on domination and submission, and his "boss lady" fantasy is something "secret," to be enacted only "every once in a while" and only in the bedroom. Proper gender roles remain in place: The onus is on the woman to fulfill the man's fantasies. As the "boss lady" reference indicates, our hierarchical social institutions, including work, the family, schools, churches, and the military, are based on someone "on top" ordering someone else around.

Such everyday hierarchies begin with the basic imbalance of power required by proper gender roles and then inevitably influence the shapes taken by our desires. Many of us do respond to social pressure to be exclusively heterosexual and/or to be aroused only by people who embody conventional masculinity or femininity. Many of us also find ourselves aroused by power inequalities. Particularly after the popularity of E. L. James's (2012) *Fifty Shades of Grey* and its two follow-ups, there is much more focus on sexualities based in what Matt Haber (2013), writing in the *New York Times*, calls a "power exchange in sexuality"—referring to so-called sado-masochistic sexual practices such as bondage, spanking, and other activities that more explicitly replicate actual torture, including waterboarding.

Those who practice what they call sexual "kink" do diverge from the traditional power imbalances (and silences) in conventional sexual relationships by putting forth an ethic of the need for open discussion and explicit consent for all sexual activities. Obviously, these should be part of all sexual relationships. Still, our ability to freely consent (or not) to specific sexual practices often remains compromised by social inequalities and hatreds (including self-hatreds) based in gender, sex, race, age, sexuality, ability, and so on. Sometimes an experience of childhood sexual abuse can result in someone learning to associate sexuality with domination and abuse, even torture, either as victim or perpetrator. *Consent* in a social context of widespread sexual abuse of children as well as adults, along with systemic gender and other inequalities, is rarely quite so simple as saying "yes."

Whatever our choice of sexual practices, I hope we can continue to consider the ways our sexualities have been and continue to be formed in an unequal world long based in sexualized hierarchies and torments. Yearning for something better, we might also continue to imagine and generate sexual desires and practices reflective of a culture based in justice, freedom, equality, community, and reverence for life—human and nonhuman.

Violence Porn

A definition of *power* as domination is inherent in normative/pornographic gender roles and also is manifested vividly in the ways slang words for sexual intercourse equate it with violence: *fucking, nailing, screwing, banging, beating up the pussy,* and so on. The first two official definitions of the verb *fuck* are "to engage in heterosexual intercourse" and "to harm irreparably; finish; victimize" (Sheidlower, 1999, pp. 117, 124). In this schema, "the man" (or masculine-identified partner) is the one doing the "fucking," and the one getting "fucked" is "the girl" (even if this partner is male). In this framework, "manhood" can never be a given but, rather, must be perpetually proven. A man must regularly demonstrate that he is the one "on top," that he has no trace of the characteristics defined as "feminine." This setup leaves boys and men constantly vulnerable and liable to humiliation, and it functions as the basis for misogyny as well as homophobia. When boys and men, and even some women and girls, sexually harass boys and men with words, they call them *woman, whore, pussy, bitch, sissy, faggot,* and *punk,* putting them in the place of the woman. To prove manhood, men, one way or another, have to assert domination, achieved most efficiently and most effectively by being violent (Gilligan, 1996).

A 2009 ad for Dockers takes on the role of the homophobic, misogynist bully, showing a male figure from the top of his head to his knees (Image 7). From the waist down, we see only pants-clad legs. Above, an outline of the body is filled in with a stream of screaming words scolding the man and proclaiming that a "genderless" society has stripped all men of their manhood and left them "stranded on the road between boyhood and androgyny." Dockers demands that all males "answer the call of manhood," take charge, and "WEAR THE PANTS." This is a resounding call for gender conformity in behavior as well as dress. In mainstream American culture since the 1960s, women have mostly been able to get away with wearing pants, but men still cannot wear skirts in most situations. Men who do cross-dress in popular representations can be acceptable only if they present themselves as obvious comic characters whose maleness and heterosexuality are still apparent. Some element of cross-dressing is allowed for women as long as it can be presented as titillating for men, and as long as the women are clearly straight, feminine, seductive, and often partly undressed. If not, they, too, are punished.

The Dockers ad is a call for sexist domination. Dockers' mandate to "wear the pants" intends to make us think of what is inside the pants and fall sway to the pornographic notion that the penis is inherently an instrument of violence. Male heroes in popular culture invariably are pictured not only wearing pants but also wielding weapons, usually guns—and the bigger, the better. In Freudian psychoanalysis, as well as popular understandings, these weapons are phallic symbols.

In 2012, Adam Lanza—a small, weak, mentally disturbed, 20-year-old White man from a wealthy family—first killed his mother and then 6 adult women and 20 children at a Newtown, Connecticut, elementary school. He used two weapons, including a Bushmaster assault rifle belonging to his mother; he then killed himself. Most such crimes are committed by White and relatively privileged young men, though often ones who do not fit a masculine ideal. It is interesting to look at the ways the Bushmaster rifle has been advertised, not to suggest that this advertising had any direct influence on Lanza but to see it as evidence of the kind of overall gender pornography that links men with violence and sets them in opposition to women. The Bushmaster rifle in earlier ads was touted as coming replete with a "man card," which would allow men to avert "complete humiliation" (Image 8). This card, the ad proclaimed, also bestowed

"rights and privileges," including being able to "belch loudly" and "leave the seat up." Implicit in this kind of language is a suggestion that women constrain, oppress, and humiliate boys and men, and that violence is a way to get revenge, if not men's "right and privilege."

On Valentine's Day 2013, the celebrated Olympic hero Oscar Pistorius (nicknamed "The Blade Runner" due to his use of two prosthetic legs) shot four bullets through a bathroom door in his home in the middle of the night, killing his girlfriend, Reeva Steenkamp, who had been spending the night with him. As of this writing, Pistorius has been arrested and charged with murder. He claims innocence, saying that he believed he was shooting an intruder and hadn't noticed that Steenkamp was no longer in their bed. Many suggest, instead, that this might have been a lethal episode of domestic violence. Ironically, a Nike ad featuring Pistorius had shown him sprinting with the caption, "I am the bullet in the chamber," together with Nike's "Just do it" slogan and logo (Image 9).

Visual metaphors and exhortations relentlessly associate being a man with being violent, contributing to a gender pornography that implies that men are "killers by nature." They try to make us forget that neither a male nor a penis is innately like a weapon—permanently hard, mechanical, and lethal. On the contrary, the penis is more often soft, always sensitive, often fertile, and, like all life, fragile (Dyer, 1993; Marcus, 2005). When the penis is represented as a weapon, rape becomes its purpose, intercourse becomes a kind of murder, and the will to hurt becomes definitive of being a man.

Rape Porn

In pornography, sexualized domination is enacted via explicit scenes that feature and promote rape. In everyday porn, these same behaviors are suggested with varying degrees of subtlety. Sharon Marcus (2005) argued that a "rape script" is coded into the ways our culture habitually represents powerful men's bodies as penetrating forces (such as bullets) and women's bodies as inner spaces that can be "gotten inside of," invaded, and owned—bodies without will or capacity for violence, including defensive violence.

These themes inform a deliberately provocative 2008 ad for an organ donor foundation, Reborn to Be Alive, that shows an underwear-clad, stiletto-heeled White woman wearing heavy eye makeup and posed in a way that suggests she is offering herself as a prostitute (Image 10). The tag line reads: "Becoming a donor is probably your only chance to get inside her." More subtly, a 2007 ad for business loans offered by J. P. Morgan Chase, set in a dress store, makes the same point (Image 11). A young, demure Asian woman stands holding at womb level a sign that reads "OPEN," her eyes and head downcast. Flanking her are frocks draped on headless mannequins. She, too, is for sale, is completely available, has no will (indicated by her lowered, submissive gaze), and has no voice to protest (suggested by the headless mannequins). A 2005 ad for St. Pauli Girl beer draws on that same rape script and indicates that alcohol facilitates the process: "It's hard to get some girls to open up. Others just need a bottle opener" (Image 12).

One of the most extreme, and notorious, rape-friendly ads is one for Dolce & Gabbana that appeared in 2007 (Image 13). It shows a blank-looking White woman in a bathing suit pinned to the ground by one White man, while four others look on. International protests ensued for its too-obvious suggestion of gang rape, and D&G pulled the ad. Within a year, the same company again took up this theme, again with an all-White male group— though this time with a young man as the victim (Image 14). There was no widespread protest. Due to homophobia and gender norms, the subject of male-on-male rape is still so locked up in denial and taboo that any outcry was foreclosed.

The Pure and the Dirty

A complex sexual double standard abides at the foundation of both patriarchal religion and pornography (Caputi, 2011). First of all, men have much greater sexual latitude than women. Hence, women are split into "pure" or "dirty," "virgins" or "whores," "keepers" or "trash," often along race and class lines. "Good girls" are proper—that is, faithful and chaste, wives and daughters, the property of just one man. "Bad girls" are defined as dirty "others"—treacherous, hypersexual, not properly feminine, fit only for prostitution and pornography, and accessible to all men. Notions of purity and dirtiness underlie not only sexism but also racism and homophobia. Those who claim to be the most "pure" tend to project all that they deny and fear in themselves onto people whom they then classify as "dirty," "savage," "morally inferior," and so on. For example, consider the many implications of an ad for liquor that shows two women, one an Asian woman wearing black, the other a White, blonde woman wearing a white dress (Image 15). They are in front of a mirror, and the Asian woman, applying lipstick, appears to be gazing directly at the viewer. She is labeled a "maneater" (the "bad girl"), while the White woman, staring off blankly, is a "vegetarian" (the "good girl").

Soap ads have a long history of projecting these sexist and racist notions (Smith, 2005, pp. 9–10). A classic expression of such notions from a 1995 ad shows an upright, young, blonde White woman in a white blouse alongside the printed word *PURE*. It looks, on the one hand, like an endorsement of female chastity. On the other, it might remind us of a neo-Nazi poster evoking racist notions of "purity" of blood (Image 16).

Alice Walker (1980, p. 103) observed that while White women are represented as "objects" in pornography, Black women are represented as "shit." This is often true in everyday pornography as well. Each year, the men's magazine *Esquire* names a "sexiest woman alive" and features her in a photo spread. In 2010 and 2012, White women were named and were shown posed in conventional ways that stressed their availability, in lingerie or in bed. But a different treatment was given to Rihanna, who was named in 2011. In her photo spread, Rihanna is naked and, in most of the pictures, seems to be outside and on the ground. Dirt is clinging to her skin, and she is covered with sticks and other sorts of debris, even what looks like wet seaweed (Image 17). These pictures arguably represent a dark-skinned woman in traditionally racist ways, as being inferior because she is supposedly "dirtier" than a White woman.

Distorted notions of purity and dirtiness also are used to foment and justify homophobia and transphobia. In March of 2005, an extraordinary interfaith alliance of male religious leaders in Jerusalem formed to try to stop an international gay pride festival in Jerusalem. One leader stated the group's aim: "We can't permit anybody to come and make the Holy City dirty" (Goodstein & Myre, 2005). A 2004 ad for gum makes a similar point (Image 18). It shows a young White woman with short brown hair and minimal makeup, wearing a button-down shirt and tie. A sewer cover is shoved into her mouth. The copy reads: "Dirty Mouth, Clean it up with Orbit." The implication here is that the cross-dresser, transman, or lesbian is dirty and should be abused, silenced, and "cleaned up."

"Dirtiness" also is the theme of a 2005 *Hustler* spread, featuring Jenna Jameson and Briana Banks in a "kinky" scene (Image 19). To immediately establish the context of "filth," the setting is a black-and-white checkered bathroom. Jameson sits on the toilet, legs spread and brandishing a whip. Banks is stretched out on the floor in front of the toilet. This "girl–girl"

scene is a regular feature of heterosexual porn, pitched to homophobic, straight-identified men who want to watch women "degrade" themselves by performing especially "dirty" and taboo sex (rather like the tormentors at Abu Ghraib who forced male prisoners to simulate supposedly "dirty" homosexual sex). Variations often appear in mainstream imagery, as in a 2009 Cesare Paciotti fashion spread featuring two glamorous White women presented as "bad girls," wearing dark clothing and makeup and enacting a vampiric form of sexuality (Image 20). (Lesbian readers, of course, might take different meanings from such images.)

This justification of violence against or stigmatization of those who are labeled as "animalistic," "dark," and "dirty" (often along gender, racial, class, and sexual lines) is linked to an overall pattern of body loathing and concomitant disrespect for nature (including human nature) and the dark Earth, the original source of *dirt* and also the source of all life as we know it. Aspects of human life, such as our animality, sexuality, defecation, emotionality, and aging, are cast as "nature" and inferior to (masculine and usually White-identified) rationality, culture, and "civilization." Accordingly, the planet Earth is treated as mere matter—body without mind, something for elite humans to exploit and use. In so doing, we forget that we are made of earth. Violence against women and girls, as well as against peoples who have been stigmatized as "dirty," "low," and "other," is part of an overall pattern of violence against the Earth.

Objectification

Patriarchal cultures commodify women's sexuality and reproductive powers and then define women as the paradigmatic "natural resource," something men can exploit to accumulate wealth and services. Patriarchal men define women as their property. This is why, historically, women go from bearing their father's name to their husband's upon marriage, and also why brides are supposed to be "virgins"—that is, unused or undamaged "goods."

One expression of patriarchal ownership of women in popular culture is what feminists identify as "objectification." To objectify someone is to treat that person as your property, to deny him or her autonomy and use him or her as a tool for your own purposes, to make that person into a kind of consumable object or replaceable commodity (Nussbaum, 1999).

In advertising, the classic symbol of objectification is the doll, mannequin, or "fembot," which appears in advertisements for everything from antidepressants to window treatments, sports gear, and liquor. A 2007 Heineken television commercial, which retains a following on YouTube, features a platinum-blonde, white-skinned robot who dances, sprouts an additional set of mechanical arms, and produces from her torso a keg of Heineken, from which she pours a glass of beer that she offers to viewers (Image 21). She then splits into three identical models. Here is the ultimate sex object—decorative, entertaining, and with no possibility of free will, existing only to serve. Numerous YouTube commentators affirm their sexual attraction to this robot, one (Dominatorxxx) deeming her the "perfect woman."[3]

Sexual objectification (treating the target of desire like a literal thing) fits perfectly into a capitalist–consumer and monocultural society. It sexualizes possession and creates a desire to buy and own, with the most luxurious items defined as the ones carrying the greatest sexual charge. Sexual objectification also defines women as in need of innumerable products and processes to measure up to desirability standards. This includes even the mutilation of her body. A 2008 ad for a center for cosmetic surgery shows an Asian woman, naked except for fetish-wear underpants (Image 22). Lines are drawn from key zones of her body, indicating where she has been worked on—for example, "breast augmentation." The headline claims: "WE CAN REBUILD HER." The unmodified female body is a turn-off to a pornographic culture steeped in misogyny, body loathing, and the technological "fix" for the supposed imperfections of matter. She must be made new, remade into the perfect consumer object.

Regularly, ads call on girls and women to be "perfect"—possessing "flawless" skin, being impossibly slender, and so on. This kind of perfectionism can be read as a form of fascism, obliterating diversity and also imposing a racial hierarchy, as is clear in a 2013 ad for Louis Vuitton (Image 23). The ad shows six women in three pairs, each pair exactly alike and all six made to seem almost interchangeable, except that the two identical White women are in the foreground, the two identical Asian women are at midrange, and the two identical Black women are in the back.

Snuff Porn

Images of mutilated and dismembered female bodies are the very stuff of slasher films, as well as the basis of the "snuff" genre of pornography, which documents actual sexual murders and mutilations. Symbolic dismemberment of female bodies has long been the norm in fashion photography (Caputi, 1987) and usually is not recognized as such, so habituated are we to it. We might notice this practice if it were being done to male bodies, but this does not occur in any comparable way. In the February 2009 issue of *Details*, a photograph illustrating a story about dating during the economic recession shows a White woman turned upside down and dumped in a garbage can (Image 24). Dismemberment is the visual motif, as all we can see is her high-heeled feet and legs, jutting up into the air. This theme of women's severed legs is a common one. When Juergen

Teller photographed Victoria Beckham in an ad for Marc Jacob's designs, he didn't present her as a glamorous celebrity but, rather, as something less than human, a kind of "living doll" (Horyn, 2008). In one photo, we see only her bare, high-heeled legs flopping spread-eagle over the side of a shopping bag (Image 25).

A "virtual snuff" sensibility informs countless images that have appeared in advertising and fashion tableaus since the 1970s. Models are showcased in positions that suggest they are dead: suffocated under plastic bags; as heads without bodies, bodies without heads; laid out in gift boxes; sprawled brokenly on stairs, streets, and boutique floors. A disturbing 2012 ad for a Canon camera shows a young Asian woman on her back, seemingly washed up at the edge of a lake (Image 26). She wears a drenched top and short skirt. Her face is blank, water is pooling up in the cavity at the base of her neck, her eyes are closed, and her head and arms, resting on the shore's edge, are flung back and out. She could be dead. A few yards away, we see a White man's head and arms as he stands in water that comes up to his neck. He is training a camera on her. The copy reads: "When was the last time something inspired you to be creative?" One possible interpretation of this bizarre scenario is that the man has killed the woman and is now documenting this act in a "snuff" photo. Her destruction becomes his "creativity."

This theme of the femicidal killer as some kind of genius or creative artist is a core element in the contemporary myth of the serial sex killer, represented throughout our popular culture as the epitome of masculine mastery. The 2013 television lineup included an unprecedented four shows focusing on male serial killers,[4] guaranteeing continuous stories about terrorized and tortured women. The standard serial-killer story (as in the Fox network show *The Following*) includes a "normal" man who identifies with the killer, often able to "think just like him" and even sharing some women with him. Patriarchal heroes and villains always have had a lot in common, as evident in their shared obsession with possessing women, wielding phallic weaponry, and making violence their way of life.

The November 2012 issue of *Vanity Fair* takes an underlying shared identity between villain and hero for granted, while also showcasing a snuff sensibility (Image 27). It displays an Annie Leibowitz photo of Daniel Craig as James Bond, referencing not the 2013 film *Skyfall* but the 1964 Bond film *Goldfinger,* and the novel (Fleming, 1959) on which the film was based. In this story, an arch-villain lusts for gold and even paints women gold (leaving a bit of skin exposed so they don't epidermally suffocate) before having sex with them. When Goldfinger wants vengeance against Bond, who has caught him cheating at cards and also seduced one of his women, Goldfinger has that woman painted gold all over, killing her. Presumably, he also rapes her. The 2012 Leibowitz photo shows Craig's smirking face set against the backdrop of the svelte and sectioned golden object/body, his head placed precisely over her sex. The message transmitted here is that male sexual gratification, as well as status, wealth, and power, derive from rape, objectification, exploitation, and possession unto death of both women and the Earth's substances.

Monica Sjöö and Barbara Mor (1991) suggest that those killed and tortured "images . . . of female flesh . . . are really our species' maps of the mutilated earth" (p. 411). A 2009 ad for Global Fruits juice shows the Earth being compressed and squeezed dry by a pair of male hands (Image 28). Paralleling the abused and murdered images of women in our popular culture are countless such images of the Earth carved up, dismembered, diminished, painted, strangled, objectified, targeted, and violated along uncannily parallel lines (Caputi, 2004).

Alternative Visions

A 2007 ad for Chanel lipstick shows a partial image of the bottom of a White woman's face (Image 29). Stretching across her mouth is a gold chain with a large pearl in the middle, held just between her teeth. This jewelry item resembles, and is being used as, a ball gag—used to force the mouth open and silence the wearer (you can see one in *Pulp Fiction* as well as in the "torture-porn" film *Hostel*). This image sums up pornographic intention to keep women (and those used in the place of women) *open* for violation and, at the same time, *shut* them up—silencing not only speech but also a resistant imagination.

So imbued is the pornographic worldview, it is extremely difficult to imagine a sexuality outside of it. This inability to imagine an alternative is itself an effect of abuse. Violence, including violence in intimate relationships, does not always take the form of physical blows. Abuse also takes an emotional/psychological form that is meant to destroy the self-esteem of the victim while enhancing that of the abuser. It appears as verbal assaults, belittlement, cultivation of anxiety and despair, humiliation, blaming, accusation, denigration, disrespect, and reality control, which includes denying the harm of the abuse, creating an atmosphere of threat, and blocking awareness of alternative ways of living and being.

Repeated negative mass representation of a group is a public form of psychological abuse. It, too, serves as a form of spirit-breaking destruction meant to squelch resistance and destroy self-esteem. It, too, feeds the dominators' sense of omnipotence. And it, too, serves as a form of reality control. It tells us that this is the only world possible, blocks awareness of alternative ways of living and being, and stifles the development of an imagination other than the pornographic one.

Numerous theorist/activists counter with alternatives. Marcus (2005) celebrated a discourse of the female body/mind as no longer "object, property, and . . . inner space" but, rather, as powerful—capable of will and even violence. bell hooks (1993) asks heterosexual women to cease sexualizing the dominating "hard man" and, instead, to eroticize equal and respectful relationships. Patricia Hill Collins (2004) puts forth an ethic of "honest bodies that are characterized by sexual autonomy and soul, expressiveness, spirituality, sensuality, sexuality, and an expanded notion of the erotic as a life force" (p. 287).

Collins draws on poet Audre Lorde (1984), who extoled what she called the "erotic," a cosmic force of connectivity and creativity that courses through unfettered sexuality as well as creative work and play. The erotic rejoins body and mind, sex and spirit and is, Lorde claimed, our birthright—our bodily access to forces of creativity, ecstasy, and connection, and also the energy source that enables us to resist oppression and transform ourselves and our world.

In ancient understandings, the erotic as a cosmic creative force was represented by the figure of a (Sex) Goddess, sometimes a bisexual divinity, sometimes a mother. She is pictured variously as naked, outside, surrounded by animals or herself part animal, and with spread legs to signify the vulva as sacred and powerful. Patriarchal religions came to power, in part, by defaming and profaning the Goddess and trying to eliminate her as a rival by turning her into pornography (Caputi, 2004). Susan L. Taylor (2006), former editorial director of *Essence* magazine, proclaimed that now is the time for the "Goddess to awaken from patriarchy's trance." She claimed that this happens every time "women step into our power." Some will resonate with this symbol; others will generate new ones. This is as it should be, for diversity—as well as fun, pleasure, joy, care, freedom, and reverence toward others—is fundamental to the erotic principle.

Notes

1. My film *The Pornography of Everyday Life*, distributed by Berkeley Media (www .berkeleymedia.com), incorporates much of this material. This chapter is an updating and revision of my article "Everyday Pornography," which appeared in the earlier edition of this anthology, as well as several other pieces, including one in Caputi (2004). I thank Lauren Walleser, Ann Scales, Shannon Gilreath, Mary Caputi, Peter Cava, Andria Chediak, Rebecca Whisnant, Nicole Calvert, and many students who gave me some of these materials and/or discussed them with me. A list of the sources of the images analyzed in this chapter appears at the end.

2. For more information, see a fact sheet compiled by the Institute on Domestic Violence in the African American Community, University of Minnesota (www.idvaac.org/media/publications/ FactSheet.IDVAAC_AAPCFV-Community%20 Insights.pdf).

3. Ad and comments available at www .youtube.com/watch?v=l-NfrBgYIEQ.

4. The shows are *Ripper Street*, *The Following*, *Bates Motel*, and *Hannibal*.

References

Benjamin, J. (2007, September). The sex he secretly craves. *Cosmopolitan*.

Caputi, J. (1987). *The age of sex crime*. Bowling Green, Ohio: Bowling Green State University Press.

Caputi, J. (2004). *Goddesses and monsters: Women, myth, power and popular culture*. Madison: University of Wisconsin Popular Press.

Caputi, J. (2011). Re-creating patriarchy: Connecting religion and pornography. *Wake Forest Journal of Law & Policy, 1:2*, 293–324.

Collins, P. H. (2004). *Black sexual politics: African Americans, gender, and the new racism*. New York: Routledge.

Dyer, R. (1993). Male sexuality in the media. In R. Dyer (Ed.), *The matter of images: Essays on representation* (pp. 111–122). New York: Routledge.

Fleming, I. (1959). *Goldfinger*. New York: Penguin.

Gilligan, J. (1996). *Violence: Reflections on a national epidemic*. New York: Random House.

Goodstein, L., & Myre, G. (2005, May 31). Clerics fighting a gay festival for Jerusalem. *New York Times*. Retrieved from http://www .nytimes.com/2005/03/31/international/ worldspecial/31gay.html

Haber, M. (2013, February 27). A hush-hush topic no more. *New York Times*. Retrieved from http://www.nytimes.com/2013/02/28/ fashion/bondage-domination-and-kink- sex-communities-step-into-view.html? pagewanted=all

hooks, b. (1993). Seduced by violence no more. In E. Buchward, P. Fletcher, & M. Roth (Eds.), *Transforming a rape culture* (pp. 351–356). Minneapolis: Milkweed.

Horyn, C. (2008, April 10). When is a fashion ad not a fashion ad? *New York Times*.

James, E. L. (2012). *Fifty shades of grey*. New York: Vintage.

Kaplan, L. J. (1991). *Female perversions: The temptations of Emma Bovary*. New York: Doubleday.

Lorde, A. (1984). Uses of the erotic: The erotic as power. In *Sister Outsider* (pp. 53–59). Trumansburg, NY: Crossing Press.

MacKinnon, C. A., & Dworkin A. (Eds.). (1997). *In harm's way: The pornography civil rights hearings*. Cambridge, UK: Harvard University Press.

Marcus, S. (2005). Fighting bodies, fighting words: A theory and politics of rape prevention. In E. Hackett & S. Haslanger (Eds.), *Theorizing feminisms: A reader* (pp. 368– 381). New York: Oxford University Press.

Nussbaum, M. C. (1999). *Sex and social justice*. New York: Oxford University Press.

Rennison, M., & Welchans, W. (2000, May). *Intimate partner violence* (NCJ 178247). Washington, DC: U.S. Department of Justice, Office of Justice Programs, Bureau of Justice Statistics. Retrieved from http://www.bjs.gov/content/pub/pdf/ipv.pdf

Sheidlower, J. (Ed.). (1999). *The F-word* (2nd ed.). New York: Random House.

Sjöö, M., & Mor, B. (1991). *The great cosmic mother: Rediscovering the religion of the Earth* (2nd ed.). San Francisco: HarperSanFrancisco.

Smith, A. (2005). *Conquest: Sexual violence and American Indian genocide*. Boston: South End Press.

Taylor, S. L. (2006, October). The goddess within. *Essence*.

Walker, A. (1980). Coming apart. In L. Lederer (Ed.), *Take back the night: Women on pornography* (pp. 95–104). New York: Bantam Books.

Williams, P. J. (1995). *The rooster's egg: On the persistence of prejudice*. Cambridge, MA: Harvard University Press.

LIST OF IMAGES

1. Abu Ghraib abuse photos. (2006, February 16). Retrieved from http://www.antiwar.com/news/?articleid=8560

2. "Bottoms UP," Photograph by Natasha Papadopoulou, *Vibe*, ca. 2002.

3. Ad for *Human Target* TV series, *New York Times*, January 3, 2010.

4. "Guilty," Gucci, *Vanity Fair*, February 2013.

5. "CK IN2U," *Cosmopolitan*, 2007.

6. "Unforgivable Woman," Sean Jean, 2007. (See the ad and read feminist commentary at http://shakespearessister.blogspot.com/2007/09/assvertising_21.html.)

7. "Wear the Pants" Dockers, © 2009 Levi Strauss & Co., *New York Times*, December 6, 2009.

8. Seitz-Wald, A. (2012, December 17). Assault rifle company issues "man cards." *Salon*. Retrieved from http://www.salon.com/2012/12/17/bushmasters_horrible_ad_campaign/

9. Busbee, J. (2013, February 14). Oscar Pistorius Nike ad takes on new, chilling resonance after tragedy. *Yahoo! Sports*. Retrieved from http://sports.yahoo.com/blogs/olympics-fourth-place-medal/oscar-pistorius-nike-ad-takes-chilling-resonance-tragedy-182235671–oly.html

10. What is this ad announcing? (n.d.). *AdWomen*. Retrieved from http://www.adwomen.org/2011/06/what-is-this-ad-announcing/

11. © JPMorganChase, 2007.

12. Pauli Girl Beer, 2005, © Imported By Barton Beers, Ltd., Chicago.

13. Dolce & Gabbana, 2007. Retrieved from http://loveyourbody.nowfoundation.org/offensiveads.html

14. Dolce & Gabbana, 2008. Retrieved from www.bilerico.com/2008/06/dolce_gabbana_sells_gang_rape.php

15. Hennessy [Vegetarian/Maneater], © 2001 Schiefflin & Somerset Co. New York.

16. "Pure," © 1994 Neutrogena Corp.

17. Rihanna is the sexiest woman alive. (2011, October 11). *Esquire*. Retrieved from http://www.esquire.com/women/the-sexiest-woman-alive/rihanna-naked-1111

18. "Dirty Mouth," © 2004 Wm. Wrigley Jr. Co.

19. © *Hustler*, 2005.

20. Cesare Paciotti, 2009.

21. "Heineken: Keg" ad, 2007. Retrieved from http://www.youtube.com/watch?v=l-NfrBgYIEQ

22. New Beauty Center, Ocean Drive, September 2008.

23. Louis Vuitton. Set Design Daniel Buren © ADAGP-Paris & DB 2012, *New York Times Style Magazine*, February 17, 2013.

24. *Details*, February 2009.

25. Photo in *New York Times*, April 10, 2008, accompanying the article by Horyn.

26. © 2012 Canon U.S.A.

27. *Vanity Fair* cover, November 2012. Retrieved from http://www.vanityfair .com/online/oscars/2012/10/daniel-craig-skyfall-november-cover-preview

28. Global Fruits, *Backpacker Magazine*, 2009.

29. © 2007, Chanel, Inc.

40

There Are Bitches and Hoes

Tricia Rose

One of the signature icons that drives commercial hip hop is the pimp. An important facet of urban street cultures and illicit economies, and once relegated to folklore, underground vernacular culture, and the margins of mainstream society, pimps have become popularized and mainstreamed. Building on the glamorization of black pimp culture in blaxsploitation films of the 1970s and on the influence of raw sexual hierarchies exported from prison culture, many rappers began drawing from pimp culture, style, slang, and attitude as part of their identities. Rappers such as Too Short, Snoop Dogg, Ice T, now deceased Pimp C, Dr. Dre, David Banner, 50 Cent, Nelly, and Lil' Pimp brag about controlling women like pimps, being stylish like pimps, and about being pimps themselves; promote pimp-based products (e.g., Nelly's energy drink, Pimp Juice); and elevate former pimps like the Archbishop Don "Magic" Juan to cult-like status. Pimp culture has saturated commercial hip hop. As T. Denean Sharplev-Whiting has put it: "The 'g's up, ho's down mentality of late 1980s hip hop laid the groundwork for the pimp-playa-bitch-ho' nexus that has come to dominate hip hop." Strippers and groupies, already praised and demeaned for their sexual actions, are now also being promoted and contained within this pimp-ho framework. Pimping style and attitude have migrated into other facets of mainstream popular culture, such as the car-customizing show *Pimp My Ride,* "Pimp and Ho" Halloween and theme parties, the film *Hustle and Flow,* and cable network programming exposing pimp culture. Pimping is everywhere these days.[1]

Despite the cuddly, fuzzy-hat image of pimps in some mainstream outlets and celebrated films like *Hustle and Flow* that attempt to generate sympathy for pimps, pimp ideology and its expression in popular culture are fundamentally exploitative to women. Dominating prostitutes and living off of their sex work, street pimps use physical violence (including rape) as well as emotional and psychological manipulation to control prostitutes. Phrases like Snoop Dogg's famous rap lyric "Bitches ain't shit but hoes and tricks" capture pimps' fundamental attitude: Women are bitches, and bitches are whores and prostitutes.

Taking a brash attitude in defense of these exploitative terms, most defenders of this trend in hip hop rely on the idea that they are talking about a reality of life and dare people to deny it. . . .

Some hip hop artists defend their endless self-aggrandizing talk about dominating "bitches and hoes" by saying that they are not talking about all women. But "bitches and hoes" are all the women they talk about. The valorization of the gangsta and pimp also highlights and celebrates the very women they degrade, encouraging young women fans to emulate the behaviors of "bitches and hoes" to get attention, to be desired, and to be considered sexy. Bitches and hoes get all the attention in hip hop. Of course, many women participate in the videos and other aspects of the culture that demeans them—and female fans emulate these behaviors, too. Some point to women's cooperation with sexism in hip hop to say that it cannot, therefore, be that bad and that women must not really mind. While being a black gangsta is the primary means of gaining recognition, money, and fame for males in hip hop, behaving in hyper-sexual ways is, for some women, the only means of making any gains at all. Men have gangs, drug dealing, and pimping; sex is the street economy open to women. Pointing to women's participation in a system that exploits them to prove it isn't sexist falsely assumes that sexism is sexism only when all women label it so. It also denies the power of socialization in creating our collusion with social relationships that hurt us. Again, since sexism socializes all men and women, we have to work against it; being anti-sexist doesn't come naturally in a system that rewards us for participating.

Because street culture and the exploitative culture on which it is based have become such key sources of black identity in the hip hop generation, many young black women parrot the sexist ideas that are so widely circulated in hip hop; it's a key to belonging. For many young black women, the language of commercial hip hop about black sexuality has influenced their understanding of black women, not just reflected it. Sexism works best when women are isolated from and pitted against one another (as detailed in the song "Bitches and Sisters"). Isolation and conflict ensure that they will sustain and internalize the terms of insult and control used to keep things as they are. Women are rewarded by men for participating in this system.

Young women are also coerced into participating by the dictates of record-industry marketing. As noted by Glen Ford, a veteran radio and rap video programmer and current executive editor of the *Black Agenda Report,* the consolidation of these limited identities is directly related to corporate pressure:

> The term "street" became a euphemism for a monsoon or profanity, gratuitous violence, female and male hyper-promiscuity, the most vulgar materialism, and the total suppression of social consciousness. A slew of child acts was recruited to appeal more directly to the core demographic. Women rappers were coerced to conform to the new order. A young female artist broke down at my kitchen table one afternoon, after we had finished a promotional interview. "They're trying to make me into a whore," she said, sobbing, "They say I'm not 'street' enough." Her skills on the mic were fine. "They" were the A&R [Artists and Repertoire] people from her corporate label.[2]

Some young women who are angered by this hyper-sexism speak out, but many do not. To be publicly and strongly against sexism in the music industry is to guarantee one's marginality. And to challenge sexism in the black community (as in larger society) is to discourage public support; in fact, doing so is often perceived as an anti-black community action and can make one a target. For black women—who are already marginal in larger society—taking a stand in a way that might alienate them from their local community is painful and difficult and often not worth it. So, instead, there is a great deal of silence or skirting of the issue, as black women try to find ways to manage what is a hurtful, insulting, and discriminatory language of belonging. One such way is to agree that "there are bitches and hoes." . . .

The constant public labeling of black women in hip hop as "bitches and hoes" has forced young women to stake out a position. Some embrace "bitch" as a term of empowerment and also try to reverse the sexual-power exchange, calling men "hoes." Women who use "bitch" in this subversive way are trying to challenge the language of sexism; men who use "bitch" are ultimately supporting such language. Many women and girls say that since they are not "bitches and hoes," these rappers are "not talking about me" because I don't "behave that way." So, "it doesn't impact me." In some cases, this kind of distorted self-defense is a valiant but tragic effort to pretend that such labeling is not hurtful to all women no matter how one acts. It's often a matter of survival to craft this defense, as the distinction is mostly a fiction. In the film *Hip Hop: Beyond Beats and Rhymes,* Byron Hurt makes the following point to a young woman who tries to use this defense: "It's funny when I hear women say, 'when these rappers are calling women bitches and ho's, they're not talking about me.'" It's like, yo, they *are* talking about you. If George Bush was to get on national TV and make a speech, and he started calling black people niggers, would you be like, 'I don't know who George Bush is talking about, but he ain't talking about me?'" . . .

Although the roots of the common portrayal of black women as ugly, aggressive, and hypersexual were formed long ago, there is a more recent term that bears importance here. The term "welfare queen," coined by Ronald Reagan in the 1980s, typecast poor black women on welfare as sexually irresponsible, money-hungry and lazy. To drum up support for drastic reductions in public welfare assistance, those who used this term accused economically limited black women of manipulating and cheating the welfare system by having babies to increase their welfare assistance payments. The label "welfare queen" relied on the already sedimented idea that black women are sexually deviant and untrustworthy. Now, as the term implied, they were whoring themselves for state assistance.

This kind of racist and sexist name-calling is pretty similar to what Snoop claims about the "bitches and hoes" in his 'hood: "that ain't doin' shit, that's trying to get a nigga for his money." It's just that he says he has a right to do it because he knows them from personal experience. Snoop's attitude about poor black women isn't any better than that of many of the conservatives who attack him.

Snoop's "I know them from personal experience" defense also uses a racial authenticity argument to justify his sexism. Snoop and many other multi-platinum rappers from tough, poor black and brown neighborhoods continue to *choose to represent a sexist perspective about reality they no longer have.* There are many men and women in the 'hood who don't hold his sexist views, and he can't legitimately rely on his so-called reality to justify his own perpetuation of this image of black women. After several years of hits and celebrity living and socializing out of the 'hood, traveling the world, and having access to nearly any and all manner of ideas, knowledge, and new forms of socialization, to act as if they have no meaningful relationship to women beyond the ones they call "bitches and hoes" is ridiculous. Like they still live in a rented apartment in the 'hood and a brigade of money hungry black women are figuring out ways to take their riches?

Rappers are not under assault by black women whose behavior they don't like. The gangsta rapper image *needs* "bitches and hoes," and so they continually invent them. Women, so labeled, add lots of status and value to gangsta and pimp images. If you can't have lots of women serving and servicing you, then how can you be a real player, a real pimp? So, the process of locating, labeling, partying with, and then discarding black women is part of the performance that enhances gangsta- and pimp-style rappers' status and, thus, their income. If, as Jay-Z raps in "99 Problems," "I got 99 problems but a bitch ain't one," then why bother telling us about her inability to give him problems—unless controlling bitches is part of his power? Similarly, Snoop and other rappers at his level don't have any reason to fraternize with women whom they feel are out to "take their money." So, if they're "just keeping it real," then they need to stop pretending that they are victims of black women out to take their money. That's nonsense. If they're so good at identifying women they insist should be called bitches and hoes, then it shouldn't be too hard to stay away from them. And, if they're able and want to stay away from them, then there's no reason to rap about them constantly.

I'm not saying that all women are above criticism. But if people want to challenge someone's behavior because they don't like it, they should talk about the behavior and say why it's problematic rather than using generalized, sexist, or racist language and labeling. The culture of women's sexual behavior promoted by hip hop videos shapes the actions of young black women in ways that will bring them attention and status. So, in a sense, hip hop is becoming a "bitches and hoes" factory, encouraging girls and young women to play the limited roles assigned to them.

Conservative responses to hyper-sexual popular culture usually involve an anti-sex agenda, one that functions to contain women's sexuality while failing to fight sexism or to work toward women's overall freedom. Rappers and corporate industry representatives highlight the sexually repressive tone and agenda of conservative attacks on hip hop in order to encourage women's complicity with their own exploitation. Indeed, the two positions—sexual exploitation and sexual repression—are birds of a feather. I am not interested in a less sexually open society or in sexual censorship, and I am not against sex workers or a gender-equal sex industry that protects women's rights and work conditions. Rather, I am concerned about black women's overall freedom and equality. This involves genuine sexual freedom of expression—not freedom of expression tied to sexist male fantasies or to male-dominated sex trades in which women are demeaned and degraded in order to appear to be sexually free. Nor does it involve women's sexual repression—a returning to sexual determination of women through sexual repression in the interests of patriarchal male control. Sexual explicitness does not have to be sexually exploitative. If we don't make this distinction when we fight against the constant barrage of "there are bitches and hoes," then we wind up with a sexually repressive call for less sexuality.

The problem in commercial hip hop as it has evolved over the past fifteen years is that terms of sexual exchange are now so exploitative and overarching that nearly everyone is cast as either a player (the one in control) or the one getting played (the one being dominated). Women are nearly always on the latter end of this exchange and their only way out is to either confine their sexuality or try to become players. Those who reverse the terms and do try to become players are often relabeled "bitches and hoes" who are "trying to take a nigga's money." So, either way, they lose. This blending of sexual explicitness with sexual exploitation is hurtful and destructive for black women and for black male/female relationships and the black community generally.

So, although hip hop isn't primarily responsible tor America's sexism, it is the most visible and extreme engine for it in black popular culture, which means that it has a special impact on black women and men who, because of the racist and sexist world in which they live, rely on black culture as a source of reflection, support, and affirmation. This is one key reason why it's important to make sure that black popular culture is not overrun by the worst forms of domination and inequality. Making sexism sexy only makes life harder for everyone, especially black women and others in the black community who already have too many unfair hurdles to overcome.

Instead, let's demand that empowered women be in charge of their own sexual imagery and give them the freedom to express themselves as they see fit. There is no evidence that most young women want to replace the more sexually explicit brand of sexism they currently manage with a repressed version of sexism. This less-repressed one gives them more day-to-day freedom, even though it is often highly exploitative. The anti-sex agenda of many conservatives is unappealing, disempowering, and uninterested in promoting women's rights or fighting sexism.

We have to work hard against what destroys who we are, what prevents us from reaching our best selves and stalls our efforts to create a truly just society. Many of the artists and executives who deflect legitimate criticism with the kinds of excuses presented here defend their constant use of highly insulting racist and sexist ideas about black women while profiting from it. We need to understand the roots of sexist images and work to reduce their impact, visibility, and perpetuation everywhere, not only in hip hop. We also have to confront the reason why these images are so successful as products sold to millions of people from all racial backgrounds. . . .

When asked about their lyrics, many rappers respond to the terms set out by conservatives who attack them, not to the many black women who have generally supported hip hop but find this escalation of highly destructive imagery a problematic betrayal. The fact that conservatives attack male rappers doesn't mean that these rappers' lyrics and their too-easy defense of their portrayals of black women are worthy of progressive defense. Save the defense for the young men and women who are willing to stand up for what is right, not for those who pander to what is clearly wrong and unjust because "it's the way it is," "other people do it," "I get unfairly attacked for it," and "conservatives don't understand or like it." We can attack the conservatives about plenty of issues, but we shouldn't marshal black people's solidarity in the service of defending sexist attacks on black women. Not in hip hop, and not anywhere else.

Notes

1. T. Denean Sharpley-Whiting, *Pimps Up, Ho's Down: Hip Hop's Hold on Young Black Women* (New York University Press, 2007), p. xvii.

2. Glen Ford, "Hip Hop Profanity, Misogyny and Violence: Blame the Manufacturer," available online at www.peacheandjustice.org/article.php/20070507114621137/print.

41

The Limitations of
the Discourse of Norms

Gay Visibility and Degrees of Transgression

Jay Clarkson

Painful.

Both my partner and I are totally straight-acting, very masculine, and when we're in mixed company with someone who's . . . um . . . well, let's just say they open their mouth & their purse falls out, well, we get rather uncomfortable.

Case in point: a big get-together of a bunch of friends last year at the local Macaroni Grille (chain Italian restaurant). Thing is, this is suburban Detroit, not the Castro, and a table full of fourteen guys in a busy restaurant full of middle-class families might get noticed of its own accord!

Add in one of our friends, let's call him "Bill." Not his real name. Bill's 23, lives at home, has no responsibilities, and is finishing up interior design school. He's emaciated thin; we think he lives on ice chips, Dolce & Gabbana anything, and Swarovski crystal trinkets. Both he and another member of our crew decided that this would be the perfect place to turn up their flames from "dull glow" to "viewable-from-space." It was all I could do not to either 1. smack him or 2. flee the building.

Because my one pet peeve, more than anything else with regards to gay men (besides the idiots who believe that HIV is a curable disease and therefore don't use protection) are fags who don't recognize the conditions of their environment. There's a time to flame out (greeting friends in the gay bar) and a time to tone it down (the sideline at an NFL game). Boys who don't change their temperament in accordance with their conditions endanger themselves and those they're with, in my opinion. (roadster_guy)

From Jay Clarkson, "The Limitations of the Discourse of Norms: Gay Visibility and Degrees of Transgression." *Journal of Communication Inquiry* (2008), 32 (4), 368–382. Reprinted with permission of SAGE Publications.

At the heart of the politics of gay representation are two intersecting considerations: the meanings and functions of visibility, and the role of gender performance in our understanding of sexuality. This chapter continues the discussion of gay visibility and gender transgression that has emerged as a key concept in recent scholarship of GLBTQ (gay, lesbian, bisexual, transgender, and queer) representation in the media. I explore the discourse of the discussion board of StraightActing.com, an Internet discussion board for self-identified straight-acting gay men, to demonstrate how current popular understandings of representational power create divisiveness among groups of gay men who seek to normalize a particular set of gender performances as acceptably gay, at the expense of other performances perceived as more transgressive. . . .

The discourse of visibility on Straight Acting.com is useful because the online space functions for self-proclaimed straight-acting gay men to make themselves visible to other gay men. Their discussions include significant debate about the nature of their and other gay men's visibility, of which I have chosen a representative sample. Their discourse mirrors critical understandings of the power of visibility and gender transgression. They demonize an effeminate gay stereotype, which they perceive as dominating media representations of gay men, because they fear that it functions to construct a normative gay identity that is promoted by other gay men and can only be undone with increased visibility of straight-acting gay men. . . .Their argument assumes that transgressive gender performance, not just same-sex desire, is the root of antigay attitudes. Homophobia in this formulation is reduced to a fear of particular gender performances, and not a deeper cultural fear of same-sex attraction. The visibility of straight-acting gay men, or men who cannot be read as gay, may challenge the notion of a hegemonic and monolithic gay identity, but they reflect the historic need

for the marginalized to remain obedient, silent, and invisible in order to be recuperated into dominant ideologies (Owen, Vande Berg, & Stein, 2007). I argue that for gay visibility to challenge the hegemonic gender regime, the acceptance of outspoken, disobedient, visible gay men and lesbians is necessary to raise acceptance of all gay people, including those who identify as straight acting, and to recognize the diversity of gay identities.

Conceptualizing Visibility

It is important to remember that visibility is not in itself an unproblematic concept. Peggy Phelan criticizes identity politics for its reliance on the assumption that a lack of media visibility of a minority group reflects and reproduces inequality, and accordingly, these groups should seek great power through increased visibility. Phelan has quipped, "If representational visibility equals power, then almost-naked young white women should be running Western Culture" (Phelan, 1993, p. 10). She recognizes that equating visibility with power is problematic, for in its supposed promise of liberation it invites increased surveillance. . . . The notion that the power visibility promises may be reduced to quantity is nonsensical, since visibility is often used to signify deviance and not to promote tolerance (see, e.g., Sloop, 2004). . . .

Gay and lesbian media critics have long recognized that media visibility of gay men and lesbians often functions only to make a certain type of homosexual natural and normal (Battles & Hilton-Murrow, 2002; Dyer, 1977; Shugart, 2003). It is important therefore for critics to analyze gay and lesbian visibility to see how it is being used by heterosexual society to define homosexuality. . . . Despite the widely accepted notion that GLBTQ people turn to the media to understand homosexuality, there remains a relative void in research detailing the ways that actual gay people conceptualize visibility in the media or in actual social practice. It is important to look beyond merely examining media texts to determine how transgressive performances may be constructed, and to actually observe how these transgressive performances are read by those who oppose them. . . .

DEGREES OF TRANSGRESSION AND THE LIMITS OF NORMALIZATION

The passage from roadster_guy that begins this chapter reveals the tension over gay visibility that exists even within gay communities.[1] In answering the question "How have your experiences with nelly men been," roadster_guy blames those who are read as gay for their own oppression and advocates invisibility for gay men. He demonstrates a homophobic, but widely accepted and repeated, view: those who do not alter their behaviors to avoid the risk of offending potentially homophobic bystanders are responsible for any disciplinary action that those homophobes may choose to inflict. Furthermore, the fact that he would consider smacking his friend for displaying any sort of gender transgression reveals his reliance on blending into a presumably heterosexual environment at any cost, and his assumption that gender performance is an overtly agentic set of choices to be made.

Given roadster_guy's obvious discomfort with Bill, even before he broadcast his flaming performance to space, it is unclear why Bill is his friend at all. His reaction does reveal how gender transgressors are disciplined differently than those who conform. Most importantly, it reveals that selective homophobia is alive and well within gay communities. It suggests that some gay men fear the gender performances they see as flaming, not only because they do not like them, but also because they fear what those performances may mean to straight people. However, it is these flaming gender performances

which represent a heightened degree of transgression that, as the visibility of gay men grows, remains a barometer for gay rights and highlights how the gender and sex regime continues to operate even within gay communities. Potentially, as Halberstam (1998) argues, these transgressors are not simply saying no to the dominant gender regime, but are in fact saying "I don't care" to the system of power, and thus it is more difficult for disciplinary forces to cope with this transgression.

I submit "degrees of transgression" as a metaphor for discussing the political potential of rethinking "normalization" of gay visibility as "conventionalization." This phrasing should remind critics that "flaming gays" remain among the most marginalized members of society, even in some gay communities. Even when these flamers are represented in the media, audiences, including gay men, often are positioned to laugh at gender transgression, not to identify with those who perform it. Furthermore, many assume that the presence of a flamer positions the reader to laugh at the transgression, even if the audience is positioned to identify with the transgressor. The flamer needs to be validated in media texts, and by media audiences, as a critical first step toward the acceptance of these gender performances as legitimate conventions of the larger and more diverse gay community. . . .

Negating Transgression in Representations of Gay Pride

The limits of normalization and the fear of heightened degrees of transgression can be observed in the discourse of Straight Acting.com. Several of its members suggest that gay visibility would improve in quality if gay pride parades were abolished and gay men implemented a strategy of being "quietly gay":

I'm not sure gay pride is working. A gay author, Dan Savage, I think, suggested that once the disease is cured, the cure becomes toxic. Once the cancer is gone, the chemo will kill you. I think the Stonewall/Gay Pride movement was a necessary cure, and brought the gay world to people's attention. But I think that what was once the cure is now toxic. I see more and more of our rights taken away, and more hate crimes, because the flamboyant elements of the gay movement have remained in power after they have ceased to be effective, IMHO.[2]

I suggest a movement called "quietly gay." I think it's important for me to be out to the people closest to me, but as for the rest of the world, they can "do the math." I don't need to be vocal or up front with the world at large. And I think the world would be more accepting if we just lived our lives in our own little world. I think that we are losing because people continue to shove their orientation in people's faces. I think a new vanguard of "normal" men living normal lives would help the movement more at this moment in time. Thought I'd toss that out for discussion. (James)

James is interpreting Dan Savage, a controversial gay columnist, correctly. Savage does argue that pride has outlived its usefulness and may be more of a hindrance than a help. The article that James is citing argues that gay pride functions to suggest that there is a unified gay community, and warns of the danger of assuming that all gay people look out for each other.

Of course, Savage is correct in asserting that not all gay people are allies, as the discourse of this Web site reveals; however, he is wrong to assume that we are at the point where a cure for societal homophobia is no longer needed. I am not arguing that pride is the solution to homophobia, but Savage's perspective that gay rights have been won is tragically optimistic and ignores the growing amount of antigay physical and political violence, as well as the overwhelming body of legislation that

has passed to prevent GLBTQ people from enjoying equal access to citizenship.[3]

James, in his post above, reveals that antigay sentiment is still quite strong among large sections of the American population. However, James attributes this sentiment, and an increase in hate crimes, to the visibility of "flamboyant" gay people, and argues that we should move toward a gay identity that conforms to normative standards of gender identity while retaining nonnormative sexual identities. His comments suggest that invisibility is his preferred strategy and that normalization of his particular gender identity is more important than the acceptance of other conventions of gay identity. James's insistence on reduced visibility for particular types of gay people does recognize that diversity exists, but his strategy of reduced visibility attempts to rhetorically douse those who perform higher degrees of transgression. . . .

James's perspective represents only one side of the debate about visibility on StraightActing.com. Xaphan is the first to challenge James's understanding of the power of gay visibility:

Ahh, but the chemo doesn't get all the cancer during the first treatment. You need to have repeated treatments and follow up to make sure it's gone. Pride is that treatment. And each year, society as a whole gets a little dose of Queer Chemo.

Pride in Boston started 35 years ago. Since that time we've become more visible, less discriminated against, have more rights, less fears, and now we can marry. We're getting to be cured of the homophobic cancer. Will it all go away? Nope. There are still people that think blacks should go back to Africa and women shouldn't be independent. But, can we improve conditions for a more equal world, yes.

So while Pride is seen by people with clouded vision (nice way of saying ignorant fools) as a show of flamboyance, it is in fact exposure, a dose of the variation of life. If Pride is a foolish display of homosexuality, then what of Mardi Gras, Carnival, and Spring Break. What do these things say of heterosexual people? What do they say of young people? And these are groups who don't require any visibility or more acceptance.

So Pride is the continuation of the homophobia chemotherapy. (Xaphan)

Xaphan recognizes that gay rights have increased since the inception of gay pride events, although whether this is as a consequence is impossible to determine. His comment reveals the assumptions of identity politics: that increased visibility results in increased power, which here is framed as acceptance and civil rights. More importantly, he reveals the power of exposing the invisible in order to challenge interpretations of the visible. His comparison of the heterosexual displays of Spring Break and Mardi Gras to the homosexual "flamboyance" of gay pride reveals the ways in which homosexuality is seen and heterosexuality remains unmarked, because these expressions of heterosexuality are contextualized, and thus seen as only one convention of heterosexuality. Few complain about the display of heterosexuality during Spring Break, although some complain about its graphic nature. Furthermore, this distinction recognizes the diversity in heterosexual sexuality—not just their straightness, but the ways that they may employ their sexuality in public or in private. However, the assumption that Xaphan is revealing is that gay sexuality is defined for the public by the gay pride events: that the norm is public displays of sex and sexuality, not that these are indicative of a particular group within the gay community.

What the discourse about gay pride reveals is not that some of these men believe that visibility does not lead to social change, but instead that they see only specific types of representation leading to social change. The flaming performances that are traditionally associated with gay pride are rejected when James

advocates that gay people should quietly emulate heterosexual relationships. In the following comment James elaborates on what "quietly gay" means to him. In doing so he assumes that one can be publicly gay without revealing the private desires that homosexuality entails:

> For me, the couples standing in line to get licenses in San Francisco was a powerful, quiet witness. It said something strong and true about the gay experience, and didn't require any costumes. I'm not asking anyone to sit down and shut up—I'm thinking of becoming visible in a different set of roles. I don't think the public at large benefits from knowing about my private desires, but they can see me working for a candidate, cleaning up a park, being a churchgoer, etc., and do the math from the way I live my life. I think the last election has shown that rather than gaining us rights, the gay pride movement is galvanizing people against us. Showing that we are the same as everybody else, and living our lives with our orientation blended in with the rest of the flavors of our lives, would do more to help the cause now, IMHO. (James) . . .

Conclusion

The important difference between norm and convention lies in the insistence on a plurality. However, the intragroup struggle over a dominant convention, revealed in the discourse of StraightActing.com, reveals the danger of the current conceptualization of visibility among gay men. The reliance on this discourse of normalization suggests that what media representations contribute to is a single norm for gay men, and all else are abnormal or less than acceptable. Formulating representational power as normalizing, and not conventionalizing, promotes divisiveness among members of the gay community, struggling over which of their identities may become normalized. Just as heterosexuality is not reduced to a single norm, with its recurring representation in MTV's variety of Spring Break specials and coverage of overt sexual display at Mardi Gras celebrations, homosexuality at gay pride parades may be thought of as contextualized within that moment. The displays of homosexuality are conventions that occur within a particular moment and do not represent homosexuality as a whole, and may not even represent the lives of those who engage in these displays at pride events. A discursive shift to conventionalization may reduce the intergroup struggle over who is represented, by assuming a wider range of degrees of transgression.

The discourse of media stereotypes of gay men reveals both pro- and anti-visibility perspectives. In their calls for inclusion, these men focus on inclusion for those men who adhere to the traditional and perhaps conventional expectations of male behavior. In this discussion group, these particular men want to see a change in the ways gay men are represented. They are angered by the seeming focus on feminine gay representations and want to shift the focus to gay men who act just like "normal" heterosexual men, thus returning feminine gay men to a closet of symbolic annihilation. Indeed, they want to return to the privileged position of seeming to be just like heterosexual men, so that they can assume some of the power that this position entails. . . .

Some of these men, as well as some media critics, argue that increased visibility of straight-acting gay men has the potential to undo what they see as the negative consequence of the prevalence of effeminate gay stereotypes and those who uphold them. They fail to recognize the liberatory potential of representing higher degrees of transgression. While their argument seems to be that their increased visibility will lead to greater acceptance of homosexuals, they fail to acknowledge that the root of homophobia remains homosexuality. They seek to normalize

gay men as "real men," but their strategy for confronting homophobia is limited to challenging the conflation of gender and sexuality, and does not seek acceptance for those whose degrees of transgression are higher. It does not challenge the fear or hatred of gayness. . . .

Notes

1. StraightActing.com is a privately funded Web site for self-proclaimed straight-acting gay men that can be read by all, but users must register (at no cost) to post. The site is based around the discussion area called the Butch Boards, but also includes a series of straight-acting quizzes and, before a massive server crash in the summer of 2004, personal ads, home pages, and other services. The Butch Boards and the quiz have been restored, but unfortunately the previous content has been irreparably lost, and the discussion boards started anew early in October 2004. In June 2005, the Butch Board included 18 forums ranging from 41 to 310 topics in each. Overall, there were slightly less than 55,000 total posts, ranging widely in length and content. While the forum descriptions suggest that the discussion topics are well organized, there is considerable overlap in topic area from forum to forum. As part of a larger study, I engaged all areas of the discussion board in order to avoid overlooking certain perspectives or favoring one forum's most active posters. This chapter focuses exclusively on the discourse of visibility in these forums.

2. IMHO is a common acronym for "In my humble opinion."

3. Five more states voted to ban same-sex marriage in the 2006 election, bringing the total number to 24.

References

Battles, K., & Hilton-Morrow, W. (2002). Gay characters in conventional spaces: *Will & Grace* and the situation comedy genre.

Critical Studies in Media Communication, 19(1), 87–106.

Dyer, R. (1977). *Gays and film.* London: British Film Institute.

Halberstam, J. (1998). *Female masculinity.* Durham, NC: Duke University Press.

Hequembourg, A., & Arditi, J. (1999). Fractured resistances: The debate over assimilationism among gays and lesbians in the United States. *Sociological Quarterly, 40,* 663–680.

Owen, A. S., Vande Berg, L. R., & Stein, S. R. (2007). *Bad girls: Cultural politics and media representations of transgressive women.* New York: P. Lang.

Phelan, P. (1993). *Unmarked: The politics of performance.* London: Routledge.

Shugart, H. A. (2003). Reinventing privilege: The new (gay) man in contemporary popular media. *Critical Studies in Media Communication, 20*(1), 67–92.

Sloop, J. M. (2004). *Disciplining gender: Rhetorics of sex identity in contemporary U.S. culture.* Amherst: University of Massachusetts Press.

Squires, C. R., & Brouwer, D. C. (2002). In/discernible bodies: The politics of passing in dominant and marginal media. *Critical Studies in Media Communication, 19*(3), 283–311.

42

Sex Lives in *Second Life*

Robert Alan Brookey and Kristopher L. Cannon

S*econd Life* (SL) is a little hard to classify. It could be classified with other massive multiplayer online role-playing games (MMORPGs), because it shares several characteristics with these games. Multiple users from all over the world log onto SL and interact in a virtual environment. Users in SL also construct avatars, characters that function as in-game proxies, as do players in other MMORPGs. And like other MMORPGs, SL has an in-game economy that allows users to buy and sell various items and goods (Castronova, 2006). But when it comes to the actual "game" the comparison breaks down. First, there are no clearly defined role-play objectives in SL: no required missions, quests, or monsters to slay. Second, while the producers of many online commercial games discourage players from changing the elements of the game, users in SL are encouraged to manipulate the environment (Bartle, 2006). Although Linden Lab, the creative force behind SL, has established some rules and guidelines, users are able to build their own buildings, create their own clothing and accessories, and are usually at liberty to shape this virtual world in any way they see fit.

Consequently, SL has been used in a variety of ways, including educational and commercial applications, and as a means to interact with other people. Given the liberty available in SL, users have the opportunity to create new relationships, and create those relationships in new and different ways. Some SL users are taking advantage of this liberty to refigure gender and sexuality; when one of us first entered SL, we came upon a very large statue with prominent breasts and an erect penis; it was a shrine to "shemales," one that celebrated the sexual viability of transsexuals. Other SL users, however, reproduce traditional gender roles and sexual norms, and sometimes do so in disturbing ways.

We see SL as a valuable space in which to study gender and sexuality in cyberspace, because unlike traditional forms of print, film, or television media (hereafter, traditional media), SL users are primarily responsible for the content.[1] In other words, users have the agency to create the gender roles and the sexual experiences that they want. In many of the existing studies of gender and sexuality in cyberspace, this agency is theorized from a liberatory perspective that sees cyberspace as a unique social arena in which traditional gender roles and sexual norms are challenged and transgressed. Unfortunately, this theoretical perspective does not account for those who use their agency to reproduce the traditional roles and norms found in real life (RL).[2] . . .

Liberatory Perspective

The idea that cyberspace is a liberatory environment is certainly not new, and other scholars have challenged this idea (Gunkel, 2001). For our purposes, we are using the phrase "liberatory perspective" to refer to a critique of cyberspace that imagines it to be an arena in which subjects have greater agency to explore and refigure gender norms and sexual roles. When scholars first began studying relationships in cyberspace, there was a great deal of optimism about the potential for virtual environments to offer users opportunities to explore multiple identities. For example, Sherry Turkle (1995) looked at how users switched genders in online social environments, and how this gender switching allowed these users to assert new identities, and develop more empathy for the opposite gender. Allcurque're Rosanne Stone (1995) argued that online environments allowed for the exploration of fragmented identities, because subjects were able to operate independently of their bodies on which gender and sexual discipline has been exercised. She claims that successful gender switching online reveals both the instability of identity, and how new *media* "presaged radical changes in social conventions" (p. 81).[3]

. . . This liberatory perspective, however, teeters on the brink of technological determinism, and unfortunately cyberspace docs not always provide an escape. Lynne Roberts and Malcolm Parks (2001) have conducted one of the few social science studies about gender switching in cyberspace, and they found that the majority of people do not switch genders online.

In addition, they found that some women switched genders in order to escape sexual harassment online. In these cases, gender switching may allow these women to escape, but this escape is merely a reaction to the reproduction of problematic RL sexual relations in cyberspace. This is not to suggest that cyberspace has not facilitated the potential for liberatory use. Indeed, scholars who have analyzed interactive online media contend that cyberspace has opened up opportunities for political resistance and community building, particularly for individuals with queer identities (Alexander, 2002; Bryson, 2004). . . .

In contrast to this liberatory perspective, queer scholars of traditional media have approached the representation of gender and sexuality with a healthy skepticism. For almost two decades, queer media scholars have examined how gender and sexual norms are reproduced, and how representation can function to exclude or contain sexual minorities (Battles & Hilton-Murrow, 2002; Brookey & Westerfelhaus, 2001; Dow, 2001; Shugart, 2003; Sloop, 2004). These studies focused on traditional forms of media, in which the agency of representation is in the hands of media producers. New media scholars, however, are often quick to point out that users have the agency of production where interactive media is concerned, and they maintain that this shift in agency is a significant difference.

Interactivity and the Docile Body

In the studies of interactive media generally, a great deal has been written about the agency of the user. Some have associated this agency with ideological resistance, suggesting that interactivity allows users to escape and challenge the influences associated with traditional media industries (Bryce & Rutter, 2002; Frasca, 2003). Other scholars question this agency (Brookey & Booth, 2006; Marshall, 2002), but where gender and sexuality are concerned, there are other influences that need to be considered. It is often the implicit assumption of queer scholars that traditional forms of media will cater to established norms in order to attract the broadest audience. Yet, these scholars acknowledge that these norms operate in larger social, cultural and political contexts, what Judith Butler (1990) would describe as a "heterosexual matrix," a grid of gender rules and sexual laws that favor and enforce procreative heterosexuality. While interactivity might create different relationships between users and media producers, interactivity does not categorically remove users from the influence of this social matrix. For example, users in SL create their own characters (avatars), give them primary and secondary sex characteristics, dress them and determine their sexual practices. Indeed, when it comes to the construction of gender and sexuality in SL, the users exercise a great deal of control. These users, however, represent subjects whose identities have been formed by the way gender and sexuality are "disciplined" in society.

In *The History of Sexuality,* Vol. 1, Michel Foucault (1978) outlines a program of discipline that explains how sexuality became a part of identity. He argues that with the rise of bourgeois society [historically, in the 19th century], there was thought to be a move to repress and censor the discussion of sex and sexuality ("the repressive hypothesis"), when in actuality a great deal of discourse emerged at this time articulating sexual norms, and delineating sexual perversity. In this discourse, sexual practice became an indicator of the psychological health of the individual, because sexuality was thought to reside in the psyche of the individual. Consequently, the individual was invested with the responsibility of maintaining proper sexual practices, and seeking out help for perverse sexual behavior. In this way, the supposed social repression of sexuality resulted in a repression of sexuality within the psyche of the individual.

Once sexuality was invested in the person, individuals aligned their sexual practices with established norms, and actively assumed the responsibility for their own sexual health. In other words, the sexual subject became a "docile body."

Foucault (1975) argues that the docile body is not passive, but rather the active embodiment of disciplinary practices, becoming a self-disciplined body. The concept of docility also informs Judith Butler's (1990) theory of gender performativity. She argues that individuals must constantly "perform" established gender norms, in order to escape the social discipline that is exercised against queer sexuality. In the repetition of the performance, the performativity of gender is forgotten, and the embodiment of gender norms is thought to be an expression of internal identity; in this way the gendered subject becomes a docile body.

Theorizing from Foucault and Butler, a fundamental problem with the liberatory perspective emerges. Although the disciplining of gender and sexuality may be exercised on the body, this discipline produces a sexual subject who imagines itself independent of the body. Liberating this subject from the body via cyberspace does not necessarily mean that this subject escapes the influential disciplinary practices that produced its identity. For example, Miroslaw Filiciak (2003, p. 100) posits that the creation of identities in cyberspace is not so much an escape from the "self" as it is "a longed-for chance of expressing ourselves beyond physical limitations." We would add, however, that these expressions might not move beyond the gender roles and sexual norms that created the "self."

Because docility is the underlying concept of performativity, we have chosen to use it in our analysis. Docility helps explain why individuals empowered with the agency to produce their own sexual world might choose to perpetuate the established norms of gender and sexuality. We have chosen SL as an environment in which to apply this critical concept, because SL is an interactive virtual world in which users are primarily responsible for creating the sexual content. Our purpose is specific: to offer an alternative to the liberatory perspective on gender and sexuality in cyberspace. Therefore our claims will also be specific; we do not offer our observations in order to generalize about the SL environment. In fact, a general analysis of SL would be beyond the scope of this chapter, because the environment is too large, and the content created by its users is too diverse. Instead, we focus on two types of sexual content created by SL users.

First, we analyze how certain users render women as sexual objects, designed to be sexually attractive, sexually available and sexually subordinate to men. Second, we show how gay, lesbian, transgender and "Furry"[4] users are marginalized in SL content, and in some instances participate in their own marginalization. To do so, we critically analyze advertisements and spaces in SL that we have found through our own exploration of SL.[5] We also analyze *The Second Life Herald,* a blog founded by University of Toronto philosophy professor Peter Ludlow, which publishes articles written by SL users and allows other SL users to comment on the articles published. We include *The Second Life Herald* in our analysis because it comprises the opinions of actual SL users, and it gives us an additional metatext to which we can compare the content we have found in SL.[6]

Virtual Objectification

The avatar is often considered the embodiment of identity in cyberspace, and SL provides various means with which to design avatars. As Linden Lab suggests:

> Second Life is about personal expression and your avatar is the most personal expression of all. After all, an avatar is your persona in the virtual world ... Despite offering almost infinite possibilities, the tool to personalize your avatar is very simple to use and allows you to change anything you like, from the tip of your nose to the tint of your skin. Don't worry if it's not perfect at first, you can change your look at any time. (Linden Research, 2006)

Clearly, Linden Lab has decided to highlight the agency that users can find in SL, and they suggest that users seem to have unlimited options available to them in the construction of their online identities. Users construct their avatars through the appearance editor in SL, which allows them to adjust their avatars' appearance including the body shape, the skin, the hair, and the eyes. Although Linden Lab may claim that there are almost infinite possibilities for the manipulation of an avatar, the ability to create an avatar is initially limited in an important way. The avatar's gender is the first trait that a user must designate before editing other aspects of the avatar body; a user must check one of two boxes: male or female. Granted, a user may switch between these two genders with relative ease (and, as we will discuss later, hermaphrodism is possible), but the default options available to users are limited to two choices. As Ann Fausto-Sterling (2000) observed, this bifurcation of gender is supported by the tendency to dichotomize biological sex, a dichotomy not supported by the biological record that includes a multiplicity of examples that defy easy categorization. In SL, this dichotomy is reproduced, and these default options introduce the user into SL in the same way that a gendered subject is introduced into a RL heterosexual world divided up into women and men.

The user can also choose "shapes" or "skins," which can cover the avatar's body. A shape will reconstruct the form of the avatar body (e.g., adding a well sculpted build to the body), while a skin allows a user to replace an avatar's skin color and can contour a body shape (e.g., skin tones that are pigmented and can contour the musculature of a shape for more depth). A user can also replace default clothing with designed pieces (e.g., clothing or other costumes purchased in shops), and can add attachments, items that can be linked to a particular part of an avatar's body (e.g., jewelry). The user can personally create clothing, body parts and attachments by constructing these objects in the SL environment; however, many users choose to purchase these objects in SL stores. . . . All transactions within SL are conducted with an in-game currency called "Linden Dollars," and users can either earn these dollars by "working" in SL, or they can buy them outright with RL currency (Linden Research 2007). SL users can transfer U.S. currency into Lindens to purchase items in SL, and users who become merchants and sell content are able to transfer Lindens into U.S. currency.

Many of the stores in SL offer clothing, swimwear and lingerie which accentuate feminine sexual attractiveness. One store sells "Evening Starr Formals," gowns that accentuate the female form with tight bodices and plunging necklines. This store also offers more casual attire, including miniskirts and tight-fitting slacks. Another store, "Liberte Fashion," offers a similar selection of clothes that accentuate the female body. It also offers a selection of bridal gowns, for those who choose to reproduce the tradition of marriage in the SL environment. The critique of marriage as a power-laden institution is well established in feminist literature, and we will not revisit it here. We would note, however, that some work has gone into the design of these wedding gowns, and at $1,500 Lindens, SL users would have to work (either in SL or RL) in order to raise the money to purchase one. In other words, a good deal of user agency is invested in the reproduction of the marriage tradition, in both the design and purchase of the dress.

Some of the clothing available for female avatars is modeled by the "Post 6 Grrls" in

The Second Life Herald. The Post 6 Grrls are female avatars that are chosen to pose for "pictures" in which they are scantly dressed, posed provocatively, and often appear in the nude. The pictures are accompanied by short biographies, in which the Grrls discuss their likes and dislikes, as if they were the "Playmate of the Month." We should note that there are "Post 6" men, and robots as well, but the biographies of some of the Post 6 Grrls are as revealing as some of their pictures. For example, Kaylia Burgess (2007, ¶ 5), the Post 6 Grrl for March 9, 2007, lists the following interests: "I love fashion, makeovers, and just getting to know those I am close with (sic). And in SL, I can wear a bikini and lay on the beach all year round." Jabra Kostolany (2006, ¶ 4), the Post 6 Grrl for November 10, 2006, discusses what she would like to accomplish in SL: "One of the ideas is to make a woman's magazine like 'Cosmopolitan' for the Second Life woman. Woman (sic) need to know how to correct them and how to build and rebuild themselves (sic), where to buy, dresses, make-up and other accessories."[7] In addition to presenting their avatars as sexual objects, these Post 6 Grrls also seem to believe that women should be valued for their appearance, and indicate that their own agency is caught up in the purchase of clothes and accessories. . . .

This same value system is also apparent in the sexual and fetish ware stores in SL. Various bondage clothing, harnesses, and other types of sexual attachments are available for purchase, and the images and advertisements that appear in the stores often depict women as sexually submissive. For example, BDSM [bondage and discipline, sadism and masochism] toys and accoutrements include objects like a bullwhip, buggy whip, cattle prod, "Gorean" slave goad, spiked paddle, wooden paddle, cane, riding whip and hand crop. Any avatar can use these various toys, but female avatars are often depicted in the subordinate role in the advertisements. . . .

Actual sexual intercourse is available through various "pose balls" found in SL. Pose balls initiate directed animation, and are demarcated by colored balls that can be found in different areas of SL. When a user clicks on a pose ball, the avatar will move into the position and begin the animation that the pose ball directs. When pose balls are activated, the avatar will continue the movement, or sexual act, until the user directs the avatar to stop. Those pose balls that animate sexual positions are often color coded in ways that denote gender; for example, blue pose balls are usually for male participants, while red or pink balls are for female participants. Sexual pose ball colors also demarcate active and/or passive roles, and often the female role is the passive one. . . .

Several advertisements illustrate pose balls that include behaviors like "blow-jobs" or "handjobs," and in these positions the female avatars service the male avatars. The sexual subjugation of women in SL is, however, perhaps best illustrated by the presence of advertisements for pose balls that allow avatars to engage in "role-play rape." For example, a series of advertisements in the "M & P Shop" depicted two men who are engaged in the rape of a woman; one placed the woman on her hands and knees while she was orally and vaginally penetrated by two men, while another showed one man holding the woman by her shoulders while the other man held her legs in the air and penetrated her. On May 31, 2007, Linden Labs declared depictions of sexual violence, including rape, to be unacceptable, and the advertisements that once appeared in the M & P Shop were replaced with a posting that listed unacceptable content. Although they are not advertised, rape pose balls can still be found in other SL spaces, including the "Back Alley" area of "Bound & Determined Fetish Club;" "Miss Lucie's Land of Fun and Fantasy" offers pose balls labeled "ravished" and "ravisher."

While the users with female avatars voluntarily participate in these rape scenes, just because the practice is volitional does not absolve it from critique. The fact that a user is complicit in the rape scene is very problematic, if we are to assume that a female user controls the female avatar. Such a scenario has implications more disturbing than the banal aspects of rape fantasy; it suggests that rape is just sexual play, in which the female is expected to say "no" even though she means "yes." Even more disturbing, however, is the possibility that the female avatar who "volunteers" for a rape scene or "ravishment" could be controlled by a man. The possible empathy generated by crossing genders withers in the light of this possibility: a man can create a female avatar with the purpose of having her submit to sexual violation and humiliation. In any case, it is important to note that users created these pose balls, and used their agency to construct a violent sexual experience.

In addition, there are the real world benefits available to SL users who have created this sexual content. Digital avatars and the content in SL become the intellectual property of their creators, and users can actually make RL money from creating and selling content in SL. . . .

Virtually Queer

When it comes to queer sexuality, it is not that such expressions are absent from SL. On the contrary, the visibility and presence of queer sexuality can be found in social spaces, sexual spaces, and market places. The "place" search function can be used to find queer spaces, just like other spaces in SL, and using this search function with the keywords "gay" or "lesbian" results in dozens of spaces and "islands." . . .

Islands in SL are similar to their RL equivalent, in that they are isolated from other areas in SL; many of these queer spaces exist on islands disconnected from other areas, and some are even further isolated within areas on islands. One example of such a space is the "Bad Boys Club" (a club for gay men on "Munford Island"), which does not allow avatars to freely move between the club and other locations on the island. This club restricts avatars from either entering or leaving the club through the conventional means of movement (walking and flying); thus this club cannot be entered unintentionally. Instead, a user must "teleport" into the club. (Teleporting occurs when a user jumps to a new location by entering spatial coordinates.) Some places in SL cannot be entered in any other way, and therefore a user must know the coordinate address to enter these spaces. When queer spaces restrict entry in this manner, it is reminiscent of early times in the gay community, when clubs, in order to protect the anonymity of their patrons, would only post the street address by the door, but offer no other signage. As then, to enter some queer spaces in SL, a user must know the exact address.

It is likely that many of these queer spaces are isolated because they rarely restrict sexual content. Sexual content permeates these queer spaces, whether they cater to males or females, and these spaces typically have sex clubs, or places for sexual activities, and contain shops that sell sexual paraphernalia. Sex clubs differ in style depending on each space and whether the content is for male or female avatars. The way that these sexual spaces are constructed is not always the same, but common elements appear. Many of the gay male spaces have a sex club within the vicinity of the dance floor, and lesbian sex spaces are often constructed similarly to gay male spaces. Many of these spaces, however, are segregated by gender; there are gay spaces that are designated for "men only," such as "Bad Boys Club" or "Devil Inside," and there are lesbian spaces that are labeled "women only," such as "Ruby Bayou Ladies Club" and "Pink Passions." The explicit segregation of genders in SL is unique to queer spaces, and ensures that the sexual activity within these spaces does not include heterosexual

behaviors. In this way, however, queers construct and congregate in spaces that ensure their isolation, and thereby reproduce their own marginalization.

Not every queer area or space includes sexual paraphernalia and/or sex clubs. "The L Word Island" is a reconstruction of a neighborhood from the Showtime cable television series The L Word, and this island does not offer any sexual content. The various shops on this island offer clothing (for both men and women), as well as skins and hair. This island is one of the few queer islands that seem to place an emphasis on relationships over sexual intercourse; the presence of a speed-dating lounge points to this emphasis. It is possible that Showtime, the owner of the island, wanted to restrict sexually explicit content, but this would suggest that the motive behind the construction of this queer space is different from other queer spaces in SL. This space has been developed to promote a television show, so restriction of sexual content may only serve the commercial interests of Showtime.

Therefore, we need to recognize that some queer sexuality in SL may not be designed for the interests of the sexual minorities represented. For example, in some of the sex clubs and dungeons that cater to heterosexuals, it is common to find pose balls for female-on-female sexual animations. While there is a prevalence of female-female and female-female-male pose balls in these spaces, male-male pose balls are not present. The absence of gay male sexual opportunities in these spaces might indicate that these particular instances of lesbian sexuality are being offered up for the pleasure of male heterosexuals. (Lesbian sex scenes are prevalent in the pornography marketed to heterosexual men, and it would seem that these lesbian pose balls are placed to create sexual acts primarily for the desires of heterosexual men, and not lesbians.) This is not to suggest that all lesbian sex in SL is served up for male heterosexual pleasure, because there are "women only" spaces where men cannot observe lesbian acts. Even in these contexts, however, we cannot assume that all of the female avatars signify female users; some may be cross-dressed male users enjoying lesbian experiences.

As we have mentioned, when a user begins SL, they can choose an avatar of the opposite sex, and use all of the clothing and attachments available in SL to construct the avatar. Not everyone, however, welcomes these transgender avatars in SL; for example, some men who patronize escorts in SL want to make certain the women they solicit have been created, and are played, by women in RL. In fact, a voice verification system has been set up so that female escorts in SL can be certified "GVF" (Gender-Verified Female) (Elliott, 2006). Therefore, voice becomes the ultimate gender signifier, separating the "real" women from the transgendered, and once again anchoring gender in biological sex.

Unfortunately for those who use SL to explore transgender experiences, voice has become an important issue. Integrated voice technology was recently made available to SL users; and this technology allows people to talk to one another, rather than using the text chat function. Some SL users who cross-dress saw this new technology as a threat to their existence in SL. For example, in *The Second Life Herald*, Prokofy Neva (2007, ¶ 15) writes about the harassment that transgender users already experience, and notes "Being forced to use a voice in a virtual world, something not of my choice, against my will . . . feels like the ultimate blow. It won't be—but you do get tired of this crap after awhile." In another *Second Life Herald* article, Aurel Miles mentions the ways that "shemales" can be identified in SL. A commenter to this article writes, "All of you are fussing over something that's going to be moot shortly anwyays (sic). As soon as Voice Chat is rolled out you'll see the number of gender benders suddenly dissolve" (realityfish, 2007, ¶ 62). As the comment reveals, this SL user looks to this

technological change as a way of reasserting heterosexuality in SL. After all, the use of voice to identify the biological sex of users is a way to ensure that biological males will only interact sexually with biological females, and in this way, voice technology can be deployed to reduce the instances of queer sex.

The issue of voice in this controversy takes on a strange irony. Voice has often been equated with agency, and the act of speaking for oneself has been characterized as an act of visibility, and a sign of political viability (Morris, 2007). This is true of marginalized groups generally, and sexual minorities specifically; the slogan of AIDS activism, "Silence = Death", illustrates the point. The deployment of voice technology will allow the transgender users to be heard in SL, and will make them visible. Unfortunately, this visibility may be turned against transgender users, so the agency of voice becomes the material for marginalization. Therefore some of these transgender users do not want their voices to be heard, because they do not want to be recognized as transgender. In this way, silence becomes a means of survival in SL, and the political potential of queer voice and visibility is turned on its head. Still, while we are sympathetic to the plight of transgender users in SL, the decision to eschew voice chat accommodates a heteronormative demand that queers should be neither heard, nor seen. . . .

Same Old Game

At the beginning of this chapter, we discussed how it was difficult to classify SL as a game. Where the issues of gender and sexuality are considered, the question may be moot because the "play" in SL is quite serious. In *Bodies That Matter*, Butler (1993) explains that the performative nature of gender does not mean that the performance of gender does not matter. On the contrary, these performances constitute our identities, and locate us as sexual subjects in society. The gender and sexual play that we have observed in SL could also be regarded as part of a game, but we would argue that it is a game that matters. The users who perform these actions are identifying themselves as sexual subjects, and identifying others as sexual objects.

Given the agency to create their own sexual experiences, some users have chosen to create experiences that objectify women and marginalize queers. The possibility that heterosexual men would construct these experiences comes as no surprise; the possibility that both women and queers might assist in the construction is more surprising. Indeed, the enactment of self-subjugation and self-marginalization would seem to be the ultimate expression of docility. Women, who have chosen to construct identities in SL only to serve themselves up as objects of sexual desire, reassert an existing belief system that limits the value of women. Queers who have cloistered themselves on an isolated island, often segregated by gender, have complied with the heteronormative demand to keep their practices private.

Consequently, our analysis illustrates some problems with the liberatory perspective. To view cyberspace as liberatory rewrites RL as inherently repressive, and this is evident in some of the comments that we have discussed, where users refer to SL as a space where they are free to express themselves. Unfortunately, if cyberspace is liberatory, and SL specifically, then how do we challenge the politically retrograde content without inviting the charge of repression? After all, complaints about "political correctness" have been used to mock and undermine feminist and queer critiques of cultural representation in RL. Foucault argued that while it was possible to resist the sexual norms of society, it was not possible to move outside of the relations of power produced by the disciplining of sexuality. Consequently, he had his own suspicions about the liberatory promise of the sexual revolution of the sixties and seventies, and he warned: "(w)e must not

think that by saying yes to sex, one says no to power" (1978, p. 157). Arguing from Foucault, we suggest that cyberspace should not be regarded as an environment that moves the user outside of the political and social matrix of gender and sexuality. Cyberspace may allow us to rework those power relationships, but we cannot assume that liberation is obtained there, nor can we overlook the instances that clearly reproduce traditional gender roles and sexual norms, and willful sexual violence.

Applying Foucault's warning to SL, perhaps we should not think that by saying "yes" to cybersex, we are saying "no" to power. Indeed, we should not look to cyberspace as a universal panacea. Granted, technology can be quite attractive, and it would be nice to imagine that escape from oppression, and relief from violence is a mere keystroke away. The problems associated with gender and sexuality are RL social problems that predate the technology of SL, and therefore we should be mindful that the solutions to those problems might lie in RL as well. If our analysis reveals anything, it is that while SL may appear new and exciting, where gender and sexuality are concerned, too often it is the same old game.

Notes

1. We recognize that the term "traditional media" increasingly becomes a problematic term as various mediums begin to converge. Yet, we make this distinction to illustrate a difference between representations that are created within media by media producers versus representations that are created by users of an interactive medium.

2. Admittedly, the term "real life" is problematic, and we are aware of the debate about surrounding the distinctions draw between the real world and the virtual one. The players of SL, however, use this term, so we are merely reproducing a distinction that is made by these players—the distinction of a virtual "second life" in contradistinction to the "first life" lived by flesh bodies.

3. Stone's observations are influenced by the work of Donna Haraway (1991), who has conceptualized the cyborg as a modern border/ed body (between animal, man, machine, and physicality) that has the potential to deconstruct hegemonic power. She specifically noted a possibility to imagine a world without gender or genesis. We do not feel, and will argue, that this rather Utopian possibility has come to fruition within SL.

4. The queerest of the queer in SL may be the "Furries." Furries are avatars that are anthropomorphic animals; they often have the body shape of humans, but the heads and fur of animals. Linden Lab has even made a furry avatar an option available to new users.

5. Both authors of this project have spent a considerable amount of time exploring the virtual SL environment. One has been a member of SL since December 9, 2006; the other has been a member since May 26, 2006. Each author has investigated various SL islands to obtain pertinent information for this article. Collectively we have spent approximately 140 hours in-world as active participants in SL. We should note that because the content in SL is user created, it is in constant flux, and we cannot be certain that the same content will be available in SL at the time of publication. Still, the content that we critique was created by users, and our argument is about the agency of creation.

6. James Gillett (2007) has demonstrated this integration of analyses of visual texts and blogs.

7. We are well aware of the fact that some of these female avatars are constructed and controlled by male players. Indeed, this possibility raises other concerns that we address later in the article.

References

Alexander, J. (2002). Homo-pages and Queer sites: Studying the construction and representation of Queer identities on the World Wide Web. *International Journal of Sexuality and Gender Studies, 7,* 85–106.

Bartle, R. (2006). Virtual worldliness. In J. Balkin & B. Novek (Eds.), *The state of play: Law, games, and virtual worlds.* New York: New York University Press.

Battles, K., & Hilton-Murrow, W. (2002). Gay characters in conventional spaces; 'Will and Grace' and the situation comedy genre. *Critical Studies in Media Communication, 19,* 87–105.

Brookey, R., & Booth, P. (2006). Restricted Play: Synergy and the limits of interactivity in "The Lord of the Rings/Return of the King" video game. *Games and Culture, 1,* 214–230.

Brookey, R., & Westerfelhaus, R. (2001). Pistols and petticoats, piety and purity: *To Wong Foo,* the queering of the American monomyth, and the marginalizing discourse of deification. *Critical Studies in Media Communication, 18,* 141–156.

Bryce, J., & Rutter, J. (2002). Spectacle of the deathmatch: Character and narrative in first-person shooters. In G. King & T. Krzywinska (Eds.), *Screenplay: Cinema/videogame/interfaces* (pp. 66–80). London: Wallflower Press.

Bryson, M. (2004). When Jill jacks in: Queer women on the Net. *Feminist Media Studies, 4,* 239–254.

Burgess, K. (2007, March 9). Kaylia Burgess-Post 6 Grrrl. *The Second Life Herald.* Retrieved on March 14, 2008, from http://www.secondlifeherald.com/ slh/2007/03/kaylia_burgess_.html

Butler, J. (1990). *Gender trouble: Feminism and subversion of identity.* New York: Routledge.

Butler, J. (1993). *Bodies that matter: On the discursive limits of "sex."* New York: Routledge.

Castronova, E. (2006). *Synthetic worlds: The business and culture of online games.* Chicago: University of Chicago Press.

Dow, B. J. (2001). Ellen, television and the politics of gay and lesbian visibility. *Critical Studies in Media Communication, 18*(2), 123–140.

Elliott, S. (2006, April 7). Escort Mission. Joystiq. Retrieved September 28, 2007, from www.1up.com/do/feature?cld=3149323&did=4

Fausto-Sterling, A. (2000). *Sexing the body: Gender politics and the construction of sexuality.* New York: Basic Books.

Filiciak, M. (2003). Hyperidentities: Postmodern identity patterns in massively multiplayer online role-playing games. In M. Wolf & B. Perron (Eds.), *The videogame theory reader* (pp. 87–102). New York: Routledge.

Foucault, M. (1975). *Discipline and punish*. A. Sheridan, trans. New York: Vintage.

Foucault, M. (1978). *The history of sexuality, Vol. 1*. R. Hurley, trans. New York: Vintage.

Frasca, G. (2003). Simulation versus narrative: Introduction to Ludology. In M. Wolf & B. Perron (Eds.), *The video game theory reader* (pp. 221–235). London: Routledge.

Gillett, J. (2007). Web logs as cultural resistance: A study of the SARS arts project. *Journal of Communication Inquiry, 31*, 28–43.

Gunkel, D. (2001). *Hacking cyberspace*. Boulder, CO: Westview Press.

Haraway, D. (1991). A cyborg manifesto: Science, technology, and socialist-feminism in the late twentieth century. In *Simians, cyborgs, and women: The reinvention of nature* (pp. 149–181). New York: Routledge.

Kostolany, J. (2006, November 10). Jabra Kostolany-Post 6 Grrl. *The Second Life Herald*. Retrieved on March 14, 2008, from http://www.secondlifehearald.com/slh/2006/11/jabra_kostolany.html

Linden Research. (2007). Second Life currency exchange. *SecondLife.com*. Retrieved May 01, 2007, from http://secondlife.com/whatis/currency.php

Marshall, P. (2002). The new intertextual commodity. In D. Harries (Ed.), *The new media book* (pp. 69–81). London: British Film Institute.

Morris, C. (2007). Introduction. In C. Morris III (Ed.), *Queering public address: Sexualities in historical discourse*. Columbia: University of South Carolina Press.

Neva, P. (2007, Feb. 27). Vox Lindeni. *The Second Life Herald*. Retrieved March 15, 2008, from http://foo.secondlifeherald.com/slh/2007/02/vox_lindeni.html#more

realityfish. (2007, April 22). Sex in SL: Dude looks like a lady. *The Second Life Herald*. Retrieved on March 15, 2007, from http://www.secondlifeherald.com/slh/2007/04/sex_in_sl_dude.html

Roberts, L., & Parks, M. (2001). The social geography of gender-switching in virtual environments on the Internet. In E. Green & A. Adam (Eds.), *Virtual Gender: Technology, consumption and identity*. New York: Routledge.

Shugart, H. (2003). Reinventing privilege: The new (gay) man in contemporary popular media. *Critical Studies in Media Communication, 20*, 67–91.

Sloop, J. (2004). *Disciplining gender: Rhetoric of sex identity in contemporary US culture*. Amherst: University of Massachusetts Press.

Stone, A. (1995). *The war of desire and technology at the close of the mechanical age*. Cambridge, MA: MIT Press.

Turkle, S. (1995). *Life on the screen: Identity in the age of the Internet*. New York: Touchstone.

43

Queering *Queer Eye*

The Stability of Gay Identity Confronts the Liminality of Trans Embodiment

E. Tristan Booth

I n 2004, I attended a home and garden show with the sole purpose of hearing a speech by Carson Kressley—the so-called "Fashion Savant" of cable's *Queer Eye for the Straight Guy*.[1] Meeting him briefly during an autograph session, I suggested that the program consider featuring a transsexual man, since men who had been socialized to enact roles in accord with their female bodies seldom had been taught the finer points of tying ties, shaving, or purchasing suits. Kressley's light-hearted response—"I hear ya"—was affirming, but I thought it unlikely that a "queer eye for the trans guy" episode would ever be filmed.

I was pleasantly surprised, if slightly apprehensive, when I heard that one such episode— officially titled "Trans-form This Trans-man"—would premiere on August 1, 2006, and I felt sure that others must have been making the same suggestion if the producers were willing to embark upon this uncommon venture. My primary concern—on behalf of an identity label that I can also claim[2]—was that the information provided about transmen be accurate. In other words, I did not want to see transmen portrayed with typical misconceptions, for example, that they are masculine women who crossdress for amusement, that they are always attracted to women rather than to men, or that they are women who live as men in order to obtain social privilege.

I also hoped that the man chosen to represent this population would acquit himself well, and in this I was not disappointed. Miles Goff, a 24-year-old college graduate, was bright and personable. He introduced the serious challenges faced by transmen without coming across as cynical or defensive. I was also relieved to find that the show's team of gay men— the so-called Fab Five—were presenting well-researched information about transmen. . . .

It struck me then that *Queer Eye*, for the first time, had taken a decidedly political turn. In fact, even the Fab Five themselves were slightly altered; though the format of the episode reflected business as usual, there were subtle deviations in the Fab Five's behavior. Granted,

From E. Tristan Booth (2011), "Queering *Queer Eye*: The Stability of Gay Identity Confronts the Liminality of Trans Embodiment," *Western Journal of Communication*, Vol. 75, No. 2, March-April 2011, 185–204. Reprinted by permission of the publisher (Taylor & Francis Ltd, http://www.tandf .co.uk/journals).

Miles Goff was not the typical makeover subject for this series, and it stands to reason that his presence would position this episode as distinct within the *Queer Eye* canon. The more cynical viewer might even see the episode as a ratings ploy—an attempt to attract viewers who had grown tired of the *Queer Eye* routine. I contend, however, that this episode represented more than simple variation. It shook the very foundation of a series premised on binary, essentialist conceptions of sex, gender, and sexuality. Despite its name, *Queer Eye* had never been particularly queer in the theoretical sense . . .

The Liminal Nature of Transsexualism

Victor Turner's (1969) famous definition of liminality—"betwixt and between the positions assigned and arrayed by law, custom, convention, and ceremonial"—is focused on cultural rites of passage that typically transport the individual from one traditional social position to another. For example, in some cultures a young male, whose accepted social identity is that of a boy, is temporarily separated from this identity in order to undergo some type of cultural ritual. During this process, he can claim no distinct social identity. Then, upon exiting this liminal state, he attains the accepted social position of a man (pp. 94–95).
. . . Prior to the Goff episode, the Fab Five had been accustomed to confronting one particular form of liminality: the period of time required to makeover a subject's appearance, behavior, and home environment. In other words, the majority of each episode was a liminal period, bookended by an introductory discussion about the makeover subject while en route to his home, and a casual denouement during which the Fab Five communed over drinks, observed their subject on a monitor, and critiqued his ability to enact the lessons they had taught. Within this liminal time frame, the subject was betwixt and between

his former disheveled self and his future debonair self. Typically, however, the *Queer Eye* subject did not inhabit a liminal social identity; in the vast majority of episodes, he was a natal (cisgender) male who identified as heterosexual.[3] The conventional liminality of *Queer Eye,* then, concerned the sartorial transformation of a man whose sex, gender, and sexuality remained stable within the conventional binaries. What the Fab Five were not accustomed to confronting was liminal embodiment and its corresponding social ambiguity. Arguably, Goff's gender identity could be described as stable on the assumption that he identified as a man even prior to beginning transition. However, his attraction to "girls and boys," as noted by his roommate Austin, could be read as a liminal (and, some would still argue, unstable) position between the conventional norms of gay and straight. Likewise, the lack of normative consonance between Goff's birth sex and gender identity, in addition to the fact that he had not received sex reassignment surgery, positioned him between hegemonic definitions for man=male and woman=female. This betweenness, I argue, renders his social identity perpetually liminal for those who are aware of his history. . . .
. . . As a man who is both transsexual and bisexual, Goff wreaks havoc with the stable notions of queer and man as the Fab Five know them. He appears to frame his gender as stable and his body as a fluid work in progress with no trace of uncertainty. For their part, the Fab Five make an effort to affirm the stability of his gender, even as they struggle to confront the queerness of his body. They are clearly attempting to accommodate his liminal status even as it destabilizes the premises on which the series is constructed.
Terrill (2006) suggests that liminality can lead to greater insight if one is willing to enter into the liminal space and accept the process without attempting to control it (pp. 166–167). . . . If the willingness to enter liminal space is, indeed, a gateway to greater insight, the perpetual liminality of the transsexual may represent an ongoing

opportunity for insight into the complexities of sex, gender, and sexuality, not only for transsexuals themselves, but also for those who interact with them. . . .

The Miles Goff Episode

Queer Eye had always provided lifestyle advice that could be utilized by its television audience. While the Fab Five's recommendations are dispensed to particular makeover subjects, viewers can also benefit from their tips on cooking, home decoration, and personal grooming. Until the introduction of Miles Goff, however, there was no overt attempt to advance a political agenda. The focus of each episode was on the welfare of the "straight guy," after all, and not on those issues specific to the gay community or any other marginalized group. Consequently, the audience had not been encouraged to consider the personal lives of the Fab Five; though these men were known to be gay, they told no tales of family rejection, discrimination, or vulnerable bodies. Their presence sought only to entertain and advise.

Goff's liminal status brought these types of issues into sharp relief, however. Unlike *Queer Eye*'s typical "straight guy," Goff was neither "straight" nor a conventionally natal male "guy." As such, he lacked the social privilege enjoyed by the vast majority of makeover subjects,[4] and this fact could not help but impact the performance of the Fab Five, as well as the production decisions impacting the contents of this particular episode. As a result, its singularity within the series positions it as a significant cultural text offering multiple disruptions: to the routine behavior of the Fab Five; to the nature of the series itself; to the social norms concerning sex, gender, and sexuality; and to the conventional lack of media representation of transmen. . . .

SPEAKING FOR THE AUDIENCE

The first obvious way in which this episode differs from the rest of the series is in the amount of careful explication. From the opening moments of the episode, the Fab Five clearly recognize that there will be many in the viewing audience who require basic information in order to understand Goff's identity. . . .

Ted [provides] a basic definition: "He was born a woman but he identifies more as a man." When Thom then asks, "He's not really a man?" Carson provides more information to further clarify Goff's identity. He explains that Goff was raised female but always felt male, that he had lived as a lesbian, and that he had decided to transition and live as a man during college. Ted then emphasizes that Goff has been taking testosterone injections that have lowered the tone of his voice. They go on to explain that Goff is a recent college graduate who has just moved to New York, that his roommate is another transman named Austin, and that he has not had any sex reassignment surgeries. . . .

Further audience confusion is preempted by a conversation between Carson and Goff's roommate Austin. Since Carson had noted earlier that Goff had previously lived as a lesbian, the audience might be inclined to assume that all transmen had done so. After establishing that Austin is attracted to women, Carson asks him, "And what about Miles?" Austin's response that Goff "likes girls and boys" differentiates the orientation of one transman from that of another, allowing Carson to educate the audience as he performs the role of educating himself: "So the whole thing about your gender identity is that it doesn't necessarily mean that it's gonna correspond to your sexual identity." The choice to interview two transmen is crucial here. An interview with only one transman might have led the audience to conclude, synecdochically, that his orientation is the standard orientation for all transmen. The comparison helps Carson to make the point that there is no necessary correspondence between gender identity and sexual orientation. In other words, a transman might identify as heterosexual, bisexual, or gay. This dispels a myth about transsexuals—that they are gay or lesbian individuals who transition in order to achieve heterosexual status—while also foregrounding the inherently liminal category of bisexuality. . . .

DEVIATIONS
IN FAB FIVE BEHAVIOR

On the customary *Queer Eye* episode, we see the Fab Five in the company of the "straight guy" with little interference from friends or relatives. Wives, children, and/or girlfriends are typically sent away from the subject's home during its renovation, and they do not often accompany him on his shopping excursions with members of the Fab Five. As Morrish and O'Mara (2004) point out, "This is a show about male bonding" where women "remain in the rear view mirror" until the subject's personal and environmental transformation is complete (p. 351). What is perhaps significant for the Goff episode is the fact that neither his previous experience living in the role of a woman, nor the sexed nature of his body structure, can be temporarily banished from the premises, as could a wife or girlfriend. These lingering remnants—ghosts of femaleness, if you will—contribute to the perpetual liminality of the transman's social identity and cannot help but impact the interaction between Goff and the Fab Five. . . .

[One] way in which nonstandard interaction is expressed verbally concerns the manner in which Goff's sexuality is addressed, or even avoided altogether. Since the typical episode involves a "straight guy" as its subject, there is generally no question as to the subject's orientation. During the opening sequence, en route to the subject's home, the Fab Five typically mention his wife or girlfriend, or the fact that he is single and therefore in need of transformation in order to attract a female partner. During the opening sequence of the Goff episode, however, Goff's orientation and relationship status are not mentioned. Later, when the subject of Goff's orientation is addressed,

the discussion takes place between Carson and Austin. Consequently, Goff is not provided with a direct opportunity to define his own sexual identity. If it is the case that Goff had addressed this subject on camera, one can only conclude that the program's editors chose not to include it.

Goff's sexuality is directly addressed in his bedroom after the apartment has been renovated. Previously, Goff had slept on an air mattress, and he was pleased to find that Thom had installed a bed. As Goff, Thom, and Ted are talking, Thom is reclining on the bed while Goff and Ted are standing to one side. Ted jokingly expresses the hope that "someday soon you'll have someone besides Thom in your bed." With fingers crossed, Goff replies, "Here's hoping." From the perspective of the nontransgender audience, the very suggestion that Goff would one day have sex with *anyone* could be read as transgressive, since it brings to mind questions regarding who that partner would be, what types of bodies would be involved, and how the activity would commence. This context makes the liminal body particularly salient for these viewers.

In a final example of nonstandard verbal interaction, the Fab Five do not engage in mock flirtation with Goff as they typically do with other makeover subjects. In addition to Carson's more outrageous demonstrations, the other four gay men frequently comment on the heterosexual man's appearance both before and after his shopping and grooming expeditions. However, in the Goff episode, there are no overt sexual jokes or innuendo. Goff's attractiveness is, of course, affirmed, since positive remarks from the team are crucial to meeting the program's objectives. However, in Goff's case, all such comments are respectful rather than salacious. Kyan, for instance, refers to Goff as "handsome."

In terms of physical interaction, the makeover subject in *Queer Eye* understands that the Fab Five are likely to suspend the customary rules of social etiquette during the course of this makeover. Westerfelhaus and Lacroix (2006) argue that the Fab Five possess a "liminal license" to "tame, tease, and touch" (p. 432) their subject for the purpose of "expressing and relieving social tensions" (p. 430). Ordinarily, for example, it would be considered rude for a gay man to request that a nongay man remove his shirt. On *Queer Eye,* however, such liberties are permitted because this type of request is understood as an attempt to relieve sexual tension by indirectly reassuring heterosexual men that the Fab Five "do not really pose actual threats to their sexuality" (Hart, 2004, p. 248). In the Goff episode, much of the physical contact initiated by the Fab Five is no different than that which takes place in other *Queer Eye* episodes, that is, placing a hand on his shoulder or offering a hug hello or goodbye. It is also typical for Carson to adjust the subject's clothing or for Kyan to touch the subject's face and hair as he provides a lesson in grooming. The one noticeable difference is the absence of sexually suggestive touch and bodily positions. In episodes featuring "straight guys," Carson has been known to pull up a subject's shirt without warning, enter his fitting room in a store, or suggestively position his own body next to the subject's. In the Goff episode, however, the physical touch is more respectful. For example, although Kyan examines Goff's haircut and beard, and while there are also numerous hugs taking place throughout the episode, there is nothing remotely sexual in the physical interactions between Goff and the Fab Five. Whereas Carson might lift the shirt of a "straight guy," he verbally suggests to Goff, "Let's take the shirt off," immediately followed by words of concern from Kyan: "Can we do that? Are you uncomfortable?"

It becomes clear from this example that the Fab Five are much more cautious in their treatment of Goff than they are with nontranssexual men. Should this caution be read as a form of respect for Goff? If so, what is it about Goff that prompts

greater respect than that given to nontrans men? One possible answer is the fact that Goff lacks the social privilege of most makeover subjects. In other words, the scenario can no longer be read as a marginalized group (gay men) teasing a member of a privileged group (straight men); instead, the Goff episode displays interactions among marginalized groups (gay men and transsexual men). On the other hand, one might also question whether or not the Fab Five are perceiving Goff as a man, since there is no way to erase their knowledge that Goff had been born into a female-appearing body. Some nontranssexuals are unable to reconcile a transman's birth body with his present identity, and they will always see him as a woman to some degree, whatever his outward appearance. In Goff's case, this problem may be exacerbated by his youth and small physical stature.

The ways in which these interactions differ from those on typical *Queer Eye* episodes demonstrate that Goff occupies a social position unlike that of the other men featured on the series. While the behavior of the Fab Five—both more polite and less suggestive—can be open to various interpretations, these deviations are likely related to Goff's liminal status as a man who is not fully "male." Since the series had always assumed a correspondence between manhood and maleness, it is possible that the Fab Five do not accept Goff's identity without some discomfort.

POLITICAL TONE

Berila and Choudhuri (2005) have suggested that the *Queer Eye* series reduces gayness to "elements of fashion and grooming, while other elements of queer culture, such as social issues, relationships, or queer resistance, remain absent" (¶ 31). Since the focus of each episode remains on the life of the makeover subject—not on the lives of the Fab Five—there seems to be little need for the political, given that the "straight guy" is almost always White, middle-class, and heterosexual. Consequently, there is virtually no reference to the daily problems faced by gay men or others within marginalized identity categories. As Clarkson (2005) states, "The relative absence of homophobia in the show assures viewers that the struggle for civil rights" is "merely symbolic" and does not "reflect a fear of material consequences" (p. 246). In fact, the series basically depicts gay as a position of privilege, since the viewer is rarely confronted with poverty, racism, discrimination, or violence. It is clear, therefore, that a self-defense lesson in the Goff episode had been included because this particular makeover subject was perceived to be at risk. The fact that other members of the Fab Five also participate in this lesson is a singular reminder that the gay body is also susceptible to attack. Self-defense is not mentioned in conventional episodes because heterosexual men are not perceived to be at risk of anything more than the loss of a relationship. In this respect, the Goff episode represents a distinct departure for the series, since the Fab Five, at long last, glance back at themselves and hint at their own vulnerability. . . .

[One] direct reference to a political issue is found in a conversation between Carson and Ted regarding Goff's explanation of gender identity disorder as a diagnosis required for physical transition. Carson remarks, "I don't like that 'disorder' word," with Ted adding, "That's not fair, to call that a disorder." These comments offer queer resistance against an established institution—in this case, the American Psychiatric Association, publisher of the *Diagnostic and Statistical Manual of Mental Disorders* (DSM)—that has stigmatized the transsexual segment of the population with a diagnosis of mental disorder, even though the hormonal and surgical aspects of treatment are outside the parameters of psychological therapy. This particular act of resistance, however, is almost always performed by transsexuals themselves. It is

therefore significant to find gay men defending a transman in this way, despite the fact that gay men, themselves, had been similarly pathologized prior to 1973.

. . . The most visible indication of political tone in the episode is the presence of Rachel Goldberg, a representative from GenderPAC. When Goff reunites with family and friends at a party to celebrate his transition, Goldberg praises Goff and offers him an internship at the GenderPAC office. While the typical *Queer Eye* episode never even mentions political advocacy, this episode presents Goff's future as inextricably linked to political activity, thus suggesting that any transgender identity is, by its very nature, political. Unlike previous episodes in which the Fab Five had assisted makeover subjects with their careers—an art gallery show for an artist, an audition for an actor—the Goff episode explicitly frames Goff's physical transition as a political act. Indeed, this offer of an internship at a trans-gender organization presumes Goff's willingness to present himself as an "out" transman, even as the Fab Five labor to assist him with an unambiguous male presentation.

The presence of a transman serves to politicize the series because the liminal nature of his social status has political implications. Men are assumed to occupy a privileged position, yet a transman's body faces a greater risk of attack than that of a heterosexual male; appropriate clothing may be absent from both men's and women's commercial lines; he is diagnosed with a mental disorder, while exhibiting no signs of mental instability; and his existence is perceived to be inherently political, even if he wishes to live a private life as an "ordinary" man.

Critical Reflection

. . . The Goff episode provides a cultural text that disrupts not only the essentialist, binary premises upon which the series was constructed, but also the cultural assumptions held by many of its viewers. As a consequence, the series is afforded the opportunity to educate at least a segment of the U.S. public about the lived experience of transmen. Though this limited representation (Goff and his roommate) obviously excludes the representation of those who identify as gender-variant or genderqueer, this is neither surprising nor inappropriate, since the purpose of the program is to provide makeovers for men. As a consequence, however, this adherence to the gender binary fails to trouble its hegemonic nature, thus maintaining the cultural expectation that all adults will identify as either men or women. Goff's orientation does queer the gay–straight binary, however, and the fact that he has had no sex reassignment surgery makes clear that one need not possess a normative male body to identify as a man.

Despite Austin's statement that Goff "likes girls and boys," Goff comes across as somewhat desexualized in this episode. For a heterosexual audience, his lack of a partner as well as his bisexuality serve to envision any future intimacy as vague and ambiguous. Given his age and small stature, some viewers could perceive Goff as young, innocent, naïve, or even confused, since both transsexualism and bisexuality are often read as evidence of confusion. Thus, a liminal status is applied, not only to his manhood, but also to his adulthood.

. . . I have suggested that the perpetual liminality of the transsexual's social identity allows for continuing insight into the complexities of sex, gender, and sexuality. However, visibility has conflicted value for the individual transsexual. In the case of transmen, society will never understand this population if it never sees them or hears their narratives. On the other hand, the transman's visibility as a transman can undermine his desire to be perceived as a man. For some, this dilemma can be reduced to a choice between the welfare of the trans community and the comfort of the individual. Fortunately for Goff, he is

not apparently inclined to live his life in stealth. (Arguably, he would not have agreed to appear on the program were that the case.) However, the nonpolitical history of the series suggests that while political activity is not required of the heterosexual or gay natal male, it is unavoidable for, and even expected of, the transsexual man.

Interestingly, while this episode was more political than any other, significant political ramifications were also neglected. Goff does not enjoy an affluent lifestyle, yet the audience is not made aware of the costs associated with counseling, medical appointments, surgery, or legal name changes, nor is there any mention of the fact that insurance rarely covers transition-related claims. Instead, there are only subtle hints of financial challenges, such as sleeping on an air mattress or having difficulty finding suitable clothing. In effect, one is given the impression that transition is no big deal: You require injections, and it's probably a good idea to know some self-defense moves, but the road is basically a smooth one. In this way, the episode frames both gay and transsexual lives as relatively unproblematic. However, this framing exists in tension with the political implications underlying self-defense lessons and diagnoses of mental disorder. All marginalized bodies, including those of the Fab Five, face a certain amount of risk and, ultimately, it took the liminality of a transman's body, as well as the corresponding liminality of his gendered social status, to bring an embodied, vulnerable queerness to *Queer Eye*.

As a cultural text, this episode of *Queer Eye* demonstrates how the introduction of liminality into a hegemonic context is likely to disrupt conventional process and behavior. An individual whose physical body and social identity are not in accord with hegemonic categories may not personally experience confusion or discomfort, yet this individual's mere presence may prompt these feelings in others. The resulting need for explanation or reassurance suggests that liminality can be used as an educational tool, but not without some risk. Transsexuals occupy a liminal position fundamentally at odds with hegemonic paradigms of sex, gender, and sexuality, and reactions ranging from fearfulness to rage have often led to discrimination and violence. The ultimate solution suggested by queer theory would be a paradigm shift away from these rigid, hegemonic structures. Arguably, however, a collective willingness to relinquish stable identity claims is far in the future, if not utopian. In the meantime, transsexuals and others who live "betwixt and between" are left to negotiate perpetual liminality in a world of ill-fitting hegemonic constructs. Through the gradual chipping away at these boundaries, they prompt others to question the unquestionable, serving an educational purpose by their very presence.

Notes

1. The original Bravo cable series was first broadcast on July 15, 2003 (Becker, 2006, p. 220), and aired its final episodes in 2007.

2. In my daily life, I identify as a gay man. In pertinent contexts, such as this essay, I also reference my experience as a transsexual man. While I do not hide my transsexual status, I am not inclined to name it as an aspect of personal identity in the same way that I name my gay orientation. I refer to the transsexual label as one that I "can" claim because I choose to make this claim contextually.

3. There was one *Queer Eye* episode in which the makeover subject was a gay man, but only the Goff episode involved the makeover of a transman. The term cisgender is a recent neologism used to designate one whose gender identity and expression reflect the normative social expectations for the designated sex of the body at birth. A cisgender man is one whose body was designated male at birth—in other words, the majority of men in U.S. culture. The Latin prefix cis translates to "on the same side" (Schilt & Westbrook, 2009, p. 461). Therefore, cisgender suggests that one's gender identity is on the same side of the

binary as one's physical sex. I prefer to use the term natal male for those whose bodies were designated male at birth.

4. On the subject of privilege, it should be noted that Goff could be read as White, given his physical appearance. As this characteristic remains unmarked, the predominant Whiteness of the Fab Five remains unmarked as well. Therefore, if the audience is led to conceptualize both gay men and transmen as White, they will also be led to think of non-White racial identities as heterosexual. In this way, each marginalized category comes to be viewed as independent, thus erasing intersectionality. Space considerations did not allow for extended comment in these areas. However, other scholars have addressed the Whiteness of the Fab Five and the majority of their makeover subjects (see Berila & Choudhuri, 2005; Heller, 2004; Muñoz, 2005; Sender, 2006). For further analysis on intersectionality, see Bérubé (2001).

References

Astraea Lesbian Foundation for Justice. (n.d.). Staff. Retrieved from http://www.astraea foundation.org/about/people/staff/#goff

Becker, R. (2006). *Gay TV and straight America*. New Brunswick, NJ: Rutgers University Press.

Berila, B., & Choudhuri, D. D. (2005). Metrosexuality the middle class way: Exploring race, class, and gender in *Queer Eye for the Straight Guy. Genders Journal, 42*. Retrieved June 14, 2008, from http://www.genders.org/g42/g42_berila_choud-huri.html

Bérubé, A. (2001). How gay stays White and what kind of what White it stays. In B. Rasmussen, E. Klineberg, I. Nexica & M. Wray (Eds.), *The making and unmaking of whiteness* (pp. 234–265). Durham, NC: Duke University Press.

Clarkson, J. (2005). Contesting masculinity's makeover: *Queer Eye,* consumer masculinity, and "straight-acting" gays. *Journal of Communication Inquiry, 29,* 235–255.

Hart, K.-P. R. (2004). We're here, we're queer—and we're better than you: The representational superiority of gay men to heterosexuals on *Queer Eye for the Straight Guy*. *The Journal of Men's Studies, 12,* 241–253.

Heller, D. (2004). Taking the nation "from drab to fab": *Queer Eye for the Straight Guy*. *Feminist Media Studies, 4,* 347–350.

Jones, K. T., Zagacki, K. S., & Lewis, T. V. (2007). Communication, liminality, and hope: The September 11th missing person posters. *Communication Studies, 58*(1), 105–121.

Morrish, L., & O'Mara, K. (2004). Queer Eye for the Straight Guy: *Confirming and confounding masculinity. Feminist Media Studies, 4,* 350–352.

Mun͂oz, J. E. (2005). Queer minstrels for the straight eye: Race as surplus in gay TV. *GLQ, 11,* 101–102.

Prosser, J. (1998). *Second skins: The body narratives of transsexuality.* New York: Columbia University Press.

Schilt, K., & Westbrook, L. (2009). Doing gender, doing heteronormativity: "Gender normals," transgender people, and the social maintenance of heterosexuality. *Gender & Society, 23*(4), 440–464.

Seidman, S. (1993). Identity and politics in a "postmodern" gay culture: Some historical and conceptual notes. In M. Warner (Ed.), *Fear of a queer planet: Queer politics and social theory* (pp. 105–142). Minneapolis, MN: University of Minnesota Press.

Sender, K. (2006). Queens for a day: *Queer Eye for the Straight Guy* and the neoliberal project. *Critical Studies in Media Communication, 23,* 131–151.

Slagle, R. A. (1995). In defense of Queer Nation: From identity politics to a politics of difference. *Western Journal of Communication, 59,* 85–102.

Terrill, R. E. (2006). Going deep. *Southern Communication Journal, 71*(2), 165–173.

Trans-form this trans-man [Television series episode]. (2006). In D. Macletchie (Producer), *Queer Eye for the Straight Guy.* Los Angeles: Scout Productions.

Turner, V. (1969). *The ritual process: Structure and anti-structure.* Ithaca, NY: Cornell University Press.

Westerfelhaus, R., & Lacroix, C. (2006). Seeing "straight" through *Queer Eye*: Exposing the strategic rhetoric of heteronormativity in a mediated ritual of gay rebellion. *Critical Studies in Media Communication, 23,* 426–444.

PART VI

GROWING UP WITH CONTEMPORARY MEDIA

The potential effects of mass media culture on children and young people have always generated much anxiety and controversy and even, on occasion, **media activism**. Educators have argued that young children are a particularly vulnerable population, given their limited experience of the world and the likelihood that their sense of the boundaries between media **representations** and the real world is less well established than (ideally) that of adults. According to Dafna Lemish (VI.44),

> Most pronounced are concerns over the effects of television violence on children, as well as the potential harm of exposure to sexual portrayals, the effects of advertising on consumer culture, and the more general concern over children's passivity and social disengagement. (p. 423)

In the age of globalizing media, concerns around children's television are now being studied on an international level. Lemish explores the current state of the research and argues,

> In summary, empirical evidence suggests that children's television around the world consists primarily of fictional animation programs not produced domestically but purchased from abroad, mainly from the United States and Canada. These programs feature mostly light-skinned characters, with an overwhelming presence of males. Therefore, the White male hegemony seems to be numerically

dominant in children's television around the world, just as it is in other aspects of popular culture. (p. 426)

Picking up on the issue of **hegemony**, Gail Dines (VI.45) argues that popular culture provides today's adolescent girls a narrow and reductive version of femininity—one centering on the **hypersexuality** that is a product of the mainstreaming of pornographic imagery and **representation**. Reminding us that "in today's image-based culture, there is no escaping the image and no respite from its power" (p. 433), she describes in particular the environment produced by celebrity hypersexual "looks." She offers a strong critique of the impact of this immersion in a "closed system of messages" on preteens and teenaged girls, who are in the critical years for developing sexual and **gender** identity. While she acknowledges that "some girls and young women conform and others resist," she points out that "alternative ideologies such as **feminism** that critique dominant conceptions of femininity are either caricatured or ignored in mainstream media," leaving those who are inclined to resist with far fewer cultural resources than their mothers had.

In another chapter on girl consumer culture, Karen Goldman (VI.46) looks back at the evolution of the Mattel Corporation's Barbie doll, which continues to reflect and construct racialized gender ideology and to attract critical analysis from media scholars and activists. The original Barbie **encoded** an idealized White American teenage girl, whose ethnic neutrality was useful for a marketing strategy that stressed a mythical "Americanness." However, over the 40 years since her first release on the toy market, in part because of a changed marketing strategy—one that targets "ethnic" U.S. consumers and a global market—Mattel has sold "more than one billion dolls" in 150 countries, making Barbie what Goldman calls "one of the world's most ubiquitous plastic objects" (p. 441). In her essay, Goldman traces the evolution of "official" Mattel representations of Latina femininity, such as Hispanic Barbie and various "Dolls of the World" Barbies. According to Goldman,

> Behind Mattel's portrayal of Latino/a identity lies a system of representation that sells itself as authentic but that ultimately either depicts Latino/a culture as homogeneous and exotic, or repackages the doll's Latinidad in an assimilated form, whether to make her more attractive to more assimilated Latinos or to market her more effectively in places where ethnic diversity is not particularly marketable. (p. 444)

No discussion of commercialized pop culture aimed at young people would be complete without a look at the impact of the Disney company on our archive of media representations that are formative in childhood. As Lee Artz (VI.47) writes, "Disney leads the world in the production and distribution of popular culture" (p. 449). In an attempt to understand why Disney animation has achieved such global dominance, Artz looks at the **political economy** of Disney, exploring it both as industry and producer of ideology. Through **textual analysis** of the **ideology** encoded in animated feature films of the past decade, Artz argues that "Disney consistently and programmatically produces 'commodities-as-animated-feature films' that promote an ideology preferred by Disney and global capitalism—an ideology at odds with democracy and creative, participatory social life" (p. 449).

So far, our chapters in this section have featured primarily text analysis, but we now turn to an audience response study that focuses on how a particular group of adolescent South Asian American girls are making sense of the popular culture in their lives. In Meenakshi Gigi Durham's words, her study (VI.48)

> explored South Asian immigrant girls' experiences of coming of age among contemporary mediascapes, through a series

of interviews that brought to the surface the dynamic intersections of body politics, culture-crossing, and myths of homeland. These issues emerged in a constant interplay with the narratives of gender and sexuality in contemporary consumer-oriented teen media. (p. 455)

Durham looked closely at how these girls consume but also critically resist some of the central messages about sexuality and romance encoded in both American TV shows and Bollywood films, using these to help them negotiate identity issues as "diaspora" adolescents—neither fully at home in the United States nor fully adopting their parents' Indian culture. In their questioning of both types of "monocultural" texts, Durham views the girls as creating "the potential for new sexual identities that have emancipatory possibilities for them as girls in-between" (p. 462).

How young audiences make meaning from media texts is also the focus of Kathleen P. Farrell's article, "HIV on TV: Conversations With Young Gay Men" (VI.49). She was specifically interested in how gay college-age men read the popular cable TV drama *Queer as Folk,* "the first television drama in the USA to deal explicitly with queer culture" by representing an almost entirely LGBTQ (lesbian, gay, bisexual, **transgender**, and queer) community in which characters lead "gay-affirming lives that center on their close friendships with one another" (p. 466). Farrell points out that in *Queer as Folk,* in contrast to other dramatic treatments of HIV/AIDS in television programs of the past, contracting HIV is not automatically presented as a death sentence. Rather, living with HIV is just one problem that characters may face, among many others, including "gay bashing, workplace discrimination, and coming out to family members" (p. 470).

Farrell's research observed how focus groups discussed a storyline in which a central character began to date someone who was HIV positive. Given that many of the focus group participants were not directly familiar with real people living with HIV, many were surprised and initially unsettled by "new ideas" suggested by the matter-of-fact presentation of HIV as a chronic disease. In Farrell's analysis, group discussions of the show also clearly provided focus group participants with an opportunity to increase their knowledge about HIV transmission. The focus group participants saw the show itself as a valuable educational tool, promoting safe-sex practices in an entertaining way, without coming across as too preachy, conservative, or critical of casual sex or gay lifestyles.

In this section considering the experience of youth growing up in daily contact with media culture, we must include substantial attention to electronic and online games, which take up such a large proportion of the leisure time of children, young people, and even older people today. As John Sanbonmatsu (VI.50) points out, "In the United States alone, an estimated 170 million people—more than half the population—play video games" (p. 473). In his provocative essay, he calls our attention to the potential dangers of the alluring, highly realistic simulations that draw so many players into these virtual worlds.

Sanbonmatsu argues that many of the most popular video games reproduce sexist and racist depictions, while also legitimizing a **consumerist** militaristic society that undermines the well-being of individuals, cultures, and the ecosystem. Placing video game playing within the socioeconomic context of our contemporary life, he questions why video games are so popular, not only with men and boys but increasingly with women and girls. For Sanbonmatsu, the answer lies in our society's many alienating problems—the increasing financial problems that working people face, a delegitimization of the state, and the destruction of the environment—all issues that people feel are out of their control. He suggests that, confronted with these problems, "we ourselves seem to hunger for escapist forms of entertainment that restore to us, albeit only in virtual form, precisely that which many of us feel we are losing in real life" (p. 474).

While it might be hard to argue for the socially or intellectually redemptive value of a commercially successful "entertainment" game such as *Grand Theft Auto,* there is increasing interest among game designers and teachers in reclaiming this compelling interactive digital technology for educational purposes. As Kevin Schut (VI.51) writes, the multifaceted, complicated, yet intuitive interaction with virtual worlds that computers make possible can potentially provide a whole new way for people to experience or learn about history. However, as Schut goes on to warn in his article, "Strategic Simulations and Our Past," we should regard even "historical simulations . . . with something of a critical eye" (p. 485). Looking at several examples of historically themed game simulation series, Schut argues that "a kind of masculine slant is exceptionally clear in game presentation of history" (p. 486). For example, he points out, while professional historians have long since broadened the scope of history to include the lives and voices of marginalized or less powerful people, most historical digital games "ignore these trends and almost exclusively focus on politics, economics, and war" (p. 486).

A conventional **masculinist** gender bias is not only displayed in the texts of most interactive digital games, as seen already, but also appears in the actual playing of games by fans. Elena Bertozzi (VI.52), who teaches digital game design, looks at observed gender differences in digital play, finding that despite increased female participation,

> researchers have documented the ways in which gender politics are reconstructed in digital worlds. . . . Given that digital play offers a considerable amount of gender plasticity through avatars, it might seem illogical for gender stereotypes and concerns to persist in digital gaming, but they do. (p. 492)

Bertozzi hypothesizes that such differences "are strongly influenced by the unwillingness of both genders to cross traditional, culturally gendered play lines" (p. 492). She is especially interested in female **resistance** to competing fiercely with men in games, because of the real-world implications of continuing to associate competitive success with masculinity. On the positive side, she reminds us, many women are now using game/play activities as a way of practicing competing "at the same level as males" (p. 492). As she writes, "If we recognize the significance and level of difficulty of challenging existing norms, we can better support their initiatives and create structures to help others join them" (p. 492).

44

The Future of Childhood in the Global Television Market

Dafna Lemish

Television and Children: A Global Issue[1]

The nature of relations between children and television is a global issue for a variety of compelling reasons. First, children of both genders and all ages, races, religions, classes, and geographic regions of the world watch television on a regular basis, enjoy it tremendously, and may well learn more about the world from it than from any other socializing agent. Few other social phenomena can be claimed with such confidence as an experience shared by most children in today's world. Whether they view TV in their bedrooms, download it on their computers or mobile phones, share the family set in the living room, or watch it in the classroom or the community center, TV is part of the taken-for-granted, everyday experiences of most children. No other cultural phenomenon has achieved such a magnitude of penetration or global status.

The global status of television can be claimed because similar debates over television's role in the lives of children have emerged globally. On one hand, high hopes and great expectations have been expressed worldwide that television would enrich children's lives, stimulate their imagination and creativity, broaden their education and knowledge, encourage multicultural tolerance, narrow social gaps, and stimulate development and democratization processes. On the other hand, there has been and continues to be great anxiety about the ability of television to numb the senses, develop indifference to the pain of others, encourage destructive behaviors, lead to a deterioration of moral values, suppress local cultures, and contribute to social estrangement.

These oppositional stances in regard to the medium of television—as a "messiah" on one hand and a "demon" on the other—have been discussed widely in public debates in every society that has absorbed the medium. Most pronounced are concerns over the effects on children of television violence, as well as the potential harm of exposure to sexual portrayals, the effects of advertising on consumer culture, and the more general concern over children's passivity and social disengagement. Media debates, public

---

This piece is an original essay that was commissioned for this volume. It has been updated from an earlier version that appeared in the 3rd edition.

forums, parent and community newsletters, legislative body hearings, educational leaders, broadcasting policymakers—all have contributed to these popular debates framed as "moral panics," exerting public pressure on governing institutions.

The relations of television and children have interested scholars worldwide, mainly in the fields of psychology, media studies, sociology, education, and health professions (see, e.g., Lemish, 2007; Pecora, Murray, & Wartella, 2007). With the advent of new media, these studies have also stimulated a more complex discussion of television as part of a process of convergence of media and multiple screens (e.g., computers, mobile phones, handheld games; Calvert & Wilson, 2008; Lemish, 2013). Their varied disciplinary homes have made a great deal of difference to the kind of theoretical underpinnings brought to their research, the questions posed, the methods applied, and, accordingly, the kinds of findings reported and their interpretation. Furthermore, in this respect, the academic field concerned with the reciprocal relationships between children and television reflects in large degree the changes that have taken place in the various disciplines nourishing this scholarly field, in general, and the study of mass media, in particular.

Psychology, the most prominent of the disciplines applied to this area, has focused on the individual child and a host of related issues, such as social learning from television, the effects of television on behavior, development of comprehension of television content, and the uses children make of television and the gratifications they acquire from their viewing behaviors. As the body of literature grew, mainly from Western academic institutions, it became clear that the "strong effects" conclusion that assumes a unidirectional television effect on children is oversimplistic. Other research demonstrated something that common sense and anecdotal data posited for a long time: Children are not passive entities, a la the proverbial "tabula rasa," upon which television messages leave their marks. On the contrary, children are active consumers of television. They react to, think, feel, and create meanings. They bring to television encounters a host of predispositions, abilities, desires, and experiences. They watch television in diverse personal, social, and cultural circumstances that also influence and are part of their discourse and interactions with television. Thus, it has become clear that asking, "What do children do with television?" is just as important a question as, "How does television influence them?"

This paradigm shift led to highlighting the need for cross-cultural research. Clearly, comparative research of this global phenomenon can illuminate many of the questions on the research agenda: Does televised violence affect children differently if they are living in a violent urban center in comparison with a tranquil, isolated village? Are children more frightened by news coverage of war when they are growing up amid armed conflict, in comparison with children for whom war is a fictitious concept? Do children react differently to actors and actresses of European descent who appear in their favorite soap operas and situation comedies if they are living in a dominantly Euro-American society, in comparison with African, Latino, or Asian societies? And what about consumerism—would children raised in rich consumer cultures amid an abundance of products from which to choose interpret advertising differently than those with no financial resources or limited personal property? Pursuing such questions related to children and television has become a global endeavor for researchers to study, as no single body of knowledge based on contextualized studies in one culture, be it as rich and diverse as possible, can provide us with the in-depth, multifaceted picture necessary to understand this phenomenon in its full global manifestation.

The topic of children and television is of global interest for an additional, crucial reason. Today, children are part of a global audience that transcends local or even regional physical and cultural boundaries in consumption of television programs. As a global phenomenon, television promotes mainly what has been termed "late-modernity" values, typified primarily by commercialism, globalization, privatization, and individualization. This is "achieved" as a result of the fact that children all over the world watch, for example, American-produced cartoons, situation comedies, soap operas, action-adventure serials, and Disney and Hollywood movies. However, they also watch programs that come from other parts of the world, such as Latin-American telenovelas, localized versions of Japanese animations, or the local coproductions of the American *Sesame Street* and the United Kingdom's *Teletubbies.* Worldwide, children complete their homework or chores to the sounds of popular music on MTV and fantasize about love and adventure while watching blockbuster movies broadcast at a later time on their local channels or downloaded to their computers. They cheer for their favorite sports team across continents and seas, follow the news of armed conflicts worlds apart, and admire many of the same celebrities—collecting their memorabilia, hanging their posters, wearing their T-shirts, and following their private lives in the magazines and websites.

Therefore, the study of media and children can no longer remain bound within national borders, as media, children, and young people's well-being are international as well as transnational phenomena involving important issues such as the political economy of media corporations; implications of the centrality of new, border-free technologies; massive migration movements; and rapidly changing understandings and theorizing of multiculturalism, cultural hybridity, and diasporic identities. The monies invested in children and child-targeted entertainment media advance a global market of enormous proportions and varying value. For huge entertainment corporations, children are not future citizens; rather, they are first and foremost consumers (Linn, 2004).

Childhood is not a distinct period in the life cycle from the commercial point of view, one that should be attended to with compassion and responsibility. Rather, on the contrary, it is a distinct market opportunity requiring strong socialization to the consumer-centered lifestyle. Thus, any attempts to advance or lobby for change in the contents of television programs and movies directed at children, to legislate Internet safety, or to develop less violent and more creative computer games for children can no longer be redressed in national isolation. Indeed, cross-cultural studies have demonstrated their potential to reveal the deep ethnocentrism and cultural biases inherent in so many of these texts, understand the complex intertwining of culture and media, and at the same time highlight those aspects of children's lives—their needs, aspirations, pleasures, and anxieties—that seem to be shared universally.

Content Characteristics of Children's Television Circulating Globally

Given this broad overview, we can discuss one of the pressing questions at the center of studies of children's television: What kind of television programs are traveling around the world? A recent analysis of children's television programs in 24 countries (Götz & Lemish, 2012) presented compelling evidence of the global flow of children's programs. The analysis of 9,000 individual programs (out of about 20,000 recorded in the sample that aired during 2,400 hours of explicit children's television) found that only 23% of the programs were produced or coproduced domestically around the world, while 77% of all fictional programs were "imported." The United States and the United Kingdom, with 83% and 67% shares of the market, respectively, were the countries with the highest percentages of local production, followed by China (53%) and Canada (45%). At the other end of the spectrum, only 1% of the programs broadcast in Hong Kong, Kenya, and New Zealand were produced domestically. The biggest export region of children's television programs was North America, where 60% of the world children's television production originated, followed by Europe with 28% and Asia with 9%.

Among the sample of programs studied, 69% were fictional shows, 17% were nonfiction, and 7% were mixed genres. Animated programs composed the main share of the fictional programs (84%). There was a much smaller share of children's programs that featured real human beings (9%), mixed formats (5%), or puppet shows (2%).

Another central finding was that there were more than twice as many male characters (68%) than female characters (32%) in children's programs. The percentage of females was much lower in programs without human characters, where creators have the most freedom to construct images (25% as animals, 21% as monsters, 16% as robots, and 13% as other fictional beings). Differences between the various countries were not significant, highlighting that this is a universally biased characteristic. In addition, on the average, 72% of all main characters were coded as Caucasian, including in countries where the dominant skin color is Black (e.g., 69% of characters in children's programming in Kenya and 81% in South Africa were White).

In summary, empirical evidence suggests that children's television around the world consists primarily of fictional animation programs not produced domestically but purchased from abroad, mainly from the United States and Canada. These programs feature mostly light-skinned characters, with an overwhelming presence of males. Therefore, the White male hegemony seems to be numerically dominant in children's television around the world, just as it is in other aspects of popular culture.

Implications for Future Childhoods Around the Globe[2]

Analysis of the characteristics of the global children's television market can be grounded in the more general discourse of critical approaches to media globalization and its influences on local cultures, indigenous traditions, heritages, and values. Globalization, in this sense, rarely means universal but, rather, refers to the spread of Western-mediated products and images around the globe.

The claim that we live in a world increasingly characterized by Americanization has been put forth repeatedly in intellectual and political thought (e.g., Bloch & Lemish, 2003; Held & McGrew, 2003; Ritzer, 1993). Most notably, in the children's television domain, there are three main American corporations (following recent purchasing and realignments) controlling the market in the United States as well as the rest of the world—the Disney Channel, Nickelodeon, and Cartoon Network ("Ratings Watch," 2009). The competition between television networks for their share of the children's market drives them to differentiate themselves from one another and to create brand identity and loyalty (White & Hall Preston, 2005), characterized, among other markers, by a specific gender and age appeal. Their global success suggests that they have succeeded in maximizing their appeal worldwide. Given these structures of market forces, what, then, are the possible implications of the dominance of North American television programs in constructing childhoods around the world? Let us consider some of the most central influences that emerged in a grounded theory of mediated childhood, via analysis of 135 interviews with producers of children's television from 65 countries around the world (discussed in detail in Lemish, 2010).

LOSS OF THE LOCAL

While this is not a new argument in the discourse of cultural imperialism (Morley,

2006), American programming for children has been strongly criticized around the world on many levels: for being stereotypical of gender and race, for being irrelevant to indigenous cultures, for being too limited in scope of content and issues for children as they mature, for unnecessarily accelerating adulthood, and for encouraging wasteful consumerism. In this study, the longing for more visibility of one's own culture is a strong theme. Exported American television for children has been blamed for its role in perpetuating inappropriate values, including flooding the children's television market with stereotypical representations of an imagined, idealized portrayal of the American way of life, with associated culturally dominant representations of gender and race roles. A partial list of the critique of values identified in the forms of American television broadcast to children around the world includes heavy consumerism, preoccupation with sex and romance, lack of respect for adults and local cultural traditions, individualism and estrangement from the collective, dominance of the English language and slang, dominance of popular culture, and celebrity adoration. Critiques also cite what is absent in these programs, including the lives, values, and concerns of lower-class children, as well as children growing up in poor-resource societies, in conflict and crisis situations, in nontraditional family arrangements, or on the streets. The lack of buying power of such populations means that they are insignificant to the industry, according to the rules by which this system operates. Accordingly, their needs, aspirations, pleasures, fantasies, and realities are not catered to or reflected on the screens to which children and youth are exposed.

Major social issues shared throughout the world that are of central concern for young people are nonexistent in the lives of the middle-class children portrayed on screens around the world—for example, schooling, life as HIV/AIDS orphans, domestic and sexual violence, safety, health, and economic survival. Rarely represented, too, are the historical values and tales, music, customs and mores, sights and sounds, foods, habits, languages, and ways of lives different from those of the "imaginary center" of the Western world (Appadurai, 1990). As a result, most young viewers see neither themselves nor their lives reflected or presented in authentic ways. Rather, among the results of the heavy dominance of the *imagined* Western world is exposure and informal socialization to a social world where they, and those like them, are marginal, unimportant, even nonexistent. Here, according to the cultivation hypothesis advanced in media studies (Signorielle & Morgan, 1990), we can argue that accumulated exposure to a particular worldview fosters an internalization of that world as an accurate and normative perspective on life. Accordingly, many scholars and media educators argue that media literacy programs should enable participants to challenge images that entrench a perspective on oneself as an "other."

THE DOMINANCE OF THE WESTERN BEAUTY MYTH

In a related argument, children's television is a partner with other industries in perpetuating an unattainable beauty model, particularly for girls. This model exemplifies the intertwining of Western gendered and racialized ideologies, and has been called "the beauty myth" by Naomi Wolf (1991): a homogenization of the desired female "look" as mostly young, thin, attractive, heterosexual, wealthy, and predominantly White. Evidence from the global study presented above (Götz & Lemish, 2012), as well as additional studies (e.g., Bramlett-Solomon & Roeder, 2008; Lemish, forthcoming; Northup & Liebler, 2010), demonstrates the priority given to selected images of Whiteness on television viewed by children, all of which convey the message that Western beauty is superior to any other racial form. Scholars claim that such media representations are disempowering for children worldwide, with impacts on self-identity, national pride, and behavior (including the purchase of products in the pursuit of the unattainable look and plastic surgery that imitates Caucasian features). Concern for young people's desire to forsake their identities and even abandon their distinct racial physical characteristics was among the sources of producer grievance around the world (Lemish, 2010).

Thus, the beauty myth has been perceived to be a well-disciplined effort to control girls, as well as a racialized form of inequity and discrimination. Indeed, Hall (1997) claimed this to be an example of "internal colonization" that occurs when adoption of a dominant representation "succeeds" so that people see and experience themselves as an Other. Black, Filipina, or Latina girls, for example, learn to see themselves through the White masculine perspective that represents and speaks for them. In doing so, they internalize an oppressive point of view of themselves and participate in a "process of whitening that attempts to modernize these identities while bleaching ethnicities" (Nayak & Kehily, 2007, p. 24). Others have referred to this as a form of discrimination based on skin color that is a process of internalized "colorism" (Banks, 2000). Thus, even skin tone may determine different "shades" of racism and create status hierarchies and inequalities within the colored community itself (Celious & Oyserman, 2001).

The struggle to attain the "Western look" also imposes an economic strain on children and their families, as it encourages heavy consumption of leisure goods that in turn fuels production of a variety of products, including clothing, fashion accessories, costly surgeries, and multiple exemplars of Western popular culture. A related concern is that the popular beauty ideals distributed by television for children promote negative self-images and glorification of thinness, as well as encouraging destructive eating disorders (Harrison & Hefner, 2006). On the other hand, the unhealthy eating habits promoted by the American "fast-food" industry paired with a passive physical life encouraged by heavy consumption of television have been found to be correlated with growing obesity among young people in Western societies (Vandewater & Cummings, 2008) and are raising anxiety over possible similar influences worldwide.

GENDER SEGREGATION

The dynamics of the television industry in the United States and the insatiable economic needs that drive them contribute in numerous ways to television's gender segregation worldwide. For example, they continue to promote a worldview through which boys and girls are encouraged to inhabit different electronic and cultural spaces. They do so through the contents offered, as well as by serving as a model for younger, resource-poor television industries. The Disney Channel, for example, with its big global hits (e.g., *High School Musical, Hannah Montana*), is clearly perceived as "girls oriented," while the Cartoon Network has been traditionally associated with action-adventure cartoons and an audience of boys. Originally, Nickelodeon was involved in extensive gender experimentation and was a somewhat gender-neutral channel. While its programming decisions have shifted, the channel retains a more balanced approach in its programming than any of the other major networks. Yet it is still perceived by industry professionals to be skewed toward girls (Lemish, 2010). This general division among the networks is strongly reinforced by the industry's working axiom: Although girls will watch boys' shows, boys will not watch girls' shows. Scholars have found that this central belief is shared throughout the industry (Alexander & Owers, 2007; Banet-Weiser, 2004; Lemish, 2010; Seiter & Mayer, 2004).

These trends are gradually shifting due to economic pressures and growing gender equity awareness of both audiences and programmers. Networks are now making an effort to address the issue of gender segregation of channels, employing strategies such as selecting lead characters from both genders, diversifying program genres and narrative styles, and modifying packaging and names. However, it is interesting to note that this increase in network efforts to expand the audience to include both boys and girls is clearly understood as primarily a marketing strategy. Take, for example, Disney's efforts to attract 6- to 14-year-old male viewers to the new Disney XD cable channel and website (Barnes, 2009). This plan does not seem to be aimed at diminishing gender segregation or erasing stereotypes; rather, on the contrary, it is geared toward offering a clearly defined "boys' world"—an X Disney—in addition to the existing girls' one.

Television professionals' construction of their young audiences as largely inhabiting two very different gendered cultural worlds draws heavily on developmental theories as well as market and academic research findings. Studies suggest that the tendency for children to segregate themselves by gender and to play more compatibly with same-sex partners is already evident in early childhood and progressively gains strength by mid-childhood. The causes and consequences of this segregation are a major topic of investigation in child psychology and education (Maccoby, 1998; Mehta & Strough, 2009). Suffice to say, for our purposes, that gender-segregated childhoods provide different contexts for children's social development. This does not necessarily prepare them for mutual understanding and collaboration. This segregation runs parallel to the current popularity of the "Mars and Venus" metaphor (Gray, 1991), according to which men and women are perceived to be essentially different beings with opposing communication styles and emotional needs. This perspective has recruited to its service key elements of the postfeminist sensibility, best represented by the slogan "different but equal" (Shifman & Lemish, 2011). Television and toy industries

seem to be capitalizing quite successfully on this popular trend, pushing it to its extremes in their pursuit of ever-expanding markets and profits worldwide.

Earlier research on the gendered nature of media consumption by children and youth found that while, overall, girls do develop an interest in traditional masculine genres, on the whole, boys continue to show no interest in female genres (Lemish, Liebes, & Seidmann, 2001). The largely descriptive evidence gathered does provide empirical support for the popular axiom applied by children's entertainment industry and media professionals cited above, but we need to provide critical analyses of the data that can unpack and identify the mechanisms creating this phenomenon. For example, according to the feminist analysis of social change, this process could be explained, at least in part, through the observation that, more generally, girls as well as women learn to gradually incorporate typical male perspectives and values into their lives while not abandoning their traditional female responsibilities and interests. This echoes other situations in which socially subordinated groups learn to adjust "up," in an effort to improve status and opportunities. Perhaps the trend of girls' interests in boys' genres (and boys' refusal after a certain age to participate in girls' genres) represents all children's growing sensitivity to the advantageous position that boys hold in societies around the world and the higher value associated with their tastes and interests.

Serving the Needs of Children: Proactive Conclusions[3]

Television programs for children that travel around the world are big business. Generating profit is the main imperative for the corporation executives who manage these programs; therefore, it is up to consumers and citizens to insist that other concerns must also shape the future of children's television globally. I submit that critical analyses of the content offerings of this major socializer raise serious questions about the industry's ethical conduct and social responsibility.

As delineated in the United Nations Convention on the Rights of the Child (1989), the rights of children include a variety of communication rights: the right to be heard and to be taken seriously, to free speech and to information, to maintain privacy, to develop cultural identity, and to be proud of one's heritage and beliefs. Yet, whether girls and boys live in deprived and resource-poor societies or in overwhelmingly commercialized and profit-driven ones, their voices are for the most part neither heard nor taken seriously. They have limited opportunities to express their needs and opinions or to access much-needed information for their healthy development. Many mass communication efforts do not respect children's privacy and dignity or foster their self-esteem and confidence. Even in the cases in which, seemingly, they are allowed to "voice" their concerns, the opportunity is often only "token" in nature, reflects adults' perspectives, and does not necessarily contribute to their holistic development or problem-solving skills (Kolucki & Lemish, 2011).

Despite cultural differences, children around the world face similar issues of personal safety, as well as anxiety over the future of the globe and their place in it. Television has a responsibility to help all children become courageous adults and active citizens of this world. It could be argued that children's television should contribute to an effort to provide children with a "safe space" that also offers advancing programs that enable them to understand what it is like to live in a society of inclusion. A diverse screen provides more realistic, humane portrayals of current societies around the world and is also central to the well-being of the children growing within those societies. It celebrates girls and boys as children who all face the same challenges and share aspirations, morality, dreams, and hopes; children who need love and friendships, have adventures and overcome difficulties; children who are curious and eager to explore their surroundings and who struggle with their multiple identities; children who try to carve out their place in the world. According to this progressive vision, children's television needs to present young persons who are self-willed, who are positive, and who share their problems and accomplishments. Breaking stereotypes and opening up the screen to blurring gender and racial differences, and offering children real choices that cut across divides can foster a safer and healthier environment for growth and development. Young viewers can be exposed to a range of possibilities relevant to their own lives that also challenge the ways they are brought up to think about their identities.

While these suggestions may seem naive given the competitive nature of the now well-established global television market, and given the critiques of how television can promote the domination of Western modernity's values in other parts of the world, it is crucial to remember that we can build on and expand many of the efforts being made worldwide by dedicated professionals who see television as a social resource that needs to be taken seriously and used responsibly. Indeed, there are professionals working, too, within the commercial world to introduce change from within the system. Others operate in organizations driven by social goals that are not solely profit motivated, as well as not-for-profit alternative and citizen media, which, collectively, offer a spectrum from the conservative to the radical, along with subversive contents (Downing, 2001). These efforts can be framed as part of media reform and democratization movements that seek not only to rebut but also to offer alternatives to the hegemonic control of media corporations (McChesney & Nichols, 2002).

Indeed, many such efforts are integrated within public broadcasting systems funded by the state, particularly in Europe. Many of these efforts in the realm of television for children are dedicated to contextualizing their productions within local cultures and children's needs (Lemish, 2010). Some of the best efforts of such work are presented in international events that bring together professionals involved in creating quality television for children around the globe, such as the Prix Jeunesse in Munich and the Japan Prize in Tokyo, among others (see Cole, 2007). Therefore, the debate over the future of public broadcasting, free journalism, and democracy (e.g., McChesney & Nichols, 2010) also has serious implications for broadcasting to children—a unique population devoid of political and economic power or opportunities to lobby, protest, or bargain for their rights.

Through incorporating concerns for children's well-being and healthy development, television can be enriching and inspiring. It can offer a diverse range of possibilities for complex characters not bound by stereotypes, and it can give voice to their multiple perspectives and experiences. It can constitute a safe environment in which to explore the full range of roles children might wish for themselves, a vision for a different reality, and aspirations for a better world.

Notes

1. This section is reprinted with some changes, with permission, from my earlier work, Lemish (2007, pp. 1–4).

2. This section draws, with permission, on my earlier work, published in Lemish (2010, Chaps. 3 and 4).

3. This section draws, with permission, on my earlier work, published in Lemish (2010, Chaps. 7 and 8).

References

Alexander, A., & Owers, J. (2007). The economics of children's television. In J. A. Bryant (Ed.), *The children's television community* (pp. 57–74). Mahwah, NJ: Lawrence Erlbaum.

Appadurai, A. (1990). Disjuncture and difference in the global economy. *Theory, Culture and Society, 7,* 295–310.

Banet-Weiser, S. (2004). Girls rule! Gender, feminism, and Nickelodeon. *Critical Studies in Media Communication, 21*(2), 119–139.

Banks, T. L. (2000). Colorism: A darker shade of pale. *UCLA Law Review, 47*(6), 1705–1746.

Barnes, B. (2009, April 14). Disney expert uses science to draw boy viewers. *New York Times.*

Bloch, L. R., & Lemish, D. (2003). The megaphone effect: International culture via the US of A. *Communication Yearbook, 27,* 159–190.

Bramlett-Solomon, S., & Roeder, Y. (2008). Looking at race in children's television: Analysis of Nickelodeon commercials. *Journal of Children and Media, 2,* 56–66.

Calvert, S. L., & Wilson, B. J. (Eds.). (2008). *The handbook of children, media, and development.* Chichester, UK: Blackwell.

Celious, A., & Oyserman, D. (2001). Race from the inside: An emerging heterogeneous race model. *Journal of Social Issues, 57*(1), 149–165.

Cole, C. F. (2007). A guide to international events in children's media. *Journal of Children and Media, 1*(1), 93–100.

Downing, J. (2001). *Radical media: Rebellious communication and social movements.* Thousand Oaks, CA: Sage.

Götz, M., & Lemish, D. (Eds.). (2012). *Sexy girls, heroes and funny losers: Gender representations in children's TV around the world.* New York: Peter Lang.

Gray, J. (1991). *Men are from Mars, women are from Venus: A practical guide for improving communication and getting what you want in your relationships.* New York: HarperCollins.

Hall, S. (1997). *Representation: Cultural representations and signifying practices.* Milton Keynes, UK: Open University Press.

Harrison, K., & Hefner, V. (2006). Media exposure, current and future body ideals, and disordered eating among preadolescent girls: A longitudinal panel study. *Journal of Youth and Adolescence, 35,* 153–163.

Held, D., & McGrew, A. (Eds.). (2003). *The global transformations reader: An introduction to the globalization debate* (2nd ed.). Cambridge, UK: Polity.

Kolucki, B., & Lemish, D. (2011). *Communication for children and youth: Good practices that nurture, inspire, excite, educate, and heal.* New York: UNICEF.

Lemish, D. (2007). *Children and television: A global perspective.* Oxford, UK: Blackwell.

Lemish, D. (2010). *Screening gender in children's TV: The views of producers around the world.* New York: Routledge.

Lemish, D. (Ed.). (2013). *The Routledge international handbook of children, adolescents, and media.* New York: Routledge.

Lemish, D. (forthcoming). Boys are . . . Girls are . . . : How children's media and merchandizing construct gender. In C. Carter, L. Steiner, & L. McLaughlin (Eds.), *Routledge companion to media and gender.*

Lemish, D., Liebes, T., & Seidmann, V. (2001). Gendered media meaning and use. In S. Livingstone & M. Bovill (Eds.), *Children and their changing media environment* (pp. 263–282). Hillsdale, NJ: Lawrence Erlbaum.

Linn, S. (2004). *Consuming kids: The hostile takeover of childhood.* New York: New Press.

Maccoby, E. E. (1998). *The two sexes: Growing up apart—coming together.* Cambridge, MA: Belknap Press of Harvard University Press.

McChesney, R., & Nichols, J. (2002). *Our media, not theirs: The democratic struggle against corporate media.* New York: Seven Stories Press.

McChesney, R., & Nichols, J. (2010). *The death and life of American journalism: The media revolution that will begin the world again.* Philadelphia: First Nation Books.

Mehta, C. M., & Strough, J. (2009). Sex segregation in friendships and normative contexts across the life span. *Developmental Review, 29,* 201–220.

Morley, D. (2006). Globalisation and cultural imperialism reconsidered: Old questions in new guises. In J. Curran & D. Morley (Eds.), *Media and cultural theory* (pp. 30–43). New York: Routledge.

Nayak, A., & Kehily, M. J. (2007). *Gender, youth and culture: Young masculinities and femininities.* Hampshire, UK: Palgrave.

Northup, T., & Liebler, C. (2010). The good, the bad, and the beautiful: Beauty ideals on the Disney and Nickelodeon channels. *Journal of Children and Media, 4*(3), 265–282.

Pecora, N., Murray, J. P., & Wartella, E. A. (Eds.). (2007). *Children and television: Fifty years of research.* Mahwah, NJ: Lawrence Erlbaum.

Ratings watch: Disney Channel, Nickelodeon. (2009, December 23). *Kidscreen.* Retrieved from http://www.kidscreen.com/articles/news/20091223/ratingswatch.html

Ritzer, G. (1993). *The McDonaldization of society.* New York: Pine Forge Press.

Seiter, E., & Mayer, V. (2004). Diversifying representation in children's TV: Nickelodeon's model. In H. Hendershot (Ed.), *Nickelodeon nation: The history, politics, and economics of America's only TV channel for kids* (pp. 120–133). New York: New York University Press.

Shifman, L., & Lemish, D. (2011). "Mars and Venus" in virtual space: Post-feminist humor and the Internet. *Critical Studies in Media Communication, 28*(3), 253–273.

Signorielle, N., & Morgan, M. (Eds.). (1990). *Cultivation analysis: New directions in media effects research.* Newbury Park, CA: Sage.

Vandewater, E. A., & Cummings, H. M. (2008). Media use and childhood obesity. In S. L. Calvert & B. J. Wilson (Eds.), *The handbook of children, media, and development* (pp. 355–380). Oxford, UK: Blackwell.

White, C. L., & Hall Preston, E. (2005). The spaces of children's programming. *Critical Studies in Media Communication, 22*(3), 239–255.

Wolf, N. (1991). *The beauty myth: How images of beauty are used against women.* New York: Doubleday.

45

Growing Up Female in a Celebrity-Based Pop Culture

Gail Dines

In today's image-based culture, there is no escaping the image and no respite from its power when it is relentless in its visibility. If you think that I am exaggerating, then flip through a magazine at the supermarket checkout, channel surf, take a drive to look at billboards, or watch TV ads. Many of these images are of celebrities—women who have fast become the role models of today. With their wealth, designer clothes, expensive homes, and flashy lifestyles, these women do seem enviable to girls and young women since they appear to embody a type of power that demands attention and visibility.

For us noncelebrities who can't afford a personal stylist, the magazines dissect the "look," giving us tips on how to craft the image at a fraction of the price. They instruct us on what clothes to buy, what shoes to wear, how to do our hair and makeup, and what behavior to adopt to look as hot as our favorite celebrity. The low-slung jeans, the short skirt that rides up our legs as we sit down, the thong, the tattoo on the lower back, the pierced belly button, the low-cut top that shows cleavage, the high heels that contort our calves, and the pouting glossed lips all conspire to make us look like a bargain-basement version of the real thing. To get anywhere close to achieving the "look," we, of course, need to spend money—lots of it—as today femininity comes in the form of consumer products that reshape the body and face. The magazines that instruct us in the latest "must-have" fashions have no shortage of ads that depict, in excruciating detail, what it means to be feminine in today's porn culture.

While the fashion industry has always pushed clothes that sexualize women's bodies, the difference today is that the "look" is, in part, inspired by the sex industry. We are now expected to wear this attire everywhere: in school, on the street, and at work. Teachers, including elementary school teachers, often complain that their female students look more like they are going to a party than coming to school. It is as if we females now have to

Republished with permission of Beacon Press, from Pornland: How Porn Has Hijacked Our Sexuality, by Gail Dines. Boston, MA: Beacon Press, 2010.

carry the marker of sex on us all the time, less we forget (or men forget) what our real role is in this society.

Among hypersexualized celebrities, Paris Hilton ranks high. The story of how she was catapulted to the A-list is one all about porn culture. Once a minor-league celebrity known mainly for her vast bank account, in 2004, her then-boyfriend, Rick Salomon—thirteen years her senior—released a videotape of them having sex, called *1 Night in Paris,* and she instantly became a household name. Thanks to that tape, Hilton is now talked about all over the porn discussion boards as "a filthy slut" who got what she deserved. The fact that Salomon was the one who orchestrated the whole thing (she sued him over the release) does not prevent her from being mocked and derided by porn users and pop culture commentators alike. Over the years, Hilton has been labeled a kind of super "slut"—a term used to demarcate the supposed good girls from the bad. Her antics have garnered a devoted following among girls and young women, as well as massive visibility as one of the most photographed women in the world. Hilton gets away with being anointed as a "slut" because she is fabulously rich; the wealth acts as a kind of upmarket cleansing cream that instantly rubs off the dirt. For most girls and women, however, especially those from the working class, the dirt sticks like mud.

Take, for example, Britney Spears. At seventeen Spears released her debut single, called "…Baby One More Time," which became an instant international success. In the accompanying video, Spears is dressed in a school uniform with a knotted shirt that reveals a bare midriff, socks, and braided hair as she writhes around asking her ex-boyfriend to "hit me, baby, one more time." Spears later went on to employ Gregory Dark to direct her videos; Dark is a longtime porn director whose films include *The Devil in Miss Jones, New Wave Hookers*, and *Let Me Tell Ya 'Bout Black Chicks*. Her meltdowns in public, together with the famous image of her sans underwear, have contributed to a kind of public humiliation: we collectively flog her for her trashy ways, yet we put her on a pedestal for embodying a kind of uncouth hot sexiness. Unlike Hilton, Spears was not born into great wealth, so the attacks on her mothering, appearance, and partying tend to carry a subtext of classism in which Spears is described as a trailer-trash slut who, despite her millions, can't escape her roots. . . .

People not immersed in pop culture tend to assume that what we see today is just more of the same stuff that previous generations grew up on. After all, every generation has had its hot and sultry stars who led expensive and wild lives compared to the rest of us. But what is different about today is not only the hypersexualization of mass-produced images but also the degree to which such images have overwhelmed and crowded out any alternative images of being female. Today's tidal wave of soft-core porn images has normalized the porn star look in everyday culture to such a degree that anything less looks dowdy, prim, and downright boring. Today, a girl or young woman looking for an alternative to the Britney, Beyonce, Kim look will soon come to the grim realization that the only alternative to looking fuckable is to be invisible.

One show that popularized porn culture was *Sex and the City*, a show that supposedly celebrated female independence from men. At first glance this series was a bit different from others in its representation of female friendships and the power of women to form bonds that sustain them in their everyday lives. It also seemed to provide a space for women to talk about their own sexual desires, desires that were depicted as edgy, rebellious, and fun. However, these women claimed a sexuality that was ultimately traditional rather than resistant. Getting a man and keeping him were central to the narrative, and week after week we heard about the trials and tribulations of four white, privileged heterosexual women who seemed to find men who take their sexual cues from porn. . . .

Nowhere is this pseudo-independence more celebrated than in *Cosmopolitan*, a magazine that claims to have "served as an agent for social change, encouraging women everywhere to go after what they want (whether it be in the boardroom or the bedroom)." It is hard to see how *Cosmopolitan* helped women advance in corporate America, given that most of the Cosmo girl's time is taken up with perfecting her body and her sexual technique. But this doesn't stop the magazine from boasting that "we here at *Cosmo* are happy to have played such a significant role in women's history. And we look forward to many more years of empowering chicks everywhere.[1] In porn culture empowering women translates into "chicks" having lots of sex, and no magazine does more than *Cosmopolitan* to teach women how to perform porn sex in a way that is all about male pleasure. . . .

With headlines every month promising "Hot New Sex Tricks," "21 Naughty Sex Tips," "Little Mouth Moves That Make Sex Hotter," "67 New Blow-His-Mind Moves," "8 Sex Positions You Haven't Thought Of," and so on, women seem to experience no authentic sexual pleasure; rather, what she wants and enjoys is what he wants and enjoys. While there might be an odd article here and there on what to wear to climb the corporate ladder, the magazine as a whole is all about "him" and "his" needs, wants, desires, tastes, and, most importantly, orgasm. In *Cosmopolitan*, as in much of pop culture, her pleasure is derived not from being a desiring subject but from being a desired object.

Women's magazines that focus on "him" are not new, as earlier generations were also inundated with stories about "him," but then the idea was to stimulate his taste buds rather than his penis. *Cosmopolitan* is the contemporary equivalent of *Ladies'*

Home Journal in that it pretends to be about women, but it is in fact all about getting him, pleasing him, and (hopefully) keeping him. For previous generations of women, the secret to a happy relationship lay in being a good cook, cleaner, and mother—for the young women of today, the secret is, well, just being a good lay. If the reader is going to *Cosmopolitan* for tips on how to build a relationship or ways of developing intimacy, she will be disappointed, as conversation only matters in the world of *Cosmo* if it is about talking dirty.

With its manipulative "We are all girls together" tone coupled with the wise older mentor approach that promises to teach young women all they need to know to keep "him coming back for more," *Cosmopolitan*, like most women's magazines, masquerades as a friend and teacher to young women trying to navigate the tricky terrain of developing a sexual identity in a porn culture. *Cosmopolitan*'s power is its promise to be a guide and friend, and it promotes itself as one of the few magazines that really understand what the reader is going through. A promotional ad for *Cosmopolitan* geared toward advertisers boasts that it is "its readers' best friend, cheerleader and shrink."[2]

In *Cosmopolitan*, hypersexualization is normalized by virtue of both the quantity of articles on sex and the degree to which they are explicit. For example, one article instructs the reader, in a somewhat clinical manner, on how to bring a man to orgasm: "While gripping the base of the penis steadily in one hand, place the head between your lips, circling your tongue around the crown. When you sense your guy is incredibly revved up, give his frenulum a few fast tongue licks." For the uninitiated, the magazine explains that the frenulum is "the tiny ridge of flesh on the underside of his manhood, where the head meets the shaft."[3]

Cosmopolitan is quick to suggest using porn as a way to spice up sex. In one article, entitled "7 Bad Girl Bedroom Moves

You Must Master," the reader is told to take "the plunge into porn" as it "will add fiery fervor into your real-life bump and grinds." The article quotes a reader who, after watching porn with her boyfriend, evidently ended up "having sex so hot that the porn looked tame in comparison." The article suggests that if the reader feels embarrassed, she should "drive to a store in another neighborhood, shop online, or go to a place that stocks X-rated."

In the world that *Cosmopolitan* constructs for the reader, a world of blow jobs, multiple sexual positions, anonymous porn sex, and screaming orgasms (usually his), saying no to his erection is unthinkable. The options on offer in *Cosmopolitan* always concern the type of sex to have and how often. What is not on offer is the option to refuse his demands since he has (an unspoken and unarticulated) right of access to the female body. Indeed, readers are warned that not having sex on demand might end the "relationship." Psychologist Gail Thoen, for example, informs *Cosmopolitan*'s readers that "constant cuddling with no follow-through (i.e., sex) can be frustrating to guys" and what's more, "he is not going to like it if you leave him high and dry all the time."[5] The reader is pulled into a highly sexual world where technique is the key, and intimacy, love, and connection appear only rarely as issues worthy of discussion. The message transmitted loud and clear is that if you want a man, then not only must you have sex with him, you must learn ways to do it better and hotter than his previous girlfriends.

That the magazine teaches women how to have porn sex is clear in an article that ostensibly helps women deal with the etiquette of how to behave in the morning after the first sexual encounter. Women are told: "Don't Stay Too Long." The article warns women that "just because he had sex with you doesn't mean he's ready to be attached at the hip for the day." Actually, the entire day seems like a long shot—"Bo" informs readers that "I was dating this girl who wanted to hang out the next morning, but after only a couple of hours with her, I realized I wasn't ready to be that close." What advice does *Cosmopolitan* have for women in this situation? "Skip out after coffee but before breakfast."[6]

Media targeted to women create a social reality that is so overwhelmingly consistent it is almost a closed system of messages. In this way, it is the sheer ubiquity of the hypersexualized images that gives them power since they normalize and publicize a coherent story about women, femininity, and sexuality. Because these messages are everywhere, they take on an aura of such familiarity that we believe them to be our very own personal and individual ways of thinking. They have the power to seep into the core part of our identities to such a degree that we think that we are freely choosing to look and act a certain way because it makes us feel confident, desirable, and happy. But as scholar Rosalind Gill points out, if the look was "the outcome of everyone's individual, idiosyncratic preferences, surely there would be greater diversity, rather than a growing homogeneity organized round a slim, toned, hairless body."[7]

This highly disciplined body has now become the key site where gender is enacted and displayed on a daily basis. To be feminine requires not only the accoutrements of hypersexuality—high heels, tight clothes, and so on—but also a body that adheres to an extremely strict set of standards. We need to look like we spend hours in the gym exhausting ourselves as we work out, but whatever the shape of the body, it is never good enough. Women have so internalized the male gaze that they have now become their own worst critics. When they go shopping for clothes or look in a mirror, they dissect themselves piece by piece. Whatever the problem, and there is always a problem—the breasts are too small, the thighs not toned enough, the butt too flat or too round, the stomach too large—the result is a deep sense of self-disgust and loathing. The body becomes our enemy, threatening to erupt into fatness at any time, so we need to be hypervigilant. What we end up with is what Gill calls a "self-policing narcissistic gaze," a gaze that is so internalized that we no longer need external forces to control the way we think or act.[8]

... Understanding culture as a socializing agent requires exploring how and why some girls and young women conform and others resist. For all the visual onslaught, not every young woman looks or acts like she take her cues from *Cosmopolitan* or *Maxim*. One reason for this is that conforming to a dominant image is not an all-or-nothing act but rather a series of acts that place women and girls at different points on the continuum of conformity to nonconformity. Where any individual sits at any given time on this continuum depends on her past and present experiences as well as family relationships, media consumption, peer group affiliations and sexual, racial, and class identity. We are not, after all, blank slates onto which images are projected.

Given the complex ways that we form our sexual and gender identities, it is almost impossible to predict, with precision, how any one individual will act at any one time. This does not mean, though, that we can't make predictions on a macro level. What we can say is that the more one way of being female is elevated above and beyond others, the more a substantial proportion of the population will gravitate toward that which is most socially accepted, condoned, and rewarded. The more the hypersexualized image crowds out other images of women and girls, the fewer options females have of resisting what cultural critic Neil Postman called "the seduction of the eloquence of the image."[9]

Conforming to the image is seductive as it not only offers women an identity that is in keeping with the majority but also confers a whole host of pleasures, since looking hot does garner the kind of male attention that can sometimes feel empowering. Indeed, getting people to consent

to any system, even if it's inherently oppressive, is made easier if conformity brings with it psychological, social, and/or material gains. Many women know what it's like to be sexually wanted by a man: the way he holds you in his gaze, the way he finds everything you say worthy of attention, the way you suddenly become the most compelling person in the world. This is the kind of attention we don't normally get from men when we are giving a presentation, having a political conversation, or telling them to do the dishes. No, this is an attention men shower on women they want sexually, and it feels like real power, but it is ephemeral because it is being given to women by men who increasingly, thanks to the porn culture, see women as interchangeable hookup partners. To feel that sense of power, women need to keep sexing themselves up so they can become visible to the next man who is going to, for a short time, hold her in his lustful gaze. ...

... Alternative ideologies such as feminism that critique dominant conceptions of femininity are either caricatured or ignored in mainstream media. Absent such a worldview and a community of like-minded people, many young women speak about feeling isolated and alone in their refusal to conform to the porn culture. The stories are the same: they have a lot of difficulty in negotiating the outsider status that they have been forced to take on. They not only refuse to sex themselves up, they also refuse to have hookup sex, which means that they have a difficult time finding men who are interested in them.

Hookup Sex as Porn Sex

One of the most noticeable shifts in girls' and young women's behavior over the last decade or so is their increasing participation in what is called hookup sex—those encounters that can be anything from a grope to full sexual intercourse but have the common feature that there is no expectation of a relationship, intimacy, or connection.[10] Sex is what you expect, and sex is what you get. In a large-scale survey of 7,000 students, sociologist Michael Kimmel found that by their senior year, "students had averaged nearly seven hookups during their collegiate careers. About one-fourth (24 percent) say that they have never hooked up, while slightly more than that (28 percent) have hooked up ten times or more."[11]

Given its lack of commitment and intimate connection, hookup sex is a lot like porn sex, and it is being played out in the real world. If porn and women's media are to be believed, then these women are having as good a time as the men. But studies are finding that women do hope for more than just sex from a hookup encounter, as many express a desire for the hookup to evolve into a relationship. Sociologist Kathleen Bogle, for example, found in her study of college-age students that many of the women "were interested in turning hookup partners into boyfriends," while the men interviewed "preferred to hookup with no strings attached."[12]

... Studies have found that women who participate in hookups have lower self-esteem and higher levels of depression, and they experience regret over the hookups.[13] Grello and her colleagues, for example, found that the more depressed females had more sex partners, and the more partners they had, the more they regretted the hookup. The authors suggest that one possible explanation for this is that "depressed females may be seeking external validation from sex. They may be maintaining a vicious depressive cycle by unconsciously engaging in sex in doomed relationships. Possibly, these females' negative feelings of self-worth or isolation may increase their desire to be wanted by or intimate with another. Thus, if they sensed a potential romance would result from the encounter, they may have engaged in sexual behavior with a casual sex partner in an attempt to feel better, at least temporarily."[14]

Probably one of the most interesting findings of this study is that males who engaged in hookup sex reported the least depressive symptoms of any group. They also reported feeling more pleasure and less guilt than the females who participated in hookups. One reason for this could be the way that masculinity is socially constructed, since the more sex partners a man has, the more he is conforming to the idealized image of manhood.

With hookup sex comes, for women and girls, an increased possibility of being labeled a slut—a term that is used to control and stigmatize female sexual desire and behavior. There is, after all, no male equivalent of a slut since men who are thought to be highly sexually active are called a stud or a player—labels most men would happily take on. What it means to be a "slut" shifts over time, as previous generations of women carried the label just for having sex before marriage. But for all of women's so-called sexual empowerment today, the effects of being labeled a slut are as devastating now as they were in the past. A study by academics Wendy Walter-Bailey and Jesse Goodman shows that these girls and young women "often resort to self-destructive behaviors such as drug and alcohol abuse, eating disorders, self-mutilation, academic withdrawal, or risky sexual conduct."[15]

Walter-Bailey and Goodman found that the girls most likely to be labeled as sluts are those who "act too casual and/or flaunt their sexuality" as well as those who "flirt too heavily, blossom too early, or dress too scantily."[16] ...

Other studies have found that women experience "unwanted sex" (in other words, rape) more frequently in hookups than in dating or long-term relationships. One study in which 178 college students were interviewed found that of the experiences students called "unwanted intercourse," 78 percent occurred during a hookup, as opposed to 8.3 percent on a date and 13.9 percent in an ongoing relationship.[17] This makes perfect sense when we think about the lack of clear borders set up during a hookup. In an ongoing relationship, couples can discuss and negotiate sexual boundaries as the relationship develops, but in a hookup, there will typically be little discussion regarding who is thinking of doing what and how far each one wants to go sexually. Talking or drawing boundaries is not what a hookup is about. . . .

The American Psychological Association's study on the sexualization of girls found that there was ample evidence to conclude that sexualizing girls "has negative effects in a variety of domains, including cognitive functioning, physical and mental health, sexuality, and attitudes and beliefs."[18] Some of these effects include more risky sexual behavior, higher rates of eating disorders, depression, and low self-esteem as well as reduced academic performance. These are the same symptoms found in girls and women who have been sexually assaulted; in terms of effect, then, we appear to be turning out a generation of girls who have been "assaulted" by the very culture they live in. And there is no avoiding the culture. The very act of socialization involves internalizing the cultural norms and attitudes. If the culture is now one big collective perpetrator, then we can assume that an ever-increasing number of girls and women are going to develop emotional, cognitive, and sexual problems as they are socialized into seeing themselves as mere sex objects, and not much else.

Where is female sexual agency in all of this? When feminists in the 1960s and '70s fought for sexual liberation, they fought for the right to want, desire, and enjoy sex—but on their own terms. They argued that their sexuality had been defined by men, and they wanted it back. What they got was not what they expected: a hypersexuality that is generic, formulaic, and plasticized. It is a sexuality that has its roots in porn and is now so mainstream that it is fast becoming normalized. One of the men interviewed by Bogle said he saw hookup culture as a

"guy's paradise."[19] Yes, Pornland is indeed paradise for these men, as it is sex with no strings attached. And for women it is business as usual: men defining our sexuality in ways that serve them, not us. Only now this sexuality is sold to us as empowering. A new twist on an old theme.

Notes

1. Jennifer Benjamin (2005). "How Cosmo Changed the World." *Cosmopolitan*, September 2005, http://www.cosmopolitan.com/about/about-us_how-cosmo-changed-the-world (accessed July 7, 2008).

2. http://www.assocmags.co.za/images/pdfs/Cosmopolitan%20Rate%20Card.pdf (accessed June 6, 2008).

3. Ronnie Koenig. "Thrill Every Inch of Him," *Cosmopolitan*, June 2006. p. 150.

4. http://www.cosmopolitan.com/sex-love/sex/420935 (accessed July 7, 2008).

5. "Cuddle Overkill." *Cosmopolitan*, June 2007, p 137.

6. "You Had Sex—Now What?" *Cosmopolitan*, June 2007, p. 76.

7. Rosalind Gill (2009). "Supersexualize Me!: Advertising and the Midriff," in Feona Attwood, *Mainstreaming Sex: The Sexualization of Western Culture*. London: I.B. Tauris. p. 106.

8. Ibid, p. 107.

9. Neil Postman, *Consuming Images* (PBS Video, 1990).

10. I would like to thank Meg Lovejoy for generously sharing her work and insights on hookup sex and for providing me with a list of resources.

11. Michael Kimmel (2008), *Guyland: The Perilous World Where Boys Become Men* (NY: Harper Books), p. 195.

12. Kathleen Bogle (2008), *Hooking Up: Sex, Dating and Relationships on Campus* (New York: New York University Press), p. 173.

13. Catherine M. Grello, Deborah P. Welsh, and Melinda S. Harper (2006), "No Strings Attached: The Nature of Casual Sex in College Students," *Journal of Sex Research* 43, no. 3):

255; Elaine Eshbaugh and Gary Gute (2008), "Hookups and Sexual Regret Among College Women," *Journal of Social Psychology* 148, no. 1: 77–90.

14. Grello, Walsh and Harper, "No Strings Attached."

15. Walter-Bailey, W. and Goodman, J. (2006). "Exploring the culture of sluthood among adolescents," in *Contemporary Youth Culture: An International Encyclopedia.* (Vol. 2). Westport, CT: Greenwood Press, 280–284. p. 282.

16. Ibid, p. 282.

17. William Flack Jr., Kimberly A. Daubman, Marcia L. Caron, Nenica A. Asadorian, Nicole R. D'Aureli, Shannon N. Gigliotti, Anna T. Hall, Sarah Kiser, and Erin R. Stine (2007). Risk Factors and Consequences of Unwanted Sex Among University Students: Hooking Up, Alcohol, and Stress Response. *Journal of Interpersonal Violence*, 22; pp. 139–157.

18. Report of the APA Task Force on the Sexualization of Girls, Executive Summary, http://www.apa.org/pi/wpo/sexualization_report_summary.pdf. p. 2 (accessed February 5, 2009). The full study can be found at http://www.apa.org/pi/wpo/sexualization.html (accessed February 5, 2009).

19. Bogle, *Hooking Up*, p. 183.

46

La Princesa Plastica

Hegemonic and Oppositional Representations of *Latinidad* in Hispanic Barbie

Karen Goldman

In the forty-some years since she emerged from her original mold, Mattel's Barbie doll has become, both as cultural icon and children's plaything, one of the world's most ubiquitous plastic objects. The doll's embodiment of a diversity of feminine images reflects Mattel's efforts to market to continuously changing and increasingly diverse groups of U.S. and international consumers. But is it true, as some observers have contended, that, given the preeminence and persistence of the image of "rich, blonde Barbie" worldwide, resistance, cultural or otherwise, to hegemonic Barbie culture is futile? Barbie scholar Erica Rand (1995) points out that there is often a wide gap between the contexts and narratives that are produced for Barbie by Mattel, which are far from monolithic themselves, and the meanings that are generated by her consumers, whether children at play, collectors, or those who find in Barbie's carefully constructed persona an irresistible target for parody and subversion (26–28). . . .

The often quoted statistics on Barbie's global presence are staggering: more than one billion dolls sold in 150 countries, representing forty-five different nationalities (Barbie Collectibles, 2002). Although there is today a multitude of manifestations of Barbie culture, both hegemonic and oppositional, the point from which they all depart is the original, blue-eyed, blonde Barbie. Barbies are marked as "ethnic" or foreign only to the extent to which they differ from the original doll. In her "unauthorized biography," *Forever Barbie* (1994), M. G. Lord begins a chapter on ethnic Barbie by drawing an analogy between the development of Ruth Handler's original doll and the creation of Caucasian, all-American Hollywood star icons by largely Jewish-run movie studios. Lord asserts that original Barbie's ethnic neutrality differs from and surpasses that of the flesh-and-blood female stars that she resembles because, unlike "real" actresses, Barbie had no biological heredity and was, in fact, better suited than a human actress to exemplify an impossible ideal: "There was no tribal taint in her plastic flesh, no baggage to betray an immigrant past. She had no navel; no parents; no heritage" (160). Barbie's plasticity afforded her creators the luxury of designing her from scratch and literally molding every aspect of her appearance.

Like Hollywood promoters, who need to "design" stars that will engage the identification of the largest number of viewers, Mattel strove to develop a Barbie that would appeal to the greatest number of the doll's target audience: white, middle-class American parents and their daughters. Thus, the company's marketing strategy involved stressing, above all else, the doll's "Americanness." She had to be, in the words of Barbie's admiring biographer, BillyBoy (1987), "the personification of the all-round American girl" (28). In the social environment of the United States of the late 1950s, this meant she had to be Caucasian, blonde, light-skinned, and free of any obvious ethnic markers.

The original Barbie's ethnic neutrality not only served to emphasize the association of middle-class Caucasian femininity with "Americanness," it also served to bolster what Erica Rand refers to as Mattel's "language of infinite possibility" (28). Citing the need to allow children to project their own imagination onto the doll, Ruth Handler went to great lengths to expunge what she perceived as distinguishing characteristics that would give Barbie a distinct look or persona. In a 1990 interview she remarked, "the face was deliberately designed to be blank, without a personality, so that the projection of the child's dream could be on Barbie's face" (quoted in Rand, 40). But, like any cultural product, and despite the claims of her inventor, Barbie has indeed "always

already" been inscribed in a manufactured narrative that is strictly circumscribed and defined by her producers. Clearly, within the rigid parameters of the doll's image as projected by Mattel, the possibilities for imagining a nonhegemonic Barbie were limited.

By 1961, Mattel had made the decision to allow Barbie to acquire a specific biography beyond her first name and the qualifier "teenage fashion model." During the early sixties, Barbie was appearing in books, records, and other texts as a blonde pony-tailed teenage fashion model with a personality, an address, a last name, and a boyfriend. While Barbie's and Ken's first names were taken from the real names of Ruth and Elliot Handler's two children, the other names are a veritable tribute to hyperbolic anglocentrism: Barbie's full name is Barbara Millicent Roberts. Ken's surname is Carson, and the two names together are, appropriately, an homage to Mattel's advertising firm: Carson/Roberts. Barbie's parents' names are identified as George and Margaret (only a minor variation of George and Martha, those archetypical grandparents of the nation). Barbie lives a glamorous but otherwise typical teenage life in a small American town called Willows.

Mattel has periodically adjusted Barbie's body, face, and hair in the interest of keeping up with styles and social realities of the day. But during the early years of her existence it was above all clothing and accessories that allowed her to (at least superficially) diversify her look. At first, the outfits marketed for Barbie fell into categories that emphasized her elegance ("Evening Splendor," "Silken Flame"), career aspirations ("Ballerina," "Registered Nurse"), leisure activities ("Ski Queen," "Movie Date"), or special occasions ("Easter Parade," "Bride's Dream"). None of these outfits departed in any substantial way from the standard of Barbie's (and later Ken's) middle-class Caucasian Americanness. By 1964, Barbie and Ken had already acquired many of the accoutrements of the American dream, for example, those appropriately named "dream" accessories: the "dream kitchen" (1964), the "dream house" (1964), and the sports car (1962). For members of the postwar American middle class who had already attained these assets, travel, particularly to an exotic location, became a status-bearing consumer item, akin to owning a nice house or car (Urry, 2002). In 1964, in a miniature reenactment of the U.S. middle-class's increasing tendency to dedicate capital and leisure time to long-distance travel, Mattel launched the Travel Costume series, and Barbie and Ken become tourists, visiting Japan, Switzerland, Holland, Hawaii, and Mexico. Each travel costume outfit included "charming traditional costumes" for Barbie and Ken, as well as a miniature storybook that narrated the pair's travel adventures.

Central to Barbie's Mexican travel experience is the fact that the dolls (with or without the storybook provided with the outfit) come with a ready-made Mattel-produced narrative that highlights the pair's status as Caucasian Americans enjoying leisure adventures, oblivious to the larger narrative that is the largely mestizo Mexican nation and its people. No images of other compete as meaning producer with the Mattel master narrative, for there are no traces of actual people (or doll personalities) in the narrative other than the costumed Caucasian Barbie and Ken. . . .

Mexico is a backdrop for Barbie's and Ken's travel adventure, not unlike the stories of the Little Theatre Costume sets that were sold concurrently, featuring Barbie as a princess of the Arabian Knights, Little Red Riding Hood, Guinevere, and Cinderella. Like the memorable figure of Donald Duck wearing a sombrero and traveling through Mexico on a flying serape in the 1989 Disney cartoon film, *The Three Caballeros*, Ken and Barbie perform their jovial masquerade against a background in which the totality of Mexico is represented as a storybook land. The story and the outfits depict folkloric or traditional elements of Mexican culture that, through caricature, are rendered no

more unfamiliar or threatening to American cultural hegemony than the storybook characters. Thus, Ken's and Barbie's masquerading in the Mexico set functions more as an affirmation of the doll's implacable whiteness than any attempt to represent a multicultural opening. . . .

Following a traditional pattern of imperialist penetration, Barbie's (and Mattel's) entry into an international, intercultural environment begins from the position of tourist, that of postcolonial traveler to exotic locations. However, and in spite of the Travel Collection's clear affirmation of the dolls as Anglo and American, even this limited acknowledgment of worlds beyond the United States points, however tenuously, to Barbie's (and Mattel's) imminent initial foray into global expansion. It marks the beginning of what would eventually become the breakup of the monolithic Barbie narrative, in which nonwhite others are not only invisible, but their existence is never even an issue, for it simply does not come into play.

By the late sixties, Barbie's privileging of Caucasian femininity as the standard of American beauty, anachronistically silhouetted against a background of the civil rights movement and increasing ethnic and racial diversity in the United States, was becoming an encumbrance to Ruth Handler's notion that all girls must be able to identify with Barbie. Mattel decided to alter its master narrative in a reversal that reined in Barbie's biography and reintroduced the "language of infinite possibility." In 1967, Mattel launched a rather unconvincing Black Francie doll, followed, in 1968, by Barbie's Black friend Christie. In 1980, Mattel introduced Black and Hispanic Barbie, as well as a "Dolls of the World" Collection. In 1988, Teresa, an Hispanic doll, was introduced, followed by a line of African American "friends of Barbie." In a 1990 interview for *Newsweek*, Mattel product manager Deborah Mitchell proudly announced, "now, ethnic Barbie lovers will be able to dream in their own image" (duCille, 1995, 554).

While it is clear that Mattel was intent on capturing the growing ethnic markets in the United States by developing dolls meant to allow identification by ethnic "others," there is much debate regarding how authentically the dolls actually represent diversity. The representation of Latinidad in the marketing of Hispanic Barbie dolls has followed the recent pattern of many products aimed at Latino consumers. Media scholar Clara Rodriguez (1997) argues that in the popular media in the United States today, Latinos are typically either absent or misrepresented. When they are represented, it is often as negative stereotypes or as exotic foreigners (13–30). Behind Mattel's portrayal of Latino/a identity lies a system of representation that sells itself as authentic but that ultimately either depicts Latino/a culture as homogeneous and exotic, or repackages the doll's Latinidad in an assimilated form, whether to make her more attractive to more assimilated Latinos or to market her more effectively in places where ethnic diversity is not particularly marketable. . . .

The first Hispanic Barbie doll's bilingual box introduced her as Barbie Hispanica (not the grammatically correct Hispaña). Like the earlier Mexico Travel Barbie, she is stereotypically dressed in a white peasant blouse and a full red skirt, a lace mantilla over her shoulders and a red rose tied around her neck. If the standard for Caucasian Barbie is light-skinned, blonde, and blue-eyed, the U.S. Hispanic version presents those contrasting physical attributes stereotypically associated with Latinas: dark hair, dark eyes, and darker skin. However, in few of the dolls designed to represent Hispanic (or Latina) women is skin tone ever darker than the suntanned Malibu Barbie dolls. Facial features never hint at indigenous or African heritage. What most prominently distinguishes the original Hispanic Barbie from any of the brunette Caucasian Barbies is the doll's paratextual items: clothing and accessories, or, more accurately, her costume. The original Hispanic Barbie, as well as subsequent special editions that celebrate occasions culturally specific to Latinos, such as the Quinceañera Barbie, all sport traditional folkloric clothing that is intended to mark them very clearly as Latinas, and therefore as foreign, exotic other.

In her physical characteristics, posture, and dress, the original Hispanic Barbie very closely resembles the international Hispanic (read: foreign) Dolls of the World, which are designed to reflect "typical" national attributes and dress in folkloric clothing. To Caucasian Barbie's quintessential Americanness, the Dolls of the World represent a quintessentially foreign counterpoint. But, as Wendy Varney argues in her convincing analysis of Australian Barbie, they are essentially American products and bear the Stamp of U.S. cultural imperialism, no matter what the guise. With respect to Latina identity, the Dolls of the World tend to negotiate difference by representing those Latinas as either hyperbolically folkloric (Mexico, Peru) or splashy and exotic (Brazil). Mattel's stated goal in offering the Dolls of the World Collection is to foster international understanding and appreciation of cultural differences. Significantly, the Andalusian Barbie and Mexican Barbie, both of whom are included in the Dolls of the World Collection, differ only superficially from U.S. Hispanic Barbie. They all have fair complexions and long dark hair, each with a large red rose tucked behind one ear. They wear full skirts and blouses, and all three dolls' clothes feature bright red as the predominant color, a characteristic that persists in Mattel's representations of Hispanics. Cultural differences among diverse groups and nationalities are elided, as Latinidad is reduced to one easily consumable, stereotypical identity-in-a-box.

The Peruvian doll, issued in 1999, provides a good example of how notions of Latin American class, race, and ethnicity play out in the real or implied narrative that frames the doll's paratextual positioning. For one thing, the doll is clearly meant to portray the identity of an indigenous Peruvian woman, with her long braids, round face, traditional woven shawl, and matching skirt. However, her facial features are wholly Caucasian, as is her rosy skin tone. In a clear and rather surprising break with standard Barbie design and Mattel's custom of representing racial differences only through what Ann duCille calls the "tint of the plastic," Peruvian Barbie carries a baby, who presumably is meant to be her own. One thing that has consistently defined the essence of Barbie has been her status as a single woman. While she is often depicted as a big sister or caring for children, and she has long been available as a bride, there has never been such a thing as a "Married Barbie," much less a maternal Barbie. Until the recent release of the "Happy Family" dolls, including a "Pregnant Midge" (not Barbie), that comes with a belly containing a removable baby, maternity has been wholly absent in the world of Barbie dolls. In the case of Midge, the issue of paternity is never in question, since, in a throwback to the early years of Mattel's use of heavy-handed biography, the doll wears a wedding ring, and her box provides a narrative identifying the father as Midge's husband, Alan.

The Peruvian doll comes with no such disclaimer. The baby is one more accessory, like Hispanic Barbie's lace mantilla, that identifies her as ethnically other. The representation of the Peruvian Barbie as mother is possible precisely because she is a Doll of the World, that is, she is foreign, and not subject to the rigid conventions of the "American" dolls. In addition, Peruvian Barbie's representation responds to principles of marketing and stereotypes that view Latinos as extremely family-oriented and conservative on the issue of nontraditional roles for women (Deanne et al., 2000). The presence of the baby, with or without an implied father, is a much more important signifier of Mattel's notion of Latina femininity than any national costume or textual commentary might be.

Following the introduction of the first Hispanic Barbie in 1980, which differed little from the "foreign" Dolls of the World, Mattel favored more culturally assimilated Hispanic dolls that differed little from nonethnic Barbies, beyond adjustments to physical characteristics such as hair color and skin tone. Hispanic Barbie and African American Barbies were simply marketed as differently tinted versions of Caucasian Barbies. Such not-*too*-ethnic dolls were attractive to both ethnic minorities and majority Caucasian buyers, and thus served the dual purpose of appearing to foster diversity while increasing profits. In 1988, Mattel introduced Teresa, a bona fide Latina friend of Barbie. Like Barbie, Teresa has been produced with a multitude of physical characteristics over the years, morphing from a doll with consistently darker skin and hair to one that is often indistinguishable from nonethnic Barbie.

Today, all ethnic Barbie dolls vary in skin tone and hair color, but they typically wear the same clothes and accessories as Caucasian Barbie. It is tempting to consider that Teresa's changing looks signal Mattel's acknowledgment of the tremendous diversity among Latino populations world-wide. But beyond the dye that is used to tint her plastic body, it is hard to appreciate any substantial difference between Teresa and brunette Caucasian Barbies. What renders them similar is far more compelling than what sets them apart. Since recent issues of the Teresa doll don't even include Spanish text on the box, the only remaining link to Teresa's Latina identity is her name, Teresa (whose echo of the distant Spanish mystic Santa Teresa does not go unnoticed by many). . . . Even when Teresa is sold in a way that culturally marks her as Hispanic— for example, as Quinceañera Teresa—she more closely resembles Caucasian Barbie than the Latin American or Spanish Dolls of the World. The ultimate confirmation of her degree of assimilation is her marketing success in regions of the United States that do not have high concentrations of Latinos.

While Mattel has been congratulating itself for promoting diversity in the United States by including Hispanic Barbie and Teresa along with other dolls of color among its products, in Latin American countries where licensed Barbies are produced by regional subsidiaries, the dolls are nearly always modeled on the traditional Hollywood-inspired brands of American beauty: Caucasian and blonde. And although Caucasian blonde Barbie is certainly popular among Latina girls in the United States (Budge, 2003), it is unusual for a Hispanic doll to be marketed in the United States that does not possess those physical characteristics typically attributed to Latinas: darker skin, hair, and eyes. That Hispanic Barbies in the United States are not generally sold as blondes, whereas they very often are in Latin America, points to some of the complexities of racial and ethnic identification and marketing in both countries. As is evident in the success of female celebrities from Eva Peron to XuXa, in Latin American popular culture it is, ironically, the Hollywood-inspired ideal of blonde feminine beauty that prevails. And, given Barbie's relatively hefty price tag in Latin America (about $20), it is precisely the mostly white elite to whom Barbie dolls are marketed. The highest proportion of Barbie ownership in Latin America (outside of Puerto Rico, where a whopping 72 percent of girls own Barbies, is in Argentina (44 percent) and Chile (49 percent), nations that also have the lowest proportion of indigenous peoples, blacks, and mestizos, and the highest proportion of European-descended Caucasians ("Barbie Dolls in Latin America," 2002). Not surprisingly, the most popular Argentine Barbies tend to be those with the most Caucasian features. . . .

Barbie's hegemonic identity and her very ubiquity have always made her an attractive target for parodical representations of subversive intent. These counterhegemonic efforts include guerrilla tactics, such as the Barbie Liberation Organization, which sabotaged toys on store shelves. Other examples include works of criticism and literature that revisit and reinterpret the Barbie image, such as *Mondo Barbie* and *The Barbie Chronicles,* works of visual art, a multitude of Internet sites such as visiblebarbie.com and distortedbarbie.com, as well as the notable 1987 film *Superstar* by Todd Haynes. This film narrates the life of pop music star Karen Carpenter, who died of anorexia in 1983, using Barbie dolls to stand in for the human figures. Like Haynes's film, the majority of these counterhegemonic and often feminist-inspired criticisms target Barbie's absurd body proportions, her flawless physiognomy, her anachronistic femininity, and the culture of consumption she promotes. Few of them problematize the issues of race, ethnicity, class, and the privileging of U.S. perceptions of foreign others in their analyses. . . .

The Internet has been a prodigious global source of Barbie resistance, parody, and criticism. Pocho.com is a Web site based on *Pocho Magazine,* which has been around since the late eighties. The site, subtitled "Aztlán's número uno source for satire y chingazos," features irreverent and biting satire, a longstanding tradition in Mexican journalism. Though *pocho* literally means faded, it is a disparaging term often used by Mexicans to describe U.S.-assimilated Mexican Americans. The magazine's and Website's appropriation of the term reflects a sentiment that has grown consistently as people of Mexican heritage in the United States proudly embrace their identity as one of fluidity and hybridity. On the site, as in the lives and cultures of Chicanos and other Latinos in the United States, English and Spanish are mixed freely, and articles on Mexican president Vicente Fox are juxtaposed with ones on Ron Unz and Monica Lewinsky. The April 28, 2000, edition featured a satirical story titled "New

Latina Barbies Unveiled," announcing that Mattel had launched a line of Barbies in the likeness of Latina celebrities Cameron Diaz, Christina Aguilera, and Jennifer Lopez, as well as a new "Hispanic Family."

The text says, in part, "These dolls accurately capture the cultural pride felt by all of these strong Latina women. . . . We hope little Latina girls feel validated each time they look at their realistic and culturally accurate Latina Barbie dolls" (Sanchez-McNulty, 2000). Of course, the joke, one that Mattel (and Hollywood) never gets, is that all of the dolls look the same; they are blonde, blue-eyed, and have perfectly symmetrical Caucasian features. Of course, this begs the question, posed by duCille with regard to black African American dolls: "What would it take to produce a line of dolls that more fully reflects the wide variety of sizes, shapes, colors, hair styles, occupations, abilities, and disabilities that African Americans—like all people—come in?" (duCille, "Dyes and Dolls," 1995, 559). Clearly, the answer to that question does not lie with Mattel, which proudly asserts that "Today, in her 43rd year, Barbie reflects the dreams, hopes and future realities of an entire generation of little girls who still see her as representing the same American dream and aspirations as when she was first introduced in 1959!" (Barbie.com, 2002).

Perhaps, as she straddles cultures, Hispanic Barbie must strive to (and be animated to) embody what Latina writer and critic Gloria Anzaldua (1999) describes as "a tolerance for ambiguity" that characterizes the new mestiza: "She learns to juggle cultures. . . . Not only does she sustain contradictions, she turns ambivalence into something else" (101). Or perhaps, as Wendy Varney suggests, the Barbie phenomenon is itself inextricably, irrevocably bound up in a white, middle-class American context (3). As such, it is hard to resist the temptation to glimpse, behind each Barbie, regardless of her skin and hair color, facial characteristics and dress, or even the language that she speaks, a little blonde blue-eyed Barbie named Barbie Millicent Robert from Willows.

References

Ananova. "Lesbian Barbie Film Banned in Mexico." http://www.ananova.com/news/story/sm_540282.html?menu=news.quirkies (accessed November 11, 2002).

Anzaldua, Gloria. *Borderlands/La Frontera: The New Mestiza* (2nd ed.). San Francisco: Aunt Lute Books, 1999.

Barbie Collectibles, http://www.barbiecollectibles.com/inciex-home.asp (accessed November 12, 2002).

Barbie.com. Mattel Corporation, http://www.barbie.com/ (accessed October 10, 2002).

"The Barbie Doll Story." Mattel Corporation, http://www.shareholder.com/mattel/news/20020428-79139.cf (accessed October 22, 2002).

"Barbie Dolls in Latin America." Zona Latina. http://www.zonalatina.com/Zldata37.html (accessed December 22, 2002).

BillyBoy. *Barbie, Her Life and Times.* New York: Crown Trade Paperbacks, 1987.

Budge, David. "Barbie Is No Living Doll as a Role Model." *Times Education Supplement,* January 7, 2003.

Deanne, Claudia, et al. "Leaving Tradition Behind: Latinos in the Great American Melting Pot." *Public Perspectives* 11, no. 3 (May/June 2000): 5–7.

duCille, Ann. "Barbie in Black and White." In *The Barbie Chronicles: A Living Doll Turns Forty.* New York: Touchstone, 1999.

———. "Dyes and Dolls: Multicultural Barbie and the Merchandising of Difference." In *A Cultural Studies Reader,* ed. Jessica Rajan and Gita Rajan. London: 1995.

"Life in Plastic." *Economist,* December 21, 20–23, 2002.

Lipsitz, George. *Dangerous Crossroads: Popular Music, Postmodernism and the Poetics of Place.* Verso: London, 1994.

Lord, M. G. *'Forever Barbie' The Unauthorized Biography of a Real Doll*. New York: William Morrow, 1994.

Pratt, Mary Louise. *Imperial Eyes: Travel Writing and Transculturation*. London: Routledge, 1992.

Rand, Erica. *Barbie's Queer Accessories*. Durham, NC: Duke University Press, 1995.

Rodriguez, Clara, ed. *Latin Looks: Images of Latinas and Latinos in the U.S. Media*. Boulder, CO: Westview Press, 1997.

Sanchez-McNulty, Maria. "New Latina Barbies Unveiled." *Pocho*. http://www.pocho.com/new/2001/barbies21200barbies31700.htm.

Urry, John. *The Tourist Gaze* (2nd edition). London: Sage, 2002.

Varney, Wendy. "Barbie Australis: The Commercial Reinvention of National Culture." *Social Identities* 4 (June 1998): 161. http://search.epnet.com/direct.asp?an=873697&db=abh (accessed October 2, 2002).

47

Monarchs, Monsters, and Multiculturalism

Disney's Menu for Global Hierarchy

Lee Artz

D isney leads the world in the production and distribution of popular culture. Although AOL–Time Warner may be the media giant in assets, none challenges Disney as the primary purveyor of entertainment nor approach its perennial popularity and box-office success in animated feature films. Indeed, animation is central to Disney's economic vitality and cultural influence. In the last decade, Disney has sold over $3 billion in toys based on characters from its animated features. Disney theme parks, featuring popular film characters and settings, now have more visitors each year than all of the fifty-four national parks in the United States.

Although Disney produces nonanimated films through its Miramax and Touchstone movie studios, its economic and cultural strength remains in animation. Using profits from its global sales of animated films, Disney has acquired the ABC television network, mass-market radio stations, and cable channels such as ESPN and A&E....

The centrality of animation to Disney's corporate success and the corresponding centrality of Disney animation to global popular culture forms and themes require some exploration. This inquiry should entail both a political-economic and a cultural studies approach, given the apparent parallels between Disney's corporate practices (from investment and workplace practices to technological production and mass distribution) and the ideological themes of Disney's animated narratives (including race and gender equality). Investigating the construction, content, and persuasive appeal of Disney animations suggests that Disney consistently and programmatically produces "commodities-as-animated-feature films" that promote an ideology preferred by Disney and global capitalism—an ideology at odds with democracy and creative, participatory social life....

From Lee Artz, "Monarchs, Monsters, and Multiculturalism: Disney's Menu for Global Hierarchy," pages 75–6, 83–4, 87–9, 91–2, 94 from *Rethinking Disney: Private Control, Public Dimensions*, edited by Mike Budd and Max H. Kirsch. © 2005 by Wesleyan University Press and reprinted with permission by Wesleyan University Press.

In a society and culture ostensibly democratic, it is unsettling to find the major distributor of global entertainment promulgating narratives that simultaneously soften and defend messages of social-class hierarchy and antisocial hyper-individualism. . . .

Naturalizing Hierarchy

Hierarchy in a social order indicates a ranking according to worth, ability, authority, or some other attribute. In Disney, these values are combined with goodness and physical appearance such that, in each animated narrative, heroes and heroines are invariably good, attractive, capable, worthy, and ultimately powerful, while in service to the narrative's social order.

From the opening "circle of life" scene in *The Lion King* we cannot mistake the social order and its validity. All species bow before the rightful king. The heavens open and a (divine?) light shines on the new lion cub. This future king is held before a multitude of reverent and bowing beasts whose happiness and very existence depend on the maintenance of the established and rightful hierarchy. The visual metaphors of good and evil are simple and transparent: a regal king and his heir; an evil uncle who covets the kingdom; and lesser passive animal-citizens overrun by social undesirables in need of leadership. The meanings are animationally inescapable—the King and his son, Simba, are brightly drawn, muscular, and smoothly curved; the villainous uncle, "Scar," is dark, angular, thin, and disfigured; the hyenas, likewise, are angular and unmistakably Black and Latino (in the voice, diction, and verbal styles of Whoopi Goldberg and Cheech Marin); the socially irresponsible meerkat and boar, more cartoonish, less naturalistically drawn, live beyond the pride lands. The dialogue and action indicate importance, as well. Mustafa speaks in the King's English, usually from on high. Scar, the villain, lurks in shape and movement, languid, lazy, and foppish, narratively manipulating other characters through deceit. The hyenas have secondary roles with fewer lines, delivered comically, with slapstick interactions that are nonetheless understood as relationships of power that are maintained throughout. . . .

The narratives of *Pocahontas, Mulan, Tarzan* and other Disney animations are formed from the same redundant template of elite hierarchy, albeit with hegemonic variation. In *Pocahontas*, the standard Disney coming-of-age romance has been updated with a feisty, independent heroine in a narrative advocating cultural tolerance but following the trail of all Western captivity narratives with its "noble" Powhatan, "savage" warrior Kocoum, and "Indian princess" Pocahontas.[1] John Smith, blond, smoothly muscular, and athletically animated, fulfills the heroic ideal in vision and plot, while Chief Powhatan appears more sedate in bold, symmetrical strokes, with slower, more dignified screen movements and dialogue. These two elites survive the actions of the reactionary Kocoum and villainous Ratcliffe. The stoic, irrational Kocoum has few lines, and dies at the hands of a naive colonialist. The Ratcliffe character reveals in dialogue that he is indulgent, pompous, greedy, incompetent, and not respected by the British nobility. He appears as the largest figure in the film, obese, with a huge nose, big lips, and pencil-thin triangular mustache. The narrative's social relations are hierarchical: lower-class Anglos work for Ratcliffe or Smith; native soldiers and villagers follow Powhatan's directives. In the end, the "good" colonialist John Smith intervenes to save Powhatan and order the arrest of Ratcliffe; Pocahontas presumably finds her true path as a peacemaker and daughter; and the rest of the natives and English adventurers assume their prescribed subordinate positions, awaiting further orders from their superiors. In *Pocahontas*, two hierarchical orders are defended and left intact, although the extended visual metaphor of John Smith saving Powhatan and wanting to civilize Pocahontas indicates that the colonial is dominant over the indigenous. . . .

While the hero and heroine are always noble and attractive by birth, villains are privileged and titled only because of the misplaced magnanimity or whim of a legitimate superior. Villains are unattractive, semi-elite social misfits. Jafar is grand vizier, adviser to Sultan; Scar is King Mustafa's disgruntled brother, ineligible for legitimate succession; and Ratcliffe's governorship is a reluctant sop from more worthy elites. Randall remains on the monsters' payroll only through his deceit, which ultimately is discovered by the hero, Sully. In each of these narratives and many others (e.g., *Little Mermaid, Beauty and the Beast, Fox and Hound*), the dominant social class has no villainy, producing only good souls who never abuse their authority. We understand this viscerally by the soft, cuddly caricatures that Disney creates. Abuse comes solely from those elevated beyond their goodness, villains who would reach beyond their status and disrupt the social order. . . . In the fairy-tale world of the dominant, class rules apply: a frog becomes a prince only if he was a prince before. Rulers may change among the elite (from Mustafa to Simba, from Sultan to Aladdin, Flik gets royal privilege), but the rules and ruled remain. And, in Disney's world, the only just rule is class hierarchy. . . .

Evil henchmen, such as Clayton's sailors or the Huns, are consistently shabbily dressed or disheveled, dark, often bearded, usually armed, speak harshly in short sentences, and mete out their brutality only as long as the villain commands. In Disney, lower-class characters do not act on their own. Large groups are often cast as mob-like in action and graphic: jeering primates terrorize Jane; wildebeest stampede without regard for others in *The Lion King;* native warriors huddle around the fire waiting for orders to attack; the Huns shout and howl above the thunder of their horses' hooves; grasshoppers and sharks indiscriminately attack. Whether African, Arabian, North American, Chinese, or nonhuman, few from the good citizenry or evil troops are individualized; even fewer have articulate voices, appearing but as replicates from two or three stencils, graphically reflective of their necessarily subordinate position in Disney's hierarchy. In sum, Disney films all play a similar refrain: a stylized, naturalized, and Westernized elite hero combats a privileged antisocial oversized villain, while cute animal sidekicks and thuggish rebels knock about in front of a shapeless, faceless humanity. Animating hierarchy centers Disney's vision, whatever the era, geography, or species.

Ordering Coercion and Power

To underscore this essential Disney law, narrative resolution in each film defends and reinforces the status quo. Nothing is resolved until the preferred social order is in place. No one lives happily ever after until the chosen one rules. All is chaos and disorder in the pride lands until Simba returns as monarch. Even nature withholds its bounty, pending the proper social hierarchy. Nemo's mistake is curiosity about another world: when he leaves the security, safety, and proper place of the coral reef, disaster strikes. Saving China is only a youthful adventure: Mulan's "place in life" is in the family garden. Even the wisest of apes knows Tarzan is superior. . . .

We all need true rulers who are wise, benevolent, and powerful. Any other arrangement is unworkable. Villains may attain power, but as nonelite, false leaders, they are ill equipped to rule. Their reign is disastrous and temporary. Soon the hero will save the day and the hierarchy. "As evil is expelled, the world is left nice and clean," and well ordered.[2] Thus, zebras bow, faceless Chinese cheer, and, in general, the working masses rejoice (and happily resume their subservience) upon the triumphant defense of the hierarchy. The pleasant narrative outcome verifies the virtue of hierarchy and models Disney's actual institutional hierarchy, in everything from animation production to cruise ships, theme parks, and town life in Celebration, Florida.[3] In its digital production, Disney replaces piecework animation artists with piecework technicians in a hierarchical structure dedicated to marketing entertainment commodities for shareholder profit—no cooperative here, no creative exchange between artists, technicians, and citizen-parents. The story scripts in narrative and in production and distribution conform to market dictates and capitalist production norms, including corporate elite control.

Preference and justification for elite control can be observed in the attributes of each narrative's leading authority: this character is morally good and invariably benevolent. The sultan may be disoriented, but he is a gentle soul, impervious to evil. A compassionate John Smith—"the perfect masculine companion"—is willing to sacrifice his own life to avoid further bloodshed.[4] In contrast to the malevolent Huns, Mulan's emperor exudes warmth to his docile subjects. Tarzan demonstrates his human compassion and species superiority in saving his ape family (and Jane). For Disney, all elite authority figures are good, caring, and protective of their wards. In a telling statistical analysis of eleven Disney animations, Hoerner found that heroic protagonists exhibit 98 percent of all pro-social behavior in the films.[5]

. . . A consistent haloing of hierarchal power as preferable for all organizes the films' moral conflicts and elite responses to challenge. In all cases, elite heroes and heroines use coercion with impunity, continuing a Disney tradition that dates back to Snow White. Elite coercion varies, from the Beast's abuse of Belle, to the colonialist's murder of Kocoum. Mulan slaughters dozens of Huns; Tarzan wrestles with Clayton, who accidentally falls to his own death.

Villains Randall, Waterhouse, Hopper, and various aliens are similarly dispatched by elite violence. In addition to coercion, elites frequently employ deceit. Everywhere and always Disney's heroic elites are stronger, smarter, and victorious in the final conflict (even when performing antisocial acts). In each case, the protagonist earns riches, power, and happiness.

In contrast, villains—who almost exclusively exhibit antisocial behavior and violence—suffer calamity or death: Jafar is imprisoned for thousands of years; Scar dies; Kocoum dies; Ratcliffe is arrested; the Hun dies; Clayton dies; Randall and Hopper are ultimately dispatched. One need not consult a literary critic to understand the moral of these stories. In all fairy tales, good triumphs over evil, but for Disney good is the exclusive genetic and social right of the elite. Elites are attractive, benevolent, good, and successful; villains are misshapen, treacherous, and evil, and cannot win. The rest of the Disney world is undifferentiated, passive, dependent on elite gratuity, and largely irrelevant, except as narrative fodder.

Community and Democracy

. . . . In focusing exclusively on individual elites, Disney dismisses group solidarity and the public interest as unimportant to the story. Although each narrative includes dozens of nonelite characters, they appear primarily as background or as proxies to the protagonists—as exhibited by Nemo's "tank guy" buddies. In fact, "every Disney character stands on either one side or the other of the power demarcation line. All below are bound to obedience, submission, discipline, humility. Those above are free to employ constant coercion, threats, moral and physical repression and economic domination."[6]

. . . . Individualism and competition—buzzwords for capitalism—are reserved for Disney's fantasy elites, who have no moral or social peer. Elite ideas and actions are right, good, and ultimately successful. Villains may have ideas and take action, but they are wrong, bad, and doomed to fail. In such a fantasy world, no other ideas or actions are needed; hence Disney's animated public seldom speaks, exhibits limited thought, and undertakes little independent action—and never, ever, does a nonelite character freely broach the question of equality, democracy, or social justice.

. . . . At most, Disney's animated populations appear as "average" characters, either acting irresponsibly as inferiors, squabbling over trifles or passively waiting for mobilization orders from a superior. Most secondary castings are not particularly bright in dialogue or graphic portrayal, except for aides, who are often mischievous but harmless, comic animals. Less enlightened nonelites tend toward antisocial behavior as thieving hyenas, tormenting monkeys, or devious monsters. Having baser instincts, "bad" nonelites (unshaven, partially dressed, usually large) are also prone to violence and easily misled by nefarious Disney antagonists: Arab bandits work for Jafar; sailors join Clayton in kidnapping; hordes follow the Hun; Randall directs his monster minions; and grasshoppers pillage for Hopper.

Predictably, according to Disney, most nonelites tacitly or enthusiastically understand that hierarchy is good and support the social order no matter who rules. The citizens of Agrabah bow to the sultan, Jafar, then Aladdin on each successive command; no animals rise up against Scar; the colonists obey Ratcliffe, then Smith; and all apes obey Kerchak, then Tarzan; the Queen rules over all bugs: long live the monarchy!

According to Disney, workers, sailors, farmers, and other producers are wretched, irrational, chaotic, and passive, unable to act in their own interests—at best they may be motivated to protect the hierarchical social order. Some may be roused to mob action under the wrong leader, but all

will be happier if the proper order is fulfilled—the hierarchical natural order of the animal kingdom, or the hierarchical social order of an Arab sultanate, Chinese empire, British or ant colony, toy room, scare factory, or ocean. Group action, in other words, occurs only at the whim of the powerful.

. . . . Moreover, in Disney animations, actions by leading characters thoroughly shred any semblance of collective interest. Aladdin deserts the orphans and his neighborhood; Pocahontas betrays her nation; Tarzan betrays his family; Mulan deceives her family and compatriots; Simba returns to the pride lands only out of royal duty; Flik imperils the colony; Marlin has no concern beyond Nemo. Disney never animates democracy or social responsibility. Disney heroes in all their wit and wisdom never seek happiness or fulfillment through commitment to improving the human condition. Instead, all Disney animated stars indicate that acting against the public interest in one's search for individual gratification is natural, legitimate, and preferred. . . .

The Realities of Fantasy

Disney is a world leader in mass entertainment implicated in the globalization of capitalism and a concerted effort to deregulate and privatize world culture. A highly proficient producer and international distributor of capitalist cultural products, Disney advances an ideological content that parallels the social and political requirements of capitalist economic activity: hierarchy, elite coercion, hyper-individualism, and social atomism.[7] In particular, Disney's animated features communicate a clear message to the world: The individual elite quest for self-gratification, adventure, and acquisition is good and just. . . .

Disney themes, characters, and animation style have been thoroughly institutionalized in practice and procedure—from the scriptwriters, animators, and technical producers, who create the actual films, to the market researchers and integrated marketing directors, who conduct product research and focus groups to spot trends and advise editors on socially sensitive issues—all are geared to maximizing corporate profits. Pixar's innovations digitally improve Disney content and productively improve Disney's market dominance. Furthermore, dominance in the production of commodified animation and its spin-offs indicates that Disney's narratives resonate with appreciative mass audiences, suggesting that Disney's hierarchical themes are also culturally acceptable, at least tacitly. Individual pleasures or meanings derived from Disney commodities reinforce, but should not be confused with, the overarching, consistent themes of self-fulfillment through consumption.

Disney's ability to market popular films and the public's delight in consuming their little pleasures can best be understood as a negotiated hegemonic activity.[8] Like modern advertising, Disney worlds are fanciful, optimistic, and tidy.[9] And like advertising, Disney has become part of everyday life, commercially and culturally institutionalized by design.[10] But in Disney's case the medium is also the advertisement. Disney products are themselves advertisements for Disney and for its ideological and cultural themes. . . .

The interpretation of Disney animation presented here is intended only as an entry to discussing Disney's vision of globalization. Understanding Disney clarifies the global intent of corporate capitalism. Without deviation Disney animates and narrates myths favorable to a corporate culture, including its own. The emerging world capitalist culture revels in the ideology distributed by Disney, an ideology that aligns the morals of every animated film to class hierarchy, thereby denigrating and dismissing solidarity, democracy,

and concern for community needs and interests. . . .

Notes

1. Michael T. Marsden and Jack Nachbar, *The Indians in the Movies: Handbook of North American Indians* (Washington, D.C.: Smithsonian Institution, 1988).

2. Ariel Dorfman and Armand Mattelart, *How to Read Donald Duck: Imperialist Ideology in the Disney Comic* (New York: International General, 1975), 89.

3. Celebration, Florida, is Disney's model perfect community located five miles from Disney World with state-of-the-art schools, pedestrian malls, and public spaces—all closely governed by the Disney Corporation.

4. Derek T. Buescher and Kent Ono, "Civilized Colonialism: Pocahontas as Neocolonial Rhetoric," *Women's Studies in Communication* 19 (1996): 117–153. (Quoted on p. 140.)

5. Keisha L. Hoerner, "Gender Roles in Disney Films: Analyzing Behaviors from Snow White to Simba." *Women's Studies in Communication* 19 (1996): 213–228. (Quoted on p. 222.)

6. Dorfman and Mattelart, *How to Read*, 35.

7. Goran Therborn, "Why Some Classes Are More Successful Than Others," *New Left Review* 138 (1983): 37–55.

8. Antonio Gramsci, *Selected Writings, 1916–1935*, ed. David Forgacs (New York: Schocken, 1988). Lee Artz and Bren Murphy, *Cultural Hegemony in the United States* (Thousand Oaks, Calif: Sage, 1990).

9. Paul J. Croce, "A Clean and Separate Space: Walt Disney in Person and Production," *Journal of Popular Culture* 23, no. 3 (1991): 91–103. (Quoted on p. 91.)

10. Pamela C. O'Brien, "The Happiest Films on Earth: A Textual and Contextual Analysis of Walt Disney's *Cinderella* and *The Little Mermaid*." *Women's Studies in Communication* 19 (1996): 155–181. (Quoted on pp. 173–75.)

48

Constructing the "New Ethnicities"

Media, Sexuality, and Diaspora Identity in the Lives of South Asian Immigrant Girls

Meenakshi Gigi Durham

To gain insight into how media narratives and images figure into the negotiation of diaspora adolescent sexuality, in this study I explored South Asian immigrant girls' experiences of coming of age among contemporary global mediascapes, through a series of interviews that brought to the surface the dynamic intersections of body politics, culture-crossing, and myths of homeland. These issues emerged in a constant interplay with the narratives of gender and sexuality in contemporary consumer-oriented teen media. . . .

In recent globalization theory, the notion of hybridization has been used to address the multiple discontinuities and meldings of global and local symbolic practices and their material implications. For diaspora women and girls, sexuality marks the locus at which competing discourses of embodiment and agency intersect, where global/local power relations play out. Deterritorialized women encounter drastic differences in the ways in which female sexuality is conceptualized and governed in different cultural contexts, and these differences have real-world physical and psychic consequences. Appadurai (1996) notes that the politics of gender and violence are deeply imbricated in global shifts and their attendant mediascapes: "as fantasies of gendered violence dominate the B-grade film industries that blanket the world . . . the honor of women becomes increasingly a surrogate for the identity of embattled communities of males" (p. 45), and female sexuality becomes an arena for power struggles.

Recent research on immigrant girls reveals that these relations of power play out in the sexual dynamics of diaspora families. For example, Espiritu (2001) found that immigrant

Filipino American families exercised a great deal of control over their daughters' sexual activity, restricting it severely, and that this "policing" led to tensions and hierarchies within the families, especially because of the differential treatment of girls and boys. Ward and Taylor (1991) found that immigrant teenagers from Vietnamese, Haitian, Hispanic and Portuguese families could not talk with their parents about sex, and that girls would be punished for evidence of sexual activity (while boys would not). Maira (2002) similarly found "a gendered double standard that is more lenient on males than females" (p. 155) among parents of second-generation immigrant South Asian youth in New York. This curtailment of girls' sexuality is tied, Maira argues, to national ideologies in which women's bodies are seen as repositories of tradition and weapons of defense against cultural violations. Gillespie (1995) made the same point in an early study of South Asian immigrant teenagers in London, noting that in this diaspora group "family honour, or izzat, ultimately depends on the chastity of daughters" (p. 152).

As Goodenow and Espin (1993) have noted, "while males are often encouraged to Americanize rather quickly, females are more frequently expected by their families to maintain traditional roles and virtues. Conflict is particularly likely to arise with regard to issues of appropriate sex role behavior and sexuality" (p. 174). Several studies indicate that female immigrants to the U.S. adapt, in general, more quickly to American sex and gender roles than men (Ghaffarian, 1989; Robinson, Ziss, Ganza, Katz, & Robinson, 1991; Tohidi, 1993); this differential adaptation tends to result in intra-familial conflict.

At the same time that immigrant families exercise rigid restraint over adolescent girls' sexuality, Western culture continues to hypersexualize girls and women of color (Parmar, 1993; Tajima, 1989; Yegenoglu, 1998). Western media promote certain displays of female sexuality—ones that call for body exposure and heterosexual voracity (McNair, 2002)—that may be in conflict with certain aspects of non-Western cultural conventions for women, while resonating with the desire for sexual agency that contemporary young women seek. . . .

All of the girls [who participated in this study] noted that their parents had either strict limits or actual prohibitions on dating and interactions with boys. These limits extended to restrictions over the girls' interactions with "American" (non-Indian) girl friends. The restrictions, the girls believed, had to do with parental fears of the possibility of sexual misbehaviors as well as other forms of delinquency, such as drug abuse or drinking. These fears played out in the form of a "discipline of the body" that extended to clothing and demeanor, and that was related to issues of sexuality.

Malini: They won't let us wear, like, short skirts or tank tops . . .

Kiran: I guess they think boys will look at us or something.

While tensions with parents are a common aspect of adolescence, not unique to the immigrant experience, these conflicts became more acute with regard to culturally specific issues. For example, all three 15-year-olds were involved in an ongoing debate with their parents about attending their school's junior prom the following year. The Indian parents had all forbidden their daughters to attend, because, the girls said, of their fears of an unfamiliar cultural ritual, understood only through salacious media frames. As Divya noted, "I can't go to prom because of what they think might happen," a view supported by Ria.

Ria: I know I'll go. I know I'm going to go. I know I'm going to go. With a boy. But my parents are like, I don't want you to go because of what's going to happen after the dance.

Researcher: What do they think is going to happen after the prom?

Ria: We're going to get all drunk and get a hotel room and have sex.

Malini: That is such a teenage movie stereotype!

Ria: I know! That's what's in all the movies about the prom, but it isn't what everybody does!

Further discussion emphasized parental fears of sexual transgressions that were, the girls believed, based on media stereotypes.

Divya: We are not allowed to go to dances because they're afraid of things that might happen. If a guy calls and my dad answers the phone and he asks to speak to me, I will hear a whole series of questions—"Who is that? What did he want? Why is he calling you?"—Oh my god, it's so crazy. And like dances . . . my mom, I don't think she cares, but my dad . . . they ask about them, and find out what we did and they don't trust me, or, I don't know, they trust me but they think I'll be tempted by drugs or alcohol and all that . . . They think that, "oh my god, everybody's doing it and she's going to get hooked on it too."

All of the girls claimed that they were on the whole prohibited from attending parties and other social events with peers, even those organized by their schools. As Ria explained,

My parents, they don't want me to go to dances. Because there's all these stories

about robberies and guns and alcohol and stuff at like schools, and like pot and stuff. My parents always ask me questions when I come home and before I go. They ask me stuff like, "was anybody smoking? Was anybody doing drugs? Was anybody in the bathroom most of the time? Did anybody come out looking funny?" Stuff like that. And I'm like, "No! Believe me! There was nothing like that!" and they go, "Do you hang out with anybody who does bad stuff?" And I'm like, "no. I don't hang out with people like that." I'll be like, "mom, why does it matter?" . . . and it really gets on my nerves. I feel like they don't trust me at all.

The girls chalked some of these restrictions up to cultural differences, but they also pinpointed the media as key factors in this parental dictum:

Malini: They never went to a prom, they don't know about things here, and they believe what's in the movies . . .

Divya: Everybody knows that those movies are nothing like real life! High school is never like that! But I think our parents believe it.

In fact, the girls perceived their parents to rely on media characterizations of American high school life in the absence of first-hand experience of it. As they pointed out, their parents were unfamiliar with the realities of the U.S. secondary school experience and so obtained their information from largely mediated sources, which the girls dismissed as unrealistic and exaggerated. . . .

Media scripts of adolescent sexuality as a crisis were identified by the girls as being particularly influential in guiding parental restrictions over the girls' activities.

Lekha: Another thing is teen pregnancy. I mean, yeah, there's a really high teen pregnancy birth rate and like all that stuff, and yeah it's pathetic, and I would never ever dream of doing that. But my parents like say, when they see commercials like that or TV shows about teens having sex, they're like, "Do you know anybody who does this? Do you do this?" and they like think I'm the worst person in the world when it comes to sex.

Kiran: They think that everything on TV totally applies to you. . . .

As Appadurai (1996) observes, the media offer a furious flow of images and texts in which reality and fantasy are mixed, and

the farther away . . . audiences are from the direct experience of metropolitan life, the more likely they are to construct imagined worlds that are chimerical, aesthetic, even fantastic objects, particularly if assessed by the criteria of some other perspective . . . (p. 35)

In these scenarios, the girls' perspectives and experiences collided with their parents' media-derived understandings of the world of the American teenager. Yet the girls themselves consumed mainstream media; while they saw themselves as more media-savvy and sophisticated than their parents, their consumption patterns indicated a different kind of reliance on media scripts, particularly of gender and sexual behavior.

Crossing Pop Culture Borders

Divya and Lekha self-defined as the heaviest users of mainstream media. Both confessed to enjoying mainstream movies and television shows. Divya said she listened to pop music, especially the Backstreet Boys and 'N Sync, but none of the others shared

those interests, which at the time of the interviews enjoyed enormous popularity among teenagers.

The other girls said they did not watch television or movies, except for the TV sitcom *Friends,* which all five girls watched regularly, participating in a fan culture that they shared with "American" friends at school. They enjoyed the show so much that they bought and exchanged DVDs of different episodes, but they consistently characterized themselves as critical viewers:

Ria: Last year I really got into the show *Friends.* Which I guess is unrealistic and I know is so stupid and stereotypical but I'm not really influenced by it, if you want to talk about media influences . . . but, I don't know, I just love watching it, I love like how fun they are and how much fun they have . . .

Divya: Sometimes they're really stupid, but it isn't as bad as *Dawson's Creek.*

Malini: Like *Dawson's Creek* is so retarded. It's just about a bunch of teens, and they do this typical teen stuff, and none of it is real . . . And I guess we like watching the stupid chick flicks, but not because we think it's real or we want to do it . . .

Ria: We think it's funny and hopefully we're not influenced by it.

Malini: We are not at all.

Again, the girls believed their own oppositional decoding of the television text was diametrically opposed to their parents' dominant reading; the latter, they felt, was unfairly transferred to their own reception of the texts.

Ria: On *Friends* they're always sleeping with different guys, and hopefully I'll never, ever do that. I don't want to use that as an example of what a relationship should be.

Divya: We own DVDs of *Friends* . . . But my parents are worried about it. They think, if they see me watching *Friends*, "oh my God, she's watching this, and she'll think they're role models, and she's going to go do all these things" . . . but it's, like, no.

Kiran: Yeah, I asked my mom to watch it with me once, and it happened to be an episode all about like, sexual stuff, and I guess it kind of revolved around sex, but not so much that that was all they talked about, and my mom was like, "oh, so you like watching this because it's all about sex" . . . [Laughter]

A significant common theme that emerged in terms of media use was the girls' critique of, and dissociation from, what they declared to be "American" media, which seemed to translate as "white mainstream" popular culture. *Friends* was the only American television show they admitted to watching regularly; while they said they enjoyed the show because it was "fun," they were dubious about their own susceptibility to the ways of life it espoused, and their use of the show was partly a matter of communicatory utility: they watched it in order to be able to converse with non-Indian peers at school. As Ria explained, "At school, if you don't have anything else to talk about, it's like, 'Oh, did you see this movie, or did you watch the Grammys or last night's *Friends?*'"

On the other hand, the girls were avid consumers of Indian popular culture, which they actively imported into their lives in various ways. They rented Indian (usually Hindi-language) movies from local Indian grocery stores and restaurants, as well as acquiring them through social networks, they downloaded Indian pop music from the Internet, and they

attended Indian movies at local showings. Music was an important arena of cultural consumption for all five of the girls; their musical tastes varied somewhat, as did the meanings they accorded to their listening practices. But all five girls expressed a predilection for Indian popular music, which was closely related to film watching.

Malini: All the CDs I own are Indian CDs, and that's all I ever listen to. All I ever listen to are Indian soundtracks and stuff, and that's what I like. It has to have a good downbeat and the words have to make sense.

Researcher: Where do you get it?

Malini: We download it off the Internet.

Ria: I *love* Hindi film songs. I *love* Hindi films songs. Even though, like, I don't even know what they mean—I mean I can understand some things, but sometimes I'm like, um, I don't know what they're saying, but I like the beat and I always end up dancing to them and stuff like that. I don't know, they're just cool, they're just better than American songs. I love listening to them.

Researcher: Do you watch the movies, too, that the songs are from?

Girls: Yeah.

Lekha: All of our . . . like my mom's friends with all these Indian people . . . like they'll all get Indian movies and we share them . . .

Researcher: Do you get together and watch them?

Girls: Yeah, we do.

Divya: I love Indian movies.

The girls' embrace of "Bollywood" films and pop culture typifies contemporary trends. Indian films are currently enjoying burgeoning popularity in the West, but their global distribution has been great for many years, particularly in the Middle East and Europe; the Indian motion picture industry produces some 800 films a year, outstripping Hollywood in its productivity and destabilizing traditional notions of West-to-East cultural and monetary flows (Aftab, 2002; Chute, 2002; Cieko, 2001; La Ferla, 2002; Murphy, 2001; Passage from India, 2000). Aftab (2002) notes that the biggest audience for Indian pop culture has, of late, been so-called "NRIs," or nonresident Indians, loosely defined as anyone of Indian heritage living outside of India. He points out that even people born abroad to Indian parents self-identify as NRIs, which, he says, "suggests that the term Indian denotes a mental rather than a physical state, the community joined up not so much by geography as by a web of shared cultural influences" (Aftab, 2002, p. 92). In Kaleem's analysis, Indian cinema is a key factor in this identificatory cultural web. In this study, too, Indian cinema and its music ranked high as a source of cultural identification.

But the girls were clear that they did not see Indian movies as any more realistic than American ones; cinema texts, for them, offered social constructions that marked the fantastic extremes of the two cultures:

Ria: The movies are not about Indian culture. It's Indian people's fantasies. Because in the movies all those people are rich and they're all, like, they always wear clothes like we do, in fact they wear shorter clothes and more expensive, it's always like a fashion show—they don't really wear Indian clothes.

Malini: I think soon enough Indian movies and American movies are going to be identical.

Significantly, while the girls partly saw Indian films as having the same sort of communicatory utility as *Friends,* they also regarded them as connecting them with the Indian community. Ria said:

The movies give us something to talk about with other Indian people, I guess. They can make us feel more like part of an Indian community, the way Bal Vihar[1] does too.

Their valorization of Indian popular culture was a marker of their need to connect to an India that was, for them, an imaginary world, as distant and unfamiliar as their American school experiences were to their parents. They were largely uncritical of Indian films and music, refusing to dismiss them as "stupid" or "retarded," as they had American cultural texts. In this, their orientation to a diasporic homeland was one of affirmation and longing. . . .

The girls saw a different role in their lives for the cinema of the South Asian diaspora. Familiar with such films as Mira Nair's *Mississippi Masala,* Gurinder Chadha's *Bend It Like Beckham,* and Piyush Dinker Pandya's *American Desi,* they expressed an emotional connection with these films that was distinctly different from the ways in which they related to other media.

Ria: If there's a film like that playing in town, I'll go see it before I go see anything else. It's like they're about us.

Malini: Those kinds of movies are more real than any others . . . I mean. I know they're exaggerations, too, but they are familiar situations.

Ria: They're sort of like inside jokes. We get them.

The girls all singled out the films' narratives of love and sex, referring specifically to the taboo relationships between Indian girls and men of different racial/cultural backgrounds in both *Bend It*

Like Beckham and *Mississippi Masala.* They identified these storylines as salient to their interests. All five girls said they envisioned eventually falling in love with and marrying men—what Malini described as a "Western marriage"—and some of the girls were certain that such a move would precipitate conflicts with their parents, an extension of the frictions they were dealing with as teenagers. Yet in a sense, these diasporic media offered hope. The girls often watched these films with their parents, and sometimes the narratives opened up topics of discussion that eased the cultural chasms between them. "My dad hates *American Desi,*" said Kiran. "He thinks we are laughing at him, when we laugh at the Indian accents and everything. But my mom likes it and we've had a lot of good discussions about what Indian girls are supposed to be like, and stuff like that." Lekha, on the other hand, found that these films further reinforced her parents' resistance to and fear of Western culture. "They think I'm about to fall in love with or sleep with every white guy who comes along. They really have no clue."

Conclusions: Media, Culture, and Difference

Overall, the girls saw themselves as outsiders to both of the spheres they inhabited; they did not self-identify as American, though all of them had been raised in the U.S. and held citizenship. They did classify themselves as Indian, but recognized that their Indianness differed from that of their parents. In fact, the issues of sexuality that marked the divisions between themselves and their parents also demarcated lines of difference between themselves and their American peers. Their grappling with these issues of culture and difference vis-à-vis the media environment demanded the exercise of an imaginative agency in carving out a space of gender/sexual identity. As two of the girls observed:

Ria: I'm figuring things out for myself. The way we have to think about this stuff is different. It's nothing like the relationships on TV, where like the popular guy and the popular girl get together . . . never in my life would I imagine that the way things are on TV are real.

Divya: When I talk to my friends about like certain things, I've even talked to guy friends about this, I've told them I think sex before marriage is wrong, and I don't want to drink. I don't want to do drugs, and they understand that, and some of them feel the same way, they accept it. And some of my other friends—I'm surprised that they can be so stupid when it comes to these things. But we, all of us here, we have to think about these things in a different way, because of Indian values and all that . . . We can talk to each other.

A number of scholars have commented on the complicated politics of race that position Indian American identities as being something between "near white" and "near black" (Maira, 1998; Mazumdar, 1989; Okihiro, 1994). Sunaina Maira's studies of second-generation Indian American youth and the New York club scene suggest that club "remix" music, which combines traditional Indian rhythms with rap, is an attempt by these youth "to mediate between the expectations of immigrant parents and those of mainstream American culture, by trying to integrate signs of belonging to both worlds" (1998, p. 360).

By contrast, the girls in this study saw both Indian and American popular culture as marking the boundaries of those two worlds, neither of which they claimed as their milieu. Rather than attempting to find a place in both cultural spheres, they recognized the need to assert a new identity position that, in a sense, rejected the options offered by Indian as well as

American media texts. As consumers, therefore, their textual readings involve a radical questioning of the sexual mores instantiated by the television shows, films, and popular music they consumed. . . .

A number of studies indicate that viewers who are socially marginalized are better able to read media oppositionally than mainstream audiences (see Bobo, 1995; Cohen, 1991; Lind, 1996; Morley, 1992). Given this, it would be a mistake to dismiss the girls' critiques of the texts as naïve or unthinking: their recognition of the identity politics at play speaks to a different interpretation of their viewing positions. . . . The girls' lives at home and at school are circumscribed and colored by the cross cultural currents that traverse them, and their experiences in these "border zones" of youth culture are not represented in the mainstream media.

In contrast, the cinema of the diaspora, with its themes of inter-ethnic love and romance within and outside of the family sphere, offered a framework that resonated with the girls. Perhaps this is because the diaspora films encapsulate and explore the themes of cultural hybridization that the girls are negotiating in their daily lives. If we think of hybridization in terms of the interlacing of the global and the local, a way of understanding the symbolic and material collisions and fusions that mark the new global landscape, then these cinematic representations offer a cultural form in which the seemingly irreconcilable differences between cultures are articulated and worked out. Monocultural forms, by contrast, as the girls observed, mark the poles and never engage in analyses of the complexities of cultural globalization. In representing sexuality, in particular, the micropolitics of cultural hybridity are invisible and therefore untenable. . . .

For the girls in this study, sexual self-identification is a political project that is articulated to gender, race, and culture. Inherent in it is a critique of the dominant discourses of assimilation, that would draw them into the culturally fetishized role of the hypersexual woman of color, and a concomitant critique of the essentialized, marginal sexual script of the Indian immigrant with its "fantasies of sexual purity and fears of polluting seductiveness [that] are part of a larger ideology of ethnic authenticity at work" in its popular culture forms (Maira, 1998, p. 361). In deploying these critiques, these adolescent girls create the potential for new sexual identities that have emancipatory possibilities for them as girls in-between, or girls embarking on the project of forging new ethnicities in the interstitial cultural spaces that allow for new imaginings of gender and sexuality.

Note

1. Bal Vihar refers to the Hindu religious educational program that three of the girls (Ria, Kiran, and Divya) attended.

References

Aftab, K. (2002). Brown: The new black! Bollywood in Britain, *Critical Quarterly*, *44*, 88–98.

Appadurai. A. (1996). *Modernity at large: Cultural dimensions of globalization.* Minneapolis: University of Minnesota Press.

Bobo, J. (1995). *Black women as cultural readers.* New York: Columbia University Press.

Chute, D. (2002). The road to Bollywood. *Film Comment, 38,* 36.

Cieko, A. (2001). Superhit hunk heroes for sale: Globalization and Bollywood's gender politics. *Asian Journal of Communication, 11,* 121–143.

Cohen, J. R. (1991). The "relevance" of cultural identity in audiences' interpretations of mass media. *Critical Studies in Mass Communication, 8,* 442–454.

Espiritu, Y. L. (2001). "We don't sleep around like white girls do": Family, culture, and gender in Filipina Americans' lives. *Signs, 26,* 415–440.

Ghaffarian, S. (1989). *The acculturation of Iranians in the United States and the implications for mental health.* Unpublished doctoral dissertation, California School of Professional Psychology, Los Angeles.

Gillespie, M. (1995). *Television, ethnicity and cultural change.* New York: Routledge.

Goodenow, C., & Espin, O. M. (1993). Identity choices in immigrant adolescent females. *Adolescence, 28*(109), 173–184.

La Ferla, R. (2002, May 5). Kitsch with a niche: Bollywood chic finds a home. *New York Times,* p. K1.

Lind, R. A. (1996). Diverse interpretations: The "relevance" of race in the construction of meaning in, and the evaluation of, a television news story. *Howard Journal of Communication, 7,* 53–74.

Maira, S. (1998). Desis reprazent: Bhangra remix and hip hop in New York City. *Postcolonial Studies, 1,* 357–370.

Maira, S. (2002). *Desis in the house: Indian American youth culture in New York City.* Philadelphia: Temple University Press.

Mazumdar, S. (1989). Racist responses to racism: The Aryan myth and South Asians in the United States. *South Asia Bulletin, 9,* 47–55.

McNair, B. (2002). *Striptease culture: Sex, media, and the democratisation of desire.* Routledge: London and New York.

Morley, D. (1992). *Television audiences and cultural studies.* New York: Routledge.

Murphy, D. E. (2001, April 27). A little bit of Hollywood starring India. *New York Times,* p. B1.

Okihiro, G. Y. (1994). Is yellow black or white? In G. Y. Okihiro (Ed.), *Margins and mainstreams: Asians in American history and culture* (pp. 31–63). Seattle: University of Washington Press.

Parmar, P. (1993). That moment of emergence. In M. Gever, J. Greyson, & P. Parmar (Eds.), *Queer looks: Perspectives on lesbian and gay film and video* (pp. 3–11). New York: Routledge.

Passage from India. (2000, October 21). *The Economist, 357*(8193), 80.

Robinson, I., Ziss, K., Ganza, B., Katz, S., & Robinson, E. (1991). Twenty years of the sexual revolution, 1965–1985: An update. *Journal of Marriage and the Family, 53,* 216–220.

Tajima, R. E. (1989). Lotus blossoms don't bleed: Images of Asian women. In Asian Women United of California (Eds.), *Making waves: An anthology of writings by and about Asian American women* (pp. 308–317). Boston: Beacon.

Tohidi, N. (1993). Iranian women and gender relations in Los Angeles. In R. Kelley, J. Friedlander, & A. Colby (Eds.), *Irangeles: Iranians in Los Angeles* (pp. 175–217). Berkeley: University of California Press.

Ward, J. V., & Taylor, J. M. (1991). Sexuality education for immigrant minority teenagers: Developing a culturally appropriate curriculum. In J. Irvine (Ed.), *Sexual cultures and the construction of adolescent identities* (pp. 51–68). Philadelphia: Temple University Press.

Yegenoglu, M. (1998). *Colonial fantasies: Toward a feminist reading of Orientalism.* Cambridge, UK: Cambridge University Press.

49

HIV on TV

Conversations With Young Gay Men

Kathleen P. Farrell

A s the current HIV epidemic in the United States continues to affect gay communities, it is important to understand how young gay and bisexual men understand this phenomenon in relation to themselves, their friends, and their futures. While in colleges and universities across the country, oftentimes far from large, established gay communities such as in New York City and San Francisco, many young gay men have never met anyone living with, or directly affected by, HIV. Instead, these students only have access to media and popular culture representations of people with HIV and the HIV epidemic, more generally.

This study draws on a unique storyline from the popular groundbreaking series, *Queer as Folk,* to address the different ways that several groups of undergraduate gay males make sense of HIV and its representation in a fictional TV storyline. This research is important since it adds to the minimal published accounts of televised HIV content by moving past textual analysis and, instead, learning from audience members how these representations are understood by them. In addition to gaining a better understanding of how some gay audiences consume these HIV related stories and incorporate them into their own lives, these findings also illuminate the possibilities for HIV prevention through entertaining television programs that appeal to young nonheterosexual audiences, as well as the possibility of focus group research as a prevention source in and of itself. . . .

A Brief History of HIV on TV

On 7 July 1981, CNN aired a story on Kaposi's sarcoma and marked the first time the syndrome, later known as AIDS, was mentioned on TV (Kinsella, 1989: 260). Two and a half years later, *St. Elsewhere* became the first prime-time drama to include a story of a gay

From Kathleen P. Farrell, "HIV On TV: Conversations with Young Gay Men." *Sexualities* (2006), 9(2), 193–213. Reprinted with permission of SAGE Publications, Ltd.

or bisexual man with AIDS, although the next gay-themed AIDS drama did not air until late 1985. During this time, networks reportedly feared that AIDS dramas would encourage backlash from both gay rights groups and right-wing activists and chose, instead, to deal with AIDS on talk shows and news programs, where audiences were often shown depictions of emaciated AIDS patients dying in hospital rooms. However, when NBC's *An Early Frost* (1985), the first TV movie to focus on AIDS, aired, it received exceptional ratings and even Emmy nominations. The timing was perfect: AIDS was headline news following Rock Hudson's confirmation of infection, and the movie provided accurate medical facts to millions of viewers who knew little of the emerging epidemic. Also around this time, ABC and CBS were working on TV movie proposals about young gay men and AIDS (Capsuto, 2000).

While NBC treated *An Early Frost* as 'a prestige piece', some gay activists criticized the film and subsequent TV AIDS dramas featured throughout the late 1980s and early 1990s for their consistent shortcomings (Capsuto, 2000; Gross, 2001; Netzhammer and Shamp, 1994; Russo, 1987; Seidman, 2002). Gross (2001) describes gay characters on television, in general, as primarily being defined by their problems and absent from any sort of larger gay culture, and these AIDS stories were no exceptions. In fact, gay and bisexual male characters with AIDS at this time were always classified by their illness, used as a 'dramatic device'.[1] In addition, a repeated feature of all TV AIDS dramas was a focus on individual people who have AIDS, and perhaps their heterosexual family, but with no recognition of gay communities or AIDS activists (Gross, 2001). Gross (2001) argues that this type of representation suggests that people with AIDS are abandoned until their birth family comes and saves them from being alone. *An Early Frost* is one such film: it focuses on how a heterosexual family deals with

their son being forced out of the closet by AIDS, but little consideration is given to the fact that this is happening to their son, *not them*, and the film does not include any attention to how this young man struggles with his illness in his own circle of friends (Russo, 1987).

Critics also note how AIDS dramas of this time period, whether 'about' gay men or not, were sanitized, often portraying 'white people with bad luck' (Gross, 2001: 144). A newspaper editorial from 1988 explains, '[o]n TV, AIDS is primarily a disease of middle-class white children, who get it from blood transfusions, and, secondarily, of middle-class white hetero sexuals, who get it from prostitutes, and middle-class white homosexuals, who get it from a single lover who committed a single indiscretion.'[2] These were the dramas that depicted the innocent victims of AIDS and their families, and were primarily 'message' scripts with lessons like 'Be nice to people with AIDS' and 'Protect yourself from HIV', reminding audiences to be compassionate to these 'victims' (Capsuto, 2000). On the other hand, Gross (2001) describes an (also unfavorable) alternative to this popular family-centered model—those films that portrayed 'AIDS villains': people who carelessly or deliberately place others at risk of becoming infected. One example, from 1988, is *Midnight Caller*, a dramatic series on NBC, which featured an episode with a bisexual man who intentionally spreads HIV to numerous unsuspecting sexual partners.

Since the 1980s, the presence of HIV on TV has been a relatively rare event, especially on shows that may appeal specifically to young gay audiences. Although Hollywood films continue to address HIV on the big screen, in such films as *Philadelphia* (1993) and the more recent *The Hours* (2002), HIV has become relegated on television to daytime programming with audiences containing large numbers of heterosexual female viewers, such as afternoon soap operas, or health/ scientific news stories on the evening news. While gay characters, in general, have become more commonplace on network television, including prime-time sitcoms, dramas, and reality TV programs, there continues to be an absence of HIV-positive gay men. Additionally, when one of these characters does appear, he is usually portrayed as one single gay person with HIV among his heterosexual and HIV-negative friends and family.

The Text: *Queer as Folk*

Queer as Folk is a weekly television drama [U.S. run was from 2001 to 2006], and one-time highest rated program on the premium cable network, Showtime. Although *Queer as Folk* centers on a group of middle-class white characters (a criticism offered by both activists and focus group participants), it also deserves recognition for its departure from the patterns of televised AIDS stories from the last two decades.

The show originated in Britain, and its American counterpart was the first television drama in the USA to deal explicitly with queer culture: almost all its primary characters are gay men and lesbians who are active members of a larger queer community including gay nightclubs and bars, stores, gyms and even gay-themed restaurants. In addition, the characters often come into contact with other gay people at their work and even on the street. In fact, one character is an advertising executive who frequently wins clients by creating advertisements that are meant to appeal specifically to gay audiences. The main characters of the show are not ashamed of their sexuality—they lead complex lives with good days as well as bad days; bad days that sometimes involve dealing with homophobia from the larger society without being portrayed as victims. Instead, this group of characters leads gay-affirming lives that center on their close friendships with one another. Although it received less controversy than initially expected, *Queer as Folk* was often considered problematic by both gay and straight audiences primarily in reaction to the abundance and explicitness of its sex scenes. Some audiences seemed to be uncomfortable with the frankness of these scenes, while other audiences criticized the stereotypical representations of gay men as hanging out in dance clubs looking for sex. Supporters of the show often argue that *Queer as Folk* simply offered a representation of one aspect of gay culture, and felt that the storylines were compelling and true to life.

Unlike television's attention to HIV in the late 1980s as an issue for the movie of the week, the American *Queer as Folk* incorporates HIV storylines throughout the series. In fact, HIV does not appear as a special dramatic topic that the show's characters encounter in one or two heart-felt episodes, but rather, it is presented simply, and matter-of-factly, as one problem with which these characters must struggle in the context of other storylines about gay bashing, workplace discrimination, and coming out to family members. Specifically, *Queer as Folk* has included stories of its leading characters being tested for the virus; an episode where a good friend of a main character dies of AIDS; an episode centered on raising money for an AIDS-care organization; and several other explicit references to condom use to protect from sexually transmitted diseases, including HIV. Also, quite notably, one of the featured characters, although not a lead role, is the uncle of the primary character Michael, Vic, who has been living with AIDS for over a decade. Although the audience is sometimes reminded that Vic has AIDS, it is not the central concern in most of his scenes. Instead, he is Michael's uncle, an older gay man who happens to have AIDS.

The Current Project

This project focuses on one of the HIV-related storylines from the second season, in which the primary character, Michael, begins to date Ben, who is HIV-positive. Audience members watch as Michael struggles to negotiate his feelings for someone with HIV, while members of his support system voice their opposition to the relationship, citing their fear that Michael will also become infected. In the story, Ben's HIV status is revealed to Michael soon after they kiss on their first official date. Michael chooses not to advance the sexual contact that night, but continues to date Ben, despite fierce confrontations with his good friend, Ted, and his mother, Debbie. When Michael and Ben are about to have sex for the first time, Michael sees Ben's HIV medications and gets too scared about the possibility of becoming infected, causing him to end the relationship with Ben.[3] However, later in the season, Michael has realized the extent of his romantic feelings for Ben, and fights to resume their relationship. Their relationship continues throughout the series, as we see them become a sexually intimate couple and work to gain approval from Debbie and Ted. We also see Ben, sick with an HIV-related complication, go to the hospital. Ultimately, he recovers and, at the end of the season, his relationship with Michael is going strong, supported by both Debbie and Ted. Michael has not become infected with the virus.

As an HIV story that focuses on the relationship between two gay men surrounded by family, gay friends and a larger gay culture, the romance of Michael and Ben is exceptional and worthy of investigation. This couple continues to be sexual, in spite of HIV (an occurrence which is rare for any gay couple on TV), and their participation in the show is not limited to the HIV aspect of their relationship. Instead, there are many accounts of Michael and Ben doing everyday things, without any mention of Ben's HIV status or of Michael's reaction and negotiations of it. This HIV storyline from *Queer as Folk*, then, provides a unique opportunity to investigate the various ways that audiences make sense of HIV and its dramatic representation. Primarily, I wanted to learn how gay undergraduate males engage with and discuss the fictional television portrayal of a serodiscordant gay couple (that is, mismatched HIV status) who are struggling with their relationship. How are these young men making sense of HIV on TV, and in their own lives?

Method

In order to gain access to the perspectives of *Queer as Folk* audience members, I organized a series of small focus groups. Each group meeting lasted 3–4 hours and took place in a seminar/conference room or an empty classroom. In these groups participants were asked to watch three separate 20-minute collections of edited clips from the second season of the U.S. *Queer as Folk*. The clips were organized so that Ben and Michael's relationship was highlighted, although some other sequences from the series were also included. After viewing each 20-minute segment, I turned the discussion over to the participants to talk about whatever interested them the most, and I recorded these interactions on audiotapes. Although I guided the conversations, and often interjected with probing follow-up questions (such as 'What did you think of that scene?' or 'Can you tell me more about why you think that?'), most of the talk took place among the focus group members and centered on their opinions of the stories and characters that they viewed. After transcribing these tapes, I carefully reviewed the conversations and coded them according to emergent themes. These focus groups proved to be a very useful way to collect rich data from my study participants. . . .

Results

TALKING ABOUT HIV (ON TV)

Like all socially constructed phenomena, the meaning of HIV in society, and in the lives of the young men I talked with, can be complex and multi-layered. In this chapter I will address several of the primary themes relating to HIV that emerged from our focus group meetings: the way that HIV was most often described in the context of our discussions (what I refer to as the social definition of HIV); how most participants recognized that the HIV storyline from *Queer as Folk* is a sharp departure from previous televised representations of HIV and their opinions of this shift; the attitudes toward condom use and safe-sex behavior in the real lives of the focus group members; as well as the safe-sex messages they perceive this TV show to be imparting. Overall, these discussions expose the many ways that these young men are making meaning of this HIV storyline in relation to their own lives and their understanding of gay culture. . . .

Despite reporting that HIV awareness and prevention has become a routine aspect of their sexual existence, study participants did not express any level of comfort or indifference when discussing their ordinary, everyday negotiations of HIV. Instead, participants referred to asking a potential sex partner's HIV status as 'daunting', 'a very sensitive situation', and one focus group member reported that asking someone's HIV status 'somehow seems like it would be rude'. Moreover, study participants did not share an understanding of HIV as a chronic illness, rather than a fatal disease.

On *Queer as Folk*, Ben, who is HIV-positive, refers to revealing his HIV status to Michael as 'dropping a bomb'. . . . Many of the focus group participants were surprised when Michael chose to continue dating Ben, and most agreed that, while Ben appeared to be a great match for Michael before he 'dropped the bomb', once his HIV status was known, Ben's attractiveness rating dropped also:

Pete: When I first heard it I guess I was disappointed because his perfect image was destroyed. And, you know, before that, he was seen as perfect: all the men were looking at him, they all wanted him, but after this happened, he's not as perfect anymore.

George: [referring to Ben's HIV status] That's a deal breaker.

While some focus group members did not fully subscribe to the thinking presented here, it became very clear through our discussions that the exposure many of these young men have had to HIV scared them. Regardless of whether participants supported Michael and Ben's relationship or not, they all expressed fear of contracting HIV; they all thought that life, as they know it, would change completely. Since all but five of the focus group participants reported that they have never known anyone, in their real lives, who is directly affected by, or infected with, HIV, it seems logical that HIV information, whether viewed in prevention literature, in schools or through the mass media, has contributed to an understanding of HIV as something extraordinary, negative and frightening. This social definition of HIV was shared by all members of my focus groups.

HIV ON TV IN 2003: LIFE WITH HIV

Many times throughout my research, participants noted how the depiction of Ben, as a character *living* with HIV, is groundbreaking. . . .

We never really see this side of the happy HIV person, that's kind of sad . . . I think it's actually a great thing that they have it on a television show, have someone talk about HIV and their life and not talk about just the end part of the cycle, rather than the middle part—about living their life and . . . that they are able to live a healthy life having AIDS, having a relationship . . . I think it's great and I really enjoy, I love, watching it.

. . . John, impressed with Ben's character not being celibate, said:

I think it is an interesting twist considering the person with AIDS [wants to have sex] which is different 'cause that's something, that isn't something, like a requirement that you'd expect someone with AIDS to have . . . I thought that was a pretty good portrayal of someone with AIDS because it shows them as being sexual people.

Pete elaborated on this by explaining that Ben, as a young, good-looking and physically fit HIV-positive character, challenges stereotypical television portrayals of people with HIV/AIDS:

I guess just the fact that he was seen as perfect sends the message that not all people with HIV are old, nasty, gay men that look sickly and everything. . . .

While academic and medical reports of HIV emphasize this fact, that HIV-positive people can live in excellent health and form for decades, study participants point out that many audience members may not be aware of this fact, and that their comprehension of HIV-positive people would be expanded through these characters. . . .

Repeatedly, focus group members described how *Queer as Folk* extended their knowledge of *people* with HIV, and criticized their formal schooling for not addressing these issues:

Mike: Like, you learn about it [HIV/ AIDS] in school, you learn about it, whatever, and it's . . . you

learned about the virus, you didn't learn about the people.

Pete: When people do learn about AIDS prevention and everything, you just are told like, 'ok, this could happen to you, and so and so and so, and you can get sick, and you'll have to take medicine, whatever,' but they don't actually tell you what happens, how you live your life and how you . . . the medical terms and everything.

. . . Generally, focus group members felt that TV shows like this help people understand that people living with HIV are living with 'one more thing to deal with,' instead of always being consumed with the possibility of death or illness. Repeatedly many of these young men reported that these were new ideas for them; they had not really considered HIV-positive people as living 'regular lives', dating HIV-negative people, promoting casual sex to their friends (as opposed to warning them of the dangers and suggesting that casual sex will inevitably lead to HIV infection), and not being particularly preachy about HIV awareness. In these ways, *Queer as Folk* has increased their understanding of the social dimensions of HIV.

Beyond what they watched on-screen, participants' knowledge about HIV was also transformed through their involvement in these focus groups. In fact, misconceptions about how HIV is transmitted, the medical implications of a positive HIV test result, and other incorrect assumptions regarding the virus and its treatment, were voiced and frequently dismantled during these focus group meetings. . . .

CONDOM USE: AN ISSUE OF TRUST

Consistently, focus group participants reported that condom use is required in order for them to have sex whenever a partner's HIV status is uncertain. Here, George describes what he was thinking, during a scene in which two of the main characters accidentally walk into a party and immediately leave, disapprovingly, when they see that many attendees were having unprotected sex:

It was just shocking, because you, for us, well, for me, anyway, you're just always going to have the image of having a condom. Like always. Like, it's like health or whatever, but you know [you need] to have a condom . . . [having sex without a condom] that's not really cool.

. . . By openly enforcing the notion that condoms are essential, focus group members are creating and recreating the sexual norms which pertain to their lives. *Queer as Folk,* as a TV show, is also contributing to these sexual scripts by including storylines containing explicit references to condom use, and by communicating, through the use of fictional characters, that unprotected sex is improper. In the context of these focus groups, both the participants and the TV show are promoting lessons about consistent condom use, by criticizing men who do not use them and praising those who do.

In reference to why some gay men do not use condoms regularly, explanations such as 'ignorance', 'stupidity', and 'because some people just don't seem to be getting it' were offered by most focus group members. However, while condom vigilance initially was reported as essential, some participants later revealed that exceptions to this rule are acceptable [when] carried out in the context of a 'serious' relationship in which the HIV status of both partners is known, or, in one participant's terminology, when he knows that his partner is 'clean'. Furthermore, focus group discussions uncovered that having sex without a condom, in a long-term romantic relationship, is the 'ultimate sign of trust' for some of these young men:

Rhyse: I think part of that has to do with trust, that, the whole HIV/AIDS issue partially is one of trust, and so, in order to say that you fully trust the person you're with, well, lose the condom. You know, I mean, if you trust them that much, and they said they don't have anything, you believe them, and you're going to prove that at any cost . . . that's not to say that the words 'I love you' or that the words 'I trust you' are meaningless, but actions speak louder than words and that's a huge action.

Elliot: And, kind of going along with that, when you put your life into somebody's hands . . . that's the ultimate sign of trust. And sexual acts without a condom, is really, there's a ton of danger that goes along with that, and you're totally putting yourself out there, in the control of someone else.

This conversation took place after viewing a scene in which one primary character, Justin, discusses how his sexual relationship allows certain behaviors, such as sex without a condom, because both he and his regular partner are both HIV-negative. In this scene, Justin is noting how a serodiscordant couple, such as Ben and Michael, will never be able to engage in these activities, due to the risk of infection. Justin's partner, Brian, immediately and emphatically corrects Justin's naive statement, expressing that unprotected sex with anyone is always a bad idea. After all, Brian argues, Ben contracted HIV from unprotected sex with a serious boyfriend who was also believed to be HIV-negative.

While some focus group members agreed that Justin's partner was speaking words of wisdom, others, such as Rhyse and Elliot, quoted earlier, did not seem to be persuaded by this on-screen lesson. What is noteworthy here is the way that the fictional story imparts a message that is counter to the risky sexual practices in which some of these young men choose to engage. There is an opportunity here for the show to begin challenging audiences' ideas regarding what types of behavior are acceptable or 'safe' and in what contexts. While many of the focus group participants already subscribed to the idea of persistent condom use outside of 'serious' relationships, there is much room for change in behavioral norms regarding the strict use of condoms within these relationships. Is there potential for a TV show to provide sexual scripts that effectively communicate this necessity?

TV as Safe-Sex Education?

. . . . Although initially attracted to the show for entertainment, many focus group members recognized that this show also functions as an educator regarding many aspects of gay culture, including HIV awareness and prevention. While a few participants, including Schyler, felt some of these informative attempts were a bit 'heavy handed', 'contrived and really irritating', most other focus group members were not bothered by these messages and, instead, had only positive things to say regarding the way that the storylines were presented. However, even some of these focus group members cautioned that the safe-sex messages could easily become 'over the top' and feel 'preachy' if handled in a more focused or explicit way. The following statements by Charles and Mikey provide instructive warnings for TV stories attempting to offer informational messages regarding HIV-positive people and/or safe sex:

Charles: If they would have elaborated on that scene [regarding condom use] I'm not sure if the audience would have liked that, because it would have put too much emphasis on the suggestion that it needs to be dealt with, and like they're trying really hard to deal with this issue, you know, trying to teach a lesson.

Mikey: I think they don't overemphasize the issue, or they don't make it too out there . . . they refer to it in very brief moments, but it's not the focus of it, that's where the entertainment comes into play. When you beat down the issues such as this, not using condoms, it just gets to be boring to the person watching it.

In fact, common published critiques of media-based HIV prevention campaigns, which rely heavily on the use of Public Service Announcements (PSAs) aired during televised commercial breaks, are that these messages often do not appeal to gay audiences; they often inspire feelings of guilt within gay communities; they are frequently perceived to be insensitive or too moral; and audiences are turned off due to feeling that they are receiving a lecture (Dejong et al., 2001; Salmon, 2000; Turner, 1997). Instead, as outlined by Charles and Mikey, entertainment-based media campaigns should be designed to incorporate responsible sexual heath messages, using more subtle, positive reinforcement strategies in TV programs that appeal specifically to their target audience (Dejong et al., 2001; Keller and Brown, 2002; Steele, 1999; Turner, 1997). The challenge here is to continue entertaining, as the educational messages are being consumed. For audiences who were learning sexual scripts through their consumption of popular culture, *Queer as Folk* provided them with attractive material from which they could begin to understand the necessity of condom use. These audiences, in a sense, were seeking out these safer-sex lessons by repeatedly tuning in on a weekly basis, where their education continued. . . .

Notes

1. In *The Celluloid Closet,* Vito Russo writes, '[i]n Hollywood films . . . homosexuals have not been people; they have been a dramatic device used to shock and sell' (Russo, 1987: 248).

2. *San Jose Mercury News,* 1988, cited in Capsuto (2000).

3. Michael's decision not to continue his relationship with Ben was followed by protests from AIDS activist groups (*Larry King Live,* 2002).

References

Capsuto, S. (2000) *Alternate Channels: The Uncensored Story of Gay and Lesbian Images on Radio and Television.* New York: Ballantine Books.

Dejong, W., Wolf, R. C. and Austin, S. B. (2001) 'US Federally Funded Television Public Service Announcements (PSAs) to Prevent HIV/AIDS: A Content Analysis', *Journal of Health Communication* 6 (3): 249–63.

Gross, L. (2001) *Up From Invisibility: Lesbians, Gay Men, and the Media in America.* New York: Columbia University Press.

Keller, S. N. and Brown, J. D. (2002) 'Media Interventions to Promote Responsible Sexual Behavior', *The Journal of Sex Research* 39 (1): 67–72.

Kinsella, J. (1989) *Covering the Plague: AIDS and the American Media.* New Brunswick, NJ: Rutgers University Press.

Larry King Live (2002) Interview with Cast of *Queer as Folk.* Air date: 24 April CNN.

Netzhammer, E. C. and Shamp, S. A. (1994) 'Guilt by Association: Homosexuality and AIDS on Prime-Time Television', in R. J. Ringer (ed.) *Queer Words, Queer Images: Communication and the Construction of Homosexuality,* pp. 91–106. New York and London: New York University Press.

Russo, V. (1987) *The Celluloid Closet: Homosexuality in the Movies* (revised edn). New York: Harper & Row Publishers.

Salmon, C. T. (2000) 'Summary Report: Setting a Research Agenda for Entertainment-Education', in Centers for Disease Control and Prevention, Office of Communication, URL (retrieved September 2003): http://www.cdc.gov/communication/eersrcha.htm

Seidman, S. (2002) *Beyond the Closet: The Transformation of Gay and Lesbian Life.* New York: Routledge.

Steele, J. R. (1999) 'Teenage Sexuality and Media Practice: Factoring in the Influence of Family, Friends, and School', *The Journal of Sex Research* 36(4): 331–341.

Turner, D. C. (1997) *Risky Sex: Gay Men and HTV Prevention.* New York: Columbia University Press.

50

Video Games and Machine Dreams of Domination

John Sanbonmatsu

The computer video game has emerged in the space of a few short decades from the shadows of "geek" subcultural obscurity to become the most pervasive entertainment medium in the industrialized world. In the United States alone, an estimated 170 million people—more than half the population—play video games (John, 2009).[1] By comparison, about 75 million go each year to professional baseball games, and 39 million play chess ("National Chess Survey," 2003). In 1980, the video game industry barely existed. Today, it dwarfs almost every other media industry. Sales of video game software, hardware, and accessories totaled about $20 billion in 2009—twice what Hollywood brought in the box office that year.

If media theorist Marshall McLuhan was right, a generation ago, to say of the new mass media of his time, television, that "the medium *is* the message," what message is being signaled by the aggressive new medium of video games? What does the popularity of technologically mediated forms of play tell us about the social forces and myths shaping life today in advanced capitalist culture? Why have video games become as pervasive as they have? Might video games *play us* as much as we play them?

While some critics have depicted video games (as well as cyberspace and the new interactive digital media more generally) as liberatory phenomena—for example, praising them as spaces where players can subvert repressive gender norms by assuming fluid identities—others have argued that, far from being a utopian force in society, the video game is both a mirror of existing relations of power and authority in society and a powerful cultural force in its own right. Thus, feminists have observed that the content of video games mirrors the worldview of the White, heterosexual men who overwhelmingly create and play them, noting that exaggerated sex stereotyping, misogyny, and simulated violence against women are the norm. The vast majority of game protagonists and heroes are male, and the latter conform closely to the hegemonic norm of masculinity—the aggressive, dominating man authorized by the wider patriarchal culture (Alloway & Gilbert, 1988; Hill, n.d.). Few games model a range of female body types for players to inhabit as avatars: Women are White and young (or exoticized women of color) with unrealistic body proportions and

This piece is an original essay that was commissioned for this volume.

depicted either semi-nude or in clinging body suits (*Lara Croft*). Games like *Dead or Alive: Extreme Volleyball* are indistinguishable from soft-core pornography; others, like *Grand Theft Auto*, invite the player to exploit women sexually. Critical race theorists similarly note the prevalence of racist representations of people of color in many games. Asians are depicted as martial arts experts or sinister villains, never as political leaders, accountants, or composers; African Americans and Latinos are depicted as drug kingpins or prostitutes, not hard-working migrant laborers or professors of literature; Arabs are blood-thirsty savages and terrorists, never citizens of particular nations and cultures, or parents with children, and so on (see Chan, 2005; Leonard, 2004).

Video games are thus potent conduits of the dominant ideologies, myths, and norms of society (i.e., those most conducive to maintaining the status quo in unequal social and property relations). Like other forms of mass media, video games do more than just represent our world; they actively *shape* that world, conforming reality to particular ideologies, social expectations, and collective fantasies. As Ian Bogost (2007) observes, "The logics that drive our games make claims about who we are, how our world functions, and what we want it to become" (p. 340). The very immersive and participatory qualities of video games make them especially persuasive mechanisms of social indoctrination and control. Anyone who has careered down the virtual streets of Chicago in *Gotham Racing* or joined a platoon of Marines patrolling the dusty streets of a Middle Eastern city in *Call of Duty 2* can attest to the visceral power of the medium—the degree to which intense player involvement heightens the psychological connection between human and machine. While the industry disavows real-world connections between kids shooting virtual humans in the head and real-life mass shootings by children in our schools, that same industry, in other market sectors, brags that video games are

without peer among media in shaping human behavior and psychology. As Penny observes, "Psychotherapists employ simulation technologies precisely because they have effect in people's lives," while the Pentagon invests heavily in game simulations because of their proven effectiveness in conditioning soldiers to kill or to learn new battlefield tactics (Penny, 2004). Computer simulations are now widely used in corporate culture—by the aviation industry to train pilots, by hospital schools to teach surgical techniques, by the finance industry to simulate trading transactions, and by companies to train sales personnel in the arts of persuasion. There is no doubt, therefore, that the simulations we ourselves enact as ordinary consumers of video games are educating our senses and structuring our perceptual world too. The question is, what are we being "educated" into?

My argument is that video game culture "hails" or conditions us into an aggressive, socially destructive form of consciousness. By training the player into an *instrumentalist* conception of human thought and action—inviting him or her to conceive of the world as little more than an arena for demonstrating his or her own mastery and control—video games facilitate the ever more fateful intrusion of capitalism, technological fetishism, and masculine fantasies of domination into the fabric of daily life. At the same time, the process of "society's ingression into the psyche," as the philosopher Herbert Marcuse termed it, could not gain traction without our own tacit collusion or consent (Marcuse, 1968, p. 254). We ourselves seem to hunger for escapist forms of entertainment that restore to us, albeit only in virtual form, precisely that which many of us feel we are losing in real life—namely, a sense of our own efficacy and power in a chaotic, terrifying, and alienating world that seems increasingly out of our control. Paradoxically, however, the more we participate in simulations of life, the less involved we become in real life, forsaking those forms of speech and action that could *matter*.

War Simulation and the Militarization of Everyday Life

To frame my discussion, I want to draw on Herbert Marcuse's analysis of how media and technology serve to integrate consciousness into the circuits of capitalism and imperialism. Marcuse argued that the repression of human libidinal or instinctual needs by Western society yields ever more destructive forms of culture. As capitalism becomes more advanced, a gap opens up between, on one hand, the creative and productive forces of society, our potential to make the world a livable one, and, on the other, pathological forms of social life and behavior that are in reality quite harmful: mobilization for perpetual war, destruction of nature, and heightened aggressiveness in all arenas of life and culture. The result is "a suicidal tendency on a truly social scale" (Marcuse, 1968, p. 268). Such a system meanwhile requires a particular form of human personality or consciousness to maintain itself. Freud believed that the repression or taming of our biological instincts was the price we paid for our entry into society. The healthy human individual channels or "sublimates" his or her instinctual needs into socially productive activities—art, work, family relations, and so on. However, Marcuse argued that in the context of a pathological social order, society might cause such strain in the individual as to produce what he termed "surplus" repression, in effect taking the individual's libidinal instincts and channeling them into socially *destructive* forms.

Technology is the characteristic mechanism of such aggression. As the distillation of an "instrumentalist" mentality, technology strengthens the life-denying system and effectively shields it from possible revolt by those whom it has stripped of power and dignity. Particularly, in the sphere of mass media, the dominant culture blurs together or integrates existential opposites—death and life, killing and culture, sadism and joy. The new "unities" then get sold back to us as commodities. As Marcuse (1968) wrote,

> The brutalization of language and image, the presentation of killing, burning, and poisoning and torture inflicted upon the victims of neocolonial slaughter is made in a common-sensical, factual, sometimes humorous style which integrates these horrors with the pranks of juvenile delinquents, football contests, accidents, stock market reports, and the weatherman. (p. 259)

Marcuse's framework is helpful in revealing the hidden meaning of contemporary video game culture. For, notwithstanding the seeming diversity of video games on the market today—for example, massively multiple-player online role-playing games (MMORPGs), puzzle and educational games, driving simulations, sports and fashion games, and so on—themes of violence, aggression, and war predominate. In 2008, the three most popular new online games were *Grand Theft Auto IV; Star Wars: Force Unleashed,* a futuristic battle game; and *Fallout 3,* a futuristic first-person shooter and combat strategy game. The other top 10 online games included the violent first-person shooter war games *Gears of War 2, Call of Duty,* and *Metal Gear Solid 4: Fable II,* a fantasy adventure game in which the hero fights various dangerous enemies; *Super Smash Mario Brothers Brawl,* a Hobbesian "war of all against all," using popular animated characters; *Madden N.F.L. '09,* a complex simulation of commercial male football; and *WWE Smackdown vs. Raw '09,* an ultraviolent simulation of the misogynistic cable program, World Wrestling Entertainment, in which players inhabit the avatars of muscular male fighters and use extreme fighting techniques to kill their opponent—by setting their opponents' bodies on fire (Freierman, 2008). As this list suggests, many of the leading games are both *masculinist* and *militaristic*. To understand why, it is essential to appreciate the institutional origins of the medium in the U.S. national security state apparatus, where patriarchal dreams of "virtuous" domination and control of others materialized into functional high-tech weapons systems.

The emergence of a permanent war economy in the United States after World War II, and with it the functional integration of capitalist industry and academic institutions into cold war nuclear war planning, led to computerization and a new culture of simulation. A watershed came in 1961 when academic researchers working for the Department of Defense at M.I.T. developed a digital game called *Spacewar.* Other researchers soon grasped the military potential of combining traditional war game simulations with computerization. In the late 1970s, the Office of Naval Research established the "Theater-Level Gaming and Analysis Workshop for Force Planning," and by the early 1980s, the United States was spending many millions of dollars on computer simulations like SIMNET, which allowed dispersed participants to engage in real-time "war" over a virtual battlefield (Lenoir & Lowood, 2005). By the 1990s, finally, the Pentagon had built an elaborate network bringing together commercial video game design companies, university researchers, and U.S. military personnel to create what critics have called a "military-industrial-academic-entertainment complex."

Today, the video game is the sine qua non of modern high-tech war fighting, an indispensable tool at all stages of conflict, from recruitment (e.g., *America's Army,* a MMORPG released by the U.S. Army in 2002 and since played by millions; Nichols, 2010) through training (e.g., *Marine Doom,* the military adaptation of the FPS video game, *Doom,* which teaches soldiers to kill unreflexively) to actual battlefield use. Among today's war game centers is DARWARS, a program funded by the Defense Advanced Research Projects Agency (DARPA) for the U.S. Joint Chiefs of Staff and Marine Corps, which uses "webcentric, simulation-based trainers

[to] take advantage of widespread PC-based technology, including multi-player games, virtual worlds, intelligent agents, and online communities."[2] Meanwhile, in Afghanistan, NATO pilots trained, perhaps, at PEO STRI (the U.S. Army's Program Executive Office for Simulation, Training, and Instrumentation, headquartered in Orlando, Florida) use computer-mediated weapons to drop real munitions on real people. And in Nevada and Arizona, U.S. Air Force pilots and CIA-sponsored mercenaries remotely operate robotic Predator and Reaper drones to launch lethal missile attacks in Syria or Pakistan, 7,500 miles away.

As Marcuse emphasizes, the form and content of technological artifacts and mass culture in a repressive or destructive order tend to serve the ideological and practical needs of that order. In this regard, commercial video games do critical ideological work in preparing the population for permanent war mobilization and military aggression, by normalizing and dehistoricizing state violence and demonizing "authorized" enemies of the U.S. state. While many Americans believe they live in a nation that uses violence as a last resort and then only in self-defense, the facts of U.S. foreign policy over the past century tell a different story, of illegal military intervention, counterrevolutionary warfare, support for pro-U.S. dictatorships around the world, and paroxysms of ruthless violence (Johnson, 2004). Yet military FPS (first-person shooter) games, including historical games depicting past wars, uncritically celebrate U.S. military and technological supremacy and depict America's enemies as dangerous savages worthy of extermination. The narrative content of many post-9/11 games in particular reiterates the values and policy assumptions of the so-called war on terror, mapping the world cognitively to prepare American soldiers and citizenry alike "for colonial exercises of spatial domination" (King & Leonard, 2010, p. 91). As Höglund (2008) observes, such games serve the interests of the U.S. state by constructing the entire Middle East "as a frontier zone where a perpetual war between U.S. interests and Islamic terrorism" can be enacted.[3] The result is a new Orientalism in which "the gamer involved in a military shooter set in the Middle East is forever performing . . . strategic containment of the Other"—the dark-skinned barbarian perpetually threatening the innocent redoubt of Western civilization.

In sum, as Kline, Dyer-Witheford, and de Peuter (2003) observe, the video "game industry, conjured into being by technologically adept and culturally militarized men, made games reflecting the interests of its creators, germinating a young male subculture of digital competence and violent preoccupations" (p. 257). What is disturbing is how widespread and "normal" such "violent preoccupations" have become, as young men and boys routinely play at war using forms of software and hardware that are functionally indistinguishable from the ones being used at DARWARS or in the Afghan "theater." Gaming culture has indeed become the central mechanism for socializing the nation's boys and young men into an unthinking, pro-U.S. military perspective. Children and adults now play at war using highly realistic virtual weapons—the AK-47, M16A4, M1 Garand, Walther PPK, sniper rifle, and so on—whose technical specs and behavior in the field mimic the real thing. (Meanwhile, to capitalize on the fact that virtually every young male growing up today attains technical prowess in destroying virtual objects and enemies using commercial game controllers, the military has begun integrating Xbox and Wii controllers into the controls of its actual weapons and robotics equipment [Derene, 2008].)

What has enabled such realism and fidelity is the seamless integration of the private video game industry with the Pentagon. Not only do designers cycle back and forth between the U.S. military and private corporations, but commercial companies scrupulously model games on the latest in U.S. military doctrine, equipment, and weaponry. Some game companies even manufacture hardware or software for actual weapon systems. SEGA, which has a lucrative contract with the Boeing corporation to produce computer boards for a real tactical fighter plane, also produces *After Burner Climax,* which invites players to select "aircraft from the F-14D Super Tomcat by Northrop Grumman to the F-15E Strike Eagle and F/A-18E Super Hornet by Boeing."

In November 2009, Activision shattered the previous record for the opening of a video game (previously held by *Grand Theft Auto IV*) with its release of *Call of Duty 2: Modern Warfare,* a military shooter game that raked in more than $300 million on its first day alone. *Call of Duty 2* was widely praised for its attention to "realism." And indeed, to see the command protocols, infrared images, the tactical ballistics, and flight characteristics of the C-130 attack aircraft experienced by the player of *Call of Duty 2* side by side with those evident in actual video footage of U.S. pilots strafing real human beings from a C-130 during a night raid in Afghanistan is to be awed by the realism.[4] But as in other games, what counts as verisimilitude is technological fetishism, not historical or psychological truth. Elided in such war simulations are the actual human consequences of combat—loss, trauma, suffering, the deaths of children, the cries of wounded soldiers and animals.

Virtual warfare is no longer limited to the military battlefield, either: Civil society itself becomes a war zone for symbolically enacting aggression and playing out the destructive "scripts" authorized by the wider culture. Violence against women (a social class whose objectification and subordination is still widely sanctioned by the society) is an especially prominent theme in some of the leading games. Thus, the popular Japanese video game *Rape-lay* consists of raping girls and young women (e.g., on deserted subway platforms), while sexual violence is one of the draws of the *Grand Theft Auto* series (a role-playing [RPG] game set in highly realistic urban settings). On YouTube, young men from different countries post homemade videos showing their favorite ways of killing prostitutes in *GTA IV*. The players' avatars drive women in the game to remote, desolate spots in the *GTA* world, and then murder them in various ways—bludgeoning them with tire irons, knifing them, shooting them in the head or stomach, burning them alive, drowning them, or dismembering them with a hand grenade. The bodies of the women writhe and fall apart in a fair simulation of the way a real woman's body might behave in real life, showing the detail that male software engineers specializing in "frag physics" lavish on simulated violations of the human body. The question here is not whether playing *GTA IV* directly causes violence against women but whether games that invite male players to participate in such simulated atrocities do not trivialize actual male violence against women—an epidemic in our and other societies—and legitimate and reinforce existing misogynistic attitudes. The evidence suggests that playing such games in fact does dull players' empathetic responses to real-world victims of violence, including women.[5]

Militarism and symbolic violence have become so pervasive that even ostensibly benign children's games are often inflected with technological aggression and masculine dreams of domination. In *Pokémon*, the player's avatar roams the world trying to enslave "as many of several hundred elusive creatures" as possible. "Once you leash one and it becomes part of your menagerie, you then train it and make it more powerful by carrying it around and deploying it in battles against other trainers" (Schiesel, 2010, p. C3). On the Arcademic Skill Builders website, meanwhile, children learn mathematical division by blasting away at a phalanx of advancing tanks ("Demolition Division") or learn multiplication by shooting at asteroids. Few children's games are in fact entirely free of militarization, and fewer from the drive to instrumentalize nature.

Capitalism and Instrumental Reason

Even when the content of games is not explicitly violent, the medium itself conveys an educative "message" that instrumental manipulation of the world, of self and other, is natural and socially productive. One striking feature of the computer video game is the extent to which the player's fundamental cognitive and behavioral modality is oriented toward *manipulation* of the representational world, rather than *receptivity* toward it. In this regard, the computer video game may represent the ideal distillation of what Marcuse and other critics have termed *instrumental reason*. By this I mean, first, the prejudice of the modern capitalist age that things in the world have no value outside of our ability to manipulate them and, second, a mode of thinking and action whereby qualitative experiences, processes, and modes of being are reduced to *quantitative* measures. Hannah Arendt (2003) observed these "typical attitudes" in *homo faber* or "Man the maker,"

> His instrumentalization of the world, his confidence in his tools and in the productivity of the maker of artificial objects; his trust in the all-comprehensive range of the means-ends category, his conviction that every issue can be solved and every human motivation reduced to the principle of utility; his sovereignty, which regards everything given as material and thinks of the whole of nature as [a mere thing to be made into whatever we wish]. (p. 364)

The roots of this "instrumentalization of the world" are deep—they go back at least as far as ancient Greek culture and myth, which celebrated the "cunning" of human reason in its capacity to master and dominate the world. With the emergence of capitalist social relations in modern Europe, Nature came to be viewed as "thing-like," as dead matter to be manipulated at will. The logic of the commodity, which is the logic of abstraction and numerary—the "mathematization of nature"—meanwhile became the dominant perceptual template through which Western culture viewed the world (Husserl, 1970). Computerization in some ways represents the ultimate triumph of this process, a victory of the quantitative over the qualitative in our encounters with the real. As critic Michael Heim (1993) notes, however, what we "gain in power" through the system of technological abstraction comes at the expense "of our direct involvement with things" (p. 18). We learn to think and perceive in fragments, to "outsource" our skills and consciousness to machinic entities, and to treat one another with brutal, offhand indifference. Reality collapses into solipsism: The world seems to organize itself around *my* needs and desires. The human and animal body—the true ground of all our experiences and ways of knowing—is diminished, as virtual reality leads to a sense of *disembodiment.*

This instrumentalist conception of the world achieves its fullest expression in first-person shooter games, where the subject's interaction with others is most likely to be represented by a disembodied weapon floating in mid-air, and in strategy games, which reduce history to instances of technological social Darwinism (groups of humans dominating and subduing one another on the basis of their artifacts; Friedman, 1999; see also Galloway, 2006). But instrumentalism stalks even ostensibly innocent games like those in the lucrative *Sims* franchise, where living processes—whether life in the suburbs or life evolving on another planet (as in *Spore*)—are reduced to a series of cost-benefit decisions. In the original *Sims,* the player lives in a middle-class White suburban neighborhood, shops, raises a family, pursues a

career, forms friendships, dates, and so on, all the while keeping an eye on quantitative status bars that allow him or her to monitor the Sims' biological functions, social status, and so on. Life is reduced to a sequence of strategic moves to maximize one's individual interests, with the Sim player assuming the role of a technocratic manager over his or her life—"controlling and predicting and directing the behaviour of a very finely tuned market niche, a 'segment of one'" (Kline et al., 2003, p. 278). As J. C. Herz (2000) writes, "Everything is an object that yields a measurable benefit when some action is performed on it" (p. G10). Other human beings are viewed in the same light, as a means for maximizing one's own self-interest. "Even having children is a means to an end," Kline et al. (2003) observe of *The Sims,* "since it is through the interaction of your Sims' kids with the neighbours that adult Sims get to know each other" (p. 276), and it is through such interactions that one builds the connections one needs to advance one's career and increase one's income.

The fact that such instrumental egoism is by no means accidental but is "formally engineered into the game-play" can be traced to the ultimate objective of commercial gaming culture, which is to integrate the player into the circuits of real-world capitalist production and consumption (Herz, 2000). Ideologically, the worldview of *The Sims* is in fact indistinguishable from neoliberal economics. As economist (and capitalist apologist) Milton Friedman once wrote, "Children are at one and the same time *consumer goods* and potentially responsible members of society" (Friedman, 2002, p. 33, emphasis added), confirming the hidden logic of capital, which is to reduce all labor, all living beings, to the status of *things.*[6] Today, the computer video game is the "ideal commodity" of post-Fordist capitalism, the paradigmatic form of a system that now requires "a ceaseless stream of new commodities with ever-shortening product cycles and life-spans" (Kline et al., 2003,

p. 66). Kline et al. (2003, pp. 60–77) relate the emergence of the video game as *the* significant consumer commodity of the 21st century to the need of the world capitalist system to stave off systemic crisis. The information revolution, they suggest, made it possible for capital to circumvent the objective limits of an older "regime" of capital accumulation. Just as the post-1980s era of speculative finance capital led banking institutions and consumers to invest wildly in "virtual" or fictive financial commodities—credit default swaps and other esoteric derivatives—the need of capital to colonize new markets led to the extension of commodity fetishism into the *virtual* realm. Where once computer games had to be tethered to bulky media like cathode-ray TVs or hulking, stationary consoles at the arcade, today they leap nimbly from cell phones and laptops to PCs and from HD televisions to the DIS (Disney Information System), heedless of spatial or temporal limits. Whereas chess can be played for free and has withstood the centuries with few modifications (and those rendered through folk adaptation), today's virtual games are expensive and designed to be obsolete within days or weeks, requiring the consumer to spend money continuously. Game content itself becomes commodified: In *Second Life,* players buy virtual clothes from the Gap or other mainstream retail chains, using real dollars, and hire real sweat-shop labor in China to mine virtual gold in *World of Warcraft* (see Castronova, 2005, pp. 170–204).

While the appeal of simulation games like *The Sims* or *Spore*—or *GTA*—is that they offer the player the illusion of complete freedom and power, in reality they tap into the thwarted libidinal energies of players and spin virtual flax into the real gold of the capitalist economy. Multinational corporate behemoths like Sony, Entertainment Arts, and Activision spend billions on marketing campaigns to manipulate the consciousness and behavior of the millions of children, teenagers, and young adults in the wealthy North who together make up the lucrative youth market (in 2000, worth up to $164 billion; Kline et al., 2003, p. 221). As Kline et al. (2003) point out,

> [When] one looks at the ... economic, technological, and cultural forces shaping *The Sims* gamer—not merely as the participant in a ... scripted and designed play scenario but also as a member of a population among which certain levels of technological familiarity are increasingly normalized, required, and rewarded, and as the target of a high-intensity marketing regime designed to elicit certain levels of consumption activity—much of [his] apparent autonomy and empowerment evaporates. The player reappears as object, not subject, the product of a system ... partially programmed ... as much played upon as player. (p. 279)

On one hand, the player himself colludes in this process, knowing full well that the real game in town is the game of consumerism and profit realization. On the other hand, he barely comprehends the degree to which his own behavior, his consciousness, his values, his desires, have been effectively commandeered and subordinated to reinforce a regime of power whose destructive features are rendering his sovereignty as a political subject, his own consciousness itself, *obsolete.*

Conclusion

The more ubiquitous the video game form becomes and the more lifelike its simulations of reality, the more its characteristic phenomenology comes to assume the form of a *paradigm,* a structuring set of knowledge practices and theories with the power to shape the way we see and experience the world. The trouble is, the more we paradoxically seek solace in the womb of the machine itself—that is, in a limitless virtual realm where the very masculinist and "instrumentalist" approach that has failed us in the real world yet retains its aura of potency—the more we flee the actual public sphere, that realm of appearances where *action and speech* might still matter. Political theorist Sheldon Wolin warns of a creeping "inverted totalitarianism" in which powerful interests rule not by whipping the masses up to a frenzied unity (as in fascism) but by turning us into quiescent spectators. Meanwhile, our own deep anger over being treated as mere things—by our employers, by our government, by the anonymous corporate bureaucracies we are forced to interact with every day—gets channeled into socially destructive forms: addictive online behaviors, simulations of atrocities, real bombs, and missiles raining on real people in foreign lands. By thus adapting life instincts to the external needs of an unjust social order, the individual in effect (to quote Marcuse again) "collaborates in his own repression, in the containment of potential individual and social freedom, [and hence] in the release of aggression" (Marcuse, 1968, p. 254). The individual comes to bear "the marks of a mutilated human being." For while the behaviors, forms of culture and play, and so on called into being and sanctioned by the system may be productive for that system itself, they are fundamentally destructive from the vantage point of actual human happiness and planetary well-being.

Notes

1. The original report was released by the NPD Group, a market research firm.

2. DARWARS website (http://www.darwars .org/about/index.html), accessed March 10, 2010. I am indebted to Nina Huntemann for her research on military uses of video game technologies.

3. As David Nieborg points out, the U.S. Army's *America's Army* MMORPG "has become a powerful vessel for disseminating U.S. Army ideology and foreign policy to a global game culture" (Höglund, 2008, p. 9).

4. Both the real C-130 footage and the simulacral footage were available on YouTube in April 2010. I want to thank Darius Kazemi for bringing this footage to my attention.

5. "In violent video games," the authors of one study of the effects of violent media on children's behavior conclude, "empathy is not adaptive, moral evaluation is often non-existent, but proviolence attitudes and behaviors are repeatedly rewarded" (Funk, Baldacci, Pasold, & Baumgardner, 2004, p. 34).

6. South Korea, a nation so obsessed with video games that some individuals have literally played themselves to death, became a tragic proving ground for this theory of human disposability when authorities there arrested a couple for child abuse and neglect after the parents left "their 3-month-old daughter to starve to death while they raised a virtual daughter online during 12-hour bouts at a cyber cafe." The couple had become addicted to *Prius Online*, a game akin to *Second Life* where players engage in virtual work and virtual relationships, and "[earn] an extra avatar to nurture once they reach a certain level." One police officer observed, "The couple seemed to have lost their will to live a normal life because they didn't have jobs and gave birth to a premature baby. . . . They indulged themselves in the online game of raising a virtual character so as to escape from reality, which led to the death of their real baby." The virtual child, ironically named *Anima* (the Latin word for "breath" or "soul," which in ancient usage meant a *living being*) flourished; meanwhile, the real baby perished from "severe dehydration and malnutrition" (Frayer, 2010). While one must be careful not to make too much of a single case, the incident nonetheless serves as a reminder of what can happen when flesh and blood human beings become subordinated to, and indeed absorbed into, the realm of virtual commodities.

References

Alloway, N., & Gilbert, P. (1988). Video game culture: Playing with masculinity, violence, and pleasure. In S. Howard (Ed.), *Wired-up: Young people and the electronic media* (pp. 95–114). London: University of London College Press.

Arendt, H. (2003). The human condition. In R. C. Scharff & V. Dusek (Eds.), *Philosophy of technology: The technological condition.* New York: Blackwell.

Bogost, I. (2007). *Persuasive games: The expressive power of video games.* Cambridge: MIT Press.

Castronova, E. (2005). *Synthetic worlds: The business and culture of online games.* Chicago: University of Chicago Press.

Chan, D. (2005). Playing with race: The ethics of racialized representations in e-games. *International Review of Information Ethics, 4*(12), 24–30.

Derene, G. (2008, May 29). Wii all you can be? Why the military needs the gaming industry. *Popular Mechanics.* http://www.popular mechanics.com/technology/military_law/4266106.html

Frayer, L. (2010, March 10). Baby starved as couple nurtured virtual kid. AOL News. http://www.aolnews.com/crime/article/south-korean-couple-nurtured-virtual-child-as-their-baby-starved-police-say/19384636

Freierman, S. (2008, November 10). Popular demand: Video games. *New York Times,* p. B10.

Friedman, M. (2002). *Capitalism and freedom* (40th anniversary ed.). Chicago: University of Chicago Press.

Friedman, T. (1999). Civilization and its discontents: Simulation, subjectivity, and space. In G. Smith (Ed.), *Discovering discs: Transforming space and place on CD-ROM* (pp. 132–150). New York: New York University Press.

Funk, J. B., Baldacci, H. B., Pasold, T., & Baumgardner, J. (2004). Violence exposure in real-life, video games, television, movies and the Internet: Is there desensitization? *Journal of Adolescence, 27,* 23–39.

Galloway, A. (2006). *Gaming: Essays on algorithmic culture.* Minneapolis: University of Minnesota Press.

Heim, M. (1993). *The metaphysics of virtual reality.* Oxford, UK: Oxford University Press.

Herz, J. C. (2000, February 10). The Sims who die with the most toys wins. *New York Times,* p. G10.

Hill, N. (n.d.). Playing with patriarchy. *Cerise Magazine.* http://cerise.theirisnetwork.org/archives/9

Höglund, J. (2008, September). Electronic empire: Orientalism revisited in the military shooter. *Game Studies: The International Journal of Computer Game Research.* 8(1). http://gamestudies.org/0801/articles/hoeglund

Husserl, E. (1970). *The crisis of European sciences and transcendental phenomenology.* Evanston, IL: Northwestern University Press.

John, T. "170 Million Americans Play Video Games, Study Finds." *Wired* Magazine, Aug. 3, 2009. (http://www.wired.com/gamelife/2009/08/npd-games/).

Johnson, C. (2004). *Blowback: The costs and consequences of American empire.* New York: Holt.

King, C. R., & Leonard, D. J. (2010). Wargames as a new frontier: Securing American empire in virtual space. In N. B. Huntemann & M. T. Payne (Eds.), *Joystick soldiers: The politics of play in military video games.* New York: Routledge.

Kline, S., Dyer-Witheford, N., & de Peuter, G. (2003). *Digital play: The interaction of technology, culture, and marketing.* Montreal, Quebec, Canada: McGill-Queen's University Press.

Lenoir, T., & Lowood, H. (2005). Theaters of war: The military-entertainment complex. In H. Schramm, L. Schwarte, & J. Lazardzig (Eds.), *Collection—Laboratory—Theater: Scenes of knowledge in the 17th century* (pp. 427–456). Berlin: Walter de Gruyter.

Leonard, D. (2004). Unsettling the military entertainment complex: Video games and a pedagogy of peace. *Studies in Media & Information Literacy Education, 4*(4).

Marcuse, H. (1968). *Negations: Essays in critical theory* (J. J. Shapiro, Trans.). Boston: Beacon.

National chess survey reveals the truth about chess: Why people play and what scares them away. (2003, December 2). *Business Wire.*

Nichols, R. (2010). Target acquired: *America's Army* and the video games industry. In N. B. Huntemann & M. T. Payne (Eds.), *Joystick soldiers: The politics of play in military video games* (pp. 39–52). New York: Routledge.

Penny, S. (2004). Representation, enaction, and the ethics of simulation. In N. Wardrip-Fruin & P. Harrigan (Eds.), *First person: New media as story, performance, and game.* Cambridge: MIT Press.

Schiesel, S. (2010, March 19). Look kids: A way to slip Pokémon past mom. *New York Times,* p. C3.

51

Strategic Simulations and Our Past

The Bias of Computer Games in the Presentation of History

Kevin Schut

Education and Historical Simulations

A growing number of educators are starting to champion the use of digital games as teaching tools.[1] Anyone who has played a substantial number of games probably already realizes that this new medium has several educational benefits. But aside from the obligatory copy of *Oregon Trail* (Learning Company, 1997) or other relatively simple and limited edutainment CD-ROMs hanging around the classroom computer, computer games have not been commonly used to teach in a systematic manner. Now an increasing number of voices are speaking up for just that.

In a recent guest editorial in *Wired* magazine, famed game designer Will Wright (2006), who designed *SimCity* (Maxis Software, 1989) and *The Sims* (Maxis Software, 2000), touts the ability of games to encourage scientific thinking. Likewise, writer Steven Johnson (2005), in his engaging book *Everything Bad Is Good for You,* argues that video games have been a perfect vehicle for encouraging increasingly complex thought patterns. This echoes recent publications in education theory. James Paul Gee's (2003) book *What Video Games Have to Teach Us About Learning and Literacy* is a very readable treatise on how good digital games model good learning practices. The book puts together a persuasive case for the ability of games to make meaning situated, to help create motivated, tailored, and incremental discoveries, and to encourage social sharing of knowledge, among other things. Although evidence-based research is still not available in large quantities—and much of what *is* available is methodologically questionable—Kurt Squire (2004b, 2005; Squire & Jenkins, 2003) is one prominent education researcher who has

From Kevin Schut, "Strategic Simulations and Our Past: Bias of Computer Games in Presentation of History." *Games and Culture: A Journal of Interactive Media* (2007) 2 (3), 213–235. Reprinted with permission of SAGE Publications.

widely published about using the game *Civilization III* (described in more detail below) in actual classrooms. Although he sees potential drawbacks, Squire believes that digital games are potentially powerful teaching tools. Gee, Squire, and others do not argue that games are a panacea for all that ails schools today; rather, these theorists see computer and video games as valuable tools when coupled with proper guidance and other media resources.

Personally, I strongly support the idea of integrating games with teaching. As a lifelong game player, I have experienced many of the benefits of gaming that Squire, Gee, and others describe. But there is no such thing as a perfect tool. Games have significant strengths and limitations. This does not mean we should abstain from historical simulations; it simply means we should approach them with something of a critical eye. The current educational research on games certainly notes the pragmatic limitations of using them in standard school settings. . . . I think, however, that these analyses could go a little further.

I take my cue for this article partly from a question asked in a recent article by the educators at the University of Wisconsin who are leading the charge for the use of games in classrooms (Shaffer, Squire, Halverson, & Gee, 2005). The authors end the piece with a call for more research on games, and specifically wonder "how inhabiting a virtual world develops situated knowledge—how playing a game like *Civilization III,* for example, mediates players' conceptions of world history" (p. 111). It is at this level that I think educators and players need to be aware of some of the limitations and tendencies of the medium.

Media Ecology and the Ideology of Games

As games have moved from niche-culture status to mainstream, intellectuals have started to pay more attention to the ideologies that a game appears to support, in spite of the apparent freedom of play. Although a digital game may seem to give greater latitude to gamers than do other media, the procedural authors of games set limits and boundaries to activity (Frasca, 2003). As Shoshana Magnet (2006) argues, in her critique of *Tropico* (PopTop Software, 2001), capitalist or ethnocentric assumptions can be built right into a game's virtual landscape (its "gamescape," as she puts it). Barkin (2002) and Chen (2003) likewise criticize *Civilization III* (Firaxis Games, 2001) for the problematic assumptions built into the game's model of culture. In their seminal textbook *Rules of Play,* Katie Salen and Eric Zimmerman (2004) also extensively talk about the possibility of specific games encoding ideologies.

Although this kind of single-game analysis is valuable, we can draw a larger picture: a consideration of the ideological implications of the medium as a whole. As Ted Friedman (1999) puts it, "Any medium . . . can teach you how to see life in new ways" (p. 133). By being able to "reorganize perception," to use Friedman's term, the digital game medium can have profound implications for how we understand the world and how it works. Educators and players in general would be well served to consider how computer and video games provide new ways to see and understand history.[2] . . .

MASCULINE HISTORY

Both computers and computer games have a strongly masculine history that still manifests itself in numerous ways. Although it is widely believed that the first computer programmer was a woman—Ada Lovelace is reputed to have written theoretical programs for Charles Babbage's never-constructed Analytical Engine—the roots of the modern computer are in thoroughly masculine contexts, such the cold war–era U.S. military, academic engineering departments of major research universities, and the early hacker culture.[3] Although the gender balance has clearly shifted during the past two or three decades, it is clear that computers are still very male items in many ways (Cassell & Jenkins, 1998). For example, recent statistics from the U.S. Bureau of Labor Statistics (2005) list women as occupying only 27.0% of positions in "computer and mathematical occupations," and a recent survey completed by the International Game Developers Association found that women form only 11.5% of the game industry's total workforce and only 5.0% of its programmers (Gourdin, 2005).

This latter statistic is not a new development: Computer games have also had a very male-dominated history. A few prominent female designers, such as Roberta Williams, have managed to make their mark on game culture, but, by and large, the people who made the digital game industry what it is today were men. A look at any list of credits today shows that although there are ever-greater numbers of women working in the game-making industry, the vast majority are still male. In short, one of the most salient features of the digital game medium—both in terms of computer technology and the game industry itself—is that it is very masculine in nature. It should be clear that there is nothing essentially masculine about either games or computers; nevertheless, a masculine bias has been a major feature of the social construction of the digital game medium throughout its history.[4]

For decades now, critical historians have struggled to counteract the manner in which the standard Western histories of Great White (dead) Men have written marginal social groups out of our cultural historical consciousness. Although the discipline of history has been busy correcting this significant problem, digital games tend to reinscribe it. A kind of masculine slant is exceptionally clear in game presentation of history. For one thing, practically all history in digital games is focused on some combination of politics, economics, and war. For another, all of the historical games examined for this article demonstrate the centrality of aggressive power and/or acquisition. The centrality of these features displays the importance of stereotypical manhood to historical simulations.

The first evidences of this masculine bias are the types of historical focuses of the game simulations. Partly as an attempt to correct the hegemonic bias of traditional historical research, the discipline of history has broadened its scope to include a great diversity of subjects. Social, cultural, and critical histories are particularly valuable for emphasizing the significance of people ignored in the traditional accounts of monarchs, merchants, and military campaigns. Most historical digital games, however, ignore these trends and almost exclusively focus on politics, economics, and war. Strategy games that are historical simulators almost always have an economic component and frequently have a political dimension as well. A major part of *Civilization* and the *Total War* games—and, to a lesser extent, *Pirates*— consists of balancing income and expenses, developing commercial trade, exploiting resources, investing in economic infrastructure, and so on. Another part of these same games is dedicated to developing and maintaining advantageous relationships with other factions or powers in the games (whether they are played by humans or the computer): making and breaking alliances, trading deals, and other diplomatic agreements. Both *Civilization* and the *Total War* games have an internal political element as well, requiring the player to keep his or her own population content enough to avoid rebellion.

More blatant than the two themes of economics and politics, however, is the centrality of war. Practically all commercial historical digital games feature some kind of military- or combat-oriented activity, even if it is not the only option available to players. *Pirates* allows the player to be a peaceful merchant instead of a bloodthirsty privateer, and the *Civilization* player may win the game without conquering anyone or anything. In both cases, however, it would be extremely challenging to make it all the way through the game without a single battle. In addition, the mechanics of these games, their manuals, and even their promotional literature clearly indicate that game makers wish violence and combat to prominently feature in gameplay. In many other historical simulations, war is the raison d'être, as clearly evidenced by the titles of the *Total War* and *Battlefield* games. Playing these games in a nonconfrontational or nonviolent way would be to deliberately subvert the games' purposes (which, of course, is possible).

Other kinds of historical focuses certainly do appear in historical representations of the past. All of the games except for the *Battlefield* series feature broader cultural issues. *Civilization* has numerous cultural and social technologies, such as mysticism or nationalism, and buildings, such as coliseums or cathedrals. In addition, its encyclopedic descriptions of the various game units, improvements, and concepts give a great deal of historical depth that often moves beyond political, economic, and military considerations. In *Pirates*, one of the major mini-games is the decidedly artistic activity of ballroom dancing. But, as a whole, these social and cultural pictures of history are subservient to the political, economic, and military focuses of the game mechanics: Their game function is to help the player become more politically, economically, and militarily successful. Successful dancing in *Pirates*, for example, leads the charmed governor's daughter to give gifts or tips about financially rewarding quests.

When culture is apparently autonomous, it ends up functioning in much the same manner as an economic system. In the last two versions of *Civilization*, a player may win the game by achieving cultural dominance. Buildings such as libraries or theaters produce "culture points." These accumulate throughout the game, extending the territory of the player and even leading to enemy cities defecting to a dominant neighboring civilization. If a player's culture is powerful enough, he or she wins the game. Although the game uses the word *culture*, this is obviously misleading: Culture in reality is a complex, particular, multifaceted phenomenon (Barkin, 2002; Chen, 2003). What we are seeing here is currency, dressed up as culture points. Even when the game tries to get away from politics, economics, and war, it cannot escape the well-worn pattern.

In fact, *Civilization*'s culture system is also a good illustration of another masculine theme: Games typically present history as a matter of aggressive power. In the *Battlefield* games, this is particularly clear: The player must kill or be killed—the player's team must physically destroy the opposition with firearms or military vehicles. In the strategy games, the focus can be on this kind of conquest-oriented militaristic power drive, but just as often, the key motive of the game is aggressive acquisition. In *Total War*, the player tries to get as much territory and as large an army as possible. In *Civilization*, the player has several options, but whether he or she chooses a military, cultural, or technological route to success, the game consists of trying to get as much stuff as possible, often forcefully. In *Pirates*, we see the modern suburban dream of acquiring a career, wife, and house with a yard, written onto a 17th century Caribbean setting; the player's score is dependent, among a few other things, on the amount of treasure acquired, the amount of land rewarded by grateful governors, and the attractiveness of the wife.[5] Again, the player achieves this primarily via sword fights, ship-to-ship combat, and ground-based invasions.

It is of course important to note that politics, economics, and even war are not inherently male spheres of life, nor do only men desire power or focus on acquisition (or that not all men wish for these things). However, all of these themes are stereotypically male; they fit widely publicized, rough masculine ideals of aggressiveness and domination (e.g., Douglas, 1999; Faludi, 1999; Jeffords, 1994). More importantly, these themes crowd out or subvert things that are not stereotypically masculine, especially in the presentation of historical games. Many, including myself, have reasonable hope that this might change. There are a growing number of popular digital games that break the hypermasculine mold—notably best-sellers *SimCity* and *The Sims*—although virtually none take place in historical settings. M.I.T.'s "Games-to-Teach" project developed a historical multiplayer role-playing game that also suggests that the representation of history in games is not locked into the stereotypically masculine interests (Squire & Jenkins, 2003). For the moment, however, the bias of the medium is pretty thoroughly in favor of one gender, and it will take work to change that. . . .

Notes

1. Discussion about the educational value of games has actually gone on for a long time (Egenfeldt-Nielsen, 2004; Squire, 2004a). According to Squire (2004a), teaching with games was somewhat in vogue during the 1970s, but these games rarely used computers, and they fell out of favor in the 1980s. What we are seeing now is a renaissance of interest from a distinctively constructivist educational theory viewpoint.

2. Squire's (2006) recent writing, "Videogames as Designed Experience," is an excellent example of a broad ideological critique of the digital game medium. He touches some of the same issues as this article does, but his main focus is on educational ideology—the way game playing and game design encode the character of learners. Another contrast with this piece is that Squire's article spends much more time talking about the performance of gameplay.

3. Although none of these observations are particularly controversial, a good game-oriented discussion of some of these issues is in *Digital Play* (Kline, Dyer-Witheford, & De Peuter, 2003).

4. Again, for a good discussion of the "militarized masculinity" in games, see *Digital Play* (Kline et al., 2003). Also see Cassell and Jenkins (1998) and Herz (1997).

5. This is actually ranked in the game; the three varieties are "plain," "attractive," and "beautiful."

References

Barkin, G. (2002, January 15). The culture of Civilization III. Message posted to http://web.archive.org/web/20020201200724/www.joystick101.org/?op=displaystory&sid=2002/1/12/222013/422

Cassell, J., & Jenkins, H. (1998). Chess for girls? feminism and computer games. In J. Cassell & H. Jenkins (Eds.), *From Barbie to Mortal Kombat: Gender and computer games* (pp. 2–45). Cambridge, MA: MIT Press.

Chen, K. (2003). Civilization and its disk contents: Two essays on civilization and Civilization. *Radical Society, 30*(2), 95–107.

Douglas, S. (1999). *Listening in: Radio and the imagination, from Amos 'n Andy and Edward R. Murrow to Wolfman Jack and Howard Stern.* New York: Times Books.

Egenfeldt-Nielsen, S. (2004). Practical barriers in using educational computer games. *On the Horizon, 12*(1), 18–21.

Faludi, S. (1999). *Stiffed: The betrayal of the American man.* New York: William Morrow.

Ferguson, N. (Ed.). (1997). *Virtual history: Alternatives and counterfactuals.* London: Picador.

Firaxis Games. (2001). Sid Meier's civilization III [Computer game]. Lyon, France: Infogrames.

Firaxis Games. (2004). Sid Meier's pirates! [Computer game]. New York: Atari.

Firaxis Games. (2005). Sid Meier's civilization IV [Computer game]. New York: 2K Games.

Fiske, J. (1987). *Television culture*. New York: Routledge.

Frasca, G. (2003). Simulation versus narrative: Introduction to ludology. In M. J. P. Wolf & B. Perron (Eds.), *The video game theory reader* (pp. 221–235). New York: Routledge.

Friedman, T. (1999). Civilization and its discontents: Simulation, subjectivity and space. In G. M. Smith (Ed.), *On a silver platter: CD-ROMs and the promises of a new technology* (pp. 132–150). New York: New York University Press.

Gee, J. P. (2003). *What video games have to teach us about learning and literacy*. New York: Palgrave Macmillan.

Gourdin, A. (2005). *Game developer demographics: An exploration of workforce diversity*. San Francisco: International Game Developers Association.

Herz, J. C. (1997). *Joystick nation: How videogames ate our quarters, won our hearts, and rewired our minds*. Boston: Little, Brown.

Huizinga, J. (1949). *Homo ludens: A study of the play-element in culture* (R. F. C. Hull, Trans.). London: Routledge and Kegan Paul. (Original work published 1938)

Jeffords, S. (1994). *Hard bodies: Hollywood masculinity in the Reagan era*. New Brunswick, NJ: Rutgers University Press.

Jenkins, H. (1992). *Textual poachers: Television fans and participatory culture*. New York: Routledge.

Jenkins, H. (2002). Game design as narrative architecture. In N. Wardrip-Fruin & P. Harrigan (Eds.), *First person: New media as story, performance, and game* (pp. 118–130). Cambridge, MA: MIT Press.

Johnson, S. (2005). *Everything bad is good for you: How today's popular culture is actually making us smarter*. New York: Riverhead Books.

King, B., & Borland, J. (2003). *Dungeons and dreamers: The rise of computer game culture from geek to chic*. New York: McGraw-Hill/Osborne.

Kline, S., Dyer-Witheford, N., & De Peuter, G. (2003). *Digital play: The interaction of technology, culture, and marketing*. Montreal, Quebec, Canada: McGill-Queen's University Press.

Latour, B. (1996). *Aramis, or the love of technology*. Cambridge, MA: Harvard University Press.

Learning Company. (1997). The Oregon trail (3rd ed.) [Computer game]. San Francisco: Author.

Magnet, S. (2006). Playing at colonization: Interpreting imaginary landscapes in the video game Tropico. *Journal of Communication Inquiry, 30*(2), 142–162.

Manovich, L. (2001). *The language of new media*. Cambridge, MA: MIT Press.

Maxis Software. (1989). SimCity [Computer game]. Eugene, OR: Broderbund.

Maxis Software. (2000). The Sims [Computer game]. Redwood City, CA: Electronic Arts.

McMahan, A. (2003). Immersion, engagement, and presence: A method for analyzing 3-D video games. In M. J. P. Wolf & B. Perron (Eds.), *The video game theory reader* (pp. 67–86). New York: Routledge.

Murray, J. H. (1997). *Hamlet on the holodeck: The future of narrative in cyberspace*. Cambridge, MA: MIT Press.

PopTop Software. (2001). Tropico [Computer game]. New York: Gathering of Developers.

Salen, K., & Zimmerman, E. (2004). *Rules of play: Game design fundamentals*. Cambridge, MA: MIT Press.

Shaffer, D. W., Squire, K. R., Halverson, R., & Gee, J. P. (2005). Video games and the future of learning. *Phi Delta Kappan, 87*(2), 105–111.

Squire, K. (2004a). *Replaying history: Learning world history through playing Civilization III*. Unpublished doctoral dissertation, Indiana University, Bloomington.

Squire, K. (2004b). Review: Sid Meier's civilization III. *Simulation and Gaming, 35*(1), 135–140.

Squire, K. (2005). Changing the game: What happens when video games enter the classroom? *Innovate Journal of Online Education, 1*(6). Retrieved June 8, 2006.

Squire, K. (2006). From content to context: Videogames as designed experience. *Educational Researcher, 35*(8), 19–29.

Squire, K., & Jenkins, H. (2003). Harnessing the power of games in education. *Insight, 3,* 5–33.

Starr, P. (1994). Seductions of Sim. *American Prospect, 5*(17). Retrieved July 18, 2006, from http://www.prospect.org/print/V5/17/starr-p.html

Suits, B. (1978). *The grasshopper: Games, life and utopia.* Toronto, Ontario, Canada: University of Toronto Press.

U.S. Bureau of Labor Statistics. (2005). *Women in the labor force: A databook* (Publication No. 985). Retrieved June 12, 2006, from http://www.bls.gov/cps/wlf-databook-2005.pdf

Wright, W. (2006, April). Dream machines: Will Wright explains how games are unleashing the human imagination. *Wired, 14*(4), 110–112.

52

"You Play Like a Girl!"

Cross-Gender Competition and the Uneven Playing Field

Elena Bertozzi

Much has been written about why females do not play the same games or as many digital games as males do. It is now estimated that females play digital games at least as often as males do, but the levels of complexity of games varies widely (Dillon, 2006). Lucas and Sherry (2004) define casual/traditional games (those preferred by females) as 'non-mental rotation games' and console or complex PC games (preferred by males) as 'mental rotation games.' These terms suggest that playing 'mental rotation' games requires an additional level of training and immersion not required by traditional games. The lack of female engagement in this sphere matters because participating in complex digital play[1] is a predictor of confidence in and competence with digital technology (AAUW, 2000; Bertozzi and Lee, 2007; Oxford, 2005). Some have suggested that the representation of women as passive sex objects prevents women from fully engaging in the medium, while others have posited that the emphasis on violent/shooting-based conflict keeps females from being interested in this type of play (Cassell and Jenkins, 1998; Heintz-Knowles, 2001; Oxford, 2005; Schleiner, 1998). For years, it has been argued that females value social behavior and positive values, and that as soon as games of this type emerge, females will play them. Over the last couple of years, several games have been published that meet these criteria (*Final Fantasy, Animal Crossing, World of Warcraft* [*WOW*], *SIMS*) and there have been significant increases in female players of these games.[2] If anything though, the popularity of these games among males demonstrates that males do not require stereotypical representations of females or violence to enjoy digital gameplay, and that they value social interaction as much as females do.

The lack of female engagement in digital play is related to deeply rooted understandings of gender differences in the culture at large. Playgrounds such as poker tables,

From Elena Bertozzi, "'You Play Like a Girl:' Cross-Gender Competition and the Uneven Playing Field." *Convergence* (2008), 14, 473–487. Reprinted with permission of SAGE Publications.

Monopoly boards or levels of Halo are affected by gender politics in the larger culture. Players can certainly make a conscious decision to avoid or ignore them, but they exist and affect the play process in both conscious and unconscious ways. It is possible that males seek to play with males and females with females in part because single gender playgrounds are arenas in which players feel somewhat freed from having to deal with the complexities of cross-gender interactions which affect every other area of their lives.

Researchers have documented the ways in which gender politics are reconstructed in digital worlds (Schleiner, 1998; Taylor, 2006; Yee, 2004, 2006). In *Everquest,* for example, players can choose to play as either male or female avatars. The gender of the avatar makes absolutely no difference to the actual abilities or capacities of the avatar. The world is constructed to be gender neutral. Players, however, are affected by the sex of the avatar, in that they treat avatars differently based on their appearance. A delicate-looking female avatar will receive more offers of help and collaboration than a male ogre avatar will. Players are very sensitive to gender politics and are often very savvy about playing as a certain type of avatar when they wish to solicit different types of reactions from other players. Many players will play as both male and female avatars under different circumstances, either for strategic advantage, or because it allows them to replay a game and experience a different set of circumstances.

Given that digital play offers a considerable amount of gender plasticity through avatars, it might seem illogical for gender stereotypes and concerns to persist in digital gaming, but they do.[3] Players of digital games are sexed and the sex of the player matters. The preponderance of male players in complex digital games makes it virtually certain that females who play these digital games will be playing against males.

This chapter considers the possibility that gender differences in digital play are strongly influenced by the unwillingness of both genders to cross traditional, culturally gendered play lines. The fact that females are routinely punished for challenging males on what is perceived to be their turf may be an important factor in deterring women from digital play. When males play against players whom they believe to be female, they are affected by a range of cultural norms including: standards of civility, their own self definition as male, and culturally sanctioned expressions of sexual desire. When females play against players whom they believe to be male, they are affected by similar issues, but from a different perspective. Analysis of gender differences in digital play behavior should consider these factors. In a huge range of game/play activities, including digital gameplay, some females are competing or attempting to compete at the same level as males. They are forging new paths in difficult territory. If we recognize the significance and level of difficulty of challenging existing norms, we can better support their initiatives and create structures to help others join them.

Civility and Chivalry

When males and females play against one another, problems arise. Although there has recently been much lamenting about the death of civility, and concern that young people are growing up without manners, we still have very strongly felt beliefs about how males and females should interact with one another. One of the most relevant, in terms of play, is that it is wrong for males to be aggressive towards females. Our cultural history includes the understanding that males should be protective of women and seek to help them. This understanding was, of course, based on the idea that females are the 'weaker sex,' and required protection and dominance from a strong male. Although we are moving past this perception to some degree, there is no question that public demonstration of violence or aggression from a male towards a female remains culturally unacceptable. Such behavior brings to mind issues of wife beating, rape and other serious crimes. Many males are thus understandably reluctant to engage in any behavior that might even suggest aggression towards a female, for fear that this might be misinterpreted (Hargreaves, 1990).

> A boy on a co-ed football squad—or playing against a co-ed squad—faces an irreconcilable conflict between his duty as a man and his duty as a player. As a man, he must never strike a woman. As a player he must strike teammates during scrimmages, and opposing players during games, fairly and within the rules, but with all the force he can muster. (Jeffrey, 2004)

It is therefore complicated to have males and females on certain types of playgrounds, participating as equals. If a male were playing against another male, he might use a number of aggressive tactics including: physical proximity, verbal taunting, feints, and actual aggression, among other things. It can be very difficult for a male to understand how much and to what degree he can use these kinds of behaviors when playing against a female opponent. In order to truly treat each other as equals, males and females have to willfully attempt to ignore years of cultural conditioning, which codifies inequality.

These difficulties can, however, be overcome if the concept of 'play' is correctly understood and applied. The philosophical premise of play is that whosoever steps onto the 'sacred space' (Huizinga, 1955) of the playing field sheds any discrimination/bias/advantage accrued to him or her outside of the playing field. Within that physical space and within the constraints of the rules of that game, contestants are measured purely by their ability to perform that particular action, in that particular place, at that particular time. The

success of females at high school wrestling, where females often compete on teams with and against males, for example, demonstrates that this can be accomplished even for contact sports.[4]

Consequences of Challenging Males

Despite the many changes in male–female relations over the past 50 years and the goals attained by women's rights movements in a variety of areas, play of almost all kinds remains rigidly gendered. From birth, children are given toys and encouraged to play in ways that reinforce cultural stereotypes of gender appropriateness (Martin and Ruble, 2004; Serbin et al., 2001). Toys "R" Us, Mattel, and other toy production and sales companies have separate product and sales teams for products aimed at separate gender markets. Studies on sex-role stereotypes demonstrate that in fact little has changed in the public's perception of what constitutes masculine and feminine traits (Broverman et al., 1972; Conway and Vartanian, 2000). Video game environments tend to emphasize the differences between gendered avatars rather than diminish them (Ray, 2004). Females often have enormous breasts, male avatars are muscular and heroic. Although this is often presented as a reason why females do not play video games, Waem et al. found that hyper-sexualized avatars are actually preferred by both male and female players (2005).

One result of Title IX legislation has been to encourage females to play more and to provide them with better equipment and better training (Dowling, 2000; Roberts, 2005). Enormous gains have been made in female sporting achievement as a result of this legislation. If anything though, these gains have further demarcated the 'separate but equal' approach to sports education in the USA. Play is fundamentally about power: who has the right to exercise it and how it is exercised (Bertozzi, 2003). Many kinds of play behavior reward aggression, competition and violence, within a system of checks and balances that control how these behaviors are expressed. Traditional male play behaviors often reward players for engaging in these behaviors appropriately. Males are taught that seeking power through socially sanctioned means is appropriate, and will result in deserved rewards. Interviews with CEOs and other successful businessmen often mention past or current participation in sporting events that helped them create a 'winning' work ethic. . . .

The tenacity of gender stereotypes becomes apparent when women attempt to cross the boundary lines and compete on the same terms as males (Roth, 2004). The fact that the female placekicker for the University of Colorado football team was subjected to constant hazing and then raped (CNN, 2004) is an example of how females can be overtly punished for putting themselves on a par with men. The response to events like these often suggests that the harm inflicted on the female in question was somehow deserved, because she put herself in a place where she did not belong:

> Only a few female kickers have played college football, but female high school players are more common. The National Federation of State High School Associations (NFHS), which represents state governing bodies for high school sports, says 1,477 girls participated on the tackle football teams last year at 306 U.S. high schools.
>
> That's a national disgrace. There is a connection between the increasing disrespect shown to women in our society and an ultra-feminist ideology that pushes teenage girls to play a brutal contact sport with teenage boys. (Jeffrey, 2004)

According to this columnist, girls are not freely choosing to participate in football. They are the unwitting pawns of feminist ideology, which places them in an arena in which they are certain to be hurt. This ignores the obvious point that the placekicker in question was not hurt on the field, but in the locker rooms and other social settings, and that she was hurt by her own teammates, not by contact with the opposing team. When Annika Sorenson dared to challenge the men of the PGA, the media hubbub went on for weeks. Some of Sorenson's male colleagues made extremely unsportsmanlike comments regarding her ability despite her clear demonstration of competence.

> WOODRUFF: . . . fans of Annika Sorenson would like to believe that golfer Vijay Singh is eating a big plate of crow for dinner tonight. He's the man who said Sorenstam—quote—'doesn't belong here with the men of the PGA Tour.' And today, Sorenstam [sic] became the first woman since World War II to play at a PGA event, the Colonial in Fort Worth, Texas. And judging by her game and her game alone, she belonged there. (CNN, 2003)

Ambivalence towards players who represent themselves as females in digital games has been reported by many players. A player using a female avatar is very frequently subject to sexual innuendo and communication from other players that focuses on aspects of the female body, clothes she is wearing and so on. In her discussion of how she was treated differently while playing as male- and female-identified avatars in online poker environments, Slimmer points out that some males become extremely aggressive when beaten by a player using a female-identified avatar, and that her decision to play as a male-identified avatar resulted in part from real fear of retaliation from enraged male players (2007). This hostility towards women who dare to challenge gender norms in play is due to the fact that their presence on the playing field calls into question the very definition of masculinity.

Masculine Cultural Play Norms

Cultural norms are often reflected in banter, jokes, idiom and insults. Despite the media presence of many strong and athletically talented women, 'You play/throw/kick like a girl' remains a potent insult. When males play in groups, gendered terms such as 'sissy,' 'pussy' and 'fag,' are used as normal and acceptable putdowns. Some males have to differentiate themselves from females in order to prove their masculinity. In a culture where male traits are valued more highly than female, this process often involves devaluing and 'dissing' females and female traits (Messner, 2002). In fact, publicly devaluing females and feminine traits is considered by some researchers to be an integral part of the development of a culturally accepted 'male' gender persona (Butler, 1990; Connell, 1987; Nelson, 1994; Tolman et al., 2003). In digital gameplay, male conversational exchanges often emphasize the establishment of maleness through choice of language and the explicit enunciation of heterosexist norms (Herring, 2001). Other researchers have argued that in digital gameplay it is even more important for males to establish aggressive masculinity through language precisely because the male body is not present and can only be elicited through speech (Alix, 2007).

When a female steps onto the playing field as an equal, it is disruptive to deeply engrained cultural norms that males are different from females, males are better/stronger/more competent than females, and that males are more aggressive/competitive than females. In cultures where heterosexist cultural norms are especially powerful, in those very few sporting/play activities where males compete on the same level as females, the sport is branded as somehow 'gay' or appropriate only for homosexual men. In the USA these activities include competitive horseback riding events, such as dressage and hunter/jumper competitions, and dance of any kind.[5] The fact that calling someone or some activity 'gay' remains an insult, further underscores the tenacity of traditional binary gender roles in both analog and digital play activities.

The devaluation of the female in the culture at large creates a dilemma when males and females do compete. The stakes are particularly high for a male in this situation, especially if there are spectators. When a male is competing against a female, he is in a lose/lose situation. If he defeats his female opponent, it is not much of a victory, because the cultural expectation is that she is weak anyway. Beating an opponent that is known to be weaker can actually be seen as a kind of humiliation for the winner in this context. If he loses to the female, however, his defeat is compounded by the humiliation of having been defeated by 'a girl.' If this occurs in front of male spectators he is likely to hear about it for a long time afterward.

Female Unwillingness to Excel at Cross-Gender Play

Can we then assume that cross-gender competition is a win/win situation for females? If the female loses against the male, she is still admired for having dared to challenge someone 'superior' to her. If she wins, however, her victory has a different sort of taint to it. There are several terms in western culture for women who dominate men: 'shrew,' 'bitch' and 'ball-breaker' are examples. A man who is dominated by a woman can be called 'pussy-whipped' among other such terms.

Although a woman who defeats a man publicly at play does enjoy the extra status of beating a 'tough' opponent, she also risks being branded with one of these extremely negatively-valenced terms. If for a male, being beaten by a female is a form of emasculation, then the female who beats him is the agent. She, by winning, risks emasculating him. This is its own sort of catch-22. The female athlete, like any other athlete, simply wants to defeat anyone else in her class. She wants to compete against, and hopefully defeat the strongest contestants in her sport. In competing against a male, however, she has other stakes to consider. If she wins, she demonstrates her own superiority and at the same time is potentially responsible for inflicting a sort of societal harm upon her opponent.

Given the cultural norms that correlate femininity with passivity, females who dare to compete and win at the same level as males often find it necessary to emphasize the fact that they remain sexually 'female.' Florence Joyner, a world record holder in track and field, was notorious for her bright pink running suits and impossibly long nails. Female tennis, a sport long associated with powerful women and lesbianism (Nelson, 1994), now has female players who emphasize their femininity with the type of clothing they wear and their off-court behavior. A recent article in the *New York Times* on top-level female chess players pointed out that the top women players are ranked not only on how well they play the game, but also on their looks (Mclain, 2005). Such behavior suggests that women are not just focusing on success in the game, but are at the same time concerned with protecting their status as sexually viable females, because they feel that this status may be threatened by their successes in play. This may in part explain why hyper-sexualized avatars are often chosen as self-representations.

Another reason for choosing not to defeat males is that the act of doing so may make it more difficult for the female athlete to have sexual relationships with males. Given that male/female sexual relationships continue to reflect cultural stereotypes, a female who is known as someone capable of defeating males (thus potentially emasculating them) may encounter difficulties finding male sexual partners off the playing field. In my game design classes, I routinely ask the males in the class if they would date someone who

is able to beat them at the games they consider themselves best at. They always say 'No,' except for the few that say 'It depends how hot she is.' Given the societal cost of defeating men, it is not a surprise that many women prefer to maintain their status as sexually attractive rather than choosing to be winners.

The 'it depends' comment just mentioned, however, does seem to indicate a change in attitudes. There has been a definite increase in the portrayal of strong, competitive athletic females as sexually attractive. Some female singers, such as Madonna, for example, include physically challenging routines in their performances that show off their sleekly muscled bodies. Advertisements for sportswear aimed at females are now often images of powerful-looking women making statements that suggest that they revel in their athletic abilities. 'Working out' is now a common activity among females both old and young, and many popular women's magazines promote a more physically powerful female self-image (*Fitness, Self,* and *Women's Health,* for example).

Some have argued, however, that the importance of fitness can be seen as just another way of pressuring women to obsess about and objectify their bodies, rather than in fact empowering women (Markula, 2001; Tiggemann and Williamson, 2000). Researchers and doctors who deal with anorexic patients have noted that there are pro-anorexia websites, where girls compete to see who can get by on the least amount of food per day and/or work out for the longest amount of time (Williams, 2006). Ryan's (1995) work on sports such as ice-skating and gymnastics found that these sports promote an ideal of fitness which is in fact damaging to a healthy adult female body, and which idealizes traditional norms of femininity:

The anachronistic lack of ambivalence about femininity in both sports is part of their attraction, hearkening back to a simpler time when girls were girls, when women were girls for that matter: coquettish, malleable, eager to please. In figure skating especially, we want our athletes thin, graceful, deferential and cover-girl pretty. (Ryan, 1995: 25)

These analyses suggest that play activities may provide women with physical, mental and emotional strength, and help them become more competent and capable in many areas of life, but that for some, the recent emphasis on fitness for women perpetuates an ethos in which females manipulate their bodies, sometimes in explicitly damaging ways, in order to be more attractive to males.

Women on Top

... Males tend to use play as a way of determining their rank and status within a group. Ranking in the group is achieved by ability/success at the game in question. Rank is mobile. A male can raise or lower his ranking by his play performance at any given time. One of the appealing things about play is that, unlike 'real life,' there is always the chance to play the game again. There is always the opportunity to make the attempt to prove yourself as better than you were the last time. DeBoer points out that although males are playing for the team, they are also always playing for themselves. Better individual performance (within limits) is better for the team overall. Males tend to want each other to excel, and respect each other for the levels of excellence achieved (DeBoer, 2004; Vincent, 2006). Competitiveness between males is overt, socially acceptable and rewarded by status.

Competitiveness between females is much more problematic. Generally it is not overt, and often it does not lead to positive outcomes. Recent books such as *Odd Girl Out* and the film *Mean Girls* (Mark Waters, UK, 2004) have documented the 'culture of hidden female

aggression' (Simmons, 2002). Overt female aggression and competitiveness have long been discouraged, but this does not signify that females are any less interested in achieving higher status and pursuing their own personal best interests. Evolutionary theory demonstrates that there is always competition for scarce resources and status within groups. Discouraged, and often punished by cultural norms, female aggression is often more subtle, nuanced and emotionally wounding. Unlike males who can publicly challenge one another to a contest, females tend to express aggression through social shunning and verbal harassment. It is much more difficult to confront this kind of aggression. It is also very complicated for an individual female to figure out how to improve her status.

Social status among young females continues to be determined by different criteria than it is among males. Rather than achieving status through physical strength, athletic skill, or intellectual achievement as is common among males, female rank is often determined by beauty, thinness, blondness, and attractiveness to males. Unfortunately, this does not appear to have changed significantly over the last 20 years. In 1984, Weisfeld et al., in a study on social dominance in adolescence, found that: 'Boys seem to strive for social success mainly through competence in athletics, and girls through cultivating an attractive appearance' (1984: 115). When Simmons asked young girls the traits of the 'ideal girl,' the top five characteristics were: 'Very thin, Pretty, Blond, Fake, Stupid' (Simmons, 2002: 124). She summarizes her results: 'The ideal girl is stupid, yet manipulative. She is dependent and helpless, yet she uses sex and romantic attachments to get power. She is popular, yet superficial. She is fit, but not athletic or strong' (Simmons, 2002: 126). In a 2003 study on the importance of facial attractiveness to social ranking, the authors found that attractiveness was a significant factor in social dominance, and particularly so among females (Gary et al., 2003).

Female status appears to be determined by factors that are difficult to change (prettiness, thinness). It is thus much more difficult for a female to raise her status in the group. If she overtly competes against other females the way males can, there are societal costs. This affects how females engage in gameplay. Not only is overt competition discouraged, but it can also be punished by social ostracism and shunning. Girls learn to be cautious about whether or not to seek improved status within a group and how to go about achieving it. They may also be reluctant to engage in any kind of activity that further diminishes their status in the female hierarchy (becoming very physically fit and/or more dominant, for example). In digital gameplay, however, these considerations disappear. Any player can choose to represent himself/herself as thin, blond, pretty and stupid, and all avatars are fake by definition. Digital play offers female players the opportunity to represent themselves in a way that makes them look like a high ranking analog female, but it also makes the ranking moot given that anyone can achieve it and many players do. . . .

In her book, *Female Chauvinist Pigs,* Ariel Levy (2005) describes . . . women who have succeeded in male dominated fields as 'loophole women' who enjoy and exploit the fact that there are few women around them, because this increases their uniqueness and cachet. They are, in fact, invested in ensuring that other women do NOT succeed in order to maintain this status.

An interview with a senior *World of Warcraft* (*WOW*) player (Lehtonen, 2007), however, suggests that the situation, at least in *WOW*, is more complicated. She points out that women who have invested a great deal of time and energy in raising their ranking in Massively-Multiplayer Online Roleplaying Games have done so generally through diligence, practice and careful construction of social relationships with other players. Hostility towards new female players does exist, but only if those females come into the game and attempt to circumvent the laborious process of earning status in the group through 'serious' gameplay. Some females come into the game and use heteronormative feminine wiles, such as flirting and sexual innuendo, to attempt to make progress in the game by bonding with higher ranked males. This kind of behavior is extremely irritating to experienced female players because it undercuts the idea that females can and should gain status by earning it, the same way males do (Lehtonen, 2007) . . . .

Changing the Paradigm

Claude Steele developed the term 'stereotype threat' to describe the experience of members of a minority group within the context of a majority group. His studies have demonstrated that dominant stereotypes about minorities will affect performance in certain group situations (Spencer et al., 1999). Elite female gamers playing a complex digital shooting game such as *Counter-Strike* against almost exclusively male opponents are clearly operating in a situation of stereotype threat. They are not just playing the game (as all the other participants are), but they are concurrently disproving a number of stereotypes about females and aggressivity, technology, and willingness to challenge males. Steele has suggested strategies of 'wise schooling' to counteract the effects of stereotype threat in academic environments (Steele, 1997). These strategies include changing attitudes and increasing numbers.

The ability of minority populations to succeed in an environment from which they were previously excluded appears to be related to percentages. Once a certain numeric threshold has been crossed, members of the minority population are less likely to feel the effects of stereotype threat. A study that sought to determine why there remain so few women at high levels of *Fortune* 500 companies found that once a critical mass of three women on the board of a company has been reached, other participants stop viewing gender as the reason underlying female recommendations (Kramer et al., 2006).

Policy Implications

. . . If game designers are aware of issues related to cross-gender play, these can be relatively easily addressed. Additionally, schools and other institutions hoping to attract women to technology might consider the following suggestions.

(1) *Normalize cross-gender play and competition by making it frequent, routine and pleasurable.* In game worlds, this can be accomplished by having many more female characters present in game narratives, and by having them engage with player avatars across a wide range of activities. Stereotype threat can be countered by increasing the number of the members of a minority population present in the majority population and by providing numerous examples of characters that counter stereotypes.

(2) *Create a broad range of non-playable female characters and female avatars who have attributes not stereotypically considered 'female.'* Certainly popular media will always include traditional, stereotypical representations of women. But by broadening the range of females depicted, female and male players alike can choose to represent themselves as a variety of types of female (muscled and timid, thin, blond and bloodthirsty, maternal and insanely competitive, and so on).

(3) *Reinforce emerging perceptions of physically strong, competitive, aggressive females as sexually desirable.* Cultural norms that penalize women for challenging men are a potent deterrent. Females (like males) want very much to be attractive to others and are unlikely to engage in behavior that they perceive as minimizing their attractiveness. By consciously creating

representations of females who successfully defy existing gender norms, new norms will be developed. Given that both male and female players will play as female avatars, perceptions can be changed across genders.

(4) *Increase the number of female players and female avatars in digital games.* Games that have large numbers of female avatars and players, *Second Life* and *Sims* games, for example, are potential models for change. . . .

Notes

1. This is to differentiate digital games such as *Solitaire, Tetris,* or other games which do not require specialized equipment, software, or training, from games including *World of Warcraft, Counter-Strike, Civilization IV* and others, which are much more complicated to learn and play.

2. It is currently estimated that 16 percent of *WOW* players are female (Yee, 2006) while a surprising 46 percent of *SIMS* players are male (Microsoft, 2004).

3. See E. Castronova's article on gendered avatar pricing for an example of how these stereotypes are concretized economically (Castronova, 2003).

4. 'In 2004–5, there were 4334 girls competing in wrestling on the high school level. This total has increased every year since 1990. This actual number is much higher, as some states that have women competitors do not report them' (Abbott, 2006).

5. The film *Billy Elliot* (Stephen Daldry, UK, 2000) explored the gender issues of ballet.

References

AAUW (2000) *Tech Savvy.* Washington, DC: American Association of University Women Educational Foundation.

Abbott, G. (2006) 'Women's High School Wrestling Continues Growth with CIF

Regional Tournaments,' *TheMat.com* (USA Wrestling), URL (accessed June 2008): http://www.themat.com/index.php?page=showarticle&ArticleID=13874

Alix, A. (2007) 'Online Game Talk and the Articulation of Maleness,' in *Flow TV 5* (special issue on video games). University of Texas at Austin. URL (accessed June 2008): http://flowtv.org/?p=53

Bertozzi, E. (2003) 'At Stake: Play, Pleasure and Power in Cyberspace,' PhD dissertation, European Graduate School, URL (accessed June 2008): http://www.egs.edu/resources/elena-bertozzi.html

Bertozzi, E. and Lee, S. (2007) 'Not Just Fun and Games: Digital Play, Gender and Attitudes Towards Technology,' *Women's Studies in Communication* 30(2): 179–204.

Broverman, I. K., Vogel, S. R., Broverman, D. M., Clarkson, F. E. and Rosenkrantz, P. S. (1972) 'Sex Role Stereo types: A Current Appraisal,' *Journal of Social Issues* 28(2): 59–78.

Butler, J. (1990) *Gender Trouble: Feminism and the Subversion of Identity*. New York: Routledge.

Cassell, J. and Jenkins, H. (1998) *From Barbie to Mortal Kombat: Gender and Computer Games*. Cambridge, MA: MIT Press.

Castronova, E. (2003) *The Price of 'Man' and 'Woman': A Hedonic Pricing Model of Avatar Attributes in a Synthetic World* (CESifo Working Paper Series No. 957). Munich: CESifo.

CNN (2003) CNN News night with Aaron Brown, 22 May, URL (accessed May 2003): http://transcripts.cnn.com/TRANSCRIPTS/0305/22/asb.00.html

CNN (2004) 'University Asks Police to Look Into Alleged Rape,' URL (accessed 5 December 2005): http://www.cnn.com/2004/US/Central/02/18/colorado.football/

Connell, R. W. (1987) *Gender and Power: Society, the Person and Sexual Politics*. Stanford, CA: Stanford University Press.

Conway, M. and Vartanian, L. R. (2000) 'A Status Account of Gender Stereotypes: Beyond Communality and Agency,' *Sex Roles* 43(3–4): 499–528.

DeBoer, K. J. (2004). *Gender and Competition: How Men and Women Approach Work and Play Differently*. Monterey, CA: Coaches Choice.

Dillon, B. (2006) E3 Panel: 'Analyzing World Markets,' *Gamasutra Industry News,* URL (accessed June 2008): http://www.gamasutra.com/php-bin/news_index.php?story=9298

Dowling, C. (2000) *The Frailty Myth*. New York: Random House.

Gary, L. A., Hinmon, S. and Ward, C. A. (2003) 'The Face as a Determining Factor for Social Manipulation: Relational Aggression, Sociometric Status, and Facial Appearance,' *Colgate University Journal of the Sciences,* pp. 93–114, URL (accessed June 2008): http://groups.colgate.edu/cjs/student_papers/ 2003/Garyetal.pdf

Hack, D. (2006) 'Dealing with the Wind is a Challenge in Hawaii,' *New York Times* Sports Section, Sunday 15 January: 2.

Hargreaves, J. A. (1990) 'Gender on the Sports Agenda,' *International Review for the Sociology of Sport* 25(4): 287–307.

Heintz-Knowles, D. K. (2001) *Fair Play? Violence, Gender and Race in Video Games*. Oakland, CA: Children Now.

Herring, S. (2001) 'Gender and Power in Online Communication,' CSI Working Paper no. WP-01–05, URL (accessed June 2008): http://rkcsi.indiana.edu/archive/CSI/WP/WP01–05B.html

Huizenga, J. (1955). *Homo Ludens: A Study of the Play-Element in Culture*. Boston, MA: Beacon Press.

Jeffrey, T. (2004) 'Ban Girls from Football,' *Townhall.com,* URL (accessed June 2008): http://www.townhall.com/columnists/TerenceJeffrey/2004/02/26/ban_girls_from_football

Kramer, V., Konrad, A. and Erkut, S. (2006) 'Critical Mass on Corporate Boards: Why Three or More Women Enhance Governance,' available from Wellesely Centers for Women's Publications, URL (accessed June 2008): http://www.wcwonline.org/

Lehtonen, E. (2007) In-person interview and email communication with author. (Lehtonen is a World of Warcraft Guild member; character: Jaspre, title: Ascent Position: 2nd Officer.)

Levy, A. (2005) *Female Chauvinist Pigs: Women and the Rise of Raunch Culture*. New York: Free Press.

Lucas, K. and Sherry, J. L. (2004) 'Sex Differences in Video Game Play: A Communication-Based Explanation,' *Communication Research* 31(5): 499–523.

Markula, P. (2001) 'Beyond the Perfect Body: Women's Body Image Distortion in Fitness Magazine Discourse,' *Journal of Sport and Social Issues* 25(2): 158–79.

Martin, C. L. and Ruble, D. (2004) 'Children's Search for Gender Cues: Cognitive Perspectives on Gender Development,' *Current Directions in Psychological Science* 13(2): 67–70.

Mclain, D. L. (2005) 'Sex and Chess. Is She a Queen or a Pawn?,' *New York Times* 27 November: 1.

Messner, M. (2002) *Taking the Field: Women, Men, and Sports*. Minneapolis: University of Minnesota Press.

Microsoft (2004) 'Women Get in the Game,' Microsoft, URL (accessed June 2008): http://www.microsoft.com/presspass/features/2004/jan04/01–08womengamers.mspx

Nelson, M. B. (1994) *The Stronger Women Get, the More Men Love Football: Sexism and the American Culture of Sports*. New York: Harcourt Brace.

Oxford, N. (2005) 'Venus or Mars: The Uneasy Relationship Between Gaming and Gender,' *1up,* URL (accessed June 2008): http://www.1up.com/do/feature?cId=3141723

Ray, S. G. (2004) *Gender Inclusive Game Design: Expanding the Market*. Boston, MA: Charles River Media.

Roberts, S. (2005) *A Necessary Spectacle: Billie Jean King, Bobby Riggs, and the Tennis Match that Leveled the Game*. New York: Crown Publishers.

Roth, A. (2004) 'Femininity, Sports, and Feminism,' *Journal of Sport and Social Issues* 28(3): 245–65.

Ryan, J. (1995) *Little Girls in Pretty Boxes: The Making and Breaking of Elite Gymnasts and Figure Skaters*. New York: Doubleday.

Schleiner, A.-M. (1998) 'Does Lara Croft Wear Fake Polygons?,' *Switch,* URL (accessed June 2008): http://switch.sjsu.edu/web/v4n1/annmarie.html

Serbin, L. A., Poulin-Dubois, D., Colburne, K. A., Sen, M. G. and Eichstedt, J. A. (2001) 'Gender Stereotyping in Infancy: Visual Preferences for and Knowledge of Gender-Stereotypical Toys in the Second Year,' *International Journal of Behavioral Development* 25(1): 7–15.

Simmons, R. (2002) *Odd Girl Out: the hidden culture of aggression in girls*. New York: Harcourt Inc.

Slimmer, J. (2007) 'Kings, Queens, and Jackasses: Playing with Gender in Online Poker,' *Flow TV 5* (special issue on video games). University of Texas at Austin, URL (accessed June 2008): http://flowtv.org/?p=52

Spencer, S. J., Steele, C. M. and Quinn, D. M. (1999) 'Stereotype Threat and Women's Math Performance,' *Journal of Experimental Social Psychology* 35(1): 4–28.

Steele, C. M. (1997) 'A Threat in the Air: How Stereotypes Shape Intellectual Identity and Performance,' *American Psychologist* 52(6): 613–29.

Taylor, T. L. (2006) *Play Between Worlds: Exploring Online Game Culture*. Cambridge, MA: MIT Press.

Tiggemann, M. and Williamson, S. (2000) 'The Effect of Exercise on Body Satisfaction and Self-Esteem as a Function of Gender and Age,' *Sex Roles* 43(1–2): 119–27.

Tolman, D. L., Spencer, R., Rosen-Reynoso, M. and Porche, M. V. (2003) 'Sowing the Seeds of Violence in Heterosexual Relationships: Early Adolescents Narrate Compulsory Heterosexuality,' *Journal of Social Issues* 59(1): 159–78.

Vincent, N. (2006) *Self-Made Man: One Woman's Journey into Manhood and Back Again*. New York: Viking.

Waem, A., Larsson, A. and Neren, C. (2005) 'Gender Aspects on Computer Game Avatars,' paper presented at the ACM SIGCHI International Conference on *Advances in Computer Entertainment Technology* at the Swedish Institute of

Computer Science, Valencia Spain, URL (accessed June 2008): ftp://ftp.sics.se/pub/SICS-reports/Reports/SICS-T—2005–06—SE.pdf

Weisfeld, G. E., Bloch, S. A. and Ives, J. W. (1984) 'Possible Determinants of Social Dominance Among Adolescent Girls,' *Journal of Genetic Psychology* 144(1): 115–29.

Williams, A. (2006) 'Before Spring Break, the Anorexic Challenge,' *New York Times* Sunday Styles 2. April: 1.

Yalom, M. (2004) *Birth of the Chess Queen: A History.* New York: HarperCollins Publishers.

Yee, N. (2004) 'Avatar: Use/Conceptualization and Looking Glass Self': Terranova Blog, URL (accessed 17 May 2006): http://terranova.blogs.com/terra_nova/2004/01/the_avatar_and_.html

Yee, N. (2006) 'WoW Gender-Bending' Daedalus Project, URL (accessed 2 April 2006): http://www.nickyee.com/daedalus/archives/001369.php

PART VII

IS TV FOR REAL?

Locating media texts within the context of the politics and economics of production helps ensure that we understand how the products we consume are rooted within a **capitalist** system that shapes, to varying degrees, the content, narratives, and **ideologies** of the text. Richard Butsch (VII.53) provides a good example of this approach in his analysis of how corporate control of the national television industry has been shaping the representations of working-class men as primarily "buffoons"—"dumb, immature, irresponsible, and lacking in common sense"—on 400 prime-time television sitcoms produced over 60 years (p. 507). Given the high cost of producing a television series such as a situation comedy, he argues that "television networks' first concern affecting program decisions is risk avoidance" (p. 510). Thus, once a formula has proved successful, "network executives have chosen programs that repeat the same images of class decade after decade" (p. 510).

While Butsch's chapter focuses on homegrown, scripted television content, Chris Jordan (VII.54) introduces us to the **political economy** of international reality TV. Using the historical example of the wildly popular *Survivor* series, this chapter explores "why reality television is a global staple of domestic and international prime time television," and concludes that such shows fit the needs of producers, networks, and advertisers in an age of global television. The formulas of a reality TV series lend themselves particularly well to international franchising. Jordan's study shows that

> *Survivor*'s relatively low cost and high ratings potential made the show imminently marketable worldwide. . . . Overseas broadcasters that have licensed the American format of *Survivor* and created their own versions include China's CCTV, the Middle East satellite

platform Gulf DTH, South Africa's SABC, Mexico's Televisa, and stations in Scandinavia, Eastern Europe, and throughout Asia. (p. 520)

For the most part, audiences understand that the content of so-called reality television is far from completely spontaneous, and, indeed, the appeal lies to a large extent in the voyeuristic expectation that we are going to catch dramatic glimpses of "real life." This makes it all the more important to look closely at such **texts** and learn how to see through and beyond their surface appearances and evaluate their claim to "reality." Our next two chapters offer readings of representations of **race** in reality show texts, the first pointing to a **progressive** potential when African American males are involved in the production of shows about African American families, and the second warning that mainstream reality-show producers continue to be looking for stereotypical "ethnic" behavior in competition-style reality shows.

Debra C. Smith (VII.55) argues that (relatively) "unscripted 'reality' television has the capacity to present . . . Black family life in 'authentically' complex ways" (p. 525). She offers a cautiously positive reading of two reality shows featuring African American fatherhood and produced by African American male hip-hop celebrities: Calvin Broadus (Snoop Dogg) and Joseph Simmons (Rev. Run, of Run-DMC). Smith sees in these cable-network reality shows the possibility of counterhegemonic imagery in a post-*Cosby* era. She points also to the capacity of reality shows to display a welcome class diversity in the portrayals of Black family life from the perspectives of the new generation of African American producers. In her view, "the 'safer' show, *Run's House,* demonstrates template-like similarities to *Cosby*, while *Father Hood* further drives behind the scenes to show the audience working-class realities consistent with Snoop's intentional opposition to *Cosby*'s reality" (p. 533).

Drawing on viewer responses from the websites for these shows, Smith analyzes

the themes of fathers' presence, fathers' disciplinary styles, and Black fathers as role models, concluding that these shows provide "much-needed visibility to alternative constructions of Black fatherhood/family" (p. 533).

On a more critical note, in the context of the competition reality show genre, Grace Wang (VII.56) shows how the familiar trope of the Asian American "model minority"—as a technically proficient but robotic performer—must be negotiated, and indeed performed, if an Asian American contestant is to succeed. Using as one example a particular season of the Bravo network's program *Top Chef*, Wang argues that "while reality TV programs open up a space for greater representation of racialized minorities, these shows also adhere to, and authenticate, racialized narratives and stereotypes by embodying them in the characters of 'real' people" (p. 537). In this example, also using interviews given by the contestant outside the context of the show, she demonstrates how the "savvy" Vietnamese American chef picked up on early comments and criticisms by the show's panel of judges, to the effect that "his food communicated neither passion nor a sense of his identity as an individual born in Vietnam," and responded by completely transforming his onscreen persona. According to Wang,

On *Top Chef*, the nuance of Hung's life story and his multilayered relationship to cuisine were compressed into an easily digestible story of immigrant success achieved through hard work, humility, gratitude, and maintaining one's ethnic heritage and "roots." (p. 541)

Many critics of reality television argue that the shows often encode the **neoliberal** discourse that is now so popular in the West, based on the key belief that, according to the formulation of Laurie Ouellette (VII.57), the "free" market is "the best way to organize every dimension of social life" (p. 546). Ouellette's chapter invites us to see the long-running and popular courtroom reality show *Judge Judy* as a fusion of "television, neoliberalism, and self-help discourse" that "attempts to shape and guide the conduct and choices of lower-income women in particular" (p. 546).

Judge Judy, the former New York family court judge Judith Sheindlin, "plays judge, prosecutor, professional expert, and punctilious moral authority, handling an average of two cases per thirty-minute episode" (p. 548). Sheindlin is known for her no-nonsense treatment of the working-class people in financial and/or family trouble who appear in her simulated TV courtroom, having agreed to accept her decision as final. As Judge Judy, she offers "citizenship lessons" to those who are constructed as failing in their economic and familial responsibilities—especially couples who live together outside of marriage and people who must apply for public assistance. As Ouellette points out, in this show's version of "reality," "all women are presumed to be capable of supporting themselves and their children financially; accepting welfare is construed not as a reflection of gender or economic inequality but as a character flaw" (p. 551).

While the concept of self-empowerment for women was first articulated within a liberal feminist discourse in the 1980s, it has since been repackaged for a **postfeminist** age, as several chapters in this part and elsewhere in the book point out. A particularly interesting example is what Sue Tait (VII.58) calls "the domestication of cosmetic surgery," in which television plays a significant role. Tait's study links the reality show *Extreme Makeover* with the edgy dramatic series *Nip/Tuck* as manifestations and media vehicles of the "culture's surgical turn"—that is, the disappearance of prior negative associations with this radical approach to improving one's appearance. In contrast to surgical reality shows, Tait argues, "*Nip/Tuck*'s response to surgical culture provides moments of resistance" (p. 563). Yet these textual gestures in the direction of a critical perspective on the **ideological** underpinnings of cosmetic surgery

"are frequently overwhelmed by the requirement to render the surgeon characters as redeemable, and by a sensationalism which prefers the dramatic over the political" (p. 563). In Tait's view, neither show challenges "a culture that is inevitably surgical," and she concludes critically, "As these two shows illustrate, feminist responses to cosmetic surgery are overwhelmed by a post-feminism which asserts our right to shape ourselves" (p. 563).

We end this part with two chapters that explore the ways television content and distribution are shifting in response to rapid technological changes in our age of **media convergence**, when the boundaries between commercial and noncommercial media formats and **platforms** have become less clear and what was formerly broadcast and then cablecast television content continues to migrate onto laptops and other mobile electronic devices, as well as the Internet.

In Chapter VII.59, Abigail De Kosnik argues that in a 21st century world, where television is facing a diminishing appeal to younger consumers, the creators of television entertainment content are "in the position of having to defend its relevance, having to rally and broadcast the reasons why it still matters" (p. 570). In this context, she analyzes a pattern in some recent prime-time programs in which fictional characters are able to find their "true selves" through moments when they "make spectacles of themselves in the eyes of others" (p. 565). As she interprets this pattern, it is television's response to anxieties about the authenticity of identity aroused by gossip culture on the Internet. As she sees it,

> TV is calling up arguments that it has used since the 1950s, arguments that add up to the fact that television is theatre and therapy all at once. . . . Ultimately television uses drama . . . as both a cure for Internet gossip and as a serious competitor for it. (p. 570)

Michael Z. Newman (VII.60) also writes about the shifts in television's appeal and status in the Internet age in his analysis of the discourse of television file sharers (those who circulate digital files of television content "free" online, among peers). Newman is gratifyingly attentive to the gendered dimension of the shift in TV's status among technically savvy file sharers, arguing that this new way of distributing television content

is one among a cluster of technologies of agency, making TV more culturally respectable by masculinizing the experience, articulating it with activity and discernment rather than the more feminized and passive characteristics that defined television from its earliest days of widespread adoption. (p. 574)

Newman also points out that while the media industries may see file-sharing as "piracy," his sample of "users find it hard to accept downloading of TV shows as free-riding or stealing, and often view advertising-avoidance in positive rather than negative moral terms" (p. 578). He argues that recent efforts by the television industry to spread content digitally through monetized means amount to "a form of protection from file-sharing and the threat it poses to the traditional business models of the TV industry" (p. 578). Thus, he has given us an interesting example of how, in a convergence era, consumers with digital tools may actually have an impact, even if temporary, on the television industry's political economy.

53

Six Decades of Social Class in American Television Sitcoms

Richard Butsch

Strewn across our mass media are portrayals that justify class relations of modern capitalism. Studies of comic strips, radio serials, television series, movies, and popular fiction reveal a persistent pattern underrepresenting working-class occupations and overrepresenting professional and managerial occupations, minimizing the visibility of the working class. Similar patterns are evident for other subordinate statuses on race, gender, and regional lines.

My own studies of class in prime-time network television family series from 1946 to 2004 (Butsch, 1992, 2005; Butsch & Glennon, 1983; Glennon & Butsch, 1982) indicate that this pattern persisted over six decades of television and roughly 400 domestic situation comedies, including such icons as *I Love Lucy*, *The Brady Bunch*, *All in the Family*, and *The Simpsons*. In only about 10% of the series were heads of house portrayed as working class (i.e., holding occupations as blue-collar, clerical, or unskilled or semiskilled service workers). Widespread affluence was exaggerated as well. More lucrative, glamorous, or prestigious professions predominated over more mundane ones. Working wives were almost exclusively middle class and pursuing a career. Working-class wives, such as the title character in *Roseanne*, who have to work to help support the family, were rare.

Throughout these decades, the few working-class men were portrayed as buffoons. They are dumb, immature, irresponsible, and lacking in common sense. This is the character of the husbands in almost every sitcom depicting a blue-collar head of house—*The Honeymooners*, *The Flintstones*, *All in the Family*, *The Simpsons*, and *The King of Queens* being the most famous examples. The man is typically well intentioned, even lovable, but no one to respect or emulate. These men are played against more sensible wives, such as Alice in *The Honeymooners* or Carrie in *King of Queens*.

For most of this history, there were few buffoons in middle-class series. More typically, both parents were wise and worked cooperatively to raise their children in practically perfect families, as in *Father Knows Best*, *The Brady Bunch*, and *The Bill Cosby Show*. The humor came from the innocent foibles and fumbles of the children. The few middle-class

This piece is an original essay that was commissioned for this volume. It is an update of an earlier version, titled "Ralph, Fred, Archie, Homer, and the King of Queens: Why Television Keeps Re-creating the male Working-Class Buffoon," that appeared in the 3rd edition.

◆ 507

buffoons were usually in the form of the ditzy wife, such as Lucy, while the professional/managerial husband was the sensible, mature partner. Inverting gender status in working-class but not middle-class sitcoms makes this a statement about class more than gender.

The 1990s brought a shift in parts of this pattern. There was a significant increase in the number and percentage of working-class families represented in domestic sitcoms: Of 42 new domestic sitcoms from 1991 to 1999, 16 featured working-class families and 9 of those were Black families. Reverting back to form, in the 2000s, only three new working-class and four African American sitcoms were added. By 2008, working-class sitcoms again disappeared ("TV's Class Struggle," 2008). The depictions of middle-class males became more diverse in these two decades, with shows such as *Home Improvement* and *Two and Half Men* featuring men who succeeded at work but at home exhibited an insistent, adolescent, macho maleness—not buffoons but not super-parents either.

Still, the portrayals of working-class men remained relatively unchanged. The successful *King of the Hill* (1997), *King of Queens* (1998), and *Family Guy* (1999), as well as several shorter-lived series throughout the decade, reproduced the traditional, stereotyped working-class man, cast opposite a capable women. In the late 2000s and early 2010s, as sitcoms increased in number, negative stereotypes of the working-class man as buffoon recurred in *The Cleveland Show, Raising Hope,* and *Working Class*. On the other hand, middle-class sitcom families and their male characters grew more diverse and complicated. Capable and successful professional men appeared in *Hank, American Dad,* and *Modern Family. Modern Family* and *The New Normal* also featured competent, professional gay couples, albeit with quirks and within unconventional families. Three other shows focused on single mothers: *Cougar Town, I Hate My Teen Daughter,* and *Malibu Country.* All in all, it appears the old stereotype of working-class men persisted, even though other shows presented a wide range of character types and were more ambiguous about class. *Plus ça change, plus c'est la même chose.*

Why has television kept reproducing the working-class male caricature across six decades, despite major changes in the television industry? How has it happened? Seldom have studies of the television industry pinpointed how specific content arises. Studies of production have not been linked to studies of content any more than audience studies have been. What follows is an effort to explain the link between sitcom production and the persistent images produced. In the words of Connell (1977), "No evil-minded capitalistic plotters need be assumed because the production of ideology is seen as the more or less automatic outcome of the normal, regular processes by which commercial mass communications work in a capitalist system" (p. 195). The outcome of complex structural and cultural factors is what shaped and continues to shape the representation of working-class men, even as the television industry has undergone remarkable changes from the 1980s on.

I will describe the factors as they worked from the beginnings of TV sitcoms in the late 1940s into the 1980s and then examine what effects on representation were wrought by the growth of cable TV and the VCR in the 1980s, computers and the Internet in the 1990s, and the concomitant restructuring of the industry into a new oligopoly of global multimedia corporations. Finally, I will examine the 2000s and 2010s, which have seen substantial growth of cable networks commissioning new television series—although mostly hour-long dramas—and the growth of new TV outlets via Internet streaming to digital televisions, computers, and smartphones through new companies such as Netflix and Hulu. I will look at three levels of organization: (1) network domination of the industry, (2) the organization of decisions within the networks and on the production line, and (3) the work community and culture of the "creative personnel." I will trace how these levels may explain the consistency and persistence of the portrayals of the working class, under-representation of the working class, and specific negative stereotypes of working-class men in prime-time domestic sitcoms.

Network Domination and Persistent Images

For four decades, ABC, CBS, and NBC dominated the television industry. Ninety percent of television audiences watched these networks. They accounted for more than half of all television advertising revenue in the 1960s and 1970s and just under half by the late 1980s (Owen & Wildman, 1992). They therefore had the money and the audience to dominate the market as the only buyers of series programming from Hollywood producers and studios. The television series market was thus an oligopsony—the buyer equivalent of an oligopoly—with only three powerful buyers of sitcoms and several sellers (Federal Communications Commission [FCC] Network Inquiry Special Staff, 1980; Owen & Wildman, 1992).

Through the 1980s, cable networks and multistation owners (companies that own several local broadcast stations) began to challenge the dominance of the "big three." Their combined rating shrank from 56.5% in 1980 to 39.7% in 1990, even including the new Fox Broadcasting network that debuted in 1986 (Butsch, 2000, p. 269; Hindman & Wiegand, 2008). By 1999, the four-network rating had slipped to 28.6% ("Upscale Auds Ease B'casters," 1999), while advertising-supported cable had grown to 23.9% ("Young Auds Seek Web, Not Webs," 1999). Still, only five cable networks had sufficient funds in the 1990s to qualify as buyers of drama programming (Blumler & Spicer, 1990). In 2000, cable networks were beginning to become a factor in the market for new drama and comedy series ("B'cast, Cable: Trading Places," 2000); yet ABC, CBS, and NBC still accounted for the development of the

overwhelming majority of new series. However, by 2008, cable networks had become major buyers of new scripted series ("TV role reversal," 2009).

Whether or not dominance by the broadcast networks has slipped, many of the same factors that shaped their programming decisions shape the decisions of their cable competitors as well. The increased number of buyers has not resulted in the innovation and diversity in program development once expected (FCC Network Inquiry Special Staff, 1980). Jay Blumler and Carolyn Spicer (1990) and Robert Kubey (2004) interviewed writers, directors, and producers, and found that the promise of more openness to innovation and creativity was short-lived. The cost of drama programming limits buyers to only a handful of large corporations and dictates that programs must attract a large audience and avoid risk. Moreover, even when cable networks became viable buyers, they did not significantly increase the number of buyers because they seek niche markets, and a given new series idea can be sold only to a cable network seeking that niche. In other words, sitcoms tend to be custom made for a particular network.

Using their market power, networks maintained sweeping control over the production decisions of even highly successful producers, from initial idea for a new program to final filming or taping (Bryant, 1969, pp. 624–626; Gitlin, 1983; Pekurny, 1977, 1982; Winick, 1961). In the 1990s, the FCC freed the broadcast networks from rules established in 1970 to reduce their power. This allowed them to increase ownership of programs and in-house production and re-create the vertical integration of television production of the 1950s and 1960s ("TV's Little Guys Stayin' Alive," 2001). It also enabled the movement of film studios into television ownership and created much larger multimedia corporations.

By the late 2000s, programs streaming via Internet to TVs, computers, tablets, and smartphones threatened TV networks. In 2007, 5% of the TV audience was viewing via DVR (Consoli & Crupi, 2007). By 2012, more than 100,000 movies and TV shows were available via Internet (Graser, 2011) and more than 20% of U.S. households had Internet-ready video devices (Lisanti, 2012). These alternative delivery systems began to seriously challenge the broadcast and even cable networks delivering to the standard television (Carr, 2013). Netflix and other Internet outlets were preparing to order their own first-run series. In 2011, first-run series were still costly and risky, but basic cable was becoming a more significant player in the market for commissioning them, although more for hour-long dramas than half-hour sitcoms. The United States, for example, by 2012 had developed a prime-time schedule full of its own hour-long drama series.

All this will further reduce the oligopsony of broadcast networks. So uniformity and persistence of representations of class are likely to be less the consequence of a concentrated market of buyers of sitcoms. But television dependence on advertising revenue and its influence on sitcom content remains. It means that more efforts will be made to prevent audiences from skipping advertising—for example, by using product placement within shows and stopping DVRs from fast-forwarding through commercials.

Network Decision Making: Program Development

Television networks' first concern affecting program decisions is risk avoidance. Popular culture success is notoriously unpredictable. The music recording industry spreads risk over many records so that any single decision is less significant (Peterson & Berger, 1971; Rossman, 2005). Spreading risk is not a strategy available to networks (neither broadcast nor cable), since only a few programming decisions fill the prime-time hours that account for most income. Networks are constrained further from expanding the number of their decisions by their use of the series as the basic

unit of programming. The benefit of the series format is that it increases ratings predictability from week to week, but it reduces the number of prime-time programming decisions to fewer than 50 for the whole season. So each decision represents a considerable financial risk, not simply in production costs but in advertising income as well. Success may produce a windfall. For example, ABC multiplied its profits fivefold from 1975 to 1978 by raising its average prime-time ratings from 16.6 to 20.7 (W. Behanna, personal communication, 1980). But mistakes can cause severe losses.

Since programming decisions are risky and costly, and network executives' careers rest on their ability to make the right decisions, they are constrained, in their own interest, to avoid innovation and novelty. They stick to tried-and-true formulas, a common complaint among successful television writers and producers (Brown, 1971; Kubey, 2004; Wakshlag & Adams, 1985). They also prefer those who have a track record of success. The result is a small, closed community of proven creative personnel (roughly 500 producers, writers, and directors) closely tied to and dependent on the networks (Gitlin, 1983, pp. 115, 135; Kubey, 2004; Pekurny, 1982; Tunstall & Walker, 1981, pp. 77–79). These proven talents then self-censor their work on the basis of a product image their previous experience tells them the networks will tolerate (Cantor, 1971; Pekurny, 1982; Ravage, 1978), creating an "imaginary feedback loop" (Dimaggio & Hirsh, 1976) between producers and network executives. These same conditions continue to characterize program development in the 1980s, 1990s, and 2000s, since the new buyers of programming—cable networks—operate under the same constraints as broadcast networks do.

To avoid risk, network executives have chosen programs that repeat the same images of class decade after decade. More diverse programming appeared only in the early days of the industry, when there were no past successes to copy—broadcast television in the early 1950s and cable in the early 1980s—or when declining ratings made it clear that past successes no longer worked (Blumler & Spicer, 1992; Turow, 1982b, p. 124). Dominick (1976) found that the lower the profits of the networks, the more variation in program types could be discerned from season to season and the less network schedules resembled one another. For example, in the late 1950s, ABC introduced hour-long Western series to prime time to compete with NBC and CBS (FCC Office of Network Study, 1965). Again, in 1970, CBS purchased Norman Lear's then controversial *All in the Family*—other networks turned it down—to counteract a drift to an audience with demographics (rural and over 50) not desired by advertisers. Increased numbers of working-class and African American sitcoms appeared in the 1990s when television executives feared that the White middle class was turning to other entertainments ("Genre-ation Gap Hits Sitcoms," 1999).

Network acceptance of innovative programs takes much longer than for conventional programs and requires backing by the most successful producers (Turow, 1982b, p. 126). *Roseanne* was introduced by Carsey-Werner, producers of the top-rated *Cosby Show*, when ABC was trying to counter ratings losses (Reeves, 1990, pp. 153–154). Hugh Wilson, the creator of *WKRP* and *Frank's Place*, described CBS in 1987 as desperate about slipping ratings: "Consequently they were the best people to work for from a creative standpoint" (Campbell & Reeves, 1990, p. 8). Even as declining ratings spurred networks to try innovative programs in the 1990s, they still tended to hire proven talent within the existing production community. The new ideas that were accepted came from (or through) established figures in the industry. As cable networks began to buy series, they contributed to this pattern by supporting programming that satisfied their niche audience but would offend some portion of the broadcast networks' mass market.

The second factor affecting network decisions on content is the need to produce programming suited to advertising. What the audience wants—or what network executives imagine they want—is secondary to ad revenue. Pay-cable networks, not bound by this constraint, have been freer to explore sexual and violent content—as in the *Sopranos*—that may have scared off advertisers but attracts an audience. In matters of content, advertising-supported networks avoid content that will offend or dissatisfy advertisers (Bryant, 1969). For example, ABC contracts with producers in 1977 stipulated the following:

> No program or pilot shall contain . . . anything . . . which does not conform with the then current business or advertising policies of any such sponsor; or which is detrimental to the good will or the products or services of . . . any such sponsor. (FCC Network Inquiry Special Staff, 1980, Appendix C, p. A-2)

Gary Marshall, producer of several highly successful series in the 1970s, stated that ABC rejected a story line for *Mork & Mindy*, the top-rated show for 1978, in which Mork takes TV ads literally, buys everything, and creates havoc. Despite the series' and Marshall's proven success, the network feared advertisers' reactions to such a story line.

An advertiser's preferred program is one that allows full use of the products being advertised. The program should be a complementary context for the ad. In the 1950s, an ad agency rejecting a play about working-class life stated, "It is the general policy of advertisers to glamorize their products, the people who buy them, and the whole American social and economic scene" (Barnouw, 1970, p. 32). Advertisers in 1961 considered it "of key importance" to avoid "irritating, controversial, depressive, or 'downbeat' material" (FCC Office of Network Study, 1965, p. 373). This requires dramas built around affluent characters for whom consuming is not problematic. Thus, affluent characters predominate, and occupational groups with higher levels of consumer expenditure are overrepresented. Even in a working-class domestic sitcom, it is unusual for financial strain to be a regular theme of the show—two exceptions being *The Honeymooners* and *Roseanne*.

A third factor in program decisions is whether the program will attract the right audience. Network executives construct a product image of what they *imagine* the audience wants—which, surprisingly, often is not based on actual market research on audiences (Blumler & Spicer, 1992; Pekurny, 1982). Michael Dann, a CBS executive, was "concerned the public might not accept a program about a blue collar worker" when offered the pilot script for *Arnie* in 1969 (before *All in the Family* proved that wrong and after a decade in which the only working-class family appearing in prime time was *The Flintstones*). On the other hand, in 1979, an NBC executive expressed the concern that a couple in a pilot was too wealthy to appeal to most viewers (Turow, 1982b, p. 123). Sitcom producer Lee Rich said, "A television series, to be truly successful, has got to have people you can identify with or dream about being" (Kubey, 2004, p. 102). For the sought-after middle-class audience, then, advertisers prefer affluent, middle-class characters.

Aside from anecdotes such as I have mentioned, almost no research has examined program development or production decisions about class content of programs. My own research found no significant differences between characters in sitcom pilots and series from 1973 to 1982, indicating that class biases in content begin very early in the decision-making process, when the first pilot episode is being developed (Butsch, 1984). I therefore conducted a mail survey of the producers, writers, or directors of the pilots from 1973 to 1982. I specifically asked how the decisions were made about the occupation of the characters in their pilot. I was able to contact 40 persons concerning 50 pilots. I received responses from 6 persons concerning 12 pilots.

Although the responses represent only a small portion of the original sample, they are strikingly similar. Decisions on occupations of main characters were made by the creators and made early in program development as part of the program idea. In no case did the occupation become a matter of debate or disagreement with the networks. Moreover, the choice of occupation was incidental to the situation or other aspect of the program idea; thus, it was embedded in the creators' conception of the situation. For example, according to one writer, a character was conceived of as an architect "to take advantage of the Century City" location for shooting the series; the father in another pilot was cast as owner of a bakery after the decision to do a series about an extended Italian family; and in another pilot, the creator thought the actor "looked like your average businessman." The particular occupations and even the classes are not necessitated by the situations creators offered as explanations. But they did not seem to be hiding the truth; their responses were open and unguarded. It appears they did not consciously consider whether they wished to portray this *particular* class or occupation; rather, to them, the occupation was derivative of the situation or location or actors they chose. They didn't think of characters explicitly in terms of class but, rather, as a personality type that may conjure up a particular occupation. This absence of any awareness of decisions about class is confirmed by Gitlin's (1983) and Kubey's (2004) interviews with industry personnel.

Thus, the process of class construction seems difficult to document given the unspoken guidelines, the indirect manner in which they suggest class, and the absence of overt decisions about class. Class or occupation is not typically an issue for discussion, as obscenity or race is. The choice of class is thus diffuse and indirect, drawn from a culture that provides no vocabulary to think explicitly and speak directly about class. To examine this further, we need to look at the organization of the production process and the culture of creative personnel.

Cable changed television markets from mass to niche so that some networks, especially those not supported by advertising, could be more risky and risqué. Yet sitcoms, due in part to production costs, were still targeting a broader mass market. By the 2000s, however, more networks and outlets, and thus more shows, were beginning to push the envelope of what was successful. Future added delivery via the Internet to computers and smartphones is likely to increase diversity of programming and characterization.

The Impacts of Time Constraints, Work Community, and Culture in Television Series Production

Within the production process in Hollywood studios and associated organizations, and in the work culture of creative personnel, we find factors that contribute to the use of simple and repetitious stereotypes of working-class men.

An important factor in television drama production is the severe time constraints of production (Kubey, 2004; Lynch, 1973; Ravage, 1978; Reeves, 1990). The production schedule for series requires that a finished program be delivered to the networks each week. Even if the production company had the entire year to complete the season's 22 to 24 episodes, an episode would have to be produced on the average every 2 weeks, including script writing, casting, staging, filming, and editing. This is achieved through an assembly-line process where several episodes are in various stages of production and being worked on by the same team of producer, writers, director, and actors, simultaneously.

Such a schedule puts great pressures on the production team to simplify as much as possible the amount of work necessary and the decisions to be made. The series format is advantageous for this reason: When the general story line and main characters are set, the script can be written following a simple formula. For situation comedy, even the sets and cast do not change from episode to episode.

The time pressures contribute in several ways to dependence on stereotypes for characterization. First, sitcoms are based on central characters rather than plot and development. These characters are coming into the living rooms of people who have to like watching the characters and to find them believable (Kubey, 2004). All this means that, to sell a new series, writers should offer stock characters (i.e., stereotypes). Writing for the same stock character, week after week, also greatly reduces the task of producing a script.

Also, time pressure encourages typecasting for the minor characters who are new in each episode. The script is sent to a "breakdown" agency, which reads the script and extracts the description of characters for that episode. These brief character descriptions, not the script, are used by the casting agency to recommend actors (Turow, 1978). Occupation—and by inference, class—are an important part of these descriptions, identified for 84% of male characters. Not surprisingly, the descriptions are highly stereotyped (Turow, 1980).

Notably, most of the production pressures and processes remain the same in the 2010s, regardless of the vast changes in the television industry landscape, including the new delivery systems of Internet streaming. The three- or four-camera method of filming in front of a live audience favored by Norman Lear in the 1970s is still widely used—notably, by the recent most successful showrunner, Chuck Lorre—even while some sitcoms on cable seeking an edgier or more "discerning" niche market have turned to single-camera filming without a live audience, closer resembling feature-film production (Bissell, 2010). Also, while time pressures may be somewhat reduced due to the dissolution of the traditional season and fewer episodes commissioned at one time, still time remains insistent, forcing production teams to rush from task to task and seek ways to make the process more efficient and less time-consuming. Lorre refers to his own production schedule as "Chuck's Inferno" for its intense pace and pressure, just as Norman Lear advised him: "You run around like a madman" (Bissell, 2010, p. 33).

Producers, casting directors, and casting agencies freely admit to stereotyping but argue its necessity on the basis of time and dramatic constraints. Typecasting is easier and much quicker. They also argue that to diverge from widely held stereotypes would draw attention away from the action, the story line, or other characters and destroy dramatic effect. In addition, stereotyped stock characters are familiar to audiences, requiring less dramatic explanation. Thus, unless the contradiction of the stereotype is the basic story idea—as in *Arnie*, whose title character was a blue-collar worker suddenly appointed as a corporate executive—there is strong pressure to reproduce existing stereotypes.

The time pressures also make it more likely that the creators will stick to what is familiar to them as well. Two of the most frequent occupations of main characters in family series up to 1980 were in entertainment and writing—that is, modeled on the creators' own lives (Butsch & Glennon, 1983)—and that trend continues today, as many sitcom stars are well-known comics and actors. The vast majority of writers and producers come from upper-middle-class families, with little direct experience with working-class life (Cantor, 1971; Gitlin, 1983; Kubey, 2004; Stein, 1979; Thompson & Burns, 1990). Moreover, the tight schedules and deadlines of series production leave no time for becoming familiar enough with the working-class lifestyle to capture it realistically. Those who have done so (e.g., Jackie Gleason, Norman Lear) had childhood memories of working-class neighborhoods to draw on.

Thus, the time pressure encourages creative personnel to rely heavily on a shared and consistent product image—including diffuse and undifferentiated images of class—embedded in what Elliott (1972) called the media culture. The small, closed community of those engaged in television production, including Hollywood creators and network executives (Blumler & Spicer, 1990; Gitlin, 1983; Stein, 1979; Tunstall & Walker, 1981; Turow, 1982a), shares a culture that includes certain conceptions of what life is like and what the audience finds interesting. According to Norman Lear, the production community draws its ideas from what filters into it from the mass media, which is then interpreted through the lens of members' own class experiences and culture, to guess what "the public" would like and formulate images of class they think are compatible (Gitlin, 1983, pp. 204, 225–226).

The closeness of this community is both reflected in and reinforced by the hiring preference for proven talent already in the community, lack of any apprenticeship system to train new talent, and the importance of social networking or, as one director phrased it, "nepotism" in obtaining work (Kubey, 2004). The production community in the 2000s continues to be small and insular, much like Hollywood as described by Leo Rosten in 1941. Stories of successes repeatedly begin with an intermediary close to a member of or in that community through whom the newcomer's work was first brought to the attention of decision makers. For example, sitcom showrunner Chuck Lorre got his first break by virtue of knowing a neighbor of perennial sitcom actress Betty White (Bissell, 2010, p. 36).

Thus, while the consistency of image, underrepresentation, and stereotyping of the working class can be explained by structural constraints, the particular stereotypes grow from a rather diffuse set of cultural images, constrained and framed by the structure of the industry. Reaching the vast majority of the population for more than half a century and seeping into everyday conversation, sitcoms have made a significant contribution to our culture's attitude toward the man who makes his living with his hands. It is an attitude based on the presumption, repeated again and again by these sitcoms, that this man is dumb, immature, irresponsible, lacking common sense, often frustrated, and sometimes angry. This legitimates his low pay and close supervision at work. Further, it is an attitude of disrespect for him everywhere else in the public realm. That disrespect is the ultimate "hidden injury" that working-class interviewees expressed to Richard Sennett and Jonathan Cobb (1972) in the early 1970s, just about the time Archie Bunker first appeared on network television. The continuing stereotype in sitcoms tells us *plus ça change* . . . the injury remains the same.

References

Barnouw, E. (1970). *The image empire: A history of broadcasting in the U.S. from 1953.* New York: Oxford University Press.

B'cast, cable: Trading places. (2000, April 24). *Variety*, p. 61.

Bissell, T. (2010, December 6). A simple medium. *New Yorker*, 33–41.

Blumler, J., & Spicer, C. (1990). Prospects for creativity in the new television marketplace. *Journal of Communication, 40*(4), 78–101.

Brown. L. (1971). *Television: The business behind the box.* New York: Harcourt, Brace.

Bryant, A. (1969). Historical and social aspects of concentration of program control in television. *Law and Contemporary Problems, 34*, 610–635.

Butsch, R. (1984). *Minorities from pilot to series: Network selection of character statuses and traits.* Paper presented at the Society for the Study of Social Problems annual meeting, Washington, D.C.

Butsch, R. (1992). Class and gender in four decades of television situation comedy. *Critical Studies in Mass Communication, 9*, 387–399.

Butsch, R. (2000). *The making of American audiences.* Cambridge, UK: Cambridge University Press.

Butsch, R. (2005). Five decades and three hundred sitcoms about class and gender. In G. Edgerton & B. Rose (Eds.), *Thinking outside the box: A contemporary television genre reader* (pp. 111–135). Lexington: University Press of Kentucky.

Butsch, R., & Glennon, L. M. (1983). Social class: Frequency trends in domestic situation comedy, 1946–1978. *Journal of Broadcasting, 27*, 77–81.

Campbell, R., & Reeves, J. (1990). Television authors: The case of Hugh Wilson. In R. Thompson & G. Burns (Eds.), *Making television* (pp. 3–18). New York: Praeger.

Cantor, M. (1971). *The Hollywood TV producer.* New York: Basic Books.

Carr, D. (2013, March 18). Spreading disruption. *New York Times*, pp. B1, B5.

Connell, B. (1977). *Ruling class, ruling culture.* London: Cambridge University Press.

Consoli, J., & Crupi, A. (2007, April 30). DVRs make their presence felt. *MediaWeek, 17*(18), 8–10.

DiMaggio, P., & Hirsch, P. (1976). Production organization in the arts. *American Behavioral Scientist, 19*, 735–752.

Dominick, J. (1976, Winter). Trends in network prime time, 1953–74. *Journal of Broadcasting, 26*, 70–80.

Elliott, P. (1972). *The making of a television series: A case study in the sociology of culture.* New York: Hastings.

Federal Communications Commission Network Inquiry Special Staff. (1980). *Preliminary reports.* Washington, DC: U.S. Government Printing Office.

Federal Communications Commission Office of Network Study. (1965). *Second interim report: Television network program procurement, Part II.* Washington, DC: U.S. Government Printing Office.

Genre-ation gap hits sitcoms. (1999, April 26). *Variety*, p. 25

Gitlin, T. (1983). *Inside prime time.* New York: Pantheon.

Glennon, L. M., & Butsch, R. (1982). The family as portrayed on television, 1946–78. In National Institute of Mental Health (Ed.), *Television and social behavior: Ten years of scientific progress and implications for the eighties* (Vol. 2, Technical Review, pp. 264-271). Washington, DC: U.S. Government Printing Office.

Graser, M. (2011, December 5). Cyber-bidding war. *Variety,* pp. 1, 35.

Hindman, D., & Wiegand, K. (2008). The big three's prime-time decline. *Journal of Broadcasting and Electronic Media, 52*(1), 119–135.

Kubey, R. (2004). *Creating television: Conversations with the people behind 50 years of American TV.* Mahwah, NJ: Lawrence Erlbaum.

Lisanti, J. (2012, May 21). Games grow home nets. *Variety,* p. 2.

Lynch, J. (1973). Seven days with *All in the Family*: A case study of the taped TV drama. *Journal of Broadcasting, 17*(3), 259–274.

Owen, B., & Wildman, S. (1992). *Video economics.* Cambridge, MA: Harvard University Press.

Pekurny, R. (1977). *Broadcast self-regulation: A participant observation study of NBC's broadcast standards department.* Unpublished doctoral dissertation, University of Minnesota.

Pekurny, R. (1982). Coping with television production. In J. S. Ettema & D. C. Whitney (Eds.), *Individuals in mass media organizations* (pp. 131–143). Beverly Hills, CA: Sage.

Peterson, R. A., & Berger, D. (1971). Entrepreneurship in organizations: Evidence from the popular music industry. *Administrative Science Quarterly, 16,* 97–107.

Ravage, J. (1978). *Television: The director's viewpoint.* New York: Praeger.

Reeves, J. (1990). Rewriting culture: A dialogic view of television authorship. In R. Thompson & G. Burns (Eds.), *Making television* (pp. 147–160). New York: Praeger.

Rossman, G. (2005). *The effects of ownership concentration on media content.* Unpublished doctoral dissertation, Princeton University.

Rosten, L. (1941). *Hollywood: The movie colony, the movie makers.* New York: Harcourt Brace.

Sennett, R., & Cobb, J. (1972). *The hidden injuries of class.* New York: W. W. Norton.

Stein, B. (1979). *The view from Sunset Boulevard.* New York: Basic Books.

Thompson, R., & Burns, G. (Eds.). (1990). *Making television: Authorship and the production process.* New York: Praeger.

Tunstall, J., & Walker, D. (1981). *Media made in California.* New York: Oxford University Press.

Turow, J. (1978). Casting for TV parts: The anatomy of social typing. *Journal of Communication, 28*(4), 18–24.

Turow, J. (1980). Occupation and personality in television dramas. *Communication Research, 7*(3), 295–318.

Turow, J. (1982a). Producing TV's world: How important is community? *Journal of Communication, 32*(2), 186–193.

Turow, J. (1982b). Unconventional programs on commercial television. In J. S. Ettema & D. C. Whitney (Eds.), *Individuals in mass media organizations* (pp. 107–139). Beverly Hills, CA: Sage.

TV role reversal. (2009, January 12). *Variety,* p. 1.

TV's class struggle. (2008, September 22). *Variety,* p. 1.

TV's little guys stayin' alive. (2001, February 19). *Variety,* p. 1.

Upscale auds ease b'casters. (1999, August 23). *Variety,* p. 34.

Wakshlag, J., & Adams, W. J. (1985). Trends in program variety and prime time access rules. *Journal of Broadcasting and Electronic Media, 29,* 23–34.

Winick, C. (1961). Censor and sensibility: A content analysis of the television censor's comments. *Journal of Broadcasting, 5,* 117–135.

Young auds seek Web, not webs. (1999, January 4). *Variety,* p. 65.

54

Marketing "Reality" to the World

Survivor, Post-Fordism, and Reality Television

Chris Jordan

This chapter analyzes the production, distribution, and consumption of *Survivor* in order to explain why reality television is a global staple of domestic and international prime time television.[1] It argues that intensifying concentration of ownership in the television industry, the worldwide proliferation of commercial television, the fragmentation of the global television audience, and the design of *Survivor*, as a thinly veiled advertisement, account for its success.

The centrifugal trends of media industry ownership concentration and global television audience fragmentation exemplify post-Fordism. . . . The Fordist system of manufacturing and marketing strove to maximize profits by making one commodity appeal to as many consumers as possible for as long as possible (Harvey 145). Under post-Fordism, capitalism responds to the global flow of labor and consumption markets within and between nation-states by transforming local and regional cultures into market segments and mobilizing citizens as consumers. By implementing a post-Fordist strategy of diversifying its products and their marketing in order to incorporate diverse locales, capitalism transforms a problem into an opportunity, as it markets products for both global markets and niche segments to take advantage of the countervailing flows of localism and globalism (Fiske, "Global" 58).

Stuart Hall contends that post-Fordism promotes democracy by globally circulating media products and other consumer goods (62). Reality television programs thus flow both ways between the United States and other nations. As John Fiske argues, globalization thus provokes localization, multiplying histories through migration and diaspora and eroding a sense of nationalism built around the interests of dominant groups ("Global"). . . .

Production of Reality Television: The Medium Is the Advertiser's Message

. . . . Charlie Parsons and former rock band singer Bob Geldof developed the concept that became *Survivor* at their British TV production company, Planet 24. When Parsons and Geldof sold Planet 24 in 1999, they retained the rights to *Survive!*, which was being produced in Sweden by the duo's Castaway Productions, under the name *Expedition: Robinson*. The next year, Parsons and Geldof licensed the *Survive!* concept to Mark Burnett, for a U.S. version that ended up launching the reality TV craze in America.

As an independent producer, Burnett faced an uphill battle in gaining access to prime time, because the relaxation of government regulations in the 1990s made it possible for networks to produce many of their own shows. In 2000, all six broadcast networks either owned or co-owned more than half of their new shows, and three of them (ABC, CBS, and WB) owned or co-owned more than 75 percent of their new programs (Schneider and Adalian 70).

Survivor appealed to CBS because the co-production deal it struck with Burnett required no deficit financing, yet offered the network a program with the high quality production values that audiences expect of prime time television. Instead of paying Burnett a fee to license the show, CBS agreed to share the show's advertising revenue with him if he pre-sold sponsorship of the program. By pre-selling the show, Burnett raised the capital necessary to produce *Survivor*, provided CBS with essentially free prime time programming, and enjoyed a hefty share of the show's advertising revenue.

Advertisers readily sponsored *Survivor* because of its design as a virtual commercial for their products. Burnett acquired eight sponsors before the commencement of principal photography during the first season, selling not only 30-second spots, but also sponsorship space in the show itself. Anheuser-Busch, General Motors, Visa, Frito-Lay, Reebok, and Target paid approximately $4 million each for advertising time, product placement in the show, and a website link (McCarthy, "Sponsors" B1). Even though *Survivor* is one of the most expensive reality shows to date, with production costs escalating from $1 million an episode for the first season to $1.5 million an episode for subsequent editions, it is profitable. With presold sponsorships covering production costs, and 30-second spots commanding $445,000 during the 2001–2002 season, *Survivor* proved that lavishly produced reality television shows could be low-risk and lucrative (Raphael 122).

Burnett's success in pitching *Survivor* to advertisers enabled the producer to circumvent the role of the advertising agency as a liaison between program creator and sponsor, making it even more cost efficient for sponsors. Producers started working directly with products' brand managers, moving away from shows such as *Temptation Island*, with overt sexual innuendo, and towards shows such as *Survivor* (see Littleton). Praised by CBS President Les Moonves as a "great pitchman," Burnett steered away from sexual sensationalism and towards themes of competitive merit, by explaining to advertisers "how much sense it would make for someone on an island a million miles from home to crave a soft drink or something to eat from home" ("Burnett Likes Mad Ave" 3).

At one time, advertisers balked at the insertion of a bag of chips or a soda into a situation comedy or drama, because it might break the audience's suspension of disbelief. However, *Survivor* host Jeff Probst's act of rewarding winners of the show's challenges with Doritos and Mountain Dew integrated the products into a circumstance that abstracted the line between programming and advertising by associating them with adventure and heroism. During *Survivor: Africa*, for example, the word "avalanche" was the answer to a reward challenge. Viewers then saw the winner driving a Chevrolet Avalanche across the African plain to deliver medical supplies to hospitals treating AIDS patients (McCarthy "Sponsors" B1). In 2001, Burnett received $14 million from marketers such as Mountain Dew and General Motors for the production of *Survivor: Africa* (McCarthy, "Also Starring" B1).

The design of *Survivor* as a virtual advertisement raises the issue of how television's goal of selling audiences to advertisers shapes the program. According to Sut Jhally, a television program must be able to attract large numbers of people. Second, it has to attract the "right" kinds of people. Not all parts of the audience are of equal value to advertisers. Television programs will also have to reflect this targeting, excluding demographic groups that lack the spending power to satisfy advertisers. Third, television must not only be able to deliver a large number of the correct people to advertisers, but must also deliver them in the right frame of mind. Programs should be designed to enhance the effectiveness of the ads in them (Jhally 76).

Survivor accomplishes all of these goals. Broadcast during prime time, it attracts a teen demographic sought by advertisers as well as a huge national audience composed of other age groups. According to *Variety, Survivor* delivered during its initial season more teens than *WWF Smackdown,* more young adults than *Friends,* more children than *Wonderful World of Disney,* and more 50-plus viewers than *60 Minutes* (Kissell 19). Rejecting the jittery hand-held camera style of public television documentaries of the 1970s, *Survivor* also boasts high quality production values that associate products woven into its text with adventure, heroism, and escape.

Survivor thus appeals to networks and advertisers because it combines high ratings with relatively low cost in comparison to comedies and dramas. The escalating cost of must-have sport and movie properties, and the success of special effects-driven docudramas such as BBC-Discovery's *Walking with Dinosaurs* during the 2000 television season, put drama budgets under scrutiny and encouraged U.S. producers to co-produce much more drama on the terms of European networks. Compounding the shift away from half-hour comedy shows and towards low-cost reality-entertainment hybrids was the lack of obvious successors to prime time smash hits such as *Seinfeld* [1989–1998] and *Friends* [1994–2004] (Fry M4). High quality production values and exotic locations became means through which *Survivor* targeted the prime time audience sought by advertisers, distinguished itself from cheaper crime-based reality shows, and blurred the line between prime time drama and reality shows ("TV's Peeper Producers Are Powerhouses" 1).

Reality television shows have thus proliferated on prime time television in recent years because they pose little financial risk for networks, yet offer prime-time-friendly production values and generate huge ratings. The use of Internet and cable television networks also attracts a young audience prized by advertisers. On this basis, *Survivor* became a valuable addition to Viacom's cradle-to-the-grave programming spectrum by enabling CBS, known for its primarily elderly audience, to capture a huge mass audience, as well as a slice of the highly coveted youth audience.

Distribution of *Survivor:* Creating a Global Franchise

.... While network television enables advertisers to target a huge audience, cable and the Internet can target specific viewer demographics and deliver them to advertisers at a lower cost. Viacom's cross-promotion of *Survivor* on CBS, its cable networks MTV and VH1, and its Internet websites CBS.com and MTV Networks Online enabled CBS to capture a young audience during the show's first episode and deliver it to advertisers along with a mass audience of 15.5 million.

During its second week, the show attracted 18.1 million viewers, a 17 percent gain (Schneider and Adalian 70). According to *Variety, Survivor* "gave CBS and Viacom tangible proof that corporate synergy works," by being the first CBS program to get the full marketing treatment from Viacom's youthful properties, MTV and VH1 (Kissell and Schneider 19).

CBS's use of the Internet also promoted interactivity between viewers and *Survivor,* allowing the network to extend the program beyond the confines of the television set, by encouraging audiences to participate in its dramatic trajectory by using other media to stay in touch with the show. Viewers stayed in touch with the program through the official *Survivor* website. Prolific coverage from established news outlets also generated several unsanctioned online homages, as the websites *Survivor* Junkie and Megadice offered winner predictions, plot spoilers, conspiracy theories, and other information of varying quality (Bing and Oppelaar 5). Mobile media, such as cellular telephones, offer additional means of promoting this interactivity and provide valuable information about the audience that is impossible to gather from any other source. Text-based advertising campaigns have been conducted in various countries by major brands, including Coca-Cola, Nike, and McDonald's (McCartney C1).

The ability of Viacom to endlessly promote *Survivor* across multiple media improved CBS's ability to quickly capture a large audience, during an era in which the network practice of ordering shows in small batches makes it imperative to transform a new show into a smash hit as quickly as possible. Variety observed that "the numbers for *Survivor* all the more amazing given that *Survivor* had only 13 weeks to generate viewer interest and such a rabid following . . ." (Kissell and Schneider 19).

Survivor's relatively low cost and high ratings potential made the show imminently marketable worldwide, especially in the wake of CBS's purchase of television syndication giant, King World, in 1999.

King World collaborates closely with international partners to produce shows carefully tailored to specific national markets, and creates customized promotional advertisements for international licensees (Compaine and Gomery 218). Overseas broadcasters that have licensed the American format of *Survivor* and created their own versions include China's CCTV, the Middle East satellite platform Gulf DTH, South Africa's SABC, Mexico's Televisa, and stations in Scandinavia, Eastern Europe, and throughout Asia (Guider 1).

The global popularity of *Survivor* is attributable, in part, to CBS's use of the economies of scale provided by the size of the U.S. television audience, to sell the program cheaply in developing countries. The proven commercial appeal of *Survivor's* format, and the relatively low cost of reality television production, also encourage foreign broadcasters to create their own versions of the program. . . .

The formation of advertising agencies with global reach provides evidence of the role of advertising in propagating the overseas proliferation of reality television. . . . Global consolidation is encouraged because the larger an advertising agency, the more leverage it has getting favorable terms for its clients with global commercial media (McChesney 86). "More and more, what (advertisers) want is to distribute their global dollars into fewer agency baskets," the *Wall Street Journal* observed in 1998 (Beatty 1).

The rise of transnational advertising agencies also enables sponsors such as Proctor & Gamble to penetrate developing countries with the offer of "free" programming, through which advertisers underwrite programming of general appeal, and provide it free of charge to financially struggling broadcasters (Schiller 330). The top 10 global advertisers alone accounted for some 75 percent of the $36 billion spent by the 100 largest global marketers in 1997 (McChesney 84). Advertising sponsorship thus plays a pivotal role in determining the type of programming made and broadcast by foreign television producers in their native markets.

The competition for audiences and advertisers created by the proliferation of broadcast, cable, and satellite television overseas has led broadcasters in other countries to seek low-cost programming with immediate ratings potential attractive to advertisers. . . .

The consequence of an increasing number of channels in formerly public television markets competing for funding and audiences is that broadcasters must spend greater and greater sums on marketing to get their shows noticed, intensifying pressures on program funding. The pressures on overseas networks to control production costs has in turn led to the concentration of television production in the hands of companies most able to supply low-cost, high volume programming. . . .

The adaptability of reality television shows to local cultures and the convertibility of the format into a virtual infomercial for sponsors' products raises a concern about the role of reality television in propagating the culture of consumption, in both the United States and other nations targeted by transnational capitalism. . . .

Consumption of Reality Television: Transforming Citizens Into Consumers

The global success of reality television is attributable to the practice of licensing the format of a show to overseas broadcasters for adaptation to specific markets. The strategy of formatting springs from the principal of product differentiation, through which network executives attempt to replicate a successful show by blatantly imitating it. Hits are so rare on network television that network executives think that a bald imitation stands a better chance of getting ratings than a show that stands alone. This results in the repackaging of old forms in slightly different permutations

(Gitlin 77–85). In the wake of *Survivor*'s success, television executives aggressively pursued imitations of it, as the number of reality television hours on broadcast television skyrocketed from four-and-a-half to 19 hours a week between Fall, 2002 and Fall, 2004 (McNary 21).

Paralleling this proliferation of reality television programming was the repetition of what the *New York Times* called a "hamsters-in-a-box" narrative design. The strategy of casting individuals on the basis of type, and forcing them to work and live together, became cross-pollinated with various genres, including game shows, gross-out contests, makeovers, dating programs, situation comedies, and satires (Nussbaum 2). The minimal difference between these many shows stems from the pressure of the marketplace to duplicate a financially successful show.

Financed by advertisers interested in cultivating new consumers abroad, the development of reality television as a format that flexibly incorporates national ideologies on a nation-by-nation basis further suggests that reality TV is first and foremost a commodity. In licensing the *Survivor* format from a British production company, CBS found a program that can be tailored on a market-by-market basis around the world, by integrating the game show and the adventure drama into a hybrid formula. Rather than democratizing global television programming, this trend organizes citizens into consumers by reifying capitalism as an ideology and a way of life. The design of *Survivor* as a game show/adventure/drama hybrid facilitates the placement of products in competitive circumstances that blend adventure and consumption.

In this way, the premise of the show— game show competitors seeking adventure in exotic locations that render global politics invisible—fuels demand for a lifestyle of conspicuous consumption around the world. The director marketing for Sony's AXN Action TV Network, on which *Survivor* airs in East Asia, exclaimed that "the focus on action and adventure is something that's really picking up—it's a new lifestyle for the young in Asia, a fact borne out by the rise in sales of four-by-four vehicles, for example" (Osborne 32).

The design of *Survivor* also affirms consumption as a way of life, both by attracting advertising and by enabling its producers to develop lucrative licensing deals that extend its shelf life. By organizing leisure time around the consumption of both these programs and pricey ancillary merchandise, *Survivor* encourages viewers to participate in a commodified system of exchange. While merchandising tie-ins have been around since the advent of television, they are now far more commonplace. There are now 150 *Survivor*-themed products available, ranging from CDs to bug spray, to board games, and bandanas (Madger 150). Reality television's organization of the audience into consumers socializes the public into behaving like a market, and as consumers rather than citizens.

Conclusion

This chapter argues that the worldwide proliferation of reality television is a product of the increasing concentration of ownership in the television industry, the globalization of commercial TV, and the fragmentation of the worldwide audience. The dependence of the U.S. and other governments on capital investment has led to the implementation of policies that enable the largest media corporations to curtail access to prime time television through in-house production and co-production, and by favoring programs that offer the lowest risk and the highest potential for ratings. The privatization of formerly public overseas broadcasters has also led television programmers in developing nations to seek out inexpensive programming capable of attracting advertisers and viewers.

The first casualty of this trend is educational programming. Television producers,

advertisers, and networks know that programs that are too long, too difficult to comprehend, or simply too boring will lead viewers to switch channels. In this way, reality television turns attention away from issues such as poverty in developing countries. The victory of a contestant from the African country of Zambia over a competitor from Tanzania on *Big Brother Africa* provided, according to *Variety,* "a welcome distraction from nationwide strikes in the impoverished country, where most people earn less than $1 a day" (De Jager 19). While some celebrate reality television's global popularity as a sign of the democratization of television production and distribution, a political economic study of reality television compels us to consider that economic determinism limits the possibilities of reality television's potential for democratic communication.

Note

1. Prime time refers to a twenty-two hour weekly period spanning 8PM to 11PM Monday through Saturday, with an extra hour on Sunday.

References

Beatty, Sally. "Survey Expects Pace of Mergers to Pick Up on Madison Avenue." *Wall Street Journal* 21 May 1998: 1.

———. "Who Owns Prime Time? Industrial and Institutional Conflict over Television Programming and Broadcast Rights." *Framing Friction: Media and Social Conflict.* Ed. Mary S. Mander. Urbana: University of Illinois Press, 1999. 125–160.

Bing, Jonathan and Justin Oppelaar. "'Rat' Race to Publish 1st Survivor Book Begins." *Variety* 28 August–3 September 2000: 4.

"Burnett Likes Mad Ave." *Advertising Age* 19 May 2003: 3.

Compaine, Benjamin and Douglas Gomery. *Who Owns the Media?: Competition and*

Concentration in the Mass Media. Mahwah, N.J.: Lawrence Erlbaum Associates, 2000.

De Jager, Christelle "Big Bro' Gives Reality New Meaning." *Variety* 15–21 September 2003: 19.

Fiske, John. "Global, National, Local? Some Problems of Culture in a Postmodern World." *Velvet Light Trap* 40 (1997): 58–66.

Fry, Andy. "Europe Secure as Leader of Reality Programming." *Variety* 25 September–1 October 2000: M4.

Gitlin, Todd. *Inside Prime Time.* New York: Pantheon Books, 1983.

Guider, Elizabeth. "Eye Floats Survivor Worldwide." *Variety* 18 January 2001: 1.

Harvey, David. *The Condition of Postmodernity.* Boston: Blackwell, 1989.

Jhally, Sut. "The Political Economy of Culture." *Cultural Politics in Contemporary Ameri*ca, Eds. Ian Angus and Sut Jhally. New York: Routledge, 1989. 65–81.

Kissell, Rick. "Survivor Fittest in All Demos." *Variety* 31 July–6 August 2000: 20.

Kissell, Rick and Schneider, M., "Summer Serves as Eye-Opener." *Variety* 28 August–3 September 2000: 19.

Littleton, Cynthia. "Dialogue: Mark Burnett." *Hollywood Reporter.* 26 May 2004. 18 Aug. 2004 <www.hollywoodreporter.com/thr/crafts/feature/display.jsp?vnu_content_id=10011523184>

Madger, Ted. "The End of TV 101: Reality Programs, Formats, and the New Business of Television." *Reality TV: Remaking Television Culture.* Eds. Laurie Oullette and Susan Murray. New York: New York University Press, 2004: 137–156.

McCarthy, Michael. "Also Starring (Your Product Name Here); Brands Increasingly Make Presence Known in TV Shows." *USA Today* 12 August 2004: B1.

———. "Sponsors Line Up Survivor Sequel." *USA Today* 9 October 2004: B1.

McCartney, Neil. "Can You Hear It Now?" *Variety* 29 March–4 April 2004: C1.

McChesney, Robert W. *Rich Media, Poor Democracy: Communication Politics in Dubious Times.* New York: The New Press, 1999.

McNarv, Dave. "Coming to Terms with Reality." *Variety* 4–10 October 2004: 21.

Nussbaum, Emily. "The Woman Who Gave Birth to Reality TV." *Variety* 22 February 2004: 2.

Osborne, Magz. "AXN Packs Reality Fare, Hopes Viewers Will Follow." *Variety* 5–11 February 2001: 32.

Raphael, Chad. "The Political Economic Origins of Reality TV." *Reality TV: Remaking Television Culture.* Eds. Laurie Oullette and Susan Murray. New York: New York University Press, 2004. 119–136.

Schiller, Herbert. "The Privatization of Culture." *Cultural Politics in Contemporary America.* Eds. Ian Angus and Sut Jhally. New York: Routledge, 1989. 317–332.

Schneider, Michael and Joseph Adalian. "Nets Get It Together." *Variety* 22–28 May 2000: 15.

"TV's Peeper Producers are Powerhouses." *Variety* 25 September–1 October 2000: 1.

55

Critiquing Reality-Based Televisual Black Fatherhood

A Critical Analysis of *Run's House* and *Snoop Dogg's Father Hood*

Debra C. Smith

The Cosby Show (*Cosby*), a network situational comedy, debuted September 20, 1984, to critical acclaim (Inniss & Feagin, 1995). From 1984 to 1992, Bill Cosby, producer and star of the show, unveiled a Black family who did not live in public housing or lament on how they would manage household expenses. In fact, scholars (Berman, 1987; Inniss & Feagin, 1995; Gray, 1995) declare that by design, the show was the first with an all-Black cast that managed to avoid racial stereotyping. Instead, the show focused on themes of family stability, heritage, and education, giving the NBC network a ratings winner, and instilling a sense of pride in Black people everywhere. Cosby himself said the show reflected his own philosophy that the Black community must take responsibility for its own fate ("The Cosby Show Legacy," 2005). Though *Cosby* was criticized as showcasing a Black family in White face that did not address racial and social issues, the show continued in the genre of happy endings, family values, and escapism, as it sauntered into the history books. The show was hailed as portraying Black men in a positive light; portraying Black families optimistically; showing Black Americans as being like other U.S. Americans; and modeling good examples for Black children (Inniss & Feagin, 1995). With its focus on parenting, values, and Black respectability, *Cosby* essentially normalized the nuclear family.

Two decades later, at least two Black families have emerged on reality television shows, both of which provide a platform from which to examine the televisual construction of Black fatherhood and family years after *Cosby*'s debut. *Run's House* and *Snoop Dogg's Father Hood* (*Father Hood*), both shows based on "real" Black families, can be interpreted in comparison and contrast to Cosby's version of upper-middle class Black fatherhood to (a) investigate constructions of Black fatherhood in a variety of positive forms, while challenging limited images of Black fathers on television; and (b) revive debates from Jhally and Lewis' (1992) book *Enlightened Racism,* as the families in the reality sitcoms simultaneously shift away from issues of race and class while still attempting to foster a strong identification with viewers. Throughout this chapter, arguments [based on the texts] will be contextualized by comments from critics and fans of the shows.

According to Brooks and Jacobs (1996), attention must be given to the potential inherent in television's ability to promote anti-essentialist and nonstereotypical images of African Americans (see Orbe, 1998). That being the case, this focus on unscripted "reality" television has the capacity to present the whole of Black family life in "authentically" complex ways. Such possibilities appear more likely—outside of traditional networks—within the cutting edge programming found on cable networks (Brooks & Jacobs). MTV has certainly enjoyed success, while supporting this argument, with its own version of Black family life portrayed in the show *Run's House,* as has *Father Hood* on E! Channel, as the stars of both shows set out to construct their own version of the twenty-first century family.

Run's House

Multiple studies (Berry, 1980; Greenberg & Atkin, 1978; Greenberg & Neuendorf, 1980; Merritt & Stroman, 1993) have analyzed the imagery of Black families on television and considered the messages that are perpetuated by the media. Some of these messages include the Black family as female-headed, characterized by conflict,

and having children in the home who experience little supervision and concern from their parents. But on Thursday, October 13, 2005, MTV debuted a Black television family that appeared to be in direct contradiction to these "realities."

Run's House is, according to the main character and "father" of the household, Joseph Simmons (Rev. Run), of Run.DMC fame, what critics consider a "real life" version of *Cosby* and *Father Knows Best* (Collier, 2006). Presiding over discussions about education, empty nesting and child anger management, Simmons and his wife, Justine, put family life on display along with their children, Vanessa, Angela, JoJo, Daniel ("Diggy"), and Russell II ("Russy"). In constructing his version of the authentic Black family, Simmons says the show is less about dismantling long-standing Black stereotypes and more about toppling stereotypes about rap music artists: "I'm just trying to give another perspective and show what rap is all about, especially for someone who knows only the negative things. Me and my family are rap all grown up" (MTV Networks, 2008). . . .

Like *Cosby,* neither *Run's House* nor *Father Hood* deals in any strong way with racism, economic distress, or other societal barriers on their shows. Instead, like their predecessor show, both build their plots around family success, humor, and harmony. This is particularly curious, considering that Simmons and Snoop Dogg represent opposite sides of the unharmonious divide between East Coast and West Coast rap artists, respectively. From the 1990s to the present, rivalry through rap lyrics between East and West Coast rappers has stimulated record sales, to help situate rap music as a $1.6 billion industry (Leland, 2002). Yet the contentious nature of their art is never reflected in either of their shows. Instead, viewers continue in the ideal world of Black families as perpetuated for the most part by both of these reality shows.

Snoop Dogg's Father Hood

The rap artist Calvin Broadus (Snoop Dogg) leads the theme song to *Father Hood* by making a direct comparison of his show and parenting style to that portrayed in *Cosby*. The title of the show itself emphasizes that Snoop, a prominent West Coast rapper, is a father from the 'hood.

Snoop Dogg came to fame in the 1990s when his debut album, *Doggystyle,* became a platinum seller in its first week (Quinn, 1996). Now, as head of household in *Father Hood*, Snoop starts the show by rapping that "this ain't *The Cosby Show* . . . and I don't make my kids eat their vegetables . . .", establishing at the inception that the structured family life of the 1980s hit show will not be replicated in the Broadus household. In fact, notions of distinguished, high-brow and dignified Blackness (Gray, 1995) and controlled representation are overwhelmed by the Broadus family's antitypical representation of family (compared with the archetypical Huxtable and Simmons families).

The selection of Snoop and the Broadus family appears a likely choice for a new reality show, especially considering the liberties television takes in its 21st-century portrayals. Robinson and Skill (2001) contend that "it is clear that TV portrayals of family are becoming more complex and diverse," and "television portrayals of the family have become less conventional" (p. 160). Obscene language, references to illegal drugs, and memories of confrontations with the law all represent material explored in *Father Hood*. In this case, it is relevant to remember that the producers of *Father Hood* have labeled the show as "real" day-to-day activity, as opposed to material created for television. Consider that the "less conventional" Broadus family challenges stagnant impressions of family life, normal TV conventions for family, and anticipated roles for adults and children in families. . . .

Conceptual/Theoretical Framework

. . . . Enlightened racism is a concept that grew out of the audience analysis work of Jhally and Lewis (1992). . . . Jhally and Lewis' seminal work argued that hypervisibility of the Huxtable family reinforced the notion of social mobility—in that they have achieved the upper echelons of the middle class. Their social mobility was made problematic in that no attention was given to the economic disadvantages and deep-rooted racial discrimination that prevent most African Americans from being socially mobile. As a result, the show contributed to a contemporary form of racism that is based on the idea that racism is no longer a problem in the United States, and that lack of African American success is caused by lack of effort and/or ability. The existence of the Cosbys—and other popular mass-mediated African American success stories, such as Oprah Winfrey, Michael Jordan, and Colin Powell—is taken as proof of this stance. The logic, then, is that "their success assures us that in the United States everyone, regardless of race or creed, can enjoy material success" (Jhally & Lewis, 1992, p. 73). If racism does exist, it is manifested within interpersonal interactions (and situated as a personal issue), with no connection to historical, institutionalized policies, procedures, and/or practices. Consequently, the media glamorization of these individuals reinforces belief in both the availability and desirability of the American Dream.

Similar to the Huxtable family, the Simmons family, from *Run's House,* can be critiqued as representing Black families "without struggle," who suggest "effortless" and "nice" Blackness (Jhally & Lewis, 1992, pp. 107, 47), further confirming the myth of easy access to the American Dream that *Cosby* started over 20 years earlier. Also, *Run's House* places emphasis on the tremendous wealth and comfortable lifestyles of the Simmonses, sustaining the fantastical "myth of social mobility" that Jhally and Lewis (1992) discuss in their work (p. 7). That is, they move, exertion-free, through their White-washed utopian lives, with little to no reference to struggle.

While *Run's House* tends to advance the notion of class trumping race, *Father Hood,* on the other hand, contends with this concept in a variety of ways. Simmons' "rap grown up" implies that he is beyond the reckless, gangster lifestyle that has, unfairly or not, characterized some rap artists. His retreat to family life in the New Jersey suburbs parallels the upper middle class existence of *Cosby.* Yet, though wealthy and famous, Snoop Dogg connects visibly on his show to working-class Black cultural "institutions," food, and environments. Snoop's reconnection to his old "hood," through frequent meals of fried chicken, and visits to soul-food chain Roscoe's House of Chicken 'n Waffles, identifies him with working-class Black people, in a way that was absent from *Cosby* and is also absent from *Run's House.* Further, Snoop's confrontations with the law are also realistic occurrences that are not addressed in the other two shows. . . .

Of *Cosby,* Jhally and Lewis said that viewers' class position, interestingly, did not diminish the vigor with which they identified with the Huxtables. In fact, they say "working class respondents were just as likely to relate the Huxtables' world to their own as middle or upper middle class respondents" (p. 24). Recognizing the world that the Huxtables lived in as one from which they could draw references to their own lives, with regard to culture, parenting styles, etc., was meaningful to audiences. Similarly, *Run's House* viewers indicated in their messages ["Run's House Official Blog," MTV website] that they too discovered a world they recognized and identified with in the wealthy Simmons'. Likewise, *Father Hood's* light treatment of real-life struggles and references to working-class culture prompted viewers to comment on *Father Hood* message boards that that Snoop "keeps it real"

and, regardless of mobility and access, is inextricably linked to his "hood."

Thus I advance the argument that despite any issues of race and class, the perception that was overriding in *Enlightened Racism* works here as well: that the Simmonses from *Run's House* and the Broaduses from *Father Hood* are—to some extent—"just like a real family" (p. 24) to their viewers, who indicate a strong identification with the wealthy families.

Black Fathers' Disciplinary Styles

RUN'S HOUSE

In *Run's House,* the theme of Black father as disciplinarian is well demonstrated in the episode where Russy has issues of anger management ("Anger Management," Season 2, Episode 9). During the course of the show, Russy takes out his frustrations on expensive hand-held video games, which he destroys and expects to be replaced by his parents. Instead, they determine that professional consultation is necessary. Later, at the behest of the therapist—much like *Cosby*'s light hand as disciplinarian—the strictest that Rev. Run gets is when he enrolls Russy in karate lessons to assist him in channeling his anger toward productivity and focus. Simmons' discipline style is considered to be positive [by a critic writing in *Jet* magazine]. Collier (2006) explains:

> Family discussions are a constant in the Simmons household. They can often be found all sitting around the sofa discussing such things as Russy's anger issues or how to resolve conflict. What fans see, in spite of some arguing and debating, is a very close-knit and respectful family. (para. 10)

Such family discussions, where children and adults were provided equal time to articulate their ideas, were thematic of

Cosby. Differently from *Cosby,* however, Rev. Run utilizes some time at the conclusion of each episode to provide the viewing audience with a covert important life lesson. For example, reflecting on Russy's problem with anger management, Rev. Run journals the following text on his Blackberry messaging device (while his voice-over verbalizes the message for the audience):

> How do you channel your personal strength? In putting forth the effort that our daily life requires, energy plus optimism equals progress, while energy plus anger results only in frustration. Do the math and you'll soon add up the difference between what's work and what's whack. God is love.—Rev Run

Comments on *Run's House*'s Official Blog indicate that viewers identify with the discipline displayed on the show and with the message that concludes the episodes. Without exception, the response was overwhelmingly positive. One person wrote: " ... Rev. Run (is) never afraid to discipline and be a parent, but always loving and fun," while another said " ... Love the way they all get along and seem to talk through issues as they come up." Still another person wrote, "This show should be required viewing for each and every family in this country. Ironically enough, a show on MTV that is promoting family values." Others lauded the reality show for featuring a Black family "with people that don't act up." In this regard, some viewers described the Simmons as an ideal family, like the person who shared: "I love this family so much ... I hope I can have a family that's something like theirs. ... The parents don't let their kids take anything for granted." Some viewers pointed to the positive nature of *Run's House,* despite not being a fan of the reality television genre as a whole: "I am not a fan of reality shows ... but this is one ... (that) shows the family in the 'FOR REAL' state ... The greatest thing about this show is that each week, there is a learning lesson behind each episode." ...

SNOOP DOGG'S FATHER HOOD

In the episode titled "Dogg Whisperer," Snoop complains that the family's more than 10 dogs have too much freedom in their home. In another episode he laments that the house is disheveled. Yet the first line of the show's theme song ("I don't make my kids eat their vegetables") provides the sense that Snoop is not a strict disciplinarian on any level. In fact, he frequently refers to his sons and others as "nigger," and uses profanity often as a matter of course. When Snoop complains that his home is untidy, the children do not react. Likewise, when their dogs run amok in the household, it is their father who hires a dog trainer to teach the dogs obedience. In comparing *Father Hood* to *Run's House,* one *Father Hood* viewer wrote: "They need to spend the day at Run's House. Please ... drop this show. They can keep their business and nasty house to themselves ... He needs to control his kids." Clearly this viewer sees a sense of order in the Simmons' household that is not visible in the Broadus'.

In another episode, Snoop's younger son, Cordell ("Rook"), rough-housing with friends, gets hit in the eye. Snoop, who had earlier cursed the kids and asked them to stop the rough activity, laughs and tells his son, "You got to be able to take a blow if you can give a blow, cuz." Despite resistance from his wife, who coddles her injured son and demands that her husband stop chiding the boy, Snoop continues to laugh and tease, rather than use the incident as a forum to display disciplinary action and teach a lesson to the children involved.

The E! Channel description of an episode featuring British soccer star David Beckham, says: "Snoop Dogg wants his kids to play soccer but they won't practice ... ," reflecting that, at times, Snoop has failed as an authoritarian. In another incident, Snoop implores older son, Corde ("Spank"), to help him stop Rook from stealing money out of his pockets in his absence. On the other hand, the episode guides—and Snoop himself—brag about Rook's infatuation with money," sending a mixed message. Finally, Snoop's style of discipline is actually highlighted in advertisements for the show. The promotional photo advertising *Father Hood* features the Broadus family, at a dinner table loaded with fried chicken, corn bread, and waffles, even as three pet dogs stand atop the table.

Snoop's "honorary" son, Anthony, fares no better in the discipline arena, often behaving like a big kid himself. In one episode, where Snoop's sons were left alone in Anthony's care, they were cited by law enforcement, and had their car towed for illegal parking, prompting them to sell Snoop's $5,000 bedroom slippers for $500 to bribe their way out of the charge. In another episode, Anthony collaborates with the Broadus brothers to have a pizza party in their parents' absence. One *Father Hood* viewer wrote:

> I think "honorary son" . . . is a terrible adult to have around any children. I saw the episode where Snoop left "honorary son" in charge of his 2 boys. He covered for Snoop's son taking money . . . He participated in taking the Porsche without permission. The worst thing was lying to Snoop (in front of his sons) . . . He helped Snoop's sons to deceive their father. "Honorary Son" is nothing but a sorry oversized child. Snoop and his wife should never allow this man to ever be alone with their children.

Martel (2007) describes Snoop as "barely (rising) to the responsibility of fatherhood" (para. 1), and Johnson (2007) quotes the rapper as saying he "likes to be more of a friend than a father figure" (para. 6), both comments being oppositional to the order found in *Cosby* and *Run's House*.

In the same manner of the wives on *Cosby* and *Run's House*, Snoop's wife Shante is seen as the primary disciplinarian on the show. Even Snoop calls her "Boss Lady." Gamble (2007) says that while Snoop "may run things in his hip-hop career . . . at home, being the 'top dogg' is another story" (para. 1). He continues describing Shante as an authority in the Broadus household by saying: "his wife and high school sweetheart, Shante, a.k.a. Boss Lady, runs the show" (para. 2). Indeed she does, as in several episodes she not only disciplines the kids but firmly regulates her husband as well. For instance, in the episode titled "The Doggs and the Bees," Shante tells Snoop to have a talk about sex and intimacy with his oldest son, which he does, but with little seriousness. This comes on the heels of Snoop's production of a video for his new sex-laden single, "Sensual Seduction." Yet what cannot be dismissed about this episode is that a real-life issue is being discussed by father and son. Issues of sex were not as prominent in either *Cosby* or *Run's House*.

Black Fathers as Positive Role Models

. . . . On *Cosby,* Cliff Huxtable's emphasis on education, and his own achievement as a medical doctor, place him in a position of influence, in what Jhally and Lewis (1992) call "demonstrating the opportunity for African Americans to be successful" (p. 94). Miller (as cited in Jhally & Lewis) describes Cosby, and his alter ego Dr. Huxtable, as verification of the access of the American Dream. Similar themes are evident in *Run's House* and *Father Hood*.

RUN'S HOUSE

The virtues of hard work and pulling one's self up by one's own bootstraps are rampant in *Run's House*. Joseph Simmons parlays humility and values to his children. Again, comparisons can be tied to *Cosby*. For example, as in *Cosby*, where the patriarch, a medical doctor, insisted that while he and his wife, an attorney, were "rich," his children had no wealth, Simmons implores his children to make their own living.

Further, Simmons' very real depiction of religious values closely aligns with those of "real" Black families. According to Pipes (1981), "preaching and churches have traditionally been a mainstay of Black families" (p. 54). As a Black father embracing religion, a key tenet of African American culture, Simmons shows the real existence of religion in a Black household in a way that *Cosby* did not. Simmons insists that religion and respect are staples of his household, whether the cameras are on or off (Collier, 2006). . . . As in *Cosby*, on the other hand, Simmons seeks the ear of his wife to recollect family issues, as the couple settles into bed for the night. Yet, a trip to a tattoo parlor with daughter Angela, a golf/spa outing with son JoJo, or a family vacation to Las Vegas so that the Simmons parents can renew their wedding vows— all simmer down to a ritual closing scene where the patriarch Simmons, amid a cozy bubble bath, emits lessons of the day via his electronic Blackberry. This "ownership" of the parental "lesson of the day," outside the influence of his wife, is the lasting impression at the close of each show.

As a Black father, then, Simmons seeks out his children to give judicious advice and coach them through obstacles they encounter. While Snoop Dogg may not achieve the same results in a fantasyland TV manner, he does make an attempt at being a role model for his children as well.

SNOOP DOGG'S FATHER HOOD

Perhaps the greatest commentary not only on Snoop Dogg's being a positive example for his children, but also on his relationship to Black working-class life, comes in the episode where he visits the Long Beach neighborhood where he grew up. This episode reflects an important point of distinction, in that such representations

of social mobility are never explicit with *Cosby* or *Run's House*.

In the episode, which aired February 2008, Snoop takes his two young sons to the neighborhood where he was raised and socialized. During the episode he is pensive about his upbringing, admitting that his mother could not teach him what it meant to be a man. He talks about growing up without a father, and how that fact motivates him to have a presence in his own sons' lives. Highlights of the boys' visit included a walk through Snoop's old high school and a conversation with his former teacher. The teacher implores them to get a good education, and Snoop laments that he wishes he had been more diligent as a student. One viewer said: "The episode that had any substance and positive influence was when Snoop took his children to Long Beach and left them alone with the principal [teacher]." Still another viewer stated that they enjoyed "the episode where Snoop speaks about how he came up without a father and how that pushes him to be a good father and how the public don't get to hear about these situations. [S]o from all us responsible fathers especially us single ones thanks."

During the episode, Snoop impressed upon his sons that they needed to understand where he came from to be able to better grasp where he is, admitting that his upbringing is not reflective of the current success he enjoys. While visiting Long Beach, the boys meet Snoop's uncle, a recovering crack cocaine addict, who advises them to stay away from drugs— but not before detailing the harsh realities of a drug addict's existence, including lying, stealing, and sexual acts to gain a fix. This lifestyle is certainly remote from the comfortable lifestyle the Broadus brothers enjoy as a result of their father's achievements in entertainment. And this conversation is like none ever seen on *Cosby* or *Run's House*. One viewer noted the show's value as an authentic representation of Black life—Black life in Long Beach, California, specifically—which was something valued by viewers, and commented on specifically on the *Father Hood* Message Board:

> This show is hilarious . . . he's definitely from "da LBC" . . . he even (has) a shack in the back like the (old) days . . . now if you don't know then you wouldn't understand . . . he's original and . . . and he definitely ain't front'n.

While Snoop's forays into his old neighborhood were meant as a lesson for his sons, he still maintains his existence as a counter image to *Cosby*. For example, in contesting the image of the faultless Black father, during yoga class he daydreams that he's lying flat on his mat as a result of a police officer's mandate—reminiscent of his real-life brushes with the law. Later, he imagines that the mellow feeling he gets from yoga is really a result of being high. In another episode, Snoop ignores the complaints of his daughter, Cori ("Choc"), that she can't concentrate on her schoolwork because his music is playing too loudly.

Viewers have conflicting views on Snoop's ability to be a positive influence as a father. One person criticized the decision to provide a venue for highlighting his behavior:

> You have got to be kidding. Now they are giving a THUG like Snoop Dogg a TV show? . . . Now we have come down to watching absolute garbage on TV with watching self proclaimed thugs and gangsters like this idiot . . . Snoop Dogg is not a mainstream citizen and all the media are doing is helping a criminal . . . look legitimate and part of mainstream society . . . let's stop glorifying these criminals and remember just because they are famous does not mean they should be admired.

Other viewers were quick to take issue with this viewer's point of criticism. One questioned the problematic nature of the label "mainstream citizen," while another pointed out that "it's the MAINSTREAM WHITE media that has labeled Snoop as a gangster, thug and criminal." This issue was also addressed by others, such as the viewer who wrote:

> . . . when did Snoop ever state that he was a criminal or thug? . . . he professes to be . . . a father, husband, rapper, who hustles . . . and if you don't know what hustles means that is a slang word for he works hard to provide a LEGAL lifestyle for himself and family.

Other viewers make a comparison between Snoop's ability as a positive role model and that of Ozzy Osbourne, another famous father and musician, who also had his own family reality show on MTV, for three years, beginning in 2002:

> If someone like Ozzy Osbourne can have a show . . . why on earth can't Snoop Dogg? . . . I originally thought he was just a typical rapper jerk. But watching . . . Father Hood show has shown his "human" side . . . I may not agree with . . . his music, but I do commend him for how he cares and provides for his family.

Despite his laidback parenting style, most viewers have a positive reaction to *Father Hood*. Though Snoop raps in the opening song that he's a nonconventional father, some of the same lessons of humility and success through education, thematic of *Cosby* and *Run's House*, are also canons in the Broadus household.

Discussion: Reality TV and Enlightened Racism in the 21st Century

. . . . As the traditional roles and values of Black family life become increasingly dynamic, televisual constructions of Black fatherhood should reflect this reality. While Snoop's style is described as a "benign older brother," with gangster appeal (Martel, 2007, para. 8), Rev. Run is a more conventional father. This examination of Black fathers in reality television confirms, contradicts and challenges images of Black fathers that exist in our culture.

Orbe (1998) asserts that the lens through which we view Black life is skewed: "Many critics have posited that the vast majority of African American media images represent portrayals of Black life as European Americans see it" (p. 33). Both Simmons and Snoop defy this view. *Run's House* is coproduced by Simmons, and Snoop's own Snoopadelic Films coproduces his show, on which he also serves as executive director. Therefore, both fathers have some degree of influence regarding their construction of Black fatherhood for reality TV. In other words, neither *Run's House* nor *Father Hood* are restricted to outsider perceptions about the Black father and family, and both make their intentions clear about what they hope to reveal through their snows. *Run's House* and *Father Hood* feature "real" daily-life activity that is actually constructed, just as *Cosby* was, to respond to a limiting view of Black fatherhood and family. Simmons' goal was to counter the negative stereotypes leveled at rappers, and though Snoop's goal was to deviate from *Cosby,* he rebuffs claims that he has "rebranded" himself as "family-friendly," instead insisting that he always was (Forrest, 2008): "I am. That's what I always been . . . People . . . always get information on me as far as when I go to jail and my criminal record . . . Negative things . . . They never hear about my football team, my wife, my kids, my standing in the community, the gang interventions that I do" (para. 26). . . .

Central to this analysis is the argument that *Run's House* and *Father Hood* work to extend the representation of successful Black fathers popularized through Cosby. The likelihood that these shows work to reinforce existing forms of enlightened

racism is strong, given three points. First, all three shows display professional and material success in environments void of any race-based obstacles. Two, the two reality sitcoms, viewed as more "real" than traditional sitcoms, lend credence to belief of the [raceless] American Dream. Third, reality TV—like the Cosby Show—has proven its ability to attract diverse audiences, which increases opportunities for White exposure to Black fathers/families.[1] While such a stance is important to articulate, this discussion works to avoid critical analyses that utilize a dichotomous approach—where the media generally, and reality TV specifically, are described in absolute terms. Instead, I advocate for more complex readings that interrogate the ways in which shows are both productive and unproductive, negative and positive, good and bad, and supportive yet resistant of enlightened racism. The remainder of this discussion is situated within this approach.

According to Jhally and Lewis (1992), the fact that White viewers of *The Cosby Show* thought of the Huxtables as unraced is not evidence that race was no longer an issue. On the contrary: their behaviors were seen as being able to transcend race as a means to be defined as "normal." In this context, viewers who described the family as "normal," "generic," and "average" were not using terms that were unraced; instead the terms were racially specific—the family was implicitly viewed as White. Jhally and Lewis found that *The Cosby Show* represented different things to its White and Black audiences. For most Whites, Bill Huxtable was a Black *father*; for most Blacks, he was a *Black* father (Jhally and Lewis). Whites saw a middle-class family that could transcend race; Blacks saw a middle-class Black family where positive images helped to counter negative media stereotypes.

Within the two reality TV shows analyzed here, interrogating the saliency of racial identity for Rev. Run and Snoop Dogg lends insight into the ways in which such upwardly mobile mass-mediated personalities can continue to centralize their presence as *Black fathers*. Both men represent "rap grown up"—albeit in diverse ways—an explicitly Black form of expression that situates their life experience in racialized ways. While this can assist in avoiding one of the building blocks of enlightened racism (i.e., race is no longer relevant), the fact that African American achievement of the American Dream is possible only through limited venues (e.g., rap music or sports) contributes to problematic existing stereotypes. . . .

One of the core elements of enlightened racism is acceptance of the desirability, and belief in the accessibility, of the American Dream. While each of the Black fathers/families analyzed within this chapter reflect "American success stories," how they live out their successes differs in significant ways. In *Father Hood,* for example, Snoop introduces how his past served as a challenge—but not a permanent barrier—for his success as a rap artist (he was cleared of a gang-related murder charge in 1993; his uncle continues to struggle with drug addiction). Interestingly, his race-, class-based struggle lends "street credibility" to his music, something that is also reflected in the ways in which he continues to live his life (e.g., "keepin' it real" by not losing his cultural edge). I would suggest that *Father Hood,* within this context, reinforces the *accessibility* of the American Dream, while simultaneously challenges its *desirability.*

. . . . Therefore, while the social mobility of both Rev. Run and Snoop Dogg is situated within their celebrity status as rap artists, their relationships to the "American Dream" are distinctly different. Snoop, as a successful *Black father,* refuses to leave behind his cultural upbringing, despite professional and material success. Rev. Run, in comparison, embraces his identity as a successful *Black father* and utilizes that success to facilitate the intergenerational transfer of wealth. (Within the multimillion dollar family of businesses instituted by Russell and Joseph Simmons, the next generation of entrepreneurs, the Simmons children, are seen getting specific instructions from their father and uncle on how to participate in, and subsequently influence, various business dealings, and working to establish themselves in music, publishing, fashion, footwear, and jewelry.) In this vein, both represent diverse ways of "rap all grown up"—which can serve the function of role model, albeit in different expressions of success.

This chapter looks to contribute to historical debates on race, class, and audience responses to Black television families. If *Cosby* is the quintessential Black family television show, what new observations and characteristics of Black fathers, Black mothers, and their families loom, post-*Cosby*? How are such constructions situated within shows that span the continuum of fictional and reality-based depictions of Black life? For starters, I would argue that *Run's House* and *Father Hood* succeed at providing a post-*Cosby* televisual look at Black fathers and families in U.S. society, while revealing further angles with which to discuss issues of race, class, and viewer identification with these shows.

The "safer" show, *Run's House,* demonstrates template-like similarities to *Cosby,* while *Father Hood* further drives behind the scenes to show the audience working-class realities consistent with Snoop's intentional opposition to *Cosby's* reality. *Run's House* and *Father Hood* are valuable in the movement against continual stereotypes about Black fathers and families, picking up the torch from *Cosby* and bringing much-needed visibility to alternative constructions of Black fatherhood/family. Jhally and Lewis (1992) suggest that "we learn to live in the dreams sold by network executives" (p. 133). Reality-based TV represents a genre that has opened the possibilities of diverse representations of Blackness—especially on cable networks that are more likely to assume the risk of less conventional programming. Within this expansion lies the potential to negotiate how diverse audiences embrace, negate, and adapt to living various forms of the American Dream.

Note

1. This point does not discount African Americans who also embrace enlightened racism. Such individuals were not explicitly evident within the work of Jhally and Lewis (1992); however, I would argue that they are increasingly prevalent in contemporary U.S. society. Ironically, Bill Cosby's recent criticism of African Americans participating in their own oppression, reflects elements of an enlightened racist ideology ("Dr. Bill Cosby speaks at the 50th Anniversary Commemoration of Brown vs. Topeka Board of Education Supreme Court Decision," n.d.).

References

Berman, R. (1987). Sitcoms. *Journal of Aesthetic Education, 2*(1), 5–19.

Berry, G. L. (1980). Children, television, and social class roles: The medium as an unplanned educational curriculum. In E. L. Palmer & A. Dorr (Eds.), *Children and the faces of television* (pp. 71–81). New York: Academic.

Braxton, G. (2001, December 4). *My Wife and Kids* is no clone of *Cosby:* Damon Wayans goes domestic but keeps the attitude in his new sitcom on ABC. *The Charlotte (NC) Observer,* p. E-01.

Brooks, D. E., & Jacobs, W. R. (1996). Black men in the margins: Space Traders and the interpositional strategy against b(l)acklash. *Communication Studies, 47,* 289–302.

Budd, M., & Steinman, C. (1992, July). White racism and *The Cosby Show. Jump Cut: A Review of Contemporary Media, 37,* 5–12. [Online]. Retrieved February 17, 2008, from http://www.ejumpcut.org/archive/onlines says/JC37folder/Cosby.html

Collier, A. (2006, August 7). *Run's House:* TV's first family of hip hop shares values and leads by example on reality show. *Jet.* [Online]. Retrieved January 19, 2008, from http://findarticles.com/p/articles/mi_m1355/is_/ai_n16620295

Cornwell, N. C., & Orbe, M. (2002). "Keepin' it real" and/or "Sellin' out to the man": African American responses to Aaron McGruder's *The Boondocks.* In R. Means Coleman (Ed.), *Say-it loud!: African American audiences, media, and identity* (pp. 27–44). New York: Routledge.

Dates, J. L., & Stroman, C. (2001). Portrayals of families of color on television. In J. Bryant & J. Alison Bryant (Eds.), *Television and the American family* (pp. 207–228). Mahwah, NJ: Erlbaum.

"Dr. Bill Cosby speaks at the 50th Anniversary Commemoration of Brown vs. Topeka Board of Education Supreme Court Decision." (n.d.). Retrieved May 10, 2008, from www.eightcitiesmap.com/transcript_bc.htm

E-Channel Message Board for *Snoop Dogg's Father Hood.* Retrieved July 25, 2008, from boards.eonline.com

Fiske, J. (1994). Ethnosemiotics: Some personal and theoretical reflections. In H. Newcomb (Ed.), *Television: The critical view* (pp. 411–425). New York: Oxford University Press.

Forrest, E. (2008, April 3). At home with the Doggs: Rapper Snoop Dogg is reinventing himself as a family-friendly father on his own reality TV show. Is he serious? Retrieved April 15 from http://music.guardiaii.co.uk/urban/story/0,,2270399,00.html

Gamble, R. (2007, December 6). *Snoop Dogg gives fans access to his family life with 'Father Hood.'* [Online]. Retrieved February 28, 2008, from http://www.ballerstatus.com/article/news/2007/ 12/3678/

Gray, H. (1995). *Watching race: Television and the struggle for Blackness.* Minneapolis: University of Minnesota Press.

Greenberg, B. S., & Atkin, C. K. (1978, March). *Learning about minorities from television: The research agenda.* Paper presented at the conference on Television and the Socialization of the Minority Child, University of California, Los Angeles.

Greenberg, B. S., & Neuendorf, K. (1980). Black family interactions on TV. In B. S. Greenberg (Ed.), *Life on television: Content analysis of U.S. TV drama* (pp. 173–181). Norwood, NJ: Ablex.

Herbert, B. (2007, October 16). Tough, sad and smart. *New York Times.* [Online]. Retrieved February 11, 2008, from http://www.nytimes.com/2007/10/16/opinion/16herbert./html?_r=18coref=slogin

Inniss, L. B., & Feagin, J. R. (1995). *The Cosby Show:* The view from the Black middle class. *Journal of Black Studies, 25*(6), 692–711.

Jhally, S., & Lewis, J. (1992). *Enlightened racism:* The Cosby Show, *audiences, and the myth of the American Dream.* Boulder, CO: Westview Press.

Johnson, C. A. (2007, December 4). Snoop gets real with kids. *The Showbuzz.* [Online]. Retrieved February 22, 2008, from http://www.showbuzz.cbsnews.com/stories/2007/12/04/tv/main 3573842 .shtml

Leland, J. (2002, November 2). Feuding for profit: Rap's war of words; in rap industry, rivalries as marketing tool. *New York Times.* Retrieved February 22, 2008, from http://query.nytimes.corn/gst/fullpage,html?res=9C0CE2DE143EF930A35752C1A9649C8B63

Martel, N. (2007, December 29). Just chillin' with Snoop Dogg: A rapper's blend of offspring and entourage. *New York Times.*

Merritt, B., & Stroman, C A. (1993). Black family imagery and interactions on television. *Journal of Black Studies, 23,* 492–499.

MTV Networks. (2008). *Run's House (Season 1)* [Online]. Available: http://www.mtv.com/ontv/dyn/runs_house_season_01/series.jhtml

Orbe, M. P. (1998). Constructions of reality on MTV's "The Real World": An analysis of the restrictive coding of Black masculinity. *Southern Communication Journal, 64*(1), 32–45.

Pipes, W. H. (1981). 'Old-time religion': Benches can't say "Amen." In H. Pipes McAdoo (Ed.), *Black families* (pp. 54–76). Beverly Hills, CA: Sage.

Quinn, M. (1996). Never shoulda been let out of the penitentiary: Gangsta rap and the struggle over racial identity. *Cultural Critique, 34,* 65–89.

Robinson, J. D., & Skill, T. (2001). Five decades of families on television: From the 1950s through the 1990s. In J. Bryant & J. Alison Bryant (Eds.), *Television and the American family* (pp. 139–162). Mahwah, NJ: Erlbaum.

Run's House Official Blog. http://www.mtv.com

"The Cosby Show legacy." (2005, August 2). *USA Today,* p. D04.

56

A Shot at Half-Exposure

Asian Americans in Reality TV Shows

Grace Wang

From the start of the sixth season of *Dancing with the Stars*, it seemed almost inevitable that ice skater Kristi Yamaguchi would win the top prize. The graceful poise and athleticism that helped her capture gold in the 1992 Winter Olympics translated well into the realm of ballroom dancing. Throughout the season, Yamaguchi appeared to have little difficulty learning and mastering new dance moves. But having the winner be a foregone conclusion on a show structured around the drama of a competition hardly seemed an ideal way to generate viewer excitement or ratings. And thus, for the Olympian who "brought golden precision to the floor," a different narrative about obstacles faced and overcome needed to be constructed about her character during the season. It soon became clear to viewers that the primary narrative arc structuring Yamaguchi's character on the show would be her inability to express emotions through her ballroom dancing and the personal barriers she would face learning to feel and show passion.

Dancing with the Stars is a popular reality TV show where an assortment of "stars" ranging from B-list Hollywood actors to professional athletes are paired with professional dancers and taught to perform a variety of ballroom dances. Each week, the judges and television audience collectively vote off a celebrity until a winner is finally chosen. Like many other reality TV programs, the show follows a fairly predictable format. Before the contestants perform their dance numbers, they are introduced in brief, easily digestible clips that provide tantalizing glimpses into their inner thoughts and personal biography. Yamaguchi, the cheerful ice skating champ turned mother of two, reflected early in the season, "It is not in my nature to be so open with my emotions." And just in case viewers failed to intuit her lack of emotion while dancing such fiery ballroom styles as the tango and rumba—dances that even casual viewers know are supposed to embody intensity, passion, and lust—a panel of expert judges was on hand to assess her performance. After Yamaguchi's tango in the third week, judge Len Goodman exhorted, "Sharp! Clean! Clear! Always delivered with extreme precision ... [but I need] more

From Grace Wang (2010), "A Shot at Half-Exposure: Asian Americans in Reality TV Shows." *Television & New Media,* 11:404–427. Reprinted with permission of SAGE Publications.

emotional engagement. Lust! I want you to be a dirty girl. Release that for us to see!" Always the model competitor, Yamaguchi does learn to "release" her emotions over the course of the season and eventually wins the coveted top prize.

I begin this essay with Yamaguchi's character construction on *Dancing with the Stars* as it offers an entry point for understanding one of the central narratives that influences Asian American representation in the reality TV format. In what follows, I argue that while reality TV programs open up a space for greater representation of racialized minorities, these shows also adhere to, and authenticate, racialized narratives and stereotypes by embodying them in the characters of "real" people.

... If reality TV has been credited with diversifying television culture, this diversification has also depended on fueling drama and conflict through the deliberate casting of disparate characters that will generate tension over the course of the season (Braxton 2009; Stanley 2007). Rather than represent a wide range of "real people" who reflect the diversity of the nation, reality TV repackages difference into comfortingly familiar stock characters and stereotypes. Individuals are chosen to represent certain types and then slotted (self-consciously or not) into a limited array of available characters: the angry black woman, the conservative Christian, the fabulous gay (usually white) man, the nonwhite immigrant grateful for the opportunities afforded to him or her in the United States, and so forth (Collins 2008). To make "real" people, who are obviously complex and contradictory, understandable to viewers in thirty- or sixty-minute time slots, reality shows turn them into "characters." Individuals frequently become stand-ins for only a few of the most visible (and charged) aspects of their identity. Contestants seeking to win a reality TV competition quickly learn to perform their racial, gender, class, and sexual identities on demand or risk being sent home.

The Technical but Unfeeling Asian: Historicizing Racialized Narratives

... Since the mid-1960s, journalists and scholars have frequently depicted Asian Americans as model minority subjects whose hard work ethic, compliant temperament, and self-sufficient nature have led to their relative material success. Much has been written about the ideological function that model minority discourses serve in disciplining other racial minority groups for their purported cultural "inferiorities" while also continuing to buttress white superiority and celebrate U.S. meritocracy (Kim 2003; Palumbo-Liu 1999; Osajima 1988). Model minority myths also help perpetuate the racial and cultural difference of Asian Americans by depicting members of this group—regardless of their generational status—as embodying "Asian" rather than "American" cultural values. Such a construction contributes to the continued elision between Asians and Asian Americans and the perpetually "foreign" status that Asian Americans hold in the U.S. racial imaginary.

While virtues such as discipline and diligence are valorized in the U.S. context, these purportedly "model" traits can become deviant when pushed to excess. Political scientist Claire Jean Kim (2003, 46) notes that during the 1980s, U.S. popular media portrayed Korean merchants as so hardworking, driven, and self-sacrificing as to seem "barely human." Taken to its zealous extreme, the unrelenting work ethic of Asians appears to evacuate them of both creativity and feeling. As Kim further observes, such narratives have a long historical precedent: "The construction of Asians/Asian Americans as self-immolating robots dates back to discussions of Chinese immigrant labor and Japanese kamikaze pilots during the 1800s and World War II respectively." Similar discourses about the North Vietnamese as "subhuman" enemies who lacked feeling and individuality and placed little value on human life also circulated in the United States during the Vietnam War.

While the construction of Asians and Asian Americans as "quasi-robots" performs a dehumanizing function, it has also been used to domesticate the success that Asians and Asian Americans achieve in the United States. During the 1980s, an era marked by U.S. anxieties over the escalating ascendancy of Japan in the global economy, the United States positioned Japan as its cultural inverse. The conformist, unfeeling, and mechanical nature of Japanese culture specifically, and Asian cultures generally, stood in implicit contrast to the United States, which promotes individuality, free thinking, and ingenuity.... Aligning Japan's high-tech advancements with a culture of robot-like efficiency, discipline, and control allowed for the threat of Japan's economic growth to be contained and managed through the framework of what David Morley and Kevin Robins have termed *technoorientalism.*[1] Within such a context of anxiety over techno-orientalism, Asians and Asian Americans become the implied foil for normative white Americans, whose balanced pursuit of work and innovation would, in the long run, prove more successful.

More recently, the specter of Asian and Asian American success has led literary critic Min Song (2008, 16) to suggest the emergence of a new construction of model minority success in U.S. popular media—the "super minority." As Song observes, in such a characterization, "Asian Americans become less of a model whose successes specifically berate blacks and other racial minorities and more a kind of, for lack of a better term, super minority whose successes berate *everyone* who fails somehow to succeed." Such a narrative can be detected in media descriptions of the "new white flight"—white families who leave high-achieving suburban school districts that have become "too Asian." In this instance, the descriptor "too Asian" becomes a referent for a broad range of racialized anxieties about the ways that

having an "overrepresentation" of Asian Americans transforms schools into excessively competitive environments, where the drive for academic achievement comes at the expense of the "whole" child (Egan 2007; Jaschik 2006; Hwang 2005).... By coding expertise in fields such as math and classical music as the consequence of discipline and relentless practice—rather than creativity, passion, or even inventiveness—what counts as talent and skill is transformed to diminish the achievements of Asian Americans. Moreover, while the unremitting drive and work ethic of Asian Americans might lead to particular types of success, these same qualities also limit their ability to reach the highest echelons of their professions, where creativity—in addition to technical mastery—is required.

Contestants need a narrative to be interesting in a reality TV competition over the course of a season, and for racialized characters these narratives frequently fall into a longer history of racialized discourses and stereotypes.... As a site that recycles and reworks racialized narratives onto "real" individuals, reality TV represents a critical new laboratory for understanding the maintenance of racial hierarchies in the contemporary U.S. context.[2] ...

Finding "Heart" and "Soul" on *Top Chef*

Hung Huynh, a Vietnamese immigrant, won the third season of *Top Chef* (original episodes aired June through October 2007, but, like other Bravo programs, the episodes constantly replay). Similar to the other contestants on the show, he arrived with an impressive resume, having worked his way through some of the nation's most celebrated restaurants. Yet few contestants matched Hung's arrogance.... Relentlessly self-centered, Hung's attitude was best summarized by his mantra: "I'm here for myself, I came here by myself, and hopefully I can win this by myself." Not just mere bragga-docio, however, Hung backed his arrogant swagger with an extensive arsenal of culi-nary skill and knowledge. His deft use of classic French techniques—depicted on *Top Chef* as representing the backbone of all fine culinary cuisine—brought him praise throughout the season.

Hung shined in challenges that focused on technique. He butchered chickens in such record time that even the head judge, chef Tom Colicchio, was left chuckling and shaking his head in astonishment.[3] In another challenge, Hung outperformed his contestants by replicating a signature dish served at the fancy French eatery Le Cirque that looked and tasted most close to the original. And in a challenge meant to showcase the competitors' knowledge of classical training, he garnered abundant praise for his beautifully presented and executed dish by a panel of culinary lumi-naries at the French Culinary Institute. At the same time, however, the adulation Hung received was tempered with reserva-tion. For while he was arguably the best chef technically, his food seemed to lack a certain elusive quality we might term "soul." Throughout the season, a swirl of questions consistently trailed Hung: Where was his passion? Where was his heart? One of the three finalists, Dale—the self-anointed "big gay chef" of the season—commented, "Hung is the best technical cook. But in my world, the best food has heart and when you don't have one it doesn't taste good."[4] This sentiment seemed to be shared by the judges, who complimented Hung for his technique but praised other contestants for dishes that "sang" and had "soul."

... In the episode before the finale, head judge Colicchio deftly summarized Hung's limitations this way: "You [Hung] are technically the best chef up here. Technically. But we don't see you in the food at all [pause ... drum sounds dra-matically in the background]. You were born in Vietnam?" Already knowing the answer, Colicchio quickly continued, "We

need to see you in the food. Somewhere, we need to see Hung." In this particular iteration, Hung became a proxy for his nation of birth. Finding Hung, and pre-sumably his soul, would involve tasting Vietnamese flavors in his food and, in so doing, returning to his "roots," his ethnic heritage, and his place of birth.

Colicchio's suggestion that Hung look "homeward" to Vietnam invoked a straightforward and accessible narrative for successfully performing "ethnic soul." For Hung to cook food that showcased his skills and knowledge in the fundamentals of classic French cuisine somehow inferred that he was not being himself. Yet similar pressures were not placed on his fellow white competitors. In fact, one of Hung's fellow finalists, a white woman from Texas, described her signature style of cui-sine as drawing on Asian flavors. Thus, while the whiteness of the other finalists insulated them from any implicit (or explicit) expectation to draw on certain influences and flavor profiles in their food, as a clearly marked "ethnic" contestant, Hung needed to authenticate himself through a narrowly defined conception of passion to win over the judges. The image of Hung facing a white judge advising him to reveal his "soul" by looking to Vietnam—a nation long colonized by France and subject to imperial blunders by the United States—visually symbolized the bind that Asian Americans face when navigating fields of culture that continue to be governed by white privilege.[5] French food, it seems, could never authenticate a Vietnamese chef's "soul," regardless of the historical relationship of colonialism that linked these two nations. Since *Top Chef* presents the techniques and standards of Europeans and white Americans as univer-sal, racialized minorities are cast either as "soulless" when they better their white counterparts at those skills or as unsophis-ticated and lacking proper training when they do not.[6]

... In the complex interplay among character construction, perception, and expectation operating in *Top Chef*, Hung appeared to be a quick study. He knew that the primary customers he needed to please were the panel of judges.[7] And if the judges wanted Hung to authenticate his passion for cooking through a particular construction of himself and his food, then he would willingly oblige. And thus, whether or not he believed himself to have a special connection to Vietnamese cuisine, Hung seemed to realize just how much authority the trope of "returning to one's roots" and cooking from one's "own" ethnic and national culinary tradition held on *Top Chef*.

On screen, Hung's persona transformed completely following judge Colicchio's caution that despite having superior technical skills his food communicated neither passion nor a sense of his identity as an individual born in Vietnam. While the process of judging on *Top Chef* demands a performance of authenticity—a declaration of love and passion—the change in Hung's character was so abrupt as to feel forced, even for a reality TV competition clearly edited to reveal, over the course of a season, the personal motivations that drive each contestant's passion for cooking. Writing about the *Top Chef* finale, Frank Bruni (2007), a restaurant critic for the *New York Times* at the time, appeared unconvinced by what he described as Hung's "transparent groveling and obsequiousness to the judges' panel. . . . On the heels of a comment that he didn't seem to cook with enough heart or soul, Hung suddenly morphed—at least semantically— into one big, red beating heart that had been marinated for 24 hours in essence of soul."

. . . The redemption of Hung's character and "soul" took place on the level of discourse—the narratives he used to frame his life story—and in the flavors contained in the dishes he promised to deliver in the finale. Arguing for his spot in the final challenge, Hung linked cooking to the very soul of his being. For the first time on the show, he spoke of a childhood spent sleeping in the kitchen and learning to cook from his mother. He described his mother as "the greatest chef in the world" and cooking as inherent to his family bloodline: "I cook with so much love and I get that from my mother. I grew up in the kitchen, sleeping in the kitchen. Cooking all my life. And when I think about my mom's food, I get so emotional. I get tingly. Because it's all about soul." The details Hung revealed about his personal background were equally compelling. His father risked his life escaping postwar Vietnam on a fishing boat headed for the United States when Hung was an infant; he did not see his father again until he was nine years old. Through hard work, sacrifice, and determination, his family eventually got off welfare by opening a restaurant. Winning the title "top chef" would, as Hung put it, make his mom proud *and* show the viewing public that "through hard work every immigrant can achieve the American Dream." And thus, whether the result of careful editing, a self-conscious recrafting of his on-screen persona, or a blend of both, by the finale Hung was less the self-centered braggart talking up his superior technique and skills and more the earnest immigrant who wanted, in his own words, to "win it for all immigrants in America." Hung scripted his family inheritance as twofold: he gained the flavors of home and family from his mother (a narrative replete with the gendered slippage between mother, food, and "homeland") and inherited the classic American story of self-reliance and immigrant success from his father.

In the final challenge, Hung showcased Vietnamese flavors in his food—palm sugar, coconut, and "ocean-scented rice"—and was rewarded not only with the title of "top chef" but also with praise for finally marrying "passion with technique." Colicchio lauded, "You put together a fabulous meal, and we're really happy to see you in your food." When the judges announced his win, an elated Hung exclaimed, "I'm so excited! I worked so hard to get here and to prove myself. And I have so much support from America."

. . . In interviews conducted outside of *Top Chef* and the Bravo network, viewers gain a sense of how Hung negotiated his television persona, as many of these interviews reveal the deliberateness with which he constructed his reality TV persona. He was media conversant enough to realize that *Top Chef* was as much a cooking competition as it was a reality TV program that depended on conflict and drama from its contestants. As Hung observed, being an interesting and outspoken character on the program would garner the most media exposure and ensure a lengthier stay on the show: "I wouldn't say I was the bad boy, but the most controversial contestant. That's the character I wanted to create from the beginning. I'm the most talked-about contestant. Either you love me or you hate me. It gets you more exposure. . . . It's a way to stay on the show, and it made good TV" (Smith 2007). Hung was clearly aware that he was playing a character crafted in concert with specific professional goals.

Hung's savvy also extended to the narratives he performed to satisfy the judges. For while he repeatedly emphasized the importance of passion, love, and soul toward the end of the *Top Chef* season, in interviews outside the show Hung continued to maintain that "technique is more important than soul and love, and creativity" (Tieu 2008). In one interview, Hung noted that he would donate a portion of his winnings to Buddhist temples and use another portion to travel to Spain and "experience life, learn, cook, [and become] *more* technical!" As he scoffed later in that interview, "When was the last time you walked out of a restaurant and said, 'That steak was so soulful, I'm definitely going back?' No. You say it was cooked perfectly, it was seasoned perfectly. . . . Why am I being dissed for having some technical skills?" (Lalli 2007). Thus, while *Top Chef* created an aura around "soul" that erased the typically racialized and immigrant labor involved in running a restaurant, such a media-constructed fantasy held less currency outside the realm of

television. As Hung noted, in the day-to-day work of running a business, dishes need to be replicated with technical precision, and "heart" will not keep a restaurant afloat: "Just because you have passion and love for the food doesn't mean you can operate a restaurant. You do need the training and the skills and the techniques to produce food for a $30 million operation. Passion just doesn't do that for you" (Smith 2007). Such media reports suggest how consciously Hung went about trying to create a television character that would not only keep him on the show but also win over the judges who ultimately controlled his fate in the competition.

Hung willingly participated in the reality TV competition and accepted the specific parameters set forth by *Top Chef*. If the television program needed him to embody the role of the grateful Vietnamese immigrant who cooks food inspired by the flavors of his homeland, he did his part and hoped that the editing process would go his way. In an article that appeared a few days before the finale aired, Hung seemed hopeful that he had performed enough "soul" and gratitude to secure the win: "Everything is going to make sense in the end, if they edit it right" (Lalli 2007). At the same time, he seemed to brace against the limitations placed on him, including the one-dimensional and expected version of ethnicity offered to him within the context of the show. For such a simplistic performance of ethnicity revealed neither the complexity of his life experience nor his food. As Hung questioned in an interview, "What does that mean when [Colicchio] says, 'We don't see Hung.'? What should I do, make sweet and sour chicken and wontons? I'm trained in French food. I love French food. That is me" (Lalli 2007).

. . . On *Top Chef*, the nuance of Hung's life story and his multilayered relationship to cuisine were compressed into an easily digestible story of immigrant success achieved through hard work, humility, gratitude, and maintaining one's ethnic heritage and "roots." Hung's narrative on *Top Chef* revealed not only how the trope of being technical but lacking "heart" and "soul" is placed on Asian Americans but also the conflicts that racialized minorities encounter competing in fields of culture that continue to be governed by white privilege. . . .

Notes

1. See Morley and Robins (1995).

2. Space limitations prevent a fuller analysis of racial representation across a range of reality TV shows. While the rapid proliferation of new reality TV programs produced each year makes it somewhat difficult for critical scholarship to keep pace, several scholars have insightfully analyzed how reality TV incorporates the tenets of multicultural discourse in the United States by celebrating racial and ethnic diversity through the mere fact of representation itself and by personalizing, decontextualizing, and containing racism to the realm of individual conflict. See, for instance, Kim and Blasini (2001) and Kraszewski (2009).

3. At the same time, Hung's impressively fast skills were also portrayed on the show as making him, quite literally, a menace in the kitchen. Contestants noted that Hung ran quickly and carelessly around the kitchen with his knives in hand, ready at any minute to accidentally slice off the limb of an unsuspecting competitor.

4. It is worth noting that while Hung reveals himself to be bisexual during the reunion show, his queerness never becomes part of his narrative arc. It might be that to foreground Hung's queerness *and* his identity as a racialized immigrant would have muddled his character construction too much for a show that depends on the easy legibility of its characters.

5. It is worth noting that included in the panel of judges is Padma Lakshmi, who is of South Asian descent. However, as the host of the show, her capital seems primarily located in her attractiveness rather than in her culinary expertise.

6. See Priscilla Ferguson (2004, 4) for a fascinating account of how the French came to dominate Western concepts of sophisticated culinary cuisine. As Ferguson notes, from the nineteenth century to the present era, French culinary customs, restaurant practices, and discourses of gastronomy have retained their special place as an "ideal of culinary. . . . French cuisine supplies a point of reference and a standard."

7. Hung, like many other *Top Chef* contestants, frequently noted the importance of pleasing the judges first and foremost regardless of the particular demographic being targeted for the challenge (which ranged from "cowboys" and "cowgirls" at a rodeo to members of the Elks club).

References

Betts, Kate. 2004. Visions from the East. *Time*, September 20. http://www.time.com/time/magazine/article/0,9171,699434,00.html.

Blasini, Gilberto Moíses and Kim, L.S. 2001. The Performance of Multicultural Identity in U.S. Network Television: Shiny, Happy, POPSTARS (Holding Hands) *Emergences: Journal for the Study of Media and Composite Cultures* 11 (2): 287-307.

Boncompagni, Tatiana. 2008. Korea opportunities. *FT.com*, January 5. http://www.ft.com/cms/s/2/3a1b5eb6-ba6b-11dc-abcb-0000779fd2ac.html.

Bourdain, Anthony. 2007. *The nasty bits: Collected varietal cuts, usable trim, scraps, and bones*. New York: Bloomsbury.

Braxton, Greg. 2009. The greater reality of minorities on TV. *Los Angeles Times*, February 17.

Bruni, Frank. 2007. The *Top Chef* finale: Of bad lobster and tame cake. *New York Times*, October 4.

Chung, Hye Seung. 2006. *Hollywood Asian: Philip Ahn and the politics of cross-ethnic performance*. Philadelphia: Temple University Press.

Cohen, Lara. 2006. In her own words: From refugee to *Project Runway*. *US Weekly*, March 20, 120–21.

Collins, Sue. 2008. Making the most out of 15 minutes: Reality TV's dispensable celebrity. *Television & New Media* 9:87–110.

Dominus, Susan. 2008. The affluencer. *New York Times*, November 2.

Egan, Timothy. 2007. Little Asia on the hill. *New York Times*, January 7.

Ellick, Adam. 2007. Boulud settling suit alleging bias at French restaurant. *New York Times*, July 31.

Elliot, Charles. 1995–1996. Race and gender as factors in judgments of musical performance. *Bulletin of the Council for Research in Music Education* 12 (7): 50–56.

Feldman, Jenny. 2006. Being a good Asian daughter, I thought I should become a buyer or work on the business side instead of trying to design. *Elle*, August.

Feng, Peter X. 2000. Recuperating Suzie Wong: A fan's Nancy Kwan-dary. In *Countervisions: Asian American film criticism*, ed. D. Hamamoto and S. Liu, 40–58. Philadelphia: Temple University Press.

Ferguson, Priscilla. 2004. *Accounting for taste: The triumph of French cuisine.* Chicago: University of Chicago Press.

Fisher, Ian. 2008. Is cuisine still Italian even if the chef isn't? *New York Times*, April 7.

Go, Kitty. 2005. Eastern exposure. *Financial Times*, January 8.

Hendershot, Heather. 2009. Belabored reality: Making it work on *The Simple Life* and *Project Runway*. In *Reality TV: Remaking television culture*, 2nd ed., ed. S. Murray and L. Ouellette, 243–59. New York: New York University Press.

Holmes, Su. 2004. "Reality goes pop!" Reality TV, popular music, and narratives of stardom. *Television & New Media* 5:147–72.

Hwang, Suein. 2005. The new white flight. *Wall Street Journal*, November 19.

Jaschik, Scott. 2006. Too Asian? *Inside Higher Ed*, October 10. http://www.insidehighered.com/news/2006/10/10/asian.

Kim, Claire Jean. 2003. *Bitter fruit: The politics of black-Korean conflict in New York City.* New Haven, CT: Yale University Press.

Kingsbury, Henry. 2001. *Music, talent, and performance: A conservatory cultural system.* Philadelphia: Temple University Press.

Kraszewski, Jon. 2009. Country hicks and urban cliques: Mediating race, reality, and liberalism on MTV's *The Real World*. In *Reality TV: Remaking television culture*, 2nd ed., ed. S. Murray and L. Ouellette, 205–22. New York: New York University Press.

Lalli, Nina. 2007. Hung speaks: "What should I do, make sweet and sour chicken?" *Village Voice*, October 1. http://blogs.villagevoice.com/food/archives/2007/10/hung_speaks_wha.php.

Manalansan, Martin. 2009. The empire of food: Place, memory, and Asian "ethnic" cuisines. In *Gastro polis: Food and New York City*, ed. A. Hauck-Lawson and J. Deutsch, 93–107. New York: Columbia University Press.

Morley, David, and Kevin Robins. 1995. *Spaces of identity: Global media, electronic landscapes and cultural boundaries.* London: Routledge University Press.

Osajima, Keith. 1988. Asian Americans as the model minority: An analysis of the popular press image in the 1960s and 1980s. In *Reflections on shattered windows: Promises and prospects for Asian American studies*, ed. G. Okihiro, 165–174. Seattle: University of Washington Press.

Palumbo-Liu, David. 1999. *Asian/America: Historical crossings of a racial frontier.* Stanford, CA: Stanford University Press.

Parasecoli, Fabio. 2009. The chefs, the entrepreneurs, and their patrons: The avant-garde food scene in New York City. In *Gastropolis: Food and New York City*, ed. A. Hauck-Lawson and J. Deutsch, 116–31. New York: Columbia University Press.

Senior, Jennifer. 2007. The near fame experience. *New York Magazine*, August 6. http://nymag.com/news/features/35538/.

Severson, Kim, and Adam Ellick. 2007. A top chef's kitchen is far too hot, some workers say. *New York Times*, January 17.

Silverstein, Michael, and Neil Fiske. 2003. *Trading up: The new American luxury.* New York: Portfolio.

Smith, Nina. 2007. *Top Chef's* controversial Hung wins—and says he deserves it. *TV Guide*, October 5. http://www.tvguide.com/news/top-chef-hung-35797.aspx

Song, Min Hyoung. 2008. Communities of remembrance: Reflections on the Virginia Tech shootings and race. *Journal of Asian American Studies* 11 (1): 1–26.

Stanley, Alessandra. 2007. The classless utopia of reality TV. *New York Times*, December 2.

Stokes, Martin. 1994. *Ethnicity, identity and music: The musical construction of place.* New York: Berg.

Tieu, Hong Hoa. 2008. Hail to the chef: Cooking his way to the top. *BN Magazine*, March 28. http://news.newamericamedia.org/news/view_article.html?article_id=4b076d2bc03de735409ee094a90255f2

57

"Take Responsibility for Yourself"

Judge Judy and the Neoliberal Citizen

Laurie Ouellette

A woman drags her ex-boyfriend to court over an overdue adult movie rental and unpaid loan. A woman is heartbroken when her best friend betrays her and ruins her credit. A smooth-talking ex-boyfriend claims money from his ex was a gift. Welcome to *Judge Judy*, queen of the courtroom program, where judges resolve "real-life" disputes between friends, neighbors, family members, roommates, and lovers on national television. For critics who equate television's role in democracy with serious news and public affairs, altercations over broken engagements, minor fender benders, carpet stains, unpaid personal loans, and the fate of jointly purchased household appliances may seem like crass entertainment or trivial distractions. But such dismissals overlook the "governmental" nature of courtroom programs like *Judge Judy*, which gained cultural presence—and a reputation for "zero tolerance when it comes to nonsense"—alongside the neoliberal policies and discourses of the 1990s.[1]

Judge Judy took the small claims–based court format from the fringes of commercial syndication to an authoritative place on daytime schedules when it debuted in 1996, the same year the U.S. Telecommunications Act was passed.[2] While the legislation has been critiqued for its deregulatory ethos as well as its affinity with the broader neoliberal forces behind welfare reform and the privatization of public institutions from the penal system to the post office, the cultural dimensions of these parallels remain less examined.[3] There is a tendency within policy studies to take the cultural impact of neoliberalism as self-evident— to presume that the laissez-faire principles codified by the Act will erode democracy in predictable ways that typically involve the decline of journalism, documentaries, and other "substantial" information formats found unprofitable by the culture industries. While such concerns have some validity, the metaphor of subversion needs to be jettisoned, for it reifies untenable cultural hierarchies, and neglects neoliberalism's productive imprint on contemporary television culture and the "idealized" citizen subjectivities that it circulates.

From Laurie Ouellette, "'Take Responsibility for Yourself': *Judge Judy* and the Neoliberal Citizen." In Susan Murray and Laurie Ouellette (eds), (2004), *Reality TV: Remaking Television Culture*. New York: New York University Press, 231–250.

◆ 545

Reality programming is one site where neoliberal approaches to citizenship have in fact materialized on television. From makeover programs (such as *What Not to Wear* and *Trading Spaces*) that enlist friends, neighbors, and experts in their quest to teach people how to make "better" decorating and fashion choices, to gamedocs (like *Survivor* and *Big Brother*) that construct community relations in terms of individual competition and self-enterprising, neoliberal constructions of "good citizenship" cut across much popular reality television. The courtroom program is a particularly clear example of this broader trend because it draws from the symbolic authority of the state to promote both the outsourcing of its governmental functions and the subjective requirements of the transition to a neoliberal society. *Judge Judy* and programs like it do not subvert elusive democratic ideals, then, as much as they *construct* templates for citizenship that complement the privatization of public life, the collapse of the welfare state, and most important, the discourse of individual choice and personal responsibility.

This chapter situates *Judge Judy* as a neoliberal technology of everyday citizenship, and shows how it attempts to shape and guide the conduct and choices of lower-income women in particular. As we shall see, *Judge Judy* draws from and diffuses neoliberal currents by fusing an image of democracy (signified in the opening credits by a gently flapping U.S. flag, stately public courthouse, and gavel-wielding judge) with a privatized approach to conflict management and an intensified government of the self. *Judge Judy* and programs like it supplant institutions of the state (for instance, social work, law and order, and welfare offices), and using real people, caught in the drama of ordinary life as raw material, train TV viewers to function without state assistance or supervision as self-disciplining, self-sufficient, responsible, and risk-averting individuals. In this way, the courtroom subgenre of reality TV exemplifies what James Hay has called a

cultural apparatus for "neoliberal forms of governance."[4]

Neoliberalism and Television Culture

To understand *Judge Judy*'s neoliberal alignments, a brief detour through the concept of neoliberalism is in order. My understanding of neoliberalism begins with political economy and the activism it inspires. From this vantage point, neoliberalism is generally understood as a troubling worldview that promotes the "free" market as the best way to organize every dimension of social life. According to activists Elizabeth Martinez and Arnoldo Garcia, this worldview has generated five trends that have accelerated globally since the 1980s: the "rule" of the market; spending cuts on public services; deregulation (including the deregulation of broadcasting); the privatization of state-owned institutions, "usually in the name of efficiency"; and "eliminating the concept of the public good or community and replacing it with individual responsibility."[5] For critics like Robert McChesney, the upshot of neoliberalism and the reforms it has spawned is that a "handful of private interests are permitted to control as much as possible of social life in order to maximize their personal profit."[6]

While I share these concerns, I have found Foucauldian approaches particularly useful for analyzing the subjective dimensions of neoliberalism that circulate on reality TV. Drawing from Michel Foucault, Nikolas Rose theorizes neoliberalism less as a simple opposition between the market (bad) and welfare state (good) than as a "changing network" of complex power relations. If neoliberal regimes have implemented an "array of measures" aimed at downsizing the welfare state and dismantling the "institutions within which welfare government had isolated and managed their social problems," they still rely on "strategies of government."[7] This manifests as various forms of "cultural training" that govern indirectly in the name of "lifestyle maximization," "free choice," and personal responsibility, says Rose. This diffused approach to the "regulation of conduct" escapes association with a clear or top-down agenda, and is instead presented as the individual's "own desire" to achieve optimum happiness and success. As Rose points out, the "enterprising" individual crafted by this discourse has much in common with the choice-making "customer" valorized by neoliberal economics. Both presume "free will," which means that those individuals who fail to thrive under neoliberal conditions can be readily cast as the "author of their own misfortunes."[8]

. . . . *Judge Judy* fuses television, neoliberalism, and self-help discourse in a governmental address to women living out what feminist philosopher Nancy Fraser has called the "postsocialist" condition.[9] The program presents the privatized space of the TV courtroom as the most "efficient" way to resolve microdisputes steeped in the unacknowledged politics of gender, class, and race, but it also classifies those individuals who "waste the court's time" as risky deviants and self-made victims who create their own misfortunes by making the "wrong" choices and failing to manage their lives properly. The imagined TV viewer is the implied beneficiary of this litany of mistakes, for one's classification as "normal" hinges on both recognizing the pathos of "others" and internalizing the rules of self-government spelled out on the program. The courtroom program has, for precisely this reason, been institutionally positioned as a moral and educational corrective to "permissive" entertainment, suggesting that the discourse of the "public interest" in broadcasting has not been squashed but rather reconfigured by neoliberal reforms. Indeed, it could be that television is increasingly pivotal to neoliberal approaches to government and the citizen subjectivities on which they depend.

"The Cases Are Real, the Rulings Are Final"

Judge Judy is not the first television program to resolve everyday microconflicts in simulated courtroom settings. The genre can be traced to 1950s programs like *People in Conflict* and *The Verdict Is Yours*. In the 1980s, retired California Superior Court judge Joseph Wapner presided over *The People's Court*, while *Divorce Court* used actors to dramatize "real" legal proceedings.[10] *Judge Judy* did, however, rework and revitalize the format, and the program's "no-nonsense" approach to family and small claims disputes generated notoriety and imitators (examples include *Judge Joe Brown, Judge Mathis, Judge Hatchet, Curtis Court,* a revitalized *People's Court,* and *Moral Court*). Well into the new millennium, courtroom programs abound on television, competing with talk shows, game shows, and soap operas for a predominantly female audience.

On *Judge Judy,* real-life litigants are offered travel costs and court fees to present their cases on national television. The price is to drop out of the public judicial process and submit to the private ruling of Judith (Judy) Sheindlin. A former New York family court judge, Sheindlin was recruited for the "tough-love" philosophy she first spelled out in an influential *60 Minutes* profile, and later expanded on in her best-selling book *Don't Pee on My Leg and Tell Me It's Raining,* which faulted the overcrowded court system as a lenient bureaucracy that reflects "how far we have strayed from personal responsibility and old-fashioned discipline."[11] Spotting ratings potential, Larry Lyttle, president of Big Ticket Television, a Viacom company, invited Sheindlin to preside over "real cases with real consequences in a courtroom on television." Called a "swift decision maker with no tolerance for excuses" by the program's publicity, Sheindlin claims to bring to her TV show the same message she advocated in the courts:

"Take responsibility for yourself, your actions and the children you've brought into the world."[12] In interviews, she situates *Judge Judy* as a public service that can solve societal problems by instilling the right attitudes and choices in individuals:

> It's a much larger audience. Whatever message I spew—"Take responsibility for your life. If you're a victim, it's your fault. Stop being a victim. Get a grip! You're the one who's supposed to make a direction in your life." All those messages I tried in Family Court to instill in people—primarily women. [The TV show] sounded like something that would not only be fun, but worthwhile as well.[13]

Like other TV judges, Sheindlin now hears noncriminal disputes that rarely exceed several hundred dollars or the equivalent in personal property. While these conflicts often speak to broader social tensions and inequalities, the program's governmental logic frames the cases as "petty squabbles" brought about by the deficiencies of individuals. Sheindlin's courtroom is filled with feuding relations and typically devoid of people who wish to sue businesses, bosses, or least of all, big corporations. This focus makes perfect sense, for the program's impetus as a technology of citizenship is to scrutinize ordinary people who require state mediation of everyday affairs, a process that hinges more on the moral radar Sheindlin claims to have developed in the public court system than on time-consuming democratic processes (she has been known to snap, "I don't have time for beginnings" and "I don't read documents"). While TV viewers are situated outside Sheindlin's disciplinary address to litigants derided as losers, cheaters, liars, and "gumbos," their status as "good" citizens presumes the desire to adhere to the neoliberal templates for living she espouses.

While the opening credits promise "real people" involved in "real cases," a male narrator differentiates the program from the public court system with the reminder: "This is Judy's courtroom," where the "decisions are final." Onscreen, Sheindlin plays judge, prosecutor, professional expert, and punctilious moral authority, handling an average of two cases per thirty-minute episode and dispensing justice at "lightning speed," according to the program's publicity. Participants must abide by the program's rules, which include speaking only when spoken to, accepting the authority of the judge ("Just pay attention, I run the show" she tells litigants), and taking humiliating remarks and reprimands without rebuttal or comment ("Are you all nuts" and "I'm smarter than you" are typical examples). More important than the details of any particular case is Sheindlin's swift assessment of the choices and behaviors of the people involved in them. . . .

Sheindlin questions litigants about their employment history, marital and parental status, income, drug habits, sexual practices, incarceration record, and past or present "dependency" on public welfare.[14] Such information transcends the evaluation of evidence as the principal means whereby Sheindlin determines who is at fault in the citizenship lesson that accompanies every ruling. Sheindlin is also known to belittle the accents of non-English speakers, accuse litigants of lying and abusing the "system," and order individuals to spit out gum, stand up straight, and "control" bodily functions to her liking. In one episode, a male litigant who denied her accusations of pot smoking was ordered to take a live drug test. *Judge Judy* thus both duplicates and extends the surveillance of the poor and working class carried out by welfare offices, unemployment centers, and other social services.[15]

Judge Judy is part of the current wave of reality TV in that "real" people (not actors) involved in "authentic" disagreements are used as a selling point to differentiate the show from fictional entertainment. While scripts are not used, reality is, as John Fiske reminds us, "encoded" at every level.[16]

The program scours small claims dockets for potentially "interesting" cases; would-be litigants must complete a questionnaire, and only those "actual" disputes that can be situated within the program's logic are presented on television. Offscreen narration, graphic titles, video replays, and teasers further frame the meaning of the cases by labeling the litigants, characterizing their purportedly real motivations to viewers and highlighting scenes from the program that reiterate Sheindlin's governmental authority. Due to increased competition for conflicts among the growing cadre of courtroom programs, viewers are now invited to bypass the courts altogether and submit their everyday disputes directly to *Judge Judy.* On-air solicitations like "Are You in a Family Dispute? Call Judy" promise an efficient, private alternative to public mediation of conflicts—and yet, individuals who accept the invitations are ultimately held responsible for their "mistakes" on cases like "The Making of a Family Tragedy."

Judge Judy's focus on everyday domestic conflicts has led some critics to denounce the courtroom program as a new twist on the sensational "low-brow" daytime talk show.[17] Yet Sheindlin insists that her program is a somber alternative to the participatory, carnivalesque atmosphere of the genre it now rivals in the ratings. Indeed, the court setting and overtly disciplinary address of the *Judge Judy* program "code" it in distinct ways that are easily distinguishable to TV viewers. Sheindlin's strict demeanor and authoritative place on the bench are accentuated by camerawork that magnifies her power by filming her from below. The silence of the studio audience, the drab, institutional-like setting of the simulated courtroom, and the presence of a uniformed bailiff also separate the court program from talk shows, a format that feminist scholars have characterized as a tentative space for oppressed groups (women, people of color, and the working classes) to discuss the politic of everyday life. . . .

On *Judge Judy,* the authority represented by the simulated courtroom setting is often enlisted to "force" . . . confessions. Sheindlin claims that her past experience as a frustrated state official has enabled her to "see through the bull" ("She can always tell if you're lying. All she has to do is make eye contact," reported *USA Today*). Litigants who refuse to "confess" to suspected actions have been subjected to live background checks, but more often than not Sheindlin simply discounts "false" confessions and replaces the version of events offered by the litigant with an expert interpretation gleaned through biographical information as much as "evidence."

Court programs also magnify the disciplinary logic present on the talk show by disallowing audience participation, controlling the flow of personal revelations, and fusing the therapeutic ethos of the "clinic" with the surveillance of the welfare office and the authoritative signifiers of law and order. This distinction, as much as the absence of the carnivalesque, is what has allowed courtroom programs to be institutionally positioned as a cultural corrective to "tabloid" television. *Judge Judy* is the "antithesis of Jerry Springer," insists Sheindlin. "Jerry Springer encourages people to show off their filthiest laundry, to misbehave. I scrupulously avoid doing that. I cut them off."[18]

The television industry has also been quick to assert that courtroom television "educates" as well as entertains—a claim to public service that is rarely made of most popular reality formats. Big Ticket's Larry Lyttle maintains that courtroom programs function as a positive moral force because unlike on talk shows, where "conflicts are aired and tossed around" a court show like *Judge Judy* "ends with a decision that someone was right and someone was wrong."[19] WCHS-TV in Charleston, West Virginia, similarly praises the program's "unique ability to act as a true moral compass for people seeking guidance, insight and resolution."[20] Characterizing the courtroom genre as a technology of citizenship that can temper the "effects" of fictional television, one TV judge explained in an interview that

> America's been looking at soap operas for going on 50 some years, and they legitimize the most back stabbing, low-down, slimeball behavior. That's gotten to be acceptable behavior. . . . We find ourselves confronted with a lot of soap-opera behavior in our courtrooms. And we resolve them and say, no, we know you may have seen this, but it's not right.[21]

Privatizing Justice, Stigmatizing "Dependency"

Judge Judy's claim to facilitate "justice at lightning speed" boldly implies that commercial television can resolve problems faster and more efficiently than the public sector. In this sense, the program affirms neoliberal rationales for "outsourcing" state-owned institutions and services. *Judge Judy* also complements neoliberal policies by conveying the impression that democracy (exemplified by the justice system) is overrun by individuals embroiled in petty conflicts and troubles of their own making. If the program feeds off of real-life microdisputes, Sheindlin chastises litigants for failing to govern their "selves" and their personal affairs. In addition to lecturing guests about their personal history, she often accuses participants of "wasting the court's time," conveying the idea that "normal" citizens do not depend on the supervision of the judiciary or any public institution for that matter. People who rely on professional judges (including TV judges) to mediate everyday problems are cast as inadequate individuals who lack the capacity or, worse, desire to function as self-reliant and personally responsible citizens.

On *Judge Judy*, citizenship lessons are often directed at people who reject marriage,

the nuclear family, and traditional values; unmarried couples who live together are of particular concern. While Sheindlin (who is divorced) does not condemn such behavior as immoral conduct, she does present rules and procedures for navigating modern relationships, which include getting personal loans in writing, not "living together for more than one year without a wedding band," and not "purchasing homes, cars, boats or animals with romantic partners outside of wedlock."[22] On *Judge Judy*, individuals are told that they must impose these rules on themselves—both for their own protection and because, as Sheindlin explains, there is "no court of people living together. It's up to you to be smart. Plan for the eventualities before you set up housekeeping." When former lovers dispute an unpaid car loan, Sheindlin takes the disagreement as an opportunity to explain the dos and don'ts of cohabitation without marriage. Sheindlin finds the couple incompatible and "irresponsible," and rules that it was an "error of judgment" for them to share an apartment together. This judgment is tied to a broader failure of appropriate citizenship when Sheindlin lectures the pair for then "asking the courts" to resolve a domestic property dispute. "You're not married—there is a different set of rules for people who choose to live together without marriage," she asserts, reiterating that people who stray from state-sanctioned conventions have a particular duty to monitor their own affairs.

If the idealized citizen-subject constructed by *Judge Judy* complements the choice-making neoliberal customer discussed by Rose, that individual is also a self-supporting worker. People who receive any form of public assistance are cast as deviants in particular need of citizenship lessons. The advice they receive evokes Nancy Fraser and Linda Gordon's observation that welfare has become cloaked in a stigmatizing discourse of "dependency" that presumes gender, class, and racial parity. As Fraser and Gordon point out, women (including single mothers) are now held accountable to the white, middle-class, male work ethic, even as they lack the advantages and resources to perform as traditionally male breadwinners. While this marks a shift away from the patronizing assumption that all women are helpless and therefore "naturally" dependent on men or, in their absence, the state, it conceals the structural inequalities that lower-income women in particular continue to face.[23]

On *Judge Judy* all women are presumed to be capable of supporting themselves and their children financially; accepting welfare is construed not as a reflection of gender or economic inequality but as a character flaw. Women are routinely asked to disclose their past or present reliance on government "handouts," and those who admit to receiving benefits are subsequently marked as irresponsible and lazy individuals who "choose" not to work for a living. Welfare recipients are also constructed as morally unsound citizens who cheat taxpayers, as was the case in an episode where Sheindlin demanded to know whether an unmarried woman with three children by the same father had "avoided" marriage merely to qualify for welfare benefits. In another episode, an unemployed twenty-something mother being sued by her baby's would-be adoptive parents was scolded for relying on public assistance to raise the child she had decided not to give up for adoption. While adoption law doesn't allow adoptive parents to reclaim monetary "gifts" to birth mothers, Sheindlin stressed the woman's "moral" obligation to repay them. Presuming that the mother had chosen poverty, Sheindlin also sternly advised her to get a job and "not have more babies she can't take care of." *Judge Judy*'s disdain for so-called welfare dependency extends to charity and other forms of assistance. If individuals are told to take care of themselves and their families, empathy and social responsibility for others are discouraged. "No good deed goes unpunished," Sheindlin advised a family friend who took in a homeless woman who had spent some time in jail.

At the societal and community level, the public good is cast in neoliberal terms, as a system of individual responsibilities and rewards. . . .

Since the litigants on *Judge Judy* are introduced by name and occupation this information also appears in onscreen titles—viewers know that individuals cast as risky are often working-class men who drive trucks, wait on tables, enter data, do construction, or perform low-paying forms of customer service. If female welfare recipients are cast as irresponsible non-workers, men lacking middle-class occupations and salaries are routinely scorned for "choosing" a life of poverty, as was the case when Sheindlin lectured a middle-aged male Wal-Mart cashier for failing to obtain more lucrative employment. In the adoption episode mentioned above, a similar evaluation of male employment was tied to a failure of citizenship. The infant's father, who had worked on and off as a gas station attendant but was currently unemployed, was characterized as a personal failure and societal menace, not just because he refused to admit "personal moral responsibility" to repay the money to the adoptive parents, but because he "refused" to enterprise himself in accordance with the middle-class work ethic.

Cases involving men who manipulate women out of money, gifts, rent, or property are a staple on *Judge Judy,* and in these cases, male unemployment and insolvency are closely tied to the detection and avoidance of romantic risk. In a case where a woman met a man on the Internet, loaned him money, and was dumped, Sheindlin fused a harsh judgment of the boyfriend's opportunism and dishonesty in his romantic relationship to an undeveloped work ethic. Demanding to know when he last "held a full-time job," she swiftly identified the man as a freeloader and "con artist," implying that men without economic means are especially dangerous and therefore not to be trusted when it comes to intimate relationships. Female litigants can also be categorized as identifiable romantic risks, as was the case in "Opportunity Knocks," where Sheindlin wanted an attractive young woman in court to resolve whether money from her ex-boyfriend was a gift or loan, accusing her of "using" the man financially with "no intention of marrying him." In most cases, though, it is lower-income men who play this role in a gender reversal of the gold digger stereotype. This complements the program's focus on solving the problem of female victimization through better self-management.

Women are typically cast as "self-created" victims in terms that articulate neoliberal currents to female self-help culture. Rejecting what she terms the "disease of victimization," or tendency to blame society for one's hardships, Sheindlin claims, in her books and on her TV program, that all women can achieve happiness and success with a little knowledge along with the right attitude. On *Judge Judy*, women's problems are blamed on their own failure to make good decisions, whether that means pulling one's self up from a life of poverty, "preparing" wisely for financial independence, or avoiding entanglement with unstable, manipulative, or abusive individuals. . . .

Women who claim to have been abused by men appear frequently on *Judge Judy*, where they, too, are lectured for creating their circumstances. Domestic abuse is never the basis of a legal case, but is typically revealed in the course of Sheindlin's interrogation of the participants involved. In a case involving cousins fighting over a family collection of knickknacks, Sheindlin determines that the man is a deranged and unstable individual, while the woman he bullied and harassed is an "adult" who has "chosen to let someone do this to her." When Sheindlin learns that an ex-boyfriend, in court over a minor car accident, has battered his former teenage girlfriend, she maintains that the girl made unwise "choices," sternly advising, "Never let a man put his hands on you." In a case involving former lovers disputing overdue phone and gas bills, the woman reveals that

in refusing to pay household expenses, her former boyfriend was addicted to heroin and had spent time in jail for assaulting a minor. She also implies that he physically abused her. Typifying the program's neoliberal solution to the problem of domestic violence as well as the complexities of gender and class, Sheindlin faults the woman for failing to accept responsibility for her own conduct. Taking the troubled relationship as the raw material for a citizenship lesson aimed at women, Sheindlin determines that "being with him doesn't speak well of your judgment." As "young as you are, you allowed someone with a criminal history and no job to live with you . . . and you want the courts to fix that?"

Judge Judy seeks to instill in women a desire to avoid the "disease" of victimization along with the overreliance on state assistance and intervention it is said to have spawned. This message carries traces of liberal feminist discourse to the extent that it promotes female independence and agency. Presuming that barriers to social and gender equality have long been dismantled, the program places the onus to achieve these goals on individuals. Sheindlin, who considers herself a positive female role model, contends that all "women have the power to make decisions, to call it as they see it, to take no guff."[24] She claims that all women, however positioned by an unequal capitalist society, can reap the benefits of happiness and success so long as they exercise good judgment and cultivate self-esteem. Economic security and "feeling good about yourself" are thus closely bound in Sheindlin's blueprint for successful female citizenship. The responsibility for cultivating self-esteem is placed not on society but on individual women, whose job it is to train themselves and their daughters "to have a profession, have a career . . . so they will never be dependent on anybody."[25] On *Judge Judy*, female litigants are advised to avoid "depending" on boyfriends and husbands for financial assistance in particular. This message has less to do with dismantling dominant ideologies and institutions than it does with ensuring that women "take care of themselves" so that the state doesn't have to. *Judge Judy* conveys the idea that women can no longer "claim" a victim status rooted in bifurcated and hierarchical gender roles; nor, however, can they expect public solutions to the inequalities that structure women's lives.

Sheindlin presents "independence" as a responsibility that all women must strive to achieve, but she also promotes the hegemony of the nuclear family, reconstituted as a two-wage-earning unit. Family troubles underscore many of the cases heard on *Judge Judy,* where mothers suing daughters, children suing their parents, and parents suing each other are the norm. This steady stream of feuding relations paints a portrait of a troubled institution that clearly isn't working, yet Sheindlin uses her authority to promote the sacred importance of family bonds. The contradiction exists in perpetual tension, as illuminated by the treatment of family in two key episodes.

In the first, a male cashier is suing his unemployed ex-fiancée for bills paid when they lived together; she is countersuing for "mental distress." After Sheindlin interrogates the woman about why she wasn't working at the time, the woman replies that she quit her job to "build a home together." She also tells Sheindlin that her fiancé stalked her and threatened to come after her with a gun when they broke up. Although this scenario contains the material to cast the male as a deviant individual, Sheindlin rejects the woman's story as an "excuse" smacking of victimization, comparing her own success as a married working woman who didn't "quit her job to pick out furniture and dishes" to the failure of the "alleged victim of harassment," she orders the woman to pay the back rent. In this episode, the female litigant's embrace of traditional family values is denounced because it includes the desire for "dependency" on a male breadwinner, thereby violating the neoliberal mantra of self-sufficiency that *Judge Judy* espouses.

In a dispute involving an estranged mother and daughter, though, the nuclear family is valorized against a woman's quest for independence. The mother, who divorced her husband when she came out as a lesbian, is implicitly cast as selfish and irresponsible for abandoning the heterosexual family unit to pursue her own personal fulfillment. While Sheindlin doesn't condemn the woman's homosexuality, she harshly criticizes her performance and "choices" as a mother, and recommends family counseling to repair the damage.

As these examples attest, *Judge Judy*'s advice to women does not seek to expand women's choices, it merely guides them in particular directions. Operating as a technology of citizenship, the program steers women toward neoliberal reforms that are presented as their own responsibilities and in their own "best interests." In this sense, *Judge Judy* seeks to transform what Rose calls the "goals of authorities into the "choices and commitments of individuals."[26]

Judge Judy and the Normative Citizen

Judge Judy constitutes the normative citizen—the TV viewer at home—in opposition to both risky deviants and "self-made" victims. By scrutinizing the dos and don'ts of everyday life as it is presumed to be lived by "troubled" populations, it promotes neoliberal policies for conducting one's self in private. It scapegoats the uneducated and unprivileged as "others" who manufacture their hardships, and thus, require nothing more than personal responsibility and self-discipline in the wake of shrinking public services. Those who reject this logic are deemed abnormal and often unreformable: "I'm not going to get through to her. I have a sense that she's a lost cause at fourteen," Sheindlin once said of a female litigant.[27] TV viewers are encouraged to distance themselves from the "deficient" individuals who seep into Sheindlin's courtroom, therefore avoiding any recognition of the societal basis of women's problems and concerns. While Sheindlin's harshest derision is aimed at the socially "unrespectable," her governmental advice is intended for all women—particularly middle-class viewers—for according to the program's neoliberal logic, their happiness and success hinges on it. . . .

Notes

1. The popular press has emphasized the "no tolerance" ethos of the programs, contributing to the cultural context in which they are received. See, in particular, Melanie McFarland, "Tough Judges Show There's Justice in Watching Television," *Seattle Times,* 30 November 1998, http://archives.seattletimes.

2. See ibid.

3. For a critical analysis of the Telecommunications Act of 1996, see Patricia Aufderheide, *Communications Policy and the Public Interest* (New York: Guilford, 1999) and Robert McChesney, *Rich Media, Poor Democracy: Communication Politics in Dubious Times* (New York: New Press, 2000).

4. James Hay, "Unaided Virtues: The (Neo)-Liberalization of the Domestic Sphere," *Television and New Media* 1, no. 1 (2000): 56.

5. Elizabeth Martinez and Arnoldo Garcia, "What Is Neoliberalism?" *Corpwatch,* 1 January 1997, www.corpwatch.org.

6. Robert McChesney, introduction to *Profit over People: Neoliberalism and Global Order,* by Noam Chomsky (New York: Seven Stories Press, 1999), 7, 11.

7. Nikolas Rose, "Governing 'Advanced' Liberal Democracies," in *Foucault and Political Reason: Liberalism, Neoliberalism, and Rationalities of Government,* ed. Andrew Barry, Thomas Osborne, and Nikolas Rose (Chicago: University of Chicago Press, 1996), 55, 58–59. For a Foucauldian approach to "governmentality," see also Graham Bruchell, Colin Cordon, and Peter Miller, eds., *The Foucault Effect:*

Studies in Governmentality (Chicago: University of Chicago Press, 1991). I have also found Toby Miller's analysis of citizenship and subjectivity helpful for thinking through neoliberal modes of government. See his *The Well-Tempered Self: Citizenship, Culture, and the Postmodern Subject* (Baltimore, Md.: Johns Hopkins University Press, 1993).

8. Rose, "Governing 'Advanced' Liberal Democracies," 57–59.

9. Nancy Fraser, *Justice Interruptus: Critical Reflections on the "Postsocialist" Condition* (New York: Routledge, 1997).

10. Judge Wapner was brought back to resolve disputes between pet owners on the Animal Channel's *Animal Court.*

11. Luaine Lee, "Judge Judy Has Always Believed in the Motto 'Just Do It'," *Nando Media,* 28 November 1998, www.nandotimes. com; and Judy Sheindlin, *Don't Pee on My Leg and Tell Me It's Raining* (New York: Harper Perennial, 1997), 3.

12. Cited on www.judgejudy.com.

13. Cited in Lee, "Judge Judy."

14. Michel Foucault, "Complete and Austere Institutions," in *The Foucault Reader,* ed. Paul Rabinow (New York: Pantheon, 1984), 219–20. See also Michel Foucault, *Discipline and Punish* (New York: Random House, 1995).

15. See Frances Fox Piven, *Regulating the Poor: The Functions of Public Welfare* (New York: Random House, 1971); and John Gillion, *Overseers of the Poor* (Chicago: University of Chicago Press, 2001).

16. John Fiske, *Television Culture* (New York: Routledge, 1987).

17. Michael M. Epstein, for example, argues that courtroom programs are an extension of the talk show to the extent that they use law and order to legitimate a sensationalist focus on personal conflict. Epstein also points out that the judge figure is construed as an "ultimate" moral authority less concerned with legal procedures than with the evaluation of personal behaviors. Presuming the "low" status of the genre and concentrating on its misrepresentation of the actual law, however, his critique overlooks the governmental nature and implications of this focus on everyday conduct and behavior. See Michael M. Epstein, "Judging Judy, Mablean,

and Mills: How Courtroom Programs Use Law to Parade Private Lives to Mass Audiences," *Television Quarterly* (2001), http://www.emmyonline.org/ tvq/articles/32–1–1.asp.

18. Cited in Barbara Lippert, "Punchin Judy," *New York Magazine,* 15 June 2001, www.newyorkmetro.com.

19. Cited in *Judge Judy* publicity, www.wchstv.com/synd_prog/iudy.

20. Cited on www.wchstv.com/synd_prog/judy.

21. Cited in McFarland, "Tough Judges Show There's Justice."

22. Judy Sheindlin, *Keep It Simple Stupid* (New York: Cliff Street Books, 2000), 2.

23. Nancy Fraser and Linda Gordon, "A Genealogy of 'Dependency': Tracing a Keyword of the U.S. Welfare State," in Fraser, *Justice Interruptus.*

24. Ibid., 105.

25. Sheindlin, cited in Lee, "Judge Judy."

26. Rose, "Governing 'Advanced' Liberal Democracies," 58.

27. The clip was replayed during an interview with Sheindlin on *Larry King Live,* CNN, 12 September 2000.

58

Television and the Domestication of Cosmetic Surgery

Sue Tait

This chapter explores the discursive production of cosmetic surgery on *Extreme Makeover* (2002–2005), the most successful of television's surgical reality shows, and *Nip/Tuck* (2003–), the first drama series about cosmetic surgery. Both US produced shows are internationally syndicated and *Nip/Tuck* is available on DVD. My analysis attends to the ways in which particular meanings of cosmetic surgery are empowered within public culture through the way in which surgery and surgical patients are visualised and narrated on television. I argue that while *Extreme Makeover* at once spectacularises and domesticates the surgical body, *Nip/Tuck*'s rendering of surgical culture attempts to disrupt the prevailing cultural comfort with cosmetic appearance work. *Extreme Makeover* illustrates the manner in which the domestication of surgical culture relies on, and elaborates, a post-feminist cultural imaginary, whereby individual consumption rather than cultural transformation is posited as the means to empower the deviant gendered body. Feminist understandings of cosmetic surgery, as a cultural phenomenon which expresses gendered inequity, get left behind. . . .

As I shall elaborate, while *Nip/Tuck*'s critique of surgical culture is frequently curtailed by sensationalism and recourse to individualist explanatory frames, the show nevertheless remains a rare space through which a dystopic view of surgery is signalled within public culture. Identifying potentially resistive frames to the domestication of surgical culture, and the manner in which these are constrained by the conventions of television drama, illustrates the limited range of subject positions available to contemporary television viewers which may be marshalled when framing their own responses to cosmetic surgery. . . .

Extreme Makeover: The Practice of Aesthetic Eugenics as Charity

Press statements released by both the American Society for Aesthetic Plastic Surgery (ASAPS) and the American Society of Plastic Surgeons (ASPS) in 2005 link the rise in the

From Tait, S. (2007). Television and the domestication of cosmetic surgery. *Feminist Media Studies*, 7(2), 119–135. Reprinted by permission of Taylor & Francis Ltd., www.tandf.co.uk/journals.

number of surgical procedures performed in 2004 to the trend in cosmetic surgery reality television. ASPS suggest that this increase is not "rampant," with the 9.2 million procedures performed in 2004, 5 per cent up on 2003 and 24 per cent up on 2000. Figures released by ASAPS differ markedly from ASPS's (which may be attributed to a different method of data collection), claiming that 11.9 million procedures were performed in 2004, a 44 per cent increase from 2003. The president of the organisation suggests this rise is connected to media coverage of plastic surgery: "[p]eople have had many more opportunities to see, first hand, what plastic surgery is like and what it can do for others. That can be a strong incentive for them to seek the same benefits by having cosmetic procedures themselves" (ASAPS 2005). The ideological labour *Extreme Makeover* performs in normalising cosmetic surgery was commented upon by a member of the "Extreme Team" on a follow-up special:

I think the show has done a wonderful thing for plastic surgery and patients because it has brought it out of the closet. It's made it okay to have plastic surgery without hiding it, and that's an incredibly liberating thing for a lot of people for whom it makes a huge difference in their lives. (Life After *Extreme Makeover* 2004)

Extreme Makeover stages the surgical transformation of candidates in a manner which not only publicises cosmetic surgery, but makes it meaningful in ways which eschew perceptions of surgery as the practice of the vain or superficial. It contributes to a post-feminist surgical imaginary by figuring surgery as the means to empower the suffering individual, a discursive production which domesticates practices of discrimination, along with their surgical solution. . . .

The opening sequence of *Extreme Makeover* introduces the candidates, who make a confession of ugliness and a confession of suffering which serve to legitimise their surgical candidacy. The candidate, friends and family, and the narrator testify to the suffering the appearance of the patient brings: David (improbably) claims his infant son finds him unattractive (season 1: episode 2); Lori and her children have been teased about Lori's "witch" nose (Lori's young daughter confesses "I feel sad that my mother can't go any places at school with me . . . because of her face and the stuff that's wrong with her") (season 3: episode 2); and James has been beaten and bullied (season 2: episode 19). Testimonies of suffering include accounts of loneliness, poor job prospects, social phobia, bullying, and the inability to find a mate. These confessions locate the physical appearance, rather than the cruelty of others, as the site which produces unhappiness, and posit surgical transformation as the most expedient cure. As Deery observes, *Extreme Makeover* may be regarded as a prime-time infomercial for cosmetic surgery which presents "individual stories which inspire empathy but short-circuit politicization" (2004, p. 212).

Viewers are often told that suffering and tragedy in the candidate's lives, or the work they do in the service of others, have taken a toll on their appearance. Kari (season 3: episode 12) has lost a son, Sandra spent 30 years caring for a disabled husband (season 1: episode 4), and Peggy claims her career in law enforcement has aged her (season 2: episode 2). These narratives are supplemented by testimony from loved ones as to the moral worthiness of the candidates, who are described as caring and self-sacrificing, kind and hardworking. This convention of the show performs important ideological labour in representing the bestowal of a make-over as an act of charity, awarded to a morally worthy recipient who has suffered unfairly. The implication is that the physical appearance of candidates does not reflect who they "truly" are, playing out the culturally produced belief that character is manifest in appearance (Sullivan 2001, p. 18). The show thus rewards a beautiful appearance to the moral individual, and in doing so makes things as they really "ought" to be.... This awarding of make-overs to the morally deserving contributes to post-feminist ideology by eliding feminist readings of surgical culture. Cosmetic surgery becomes about "justice"; it is framed a cure for suffering, eliding the feminist contention that "it is a significant contributory cause of women's suffering by continually upping the ante on what counts as an acceptable face and body" (Bordo 1997, p. 43).

The confession of ugliness which produces suffering is elaborated through sequences in each show where candidates describe and demonstrate their flaws before the camera. This stages the unruly and deviant body that may be redeemed through medical technologies. This is not so much a ritual in humiliation (Weber 2005); rather it is a visualising of proof central to the confession of suffering. These sequences function to recruit the viewing audience to share the candidate's assessing and disciplinary gaze and assent with the identification of the aberrant features of the displayed body. This ostensibly "proves" that surgical intervention is warranted, through implicit comparison to the bodies which are usually spectacularised within consumer and televisual culture: the hegemonic bodies which do not bear the traces of childbirth, aging or poverty. This demonstration of the pre-surgical body performs a pedagogy of defect (Bordo 1997, p. 37), inviting the viewing audience to compare themselves with the body on screen. The candidate's assessment of their body is subsequently confirmed by the surgeon, who names the aberrant features and prescribes surgical remedy....

The boundary between the reconstructive and cosmetic procedure is further blurred on *Extreme Makeover* through the inclusion of candidates with deformities,

both congenital and resulting from illness. Several cleft palates have been treated, replacement breasts awarded to a breast cancer survivor, and state-of-the-art hearing aids fitted for a woman with a hearing impairment. These procedures, which restore function, intensify the charitable dimension of the show, and render all surgical intervention equivalent. A patient who receives an operation to restore function also receives multiple cosmetic operations. As Brenda Weber notes:

[b]y pairing those with "legitimate" defects and those with "aesthetic" flaws, the show effectively collapses the difference between the two—if a cleft palate merits surgery, so does a weak chin. The subjects are not selected, then, according to their relative degree of "deformity," since all aesthetic anxieties signal crippling disabilities. (2005, p. 16)

The confession process continues in the surgeon's office, where the patient's defects are named and surgical solutions explained. These consultations with the surgeon function to extend the surgeon's gaze into the culture. Belling (1998) discusses the creation of "expert" patients via reality television depicting medical operations. Surgical make-over shows similarly offer a pedagogy which equips the viewer for the surgeon's office. This was illustrated in an episode of *Extreme Makeover* where, after listing the six facial operations she would like to receive, Kim's surgeon asked "Now, where did you learn about these procedures, from watching the show?" to which she replied, "Definitely!" (season 3: episode 9). The sharing of the surgeon's specialist language and aesthetic sensibility does not diminish his power—rather it multiplies it by enabling participation in surgical culture. Thus surgical television democratises knowledge of cosmetic surgery; its specialist discourse circulates beyond disciplinary confines and functions to authorise and extend its discursive field. Viewers may thus become experts, within a discourse which can identify a chin which "needs" an implant to "balance" a face, and this consent to the surgeon's expertise intensifies his authority.

As Sarah Banet-Weiser and Laura Portwood-Stacer observe, according to the post-feminist ideology of surgical television:

> The submission of one's body to a group of cosmetic surgeons to be reworked and redefined is never positioned as an issue about gender inequity or unattainable femininity—indeed, shows such as *The Swan* and *Extreme Makeover* provide "evidence" that *any* body is possible, if one simply has the desire. (2006, p. 269)

Of course, while any body may be possible, only particular kinds of body will do. Surgery for men is rendered as bestowing or restoring virility (indeed, one candidate received a reverse vasectomy), and descriptions of the effect procedures will have on the appearance often refer to gendered ideals: a chin implant will make a face more "masculine," a woman's nose may be rendered more "delicate" and "feminine," and the procedure most requested by female candidates is breast implants. During Mike's make-over, analogies were drawn between his surgeries and automotive body work (season 2: episode 20). Post-surgically, Dan exclaimed, "Oh my God, I look like an action hero" (season 2: episode 1), while the make-overs of female contestants are sometimes described as real-life "fairy tales."

Occasionally, people of colour are selected for a make-over. Angela's confession is an account of her experiences of racism: of being called "big nose," "big lips" and "monkey girl" (season 2: episode 12). It is reiterated again and again, by her surgeon (who is black) and the narrator, that Angela's surgery is not about race; that it is not an attempt to conceal her ethnic identity—rather it is about beauty and proportion. However, as Padmore instructs, "it is vital to interrogate the idea of cosmetic surgery as a movement towards 'better' looks. The phrase implies there is a universal aesthetic paradigm; a series of features which 'everybody' knows are beautiful or ugly" (1998, p. 6). As Balsamo (1996) explains, this paradigm is shaped through particular raced, gendered and ageist sensibilities. The assertions that Angela's make-over is not about "race" are disingenuous on a fundamental level: Angela's experience of her body has been produced by a racism which codes her features as "too black." While Angela's make-over brings her happiness, at her reveal we see that her four children share their mother's original facial features. This highlights the impoverished form of power the individual's transformation consists of. It does nothing to unsettle, and may in fact reproduce, the cultural meanings of difference which "often offer a pedagogy directed at the reinforcement of feelings of inferiority, marginality, ugliness" (Bordo 1993, p. 262).

Extreme Makeover devotes scant screen time to the surgeries themselves. During these sequences the carnality of surgery is elided: incursions into the body are concealed as camera and editing coyly avoid shots of instruments or hands entering flesh, the presence of blood, or the opened body. Instead, up-beat narration accompanies close-ups of the surgeon's face and long shots, which signify surgical performance but mystify its specificities. This effacement of carnality, and, as the patients recover, pain, trivialise these aspects of the surgical process. Instead, narrative momentum builds towards the "reveal," the climax of each show where the transformed candidates are restored to friends and family. It is the "reveal" which demonstrates most graphically that cosmetic surgery "works" to heal the psyche. The candidates are invariably ecstatic, as they parade before assembled guests. Shame deriving from one's appearance has transformed into a desire to be looked at. Candidates testify to new, empowered subjectivities: Pam claims "I'm the person I always wanted to be on the outside, and that's completed me and made me whole" (season 2: episode 9).

The transformations performed on *Extreme Makeover* render the body "cultural plastic" (Bordo 1993; Brush 1998). As one patient expressed in relation to his presurgical body: "I'm just starting to understand that the limitations I thought I had, are not there" (season 2: episode 1). . . . Feminism, as a means to think beyond the body of the individual to the culture which produces the body's significance, becomes further displaced by a post-feminist logic of plasticity. By staging an ease and acceptability of cosmetic surgery, facial and bodily features which are culturally reviled become increasingly contingent: "ugliness" becomes our choice and responsibility.

Nip/Tuck: Melodrama and the Limits of Cultural Critique

Nip/Tuck is a melodrama about two philandering male plastic surgeons which has been condemned by both ASAPS and ASPS (Hopkins Tanne 2003). *Nip/Tuck* disrupts the culture's domestication of cosmetic surgery through the graphic realism of its depiction of surgery and through its ambivalent exploration of the impact of surgical culture on its gendered subjects. On *Extreme Makeover*, narrative drama is produced through the "before" and "after," and the attendant cultural assumption that the transformed appearance will transform the psyche. The boundary between reconstructive and cosmetic surgery is effaced and the carnality of surgery elided. *Nip/Tuck* eschews and inverts these conventions of the makeover: the surgery in between is the source of dramatic impact, the boundary between reconstructive and cosmetic surgery actively negotiated, and the latter is rendered as narcissistic; a practice through which "people externalise the hatred they feel about themselves" (season 1: episode 1). . . .

Nip/Tuck's surgical scenes display the intervention into healthy (though sometimes disfigured) bodies, and rather than drawing the viewer towards a narrative outcome (the patient is saved), these scenes function as a display of the surgical as gruesome aesthetic. During these sequences, dialogue is replaced by a musical track which frequently functions as an ironic counterpoint to the surgery on screen. In the episode "Sean McNamara" (season 2: episode 1), the track "Eyes Without a Face" plays, while a large strip of flesh is sliced from the patient's leg in order to reconstruct the damage a gun shot has done to her face. This two minute sequence consists of quick edits cut in time to the music. The face is sliced above the brow and the flesh peeled down over the eye. A metal plate is screwed into the skull via the wound site. A scalpel slices through the flesh along the jawline and scissors are used to snip through the underlying layers of tissue to reveal a metal plate, which is removed. One of the surgeons peers through a large microscope, and our point of view follows his gaze upon his performance of a delicate microsurgery performed within a field of red. The lay viewer does not actually know the specifics of what is being performed here—rather, we are privy to a specialist, mystified, carnographic spectacle.

A facelift performed in the same episode is similarly graphic: skin is sliced and flesh loosened from the forehead, pulled, and stitched. These procedures, which are staged using elaborate prosthetic effects, are so realistic they prompted one reviewer to assume real life surgical footage was incorporated into the fictional text (Dumenco 2003). The realism here does not serve to facilitate communication between prospective patient and surgeon, as Belling (1998) argues may be the case for surgical reality television—rather, it draws a fascinated gaze upon the carnographic which is intended to reveal the mystification implicit in the term "cosmetic" surgery. As Ryan Murphy, creator of *Nip/Tuck* explains:

When I was researching the show, one plastic surgeon told me that getting your face done is basically the equivalent of going through a car window at 70 miles an hour and surviving. I wanted to do a show that really shows you: if you really want to have this done, there's a price to be paid on every single level. Surgeries are brutal. (Ryan Murphy cited in Mim Udovitch 2003, p. 22)

Murphy's agenda mirrors the agenda of feminist commentators who similarly underscore the violence of going under the knife. Murphy opens her critique of surgical culture with an illustration of surgical instruments: scalpels, knives, needles, and scissors, and directs the reader, "Now look at the needles and the knives. Look at them carefully. Look at them for a long time. *Imagine them cutting into your skin*" (1991, p. 26). Finkelstein (1991) provides detailed descriptions of surgical procedures, including face and eye lifts, rhinoplasty and chemabrasion, illustrating that rather than "cosmetic" procedures, a term which implies superficial ministrations, these are medical operations which rely on the slicing, pulling and grinding of flesh. In these feminist accounts, and on *Nip/Tuck*, graphic imagery works against the trivialization and domestication of cosmetic surgery within the culture. However, the feminist analyses are part of an explicit critique of the ideological, cultural and political implications of the pursuit of youth and beauty, while such an agenda on *Nip/Tuck* is sporadic. The graphic sequences, which are a signature of the show, are bracketed from the narrative, rarely advancing this resistive gesture into weightier critique. Through repetition, these scenes may even lose their shock value and instead train the viewer to look. Fascination may displace repulsion; awe at the skill of the *surgeons* may overwhelm the intended politics of the gruesome spectacle.

The spectacle of surgery on *Nip/Tuck* expresses a political posture, but this is rarely supported by sustained narratives which politicise surgical culture. Rather, while issues regarding the raced and gendered politics of cosmetic surgery may be raised, the sensational is routinely favoured over coherent critique. For example, in the episode "Kurt Demsey" (season 1: episode 5), a white man wants his eyelids refashioned so that he can "pass" as Japanese and win the approval of a xenophobic prospective mother-in-law. Rather than tell a story of the "Westernisation" of the "Oriental" eye, thus politicising the manner in which race is in play within surgical culture (Balsamo 1996; Gilman 1999; Haiken 1997; Padmore 1998), the show opts to tell the story of an individual prepared to go to great lengths to prove his love. Nevertheless, Liz, the practice's anaesthesiologist, poses the procedure as an ethical, and political issue: "Does anyone here besides me think there is anything morally reprehensible about a white man trying to pass himself off as a victim of the American racial hierarchy?" Sean's response is that their job is to "alleviate pain," to which Liz replies "That's your answer? So why don't we turn everyone white and hetero?"

Liz acts as the show's moral compass. She routinely pops up, like a Shakespearian chorus, to espouse a feminist line on cosmetic surgery. The paradox that Liz works within an industry she so explicitly distains is never reconciled, and her complicity with the industry, coupled with the often caricature-like quality of her commentary, cast her criticism of surgical culture as ineffectual. Feminism is rendered as an opinion, rather than a means of intervening into the reproduction of surgical culture. As a patient lies on the table prior to the removal of her breast implants, Liz comments "every time I see what women do to themselves with these tit jobs, it makes me ashamed of what I do for a living" (season 1: episode 12). The audience is directed to concur as we watch an incision being made beneath a breast which slices the lower portion from the body. An instrument resembling a crow bar is used to prise the flesh from the chest, so that an entire hand can enter the body and pull the bloody implants from the breast cavity.

Nip/Tuck frequently explores the gendered cruelties of appearance work through the breast, rendering implants as dangerous and a site of exploitation. One storyline featured drug mules who trafficked heroin in breast implants in return for the promise of a modelling career in the U.S. (season 1: episode 12). A surgery depicting the removal of ruptured silicone implants showed the sticky silicone being pulled like taffy, slurping, from inside the breast (season 3: episode 1). Megan O'Hara's implants weakened her immune system and were cited as the reason for the return of her cancer (season 1: episode 10), and Julia McNamara's decision to have breast augmentation in a bid to win back her husband was met with derision (she subsequently had the implants removed). Responding to her mother's criticism of her new implants, Julia asks "You had a face lift, mother, what's the difference?" Her mother conjures the pornographic-ness of implants by responding "I did it for professional reasons. The only professional reason for that is to look better dancing on a pole" (season 2: episode 11). The unevenness of *Nip/Tuck*'s critique of cosmetic surgery is illustrated through this exchange: the pathologising of female aging is not addressed here, and the fact that Julia's mother is a psychiatrist adds weight to the arbitrary distinction she draws.

Kimber Henry is a recurrent character through whom a dystopian narrative of becoming surgical is presented. In the morning following their initial sexual encounter, Christian ranks Kimber's attractiveness as "an eight," promising that with surgery he can make her "a ten" (season 1: episode 1). Christian takes her red lipstick and marks her face and body with vivid gashes, which prefigure the blade that will follow. Thus Kimber's decision to become surgical is rendered as a product of shame and humiliation; a response to the violent misogyny of an unethical surgeon. Following her surgery, Kimber retains Christian's interest only intermittently (at one point he trades her to a colleague for a sports car), her success as a model and mainstream actor is short lived, she becomes addicted to cocaine and ends up working in the porn industry.

Kimber's character is used to tell a cautionary tale about the excesses of surgical culture, but the show's preference for the prurient over the political limits this critique. In a second season episode, "Kimber Henry" (season 2: episode 10), Kimber asks the partners to make modifications to the vagina of a silicone sex doll made in her image. She explains: "The vagina looks too generic to me. I'd like it to be appealing and pretty. The folds are too fleshy." As Sean makes the mould of Kimber's vagina she asks him to "cheat" and "make the labia just a touch more delicate" than her own: "I'd like my vagina to be prettier." Rather than politicising the growing trend in cosmetic labia plasty, produced through women's subscription to increasingly pornographic beauty ideals (Braun 2005; Weil Davis 2002), women's literal embodiment of a pornographic aesthetic is displaced onto the doll.

Unlike *Extreme Makeover,* where the boundary between reconstructive and cosmetic surgery is elided, *Nip/Tuck* frequently asserts this boundary. However, the heroism through which reconstructive work is rendered at times deflects criticism from the practice of cosmetic surgery, rendering the individual's vanity as the appropriate target of critique. . . .

While *Nip/Tuck*'s critical sensibility is erratic in its target, there are rare moments at which it interrogates the logic behind the domestication of surgical culture. Mrs. Grubman, a polysurgical addict, blackmails the partners into performing her numerous surgeries. While on one level her vanity is punished—she suffers a stroke during a procedure and becomes partially paralysed—she is ultimately rendered sympathetically, and a broader cultural critique is levelled (season 2: episode 4). It emerges that Mrs. Grubman is clinically depressed because she is aging, and we are directed to consider both the way in which the culture pathologises female aging, and the folly in attempting to address a psychological problem with a surgical cure.

Conclusion

This chapter has examined what television offers publics to think about cosmetic surgery. *Extreme Makeover* domesticates cosmetic surgery by publicising its practice, and in so doing authorising synthetic beauty ideals. Surgery is rendered as an increasingly normative practice, and the post-feminist spectacle of transformation as a cure for suffering and a route to empowerment distances its practice from negative associations with vanity and gendered oppression. The imperative to conceal surgery as a mark of inauthenticity dissipates, as transformation is celebrated as self-actualisation. Surgical reality television provides viewers with tools for imagining themselves as clients of surgical services: a language for naming procedures, knowledge of the suitability of candidates, ways to imagine surgeons, and testimonials that surgical intervention "works" to cure suffering. *Extreme Makeover* further domesticates cosmetic surgery by eliding surgery's intervention into the body, and by constituting it as family entertainment. In conflating surgery and charity, the former is imbued with a moral dimension, rendering invisible concerns that may be raised about the commercialisation of medicine (Sullivan 2001), the risks people take for an altered appearance, and the cultural consequences of positing surgery as the means to remedy psychic distress. . . .

Nip/Tuck attempts to unsettle the domestication of cosmetic surgery by rendering its carnality and invoking its raced, gendered and ageist practices. The show represents the limited efficacy of feminist critique, within a culture which has embraced the post-feminist logic of the surgical cure. *Nip/Tuck*'s response to surgical culture provides moments of resistance, but these are frequently overwhelmed by the requirement to render the surgeon characters as redeemable, and by a sensationalism which prefers the dramatic over the political. . . .

Nip/Tuck's gestures towards a feminist sensibility serve to stage conflict between characters and, through the surgical scenes, render novel televisual spectacles which are rarely linked to sustained frameworks that coherently articulate the cultural consequences of the domestication of cosmetic surgery. Thus while *Nip/Tuck* conjures feminist critique, it is ultimately part of a post-feminist mediascape, where feminism is an occasional voice within a culture that is inevitably surgical. As these two shows illustrate, feminist responses to cosmetic surgery are overwhelmed by a post-feminism which asserts our right to shape ourselves. The individual's choice to transform their body is uncoupled from potential collective agendas to locate, and intervene on, a source of suffering outside of the individual's pre-surgical body.

References

American Society for Aesthetic Plastic Surgery (2005) '11.9 million cosmetic procedures in 2004', [Online] Available at http://www.surgery.org/pre/news-release.php?iid=395 (18 Oct. 2006).

American Society of Plastic Surgeons (2005) '9.2 million cosmetic plastic surgery procedures in 2004—up 5% growth paces US economy despite reality TV fad', [Online] Available at: http://www.plasticsurgery.org.news_room/Press_release/2004-Wverall-statistics (18 Oct. 2006).

Balsamo, Anne (1996) *Technologies of the Gendered Body: Reading Cyborg Women*, Duke University Press, Durham.

Banet-Weiser, Sarah & Portwood-Stacer, Laura (2006) "I just want to be me again!": beauty pageants, reality television, and post-feminism. *Feminist Theory,* vol. 7, no. 2, pp. 255–272.

Belling, Catherine (1998) 'Reading The Operation: television, realism, and the possession of medical knowledge', *Literature and Medicine,* vol. 17, no. 1, pp. 1–23.

Bordo, Susan (1993) *Unbearable Weight Feminism, Western Culture, and the Body,* University of California Press, Berkeley.

Bordo, Susan (1997) *Twilight Zones: The Hidden Life of Cultural Images,* University of California Press, Berkeley.

Braun, Virginia (2005) 'In search of (better) sexual pleasure: female genital "cosmetic" surgery', *Sexualities,* vol. 8, no. 4, pp. 407–424.

Brush, Pippa (1998) 'Metaphors of inscription: discipline, plasticity and the rhetoric of choice', *Feminist Review,* vol. 58, no. 1, pp. 22–43.

Deery, June (2004) 'Trading faces: the makeover show as prime-time infomercial', *Feminist Media Studies,* vol. 4, no. 2, pp. 211–214.

Dumenco, Simon (2003) 'Their bodies, ourselves: why we like (not love) to watch plastic surgery on TV', *New York Magazine,* 6 Oct., [Online] Available at http://newyorkmetro .com/nymetro/health/bestdoctors/cosmetic surgery/2003/n_ 9285/ (18 Oct, 2006).

Extreme Makeover (television series) (2002–2005) Burbank, California, Lighthearted Entertainment.

Finkelstein, Joanne (1991) *The Fashioned Self,* Temple University Press, Philadelphia.

Gilman, Sander (1999). *Making the Body Beautiful: A Cultural History of Aesthetic Surgery.* Princeton University Press, Princeton.

Haiken, Elizabeth (1997) *Venus Envy: A History of Cosmetic Surgery,* The Johns Hopkins University Press, Baltimore.

Hopkins Tanne, Janice (2003) 'New US drama outrages plastic surgeons', *British Medical Journal,* vol. 327, 2 Aug, p. 295.

Life after Extreme Makeover (television series) (2004) Burbank, California, Lighthearted Entertainment.

Nip/Tuck (television series) (2003–) USA, Hands Down Entertainment.

Padmore, Catherine (1998) 'Significant flesh: cosmetic surgery, physiognomy, and the erasure of visual difference(s)', *Lateral* no. 1, pp. 1–22, [Online] Available at http:// pandora.nla.gov.au/nph-arch/1999/ 01999-Jul-2/ http://www.latrobe.edu.au/ www/english/lateral/simple_cpl.htm (18 Oct. 2006).

Sullivan, Deborah A. (2001) *Cosmetic Surgery: The Cutting Edge of Commercial Medicine in America,* Rutgers University Press, New Brunswick.

The Swan (television series) (2004–5), USA, Galan Entertainment.

Udovitch, Mim (2003) 'The cutting edge of television: A bloody scape!', *The New York Times,* 3 Aug., p. 22.

Weber, Brenda (2005) 'Beauty, desire, and anxiety: the economy of sameness in ABC's *Extreme Makeover*', *Genders,* no. 41, [Online] Available at: http://www.gender .org/g41/g41_weber.html (18 Oct. 2006).

Weil Davis, Simone (2002) 'Loose lips sink ships', *Feminist Studies,* vol. 28, no. 1, pp. 7–35.

59

Drama Is the Cure for Gossip

Television's Turn to Theatricality in a Time of Media Transition

Abigail De Kosnik

Introduction

... Prime-time television programs of the past few years have been rife with instances of individuals achieving self-realization ("finding themselves") through acting, singing, and/ or dancing in front of audiences—not just for television audiences at home, who watch their antics from a distance, but for audiences who exist within the narratives of the show and who are the performers' immediate witnesses. In other words, these (fictional) people consciously make spectacles of themselves in the eyes of others, and by exposing themselves in this way, they realize and reveal core truths about themselves.

... This chapter is concerned with the question of why it has recently become a priority for U.S. television to depict the existence of a "true" self, which is, for the most part, hidden or concealed (sometimes even from the characters themselves), a self that is then exposed through theatrical performance. ...

Theatricality as Self-Discovery in Contemporary TV Dramas and Comedies

The CW series *Gossip Girl* (2007–present) concerns a specific sliver of high society, a group of super-rich youths in Manhattan's Upper East Side (UES), who plot and scheme with and against one another as they struggle with issues of family, friendship, sex, school

From Abigail De Kosnik (2010), "Drama Is the Cure for Gossip: Television's Turn to Theatricality in a Time of Media Transition." *Modern Drama*, Vol. 53, No. 3, 370–389. Reprinted with permission from University of Toronto Press (www.utpjournals.comj).

success, and social standing. In a plot device that recurs in each episode, the title character, Gossip Girl, an anonymous blogger who operates as a clearing house for all the rumours that swirl around the UES crowd, posts blog entries and sends out mobile device "blasts" that make public the characters' secrets and expose any falsehoods they have constructed. Despite all of the money and power wielded by *Gossip Girl*'s privileged characters, therefore, gossip is the most important currency in their world: the UES teens who artfully deceive adults and peers alike in order to further their own interests can be brought low instantly by a Gossip Girl blast; they can also ruin one another by sending Gossip Girl some insider information.

Viewers are asked to identify with the UESers who are the series' main focus, and what we learn, episode after episode, is that they are not reducible to their intrigues. The gossip that circulates about them does not tell the complete story of any of them. *Gossip Girl* illustrates a predicament increasingly common today: people who have online reputations find that, while Internet rumours circulated about them tell some portion of the truth, it is never the whole truth. Celebrities are closely analysed on various Hollywood Web sites (*TMZ* .com, justjared.buzznet.com, People.com, or EW.com, among others), university instructors are reviewed on RateMy Professors.com and various review sites, and managers at all levels are ranked in a wide range of employment-related Internet forums. While readers of the gossip posted on these sites have a sense that they are privy to many facts about the people discussed, they do not really *know them*. A superfluity of online rumours can coalesce around almost anyone, with the result that all of us need to be watchful custodians of our reputations. If we do not craft our online personae carefully, we risk allowing Internet gossip to define "who we are."

Using theatrical performance as a plot device, *Gossip Girl* dramatizes the conundrum of how to establish who one "really is" in a gossip-saturated society. In fact, the characters never successfully combat Gossip Girl's rumour mill or win the right to define their public reputations, but their consolation is that, through the show's narrative, they can at least discover their true selves for their own sakes. On the one hand, the main characters on the show are constantly engaged in performance: their machinations typically involve a great deal of artful dissembling. On the other hand, these planned performances generally end in disappointment or crisis, as Gossip Girl, drawing on the surveillance of anonymous tipsters who track every movement of the UESers, uncovers all of their ploys. But the main characters also put on different kinds of performances, which are wholly improvised and through which they surprise even themselves.

The most prominent examples of improvised drama leading to a character's self-discovery involve Blair Waldorf, who is equal parts heroine and villainess in the *Gossip Girl* universe. Blair, the queen bee who reigns over the social scene of her elite private high school, strives for excellence in all of her activities and plans out in great detail most of her life's major events. Her own deflowering is no exception. In the series' early episodes, Blair sets up several scenarios that she thinks will encourage her long-time boyfriend, Nathaniel (Nate) Archibald, to finally seduce her, but Nate (who is secretly in love with Blair's best friend) balks at each of these carefully orchestrated productions and leaves Blair untouched.

In episode "Victor, Victrola," Blair finally accepts that Nate does not love her and breaks up with him. Her first stop after the break-up is the burlesque club Victrola, owned by Nate's best friend, the debauched and rakish Chuck Bass. There, on a dare from Chuck, Blair takes the stage alongside the scantily clad burlesque dancers and spontaneously performs with them. She sways seductively to the music as she strips down to her slip. "Who is that girl?" a waiter asks Chuck, gesturing at

Blair on the stage, who is earning cheers and catcalls from the mesmerized club-goers. "I have no idea," Chuck replies, a look of awe on his face, as he stands and raises his champagne glass in a toast to Blair.

Later that night, Blair loses her virginity to Chuck in the back seat of his limousine. Blair's "first time" is completely unplanned (unlike all of the "first times" she tried to coordinate with Nate). That she should choose Chuck as her partner and that he should desire her comes as a great surprise to both of them. What Blair's impromptu performance on the Victrola stage has revealed to both is *herself*, the core of per-sonality, which is far more daring, sensual, and risk-taking than her rigid, carefully controlled fac̦ade would suggest. Until the moment that Blair literally and meta-phorically strips off her outer covering, Chuck "has no idea" who she is. Chuck falls hard for the Blair who suddenly reveals herself to him, and the night in the limousine is the start of a tumultuous affair that continues to be *Gossip Girl*'s central love story into the show's third season. When Blair performs spontane-ously on Victrola's stage, she finds not only her true self but also her true love. . . .

The FOX musical comedy series *Glee* (2009–present) similarly equates stage per-formance with self-realization. Glee oper-ates on the premise that, when an individual performs before a live audience, she is exposing her truest self to the world. The high school students in the universe of *Glee* can be either misfits on the lowest rung of the social ladder or the rulers of school society, but when they perform as members of the glee-club, the overlooked coolness of the pariahs is revealed and the often suppressed egalitarianism and open-mindedness of the football players and cheerleaders come to the surface. The mes-sage of *Glee* is that, no matter how awk-ward or cynical you may appear in everyday life, you can slough off your outer skin—your social persona—and show off how smart, fair, kind, brave, and

talented you are if only you dare to sing show tunes in front of witnesses.

Glee also showcases theatrical perfor-mance as a means by which its gay and disabled characters can express their inner-most selves, which are often invisible in everyday social settings. One member of the glee-club, Kurt, blatantly marks himself as queer whenever he sings and dances, but (at least, for the show's first few episodes) must conceal his homosexuality from his father and make excuses when his father catches him practising routines. Another glee-club member, Artie, is confined to a wheel-chair and is a social outcast in the high school; however, in glee-club, Artie is able to dance (by performing choreo-graphed, energetic moves in his wheel-chair), sing, and play instruments, revealing to audiences his extroverted nature. In the halls of the school, Artie's charisma and talents go unseen; onstage, Artie's virtuoso movements and musicality are often the focus of attention. . . .

Internet Gossip Culture

Why does contemporary TV so fre-quently . . . show characters discovering who they "really are" through performing live in front of audiences?

One possible reason is television's desire to respond to the Internet, which is regarded in some corners of the television industry as a formidable threat to TV as it competes for media consumers' attention and advertisers' dollars. Recent research indicates that increasing use of the Internet has not, in fact, decreased television viewing (Nielsen), and television and the Internet do converge at points: TV fans participate in fan com-munities online; increasingly, TV viewers watch TV at the same time as they surf the Web; many people watch television content on Web sites such as *Hulu and Fancast*; and most TV networks produce Internet-specific content, such as supplementary "webisodes" or interviews with actors and writers of popular shows. Nevertheless, even as the TV industry strives to expand its consumer base and revenue through the Internet, television and the Internet are undeniably rivals on at least one level: for five decades (from the 1950s through the 1990s), television was what Philip Auslander calls "the cultural dominant" (xii), and since the millennium, it has appeared increasingly likely that the Internet will supplant TV in that role. At present, Auslander states, "[T]here is an ongoing, unresolved struggle for dominance among television, telecommunications, and the Internet. The principal players behind each of these would like nothing better than to be your primary source of news, entertainment, art, conversation, and other forms of engagement with the world" (xii). The television industry may partner with the Internet in many ways, but it also struggles to prove that TV offers media audiences benefits that the Internet does not and that TV will continue to be relevant to mass society even if the Internet displaces it as the cultural dominant.

In light of this rivalrous, or at least complex, relationship between contemporary TV and the Internet, we can interpret television's persistent equation of theatricality with self-authentication as a serious critique of Internet culture. One common criticism of the Internet is that the anonymity of online communications enables people to be uncivil and dishonest, far more so than they would be in face-to-face interactions, and that, as a result, Internet culture is largely gossip culture. Solove writes,

> [A]nonymity can make lying easier ... Anonymity also facilitates deception ... As sociologist Robert Putnam observes: "Anonymity and fluidity in the virtual world encourage 'easy in, easy out' 'drive-by' relationships ... If entry and exit are too easy, commitment, trustworthiness, and reciprocity will not develop." In other words, anonymity inhibits the process by which reputations

are formed, which can have both good and bad consequences. Not having accountability for our speech can be liberating and allow us to speak more candidly; but it can also allow us to harm other people without being accountable for it. (141)

The Internet, whose content is largely user-generated, facilitates rumourmongering far more than television does, as it is a one-way broadcasting medium and is hence closed to viewer contribution or participation. A great deal of what the Internet offers media consumers as entertainment is gossip, primarily concerning celebrities but also concerning average people, whose colleagues, students, family members, and acquaintances can post gossip about them on review sites, blogs, and message boards without encountering any negative consequences.

> Somebody you've never met can snap your photo and post it on the Internet. Or somebody that you know very well can share your cherished secrets with the entire planet. Your friends and coworkers might be posting rumors about you on their blogs ... You could find photos and information about yourself spreading around the Internet like a virus. (Solove 2)

Internet gossip culture can build up or ruin individuals' public reputations. People who have online reputations, which is anyone whose name has been mentioned on any Web site and who can, therefore, be "Googled" or looked up on Internet search engines, must take care to defend those reputations, which can be difficult, given how vulnerable they are to anonymous users in the network. "Few things are more valuable than reputation, or more consequential for the success of new ventures," Burt writes. "[R]eputations emerge not from what we do, but from people talking about what we do. It is the positive and negative stories exchanged about you, the gossip about you, that defines your reputation" (1).

Human societies have probably always given rise to fears about possible differences between individuals' public and private identities, and the question of how to ascertain the nature of one's true self has been a problem for philosophers, ever since at least ancient Greek times, but the Internet may be generating new levels of anxiety about personal identity.

... Constructing and safeguarding one's online reputation depends on a multitude of performances. . . . We must exert ourselves in order to define who we are to others. Human beings have always had to perform, signal, or work in this way, but the amount of identity signaling required by each of us today is greater than before, and there is a higher risk of failure, for, in addition to safeguarding our real-life identities, we must do the same for our online identities, and those identities are susceptible to sudden, anonymous attacks.

Responding to this climate of anxiety around identity, contemporary television offers viewers the fantasy of not having to work to construct themselves. Characters on fictional television shows, as they engage in dramatic action, breaking away from their ordinary routines in order to perform before a "live" audience, appear on viewers' TV screens as instantaneous and seemingly effortless, or at least "natural." Getting up on a stage to perform reads on these shows as a kind of doing-without-thinking, and the connection with self that results is produced automatically, without conscious effort on the part of the performer. . . .

Thus, television shows today acknowledge the substantial costs of our having to produce/perform/signal our identities online, under threat of being undermined by the gossip culture that is endemic to the Internet, and present media users with a fantasy of *easy identity*. In television

narratives, one does not have to create one's identity, for one's most real and true self is buried deep inside; one does not have to work hard to communicate one's identity to others, for they are present in the room at the moment of one's greatest self-revelation; and one does not have to labour at deciding or shaping one's identity because, even if the "true self" seems difficult to reach, one need only be willing to make a sudden departure from one's usual routine. That departure is portrayed as literally and affectively *dramatic* —happening in an instant, requiring no planning, frictionless and spontaneous and simple, and coded as theatrical performance. After engaging in these dramatics, the individual has self-knowledge: she is in full possession of her identity. . . .

The Promise of Gossip Versus the Promise of Authenticity

. . . Television dramas and comedies today offer fantasies not only of easy identity but also of absolute certainty. The concepts promoted by these TV shows—that each of us has a core self that we can know, be completely sure of, and effectively display to others and that exposing that self yields only happy outcomes . . .—may currently have mass appeal because of the confusions, complexities, and even dangers inherent in Internet gossip. Television characters know, for sure, what constitutes their "real selves," and they meet with positive results every time they express this certain knowledge. Internet users rarely know what gossip is real and can never be certain of the ramifications of their writing or reading online rumours. As the Internet has established itself as the provider of entertainment comprised of gossip, television has become increasingly a provider of entertainment comprised of fantasies of authenticity and security. . . .

Television's Ties to Theatre and Therapy

. . . The television industry has attempted for decades to convince audiences that watching TV is, itself, a form of therapy. White (1992) mentions a number of articles published in *TV Guide* during the 1980s that promote "the idea that television functions therapeutically within a familial and interpersonal context. Watching television can help or hinder your relationship with your spouse and children. Television can speak a therapeutic discourse" (25). She quotes one *TV Guide* author who writes, "TV can provide current information on common problems. It can, while respecting privacy, encourage the discussion of feelings" (29). All of the equivalences to therapy that belonged to TV in the past—the structuring of the television narrative as a confession, the making public (televising) of the therapist's interaction with patients, the theory that the act of watching TV can lead one to undergo therapy—are seemingly combined in the theatricality-as-authenticity convention that recurs on various TV shows currently.

What contemporary television producers appear to be aiming at, then, in highlighting TV's closeness to both theatre and therapy and in making theatre-as-therapy a central trope in their narratives, is a link to TV's historically successful value propositions. Television is currently in a highly transitional phase of its evolution. If it does not want to disappear as a business and lose its mass appeal, then it needs to prove to media consumers that it has worth that cannot be duplicated by the Internet. . . .

Television, which was the cultural dominant for fifty years, finds itself, in the twenty-first century, in the position of having to defend its relevance, having to rally and broadcast the reasons why it still matters. To this end, TV is calling up arguments that it has used since the 1950s, arguments that

add up to the fact that television is theatre and therapy all at once. Television narratives display people's most intimate journeys—their inward journeys, their diving into their innermost core to discover their authentic selves—as public performances, and this is simultaneously a critique of anonymous Internet gossip culture, with its lack of intimacy and cool distance from its subjects, and an attempt to proffer much better gossip than the Internet can, in the form of high personal drama. Ultimately, television uses drama . . . as both a cure for Internet gossip culture and as a serious competitor to it.

Works Cited

Auslander, Philip. *Liveness: Performance in a Mediatized Culture.* New York: Routledge, 2008.

Buckley, Michael. "Stage to Screens: Carla Gugino, David Hyde Pierce, and 'In Treatment' Writer Leight." *Playbill 4.* May 2009. 24 May 2010, http://www.playbill.com/features/article/128890-STAGE-TO-SCREENS-Carla-Gugino-David-Hyde-Pierce-and-In-Treatment-Writer-Leight.

Burt, Ronald S. "Gossip and Reputation." *Management et re´seaux sociaux: ressource pour l'action ou outil de gestion? [Management and Social Research: Resource for Action or Tool for Corporations?]* Ed. Marc Lecoutre and Lievre Pascal. Cachan: Hermes–Lavoisier, 2008. 24 May 2010, http://faculty.chicago booth.edu/ronald.burt/research/GR.pdf.

Butler, Judith. *Gender Trouble.* New York: Routledge, 1990.

De Kosnik, Abigail. "Soaps for Tomorrow: Media Fans Making Online Drama from Celebrity Gossip." *The Survival of Soap Opera: Transformations for a New Media Era.* Jackson: UP of Mississippi. Unpublished manuscript.

Donath, Judith. "Signals, Cues and Meaning." *Signals, Truth and Design.* Cambridge, MA: MIT, 2010. Unpublished manuscript.

24 May 2010, http://smg.media.mit.edu/papers/Donath/SignalsTruthDesign/Signals.distribute.pdf

Foucault, Michel. "Technologies of the Self." *Technologies of the Self: A Seminar with Michel Foucault.* Ed. Luther H. Martin, Huck Gutman and Patrick H. Hutton. Amherst: U of Massachusetts P, 1988. 16–49.

Gaskell, Stephanie. "Brad Pitt and Angelina Jolie to Sue British Tabloid, *News of the World,* over Split Rumors." NY Daily News 8 Feb. 2010. 24 May 2010, http://www.nydailynews.com/gossip/2010/02/08/2010–02–08_brad_pitt_and_angelina_jolie_to_sue_british_tabloid_news_of_the_world_over_split.html

Grotowski, Jerzy. *Towards a Poor Theatre.* New York: Simon, 1968.

Harrison, John R. "Therapy Vicariously – Watch HBO's *In Treatment.*" Ezine 20 Aug. 2009. 24 May 2010, <http://entertainment.ezinemark.com/therapy-vicariously-watch-hbo-s-in-treatment-4f42b9f17fc.html

Heidegger, Martin. "The Origin of the Work of Art." *The Continental Aesthetics Reader.* Ed. Clive Cazeaux. London: Routledge, 2000. 80–101.

Milian, Mark. "Waiter Gets Canned after Twittering about 'Hung' Actress Jane Adams." *Brand X* 30 Sept. 2009. 24 May 2010, http://www.thisisbrandx.com/ 2009/09/jane-adams-twitter.html

Mills, Elinor. "Yelp User Faces Lawsuit over Negative Review." CNET 6 Jan. 2009. 24 May 2010, http://news.cnet.com/8301–1023_3– 10133466 –93.html

Nielsen. "Three Screen Report: Media Consumption and Multi-Tasking Continue to Increase across TV, Internet, and Mobile." *Nielsen Wire* 2 Sept. 2009; updated 18 Dec. 2009. 24 May 2010, http://blog.nielsen.com/nielsenwire/media_entertainment/three-screen-report-media-consumption-and-multitasking-continue-to-increase.

Rose, Brian G. *Television and the Performing Arts: A Handbook and Reference Guide to American Cultural Programming.* New York: Greenwood, 1986.

Shklovsky, Victor. "Art as Technique." *Russian Formalist Criticism: Four Essays.* Ed. Lee T. Lemon and Marion J. Reis. Lincoln: U of Nebraska P, 1965. 3–24.

Solove, Daniel J. The *Future of Reputation: Gossip, Rumor, and Privacy on the Internet.* New Haven: Yale UP, 2007.

Spigel, Lynn. *Make Room for TV: Television and the Family Ideal in Postwar America.* Chicago: U of Chicago P, 1992.

Stanley, Alessandra. "Patients in Therapy, Therapist in Trouble." *New York Times* 2 Apr. 2009. 24 May 2010, http://tv.nytimes.com/2009/04/03/arts/television/03trea.html

Wertz, Diane. "Gabriel Byrne in HBO's *In Treatment.*" *redOrbit* 28 Jan. 2008. 24 May 2010, <http://www.redorbit.com/news/entertainment/1232364/review_gabriel_byrne_in_hbos_in_treatment/index.html

White, Mimi. *Tele-Advising: Therapeutic Discourse in American Television.* Chapel Hill: U of North Carolina P, 1992.

60

Free TV

File-Sharing and the Value of Television

Michael Z. Newman

Television has been free since its earliest days of broadcasting, following the advertising-sponsorship model of radio to gather up audiences whose attention could be sold to companies eager to spread commercial appeals. Despite the penetration of subscription services, DVD, and other forms of distribution dependent on consumer expenditure, many millions of viewers still receive their television content as a free broadcast signal. More importantly, no matter how content is received, the cultural status of television—despite shifts in recent years toward greater legitimacy—endures as a product of the over-the-air model. Free TV is of course commercial media, and the audience pays indirectly by consuming goods and services and inhabiting a consumerist society. But in the digital age, a new kind of free TV has emerged that is removed from the commercial circuit. Television shared as files among peers using BitTorrent and other online means removes media from the commercial sphere. TV becomes freer in some ways than it ever was when shared among peers (though users might spend considerable sums on digital hardware and high-speed network access).

The emergence of this new mode of distribution poses a challenge to our conception of television as a technology, medium, and set of social practices. File-sharing of TV content is one of the many developments in our era of media convergence, prompting a renewal of television's place in the "popular imagination" (Boddy 2004). Thus my title is meant to have two distinct senses. P2P TV is free to the consumer, but it also promises to free television from its old identity, from old modes of viewing rooted in earlier technological ensembles. By considering its conflicted cultural implications, this essay's aim is to understand TV file-sharing as one term in the negotiation of television's value during the era of its digital convergence. . . .

In particular, the analysis to follow considers the discourses of television file-sharers as they are expressed in online sites of discussion and commentary. Looking at postings to message boards and blog entries, we find that users of file-sharing networks make ethical

---

From Michael Z. Newman (2011), "Free TV: File-Sharing and the Value of Television." *Television & New Media* 13:463–479. Reprinted with permission of SAGE Publications.

calculations, formulating clear valuations of different kinds of media and ways of accessing them. For instance, users see television sharing in some ways as a different ethical matter than P2P circulation of music or movies. We can appreciate the value added to the television text as expressed in these discourses as a form of commons-based peer distribution, solving some of the problems of television consumption such as asynchronous global airing of fan-favorite shows. However, we also observe a contradictory ideological positioning as file-sharing is constructed as a more legitimate, sophisticated, cosmopolitan, and masculinized form of television consumption. The analysis concludes by considering the response to file-sharing of the American television industry as it seeks to negotiate the protection of legacy business models while also exploiting the opportunities of new technologies such as web video. Rather than see file-sharing as a legal, moral, or industrial problem in need of solving, I propose that we consider this new form of free TV as a way of understanding the medium's contemporary cultural status. I argue that discourses of file-sharing at once challenge the historical low valuation of television, and reaffirm the medium's lesser status.

Three Problems of Value

. . . In its traditional identity rooted in the network era, television's cultural status was as feminized mass culture (Spigel 1992). Shows were rarely considered as aesthetic works and the medium's value was often seen in negative terms, as a threat to intellectual culture, childhood development, and social cohesion. Television was constructed as culturally lesser than other media, such as books and films—as more disposable and less artistic. But in some ways the introduction of television into P2P networks, alongside other technological developments of the convergence era, bespeaks the high value of some forms of TV to media consumers eager to locate and select episodes and to devote time and resources to their acquisition and experience. The availability of TV series alongside movies and music, as well as books, games, software, and other forms of content, is a factor in the rising legitimacy of TV, now seen as equivalent to other media at least in the context of some forms of convergent distribution (Newman and Levine 2011). The kinds of television shared in P2P networks tends to be the most highly valued and aestheticized, scripted prime-time comedies and dramas addressed to younger, more affluent, and masculine audiences. During one week in 2009, more than 1.7 million people accessed the latest episodes of *Heroes* and *Lost* using BitTorrent. Other heavily shared shows included *24*, *The Big Bang Theory*, and *Battlestar Galactica* (Ernesto 2009). TV apparently accounts for half of BitTorrent traffic, and clearly many viewers are substituting downloads for other forms of access (Ernesto 2008a). In 2008, *Lost* was the most torrented show and its most popular episode was downloaded more than 5.7 million times (13.4 million American viewers tuned in the old-fashioned way, according to Nielsen) (Ernesto 2008b).

Users of P2P networks might come in all shapes and sizes, but the practice is typically linked to youth, technological sophistication, and masculinity. Torrent tracker sites often serve ads for pornographic or sexual content and services; for example, a tagline for a site advertising on The Pirate Bay calls out: "Beautiful Russian Girls Want to Meet You!" Such sites are clearly addressing a straight, young, male consumer and contributing to a culture that excludes girls and women (Sarkeesian 2010). It may not be possible to know the gender of online commenters, but the masculine character of the discussions from which I will quote below is apparent. Furthermore, one seldom finds the less legitimate and more ephemeral forms of television, feminized and devalued genres such as daytime talk shows and local news, circulating in P2P networks. The existence of files of shows available for sharing is itself a token of the value of certain kinds of television. Traditionally, television has been a medium of mass culture, a domestic appliance in family spaces, and a cultural form addressed to audiences including women, children, the elderly, and those of lesser class status. The construction of the television audience in BitTorrent sites and in the communities that use them is markedly different. By articulating television consumption to technological sophistication and masculinity, file-sharing communities participate in the renegotiation of the medium's cultural status.

The supposedly liberating potential of the BitTorrent experience is further legitimating by transforming the audience for television from supposedly passive viewers into active users, a discursive shift with class and gender implications. The ability of users to program their own viewing rather than being "slaves to the schedule" of broadcasters, and the possibility of watching television shows purged of commercials and promotions, function to legitimate television (Newman and Levine 2011). Our culture masculinizes technical competence, and the know-how required to download files online is greater than that required to use more conventional technologies. Sharing files of episodes is one means, along with DVD and DVR usage, of the viewer becoming an advertising-avoiding television programmer. Thus the P2P distribution of television is one among a cluster of technologies of agency, making TV more culturally respectable by masculinizing the experience, articulating it with activity and discernment rather than the more feminized and passive characteristics that defined television from its earliest days of widespread adoption (Spigel 1992; Tichi 1992).

However, the culture of file-sharing also articulates television content with the broadcasting or cable and satellite models of TV distribution, which construct the television text as an object with no price. In some ways, file-sharing confirms the value of television as ephemeral and disposable even as it arrests the "flow" of the broadcast/ network era to make possible sharing of TV shows as files.... The agenda of the television industry to extract a revenue stream from every experience of television runs up against the expectations of television viewers to be entitled to a free-flowing stream of content. In this way, the enduring idea of TV as free of charge runs up against the newly legitimated status of TV texts as worth paying to own, as in discourses of TV on DVD (Hills 2007; Kompare 2006). The contemporary cultural status of the television text is contradictory and unstable....

As with the instability over television's status as a public or private good, the transition from local/national to global distribution of TV requires new negotiations over television's value, thinking of it now more as a cosmopolitan global culture and less as a source of cohesion for communities defined by geographical regions and state policies and institutions.

In some respects, then, discourses of P2P circulation of television recycle a residual conception of TV, rooted in the network era, as a local/national public good but one of low value as culture. In other respects, P2P TV discourses are part of the newly upgraded cultural status of television, which is in part a consequence of convergence.... The file-sharing of TV content is thus a practice and discourse wherein television's cultural value can be contested and reassessed as the medium's identity is renewed. The remainder of this essay considers the terms of this renewal in the discourses of television file-sharing, both those of its communities of users and of TV industry circles.

User Rationales and the Value of Television

The television audiences who turn to BitTorrent and other legally questionable means of accessing programs they want to watch do so at some acknowledged personal risk, and their practices are products of a moral, political, and economic calculus as well as ways of satisfying personal and social needs. TV file-sharing offers an opportunity to consider emergent practices of media consumption in the context of convergence and thereby examine the ideological clashes they expose. These practices of consumption are revealed in the discourses of TV file-sharing communities such as message board postings and comments threads, which frequently make arguments in favor of file-sharing in self-consciously value-laden and often ethical terms. They can also be traced in the popular and trade press. The grounded, practical ethical theories of P2P users offer evidence of ways of thinking about television and its value as new technologies introduce problems and possibilities never before faced by television consumers. The discourses of P2P community members express resistance to the hegemony of media industries imposing distribution practices on consumers who deem them unacceptable. But these discourses are ideologically contradictory insofar as they also promote a sophisticated, masculinized notion of media consumption, distinguishing a newly legitimate mode of television viewing from the backward ways of ordinary viewers and technologies.

P2P users rationalize their behavior in terms of costs and benefits, and justify their practices not only in terms of legal categories like fair use but also in terms of judgments about right and wrong, about the appropriateness of their actions in given contexts and in relation to the practices of media companies. For instance, they might reason that it is ethical (or should be) to download content not otherwise or legally available, or to sample a product before committing to it. Many believe that downloading is justified when one has also paid for the content in another format. Some rationales for file-sharing, like "try before you buy" might justify any of the media accessed through

P2P networks. But TV downloaders, like the ones who comment at the news aggregator site Digg, often defend their practice in ways that establish specific norms and conditions for television. They reason that those already paying for cable are entitled to download. In a nightly.net forum thread ("Do you consider downloading TV shows to be 'stealing?'" February 23, 2009), commenter D-Ray Kenobi explains, "I personally don't hold a lot of guilt for using BitTorrent to download shows. Everything I've downloaded using it is something I've technically paid for in my satellite bill." Sharers also insist that DVR recordings and downloads are ethically equivalent. The difference between recording a show oneself using a VCR or DVR and skipping commercials and downloading a commercial-free file via BitTorrent is regarded as ethically insignificant. . . . The nature of broadcast television's advertising-driven business model makes sharing different from music or movies, especially when considering network programming for which no one pays a subscription fee. As scottykempf explains in a Digg thread ("BitTorrent in Focus: TV-series are Hot," May 17, 2007): "The networks BROADCAST their shows, sending them out FOR FREE into the air all over the country. How can they claim that I am stealing if they are giving it away for free?"

A multitude of rationales exist for file-sharing, and some might be more noble than others. For some users, avoiding the cost of cable or satellite subscription, of DVD purchase or rental, or even of owning a television might be paramount. There might also be value found in having a way to watch TV without some of the traditional cultural associations constructing television as degraded and shameful. A 2008 reddit discussion on the question "How many redditors don't watch TV?" (undated, c. 2008) inspired a number of telling confessions from community members. In some quarters, especially in elite circles, the boast of not having or watching a television set is something of a cliché, but the legitimation of the convergence era has opened up new opportunities for television appreciation while distancing a new conception of TV from its old cultural construction. The following selection of contributions to this thread (commenters' screen names are given in parentheses) reveal much about the motivations and values of file-sharing participants, or at least the ones active on reddit:

–I don't watch TV but I do download some TV shows. (Xet)

–I watch a few TV shows but I mostly download them so you could say I watch Laptop. (eMigo)

–My TV is called Pirate's Bay. (MasterMahan)

–I love TV. I don't have cable cause I'm poor so I download. (nerve)

–TV rules. You just have to know where to look. It's also better to download or DVR shows rather than watch them live. Watching TV when it's on kinda blows. (funkah)

–I was going to ask if torrents of TV shows counted.

–No waiting for the local station to pick up a program

–No loud annoying commercials

–You can download an entire season at a time (mbm)

The ideal of television as it is most typically experienced reflected in these comments is clearly a residual conception of TV rooted in the technologies of an earlier period. The superiority of new technologies is given as self-evident and as distinguishing a youthful, masculine, and technologically adept community from the mainstream of television audiences. Many qualify that if they watch TV it is not really watching TV, in ways similar to HBO's elitist tagline, "It's not TV. It's HBO." . . . The user is able to present his mode of consumption in a positive light, even if it is morally questionable in the wider mainstream culture, because of its amelioration of some of television's most basic problems. Within the community of file-sharers, overcoming these issues is good, indeed, doing so has the potential to recuperate television from its low cultural status and make watching TV more legitimate, as other digital technologies such as TV on DVD have done (Hills 2007; Kompare 2006).

The use of BitTorrent and other ways of sharing television functions as one of many technologies of agency, the means by which television viewers are able to program their own viewing. The use of these technologies can itself be presented as an ethical choice, a kind of imperative for the improvement of cultural consumption by empowering individuals to take control over the process. TiVo and TV on DVD are often presented as saviors of television in quasi-religious terms—redemptive Godsends to the viewing public (Boddy 2004, 123; Newman and Levine 2011). In many ways torrenting improves on these technologies by overcoming further obstacles to the availability of any and all content to anyone, anywhere, anytime. Even with DVRs and other legally legitimate technologies of agency, there are obstacles standing in the way of some consumers accessing TV content on their own terms. Shows are not released in all countries simultaneously, and in many countries some desirable content is not available at all. . . . For reasons of protecting intellectual property, web content such as webisodes and streaming video of previously aired content is routinely geo-blocked: some sites will work only in some territories. Hulu, a joint venture of NBC Universal, Fox, and ABC streaming recent episodes of many popular shows (as well as movies and other video content), has not been available outside the United States. Users abroad are greeted at such sites with a "not available in your region" message, which has evidently frustrated many file-sharers who might otherwise avail themselves of such legally sanctioned services. . . .

. . . As Ira Wagman and Peter Urquhart argue, Canadians are constantly made to suffer delayed gratification when it comes to American consumer products. Geo-blocking, they observe, is one among many forms of Canadians' deprivation of popular culture, and whether in the name of business-minded IP agreements or nationalist cultural protectionism, the experience of Canadians can be characterized by frustration and resentment over the inability to share a common culture with those beyond Canada's political borders (Wagman and Urquhart, forthcoming). The access of television shows available online through file-sharing networks functions to ameliorate this sense of being wronged by cultural institutions. Insofar as it finds ways around the legally legitimate obstacles to access, then, file-sharing in Canada and elsewhere is constructed as ethically legitimate because of a sense of justified entitlement to television and other forms of popular culture, as well as a sense of the illegitimacy of this access's denial. This returns us to a sometimes lost sense of popular culture as culture belonging to the people rather than the corporations who produce and disseminate it. Preserving the people's access to their culture in the face of corporate and state interference might be a more ethical gesture than preserving intellectual property rights in the name of corporate profits and national sovereignty. By framing TV as popular culture in this sense, rather than as disposable trash or commodified mass culture, the communities of TV fans downloading their shows express a valuation of television as central to their cultural experience. . . .

The global, cosmopolitan flow of television thus produces a justification for file-sharing as a resource for binding communities of popular culture consumers. Along with the legitimation of television, the sense that TV is a worthwhile and artistic form of culture, comes the globalization of its content. The sharing economy of the internet facilitates the simultaneity of distribution in ways that media corporations and their state regulators have not yet achieved. In this way, the peer networks function as productive institutions, and not the kinds of uncaring and selfish criminals imagined by the media corporations and their friends in government. Yochai Benkler (2006, 60) speaks of Wikipedia and open-source software as the work of "commons-based peer production" and along these lines we might think of BitTorrent and other communities as commons-based peer *distribution*, which also makes value outside of the traditional commercial sphere. Rather than lawless pirates (though some do "own" that term), participants in peer networks are informed practitioners who assume known risks in exchange for clearly valued benefits. They add value to the television text and experience. Although in some ways they might function as parasites on the commercial economy, we might also regard their work as adding value to television by recirculating it on the terms desired by a segment of the audience—available anywhere and anytime for no monetary payment, stripped of commercials and promotions, labeled with episode information, and re-circulated under the terms of the gift economy (Lessig 2008; Jenkins, Li, and Krauskopf 2009). Moreover, television file-sharing is also a form of production, in the sense that the labor of P2P networks not only distributes shows but also produces easily shared files of them stripped of commercials and other unwanted parts, saved in formats that will play easily on users' computers, as well as metadata that allow for efficient online organization and search, and comments on torrent tracking websites attesting to the reliability of the video file (some files contain malware or are not what they appear to be). They add value to the text through this productive labor in service of a popular culture community whose desires they satisfy. Thus we can appreciate television's value in a number of ways, from a number of perspectives, and appreciate the clashes, contradictions, and changes in its valuation. In some ways, the value of community cohesion and of culture being under the people's power is more significant than the commercial value of media from the perspective of institutions who benefit from a capitalist market in cultural goods. The global dimension of this community, this cosmopolitan populace, further complicates the traditional functioning of these institutions, situated as they are in national industries and regulatory regimes.

A consideration of file-sharing thus reveals a number of new positive valuations of television in the context of digital convergence: as more culturally legitimate than it had been, and as a form of global popular culture that finds a hospitable site of community cohesion on the internet. At the same time, however, the residual reputation of TV as a form of low culture, and the efforts of media corporations to extract revenue from every experience of mediated culture, also inform the valuation of television evident in the case of file-sharing.

... A "Don't Make Me Steal: Digital Media Consumption Manifesto" circulating online in 2011 sets clear values for television and movies. The point of this online petition is to encourage practices for media corporations to follow to make legitimate alternatives preferable to file-sharing. Among these is reasonable pricing of media products. These include making a television series cost one-third the price of a film, and insisting that content be advertising-free. As we have seen, the conception of TV as free of charge has a strong effect on the ethical calculation involved in sharing television. Users find it hard to accept downloading of TV shows as free-riding or stealing, and often view advertising-avoidance in positive rather than negative moral terms, which serves to maintain the lesser reputation of an advertising-driven, feminized medium. Of course the media industries don't see it this way, and have responded to the illegal circulation of television shows online in part by

waging a legal and propaganda campaign, but also by adopting some of the strategies of internet culture to "learn from piracy" and thereby avoid the fate of the recording industry.

Industry Countermeasures and the Value of the Audience

To a considerable extent, ... television content has spread from the channels and networks transmitting over the air and via cable and satellite systems to websites and other digital outposts. This is in response to consumer demand and a growing sense of opportunity for new distribution windows to monetize or to function promotionally. But perhaps more significantly, it can also be viewed as a form of protection from file-sharing and the threat it poses to the traditional business models of the TV industry. The networks and studios have offered their content in ad-supported free streaming browser windows, under the terms of monthly subscription services like Netflix, and as pay-per-view downloads via iTunes and other retailers. These forms of access offer legally sanctioned means of online access to TV. In some instances, they appeal to consumers as simpler and more straightforward processes of access than BitTorrent and other online channels.

... If file-sharing is sometimes figured in the media industries as a criminal, even terrorist threat, it is sometimes also seen as good promotion (Kravitz 2009). The media industries see an opportunity in piracy because it indicates the terms by which audiences desire access to content, and it signals the objects of their desires. ...

The legal online alternatives to P2P distribution find themselves, much like file-sharing, at a meeting point of contradictory values. They seek revenue from the online audience, but perhaps if they prevent piracy from gaining ground this is sufficient for the TV industry for the time being. Media companies aim to protect their legacy business model of advertiser-supported network and cable distribution, as well as subscriptions and ancillary home video sales, while also opening up the internet as a new distribution site. But unlike the file-sharing community, their conception of value is always, in the last analysis, commercial. Among other practices of the convergence era, file-sharing has revealed television's value to be multiple, unstable, and in transition just as television's technologies and cultural status are in transition. If peer distribution of television shows has shown us anything, it is the passion with which some consumers of TV devote themselves to the circulation and experience of some of television's texts. This occurs apart from television's official and traditional institutions, but it is familiar as a set of practices within the new, networked cultures of the internet.

References

Benkler, Y. 2006. *The wealth of networks: How social production transforms markets and freedom.* New Haven: Yale University Press.

Bjarkman, K. 2004. To have and to hold: The video collector's relationship with an ethereal medium. *Television & New Media* 5: 217–46.

Boddy, W. 2004. *New media and popular imagination: Launching radio, television, and digital media in the United States.* Oxford: Oxford University Press.

Ernesto, 2007a. Television studios embrace BitTorrent. *Torrent Freak*, August 7.

Ernesto. 2007b. Massive leak of pre-air TV shows: Piracy or promotion? *Torrent Freak*, July 24.

Ernesto. 2008a. 50% of all BitTorrent downloads are TV shows. *Torrent Freak*, February 14.

Ernesto. 2008b. Top 10 most pirated shows of 2008. *Torrent Freak*, December 23.

Ernesto. 2008c. MPAA demands $15 million from The Pirate Bay. *Torrent Freak*, August 5.

Ernesto. 2009. Top 10 most pirated TV shows on BitTorrent. *Torrent Freak*, April 11.

Gillespie, T. 2007. *Wired shut: Copyright and the shape of digital culture.* Cambridge, MA: MIT Press.

Green, J., and H. Jenkins. 2009. The moral economy of Web 2.0. In *Media industries: History, theory and method*, edited by J. Holt and A. Perren, 213–25. Malden, MA: Wiley-Blackwell.

Hills, M. 2007. From the box in the corner to the box set on the shelf: TVIII and the cultural/textual valorizations of DVD. *New Review of Film and Television Studies* 5: 41–60.

Jenkins, H. 2008. *Convergence culture: Where old and new media collide*, rev. ed. New York: New York University Press.

Jenkins, H., X. Li, and A. Domb Krauskopf, with J. Green. 2009. If it doesn't spread it's dead (part four): Thinking through the gift economy. *Confessions of an Aca-Fan*, February 18.

Kompare, D. 2006. Publishing flow: DVD box sets and the reconception of television. *Television & New Media* 7: 335–60.

Koulikov, M. 2010. Fighting the fan sub war: Conflicts between media rights holders and unauthorized creator/distributor networks. *Transformative Works and Cultures* 5.

Kravitz, D. 2009. Hollywood-funded study concludes piracy fosters terrorism. *Wired.com*, March 3.

Leaver, T. 2008. Watching *Battlestar Galactica* in Australia and the tyranny of digital distance. *Media International Australia* 126: 145–54.

Lessig, L. 2004. *Free culture: The nature and future of creativity.* New York: Penguin.

Lessig, L. 2008. *Remix: Making art and commerce thrive in the hybrid economy.* New York: Penguin.

Litman, J. 2001. Digital copyright: Protecting intellectual property on the Internet. *Amherst*, NY: Prometheus.

Newman, M. Z., and E. Levine. 2011. *Legitimating television: Media convergence and cultural status.* New York: Routledge.

Pesce, M. 2005. Piracy is good? How *Battlestar Galactica* killed broadcast TV. *Mindjack*, May 13.

Roetggers, J. 2009. Is Hulu driving people back to piracy? *New Tee Vee*, February 21.

Sarkeesian, A. 2010. No girls allowed: File sharing culture and BitTorrent. *Bitch Media blog Mad World*, July 20.

Song, W. 2008. U.S. TV dramas hot in China. *China Today*, March.

Spigel, L. 1992. *Make room for TV: Television and the family ideal in postwar America.* Chicago: University of Chicago Press.

Strangelove, M. 2005. *The empire of mind: Digital piracy and the anti-capitalist movement.* Toronto: University of Toronto Press.

Stelter, B., and B. Stone. 2010. Successes (and some growing pains) at Hulu. *New York Times*, March 31.

Tichi, C. 1992. *Electronic hearth: Creating an American television culture.* New York: Oxford University Press.

Vaidhyanathan, S. 2001. *Copyrights and copywrongs: The rise of intellectual property and how it threatens creativity.* New York: New York University Press.

Wagman, I., and P. Urquhart. Forthcoming. This content is not available in your region: Geoblocking culture in Canada. In *Dynamic fair dealing: Creative Canadian culture online*, edited by R. Coombe, D. Wershler-Henry, and M. Zelinger. Toronto: University of Toronto Press.

PART VIII

INTERACTIVITY, VIRTUAL COMMUNITY, AND FANDOM

As discussed elsewhere in this book, there is a robust debate within media studies regarding the degree to which consumers internalize mediated messages into the way they make sense of the world. Those scholars working within the more **Marxist**-based paradigm of **political economy** tend to focus on the powerful impact that **hegemonic ideology** has on the way consumers construct their notions of reality, identity, and even commonsense. However, in recent years, there has been a shift toward emphasizing not only the **active audience** but also in particular the **fans**, those consumers who are most highly engaged in making new meanings out of given cultural **texts**—sometimes producing not just unintended interpretations but also new texts of their own. In this part, we focus on consumer productive activity and on **activism**—showing some of the many ways that people go beyond a passive relation to mass media culture. We also include chapters that are critical of an overemphasis on the active-audience model.

We set these studies of audience activism, participation in production, and political lobbying to reshape mainstream media within the context of 21st-century media with the help of Henry Jenkins, a theorist of what is sometimes called **media convergence**. According to Jenkins (VIII.61),

Media convergence ... involves the introduction of a much broader array of new media technologies that enable consumers to archive, annotate, transform, and recirculate media content ... it alters the relationship between existing technologies, industries, markets, genres, and audiences. (p. 588)

In his view, we need to attend to the way in which two kinds of media convergence interact if we are to understand the dizzyingly unstable contemporary world of media production and consumption:

Corporate convergence—the concentration of media ownership in the hands of a smaller and smaller number of multinational conglomerates who thus have a vested interest in ensuring the flow of media content across different platforms and national borders.

Grassroots convergence—the increasingly central roles that digitally empowered consumers play in shaping the production, distribution, and reception of media content. (p. 588)

Jenkins, a pioneer in the field of fandom studies (see his influential article on *Star Trek* fan fiction, I.8), questions the "media imperialism" argument, which holds that giant media corporations and cultural products based in the West completely dominate global media production and consumption. Applying the same principle by which audience and fandom studies complicated our understanding of the power dynamics between consumers and texts, he urges us to look carefully, through ethnographic study, at the ways in which regional and local audiences may actually read imported cultural texts like Disney goods "in radically different ways . . . against the backdrop of more familiar genres and through the grid of familiar values" (p. 589). And beyond simply looking in more nuanced ways at how U.S. cultural texts are received in other nations, Jenkins points to

the importance of understanding "grassroots convergence"—the digitally assisted ways in which U.S. media consumers, particularly the sophisticated group he calls "pop cosmopolitans," now embrace, appropriate, and help to circulate imported Asian cultural goods, such as Japanese anime and manga or Bollywood films.

In recent years media scholars with a critical political economy perspective have been taking a closer look at how Internet-based fan activities operate within the context of corporate domination of Internet. (This critical perspective is laid out by Foster and McChesney, in I.5.) These critical analyses take into account the whole range of individual and group user involvement, from enthusiastic consumption of online cultural products and creation of community based on that consumption; through the production and distribution of new narratives like fan fiction or remixed videos or the creation of online identities through social media and virtual reality websites.

Picking up on the term "prosumer" introduced by Alvin Toffler in the early 1980s—to indicate "the progressive blurring of the line that separates producer from consumer"—Christian Fuchs (VIII.62) looks at the political economy of Facebook, and in particular at its privacy policy, which enables it to gather, store, and own personal information and cultural products provided by its users. In contrast to what some media scholars refer to as "celebratory" studies of participatory culture on the Internet, Fuchs emphasizes not the creativity or pleasure of the productive internet consumer but the corporate profit derived from that person's labor. He writes uncompromisingly "that prosumption is used for outsourcing work to users and consumers, who work without pay. In this model, corporations reduce their investment costs and labor costs, destroy jobs, and exploit consumers who work for free" (p. 594). He cites the example of the thirteen-year-old Facebook user who notes targeted advertisements on his Facebook page that are obviously based on personal data sold by Facebook, and calls this boy "the prototypical Facebook child worker."

Fuchs follows his incisive critique of Facebook's "use of targeted advertising and economic surveillance" ("legally guaranteed by Facebook's privacy policy") with an appeal to readers to think about a contrasting "socialist internet privacy politics." He offers several strategies for "advancing the decommodification of the internet, from the relatively modest policy of "opt-in online advertising" through the development and support of "corporate-watch" organizations and non-commercial collectively organized "alternative internet platforms" (p. 596).

The evolving corporate efforts to control autonomous fansites is also critiqued in Kelly Kessler's chapter, "Showtime Thinks, Therefore I Am: the Corporate Construction of 'The Lesbian' on sho. com's the *L Word* Site" (VIII.63). Like several other writers in this edition of our book, Kessler is wary of the "power of the purse strings" that "allows those with creative and economic control to tweak fanbase identities and define who is worthy to engage in *seemingly* independent conversations" (p. 601). In this case, a study of a fan website launched by the Showtime Channel for the lesbian-themed drama, *The L Word*, the corporation had a fairly good reputation for producing "GLBT-friendly television," but as Kessler points out, "it still played safe by relying heavily on **heteronormative** or **hypersexualized** images . . . and programming its lineup to include only one gay show at a time" (p. 603).

Kessler traces the show's website evolution over time, from low-tech, bare-bones bulletin board of open comments, in which a good diversity of lesbian types and styles was visible, into more heavily designed restrictive online spaces "far from equally hospitable to everyone" (p. 605). Giving us a bit of her own frustrating experience trying to create an appropriate avatar on the

Second Life virtual reality portal of *The L Word*, Kessler humorously presents a serious issue: the increasingly "safe" representational regime possible in corporation-controlled cyber space:

> Unsurprisingly, the network-sponsored sites erased the butch, the bi, the trans, the working class, the Midwestern, and the rural, all in favor of creating a largely idealized and marketable (to both men and women) image of lesbianism. This corporate creation of the lesbian community basically legitimized a new closet, one in which lesbianism was accepted, but only a narrow vision thereof. (pp. 606–607).

We turn next to two studies of digitally enabled fan media productivity. In a direct line of descent from Janice Radway's well-known study of romance novel readers (her article title suggests a tip of the hat to Radway's book, *Reading the Romance*), Eve Ng (VIII.64) has explored how a small group of fans of the popular American daytime soap opera *All My Children* were able to create and circulate music videos that "rewrote the romance" of Bianca Montgomery and Lena Kundera, who shared a temporary lesbian relationship on the show. Lesbian fans may have particularly experienced disappointment with the way the soap writers had handled the relationship, which at that time (2003) was "the first and only lesbian romance on U.S. daytime television." According to Ng, "one reason was that physical and sexual intimacy between Bianca and Lena was depicted much less explicitly than is commonly seen between soap opera couples" (p. **613**). In response, fans digitally edited together clips emphasizing the physical as well as emotional moments from the show "that would appeal to viewers looking for a text in which Bianca and Lena were the primary figures, with their love for each other apparent" (p. **615**), and created the imagined possibility of a "happy ending" as an alternative to the unsatisfying narrative offered by the show's writers.

Fan alternative text production and distribution in cyberspace does often enable marginalized groups both to make themselves more visible to other cultural consumers and to push against the boundaries of mainstream **representations**, as this example shows. However, another study of fan productivity, this time in relation to *World of Warcraft*, the massively multiplayer online role-playing game (MMORPG), suggests that there are significant limits to the progressive potential of participatory media. Lisa Nakamura's essay (VIII.65) examines how the hostility that many players feel about the game's unintended subsidiary practice of "gold farming, or selling in-game currency to players for real money," has taken a visual and specifically racialized (anti-Chinese) form. Fan-produced *machinima* (homemade music videos using visuals appropriated from within the online world and distributed on the Internet outside the game) stereotype the "gold farmers" as faceless Chinese worker multitudes, a threat to the leisure players who cannot hope to compete with their relentless labor. She argues that in this case, participatory media, often seen by enthusiasts as able to extend the world of mainstream texts "in truly liberatory ways," can also be used by fans in destructive and divisive ways:

> If indeed machinima extend the world of gameplay, how are players co-creating this world? . . . A closer look at user produced content from Warcraftmovies.com reveals a contraction and retrenchment of concepts of gender, race and nation rather than their enlargement. (pp. 623–624)

Another way to become active as a fan of a particular media cultural product is to organize and lobby on behalf of its existence when threatened by economically driven decision making by its producers. Televised soap operas, another example of

a cultural form heavily derided as "low culture" in the past, have played a major role in the imaginative lives of their predominantly female viewers for many years. In Melissa Scardaville's study (VIII.66) of activism around the 1999 cancellation of the 35-year-old daytime drama *Another World*, she shows how

> soaps may be seen as an apolitical medium enjoyed only by complacent viewers, but in actuality, daytime television provides a powerful platform for activism. (p. 636)

While soap fan activism is not a new phenomenon, as Scardaville shows, a series of campaigns on behalf of this show were aided substantially by the Internet, which provided instant communication among potential fan activists as well as between fans and mainstream industry insiders (e.g., actors and executives). Although in this instance, the campaign to keep *Another World* on the air ultimately failed, Scardaville finds that "What is extremely meaningful about these movements . . . is not their success or failure but the soap opera genre's ability to create these accidental activists" (p. 636). Most of the fans contacted by Scardaville were motivated to get involved in activism because of "their perception of the show as an extended family."

The chapter by Lori Kido Lopez (VIII.67) offers another interesting example of the ways in which media fan communities can use the Internet to "transition from everyday fans to political activists" (p. 641). In this case, in 2008 a "firestorm of criticism" greeted the casting decisions of producers of a film adaption of a Nickelodeon cartoon that had originally seemed set in an "Asian" imaginary world. When white actors were tapped for all four lead roles, fan activists, arguing in a letter-writing campaign facilitated by the online *Live Journal* social networking platform that "Asian" actors should have been cast in these roles, faulted the producers for "race-bending": whitening the characters for economic reasons. When the film was scheduled for release the leaders urged the group's members to boycott it and attend various protest actions to promote the broader cause of increasing film companies' hiring of Asian American film actors. Lopez closely studied the dynamics of the fan activism through 2010, and while she points out problematic aspects (such as the "essentialized" discourse of race in general and "Asianness" in particular") she also points out "how the set of skills exercised and utilized by fan communities have the potential to translate effectively into skills for a new mode of activism that takes place largely online" (p. 640). While it was in some cases difficult to get members of the online activist community to participate in "real-life protest activities" at events such as rallies, she concludes that

> The group is still participating in important discursive and educational work . . . Further, they have moved their mission toward general casting and racial representation issues that are not even related to their original fan object—a trend that can only be seen as political, since it no longer relies on the affective ties of fandom—and through this shift, they have been a part of important conversations with industry executives. (p. 644)

In addition to facilitating online organizing by fans, web sites created by users of social media platforms like *Live Journal* or *Second Life* can provide opportunities to some marginalized groups for online alternative community formation and maintenance, as is demonstrated in the chapter by Cole et al. (VIII.68), "GimpGirl Grows Up: Women With Disabilities Rethinking, Redefining, and Reclaiming Community." Employing auto-ethnographic writing by the founding member Jennifer Cole, as well as archival materials, the authors document the evolution of a forum for women with disabilities, run by women with disabilities, as the technologies changed and

made different tools available. The authors view information and communication technologies as "an opportunity" for the GimpGirl Community members "to move beyond externally imposed definitions of who they are, experiment with self-representation and forge their own sense of identity" (p. 654).

In one example of the way members using the online platforms "develop a capacity to perform as agents of self- and social transformation," Jennifer Cole tells us that she can use "an avatar with a wheelchair when speaking to non-disabled people about the GGC, and an able-bodied avatar when speaking to her peers." She writes:

> My avatar looks very much like me in real life, minus the signs of disability that I rarely display in *Second Life* because in my head I don't really picture myself as disabled. (p. 653)

While the new media technologies can enable community development and cohesion, it is important to remind ourselves of the potential damage communities can suffer when the Internet amplifies the politics of hate and fear. In the chapter by Flores-Yeffal et al. (VIII. 69), a description and analysis is offered of what is termed "the Latino Cyber-Moral Panic Process in the United States."

Defining "moral panic" as "the reaction of a society against a specific social group based on beliefs that the subgroup represents a major threat to society," these authors use the case of anti-immigrant sentiment directed against Latinos to show how the online technology has enabled a rapid and widespread panic. This study combined an online **ethnography** with a **content analysis** of anti-immigrant websites, and it observed not only that the "classic moral panic stages were effectively promoted online, but also that the Internet enabled a new stage which the authors called "a call for action"—through requests for donations and the promotion of particular political and civil activities. The chapter is an important reminder that the new online technologies potentially enable social activism of all kinds—not just that which would tend to democratize and decrease inequalities in society.

We end this part with a chapter by Christine Bacareza Balance (VIII.70) that shows the way in which the video-sharing website *YouTube* has enabled the emergence of Asian American performers into public visibility and has become "an alternative avenue of cultural production" (p. 670). Beginning her chapter with the story of an undergraduate student's satirical response video, mocking white racial stereotyping of Chinese immigrants in another student's video, Balance discusses the various ways in which Asian American *YouTube* performers have contributed to and benefited from "social media's democratic promise" (p. 672). First she notes the prominence of Asian Americans in viral video production:

> All but absent in the Hollywood star system and on the Billboard charts, Asian Americans . . . dominate YouTube's Most Subscribed lists. . . . Today's Asian American creative hopefuls do not merely accede to but actively exploit social media and information sharing platforms such as YouTube, Facebook, Twitter and blogs . . . as their new "calling card". (p. 670)

Beyond the boost that the viral capability of these platforms has given to the independent artists, she explores how *YouTube* captures such a large Asian American audience, through speaking "to the simultaneously virtual and material aspects of Asian American identity" (p. 672). In the context of frustration with "the model minority myth's discursive containment," she argues, Asian American youth audiences may be hungry to see and hear expressions of the "paradoxical feelings of Asian America: cultural alienation and, yet, the desire to belong" (p. 675).

In this last section of our book, we have seen that despite increasing conglomeration and monopolization of media industries by giant corporations, there are still spaces left where individuals and communities can build affirmative identities, have a voice in creating and distributing cultural representations of themselves and others, and in general resist hegemonic representations. There are even opportunities to use Internet platforms for organizing media activism and social activism more generally. Nevertheless, we end with the caveat that no amount of participatory production, consumption, and distribution via the Internet can stand in for what our society still needs: fair and equal access for noncorporate entities, individuals and groups, to the whole range of cultural production.

Broader political efforts are still necessary to pressure mainstream producers and owners to create and distribute different kinds of representations. Certainly, achieving a more democratic system of media ownership and access will require a very high and sustained level of citizen activism—including working to change public media policies favoring corporate control, such as the deregulation of broadcast media. Still, for those interested in the relationship of media to cultural democracy, active audiences and media activism are welcome exercises of media consumer power.

61

Pop Cosmopolitanism

Mapping Cultural Flows in an Age of Media Convergence

Henry Jenkins III

If there is a global village, it speaks American. It wears jeans, drinks Coke, eats at the golden arches, walks on swooshed shoes, plays electric guitars, recognizes Mickey Mouse, James Dean, E.T., Bart Simpson, R2-D2, and Pamela Anderson.

Gitlin 2001

The twain of East and West have not only met—they've mingled, mated, and produced myriad offspring, inhabitants of one world, without borders or boundaries, but with plenty of style, hype, and attitude. In Beijing, they're wearing Levis and drinking Coke; in New York, they're sipping tea in Anna Sui. While Pizzicato Five is spinning heads in the U.S., Metallica is banging them in Japan.

Yang, Gan, Hong and the staff of A. Magazine, 1997

I have spent my career studying American popular culture, adopting an approach based on older notions of national specificity. In recent years, however, it has become increasingly difficult to study what's happening to American popular culture without understanding its global context. I mean this not simply in the predictable sense that American pop culture dominates (and is being shaped for) worldwide markets but also in the sense that a growing proportion of the popular culture that Americans consume comes from elsewhere, especially Asia. This chapter represents a first stab at explaining how and why Asian popular culture is shaping American entertainment.

The analysis must start with the concept of media convergence. Most industry discourse about convergence begins and ends with what I call the black box fallacy: sooner or later all media are going to be flowing through a single black box in our living rooms, and all we have to do is figure out which black box it will be. Media convergence is not

From Jenkins, H., "Pop Cosmopolitanism: Mapping Cultural Flows in an Age of Convergence." In Marcelo M. Suarez-Orozco and Desiree Baolian Qin-Hilliard (eds) (2004), *Globalization: Culture & Education in the New Millennium*. Berkeley: University of California Press.

an end-point; rather, it is an ongoing process occurring at various intersections among media technologies, industries, content, and audiences. Thanks to the proliferation of channels and the increasingly ubiquitous nature of computing and telecommunications, we are entering an era when media will be everywhere and we will use all kinds of media in relation to each other. We will develop new skills for managing that information, new structures for transmitting information across channels, new creative genres that exploit the potentials of those emerging information structures, and new modes of education to help students understand their impact on their world. Media convergence is more than simply the digital revolution; it involves the introduction of a much broader array of new media technologies that enable consumers to archive, annotate, transform, and recirculate media content. Media convergence is more than simply a technological shift; it alters the relationship among existing technologies, industries, markets, genres, and audiences. This initial wave of media changes exerts a destabilizing influence, resulting in a series of lurches between exhilaration and panic. Yet media convergence is also sparking creative innovation in almost every sector of popular culture; our present media environment is marked by a proliferation of differences, by what Grant McCracken calls "plenitude" (see McCracken 2003). . . .

In this chapter I focus on the interplay between

Corporate convergence—the concentration of media ownership in the hands of a diminishing number of multinational conglomerates that thus have a vested interest in ensuring the flow of media content across different platforms and national borders

and

Grassroots convergence—the increasingly central roles that digitally empowered consumers play in shaping the production, distribution, and reception of media content.

These two forces—the top-down push of corporate convergence, the bottom-up pull of grassroots convergence—intersect to produce what might be called global convergence, the multidirectional flow of cultural goods around the world. Ulf Hannerz is describing global convergence when he writes: "[World culture] is marked by an organization of diversity rather than by a replication of uniformity. . . . The world has become one network of social relationships and between its different regions there is a flow of meanings as well as of people and goods" (Hannerz 1990, p. 237).

Global convergence is giving rise to a new pop cosmopolitanism.[1] Cosmopolitans embrace cultural difference, seeking to escape the gravitational pull of their local communities in order to enter a broader sphere of cultural experience. The first cosmopolitans thought beyond the borders of their village; the modern cosmopolitans think globally. We tend to apply the term to those who develop a taste for international food, dance, music, art, or literature—in short, those who have achieved distinction through their discriminating tastes for classical or high culture. Here, I will be using the term pop cosmopolitanism to refer to the ways that the transcultural flows of popular culture inspire new forms of global consciousness and cultural competency. Much as teens in the developing world use American popular culture to express generational differences or to articulate fantasies of social, political, and cultural transformation, younger Americans are distinguishing themselves from their parents' culture through their consumption of Japanese anime and manga, Bollywood films and bhangra, and Hong Kong action movies. This pop cosmopolitanism may not yet constitute a political consciousness of America's place in the world (and in its worse forms, may simply amount to a reformation of orientalism), but it opens consumers to alternative cultural perspectives and the possibility of feeling what Matt Hills calls "semiotic solidarity" with others worldwide who share their tastes and interests (Hills 2002). . . .

Pop cosmopolitanism cannot be reduced to either the technological utopianism embodied by Marshall McLuhan's "global village" (with its promises of media transcending the nation-state and democratizing cultural access) or the ideological anxieties expressed in the concept of media imperialism (with its threat of cultural homogenization and of "the West suppressing the Rest," as Ramaswami Harindranath describes it [see Harindranath 2003, p. 156]).

The media imperialism argument blurs the distinction between at least four forms of power—economic (the ability to produce and distribute cultural goods), cultural (the ability to produce and circulate forms and meanings), political (the ability to impose ideologies), and psychological (the ability to shape desire, fantasy, and identity). Within this formulation, Western economic dominance of global entertainment both expresses and extends America's status as a superpower; the flow of cultural goods shapes the beliefs and the fantasies of worldwide consumers, reshaping local cultures in accordance with American economic and political interests. The classic media imperialism argument ascribed almost no agency to the receiving culture and saw little reason to investigate actual cultural effects; the flow of goods was sufficient to demonstrate the destruction of cultures.[2] Ethnographers have found that the same media content may be read in radically different ways in different regional or national contexts, with consumers reading it against the backdrop of more familiar genres and through the grid of familiar values. Even within the same context, specific populations (especially the young) may be particularly drawn toward foreign media content while others may express moral and political outrage. Most will negotiate with this imported culture in ways that reflect the local interests of media consumers rather than the global interests of media producers.

To be sure, there is probably no place on the planet where one can escape the shadow of Mickey Mouse. Entertainment is America's largest category of exports. The Global Disney Audiences Project, for example, deployed an international team of scholars to investigate the worldwide circulation of Disney goods. They found that in eleven of eighteen countries studied, 100 percent of all respondents had watched a Disney movie, and many of them had bought a broad range of other ancillary products (Wasko, Phillips, and Meehan 2001). But while still strong, the hold of American-produced television series on the global market has slipped in recent years (Foroohar 2002; Klein 2002). Local television production has rebounded, and domestic content dominates the prime evening viewing hours, with American content used as filler in the late-night or afternoon slots. Hollywood faces increased competition from other film-producing nations—including Japan, India, and China—that are playing ever more visible roles within regional, if not yet fully global, markets. Major media companies, such as Bertelsmann, Sony, and Universal Vivendi, contract talent worldwide, catering to the tastes of local markets rather than pursuing nationalistic interests; their economic structure encourages them not only to serve as intermediaries between different Asian markets but also to bring Asian content into Western countries. Many American children are more familiar with the characters of Pokemon than they are with those from the Brothers Grimm or Hans Christian Andersen, and a growing portion of American youth are dancing to Asian beats. With the rise of broadband communications, foreign media producers will distribute media content directly to American consumers without having to pass by U.S. gatekeepers or rely on multinational distributors.

At the same time, grassroots intermediaries will play an increasingly central role in shaping the flow of cultural goods into local markets.

Adopting a position that if you can't beat them, merge with them, the American entertainment industry has become more aggressive in recruiting or collaborating with Asian talent. Sony, Disney, Fox, and Warner Brothers have all opened companies to produce films—aimed both at their domestic markets and at global export—in Chinese, German, Italian, Japanese, and other languages. American television and film increasingly remake successful products from other markets, ranging from *Survivor* and *Big Brother,* which are remakes of successful Dutch series, to *The Ring,* a remake of a Japanese cult horror movie, and *Vanilla Sky,* a remake of a Spanish science fiction film. Many of the cartoons shown on American television are actually made in Asia (increasingly in Korea), often with only limited supervision by Western companies.

Some have argued that Hollywood entertainment has always been global entertainment. Whereas many national cinemas respond to a relatively homogenous local market, Hollywood has had to factor in the tastes of a multicultural society. Richard Pells writes: "The United States has been a recipient as much as an exporter of global culture. . . . American culture has spread throughout the world because it has incorporated foreign styles and ideas. What Americans have done more brilliantly than their competitors overseas is repackage the cultural products we received from abroad and then retransmit them to the rest of the planet" (Pells 2002; also see Olson 1999). Pells sees this as an ongoing development that has shaped the evolution of American pop culture, not simply a cosmetic shift in response to recent economic trends or cultural developments.

These shifts complicate any simple mapping of the relationship among economic, political, and cultural power. We still must struggle with issues of domination and with the gap between media have and have-not nations, but we do so within a much more complicated landscape. . . . Arjun Appadurai writes, "Electronic mediation and mass migration . . . seem to impel (and sometimes compel) the work of the imagination. Together, they create specific irregularities because both viewers and images are in simultaneous circulation. Neither images nor viewers fit into circuits or audiences that are easily bound within local, national, or regional spaces" (Appadurai 1996, p. 4).

Strategies of Corporate Convergence

The flow of Asian goods into Western markets has been shaped through the interaction of three distinct kinds of economic interests: (1) national or regional media producers who see the global circulation of their products not simply as expanding their revenue stream but also as enhancing national pride; (2) multinational conglomerates that no longer define their production or distribution decisions in national terms but seek to identify potentially valuable content and push it into as many markets as possible; and (3) niche distributors who search for distinctive content as a means of attracting upscale consumers and differentiating themselves from stuff already on the market. For example, in the case of world music, international media companies, such as Sony, identify international artists and market them aggressively in their local or regional markets. As those artists are brought westward, the companies make a commercial decision whether they think the musicians will open mainstream, in which case the companies retain distribution rights within the United States, or niche, in which case they subcontract with a boutique label or third-party distributor (Levin 2002).

In a compelling analysis of the impact of Japanese transnationalism on popular culture, Koichi Iwabuchi draws a distinction between the circulation of cultural goods that are essentially "odorless," bearing few traces of their cultural origins, and those that are embraced for their culturally distinctive "fragrance" (Iwabuchi 2002). In some cases, mostly where these goods are targeting niche or cult audiences, these goods are strongly marked as coming from some exotic elsewhere; in other cases, especially where they are targeted to the mainstream, their national origins are masked and the content retrofitted to American tastes.

As Iwabuchi has documented, Japanese media industries sought ways to open Western markets to their "soft goods," or cultural imports, based on the overseas success of their hardware and consumer electronics. Seeking global distribution for locally produced content, Japanese corporations such as Sony, Sumitomo, Itochu, and Matsushita bought into the American entertainment industry. They saw children's media as sweet spots in Western societies. Much as Hollywood's ability to compete in international markets rests on its ability to recoup most of its production costs from domestic grosses, the success of Japanese-made comics and animation meant that these goods could enjoy competitive prices as they entered Western markets. In Japan, manga constituted 40 percent of all books and magazines published, and more than half of all movie tickets sold were to animated films (Ahn 2001). More than two hundred animation programs were aired each week on Japanese television, and about seventeen hundred animated films (short or feature length) were produced for theatrical distribution each year. Japanese media producers had created a complex set of tie-ins among comics, animated films and television series, and toys, which allowed them to capitalize quickly on successful content and bring it to the largest possible audience. They hoped to export this entire apparatus—the programs, the comics, and the toys—to the West. In the domestic market, anime and manga appealed to a broad cross-section of the public, but as they targeted the West, Japanese media companies targeted children as the primary consumers of their first imports. As this generation matured, the companies anticipated that they would embrace a broader range of Japanese-made media. . . .

Tactics of Grassroots Convergence

. . . . Grassroots convergence serves the needs of both cosmopolitan and local. A global communication network allows members of diasporic communities to maintain strong ties with their motherlands, ensuring access to materials and information important to their cultural traditions and preserving social connections with those they left behind (Punathambekar 2003). Cosmopolitans use networked communication to scan the planet in search of diversity and communicate with others of their kind around the world. . . .

The pop cosmopolitan walks a thin line between dilettantism and connoisseurship, between orientalist fantasies and a desire to honestly connect and understand an alien culture, between assertion of mastery and surrender to cultural difference.

These same paradoxes and contradictions surface when we turn our attention to American fans of Japanese anime, the otaku. Otaku is a Japanese term used to make fun of fans who have become such obsessive consumers of pop culture that they have lost all touch with the people in their immediate vicinity. American fans have embraced the shameful term, asserting what Matt Hills calls a "semiotic solidarity" with their Japanese counterparts (Hills 2002); constructing their identity as "otaku" allows them to signal their distance from American taste cultures and their mastery over foreign content. While a minority of otaku are Asian or Asian American, the majority have no direct ties to Japan. . . .

Initially, anime, like Bollywood videos, entered the United States through small distributors who targeted Asian immigrants. Fans would venture into ethnic neighborhoods in search of content; in New York and San Francisco they turned to a handful of Japanese bookstores for manga that had not yet been translated or distributed in North America.[3] The Web enabled fans to start their own small-scale (and sometimes pirate) operations to help import, translate, and distribute manga and anime. . . .

Ethnographers who have studied this subculture disagree about the degree to which otaku seek any actual connection with real-world Japan or simply enter into an imaginary world constructed via anime genres. As Susan Napier writes, "the fact that anime is a Japanese . . . product is certainly important but largely because this signifies that anime is a form of media entertainment outside the mainstream, something 'different'" (Napier 2000, p. 242; see also Newitz 1994; Tobin 1998). Napier suggests that fans are attracted to the strange balance of familiar and alien elements in Japanese animation, which openly appropriates and remakes Western genre conventions. Some anime fans do cultivate a more general knowledge of Japanese culture. They meet at sushi restaurants; clubs build partnerships via the Internet with sister organizations in Japan. Members often travel to Japan in search of new material or to experience the fan culture there more directly; some study the Japanese language in order to participate in various translation projects. As American fans go online and establish direct contact with their Japanese counterparts, they create an opening for other kinds of conversation. Discussion lists move fluidly from focus on anime- and manga-specific topics onto larger considerations of Japanese politics and culture.

These different degrees of cultural engagement are consistent with what Hannerz has told us about cosmopolitanism more generally: "[In one kind of cosmopolitanism], the individual picks from other cultures only those pieces which suit himself. . . . In another mode, however, the cosmopolitan does not make invidious distinctions among the particular elements of the alien culture in order to admit some of them into his repertoire and refuse others; he does not negotiate with the other culture but accepts it as a package deal" (Hannerz 1990, p. 240). What cosmopolitanism at its best offers us is an escape from parochialism and isolationism, the beginnings of a global perspective, and the awareness of alternative vantage points. . . .

Notes

1. For another take on what I am calling pop cosmopolitanism, see Roberts 2001.

2. For overviews of the debates on media imperialism, see Tomlinson 1991, Howe 1996, Liebes and Katz 1990, and Featherstone 1996.

3. On manga fandom, see Schodt 1996; Kinsella 2000; and Macias and Horn 1999.

References

Ahn, J. (2001). Animated subjects: On the circulation of Japanese animation as global cultural products. Paper presented at the Globalization, Identity and the Arts Conference, University of Manitoba, Winnipeg.

Appadurai, A. (1996). *Modernity at large: The cultural dimensions of globalization.* Minneapolis: University of Minnesota Press.

Featherstone, M. (1996). Localism, globalism and cultural identity. In *Global local: Cultural production and the transnational imaginary.* Rob Wilson and Wimal Dissanayake, eds. Durham: Duke University Press.

Foroohar, R. (2002). Hurray for Globowood: As motion-picture funding, talent and audiences go global, Hollywood is no longer a place, but a state of mind. *Newsweek International,* May 27.

Gitlin, T. (2001). *Media unlimited: How the torrent of images and sounds overwhelms our lives.* New York: Metropolitan.

Hannerz, U. (1990). Cosmopolitans and locals in world culture. In *Global culture: Nationalism, globalization, and modernity.* M. Featherstone, ed. London: Sage.

Harindranath, R. (2003). Reviving "cultural imperialism": International audiences, global capitalism and the transnational elite. In *Planet TV.* L. Parks and S. Kumar, eds. New York: New York University Press.

Hills, M. (2002). Transcultural Otaku: Japanese representations of fandom and representations of Japan in Anime/Manga fan cultures. Paper presented at Media-in-Transition 2: Globalization and Convergence Conference, Massachusetts Institute of Technology, Cambridge, MA.

Howe, D. (1996). Commodities and cultural borders. In *Cross-Cultural Consumption: Global Markets, Local Realities.* London: Routledge.

Iwabuchi, K. (2002). *Recentering globalization: Popular culture and Japanese transnationalism.* Durham: Duke University Press.

Kinsella, S. (2002). *Adult Manga: Culture and power in contemporary Japanese society.* Honolulu: University of Hawaii Press.

Klein, C. (2002). The globalization of Hollywood. Paper presented at the Modern Language Association conference, New York, NY.

Levin, M. (2002). Independent distributors and specialty labels move product in the U.S. by such international artists as Shakira. Copyright 2002 BPI Communications, Inc. Used with permission from Billboard, November 2.

Liebes, T., and E. Katz (1990). *The export of meaning: Cross-cultural readings of* Dallas. Oxford, UK: Oxford University Press.

Macias P., and C. G. Horn, eds. (1999). *Japan edge: The insider's guide to Japanese pop subculture.* San Francisco: Cadence Books.

McCracken, G. (2003). Plenitude. http://www.cultureby.com/books/plenit/cxc_trilogy_plenitude.html.

Napier, S. (2000). *Anime from Akira to Princess Mononoke: Experiencing Japanese animation.* New York: Palgrave.

Newitz, A. (1994). Anime Otaku: Japanese animation fans outside Japan. *Bad Subjects* 13. http://eserver.org/bs/13/Newitz.html.

Olson, S. R. (1999). *Hollywood planet.* New York: Lawrence Erlbaum.

Pells, R. (2002). American culture goes global, or does it? *Chronicle of Higher Education,* April. http://chronicle.com/free/v48/i31/31boo701.htm.

Punathambekar, A. (2003). *Bollywood bytes: A story of how I found an Online Adda.*

Roberts, M. (2001). Notes on the Global Underground: Subcultural Elites, Conspicuous Cosmopolitanism. Paper presented at the Globalization, Identity and the Arts Conference, University of Manitoba, Winnipeg, http: //www.umanitoba.ca/faculties/arts/english/media/workshop/papers/roberts/roberts_papcr.pdf.

Schodt, F. (1996). *Dreamland Japan: Writings on modern Manga.* Berkeley, CA: Stone Bridge.

Tobin, J. (1998). An American Otaku or, a boy's virtual life on the Net. In *Digital diversions: Youth culture in the age of multimedia.* J. Sefton-Green, ed. London: University College of London Press.

Tomlinson, J. (1991). *Cultural imperialism.* Baltimore: Johns Hopkins University Press.

Wasko, J., M. Phillips, and E. R. Meehan, eds. (2001). *Dazzled by Disney? The global Disney audiences project.* London: Leicester University Press.

Yang, J., and D. Gan, T. Hong, and the staff of A. Magazine, eds. (1997). *Eastern Standard Time: A guide to Asian influence on American culture from Astro Boy to Zen Buddhism.* Boston: Houghton Mifflin.

62

The Political Economy of Privacy on Facebook

Christian Fuchs

The Political Economy of Facebook

Alvin Toffler (1980) introduced the notion of the prosumer in the early 1980s. It means the "progressive blurring of the line that separates producer from consumer" (Toffler 1980, 267). Toffler describes the age of prosumption as the arrival of a new form of economic and political democracy, self-determined work, labor autonomy, local production, and autonomous self-production. But he overlooks that prosumption is used for outsourcing work to users and consumers, who work without pay. In this model, corporations reduce their investment costs and labor costs, destroy jobs, and exploit consumers who work for free. Free labor produces surplus value that is appropriated and turned into corporate profit. Notwithstanding Toffler's uncritical optimism, his notion of the "prosumer" describes important changes in media structures and practices that can therefore be adopted through critical studies....

... New media corporations do not (or hardly) pay users for the production of content. A widely-used accumulation strategy is to give the users free access to services and platforms, let them produce content, and to accumulate a mass of prosumers that are sold as a commodity to third-party advertisers. No product is sold to the users; the users are sold as a commodity to advertisers. The more users a platform claims, the higher the advertising rates. The productive labor time that is exploited by capital involves, on one hand, the labor time of paid employees, and, on the other hand, all of the time spent online by users. New media corporations pay salaries for the first type of information labor, but not for the second type....

What does it mean that Facebook prosumers work for free and are exploited? Adam is a thirteen-year-old pupil and heavy Facebook user. He has two thousand Facebook friends, writes fifty wall postings a day, interacts with at least forty of his close contacts and colleagues over Facebook a day, updates his status at least ten times a day, and uploads annotated videos and weekend photos, often showing him with his girlfriend in the countryside. Yet there is one thing that puzzles him. The advertising at the right-hand side of his profile frequently relate to what he has done last weekend or what he intends to do next weekend.

From Christian Fuchs (2012), "The Political Economy of Privacy on Facebook," *Television & New Media*, 13 (2), 139–159. Reprinted with permission of SAGE Publications.

Adam wonders how this happens and feels uneasy about the fact that his personal data obviously serves inscrutable economic ends that he cannot control in terms of which personal data and usage behaviors are stored, assessed, or sold. The answer to Adam's dilemma is that Facebook closely monitors all of his contacts, communication, and data, selling this information to companies, which then send targeted advertisements to him. Facebook thus profits and could not exist without the unpaid labor that Adam and millions of his fellow Facebook workers conduct. Adam is the prototypical Facebook child worker.

. . . With the rise of user-generated content, open access social networking platforms, and other ad-based platforms, the web seems to approach TV or radio in their accumulation strategies. The users who upload photos and images, write wall posting and comments, send mail to their contacts, accumulate friends, or browse other profiles on Facebook constitute an audience commodity that is sold to advertisers. The difference between the audience commodity for traditional mass media and for the internet is that, in the latter case, the users are also content producers who engage in permanent creative activity, communication, community building, and content-production. In the case of Facebook, the audience commodity is an internet prosumer commodity.

Surveillance of Facebook prosumers occurs via corporate web platform operators and third-party advertising clients, which continuously monitor and record personal data and online activities. Facebook surveillance creates detailed user profiles so that advertising clients know and can target the personal interests and online behaviors of the users. Facebook sells its prosumers as a commodity to advertising clients; their exchange value is based on permanently produced use values, that is, personal data and interactions. . . .

Data surveillance is the means for Facebook's economic ends. Facebook permanently monitors users for economic ends, which means that no economic privacy is guaranteed to them. Since it remains unknown to users what specific information and data contributes to targeted advertising, they cannot control their data use or protect themselves from its commodification.

The use of targeted advertising and economic surveillance is legally guaranteed by Facebook's privacy policy (Facebook privacy policy, version from December 22, 2010, http://www.facebook.com/policy.php, accessed on May 29, 2011). Facebook's privacy policy is a typical expression of a self-regulatory privacy regime, in which businesses define their own personal user data processes. In general, U.S. data protection laws cover government databanks, leaving commercial surveillance untouched in order to maximize its profitability (Ess 2009, 56; Lyon 1994, 15; Rule 2007, 97; Zureik 2010, 351). Facebook's terms of use and its privacy policy are characteristic for this form of self-regulation. When privacy regulation is voluntary, the number of organizations protecting the privacy of consumers tends to be very small (Bennett and Raab 2006, 171).

Socialist Privacy Ideals and Social Networking

. . . What could socialist privacy protection policies on Facebook look like? One basic insight here is that the protection of consumers', prosumers' and workers' privacy can only be achieved in an economy that is not ruled by profit interests, but is controlled and managed by prosumers, consumers, and producers, thereby ending the need for privacy rules that protect us from domination. If there were no profit motive on internet platforms, then there would be no need to commodify the data and behaviors of internet users. Achieving such a situation is not primarily a technological task, but one that requires changes in society.

. . . The overall goal of socialist internet privacy politics is to drive back the commodification of user-data and the exploitation of prosumers by advancing the decommodification of the internet. Three strategies for achieving this goal are the advancement of opt-in online advertising, the civil society surveillance of internet companies, and the establishment and support of alternative platforms.

OPT-IN PRIVACY POLICIES

Gandy (1993) argues that an alternative to opt-out solutions for targeted advertising are opt-in solutions that are based on the informed consent of consumers. . . .

Opt-in privacy policies are typically favoured by consumer and data protectionists, whereas companies and marketing associations prefer opt-out and self-regulation advertising policies in order to maximize profit (Bellman et al. 2004; Federal Trade Commission 2000; Gandy 1993; Quinn 2006; Ryker et al. 2002; Starke-Meyerring and Gurak 2007). Socialist privacy legislation could require all commercial internet platforms to use advertising only as an opt-in option, which would strengthen the users' possibility for self-determination. Within capitalism, forcing corporations by state laws to implement opt-in mechanisms is certainly desirable, but at the same time it is likely that corporations will not consent to such policies because they would likely reduce the actual amount of surveilled and commodified user data significantly, resulting in a drop of advertising profits. Organizing targeted advertising as opt-in instead of as opt-out (or no-option) does not establish economic user privacy, but is a step toward strengthening the economic privacy of users.

CORPORATE WATCH-PLATFORMS AS FORM OF STRUGGLE AGAINST CORPORATE DOMINATION

To circumvent the large-scale surveillance of consumers, producers, and consumer-producers, movements and protests against economic surveillance are necessary. . . .

Critical citizens, critical citizens' initiatives, consumer groups, social movement groups, critical scholars, unions, data protection specialists/groups, consumer protection specialists/groups, critical politicians, and critical political parties should observe closely the surveillance operations of corporations and document these mechanisms and instances, in which corporations and politicians take measures that threaten privacy or increase the surveillance of citizens. Such documentation is most effective if it is easily accessible to the public. The internet provides means for documenting such behavior. It can help to watch the watchers and to raise public awareness.

In recent years, corporate-watch organizations that run online platforms have emerged.[1] Transnationale Ethical Rating aims at informing consumers and research about corporations. Its ratings include quantitative and qualitative data about violations of labor rights and human rights, employee layoffs, profits, sales, earnings of CEOs, boards, president and managers, financial off-shore operations, financial delinquency, environmental pollution, corporate corruption, and dubious communication practices. Dubious communication practices include an "arguable partnership, deceptive advertising, disinformation, commercial invasion, spying, mishandling of private data, biopiracy and appropriation of public knowledge" (http://www.transnationale.org/aide.php, accessed on March 21, 2011). The topics of economic privacy and surveillance are here part of a project that wants to document *corporate social irresponsibility*. Privacy is not the only issue addressed here, but corporate watch platforms can be situated in the larger political-economic context of corporate social irresponsibility (the counterpart of the CSR ideology).

ALTERNATIVE INTERNET PLATFORMS

. . . It is not impossible to create successful nonprofit internet platforms, as the example of Wikipedia, which is advertising-free, open access, and donor financed, shows. Diaspora is the best-known alternative social networking site that has developed an open-source alternative to Facebook. It is a project created by four New York University students, Dan Grippi, Maxwell

Salzberg, Raphael Sofaer, and Ilya Zhitomirskiy. Diaspora defines itself as "privacy-aware, personally controlled, do-it-all, open source" (http://www.joindiaspora.com, accessed on November 11, 2010). It is not funded by advertising, but by donations. Three design principles of Diaspora are choice, ownership, and simplicity: "Choice: Diaspora lets you sort your connections into groups called aspects. Unique to Diaspora, aspects ensure that your photos, stories, and jokes are shared only with the people you intend. Ownership: You own your pictures, and you shouldn't have to give that up just to share them. You maintain ownership of everything you share on Diaspora, giving you full control over how it's distributed. Simplicity: Diaspora makes sharing clean and easy—and this goes for privacy too. Inherently private, Diaspora doesn't make you wade through pages of settings and options just to keep your profile secure" (http://www.joindiaspora.com, accessed on March 21, 2011).

The Diaspora team is critical of the control of personal data by corporations. It describes Facebook as "spying for free" and the activities of Facebook and other corporate internet platforms in the following way. Salzberg opined, "When you give up that data, you're giving it up forever. . . . The value they give us is negligible in the scale of what they are doing, and what we are giving up is all of our privacy" (http://www.nytimes.com/2010/05/12/nyregion/12about.html). In an online video Zhitomirskiy added, "For the features that we get on blogs, social networks and social media sites, we sacrifice lots of privacy. . . . The features that we get are not anything special. . . . What will happen. . . . when one of these big large companies just goes bust, but has as one of its assets all of your personal data and all of our personal data, our communications, our photos, our comments? . . . They are in power to do what they please with it" (http://vimeo.com/11242604).

The basic idea of Diaspora is to circumvent the corporate mediation of sharing and communication by using decentralized nodes that store data that is shared with friends. Each user has his or her own data node that he or she fully controls.

Diaspora aims to enable users to share data with others, and, at the same time, to protect them from corporate domination by sacrificing their data to corporate purposes in order to communicate and share. Diaspora can therefore be considered as a socialist internet project that practically tries to realize a socialist conception of privacy.

. . . There are diffuse feelings of discontent with Facebook's privacy practices among many users. These have manifested into groups, such as those against the introduction of Facebook Beacon, news feed, mini-feed, as well as the emergence of the web 2.0 suicide machine (http://suicidemachine.org/), and the organization of a Quit Facebook Day (http://www.quitfacebookday.com/). These activities are mainly based on liberal and Luddite ideologies, but if they were connected to ongoing class struggles against neoliberalism (such as those of students in the aftermath of the new global capitalist crisis and the protests against austerity measures, unemployment and inequality in countries like Greece, Spain, Portugal, etc.) and the commodification of the commons, they could grow in importance. Existing struggles could be connected to the attempts to establish opt-in policies, corporate social media watchdogs, and alternative social media. . . .

Notes

1   Examples of corporate watch organizations are: CorpWatch Reporting (http://www.corpwatch.org), Transnationale Ethical Reporting (http://www.transnationale.org), The Corporate Watch Project (http://www.corporatewatch.org), Multinational Monitor (http://www.multinationalmonitor.org), Crocodyl: Collaborative Research on Corporations (http://www.crocodyl.org), Endgame Database of Corporate Fines (http:///.endgame.org/corpfines.html), Corporate Crime Reporter (http://www.corporatecrimereporter.com), Corporate Europe Observatory (http://www.corporateeurope.org), Corporate Critical Database (http://www.corporatecritic.org).

References

Andrejevic, Mark. 2002. The work of being watched. *Critical Studies in Media Communication* 19 (2): 230–48.

Arendt, Hannah. 1958. *The human condition*, 2nd ed. Chicago: University of Chicago Press.

Bellman, Steven, Eric J. Johnson, Stephen J. Kobrin, and Gerald L. Lohse. 2004. International differences in information privacy concerns: a global survey of consumers. *Information Society* 20 (5): 313–24.

Bennett, Colin, and Charles Raab. 2006. *The governance of privacy*. Cambridge, MA: MIT Press.

Bolin, Göran. 2005. Notes from inside the factory. *Social Semiotics* 15 (3): 289–306.

Bolin, Göran. 2009. Symbolic production and value in media industries. *Journal of Cultural Economy* 2 (3): 345–61.

Bruns, Axel. 2008. *Blogs, Wikipedia, Second Life, and beyond. From production to produsage*. New York: Peter Lang.

Culnan, Mary J., and Robert J. Bies. 2003. Consumer privacy. Balancing economic and justice considerations. *Journal of Social Issues* 59 (2): 323–42.

Dussel, Enrique. 2008. The discovery of the category of surplus value. In *Karl Marx's Grundrisse: Foundations of the critique of the political economy 150 years later*, edited by Marcello Musto, 67–78. New York: Routledge.

Ess, Charles. 2009. *Digital media ethics*. Cambridge, UK: Polity.

Etzioni, Amitai. 1999. *The limits of privacy*. New York: Basic Books.

Federal Trade Commission. 2000. *Privacy online: fair information practices in the electronic marketplace*. http://www.ftc.gov/reports/privacy2000/privacy2000.pdf.

Fuchs, Christian. 2009a. Information and communication technologies and society. A contribution to the critique of the political economy of the Internet. *European Journal of Communication* 24 (1): 69–87.

Fuchs, Christian. 2009b. *Social networking sites and the surveillance society. A critical case study of the usage of studiVZ, Facebook, and MySpace by students in Salzburg in the context of electronic surveillance*. Salzburg/Vienna: Research Group UTI.

Fuchs, Christian. 2010a. Labour in informational capitalism. *Information Society* 26 (3): 179–96.

Fuchs, Christian. 2010b. Social networking sites and complex technology assessment. *International Journal of E-Politics* 1 (3): 19–38.

Fuchs, Christian. 2010c. Some reflections on Manuel Castells' book "Communication Power." *tripleC* 7 (1): 94–108.

Fuchs, Christian. 2010d. studiVZ: social networking sites in the surveillance society. *Ethics and Information Technology* 12 (2): 171–185.

Fuchs, Christian. 2011a. A contribution to the critique of the political economy of Google. *Fast Capitalism* 8 (1).

Fuchs, Christian. 2011b. *Foundations of critical media and information studies*. New York: Routledge.

Fuchs, Christian. 2011c. The political economy of WikiLeaks: Power 2.0? Surveillance 2.0? Criticism 2.0? Alternative media 2.0? *Global Media Journal—Australian Edition* 5 (1).

Gandy, Oscar H. 1993. *The panoptic sort. A political economy of personal information*. Boulder, CO: Westview.

Habermas, Jürgen. 1989. *The structural transformation of the public sphere*. Cambridge, MA: MIT Press.

Hearn, Alison. 2010. Reality television, the Hills, and the limits of the immaterial labour thesis. *tripleC* 8 (1): 60–76.

Held, David. 1996. *Models of democracy*. Cambridge, UK: Polity.

Hesmondhalgh, David. 2010. User-generated content, free labour and the cultural industries. *Ephemera* 10 (3/4): 267–84.

Jenkins, Henry. 2008. *Convergence culture*. New York: New York University Press.

Jhally, Sut. 1987. *The codes of advertising*. New York: Routledge.

Jhally, Sut, and Bill Livant, Bill. 1986. Watching as working: The valorization of audience consciousness. *Journal of Communication* 36 (3): 124–43.

Johnson, Deborah G., and Kent A. Wayland. 2010. Surveillance and transparency as sociotechnical systems of accountability. In *Surveillance and democracy*, edited by

Kevin D. Haggerty and Minas Samatas, 19-33. New York: Routledge.

Karatani, Kojin. 2005. *Transcritique: On Kant and Marx*. Cambridge, MA: MIT Press.

Kücklich, Julian. 2005. Precarious playbour. Fibreculture Journal 5, http://five.fibrecul turejournal.org/fcj-025-precarious-play bour-modders-and-the-digital-games-industry/.

Lee, Micky. 2011. 2011. Google ads and the blindspot debate. *Media, Culture & Society* 33 (3): 433–47.

Livant, Bill. 1979. The audience commodity. *Canadian Journal of Political and Social Theory* 3 (1): 91–106.

Lynd, Staughton. 1965. The new radicals and "participatory democracy." *Dissent* 12 (3): 324–33.

Lyon, David. 1994. *The electronic eye. The rise of surveillance society*. Cambridge, UK: Polity.

Macpherson, Crawford Brough. 1973. *Democratic theory: Essays in Retrieval*. Oxford, UK: Clarendon Press.

Manzerolle, Vincent. 2010. Mobilizing the audience commodity: Digital labour in a wireless world. *Ephemera* 10 (3/4): 455–69.

Marcuse, Herbert. 1955. *Eros and civilization*. Boston, MA: Beacon Press.

Marx, Karl. 1843a. Critique of Hegel's doctrine of the state. In *Early writings*, 57–198. London: Penguin.

Marx, Karl. 1843b. On the Jewish question. In *Writings of the young Marx on philosophy and society*, 216–48. Indianapolis, IN: Hackett.

Marx, Karl. 1867. *Capital. Volume 1*. London: Penguin.

Meehan, Eileen. 1993. Commodity audience, actual audience. The blindspot debate. In *Illuminating the blindspot*, edited by Janet Wasko, Vincent Mosco, and Manjunath Pendakur, 378–97. Norwood, NJ: Ablex.

Mill, John Stuart. 1965. *Principles of political economy*. 2 vols. London: University of Toronto Press.

Moglen, Eben. 2003. *The dotCommunist Manifesto*. http://emoglen.law.columbia .edu/publications/dcm.html

Murdock, Graham. 1978. Blindspots about Western Marxism. *Canadian Journal of Political and Social Theory* 2 (2): 109–19.

Negri, Antonio. 1991. *Marx beyond Marx*. London: Pluto.

Nissenbaum, Helen. 2010. *Privacy in context*. Stanford, CA: Stanford University Press.

Pateman, Carole. 1970. *Participation and democratic theory*. Cambridge: Cambridge University.

Press. Quinn, Michael. 2006. *Ethics for the information age*. Boston: Pearson.

Rule, James B. 2007. *Privacy in peril*. Oxford: Oxford University Press.

Ryker, Randy, Elizabeth Lafleur, Chris Cox, and Bruce Mcmanis. 2002. Online privacy policies: an assessment of the fortune E-50. *Journal of Computer Information Systems* 42 (4): 15–20.

Smythe, Dallas. 1977. Communications: Blindspot of Western Marxism. *Canadian Journal of Political and Social Theory* 1 (3): 1–27.

Smythe, Dallas W. 1978. Rejoinder to Graham Murdock. *Canadian Journal of Political and Social Theory* 2 (2): 120–27.

Smythe, Dallas W. 1981/2006. On the audience commodity and its work. In *Media and cultural studies*, edited by Meenakshi G. Durham and Douglas. M. Kellner, 230–56. Malden, MA: Blackwell.

Starke-Meyerring, Doreen and Laura Gurak. 2007. Internet. In *Encyclopedia of privacy*, edited by William G. Staples, 297–310. Westport, CT: Greenwood Press.

Tännsjö, Torbjörn. 2010. *Privatliv*. Lidingö: Fri Tanke.

Tavani, Herman T. 2008. Informational privacy: Concepts, theories, and controversies. In *The handbook of information and computer ethics*, edited by. Kenneth Einar Himma and Herman T. Tavani, 131–64. Hoboken, NJ: Wiley.

Toffler, Alvin. 1980. *The third wave*. New York: Bantam Books.

Turow, Joseph. 2006. *Niche envy. Marketing discrimination in the digital age*. Cambridge, MA: MIT Press.

Zureik, Elia. 2010. Cross-cultural study of surveillance and privacy: Theoretical and empirical observations. In *Surveillance, privacy and the globalization of personal information*, edited by Elia Zureik, Lynda Harling Stalker, Emily Smith, David Lyon, and Yolane E. Chan, 348–59. Montreal: McGill-Queen's University Press.

63

Showtime Thinks, Therefore I Am

The Corporate Construction of "The Lesbian" on Sho.Com's *The L Word* Site

Kelly Kessler

The expansion of net access, computer literacy, and media convergence continues to provide new means and spaces for individuals who may have once felt isolated by identity or fannish fixation. Where once fans of *Doctor Who* or Farrah Fawcett were left to enjoy their obsessions in solitary or pursue each other through conventions or hard-to-find fan clubs, they now need only log on to find a stream of others similarly passionate about their objects of desire. Scholars such as Henry Jenkins (2008) and Sharon Ross (2008) have focused heavily on the dynamics and politics of both this new-found access to like-minded people and media creators'/producers' drive to make the most of escalating convergence.[1] As the internet has provided fans easy access to each other, it also continues to allow members of once-isolated groups convenient ways to find and chat with each other. Members of the gay, lesbian, bi, trans (GLBT) community, for example, once relegated to finding like individuals through community outreach or bars (if even available) need only jump online to find thriving communities that self-identify as queer. In addition to an array of GLBT dating and sex sites, websites such as *Gay.com* and *AfterElton.com* provide varying forms of queer entertainment information, political commentary, and social networking.

Along with this popularity, visibility, and access comes the corporate recognition that this audience is a lucrative one. Acknowledging in the nineties that gay dollars were just as worthy as straight ones, companies started overtly targeting the "good" GLBTs through subtle advertisements and an increased presence of GLBTs in mainstream television and film (Becker 1998; Fejes 2002; Oakenfull et al. 2008; Seidman 2002). This desire to sell did not coincide with a sudden change of heart toward the entire GLBT community; rather the value of upwardly mobile purchasers (who happened to be GLBT) merely

From Kelly Kessler (2011), "Showtime Thinks, Therefore I Am: The Corporate Construction of 'The Lesbian' on Sho.Com's *The L Word* Site." *Television & New Media*, December 1, 2011, 1–23. Reprinted with permission of SAGE Publications.

trumped what may have still been seen as problematic identity politics. Shows such as *The L Word* and *Queer as Folk* provide stellar evidence of who "good gays" are (or who they should want to be)—good-looking, flashy, upwardly mobile purchasers—and the online spaces discussed in this article further illustrate the media industry's investment in those desirable characteristics through their choices in interface, staffing, and overall design.[2]

The power of the purse strings not only determines which audience is valuable enough to target, but through the corporate control of television-related fansites, it also allows those with creative and economic control to tweak fanbase identities and define who is worthy to engage in *seemingly* independent conversations about who she or he is and what she or he desires. (After all, companies are not using their resources simply to build an online play land for visitors, but to further hawk their wares.) As media companies take control of and fill fansites with all of the latest bells and whistles, an increased level of policing of fan products and interactions works to curtail fan activity. Not always strong-arming fans into submission, a more subtle control emerges as fans trade increased visibility for complicity in a vision conducive to the industries' own economic or ideological goals.

A Butlerian (1990) notion of personal performance suggests that only through repetition do gender and gender norms become socially legible; as interactive websites recurrently promote specific images of queerness (and marginalize others), they consequently render legitimate or readable a similarly limited "lesbian" or "gay male." Through website/game construction the creators/sponsors choose which identities are easily accessible as they feature specific bloggers' voices, choose predetermined subject headings for conversations, and make specific gendered visages more visibly present or easily available than others during site design or avatar construction. In order

to partake in the newest and sexiest online toys, fans are encouraged to conform—wittingly or no—and define themselves in ways most conducive to the corporation's predetermined vision. While not all overt calls toward legitimizing "the lesbian" or "the gay male" image most attractive to the moneymakers will succeed, such choices in style and message favor—while not guaranteeing—a reading/fan performance that privileges the "good gays."

This article explores this concept of corporate control and its resultant homogenization of the conceived audience through a look at the evolution of the Showtime-sponsored *L Word* (2004–2009) websites. More than a study of fan activities, this is a study of the construction of spaces. I am ultimately interested in how Showtime, *The L Word*'s cast and creative team, and The Electric Sheep Company (the Showtime-hired *Second Life* portal design company) created sites that would textually and formally project a relatively stable notion of the "good gay." The online activities and spaces provided to further advertise the show projected a welcoming space of lesbian freedom, but one far from equally hospitable to everyone. . . .

Showtime's foray into Sapphic cyberspace began in 2004 when they launched their dyke drama with a less-than-stellar website that allowed fans to login and talk about the show (or whatever). Over time, Showtime augmented *The L Word*'s online presence with all of the trendy accessories: blogs, social networking, *SL* portal, wiki, online-only video materials, and message boards. Along with these changes came an increasingly rigid sense of how the network and *The L Word* defined "lesbian" and to whom they hoped to speak (or how they hoped fans might come to see themselves). In a promo, cast member Jennifer Beals (Bette) describes the social networking site—*OurChart*—as "for gay women, [and] a safe place for them to go and be themselves and meet new people, people who they probably wouldn't meet otherwise."[3] Kate Moennig (Shane) then says "I'm just really looking forward to being part of something so exciting that can create community." This fan–star interaction positioned online fans as possessing a heightened sense of "access" or "democratic agency" (Moore 2009b). Although their closeness to and (assumed) two-way communication with the stars provided a sense of access to and control over both the show's diegetic community and a burgeoning star-studded online one, the site as designed fell short of such utopic promises of empowerment.

. . . At the heart of my study of these sites lies an examination of their strict reins on identity construction as produced by their texts, interfaces, inclusions, and striking omissions. Ultimately, I hope to shed some light on the more subtle means by which corporate participation in and design of fan spaces can lead to fans (perhaps unwittingly) bending to corporate designs and playing on a field skewed to corporate rather than personal advantage.

The L Word, "L" Is for Less Than Realistic

The tweaking of *The L Word*'s fanbase identity does not come as a complete surprise. Critics, scholars, and viewers complained since the show's 2004 premiere about its unrealistic or narrow projection of the lesbian community (Chambers 2006; Jonet and Williams 2008; Moore and Schilt 2006). The show centers on the lives of a handful of (mostly) feminine, (almost entirely) white, and (unrealistically) economically flush lesbians living in Los Angeles. Always at the center of the action stand Bette, a sassy bi-racial art curator/academic dean; Tina, Bette's on again/off again movie executive longtime companion and coparent; Jenny, a hypersexual and emotionally imbalanced writer;

Shane, the show's token butch street-smart hairdresser—who only seems butch in the context of her highly feminine cast mates; and Alice, the group's token bisexual, wacky radio/blogging pioneer.[4] Not so removed from straight-targeted lesbian pornography or the show's soap opera foundation, traditionally hot/heteronormative women cavort, swim, and have liaisons (occasionally with men) in sexy LA (Allen 1985; Beirne 2007; Moore 2009a; Williams 1989).

On the fansite boards and elsewhere, viewers scorned the show's creators for their reinforcement of dominant norms and the continued invisibility of nonwhite, butch, and middle- and working-class lesbians. Jumping to her own defense, creator Ilene Chaiken described the show as a representation of her own specific Los Angeles lesbian community. Sure, butches, lesbians of color, lesbians of different body types, trans folks, as well as pretty much anyone identified as middle class or nonurban are largely absent from the narrative, but as director Rose Troche is quoted as rationalizing in a 2004 *The Advocate* article, "These characters are not every woman. They are not every lesbian. They are a very real depiction of a group of L.A. lesbians based on Ilene's own experiences" (Hensley 2004, 46).

Showtime's role in the development of the show is less frequently considered. Their transtextual participation and the economic stakes thereof, however, are of ultimate importance in this examination of the ideological ramifications of *OurChart* and *The L Word*'s SL portal. Although the network has prided itself on the production and airing of GLBT-friendly television—*Queer as Folk, Tales of the City* mini-series installments, *The L Word, The United States of Tara*—it nevertheless exists as a premium cable channel, part of a major media conglomerate, and within a capitalist television model. When the show launched, Showtime was part of Viacom. On the CBS/Viacom split of 2006, the network fell to CBS.

Regardless of parent, it overall exists as part of a major media corporation whose primary goal is drawing eyeballs. Despite Showtime's gay-friendly programming, it still played it safe by relying heavily on heteronormative or hypersexualized images, constructing shows around traditional generic norms, and programming its lineup to include only one gay show at a time.[5] . . .

"L" Is for Let Me Tell You Who I Am

The drive for marketability and a tendency toward the femme-imperative (or at least the "good gay") emerged quickly as Showtime and the show's creative team committed fully to branching out from *The L Word*'s early rudimentary online presence and its original *sho.com* site. In early 2004, the interactive element of the show's fan site mirrored boards common to those on television-related sites at the time: low-tech, user friendly, and user driven. Generalized in its setup and not really directing viewers toward any specific kind of commentary—other than being about the show—the boards appeared as just that: message boards on which to discuss Showtime's new hopefully hit show. What emerged out of these early message boards was a vibrant community who used this assumed lesbian space to discuss their mutual object of mediatized affection, chat about ways in which the show's plotlines related to and deviated from their own lives, and ask for, offer, and receive advice as posters used this space to come out, discuss problems, and ask others for help. . . .

The largely undirected nature of the original boards encouraged show support and critique equally, and appeared to project an assumed safe lesbian space. Perhaps by accident, Showtime created a forum where lesbians could meet, discuss feelings, and engage in a virtual lesbian community. Early threads often wholly deviated from the show itself. Members instead inquired/shared, "What City and State are You Watching From?," "MY LIST OF LESBIAN FILMS," "Married bi women.....need to know," "Can't enjoy sex (minus love) with a woman, but can enjoy it with a man..What's up with that??," or "Any single Lesbians out there who would like to become pen pals and share thoughts of the show as well as anything else??" . . .

More than simply serving as a site to stir one's love for the dyke drama, the early boards functioned as a safe (assumed) lesbian gathering space. With all posts falling under a general forum slated for responses to the episodes, the site's construction aided in the creation of a community where everyone had the potential for equal—spatial and discursive—footing.

"L" Is for Lack of Cargo Shorts and Pool Tables

While the early boards welcomed all minimally computer literate participants with their simple interface and user-created threads, later network sponsored forays into cyberspace would fail to do so. In early 2007, *The L Word*'s Emmy-winning virtual reality *SL* portal would overtly disinvite those who possessed questionable technical savvy, lacked economic means, and/or deviated from a predetermined vision of gender performance. Like the rest of *SL*, the *L Word* portal functioned as a virtual world where residents could join (for free), create their own self-designed or self-modeled characters (or avatars), use real money to purchase property, clothes, et al., or even make real money by creating sellable objects or performing a service. Developed by the (ironically named) Electric Sheep Company, Showtime's virtual incarnation of the dyke drama allowed fans to step into the lush surroundings of *The L Word* to live, chat, dance, and hangout. Per the network's *SL* advertisement, this experience would only increase fans' opportunities to "be whoever you want to be." Instead of welcoming such promised inclusiveness, however, its complex and limited interface and money-reliant culture ultimately reinforced qualities critiqued about the show and embraced the characteristics of the "good gay"—attractiveness, youth, wealth, leisure, and education. . . .

To look at the Showtime-produced advertisement for *The L Word* in *SL* or images posted on various websites, one would think dyke-friendly visages were readily available.[6] To the contrary, Electric Sheep Company and the folks at Showtime appeared to have had little concern about tweaking the interface such that visitors could easily assume the appearances flaunted in the ad. Instead, the default female avatar came big busted, big haired, Caucasian, and sporting funky sandals, a bare midriff top, and low-rise jeans. On my arrival, I fussed with the avatar options attempting to settle on a cyber-me that remotely represented the (relatively computer literate) soft-butch I am. After much struggle I settled for a crazy looking, short hair sporting, and almost-belly shirt wearing figure totally unrepresentative of me. The most difficult part of this process was manufacturing short hair when the program tended to equate short hair with baldness. As I tried to escape the default flowing locks, I repeatedly created unattractive bald spots on my avatar, Agnes. After a bit of travel through the welcome area, I discovered a few outfits that newbies could choose to wear: six women's and two men's. Although these women's outfits provided some options—jeans, dresses, capri pants, strappy heels, tank tops, spaghetti strap tops, etc.—they all screamed "I enjoy being a girl." I was eventually able to find an outfit less awkward for my avatar to wear by donning clothes they identified as men's.

Assumedly, once the gamer created her avatar, she could go on to the good part of the program: becoming part of a community. Instead, what Agnes/I found was a rather standoffish group of people with little patience for newbies and which was suspect of Agnes's butch appearance. More than once she was defensively asked if she was a man. Upon revealing she was a woman, she was met with hostile dialogue regarding men and their less-than-welcome presence in this *SL* portal. In a community known for its diversity and in a fan community vocally disturbed by the absence of narrative butches, this aggression came as a shock. Perhaps I should have been less shocked in a portal where developing a newbie butch avatar was such a challenge. (After all, the only way to produce a "butch" avatar early on was to disavow one's female-ness and choose to *be* a man.) Regardless, it quickly became clear that to some degree gamers had internalized (or at least settled on visually projecting) the traditionally feminine image, one encouraged by the show and the interface equally.

Surely, not all women who visited the site would want to build a butch avatar—a thought just as essentialist as the one guiding the actual interface—but where was the option? . . .

"L" Is for Let Me Tell You Who You Are

. . . In the same year (2007) that Showtime rolled out its high-tech, dyke-friendly *SL* portal, they marginalized their largely fan-driven message boards. Where once the Showtime show site had included mainly show information, low-tech boards, a few show extras, and links to *L Word* merchandise, the new highly designed and interactive *OurChart* site presented fans with more *L Word* extras, dyke-friendly (but show divergent) webisodes like *GirlTrash!* (2007), games, the show-based Sapphic social networking site, and new and fancier blogs and boards. . . .

... The website described itself in the following terms:

> *OurChart* is the new site where women can connect, share and hang out with friends of all shapes, stripes, genders and orientations. Launched from an idea in the Showtime hit "The L Word," *OurChart* provides unreleased gems from the show, along with exclusive original editorial and multimedia content from some of the most excellent creative folks out there. *OurChart* will also let folks create their own chart of friends, lovers, and everyone else in their own L worlds.
>
> *OurChart* was founded by several of the people behind the innovative TV show, along with a few professional homosexuals and a crack team of queer-at-heart geeks, designers and writers. Rumor has it the site was created in order to fulfill item 197 on the Homosexual Agenda, but we're not gay enough to see the document, so we have no idea if it's true or not.
>
> Most of the staff is based in Los Angeles and San Francisco, but like the gays, we're everywhere. Snap. (OurChart 2007)

Tongue in cheek, *OurChart*'s mission mocks the Right's paranoia regarding the homosexual agenda, while merely setting the site up as a queer-friendly place to meet and gather. . . . . Between the promo and the site's listed mission, the founders position *OurChart* as transcending the narrow view of lesbian life the show so often had been critiqued for espousing. The mission statement evokes the popular mantra "we are everywhere" as it jokingly positions its founders as edgy folks looking out for the lesbian community (although it simply says "for women"). Chaiken and Moennig bring to mind the transcendent quality of the site and its ability to bring fans in to join in good clean fun, especially those otherwise lacking a lesbian community.

Contrary to the founders' publicized aspirations, the site suffered from the same weaknesses as the series. The chart itself functioned much like other social networking sites where members develop profiles, seek out connections, and make visible their own likes, dislikes, and social networks.[7] As would be expected, *OurChart* members developed profiles and sought out friends (through connections or blog entries). After its initial launch, designers added a "friends plus" component to mirror Alice's sexual encounter-driven "Chart."

... When a viewer entered the *OurChart* site, she could choose to enter the profiles or visit the blogs, forums, or video areas. Upon traveling to the blogs, she could choose to read the latest featured blogs or enter one of the general topic areas: "Hook Up" (messages from the editors), "Feel Up" (culture and entertainment), "Touch Up" (health and beauty), "Wake Up" (politics), "Sex Up," or "The Chart Report" (gay news stories). Featured blogs visually dominated the space, with links to the most read blogs by everyday users identified by small profile pictures off to the right. The featured blogs dwarfed those of everywoman bloggers both in size and overall prominence within the site's visual design, as they consistently appeared on the homepage as a hello for visitors. Individuals hired/appointed by the *OurChart* powers that be—ranging from creator Ilene Chaiken and author/radio personality Diana Cage to urban designer Mitch McEwan and *OurChart* editor Lisa Bang—authored these more prominent blogs.[8] (Notably, many of the celebrities and pseudo-celebrities would only be recognized by those "in the know," placing those visitors not hip to dyke culture at a disadvantage.) Unlike the "we're all equal in the board's eyes" feel of the old site, the new format framed these bloggers as the chosen ones (both literally and figuratively).

By mid-2008, *OurChart*'s thirteen featured bloggers included two writers, two radio hosts, a performance artist, urban designer, magazine founder, comic, music industry insider, personal trainer, and the *OurChart* site editor. Pictured on the page—larger than the everywoman bloggers—they headlined the main editorial content of the sexual, political, and cultural themed headings. Of the thirteen, all but one resided in New York, Boston, or California. Although *OurChart* was launched for lesbians "everywhere," the voices who constructed the face of *OurChart* excluded many of the same individuals excluded from the series. Despite including African Americans more fully than the series, the bloggers remained largely American and white. Living in Canada, Leah Beckingham provided *OurChart* with its only blogger living outside of the United States. Lenelle Moise and Parisa Parnian, Haitian and Iranian respectively, served as the only non-Americans (although North American coastal residents). These thirteen women's prominent voices and social profiles define the site's image of the "good lesbian" or she who is worthy of address. Despite some diversity, the overall range of valid lesbian voices wholly excluded those who might identify as rural, suburban, Southern, Midwestern, conservative, or working-class to name a few.

Like the show, whose main characters are filmmakers, hair designers to the stars, and star athletes, the bloggers/anointed opinion leaders brought glamour and cultural capital to the table. Simultaneously, visible bi, butch, and transgendered voices failed to emerge through the design of the featured community. Only African American blogger and self-identified dyke Mitch McEwan (sporting short cropped hair, sport coat, and sweater) would have been visibly identified as butch; none of the bloggers self-identified as trans or bi.[9] . . .

. . . While in no way curtailing who can read the *OurChat* blogs, the choices in featured bloggers surely refine the *who* that the site hails: one who fits the definition of a specific lesbian, rather than particularly queer.

Users could surely find other (assumed) lesbians to talk to aside from the featured

bloggers, but those who reflected their own political, economic, and regional backgrounds (if divergent from the in-site established norms) were perhaps hard to find. True, members could create their own blogs, as well as reply to those of nonfeatured bloggers, but while pictures of and links to the featured bloggers graced the blog homepage the site's design marginalized member-driven blogs and replies. Only by searching a secondary link under "profiles" or a small "browse member blogs" link in the bottom corner of the homepage could visitors explore the musings of the larger spatially closeted community—and that beyond the urban intelligentsia. Reflecting a common design-oriented "pseudo-closeting gesture" discussed in Jonathan Alexander's (2002, 92) exploration of "homo-pages," *OurChart* forced visitors to *seek out* divergent voices, rather than—as in the early boards—featuring them equally. . . .

"L" Is for Better Luck Next Time or Lookin' Out for the Man

Through each of these fan-directed and somewhat fan-driven activities/meeting grounds tied to Showtime's and *The L Word*'s (2004–2009) investment in media convergence, the same issues of minority marginalization or assimilation emerged that had been critiqued for decades regarding film, television, and the internet. The issue of ultimate importance in this and other cases relating to user participation in corporate-created interactive spaces—specifically those targeting marginalized, minority, or isolated groups—is the fact that the fans themselves are so highly complicit in their own invisibility. In short, while these sites were (like the show) totally sexy, the images and voices presented as natural options were narrow depictions of a diverse community.

Unsurprisingly, the network-sponsored sites erased the butch, the bi, the trans, the working class, the Midwestern, and the rural, all in favor of creating a largely idealized and marketable (to both men and women) image of lesbianism. This corporate creation of the lesbian community basically legitimized a new closet, one in which lesbianism was accepted, but only a narrow vision thereof. This type of site, behavior, and fan-creation goes beyond the television industry's historically problematic production of limited images of non-whites and non-upwardly mobile characters. This type of user-driven activity, instead provides a façade of visibility, ownership, equality, and agency though its interactivity, rending less visible the individuals omitted from its virtual guest list or kept just behind the velvet ropes.

Although these same users can storm the dance club by trampling through the ropes, they may lack the self-assuredness (that scholars argue an inclusive site would help foster) or the technical know-how to do so. I hope that work such as this and further interrogations of the economic, racial, gendered, and sexual ramifications of television/film-linked media convergence continue to examine such "liberation" and that both scholars and users develop a keener eye toward the limited options being presented by the big corporations in the guise of community development and harmless branding. . . .

Notes

1. For more on this see Jenkins' Fans, Bloggers, and Gamers (2006) and his website The Confessions of an Aca-Fan: The Official Weblog of Henry Jenkins (2009).

2. Alexandra Chasin's Selling Out (2000) provides a close read of how in the 1990s advertisers both recognized and capitalized on the marketability of the gay and lesbian market and constructed them as a group who could achieve the American dream through consumption.

3. Notably, when the site was created, Co-Founder Hillary Rosen stated "Our future is not wed at all to the show" (Levy 2007, 7). By late 2008, OurChart had laid off its bloggers and was functioning almost solely as a user-content-driven queer Facebook. By January 2009, the site had been discontinued and users rerouted to a watered-down version at sho.com. Chaiken (2009) linked the change to the show's close relationship with Showtime and the network's selfless commitment to GLBT television.

4. Although the core ensemble remained relatively stable over the show's six seasons (with minor changes here and there), femme on-again-off-again duo Bette and Tina and hypersexual/bi bad-girl Jenny surely garnered more than their fair share of screen time.

5. Notably, despite being the leading American network of gay-themed programming during these years, Showtime managed its overall gayness by only airing only one gay program at a time (e.g., Queer as Folk and The L Word would run during two separate times of the year, and when Tales of the City aired, Queer as Folk would go on hiatus).

6. Examples of such diversity can be seen in online articles/ads such as the following: http://www.wired.com/underwire/2007/06/im_not_a_lesbia/, http://secondlife.reuters.com/stories/2008/01/10/showtime-mulls-expansion-of-sl-presence/index.html, http://www.youtube.com/watch?v=cTOxq4ZKVVY.

7. I actually found this site more off-putting than MySpace or Facebook, as one's friends list appears in chart form. The format visually amplified the fact that I had relatively few friends. Despite a relatively interesting profile, I looked a little pathetic. For an overview of the history of social networking and related scholarship see Danah M. Boyd and Nicole B. Ellison's (2007) "Social Network Sites: Definition, History, and Scholarship."

8. At the time of this study, the thirteen bloggers were Diana Cage (writer/radio host), Grace Moon (magazine founder), Ilene Chaiken (The L Word creator), Mitch McEwan (architect/ urban designer), Leah Beckingham (trainer), Lenelle Moise (poet/playwright), Parisa Parnian (fashion designer), Lisa Bang (OurChart editor), Gloria Bigelow (standup comic/writer), Katie

Liederman (freelance writer), Cynthia Galindo (??), Kelly McCartney (LA music scene staple), and Sabrina Artel (radio talk show host).

9. Although bloggers Michelle Tea (a blogger at a later date) and Diana Cage are known to have dated transmen and could therefore be positioned as allies, this still renders the community present only through a proxy.

References

Alexander, J. 2002. Homo-pages and queer sites: Studying the construction and representation of queer identities on the World WideWeb. *International Journal of Sexuality and Gender Studies* 7: 85–106.

Allen, R. C. 1985. *Speaking of soap operas.* Chappell Hill: University of North Carolina Press.

Altinay, R. 2008. "Be a gay with a soul of a man, don't be feminine!" Constructing masculinity in gay online dating websites. *Feminist Media Studies* 8(2): 218–20.

Becker, R. 1998. Prime-time television in the gay nineties: Network television, quality audiences, and gay politics. *Velvet Light Trap* 42(fall): 36–47.

Beirne, R. 2007. Lesbian pulp television: Torment, trauma and transformations in The L Word. *Refractory*, September 4. http://refractory.unimelb.edu.au/2007/09/04/lesbian-pulp-television-torment-trauma-and-transformations-in-the-l-word-rebecca-beirne/ (accessed August 15, 2011).

Boostrom, R. 2008. The social construction of virtual reality and the stigmatized identity of the newbie. *Journal of Virtual Worlds Research* 1(2): 1–19.

Boyd, D. M., and N. B. Ellison. 2007. Social network sites: Definition, history, and scholarship. *Journal of Computer-Mediated Communication* 13(1). http://jcmc.indiana.edu/vol13/issue1/boyd.ellison.html (accessed December 1, 2010).

Bryson, M. 2004. When Jill jacks in: Queer women and the net. *Feminist Media Studies* 4: 239–54.

Burns, M. 2009. The power of real-world gender roles in Second Life. *Pixels and Policy*, November 2. http://www.pixelsandpolicy.com/pixels_and_policy/2009/11/female-avatars.html (accessed August 15, 2011).

Busse, K. 2006. My life is a WIP on my LJ: Slashing the slasher and the reality of celebrity and internet performances. In *Fan fiction and fan communities in the age of the internet*, edited by K. Hellekson and K. Busse, 207–24. Jefferson, NC: McFarland.

Butler, J. 1990. *Gender trouble.* New York: Routledge.

Castronova, E. 2005. *Exodus to the virtual world: How online games will change reality.* York: New Palgrave/MacMillan.

Castronova, E. 2006. Synthetic economies and the social question. *First Monday* (Special Issue #7). http://www.firstmonday.org/ISSUES/special11_9/castronova/index.html (accessed December 1, 2010).

Castronova, E. 2007. *Synthetic worlds: The business and culture of online games.* Chicago: University of Chicago Press.

Chaiken, I. 2009. A new year a new OurChart. http://www.sho.com/site/lword/popup.do?content=ourchart_info (accessed December 1, 2010.)

Chambers, S. A. 2006. Heteronormativity and The L Word. In *Reading The L Word: Outing contemporary television,* edited by K. Akass and J. McCabe, 81–98. London: I.B. Tauris.

Chasin, A. 2000. *Selling out: The gay and lesbian movement goes to market.* New York: St. Martin's.

Correll, S. 1995. The ethnography of an electronic bar: The lesbian café. *Journal of Contemporary Ethnography* 24(3): 270–98.

Dumitrica, D., and G. Gaden. 2009. Knee-high boots and six-pack abs: Autoethnographic reflections on gender and technology in Second Life. *Journal of Virtual Worlds Research* 1(3): 3–23.

Fejes, F. 2002. Advertising and the political economy of lesbian/gay identity. In *Gender, race, and class in media,* edited by G. Dines and J. Humez, 212–22. Thousand Oaks, CA: Sage.

Gregg, M. 2008. Testing the friendship: Feminism and the limits of online social networks. *Feminist Media Studies* 8(2): 206–9.

Hensley, D. 2004. L is for Leisha. *The Advocate,* February 17, 41–53.

Hoyt, C., J. Blascovich, and K. Swinth. 2003. Social inhibition in immersive virtual environments. *Presence* 12: 183–95.

Hussain, Z., and M. Griffiths. 2008. Gender swapping and socializing in cyberspace: An exploratory study. *Cyber Psychology and Behavior* 11(1): 47–53.

Jenkins, H. 2006. *Fans, bloggers, and gamers.* New York: New York University Press.

Jenkins, H. 2007. How Second Life impacts our first life... Confessions of an Aca-Fan: The official weblog of Henry Jenkins, March 13. http://www.henryjenkins.org/2007/03/my_main_question_to_jenkins.html (accessed December 1, 2010).

Jenkins, H. 2008. *Convergence culture.* New York: New York University Press.

Jensen, E. 2006. *The L Word* spins off its chart. *The New York Times,* December 18: C1.

Jonet, C., and L. A. Williams. 2008. "Everything else is the same": Configurations of *The L Word.* In *Televising queer women: A reader,* edited by R. Beirne, 149–62. New York: Palgrave-Macmillan.

Levy, S. 2007. Uncharted terrain: "The L Word" spawns a network for gay women. *Newsweek* May 28, 7.

Lothian, A., K. Busse, and R. A. Reid. 2007. Yearning void and infinite potential: Online slash fandom as queer female space. *English Language Notes* 45: 103–12.

Moore, C. 2009a. Having it all ways: The tourist, the traveler, and the local in *The L Word. Cinema Journal* 46(4): 3–23.

Moore, C. 2009b. Liminal places and spaces: Public/private considerations. In *Production studies: Cultural studies of media industries,* edited by V. Mayer, M. J. Banks, and J. T. Caldwell, 125–38. New York: Routledge.

Moore, C., and K. Schilt. 2006. Is she man enough? Female masculinities on The L Word. In *Reading The L Word: Outing contemporary television,* edited by K. Akass and J. McCabe, 159–71. London: I.B. Tauris.

Nakamura, L. 2002. *Cybertypes: Race, ethnicity, and identity on the internet.* New York: Routledge.

Oakenfull, G., M. McCarthy, and T. Greenlee. 2008. Targeting a minority without alienating the majority: Advertising to gays and lesbians in mainstream media. *Journal of Advertising Research* 48: 191–98.

OurChart: The official social network of The L Word. 2007. http://www.ourchart.com/about.

Pratt, M. 2008. "This is the way we live... and love!": Feeding on and still hungering for lesbian representation in *The L Word.* In *Televising queer women: A reader,* edited by R. Beirne, 135–48. New York: Palgrave-Macmillan.

Rak, J. 2005. The digital queer: Weblogs and internet identity. *Biography* 28: 166–82.

Ross, S. 2008. *Beyond the box.* Malden, MA: Blackwell.

Russo, J. L. 2009. Cyberorganize's journal. http://cyborganize.livejournal.com/33253.html (accessed July 25, 2011).

Schiller, G. 2006. Our space: Net gain for L Word. Hollywoodreporter.com, December 18. http://www.hollywoodreporter.com/news/space-net-gain-l-word-146834 (accessed August 15, 2011).

Seidman, S. 2002. *Beyond the closet: The transformation of gay and lesbian life.* New York: Routledge.

Terra nova. 2010. http://terranova.blogs.com (accessed December 1, 2010.)

The L Word. 2004-2009. Showtime Productions.

The L Word website. 2004. http://www.sho.com/site/lword (accessed December 1, 2010).

The L Word Ourchart.com promo. 2007. http://www.youtube.com/watch?v=W4Ln-3PFAC8 (accessed December 1, 2010).

The L Word message boards. 2004. http://www.sho.com/site/message/boards.do?groupid=12 (accessed December 1, 2010).

The L Word Second Life promo, 2007. http://www.youtube.com/watch?v=cTOxq4ZKVVY (accessed December 1, 2010).

Turkle, S. 1995. *Life on the screen: Identity in the age of the internet.* New York: Simon & Schuster.

Williams, L. 1989. *Hard core: Power pleasure and the "frenzy" of the visible.* Berkeley: University of California Press.

64

Reading the Romance of Fan Cultural Production

Music Videos of a Television Lesbian Couple

Eve Ng

On April 23, 2003, viewers of ABC's *All My Children* (1970–present) saw Bianca Montgomery (Eden Riegel), daughter of cosmetics magnate Erica Kane, and Lena Kundera (Olga Sosnovska), a woman Bianca had first met as her mother's employee, close that day's episode with the first same-sex romantic kiss on an American daytime soap. Several years later, with their relationship having ended in November 2004, footage of this kiss, invariably among the favorite scenes of Bianca/Lena devotees, continues to circulate online, especially as incorporated with other clips into fan-made music videos focusing on Bianca and Lena's relationship. . . .This chapter argues that theories of fan cultural production and queer media representation are fruitfully extended by considering the characteristics and meanings of contemporary fan texts such as the Bianca/Lena videos, and how they are positioned in relation to dominant discourses, as they renegotiate the canon* in particular ways.

The sharing of fan videos online points to technology as one obvious dimension of difference characterizing the Bianca/Lena—or "Lianca"— fandom, compared to the first fan videos. These had used relatively expensive audiovisual equipment to physically splice together videotape clips and synchronize them with a soundtrack; duplicating the resulting music video required tape-to-tape copying, with distribution usually occurring in person at fan conventions. Digitization technology and the Internet now mean that fans can create their videos using readily available computer software, publicize these at online message boards, and share them via YouTube or various other Web sites. . . .

From Ng, E. (2008). Reading the romance of fan cultural production: Music videos of a television lesbian couple. *Popular Communication*, 6(2), 103–121. Reprinted by permission of Taylor & Francis Ltd., www.tandf.co.uk/journals.

Particularly pertinent to analyses of the Lianca fandom is another change in popular media: the increased regular or recurring presence of LGBT people on U.S. television, and not only as guest characters who often met untimely ends or who advance the dramatic trajectory for characters other than themselves (Gibson, 2006; Gross, 2002; Tropiano, 2002). Significant as this is, it also comprises and reflects the mainstreaming of gay culture that queer theorists such as Warner (1999) have argued seeks to assimilate a limited set of nonheterosexual identities and practices, while continuing to exclude others. . . . The Bianca/Lena romance on *All My Children* cannot be assumed to be unproblematically progressive. At the same time, the Lianca videos belong to a genre that has traditionally constructed narratives against the grain of the canon. Thus, a key question is what the implications of lesbian canonicity are for the versions of queer representation these texts offer as particular fan negotiations of mainstream media.

As scholars such as Russo (1987) and Doty (1993) have argued, even in periods when canonical depictions of same-sex romantic relationships were rare, popular cultural texts have hardly been devoid of queerness, with queer discourses constitutive of particular genres such as horror, and alternative readings of texts in general available to subtextual interpretations. Fan videos of the 1980s and early 1990s were often instances of *slash,* originally defined as involving two canonically heterosexual characters of the same sex who were paired romantically in fan narratives (Bacon-Smith, 1992; Jenkins, 1992; Penley, 1991; Russ, 1985). Initially most slash fiction circulating among fans featured two men and was usually written by straight women. From one queer analytical perspective, this sort of slash critically interrogates conventional understandings of gender and sexuality, with men's interactions typically depicted as more physically

tender and emotionally open than dominant norms around masculinity would dictate, and the pairing of characters who have sexual histories with women implying a more flexible view of sexuality than a strict heterosexual/homosexual divide (e.g., Cicione, 1998; Green, Jenkins, & Jenkins, 1998; Jung, 2004; Woledge, 2005). However, Scodari (2003) countered that the impulse to read or write slash does not necessarily stem from a politically progressive position with respect to gender, and Jenkins (1992) noted that even some fans found certain conventions of slash fiction problematic, including common disavowals of gay identity by the characters, lack of engagement with structural-level political issues, and "an often thinly veiled distaste for female sexuality and feminine bodies" (p. 219).

The counter-hegemonic dimensions of same-sex romance narratives based on canonical couples and produced by queer fans are also complex, though in different ways. First, the predominance of queer women in the Lianca creative fandom is part of an increase in the proportion of slash[1] authors who are not heterosexually-identified (Boyd, 2001; Russo, 2002; Wilder, 1998), a trend most fueled, at the outset, by a significant lesbian following for *Xena: Warrior Princess* (syndicated, 1995–2001). The ambiguity of the intensely devoted friendship between Xena and Gabrielle on the canonical show inspired a huge volume of fan fiction in which the relationship between the two was explicitly romantic. Many viewers also have been motivated to produce fan narratives for textually lesbian relationships on other television shows,[2] especially when the canon is found to be deficient in various ways.

As texts that generally end happily or hopefully, fan cultural forms such as the Lianca music videos constitute rearticulations that are what fans want in queer narratives, at least some of the time. In her groundbreaking ethnography,

Radway (1984) argued that readers derived meaning from romance novels that helped them imagine women as strong, intelligent, and able to attain their goals; thus, their consumption of this denigrated genre was not simply an example of acquiescence to discourses of female inferiority and dependence on men. A parallel can be drawn with the typical Lianca video, which refuses the narrative of sad, lonely queers, creating instead a text in which lesbians find the love that soap opera logic—and mainstream culture more generally—suggests is necessary for happiness. . . .

Fan texts, then, do not fully depart from conventional ideas and values about human relations, and compared to fan fiction, fan videos are particularly dependent on the canonical texts as source for their visual material. A fan fiction author can have characters engage in actions that have never been portrayed or described in the canon, as well as create new characters, settings, and situations. On the other hand, in most fan videos, "neither the sights nor the sounds . . . originate with the fan artists; the creator's primary contribution, in most cases, comes in the imaginative juxtaposition of someone else's words and images" (Jenkins, 1992, p. 225). . . .

It is certainly possible for fan videos to incorporate or produce various sorts of video outside of "official" sources, a common practice for some users of other media, such as creators of interactive Internet applications known as mashups[3] (Merrill, 2006), or video gamers who use commercially released software to create their own distinctive animations and narratives (Herman, Coombe, & Kay, 2006; Jones, 2006). Why the majority of television fan video makers do not do so probably has to do with audience expectation, with viewers of these videos generally looking for something that fits sufficiently within the confines of the visual and cultural world familiar to them from the show, even as narrative sequences are being reworked. As Stein (2006) argues, fan texts may be shaped not just by their canonical sources, but also by "shared understandings of generic codes and tropes" that "contribute story possibilities and yet also limit the ranges of types of stories told" (p. 248). The development of these generic codes warrants further investigation, but they surely draw not just on elements of fan cultures—the delight in slashing canonically straight men, for example, or the popularity of the hurt-comfort dynamic[4]—but are also shaped by more mainstream norms, particularly those around relationships, sex, and gender. . . .

All My Children and the Bianca/Lena Relationship

Bianca and Lena's relationship played out onscreen on one of the longest-running soap operas of U.S. television, ABC's *All My Children,* set in the fictional town of Pine Valley, Pennsylvania. Bianca Montgomery was introduced in 1988 as the baby daughter of series matriarch Erica Kane, but was not written as lesbian until 2000 when, with a revised birth year of 1984, the character was aged to 16. At that time, Bianca became the first regular character on a U.S. daytime soap to come out (see Harrington, 2003a, b), and, like most lesbians on U.S. television, she fit dominant standards of female attractiveness: thin, long-haired, wearing make-up and feminine attire. Lena Kundera, also conventionally feminine, had first appeared on the show at the end of 2002 as a shadowy figure, and came to work at Erica Kane's cosmetics company, Enchantment, in January 2003. It became apparent a couple of months later that she was actually a spy for—and the lover of—Michael Cambias, a business rival of Erica's. In the course of Lena's espionage, she and Bianca met and fell in love, culminating in their first kiss in April 2003, and a couple of weeks later, a morning-after scene. The couple broke up and made up a couple of times in the next few weeks, primarily due to revelations about Lena's associations with Michael, and the fact that she was directed by him to seduce Bianca for strategic purposes. However, in early July, Bianca and Lena appeared headed toward a romantic vacation together—until Bianca was raped by Michael.

Bianca was, predictably, traumatized by her rape; she destroyed evidence of the attack and did not tell anyone about it for weeks. Various people close to her realized there was something wrong, but Bianca pushed them away, including Lena, with whom she ceased all intimacies and, indeed, meaningful conversation for months. Bianca's main storylines came to revolve around the pregnancy resulting from the rape; the murder of Michael Cambias, for which both Bianca and Lena were suspects; and the birth and then apparent death of her daughter Miranda (Miranda had actually been secretly given to another couple). Bianca and Lena appeared to have a mini-reconciliation around New Year's Eve, having slowly moved back to one another, and by March 2004 Lena noted that the two were "dating," but it was not clear that they ever resumed a sexual relationship. In April 2004, Lena was written out of the show, and the couple had a phone break-up in November, when Bianca, feeling an inexplicable tie to Pine Valley, refused to join Lena in Poland, where Lena was tending her ailing mother and in desperate need of Bianca's support.

Bianca has also been involved with Maggie Stone (Elizabeth Hendrickson), a young woman who first appeared on the show in early 2002. While Bianca's feelings for Maggie were mostly unreciprocated for the bulk of their time together in Pine Valley, they left for Paris in early 2005 as close friends open to a romantic relationship, and when Bianca showed up for a short stay around Christmas that year, viewers learned that the two had become lovers. Bianca returned to the show in October 2006 for a six-month stint, during which time she and Maggie broke up, due to Maggie's (off-screen) infidelity, and Bianca became attracted to Zarf/Zoe (Jeffrey Carlson), an MTF (male-to-female) transgender character. Support for a Bianca/Maggie pairing preceded Lena's arrival,[5] and throughout the Bianca/Lena relationship, there were still fans in favor of Bianca getting together with Maggie. Still, many switched their allegiance to Lianca, and die-hard Lianca fans have remained active at online message boards, if with varying degrees of disillusionment, through Bianca's other onscreen romantic attachments.

At the outset of Bianca and Lena's relationship, viewer reaction among a wide cross-section of viewers was, on the whole, positive, according to Eden Riegel, Olga Sosnovska, and the *All My Children* producers (Warn, 2003b). Bianca's long period of celibacy had been a source of discontent to many fans; at the time of Lena's arrival on the show in December 2002, it had been over two years since Bianca had come out, and she had consistently fallen in love with women who did not return her feelings (Maggie being, at the time, only one of several). Before Bianca and Lena's first kiss, *All My Children* head writer, Agnes Nixon, and the head of ABC daytime programming, Brian Frons, had made supportive public statements about the upcoming romance, so fans seemed to have good reason to be hopeful, protests from conservative groups such as Concerned Women for America notwithstanding (Kleder, 2003).

However, it is not hard to see why the portrayal of the relationship was ultimately found wanting by many fans. One reason was that physical and sexual intimacy between Bianca and Lena was depicted much less explicitly than is commonly seen between soap opera couples, and this was particularly galling when compared to the portrayal of Bianca's rape, where Michael was shown holding Bianca very closely for some time as well as touching her bare skin. Furthermore, for the months following the rape, Bianca, along with her relationship with Lena, were effectively desexualized, with only some scenes of prolonged eye contact, hand-holding, and hugging between the two before they shared a brief New Year's Eve kiss. Perhaps as disturbing to many fans was the loss of even emotional connection between Bianca and Lena. As others have noted, rape happens all too often to women onscreen, especially in soap operas, and these storylines frequently draw on and reinscribe problematic gender discourses (see Dutta, 1999; Projansky, 2001). However, the partners of straight characters who are raped aren't generally shut out of their recovery the way that Lena was; Bianca was shown opening up to her friend Maggie and to her mother Erica about the rape, but not to Lena.

Furthermore, the general characteristics of soap operas often frustrate fans of a particular character or couple. U.S. daytime soaps are generally ensemble shows, so screen time must be shared with other characters and storylines. Also, although *All My Children* is aired for an hour five days a week, the narrative proceeds slowly in typical soap opera fashion. Thus, although Bianca was a main character, she might appear on only three or four episodes a week without being the focus of all of those episodes, and Lena had even less screen time than Bianca.[6] Of course, viewers are often unhappy with how television shows depict relationships in which the fans are invested. However, the Bianca/Lena relationship was at the time the first and only lesbian romance on U.S. daytime television, and indeed was one of the few ongoing lesbian relationships on U.S. television at all. In other words, for many fans, it was not simply a matter of tuning off *All My Children* and moving onto programs with better depictions of lesbian characters. Although some posters at message boards did vow in disgust that they would never again watch *All My Children*

after Bianca's rape, others continued seeing how the story unfolded on the canonical show, even as they expressed their criticism. A number of viewers also turned to existing fan genres, including music videos, for more satisfying narratives.

The Lianca Music Videos

The Lianca fandom, like others devoted to a series couple, has been a passionate one, but it was always relatively small, making the creative output of Lianca fans more easily surveyed than those produced by the huge followings for other shows, such as *Buffy, The X-Files,* or the *Star Trek* series. Bianca/Lena music videos have usually been publicized at either or both of the message boards associated with the Riegel Rebels and the Sosnovska Symposium Web sites, (named for the actors playing Bianca and Lena, respectively).

. . . . Based on my observations at Bianca/Lena Web sites and online interviews with three video makers,[7] they, like the majority of Lianca fans, are mostly lesbian women.[8] A few of the Bianca/Lena *vidders* (as they are sometimes known in fan cultures) were also fairly frequent posters in discussion threads at the message boards, but others were most visible through their video productions. Vidders may be somewhat more computer/tech-literate than many other fans; one Lianca video maker was a computing major who later became a software engineer, while another was familiar with video editing techniques from her work. While vidders occasionally chose a song based on the requests of other fans, they were more often inspired when a certain song struck them as particularly appropriate for Bianca and Lena's relationship.[9] Feedback from video viewers was usually expressed on message board threads after the video had been publicized and distributed, and was invariably positive (nor did any of the video makers I interviewed recall receiving any negative feedback privately). Thus, the Lianca vidders had a good sense of what other fans wanted, and skillfully put together scenes and music that would appeal to viewers looking for a text in which Bianca and Lena were the primary figures, with their love for each other apparent.

Jenkins (1992) noted that a fan music video was almost always set to a contemporary popular song, and this is true of the Lianca videos.[10] In most of them, the songs are about love relationships and/or their associated difficulties, often falling into the "ballad" genre; thus, both the lyrics and the melody tend to conform to cultural understandings of emotionality. Crucially, with their compression and focus, music videos facilitate a unique intensity of media engagement: viewing a three-five minute video, where all or nearly all the images feature the characters and relationships in which a viewer is invested, is an experience that cannot be derived from watching the show. Also, as digital files on personal computers, music videos can easily be replayed. Fans sometimes comment that their consumption of fan texts is so much more pleasurable that they have replaced their viewing of the show with reading fan fiction or watching fan videos.

Unlike, for example, the Kirk/Spock music videos discussed by Jenkins and others, Lianca videos do not re-contextualize images to suggest a romantic relationship. Rather, the techniques of non-canonical sequencing and association of clips with a fan-selected song constitute a refusal of the loss of significant communication between Bianca and Lena that plagued them for months on *All My Children* after Bianca's rape; even when a video shows the women upset or angry, they are generally still interacting, or at least in the same frame together. In terms of clip selection, it obviously isn't possible to detail all of them here, but the following summary of some commonly used scenes should suffice to give the flavor. First and foremost are three kisses between Bianca and Lena: their first kiss, which occurs at the airport as Lena seemed about to leave Pine Valley, their second as they end a slow dance at midnight on New Year's Eve, and their last one in Lena's final onscreen appearance. Also popular are excerpts from Bianca and Lena's first (and only onscreen) date in March 2003, which involves touching hands, significant eye contact, and a long hug; a scene from a July 2003 episode when Bianca and Lena sit closely on a bench in a moonlit park, talking and touching each other tenderly; and clips from a November 2003 episode when Bianca is visiting Lena in jail, during which the two hold hands through the bars and look at each other intensely. Also, in an August 2003 episode, with Bianca having inexplicably pushed her away (after the rape), Lena has a daydream in which the two are dressed in faintly bride-like garb, with close-ups of their clasped hands showing both wearing the commitment rings that Lena had offered to Bianca a couple of weeks prior (and which in reality, Bianca had declined).

Extracts from one of these scenes conclude 20 of the 29 Lianca videos I have, and another four videos end with a clip that suggests that Bianca and Lena are or will be together. This is a key narrative characteristic that distinguishes the videos from the Bianca/Lena relationship as it was depicted on the canonical show for much of the time. An upbeat final clip is frequently used, even in videos in which much of the visual narrative and the song's lyrics suggest a less heartening outlook on love and relationships. For example, one video set to 3 Doors Down's *Here Without You* (2002) mostly features clips of Lena being sad after Bianca had spurned her, yet it ends with Bianca lying in Lena's lap (a clip from a March 2004 episode); similarly, the second half of a video that uses *Why They Call It Falling* (2002) matches the disillusionment with love that Lee Ann Womack sings about, except for Bianca and Lena's New Year's Eve kiss in its final moments, a contrast to the song's more bittersweet tenor. Thus, a Lianca video with a generally downbeat tone that nevertheless closes with a moment of connection between the two women is one way that fans could assert the possibility, as well as the desirability, of this couple ending up together, even in the face of pain and other relationship difficulties. . . .

In the context of fan videos more generally, to some extent Lianca videos are like those centered on other canonical, and hence usually heterosexual, television pairings: creative efforts that allow fans to fashion narratives about their preferred couples that provide additional and often more rewarding viewing experiences than watching the show. On the other hand, the Bianca/Lena romance is one of several same-sex relationships on U.S. television that has disappointed viewers, and in that light, the Lianca video oeuvre has continuity with slash from an earlier generation of fan culture, in constructing more satisfying stories about queer relationships than those told by heterocentric and heterosexist television shows.

Still, analyses of male/male slash, as motivated, in part, by a theoretically interesting and politically significant impulse to re-imagine gender, do not apply to the Lianca videos as a whole. On *All My Children,* Bianca and Lena may have been in a lesbian relationship, but except for each woman's choice of another woman as a romantic partner, neither character departed from fairly conventional gender roles for female characters—Bianca the loving daughter, sister, and then mother; Lena starting out as a femme fatale, and then becoming the loyal would-be lover who seemed to have little of importance to do outside of her relationship with Bianca. Nor were Bianca and Lena's intimate interactions significantly different from what we are accustomed to seeing between other women onscreen—talking, touching, and hugging, with only a few kisses in the whole year of their relationship. . . .

Alternative modes of sexual expression—couplings motivated by sexual pleasure or multi-partner encounters, for example—remain backgrounded in much of popular fandom, as is true in the dominant culture. While popular media representation is only one domain in which normativity is constructed and contested, it is a significant one. With the fight for same-sex marriage occupying center-stage in the American gay rights movement, at the expense of a broader reconsideration of social strictures on sexual and gender expression, the Lianca music videos are also texts that reproduce and reinforce the dominant liberal defense of same-sex relationships—that they are (and should be) about love and long-term commitment. In writing about the formation of the gay commercial market in the United States, Sender (2004) notes that it was "constituted in part through the political marginalization of GLBT people" (p. 240) who did not fit the mould of ideal gay consumers. A comparable phenomenon of marginalization exists in lesbian fan culture, in which dominant norms often remain uninterrogated. . . .

Notes

*["The canon" and "canonical" refer throughout this chapter to the officially authorized texts of *All My Children* episodes, as broadcast by ABC, as opposed to unauthorized, fan-produced materials making use of those texts in new ways. Ed.]

1. Although scholars have applied the term "slash" to narratives about both male-male and female-female relationships, authors of lesbian fan fiction often do not use the term. In the *Xena* fandom, for example, the categories Gen(eral) and Alt(ernative) emerged, with the first indicating heterosexual relationship and the second, same sex-relationships. Some writers use the term "femslash," while other consider stories about canonical relationships to not be slash at all. For convenience, I use "slash" to refer to narratives about both canonical and non-canonical same-sex pairings.

2. Post-*Xena,* besides Bianca and Lena on *All My Children,* these have included Willow

and Tara on *Buffy the Vampire Slayer* (WB, 1997–2001; UPN, 2001–2003), Kerry and Kim on *ER* (NBC, 1994–present), Spencer and Ashley on *South of Nowhere* (The N, 2005–present), Paige and Alex on *Degrassi: The Next Generation* (CTV, 2001–present and The N, 2002–present), as well as couples on *Bad Girls* (first on Britain's ITV, 1999–2006; currently in North America on Logo, 2006–present), *The L Word* (Showtime, 2003–present), and other premium cable shows such as *Queer as Folk* (Showtime, 2000–2005) and *The Wire* (HBO, 2002–present).

3. "Mashup" also refers to audio products from musical blending, usually involving coupling the vocals from one song with the instruments from another (Cruger, 2003; Frere-Jones, 2005).

4. Hurt-comfort is a genre of fan fiction, although the basic elements are also often present in the narratives of source texts, particularly action-adventure shows. Generally, one character is physically and/or psychically injured, and another character cares for them, creating a context of greater intimacy and intensity of relating than usual.

5. Self-designated "BAMmers/bammers" (i.e., people in support of a Bianca und Maggie romantic relationship), these fans undertook a campaign aimed at the *All My Children* writers and ABC daytime drama executives that, although not at the time successful in terms of having Bianca and Maggie get together, did alert ABC and *AMC* that there was interest in having Bianca depicted in a relationship with another woman, and helped pave the way for the introduction of Lena as Bianca's love interest (see Warn, 2003a).

6. Olga Sosnovska did not sign a contract as a regular with *All My Children* until May 2003; before that she had been a guest star.

7. This message board used to be officially associated with Olga Sosnovska, but at her request, this relationship was cordially terminated, and after some debate, the board moderators re-named it "The Symposium" in early 2006. Technical issues in 2007 resulted in the loss of many threads, including those which had publicized fan videos.

8. I recall a few posters at the message boards identifying themselves as male and/or straight in the context of pertinent discussions (e.g., threads about how broadly Lianca appealed to the *All My Children* audience), but most spoke of themselves as lesbians for whom much of the appeal of the Bianca/Lianca relationship was that it was a romance between two women.

9. For example, one Lianca vidder recalled that, for the sole Lianca music video she made, "I heard the Lianca story, from Lena's point of view, in Jonathan Brooke's song. It struck me that many of the lyrics could describe scenes shared by Lena and Bianca. It was just something that I saw in my head every time I heard the song, so I decided to create it for others to see." In a similar vein, another vidder, who made several Lianca videos, wrote that "I would just hear a song and start seeing clips. I would be driving down the road and it would just hit."

10. Twenty-six of the videos used a popular song released 1998 or later (i.e., within about five years of the time that most videos were made); eight used a song released 1990–1997 and one a song released in 1989; the other two were set to instrumental pieces. The songs included *Because I Told You So* (1997), sung by Jonathan Brooke; *Have You Ever Been in Love* (2002), sung by Celine Dion; *Mime* (1990), sung by Heart; *The Reason* (2003), sung by Hoobastank; *Loneliness* (2001), sung by Annie Lennox; *When I Found You* (2001), sung by Britney Spears; and *Just Another* (2001), sung by Pete Yorn.

References

Bacon-Smith, C. (1992). *Enterprising women: Television fandom and the creation of popular myth*. Philadelphia: University of Pennsylvania Press.

Boyd, K. S. (2001). "One index finger on the mouse scroll bar and the other on my clit": Slash writers' views on pornography, censorship, feminism and risk. PhD dissertation, Simon Fraser University. Retrieved June 15, 2007, from http:www.collectionscanda.ca/obj/s4/f2/dsk3/ftp04/mQ61537.pdf

Cicione, M. (1998). Male pair-bonds and female desire in fan slash writing. In C. Harris & A. Alexander (Eds.), *Theorizing fandom; Fans, subculture and identity* (pp. 153–177). Cresskill, NJ: Hampton Press.

Cruger, R. (2003, August 9). The mash-up revolution. *Salon.com.* Retrieved June 15, 2007, from http://dir.salon.com/story/ent/music/feature/2003/08/09/mashups_cruger/index_ np.html?pn=1

Doty, A. (1993). *Making things perfectly queer: Interpreting mass culture.* Minneapolis; University of Minnesota Press.

Dutta, M. B. (1999). Taming the victim: Rape in soap opera. *Journal of Popular Film and Television, 27*(1), 33–39.

Frere-Jones, S. (2005, January 10). 1 + I + 1 = 1: The new math of mashups. *New Yorker.* Retrieved June 15, 2007, from http.//www.newyorker.com/archive/2005/01/10/050110crmu_music

Gibson, R. (2006). From zero to 24–7: Images of sexual minorities on television. In L. Castaneda & S. Campbell (Eds.), *News and sexuality: Media portraits of diversity* (pp. 256–277). Thousand Oaks, CA: Sage.

Green, S., Jenkins, C., & Jenkins, H. (1998). "The normal female interest in men bonking": Selections from *The Terra Nostra Underground* and *Strange Bedfellows.* In C. Harris & A. Alexander (Eds.), *Theorizing fandom: Fans, subculture, and identity* (pp. 9–38). Cresskill, NY: Hampton Press.

Gross, L. (2002). *Up from invisibility: Lesbians, gay men, and the media in America.* New York: Columbia University Press.

Harrington, C. L. (2003a). Lesbian(s) on daytime television: The Bianca narrative on *All My Children. Feminist Media Studies, 3*(2), 211–232.

Harrington, C. L. (2003b). Homosexuality on *All My Children:* Transforming the daytime landscape. *Journal of Broadcasting & Electronic Media, 47,* 216–235.

Herman, A., Coombe, R., & Kaye, L. (2006). Your second life? Goodwill and the performativity of intellectual property in online digital gaming. *Cultural Studies, 20*(2–3), 184–210.

Jenkins, H. (1992). *Textual poachers: Television fans and participatory culture.* London: Routledge.

Jones, R. (2006). From shooting monsters to shooting movies: Machinima and the transformative play of video game fan culture. In K. Hellekson & K. Busse (Eds.), *Fan fiction and fan communities in the age of the Internet* (pp. 261–280). Jefferson, NC: McFarland & Company.

Jung, S. (2004). Queering popular culture: Female spectators and the appeal of writing slash fan fiction. *Gender Forum Gender Queeries, 8,* Retrieved June 15, 2007, from http://www.genderforum.uni-koeln.de/queer/jung.html

Kleder, M. (2003). Daytime goes pay time: *All My Children* features lesbian affair. Retrieved June 15, 2007, from http://www.cwa.org/articles/3814/CFI/cfreport/index.htm

Merrill, D. (2006, October 16). Mashups: The new breed of Web app. Retrieved June 15, 2007, from http://www.ibm.com/developerworks/xml/library/x-mashups.html

Penley, C. (1991). Brownian motion: Women, ladies, and technology. In C. Penley & A. Ross (Eds.), *Technoculture* (pp. 35–161). Minneapolis: University of Minnesota Press.

Projansky, S. (2001). *Watching rape: Film and television in postfeminist culture.* New York: New York University Press.

Radway, J. (1984). *Reading the romance: Women, patriarchy, and popular literature.* Chapel Hill, NC: University of North Carolina Press.

Russ, J. (1985). Pornography by women for women, with love. In J. Russ (Au.), *Magic mommas, trembling sisters, puritans & perverts: Feminist essays* (pp. 79–99). Trumansburg, NY: Crossing Press.

Russo, J. L. (2002). NEW VOY "cyborg sex" J/7 [NC-I7J 1/1: New methodologies, new fantasies]. Retrieved June 15, 2007, from http://j-1-r.org/asmic/fanfic/print/jlr-cyborgsex.pdf

Russo, V. (1987). *The celluloid closet: Homosexuality in the movies.* New York: Harper.

Scodari, C. (2003). Resistance reexamined: Gender, fan practices, and science fiction television. *Popular Communication, 1*(2), 111–130.

Sender, K. (2004). *Business, not politics: The making of the gay market.* New York: Columbia University Press.

Stein. L. (2006). "This dratted thing": Fannish storytelling through new media. In K. Hellekson & K. Busse (Eds.), *Fan fiction and fan communities in the age of the Internet* (pp. 245–260). Jefferson, NC: McFarland & Company.

Tropiano, S. (2002). *The prime tune closet: A history of guys and lesbians on TV.* New York: Applause Books.

Warn, S. (2003a). The battle for Bianca and Maggie on *All My Children.* Retrieved June 15, 2007, from http://www.afterellen.com/archive/TV/ame-bam.html

Warn, S. (2003b). *All My Children:* A lesbian kiss to build a dream on? Retrieved June 15, 2007, from http://www.afterellen.com/archive/ellenTv/amc-kiss.html

Warner, M. (1999). *The trouble with normal: Sex, politics, and the ethics of queer life.* Cambridge, MA: Harvard University Press.

Wilder, J. C. (1998, October) Romancing the fan: Romance and Xena fan fiction. *Whoosh,* 25. Retrieved June 15, 2007, from http://whoosh.org/issue25/wilder.html

Woledge, E. (2005). From slash to the mainstream: Female writers and gender blending men. *Extrapolation, 46*(1), 50–65.

65

"Don't Hate the Player, Hate the Game"

The Racialization of Labor in *World of Warcraft*

Lisa Nakamura

Massively Multiplayer Online Role Playing Games (MMOs) such as *World of Warcraft* (*WoW*), *Lineage II*, and *Everquest* are immensely profitable, skillfully designed, immersive and beautifully detailed virtual worlds that enable both exciting gameplay and the creation of real time digitally embodied communities. This year, *World of Warcraft* surpassed 10 million users, confirming games economist Edward Castronova's (2005) predictions for exponential growth, and these players are intensely interested in and protective of their investments in the virtual world of Azeroth. This stands to reason: as Alexander Galloway (2006) writes, "virtual worlds are always in some basic way the expression of Utopian desire." One of their primary rallying points as a group has been to advocate strongly that Blizzard regulate cheating within the game more stringently; however, the definition of cheating is unclear, despite the game's End User License Agreement (EULA), since many players break these rules with impunity, a state of affairs which is actually the norm in MMO's.[1] As Mia Consalvo (2007) argues, it makes much less sense to see cheating within games as a weakness of game design or a problem with player behavior than to see it as an integral part of game culture, a feature that keeps players from getting "stuck" and quitting. "Cheating" thus benefits players and the game industry alike. However, cheating is as varied in its forms as is gameplay itself, and some varieties are viewed by players as socially undesirable, while others are not.

Though Consalvo (2007) stresses the extremely subjective ways that MMO players define cheating, asserting that "a debate exists around the definition of cheating and

From Nakamura, L. (2009). "Don't hate the player, hate the game": The racialization of labor in *World of Warcraft. Critical Studies in Media Communication*, 26(2), 128–144. Copyright © National Communication Association, reprinted by permission of Taylor & Francis Ltd. (http://www.tandfonline.com) on behalf of The National Communication Association.

whether it actually hurts other players [and] players themselves see little common ground in what constitutes cheating" (p. 150), real-money trading (RMT), or buying and selling in-game property for real money, is widely considered the worst, more morally reprehensible form of cheating. In particular, the practice of gold farming, or selling in-game currency to players for real money, usually through resellers such as IGE or EBay, is especially disliked. Leisure players have been joined by worker players from poorer nations such as China and Korea who are often subject to oppression as both a racio-linguistic minority, and as undesirable underclassed social bodies in the context of game play and game culture.[2] These "farmers," as other players dismissively dub them, produce and sell virtual goods such as weapons, garments, animals, and even their own leveled-up avatars or "virtual bodies" to other players for "real world" money. As Consalvo (2007) writes, the "gill-buying practice is viscerally despised by some players" (p. 164). . . .

Though as T. L. Taylor (2006) notes, MMOs are distinguished by their "enormous potential in a fairly divisive world," the "fact that people play with each other across regions and often countries" as often as not results in ethnic and racial chauvinism: "as a tag the conflation of Chinese with gold farmer has seemed to come all too easy and now transcends any particular game" (p. 321). Robert Brookey (2007) expands upon this claim; in his analysis of gaming blogs, he discovered "overt racist attitudes" towards Chinese farmers; most importantly, that "some players, who harbor negative feelings toward Chinese farmers, do not believe that these feelings denote racial discrimination." Thus, though it is the case that players cannot see each others' bodies while playing, specific forms of gamic labor, such as gold farming and selling, as well as specific styles of play have become racialized as Chinese, producing new forms of networked racism

that are particularly easy for players to disavow.

Unlike the Internet itself, MMOs have *always* been a global medium, with many games originating in Asia.[3] Korea has been a major player in the industry from its beginning, but Asian players are numerous even in American-run MMOs such as Blizzard's *WoW*; in 2008, the number of simultaneous players on Chinese *WoW* servers exceeded 1 million, the most that have ever been recorded in Europe or the U.S. ("Blizzard," 2008). Thus, though gold farmers are typecast as Chinese, most Asian players are "leisure players," not player workers. . . .

Perhaps because most digital game scholars are players themselves, the economics of gold farming are usually discussed in the scholarly literature in terms of their negative impact upon the "world" of leisure players, who buy gold because they lack the time to earn virtual capital through "grinding" or performing the repetitive and tedious tasks that are the basis of most MMOs. However, as Toby Miller (2006) has advocated, digital games scholars need to attend to its medium's political economy, and to "follow the money" to its less glamorous, less "virtual" places, like games console and PC manufacturing plants, gold farmer sweatshops, and precious metals reclamation sites—in short, to China. Yet while many players are fairly unaware that their computer hardware is born and dies, or is *recycled*, in China, they are *exceptionally* aware of the national, racial, and linguistic identity of gold farmers. Gold farmers are reviled player-workers whose position in the gamic economy resembles that of other immigrant groups who cross national borders in order to work, but unlike other types of "migrant" workers, their labors are offshore, and thus invisible—they are "virtual migrants."[4] However, user generated content in and around MMOs actively visualizes this process. Machinima fan-produced video production racializes this reviled form of gameplay as "Oriental" in ways that hail earlier visual media such as music videos and minstrel shows. Gold farming, a burgeoning "grey market" labor practice in a disliked and semi-illegal industry that as Consalvo (2007) notes, may soon outstrip the primary games market as a source of revenue, has become racialized as Asian, specifically as Chinese. . . .

WoW and other virtual worlds have been touted for their democratic potential—as Castronova (2005) puts it:

> People entering a synthetic world can have, in principle, any body they desire. At a stroke, this feature of synthetic worlds removes from the social calculus all the unfortunate effects that derive from the body . . . all without bearing some of the burdens that adhere to the Earth bodies we were born with. (pp. 25–26)

The social calculus of race, nation, and class are burdens borne by Chinese gold farmers, Chinese leisure players, and ultimately, the gaming community as a whole. Hatred of Chinese gold farmers drives *WoW* users to produce visual and textual media that hews closely to earlier anti-Asian discourses, media that they broadcast to other users through forums, general chat in-game, and "homemade" videos.

World of Warcraft is a virtual world where significant numbers of people are conducting their psychic, financial, and social lives. This massively multiplayer online game continues to roll out content for its users in the form of expansion packs, frequent software updates, action figures and a feature film in development, and an extensive content-rich and frequently updated website for its community of users. Users are invited by Blizzard to get involved in some aspects of this world's production by contributing interesting screenshots, machinima, personal narratives, and advice on gameplay to their site, and even in cases when they are not, players actively produce in defiance of its

wishes. Topics that the game industry may wish to avoid because they may seem divisive, or may reflect badly on the virtual world, are confronted frequently in participatory media created by its users.

Machinima as User-Generated Racial Narrative: The Media Campaign Against Chinese Player-Workers in *WoW*

Machinima is a crucial site of struggle over the meaning of race in shared digital space, and it is a central part of the culture of MMOs such as *World of Warcraft*. Machinima has recently become the object of much academic interest because it exemplifies the notion of participatory media, an influential and useful formulation that is the basis for Jenkins' (2006) book *Convergence Culture*. In it, Jenkins describes how machinima are prime examples of users' seizing the right to contribute to media universes in defiance of industry wishes, standards, and control; their value lies in the ability to produce counternarratives whose impact lies in their active subversion of the narrow messages available in many dominant media texts. Machinima literally extend the storyspace of the games upon which they are based, and the most interesting of these actively work to reconfigure their original meanings in progressive, socially productive ways. Jenkins explains that transmediated storyspaces which exist across media platforms permit increased opportunities for engaged users like fans to insert their own content into these "synthetic worlds," to use Castronova's (2005) phrase—while game developers like Blizzard provide limited, licensed, and fairly tightly controlled virtual space for players to navigate, users extend this space by writing fan fiction, creating original artwork, and making their own movies or machinima using images, narratives, and tropes from the game.

While part of the pleasure of *World of Warcraft* consists in navigating its richly imaged, beautifully rendered spaces, users must rely upon the company to provide more of this valuable commodity in the form of expansion packs such as "The Burning Crusade" and "The Wrath of the Lich King," eagerly anticipated and extremely profitable products for which users are willing to stand in line for days at a time. Machinima permits users to expand this space for free; while navigable space is still tightly controlled by the company—unlike in *Second Life*, users are unable to build their own structures or objects to insert in the world—machinima allows users to extend its representational or narrative space, creating scenarios that are genuinely new because they depict activities or behaviors impossible in the space of the game. This is a fascinating area of study, and one that is a thriving and integral part of *WoW* in particular. The struggle for resources integral to the structure of MMOs can also be re-envisioned as the struggle to own or claim virtual space and to police national boundaries as well.[5] Player-produced machinima accessed from Warcraftmovies.com make arguments about race, labor, and the racialization of space in *World of Warcraft*.[6] These highly polemical texts employ the visual language of the game, one of the most recognizable and distinctive ever created for shared virtual play, to bring into sharp relief the contrast between the privileges of media production available to empowered players with the time and inclination to create machinima, and those who are shut out of this aspect of *WoW* by their status as worker players. Participatory media is a privilege of the leisure class; active fandom is too expensive a proposition for many digital workers, who as Dibbell explains poignantly, can't afford to *enjoy* the game that they have mastered, much less produce media to add to it.[7]

Unsurprisingly, there are two tiers of this type of user production—Blizzard frequently solicits screenshots, holds art contests, and showcases user-produced machinima that become part of the "official" canon of the game. However, there is extensive traffic in content that is not endorsed by the developer, but which is nonetheless part of the continuing rollout of the world. Racial discourse is a key part of this rollout. If the official *World of Warcraft* game is a gated community, one that users pay to enter, its covenants consist in its EULA [End-User License Agreement]. However, part of Jenkins' (2006) argument is that media technologies such as the Internet have made it impossible to "gate" media in the same way. The "underground" machinima I will discuss in this chapter build and expand the world of *WoW* in regards to representations of race in just as constitutive a way as its official content. As Lowood (2006) notes, *WoW* players have been creating visual moving image records as long as, or perhaps even longer than, they have been playing the game. Thus, machinima is anything but a derivative or ancillary form in relation to *WoW*, for its history runs exactly parallel, and in some sense, slightly in advance of the game itself—as Lowood notes, users were employing the beta version of *WoW* to make machinima before the game was available to the public. Lowood claims, "*WoW* movies, from game film to dance videos, have become an integral part of the culture shared by a player community" (p. 374).

If indeed machinima extend the world of gameplay, how are players co-creating this world? Anti-farmer machinima produces overtly racist narrative space to attach to a narrative that, while carefully avoiding overt references to racism or racial conflict in our world, is premised upon a racial war in an imaginary world—the World of Azeroth. While Jenkins (2006) celebrates the way that fans, particularly female fans, have extended the worlds of *Star Trek* in truly liberatory ways, inserting homosexual narratives between Captain

Kirk and Spock that the franchise would never permit or endorse, a closer look at user produced content from Warcraftmovies .com reveals a contraction and retrenchment of concepts of gender, race, and nation rather than their enlargement.

Warcraftmovies.com, the most popular *World of Warcraft* machinima website, organizes its user generated content under several different categories. "Underground" machinima deals with topics such as "bug/exploit," "exploration," and "gold farming." "Ni Hao (A Gold Farmer's Story)" by "Nyhm" of "Madcow Studios" has earned a "4 x Platinum" rating, the highest available, from Warcraftmovies.com, and it is also available on *YouTube,* where it has been viewed 533,567 times, has been favorited 1,998 times, and has produced 981 comments from users ("Ni Hao"). This extremely popular, visually sophisticated machinima music video features new lyrics sung over the instrumental track of Akon's hit hip hop song "Smack That." This polemical anti-Asian machinima's chorus is:

> I see you farmin' primals in Shadow moon Valley, 10 cents an hour's good money when you are Chinese, I buy your auctions you sell my gold right back to me, feels like you're bendin' me over, you smile and say "ni hao" and farm some gold, "ni hao" it's getting old, ni hao, oh.

The claim that "10 cents an hour's good money when you are Chinese" displays awareness that the farmers' incentive for exploiting or "bending over" better-resourced players comes from economic need. Another part of the video shows a "farmer" shoveling gold into a vault, with the subtitled lyric "IGE's making bank now." The International Gaming Exchange is one of the largest re-sellers of gold, avatar level-ups, and other virtual property, and it is an American business, not an Asian one. Nonetheless, this commentary on the gold farming economic system resorts to the full

gamut of racial stereotypes, including a Chinese flag as the background for a video scene of a sexy singing female Troll in a scanty outfit flanked by the human "farmers" wielding pickaxes and shovels.

Later in the video, a Chinese gold farmer is killed by another player, who comments as he kneels next to the corpse that "this China-man gets fired, that's one farmer they'll have to replace, not supposed to be here in the first place." . . . Clearly, Asian players, specifically those suspected of being "farmers" but as this image [suggests], all "China-men" have a diminished status on *WoW:* many American players fail to see them as "people." . . . The video depicts them as all owning exactly the same avatar, a male human wearing a red and gold outfit and wielding a pickaxe. This dehumanization of the Asian player—they "all look the same" because they all *are* the same—is evocative of earlier conceptions of Asian laborers as interchangeable and replaceable. . . .

Conclusion

The anti-Asian racial discourse in "Ni Hao," as well as that noted in Brookey's (2007), Steinkuehler's (2006), and Taylor's (2006) research are not necessarily representative of the *WoW* population as a whole (though it must be said that while *YouTube* and Warcraftmovies are full of machinima or trophy videos of farmer-killing replete with racist imagery, there are no pro-farmer user-produced machinima to be seen).[8] Machinima is a breakthrough medium because it differs from previous mass forms of media or performance; it is the product of individual users. However, like the minstrel shows that preceded it, it shapes the culture by disseminating arguments about the nature of race, labor, and assimilation. . . .

Similarly, it is certainly not the case that games must be entirely free of racist discourse in order to be culturally important or socially productive, in short, to be "good." No multiplayer social game could meet that criterion at all times. On the other hand, if we are to take games seriously as "synthetic worlds," we must be willing to take their racial discourses, media texts, and interpersonal conflicts seriously as well. As Dibbell (2006) claims, it is constraint and scarcity—the challenge of capital accumulation—that makes MMOs pleasurable, even addictive. Game economies based on cultures of scarcity engender Real Money Transfer, and as long as this form of player-work is socially debased and racialized, it will result in radically unequal social relations, labor types, and forms of representation along the axes of nation, language, and identity. Asian worker players are economically unable to accumulate avatarial capital and thus become "persons"; they are the dispossessed subjects of synthetic worlds. As long as Asian "farmers" are figured as unwanted guest workers within the culture of MMOs, user-produced extensions of MMO-space like machinima will most likely continue to depict Asian culture as threatening to the beauty and desirability of shared virtual space in the *World of Warcraft*.

Notes

1. Players of *WoW* regularly use an arsenal of "mods" and "add-ons" that are circulated on player boards online; though these are technically in violation of the End User License Agreement (EULA), many players consider the game unplayable without them, especially at the terminal or "end game" levels. Blizzard turns a blind eye to this, and in fact tacitly condones it by posting technical updates referring to the impact of add-ons on game performance.

2. See T. L. Taylor (2006), on in-game language chauvinism and the informal enforcement of "English only" chat in *WoW* even by players of non-Anglophone nationalities.

3. See Chan (2006), as well as the January 2008 special issue of *Games and Culture* on Asia, volume 3, number 1, in particular Hjorth's (2008) introductory essay "Games@Neo-Regionalism: Locating Gaming in the Asia-Pacific."

4. See (Aneesh, 2006).

5. As Brookey (2007) argues, national boundaries have been reproduced in cyberspace, and the location of the servers that generate these virtual environments are used to demarcate the borders. These respondents claim that if Chinese players experience discrimination on U.S. servers, it is because they have crossed the border into territory where they do not belong and are not welcome.

6. The phrase "player-produced machinima" is in some sense a redundant one, since machinima is from its inception an amateur form; however it is becoming an increasingly necessary distinction as professional media producers appropriate it. *South Park*'s "Make Love Not Warfare" was co-produced with Blizzard Entertainment, and Toyota has aired a 2007 commercial made in the same way. See http://www.machinima.com/film/view&id= 23588. In an example of media synergy, *South Park* capitalized on the success and popularity of the episode by bundling a *World of Warcraft* trial game card along with the DVD box set of its most recent season.

7. See Dibbell (2007) for an eloquent account of "Min," a highly skilled worker player who took great pride in being his raiding party's "tank," a "heavily armed warrior character who . . . is the linchpin of any raid" (p. 41). His raiding team would take "any customer" into a dangerous dungeon where a lower level player could never survive alone and let them pick up the valuable items dropped there, thus acting like virtual African shikaris or Nepalese porters. Min greatly enjoyed these raids but was eventually forced to quit them and take up farming again when they proved insufficiently profitable.

8. UC San Diego doctoral candidate Ge Jin's distributive filmmaking project on the lives of Chinese worker players in MMOs can be viewed at http://www.chinesegoldfarmers.com .His films, which can also be viewed on *YouTube*, contain documentary footage of Chinese worker

players laboring in "gaming workshops" in Shanghai. His interviews with them make it clear that these worker players are well aware of how despised they are by American and European players, and that they feel a sense of "inferiority" that is articulated to their racial and ethnic identity.

References

Aneesh, A. (2006). *Virtual migration: The programming of globalization.* Durham, NC: Duke University Press.

Blizzard Entertainment's *World of Warcraft*: The Burning Crusade surpasses one million peak concurrent player milestone in mainland China. (2008). *PR Newswire: United Business Media.* Retrieved May 28, 2008, from http://ww.pmewswiie.com/news/index-mail.shtml?ACCT=104&STORY=/www/story/04–11–2008/000479086&EDATE=

Brookey, R. A. (2007, November). *Racism and nationalism in cyberspace: Comments on farming in MMORPGS.* Paper presented at the National Communication Association Annual Convention, Chicago.

Castronova, E. (2005). *Synthetic worlds: The business and culture of online games.* Chicago: University of Chicago Press.

Chan, D. (2006). Negotiating Intra-Asian games networks: On cultural proximity, East Asian games design, and Chinese farmers. *Fibreculture, 8.* Retrieved May 28, 2008, from http://journalfibreculture.org/issue8/issue8_chan.html

Consalvo, M. (2007). *Cheating: Gaining advantage in videogames.* Cambridge, MA: The MIT Press.

Dibbell, J. (2006). *Play Money.* New York: Basic Books.

Dibbell, J. (2007, June 17). The life of the Chinese gold farmer. *The New York Times Magazine,* 36–41.

Galloway, A. (2006). Warcraft and Utopia. *1000 days of theory.* Retrieved April 11, 2008, from ctheory.net/printer.aspx?id=507

Hjorth, L (2008). Games@Neo-regionalism: Locating gaming in the Asia-Pacific. *Games and Culture, 3*(1), 3–12.

Jenkins, H. (2006). *Convergence culture: Where old and new media collide.* New York: New York University Press.

Lowood, H. (2006). Storyline, dance/music, or PvP? Game movies and community players in *World of Warcraft. Games and Culture, 1*(4), 362–382.

Miller, T. (2006). Gaming for beginners. *Games and Culture, 1*(1), 5–12.

Ni Hao: A Gold Farmer's Story. Retrieved November 7, 2007, from http://youtube.com/watch? V=odllf5NEI00

Steinkuehler, C. (2006). The mangle of play. *Games and Culture, 1*(3), 199–213.

Taylor, T. L (2006). Does *WoW* change everything? How a PvP server, multinational player base, and surveillance mod scene cause me pause. *Games and Culture, 1*(4), 318–337.

66

Accidental Activists

Fan Activism in the Soap Opera Community

Melissa C. Scardaville

History of Organized Fandom

The origin of organized media fandom is considered by many scholars to be *Star Trek* fans mobilizing in the late 1960s to pressure NBC to keep and later return their show to the airways (Jenkins, 1992, p. 28). Although the *Star Trek* movement provided a model for future television advocacy campaigns (Jenkins, 1992), it is important to note that local pockets of soap fans had successfully lobbied against cancellation as early as 1941 (Cantor & Pingree, 1983).

In fact, soap fans have a long history of being active. During soaps' radio days (from the 1930s to the 1950s), many listeners would respond to certain events by sending cards and/or gifts to the characters, although the frequency with which this occurred is hard to determine because "in those days the severely embarrassed networks had a hush-hush policy about such identity-confusions on the audience fringe" (LaGuardia, 1974, p. 68). By the late 1950s, soap fans routinely contacted the network, most often when a character suddenly died. In 1958, outraged *Guiding Light* fans contacted CBS in droves when a wheelchair-bound character was killed after she was knocked into oncoming traffic (Schemering, 1986, p. 31). When a beloved *Edge of Night* heroine, Sara, was killed in 1961, CBS was hit with 8,000 telegrams and letters, 260 while the day's show was airing (LaGuardia, 1974, p. 119; Schemering, 1987, p. 90). The following year, the same network was bombarded by feedback from viewers protesting the death of a long-term *As the World Turns* character, Jeff, so much so that "TV Guide called the uproar 'the automobile accident that shook the nation'" (Schemering, 1987, p. 31).

The main difference between science fiction activism and soap opera activity lies in their degree of organization (and, hence, why large-scale organized fandom sees its birth

From Melissa C. Scardaville, "Accidental Activists: Fan Activism in the Soap Opera Community." *American Behavioral Scientist* (2005), 48 (7), 881–901. Reprinted with permission of SAGE Publications.

in science fiction, not soaps). Throughout much of soaps' history, there was no overarching structure that provided guidelines to the protestor and, perhaps even more important, a space where fans could gather. The first daytime fan clubs, most of which were not show- but actor-specific, were not established until the early 1970s. Large-scale gatherings occurred almost concurrently; the most common of which were when two or more actor-driven fan clubs joined forces to host a luncheon in New York City, the place where most soaps then taped. The main point of these clubs, and indeed their modern-day counterparts, was to operate as a publicity tool—as opposed to providing means for critical discourse (Bielby et al., 1999, p. 40). By the time *Star Trek* fans began to mobilize in the late 1960s, local, national, and global organizations dedicated to the science fiction fan had been in place for more than three decades, and these clubs had a long-established history of blending politics and activism into their activities (Lynch, 2001).

Soap fans may not have formed collective groups as early for one or two possible reasons. First, soap operas had the ability to address any fan outrage quickly, in part because they were broadcast live or taped very shortly in advance until 1975 (Cantor & Pingree, 1983, p. 61). In the case of *Edge of Night* character Sara, the producers, concerned that viewers were confusing reality and fiction, put the actress on television the day after her character was killed so she could inform the audience that it was her choice to leave (LaGuardia, 1974, pp. 119–20). When *Days of Our Lives* character Addie was diagnosed with cancer in 1973, letters poured in until the show's creator changed the direction of the story and Addie lived, albeit temporarily (LaGuardia, 1983, p. 6). . . .

In addition, research done on the early soap audience reveals several key points: The majority were 18- to 49-year-old married women who stayed at home while their spouses worked, had no postsecondary education, were most likely to have been affected by the Great Depression, and lived in a rural area (Matelski, 1988, pp. 36–40). Resources—mainly time, space, and money—were not readily available to these women; any networking that did occur was limited. What soap fans needed was a space where they could gather to communicate about the show, a place that was eventually found on the Internet.

Online Communities and E-Activism

Soap communities exploded online in the 1990s, most specially, rec.arts.tv.soaps (r.a.t.s.), Usenet newsgroups dedicated to soap operas. During the early 1990s, out of almost 5,000 Usenet newsgroups, r.a.t.s. ranked in the top 15 of the highest traffic groups (Baym, 1995, p. 138).

Within this virtual space, fans bonded and could engage in faster and potentially more personal communication with executives and actors. For instance, when Brian Frons took over as head of ABC Daytime in 2002, he immediately began answering fan e-mails addressed to him. On personal Web pages, actors frequently began announcing storyline information before it was released to the press, posted messages to their fans, and established forums about their on- and off-screen lives. Actors not officially tied to a board still have chosen to post to a particular site. For those who preferred to remain anonymous, the Internet provided a relatively safe way to leak news soon after it occurred, particularly crucial now because soaps tape at least 3 weeks in advance. Whereas in the early days of soaps, a death would often take the audience by surprise, an active fan on the Internet could now be alerted to story points before they took place on air. The rapid-fire release and broad transmittal of that information virtually closed the gap between action and audience response. Moreover, because more behind-the-scenes happenings were revealed in another place (and arguably more often, and in more detail) than the soap press, often by those experiencing it firsthand, fans became more aware of what went into the decision-making process—such as an actor's likeability, who stormed off the set, and the data culled from a focus group. . . .

The Internet not only enabled fans to connect more easily with one another but also, according to Connie P. Hayman (personal communication, May 3, 2004), journalist and former opinion writer for *Soap Opera Weekly*, "[Fans] were emboldened by one another." Although Sloane believes that fan feedback is most likely to be incorporated when the show is struggling with ratings, or the fans' goals overlap with the course of action planned, she believes that "fans have much more power now, and it's because of the availability of the information. [For executives], it's like having a focus group right at your fingertips on the Internet" (S. Sloane, personal communication, May 14, 2004). . . .

Method

Ien Ang (1989) argued that any examination into television viewer activity would benefit from the author revealing how she or he is connected to the participants. To understand the genesis of this study, a brief look into my own history with soap fandom is warranted. In 1998, determined to save the show I had watched for 10 years, I joined the Save *Another World* campaign, after reading online rumors suggesting the show was in danger. After connecting with other campaign members, I quickly learned that other fans had been engaged in an organized fight to keep the show on the air since 1993. In April 1999, NBC announced that they were indeed canceling the show; the final episode aired 2 months later. Shortly thereafter, I heard from a group of online fans that *Soap Opera Digest* online was holding an essay contest titled "What

Another World Means to Me." I entered and won, and one of my prizes was a tour of the magazine's headquarters. While there, the editors suggested I send them a résumé. Two months later, I began working at the magazine as the show editor for another Procter & Gamble (P&G) soap opera.

After working at the magazine for several years—and encountering many of the same difficulties described by Bacon-Smith (1992) and Jenkins (1992) as when a science fiction fan/writer attempts to enter the world of professional authors—I desired to get a better understanding of the *AW* campaigns and their members. To that end, I designed a questionnaire with both closed and open questions to measure attitudes about soap opera activism. I sent the survey to fans I had known and who were willing to participate, including the various campaign leaders. They, in turn, put me in touch with other former members. . . .

Analysis

As for *AW* grassroots activism, the first of four distinct yet overlapping campaigns begin in 1993, when the Seattle affiliate pulled *AW*. This sparked a regional campaign to get it back on the air, and after that goal was realized, the group grew into a national organization, one that lobbied for a quality show and put pressure on NBC and P&G when the soap's contract was up for renewal. By 1998, the campaign had morphed into the version that existed through the actual end of the show.

Post-cancellation, the group continued to evolve, first focusing on bringing *AW* back to the air, and then lobbying for particular actors to find work on other soaps. Eventually it evolved into an advocacy group for all of daytime television, but by 2002, it had officially disbanded.

Each *AW* campaign had its own leaders, and although most members wore multiple hats, responsibilities were divided (such as designation of regional media contacts). Each group maintained a Web page that contained information about current activities, and usually had a listserver that distributed news updates and courses of action for the members. Other *AW*-orientated groups often would link their pages to the campaign's site. No monies were collected from members. Generally, only one *AW* campaign existed at a time, the new campaign usually arising when a leadership change occurred.

WHY A CAMPAIGN?

The reasons respondents gave for joining a campaign, as opposed to acting on their own, echoed the theme of Montgomery's (1989) work: They believed that speaking as a group amplified their voices. One respondent observed that

> it wasn't really important to be a "part" of anything. It was just important to me to make my own voice heard. I felt it might have a greater impact coming at the same time a lot of other people were making noise, too.

Being around like-minded individuals was also viewed as a relief. Said another respondent, "It was nice to know I wasn't the only person in the universe that was upset with the-powers-that-be at NBC daytime." Sympathetic insiders, usually actors, would pass information ranging from letter-writing strategies, to the status of a show's contract negotiations, to morale on set. These insider tips provided the same essential benefits as they had to the gay lobby with regard to primetime media, and allowed the *AW* campaigns to operate from an interesting gray area—they were fans who, at many times, possessed the knowledge and skills of insiders.

The tenuous identity of fan/insider also owes its formation to the extensive online networks the campaigns had created. Of those surveyed, all but one learned of the existing *AW* movements online, and the members communicated almost exclusively via the Internet. Moreover, the anonymity of the Web afforded interested *AW* cast and crew and NBC employees to contact the group to offer advice or advance warning. Use of Web pages, discussion forums, and real-time chat allowed more seasoned activist fans to quickly educate neophytes, exchange information on behind-the-scenes happenings, and develop strategies for protest, regardless of geography.

Although the Web was the site to gather and disperse information, most activist activities were carried out offline: petitions, wearing specific ribbons, placing calls to networks, talking to reporters, and boycotting or supporting particular P&G products. Non-virtual actions were selected so that those at NBC and P&G would take the group seriously, and not chalk up this movement to a small number of disgruntled Internet fans. In this way, group members themselves fought against the anonymity of the Web to put a face on fandom; power came from identifying who one was and that he or she was a fan. Centralization of information and leadership were similarly employed in primetime movements, yet not universally seen in Web-based movements. The interlocking identities of fan and activist in this case study are salient in the current cancellation-based primetime advocacy but definitely not present throughout the history of nighttime activism.

Before the Internet, soap fans typically gathered in one of two ways, which corresponded to the way people generally watched soaps—by show (such as the *AW*–fan club luncheon) or by network (such as NBC daytime stars' charity softball games). Both types of events were network and production-company sanctioned, where the focus was not on fan interaction but on the presence of actors. Ironically, this network division may have helped mobilized *AW* fans. Since *AW*'s debut in 1964, NBC had canceled more daytime soap operas than either ABC or CBS. Notably, 9 of the respondents had experienced the cancellation of at least one other NBC soap before. Just as soap watchers decode the fictional messages and devices used to tell these particular stories (Allen, 1985), and many media fans express interest in behind-the-scenes activities (Jenkins, 1992, p. 65), activist fans learn the codes of the network, the production company, the show executives, the ratings system, and the advertiser mentality—in effect, the soap behind the soap. Fans watched what, in retrospect, became precursors to cancellation—affiliates dropping the program, low ratings, storylines departing from themes traditionally associated with the show—occuring on NBC soaps such as *The Doctors*, *Search for Tomorrow*, and *Santa Barbara*. These viewers could now better recognize the red flags when they happened to *AW*—much like what happened with primetime *Arrested Development* fans. The survey suggests that going through these prior soap cancellations created an atmosphere of tension and distrust of the network that needed only a grassroots meeting place, where like minds could gather and find empowerment for community and action. . . .

WHY GET INVOLVED IN THE MOVEMENT—ANGER

> In my opinion, NBC's refusal to acknowledge the fans was basically telling all *AW* fans, "You don't matter to us anymore."
>
> —34-year-old male respondent

Perhaps more so than with any televised medium, soap opera fan feedback has played an essential role in shaping what is seen on-screen. Audiences' impact has ranged from influencing content (for an *AW* example, see Scodari, 1995) to helping reinstate fired actors (Hayward, 1997, p. 165).

In fact, show-initiated projects have long been designed to encourage, or at least support the illusion of, fan influence. The soap media also contribute to this participatory culture, as daytime television magazines have devoted more and more space to viewer feedback (Harrington & Bielby, 1995). How often and to what extent the shows listen to the fans is debatable (Harrington & Bielby, 1995, pp. 161–165), but the precedent that fans can and do have influence has been established.

The members of the *AW* campaign were first and foremost fans of the soap, and they acted precisely because they identified as fans. All survey respondents were regular viewers of *AW* and had watched an average of 22.7 years before they joined a campaign. From their point of view, this was their program and they needed to save it. The majority of respondents (15) had contacted the show prior to their campaign involvement, to express outrage at management decisions they feared would weaken *AW* and further depress ratings. In that sense, when one joined a campaign, his or her activity was a continuation and amplification of an established means of action. Given the climate of encouraged fan response, the respondents—whether they were campaign members at the time or not—became angry that the scope of their influence often appeared very limited. Then, for executives to say, on cancellation in 1999, that *AW* was a "lost cause" was seen by these fans as a slap in the face, because they had protested the very decisions that caused the show to decline. This declaration became an undercurrent for many fans that had not joined a campaign before cancellation to now do so.

Unlike their counterparts in the primetime sphere, according to those surveyed, the *AW* campaigns were not viewed as legitimate by broadcast or advertising executives, perhaps in part because the activism was so closely tied with their members' devalued status as soap fans (Harrington & Bielby 1995, p. 112). Their supporters within the industry were not in a position of power to affect larger, industry opinion of these groups, and the campaigns were not consulted on any P&G/NBC-sanctioned level. Said one member-respondent, "NBC hated what the campaigns were doing. NBC did its best to ignore, aggravate and dissipate AW's fan base any way it could. P&G refused to defend or support its show." AW-campaign members were more often seen as the antagonists, which, as shown below, affected their notions of success.

The executives' response also initiated anger of another kind that led to membership. The network explained that the show was cancelled simply for business reasons, meaning that it was not generating enough profit to justify NBC continuing its arrangement with P&G. Soap opera profit comes indirectly from the Nielsen Ratings, which provide data to advertisers. In the advertising world, some watchers—namely American women age 18 to 49—are more valuable than others. Of the survey participants, 32% indicated that the [industry subservience to] demographics—and the fact that they, the fans, were not members of the "desired demographic"—was a factor that drove them to join an AW campaign. They had begun watching the show while in the desired age range and now, because they had continued to be loyal viewers, had aged out of that demographic.

This presents an interesting conundrum, because soap opera itself was born out of advertising. When it debuted on radio, serial fiction was not targeted to a daytime audience (i.e., women) because it was thought that housewives would not be able to fulfill their duties if distracted (Simon, 1997, p. 15). Irna Phillips melded narrative and advertising and, thus, created soap operas—drama sponsored by and tied into corporate productions (Simon, 1997, p. 18). For instance, a piece of jewelry that the listener could acquire from the sponsor would be incorporated into the script as characters described the lovely broach (LaGuardia, 1974, p. 72). In the late 1930s, production companies,

rejoicing at the windfall profit that the soaps were generating, moved their headquarters from Chicago to New York, to be at the center of the entertainment and advertising world. Soap audiences quickly became well known for their steadfast loyalty to a program, even as it suffered the inevitable creative ups and downs—an advertiser's dream come true. The close relationship between the show and its advertisers may be another reason, in this case, why soap activists relied on numbers. The success of a program is tied to how many of what kind of people watch, therefore encouraging, as these campaigns did, those who represented the "right" demographics to indicate such on their correspondence to the executives, in an attempt to counter low ratings. In other words, the movement tried to say that the ratings system was broken, because they had proof that not only did many of the right people watch, but also there was an untapped audience of males and older female viewers who had discretionary income. . . .

WHY GET INVOLVED IN THE MOVEMENT—OWNERSHIP

It was not "my" Another World anymore.

—40-year-old female respondent

Soaps are designed to appear as if no one author creates the text (Allen, 1985), which leads to the phenomenon Harrington and Bielby (1995) called a "moral author," meaning that a viewer feels a claim to a program, even though he or she did not create it (pp. 155–161). Add to this the incredible longevity of soap operas—because a soap may survive for years, even decades, those who are with the show the longest are often the fans. Take, for instance, that during the years the AW campaign operated, the show had six different executive producers, and 11 head writing teams. Hence, once cancellation was announced, the desire for activism became even more salient—just whose show was it to cancel?

For an American soap opera, as opposed to other forms of serial media such as Latin telenovelas, reaching the end of its run violates its structure, because one of the basic tenets of this kind of daytime drama is its resistance to narrative closure (Allen, 1985). In primetime programming, broadcasting a show's 100th episode is a celebrated event. Yet eight out of the nine current soaps have been on the air 15 years or more; the oldest debuted in 1937, and each churns out 260 episodes a year. Therefore, the pay-off for viewing is not closure but, instead, the ability to watch the next episode with a deeper understanding of the events taking place (Brown, 1994; Hayward, 1997; Modleski, 1979). If there were nothing more to see, what value would one's dedication to, and knowledge of, the show now have?

What is tricky about that question is that, in theory, there was more to see. Like all soaps, AW's stories were not designed to end, a concept best illustrated when looking at a soap's final episodes (Allen, 1985; Modleski, 1979). Most canceled soaps continue to pose new questions or introduce new elements, even in their final hour. In the case of AW, the reappearance of a presumed dead villain in the last episode created the possibility that he would once again stir up trouble in Bay City. In this sense, the fictional universe continues to exist, but viewers have lost access to it. The cancellation of AW seemed to say to fans that the network and sponsor had mishandled a fully functioning universe; access to Bay City could continue or be reinstated, if only the show were in more capable hands.

Because knowledge of a show's history is deeply valued by soap fans, for reasons herein explained (see also Harrington & Bielby, 1995), an AW fan's years of watching no longer held the same meaning after cancellation, or after the show had, in the

fan's mind, veered so far off course that it rarely referred to or built from its own history. This cultural capital of AW knowledge could neither be translated into symbolic capital—for example, becoming a soap writer or television executive—nor exist in its own right, because the universe that imbued it with meaning was now gone (Seiter, 2001, p. 26). So an undercurrent to many of the participants' responses was that the campaign became a means of validating their cumulative history as fans, and a way to reinvest meaning into something that had been devalued.

WHY GET INVOLVED IN THE MOVEMENT— EXTENDING THE FAMILY

> I felt protective of the actors that were on the show, as if it was almost like a family splitting up.
>
> —29-year-old female respondent

The most cited reason the respondents gave for their activism related to their perception of the show as an extended family. This motivating factor is a reason given by soap fans for why they continue to watch (Hayward, 1997, p. 164), so it is not surprising that this becomes a point of galvanization toward activism. This concept of family does not suggest an inability to separate reality from fantasy—a task at which soap fans excel (Harrington & Bielby, 1995)—rather, it demonstrates the distinct relationship that develops between a soap opera and its viewers.

For some respondents, they felt indebted to a group of actors or a show as a whole. "I felt I owed AW and some of the stars my life, and I wanted to do something to honor and thank them," explained one member-respondent. For others, they did not want to sever their connection to the show, either because it was a familiar constant or because its demise would trigger another loss—one's daily habit of watching

AW was keeping something or someone else alive. Watching over the years gives one knowledge of the show's history; the act of watching creates a history of the self—the 6-year-old who watched with her mother, the 18-year-old who watched during college, the 45-year-old who watched on her lunch break. Being a fan becomes a through-line to one's life, and joining the campaign, especially after cancellation, enabled some to extend that *AW* metanarrative, even though the show itself was gone. One respondent observed that *AW*

> represented a different time, kept alive my relationship with my grandmother and certainly was a topic of conversation with my mom over the years. . . . Letting go was hard because it was like letting go a piece of my family.

Another respondent said,

> When I was in junior high and high school, I didn't get home until 2:30 and my grandmother used to watch it for me (pre-VCR days) and tell me everything I missed. She died in 1998, and I felt like I was losing another connection to her.

The characters, too, became as close as family members to some viewers. "Victoria Wyndham [who played Rachel] seemed like a member of my family since I was so used to seeing her face on my TV screen," explained a member-respondent.

Other Activism Experiences

THE MOVEMENT'S RESULTS

. . . . Although fan activism may have prolonged *AW*'s life, ultimately it did not save it. Despite this, 13 of the 20 respondents deemed the campaign successful. Their answers about success were the most diverse. Perceptions ranged from those who rated the campaign as extremely successful to those who felt the exact opposite,

as well as every combination in between. The variety in replies may be linked to the proliferation of diverse campaign goals. Although almost everyone agreed that the initial objective was to keep *AW* on the air, especially after cancellation, people's goals splintered and transformed into a multitude of agendas. For some, the fight was over and they had lost. For others, they were intent on reviving *AW* on another network. Some wanted to punish NBC for its decision; others wanted to segue into a fan-based advocacy group for all of daytime television.

Within this diversity, however, a strong linkage did emerge: Those who considered the campaign successful also indicated that it had a major impact on their lives. "It gave me a voice and made me feel a bit more secure in myself and my opinions," said a member-respondent. Another shared, "I found myself speaking out and expressing my feelings to people I had never met before. I'm basically a shy person and the fact that the cancellation of a soap opera was bringing this part out actually surprised me." Stated one respondent, "The campaign gave me a sense of purpose and caused me to spend less time dwelling on myself. It came at a very low point in my life and . . . showed me that I had not lost my edge."

Their involvement helped them feel empowered and allowed them to discover dormant or previously unknown skills. In addition to personal impact, most of these individuals felt that their collective actions had changed the landscape of daytime television, even if it was only temporary. As one respondent stated, "I think fans, for many programs have become more radicalized [as a result] and see the public airwaves as owned by the consumer, not the broadcast company."

Conversely, 7 respondents felt that the campaigns were not successful and/or had no impact on soaps as a whole. "I doubt anyone even cared," remarked one respondent. The common threads uniting these participants were that they tended to focus on having *AW* exist only in the form they loved (e.g., no spin-off or reruns), that their involvement decreased with time, and that they shared the belief that they were rarely, if ever, heard by the network or P&G.

The level of success also correlated to whether friendships and the sense of belonging to a community had developed out of their involvement. Of the 7 respondents who did not feel their efforts were successful, 5 reported that they made no lasting friendships because of their participation, and did not become more involved in the daytime television community. Everyone else stated that new friendships and increased ties to the community were highly valued by-products. A sentiment echoed by many is summed up in the following answer by one respondent: "I had never participated in such an activity before, and it gave me such a feeling of kinship to other viewers." The desire to be part of a large network of fans motivated many individuals to join, not realizing that the connections that developed would give new meaning to their activity and mitigate the loss of their personal relationship to the show. . . .

As for other kinds of activism, 13 respondents indicated that their *AW*-campaign involvement increased their interest in other movements, but only 4 were somehow involved in any current efforts, and all but 1 of these respondents had been politically active before getting involved in the *AW* campaigns. Why have not more participants become active activists? For some, the reason stems from the fact that they are no longer daytime television viewers; 8 respondents stopped watching soaps after the cancellation of *AW*; none watched its replacement, *Passions*. For others, their involvement soured them on any future activism. Even if they deemed the campaign successful, they came to the conclusion that fan mobilization will never be taken seriously, and the emotional roller coaster that is campaigning would not be worth it. In fact,

the reason given by those respondents who no longer watch soaps was that they did not want to be emotionally invested in any program again. The loss of *AW* hit viewers on a very personal level, and without that attachment, many would not be inspired to act because of one of the two perceptions they took with them: "You can't fight city hall" or "You can fight city hall, but it's going to take everything out of you." Therefore, an issue would have to arise that invoked a personal response that superceded the perceived toll that one's involvement would take financially and especially, emotionally.

Conclusion

This case study offers another example of the manner in which many soap fans defy the popular cultural myths about them. In this sense, soap activism is not an evolutionary step on the fan activity ladder but instead, one of many tools employed by fans who want to take action. Under other circumstances, several of the survey participants would not have been propelled to mobilize, but their connection to *AW* inspired them to do so. Despite numerous obstacles, many of these viewers felt, at least for a time, empowered.

Although daytime activism and primetime activism certainly share similarities—most notably the way the groups form and the various methods of protest employed—they cannot be seen as interchangeable phenomena. The reasons why daytime television fans unite are tied directly to the genre itself, and the industry response to these soap activists is nowhere near as benign or accommodating as it has been to primetime television movements. As daytime television continues to lose ratings, placing more soaps in danger of cancellation, researchers may want to look to this arena, to investigate how viewers cope with the loss of their shows. The prior presumption in daytime television programming was that if a soap was cancelled, most people would simply watch the replacement. This case study provides evidence to the contrary and suggests that there may be a relationship between the rate at which shows are canceled and declining ratings for other programs.

Also, these results point to a possible new explanation for [industry investment in] primetime television's current reality show programming—programs where viewers' influence is either minimal or very carefully prescribed. The more activist media fans become, the less programming will be developed that can be subject to their input. Soaps may be seen as an apolitical medium, enjoyed only by complacent viewers, but in actuality, daytime television provides a powerful platform for activism. What is extremely meaningful about these movements, however, is not their success or failure, but the soap opera genre's ability to create these accidental activists.

References

Allen, R. C. (1985). *Speaking of soap operas*. Chapel Hill: University of North Carolina Press.

Ang, I. (1989). Wanted: Audiences. In E. Seiter, H. Borchers, G. Kreutzner, & E. Warth (Eds.), *Remote control* (pp. 96–115). New York: Routledge.

Bacon-Smith, C. (1992). *Enterprising women*. Philadelphia: University of Pennsylvania Press.

Baym, N. K. (1995). The emergence of community in computer-mediated communication. In S. G. Jones (Ed.), *Cyber society* (pp. 138–163). Thousand Oaks, CA: Sage.

Bielby, D. D., Harrington, C. L., & Bielby, W. T. (1999). "Whose stories are they?" Fans' engagement with soap opera narratives in three sites of fan activity. *Journal of Broadcasting & Electronic Media, 43*(1), 35–52.

Brown, M. E. (1994). *Soap opera and women's talk: The pleasure of resistance*. Thousand Oaks, CA: Sage.

Cantor, M. G., & Pingree, S. (1983). *The soap opera*. Beverly Hills, CA: Sage.

Harrington, C. L., & Bielby, D. D. (1995). *Soap fans: Pursuing pleasure and making meaning in everyday life*. Philadelphia: Temple University Press.

Hayward, J. (1997). *Consuming pleasures: Active audiences and serial fictions from Dickens to soap opera*. Lexington: University Press of Kentucky.

Jenkins, H. (1992). *Textual poachers: Television fans and participatory culture*. New York: Routledge.

LaGuardia, R. (1974). *The wonderful world of TV soap operas*. New York: Ballantine Books.

Lynch, R. (2001). *Fan history book of the 1960s*. Retrieved August 2, 2004, from http://www.jophan.org/1960s/

Matelski, M. (1988). *The soap opera evolution: America's enduring romance with daytime drama*. Jefferson, NC: McFarland & Company.

Modleski, T. (1979). The search for tomorrow in today's soap operas. *Film Quarterly, 33*(1), 12–21.

Montgomery, K. C. (1989). *Target: Primetime*. New York: Oxford University Press.

Schemering, C. (1987). *The soap opera encyclopedia*. New York: Ballantine.

Scodari, C. (1995, May). *He's May. She's September, but are they both from* Another World? *Mass media, soap opera and the older woman/younger man taboo*. Paper presented at the International Communication Association Conference, Albuquerque, NM.

Seiter, E. (2001). *Television and new media audiences*. Oxford, UK: Oxford University Press.

Simon, R. (1997). Serial seduction: Living in other worlds. In *Worlds without end: The art and history of soap opera* (pp. 11–39). New York: Museum of Television and Radio.

67

Fan Activists and the Politics of Race in *The Last Airbender*

Lori Kido Lopez

I n December 2008, producers of the film adaptation of the Nickelodeon cartoon *Avatar: The Last Airbender* set off a firestorm of criticism when they announced their casting decisions. Despite the fact that the television show seemed to have appropriated cultural practices, architecture, religious iconography, costumes, calligraphy, and other aesthetic elements from East Asian and Inuit cultures, four white actors had been cast in the lead roles. Many fans became irate, demanding that the roles go to Asian actors because they had always imagined that the characters were racially Asian. When one of the lead actors dropped out of the project he was replaced with Dev Patel, who is of Indian descent, as is the film's director, M. Night Shyamalan.[1] But fans pointed out that the nation his character belonged to were the villains of the series, so now the problem was that three white stars were heroes and the non-white actor and his people villains. These conversations continued in heated online debates and culminated in a number of protest activities, ranging from the creation and spread of counter-media to a boycott of the upcoming film. . . .

In this case we can see that fans of *The Last Airbender* are able to transition from everyday fans to political activists—but, more significantly, we can see the way that this transition is facilitated through the language and culture of fandom itself. Some of the organization's strongest and most effective tactics rely on the skills developed as members of the fan community: honing their arguments through community discussions, producing and editing multimedia creations, educating themselves about every facet of their issue, and relying on their trusted networks to provide a database of information. Through interviews with leaders of the movement, textual analysis of the group's online communities, and an 18-month long ethnographic investigation of the group's leaders in action, I consider the ways that the fascination and frustration of fans can be potentially harnessed in promoting civic engagement, as well as wider conversations about racial representations and Asian American identities.

From Lori Kido Lopez (2011), "Fan activists and the politics of race in *The Last Airbender*," *International Journal of Cultural Studies*, 15:431–445. Reprinted with permission of SAGE Publications, Ltd.

Enraged Fans Take Action

When the news broke that white actors would be playing the starring roles of Aang, Katara, Sokka and Zuko, one of the first responses was from artists who had worked on the show. Under the handle 'Aang Ain't White', they anonymously created a Live Journal website and initiated a letter-writing campaign. Although hundreds of fans and non-fans learned about the issue through the site and mailed letters, most were returned to sender unopened. Soon thereafter, casting for the film was completed and production began with no changes to the cast. One consequence of creating this forum, however, was that like-minded participants had a chance to meet each other in this virtual arena and establish a basis for future conversations. Two such individuals, known on the site as glockgal and jedifreac, decided to start their own forum. They created a site called Racebending.com, as well as a corresponding community on LiveJournal. The name was a playful riff on the notion of 'bending' that was an important part of the universe of *The Last Airbender*—each tribe is based on a natural element, and individuals known as 'Benders' have the ability to manipulate that element.

The creation of this term can be read as an example of 'textual poaching' (Jenkins, 1992) or the act of fans repurposing ideas from their beloved texts to demonstrate resistance and agency. By referencing 'bending' the activists mark their fandom and attachment to the world of the franchise, even as they use the same term to articulate their frustration with an industry where roles are systematically taken from Asian Americans and given to white actors. The filmmakers seemed to be saying that audiences would only support movies starring white actors, and, as dedicated fans of a fantastical world populated by multiracial, multicultural peoples, they knew that this was not the case.

Members of the community also noted that the casting call had used the phrase 'Caucasian or any other ethnicity' when looking for these lead roles, which they found troubling and discriminatory, as it seemed that Paramount Pictures had specifically sought out white actors. In this sense, their definition of 'racebending' can be seen as more than simply changing the race of a character: it is changing the race of characters of color to white for reasons of marketability.[2]

By the spring of 2009, the Racebending .com website was managed by six main contributors, including three based in Los Angeles, one in British Columbia, one in New York, and one in Washington. Out of the six leaders of the movement, only one had been an active fan, participating in fan communities and engaging in fannish practices such as fan art and fan fiction. Four considered themselves general fans of the show but not at a serious level, and one had never seen an episode of the show and only joined the group to protest the casting. Nevertheless, the leaders of the group relied heavily on fan communities to provide the base for rallying individuals to take action. In an informal poll of 1200 Racebending.com supporters, the movement is seen to be spread across 50 countries, and racially nearly half of their supporters are white, with only a quarter of their participants identifying as Asian.[3] Although the website has gone through a few different incarnations, it generally serves as a place for newcomers to learn about the controversy, discover ways of becoming involved and read updates on the latest news. . . .

'Whiteness' and 'Asian-ness'

The practice of using white actors to tell the stories of people of color has a long cinematic history. In the specific case of Asian Americans, there are countless examples of white actors taking on Asian characters such as Fu Manchu, Charlie Chan, or, famously. Mr Yunioshi in *Breakfast at Tiffany's*. Similar to the adoption of 'blackface', the white actors participate in 'yellowface' by wearing prosthetics over their eyes, buck teeth, and garish costumes, often speaking in an exaggerated accent. Unfortunately, such practices have not disappeared; white actor David Carradine beat out Bruce Lee for the lead role of a Shaolin monk in the 1970s television show *Kung Fu*, and Rob Schneider played an offensively stereotypical Asian nerd in *I Now Pronounce You Chuck and Larry* in 2007. Beyond this practice of using costume and make-up to approximate Asian-ness, Asian actors are also systemically excluded from mainstream media through the less overt practice of whitewashing. In the case of whitewashing, Asian stories are embodied by white actors without even hinting at the erasure that is occurring, as if whiteness can adequately stand in for all racial difference. Some examples include the movie *21*, wherein white actors were cast to play the Asian Americans who actually participated in beating the casinos in Vegas, or the recent film *Extraordinary Measures*, whose star Harrison Ford portrays the real life Asian American doctor who developed the cure for Pompe disease.

The practice of whitewashing is particularly dangerous because of the way that these representations reify whiteness as both invisible and dominant. As Dyer argues, 'this property of whiteness, to be everything and nothing, is the source of its representational power' (1999: 458). Whiteness is seen as the lack of ethnicity and color, as if it is not part of its own representational category. While we may not know the reasons behind Paramount's casting decisions in *The Last Airbender*, it is nonetheless clear that the film participates in maintaining the cultural hegemony of whiteness—perhaps even to the extent that film studios assume that minority audiences prefer to watch white actors rather than actors who share their own

racial backgro
primary narra
white actors
extraneous pe
ture cannot b

Although t
created by tv
DiMartino an
the show had always been particularly attuned to the Asian aspects of the show. They proudly noted that the visuals were remarkably accurate in their portrayal of Chinese, Japanese, Korean and Inuit cultures, even though the story took place in a somewhat mythical, alternate world. Despite the fact that the race of animated characters can be underdetermined, ambiguous, or deliberately obscured (Lu, 2009), operating under the Japanese idea of *mukokuseki*, or 'lacking any nationality' (Iwabuchi, 2004), many fans actively searched for proof that these characters were actually Asian. To that end, there are countless video montages on their websites showing images from the show and comparing them to ethnographic photographs of Japanese clothing, Inuit housing, Chinese calligraphy, and other evidential images from those cultures. Within these comparisons there is a relentless insistence that we can pinpoint what Asia and Asian culture[4] are by looking at these visual artifacts.

Yet we must consider how this discourse contributes to an essentialized or fixed notion of Asia. Not only do these images suggest that an escalating pile of artifacts can be used to ascertain what is really Asian and what is not, as if Asian identities cannot exist outside of these artifacts, but we are to use this evidence to match a racialized body to this perfect image of Asianness. This becomes somewhat difficult given that the show seemingly appropriates and mixes cultural artifacts from a wide range of Asian cultures, none of which could be accurately represented by any single actor. Moreover, who and what constitutes 'Asia' is also a debatable topic, given that the geographical, ultural boundaries surrounding might consider 'Asia' are shifting ntextually constructed (Chuh, 2003; o, 1995). The demand for an Asian actor to play the role of Aang also assumes that identity and representation can be collapsed within an actor's body, when representation is always a mediation and our identities can rarely be straightforwardly mapped out without any complexity or shading.

This fixing of Asian culture as a specific set of material practices and a particular physicality is made even more problematic when accusations of Orientalism arise within the group. On the LiveJournal community, one contributor posted the following message:

> I have a friend who says that the Last Airbender race fail does not bother him because he does not see it as whitewashing because he does not see the Avatar world as Asian in the first place. To him, the world and its cultures do not code as Asian, but as more in the vein of white Orientalism. It's characters putting on Asian costumes in an exotic Asian world, for white people. Essentially, to cast the characters as white is only fitting.[5]

In the discussion that follows this posting, the participants debate whether or not the show is, at its core, authentically Asian or superficially Asian, as well as who gets to arbitrate such a debate given the diverse positionalities of those who are arguing each position. Given that over half of the fans and most active Racebending.com participants are not Asian, they would likely not want to detract from their own ability to participate in the Asian fantasy of the show. One contributor further adds, 'there's the undeniable fact that Avatar: The Last Airbender is a hybrid ... [it] is Asian American, and of course Asian Americans come in different flavors'.[6] These debates, which begin to spiral out of control rather than reaching resolutions, point to the slipperiness of authenticity and identity, and

perhaps the weakness in the group relying so heavily on these discourses. . . .

From Fans to Fan-Activists

. . . From this case study we can see how the set of skills exercised and utilized by fan communities have the potential to translate effectively into skills for a new mode of activism that takes place largely online. Van Zoonen (2004) makes a strong case for the similarity between fan communities and political constituencies, arguing that their emotional investments are both a result of performance, and that their activities are similarly concerned with things like knowledge, discussion and participation. But the mobilization of fans around this particular issue takes us one step further—not only do the activities and affective realities of fans resemble those of political constituencies, but fan activities can be seen to facilitate the development of a set of skills that are particularly suited to political activism in the era of Web 2.0.

The first move that the leaders of the community made toward engaging with fans of the show was to create a website called Racebending.com and a community on LiveJournal. LiveJournal, a blogging website that has been a platform for fan communities since 2003 (Derecho, 2006), was already a hub of fan activity surrounding *The Last Airbender*, so the community quickly grew in popularity. The Racebending.com leaders were able to tap into an already existing network of individuals who had a strong connection to the show. If they could make the argument that their beloved property was being mistreated, that passion could be redirected against the live action film. We can see that this move has been extremely effective— the LiveJournal community continues to be the most active site for conversation surrounding the issue, with daily posts written by a large number of community members and an extremely active base of commenters turning each post into a rousing debate. It is not uncommon for a single post to have anywhere from 40 to 80 comments following it.

The Racebending.com community on LiveJournal makes use of the already existing online network of individuals, but also puts them to work in sorting through and accumulating new information about the issue at hand. Fans have long been known as great collectors of information about their fan object; in an exploration of the wiki called *Lostpedia*, Mittell finds that the community website's 'core function is as a shared archive of data, culling information from the show, its brand extensions, and its cultural references to make sense of the show's mysteries and narrative web' (Mittell, 2009). The high level of fascination and attention to shows like *Lost* are multiplied when fan communities unite to pool their resources, making their data set incredibly comprehensive and detailed. Jenkins (2006) further expands on this phenomenon, comparing the advantages of Pierre Levy's notion of collective intelligence to Peter Walsh's more traditional 'expert paradigm'. He argues that there are many pleasurable reasons for people to participate in the production of collective knowledge: the exercise of generally unacknowledged skills, the assumption that individuals have something worthwhile to contribute, and the generally democratic principles that lead to a dynamic process of acquiring knowledge. This notion of collective labor maps perfectly onto the case of Racebending.com, where it is not always the leaders who provide the latest news regarding the production and promotion of the film. Rather, it is a collective of motivated individuals who sporadically contribute, leaving no stone unturned in their search for new details and developments.

Beyond updates on the making of the film, the site is also a place for a host of related discussions, including questions about racial politics, re-examinations of episodes of the show in the context of this new politicization, and the drawing of attention to similar issues in other media representations. In his examination of the cultural economy of fandom, Fiske finds that fans are 'particularly productive', and that 'all such productivity occurs at the interface between the industrially-produced cultural commodity . . . and the everyday life of the fan' (1992: 37). He specifically outlines three kinds of productivity, two of which we see in action here—enunciative productivity, or fan talk, and textual productivity, or fan art. With regard to enunciative productivity, we can see these regular conversations and debates on LiveJournal as evidence that fan talk is productive of deeper knowledge about the text itself, as well as the political implications of the way that the film has been cast. Through these discussions and debates, participants are able to sharpen their own arguments and solidify their stance on what is clearly a politically fraught issue.

With regard to textual productivity, we can look to the copious production of fan artwork and fan videos as additional components of knowledge creation. Coppa defines vidding as, among other things, 'a visual essay that stages an argument' (2008), and indeed the videos made by Racebending.com participants articulate nuanced arguments through their humorous montages, sarcastic rants, and compelling collections of evidence. There has also been a movement to create videos of individuals stating why they are participating in a boycott of the movie, which can contribute to a show of strength in numbers. In addition to these videos on YouTube, many fan artists have turned their visual arts skills toward the cause, creating original works of art that can be used as banners, t-shirts, buttons, icons, or personalized avatars. In this way, the artistic and creative skills that fans regularly employ in the creation of fan art and vids has been used to propel the arguments of the Racebending.com cause.

The group's collective use of 'comment-bombing' can also be seen as related to Fiske's notion of 'enunciative productivity'. Any time that a news organization publishes information about the upcoming film, new behind-the-scenes information, interviews with actors and cast members, or promotional material for other white-washed projects, Racebending.com participants will direct members of the community to post comments. The community is very comfortable with the act of commenting since they participate in regular online dialogues with members of their own community, and dozens comply with these requests, overwhelming the article with their viewpoint and offering counterpoints to any opposing arguments. In the era of online newswriting, comments can be seen as an important component of online discourse, and can even contribute to the creation of further legitimized conversation. For instance, *The Los Angeles Times* wrote an article based on an interview with director M. Night Shyamalan, and members of the Racebending.com community were encouraged to comment on the article. This action led to the writing of another article with the headline 'The Last Airbender is causing a casting commotion',[7] which was published in the *Los Angeles Times* blog. Although this blog often focuses on discussions that take place in the online comments, the fact that a respected newspaper like the *Los Angeles Times* would take note of online comments legitimates the commenting arena as important and worthy of concern.

Conversations around commenting are also important to note because they serve the purpose of policing the boundaries of acceptable fan behavior. This helps the group to retain their image as a respectable group of activists rather than flamers or trolls who are only interested in inciting anger or stymieing discourse. One LiveJournal post directing individuals to comment on a recent blog post included the warning, 'Just remember to be polite and keep your cool. If you come off as angry (Season 1 Zuko!) they have yet another excuse to dismiss you. Make your points calmly and confidently.'[8] Since fan communities spend so much time engaging in online discourse, there are often strict rules about the kinds of participation that are allowed and the kinds that are discouraged. In her examination of soap opera communities, Baym finds:

> Politeness is a criterion of communicative competence . . . . If conflicts were to become personal (or degenerate into 'flame wars'), people would be inhibited from contributing potentially controversial opinions, and the primary function of the group as an interpretive forum would be disrupted. (1997: 117)

If we apply this logic to the Racebending.com community, we can see that a similar desire for the primary function of the group—propelling the cause into mainstream media and convincing viewers to boycott the film—could be inhibited by allowing a lack of respect and decorum.

The leaders of the Racebending.com movement have conducted a fair amount of research into academic venues as well. Together they have accumulated an impressive amount of information on the topics of historical yellowface, the scarcity of Asian Americans in the media, the negative effects of racial stereotyping on children, the perils of a 'post-racial' rhetoric, and other issues. This knowledge has been gained through internet research, trips to local university libraries, and conversations with professors. For instance, two members of Racebending.com conducted a phone interview with Rebecca Bigler, PhD, who studies developmental psychology at the University of Texas at Austin. Although some of the conversation revolves around findings from Bigler's study entitled 'A developmental intergroup theory of social stereotypes and prejudice', their conversation never delves into the 'mechanisms and rules that govern the processes by which children single out groups as targets', as the study does. Rather, the interviewers ask where children learn about stereotypes, and Bigler responds that children recognize the racial segregation of kids sitting together in the cafeteria, and then slowly start to come up with their own explanations for racial difference. The published interview continues in this straightforward, jargon-free language, and includes pull-out quotations that help to summarize the main points.[9] Interviews like these clearly contribute to the factual basis for responses to Racebending.com's long list of Frequently Asked Questions, such as 'Why is Racebending.com so concerned over just a kid's movie?'[10] As with this interview, much of the material found on Racebending .com organizes and translates academic research into more easily understood language that helps everyday fans to better equip themselves for arguing their case.

Politicizing Beyond
The Last Airbender

The group focused on two main goals during the course of this study: the first was to affect casting, and the second was to affect ticket sales after the summer 2010 release and derail plans for a second and third movie. But beyond these goals that are directly connected to *The Last Airbender*, they have also begun to take on the cause of promoting the general casting of Asian Americans and other minorities. As Scardaville finds, many fan activism groups share a common origin story: 'A single act or a pattern of offending acts mobilize individuals to unite. After the goal is either achieved or no longer attainable, the protesting group may, with time, evolve into a watchdog organization' (2005: 886). The Racebending.com movement seems to follow this typology, since the casting decision led to the mobilization of the group, but the ongoing issue of racism in representation is what continues to motivate their collective. The Racebending.com website

lists as their mission: 'We are a coalition and community dedicated to encouraging fair casting practices. As a far-reaching movement of consumers, students, parents, and professionals, we promote just and equal opportunities in the entertainment industry.'[11] This statement clearly moves beyond the film itself to advocate for a change in casting practices in general.

One campaign that epitomized this expanded goal was against the white-washing of a comic book called *The Weapon*. The comic book starred an Asian American hero named Tommy Zhou, but when the story was set to be remade into a film, a white actor was cast to play him. Members of the Racebending.com communities were very supportive of efforts to protest this casting. The coordinators wrote a letter condemning the decision in the name of Racebending.com, and one coordinator actually had an extended phone conversation with the executive producer of the film to convey their message. The group's support for these actions revealed an interest in working on projects outside of *The Last Airbender*. Overall, in the period between the movie's production and the premiere, the majority of new posts were about issues outside the world of *The Last Airbender*, and only infrequent contained updates on the progress of the film's promotion or the occasional tidbit of new information from the main contributors.

Yet it is also important to examine some of the group's struggles; for instance, members of the Racebending.com community have been difficult to call into action with regard to real-life protest activities—particularly early in the course of their organizing—such as attending rallies or collecting pen-and-paper signed petitions. A Racebending.com leader in New York organized a protest at the film's casting call for background actors in March 2009, but only a handful of people showed up. Together they held signs and tried to gain visibility, but with the lack of bodies their impact was minimal. Similarly, the Los Angeles 'Street Team' organized a group of Racebending.com supporters at Comic-Con in San Diego in July 2009, but the two leaders ended up doing most of the work by themselves, 'full-on yelling into the crowd, handing out flyers and buttons, getting signatures',[12] with little support from their fellow Racebending .com members. Another missed opportunity for on-the-ground activism came when the Media Action Network for Asian Americans (MANAA) organized a protest at Paramount Studios against an offensive scene in their recent film *The Goods: Live Hard, Sell Hard*. MANAA approached Racebending.com to see if they wanted to use the protest to promote their cause, since Paramount was also the studio producing *The Last Airbender*, but only one member of the Los Angeles Street Team showed up to the protest. Although enthusiasm for the cause is seemingly boundless in online forums, it has been difficult to get even the most vocal members of the group to put a name to their face and show up for a local event.[13]

These examples of the group's less successful campaigns are interesting to view in the context of the successful utilization of fan skills for activism. It is possible that these more traditionally political activities veer too far from the everyday activities of fan communities, and this is why they have floundered. Like many fan communities, this particular community resides largely online, with very few members ever having met face to face, so it makes sense that their most successful collective actions take place virtually. Malcolm Gladwell has suggested that demonstrations and protests, or what he calls 'high-risk activism', are reliant on strong ties that cannot be built or activated using social media. In a provocative *New Yorker* article, Gladwell (2010) asserts that 'Facebook activism succeeds not by motivating people to make a real sacrifice but by motivating them to do the things that people do when they are not motivated enough to make a real sacrifice'. The example of Racebending.com

is a rich example for exploring Gladwell's claims, given the group's reliance on social media as well as its struggles to organize in-person actions. We might worry that the work of this group is all talk and no outcome, and that their 100 percent virtual set of activities is somehow a weakness. Yet we must be careful about suggesting that their lack of face-to-face mobilizing represents a failure to become truly politicized, or that the group cannot be considered to be engaged in 'real activism'. Although disputing the casting of a film may not be as significant an action as Gladwell's examples from the civil rights movement, where physical violence and legal battles were imminent threats, the group is still participating in important discursive and educational work. As we have seen in this discussion, the group effectively propagates their message using online organizing and has communicated their message to a broad audience of fans and non-fans. Further, they have moved their mission toward general casting and racial representation issues that are not even related to their original fan object—a trend that can only be seen as political, since it no longer relies on the affective ties of fandom—and that through this shift, they have been a part of important conversations with industry executives.

Conclusion: Fan-Activism and the Consumer-Citizen

As we consider this movement of fans toward politicized organizing and activist movements that extend beyond the text of *The Last Airbender* itself, it is important to consider the ways that their project can be framed as a consumer movement. As fans they may want to see their favorite text represented accurately, and as activists they may want to see people of color telling their own stories, but we cannot neglect their identities and motivations as consumers as well. Because the film and *The Last*

Airbender franchise are both commercial entities, at the core of this protest is the idea that the fans want to be able to spend their dollars on their favorite text. As mentioned earlier, the term 'racebending' itself was poached from the media world, so even as the fans are attempting to impact the bottom line at Paramount they are still supporting the franchise in many ways. As consumer-citizens, they use consumption as a site for enacting their politics—their central goal is to impact the film industry through the collective power of their boycott, and in doing so, convey a message about how important racial politics are to them.

From the perspective of Paramount, of course, the creation of the film is not premised on the ethics of the racial dynamics of casting in Hollywood, but simply on the commercial viability of their multi-million dollar business venture. We can see the tensions between these two motives in conversations within the Racebending .com community that revolve around the marketability of Asian American actors and actresses in the American and international media landscape. Many prominent members of the Asian American community have propagated the narrative that one of the reasons why Asian Americans are marginalized within Hollywood is because of the spending patterns of Asian American audiences. One writer and activist stated:

> Unlike black and Latino audiences, Hollywood doesn't even track Asian audiences separately. They don't need to; we essentially have the same consuming patterns as white audiences. If a studio releases an 'Asian American' film, our community is about as likely to support that as a white audience. (Chung, 2007)

Although it is unclear whether or not this statement is true, Chung nevertheless asserts the importance of Asian American consumption in the ethical imperative of the Racebending.com movement. The argument that an 'Asian American' film—or a film that stars Asian Americans, as Racebending.com members would like *The Last Airbender* to be – would draw a diverse audience only helps to strengthen their argument that their representation is important, and that the only way we will know it is important is through consumption. In an entry on the Racebending .com community on LiveJournal, jedifreac writes:

> There are about 18.9 million people of Asian descent in the United States and Canada, and about 3.5 million people of American Indian/Alaska Native/First Nations/Inuit/Métis descent. . . . So to all the people who argue that Asian Americans and Native Americans are 'too small of a group' to deserve to be represented in movies or to have any purchasing power . . . that it's not worth it for Paramount to represent people from those groups in lead roles, well . . .

It is clear that 'the numbers game' has played a role in the rhetoric of the movement. But we must also remember that the numbers game is not the only way in which the group hoped to measure their success. Although much of their activism was explicitly oriented toward impacting ticket sales, they realized that it would be difficult to measure the effect of their outreach as opposed to, for instance, the film's terrible critical reception. The group also focused on much smaller goals, none of which are numerical: they hoped to meet with the production, to stage a protest at the premiere, to contact media outlets, and to sustain and expand their movement. As one leader stated

> It's not about the battle and we're not going to change Hollywood overnight. It's not about one individual fight, it's about the trajectory of the next ten or twenty years, and the one thing we can do to guarantee we lose in the long run is to sit back and stay quiet.

... This case demonstrates the complications that can arise in engaging with the racial politics of representation. We see that a fannish preoccupation with authenticity can be limiting if it becomes affixed to a relationship between racialized or otherwise marked bodies and the stories they can tell. ... This example also demonstrates the possibility for an organization to strategically rely on fan skills as a mode for engaging participants in political activity—growing their online community using a base of individuals who were already engaged in similar communities, relying on the group's far reach to stay on top of all developments, creating original and multimedia artwork to promote the cause, encouraging members to spread their message through well-worded and thoughtful dialogue, and seeking to bolster their own knowledge from a wide arena. Each of these tactics is particularly well suited for the group's goal of spreading knowledge about the movie and encouraging everyday movie viewers to join the boycott. It is unclear whether or not a different sort of campaign—for instance, a campaign to change governmental policy, or prison reform—could benefit from these fannish skills, or that this model could be usefully imported to work on another cause, given the complexity of this narrative. Yet it is clear that participatory cultures like those around fan communities offer a potential space and set of tools for shifting conversations from fictional texts to the realities that they impact and rely upon.

Notes

1. To be precise, Patel was born to Gujarati parents who were from Kenya, and he was raised in England. Shyamalan was born in India but raised in Pennsylvania from the age of six weeks.

2. The group is identified throughout as members or participants of Racebending.com —an important distinction, since they are actually 'against racebending'.

3. See: http://www.racebending.com/v3/press/demographics-of-racebending-com-supporters/ (consulted 26 July 2010).

4. Although the Racebending.com supporters also argue that Inuit culture is being represented in *Avatar: The Last Airbender* and thus should be represented in the film, the majority of their arguments focus on Asians and Asian Americans.

5. See: http://community.livejournal.com/ontd_political/4893219.html (online comment, 22 December 2009, consulted 24 July 2010).

6. See: http://community.livejournal.com/racebending/133219.html?thread=4072803#t4072803 (online comment, 23 December 2009, consulted 24 July 2010).

7. See: http://latimesblogs.latimes.com/comments_blog/2010/04/the-last-airbender-causes-acasting-commotion.html (online post, 7 April 2010, consulted 25 July 2010).

8. See: http://community.livejournal.com/racebending/155803.html (online comment, 10 February 2010, consulted 24 July 2010).

9. See: http://www.racebending.com/v3/interviews/rebecca-bigler-developmental-psychologist/ (website, consulted 1 November 2010).

10. See: http://www.racebending.com/v3/faq/ (consulted 1 November 2010)

11. See: http://www.racebending.com/v3/about/ (website, consulted 24 July 2010).

12. See: http://community.livejournal.com/racebending/81024.html (online post, 27 July 2009, consulted 24 July 2010).

13. Members of Racebending.com successfully partnered with the Media Action Network for Asian Americans, National Korean American Service & Education Consortium, and Korean Resource Center for a protest on 1 July 2010 outside a movie theatre in Los Angeles. Over 100 people gathered, and many news outlets covered the protest. Reviews of the film—although largely focused on technical failings—also paid a considerable amount of attention to the issue of race and casting, often including interviews with members of Racebending.com. Analysis of the protest and other events surrounding the

premiere of the film are not included in the study, but deserve serious analysis in the future.

References

Baym NK (1997) Interpreting soap operas and creating community: inside an electronic fan culture. In: Kiesler S (ed.) *Culture of the Internet*. Mahwah, NJ: Lawrence Erlbaum Associates, 103–120.

Chung P (2007) Where are the APA movie stars? *AsianWeek*, 14 December.

Chuh K (2003) *Imagine Otherwise: On Asian Americanist Critique*. Durham, NC: Duke University Press.

Chvany P (2003) 'Do we look like ferengi capitalists to you?' *Star Trek's* Klingons as emergent virtual American ethnics. In Jenkins H, McPherson T and Shattuc J (eds) *Hop on Pop: The Politics and Pleasures of Popular Culture*. Durham, NC: Duke University Press.

Coppa F (2008) Women, *Star Trek*, and the early development of fannish vidding. *Transformative Works and Cultures* 1. Available at: http://journal.transformative works.org/index.php/twc/ article/view/44/64

Derecho A (2006) Archontic literature: a definition, a history, and several theories of fan fiction. In: Hellekson K and Busse K (eds) *Fan Fiction and Fan Communities in the Age of the Internet: New Essays*. Jefferson, NC: McFarland and Co., 61–78.

Dyer R (1999) White. In: Evans J and Hall S (eds) *Visual Culture: The Reader*. London: Sage, 457–467.

Earl J and Kimport K (2009) Movement societies and digital protest: fan activism and other nonpolitical protest online. *Sociological Theory* 27(3): 220–243.

Fiske J (1992) The cultural economy of fandom. In: Lewis L (ed.) *The Adoring Audience: Fan Culture and Popular Media*. London: Routledge, 9–29.

Gladwell M (2010) Small change: why the revolution will not be tweeted. *The New Yorker*, 4 October.

Iwabuchi K (2004) How 'Japanese' is Pokemon? In: Tobin J (ed.) *Pikachu's Global Adventure: The Rise and Fall of Pokemon*. Durham, NC: Duke University Press, 53–79.

Jenkins H (2006) *Convergence Culture: Where Old and New Media Collide*. New York: New York University Press.

Jenkins H (1992) *Textual Poachers: Television Fans and Participatory Culture*. New York: Routledge.

Levi A (2006) The Americanization of anime and manga: negotiating popular culture. In: Brown S (ed.) *Cinema Anime: Critical Engagements with Japanese Anime*. New York: Palgrave Macmillan, 43–64.

Lu AS (2009) What race do they represent and does mine have anything to do with it? Perceived racial categories of anime characters. *Animation* 4(2): 169–190.

Mittell J (2009) Sites of participation: wiki fandom and the case of Lostpedia. *Transformative Works and Cultures* 3. Available at: http://journal.transformativeworks.org/index.php/twc/article/view/118

Ono K (1995) Re/signing 'Asian American': rhetorical problematics of nation. *Amerasia* 21(1): 67–78.

Scardaville M (2005) Accidental activists: fan activism in the soap opera community. *American Behavioral Scientist* 48: 881–901.

Scodari C and Felder JL (2000) Creating a pocket universe: 'shippers', fan fiction, and *The X-Files* online. *Communication Studies* 51(3): 238–258.

Tabron J (2004) Girl on girl politics: Willow/Tara and new approaches to media fandom. *Slayage: The Online International Journal of Buffy* 13. Available at: http://slayageonline.com/essays/slayage13_14/Tabron.htm

Van Zoonen L (2004) Imagining the fan democracy. *European Journal of Communication* 19(1): 39–52.

68

GimpGirl Grows Up

Women With Disabilities Rethinking, Redefining, and Reclaiming Community

Jennifer Cole, Jason Nolan, Yukari Seko,
Katherine Mancuso, and Alejandra Ospina

Introduction

... This study explored the key members, events, issues, and technologies of GimpGirl Community (GGC) (http://gimpgirl.com), which was founded in 1998 as a forum for women with disabilities, run by women with disabilities. We focused on the lived experiences of GGC members: how they actively shape and nurture this online community for like-minded individuals; how they maintain and moderate social interaction among members; and what path the community has taken in the past twelve years. The study could be considered a reflective narrative inquiry and learning exercise in which key members of the GGC took initiative in setting the research agenda, conducted their own inquiry, and organized and presented their analysis in collaboration with co-authors/academic mentors who wanted to help the group share their story with the academic community. By documenting the organizing efforts of GGC moderators and their learning experiences over the past decade, we were able to inquire into the connections between online technologies and the capabilities people need to develop and maintain communities.

From Jennifer Cole, Jason Nolan, Yukari Seko, Katherine Mancuso, and Alejandra Ospina (2011), "GimpGirl Grows Up: Women with Disabilities Rethinking, Redefining and Reclaiming Community." *New Media & Society* 13:1161–1179. Reprinted with permission of SAGE Publications, Ltd.

Initiating Inquiry

We were particularly interested in what initially drove GGC members to develop an online community, how the community solved problems, and how various online technologies (from text-based to more recent mixed-media virtual environments) were adapted to meet the diverse needs of members. Our investigation was inspired by the method of narrative inquiry: qualitative research that examines narratives to understand the meanings people ascribe to their experiences (Trahar, 2009). Narrative inquiry takes diverse modes of filed texts—oral, written, visual—as data sources to look for deeper understanding of 'lived experience' (Clandinin and Connelly, 2000; van Manen, 1997). We saw the value of how, based on various narrative elements, narrative inquirers interrogate how the life experiences of individuals get woven into a story, for whom and for what purpose, and what cultural discourses it draws upon.

... For our inquiry, digital archives of the twelve years of GGC activity constituted archived texts that include postings to the community listservs, blog entries, minutes from staff meetings, and online dialogues among the members. Formulation of this article took place solely online with members in different parts of the world, and incorporated recent scholarly contributions from the group (Cole, 2009; Cole and Mancuso, 2009; Mancuso and Cole, 2009; Ospina et al., 2008).

Along with archival materials, we chose to focus on auto-ethnographic reflections of the founding member Jennifer Cole, as her experiences best portray the overall structure and development of the community. It is not unusual for an author of an auto-ethnography to consult with various other people and materials, but it is less common for multiple authors to agree on a single voice to represent a community. Lather (1995) used this approach and noted the challenges of telling stories on behalf of marginalized individuals, as well as the concomitant necessity to do so. Jennifer's auto-ethnographic writings were nurtured by online discussions and one-on-one dialogues between the co-authors, as they collaboratively reconstructed memories of the community. . . .

... By investigating Jennifer's narrative in the context of various episodes and incidents in the collective life of the GGC, we explored issues of inclusivity and exclusivity crucial for maintaining a safe and open space for participants, as well as the experiments in identity construction performed by some GGC members. These experimentations presented a counterpoint to conventional assumptions about women with disabilities that construct them as asexual service recipients without autonomy or agency.

Genesis of the GGC

Inspired by her participation in the DO-IT program for teens with disabilities (http://www.washington.edu/doit/), Jennifer and her mentor Len Burns founded The Center for Breaking Away, a non-profit organization for disabled youth transitioning to adulthood. This organization originally housed the GGC project, but was dissolved after the GGC project outgrew the center. The GGC was founded in 1998 as a collaboration of young women with disabilities who shared a dissatisfaction with pre-existing services and communities, which appeared incapable of fulfilling the needs of these youth in transition to adulthood. For Jennifer, a chief motivation for creating the GGC was to fight back against abusive situations she had encountered, and to counterbalance her early heteronomous role of being a passive daughter/child with a disability. She noted in an online conversation with the co-authors:

> I started it [the GGC] when I was 18 or 19 I think. Just after I left an abusive

home. It started as me battling back against that and forming community to help each other through those tough times. Many people with disabilities feel like when we are no longer cute kids, we get thrust out into the world without much support. This is what the GGC was made for, to offer direct peer-to-peer support . . . .Interestingly, we came across many women who were just out of abusive situations or actively in abusive situations and I was so glad that they found somewhere to go and didn't have to create it.

The GGC was intended as an online-based group connecting isolated members with shared interests. Most of the founding members were teens who had met each other through the DO-IT program or similar organizations, and so the GGC was initially founded by and for young women, who created a safe and informal space for sharing ideas and experiences, discussing issues involved in the transition to adulthood, and for offering information and peer-to-peer support unavailable in formal settings. The domain gimpgirl.com was registered in February 1998; this was initially Jennifer's personal website, but was almost immediately given over to GGC. Jennifer was the first leader, though governance changed over time. She thought of herself as running and growing a nonprofit.[1] The GGC website was one of the first sites dedicated to women with disabilities based on self-diagnosed disability, without restrictions on age, sexual orientation, or types of disability. The website included links to news from the disability community and resources for women with disabilities. Other areas showcased art and writing of members, as well as fun activities such as quizzes and polls.

. . . The name 'GimpGirl' originated as a nickname Jennifer's friends called her when she was a teenager: '[The nickname] didn't have any particular meaning other than who I was, and a big part of who I am is getting beyond terminology, which still carries in what we do today.' By sharing her nickname with the group, Jennifer motivated herself and other GGC members to 'get each other through life' beyond any given terminology. Jennifer suggested that what underlies the active use of controversial language was a challenging spirit against conventional discourse surrounding women with disabilities. She noted:

[The term 'GimpGirl' was] Not offhand. I know even before we started [the group in 1998], people in the disability community were calling themselves gimps (mostly on the West Coast) and crips (mostly on the East Coast). It was a source of 'cheeky' pride . . . . While the language we use has definitely sparked some controversy, it is who we are and so it has withstood the controversy. Within the disabilities community there always seems to be some set of politically acceptable language that we are supposed to use to make people feel better, and part of our stand is that we can choose how we react to whatever language people use. Our goal is not to be popular or be politically acceptable, but to get each other through life.

Jennifer's subversive moniker also mirrored her expectation that the name and logo of the community would remind participants that they are the ones who give power to words, and would encourage them to distance themselves from the ever-changing 'politically correct' institutional language that defines and shapes much of the identity of women living with disabilities. . . .

. . . GGC members and their families became increasingly accepting; one mother of a GGC member sent an email to Jennifer, commenting: '[At first,] "GimpGirl" seems rude but when I think more on the term, it is upfront and confident and takes away any sense of pity.'

The Growth of the GGC and Use of Online Technology

One important characteristic of the GGC is its active search for, and implementation of, new technologies to facilitate member participation in community development and maintenance. The community has transcended any specific technology and has morphed through listservs, interactive virtual worlds, websites, blogs, and various social networks. Rather than abandoning old tools and moving onto new ones, the GGC has actively sought effective technologies to develop and deliver desirable content for its members. Before adopting a new form of communication, staff consults with board members and the community to see how many are already using a particular technology and how accessible they found it. The administrators then further research the technology with regard to usability and accessibility, to ensure that a benefit to some would not exclude others. . . .

. . .On 18 July 2003, the GGC created an account on the LiveJournal platform (http://gimpgirl.livejournal.com/) in an effort to rejuvenate and diversify access and to reduce duties for moderators. The GGC later transferred all existing lists to this social networking platform, making the LiveJournal group the main venue for communal activities. In this system, users were able to maintain their own accounts and benefited from a variety of available communities. LiveJournal also had community archives that were more immediate and engaging to new members. . . . Even after the GGC opened facilities in Second Life in 2008, the GimpGirl LiveJournal community remains the GGC's third largest community, with over 275 members worldwide who discuss wide-ranging subjects from bras and yeast infections to discrimination and victories.

The GGC's next major evolution came when Dr Mark Dubin of 3D Embodiment (http://3demb.com/) donated a quarter-sim parcel in *Second Life,* September 2007. The parcel was designed as a multi-use campus, with meeting rooms, a dance and pool area on the roof, an amphitheatre for presentations and events, a mall where members could sell items they had created, and a small apartment building where some members have homes. By February 2008, the parcel was fully developed and opened to the public, just in time for the GGC's tenth anniversary. This event was highly successful; members and supporters showed up to celebrate and hang out with their peers in this synchronous environment. After a decade of transitional homes, this incarnation marked a coming-of-age for the GGC, an all-volunteer group that had always worked on the fringe of the disability community without institutional support or formal funding. The launch was so successful that by March 2008 the parcel was redesigned by new volunteers to further increase accessibility and services. It also attracted support from Ryerson University's Experiential Design and Gaming Environment lab.[2]

. . . Expansion into *Second Life* sparked another wave of development in membership, activities, and staff. *Second Life* helped bring in outside resources by allowing a broader network of supporters from the large group of pre-existing disability and non-profit communities. As social networks become more popular to keep in touch with friends and family (Wellman et al., 2006), more people and organizations are willing to venture into virtual environments such as *Second Life.* The GGC was initially composed of a close-knit community of women who knew one another, but now it has extended to a larger community.

Since expanding to *Second Life* in 2008, the GGC has worked to expand and govern the community, and is using online community building tools to reach a wider range of women with disabilities and form a rich and nuanced web of people and resources. It has hosted a series of online public forums on *Second Life* in which the members join professionals or scholars outside the membership; this has raised the GGC's public profile, engaged a wider range of dialogue, and clarified the complex issues surrounding women with disabilities. The GGC also extended its presence to Facebook and MySpace (later deleted due to inactivity and usability issues) on 17 February 2008 and later opened a Twitter account 2 April 2008. Meanwhile, the GGC redesigned its main website, utilizing the open-source Moodle software to add forums, a wiki, and a membership system. The website re-release was announced on 12 April 2008. . . .

Beyond the Myth of Normativity: Community, Identity, and Technology

A consistent theme throughout this inquiry is the notion of being doubly marginalized: living as women and as individuals with disabilities. From a Foucauldian perspective, people with disabilities live immersed in a pathological discourse of disability, as an object of disciplinary power. They are forced to become the subject matter of professional groups, who constantly define the meaning of living with disabilities, resulting in the systematic closure of opportunities for agency. . . . The possibility of autonomy in day-to-day life is highly dependent on the willingness and ability of service providers and personal care assistants to see them as individuals with unique needs and goals. With potentially limited mobility and access to resources necessary to independently claim their own identity, they are often designated as the 'docile' population. . . . GGC members have strived to overcome the 'double silence' of women with disabilities by resisting the stereotypical view of living with disabilities, thereby claiming the status of

subjects with agency (Ferri and Gregg, 1998: 433). . . .

. . . While the community has successfully maintained an openness to all forms of disability by intentionally educating themselves about the needs of members, staff members have had to work in uncharted territory without models to emulate or apply. The need to create a safe and nurturing space for members must be balanced by a concomitant act of social engagement with larger disability communities, academic and medical communities, and the public at large. Because the goal of the community was to be inclusive and to give voice to those under-represented or marginalized, its model could not be fixed, but had to remain fluid and open to continual re-assessment and reconfiguration to ensure that power remained with all members. As the community has grown, the GGC has needed not only to consider the safety of members but also to reach outside its walls to interface with the public and advocate for public support and communication.

By using a variety of online tools, the GGC has helped members develop a capacity to perform as agents of self- and social transformation. The system also helps empower participants to involve themselves in their own lives by providing information and broadening their experience with others in similar situations. Meanwhile, staff members are aware of the potential exclusivity of ICTs, due to financial requirements and other factors involved in getting online. To participate, members must purchase a computer and have access to the internet (financially difficult for many women with disabilities) and be technically savvy enough to interact with others via online-mediated platforms. This, according to Jennifer, may explain why many of the GGC members are 'computer geeks.' Despite these limitations, ICTs are the only way for many GGC members to shift discourse from an institutional/medical location to a community of their own. By doing so, Jennifer and other members have developed their own skills and strategies for using various forms of online technology, structuring community, negotiating participation, developing and maintaining community standards, and resolving conflict. Jennifer noted:

> While online technologies certainly exclude a huge population, at the same time they are also very inclusive to many people because they reach into where they are. Many of us who are bedbound (like myself most days) and don't always have the same opportunities to be involved in face-to-face groups. Also for people who have issues socializing in face-to-face situations, either because of shyness or communication issues (for whatever reason), online environments are much easier.

Another challenge related to the use of online platforms is the issue of validity, stemming from the lack of face-to-face interaction among participants. While online forums are a good way to get a broad range of input from different people, participants accustomed to face-to-face interactions occasionally voiced concern about the GGC's fundamental reliance on online media. One former volunteer explained that some saw the GGC as 'not real enough,' because members rarely saw one another face-to-face. The concern is valid, because the GGC does not have an office, and members interact using text and avatars, sometimes supplemented by voice/video chat. However, the situation has been gradually changing, as the administrators have consistently encouraged other members to balance online and offline relationships. Drawing on her experience of gaining support from people she first met online, Jennifer explained how online technologies can help users overcome isolation in real life:

> I think a lot of us who have issues [with socializing in face-to-face situations]

eventually use [online platforms] to make friends face-to-face. Not all of us, obviously. But it's definitely a tool. In meetings we talk a lot about what people can do to meet friends face-to-face, how to find other support groups, how to socialize, etc. Not that I'm any great expert myself, but it's something we try to encourage to help people balance their lives.

Interactive platforms such as *Second Life* encourage members to work within a synchronous open-ended environment where they can directly interact with others via avatars. Having a visible representation of oneself on *Second Life* certainly allows members to explore their identity in a more 'realistic' environment. Members visualize their online identity in various ways; some members incorporate their real-life disabilities in their avatars, while others do not, and still others fluctuate from one choice to another. Alejandra changes her avatar's appearance depending on the representation she wants to portray, using an avatar with a wheelchair when speaking to non-disabled people about the GGC, and an able-bodied avatar when speaking to her peers. Jennifer describes her avatar:

> My avatar looks very much like me in real life, minus the signs of disability that I rarely display in Second Life because in my head I don't really picture myself as disabled. It's not part of my personal image of myself, not because I think appearing with a disability is in any way less of an option. It's just what feels comfortable to me most of the time.

Jennifer's story invites a particular and resisting reading of ICT policy, with the goal of encouraging disabled people to live 'normal' and 'integrated' lives (Moser, 2006). For Jennifer and other members, visual representations of self in the form of a *Second Life* avatar can vividly reflect how they understand their disability and identity in a variety of ways, as well as how they teach others about the disability community. Alejandra's occasional use of different avatars and Jennifer's disinclination to picture herself 'as disabled' exemplify how the *Second Life* virtual platform allows GGC members to express a subjective understanding of disability, unbounded by the stigmas ascribed to their real-life bodies. In other words, the ability to choose how to present themselves allows the members to express their identity in ways that work for them, without relying on conventional narratives of medical intervention or rehabilitation. Given *Second Life's* role as identity playground, the members become capable of creating their own meanings, to open up rather than close down the meaning of living with disabilities. By working toward transcending the myths of 'normativity' and thus being perceived as something other than helpless, they reconstruct their way of being-in-the-world as one of the privileges of life. For GGC members, who are often defined by institutions and medical definitions of their disability with limited opportunities for autonomous social exploration, ICTs represent an opportunity to move beyond externally imposed definitions of who they are, experiment with self-representation and forge their own sense of identity.

Looking Forward

... The GGC has much to share on many levels: as a model of a self-sustaining online community; a community that maintains itself across a myriad of intersecting ICTs simultaneously; an example of how to resist institutional appropriations of identity and definitions of self for women with disabilities; and as an inclusive women-centered space that tailors itself to the needs of its members wherever they are and however they define themselves. The GGC is a unique community that has had the opportunity to come into its own and grow alongside the proliferation of the Web 2.0 phenomenon. Members of the community have made choices regarding the technologies they use and how they integrate them in order to meet the needs of as many members as possible. Over the past decade, the GGC and its members have changed their lives, and have been shaped by the choices they have made in how they engage in ICTs. With the wider adoption of ICTs by society at large, we will continue to look for new ways in which to challenge institutional/medical discourses, as well as public perceptions of women with disabilities. As well, we consider the further exploration of various ICT tools central to our goal of bringing women with disabilities together in order, not only to share our stories and co-construct community, but to discover and create new opportunities for us to engage more fully with the world around us, both socially and economically. . . .

Notes

1. After 12 years of activity, the GGC finally achieved this goal in January 2010. The GGC officially became a program of People Helping People (http://www.phpnw.org) to give the GGC 501(c)3 nonprofit status and the support of an organization with the same goals and passion to support the independence of people with disabilities.

2. Just before this article was published the GGC parcel in *Second Life* moved to the EDGE lab's sims at http://slurl.com/secondlife/Research%20Edge/50/58/282

References

Barron K (1997) The bumpy road to womanhood. *Disability & Society* 12(2): 223–240.

Bowker N and Tuffin K (2002) Disability discourses for online identities. *Disability and Society* 17(3): 327–344.

Chen W and Wellman B (2005) Minding the cyber-gap. The Internet and social inequality. In Romero M and Margolis E (eds) *Blackwell Companion to Social Inequalities*. Oxford: Blackwell.

Clandinin DJ and Connelly FM (2000) *Narrative Inquiry*. San Francisco, CA: Jossey-Bass.

Cole J (2009) GimpGirl Community: Supporting the lives of women with disabilities. Paper presented at Sex::Tech Conference, San Francisco, CA, 22–23 March.

Cole J and Mancuso K (2009) GimpGirl Community: Women with disabilities. Paper presented at 2nd Virtual Praxis, Online, 21–22 November. Available at: http://people .cohums.ohio-state.edu/collingwood7/ minerva/conference09_jennylin.html (consulted March 2010).

Dobransky K and Hargittai E (2006) The disability divide in Internet access and use. *Information, Communication and Society* 9(3): 313–334.

Ferri BA and Gregg N (1998) Women with disabilities: Missing voices. *Women's Studies International Forum* 21(4): 429–439.

Finn J (1999) An exploration of helping processes in an online self-help group focusing on issues of disability. *Health and Social Work* 24(3): 220–231.

Haythornthwaite C (2008) Learning relations and networks in web-based communities. *International Journal of Web Based Communities* 4(2): 140–158.

Hine C (2000) *Virtual Ethnography*. London: Sage.

Hughes B (2005) What can a Foucauldian analysis contribute to disability theory? In Tremain S (ed.) *Foucault and the Government of Disability*. Michigan: University of Michigan Press.

Katz J and Rice R (2002) *Social Consequences of Internet Use: Access, Involvement, and Interaction*. Boston, MA: MIT Press.

Kendall L (1996) MUDder? I hardly know 'Er! Adventures of a Feminist MUDder. In Cherny L and Weise E (eds) *wired_women*. Seattle, WA: Seal, 207–233.

Lambek M (2005) Our subjects/ourselves: A view from the back seat. In Meneley A and Young DJ (eds) *Auto-ethnographies*. Toronto: Broadview Press, 229–240.

Lather P (1995) The validity of angels: Interpretive and textual strategies in researching the lives of women with HIV/ AIDS. *Qualitative Inquiry* 1(1): 41–68.

Mancuso K and Cole J (2009) GimpGirl community's best practices for facilitating an accessible community in a virtual world. Poster presented at IEEE Accessing the Future Conference, Boston, MA, 20–21 July. Available at: http://ewh.ieee.org/conf/ accessingthefuture/documents/mancuso.pdf (consulted July 2009).

Mazar R and Nolan J (2009) Hacking say and reviving ELIZA: Lessons from virtual environments. *Innovate* 5(2). Available at: http://www.innovateonline.info/index .php?view=article&id=547 (consulted July 2009).

Morris M and Ogan C (1996) The internet as mass medium. *The Journal of Communication* 46(1): 39–50.

Moser I (2006) Disability and the promises of technology: Technology, subjectivity and embodiment within an order of the normal. *Information, Communication and Society* 9(3): 373–395.

Nolan J and Weiss J (2002) Learning cyberspace: An educational view of virtual community. In Renninger A and Shumar W (eds) *Building Virtual Communities*. Cambridge: Cambridge University Press.

Ospina A, Cole J and Nolan J (2008) GimpGirl grows up: Women with disabilities rethinking, redefining, and reclaiming community. Paper presented at Internet Research 9.0, Copenhagen, 15–18 October.

Pendergrass S, Nosek M and Holcomb J (2001) Design and evaluation of an internet site to educate women with disabilities on reproductive health care. *Sexuality and Disability* 19(1): 71–83.

Rheingold H (1994) *The Virtual Community: Homesteading on the Electronic Frontier*. Reading, MA: HarperPerennial.

Sponaas-Robins R and Nolan J (2005) MOOs: Polysynchronous collaborative virtual environments. In Zemliansky P and Amant K St (eds) *Workplace Internet-based*

Communication. New York: Idea Group, 130–156.

Trahar S (2009) Beyond the story itself: Narrative inquiry and autoethnography in intercultural research in higher education. *Forum Qualitative Sozialforschung / Forum: Qualitative Social Research* 10(1): Art 30. Available at: http://www.qualitative-research .net/index.php/fqs/article/view/1218/2654 (consulted September 2010).

Valentine G and Skelton T (2009) An umbilical cord to the world. *Information, Communication and Society* 12(1): 44–65.

van Dijk J and Hacker K (2003) The digital divide as a complex and dynamic phenomenon. *The Information Society* 19: 315–326.

van Manen M (1997) *Researching Lived Experience*. London, Ontario: Althouse.

Young DJ and Meneley A (2005) Introduction: Auto-ethnographies of academic practices. In Meneley A and Young DJ (eds) *Auto-ethnographies*. Toronto: Broadview Press, 1–22.

Wellman B, Hogan B, Berg K et al. (2006) Connected lives: The project. In: Purcell P (ed.) *Networked Neighbourhoods*. London: Springer, 161–216.

658 ■ PART

Chavez
'Latino Th
tradition
immig
impa
that
ali

69

The Latino Cyber-Moral Panic Process in the United States

Nadia Yamel Flores-Yeffal,
Guadalupe Vidales, and April Plemons

According to Cohen (1972), 'moral panic' is the reaction of a society against a specific social group based on beliefs that the subgroup represents a major threat to society. Usually, the information spread is exaggerated or fabricated by what Becker (1963) calls 'moral entrepreneurs' who create a threatening situation with inflated rhetoric and develop a sense of fear against the subgroup. Commonly, this rhetoric is spread with the use of popular and mass media (e.g. newspaper headlines, radio shows, television programs, websites, weblogs, and/or discussion forums). Such outlets divert society's attention from more pressing issues affecting American society and those who are in control utilize resources such as 'politics, social status, gender, wealth, religious beliefs, and mobilization of the masses' to dominate, both, 'materially and ideologically', the information targeting the subordinate group (Adler & Adler 2009, p. 152).

Today, an immigrant subgroup is being targeted and victimized by a moral panic—Latinos/as, particularly, Mexican immigrants (Massey 2007; Chavez 2008; Perez *et al.* 2008). Such demonization of a specific subgroup of immigrants is not new in the United States. Throughout history, US immigration policies have been described as unfair and capricious procedures in which the US government acts without any regard to the immigrant's rights and needs (Calavita 1992, 1996; Ngai 2004; Massey 2007). First, the United States enacted the Chinese Exclusion Act in 1882, which discriminated against Chinese immigrants. Then, European immigrants at the turn of the twentieth century, such as Russian Jews, German Catholics and Italians, faced a second wave of discrimination where the same rhetoric previously used against the Chinese was also utilized to demonize and dehumanize these new immigrants (Brodkin 1999; Foner 2000; Ngai 2004; Portes & Rumbaut 2006).

From Nadia Yamel Flores-Yeffal et al. (2012), "The Latino Cyber-Moral Panic Process in the United States." *Information, Communication and Society*, 14:4, 568–589. Reprinted by permission of the publisher (Taylor & Francis Ltd, http://www.tandf.co.uk/journals).

(2008) states that the new
reat Narrative is part of a grand
of alarmist discourse about
ants and their perceived negative
t on society' (p. 3). He further argues
immigrant Latinos are labeled 'illegal
ens' to emphasize their criminal status,
which presents them as a group of criminal outsiders unworthy of social services,
educational support and legalization.

... Due to online technological
advances, this negative perception has
increased and become more pervasive;
'moral entrepreneurs' have facilitated the
spread of information in ways never imagined against Latinos. The near instantaneous spread of cyberspace information
directly affects the process in which contemporary moral panics take place. In
this chapter, we use the case of the anti-
immigrant sentiment against Latinos in
the United States to explore the extent to
which online technology influences the
classic moral panic stages as previously
presented by scholars before the use of
internet technology. . . .

The Classic Moral Panic Stages

According to the classic moral panic process framework, a full-blown moral panic
is the final stage in the moral campaign
process: awareness, moral conversion, and
moral panic. Through these stages, public
morality can be constructed, manufactured, and spread. In the 'awareness' stage,
a message is generated in relation to a
problem by citing statistics, case examples,
presenting 'experts' to justify their claims,
and using intense rhetorical methods. The
second stage, 'moral conversion' draws
upon 'elements of drama, novelty, or cultural myths' in which entrepreneurs utilize
wide media coverage and often seek celebrities or political leaders to convince the
masses (p. 149). Through these surrogate
sponsors, moral entrepreneurs legitimize

their claims and convince the public to join
the movement. In the final stage, 'moral
panic', there is a temporary and widespread concern about a problematic issue
promoted both by the media and legislative
attention. Furthermore, formal and informal communication outlets draw attention
to a specific targeted group, or 'folk devils',
who become the scapegoats for larger
social ills. . . .

The Construction of
Latinos as a Threat

Prior research demonstrates that people of
color are commonly perceived as a possible threat to society (King & Wheelock
2007), and Latino immigrants are not an
exception. Huntington (2004) published
'The Hispanic Challenge', in which he
asserts that Latinos, especially Mexicans,
represent an extremely dangerous threat
to the United States and its culture because
of their failure to assimilate, failure to
learn English, and failure to adopt the
Protestant values. Then, a 2005 report
from the Pew Hispanic Center announced
there were 12 million unauthorized immigrants living in the United States, and 75
percent were Hispanic (Passel 2005).
More recently, the 2006 HR 4437 law,
also called 'the Border Protection,
Antiterrorism, and Illegal Immigration
Control Act', was the catalyst for immigration marches where millions of people
marched on the streets in protest of the
proposed legislation and calling for immigration reform. These marches were
broadcasted globally, and it has been
claimed that an anti-immigrant backlash
against Latino immigrants began as a
result of the 2006 immigrant Marches
(Perez et al. 2008). In 2006, the US Census
Bureau announced in major newspapers
that the US Hispanic population was 'projected to nearly triple, from 46.7 million
to 132.8 million, from 2008 through

2050. Its share of the total US population was expected to double from 15 to 30 percent by the year 2050; thus, one in three US residents would be Hispanic' (Broughton 2008). Given this, Latino immigrants would outnumber all the other racial and ethnic groups in the United States, including the non-Hispanic White population, therefore, representing a possible numeric threat to the nation (Chavez 2008; Feagin 2009).

American nativist rhetoric was strongly associated with issues related to the preservation of national sovereignty, such as the protection of US territory from an invasion (Chavez 2001). The immigrants' utilization of the Mexican flag as a symbol of their nation is perceived as a racial threat and the 'browning' of United States. Also, other problems are perceived as a threat such as the economic burden that immigrants represented and the multiculturalism agenda they embraced. . . .

In addition, immigrant groups have been described as 'contaminated communities', and 'popular rhetoric about immigration often operates by constructing metaphoric representations of immigrants that concretize the social "problem"' (Cisneros 2008, p. 569). Immigrants also have been identified in cyberspace as 'the immigrant problem' (Sohoni 2006). In this way, immigrants become degraded images and not human beings. Goode and Yehuda (1994) argue 'folk devils' are used as metaphors or symbolic representations of moral panics; they are shrouded in myths and empirical falsehoods. Therefore, in this paper, we introduce the term *Latino cybermoral panic*, in which we claim that the use of cyber technology has provided a dangerous platform in which the already existent anti-immigrant movement has become more dangerous against Latinos. Here, false and manipulated information transforms Latino immigrants into the contemporary American 'folk devils', or those perceived as threatening the social order and blamed for much of society's problems (Cohen 1972).

Moral Entrepreneurs and the Use of Internet Technology

Media outlets tend to include such allegations against the subgroup, in this case against the Latino immigrants in the United States, into their media content and emotionally charging otherwise dispassionate subjects to maximize their audiences (McRobbie & Thornton 1995). Also Shoemaker and Reese (1996) note that 'the more deviant people or events are, the more likely they are to be included in media content and the more likely they are to be stereotyped' (p. 270). Alarmist websites, internet blogs, social networking sites such as Twitter and Facebook, internet forums, television programs, video hosting sites such as YouTube, radio talk shows and billboard propaganda, among other types of public free expression in the era of the reflexive and interactive Web 2.0, are utilized to spread the information, which generally includes hate content instantaneously at low cost, and to an even larger audience than newspaper and TV consumers. As Castells et al. (2008) state, the 'public sphere' is culturally and politically critical because it is the 'space where people come together as citizens and articulate their autonomous views to influence the political institutions of society' (p. 2). The public sphere refers to the ability to form social opinions as a result of rational public debate (Habermas 1991[1973]) which has been revived with the use of the internet technology (Papacharissi 2002). In addition, the internet allows for the access to tools which permit individuals to engage in new social and political action, have instant access to social network outlets and exchange of information at a distance (Bowen 1996; DiMaggio et al. 2001; Castells et al. 2007; Van Laer & Van Aelst 2010).

Actors at the top of the power structure who are active in the movement and who enjoy greater access to the internet utilize different features, such as derogatory images, exaggerated pictures and discriminatory cartoons to effectively spread the Latino cyber-moral panic to others, which is then reproduced and transmitted by individuals mainly also via cyberspace. Social power online is no longer simply at the hands of the few or elite. While moral entrepreneurs and politicians can exert 'considerable influence' over media and social thought, the audience is equally as active in creating, reproducing, and influencing content (Castells 2007). In either case, the internet allows a new form of cyberspace socialization containing a number of technological advances used as outlets for people to exchange information, enjoy relative anonymity and share their social views and values to untapped mass audiences (DiMaggio et al. 2001; Bergh & McKenna 2004).

The moral entrepreneurs penetrate the mass media using alarmist reports often cited by major newspapers. Such alarmist news produced by those reports help sell more newspapers and reach a larger audience given that, at the time of writing this paper, most newspapers were published via cyberspace which is now playing a more 'decisive role' in shaping social movements (Castells et al. 2008). . . .

The Study

We utilized a multi-method approach in cyber space consisting of online ethnographic research followed by content analysis of anti-immigrant websites. . . .

Our online ethnography consisted of online participant observation, field notes and data documentation from various cyber social networks including anti-immigrant and pro-immigrant websites, US government websites, documents and reports about immigration online, blogs and forums (both pro-and anti-immigration), online newspaper articles, forums, Facebook, *YouTube,* emails and online video hosting since May 2006. The authors have observed evidence of the moral panic through visiting these sources. For example, one of the authors has been an online participant-observer of an anti-immigration forum which began before the 2006 immigrant marches and spent an average of two hours per day discussing immigration issues and gathering information from other websites, blogs, forums, and news articles mostly available online and posted by other forum participants. She also obtained information concerning the main sources and how arguments that supported the anti-immigrant sentiment were originated. In addition, the three authors have been conducting content analyzes of several talk radio programs and political news television shows, and collecting data from talk radio websites, Twitter posts, and Facebook updates also related to the same television and radio programs, where the discussion of anti-immigrant issues are the norm.

. . . During the preliminary stages of our research, while constructing our snowball sample of websites, we unintentionally discovered the anti-immigrant movement in cyberspace is led by the following three 'think tank' organizations via their websites:

1. The Center for Immigration Studies (CIS)

2. NumbersUSA

3. The Federation for American Immigration Reform (FAIR).

We realized most of the sites, if not all, had links to the three think tanks named above, which illustrates the degree of the trio's influence. Others identified the 'trio' as very influential in the anti-immigrant movement (Beirich 2009), and noted that their websites did not utilize nativist language (Sohoni 2006). These are what Daniels (2009) refers to as 'cloaked websites', because the anti-immigrant agenda is not apparent to online visitors. We argue the founders, board of directors, supporters and site creators or moderators are, in fact, the moral entrepreneurs leading the incrimination against Latino immigrants. Other moral entrepreneurs are from media outlets, such as political commentators, talk radio hosts, and politicians, but the data suggested the central moral entrepreneurs behind the cyberspace movement are FAIR, NumbersUSA and CIS, all three in particular.

The content analysis of the anti-immigrant website subsample revealed that one of the main strategic processes in attacking the subgroup was with the creation of metaphors and extensive use of images portraying Latino immigrants as 'folk devils'. This strategy increases the phobia by presenting the immigrants as inhumane and inferior to Americans. Another awareness-promoting strategy was the use and manipulation of images and words in order to portray an extremely negative image of the Latino immigrants to site visitors. For example, Latino immigrants were portrayed as dangerous, possible terrorists, killers, drug addicts and were accused of spreading diseases, such as the H1N1 virus, being dirty and living in crowded and unsanitary conditions. They were blamed for taking the jobs of Americans, reducing their wages, being a burden to society by not paying taxes, stealing identities, utilizing medical facilities, asking for welfare financial benefits, Medicaid, food stamps, or using fraudulent documents to vote among other claims.

Most sites posted claims together with other text disclosures stating that the sites and arguments had 'nothing to do with race' or being negative toward immigrants, but rather that their goals were only making people aware of the sudden increase in immigration statistics and the possible burdens this could represent to the American society. Most provided neither empirical evidence, nor empirical statistics to support

their claims, but instead provided inflated statistics and pictures (which were altered and/or fabricated) that were posted next to each claim. For example, websites commonly juxtapose pictures of a young, smiling, blond haired child with one of a brown-skinned person's criminal mug shot, followed by a picture of a coffin to imply the child was murdered by an immigrant. However, there is no evidence of the picture's validity, or if the story's circumstances are even accurately associated with the people in the images.

User-created posts and comments and blogs linking to anti-immigrant sites revealed that, in general, site visitors rarely questioned the claims or content of the images. On the contrary, visitors began reproducing the links of exaggerated claims on additional blogs, forums, Facebook or Twitter pages and private sites to spread awareness to others, which exponentially spread the information in today's participatory, often user-created, Web 2.0. For example, a hoax about immigrant statistics (found by us in 2006) was circulating online that was said to have been published by *Los Angeles Times,* but the *Los Angeles Times* (2007) published a disclaimer (Internet Immigration Hoax 2007; http://latimesblogs.latimes.com/readers/2007/11/internet-immigr.html) stating this was false. The statistics stated that, '95% of warrants for murder in Los Angeles are for illegal aliens', and, that 'Over 300,000 illegal aliens in Los Angeles County are living in garages'. The hoax targeted Latinos, as it was supposed to have been published by *Los Angeles Times* and included statistics about Spanish speaking radio stations, etc. These false statistics spread online via anti-immigrant websites and newcomers believed the statistics enough to copy and paste them over and over in other forums, blogs, private websites, etc without questioning their validity or fact-checking. The claim appeared legitimate since it cited the *Los Angeles Times,* and, as of 13 September 2010, we found the phrase, 'Over

300,000 illegal aliens in Los Angeles County are living in garages' resulted in 1,570,000 hits from the Yahoo search engine, and the phrase 'of warrants for murder in Los Angeles are for illegal aliens' yielded 9,690,000 results. Therefore, internet users spread the information and fear to others on the internet in order to make everyone else aware of the Latino threat (Chavez 2008). . . .

Given that their claims could not be supported by any academic empirical evidence or governmental reports, the moral entrepreneurs, led by the three organizations listed above (FAIR, CIS, and NumbersUSA) created a system of revolving information that we call the *Recycling Factory* in cyberspace. In this original process, each organization creates statistical reports and recycles them continuously to the other organizations. Each cites the other, and almost all of the sites used the reports to support their unsubstantiated statements. . . .

The content analysis of our sub-sample revealed a new stage that is absent in Adler and Adler's original three stages of the moral campaign process. We name this new stage the '*Call for civil action*' which includes various forms of calls for action, either civil or political. It is through this stage that individuals personally participate and directly contribute to the anti-immigrant movement. Prior moral panic research has never before identified at this stage, the direct participation by the individuals being converted. The internet is providing a new 'meta-medium' in which the public sphere can be utilized as a means to gather financial, political, social, and cultural support (DiMaggio et al. 2001).

. . . Some urge the boycott of American companies supporting immigration by offering detailed information about how and why to carry it out. Others invite citizens to become "minutemen"[1] and/or volunteer to protect the borders, as well as the reporting of undocumented immigrants. In fact, we found minuteman websites for almost every state in the nation, even those not in close proximity to the border. There were calls for donations which can be paid with a credit card or PayPal (a secure form of online payment). Some sites, such as FAIR also provide site visitors with information on how they can make recurrent donations to the organization. In fact, aside from making one-time donations, a person can contribute to FAIR's cause literally from the moment they join the work force until after their death. From 401K plans (where donations will be matched dollar for dollar) to endowments, FAIR provides information on how one can include their organization and cause as a beneficiary of a life insurance policy or will. Site visitors are asked to directly participate in funding, supporting, and furthering the movement through this new stage, a call to action (found at: http://www.fairus.org/site/PageNavigator/support/other_ways_ to_give.html).

Other forms of obtaining money from upset citizens was through the sale of minuteman videos, gold or silver coins, documentaries about immigration, hats, shirts, and bumper stickers with various patriotic anti-immigrant phrases, such as 'no amnesty' or 'no invasion'. A more extreme case sought donations to construct billboards all over the nation with the message, 'Stop the Invasion, Protect our Borders' (Melamed 2006). More importantly, revenue accumulated from these sites can be used to 'make campaign contributions and sway political candidates, to fund research favorable to their [movement] and to lobby against unfavorable legislation' (Adler & Adler 2009, p. 152).

. . . A successful tactic utilized by the cyberspace movement is the invitation to engage in political action by contacting politicians. This pervasive strategy includes elaborate information charts about how to contact legislators, current legislation for congressmen to vote on, petitions to sign, and where to rally in favor of or against a political proposition related to immigration, etc. They even include direct links to legislators and offer ready-to-send messages which can be sent asking for immediate action related to immigration issues. For example, visitors can browse their state's list of congressmen to find out their stance and voting records on anti-immigration legislation. At NumbersUSA, those congressmen with highest regard, or the 'best' anti-immigration voting records, win the title of 'True Reformers'—those who 'promise to support all or nearly all of NumbersUSA's top immigration priorities'. Of course, site visitors are provided a link to that congressman's personal website and encouraged to contribute to the 'True Reformer's' political campaign, in the hope of ensuring their re-election and support for the nativist movement (http://www.numbersusa.com/content/true-reformers.html).

Finally, evidence from the sites' content analysis revealed that most sites posted evidence of the movement's successes. . . .

For example, FAIR's annual report claims that their number of site visitors in 2007 surpassed the 1 million mark and received over 6 million views, a significant increase from previous years (FAIR Annual report 2007). Evidence of the pro-immigrant movement's failures was commonly seen in reminders of the lack of immigration reform, successes of government intervention and new legislation, and the massive raids and deportations that have taken place in the past few years (Moreno 2007). Reports also show lower numbers of Mexican immigrants crossing the border to the United States, although Mexican immigrants in the United States are not returning to Mexico (Passel 2005; Passel & Cohn 2009). Unfortunately, the number of hate crimes which result from the Latino cyber-moral panic movement has yet to be measured. One example of a hate crime, which resulted as a consequence of this movement, is the case of a minuteman activist who was accused of killing a man and child in their own home:

An outspoken anti-immigration activist who was at the center of a series of violent crimes in Everett earlier this year now stands accused of the home-invasion killings of an Arizona man and his 9-year-old daughter. Shawna Forde, 41, and two associates in her Minuteman American Defense group are charged with two counts of first-degree murder, one count of first-degree burglary and one count of aggravated assault, according to the Pima County Sheriff's Department in Arizona. (North et al. 2009)

Shawna Forde, the activist mentioned above, besides being a minuteman volunteer, was also found to be one of the executive directors of FAIR. Forde, who further jeopardized the organization's reputation for the murders of the immigrants, was ultimately found guilty and sentenced to death ('Jury decides on death penalty for woman who headed vigilante squad' 2011). . . .

Conclusion

. . . In this research, we used as an example, the Latino cyber-moral panic and found empirical evidence to support that Adler and Adler's three classic moral panic stages have taken place, but in a more effective manner with the use of new online technologies.

A new stage not previously identified was conceptualized called a *'call for action'*, where donations, political action, and civil action are promoted and enforced via cyberspace. Through calls for donations, moral entrepreneurs collect funds from the movement's panic victims to pay for other forms of propaganda and further spread the moral panic. Similar internet tools have already been identified as being key instruments for the direct participation of individuals in other political and social movements around the world (Bowen 1996; Van Laer & Van Aelst 2010).

... The results presented here indicate that the continually evolving online technologies, if used in a negative way, can be extremely dangerous against specific subgroups of people. Future moral panics could occur and progress even faster than today and more efficiently could aid in the creation of legislation, hate crimes, and social suppression against the 'folk devils' being targeted. Furthermore, if moral panics indeed provide an avenue for social reproduction of particular ideologies (Beisel 1997; Gatson 2007), then cybermoral panics could then become a dangerous never-ending source of social reproduction of suppressing and discriminatory ideologies against specific subgroups of people. Future research should be conducted to examine the role of politicians as a type of secondary moral entrepreneurship with the goal of political benefit. . . . In addition, more research should explore the power of civil and political action with the help of cyberspace technology, and whether it can also be used for a more positive cyber movement in which the targeted groups, instead, could acquire some kind of benefit which could help them to succeed instead of placing them in a disadvantaged position in society.

Note

1. According to Chavez (2008), the Minutemen are a group of civilians whose final goal is 'to monitor the Arizona–Mexico border in the hopes of locating clandestine border crossers. However, this surveillance operation also had a larger objective: to produce a spectacle that would garner public media attention and influence federal immigration polices' (p. 132). According to the Minuteman Project Command Center, their organization is 'a multiethnic, immigration law enforcement advocacy group.—Operating within the law to support enforcement of the law.—The power of change through the power of peace' http://www.minutemanproject.com/ organization/about_us.asp.

References

Adler, P. & Adler, P. (2009) 'Constructing deviance', in *Constructions of Deviance: Social Power, Context, and Interaction*, eds P. Adler & P. Adler, Wadsworth, Belmont, California, pp. 147–154.

Arsenault, A. & Castells, M. (2006) 'Conquering the minds, conquering Iraq: the social production of misinformation in the United States—a case study', *Information, Communication & Society*, vol. 9, no. 3, pp. 284–307.

Bakardjieva, M. & Feenberg, A. (2001) 'Involving the virtual subject: conceptual, methodological and ethical dimensions', *Journal of Ethics and Information Technology*, vol. 2, no. 4, pp. 233–240.

Baker, P. (2001) 'Moral panic and alternative identity construction in Usenet', *Journal of Computer-Mediated Communication*, vol. 7, no. 1.

Becker, H. S. (1963) *Outsiders: Studies in the Sociology of Deviance*, Free Press, New York.

Beirich, H. (2009) 'The Nativist lobby: three faces of intolerance' in *A Report from the Southern Poverty Law Center*, ed. Mark Potok, Montgomery, Alabama, pp. 1–21 [Online] Available at: http://www.splcenter.org/sites/default/files/downloads/splc_nativistlobby.pdf (10 January 2011)

Beisel, N. (1997) *Imperiled Innocents: Anthony Comstock and Family Reproduction in Victorian America*, Princeton University Press, Princeton, NJ.

Ben-Yehuda, N. (1986) 'The sociology of moral panics: toward a new synthesis', *The Sociological Quarterly*, vol. 27, no. 4, pp. 495–513.

Bergh, J. A. & McKenna, K. Y. (2004) 'The Internet and social life', *Annual Review of Psychology*, vol. 55, pp. 573–590.

Berry, D. M. (2004) 'Internet research: privacy, ethics and alienation—an open source approach', *The Journal of Internet Research*, vol. 14, no. 4, pp. 323–332.

Bowen, C. (1996) *Modem Nation: The Handbook of Grassroots American Activism Online*, Random House, New York.

Brodkin, K. (1999) *How Jews Became White Folks and What That Says About Race in America*, Rutgers University Press, New Brunswick, NJ.

Broughton, A. (2008) 'Minorities expected to be the majority in 2050', *CNN.com*, [Online] Available at: http://edition.cnn.com/2008/US/08/13/census. minorities/index.html (11 August 2009).

Calavita, K. C. (1992) *Inside the State: The Bracero Program, Immigration and the INS*, Rutledge, Chapman and Hall, Inc, New York.

Calavita, K. (1996) 'The new politics of immigration: "balanced-budget conservatism" and the symbolism of proposition 187', *Social Problems*, vol. 43, pp. 284–305.

Castells, M. (2007) 'Communication, power and counter-power in the network society', *International Journal of Communication*, vol. 1, pp. 238–266.

Castells, M., Qui, J., Fernandez-Ardèvol, M. & Sey, A. (2007) *Mobile Communication and Society: A Global Perspective*, MIT, Cambridge, MA.

Castells, M., Qui, J., Fernandez-Ardèvol, M. & Sey, A. (2008) 'The new public sphere: global civil society, communication networks, global governance', *The ANNALS of the American Academy of Political and Social Science*, vol. 616, no. 1, pp. 78–93.

Chavez, L. (2001) *Covering Immigration Popular Images and the Politics of the Nation*, University of California Press, Los Angeles.

Chavez, L. (2008) The *Latino Threat: Constructing Immigrants, Citizens, and the Nation*, Stanford University Press, Palo Alto, California.

Chou, R. S. & Feagin, J. R. (2008) *The Myth of the Model Minority: Asian Americans Facing Racism*, Paradigm Publishers, Boulder, CO.

Cisneros, D. J. (2008) 'Contaminated communities: the metaphor of immigrant as pollutant in media representations of immigration', *Rhetoric & Public Affairs*, vol. 11, no. 4, pp. 569–602.

Cohen, S. (1972) *Folk Devils and Moral Panics*, Routledge Press, London.

Cornwell, B. & Linders, A. (2002) 'The myth of "Moral Panic": an alternative account of LSD prohibition', *Deviant Behavior*, vol. 23, pp. 307–330.

Daniels, J. (2008) 'Searching for Dr. King: teens, race & cloaked websites', in *Electronic Techtonics: Thinking at the Interface*, eds Erin Ennis Harry Halpin, Paolo Mangiafico, Jennifer Rhee et al., Lulu Press, Durham, NC, pp. 94–116.

Daniels, J. (2009) *Cyber Racism: White Supremacy Online and the New Attack on Civil Rights*, Rowman & Littlefield, Lanham, MD.

DiMaggio, P., Hargittai, E., Neuman, W. R. & Robinson, J. P. (2001) 'Social implications of the internet', *Annual Review of Sociology*, vol. 27, pp. 307–336.

Feagin, J. (2009) *The White Racial Frame*, Routledge Press, New York.

Federation for American Immigration Reform. (2007) 2007 *Annual Report, FAIRUS.org* , Washington DC, [Online] Available at: http://www.fairus.org/site/ DocServer/2007_Annual_Report.pdf?docID=2402   (18 October 2009).

Federation for American Immigration Reform (2009) 'US Immigration Policy and Legislation', *FAIRUS.org* , [Online] Available at: http://www.fairus.org/site/ PageNavigator/legislation (18 October 2009).

Federation for American Immigration Reform (2010) 'The fiscal burden of illegal immigration on United States taxpayers', *FAIRUS.org*, [Online] Available at: http://www.fairus.org/site/DocServer/USCostStudy_2010.pdf?docID=4921 (23 November 2010).

Fisher, D. R. & Boekkooi, M. (2010) 'Mobilizing friends and strangers: understanding the role of the internet in the step it up day of action', *Information, Communication & Society*, vol. 13, no. 2, pp. 193–208.

Foner, N. (2000) *From Ellis Island to JFK: New York's Two Great Waves of Immigration*, Russell Sage Foundation, New York.

Fox, N. & Roberts, C. (1999) 'GPs in cyberspace: the sociology of "virtual community"', *The Sociological Review*, vol. 47, no. 4, pp. 643–671.

Gajjala, R. (2000) 'Cyberethnography: reading each "Other"', [Online] Available at: http://personal.bgsu.edu/~radhik/

Cyberethnography.pdf (10 September 2010).

Gajjala, R. (2002) 'An interrupted postcolonial/ feminist cyberethnography: complicity and resistance in the "Cyberfield"', *Feminist Media Studies*, vol. 2, pp. 177–193.

Garcia, A. C., Standlee, A. I., Bechkoff, J. & Cui, Y. (2009) 'Ethnographic approaches to the internet and computer-mediated communication', *Journal of Contemporary Ethnography*, vol. 38, no. 1, pp. 52–84.

Gatson, S. (2007) 'The body or the body politic? Risk, harm, moral panic, and drug use discourse online', in *Real Drugs in a Virtual World: Drug Discourse and Community Online*, eds Edward Murguia, Melissa Tackett-Gibson & Ann Lessem, Lexington Books, Lanham, MD, pp. 23–44.

Gerstenfeld, P. B., Grant, D. R. & Chiang, C. P. (2003) 'Hate online: a content analysis of extremist internet sites', *Analyses of Social Issues and Public Policy*, vol. 3, no. 1, pp. 29–44.

Goode, E. & Yehuda, N. B. (1994) *Moral Panics: the Social Construction of Deviance*, Blackwell, Massachusetts.

Habermas, J. (1991 [1973]) 'The public sphere', in *Rethinking Popular Culture: Contemporary Perspectives in Cultural Studies*, eds C. Mukerji & M. Schudson, University of California Press, Berkeley, CA, pp. 398–404.

Hine, C. M. (2000) *Virtual Ethnography*, Sage Publications Ltd, Thousand Oaks, CA.

Huntington, S. (2004) 'The Hispanic challenge', *Foreign Policy*, vol. 141, pp. 30–45.

Internet Immigration Hoax (2007) 'A conversation on newsroom ethics and standards', *Los Angeles Times* , 28 November, [Online] Available at: http://latimesblogs. latimes .com/readers/2007/11/internet-immigr.html (12 November 2009).

Jury decides on death penalty for woman who headed vigilante squad (2011) CNN Justice News, February 22, 2011, [Online] Available at: http://articles.cnn.com/ 2011-02-22/justice/arizona.double.killing_1_ shawna-forde-death-penalty- anti-illegal-immigration?_s=PM:CRIME (25 February 2011).

King, R. D. & Wheelock, D. (2007) 'Group threat and social control: race, perceptions of minorities and the desire to punish', *Social Forces*, vol. 85, pp. 1255–1280.

Los Angeles Times (2007) 'Internet immigration hoax', [Online] Available at: http://latimes-blogs.latimes.com/readers/2007/11/internet-immigr.html (10 September 2010).

Marwick, A. E. (2008) 'To catch a predator: The Myspace moral panic', *First Monday* , vol. 13, no. 6, [Online] Available at: http://first monday.org/htbin/ cgiwrap/bin/ojs/index .php/fm/article/viewArticle/2152/ 1966#author (12 November 2010).

Massey, D. S. (2007) *Categorically Unequal: The American Stratification System*, Russell Sage, New York.

McRobbie, A. & Thornton, S. (1995) 'Rethinking "Moral Panic" for multi-mediated social worlds', *British Journal of Sociology*, vol. 46, no. 4, pp. 559–574.

Melamed, S. (2006) 'Politics writ large: illegals go home', *MediaLifeMagazine.com,* [Online] Available at: http://www.medialifemagazine .com/artman2/ publish/Alternative_media_ 43/Politics_writ_large_Illegals_go_home_ 5721_printer.asp (18 October 2009).

Moreno, S. (2007) 'Immigration raid leaves Texas town a skeleton', *Washington Post*, [Online] Available at: http://www.gorena.org/ pdf/287g-Cactus.pdf (18 October 2009).

Ngai, M. M. (2004) *Impossible Subjects: Illegal Aliens and the Making of Modern America*, Princeton University Press, Princeton, NJ.

North, S., Holtz, J. & Writers, H. (2009) 'Activist Shawna Forde charged in double slaying: woman with troubled past in Evertt now accused in Arizona', *The Herald*, [Online] Available at: http:// heraldnet.com/article/20090613/ NEWS01/706139922/1054#Activist. Shawna.Forde.charged.in.double. slaying (13 August 2009).

Papacharissi, Z. (2002) 'The virtual sphere: the internet as a public sphere', *New Media & Society*, vol. 4, no. 1, pp. 9–21.

Passel, J. S. (2005) *Estimates of the Size and Characteristics of the Undocumented Population*, Pew Hispanic Center, Washington, DC.

Passel, J. S. & Cohn, D. (2009) *Mexican Immigrants: How Many Come? How Many Leave?* Pew Hispanic Center, Washington, DC, [Online] Available at: http:// pewhispanic.org/reports/report.php?ReportID=112 (18 October 2009).

Perez, H. L., Benavides, C., Malagon, M., Velez, V. & Solorzano, D. (2008) 'Getting beyond the "symptom", acknowledging the "disease": theorizing racist nativism', *Contemporary Justice Review*, vol. 11, no. 1, pp. 39–51.

Portes, A. & Rumbaut, R. (2006) *Immigrant America: A Portrait,* 3rd ed, University of California Press, Los Angeles.

Rheingold, H. (1993) *The Virtual Community: Homesteading on the Electronic Frontier*, Addison-Wesley, Reading, MA.

Schafer, J. A. (2002) 'Spinning the web of hate: web-based hate propagation by extremist organizations', *Journal of Criminal Justice and Popular Culture*, vol. 9, no. 2, pp. 69–88.

Shoemaker, P. J. & Reese, S. D. (1996) *Mediating the Message: Theories of Influences on Mass Media Content*, Longman, New York.

Sohoni, D. (2006) 'The "Immigrant Problem": modern-day nativism on the web', *Current Sociology*, vol. 54, no. 6, pp. 827–850.

US Census Bureau. (2006) 'The Hispanic population in the United States: 2004 detailed tables', Census.gov. [Online] Available at: http://www.census.gov/ population/www/ socdemo/hispanic/cps2004.html (10 October 2009).

Van Laer, J. & Van Aelst, P. (2010) 'Internet and social movement action repertoires: opportunities and limitations', *Information, Communication & Society*, vol. 13, no. 8, pp. 1146–1171.

Ward, K. (1999) 'The cyber-ethnographic (Re) construction of two feminist online communities', *Sociological Research Online*, vol. 4, no. 1, [Online] Available at: http:// www.socresonline.org.uk/4/1/ward.html (21 December 2010).

70

How It Feels to Be Viral Me

Affective Labor and Asian American YouTube Performance

Christine Bacareza Balance

O n March 15, 2011, just days after University of California–Los Angeles undergraduate Alexandra Wallace posted (and subsequently took down) her incendiary "Asians
in the Library" video log (vlog) on YouTube, another video set ablaze Facebook walls and
Twitter accounts. Jimmy Wong's "Ching Chong! Asians in the Library Song"—a satirical
love song addressed to Wallace—distinguished itself from the hundreds of other ranting and
remix response videos. Opening with an excerpt from the offending party's original post—
as she mockingly renders a scene of Asians answering their cell phones in the library with
an "Ooooh, Ching Chong Ling Long Ting Tong," Wong's video quickly shifts into a style
and staging commonly associated with online vlogs. Seated and directly addressing the
camera, he is framed by his home studio's accoutrements: computer and electronic keyboard
on his left side and a row of cables neatly hanging on the wall behind him. Stuttering in a
thick Asian accent and, in turn, deriding Wallace's own orientalist rendition, a guitar-
strapped Wong introduces his song into a boom microphone that hangs near his face:
"Greetings, Miss Alexandra Wallace. I'm not most... how you say... politically correct person. So please..." (head bows quickly) "do not take offensive. Thank you."

Viewers familiar with the "Asians in the Library" video would recognize that this introduction riffs on Wallace's own preface: while she is not the most "politically correct person," she *does* have Asian friends, and hopes, in the end, that viewers do not take offense.
Wong strums a single chord, signaling a magical transformation, as the video again cuts
to Wong, now guitarless but seated in the same position. This new version of Wong purrs
into the microphone without an Asian accent or tone of deference. With his recording

studio–style headphones on, his seductive vocal style recalls Asian American radio disc jockey Theo Mizuhara ("Theo" on Los Angeles R&B/hip-hop station 92.3 the Beat), often assumed to be African American by unsuspecting listeners because of his deep and soothing voice. This sexier Wong calls to Wallace—"Oooh girl"—before launching into his own rendition of her library scene: "Don't think I didn't see you watching me talking on my phone yesterday . . . all sexy . . . All Ching Chong Ling Long . . . Baby, it's just code . . . It's just the way that I tell the ladies that it's time for me to get funky."

For Wong, "getting funky" means launching into an acoustic ode to Wallace, a remix and reclamation of words and phrases lifted from her original video post. The song culminates in a repeating chorus, one that "wrings the musicality of the original Ching Chong" bit while satirizing its incommensurability: "Ching Chong . . . It means I love you . . . Ling Long . . . I really need you . . . Ching Chong . . . I still don't know what that means." The song's arrangement of vocal melody and harmony, acoustic guitar, and lo-fi percussion are simple and catchy. Yet the video's visual elements—the main frame of Wong is surrounded by small boxes or PiPs (picture in pictures) of him performing each portion of the music—requires a professional style of multichannel editing. Here, Wong's video evidences the unstable divisions between amateur and professional that is characteristic of the video-sharing website YouTube, ones that have helped redefine contemporary media production.

Since its initial posting, "Ching Chong! Asians in the Library Song" has garnered almost 4 million hits worldwide, received coverage from both Asian American and mainstream U.S. press outlets, and landed the twenty-three-year-old actor/musician a role in an upcoming indie film. As a video that was able to spread quickly and across many screens, the "Ching Chong! Asians in the Library Song," in all respects, was a viral hit. While its popularity must be characterized as unexpected or accidental, in order for a YouTube video to "go viral," it must actually incorporate emotional hooks: key signifiers that catch the attention and sensibility of a particular audience. While sites like YouTube, by hosting such videos, enable the process of viral video making, these videos' successful transmission—from one user to the next—requires what media scholar Henry Jenkins has termed a larger participatory culture of related blogs, social networking sites, and mass media coverage (Jenkins 2006).

With these paradoxical and performative features, viral media has ushered in, according to journalists and industry insiders, a new generation of "Asian American YouTube stars." All but absent in the Hollywood star system and on the Billboard charts, Asian Americans—such as Ryan Higa (NigaHiga), Kevin Wu (KevJumba), and Wong Fu Productions—dominate YouTube's Most Subscribed lists.[1] Paying serious attention to this phenomenon of Asian American YouTube stars, either lauded for its democratizing potential (giving Asian American "unseen talents" a performance stage) or disparaged for its industry-driven tendencies (making visible an otherwise "unseen niche market"), I instead imagine other types of value that the stars hold for their youth audiences. It requires that we revisit this phenomenon, one branded as unforeseen, and locate it within a longer cultural history produced by the laborious acts of "feeling Asian American." As "production(s) defined by combination of cybernetics and affect" (Hardt 1999, 97), these YouTube performances—vlogs, webisodes, and musical covers—function as forms of affective labor for young Asian Americans today. While I respectfully engage the analytical language of media studies, my purpose falls more in line with a central theoretical concern of performance studies: to envision what these enactments might *mean* for their audiences. It is a perspective that falls out of reception studies' qualitative scope and one often concealed by the whitewash of fan studies.

I also want to think beyond a prevalent discourse that celebrates YouTube as a means for Asian Americans to infiltrate the mainstream and, therefore, "change da game."[2] With breakthrough celebrities such as Legaci (pop star Justin Bieber's touring backup vocalists) and Charice Pempengco (child star turned daytime television darling), many critics have heralded YouTube as a launching pad for Asian Americans, a group otherwise lacking representation in U.S. mainstream pop culture. Yet others maintain the opposite view: it is actually young Asian Americans whose "aesthetics and business sense have helped change the face of online video" (Kun 2010). As illustrated in discussions at the Conference for Creative Content (C3), which took place in June 2011 at Visual Communications' annual Los Angeles Asian American film festival, today's Asian American creative hopefuls do not merely accede to but actively exploit social media and information-sharing platforms such as YouTube, Facebook, Twitter, and blogs as what was described at C3 as their "new calling card." To further aid this generation in "negotiating and navigating between community and commerce," C3 panels focused on the entrepreneurial nuts and bolts necessary to succeed online: copyright and intellectual property rights; effective modes of branding, distribution, and news reporting; and crafting performances to capture audiences. And if their hands-on approach to "becoming a YouTube star" was not enough of a draw, the organizers also summoned Asian America's celebrity power as panelists—bloggers Phil Yu and Diana Nguyen, YouTube trendsetter Wong Fu Productions, and *Glee* star Harry Shum.

Along with its ability to infiltrate and infect, the viral has the power to replicate. So, while some journalists and media organizations view YouTube as an open stage for Asian American performers, artists themselves look to the website as an alternative avenue of cultural production. As twenty-four-year-old Korean American rapper Dumbfoundead (Jonathan Park) noted in a recent *Koream* magazine article, "Asians got tired of waiting to get into the mainstream. With YouTube, you don't have to wait for somebody to sign you, or give you a budget of millions of dollars to make a film; you can just do it. We're like, 'YouTube's here. We're going to smash it up with this YouTube thing'" (Eun and Ma 2010). With "no third party, no money-sucking managers, or closed-minded Hollywood executives," Asian Americans do not simply leverage but actually dominate YouTube's topten-channel lists, designating them as celebrities on the video-sharing site. Encompassing "highly visible and successful 'homegrown' performers and producers," as defined by Joshua Green and Jean Burgess, the category of "YouTube celebrity" or "YouTube star" consists of entrepreneurial vloggers such as Jimmy Wong, cultural producers who collaborate with other artists and partake in the site's daily life as active consumers (2009, 91). As a communication genre, vlogs derive from such media antecedents as "webcam culture, personal blogging, and the more widespread 'confessional culture' that characterizes television talk shows and reality television—while also adhering to current social media mandates to 'invite critique, debate, and discussion'" (94). At the same time, while "digital visuality" online "can reinstate an understanding of race as always visible and available to the naked eye," according to media scholar Lisa Nakamura, on the Internet (unlike in cinema) "users have the option to perform their identities in ways that are not possible elsewhere" (2008, 205). No longer simply broadcasting media, YouTube's celebrity system also requires its stars to post responses to their viewers' comments, follow other users' videos, and maintain public profiles through other Web 2.0 channels (Facebook, Myspace, Twitter). Tapping into and taking part in the "affective economies" of these media and networking platforms, YouTube stars are often required to extend their performances beyond these virtual arenas.[3]

To succeed in today's participatory culture, with its own logic of affective economics, the larger U.S. entertainment industry has had to rethink how it does business. No longer able to merely distribute content in a top-down fashion, organizations and performers—whether amateur or professional, nonprofit or profit driven—are forced to devise new forms of audience outreach and engagement. In Asian America, the International Secret Agents (ISA) showcase and nonprofit organization Kollaboration are two grassroots examples of this new affective economics model as they both capitalize on a niche audiences' emotional attachment to performers ("people like me") by presenting YouTube celebrities live in performance. Started in 2008 by Southern California's Wong Fu Productions and hip-hop group Far East Movement, ISA has since showcased popular Asian American performers, from YouTube celebrities A. J. Rafael, Ryan Higa, and Jennifer Chung to reality TV contestants/ hip-hop dance crews Quest Crew and Poreotics, in cities such as Seattle and New York as well as the Los Angeles ethnoburbs San Gabriel and Cerritos. With five sold-out concerts in the past three years, according to Wong Fu Productions' website, ISA "prov[es] that there is a voice, face, and desire for Asian Americans in the mainstream world" (see ISA [http://isatv.com/?page_id=66]). While both ISA and Kollaboration employ YouTube for the purposes of publicizing and programming their events, Kollaboration—with its tagline "Empowerment Through Entertainment"—actually auditions brand-new performers on YouTube for its seasonal acoustic as well as electric concert-competitions. Established eleven years ago

in Los Angeles' Koreatown (where its headquarters are still based), Kollaboration has spread across the nation, with local chapters, or Kollaboration Cities, in Asian American centers: San Francisco, Seattle; New York; Washington, DC; Toronto; Chicago; Atlanta; Houston; and Tulsa. Extending the reach of YouTube stars— from home computer screens onto concert stages—ISA and Kollaboration's community-based efforts also map today's Asian America.

According to *Koream* writers Elizabeth Eun and Julie Ma (2010), before YouTube's advent in 2005, "it all seemed self-indulgent and borderline narcissistic. . . . uploading videos of yourself belting out pop songs or talking to an invisible audience." Yet despite the ways online media has changed the aesthetics and business of entertainment, most YouTube video performances are still popularly perceived as being amateurish in their look and feel—"narcissistic" and "self-indulgent" musical or spoken solo performances addressed to a built-in computer camera, with little else in terms of lighting, backdrop, or editing. These are consumer-based productions. However, as critics have noted, the probability of a YouTube video's "going viral" hinges precisely on the qualities of authenticity and earnestness. "Not targeted nor read as necessarily containing material for general audiences," Patricia Lange notes, these viral hits often contain "stereotypical, spontaneous, and... numerous in-jokes and references that many general viewers would not understand in the way the creators intended" (2009, 73). In other words, to catch an already distracted viewer's attention, viral videos must exude an air of amateur production—versus the slick, professional, and therefore controlled aesthetics of mainstream Hollywood or television sources—and mobilize key signifiers that resonate with a particular community or subculture.

Once struggling in a constrictive media system that viewed its films and performances as unprofitable and the idea of an Asian American audience as moot, indie Asian American artists have reaped the most benefit from social media's democratic promise. Already engaged in analog forms of virality (such as DIY filmmaking, word-of-mouth advertising, and informal networks of production), Asian American artists and entrepreneurs have easily shifted into digital mode. In the nonprofit sector, Asian American theaters and arts organizations mobilize social media in order to publicize upcoming productions, assist in fund-raising campaigns, and archive highlights from past productions or major events. At the same time, some of the most successful Asian American artists on YouTube—Wong Fu, Legaci, Charice, and KevJumba, for example—had years of performance experience and training under their belt before uploading their first YouTube video. In the case of Wong Fu Productions, which started circulating its work via email in the late 1990s, the video-sharing website was merely a cheap and easy alternative for sharing film shorts and music videos, especially with friends who lacked high-speed Internet connections. In all these cases, YouTube was the means, not the ends, to producing and distributing their work.

Yet how do we account for the popularity of YouTube stars and their performances among today's Asian American youth? In other words, besides just continuing a tradition of DIY cultural production, what purpose do these Asian American YouTube performers—their videos and the ways in which they are shared—actually serve? These questions arise for me not only in the space of this essay or during my private moments of writing and researching but also, and more so, in the public spaces of teaching, when students share and retell their fandom for certain YouTube performers and performances—or when I notice swooning from thirty-and-under Asian Americans huddled around computer screens, see them standing in line for tickets to a YouTube college tour show, or

hear them screaming from their seats at a recent Kollaboration Acoustic 5 showcase. Is there something about YouTube—a genre of new media dependent upon the viral, as a "politics of form and form of politics"—that speaks to the simultaneously virtual and material aspects of Asian American identity?[4]

At once an all-too-easy catchall term (among census takers, public health researchers, and marketers) for an endlessly diverse population—of various ethnicities, nations, and classes, fluent in a number of different languages/dialects and with divergent immigration histories—"Asian American" originated as a highly contested, simultaneously political and cultural term during the civil rights, anti–Vietnam War, and student movements of the 1960s and 1970s. Purposefully pan-ethnic, it signaled the interlocking, oft-forgotten histories of U.S. war and empire in Asia and earlier Asian immigration to the United States as well as the mutually material and representational effects of these historical events and conditions. According to early Yellow Power proponents, while early twentieth-century U.S. popular representation of Asians focused on "contagious divides"—the discursive lines between U.S. modernity and Orientalized otherness drawn across Asian bodies—since the end of World War II and the Cold War's onset, one particular myth of racialization has prevailed (Shah 2001). Published in 1966, in the aftermath of the Moynihan report and amid rising domestic racial tensions, the main themes of the *U.S. World and News Report* article "Success Story of One Minority Group in the U.S." continue on in the "model minority" myth. Painting a portrait of the Chinese and Japanese as hardworking, obedient, self-reliant individuals whose drive toward assimilation is matched only by their fervent adherence to "traditional Asian values"—filial piety, humility, and sacrifice—the model minority myth is a neoliberal form of racialization.[5] It at once promises U.S. citizenship and belonging to those Asian subjects ("obedient, self-reliant individuals) who must also perform a racialized script that marks them as forever foreign ("traditional Asian values"). In this frequent collapse between "Asian" and "Asian American," model minority discourse has prescribed the parameters of Asian American-ness, setting the terms for political debate within Asian America.[6]

Against this discursive containment, scholars such as Kandice Chuh, Laura Kang, Lisa Lowe, and Karen Shimawaka have helped us fine-tune a working definition of "Asian American," one that reminds us of its supple and performative nature, an identity constituted by multiple and competing epistemologies. . . . . As Lowe eloquently outlined in her seminal *Immigrant Acts*, Asian American culture is a "countersite to U.S. national culture" where "contradictions are read, performed, and critiqued"; it functions as a "medium of the present" that "mediates the past," remembering fragmented histories while reimagining political futures (Lowe 1996, 65). Likewise, against community-based discursive containment—the kind that espouses notions of Asian Americans as culturally, socially, and politically homogeneous, attempts to expel radical Asian otherness through anti-immigrant sentiments, or even falls prey to the assimilationist lure of performing "model minority"-ness—I want to consider the political potential and critical possibilities offered by Asian American YouTube performances, as staged and everyday performances of affect and participation.

. . . As mentioned above, the success of viral media depends upon (1) a niche or subculture's active participation through online networks (i.e., websites, blogs, and social networking directed at its particular needs/ concerns) and (2) its knowledge of and ability to craft emotional hooks, key signifiers that touch upon a shared set of affective investments and affiliations. Asian America's particular use of viral media points to this virtual diaspora's simulated and representational elements

and, in turn, to the performative and affective dimensions of the "symbolic ethnicity" of Asian Americans.

A 2001 Pew Internet and American Life Project reported that "fully 75% of English- speaking Asian-American adults have used the Internet," surpassing the numbers for all other English-speaking ethnic and even white American groups and making them "the most wired racial or ethnic group in America," "the young and the connected" (Spooner 2001, 2). Unlike their ethnic or even white counterparts, Asian American Internet users were "proportionally much more likely than others to get information about financial matters, travel, and political information" as well as "to use the Internet as a resource at school or at work" (2). In this comparative race-based research study, the report's author cites the challenges to surveying and collecting coherent data within this pan-ethnic community: heterogeneity of languages, high levels of language retention, and a lack of proper translation services. Thus, with its English-only survey, the Pew report depends upon and, in turn, perpetuates a limited definition of "Asian American."

Alongside a critique of this domesticating discourse, the trope of Asian American "hyperconnectivity" requires a deeper inquiry into the causes and effects of this group's long-standing Internet use and early adoption of Web 2.0 technologies— social networking sites like Friendster, Myspace, Facebook; short message services; and Internet telephone providers such as Skype. For both U.S. and foreign-born Asian Americans who maintain connections to homeland politics and family networks, these digital technologies allow for quick, inexpensive communication across time zones and national borders. Therefore, as Linda Leung has noted, the Asian diaspora is an imagined community "experienced largely over the Internet" and best "characterized as 'virtual'" (2008, 10). While the virtuality of Asian America traffics in both the simulated and representational, it also gestures toward an extensive cluster of real-world implications and everyday situations. The explosion of Korean pop (K-pop) culture globally, in the past decade, exemplifies this interplay between the virtual and material. Although the Internet's role in disseminating state-sponsored and market-driven forms of K-Pop culture is vital, as cultural anthropologist Jung-Sun Park observes, Korean American youth (U.S.-born and 1.5 generations as well as *yuhak-saeng*, students who study abroad) and their "consumption, dissemination, and to some extent, creation of trans-Pacific popular culture"—as they participate in K-Pop-oriented websites and forums and share with friends, family, and other fans the latest news and songs from abroad—plays an equally crucial role (2008, 161). Alienated from mainstream U.S. popular culture, the Korean American youth whom Park interviews find a sense of belonging, a "feeling at home," in K-Pop's style and culture.

In the registers of emotion and affect, Asian American youth also work through and against the specter of the model minority as a prescriptive racial fiction. Throughout its popular cultural history, Asian America has propagated the "grander passions" of anger, rage, and shame (Ngai 2005, 6). Like today's YouTube videos, 'zines of the 1990s yesteryears, with their espousal of punk and indie subcultures' DIY credo, also toed the lines "between commercial and D.I.Y., between mainstream and marginal" (Rubin 2003, 14). In the case of highly successful print publications that survived their digital transformation into online 'zines—Eric Nakamura and Martin Wong's *Giant Robot*, Mimi Thi Nguyen's *Exoticize This!*, and Sabrina Alcantara-Tan's *Bamboo Girl*—the tone of Asian America's talk-back to mainstream U.S. industries and representation took on the punk aesthetic of "gleeful opposition to decorum and propriety" by expressing itself in ways that "fl[y] directly in the face of the 'polite

Asian' stereotype" (Rubin 2003, 15–16). If model minority status was maintained through deference, then these cultural forerunners instead chose to express anger and rage, emotions falling outside the boundaries of this racial fiction. Ironically, model minority rhetoric actually figures Asians as *unfeeling* or, as Wesley Yang vividly described in his recent *New York* magazine article "Asian Like Me," "a mass of stifled, repressed, abused, conformist quasi-robots" (2011, 22). Derived as they are from this 'zine publishing tradition, it is no wonder that some of today's most popular Asian American blogs still contain emotionally charged terms—the blogs *Angry Asian Man*, *Disgrasian*, and *You Offend Me You Offend My Family* (*YOMYOMF*). Through these particularly salient examples, we might hone our understanding of Asian American as a "symbolic ethnicity." According to Rachel Rubin, the categorical term of "Asian American" is "symbolic, because of its rhetorical and deliberative nature, but, nonetheless possessed of real-world implications" (2003, 5). As a mode of identification, it holds the possibility of being a "deliberative and motivated thing: experiential rather than biological, grounded in the present as much or more than in the past" (5). For Asian American 'zine writers, this "deliberative and motivated thing" registered as an "attitude," a particular way of expressing one's being-in-the-world. In the case of YouTube performances, such as Jimmy Wong's "Ching Chong! Asians in the Library" parody, the Asian American attitude today references a broader set of emotions than just anger and rage but still performs the affective labor of transforming alienating episodes into a common understanding. . . .

For Davis Jung, producer of the recent Conference for Creative Content, Wong Fu Productions' 2006 "Yellow Fever"—the group's first You-Tube video and response to the common narratives of Asian American masculinity—arrived at a critical point in his life. In his online essay

"How New Media Gave Me a Voice," Jung narrates familiar tales for Asian Americans—the perpetual mispronunciation of one's name, the attempt to cultivate a love for genres of whiteness (country music, Classical Civilization major), and, of course, the lack of "role models" or "words" to articulate one's self—in order to capture the paradoxical feelings of Asian America: cultural alienation and, yet, the desire to belong. Bored and procrastinating, one fall evening in 2007, the then college-age Jung stumbled upon the University of California–San Diego collective's video link and clicked it. "I cannot tell you how many times I watched that video. It reached out and shook me. It made me laugh, and later on, it made me cry. It excited me, it incited me. It made me question everything that I had ever assumed about myself. It made me question what it meant to be 'normal'."

Appearing at the end of his essay, this moment of cultural discovery serves as Jung's final word, his response to the question continually raised regarding the value of YouTube for Asian Americans. Pivoting between the dualities of culture and commerce, business and cultural resource, node and network, the rhetoric regarding the content-sharing website vacillates between characterizing it as "culturally generative" (for the several roles it plays as "high volume website, broadcast platform, media archive, social network") and seeing it as merely another "'top-down' platform for distributing popular culture" (Snickars and Vondereau 2009, 13). Yet, as Jung's anecdote so vividly reminds us, we need another set of protocols: an audience-centered analysis of the value of Asian American YouTube performances. By invoking a certain set of shared affects for these Asian American youth audiences, these YouTube stars' vlogs, song parodies, skits, and cover performances produce something "intangible: a feeling of ease, well-being, satisfaction, excitement, passion—even a sense of connectedness or community" (Hardt 1999,

96). Breaking out of the model minority myth's discursive containment, these emerging online personalities restage and respond to the banal and ridiculously racist moments of Asian America's everyday life, performing the affective labor of transforming alienation into humor, hate into love. Unexpectedly, a story or a song might catch us. Moved by these performances, we cannot help but share them, infecting others with the feeling.

Notes

1. The most spectacular examples: comedic vlogger "KevJumba" (Kevin Wu): no. 9 Most Subscribed Comedian (All Time), 1.4 million subscribers, over 150 million views; character actor/comedian "NigaHiga" (Ryan Higa): YouTube no. 1 Most Subscribed (All Time), 3.4 million subscribers, over 746 million views; directorial/writing collective Wong Fu Productions (Wesley Chan, Ted Fu, and Philip Wang): 785,394 subscribers, over 95 million views.

2. From the title of a panel at the 2010 San Francisco Asian American Film Festival: "Changing da Game: YouTube Legends and the Future of Online Media" (Center for Asian American Media 2010).

3. In this particular case, I am referencing Burgess and Green's use of "affective economies" to describe the participatory culture of emotional attachments and investments expressed on YouTube. Other scholars such as Sara Ahmed and Henry Jenkins have also written about the "affective economies" of political language and actions between racialized individuals within the nation-state (Ahmed 2004) and the logics of "affective economics" as propagated and perpetuated by reality television shows such as *American Idol* (Jenkins 2006).

4. I am borrowing this notion of "the politics of form and the form of politics" to discuss the critical and political work enacted by cultural productions from Jodi Kim's (2010) recently released *Ends of Empire: Asian American Critique and the Cold War.* Thanks

also to Joshua Chambers-Letson (2009) for his essay "Contracting Justice: the Viral Strategy of Felix Gonzalez-Torres," which models different ways that a term such as the "viral" can be mobilized as a conceptual meeting point for an interdisciplinary discussion of bodies, the law, and artistic form.

5. In some aspects, the political difficulties faced by a term such as "Asian American" find a kinship with the similarly vexed identity category of "Latino." As Jose Esteban Muñoz has questioned, "Latino does not subscribe to a common racial, class, gender, religious, or national category, and if a Latino can be from any country in Latin America, a member of any race, religion, class, or gender/sex orientation, who then is she? What, if any, nodes of commonality do Latinas/os share?" (Muñoz 2000, 67) Yet, in other ways, "Asian American" has historically served as an umbrella term that has unified seemingly disparate groups. For the purposes of this essay, I draw on the spirit of Muñoz's focus on affective performances, or ways of "feeling brown," as a site for mobilizing different forms of what Norma Alarcon (1996) has designated an "identity-in-difference."

6. It bears repeating here that, within this containment logic of the "model minority," "Asian" more often refers to East Asian Americans (i.e., Chinese, Japanese, and sometimes Korean) rather than Asian/Asian American ethnicities such as Filipinos, South Asians, and Southeast Asians.

Works Cited

Ahmed, Sara. 2004. "Affective Economies." *Social Text* 22(2):117–39.

Alarcon, Norma. 1996. "Conjugating Subjects in the Age of Multiculturalism." In *Mapping Multiculturalism*, ed. Avery F. Gordon and Christopher Newfield. Minneapolis: University of Minnesota Press.

Bryman, Alan. 2004. *The Disneyization of Society*. Thousand Oaks, CA: Sage.

Burgess, Jean, and Joshua Green. 2009. "The Entrepreneurial Vlogger: Participatory Culture Beyond the Professional-Amateur Divide." In *The YouTube Reader*, ed. Pelle Snickars and Patrick Vondereau. Stockholm: National Library of Sweden.

Center for Asian American Media. 2010. "Changing da Game: YouTube Legends and the Future of Online Media." http://www.youtube.com/watch?v=98ayDYfUMtk

Chambers-Letson, Joshua. 2009. "Contracting Justice: The Viral Strategy of Felix Gonzalez-Torres." *Criticism* 51(4):559–87.

Chuh, Kandice. 2003. *Imagine Otherwise: On Asian Americanist Critique*. Durham: Duke University Press.

Eun, Elizabeth, and Julie Ma. 2010. "How YouTube Transformed the Asian American Arts Scene." *Koream*, September. http://iamkoream.com/coverstory-youtube-stars/

Hardt, Michael. 1999. "Affective Labor." *boundary 2* 26(2): 89–100.

Hyon, Soyoung Sonjia. 2011. "Anxieties of the Fictive: The Immigrant and Asian American Politics of Visibility." PhD diss., University of Minnesota.

Jenkins, Henry. 2006. *Convergence Culture: Where Old and New Media Meet*. New York: New York University Press.

Jung, Davis. 2011. "How New Media Gave Me a Voice." http://asianfilmfestla.org/2011/films-events/c3-conference-for-creative-content/how-newmedia-gave-me-a-voice/

Kang, Laura. 2003. *Compositional Subjects: Enfiguring Asian/American Women*. Durham: Duke University Press.

Kim, Jodi. 2010. *Ends of Empire: Asian American Critique and the Cold War*. Minneapolis: University of Minnesota Press.

Kun, Josh. 2010. "Unexpected Harmony: YouTube Helps Legaci's Breakout." *New York Times*, June 18, AR1.

Lange, Patricia. 2009. "Videos of Affinity on YouTube." In *The YouTube Reader*, ed. Pelle Snickars and Patrick Vondereau. Stockholm: National Library of Sweden.

Leung, Linda. 2008. "From 'Victims of the Digital Divide' to 'Technoelites': Gender, Class, and Contested 'Asianness' in Online and Offline Geographies." In *South Asian Technospaces*, ed. Radhika Gajjala and Venkataramana Gajjala. New York: Peter Lang.

Lowe, Lisa. 1996. *Immigrant Acts: On Asian American Politics*. Durham: Duke University Press.

Muñoz, Jose Esteban. 2000. "Feeling Brown: Ethnicity and Affect in Ricardo Bracho's *The Sweetest Hangover (and Other STDs)*." *Theatre Journal* 52(1): 67–79.

Nakamura, Lisa. 2008. *Digitizing Race: Visual Cultures of the Internet*. Minneapolis: University of Minnesota Press.

Ngai, Sianne. 2005. *Ugly Feelings*. Cambridge: Harvard University Press.

Park, Jung-Sun. 2008. "Korean American Youth and Transnational Flows of Popular Culture Across the Pacific." In *Transpop: Korea Vietnam Remix* (exhibition catalogue), ed. Viet Le and Yong Soon Min. Seoul: Arko Art Center, Arts Council Korea.

Rubin, Rachel. 2003. "Cyberspace Y2K: Giant Robots Asian Punks." Occasional Paper, Institute for Asian American Studies. Boston: Institute for Asian American Studies, University of Massachusetts Boston.

Shah, Nayan. 2001. *Contagious Divides: Epidemics and Race in San Francisco's Chinatown*. Berkeley: University of California Press.

Shimakawa, Karen. 2002. *National Abjection: The Asian American Body Onstage*. Durham: Duke University Press.

Snickars, Pelle, and Patrick Vondereau. 2009. "Introduction." In *The YouTube Reader*, ed. Pelle Snickars and Patrick Vondereau. Stockholm: National Library of Sweden.

Spooner, Tom. 2001. "Asian Americans and the Internet: the young and the connected." Pew Internet and American Life Project. Washington, DC: Tides Center.

Visual Communications. 2011. "C3 Conference" (schedule). http:// asianfilmfestla.org/2011/films-events/c3-conference-for-creative-content/

Yang, Wesley. 2011. "Asian Like Me." *New York*, May 16, 22–29.

ALTERNATIVE CONTENTS INDEX

RESOURCES AND MEDIA ACTIVIST ORGANIZATIONS

Activist and Advocacy Organizations

Many organizations address media culture. This list selects nonprofits, educational organizations, and web and print publications that have provided trusted critical media analysis related to gender, race, and class. Organizations in this section provide a mix of educational materials for young adults and educators, opportunities to engage in media activist and advocacy initiatives, and critical media analysis and reporting. This section lists organizations along with their mission, a brief description of their available resources and activities, and information on how to connect with their content and initiatives.

ABOUT FACE

About Face equips women and girls with tools to understand and resist harmful media messages that affect their self-esteem and body image. About Face offers real-world and online media literacy and media activism for teen girls. Its website provides educational resources, action guides, and a gallery of media complete with critical analysis and actionable information about the media producers.

About Face offers many ways to engage, from providing information for conducting letter-writing campaigns to educational resources for adult advocates and educators. This organization also offers workshops and speaking engagements in the San Francisco area.

Contact About Face via the organization's website (www.aboutface .org) or About-Face, P.O. Box 77665, San Francisco, CA.

ACTION COALITION FOR MEDIA EDUCATION

The Action Coalition for Media Education (ACME) is a network of media educators and other stakeholders working to extend media literacy through education, media reform, and media activism. The organization is open to educators, students, activists, health professionals, and media producers.

ACME offers a wide variety of media education materials to educators and students, and hosts an informational network online and regular summits for members both nationally and regionally.

ACME can be reached at 2808 El Tesoro Escondido NW, Albuquerque, NM 87120, or through www.acmecoalition.org.

ADBUSTERS

Adbusters is a global network of culture jammers and creatives working to change the way information flows, the ways corporations wield power, and the way meaning is produced in our society.

Adbusters publishes six issues per year and maintains an active web community that provides critical action tools for culture jamming (www.adbusters.org).

ADIOS BARBIE

Adios Barbie's mission is to broaden the concepts of body image to include people of all ages, cultures, gender abilities, sexual orientations, races, and sizes. It creates articles, campaigns, lectures, and events that redefine perceptions of beauty. Adios Barbie can be found online at www.adiosbarbie.com.

ALLIANCE FOR COMMUNITY MEDIA

The Alliance for Community Media promotes civic engagement through community media.

The alliance serves students, professionals, and institutions concerned with local-access media. The organization advocates for public policy supporting media access for all citizens. It supports local media producers with resources, events and conferences, the annual Hometown Film Festival, and a job board for students and media professionals. This organization also offers scholarship awards.

The national website for the Alliance for Community Media is located at www.allcommunitymedia.org. Additionally, the alliance has members divided into five regions across the country, each with its own site listed under the "Regions" section of the main website.

ALLIANCE FOR WOMEN IN MEDIA

The Alliance for Women in Media advances the influence and impact of women in all forms of media by facilitating collaboration, education, and innovation.

The alliance is a professional organization for media professionals interested in gender equity behind the camera and quality representation in front it. Membership is open to women and men working in the media field or related professions. This organization is also open to students interested in pursuing a career in media. Annual Gracie Awards celebrate women in media, and travelling symposiums address relevant industry topics. Student scholarships are available through this organization.

Connect to the alliance at its national headquarters, 1760 Old Meadow Road, Suite 500, McLean, VA 22102, or online at www.allwomeninmedia.org.

ASSOCIATION FOR MEDIA LITERACY

The Association for Media Literacy is made up of teachers, librarians, consultants, parents, cultural workers, and media professionals concerned about the impact of the mass media on contemporary culture.

It seeks to help people develop a more informed and critical understanding of the nature of media. The association offers lesson plans for teachers and a resource section online, and workshops and speakers offline.

Connect with the Association for Media Literacy at www.aml.ca.

CALIFORNIA NEWSREEL

California Newsreel is the oldest nonprofit social issue documentary film center in the country. California Newsreel has a large library of social justice documentaries, with a heavy emphasis on issues of race and justice. California Newsreel hosts outstanding documentaries on race, such as the collected works of Marlon Riggs, including *Black Is . . . Black Ain't* and *Ethnic Notions and Race: The Power of An Illusion.*

Find California Newsreel's documentary catalog and educational support materials at www.newsreel.org.

CENTER ON MEDIA AND CHILD HEALTH

The Center on Media and Child Health educates parents and the public on media and their effects on the physical, mental, and social health of all children.

The center provides a database of research on children and media. It hosts a searchable database, along with active social media sites with daily info for parents.

Access the center's website, including the research database, at www.cmch.tv.

CENTER FOR MEDIA DEMOCRACY

The Center for Media Democracy is a nonpartisan media watchdog group focused on exposing corporate spin and government propaganda. The center's reporting group produces award-winning investigative journalism covering politics, corporations, environmentalism, the justice system, and other issues of social justice for its three publications: *PR Watch*, *SourceWatch*, and *Bankster*.

The Center for Media Democracy and its publications can be found at www .prwatch.org.

CENTER FOR MEDIA LITERACY

The Center for Media Literacy is an educational organization that provides leadership, public education, professional development, and educational resources nationally and internationally. A great resource for students is the center's reading room, hosted on its website, which catalogs hundreds of articles on media culture. The center also offers a large number of curriculum and educator resources.

The Center for Media Literacy can be reached at 22631 Pacific Coast Highway #472, Malibu, CA, or online at www .medialit.com.

CENTER FOR PUBLIC INTEGRITY

The mission of the Center for Public Integrity is to enhance democracy by revealing abuses of power, corruption, and betrayal of trust by powerful public and private institutions.

The organization provides nonpartisan, original reporting on a wide range of issues in the United States and abroad, with a special focus on politics, the environment, and social justice.

Access the Center for Public Integrity via www.publicintegrity.org.

COLOR OF FILM COLLABORATIVE

The Color of Film Collaborative is a nonprofit organization that works to support media makers of color and others who have an interest in developing and creating new, diverse images of people of color in film, video, and the performing arts.

The collaborative supports independent filmmakers of color with production support, screening and distribution, and workshops. It also hosts the Roxbury International Film Festival each summer.

Find the Color of Film Collaborative at www.coloroffilm.com. Access the Roxbury International Film Festival, including submission information and the winners archive, at www.roxburyfilmfestival.org.

COMMON SENSE MEDIA

Common Sense Media is dedicated to improving the lives of kids and families by providing trustworthy information, education, and the independent voice they need to thrive in a world of media and technology.

Common Sense Media provides age-based ratings and reviews of media, including videos, apps, and games for parents and families. It also offers educator programs and advocates on behalf of families to promote digital literacy and improve media rating systems to empower parents.

Find Common Sense Media reviews and resources at www.commonsensemedia.org.

FAAN MAIL

FAAN Mail is a media literacy and activist project formed by and for women of color. The organization works to engage corporate media producers in critical dialogue and to engage communities through education, dialogue, and activism.

FAAN Mail provides an active hub for those interested in addressing media representations and misrepresentations of women of color. It provides a vibrant online community both through its website and through social network engagement on Facebook and Twitter. It also provides workshops to colleges and community organizations interested in learning more about and addressing the representations of women of color in the media.

FAAN Mail holds and posts talk-back sessions, in which members address media constructions in real time and share analysis with the wider community. FAAN Mail also offers workshops and speakers.

Find the FAAN Mail portal at www .faanmail.wordpress.com.

FAIRNESS AND ACCURACY IN REPORTING

Fairness and Accuracy in Reporting (FAIR), the foremost national media watch group, has been offering well-documented criticism of media bias and censorship since 1986. It works to invigorate the first amendment by advocating for greater diversity in the press and by scrutinizing media practices that marginalize public interest, minority, and dissenting viewpoints.

FAIR offers excellent and extensive independent reporting and analyses of media across the whole spectrum of public interest issues affecting youth, minorities, the elderly, and the environment—online, on the radio, and via its YouTube channel. It also offers its audience opportunities to take action through regular action alerts.

Access FAIR and its related publications and productions through www.fair.org.

FREE PRESS

Free Press is a national, nonpartisan nonprofit advocating for universal and affordable Internet access, diverse media ownership, vibrant public media, and quality journalism.

Free Press is an active organization fighting restrictive media ownership policies and advocating for wider dissemination of the tools for media production, including starting low-power FM stations. Free Press offers a multitude of ways readers can advocate for a better media environment, from online petitions to support for community media startup projects.

Connect with Free Press at www .freepress.net.

GEENA DAVIS INSTITUTE ON GENDER AND THE MEDIA

The mission of the Geena Davis Institute on Gender and the Media is to spotlight gender inequities in every media and entertainment company through cutting-edge research, education, training, strategic guidance, and advocacy programs to dramatically alter how girls and women are reflected in media.

The organization advocates within the media industry for improved representation. It offers a variety of media education tools online, including research on media representation of women and girls, content for adults and young people, and curriculum for educators, at www.seejane.org.

MEDIA LITERACY PROJECT

Formerly the New Mexico Media Literacy Project, this organization transforms people into critical consumers and engaged media justice advocates through education, programs, and grassroots campaigns.

The project offers educational materials and resources, including curriculum, an ad deconstruction gallery online, and events and presentations around the country.

The Media Literacy Project is located at 6400 Wyoming Blvd. NE, Albuquerque, NM 87109, and online at www.medialiteracy project.org.

MEDIA WATCH

Media Watch's mission is to challenge, through education and action, abusive stereotypes and other biased information commonly found in the media.

Media Watch is a nonprofit that publishes a monthly newsletter focusing on media depictions of gender and race. It creates educational media literacy videos focused on the harms of gendered representations and hosts a media literacy education blog and public lectures.

Media Watch publishes its newsletter monthly, hosts its blog, and offers other educational materials at www.mediawatch .com.

NATIONAL ALLIANCE FOR MEDIA ARTS AND CULTURE

The National Alliance for Media Arts and Culture fosters and fortifies the culture and business of independent media arts. Through dialogue, collaboration, research, and advocacy, it connects, organizes, and develops organizations.

The alliance is a membership organization that supports artists and individuals creating digital media. For people interested in producing alternative media, it offers a host of supports, including leadership training and regular convening events. It hosts regional conferences as well as a large annual conference. It also conducts policy advocacy on behalf of its members.

The alliance maintains a national office at 145 9th Street, Suite 230, San Francisco, CA 94103, and a website at www.namac .org.

NATIONAL ASSOCIATION FOR MEDIA LITERACY EDUCATION

The National Association for Media Literacy Education's mission is to expand and improve the practice of media literacy education in the United States.

The association is an active membership organization made up of educators, students, and media activists. It provides opportunities for networking and professional development among members through conferences, a resource hub, and the *Journal of Media Literacy Education*.

The association is online at www.namle .net, and the journal is online at www .JMLE.org.

NATIONAL TELEMEDIA COUNCIL

The National Telemedia Council is a national nonprofit that has been promoting the concept of media literacy for five decades.

The organization publishes the *Journal of Media Literacy*, the country's oldest journal dedicated to media literacy.

The journal and submission guidelines can be found at www.journalofmedialiteracy .org.

PAPER TIGER TELEVISION

Paper Tiger Television is an open nonprofit volunteer video collective. The organization believes that increasing public awareness of the negative influence of mass media and involving people in the process of making media is mandatory for our long-term goal of information equity.

Paper Tiger Television produces short videos on critical media literacy and other social justice issues. It also offers community workshops and materials for those interested in hosting their own community screenings.

Find Paper Tiger Television at 339 Lafayette Street, New York, NY or online at www.papertiger.org.

SNOPES

Snopes has been operating since 1995 and is the Internet's go-to source for urban legend information. Snopes publishes on only its website, www.snopes.com, providing reliable analysis of urban legends and Internet rumors. This is an excellent source for debunking viral stories.

SPY HOP

Spy Hop's mission is to mentor young people in the digital arts to help them find their voices, tell their stories, and be empowered to effect positive change in their lives.

Spy Hop works with youth to produce film, music, and design. The organization offers education workshops for youth and educators, and maintains a website rich with high-quality youth media.

Spy Hop operates at 51 West 200 South, Salt Lake City, UT 84101, and online at www.spyhop.org.

STOP PORN CULTURE

Stop Porn Culture is an action-oriented, feminist organization concerned with educating the public on the issue of pornography, its influence on pop culture, and its effects on women, children, and men. The website provides a long list of resources and downloadable PowerPoint presentations on the harms of pornography, and holds an annual conference that offers workshops and trainings on how to become an activist. For details, go to stoppornculture.org.

UNDERSTAND MEDIA

Understand Media's intention is to educate the public about media. The website provides media literacy information in Spanish as well as English.

Understand Media is a web portal providing media literacy information for students, teachers, and adults. The site features media literacy video lessons, a podcast, and a blog on media issues.

Access Understand Media via www .understandmedia.com.

VISION MEDIA MAKERS

Vision Media Makers shares with the world native stories that represent the cultures, experiences, and values of American Indians and Alaska Natives.

This organization offers training, support, and distribution to help native media makers share stories via public broadcasting. Its website also offers educational guides for native-themed productions suitable for higher ed.

Contact Vision Media Makers at 1800 N. 33rd Street, Lincoln, NE 68503, or online via www.nativetelecom.org.

WOMEN ACTION AND MEDIA

Women Action and Media is an independent North American nonprofit dedicated to building a robust, effective, inclusive movement for gender justice in media.

This organization is a grassroots organizing and advocacy group that encourages participants to take action to increase gender representation of women in front of and behind the camera, including increasing their ownership and roles in media production.

It offers multiple ways to engage, from joining an established local chapter to creating one's own. The website provides visitors information for attending events, hosting their own, or participating in media activism and active dialogue on any number of social networking platforms.

Find Women Action and Media at www.womenactionmedia.org, or at one of its local chapters in Boston; Chicago; Washington, D.C.; Los Angeles; New York; Ottawa; or Vancouver.

WOMEN MAKE MOVIES

Established in 1972 to address the underrepresentation of women in the media industry, Women Make Movies is a multicultural, multiracial, nonprofit media arts organization that facilitates the production, distribution, and exhibition of independent films and videos by and about women. The organization serves both established and emerging artists.

Women Make Movies fosters feminist media by providing distribution services, funding and support, and workshops for women to produce independent feminist media. Interested participants can submit completed materials or apply for production support.

Contact Women Make Movies at 115 W. 29th Street, Suite 1200, New York, NY, 10001, or online at www.wmm.com.

YOUNG AFRICAN AMERICANS AGAINST MEDIA BIAS

Young African Americans Against Media Bias is a nonprofit organization whose mission is to scrutinize media coverage for fairness and accuracy in representing race and culture.

Its online site is devoted to examining racial stereotypes. Originally focused on stereotypes against African Americans, the organization has expanded to include racial stereotypes against all groups. The online community provides blogs, a podcast, and research resources. The organization produces witty commentary on media, music news, and pop culture. Regular podcasts are available by subscription.

Connect to this organization via www .yaaams.org.

Documentaries

This section provides a short summary of recommended documentaries related to race, class, and gender representations. Most of the documentaries listed are available from a number of sources and may be purchased or streamed online. Film summaries are taken from the films' websites and edited for brevity.

BEYOND GOOD AND EVIL: CHILDREN, MEDIA AND VIOLENT TIMES

This video examines how the "good and evil" rhetoric, in both the entertainment and the news media, has helped children dehumanize their enemies, justify their killing, and treat the suffering of innocent civilians as a necessary sacrifice.

THE BRO CODE

The Bro Code looks at the forces in male culture that condition boys and men to dehumanize and disrespect women. It makes a powerful case that there's nothing normal, natural, or inevitable about the toxic ideal of American manhood, and challenges young people to fight back against the resurgent idea that being a "bro"—and a man—means glorifying sexism, bullying, and abuse.

CLASS DISMISSED: HOW TV FRAMES THE WORKING CLASS

Class Dismissed navigates the steady stream of narrow working-class representations, from American television's beginnings to today's sitcoms, reality shows, police dramas, and daytime talk shows. It breaks important new ground in exploring the ways race, gender, and sexuality intersect with class, offering a more complex reading of television's often one-dimensional representations.

THE CODES OF GENDER: IDENTITY AND PERFORMANCE IN POP CULTURE

The Codes of Gender offers important insights into the social construction of masculinity and femininity, the relationship between gender and power, and the everyday performance of cultural norms, by looking beyond advertising as a medium that simply sells products and beyond analyses of gender that tend to focus on either biology or objectification.

CONSUMING KIDS

Consuming Kids traces the evolution and impact of the multibillion-dollar youth marketing industry. Drawing on the insights of children's health experts, media critics, and industry insiders, it blows the lid off the youth marketing industry's stealth tactics and explores the effects of consumerism on the imaginative lives of children.

DREAMWORLDS 3

Dreamworlds 3 takes a clarifying look at the warped world of music videos. Ranging across hundreds of images and stories from scores of music videos, Sut Jhally uncovers a dangerous industry preoccupation with reactionary ideals of femininity and masculinity, and shows how these ideals have glamorized a deeply sexist worldview in the face of the women's movement and the fight for women's rights.

THE ELECTRONIC STORYTELLER: TV AND THE CULTIVATION OF VALUES

George Gerbner clearly and comprehensively outlines the way the universal storytelling function of human societies has been colonized by corporate media. Through a concrete focus on the stories of gender, class, and race, Gerbner provides us with an analytical framework to understand what is at stake in the debates about the media.

FURTHER OFF THE STRAIGHT AND NARROW

Further Off the Straight and Narrow takes a close look at sitcoms, reality shows, and premium cable programming as it explores how representations of LGBTQ (lesbian, gay, bisexual, transgender, and queer) characters have become more complex and varied in recent years. The film acknowledges the expansion of LGBTQ representation on television and also raises questions about how this queer presence on television is shaped by the imperatives of the commercial media system.

HIP-HOP: BEYOND BEATS AND RHYMES

Hip-Hop: Beyond Beats and Rhymes provides a riveting examination of manhood, sexism, and homophobia in hip-hop culture. The film pays tribute to hip-hop while challenging the rap music industry to take responsibility for glamorizing destructive, deeply conservative stereotypes of manhood.

KILLING US SOFTLY 4: ADVERTISINGS IMAGES OF WOMEN

Jean Kilbourne uncovers a steady stream of sexist and misogynistic images and messages in media, laying bare a world of frighteningly thin women in positions of passivity and a restrictive code of femininity that works to undermine girls and women in the real world. At once provocative and inspiring, *Killing Us Softly 4* stands to challenge yet another generation of students to take advertising seriously and to think critically about its relationship to sexism, eating disorders, gender violence, and contemporary politics.

LATINOS BEYOND REEL

In *Latinos Beyond Reel*, filmmakers Miguel Picker and Chyng Sun examine how U.S. news and entertainment media portray—and do not portray—Latinos. Drawing on the insights of Latino scholars, journalists, community leaders, actors, directors, and producers, they uncover a pattern of gross misrepresentation and gross underrepresentation—a world in which Latinos tend to appear, if at all, as gangsters and Mexican bandits, harlots and prostitutes, drug dealers and welfare-leeching illegals.

MANUFACTURING CONSENT: NOAM CHOMSKY AND THE MEDIA

This film showcases Noam Chomsky and illustrates his message of how government and big media businesses cooperate to produce an effective propaganda machine to manipulate the opinions of the U.S. populous.

THE MEAN WORLD SYNDROME

The Mean World Syndrome offers a timely and clear-eyed take on the origins of some of our most irrational and unrelenting fears. Taking dead aim at a commercial media system that thrives on violence, stereotypes, and the cultivation of anxiety, the film argues that the more television people watch, the more likely they are to be insecure and afraid of others—and shows how these media-induced fears and anxieties provide fertile ground for intolerance, extremism, and a paranoid style of politics that threatens basic democratic values.

MEDIA EDUCATION FOUNDATION DOCUMENTARIES

These documentaries may be found online at www.mediaed.org.

MICKEY MOUSE MONOPOLY: DISNEY, CHILDHOOD AND CORPORATE POWER

Mickey Mouse Monopoly takes a close and critical look at the world Disney films create and the stories they tell about race, gender, and class, and reaches disturbing conclusions about the values propagated under the guise of innocence and fun.

NO LOGO

No Logo shows how the commercial takeover of public space, destruction of consumer choice, and replacement of real jobs with temporary work—the dynamics of corporate globalization—impact everyone, everywhere. It also draws attention to the democratic resistance arising globally to challenge the hegemony of brands.

THE OVERSPENT AMERICAN: WHY WE WANT WHAT WE DON'T NEED

Juliet Schor scrutinizes what she calls "the new consumerism"—a national phenomenon of upscale spending that is shaped and reinforced by a commercially driven media system. She argues that "keeping up with the Joneses" is no longer enough for middle- and upper-middle-class Americans, many of whom become burdened with debilitating debt as they seek to emulate materialistic TV lifestyles.

PRICE OF PLEASURE: PORNOGRAPHY, SEXUALITY AND RELATIONSHIPS

This eye-opening and disturbing film places the voices of critics, producers, and performers alongside the observations of men and women as they candidly discuss the role pornography has played in shaping their sexual imaginations and relationships.

REEL BAD ARABS: HOW HOLLYWOOD VILIFIES A PEOPLE

Reel Bad Arabs explores a long line of degrading images of Arabs—from Bedouin bandits and submissive maidens to sinister sheikhs and gun-wielding "terrorists"—along the way offering devastating insights into the origin of these stereotypic images, their development at key points in U.S. history, and why they matter so much today.

SHOP 'TIL YOU DROP: THE CRISIS OF CONSUMERISM

Shop 'Til You Drop moves beneath the seductive surfaces of the commercial world to show how the flip side of accumulation is depletion—the slow, steady erosion of both natural resources and basic human values.

TOUGH GUISE

Jackson Katz argues that the epidemic of male violence that plagues American society needs to be understood and addressed as part of a much larger cultural crisis in masculinity. *Tough Guise* gives special attention to how American media have glamorized increasingly regressive and violent masculine ideals in the face of mounting social and economic threats to traditional White male heterosexual authority.

Other Recommended Documentaries

AMERICA IN PRIMETIME

America in Primetime is structured around the most compelling shows on television today, unfolding over 4 hours and weaving between past and present. Each episode focuses on one character archetype that has remained a staple of primetime through the generations—the Independent Woman, the Man of the House, the Misfit, and the Crusader—capturing both the continuity of the character and the evolution.

AMERICA THE BEAUTIFUL

Filmmaker Darryl Roberts goes on a 2-year journey to examine America's new obsession: physical perfection. In *America the Beautiful* we see how these increasingly unattainable images contribute greatly to the rise in low self-esteem, body dysmorphia, and eating disorders for young women and girls, who also happen to be the beauty industry's largest consumers.

BLACK IS . . . BLACK AIN'T

The final film by filmmaker Marlon Riggs, *Black Is . . . Black Ain't*, jumps into the middle of explosive debates over Black identity. This film marshals a powerful critique of sexism, patriarchy, homophobia, colorism, and cultural nationalism in the Black family, church, and other Black institutions.

COVER GIRL CULTURE

Cover Girl Culture pairs images of girls and women in television and print ads with footage from the catwalks and celebrity media. The filmmaker is given rare access to women editors from major magazines, such as *Teen Vogue* and *ELLE*, who provide a shocking defense of the fashion and advertising worlds. The film juxtaposes these interviews with revealing insights from models, parents, teachers, psychologists, body image experts, and, most important, the heartfelt expressions of girls themselves on how they feel about the media that surround them.

THE FURIOUS FORCE OF RHYMES

Traveling through four continents and six countries, *The Furious Force of Rhymes* is a fascinating look at hip-hop as transnational protest music.

MISS REPRESENTATION

Miss Representation exposes how mainstream media contribute to the underrepresentation of women in positions of power and influence in America. The film challenges the media's limited and often disparaging portrayals of women and girls, which make it difficult for women to achieve leadership positions and for the average woman to feel powerful.

SEEING THROUGH THE MEDIA MATRIX

This is an in-depth, 60-minute program based on the topics and solutions examined in *Cover Girl Culture*, with newly released footage of key insights, wisdom, and tips from the experts, presented in short movie clips on more than 20 topics. Each clip includes activities or thought-provoking messages for educators to use in classrooms, about how to help young girls see through the media matrix and reclaim their power, increase their critical thinking and self-esteem, and enrich their sense of worth.

STARSUCKERS

Starsuckers is a feature documentary about the celebrity-obsessed media that uncovers the real reasons behind our addiction to fame and blows the lid off the corporations and individuals who profit from it. Using a combination of never-before-seen footage, undercover reporting, stunts, and animation, the film reveals the toxic effect the media is having on us all, and especially on our children.

WIRED FOR SEX, LIES, AND POWER TRIPS: IT'S A TEENS' WORLD

An inside look at the culture of sexual harassment and bullying widespread among many teens today, this unique and compelling program examines the price that adolescents, especially girls, pay to be cool, hip, and popular in our brave new wired world. Three different groups of culturally diverse teenagers share personal stories of navigating their hypersexualized, high-tech environment, where the online posting of racy photos, raunchy videos, and explicit gossip and lies is as commonplace as bombardment by provocative media messages that degrade and objectify women.

GLOSSARY OF TERMS

Active audiences. See *Audience, active audience, audience reception.*

Activism, media activism. Media activists include those who organize, educate, and lobby to challenge the mass media imagery or representations they consider harmful to society or derogatory to particular groups. Some media activists also produce *counterhegemonic* media texts as a way to raise consciousness about the economic, social, and political inequalities inherent in capitalism. Others act as public interest advocates who urge policymakers to ensure public access to broadcast media to historically disenfranchised groups.

Address, subject address. See *Subject position.*

Agency. See *Resistance.*

American Dream ideology. This refers to the belief, particularly strong for immigrants in the 19th and 20th centuries, that the United States offers unlimited opportunities for freedom, economic success, and happiness for all who are willing to work hard. In the context of media studies, this ideology is often discussed along with individualism and neoliberalism.

Appropriation. This term can refer, in a neutral sense, to how we make sense of the meanings encoded into cultural texts and incorporate these into our daily lives. It is frequently used by cultural critics to highlight power relations in an unequal society. Thus, appropriation can refer to the process whereby members of relatively privileged groups "raid" the culture of marginalized groups, abstracting cultural practices or artifacts from their historically specific contexts. Frequently this involves *co-optation,* by which a cultural item's resistant or *counterhegemonic* potential is lost through its translation into the dominant cultural context. Adding insult to injury, appropriation frequently means profit for the appropriator.

Audience, active audience, audience reception. Developed partly in response to the classical Marxist notion that ideology is all-powerful and, hence, audience members are at the mercy of the ideas of the ruling class, the concept of the *active audience* stresses the ways audiences are involved in actively constructing meaning from the *text*. There is debate within media studies as to just how much agency audience members have to construct their own meaning. Some scholars argue that given the *polysemic* nature of all texts, there are multiple ways to *decode* the *ideological* messages embedded in the texts. Others, most notably those within more critical *cultural studies*, follow Stuart Hall and argue that there are three main possible audience responses: dominant reading, preferred reading, and oppositional reading (see *encoding/decoding* entry). Today, some media scholars apply the concept of the active audience to those who produce their own media across a range of media platforms as a way to disrupt or play with the hegemonic meanings embedded in corporate-controlled media.

Binary. In critical race and gender studies, this refers to the "either/or" conceptualization of "race" as Black/White or "gender" as masculinity/femininity, in contrast to a system allowing for multiple racial or gender identities.

Black feminist perspective. See *Feminism, Black feminism, feminist media studies.*

Capitalism. An economic system based on private (rather than public or collective) ownership of the means of production, the market exchange of goods and services, and wage labor. This book tends to adopt a perspective critical of the ways capitalist ownership of the media shapes and limits content.

Class, social class. A much-debated term in both sociology and economics. It tends to be used by sociologists to refer to a social stratum whose members share certain social, economic, and cultural characteristics. However, critical sociologists use a modified version of the class Marxist usage, which defined *class* as a group of people occupying a similar position within the social relations of economic production. Whereas Marx argued that there are only two major classes under capitalism, the bourgeoisie (owner class) and the proletariat (worker class), critical sociologists distinguish five: the ruling class, the professional/managerial class, small-business owners, the working class, and the poor.

Codes, semiotic codes, media codes. A term used in *semiotics*-influenced media studies to refer to rules and conventions that structure representations on a number of levels—some specific to certain media, such as narrative film or advertising photographs, and others shared with different modes of communication. Audiences learn to "read" the conventional verbal, visual, and auditory features that make up the "languages" or "sign systems" of media and other cultural forms in much the same way children learn the complex, often arbitrary systems of meaning in natural languages. See *Semiotics* and *Encoding/decoding.*

Commodity. Any object or service that can be bought and sold in the marketplace. Marxists argue that capitalism reduces all aspects of life to commodities.

Conglomeration, conglomerates. In the context of media studies, this refers to the merging of two or more large media corporations into mega-corporations with great economic and cultural power.

Consumerism/consumerist. Consumerism is an economic system and set of cultural values that encourages the production of consumer products and services, and accords social status to their purchase, display, and consumption. Consumerism is often associated with the *capitalist* system that relies on rising production and sales, achieved through branding, promotion, and mass media advertising. The term *consumerism* is frequently used in a critical manner, especially in the context of media and *cultural studies*, to suggest the excesses of materialist culture and conspicuous consumption, as well as the negative environmental impacts of rising production and waste. Consumerism can also refer to a movement to use information and laws to protect consumers from false advertising and dangerous or defective products.

Content analysis. A social scientific method of describing and analyzing the "content" of a range of media texts, either in qualitative or quantitative terms. Quantitative content analysis (counting the number of times certain types of material appear) is especially useful for describing the broad contours of a large quantity of texts, but it tends to miss the more subtle and complex ways texts construct meaning.

Convergence, media convergence. This term has been used, confusingly, to refer to many different processes in the current fast-changing media business environment. Henry Jenkins (2006) has usefully clarified the term this way: "the flow of content across multiple media platforms, the cooperation between multiple media industries, and the migratory behavior of media audiences who will go almost anywhere in search of the kinds of entertainment experiences they want" (p. 2).

Co-opt, co-optation. See *Appropriation.*

Counterhegemonic, antihegemonic. See *Hegemony, hegemonic.*

Critical race theory. In contrast to older approaches to "race" that assumed "White" or Euro-American norms and focused on "non-White" identities as "the problem," critical race studies are based on the assumption that the proper object of study is the construction of hierarchical racial categories by which "White privilege" came to seem "natural." Critical race theorists are particularly concerned with challenging the Black/White *binary* that has dominated U.S. academic discourse on "race," rendering invisible anyone who cannot be made to exemplify one of these two artificially constructed categories. In general, critical race theorists view "race" as a purely historical construct in the service of political goals. See Omi and Winant (1993).

Critical theory, critical media theory, critical media pedagogy. Also see *Marxism.* This is an approach to the analysis of social and cultural phenomena that highlights the dominant role of a capitalist economic system and the resulting economic and social inequalities.

Cultural studies. An approach to the study of communications in society that is drawn from a number of sources, including Marxism, semiotics, literary and film analysis, psychoanalysis, feminism, and critical race and postcolonial theory. As used in this book, it locates the production, textual construction, and consumption of media texts in a society characterized by multiple systems of inequality. Of key importance is the study of the role media forms play in the production and reproduction of these systems of inequality. See Chapter 1 in this reader for an extended discussion of this approach.

Culture. A term with many different meanings, depending on the school of thought in which it occurs. In anthropology, it refers to everything created by humans, including artifacts or objects, ideas, institutions, and expressive practices. In traditional humanities fields such as art history and literature, *culture* has tended to be conceptualized as the highest-status arts of the wealthy and socially dominant, such as oil paintings, opera, or poetry. *Cultural studies* rejects this view of culture as elitist, replacing it with the more anthropological usage. In particular, cultural studies takes as its area of study all the expressive, meaningful, interactive aspects of everyday life in an industrial society.

Decode. See *Encoding/decoding.*

Deconstruct. To deconstruct (or analyze, "take apart") a cultural *text* is to first understand that texts are constructed within a political, economic, and social context that to greater or lesser degrees shapes the *encoded* meaning of the text. Texts are seen as holders of meaning and, as such, need to be carefully deconstructed using an array of methods. Over the years, however, media scholars have recognized that audiences don't necessarily make the dominant reading and have explored, often using *ethnographic* methods, the ways audiences deconstruct or unpack the texts. While scholars may deconstruct the text using different methodologies, it is only by careful research of the audience that we can understand the connection, or lack of it, between the encoding and decoding ends of the communication chain.

Discourse(s), discourse analysis, discursive. Within *cultural studies*, discourse analysis shows how power relations in societies are sustained by and reflected in a variety of specialized ways of speaking and writing, such as those of elite institutions and groups—for example, medical professionals, religious institutions, and academics—as influentially articulated in French historian Michel Foucault's *The History of Sexuality.*

Discursive. See *Discourse(s), discourse analysis, discursive.*

Encoding/decoding. "Encoding/Decoding" is the title of an influential article by British *cultural studies* writer Stuart Hall (1980). It proposes that meaning does not simply reside in a *media text's codes* but is the result of a complex *negotiation* between specific audiences and texts. In contrast to former critical media theorists who assumed that audiences had little control over meaning and were vulnerable to being "brainwashed" by the media, Hall proposed three possible audience responses to the dominant ideology contained in the media text's codes, or three distinct reading positions corresponding to audiences' different social situations: *dominant reading* (accepting the *preferred meaning*), *negotiated reading* (accepting aspects of the preferred meaning but rejecting others), and *oppositional reading* (rejecting the preferred meaning).

Ethnography. This is a social research method first used by anthropologists and now adopted by some *cultural studies* scholars for understanding the role of media audiences in the production of meaning. In ethnographic media studies research, audience members are typically interviewed about their understandings of the media text, or they participate in guided discussions in focus groups. The study can also involve participant observation, which requires that the researcher become a part of the group studied for a specified period to understand directly the context in which the media text reception takes place. For an example of an ethnographic media study, see Chapter 7 in this reader. Also see the entry for *Audience, active audience, audience reception.*

Fans, fandom studies. Ethnographic media audience studies sometimes focus on specialized groups of audiences—the enthusiasts or fans, who seem to exemplify the "active audience" phenomenon in a particularly intensive way. As Henry Jenkins showed in his original study of *Star Trek* fans, excerpted in this volume (Chapter 8), a fan community can go beyond consumption of a media text to a more active relationship, in which new texts are created by fans who borrow ("poach") from and creatively rewrite aspects of commercial media texts, especially when the original texts are found lacking in some way. Fans can bond with one another over their strong relationships with selected media texts, using passionate and interactive revision of such texts as one basis for community. Fandom studies tend to emphasize the potential of grassroots media culture productivity to undermine or challenge the dominance that corporate producers exercise over media culture.

Feminism, Black feminism, feminist media studies. A multidisciplinary approach to social analysis, rooted in the contemporary women's movement(s) and the lesbian/gay/bisexual/transgender/queer (LGBTQ) liberation movement. Emphasizing gender as a major organizing feature of power relations in society, feminists argue that the role of the media is crucial in the construction and dissemination of gender ideology and, thus, in gender socialization. Feminists of color have critiqued the tendency in some feminist theory to privilege gender over other categories of experience; in particular, cultural analysts with a *Black feminist* (sometimes called "womanist") *perspective* have brought to the foreground the ways gender is "inflected" or modified by race and class factors. See Patricia Hill Collins (2000).

Feminist film theory. This strand of *cultural studies*, which was particularly influential in the 1980s, combines a feminist view of the centrality of gender in cultural analysis with a generally psychoanalytic orientation to the study of audience reception of film. Feminist film theorists working through textual analysis have explored such issues as *gendered spectatorship,* the ways the film text, through its formal codes, "addresses" or speaks directly to the hypothetical or ideal viewer as either male or female. An early formulation by Laura Mulvey (1975) asserted that any viewer of classic Hollywood narrative film was encouraged by both plot and camera work and editing to adopt a "masculine subject position" and share in the *male gaze* of both protagonist and camera at a female object of desire.

Gay and lesbian studies, lesbian/gay/bisexual/transgender/queer studies (LGBTQ). See *Queer theory, queer studies.*

Gaze, male gaze. See *Feminist film theory.*

Gender, gendering, gendered. Whereas sex differences (anatomical and hormonal) between genetic males and genetic females are biological in nature, *gender* is a social concept by which a society defines as "masculine" or "feminine" one particular set of characteristics and behaviors and then socializes children accordingly. These criteria can vary tremendously over time and between cultures, and even between different social groups within the same culture. Some contemporary scholars argue that both gender and *sexuality* (erotic desires and identities, sexual object choice, sexual practice) are more accurately understood as continuums, rather than in binary (only two, either/or) categories. Gender is now commonly understood to be constructed in "intersectional" relationships with other aspects of social identity, such as race and class. Media theorists and critics generally try to locate their gender analysis within specific social contexts, distinguishing, for example, representations of Black middle-class masculinity of a particular time and place from other masculinities.

Gendered subjectivity, sexual subjectivities. See *Gender, gendering, gendered* and *subject position.*

Genre. Genre comes from the French word meaning "type" or kind. In media studies, it refers to a collection of *texts* categorized according to their similar content and style. A specific text is part of a genre when it uses certain *codes* and conventions that are familiar to viewers. Examples of media genres discussed in this book include reality TV shows, advertisements, and hip-hop videos. Genres are not always discrete entities, because the codes and conventions of one genre can leak into another—as in the case of pornography, where pornographic codes and conventions of representing women's bodies have seeped into pop culture, resulting in what some scholars call *hypersexualization* of media.

Globalization, global media. In this age of giant multinational media conglomerates and new digital and Internet technologies that allow for wide distribution of corporate-produced cultural products from the richer nations across the globe, the term *globalization* means different things for different media critics. Some, such as Robert McChesney (2008), warn of the dangers of cultural imperialism, which they see as threatening the integrity and autonomy of local cultures around the world, particularly those in the Global South that lack the wealth and industrial technology necessary to compete with the onslaught of Hollywood-produced imagery. Others, including Henry Jenkins (2006), argue that the process is more one of cross-cultural "flow" and see the imperialistic model as too deterministic. Also see *Convergence, media convergence.*

Hegemony, hegemonic. A term developed by Italian Marxist theorist Antonio Gramsci to refer to the process by which those in power secure the consent of the socially subordinated to the system that oppresses or subordinates them. Rather than requiring overt force (as represented by the military or police), the elite, through their control of religious, educational, and media institutions, attempt to persuade the populace that the hierarchical social and economic system is fixed and "natural," and therefore unchangeable. According to Gramsci, however, such consent is never secured once and for all but must continually be sought, and there is always some room for *resistance* through subversive (*counterhegemonic*) cultural work.

Heterocentrism, heteronormativity. These terms refer to the placing of heterosexual experience at the center of attention, or the routine assumption that heterosexuality is "normal" and any other expression of sexuality is "deviant."

Heterosexism. A term coined by analogy with *sexism*, the dictionary defines *heterosexism* as "discrimination or prejudice against gay or homosexual people by heterosexual people." As with *racism* and *sexism*, this book takes the view that structural or institutional forces underpin social inequalities, rather than individual prejudiced attitudes. Thus, heterosexism would refer to the heterosexual ideology that is *encoded* into and characteristic of the major social, cultural, and economic institutions of our society. *Heterocentrism*, similarly, refers to the centrality of the heterosexual perspective in a society. See *Race, racism, postracial* and *Sexism.*

Homophobia. A psychological concept, referring to deep-seated fear of homosexuality, in others or in oneself. Also see *Heterosexism* and *Heterocentrism, heteronormativity.*

Hypersexuality. A controversial term in media studies used to describe the increasingly sexualized imagery of young women found in pop culture. Some scholars argue that these images represent female sexual empowerment, while others see them as the outgrowth of a culture steeped in pornographic *codes* and conventions. Feminists have pointed out that this new hypersexual look is formulaic in that it requires strict adherence to a set of codes and conventions that are difficult for most women to conform to, especially women who are disabled, fat, or older. In her chapter in this book, Rosalind Gill argues that the increasing hypersexuality of images results in a "self-policing narcissistic gaze," where "the objectifying male gaze is internalized to form a new disciplinary regime" (p. 287).

Ideology. This term was traditionally used by Marxists to refer to ideas imposed on the proletariat (working class) by the bourgeoisie (owners of the means of production) to get the subservient classes to consent to their own oppression. Today, critical theorists tend to use a broader concept of ideology that emphasizes the way ideas embedded in all our social institutions (legal, educational, economic, military, etc.) create a dominant commonsense understanding of reality that supports the status quo. For a definition of *ideology*, see the essay by Stuart Hall in this reader (Chapter 11).

Image, media image. This term refers to any *representation* of social reality in media culture, as in "images of women in advertising." However, the word *image* as commonly used—as in "mirror image"— tends to suggest a more direct, uncomplicated, and less artificial or constructed relationship with "reality" than most scholars now propose for media representations. *Image* also refers, of course, to a

specifically *visual representation.* See Sut Jhally's reading (IV.26) in this volume.

Individualism. Individualism is a political philosophy, moral stance, or ideology that accords primacy to individual interests and desires. It is also a methodology that takes individual people, rather than social groups, classes, or nations, as the unit of analysis. Individualism is often contrasted with socialism or communitarianism, in which the society or community has systemic qualities with values and attributes that cannot be reduced to the level of individuals. Proponents of individualism generally presume that people are sovereign individuals capable of making informed decisions in their own interests, that the pursuit of individual interests does not have a major negative impact on others, and that efforts to regulate individual behavior are intrusive, immoral, or counterproductive.

Intersectionality. An approach to describing and analyzing social identity that recognizes multiple strands that intersect with one another in complex ways. In a world characterized by race, class, gender, and sexual inequalities, among others, an intersectional analysis allows us to study how different forms of inequality work together to limit the life chances of oppressed groups. Adopting such an approach has implications for social activism because it demands building coalitions of groups to form social movements that can address multiple oppressions.

Intertextuality. John Fiske (1987) has explicated a theory of *intertextuality* to help explain the way audiences experience a wide variety of media texts as interrelated, allowing their knowledge of one to influence their reading of another. For example, if a *primary media text* is a specific book, film, or television show, then a *secondary text* might be "studio publicity, journalistic features, or criticism" about the primary text, and *tertiary texts* might include viewers' letters, gossip, and conversation about the primary text (Fiske, 1987, pp. 108–109). *Commercial intertextuality* refers to the practice of media text promoters' using a multiplicity of media platforms to make a particular text highly visible and attractive to the intended target audience. Also see *Text, media text*.

Lesbigay, LGBTQ. See *Queer theory, queer studies*.

Liberatory. Like *emancipatory* or *progressive*, this term is used in critical *cultural studies* to indicate what the critic sees as a positive political impact, in which a socially subordinate group gains greater power or freedom (liberation or emancipation from oppression).

Liminal, liminality. A term used by anthropologists and *cultural studies* scholars to mean an area or condition of ambiguity or mixture, at the border between two different conditions.

Marxism, Marxist, Marxian. A general theory of historical change originally developed by 19th-century German philosopher Karl Marx. Marx argued for the centrality of economics in social history and developed a critique of capitalism that has had a major influence on political theory and on social revolutions in the 19th and 20th centuries. In the realm of *cultural studies*, classic Marxism argued that the economic structure of society (the "base") shapes major cultural institutions (the "superstructure"), including the military, legal system, educational system, arts, and media. This is because, according to Marx, "the class which has the means of material production at its disposal has control over the means of mental production" (Marx & Engels, 1938). For a

modification of classic Marxist ideas of this relationship, see *Hegemony*.

Masculinities. See *Gender, gendering, gendered*.

Media, mass media, mass communications media, mediated. The term *media* is originally the plural of *medium* (communications medium). It has become a shorthand way of referring to the whole range of technologically assisted means by which images and messages can be created and distributed by producers for later consumption by "the masses" (vast numbers of people). "The media" is sometimes a shorthand way of referring to news media in particular, but in the context of this book, we are referring primarily to entertainment media culture. To say that communication is "mediated" is to draw attention to its highly secondhand character (as opposed to real-time, face-to-face, traditional cultural forms, such as storytelling, live theater, acoustic musical performances for live audiences, etc.).

Media literacy/media literacy skills. The goal of media literacy is to educate people to think critically about the way media texts are produced, constructed, and consumed, and to provide skills that help deconstruct the ideological messages encoded in texts. Critical media literacy includes an analysis of political economy where the study of the production, consumption, and distribution of the text is located within the wider context of capitalist control of media institutions. Recently, many media literacy experts have argued that a major component of media literacy is to teach actual media production skills as a way to deepen an understanding of how mainstream media is constructed and to encourage people to create independent (noncorporate) media that challenge the hegemonic representations of corporate-owned media.

Media platforms. This refers to the technical mechanisms by which communications are presented to consumers. These can include traditional platforms such as television, newspapers, and radio, as well as relatively new social media platforms on the Internet, such as Facebook, Twitter, and online news sources. In media studies, the concept of media platforms is significant because the use of different platforms has implications for ownership, control, privacy, influence, and access.

Misogyny. Literally, this word means "hatred of women," and its use emphasizes the emotional or psychological basis for *sexism.* Feminist cultural critics analyze ways misogyny and sexism are embedded in culture, often in ways that make historically specific constructions and social arrangements in which males are allocated social and cultural supremacy over females seem natural or inevitable.

Multicultural, multiculturalism. As used in this book, *multiculturalism* refers to a movement affecting curricula, teaching methods, and scholarship in a variety of fields within universities and colleges in the United States. The broad objectives of activists in this educational movement include democratizing knowledge and education by bringing to the foreground and validating the experiences and perspectives of all those groups formerly marginalized or culturally and socially dominated in our society.

Multidisciplinary, interdisciplinary. An approach that encourages students and teachers to cross the boundaries between traditional academic disciplines or areas of knowledge (such as history, sociology, philosophy, economics, or political science) to be better able to capture the complexity of the subject studied.

Negotiated reading. See *Encoding/decoding.*

Neoliberalism. This term refers to an economic ideology that has become widely influential in the economic policies of the wealthier nations and of international lender organizations such as the World Bank in the past several decades. Unlike the economic theories of John Maynard Keynes, which emphasized the role of government intervention in the economy when necessary to promote the well-being of citizens, this view greatly emphasizes (and some would say exaggerates) the beneficial workings of the unregulated private sector, through the magic of the workings of the free market. Embedded in this ideology is the idea that every individual is equally able to protect herself or himself from economic disaster—an idea that easily leads to "blaming the victim" when individuals do not achieve economic stability. In the context of *cultural studies,* critics argue that certain types of media texts, such as makeover reality TV, *Judge Judy,* or *The Oprah Winfrey Show,* encode and promote neoliberal ideas, teaching that the individual can and must empower herself or himself without government support.

New media. This term generally refers to communications technologies that enable users or consumers to interact with one another and with the media texts, in contrast to traditional, older mass media technologies such as newspapers, radio and television broadcasts, films, and recorded music. New media would include blogs, social networking sites, online games, interactive websites such as YouTube, and many other examples that will be current by the time you read this book.

Objectify, objectification, objectifying. Literally, "to make into an object"; more figuratively, to depersonalize and dehumanize someone. In the context of feminist theory, objectification of women is implied by excessive emphasis on body parts and external appearances, especially in media representations designed to sexualize female bodies.

Oppositional reading. See *Encoding/ decoding.*

Patriarchal, patriarchy. Literally meaning "rule by the father" and referring to family (and clan) systems in which one older man had absolute power over all members of the group, including women, children, and younger male relatives and servants. As used by contemporary feminists, it is a concept developed to examine and critique continuing male domination of social institutions such as the family and the state, the educational system, and the media.

Political economy. In critical theory, a perspective that "sets out to show how different ways of financing and organizing cultural production have traceable consequences for the range of discourses and representations in the public domain, and for audiences' access to them" (Golding & Murdoch, 1991, p. 15). This often involves studying who owns the media industries and analyzing how ownership influences media content.

Polysemic text. One that is "open" to various readings or has multiple meanings. *Cultural studies* scholars currently disagree regarding how "open" texts are. See *Encoding/decoding.*

Pornification. Journalist Pamela Paul is often credited with introducing this term in her book *Pornified: How Pornography Is Damaging Our Lives* (2006). It refers to the way pornography, as both a discourse and an industry, has increasingly come to dominate our cultural landscape and shape

sexual relationships. Within the feminist community, there is a long-standing debate regarding the degree to which pornification is an expression of misogyny, or an example of women's sexual agency. This book, working within the critical *cultural studies* paradigm, contains articles that see pornification as inextricably linked to the increasing commodification of all aspects of our lives, and the attendant erosion of sexual agency and creativity.

Pornography. Most broadly, this refers to sexually explicit graphic and/or written texts designed to produce sexual arousal in consumers. The definition has been politicized and was strenuously contested during the 1980s, when feminists proposed city ordinances by which the production and distribution of certain classes of pornography could be prosecuted as civil rights violations, rather than under traditional anti-vice criminal law. Anti-pornography feminists argued that pornography is a form of violence against women in its production and consumption. Against this position, there are some who argue that pornography provides a space for sexual creativity and exploration for women.

Postcolonialism. A critical approach to the legacy of colonialism and imperialism, primarily by European powers, in terms of the political, cultural, and economic impacts on formerly colonized countries, and the enduring inequalities in relations between them and Western countries. Postcolonialism draws from postmodernism to understand how colonialism was not just a military phenomenon but, rather, was structured and legitimated through media and cultural representations that portrayed the superiority of Western civilization, arts, and science, and the inferiority of colonized people and their cultures. Postcolonialism investigates how many of the traditional conceptions of superiority and inferiority are perpetuated in media images and texts, and how these contribute to ongoing economic inequalities, immigration policies, military interventions, and other phenomena.

Postfeminism. This term has been used to describe and critique an apparent period of reaction against feminism that began in the 1980s, when some women sympathetic to the goals of feminism nevertheless refused to name themselves as feminists. As used by feminist media critics, however, it tends to refer to the idea embedded in some cultural texts that all the goals of the women's movement have already been achieved. In this way, it is parallel to *postracial discourse* (see *Race, racism, postracial*).

Post-Fordism. This refers to the strategies adopted by multinational corporations in seeking to maximize profits by diversifying products and marketing them in new ways in response to global flows of labor and consumption patterns. (It contrasts with "Fordism," which was the 20th-century mass production and distribution system developed by auto manufacturer Henry Ford, based on standardizing factory production of goods for mass consumption.) In the context of *global media,* post-Fordism refers to changes in the ways producers and distributors of media products must operate as they seek to capture both national mass audiences and diverse local and niche markets in other parts of the world.

Postmodernism. Literally meaning "after modernism," this term describes an influential philosophical movement of the late 20th century that has reacted to and challenged many dominant 19th-and earlier 20th-century Western ideas based on "modern" scientific certainty and authority, including faith in social progress driven by science and reason. The postmodern era (roughly corresponding to the years after World War II, though some theorists would point to earlier 20th-century roots) is characterized by fragmentation of states and sources of authority and a general skepticism regarding scientific progress and large-scale social projects and ideologies, whether religious or political. In the postmodern era, it is claimed that there is a greater awareness of the *intersectionality* of identities—that people are constructed, for example, through categories such as nation, ethnicity, class, and gender, and that these categories might be unstable and fluid. Postmodernism also claims that mass media such as movies, television, and magazines do not merely reflect a preexisting reality; rather, these *texts* construct our notions of common sense, our systems of meaning, our identities, and the larger social reality. From a postmodern perspective, however, this role does not lead to large-scale ideological manipulation or brainwashing, because the interaction of fragmented media sources with people with complex identities cannot lead to predictable or determinate outcomes.

Postracial discourse. See *Race, racism, postracial.*

Preferred reading. A concept developed by Stuart Hall to circumscribe the degree of "openness" (*polysemy*) of media texts. According to Hall (1980), the structure of mainstream media texts always "prefers" or strongly suggests a single "correct" meaning that tends to promote the dominant ideology. Within *cultural studies,* there continues to be a lively debate over whether a preferred meaning can be said to be a property of the text; some would argue that the making of meaning ultimately resides with audiences. Also see *Encoding/decoding.*

Progressive. The term *progressive*, when applied to politics, has a long and varied history. For the purposes of this book, it is used to describe a particular approach to understanding both how society is structured and a way of thinking about how to bring about social change. Progressive thinkers tend to be more left-wing in their belief that society is based on an unjust and unequal economic system. Progressives argue for a more fair distribution of economic, cultural, and political resources, and believe that only by organizing and movement building can we bring about macro social change.

Queer theory, queer studies. An interdisciplinary and politically radical approach to *cultural studies* that emphasizes the instability and fluidity of gender and sexuality categories, in contrast to the view that sexual identity is a fixed, permanent "essence." The term *queer* is adopted to reclaim it in a positive sense from derogatory usage, as well as to create a more inclusive vision of the areas of study.

Race, racism, postracial. Also see *critical race theory.* Although the political importance of "race" as a social category is evident in today's world, most scholars agree that "race" is a convenient fiction with complex historical significance but no biological reality. In everyday usage, *racism* can be used to mean holding or displaying prejudiced or bigoted attitudes or indulging in discriminatory behavior toward someone else (usually people of color, but sometimes Whites as well), on the basis of that person's apparent race, ethnicity, or skin color. However, in critical theory, and in this book, we use the term to refer specifically to the White-supremacist ideology encoded into and characteristic of the major social, cultural, and economic institutions of this society. *Postracial discourse* is based on the view that in the post–civil

rights era, race is no longer a major factor in determining one's access to resources and respect. This view is linked with the ideology of meritocracy, which assumes that individuals inevitably succeed in life and are rewarded in society as a result of hard work and motivation. Those who critique these concepts argue that such a view fails to see and acknowledge "structural inequalities" in our society, such as White privilege or class privilege, that provide hidden advantages to people from some groups from birth.

Representation, cultural representation, media representation. Representation is a current term used to include all kinds of media imagery (through words, pictures, or both) that, no matter how convincing their likeness to everyday social reality, are always to be recognized as illusions. More technically, media representations such as events seen on reality television shows or depictions of gangster life in the 'hood contained in hip-hop rap videos should be understood not as direct mirrorings of "real life." Rather, they are always the result of artistic and business judgments by their producers, "constructions taken from a specific social and physical viewpoint, selecting one activity or instant out of vast choices to represent, and materially made out of and formed by the technical processes of the medium and its conventions" (King, 1992, p. 131).

Resistance. In critical *cultural studies*, this can refer to the refusal of the reader, viewer, or audience to take up or accept the *preferred reading* and/or the *subject position* encoded into the media text, therefore resisting its power to reinforce hegemonic ideas. There is still debate among cultural studies scholars on how much opportunity to resist the text offers (how "open" or *polysemic* it is). Many scholars have criticized a tendency to "romanticize" the idea of the interpretive community's resistance. Others question the notion that audience *resistance* is in and of itself positive, citing the resistance of those with conservative social ideologies to texts whose preferred meaning is politically *progressive*. Finally, it has been asserted that "resistive readings" of specific texts do not necessarily translate into political resistance to cultural *hegemony*. (A related term, *agency*, refers to the degree to which a consumer of culture can be understood to be a free agent whose choices must be respected by the cultural critic, as opposed to merely being a passive victim of cultural brainwashing.)

Semiotics, semiology. Semiotics is a linguistics-based field of study that has had an important influence on the way *cultural studies* scholars discuss the *codes* in media texts. It is concerned with the study of "signification," or the ways both languages and nonlinguistic symbolic systems operate to associate meanings with arbitrary *signs*, such as words, visual images, colors, or objects. Signs actually consist of two elements—that which is *signified* (the meaning) and that which signifies (the *signifier* or symbol itself). See *Encoding/decoding.*

Sexism. Coined by the women's movement in an analogy with *racism,* sexism is also used several ways. In common usage, it can refer to prejudicial or disrespectful attitudes or discriminatory behavior on the part of individuals toward others on the basis of gender. In this book, we use it to refer specifically to male-supremacist or patriarchal ideology encoded into and characteristic of the major social, cultural, and economic institutions of a society.

Sexuality, sexualities, heterosexuality. Erotic identities, desires, and practices. Historians have established that *heterosexuality* emerged as a normative or hegemonic concept in response to the discovery by 19th-century medical discourses of variant or what were then called "perverse" sexualities. See D'Emilio and Freedman (1998). Also see entry for *Gender, gendering.*

Signifier, signified. See *Semiotics, semiology.*

Social networking. Social networking on the Internet refers to the use of interactive websites that provide a forum for social interaction among users who share interests or are otherwise connected. Social networking sites such as Facebook, LiveJournal, Pinterest, and LinkedIn invite users to provide information about themselves through a personal profile and then interact with others through chat and messaging, forming groups of "friends," sharing pictures and video, or posting about personal activities or current events. Social networking is widely acknowledged to be causing far-reaching changes in contemporary culture, social interaction, and the structure of communities, though there is considerable disagreement regarding the nature and overall benefits of these changes.

Spectacularize. Literally, "to make spectacular," this word was coined for use in media studies to refer critically to the tendency of contemporary mass media, especially news and sports media, to create ever more visually entrancing and emotionally exciting events (spectacles) to attract and retain audiences. Generally, it is argued that media spectacles increasingly replace the kind of substantive and thoughtful discourse needed to ground an authentic democracy. See Kellner (2005).

Spectatorship. See *Feminist film theory.*

Stereotype. This popular term was often used in 1970s media criticism and activism to describe and critique reductive, much-repeated social imagery (as in "Uncle Tom and Aunt Jemima are racist stereotypes";

"Aunt Jemima and the Playboy Bunny are sexist stereotypes").

Subject position. A concept developed within literary and film criticism, which claims that narrative texts themselves produce through their codes an ideal "viewing position" or subject position, from which the narrative is then experienced by any viewer/reader. A male viewer could be invited by a particular text to view it from a feminine subject position, for example, just as a heterosexual reader might temporarily occupy a queer subject position. A related term for this process is *interpellation*—which means that the text can be read as figuratively "hailing" or "calling out to" a particular ideal type of reader.

Text, media text. This term is used broadly and can refer to any communicative or expressive media product, from a song lyric or magazine ad to a dramatic TV show or online video game. *Textual analysis,* or a close examination of how particular media texts generate meaning, is one of the key activities of contemporary *cultural studies.*

Textual analysis. See *Text, media text.*

Transgender. This is an umbrella term for individuals whose gender identity does not match their assigned birth gender and whose gender identity, expression, or behavior is not consistent with that culturally associated with their assigned sex at birth. The existence of trans people is often seen as an example of the fluid nature of gender identity; at the same time, there is debate within the scholarly community regarding the degree to which conformity to any socially defined gender is either *counterhegemonic* or *hegemonic.* Also see entry for *Gender, gendering, gendered.*

Transgressive. A term often used positively in cultural criticism to indicate the writer's approval of an act that transgresses by challenging traditional (oppressive) rules or social or cultural hierarchies.

Whiteness. Using critical race theory, many media scholars seek to highlight the economic, legal, and cultural construction of White people as a social and material category. It is argued that Whiteness has been developed as a social category to legitimize racism by arguing that people with "white skin" are naturally and biologically superior. In media studies, theorists examine how media images help normalize Whiteness through its overwhelming presence, which paradoxically renders it "invisible" and thus less likely to be critically examined.

Womanism. A term coined by novelist and essayist Alice Walker to refer to Black feminism. See *Feminism, Black feminism, feminist media studies.*

Glossary References

Collins, P. H. (2000). *Black feminist thought: Knowledge, consciousness, and the politics of empowerment* (2nd ed.). New York: Routledge.

D'Emilio, J., & Freedman, E. (1998). *Intimate matters: The history of sexuality in America.*

Fiske, J. (1987). *Television culture.* London: Methuen.

Golding, P., & Murdoch, G. (1991). Culture, communications and political economy. In J. Curran & M. Gurevitch (Eds.), *Mass media and society* (pp. 15–32). London: Edward Arnold.

Hall, S. (1980). Encoding/decoding. In S. Hall, D. Hobson, A. Lowe, & P. Willis (Eds.), *Culture, media and language* (pp. 128–138). London: Hutchinson.

Jenkins, H. (2006). *Convergence culture: Where old and new media collide.* New York: New York University Press.

Kellner, D. (2005). *Media spectacle and the crisis of democracy.* Boulder, CO: Paradigm.

King, C. (1992). On representation. In F. Bonner, L. Goodman, R. Allen, L. Janes, & C. King (Eds.), *Imagining women* (pp. 131–139). Cambridge, UK: Open University Press.

Marx, K., & Engels, F. (1938). *German ideology* (R. Pascal, Trans.). London: Lawrence & Wishart.

McChesney, R. W. (2008). *Communication revolution: Critical junctures and the future of media*. New York: New Press.

Mulvey, L. (1975). Visual pleasure and narrative cinema. *Screen, 16*(3), 6–18.

Omi, M., & Winant, H. (1993). On the theoretical concept of race. In C. McCarthy & W. Crichlow (Eds.), *Race, identity, and representation in education* (pp. 3–10). New York: Routledge.

Paul, P. (2006). *Pornified: How pornography is damaging our lives*. New York: Henry Holt.

AUTHOR INDEX

SUBJECT INDEX

ABOUT THE EDITORS

Gail Dines is professor of sociology and women's studies at Wheelock College in Boston, where she is also chair of the American Studies Department. She has been researching and writing about the pornography industry for well over 20 years. She has written numerous articles on pornography, media images of women, and representations of race in pop culture. Her latest book is *PORNLAND: How Pornography Has Hijacked Our Sexuality* (2011). She is a cofounder of the activist group Stop Porn Culture!

Jean M. Humez is Professor Emerita of women's studies at the University of Massachusetts, Boston, where she taught courses in both women's studies and American studies and chaired the Women's Studies Department. She designed and taught an undergraduate "Women and the Media" course early in her career and, through her interest in media text analysis, came to collaborate with Gail Dines on this book. She has also published books and articles on African American women's spiritual and secular autobiographies and on women and gender in Shaker religion. Her most recent book is *Harriet Tubman: The Life and the Life Stories* (2004).

ABOUT THE CONTRIBUTORS

Mark Andrejevic is deputy director and research fellow at the Centre for Critical and Cultural Studies at the University of Queensland. His research interests focus on new media, popular culture, and the ways forms of surveillance and monitoring enabled by the development of new media technologies impact the realms of economics, politics, and culture. His latest book is *Infoglut: How Too Much Information Is Changing the Way We Think and Know* (2013).

Lee Artz is an associate professor in the Department of Communication and Creative Arts at Purdue University Calumet. He has written numerous articles on cultural diversity and democratic communication for leading journals. His most recent books are *Public Media and the Public Interest* (2002, with Michael McCauley, Eric Petersen, and Dee Dee Halleck), *Communication and Democratic Society* (2001), and *Cultural Hegemony in the United States* (2000, with Bren Murphy).

Christine Bacareza Balance is an assistant professor of Asian American Studies in the School of Humanities at the University of California, Irvine. Her research interests include Filipino American studies, performance studies, popular music studies, Asian American cultural studies, queer/feminist theory, and U.S. popular culture. In 2012 to 2013 she was a Ford Foundation Postdoctoral Fellow.

Elena Bertozzi teaches game analysis, design, and development in the Media Arts & Game Development program at the University of Wisconsin, Whitewater. She is the director of the Engender Games Group lab, which is currently developing the Emergency Birth Game, aimed at teaching players how to safely deliver a baby in the absence of a physician. Her latest book is *The Clitoris and the Joystick: Play, Pleasure, and Power in Cyberspace* (2012).

E. Tristan Booth is an instructor at Arizona State University. His specialties include rhetorical strategies of individuals and groups claiming marginalized social identities, particularly those relating to gender, sex, and sexuality; the tension between post-structural theories of identity and concepts of stable identity as related to social movements; and collective identity politics, as well as corporeal rhetoric.

danah boyd is a senior researcher at Microsoft Research; a research assistant professor in media, culture, and communication at New York University; a visiting researcher at Harvard Law School; a fellow at Harvard's Berkman Center; and an adjunct associate professor at the University of New South Wales. Her research examines social media, youth practices, tensions between public and private, social network sites, and other intersections between technology and society. She is also a coeditor of *Hanging Out, Messing Around, Geeking Out: Living and Learning With New Media* (2009).

Robert Alan Brookey is an associate professor of communication at Northern Illinois University. His research investigates the way traditional forms of entertainment media are responding to an emerging digital market, and his work has appeared in journals such as *Games and Culture*, *Convergence*, and *Critical Studies in Media Communication*. He is coeditor of *Introduction to Communication Studies: Traditional and Contemporary Readings* (2012).

Richard Butsch is a professor of sociology, American studies, and film and media studies at Rider University, and teaches in the areas of media, culture studies, and social psychology. He is author of *The Citizen Audience: Crowds, Publics, and Individuals* (2007) and editor of *Media and Public Spheres* (2009). He is currently writing a history of screen culture, and a book on the representation of manual labor and laborers in 20th-century America.

Kristopher L. Cannon is a PhD candidate in the moving image studies program, in the Department of Communication at Georgia State University. His research explores manifestations of bodies and queerness in new media and film. He has recently published "Cutting Race Otherwise: Considering Michael Jackson" in *Spectator* and is working on his dissertation, tentatively titled "Oblique Optics: Illuminating the Queerness of Images in Mediation."

Jane Caputi is a professor of women, gender, and sexuality studies, and communication and mass media at Florida Atlantic University. She is the author of several books, most recently *Goddesses and Monsters: Women, Myth, Power and Popular Culture* (2004). She also produced the educational documentary *The Pornography of Everyday Life*, distributed by Berkeley Media (www.berkeleymedia.com).

Dianne C. Carmody is an associate professor of sociology and criminal justice at Old Dominion University. Her research interests include intimate partner violence, school violence, and rape victimization. She has published numerous articles on violence against women in journals such as *Justice Quarterly*, *American Journal of Criminal Justice*, and *Affilia: Journal of Women and Social Work*.

Jay Clarkson is an assistant professor of electronic media at Indiana State University. He studies media representations of gender and sexuality and the proliferation of addiction narratives to explain media consumption patterns. He is author of several articles, including "Contesting Masculinity's Makeover: *Queer Eye*, Consumer Masculinity, and 'Straight-Acting' Gays" (2005).

Jennifer Cole is a founding member and director of the online GimpGirl Community. She is also an undergraduate studying cultural anthropology at Oregon State University and a research associate in the Experiential Design and Gaming Environments (EDGE) Lab at Ryerson University. She has worked with Oregon Public Health to create state policy recommendations around women with disabilities and sexual health.

Victoria E. Collins is an instructor in the Department of Sociology and Criminal Justice and a research and administrative assistant at the International State Crime Research Consortium at Old Dominion

University. She is also an instructor at the Samaritan House/Virginia Beach Law Enforcement Training Academy. Her research interests include state crime, transnational crime, and violence against women. She has published numerous articles in journals such as the *International Criminal Justice Review* and *Contemporary Justice Review*.

David P. Croteau taught about the sociology of media as an associate professor (retired) in the Department of Sociology and Anthropology at Virginia Commonwealth University. His most recent book, with longtime coauthor William Hoynes, is *Experience Sociology* (2013).

Lisa M. Cuklanz is professor and chair of the Communication Department at Boston College. She is author of two books published by the University of Pennsylvania Press, as well as numerous articles published in journals such as *Critical Studies in Mass Communication, Communication Quarterly, Journal of Gender Studies, Women's Studies in Communication*, and *Communication Studies*. She is coeditor, with Sujata Moorti, of *Local Violence, Global Media: Feminist Analyses of Gendered Representations* (2009).

Marlo David is an assistant professor of English and women's, gender, and sexuality studies at Purdue University and does research in contemporary African American literature and culture, African Diaspora literatures, and gender and sexuality studies. Her current project—"Mama's Gun: Maternal Figures, Black Women and the Politics of Transgression"—is a study of post–civil rights era representations of Black mothers and motherhood in literature and film. Her essays have appeared in *The African American Review, Black Camera: An International Film Journal, Tulsa Studies of Women's Literature, Home Girls Make Some Noise: A Hip Hop Feminist Anthology*, and *Black Woman & Child Magazine*.

Emily M. Drew is an associate professor of sociology and ethnic studies at Willamette University, where she teaches courses about racism, race and ethnicity, urban sociology, mass media, and social change. Her primary areas of research involve understanding how race and racism operate inside of social institutions, particularly higher education, media, and urban planning. She has been actively engaged in antiracism organizing and activism for almost 20 years, and serves as a cotrainer of "Understanding Institutional Racism" workshops for Crossroads Anti-Racism Organizing and Training.

Meenakshi Gigi Durham is a professor in the School of Journalism and Mass Communication at the University of Iowa. She is the author of *The Lolita Effect* (2008) and coeditor (with Douglas Kellner) of *Media and Cultural Studies: Key Works* (2001; revised 2006). Her research engages feminist critical and cultural studies to interrogate media representations of women's and girls' sexuality. She has published extensively in leading scholarly journals in media studies.

Kirsty Fairclough-Isaacs is a lecturer in media and performance in the School of Arts and Media at The University of Salford, United Kingdom. Her research is focused on the analysis of contemporary media, in particular the phenomenon of celebrity and how it impacts everyday life. She is coeditor, alongside colleagues Ben Halligan and Rob Edgar, of *The Music Documentary* (2013), the first full-length study of music documentaries, from rockumentary to mockumentary.

Kathleen P. Farrell is an associate professor of social sciences and education at Colby-Sawyer, New London, New Hampshire. Her primary research and teaching interests include gender and sexualities, with an emphasis on inequality studies. She is coeditor (with Nisha Gupta and Mary Queen) of *Interrupting Heteronormativity: Lesbian, Gay, Bisexual and Transgender Pedagogy and Responsible Teaching at Syracuse University* (2004).

Nadia Yamel Flores-Yeffal is an assistant professor of sociology at Texas A&M University in College Station. She specializes in

Latin American demography, Mexican–U.S. migration, and international migration from El Salvador. Her research focuses on the social networks of migrants from Latin America, the use of the Internet to spread the anti-immigrant sentiment in the United States, and human capital transferability among migrants from Latin America.

John Bellamy Foster is a professor of sociology at the University of Oregon, and also editor of *Monthly Review*. His writings focus on the political economy of capitalism and economic crisis, ecology and ecological crisis, and Marxist theory. He has published more than 100 articles, written and edited more than a dozen books, and received numerous awards and honors. His latest book (with Robert McChesney) is *The Endless Crisis: How Monopoly-Finance Capital Produces Stagnation and Upheaval From the USA to China* (2012).

Christian Fuchs is a professor of social media at the University of Westminster Communication and Media Research Institute. He is editor of the journal *tripleC: Communication, Capitalism & Critique*. His research interests include social theory, critical theory, and critique of the political economy of media. He is the author of *Foundations of Critical Media and Information Studies* (2011).

Rosalind Gill is a professor of social and cultural analysis at King's College London. Her research interests include gender and media, cultural work, new technologies, and mediated intimacy. The author of numerous articles on media and sexualization, she is currently working on a 4-year Marsden (Royal Society) project exploring how "tween" (9- to 12-year-old) girls negotiate living in an increasingly sexualized culture.

Karen Goldman is an assistant director for outreach for the Center for Latin American Studies and a research associate for the Department of Hispanic Languages and Literature at the University of Pittsburgh. She has published several journal articles and book chapters on gender themes in Spanish and Latin American film.

Stuart Hall was one of the founders of British cultural studies and was director of the Centre for Contemporary Cultural Studies at Birmingham University for many years. He has written numerous articles and books on cultural studies, race, and representation, including *Encoding and Decoding in the Television Discourse* (1973), *Cultural Studies: Two Paradigms* (1980), and *Cultural Representations and Signifying Practices* (1997). Hall retired from the Open University in 1997 and is now a Professor Emeritus.

Chong-suk Han is an assistant professor of sociology and anthropology at Middlebury College in Vermont. His areas of expertise are race and sexuality, particularly the ways categories of race and sexuality are socially constructed and the way multiple identities intersect. An award-winning journalist, he is the author of numerous articles.

Jonathan Hardy is senior lecturer in media studies at the University of East London. He writes on media and advertising, communications regulation, and international and comparative media. His books include *Cross-Media Promotion* (2010), *Western Media Systems* (2008), and *The Advertising Handbook* (2009; coedited). He is secretary of a U.K. media reform group, the Campaign for Press and Broadcasting Freedom (www.cpbf.org.uk).

William D. Hoynes is a professor of sociology and former director of the Media Studies Program at Vassar College in Poughkeepsie, New York, where he teaches courses on media, culture, and social theory. He is the author of *Public Television for Sale: Media, the Market, and the Public Sphere*. His most recent book, with longtime coauthor David Croteau, is *Experience Sociology* (2013).

Henry Jenkins III is the Provost's Professor of Communication, Journalism, and Cinematic Arts at the University of Southern

California and was previously the director of the MIT Comparative Media Studies Program and the Peter de Florez Professor of humanities. He is the author and/or editor of 12 books on various aspects of media and popular culture, including *Convergence Culture: Where Old and New Media Collide* (2006). His latest book (coauthored with Sam Ford and Joshua Green) is *Spreadable Media: Creating Value and Meaning in a Networked Culture* (2013).

Sut Jhally is a professor of communication at the University of Massachusetts at Amherst and founder and executive director of the Media Education Foundation. He is the author of numerous books and articles on media, including *The Codes of Advertising* (1990) and *Enlightened Racism* (1992). He is also the producer and director of a number of media-literacy films and videos for classroom use, including *Dreamworlds: Desire/Sex/Power in Music Video*; *The Price of Pleasure: Pornography, Sexuality and Relationships*; and *Hip Hop: Beyond Beats and Rhymes*.

Helen Johnson is an honorary research fellow in the School of Social Science at The University of Queensland. Her articles have appeared in a range of national and international journals. She has contributed to significant publications, particularly those focusing on issues of gender and development, and she has written policy and reports for a number of governments and companies.

Chris Jordan is an assistant professor of film studies in the Department of Theatre, Film Studies, and Dance at St. Cloud State University. He is the author of *Movies and the Reagan Presidency: Success and Ethics* (2003), and essays and articles on film and television. His latest scholarly research is on the history of the Motion Picture Association of America.

Jackson Katz is an educator, author, and international lecturer in the fields of gender violence prevention education and critical media literacy. He is cofounder of Mentors in Violence Prevention (MVP),

one of the original "bystander" programs and the most widely utilized sexual and domestic violence prevention initiative in college and professional athletics in North America. He is the creator of the *Tough Guise* film series, author of *The Macho Paradox* (2006) and *Leading Men: Presidential Campaigns and the Politics of Manhood* (2013), and a blogger on masculinities and politics for *The Huffington Post*. He lectures widely in the United States and around the world on violence, media, and masculinities.

Douglas Kellner holds the George Kneller Chair in the Philosophy of Education at UCLA, and is author of many books on social theory, politics, history, and culture, including works in cultural studies such as *Media Culture and Media Spectacle* (2003). His book *Guys and Guns Amok: Domestic Terrorism and School Shootings From the Oklahoma City Bombings to the Virginia Tech Massacre*, won the 2008 AESA award as the best book on education. He has also published *Cinema Wars: Hollywood Film and Politics in the Bush-Cheney Era* (2009), and *Media Spectacle and Insurrection, 2011: From the Arab Uprisings to Occupy Everywhere!* (2012). His website is at www.gseis.ucla.edu/faculty/kellner/kellner.html.

Kelly Kessler is an assistant professor of media and cinema studies at DePaul University. Her research interests include the intersection of genre and gender and the mainstreaming of lesbianism in television and film. Her investigations of the intersection of queerness and television and film narrative can be found in *Film Quarterly*, *Televising Queer Women: A Reader*, and *The New Queer Aesthetic on Television: Essays on Recent Programming*. Her latest book is *Destabilizing the Hollywood Musical: Music, Masculinity and Mayhem* (2010).

Abigail De Kosnik is an assistant professor in the Berkeley Center for New Media (BCNM) and the Department of Theater, Dance and Performance Studies, and is an affiliated faculty member of gender and women's studies. She researches popular media, particularly digital media, film and television, and fan studies. She is particularly interested in how issues of feminism, queerness, ethnicity, and transnationalism intersect with new media studies and performance studies. She coedited *The Survival of Soap Opera: Transformations for a New Media Era* with Sam Ford and C. Lee Harrington (2011).

Michael J. Lee is an assistant professor of communication at the College of Charleston and has had several award-winning conference papers in his research area of political communication. His work has been published in such journals as the *Quarterly Journal of Speech* and the *Journal of Applied Communication Research*.

Dafna Lemish currently serves as interim dean of the College of Mass Communication and Media Arts at Southern Illinois University. She is the founding and current editor of the *Journal of Children and Media* and combines her interests in children with gender representations and feminist theory in her investigation of the gendered nature of mediated childhoods. She has published seven books and more than 100 refereed journal articles and book chapters in several languages, and is the editor of *The Routledge International Handbook of Children, Adolescents and Media* (2013).

George Lipsitz is a professor of Black studies and of sociology at the University of California at Santa Barbara and studies social movements, urban culture, and inequality. He is the author of more than half a dozen books and numerous articles, and his latest book (coauthored with Daniel Fischlin and Ajay Heble) is *The Fierce Urgency of Now: Improvisation, Rights, and the Ethics of Cocreation* (2013).

Sean Lockwood is an assistant professor of ancient history and classics at Trent University in Canada. He specializes in funerary monuments in Anatolia dating from the Persian Empire to the early Roman Imperial period. He investigates the identities of those who created these monuments through analyses of ancient textual and archaeological evidence.

Lori Kido Lopez is an assistant professor at the University of Wisconsin–Madison. Her research examines the way minority groups use media in the fight for social justice. This includes battles to improve the representation of disenfranchised groups within mainstream media as well as examinations of the different ways grassroots/activist media, participatory cultures, and commodity cultures all can play a role in transforming identities and communities. She is working on a book that examines the efforts of Asian Americans to impact the way their community has been represented.

James Lull is Professor Emeritus of communication studies at San Jose State University, California, specializing in media and cultural studies. He has published 12 books, as well as dozens of journal articles, chapters, and essays, and has lectured throughout the world on the interplay between communication and culture. His latest book (coauthored with Eduardo Neiva) is *The Language of Life: How Communication Drives Human Evolution* (2012).

Katherine Mancuso is a social media consultant and instructor at Tech Liminal and a volunteer community liaison for Gimp-Girl Community (online). Her interests include digital media, online education, community building, and accessibility.

Alice Marwick is an assistant professor at Fordham University in the Department of Communication and Media Studies, where she teaches classes on social media and digital culture. Previously, she was a postdoctoral researcher at Microsoft Research in Cambridge, Massachusetts, where she worked closely with danah boyd, studying social software. Her new book is *Status Update: Celebrity and Attention in Social Media* (2013).

Robert W. McChesney is the Gutgsell Endowed Professor in the Department of Communication at the University of Illinois at Urbana-Champaign. In 2002 he was the cofounder of Free Press, a national media reform organization (www.free press.net). He served as its president until April 2008, and remains on its board of directors. He has written numerous books and articles, including *Rich Media, Poor Democracy: Communication Politics in Dubious Times* (2000), and his work has been translated into 30 languages. His latest book is *Digital Disconnect: How Capitalism Is Turning the Internet Against Democracy* (2013).

James McKay is a professor and honorary research consultant at the Centre for Critical and Cultural Studies at The University of Queensland. He has published widely on topics such as gender, race, nationalism, globalization, and popular culture. He is a former editor of the *International Review for the Sociology of Sport* and is on the editorial board of *Men & Masculinities*. His most recent publication is "Larrikins and Mates: Hegemonic Masculinities in Australian Beer Advertisements," in *Sport, Beer, and Gender in Promotional Culture: Explorations of a Holy Trinity*, edited by L. A. Wenner and S. J. Jackson (2009).

Stefania Milan holds a PhD in political and social sciences from the European University Institute, Italy. She has taught courses on global media and democracy, communications governance, and technology and society at several European universities. She has published widely on social movement media and participatory governance. Her latest book is *Social Movements and Their Technologies: Wiring Social Change* (2013).

Candace Moore is an assistant professor in the Department of Screen Arts and Culture at the University of Michigan. Her research and teaching interests include film history, cultures of consumption, and feminist and queer media studies. She has published a number of articles on Showtime's *The L Word*.

Sujata Moorti is a professor of women's and gender studies at Middlebury College in Vermont. She is coeditor of *Global Bollywood: Travels of Hindi Song and Dance* (2008) and coeditor (with Lisa M. Cuklanz) of *Local Violence, Global Media: Feminist Analyses of Gendered Representations* (2009).

Leigh Moscowitz is an assistant professor in the Department of Communication at the College of Charleston. Her research focuses on the various ways gendered and sexual identities are represented in news and popular culture. Her current research projects include coverage of child abductions in the news as well as the televisual production of class and gender in popular shows. Her latest book is *The Battle Over Marriage: Gay Rights Activism Through the Media* (2013).

Dara Persis Murray is a part-time lecturer and doctoral student in the School of Communication and Information at Rutgers University. She has published articles in *Feminist Media Studies* and *Celebrity Studies*.

Lisa Nakamura is a professor in the Department of American Cultures and the Department of Screen Arts and Cultures at the University of Michigan, Ann Arbor. She is the author of *Digitizing Race: Visual Cultures of the Internet* (2007) and *Cybertypes: Race, Ethnicity, and Identity on the Internet* (2002), as well as many journal articles. She is also coeditor of *Race in Cyberspace (2000)* and *Race After the Internet (2011)*.

Michael Z. Newman is an assistant professor in the Department of Journalism and Mass Communication at the University of Wisconsin–Milwaukee. His research interests include American cinema, television, and video games; and media history, theory, and criticism. His latest book is *Legitimating Television: Media Convergence and Cultural Status* (2012), coauthored with Elana Levine.

Eve Ng is an assistant professor in the School of Media Arts and Studies at Ohio University. Her areas of research interest include manifestations of taste and distinction in "progressive" contexts; the relationships between LGBT representations and identities; and consumer–producer dynamics in contemporary cultural production. Her latest publication is "A 'Post-Gay' Era? Media Gaystreaming, Homonormativity, and the Politics of LGBT Integration," in *Communication, Culture, and Critique* (2013).

Jason Nolan is an assistant professor in the School of Early Childhood Studies at Ryerson University. He is founding coeditor of the journal *Learning Inquiry* and coeditor of the *International Handbook of Virtual Learning Environments*. His areas of research include concept development in science, social technologies for young children, identity construction online, critical thinking and reflective practice, teacher education, and children's information privacy online in social networks.

David Nylund has been a practicing therapist with more than 25 years of clinical experience in a broad array of settings, including community mental health, nonprofit agencies, managed care, and private practice. Dr. Nylund is also an associate professor of Social Work at California State University, Sacramento. He is the author of several books, including *Beer, Babes, and Balls: Masculinity and Sports Talk Radio* (2007).

Alejandra Ospina is a liaison for GimpGirl Community. She has spoken about Gimp-Girl in a number of forums, including interviews and virtual and on-site presentations. She presented a version of "Gimp-Girl Grows Up" at the Ninth Association of Internet Researchers (AoIR) Conference, prior to its publication.

Laurie Ouellette is an associate professor in the Department of Communication Studies at the University of Minnesota, Twin Cities, where she teaches critical media studies and cultural theory. She is the author of *Viewers Like You? How Public TV Failed the People* (2002) and coauthor of *Better Living Through Reality TV: Television and Post-Welfare Citizenship* (2008). She is coeditor (with Susan Murray) of *Reality TV: Remaking Television Culture* (2008). Most recently, she edited *The Media Studies Reader* (2010).

Gilad Padva teaches in the Department of Film and Television at Tel Aviv University. He publishes extensively about cinema and television studies, gender and queer theory, media aesthetics, visual communications, camp subculture, and popular music. His articles have appeared in many journals, including *Cinema Journal, Feminist Media Studies, Sexualities, Journal of Communication Inquiry*, and *Women and Languages*.

Gareth Palmer is a professor of media in the School of Media, Music and Performance at the University of Salford, in Manchester, United Kingdom, and he has published widely on reality television and surveillance. He is coeditor of *Exposing Lifestyle Television* (2008) and editor of the long-running *Journal of Media Practice* (Intellect). He is also co-organizer of the Salford Sampler, a new venture designed to develop the storytelling capabilities of local people.

Anne Helen Petersen is an assistant professor at Whitman College, Washington, where she teaches classes in television, stardom, feminist media studies, and theory. She has published articles in journals such as *Feminist Media Studies, Television and New Media* and *Celebrity Studies*. Her first book is *Scandals of Hollywood* (2014).

April Plemons teaches courses in sociology and women's and gender studies at Texas A&M University. Her research and teaching interests include sexuality studies, gender, deviance/crime, and media. She is author of the article "Commodifying Fido: Pets as Status Symbols" (2012).

Janice Radway is a professor of literature at Duke University, North Carolina, and is past president of the American Studies Association. Her current research interests are in the history of literacy and reading in the United States, particularly as they bear on the lives of women. She is presently working on a book titled *Girls, Zines, and Their Afterlives: Sex, Gender, Capitalism, and Everyday Life in the Nineties and Beyond.*

Momin Rahman is an associate professor of sociology at Trent University in Ontario, Canada. His research interests include sexuality and citizenship, and celebrity culture, and he teaches courses on the relationship between Muslim cultures and gender/sexuality politics. He is coauthor of *Gender and Sexuality: Sociological Approaches* (2010).

Mary F. Rogers, a longtime professor of sociology and anthropology at the University of West Florida, and a pioneer in women's studies, died unexpectedly in 2009. She taught courses in feminist theory, social change and reform, social justice and inequality, and qualitative research. She was the author of *Barbie Culture* (1999, 2002), as well as *Contemporary Feminist Theory: A Text Reader* (1997). She was coauthor, with C. D. Garrett, of *Who's Afraid of Women's Studies: Feminisms in Everyday Life* (2002). With Susan E. Chase, she coedited *Mothers and Children: Feminist Analyses and Personal Narratives* (2001).

Tricia Rose is a professor and chair of Africana studies at Brown University. She specializes in 20th-century African American culture and politics, social history, popular culture, gender, and sexuality. Her scholarly interests include Black cultural production, the role of new technologies and ideologies about race in U.S. life, and the politics of intimacy and social justice. Her publications include *Black Noise: Rap Music and Black Culture in Contemporary America* (1994); *Longing to Tell: Black Women Talk About Sexuality and Intimacy* (2004); and *The Hip Hop Wars: What We Talk About When We Talk About Hip Hop and Why It Matters* (2008).

John Sanbonmatsu is an associate professor of philosophy at Worcester Polytechnic Institute in Massachusetts. He is author of *The Postmodern Prince: Critical Theory, Left Strategy, and the Making of a New Political Subject* (2003), and he is editor of the anthology *On the Animal Question: Essays in Critical Theory and Animal Liberation* (2011).

Melissa C. Scardaville is a doctoral candidate in sociology at Emory University, where she studies media, gender, and organizations. Formerly on the staff of *Soap Opera Digest*, she has also published an article about her soap opera research in the journal *Poetics*.

Juliet Schor is a professor of sociology at Boston College. Her research over the past 10 years has focused on issues pertaining to trends in work and leisure, consumerism, the relationship between work and family, and women's issues and economic justice. The author of numerous articles, her most recent books are *Born to Buy: The Commercialized Child and the New Consumer Culture* (2004) and *True Wealth: How and Why Millions of Americans Are Creating a Time-Rich, Ecologically-Light, Small-Scale, High-Satisfaction Economy* (2011).

Kevin Schut is chair and an associate professor at the School of Arts, Media, and Culture at Trinity Western University in British Columbia, Canada. He writes about the intersection of communication, culture, media, technology, and faith. He has published articles or chapters on fantasy role-playing computer games and masculinity, on computer games and myth, and on the presentation of history in computer games. His latest book is *Of Games and God: A Christian Exploration of Video Games* (2013).

Yukari Seko obtained her PhD in the Communication and Culture Programme at York and Ryerson Universities, Ontario, Canada. Her research interests include user-generated content on social media, identity practice online, multimodal self-expression, digital surveillance, and aesthetics of pain. Her dissertation theorizes photographs of self-harm on Flickr as a form of aesthetic self-disclosure.

Raka Shome recently (2011–2012) served as the Margaret E. and Paul F. Harron Endowed Chair in Communication at Villanova University, Pennsylvania. She is the author of numerous articles, and her current interests are exploring new relations of postcoloniality; Asian modernities; the rhetoric of "new India"; and Whiteness, particularly new formations of Whiteness and White femininity.

Kay Siebler is a professor of English and the coordinator of the new gender and power studies minor at Missouri Western State University in St. Joseph, Missouri. She is currently working on a book titled *Queer Identity in the Digital Age.*

Debra C. Smith is an associate professor of Africana studies at the University of North Carolina, Charlotte. Her research and teaching interests include e-Black studies; African Americans in communication and popular culture; minority images in the media; contemporary African American folklore; and developing teaching strategies that incorporate popular culture, language, and power. She is author of *The Words Unspoken: The Hidden Power of Language* (2008). Her website is at www.debracsmith.com.

Gloria Steinem is a well-known feminist activist, organizer, writer, and lecturer. Steinem was a founder in 1972 of *Ms. Magazine,* the first national women's magazine run by women, and she continues to serve as a consulting editor. She has been published in many magazines and newspapers here and in other countries, and is also a frequent guest commentator on radio and television. Her books include *The Revolution From Within: A Book of Self-Esteem* (1992), *Outrageous Acts and Everyday Rebellions* (1983), *Moving Beyond Words* (1993), *Marilyn: Norma Jean* (1986), and, most recently, *Doing Sixty and Seventy* (2006). She is also an editor of *The Reader's Companion to U.S. Women's History* (1998).

Sue Tait is a senior lecturer in media and communication at the University of Canterbury, New Zealand. She is currently researching celebrity advocacy and practices of bearing witness through media. She has recently published articles on media representations of death in scholarly journals such as *Feminist Media Studies, Science as Culture,* and *Critical Studies in Media Communication.*

Guadalupe Vidales is an assistant professor of criminal justice at the University of Wisconsin at Parkside. She is the author of "Arrested Justice: The Multifaceted Plight of Immigrant Latinas Faced With Domestic Violence," in *Journal of Family Violence* (2010).

Grace Wang is an assistant professor in American studies at the University of California at Davis. Her research and teaching focus broadly on race, immigration, transnationalism, multiethnic U.S. literature, music, and popular culture. She is currently working on a book, *Soundtracks of Asian America*, that critically interrogates the cultural role music plays in the production of Asian American identities.

Jamie Warner is a professor at Marshall University in West Virginia. Her research interests include the intersection of political theory and political communication—specifically, how irony, parody, and humor work within a democratic system. She has published articles in both political science and communications journals, including *Polity, Popular Communication,* and *Politics & Gender.* She is currently at work on a book on political culture jamming.

⑤SAGE research**methods**

The essential online tool for researchers from the world's leading methods publisher

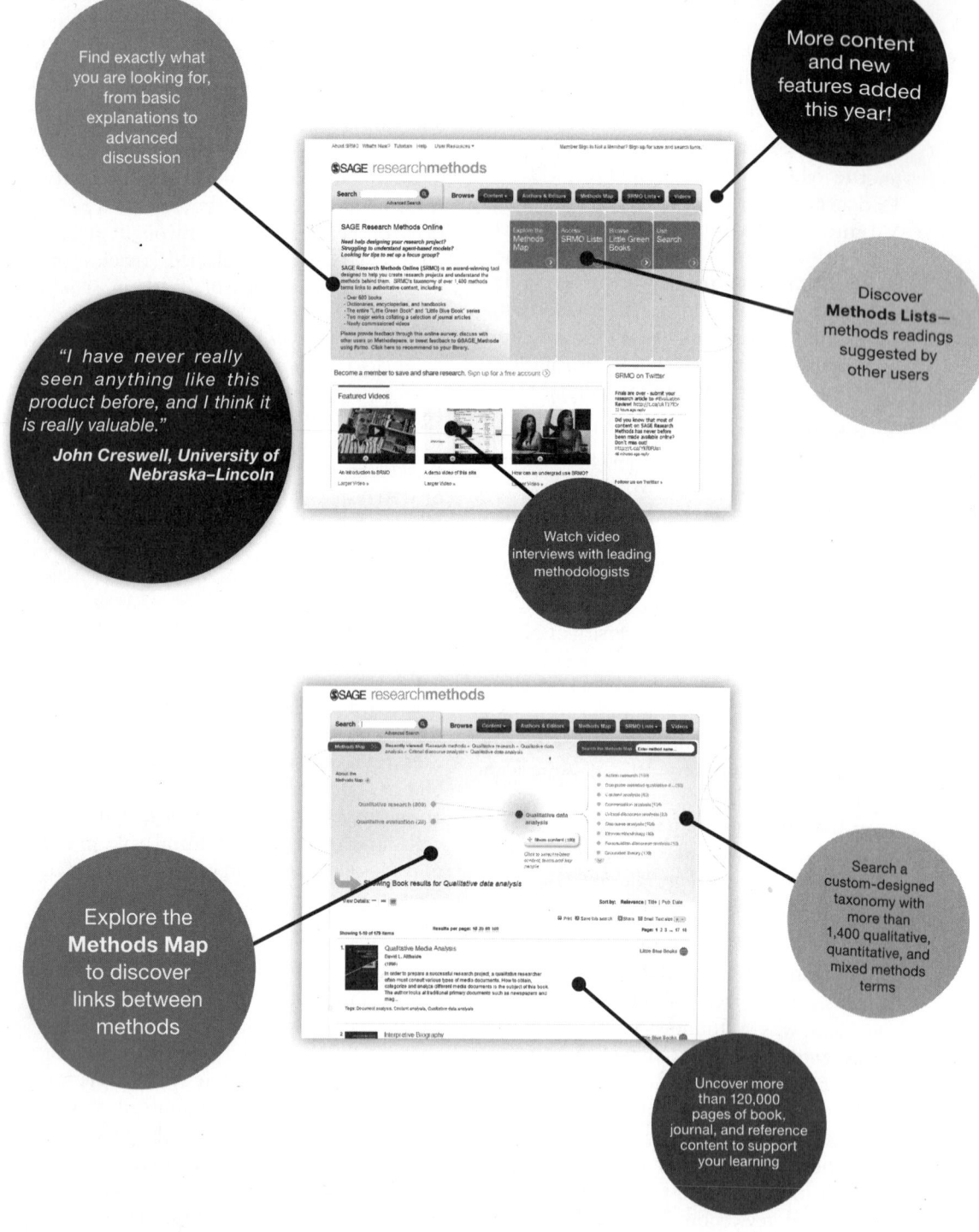

Find exactly what you are looking for, from basic explanations to advanced discussion

More content and new features added this year!

"I have never really seen anything like this product before, and I think it is really valuable."

John Creswell, University of Nebraska–Lincoln

Discover **Methods Lists**—methods readings suggested by other users

Watch video interviews with leading methodologists

Explore the **Methods Map** to discover links between methods

Search a custom-designed taxonomy with more than 1,400 qualitative, quantitative, and mixed methods terms

Uncover more than 120,000 pages of book, journal, and reference content to support your learning

Find out more at
www.sageresearchmethods.com